TWENTIETH CENTURY IMPRESSIONS OF CEYLON

TWENTIETH CENTURY IMPRESSIONS OF
CEYLON

ITS HISTORY PEOPLE, COMMERCE, INDUSTRIES, AND RESOURCES.

FIRST PUBLISHED 1907

ARNOLD WRIGHT

GYAN

Published by

GYAN

Gyan Publishing House
5, Ansari Road
Daryaganj, New Delhi-110002
Phone: 011-47034999, 9811692060
E-mail: books@gyanbooks.com

Distribution Network
gyanbooks.com
India, USA, Canada, UK, Australia, France

ISBN : 978-81-212-3225-8 (PB)
First Published, London, 1907

2nd Impression 2020

Printed at: Gyan Press, Delhi.

Twentieth Century Impressions of Ceylon
Author: Arnold Wright

HIS EXCELLENCY THE GOVERNOR AND COMMANDER-IN-CHIEF OF CEYLON,
VICE-ADMIRAL SIR HENRY ARTHUR BLAKE, G.C.M.G., F.R.C.I.

LADY BLAKE.

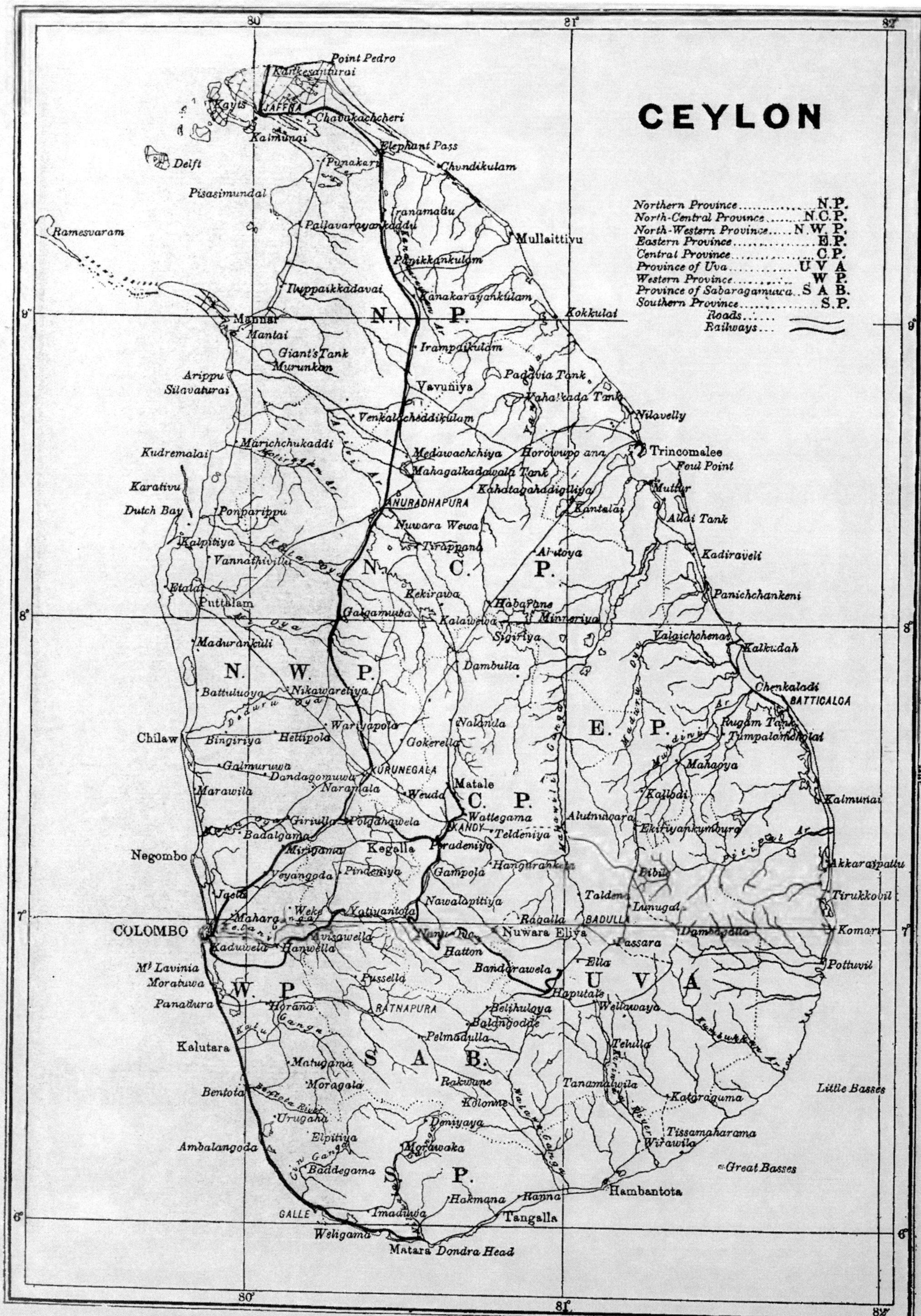

CEYLON
Northern Province N.P.
North-Central Province N.C.P.
North-Western Province N.W.P.
Eastern Province E.P.
Central Province C.P.
Province of Uva U V A
Western Province W.P.
Province of Sabaragamuwa S A B.
Southern Province S.P.
Roads
Railways
Point Pedro
Kankesanturai
Kayts
JAFFNA
Chavakachcheri
Kaimunai
Elephant Pass
Delft
Punakeri
Chundikulam
Pisasimundal
Iranamadu
Rameswaram
Pallavarayankaddu
Mullaittivu
Panikkankulam
Iluppaikkadavai
Kanakarayankulam
Mannar
Mantai
Kokkulai
Irampaikulam
Giant's Tank
Murunkan
Arippu
Silavaturai
Padavia Tank
Vavuniya
Vahalkada Tank
Nilavelly
Venkalacheddikulam
Marichchukaddi
Kudremalai
Medawachchiya
Horowupo ana
Trincomalee
Foul Point
Mahagalkadawala Tank
Karativu
Kahatagahadigiliya
Muttur
ANURADHAPURA
Dutch Bay
Ponparippu
Kantalai
Allai Tank
Nuwara Wewa
Kalpitiya
Tirappane
Vannathivillu
Alutoya
Kadiraveli
N. C. P.
Etalai
Kekirawa
Puttalam
Habarane
Panichchankeni
Galgamuwa
Kalawewa
Minneriya
Sigiriya
Madurankuli
Valaichchenai
Kalkudah
N. W. P.
Dambulla
Batuluoya
Nikawaretiya
Chenkaladi
BATTICALOA
Nalanda
E. P.
Chilaw
Wariyapola
Rugam Tank
Bingiriya
Hettipola
Tumpalanchcholai
Gokerella
Galmuruwa
Mahaoya
KURUNEGALA
Dandagomuwa
Marawila
Naramala
Matale
Weudu
C. P.
Kallodi
Kalmunai
Wattegama
Alutnuwara
Giriulla
Polgahawela
KANDY
Teldeniya
Badalgama
Ekiriyankumbura
Mirigama
Kegalla
Peradeniya
Negombo
Hanguranketa
Akkaraipattu
Pindeniya
Gampola
Veyangoda
Bibile
Ja-ela
Taldena
Tirukkovil
Nawalapitiya
Lunugala
Mahara
Yatiyantota
Ragalla
BADULLA
COLOMBO
Komari
Avisawella
Nanu Oya
Nuwara Eliya
Passara
Dambagalla
Kaduwela
Hanwella
Hatton
Ella
Mt Lavinia
Pottuvil
Bandarawela
Moratuwa
Pussella
U V A
W. P.
Haputale
Panadura
Horana
RATNAPURA
Belihuloya
Wellawaya
Balangoda
Pelmadulla
Kalutara
Telulla
Matugama
S. A. B.
Moragala
Rakwana
Tanamalwila
Kataragama
Little Basses
Bentota
Bentota River
Kolonne
Urugaha
Deniyaya
Tissamaharama
Elpitiya
Wirawila
Ambalangoda
Morawaka
Great Basses
Baddegama
S. P.
Hakmana
Ranna
Hambantota
GALLE
Imaduwa
Tangalla
Weligama
Matara
Dondra Head
80°
81°
82°
9°
8°
7°
6°

PREFACE

THIS work is the outcome of an enterprise designed to give in an attractive form full and reliable information with reference to the outlying parts of the Empire. The value of a fuller knowledge of the "Britains beyond the Sea" and the great dependencies of the Crown as a means of tightening the bonds which unite the component parts of the King's dominions was insisted upon by Mr. Chamberlain in a memorable speech, and the same note ran through the Prince of Wales's impressive Mansion House address in which His Royal Highness summed up the lessons of his tour through the Empire, from which he had then just returned. In some instances, notably in the case of Canada, the local governments have done much to diffuse in a popular form information relative to the territory which they administer. But there are other centres in which official enterprise in this direction has not been possible, or, at all events, in which action has not been taken, and it is in this prolific field that the publishers are working. So far they have found ample justification for their labours in the widespread public interest taken in their operations in the Colonies which have been the scene of their work, and in the extremely cordial reception given by the Press, both home and Colonial, to the completed results.

Briefly, the aim which the publishers keep steadily before them is to give a perfect microcosm of the Colony or dependency treated. As old Stow with patient application and scrupulous regard for accuracy set himself to survey the London of his day, so the workers employed in the production of this series endeavour to give a picture, complete in every particular, of the distant possessions of the Crown. But topography is only one of the features treated. Responding to modern needs and tastes, the literary investigators devote their attention to every important phase of life, bringing to the elucidation of the subjects treated the powerful aid of the latest and best methods of pictorial illustration. Thus, a work is compiled which is not only of solid and enduring value for purposes of reference and for practical business objects, but is of unique interest to all who are interested in the development of the Empire.

Following closely upon the lines of the earlier works of the series on Western Australia and Natal, this volume, dealing with the beautiful island Colony of Ceylon, embodies a great mass of information by writers who are recognised experts in the particular subjects with which they deal. The pages speak for themselves, but a few of the more notable sections may be briefly indicated here. As befits an island so rich in ancient lore as Ceylon, special prominence has been given to the historical matter, and the reader will be able to trace through the ages the chequered and romantic course of Sinhalese power to its tragic close in the squalid despotism of the Kandyan kings. Similarly, the investigator may, with the aid of the work, follow step by step the story of European domination, from the time when the Portuguese galleys appeared off the island until the present day, when His Majesty King Edward VII. reigns with undisputed sway over a highly civilised and intensely progressive community.

In Ceylon the religious element has always been closely associated with the dynastic and political. As the great seat of Buddhist learning, the centre in which the doctrines of the great Teacher were first committed to

PREFACE

writing, it enjoys a position of peculiar sanctity in the minds of many millions of the world's population, and due regard has been given to the fact in the preparation of the work. The introductory historical article and the special articles dealing with Buddhist lore, literature, and customs, will be found highly instructive and deeply interesting monographs upon the subjects with which they deal.

While in these and other directions due regard has been had to the historic claims of this singularly interesting Colony, its modern aspects have been fully treated from every point of view—topographical, administrative, judicial, educational, municipal, and commercial. Incidentally the lighter phases of life have been illustrated, and the volume embodies a comprehensive record of social institutions, together with a mass of information, in special articles and other contributions, on sports and pastimes. The modern religious institutions of the Colony, too, have been exhaustively and impartially dealt with, both on the side of missionary effort and in the domain of ordinary church work. A special note should be made of the biographical element in the book. The list of subjects embraces practically every personage of importance in the island, and as the most scrupulous care has been taken to compile the notices, it may be claimed for the feature that it will be of enduring value.

On the commercial side the volume has exceptional claims to attention as an accurate and absolutely complete record of the manifold interests of the island. The great tea industry, the new and rapidly developing rubber industry, the widely diffused coconut interest, the banks and kindred financial agencies, the shipping and the multifarious trade enterprises which centre in a thriving Colony like Ceylon—all have their share of space, and in the result is produced a record which may be consulted with advantage by every business house in Europe which desires to extend its connections in the East. A certain monotony, inevitable in the circumstances, may be found in the details of this section. But, on the other hand, it may be pleaded that a picturesque interest attaches to the illustrative features of these pages. The commercial operations of the island, whether on the tea or rubber estate or in the more prosaic field of retail trade, have a distinctiveness which redeems the views from the commonplace, while the portraiture reveals the domestic side of Ceylon life in a way which must be appreciated by all who are attracted by the East. Indeed, we may go further and say that it constitutes a gallery of pictures of the homes of Ceylon which for living interest has never been equalled and is not soon likely to be surpassed.

Generally it may be stated that in carrying through the work no pains or expense have been spared to ensure completeness and accuracy. On the one hand the local resources have been taxed to the uttermost to secure the material upon which to build the structure of the book; on the other, all facts have been sifted and re-sifted in order to secure that no error should creep in to mar the usefulness of the pages. This work, conducted in a tropical climate, where many of the resources of Western countries for conducting literary enterprises are not available, has been necessarily arduous. But the Editor feels it a pleasure to acknowledge that his task has been materially lightened by the cordial goodwill which he has encountered on all hands. No important request has been refused, while from many quarters has come assistance, in some instances spontaneously tendered, which has been of signal value in the working out of the plans.

His Excellency Sir Henry Arthur Blake, G.C.M.G., the Governor and Commander-in-Chief of the island, has taken a deep and abiding interest in the work in its various stages, and the Editor has to gratefully acknowledge not only the goodwill which His Excellency has manifested, but also the practical suggestions tendered by His Excellency, which, having been acted upon, have added greatly to the value of the book as an authentic record of the life of the Colony. The Editor has also to express his thanks to the heads of the various Government departments and to the leading officials of public bodies and institutions, who have materially lightened his duties by a ready compliance with his requests for information.

It is desirable to state in conclusion that there is no standard way of spelling names in Ceylon. The only rule observed is the phonetic one, and provided this is followed, no ground of criticism is considered to lie. To such length is this etymological laxity carried that often members of the same family adopt different forms in the spelling of their surnames.

The word "Singalese" or "Singhalese," as it is usually incorrectly rendered, is written throughout in the form adopted by Government—Sinhalese.

COLOMBO, JANUARY, 1907.

CONTENTS

PAGE

History of Ceylon. By C. M. Fernando, M.A., LL.M. (Cantab.), M.R.A.S., J.P., *Barrister-at-Law, Crown Counsel for the Island* 13

Part I. The Pre-Vijayan Period 13
Part II. Ancient References to Ceylon 16
Part III. The Mahavansa: 543 B.C. to 360 B.C. 20
Part IV. The Introduction of Buddhism 22
Part V. The Mahavansa: 257 B.C. to 304 A.D. 24
Part VI. The Suluvansa: 304 A.D. to 1152 A.D. 28
Part VII. The Epic of Parakrama Bahu the Great 33
Part VIII. The Later Sinhalese Kings: 1197 A.D. to 1215 A.D. 38
Part IX. The Life and Times of Alakesvara 40
Part X. The Disestablishment of the Sinhalese Power 43
Part XI. The Portuguese Period 43
Part XII. The Dutch Occupation 55

Ceylon under British Rule: 1796–1906. By Edward W. Perera, *Advocate of the Supreme Court of Ceylon, Member of the Royal Asiatic Society of Ceylon* 60

Constitution and Law. By Don Adrian St. V. Jayewardene, *Barrister-at-Law (Inner Temple), Advocate of the Supreme Court of Ceylon* 85

Part I. The Constitution 85
Part II. The Law 86
Part III. The Administration of Justice 88

Legal and Judicial and Administrative Establishments 99
Archæology. By John Still, *Assistant Archæological Commissioner of Ceylon* 139
Geographical and Meteorological Features 154
Fauna. By W. A. Julius 157
Botany. By J. C. Willis, Sc.D., F.L.S., *Director of the Royal Botanic Gardens, Peradeniya* 161
Irrigation. By H. T. S. Ward, *Director of Irrigation* 169
Forests 173
Geology and Mineralogy. By Dr. A. K. Coomaraswamy, D.Sc., F.G.S., F.L.S., M.R.A.S., *Director of the Mineralogical Survey of Ceylon* 178
Native Arts and Handicrafts. By Dr. A. K. Coomaraswamy, D.Sc., F.G.S., F.L.S., M.R.A.S. 180
Native Ceremonial Observances. By D. J. Subasinha 189
Railways 195
Information for Tourists. By H. B. Smith 204
Post and Telegraphs 207
Local Government 209
Financial. The Colonial Treasury. By Hon. Mr. H. C. Nicolle 213
Education 219
The Medical Department. By Sir Allan Perry, M.D. 225
The Pearl Fishery. By James Hornell, *Late Marine Biologist to the Ceylon Government* 227

CONTENTS

	PAGE
RUBBER. By HERBERT WRIGHT, A.R.C.S., F.L.S.	234
CACAO. By HERBERT WRIGHT, A.R.C.S., F.L.S.	242
THE TEA INDUSTRY. By KELWAY BAMBER, M.R.A.C., M.R.A.S., F.C.S.	248
COCONUT CULTIVATION	251
LABOUR ON ESTATES. By EDGAR TURNER, *Secretary of the Planters' Association of Ceylon*	254
SPORT. By H. WOOSNAM MILLS, *Co-Editor "Times of Ceylon"*	255
ECCLESIASTICAL	268
KANDY AND THE KANDYANS. By MAJOR FRANK MODDER, F.R.G.S.	293
LAND SURVEY	299
THE PRESS	301
SPICES AND OTHER PRODUCTS	320
POPULATION. By THE HON. MR. P. ARUNACHALAM, M.A. (CANTAB.); *Ceylon Civil Service, Member of the Legislative Council of Ceylon; Barrister-at-Law, Lincoln's Inn*	323
AGRICULTURE	355
SALT	362
THE CHAMBER OF COMMERCE	363
SHIPPING, COMMERCE, AND CUSTOMS	369
CEYLON HARBOURS. By CAPTAIN J. A. LEGGE, *Master Attendant*	373
OPIUM	392
COLOMBO	393
COLOMBO COMMERCIAL: FORT SECTION	425
COLOMBO COMMERCIAL: GENERAL	466
COLOMBO PROFESSIONAL AND SOCIAL	521
PLUMBAGO. By E. MANNHEIMER, A.M.T.I.M.E.	585
THE PUBLIC WORKS DEPARTMENT	628
FISHERIES	632
ARRACK AND TODDY	635
THE PROVINCIAL ADMINISTRATIONS	637
WESTERN PROVINCE	640
NORTH-WESTERN PROVINCE	716
SOUTHERN PROVINCE	751
NORTH-CENTRAL PROVINCE	776
EASTERN PROVINCE	780
NORTHERN PROVINCE	781
SABARAGAMUWA PROVINCE	791
CENTRAL PROVINCE	798
UVA PROVINCE	847
MILITARY AND VOLUNTEERS	857
CONCLUSION	863
TABLE OF RELATIVE CEYLON TIME	864
TABLES OF CURRENCY	864
TABLES OF NATIVE WEIGHTS AND MEASURES	864
INDEX	865
APPENDIX	869

Twentieth Century Impressions of Ceylon:

ITS HISTORY, PEOPLE, COMMERCE, INDUSTRIES, AND RESOURCES

HISTORY OF CEYLON

By C. M. FERNANDO, M.A., LL.M. (Cantab.), M.R.A.S., J.P.,
Barrister-at-Law, Crown Counsel for the Island.

PART I.

THE PRE-VIJAYAN PERIOD.

THE written history of Ceylon commences from the year 543 B.C. Ceylon is rich in its chronicles, and richer still in the ancient references made to her by writers of other countries. "There is no island in the world," says Sir Emerson Tennent, the eminent writer on Ceylon, "Great Britain itself not excepted, that has attracted the attention of authors in so many different countries as Ceylon. There is no nation in ancient or modern times possessed of a language and a literature, the writers of which have not at some time made it their theme. Its aspect, its religion, its antiquities and productions have been described as well by the classic Greeks as by those of the Lower Empire; by the Romans; by the writers of China, Burma, India, and Kashmir; by the geographers of Arabia and Persia; by the mediæval voyagers of Italy and France; by the annalists of Portugal and Spain; by the merchant adventurers of Holland; and by the travellers and topographers of Great Britain."

Prior to the landing of Vijaya, however, in the sixth century before Christ—from which date the written history of Ceylon begins—it is now conceded that the island was peopled by advanced races, and that its actual history as a civilised country dates back many centuries from Vijaya's occupation. The evidence of the Sinhalese chronicles proves the existence of a civilised community at the time of the Vijayan occupation; and in respect of the authenticity of these chronicles, George Turnour, an able scholar and the first translator of the Mahavansa (the history of the Great Dynasty), has said that "they are authenticated by the concurrence of every evidence which can contribute to verify the annals of any country." True it is that the Mahavansa and the Dipavansa (the history of the Island Dynasty) were written less as history of current events than as a glorification of the Buddhistic religion; but even in such chronicles it was found necessary to interweave incident with fact in the history of the religion; and these incidents and facts are, as Turnour says, authenticated in the fullest possible manner. For example, we find that where the Sinhalese records depict the glories of a king or the greatness of his court, the facts are corroborated by a Latin historian, who describes an embassy sent by the same king to the court of Rome. Again, where the chronicle refers to the building of a stupendous structure at a certain place by a certain king, we have confirmation of the historian's statements in the narrative of a foreign traveller; while the existence of the structure itself at the present day and the inscriptions yet to be found upon it remove any lingering doubts as to the authenticity of the ancient record. In fine, as there was a Rome more ancient than that which Romulus and Remus founded, so Vijaya, the accepted founder of the Sinhalese race, was preceded by Lanka. Tennent has hazarded the opinion that the pre-Vijayan inhabitants of the island were wild men, who, during the Vijayan occupation and for some centuries afterwards, subsisted on fruits, honey, and the products of the chase. The remains of such a race are still to be found in the Veddahs, who dwell in the solitudes of the eastern portion of Ceylon. These wild men were not, however, the Yakkus ("demons") who were described as being in possession of the country when Vijaya arrived. There seems to have been a pre-Aryan colonisation of Ceylon cotemporaneous with the original Aryan colonisation of Southern India; and when Vijaya landed in the island he found the country ruled by a number of petty princes, as England was during the days of the Heptarchy.

The ancient books of India contain references to the history of Ceylon and incidents of warfare in the island which can safely be said to have occurred at least five centuries before the landing of Vijaya. The two great Indian epics—the Mahabharata and the Ramayana—like all epics of ancient times, contain much that is mythical and fanciful; but like other ancient epics, whether of the West or of the East, they are founded upon actual facts of history, overlaid with a considerable veneer of poetic exaggeration and invention. As a narrative of events these poems may be of little account, but they are of value in that they prove that the poet—and therefore the society in which he lived—knew of the existence of the island, while they also throw many a sidelight on the state of ancient society in the countries in which the scenes are laid. We know from Indian history that long prior to Vijaya the wave of Aryan conquest flowed and inundated Southern India. The long and bloody war which Rama waged against Ravana, the king of Ceylon, seems to have been on the line of this irresistible wave from Southern India into Lanka. Stripped of its gorgeous Oriental trapping, the story runs as follows: Ravana, king of Lanka, hearing of the beauty of Sita, the wife of Rama (then in exile), carried her off to Ceylon. After tedious search Rama obtained a clue as to her whereabouts, and having allied himself with the non-Aryan races of Southern India, he crossed over to Ceylon, gave battle to Ravana, defeated him, and recovered Sita. The non-Aryan tribes of Southern India are described in the poem as "monkeys" and "bears," probably because their religion must have been some form of animal worship, just as the inhabitants of Lanka are described as "Yakkus" ("demons") because they must similarly have been demon worshippers. Reminiscences of this ancient invasion are yet found in the traditions which cluster around the island of Rameswaram, while the ancient city of Sitavaka and the plateau of Sita Eliya still preserve the memory of Sita's captivity in Ceylon. It follows that we can gather from the Indian epics that kings—and therefore an organised state of society—were known in Ceylon centuries before Vijaya, that weapons were used, forts built, and that the value of other accessories of civilised warfare was known to the pre-Vijayan inhabitants of Ceylon. This condition of affairs is irreconcilable with a people subsisting on fruits, honey, and the products of the chase. To quote Mr. George Wall: "Such a state of things is incompatible with the nomadic life of tribes who live by the chase, as is conclusively proved by our experience of several races still living in that way in different parts of the world. The Red Indians of America, the Bushmen of Australia, the Hottentots of Africa, and the Veddahs of Ceylon, all afford examples of the wandering, unsettled mode of life proper to such pursuits and manner of subsistence. In none of these races do we find cities and settled forms of government, or any approach to the conditions prevailing in the island when Vijaya arrived."

Tennent, curiously enough, himself proves the contrary when he maintains—and with much plausibility—that the modern port of Galle is identical with the ancient seaport of Tarshish mentioned in the Scriptures. It was from Tarshish that the ships of King Solomon brought to him once in three years an abundance of wealth. References to Tarshish in the Old Testament are numerous. The following three may be given by way of example:—

"For the king had at sea a navy of Tarshish with the navy of Hiram; once every three years came the navy of Tarshish, bringing gold and silver, ivory, apes, and peacocks" (1 Kings x. 22).

"For the king had ships that went to Tarshish with the servants of Hiram; once every three years came the ships of Tarshish, bringing gold and silver, ivory, and apes, and peacocks" (1 Chron. ix. 21).

"Silver spread into plates is brought from Tarshish, and gold from Uphaz, the work of the workman, and of the hands of the founder; blue and purple is their clothing; they are all the work of cunning men" (Jer. x. 9).

It will be seen from the above quotations that Tarshish was known to be situated in an island; that the island was governed by kings; and that it was rich in gold, silver, ivory, apes, and peacocks. Thus speaks Tennent: "A subsequent investigation has served to establish the claim of Malacca to be the 'golden land' of Solomon, and Tarshish, which lay in the track between the Arabian Gulf and Ophir, is recognisable in the great emporium of south Ceylon. The ships intended for the voyage were built by Solomon at Ezion-Geber, on the shores of the Red Sea. The rowers coursed along the shores of Arabia and the Persian Gulf, headed by an east wind. Tarshish, the port for which they were bound, appears to have been situated in a land governed by kings and carrying on an extensive foreign trade. The voyage occupied three years in going and returning through the Red Sea, and the cargo brought home to Ezion-Geber consisted of gold and silver, ivory, apes, and peacocks. Gold could have been shipped from Galle from the vessels which brought it from Ophir: 'silver spread into plates,' which is particularised by the sacred historian as an export of Tarshish, is one of the substances on which the sacred books of the Sinhalese are even now inscribed; ivory is found in Ceylon, and must have been both abundant and full-grown before the discovery of gunpowder, which led to the wanton destruction of elephants. Apes are indigenous to the island, and peafowl are found there in prodigious numbers. It is very remarkable, too, that the terms by which these articles are designated in the Hebrew Scriptures are identical with the Tamil names by which some of them are called in Ceylon to the present day; thus '*tukiyim*,' which is rendered 'peacocks' in our version, may be recognised in '*thokai*'—the modern Tamil name for these birds; and '*kapi*' (apes) is the same in both languages; and the Hebrew for 'ivory,' or rather '*habbim*' (elephants) is identical with the vernacular. Thus, by geographical position, by indigenous productions, and by the established fact of its having been from time immemorial the resort of merchants from Egypt, Arabia, and Persia, on the one side, and India, Java, and China, on the other, Galle seems to present a combination of every particular essential to determine the problem so long undecided in Biblical dialectics, and thus to present data for inferring its identity with the Tarshish of the sacred historian—'the great Eastern mart, frequented by the ships of Tyre and Judæa.'"

Before proceeding to review the conditions of life in Lanka at the time of the Vijayan invasion, it would be as well to state something about Vijaya himself. It is said that a king of Bengal once married a daughter of the king of Orissa. Their daughter, the Princess Suppadevi, mated with a lion, and gave birth to twins—a son and a daughter. The son, named Sinhabahu, afterwards became the powerful king of a large tract of Bengal and had many children, the eldest of whom was Vijaya. The Rajavaliya (chronicle of the kings) says of him: "Be it known that on the day of Vijaya's birth seven hundred men-children were born in the same city; because he was destined to destroy the demons in illustrious Lanka, and assume sovereignty by the power of the merit of his birth." On coming of age, Prince Vijaya was created sub-king, Uvaraja; but, like Prince Hal, the roistering youth who afterwards became the wise and brave King Henry V. of England, Vijaya showed such strong symptoms of a wild and reckless disposition as to jeopardise the security of his father's government. The king, fearing on the one hand the danger of a civil war, and on the other loath to sacrifice his son to the violence of an enraged people, put Vijaya and his followers (seven hundred in number) into a fully equipped ship, ordering them to seek their fortunes in some country across the ocean. Thus he came to Lanka, and with his followers landed in this ancient isle and founded that line of monarchs which for length of years is unequalled in history.

The Mahavansa recites how Vijaya landed in Ceylon, and how he met a Yakkini queen, named Kuveni, seated at the foot of a tree spinning thread. Vijaya, according to the narrative, consented to marry Kuveni and make her his queen, and it is said that she distributed among Vijaya and his followers "rice and a variety of other articles." She then procured a splendid bed, "curtained as with a wall and fragrant with incense," for the repose of the king. In the night the king heard the sounds of song and music, and inquired from the queen whence they proceeded. She replied, "In the city Sirivattha, in this island, there is a Yakku sovereign, Kalasena, and in the Yakku city, Lankapura, there is another sovereign. Having conducted his daughter Pusamitta thither, her mother, Kondanamika, is now bestowing that daughter at a marriage festival on the sovereign there. From that circumstance there is a great festival in an assembly of Yakkus. That great assemblage will keep up that revel without intermission for seven days; this revel of festivity is in that quarter. Such an assemblage will not occur again. Lord! this very day extirpate the Yakkus!" The king, accepting this advice, proceeded to the scene of the festival with his followers, and destroyed the Yakkus. He assumed the court dress of the Yakku chief, Kalasena, and his retinue donned the vestments of the other Yakkus. After this victory, Vijaya founded the city of Tambapanna, which he made his future home. Then the chronicle proceeds to describe how the followers of the prince formed separate establishments all over Lanka—Anuradha, Upatissa, Uruvela, and Vijita, each of them establishing a city. Afterwards, when the settlements had been formed, his followers beseeched the prince to assume the office of sovereign, which the king refused to do, alleging that he could do so only on his securing a queen consort of equal rank to himself. "All these chiefs," says the chronicle, "incited to exertion by their anxiety for the installation of the prince, sent to Madura a deputation, with gems and other presents." They obtained audience of Pandava, the king of Madura, and explained to him that their mission was to search for a royal maiden as queen to Sinhabahu, named Vijaya, the conqueror of Lanka. Said they, "To admit of his installation, bestow thy daughter on us." Pandava then sent to Vijaya his own daughter, and for the retinue of that king seven hundred daughters of his nobility. As dowry, King Pandava bestowed elephants, horses, chariots, and slaves. Vijaya then discarded Kuveni, the Yakkini princess, made the royal maiden his wife, and was inaugurated the sovereign of Lanka. The chronicle proceeds: "All the nobles, having assembled, in due form inaugurated Vijaya into the sovereignty, and solemnised a great festival of rejoicing. Thereafter the monarch Vijaya invested with great pomp the daughter of King Pandava with the dignity of queen-consort. On his nobles he conferred riches; on his father-in-law he bestowed annually chanks and pearls, in value two lakhs. This sovereign

AN ANCIENT CAVE INSCRIPTION AT AMBALAKANDA.
(One of the earliest to be found in the island. Date prior to fifth century A.D.)

Vijaya, relinquishing his former vicious course of conduct, and ruling with perfect justice and righteousness over the whole of Lanka, reigned uninterruptedly for thirty-eight years in the city of Tambapanna."

Here we have a short account of the conditions existing in Ceylon at the time of and immediately after Vijaya's conquest—conditions which belie the theory that he came among a race of wild men such as the Veddahs are now. It would be difficult to imagine how seven hundred warriors, landing in an uncivilised, barbarous country, could, within a short time, run up gigantic cities and build gigantic tanks without having at their disposal the surplus wealth of the country; and that phrase, as Mr. George Wall has pointed out in a series of papers in the *Journal of the Royal Asiatic Society*, can have no meaning unless the country was a civilised one. In fact, it is only in a land in which society has emerged from barbarism that organised labour is available for the building of large cities and the erection of gigantic monuments: it is only in the civilised state that surplus wealth is at hand for the payment of labour and for the indulgence of luxuries, such as curtained beds, incense, jewels, and the like.

There is the further test of language. Formerly, with the early writers of Ceylon, the belief was current that the Sinhalese language originated with Vijaya, that the language (if any) of the wild tribes who inhabited Ceylon died out on their extirpation by their conquerors, and that the language of the conquerors became the language of the country. This is no more true than to say that the English language was introduced by William the Conqueror. The language that Vijaya spoke in his home in India was a corrupt and colloquial form of Sanskrit, one of the many Prakrit dialects which are the founders of many a modern Indian language, such as Hindi and Mahrati. Vijaya brought this Prakrit into Ceylon just as the Normans brought their Norman-French into England. Later, the Buddhistic language, Pali, twin-sister of Sanskrit, came to Lanka with the Buddhist religion; and itself, like the Prakrit of Vijaya, coalesced with the common stock of the Sinhalese language. Sinhalese words are thus of a twofold character—those which can be traced to Sanskrit and Pali and those which cannot be so traced. The latter were the words spoken by the pre-Vijayan Aryan inhabitants of Ceylon, just as the Anglo-Saxon words of the English language existed before the Battle of Hastings. It is noteworthy that some of these latter words, which are not to be found in Sanskrit or Pali, are traceable to some of the other Aryan languages, including English. An example—and a very striking one—is supplied by the word "*watura*," equivalent to the English word "water," and the word "*linde*," "well" or "pool," identifiable with the Anglo-Saxon "*lynn*." Here we have testimony which philology attests in favour of the fact that the pre-Vijayan inhabitants of Ceylon had a settled language apart from that of their conquerors—a language which stood the test of the Vijayan invasion, and which drew into its vocabulary an abundant supply from the tongue of their conquerors.

Far from the aborigines having been extirpated by their conquerors, everything points to their having accepted the yoke of Vijaya with cheerfulness, not to say with alacrity. One can imagine the state of Lanka when Vijaya landed—the country inhabited by a population scattered over its area; towns and cities interspersed throughout its extent, with no central government, and with chieftains ruling isolated districts. Vijaya's work was to centralise the government of Ceylon and to unite the people into one harmonious whole. Evidently, his followers did not exactly found new cities, but took the place of the chieftains who ruled over the destinies of each. Having succeeded after his first victory in peacefully substituting his followers in place of the Yakku chiefs, Vijaya sought and won a royal bride, and consolidated as one kingdom under his sovereignty what used before his day to be the petty principalities of the island. This was less a work of conquest and extermination of wild barbarians than of the consolidation and inauguration of a central government in the island over which he was destined to rule. Rome was not built in a day; nor did the Sinhalese kingdom originate in one moment, with one stroke of Vijaya's magic wand. Rather shall we regard Vijaya as the first king known to history of united Lanka; and, as such, the Sinhalese race ever revere and honour his memory.

PART II.

ANCIENT REFERENCES TO CEYLON.

THE earliest information on record respecting Ceylon which seems to have reached the Continent of Europe is contained in the writings of Nearchus and Onesicritus, the admirals of the fleet of Alexander the Great despatched from the Indus to the Persian Gulf. They wrote from hearsay, having met and conversed with travellers who had visited the island and who had magnified by many times its real size. Ceylon was described by them under the name of Taprobane, which is identical with the Tambapanna of Vijaya's followers and its Sanskrit equivalent, *Tambrapanni.* The Mahavansa thus accounts for the name: "At the spot where the seven hundred men with the king at their head, exhausted by (sea) sickness and faint from weakness, had landed out of their vessel, supporting themselves on the palms of their hands pressed on the ground, they sat themselves down; hence, their palms became copper-coloured (*tamba-pannayo*), and from this circumstance that wilderness obtained the name of Tambapanna. From the same cause, also, this renowned land became celebrated under that name."

The geographer Dionysius alludes to Ceylon by the same name in respect of its renown for elephants—

Μητερα Ταπροβανην Ασιηγενεων ελεφαντων.

The poet Ovid regards Taprobane as one of the remotest places on earth. What boots it, says he, if his fame were to reach there?—

> "*Quid tibi si callida prosit laudere Syena,*
> *Aut ubi Taprobane Indica cingit acqua?*"

In "De Mundo," a treatise generally ascribed to Aristotle, Taprobane is described as being less in size than Britain.

Seleucus Nicator, successor of Alexander the Great, deputed the historian Megasthenes to be his ambassador at the court of Chandracottus, the king of the Prasii—the Chandragupta of Indian history. It was from his realms that Vijaya and his followers sailed for Ceylon some two hundred years before. Megasthenes thus obtained some information which he embodied in his book. He described the island as being divided by a river (presumably the Mahaveli Ganga) into two parts—the one the home of wild beasts and the other rich in gold and gems. The people he called *Palægoni,* "descendants of the Pali."

A curious incident in the first century of the Christian Era brought Ceylon into intimate touch with the court of Rome. The historian Pliny relates the story, and gives an interesting account of the island. A freed man of Rome, Annius Plocanus by name, having farmed the Red Sea revenues of the Roman Empire, set sail thither in a vessel. Meeting with a hurricane off the coast of Arabia, he was driven by stress of weather, after fifteen days' sailing, to the port of Hipporos (the modern Kuduramala, "horse-hill") in the island of Taprobane. He was well received by the people, conducted to the king, and enjoyed his hospitality during a stay of six months. He evidently expatiated to the king upon the greatness and power of the Roman Empire, with such success that the king despatched to the court of Claudius Cæsar an embassy consisting of four persons, the chief of whom the historian Pliny describes as *Rachia—"Legatos quattuor misit principe corum Rachia."* The king of Ceylon at that time (*circa* 50 A.D.) was Sandamukha Siva or Sandamuhune ("the moon-faced one"). From these ambassadors Pliny obtained the information which he has recorded in his history. Tennent seems to think that "Rachia" is a Roman corruption of Rajah; but Casie Chetty, the erudite author of the "Ceylon Gazetteer," suggests that by "Rachia" is meant "Arachchi" (chieftain), and cites in support of his view that in later history an Arachchi was despatched by King Bhuvaneka Bahu VIII. as ambassador to the court of Lisbon. The latter view seems to be generally accepted. Pliny gathered from these men that there were five hundred cities in their country, the chief of which was called "Palæsimundo," the residence of the sovereign, with a population of two hundred thousand inhabitants, and that the people had commercial dealings with a race called the *Seres*—"men of a huge size, with red hair, blue eyes, and shrill voice, and an unintelligible language." Their trade with the *Seres,* they said, was carried on by each party depositing in a certain place the goods which they desired to barter, and the barter was effected when a satisfactory equivalent had been obtained by each. They spoke of the great lake which adjoined their capital (possibly Tissawewa, in the outskirts of Anuradhapura). Of natural productions they mentioned coral from the Gulf of Mannar, marble of the colour of tortoise-shell, and pearls and precious stones of many kinds. They dwelt upon the great fertility of the soil, the abundance of all kinds of fruits (excepting the vine), the excellence of the government, the happiness of the people, and the average duration of life, which they made out to be considerably longer than in Europe. The institution of slavery was unknown. "They did not take any repose after sunrise or during the day," says Pliny. "Their houses were of moderate height; provisions were never at an extravagant price." "For the king they chose from among the people one who was venerable for his years and his humanity, and who was without a family; but if he had children they compelled him to resign the sovereignty, lest the kingdom should become hereditary. The sovereign had a council of thirty persons assigned to him by the people. If the king committed any outrage against his duty as a sovereign, he was condemned to suffer" (not by the hand of violence, as, for example, in the case of Charles I. of England) "by the universal detestation which he experienced. Every individual avoided his company, and he was left to perish in silence and solitude. Their festivals were devoted to the chase, and they delighted most in that of the tiger and the elephant. They had no grapes, but an abundance of apples, and it was not uncommon for them to attain the age of a hundred years."

Here we have before us an ideal Utopia—a monarchy more democratic than a republic, with a greater measure of liberty, of regard for popular rights, and of safeguards against the abuse of power than exists in any modern State. There can be no doubt that the capital which Pliny calls "Palæsimunda" refers to the royal city of Anuradhapura. It is probably, as Laessen conjectures, the Roman form of the Pali word used by the ambassadors—*Pali-simanta,* the head of the Sacred Law, the city being held in veneration as the then chief centre and stronghold of Buddhism. By the race of the *Seres* must have been meant the Chinese, with whom there was intercourse in Ceylon from very ancient times. Tradition has it that the southern port of Seenimodera, near Tangalle, is so called as being the port at which the Chinese anchored their vessels. Pliny further mentions the fact that the vessels which navigated the seas to the west of Taprobane had prows at either end to avoid the necessity of tacking. This description seems to point to the Ceylon canoe, with its quaint outrigger, which enables it to move with either end foremost, a kind of vessel which is probably not to be found in use anywhere else in the world.

This embassy was not the only embassy to Rome of which we have authentic historical mention. Ammianus Marcellinus speaks of another embassy which came from Ceylon in the time of the Emperor Julian (*circa* A.D. 375). This must have been in the reign of King Upatissa. It was about this time that the Sinhalese court most adopted the practice of sending embassies to distant places—even to China. An interval of a little over half a century intervened between the death of Pliny and the production of the great geographical work by the Egyptian writer, Ptolemy, who flourished in Alexandria in the middle of the second century of the Christian Era. During this interval the navigators of Rome and Egypt had made wonderful strides. The Indian seas were to them no longer a sealed book. The "system of geography" of Ptolemy proves that Ceylon must have been carefully circumnavigated before he wrote his work. The flourishing port of Alexander was in constant communication at this period with Lanka. Alexandrian merchants exhibited their wares in the shops of Anuradhapura; horses from Alexandria found here a ready market, while ivory and pearls and gems from here were sought after in Egypt. Ptolemy must thus have had ample opportunity for obtaining information from Alexandrian merchants with regard to Ceylon, and with such success that he was enabled to lay down on his map of Ceylon the position of eight promontories on its coast, the mouths of five principal rivers, four bays and harbours, and, in the interior, he had ascertained that there were thirteen provincial divisions and nineteen towns, besides two emporiums on the coast; he also mentions five great estuaries, which he terms lakes, two bays, and two chains of mountains, one of them, which he designates as *Malœa*, being in curious conformity with the Mahavansa, in which the country surrounding Adam's Peak is described as the kingdom of Malaya. Of the five rivers on Ptolemy's map, four may be recognised in their modern form as the Arippoo, the Deduru-Oya, the Mahaveli Ganga and the Bentota river. Anuradhapura he describes as "Anurogramma" ("the town of Anuro"), and the metropolis, he says, was "Maagrammum," by which name he must have meant the once populous city of Bintenne, known in the old days as "Mahayangama." The country assigned by him to the Rhogandani is the present Rayigam Korale, and his Nagadivi is the neighbourhood of Trincomalee—the Nagadivi of the Mahavansa. The little islands which he has depicted as the "Bassa" are the Basses. The south of the island, in and about the district of Matara, he describes as the great elephant feeding grounds or plains. It is a striking fact that even up to the time of the Portuguese and the Dutch this was the district for the kraaling of elephants, over which the "Gajanayaka Mudaliyars" (elephant chiefs) had special charge. Ptolemy gives the name *Salike* to

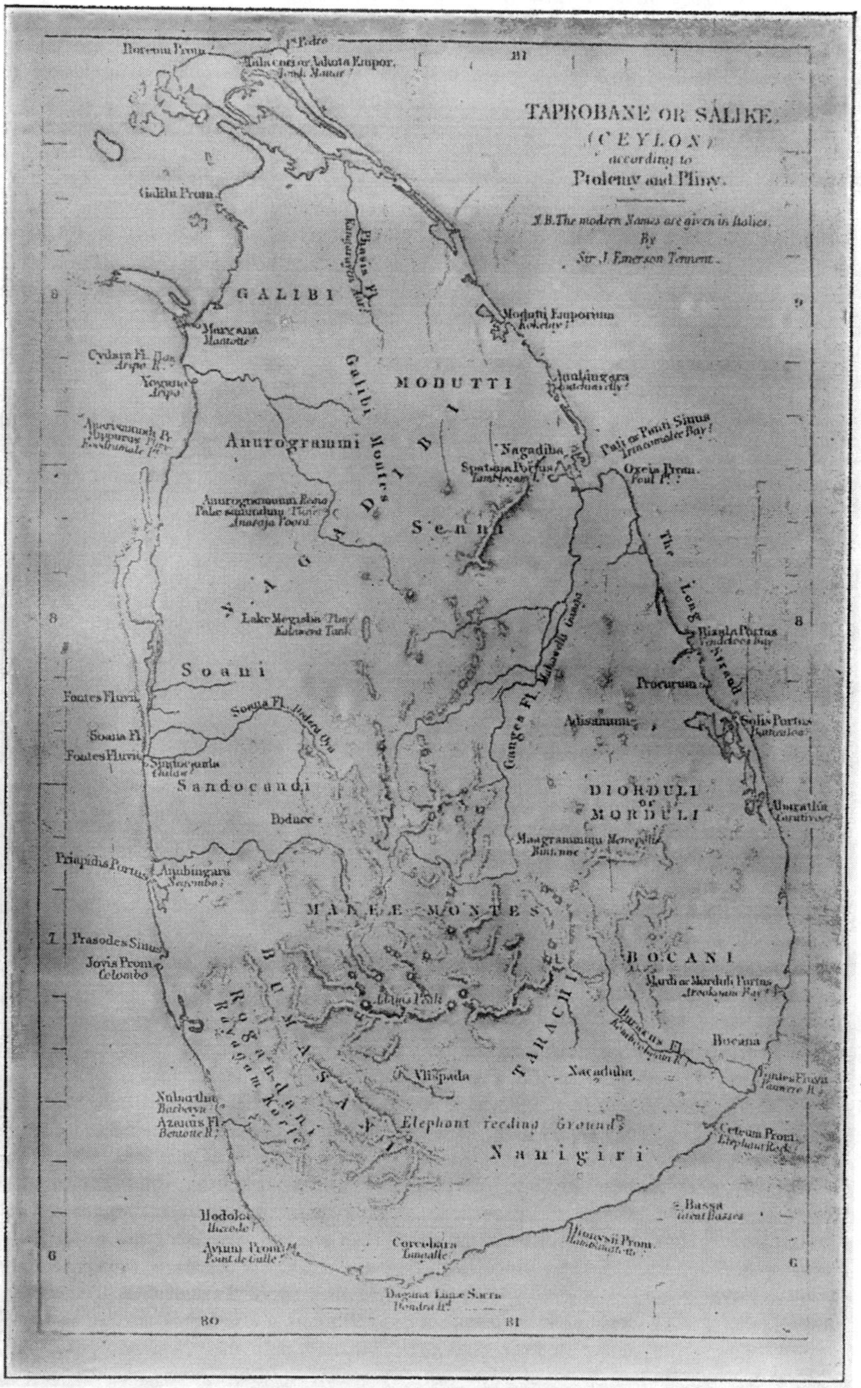

PTOLEMY'S MAP OF CEYLON.

the island. The generally accepted opinion is that it is a corrupt form of *Sihala*. Tennent, however, suggests an Egyptian origin, "*Siela-keh*," "the land of Siela." Ptolemy makes mention of the fact that the natives of the island wore their hair long, as they do up to the present time, which gives them the appearance of women :—

Μαλλοις γυναικοις εἰς ἄπαν ἀναδεδμενος.

Agathemerus, supposed by some historians to have been a contemporary of Ptolemy, and by others to have lived immediately after Ptolemy, alludes to the same fact, and describes the method of dressing the hair. "Men," he says, "who inhabit Ceylon allow their hair an unlimited growth, and bind it on the crown of their heads, after the manner of women." In this description will be recognised the *conde* (knot of hair) of the Sinhalese.

The ancient Chinese books show that at a very early period the Chinese had acquired an intimate knowledge of Ceylon. For this the commercial instincts of the Chinese must, at the outset, have been responsible, succeeded afterwards by the community of religion, which naturally brought the two nations into closer touch. The Sinhalese ambassadors who went to Rome in the time of Pliny related that their ancestors found their way to China through India, over the Himalayan Mountains, long before the sea-route was known. Sang-Shoo, in his history of the northern Shung dynasty, records the purport of the address made by the then king of Ceylon, Mahanama, (A.D. 428) to the emperor of China, through the former's envoy. This address indicates that at this time both the sea and the land routes were known and in use. The first authentic record of a Chinese traveller's experiences and observations in the East Indies is that of Fa Hian. This traveller was a Buddhist pilgrim, who, deploring the imperfect rules of discipline of the Buddhist monks of his country, and their ignorance of the Buddhistical writings, set out for India, and wandered about for many years in search of original copies of these writings. On his return he wrote an account of his exile in foreign lands. He came here in the reign of Mahanama, about A.D. 413, and resided in the island for two years. His observations are interesting, for they present an account of the condition of the island as seen through Chinese spectacles fifteen hundred years ago. His impressions will best be conveyed in his own words :—

"This kingdom of lions is situated on a great island. From east to west it is fifty *yojanas* and from north to south thirty *yojanas*. On every side of it are small islands, perhaps amounting to one hundred in number. They are distant from one another ten to twenty *li* and as much as two hundred *li*. All of them depend on the great island. Most of them produce precious stones and pearls. The *mani* gem is also found in one district, embracing a surface, perhaps, of ten *li*. The king sends a guard to protect the place. If any gems are found, the king claims three out of every ten."

The "kingdom of lions" is of course "Sinhaladwipa," from which the name "Serendib" is derived. The small islands referred to are most probably the Maldives. The *mani* gem must be connected with the Sinhalese word *manika*, and is probably the carbuncle.

"The kingdom had originally no human inhabitants, but only demons and dragons dwelt in it." Here we have the Yakkus and

A SINHALESE MAN WITH CONDE (KNOT OF HAIR).

Nagas of the Mahavansa. "Merchants of different countries resorted here to trade. At the time of traffic the demons did not appear in person, but only exposed their valuable commodities with the value affixed to them. Then the merchantmen, according to the prices marked, purchased the goods and took them away." Note here the conformity of this method of barter with the description by Pliny of the mode of trading between the Sinhalese and the Chinese. "But in consequence of these visits, and the sojourn of the merchants in the country, men of other countries also hearing of the delightful character of the place flocked in great numbers, and so a great populous community was formed. This country enjoys an equable climate without any extremes of temperature either in winter or in summer." "The plants and trees are always verdant. The fields are sown just according to men's inclination; there are no fixed seasons for doing so. Buddha came to this country (in the first instance) from a desire to convert a malevolent dragon. By his spiritual power he planted one foot to the north of the royal city and one on the top of a mountain, the distance between the two being fifteen *yojanas*. Over the impression (on the hill) to the north of the royal city is erected a great tower, in height four hundred and seventy feet. It is adorned with gold and silver, and every precious substance combines to make it perfect. By the side of this tower, moreover, is erected a *sangharama*, which is called 'Abhayagiri' ('the mountain without fear'), containing five thousand priests. They have also built here a Hall of Buddha, which is covered with gold and silver engraved work, conjoined with all the precious substances. In the midst of this Hall is a jasper figure (of Buddha), in height about twenty-two feet. The entire body glitters and sparkles with the seven precious substances, whilst the various characteristic marks are so gloriously portrayed that no words can describe the effect. In the right hand it holds a pearl of inestimable value."

"A former king of this country sent an embassy to mid-India to procure a slip of the Pei-to (Bodhi or Bo) tree. This they planted by the side of the Hall of Buddha. When it was about two hundred and two feet high, the tree began to lean towards the south-east. The king, fearing it would fall, placed eight or nine props round the tree to support it. Just in the place where the tree was thus supported it put forth a branch, which pierced through the props, and descending to the earth, took root. This branch is about twenty inches round. The props, although pierced through the cenfre, still surround the tree, which stands now without their support, yet men have not removed them. Under the tree is erected a chapel, in the middle of which is a figure of Buddha in a sitting posture. Both the clergy and the laity pay reverence to this figure with little intermission. Within the capital, moreover, is erected the chapel of the Tooth of Buddha, in the construction of which all the seven precious substances have been employed. The king purifies himself according to the strictest Brahmanical rules, whilst those men within the city who reverence (this relic) from a principle of belief also compose their passions according to strict rule. This kingdom, from the time when this chapel was erected, has suffered neither from want, famine, calamity, nor revolution. The treasury of this congregation of priests contains numerous gems, and a *mani* jewel of inestimable value. Their king once entered the treasury, and going round it for the purpose of inspection, saw there this *mani* gem. On beholding it, a covetous feeling sprang up in his heart, and he desired to take it away with him. For three days this thought afflicted him, but then he came to his right mind. He directly repaired to the assembly of priests and, bowing down his head, repented of his former wicked purpose, and addressing them, said: 'Would that you make a rule from this time forth for evermore, on no account to allow the king to enter your treasury to look at the jewels, except he be a member of the fraternity and of forty years of age; after that time he may be permitted to enter.'

"There are many noblemen and rich householders within the city. The houses of Sa-pho (Sabæan) merchants are very beautifully adorned. The streets and passages are all smooth and level. At the head of the four principal streets there are preaching halls; on the eighth, fourteenth, and fifteenth day of the month they prepare a lofty throne within each of these buildings, and the religious members of the community of the four classes all congregate to hear the preaching of the Law. The men of this country say that there are in the country altogether fifty or sixty thousand priests, all of whom live in community (take their meals in common). Besides these, the king supplies five or six thousand persons within the city with food. These persons when they require take their alms-bowls and go (to the appointed place), and according to the measure of the bowls, fill them and return. They always bring out the Tooth of Buddha in the middle of the third month. Ten days beforehand, the king magnificently caparisons a great elephant and commissions a man of eloquence and ability to clothe himself in royal apparel, and, riding on the elephant, to sound a drum and proclaim as follows: 'Bodhisatva, during three *asankya kalpas* (myriads of years), underwent every kind of austerity; he spared himself no personal sufferings; he left his country, wife, and child; moreover, he tore out his eyes to bestow them on another; he mangled his flesh to deliver a dove (from a hawk); he sacrificed his head in alms; he gave his body to a famishing tiger; he grudged not his marrow or brain. Thus he endured every sort of agony for the sake of all flesh. Moreover, when he became perfect Buddha, he lived in the world forty-nine years preaching the Law, and teaching and converting men. He gave rest to the wretched; he saved the lost. Having passed through countless births, he entered Nirvana. Since that event is 1,497 years. The eyes of the world were then put out, and all flesh deeply grieved. After ten days the Tooth of (this same) Buddha will be brought forth and taken to the Abhayagiri vihara. Let all ecclesiastical and lay persons who wish to lay up a store of merit prepare and smooth the roads, adorn the streets and highways; let them scatter every kind of flower, and offer incense in religious reverence to the relic.'

THE KANDY PERAHERA PROCESSION.

(The modern prototype of the ceremony described by Fa Hian, the Chinese traveller who visited Ceylon about 413 A.D.)

This proclamation being finished, the king next causes to be placed on both sides of the road representations of the five hundred bodily forms which the Bodhisatva assumed during his successive births. For example, his birth as Su-jin-ho; his appearance as a bright flash of light; his birth as the king of the elephants, and as an antelope. These figures are all painted beautifully in divers colours and have a very life-like appearance. At length the Tooth of Buddha is brought forth and conducted along the principal road. As they proceed on the way, religious offerings are made to it. When they arrive at the Abhayagiri vihara, they place it in the Hall of Buddha, where the clergy and laity all assemble in vast crowds and burn incense, light lamps, and perform every kind of religious ceremony both night and day without ceasing. After ninety complete days, they again return it to the vihara within the city. This chapel is thrown open on the chief holidays for the purpose of religious worship, as the Law of Buddha directs. Forty *li* to the east of the Abhayagiri vihara is a mountain on which is built a chapel called Po-ti (Bodhi); there are about two thousand priests in it. Amongst them is a very distinguished *Shaman* called Ta-mo-kin-ti (Dhammakoti or Dharmagupta). The people of this country greatly respect and reverence him. He resides in a cell, where he has been able to tame the serpents and mice, so that they stop together in one habitat, and are not mutually injurious one to another. Seven *li* to the south of the capital is a chapel called Maha vihara, in which there are three thousand priests."

PART III.

THE MAHAVANSA: 543 B.C. TO 360 B.C.

THE reign of Vijaya lasted uninterruptedly for thirty-eight years, his capital being the city of Tambapanna. "This great monarch," says the chronicle, "when he arrived at the last year of his existence, thus meditated: 'I am advanced in years, and no son is born unto me; shall the dominion acquired by my exertions perish with my demise? For the preservation of the dynasty I ought to send for my brother Sumitta.' Thereupon, consulting his ministers, he despatched a letter of invitation to him, and shortly after having sent that letter, he went to the world of the *devas* (gods)."

Previous to this, Sinhabahu, the father of Vijaya, had died, leaving his throne to his second son, Sumitta, and the latter, unwilling to resign the kingship of so powerful a kingdom, sent instead his younger brother, Panduvasa, to succeed Vijaya on the throne of Lanka. On Vijaya's death, the minister Upatissa governed the kingdom for a year, until the arrival of Panduvasa. Panduvasa and thirty-two noble youths, disguised as devotees, landed at the mouth of the Mahakandara river. The regent Upatissa received him with open arms, and Panduvasa, like his predecessor, sought a consort from India, the daughter of the Sakya prince, Amitodana. Panduvasa was then duly inaugurated king and his consort elevated to the rank of queen. The queen gave birth to ten sons and one daughter, the eldest of whom was Abhaya, and the youngest (the daughter) Çitta. It is said that the soothsayers predicted that Çitta's son would destroy his maternal uncles and usurp the throne. Abhaya, while refusing to carry out the wishes of his brothers that the sister should on this account be put to death, yet thought it prudent to confine her in an apartment in the palace. Her confinement did not, however, prevent her from falling in love with a nephew of Panduvasa, with whom she carried on a secret correspondence. This becoming known to Abhaya, who was now king (474 B.C.), he gave his consent to the marriage, intending the destruction of any male offspring that might be born of the union. A son was born to her, Pandukabhaya, and the princess, fearing for his life, substituted for the real child a female child, while the prince was brought up under the care of a Brahman. When he grew up, the prince gathered round him an army, and took up his stand in an almost impregnable position near the Mahaveli Ganga. Here he remained for four years, in spite of all attempts to dislodge him, until, hearing of the erection of a fortress elsewhere, he suddenly abandoned his camp, defeated the army of Abhaya, and captured the new fortress. After some years of fighting, Pandukabhaya, with the assistance of the Yakkus, succeeded in crushing the forces of his uncles, dethroned Tissa, who had succeeded Abhaya, and ascended the throne himself (B.C. 437). He then transferred the seat of government to Anuradhapura, and by the erection of magnificent buildings and tanks in and around that city, he made proper provision for the sanitation and good government of the country. Çando, son of the Brahman to whose kindness he owed so much, he raised to the rank of Purohita (chief minister). Several hundreds of the lower classes he employed as scavengers of the city by night and by day. He made arrangements for the proper interment of the dead; he divided the whole of the island into villages, fields, and gardens. According to the Mahavansa, this king reigned seventy years, and was succeeded by his son, Mutasiva. Mutasiva constructed the delightful royal garden Mahamegha, adorned with all varieties of fruit and flower bearing trees, and so called from the heavy shower of rain which fell while it was being planted. His reign was a reign of peace and lasted for sixty years. He was succeeded by his son, the great Devanampiya Tissa ("Tissa the delight of the gods"). Around this king and his eventful reign there cluster many legends and much romance. Miracles were said to have taken place on his accession; gems and precious stones rose to the surface of the earth; treasures lying at the bottom of the sea placed themselves on the shores of Lanka; and everything pointed to the beginning of an extraordinary era. During this time the great Asoka was ruling in Maghada, one of the most powerful and enlightened kingdoms of India at the time. Tissa despatched an embassy to the court of Asoka, with valuable presents of gems and pearls. His ambassadors were his maternal nephew, Maha Arita; the Brahman Talihabbata; Malla, his minister of state; and Tissa, his chief accountant. After a voyage of seven days and a journey of seven days, they delivered their presents to Asoka. That monarch, highly appreciating the gifts, conferred ranks on the ambassadors, and, not to be outdone in generosity, sent back gifts, an enumeration of which may serve to illustrate the advanced state of civilisation in the two countries. They consisted of a *chowrie* (a royal fly-flapper); a diadem; a sword of state; a royal parasol; golden slippers; a head ornament; a golden vase; costly clothes that required no washing; a chank, with whorls to the right, containing water from the Ganges river; a royal virgin of great personal charms; sundry golden vessels; a costly howdah (seat placed on an elephant's back); precious medicinal drugs; one hundred and sixty loads of hill paddy—all these being articles necessary for the inauguration of Tissa—together with a complete suite of royal attendants. On the return of the ambassadors, Devanampiya Tissa was inaugurated king of Lanka. The inauguration ceremony was known as *abhiseka*. The word "*abhiseka*" literally means "sprinkling," and as the sprinkling of the sacred water of the Ganges formed the chief feature of the ancient ceremony of the royal inauguration, the ceremony itself was called *abhiseka*. The following description of the ceremony is contained in the Pali commentary on the Mahavansa, known as the Mahavansa Tika, in which it has been embodied from an ancient Buddhist work. Apart from its inherent interest, it affords an instructive glimpse into the constitution of ancient society in Lanka.

"Thus it is written in the Sinhalese commentary on that portion of the Majjhimanikaya known as Cullasihanadasuttavannana: 'He who wishes to be duly inaugurated as king should obtain for this purpose three chanks, golden or otherwise, of water from the Ganges river, and a maiden of the Kshattriya (warrior) race. He himself must be ripe for the ceremony and be a Kshattriya of noble lineage, and must sit on a splendid *udumbara* (*Ficus glomerata*) chair, well set in the middle of the pavilion, made of *udumbara* branches, which is itself in the interior of a hall gaily decked for the ceremony of *abhiseka*.

"'First of all the Kshattriya maiden of gentle race, clothed in festival attire, taking in both her hands the right-handed sea-chank, filled with water from the Ganges, raises it aloft and pours the *abhiseka* water over his head, saying as follows: "Sire, by this ceremony of *abhiseka* all the people of the Kshattriya race make thee their maharaja (sovereign), for their protection; do thou rule over the land in uprightness and imbued with the ten royal virtues; have thou for the Kshattriya race a heart filled with paternal love and solicitude; let them (in return) protect and guard and cherish thee." Next, the royal chaplain, splendidly attired in a manner befitting his office, taking in both his hands a silver chank, filled with water from the Ganges, and raising it aloft, pours the *abhiseka* water over his head, and says as follows: "Sire, by this ceremony of *abhiseka* all the people of the Brahman race make thee their maharaja, for their protection; do thou rule over the land in uprightness and imbued with the ten royal virtues; have thou for the Brahman race a heart filled with paternal love and solicitude; let them (in return) protect and guard and cherish thee." Next, he who holds the office of Setthi, attired in a suitable manner, taking in both his hands the golden chank filled with water from the Ganges, and raising it aloft, pours the *abhiseka* water over his head, and says as follows: "Sire, by this ceremony of *abhiseka* all the Grahapati for their protection make thee their maharaja; do thou rule over the land in uprightness and imbued with the ten royal virtues; have thou for the Grahapati a heart filled with paternal love and solicitude; let them (in return) protect and guard and cherish thee."

"'Those who address the above form of words pronounce, as it were, a curse upon the king, as if they should say: "It is meet that thou shouldst rule the land in accordance with these our words; should it not be so, mayst thy head split in seven pieces!"

"'In this island of Lanka, be it known that a Kshattriya princess, sent by Dharmasoka, performed the ceremony of *abhiseka* over the head of Devanampiya Tissa, with the right-handed sea-chank filled with water from Lake Anotata.'"

To be "ripe for the ceremony" meant that the king should have passed his sixteenth year of age. The "ten royal virtues" were: *dhanam* (almsgiving), *silam* (observance of the precepts), *pariccaga* (generosity), *akkodha* (freedom from wrath), *avihimsa* (mercy), *khanti* (forbearance), *ajjavam* (rectitude), *maddavam* (mildness), *tapa* (self-mortification), and *avirodhana* (freedom from enmity).

The royal chaplain was called Purohita. He was always a Brahman and was the king's domestic chaplain. The "Setthi," generally a wealthy merchant, was the king's treasurer; "Grahapati" was the head of a household; "Lake Anotata" was the name of one of the seven great lakes of the river Ganges.

It would thus appear that the king in these ancient times was regarded less in the light of a ruling despot than in that of a representative and leader of the people. Himself a Kshattriya, he was the leader of that noble race; to him was entrusted the care of the priestly Brahmans and the welfare of the rest of his subjects generally. As regards the latter, the fact that their spokesman was the most influential of the Grahapati confirms the theory propounded by Sir Henry Maine and others, that ancient Ceylon formed no exception to the rule that in archaic society the unit of the State was the family and not the individual.

It would also appear from the above extract that the introduction of the *abhiseka* ceremony into Ceylon was cotemporaneous with the adoption of Buddhism as her State religion. But there is no reason to suppose that the ceremony was purely of Buddhistic origin. A new religion seldom adopts an entirely fresh ritual so as to suit the new circumstances; and in the *abhiseka* ceremony one sees but a revised edition of the Vedantic ceremony of the royal inauguration. From what can be gathered from Vedantic literature, the Hindu ceremony of the royal inauguration, which must have been the one performed on Vijaya, was but the parent of the Buddhist ceremony. Here is an extract from the Aitareya Brahmana, viii. 6–9:—

"He (the priest) spreads the tiger skin on the throne in such a manner that the fur is on the outside and that part which formed the neck is turned eastward; for the tiger is the *Kshattra* (royal power) of the beasts in the forests. The king, when taking his seat on the throne, approaches it from behind, turning his face eastward, kneels down with crossed legs, so that his right knee touches the earth, and holding the throne with his hands, prays over it a proper mantra. The priest then pours the holy water over the king's head and repeats the following: 'With these waters, which are happy, which cure everything, increase the royal power, the immortal Prajapati sprinkled Indra, Soma sprinkled the royal Varuna, and Yama sprinkled Manu, with the same I sprinkle thee. Be the ruler over kings in this world,' &c. At the conclusion of the ceremony the king partakes of a drink of wine made out of soma juice, which the priest hands to him."

Buddhism, with its hatred and abhorrence of the slaughter of animals and of the use of wine, has eliminated the tiger skin and the soma juice, while it has retained the pouring of the sacred water. In both instances was the newly inaugurated king exhorted to do his duty by his subjects. "They that wish to be rulers, then, from this day judge the strong and the weak with equal justice, resolving on doing good incessantly to the public and protecting the country from all calamities" (White, "Yajur Veda," x. 27).

PART IV.

THE INTRODUCTION OF BUDDHISM.

ASOKA, the king of Maghada, in his desire to introduce Buddhism into Ceylon, sent his son Mahinda, the prince-priest, to help Devanampiya Tissa to establish on a permanent foundation the faith of Buddha. The legends of his arrival in the island narrate that while the king was out elk hunting, taking with him a retinue of forty thousand men, he chased an elk which he had spied. The elk fled to the mountain and disappeared, and in its place the king found a Thera (Buddhist priest). The Thera accosted the king and announced himself as the minister and disciple of the Law of the True Faith. Laying aside his bow and arrow, the king conversed with the priest, and that moment the king's retinue as well as the priests who formed the retinue of the Thera arrived simultaneously. The Thera was Mahinda, the son of Asoka. For the purpose of ascertaining the intelligence of the sovereign, the Thera interrogated him, and the following quaint dialogue ensued :—

"O king," asked Mahinda, "what is this tree ?"

"It is called the *amba* (mango) tree," answered the king.

"Besides this one, is there any other *amba* tree ?"

"There are many *amba* trees," replied the king.

"Besides this *amba* and those other *amba* trees, are there any other trees on earth ?" inquired the Thera.

"Lord, there are many trees, but there are not *amba* trees."

"Besides the other *amba* trees and the trees that are not *amba* trees, is there any other tree ?"

"Gracious lord, this *amba* tree !"

"Ruler of men," said the Thera, "thou art wise."

Pursuing the conversation further, the Thera asked :

"King, have you any relations ?"

"Lord, I have many," said the king.

"King, are there any persons not thy relations ?"

"There are many who are not my relations," replied the king.

"Besides thy relations and those who are not thy relations, is there or is there not any other (human being in existence) ?"

"Lord," answered the king, "there is myself !"

"Ruler of men," said the Thera, "sadhu ! thou art wise !"

Mahinda, thus satisfied of the more than ordinary intelligence of the king, discoursed with him on Buddhism, and converted him. The Thera was then invited to preach in the royal city and the pleasure garden of the king. All the people congregated to hear him. Even the women-folk gathered in large numbers to listen to the divine message, and, convinced by the force of his eloquence, they, led by the king's sister-in-law, demanded to be made priestesses. The crowd was so great that even the royal stables where the king's elephants were kept had to be thrown open to the people. Mahinda, unable to accede to the request of the would-be priestesses, urged them to invite his sister, Sanghamitta, who was a celebrated priestess. The prime minister was thereupon sent on a second embassy to Asoka for this purpose ; but the latter, having already lost his son, was unwilling to lose a daughter as well. The devotion of Sanghamitta to her religion, however, overcame her filial love, and Asoka reluctantly consented to her departure to Ceylon. Sanghamitta brought with her a branch of the sacred Bo-tree (*Ficus religiosa*) under which Gautama Buddha was wont to meditate. On her arrival in Ceylon, she and the sacred gift that she brought with her were received with great honour. From the seashore to Anuradhapura they were accompanied by a dense multitude, and the branch planted by her (*circa* B.C. 288) still stands as the great Bo-tree of Anuradhapura—still, as it used to be twenty-one centuries ago, an object of veneration and worship, not only by the Buddhists of Ceylon, but by the Buddhists of the world. The queen herself became a candidate for the priesthood. Religious houses were established ; dagobas and viharas multiplied ; rock temples and cells for priests were scattered over the whole island. The chief of the religious buildings erected during this reign was the Thuparama dagoba, the ruins of which still attest its great beauty. The Mahamegha pleasure gardens were made over to the priesthood. The Maha vihara, the first great temple of the island, was built. Tissa reigned for forty years. Says the chronicle: "The island was plenteous during this king's reign, and delighting in the exercise of his benevolence during the whole of his life, he performed many acts of merit."

The mountain on which Mahinda met the king, and which subsequently became the scene of his meditation, is identical with the present Mihintale. The cell in which he lived and the stone bed on which he slept are still to be seen, and have been the objects of veneration by millions of people, as is testified to by the worn state of the one thousand two hundred stone steps of the gallery leading to the top of the mountain.

At this time Ceylon had been split up into three geographical divisions, due primarily to the fact that Vijaya permitted the formation of petty kingdoms in various districts of the island. All the country north of the Mahaveli Ganga was Pihitirata or Rajarata, so called from the circumstance that the ancient capital and residence of the emperor was situated in it. In the south was Ruhunurata, being bounded on the south and east by sea, by the Mahaveli Ganga on the north, and Kalu Ganga on the north and west. On the east was Mayarata, of which the northern boundary was the Deduru-Oya, and the southern the Kalu Ganga. While Anuradhapura was the chief city and the capital of Pihitirata, the ancient city of Magama was the capital of Ruhunurata, and Kelaniya was capital of Mayarata. The kings of Mayarata and Ruhunurata used regularly to pay an annual tribute to their lord at Anuradhapura.

On the death of Devanampiya Tissa he was succeeded by his brother Uttiya (B.C. 267). His was an uneventful reign. In the eighth year of his reign the great Apostle of Ceylon, Mahinda, died at Mihintale. King Uttiya was overpowered with grief on hearing of his death, and the body, embalmed in scented oil, was deposited in a golden coffin filled with spices and perfumes, which was then placed in a second coffin of sandal wood. The body was brought to the capital in magnificent procession. The Maha vihara and the space of three-*yojanas* round it were ornamented with triumphal arches, banners, and flowers. Immense crowds surged through the streets of Anuradhapura. The king himself set fire to the funeral-pyre, and the ashes of the deceased missionary were enshrined in the dagoba of Mihintale. A year later, Sanghamitta, the female apostle and sister of Mahinda, died, and similar honours were paid to her. Their names are still household words among the Sinhalese.

VIEWS OF MIHINTALE AND ANURADHAPURA.

MIHINTALE.
The Ambastale Dagoba, in which the ashes of Mahinda, the Great Apostle of Buddhism, were deposited, according to tradition.

MIHINTALE.
First flight of the famous stone steps to the summit of the sacred hill.

MIHINTALE.
Under the cavity in the large boulder to the left is Mahinda's Bed, so called.

MIHINTALE.
The third and narrowest flight of steps.

ANURADHAPURA.
The Sacred Bo-Tree,

PART V.

THE MAHAVANSA: 257 B.C. TO 304 A.D.

UTTIYA died after reigning ten years, and was succeeded by Mahasiva, a younger brother of Uttiya, who himself reigned ten years (257 B.C. to 247 B.C.). He is described by the chronicler as the "patron of righteous men." Suratissa then came to the throne (B.C. 247). He was the younger brother of Mahasiva. He erected many beautiful viharas, and is described as "the delighter in acts of piety." Whether it was that he feared rebellion among his own people, or whether it was that he merely intended to increase the pomp and pageantry of his court, he welcomed, if he did not invite, to his service two generals of cavalry, Sena and Guttika, with their followers. They came from the neighbouring continent, and in course of time murdered Suratissa and usurped the throne. They are described as two "demala (Tamil) youths, powerful in their cavalry and navy, who put to death this protector of the land, who righteously reigned for twenty-two years." In 215 B.C. Asela, the son of Mutasiva, fought and put to death the usurpers and restored the royal line in his person. But the Tamils had tasted the sweets of Lanka, and, loath to suffer it to pass out of their hands, banded themselves together under Elala, a powerful chieftain of Tanjore (on the Coromandel Coast) and determined to meet the vanquisher of Sena and Guttika and to recover the throne of Lanka. Landing a large force at the mouth of the Mahaveli Ganga, Elala marched straight to the city of Anuradhapura, attacked and captured it, and put to death the king Asela. He assumed the reins of government, fortified Anuradhapura, and erected thirty-two fortresses for the Tamils. His authority was acknowledged by the native chiefs in the island, except those of Ruhunurata, the southern division, which was still governed by a branch of the old royal family. It was from here that opposition came. In the time of Devanampiya Tissa, Mahamegha was king of Ruhunurata, and paid tribute to Tissa. His grandson, Kavantissa, had two sons, Gamini and Tissa. Gamini, chagrined at the dethronement of the older branch of the royal family, determined to devote his life to regaining the throne. His method of collecting an army was unique. Having selected ten warriors of the greatest prowess, each of them was required to enlist ten men; each of the latter, in like manner, enlisted ten men, and by the repetition of the process Gamini's army grew to be a body of ten thousand men. Gamini's eagerness to fight was damped by the caution of the king, his father, who feared the results of a war with Elala. Gamini, however, enraged at his father's cowardice, despatched a number of female ornaments to him, bidding him don them as more befitting his character! He evaded the consequences of his act by flight to Udapalata, among the mountains, and by his disobedience earned the name of Duttagamini (disobedient Gamini). His father's death occurring soon after, he immediately advanced to Magama, his father's capital, but only to find that his younger brother had proclaimed himself king in the Batticaloa district. He then marched against Tissa, and defeated him in a sanguinary battle. By a second battle, in which the brothers came in personal conflict, Tissa was convinced of the futility of opposing Gamini, and by the intervention of the priests they were reconciled. Leaving Tissa as his sub-king at Magama, Gamini now gathered together his great army—the "fourfold army" as the chroniclers describe it—infantry and chariots. Crossing Mahaveli Ganga, he arrived at Vijitapura, the city founded by the brother-in-law of Panduvasa three hundred years before. The siege of Vijitapura is said to have lasted for several months, and was brought to a close by a general assault. The outer entrenchments were captured, but the big iron gate leading to the centre of the city resisted for a long time the efforts of the besieging army. The most powerful elephant in Gamini's army, long inured to war, was forced against the gate, only to receive on his body a stream of molten lead and stones. But the infuriated animal was then covered with buffalo hide and once more rushed the gate and burst it open. After the capture of Vijitapura, Gamini, with a view of taking Anuradhapura, threw up fortresses at Kasagalyana and halted there. The following account of the great and decisive battle which ensued is from the Sinhalese chronicle, the Rajavaliya:—

"King Elala, on hearing that King Duttugemunu (Duttagamini) was halting at Kasagalyana, and had encamped there, sent for the Sinhalese ministers who were then in the Tamil city, and addressing himself to them, said, 'What think ye, my ministers? King Duttagemunu has reduced thirty-two fortresses, commencing with Majurguna, and having attacked Vijitapura, has reduced it and taken up his quarters at Kasagalyana. How shall we conduct the war?' The ministers replied, 'Let us take the fourfold army and go out to battle to-morrow.' King Elala thereupon sent a letter written in the following terms: 'King Duttugemunu, what profiteth it to you to stay at Kasagalyana? Come out to-morrow to battle.' When the letter sent by King Elala was brought and given to Duttugemunu, he read it, and in reply wrote, 'We were coming; come ye.' Having written and sent the above answer, he called together the ten great champions and asked them, 'Shall we go out to-morrow to fight with the twenty mighty champions of the great King Elala, with his army, which is like the army of Mara, or shall we forbear?' The ten great champions answering said, 'Even if the royal armies of the whole of Dambadiva were to come out, they should not gain a victory when we are present, let alone the army of one king, Elala. Fear not, O great king!'

"King Elala, attended by his fourfold army which resembled Mara's host, and by Dighajantu and the rest of his twenty great champions, set out from Anuradhapura and came to fight. King Gemunu, standing in the midst of his fortress with his pearl *sata* (canopy) raised over him, caused the couch and shield to be held on either side, had sixty-four drums beaten, making a mighty uproar like a thunder-clap on Yughandara rock; caused Nandimitra to stand on the right side and Nirmalaya on his left; and having posted the rest of the champions for the attack, he stood his ground with his fourfold army in readiness. King Elala, mounted on the elephant called Maha Parvata, went out and examined the camp at Kasagalyana. The flag-bearing captain, Dighajantu, who was the chief among the twenty champions, saw the pearl *sata* in the place where King Gemunu was standing, and thinking within himself, 'I will first strike down the king and then attack the army,' having sprung eighty cubits into the air, was coming down to strike the king, when the champion Nirmalaya took up the sword and shield and rushed out, saying, 'Where goest thou, worthless Tamil?' On hearing these words, Dighajantu, instead of approaching the king, ran towards Nirmalaya and cut at him with his sword. The champion Nirmalaya, when he was (about to be) struck, held out his shield, whereupon, the blow having alighted on the shield, Dighajantu hurt his hand, and his sword fell to the ground; while he was stooping to grasp it again, Nirmalaya struck him, cutting him in twain. The ten mighty champions and the army of Gemunu rushed into the midst of the Tamil army, and killed so many that the blood which flowed from them united and filled a tank.

"King Gemunu having given orders not to kill Elala, mounted on the *Kodol* elephant, pursued him, caused the two elephants to gore each other with their tusks, and hurled a javelin at King Elala, which pierced and killed him. In the place where he was killed he set up a stone pillar inscription to this effect:

'Let no prince in future pass this way riding in palanquin or litter or with the beating of drums.' And after having cremated the body of Elala, he entered the city of Anuradhapura as if he had been the god-king, Sakra."

Thus fell Elala, usurper though he was, yet of royal race and of indomitable courage. For twenty-two years he ruled the country wisely and dealt justice to all without distinction. His solicitude for the welfare of his subjects was so great that their grievances were personally inquired into by him. He kept a bell near his head with a cord attached to it, that those who desired to see him at night might obtain audience by ringing it. His gallant foe, Gamini, summoning within the city the whole of the inhabitants of the district, held a festival in honour of King Elala. The chronicler of the Mahavansa, writing in the fifth century of the Christian Era, notes that "even unto this day, monarchs who succeed to the throne of Lanka, on reaching that quarter of the city in procession, paid the same honour and silenced their musical band." And in later times, in 1826, Pilimi Talawwa, a scion of an ancient Kandyan house, when escaping through Anuradhapura after the failure of the rebellion against the British Government in which he had been engaged, alighted from his palanquin, although he was in a severe state of fatigue and exhaustion, and, though unaware of the precise spot wherein was Elala's tomb, proceeded on foot until he was sure he had passed far beyond this ancient memorial.

During the siege of Vijitapura, King Elala had sent messages to his kinsfolk in India, informing them of the insecurity of his throne and of the war that was being waged by Duttagamini. In consequence of this information, his younger brother, Bhaluka, set out from the continent with an army of thirty thousand Tamils. On his arrival in Ceylon he was apprised of the death of his brother, whereupon he swore an oath that he would not return to his country without avenging his brother's death, and having written a letter in this strain to King Gamini, he awaited the attack. In the very first encounter, however, the invader was slain, and the Tamils, thus bereft of their leader, were easily routed. The success of this battle and the utter overthrow of the Tamil invaders were followed by festivals of great rejoicing and religious ceremonies, and rewards and marks of royal favour were lavishly distributed among the conquerors. "Subsequently," says the Mahavansa, "while seated on his throne, which was covered with drapery of exquisite value and softness, in the state apartment, lighted up with aromatic oils and perfumed with every variety of incense and spread with the richest carpets, attended by musicians and choristers, this monarch was pondering over his exalted royal state and calling to his recollection the sacrifice of countless lives he had occasioned, and peace of mind was denied to him." It will thus be seen that the elation consequent upon Gamini's succession was followed by a reaction in which he was reminded of the number of lives lost in the wars for which he was responsible; and fearing that thereby he might have forfeited his own hope of mercy, he consulted a deputation of eight priests of great sanctity. The king prostrated himself before these saintly men, and after washing their feet and anointing them with fragrant oil, made them sit upon the throne, and in deep obeisance explained to them the cause of his trouble. The wise men answered, after hearing his confession, that he was only responsible for the lives of two human beings who had been Buddhists; the rest being heretics and sinners, and their destruction having been with a view to preserving the religion of Buddha, there would be no impediment to the king's attainment of *sagga* (heaven). The priests advised him, therefore, to devote himself to tasks which would glorify and propagate Buddhism. In fulfilment of this behest the king spent the remainder of his life, and devoted his immense resources to the building of temples, dagobas, and houses for the priests. He built the Lowa Maha Paya, or the "Great Brazen Palace," which measured two hundred and twenty-five feet square and was of an equal height. The apartments rested on sixteen hundred granite pillars placed in forty parallel columns of forty pillars each. Over these were nine storeys, each storey containing one hundred apartments, and the whole edifice was roofed with brass —hence the name of "Brazen Palace." The ruins of this stupendous structure as they stand at the present day testify to its grandeur. The interior of the edifice was magnificent. A spacious hall, adorned with statues of lions and elephants, all of gold, occupied the centre. At one end was raised an ivory throne of singular beauty, flanked on either side by emblems of the sun and the moon. He also built the Ruanveli Seya, or the "Mahathupa" as it was called, which was two hundred and seventy feet in height—so called because the outside of the edifice was ornamented with gold-dust. Its ruins now form a conical mass and rise to a height of nearly a hundred and ninety feet. It originally stood in a large square paved with stones of dressed granite and surrounded by a fosse seventy feet broad. This huge dagoba Gamini did not live to complete. But his love for the structure was such that he had himself carried to a spot facing the dagoba, so that his dying eyes might be gladdened by its sight. And there, after twenty-four years of unparalleled sovereignty, his career was ended. His last remark was that, though he had overcome all his enemies, death was an antagonist he could not vanquish; and over his life the chronicler draws this moral: "Thus, he who is ever intent on good works and does them, covers a multitude of venial sins, and enters into heaven as freely as he does into his own house. Therefore should the man of wisdom be constantly diligent in good works."

Gamini's only son, Sali, failed to inherit the ambition or the capacity of his father. Becoming enamoured of a beautiful woman of the Çandala (scavenger) class, Sali preferred domestic happiness to royal sway, and gave up the succession to his uncle, Saddhatissa, the brother of Gamini. Saddhatissa's reign was peaceful and uneventful, except for the fact that he vigorously continued his brother's policy, constructing tanks and building dagobas. On his death (B.C. 119) the priests declared in favour of his brother Tuluna; but his reign was short-lived, for the rightful heir, Laminitissa, the son of Saddhatissa, defeated and slew his uncle and seized the throne. Laminitissa's reign, which lasted till B.C. 112, was uneventful, and he was succeeded by his brother Kalune, who reigned for six years, when he was assassinated by his minister, Maharattaka. But his death was avenged by his brother, Valagambahu, who thus cleared his way to the throne. He adopted as his own son Mahakula, the son of the late king, and conferred on his mother, Anula, the royal title of queen, in consequence of which the people gave him the appellation of "father-king." A Brahman youth named Tiya, in the city of Nakula, in Ruhunurata, believing the prophecy of a foolish Brahman who predicted that he would become king, raised the standard of revolt in the south and succeeded in gaining a large number of followers, during this reign. About this time also seven Tamil chieftains with an army of seven thousand men from the Choli country, in the neighbouring continent, landed in Lanka, and made common cause with Tiya. Tiya and the Tamil chieftains thereupon despatched a letter to the king demanding the surrender of the sovereignty, to which the king sent this shrewd reply: "The kingdom is thine from this day if thou but subduest the Tamils!" Tiya then attacked the Tamils, and had the misfortune to be beaten and made prisoner The Tamils then waged war against the king, defeating him in a great battle which compelled him to leave the capital and take shelter in Ruhuna. The queen Anula succeeded in escaping to the king, but the queen Somadevi fell into the hands of the Tamils. For fourteen years the Tamil chiefs governed the island, but differences having arisen amongst them, they slew each other in their struggle for precedence and supremacy, until there was one left, whom Valagambahu finally overcame and recovered his queen and crown (B.C. 89). In thanksgiving, the king built the Abhayagiri dagoba of four hundred feet in height, and the largest of the dagobas in Lanka, as also the Dambulla vihara, which exists to the present day. It was in the reign of this king that the Tripitaka ("Threefold collection")—the first religious books of Buddhism—were committed to writing. He is also the first king known to Sinhalese history who issued coined money. The coins were of an oblong shape and made of copper, bearing on their obverse the figure of a human being, and on their reverse a modification of the ancient *swastika* emblem. His successor was his son Mahakula, who reigned for six years, until B.C. 62, and was in turn succeeded by his brother, Coranaga, who reigned for twelve years, when his son Kudatissa came to the throne. The latter's reign only lasted three years; he was poisoned by his mother, the queen Anula, in 47 B.C. The act was prompted by an unholy passion which the queen had conceived for an obscure Tamil, named Watuka. Her design was to raise this individual to the throne. But the fickle queen soon turned from her paramour, and ultimately his life was sacrificed in order that she might more readily carry on a new intrigue which she had entered upon with a firewood carrier who served in the palace. Anula's career throughout was marked by illicit passion, leading to deeds of villainy and murder. Within her short reign of six years she married and got rid of no less than thirty-two husbands! Makalantissa, her son by Kudatissa, had early in life taken to the religious habit through fear of his mother. But hearing of the cruelties perpetrated by his mother, he disrobed himself, and collecting an army, successfully besieged and captured the city of Anuradhapura. Anula, unwilling to capitulate, was burnt in the flames which consumed the palace. On every side there were grounds for dismay owing to the disorganised state of the kingdom. The fortifications of Anuradhapura demanded the king's earliest attention; and he erected a stone rampart 10½ feet high round the sixteen miles which formed the perimeter of the city. The rampart is said to have encompassed a space of two hundred and forty-four square miles. Seven miles from the modern city of Anuradhapura is still to be seen the west face, running north and south of this ancient structure. This king also built a stone dagoba at Mihintale, and during his peaceful and prosperous reign of twenty-two years he caused to be constructed several tanks and public buildings. He was succeeded (B.C. 20) by Bhatiyatissa, his son, known as Bhatiya the Pious, who reigned for ten years. He set apart a portion of the revenue for the repair of the public buildings and daily fed a thousand priests. As evidence of his great piety, the marks of his knees on the granite pavement surrounding the Ruanveli dagoba are still shown. It is believed by the Buddhists that this king obtained supernatural assistance which enabled him to open the underground entrance leading to the interior of the dagoba, so that he might worship the many sacred relics of Buddha which it contained. A stone slab 12½ feet long by 9½ feet broad is to be seen a little way from the outer enclosure of the dagoba, and is supposed to cover the secret entrance by which the pious king gained admittance to the interior. After a reign of twenty-nine years, Bhatiya died in the ninth year of the Christian era.

The reigns of the next nine kings were uneventful, and may be summarised as follows:—

Mahadailiya (A.D. 9–21), son of Bhatiyatissa;

Addagaimunu (A.D. 21–30), son of Mahadailiya, murdered by his brother, Kinihiridalla;

Kinihiridalla (A.D. 30–33), son of Mahadailiya;

Cholabhaya (A.D. 33–34), son of Addagaimunu;

Sivala (queen—A.D. 34), sister of Chola, murdered by her son, Elluna;

Elluna (A.D. 34–40), son of Kinihiridalla;

Sandamuna (A.D. 40–49), son of Elluna, murdered by his brother, Yatalaka Tissa or Yassa Sila;

Yassa Sila (A.D. 49–56), brother of Sandamuna, murdered; and

Subbho (usurper—A.D. 56–62), defeated and slain by Vasabbha.

Vasabbha came to the throne in 66 A.D. and reigned for forty-four years. This king dedicated his life to the service of religion and the erection of religious buildings. The rampart round Anuradhapura he raised to the height of eighteen cubits, and he constructed twelve large tanks in various parts of the island. He built a circular relic house at the Thuparama dagoba, and after a long and peaceful reign left his son, Vankanasika Tissa, to the tranquil possession of the throne. During the reign of this prince the king of the Soli country landed in the north-west of the island, ravaged that part of the country, and coming up within sight of Anuradhapura, retired with an immense quantity of plunder and twelve thousand Sinhalese captives. This insult was not avenged during this short reign of three years, and it was left to his son Gajabahu, who succeeded him in 113 A.D., to take measures for the removal of the stigma. This the young prince did, and not only were the Solians severely punished for the outrages committed by them in the island, but twelve thousand of their number were taken captives and brought to Ceylon as prisoners-of-war, most of them being interned in the north-western portion of the island.

The successor of Gajabahu was his maternal cousin, Mahalu Naga—so called from the great age at which he ascended the throne. He reigned for six years and constructed seven viharas. In 141 A.D. he was succeeded by his son, Bhatiyatissa II. This prince, too, added to the number of viharas and tanks in his kingdom. It was in his reign that one of the chieftains named Nala Mudaliyar created a rebellion. To suppress him the king sent to India for mercenaries, who, consisting of cavalry, infantry, and artillery, with nine distinguished generals in command, arrived from Ayodhapatnam, and landed at Kuduramala (the Hipporos of Pliny). The Ayodha here referred to is not the modern Oudh, but a seaport of the same name in the west of India. These regiments were successful in defeating Nala Mudaliyar and quelling the rebellion, and the king, in gratitude, granted them the whole of the territory lying between the Kala-Oya and the Maha-Oya. These facts are recorded in the Wanni Rajavaliya chronicle, and it is noteworthy that this is the first historical mention of artillery in Sinhalese warfare The long reign of Bhatiyatissa II. was followed by the longer reign of his brother, Kanittha Tissa. This king reigned for twenty-eight years, and, following the example of his predecessors, improved the Abhayagiri vihara and enclosed it with a wall. He constructed a covering for the Thupa at the Dakkhina vihara, and levelling the buildings within the Mahamegha garden, built a huge refreshment hall. His son, Chula Naga, only reigned two years, and was succeeded (A.D. 195) by his younger brother, Kuda Naga. The brother of his queen, named Siri Naga, who was the commander-in-chief, turned traitor to him, and at the head of a very powerful army defeated and killed the king, and as Siri Naga I. reigned for nineteen years. On his death, in 215 A.D., his son, Abhaya Tissa, succeeded to the throne. He is described as having been thoroughly conversant with the principles of justice and equity, and ruled for twenty-two years. He abolished the practice of inflicting torture which up to this time had been in vogue, thus acquiring the appellation of Voharaka Tissaraja. It was in the reign of this king that the Wytulian heresy made an effort to engraft itself on the Buddhist Church in Ceylon. By the instrumentality of the minister, Kapila, he suppressed the heresy and punished the impious members. Ultimately he fell a victim to the passion of his younger brother, Abhaya Tissa, who had conceived an affection for his queen, and who, advancing at the head of a large army on the capital, seized it and captured the king and queen at Malaya. He put the former to death, and with the queen returned to the capital

THE THUPARAMA DAGOBA, ANURADHAPURA.

and reigned for eight years (A.D. 237–245). His reign was uneventful, and so was that of his successor, his nephew, Siri Naga II. Then Vijaya II. came to the throne (247 A.D.). He was, however, soon put to death by Sanga Tissa, the commander of his army. This king is said to have placed a glass pinnacle on the spire of the Ruanveli dagoba, to serve as a protection against lightning—a fact which speaks well for the advanced state of Sinhalese science at this early period. Sanga Tissa was succeeded in 252 A.D. by Sri Sangha Bodhi, who is regarded by Buddhists as a saintly king. In his reign famine and pestilence ravaged the country and thinned the population, and the misfortune was attributed to the wrath of a demon "with red eyes," to placate which a dance—the origin of the modern devil-dance—was introduced. A minister of this king, named Gotabhaya, having conspired to remove him from the throne, the king left the city in solitude, abhorring the idea of a civil war, taking with him only his water strainer. His end is thus described by the Mahavansa chronicler: "The man who was travelling along with him on the road, carrying his meal of dressed rice with him, over and over again entreated of the raja to partake of the rice. This benevolent character, having strained the water he used to drink and made his meal, in order that he might confer a reward on him who presented the repast, thus addressed him: 'I am the raja Sangha Bodhi; beloved, taking my head, present it to Gotabhaya; he will bestow great wealth on thee.' The peasant declined to do so; but the monarch, for the purpose of benefiting that individual, bequeathing his head to him by detaching it from his shoulder, expired without rising on the spot on which he had taken his meal. The peasant presented the head to Gotabhaya; and, astonished at the statement made by the peasant, he conferred great wealth on him, and rendered him all the kind offices a monarch could bestow." Sangha Bodhi's reign has been a subject around which clusters many a tradition, and kings of the later period who ruled in Kotta, and who claimed descent from him, wore as their proudest title that of "Sri Sangha Bodhi."

During the reign of Gotabhaya the Wytulian heresy again reared its head and called forth a good number of the priesthood, including Sanghamitta, the tutor of the king's sons. The elder son, Makalantissa, refused to be influenced by the new doctrine, and on succeeding to the throne, whereon he ruled for ten years up to 277 A.D., protected the established religion by every means in his power. But his good work was set at naught by his younger brother, Maha Sen, who succeeded him, and who adopted the new doctrines. Maha Sen established the new sect as the State Church, and forbade the bestowal of offerings on the priests who refused to conform to his views. Thus deprived of food, the latter in their distress took refuge in Ruhunurata. Inflamed with anger at their obstinacy in adhering to their old doctrines, Maha Sen demolished their temples and houses. The Brazen Palace was rased to the ground, its site ploughed up and sown with rice; and with the materials of this and over three hundred and sixty other ecclesiastical buildings he built temples for the service of the new sect. He recalled the priests in exile whom his father had banished, and gave them Mihintale, and employed every device to establish the heresy on a permanent footing. But things were becoming very serious, and a rebellion of his subjects seemed imminent in consequence of the iconoclastic acts he had perpetrated. A powerful minister who had been in his service resolved on an appeal to arms, and concentrated his camp in the mountainous district round Adam's Peak. Maha Sen had to choose between the loss of his crown and the change of his religion. He thought the latter preferable, and recalled the rebellious minister to favour, beheaded his tutor Sanghamitta, and restored the old religion. He now became as eager to restore the old religion as he had once been to destroy it. He rebuilt all the temples he had pulled down, recalled the priests from exile, and reconstructed their houses. He also built sixteen tanks, and a large canal which served to irrigate twenty thousand fields. He is known in Sinhalese history as the last of the Mahavansa or "Great Dynasty" of the island.

PART VI.

THE SULUVANSA: 304 A.D. TO 1152 A.D.

THE next king, Kitsiri Nivana, the successor of Maha Sen, is known to history as the first sovereign of the Suluvansa, or "Lower Dynasty." The distinction here sought to be drawn is of the chronicler's own making, and does not arise out of the internal supersession of the reigning line or as a result of foreign usurpation or conquest. The break in the annals does not affect the continuity of the narrative, and is a change only in name; while the dynasty itself, though differentiated from the Mahavansa as "Lower," has, in point of fact, greater claims to remembrance in respect of the valour and exploits of Sinhalese power in its era and of the zenith to which that power attained.

Kitsiri Nivana continued the work of restoration zealously. In the ninth year of his reign a Brahman princess brought to Ceylon the famous Tooth Relic of Buddha from Kalingarata in India. The monarch received charge of it himself, and with great reverence and the highest honours deposited it in a precious casket and lodged it in a building erected by King Devanampiya Tissa, known as the *Dhama Chakka.* His son, Jettha Tissa II., succeeded him, and the new king rebuilt the Brazen Palace. He was possessed of considerable skill in painting and sculpture. A statue of Buddha of exquisite workmanship is said to have been the work of his hands. His successor was his son, Buddhadasa (241 A.D.), who was a celebrated student of surgery and rural economy. He is described in the chronicle as a "mine of virtues and an ocean of riches." He is said to have effected astonishing cures. A treatise by him on the art of healing, written in Sanskrit, is still extant. To every district of ten villages he appointed a medical man, an astrologer, a priest, and a devil-dancer. He built hospitals and asylums for the maimed and deformed and poverty-stricken. Intense love for humanity and administrative capacity of a high order were the characteristic features of this great king. His son, Upatissa II., succeeded him in 370 A.D. He was a devout prince, and devoted himself to the advancement of religion and the welfare of the priesthood. He built the splendid temple at Attanagalla, in the Western Province, the history of which has been translated into English by the late Hon. Mr. James de Alwis. The Topawewa tank is also ascribed to him. He fell a victim to his wife, who murdered him to satisfy the affection she had formed for her brother-in-law, Mahanama, who, mounting the throne in 412 A.D., reigned for eighteen years. It was in this reign that the celebrated Fa Hian—allusion to whom has been made previously—visited Ceylon. Another illustrious visitor, in the person of Buddhaghosa, came from India. This latter was a learned Buddhist priest and author of some scholarly commentaries on the Buddhist scriptures. On Mahanama's death, his son, Sothi Sena, the lawful heir to the throne, was assassinated by his sister on the day of his accession in order to make room for her husband, Laminitissa. The latter's reign was also a short one, and he was succeeded by Mitha Sena, who had no sooner ascended the throne than the island was invaded by a number of Malabar chiefs, who dethroned him and put him to death. A majority of the Sinhalese chieftains, however, proved faithful in their allegiance to their king, and, fleeing to Ruhunurata, maintained their independence under Dhatusena. For twenty-six long years the struggle ensued, but at the end of that time Dhatusena overcame all opposition and recovered for himself the throne of his ancestors. He extirpated every Tamil in the island, confiscated the lands of their Sinhalese followers, and bestowed them on the nobles who had rallied round him in his exile at Ruhuna. Peace was restored and the old order of things resumed its sway once more. The Mahavansa chronicle, from the date of Vijaya's arrival till the death of Maha Sen, was composed in his reign, the writer being Maha Sen's uncle and tutor, Mahanama, a priest in high office.

Dhatusena had two sons and a daughter, who was married to the Adigar, his sister's son. Being enraged at some ill-treatment which his daughter had suffered at the hands of her husband, the Adigar, King Dhatusena retaliated by putting to death his sister, the Adigar's mother. This created a breach in their relations, and the king's eldest son, Kasyapa, took sides with the Adigar, and avenged the death of his aunt by heading a force against his father, with the assistance of which he dethroned him and finally slew him.

Kasyapa, the parricide king, was not, however, long left in peaceable possession of the throne which he had wrested from his father, for his younger brother, Moggalana, determined to avenge his father's death, and departed to the continent with the idea of collecting an army. Kasyapa, fearing a general outbreak and apprehensive of public sympathy with his brother, left his capital of Anuradhapura and established himself on the rock of Sigiri, which he fortified and converted into a city. Being shaped like a lion, it was called Sigiri, or the "lion rock." It was surrounded by a rock rampart with galleries built into it. Here he lodged his treasures and his regalia. The ruins of Sigiri have recently been almost entirely restored, and afford striking examples of ancient art. In a cave leading out of one of the galleries is to be found to-day, in a fair state of preservation, a number of mural paintings which indicate the high style of art practised in the early days of Sinhalese rule. These paintings are unique in style, and are absolutely unlike the more recent frescoes to be found in Buddhist viharas of Ceylon. Strange to say, however, there are to be found in the caves of Ajanta, in the Deccan (India), similar paintings which indicate the same school of art. These latter are cotemporaneous with the paintings of Sigiri, and a number of them depict incidents in Sinhalese history, such as the preaching of the Arhat (Saint) Mahinda and the bringing of the Tooth Relic to Ceylon. This coincidence suggests that the two sets of paintings were done, if not by the same artist, at least by the same school of artists, and that it was very probably Sinhalese art.

For eighteen years Kasyapa succeeded in evading the vengeance of his brother, but in 497 A.D. Moggalana landed in Ceylon with a large army from India, and a pitched battle ensued between the brothers, in the course of which Kasyapa, finding that the battle was going against him, committed suicide by cutting his throat. It would appear that the commission of suicide by kings and princes in despair, after defeat or at the prospect of defeat in the field of battle, was common at this period, and was regarded as an act of chivalry. On the accession of Moggalana to the throne, his first thought was of revenge, and the Adigar, who was responsible for his father's death, and more than a thousand of his adherents were put to death. This reign was made famous in the annals of the island by the arrival in Ceylon of the sacred Hair Relic of Buddha, which was brought by a young merchant from Benares, and received by the king with great pomp and ceremony. Moggalana was succeeded in 575 A.D. by his son, Kumaradasa, a prince who was devoted to literature, especially to poetry. The celebrated Indian bard named Kalidasa was attracted to his court, and having learnt the Sinhalese language, gained the friendship of his brother-poet, the king, and was by him held in the highest esteem. One night, when Kumaradasa was in the house of a courtesan of whom he was very fond, he saw a bee light on a water-lily, which, on closing, held it captive. The king, deeming he was in a similar position in regard to the courtesan, wrote the following lines on the wall of her house, together with an intimation that any one who should finish the verse, directly interpreting the riddle, would be granted any request he might make :—

> "Wana bambara malanotala ronataveni !
> Mala dedara panagalawa giya seveni !"

Kalidasa was once spending a day in the same house when he saw the king's lines, and completed the verse by prefixing the following couplet :—

> "Siya tambara siyatambara siya seveni !
> Siya sapura nidi nolaba un seveni !"

The king's lines, being translated, would run thus :—

> "If all night long the lotus keeps the bee,
> The morn beholds him gay, unhurt, and free !"

while Kalidasa's couplet solves the riddle in this manner :—

> "By beauty's grasp in turmoil uncomposed,
> He's kept a prisoner with eyes unclosed !"

THE SIGIRI (OR LION) ROCK (GENERAL VIEW FROM THE SOUTH-EAST ACROSS THE TANK).
(In this fortress Kasyapa, the parricide king, established himself after the murder of his father.)

The courtesan, covetous of the prize offered by the king for the competition in verse, murdered the poet, buried him beneath her house, and alleged herself to be the author of the lines. The king, however, feeling sure that no other than Kalidasa could have solved the riddle so successfully, ordered a search to be made for him, which led to the discovery of the body. The body was exhumed and cremated in great state in the presence of the king and the whole court. The king was so distracted with grief that he threw himself into the funeral-pyre and was burnt to death, his example being followed by his five queens, who all perished in the flames. Kumaradasa's immediate successor was Kirtisena, but he was assassinated by his maternal uncle, Sivà, who seized the throne, but was in turn murdered by his brother-in-law, who succeeded to the throne in 525 A.D. as Upatissa III. He was a blind prince, and was remarkable for his melancholy temperament. His son-in-law, Silakala, aimed at subverting the authority of the king, and Upatissa died of grief. Silakala came to the throne in A.D. 526, and after a reign of thirteen years was succeeded by his son, Dapula (539 A.D.). Dapula's reign was terminated by his suicide in the following year, and his elder brother, Moggalana II., then came to the throne and reigned for twenty years, giving place to Meghawarna. He reigned only for one year, and was put to death by his successor, Mahanama, who was descended from a branch of the royal family settled in Ruhunurata. In 564 A.D., by his death, he gave place to his maternal nephew, Agrabodhi I. This king restored order in the country, built the Kurunduwewa and several other tanks, cut a great canal to the tank at Minneriya, and built many religious edifices. He was a great patron of learning, and during his long reign of thirty-four years, twelve great poets are said to have flourished in his court. He was succeeded in 598 A.D. by his son-in-law, Agrabodhi II., who reigned for ten years, after which Sanga Tissa came to the throne, only to have his head cut off by Agrabodhi's general, Dala Moggalana, who was killed in battle the same year.

The next few reigns are steeped in civil war, and it is difficult to say who really wielded the royal power until 624 A.D., when Agrabodhi III. recovered the kingdom and ascended the throne. After his reign of sixteen years came Dathpotissa to the throne. This usurper began his reign by plundering the temples and dagobas and by other acts of devastation. Kasyapa, brother of Agrabodhi III., marched against him from Ruhuna, and gave him battle, and the usurper was slain; after a reign of nine years Kasyapa left the sovereignty to his son, Dapula. Dapula, fearing the intrigues of the Tamils, determined to drive every one of them from the capital city; but they resisted, and invited to Ceylon Hatha Dattha, a prince of the Lamini family, who was an exile in India. That prince landed on the southern coast and marched against Dapula, who now, threatened both within and without, abandoned all hope and fled from Anuradhapura, and established himself in Ruhuna. The victorious

THE SIGIRI ROCK (VIEW FROM THE SOUTH-EAST, SHOWING FRESCOES).

THE SIGIRI ROCK (VIEW LOOKING EAST, SHOWING THE TERRACES).

prince was known as Dathpotissa II., and is described as a righteous ruler. He gave place to his brother, Agrabodhi IV., in 673 A.D. This prince performed many acts of charity and erected a number of sacred buildings. In the latter part of his reign he abandoned Anuradhapura and established himself at Polonnaruwa. His successor, Mahinda II., however, brought back the capital to Anuradhapura. His son, Dapula II., succeeded him, and was, in turn, succeeded by Mahinda III., his cousin, and Agrabodhi VIII. The two following reigns of Dapula III. and Agrabodhi IX. are not of much interest. Sena I. came to the throne in 846 A.D. In this reign the Tamils, the inveterate foes of Ceylon, again invaded the island, and taking advantage of the time lost by the King in concentrating his forces, made themselves masters of the northern districts. They attacked the king's army and his entrenchments at Mapilagama, but failed to dislodge him. The king sought refuge in flight, and raised a fresh army to march against the invaders, with equally disastrous results. The capital, Polonnaruwa, was besieged and taken by the Tamils, and the sacred ornaments of the temples, including the sacred cup of Buddha, were sent to the Pandian country. Plunder, rather than permanent retention of the country, seemed to be the object of the invasion, for the kingdom was given back to Sena for a suitable ransom. In this reign was built the Topawewa tank. The next king was Sena II., grandson of Sena I., and his prolonged reign of thirty-five years was, on the whole, a prosperous one. In this reign the son of the king of Pandia, having rebelled against his father, took refuge in Ceylon. Sena took up his cause and despatched to India a large army, which, disembarking, marched against Madura, the capital of the Pandian kingdom, which was carried after some resistance. The king was put to death, and the son was placed on the throne. Sena's son, Udaya, then came to the throne, and reigned for eleven years. His reign is conspicuous by the furtherance of national works and works of irrigation. A rebellion led by the Dissawa of Ruhuna was easily quelled. Kasyapa IV. succeeded Udaya, and in his reign the government of Ruhuna again revolted; but the issue of the battle that was fought in consequence was decisive in favour of the king. Kasyapa, with strange clemency, pardoned the rebel chief and gave him one of his daughters in marriage. The king's son-in-law, Kasyapa V., then came to the throne (929 A.D.). He devoted himself to the protection and purification of the church, and enforced religious discipline by royal act. He created his son, Senapati, general-in-chief, and sent him with a large army to the assistance of the king of Pandia, who was then at war with the king of Choli; but the expedition proved a failure for two reasons—the cowardice of the king of Pandia, and disease, which devastated the Sinhalese army.

The next king was Dapula IV., son of Kasyapa V., who, after a brief reign, was succeeded, in 940 A.D., by his brother, Dapula V. The king of Pandia, who had been so long struggling against his more powerful antagonist, the king of Choli, found himself at the end of his resources, and being unable to continue the conflict, betook himself to Ceylon. He landed at Mantotta, and was received by Dapula with the honours due to a sovereign. A palace near Anuradhapura was placed at his disposal, where he was entertained as the guest of the king. It is said that while the king of Lanka was preparing for war with a view to restore the king of Pandia to his throne, a plot was discovered between the exiled king and certain of the Sinhalese nobility against Dapula himself. Before Dapula's vengeance could reach the king of Pandia, the latter precipitately removed himself from Ceylon, leaving behind him his crown and regalia. Dapula died after a reign of twelve years, and was succeeded by a prince of the name of Udaya. He is described as a tyrannical prince, against whom a conspiracy was formed by the nobles and the people at the very outset of his reign. The charge of tyranny, however, seems to be based only on the fact that he pursued, and put to death, the rebel chieftains who plotted against his predecessor. "The holy ascetics," says the Mahavansa, "were sorely disgusted with this deed, and they left the country and went to Ruhuna, whereupon the people of the country, the dwellers of the city and all the men of war, were roused to anger, like the sea raging in a fierce storm, and they ascended the Ratanapasada at the Abhayagiri vihara, and after they had terrified the king and overawed him greatly, they cut off the heads of the ministers who had taken part in the crime at the Tapodana, and threw them out of the window."

Eventually, the king and his followers betook themselves to Ruhuna, and when the fury of the army was appeased and the ascetics had been prevailed upon to forgive the wrongdoers, the king came back from Ruhuna, and meeting the priesthood on the way, obtained their pardon. The people, having obtained from the king certain concessions, were at length appeased, and the old order of things was restored. Udaya died in the third year of his reign. Sena II., his successor, proved in character the very reverse of his predecessor. Sena was as remarkable for his charity and amiability as Udaya had been for his cruelty and bad temper. He appointed a friend of the name of Udaya as his sub-king, and nominated him to the succession, which he obtained in 972 A.D. In this reign ambassadors came to Ceylon from the king of Choli to demand the regalia of the dethroned king of Pandia—a demand which Udaya declined to comply with. The king of Choli, elated by his victories over his Pandian rival, was disinclined to temporise. A powerful army arrived from India, and meeting the forces collected by Udaya, defeated the latter and obliged the prince to retire to Ruhuna. Udaya, however, was not long inactive. Taking the field with a fresh army from Ruhuna, he obtained a decisive success against the invaders, and expelled them from the island. The reigns of his successors, Sena and Mahinda, are by no means remarkable. The successor of Mahinda was Sena V., who was only twelve years of age when he came to the throne; the chief Adigar of the late king was appointed

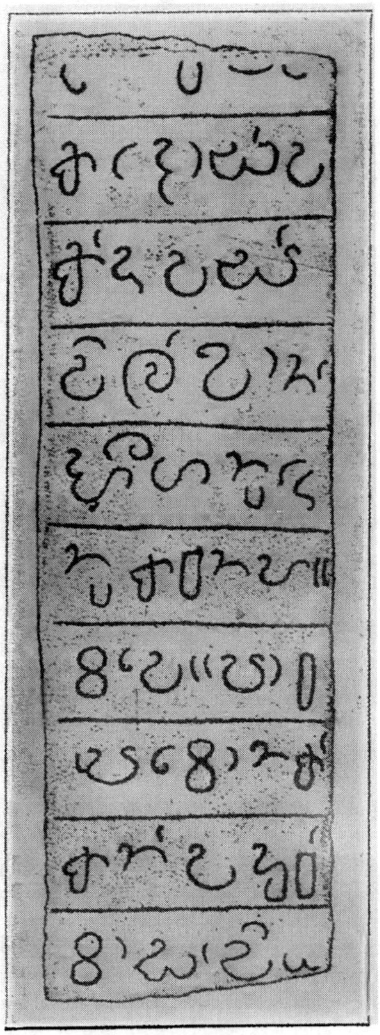

ANCIENT SINHALESE INSCRIPTION AT PARAPE.
(Tenth to eleventh century.)

regent during his minority. There was a good deal of internal trouble, due to the jealousy of the regent, which was at length patched up by a reconciliation between the monarch, who had been compelled to flee to Ruhuna, and the regent. Sena returned to Polonnaruwa, his capital, where he died in the tenth year of his reign. His brother, Mahinda V., followed him on the throne. He transferred the seat of government from Polonnaruwa to Anuradhapura, and had hardly taken up the reins of government when troubles commenced to harass him. The foreign residents of the island had increased in alarming numbers during the late reigns, which may well be called the dark ages of Ceylon. They were now so powerful that they menaced the very throne by their seditious conduct. The king's palace was surrounded by a mob bent on his destruction, and the king was obliged to flee in disguise to Ruhuna, where he fortified the place he had taken refuge in, and lived for twenty-six years; here a son, named Kasyapa, was born to him. During all that time the island was at the mercy of the anarchists. An army of Cholians landed, plundered the country, and revenged themselves on the unfortunate Sinhalese. Anuradhapura was taken, and even the fastnesses of Ruhuna were invaded, and Mahinda and his queen made captives. The king and queen, together with an immense quantity of gold, precious stones, images, &c., were sent to Choli, where they died in imprisonment. Their son, Kasyapa, however, succeeded in concealing himself in Ruhuna, and waited for an opportunity to assert his hereditary right to the throne. The Cholian governor who ruled at Polonnaruwa was apprehensive of the influence of this prince, and with a view to secure his person despatched a large army into Ruhunurata. This army was met by the army of Kasyapa's adherents, and after a deal of guerrilla warfare the Cholians withdrew themselves. The young prince now made a vigorous effort to recover his throne, but whilst taking energetic measures for this purpose, in the very midst of his preparations, he was seized with a fit and expired.

Ceylon now consisted of two separate provinces—the northern, which was the larger and the wealthier, was occupied by the Cholians, while the southern, uncultivated and rugged, was still in the possession of the native princes. Strife and dissension prevailed in both provinces for over twelve years, till, in 1052, the Sinhalese people crowned the infant son of Vikrama Bahu king of Ceylon. Ambassadors were despatched to the court of Siam, and, as a nation professing the same faith, the Buddhists were implored to provide assistance against the Tamil enemy. The embassy was successful, and the ambassadors returned with a large quantity of money and treasure. The country was, however, soon disturbed by the rebellion of a prince of the royal lineage, named Kasyapa, against the crowned king, now known as Vijaya Bahu. The rival forces met, and the young king was successful in his first venture in defeating Kasyapa. Flushed with victory, he now turned his armies against the Cholians. After much desultory warfare, owing to the rugged nature of the country, Vijaya Bahu brought matters to an issue by besieging Polonnaruwa. The battle that followed was fought within the very walls of this city. The Cholians were defeated and driven within it, and after a blockade of six weeks the fortress was carried by storm. The Cholians, apprised of this victory, speedily betook themselves to their country. Vijaya Bahu, now firmly established on the throne, was soon recognised over the whole of the island, and his renown extended even over India. The Tamils having been driven away, time was now found for the king to devote himself to the administration of the country. The degenerate condition of the church first attracted his attention. He made a state entry into Anuradhapura, and made this city once more the capital of the island, and there he was formally crowned king of Lanka. He ordered the repair of temples, reinstated neglected ceremonies, and brought about the ordination of a large number of priests, some of whom were obtained from foreign countries. The din of war was, however, once more heard in Ceylon. The king of Choli was enraged at hearing that Vijaya Bahu gave precedence in his court to the Siamese envoy. This was natural, considering the power and importance of the country which was represented and the close ties which bound the two countries together. Believing this to be a slight on his dignity, the Cholian king ordered the nose and ears of the Sinhalese ambassador at his court to be cut off. Hearing of this, Vijaya Bahu declared war against the king of Choli, and while he was preparing to embark from Mantotta, the fleet of the Cholians hove in sight. Their army landed, and Vijaya Bahu, suffering a defeat, retired to Polonnaruwa. The Cholians attacked the capital, and Polonnaruwa fell into the hands of the invaders, the king's palace being rased to the ground. Vijaya Bahu, however, did not lose hope, and raised a second army, giving command of it to Prince Vira Bahu. Polonnaruwa was once more besieged, and once more was it taken. The Cholians retired to the coast in hot haste. Soon after this Vijaya Bahu invaded the Cholian country, and revenged himself upon its inhabitants for the injuries which had been inflicted on the Sinhalese. But again the appearance of disease among the troops, and the shortness of provisions, compelled the Sinhalese forces to return to the island, and Vijaya Bahu resumed the improvement of the internal administration of the country, which had been so rudely interrupted. After a long reign of fifty-five years, Vijaya Bahu died in 1120 A.D., having brought Lanka under the canopy of one dominion. Says the Mahavansa: "Thus did Vijaya Bahu, the ruler of men, hold the reins of government without any fear in his hands for fifty and five years more, and when he had improved the religion of the land and the country, which was sore distressed by the wicked Tamils, he ascended up to heaven, as if to behold the great reward arising out of his good deeds on earth."

PART VII.

THE EPIC OF PARAKRAMA BAHU THE GREAT.

AFTER the death of Vijaya Bahu, his brother, Jaya Bahu, came to the throne, but did not possess it for long, as almost immediately on his accession his right was contested by Vikrama Bahu, the son of Vijaya Bahu I. The country was again divided into two factions, each supporting one of the claimants to the throne. Jaya Bahu was unable to resist the advance of his nephew, and finally Vikrama Bahu was declared king in 1121 A.D. The son-in-law of Vijaya Bahu, Manabharana, who was with the defeated party, betook himself to the southern districts of the island, and there reigned as king. The reign of Vikrama Bahu was continually disturbed by a war between himself and Manabharana, as also by an invasion from India, under Vira Deva. Vikrama Bahu, incurring a defeat at the hands of Vira Deva, immediately took refuge in his mountain fastnesses; and having collected a large army, again took the field and gave battle to Vira Deva, when the latter was defeated and killed. Vikrama Bahu then seems to have become reconciled to Manabharana and his two brothers, and each of them ruled his own territory. These kings did not pay that respect to religion and the nobles which their predecessors were wont to pay. Says the Mahavansa: "Nor were these four lords of the land able to bring the country under one canopy, even though they strove hard thereto. And because they were imprudent, they degraded the nobles and appointed base men in their places, such as they chose. These foolish men gave no heed to religion, neither cared they aught for their subjects, whom the king Vijaya Bahu had prospered in divers ways. The possessions of honourable men also they took away by force, even though there was no fault to find in them. And for their avarice and covetousness, they oppressed their subjects and levied grievous taxes on them, yea, even as the mill extracts juice from the sugar cane.

"Thus lived these lords of the land, transgressing all the established customs of the country. Like greedy owners of the land, they were always cruel. Their hearts were wholly bent on evil. They felt not the dignity of kings, and although placed in high offices of trust, wherein they might seek their own good and the good of others, yet lacked they even noble ambition."

We now come to the period of the greatest king that ever ruled Ceylon—Parakrama Bahu the Great. The story of his life is related in the Mahavansa in a manner which has compelled the poem to be regarded as a classic; the narrative of Parakrama the Great particularly excels, not merely in historical value, but in literary charm. Dr. Copleston, the Metropolitan of India, has contributed to the *Journal of the Royal Asiatic Society of Ceylon* an article on this king, entitled the "Epic of Parakrama." "Parakrama the Great," says he, "was the most prominent figure in Ceylon history and the hero, *par excellence*, of Sinhalese history." He holds that the vivid narrative of this period was written by an eye-witness of the splendid exploits of the king. The writer describes him under various conditions and with different characteristics—as a monarch, as a popular hero, as a lover of fun and sport, as a man of great charity, and as a soldier of reckless daring. "I fancy I perceive in these chapters," says Dr. Copleston, "in spite of the conventional turns of phrase, the feeling which in a modern might have prompted the exclamation:

"'Oh, was there ever such a knight, in friendship or in war,
As our sovereign lord, King Henry, the hero of Navarre?'"

For these reasons one cannot do better in describing the romantic and adventurous history of this king than to quote largely from the words of the poet himself. A whole chapter is devoted, as in most epic poems, to the marvellous incidents connected with his birth, which are thus described:—

"And it came to pass that King Jaya Bahu and his queen, Mitta, died while they yet dwelt at Ruhuna ; and Sugala, the wife of Sri Vallabha, gave birth to two children, namely a son, Manabharana, and a daughter, Lilavati. Likewise, the queen Ratanaveli, the consort of Manabharana, had two daughters, Mitta and Pabhavati. And the chief governor, Vira Bahu (Manabharana), seeing that he had only two daughters (and no sons), thought in this wise : 'We, who are descended from the pure race of the Moon, which is considered by the whole world as the head of the generation of all kings, are indeed placed in a very enviable position, being full of all power and might, expert in various wars, and skilful in the management of horses and elephants. Nevertheless, we three (brothers) have been again and again defeated by Vikrama Bahu, even by him singly ; and yet, there seemeth not any likelihood of the coming to us of a son who would be able to wipe off this stain. Alas ! how grievous is our lack of fortune ! What doth it profit me a kingship, stained with the reproach of the world ? Now, therefore, it seemeth good that I should give up my attachment to the pleasures of state, and spend my days diligently in the performance of good deeds.' Having thus communed with himself, he gave up all the business of the kingdom to his ministers, and lived there (in quietness) for seven or eight months. And one day, wrapt in serene thought, after keeping the holy precepts, he lay down to sleep in the temple of the king of the gods. And, lo ! in the early hours of the morning the king saw in a dream an angel of great majesty, arrayed in gorgeous apparel, adorned with scents and flowers, of exceeding great size, like unto the sun that has ascended up to the sky, making every side radiant with the glory of his body. And he spake unto the king, saying : 'Hail, lord of the land, who art favoured by fortune ! Rejoice and be exceeding glad, for ere long there shall be born unto you a noble son, endued with marks of greatness, able to accomplish all his desires, refined in mind, whose glory and dominion will be spread throughout the vault of heaven, resplendent with power and fame and glory, a mine of virtue, and one who shall raise up his people and the religion of the land. Now, therefore, arise and go quickly into the city where thy wife and thy children dwell.' Thereupon the chief of men awoke with a feeling of great joy, and when the dawn succeeded the night, he returned to Punkhagama. And the king told the pleasant dream just as he had seen it to the queen and to his ministers, and he lived with his queen, expecting a son of great renown, and heaped up good deeds of divers kinds by bestowing alms and observing the precepts of religion.

"And, again, it came to pass that while it was yet dawn, he saw in a dream a lovely young elephant, tame and wholly white, and endued with every mark of beauty. And it seemed to him as if he were leading it fondly into the bedchamber of his queen. Having seen this, he awoke and rose from his stately bed, and with a heart full of pleasure and joy entered the queen's bedroom at that very instant and told her the dream just as he had seen it. Thereupon the queen spake to him and said, 'I also have seen in a dream a young elephant like unto it, walking round my bed, and I caught him by his trunk and drew him up to my bed and fondly embraced him.' Having told each other all which they had seen, they remained awake until the break of day. And in the morning, when the household Brahman came to minister and the soothsayers also, they (the king and queen) inquired of them (the meaning of the dream), and when they heard the dreams they were glad, and interpreted them, saying, 'Of a surety there will be born unto you ere long a son richly endued with marks of good fortune. And when the king and his ministers and the citizens heard this interpretation, they all joined in a great festival of joy. From that time forth the king looked for the promised favour, and caused many prayerful blessings to be pronounced on him by the order of monks. And he daily gave away in divers ways unto the poor at the gate of charity gifts of exceeding great value, such as gems, pearls, and the like. He also caused Brahman priests who were versed in the Vedas and Vedangas to perform the religious rites, such as Homa and others, that were regarded as acts that bring blessings on men. Moreover, he appointed the king's workmen to repair the viharas and relic-chambers that had been much decayed and the tanks that had been ruined, and thus, while the king was spending his days in the performance of good deeds, a noble child was conceived in the womb of the queen. And the king, having been informed thereof, rejoiced and was exceedingly glad, and took great care of her during the period of her pregnancy. And when the full time of her delivery had come, she brought forth a son at a lucky hour when the stars were favourable. And straightway every region of the country was filled with gladness, and sweet and gentle and cooling winds blew everywhere ; and the courts of the palace resounded with the trumpeting of elephants and the neighing of horses, and were filled with great noise and confusion. And when King Manabharana heheld the various marvels that had been manifested unto him, he stood amazed. But when it was told him soon after of the birth of his son, he was filled with a fulness of joy, even as if he had been anointed with the oil of immortality. He then ordered a great many captives who were shut up in prison to be set free, and caused alms to be given in great plenty to monks and Brahmans. And the inhabitants of the city, led by the king's ministers, adorned the whole capital with arches of plantains, and in divers other ways, and, attired in their best robes and ornaments, they kept up a great and joyous feast for many days. Moreover, the king, having observed all the ceremonies regarding the prince that were connected with the birth of children in the manner set forth in the Vedas, sent unto the household Brahmans and others who were skilled in divination by signs. And when he had treated them with much kindness and respect, he commanded them to examine the signs on the body of the prince. And they examined all the signs on the hands and the feet and other parts of the prince's body with great care, and then, in the presence of the ministers that were assembled together, with great joy, they declared thus unto the king and queen : 'This prince hath power to subdue not only the island of Lanka but even the whole of India under the dominion of one canopy, and to enjoy it withal.' Then, when he had again gratified them with presents and shown them kindness, the king questioned them further whether there appeared any evil whatsoever that might happen to the child. And they answered and said : 'The prince will have a long life ; but there is a conjunction of stars that of a certainty meaneth evil to the father.' Thereupon the king gave the child the name of Parakrama Bahu, which signified that he would have an arm endued with strength to humble his enemies. And as he had a knowledge of rites and ceremonies, he caused the due performance of the feast of boring the ear and the feast of feeding the child with rice to be held according to the customs, and sent his messengers unto the king Vikrama Bahu at Pulatthi (Polonnaruwa), to convey unto him the tidings of the birth of his son. And Vikrama Bahu, having heard from them about the great good fortune that was foretold concerning the son of his fair sister and the evil that was in store for the father of the child, spake these words : 'He hath begotten unto me a fortunate nephew, who will be like a sparkling central gem in the chain of kings, beginning with Vijaya. Let the prince, therefore, grow up here, even with me, so that no evil befall him. For this my son, Gaja Bahu, is nowise able to acquire that which he has not gotten, or to retain that which he has got ; and Mahinda, my other son, although he possesses valour and other virtues, is not meet to succeed me in the kingdom, being inferior in rank on his mother's side. Therefore, of a surety, shall my nephew become the heir to my kingdom, which teemeth with riches that have been heaped up by me.' And with his mind full of such thoughts, he sent messengers with presents of princely ornaments and other valuable gifts to fetch the young prince. And the king Vira Bahu (Manabharana), having heard everything from the mouths of the messengers, said unto himself: 'The words that he hath spoken are the words of truth and wisdom, intended to profit me; nevertheless, it doth not behove me to part with a son begotten of my body that so I may turn aside the evil that impendeth on me. Moreover, if the prince be removed thither (Pulatthi), the part of Vikrama Bahu will, like a fire that burneth stronger before a fierce gust of wind, shine forth with an exceeding great blaze of glory, and our house will of a surety suffer in every wise a great loss.' Having pondered thus within himself, he withheld his son from the messengers that came to fetch him, and dismissed them after that he had gladdened their hearts with gifts of great value.

"And that lord of men (Manabharana), while he dwelt there in peace and harmony with his wife and children, was smitten with a severe disease, and quitted his body and kingdom together."

On the death of Manabharana, Kirti Sri Megha took possession of his elder brother's country, and to his brother Sri Vallabha he assigned the rest of the island over which he himself had been ruling, so that during Parakrama's youth, in addition to these two kings, Gaja Bahu was in possession of the country the capital of which was Polonnaruwa.

Much care was bestowed on the education of Parakrama. The young prince was first placed under the care and tutelage of an accomplished and learned prince, by whom he was taught the literature and the religion of the Buddhist faith. He was further instructed in logic, grammar, poetry and music. This course of mental instruction was accompanied by bodily exercises, gymnastics, horsemanship, archery, and the guidance of elephants. After the prince had imbibed these numerous accomplishments, his education was crowned by a course of foreign travel, in which he was attended by a retinue of Sinhalese nobles. On his return he felt much discontented at the disrupted state of the ancient kingdom of Ceylon, and embarked on that great aim of his life which he did not fail to fulfil, namely, the bringing together of the disunited parts under the canopy of one dominion. The king had been considering how men of high rank and valour valued glory more than life itself. Recalling the exploits recorded in the Ummagga, the Mahabharata and the Ramayana, he cried: "All these great deeds, though the doers are here no longer, are famous in the world to this very day. Life is worth living to those who have the capacity to achieve a rare and surpassing career like theirs. For me, born of Kshattriya race, if I do not something worthy of Kshattriya heroism, in vain will my life be. They were blessed, it is true, with times far more favourable; but in wisdom and all other gifts, why should they be better than me?"

The first step to the fulfilment of his ambition would naturally be to gain Polonnaruwa and the rest of his uncle Gaja Bahu's kingdom. Looked at from the point of view of the time, this would appear to have been more than an Herculean task, but Parakrama was content to set about it patiently and to make the attempt only when he had trained soldiers and captains and had collected what have been, at all times, considered the sinews of war. To do this with any chance of success, he felt that the first requirement was a knowledge of the extent of Gaja Bahu's strength and the degree of affection and attachment towards him of his ministers and people. Parakrama accordingly set forth to visit his uncle with the deliberate purpose of spying out the northern kingdom, and in doing so to train a body of followers who would have full confidence in his fortune and his prowess. The realm from which he set forth was that of his uncle Sri Megha, who had his capital in Buttala district, somewhere near the modern village of Velassa. Arriving at Badulla, which was under the care of a certain general named Sankha, he disclosed to Sankha some of his plans and ambitions. This general, cautious man that he was, did not encourage the young prince, and proceeded to steer a middle course. While entertaining the nephew, he communicated with the uncle. Parakrama, becoming aware of this duplicity, put the general to death—an act which, while it showed the resolution of the prince, savoured much of the character of a rebellion. The result was that for some little while he lived the life of an outlaw, during which he surprised his men and won their hearts by many a display of courage. The following is an instance:—

"And while he (Parakrama) dwelt there for some days, the people of that country joined together, saying, 'We shall capture the prince'; and so they surrounded that village. And being desirous to commence the fight, they ceased not to pour forth a shower of arrows with great determination. Thereupon, the soldiers who had come with the prince, saying, 'Our lives even will we sacrifice if it profit us aught,' were sore afraid, save the prince's own attendants who carried his sword and umbrella, and ran hither and thither even in sight of the prince. And the prince, seeing his soldiers fleeing, laughed and said, 'Now is there an occasion for me to show an act of great courage, for I shall terrify them and put them to flight with my single weapon.' So the prince gave a fierce cry, saying, 'Give me my sword!' and he had hardly uttered the words in a deep tone of voice that resounded on all sides like the blast of a conch of victory, which was heard by the soldiers that were fleeing, when they saw the heads fall of the bravest leaders of the enemy, who were being cut down (by the prince). Thereupon the soldiers at first rallied and fought with the enemy, who numbered several thousands, and having put them to flight, they surrounded the prince and praised his great valour, and gave him alone all the praise of their victory."

While the prince was staying at Bodhigama, he was bold enough to send for one of Gaja Bahu's generals, Gokanna by name, who was dwelling at Kalvapi, and despatched one of his men with a letter to him. Gokanna on receiving the letter was afraid to disobey the prince's command, and heedless of his duty to Gaja Bahu, promptly proceeded to Bodhigama, but not without providing himself with a considerable bodyguard, being mindful of the fate of the Badulla general. Parakrama received him with all honours. "It is known to you," said he, "how I have come away from the presence of my father, the king, and how I have dared to cause his powerful general to be slain. Hearing these things, you have come before me without even giving a thought to learn the wishes of your king, and without any knowledge beforehand of me, but simply on seeing the messenger and the letter that I sent you. In doing thus you have done well." He then bestowed on him many presents, and to his chief soldiers he gave ornaments and ear-rings of value, and provided them with food and lodging. But in the night Gokanna dreamed a dream. He thought he saw his bed surrounded by armed men who had come to kill him. With a cry of terror he leapt out of his bed, and leaving behind him his retinue, his sword, and his standard, he ran out into the jungle, and after wandering the night long, at dawn he ran away to his own village. His soldiers, seeing that their master had fled, followed in equal panic, and found themselves the next day in their master's village. When Parakrama heard the tidings of the general's flight, he smiled thereat and tarried in the same place a few days. After this incident, whenever fatigue overcame him this pleasant story was told him, and as it was in itself a pleasant thing, it removed the weariness of the prince, for he had a great love for pleasantry. After these preliminary adventures, Parakrama proceeded northwards—not without contests, in which he was invariably successful—and finally entered his cousin's kingdom, a fact which the poet has emphasised. "He entered it with a bound," says

Dr. Copleston, "as Cæsar put spurs to his horse and leapt over the Rubicon." King Gaja Bahu, who had been much disturbed by the manner of Parakrama's coming, took counsel with his ministers and determined to put a good face on the matter. He sent to Parakrama presents of garments and jewellery, with a message of welcome, animadverting on a "father who maketh not a jewel of a son like unto you," and hailing his arrival as his own good fortune, because, if they were both united, no enemy would dare to make war against them. On receiving this message, the prince, deeming it hard to fathom the wiles of princes, sent in advance a crafty officer, Nimmala by name, and having learned from him the true disposition of the king, proceeded to the neighbourhood of Polonnaruwa. Gaja Bahu came forth to meet him, surrounded by his army, and Parakrama was received with great respect. Gaja Bahu made the young prince mount the elephant on which he himself rode, and took him in state through the city, entering the royal palace. "Parakrama's life at his cousin's court was a triumph of dissimulation, but it is a remarkably picturesque scene; not only did he ingratiate himself with the king, for whom he obtained his own sister's hand, and with all his nobles, but went about continually among the common people, entering with sympathy into all their needs and, without appearing to do so, fostering all their grievances. A device which he used for gaining access, without appearing to seek it, to their houses, is too curious to be left unnoticed. He kept an elephant which he trained to run at him, and when he was near the house of any one whom he wished to win over, he would pretend to be charged by the elephant and would run for shelter into the house." He kept a perfect army of spies—men who were clever in many devices and skilled in various languages. Such as were learned in poisons went about as snake charmers; some acted as fortune-tellers; others as harp-players, dancers and singers, and puppet-showmen; some would equip themselves with umbrella and staff and pretend to be ascetics, visit the shrines of the neighbouring villages, and go about everywhere, bringing to Parakrama accurate reports of the state of feeling in the country and of the grievances of the people. As a result of these inquiries, the time came when Parakrama knew the mind of every courtier and almost of every commoner in the kingdom he desired to win over. He had friends in every part of the state, and every path in the jungles was familiar to him. When he had acquired all the necessary information, he returned to his uncle's court at Sankhatthali. He was not there long when Kirti Sri Megha died, and Gaja Bahu was pleased to see his young cousin established on the neighbouring throne. Conscious of the smallness and poverty of his kingdom, Parakrama's first duty was to develop its resources and to extend its frontiers. He placed encampments from Adam's Peak to the sea. He drained the marshes of the Pasdun Korale and built a causeway across the Deduru-Oya. The high conception of the duties of kingship as observed by Parakrama are set forth by him in these words: "All throughout this realm that belongs to me," he said to his ministers, "besides the many corn lands that are ripened by the water of the rain clouds, the fields maintained in dependence on the rivers whose waters fail not and on mighty reservoirs are few; and the kingdom includes very many rocky mountains and thick forests and great far-stretching marshes. In such a land as this not even the least drop of the water that the rain supplies should go to the ocean without bringing help to man; except places where the mines are, of gems and silver and such-like precious things, in every spot provision must be made for maintaining fields. Not to live for the people's good, but merely to enjoy the good things that have come to our hand—such a life is utterly unfit for me!" "Let there not stand in my realm in any spot whatever even the space of one small plot of ground that is not of use."

In the meantime, he kept on making preparations for the great object he had in his mind. By the sale of gems he was accumulating money, and as his hope of national unity lay in the training of native troops, he established military schools in many parts of his kingdom. He brought up in his own palace the sons and brothers and grandsons of many nobles, so that they might become familiar with the management of horses and elephants, and with fencing, with languages, music, and dancing. "In this way, when he had improved his resources and when he found himself at the head of a great army with plenty of money and grain, 'Now,' thought he, 'it is not difficult for me to subdue the continent of India, much less the island of Sihala (Ceylon).'" Then began the war with Gaja Bahu. It is needless to go through the tedious list of victories which characterised this campaign. Gaja Bahu was ultimately taken prisoner, and Parakrama found himself in the capital of Polonnaruwa. As far as Parakrama was concerned, the war was conducted with moderation, but he was not able to altogether curb the feelings of his soldiers for vengeance. Gaja Bahu having invited the assistance of Manabharana, the king of Ruhuna, the latter thought that this was his opportunity to become king of all Lanka. He came forward with his army in the first instance to assist Gaja Bahu to repel Parakrama, and in the second instance to wrest the throne from Gaja Bahu for himself. Joining his forces with those of Gaja Bahu, Manabharana inflicted a severe defeat on Parakrama, and treacherously seizing Gaja Bahu, proposed to put him to death. Parakrama soon repelled Manabharana and had Gaja Bahu at his mercy. But he exercised a splendid generosity in giving back his freedom to Gaja Bahu. The defeated king, crushed as much by the defeat as by the generosity of his enemy, entreated the Buddhist monks of Polonnaruwa to intercede for him. Parakrama capped his heroic generosity by giving back to his vanquished opponent the kingdom which he had wrested from him. Touched by this act, Gaja Bahu, by solemn gift, gave back the kingdom to his cousin. The inscription recording this act is still to be seen on a stone tablet in the vihara of Polonnaruwa, "I have given the royal country to Parakrama." Gaja Bahu did not long survive this event, and Parakrama took possession of Polonnaruwa. There was still much fighting to be done before Manabharana was finally subdued, and with his subjection we come to the termination of the first part of Parakrama's reign, which was the unification of Lanka. "It was given to him," says Dr. Copleston, "to unite the careers of a Julius and an Augustus. We have followed him to the point at which the greater Roman's course was cut short, and leave our hero prepared to inaugurate the Augustan Age of Lanka."

Now that tranquillity was restored, Parakrama resolved upon being publicly crowned emperor of Lanka. On a day fixed by the astrologers, the king, mounted on his state elephant and attended by his nobles, marched in magnificent procession and saluted the multitudes who crowded the line of march. A canopy emblazoned with the royal arms was held over his head; musical instruments resounded on all sides; delicate perfumes were sprinkled, and banners gaily floated all along the streets. Following the king and queen there came on foot the leaders of the late rebellion; at the close of the procession he was publicly crowned king, and the chief nobles swore to him fealty.

He next devoted his attention to the purification of religion. He ordered a great assembly of the monks who belonged to the three fraternities, and enunciated rules for their guidance and discipline. He founded a large establishment for the distribution of alms in his capital city at Polonnaruwa, and built a large hospital for the sick. It is thus described: "This ruler of men built further a large hall that could contain many hundreds of sick persons, and provided it also with all things that were needful; to every sick person he allowed a male and female servant that they might minister to him by day and by night and furnish him with the physic that was necessary and with divers kinds of food. And many storehouses did he build therein, filled with grain and other things, and with all things that were needful for medicine. And he also made provision for the maintenance of wise and learned physicians who were versed in all knowledge and skilled in searching out the nature of diseases. It was his custom on the four sabbaths of every month to cast off his king's robes, and after that he had solemnly undertaken to observe the precepts, to purify himself and put him on a clean garment, and visit that hall together with his ministers; and being endued with a heart full of kindness, he would look at the sick with an eye of pity; and being eminent in wisdom and skilled in the art of healing, he would call before him the physicians that were employed there and inquire fully of the manner of their treatment. And in this manner, indeed, did this merciful king, free from disease himself, cure the sick of their divers diseases from year to year."

A curious incident is also related of the king's kindness to animals. "But there yet remaineth another marvel to relate, the like of which had neither been seen nor heard of before. A certain raven that was afflicted with a canker on his face, and was in great pain, entered the hospital of the king, whose store of great goodness was distributed to all alike. And the raven, as if he had been bound by the spell of the king's great love for suffering creatures, quitted not the hospital, but remained there as if its wings were broken, cawing very piteously. Therefore the physicians, after they had found out what its true disease was, took him in by the king's command and treated him. And when he was healed of his disease, the king caused him to be carried on the back of an elephant round the whole city, and then set free. Verily, kindness such as this, even when shown unto beasts, is exceeding great. Who hath seen such a king, or where or when hath it been heard before?"

He spent much money in improving the fortifications of Polonnaruwa. He caused a chain of ramparts to be built round the town, and covered them with plaster work, "so that it was white like a cloud in autumn." He built a palace of great splendour called "Vijayanta." It consisted of seven storeys, and contained one thousand chambers supported by thousands of beautiful pillars. It was surmounted by hundreds of pinnacles, adorned with beautifully designed scroll work. Its gates and doors and windows were made of gold. The splendour of the king's bedchamber is thus described: "Full of perfume of flowers and incense, it was made beautiful with rows of large lamps of gold, and made exceedingly lovely by reason of the garlands of pearls of great size which were hung at the four corners thereof—pearls white like the rays of the moon, and which, as they waved to and fro, seemed to smile with scorn at the beautiful ripples of the river of heaven. And the network of tinkling bells of gold that hung here and there in the palace and sent forth sounds like unto fine instruments of music seemed to proclaim the unlimited glory of the merits of the king." He built a house of worship for the sole use of the Brahmans, and also a public theatre, "Sarasvati Mandapa," so that he might listen to the sweet and melodious voices of great singers and witness their delightful dances. Its walls were painted with frescoes descriptive of the events of his own life. He caused to be erected an open hall of recreation; he opened out a royal park and planted it with trees entwined with creepers of jessamine. Many ponds and baths did he construct for the people. In his time the city of Polonnaruwa was four leagues long and seven leagues broad, traversed with streets great and small. Having perfected the building of his capital city, he turned his attention to the restoration of the ancient capital of Anuradhapura.

About this time, Sinhalese merchants were carrying on trade with the kingdom of Ramanna, which is the country between Arakan and Siam, and a number of them were plundered by the king of that country, who, in addition, insulted the Sinhalese ambassador at his court, and detained some Sinhalese vessels on board of which were some Sinhalese ladies of rank. Parakrama, hearing of these wrongs, determined to send an expedition to obtain redress. All the country round about the coast seemed like one great workshop busied with the constant building of ships. Five hundred vessels and a large military force, commanded by a general of high rank, named Aditya, were despatched to the scene of operations. The force was fully provisioned for twelve months. They landed on the island of Kakkha, encountered the enemy, whom they routed, and captured the greater part of the island with a large number of prisoners. Operations were then directed against Cambodia itself. Disembarking at the port of Kusumi, they found a large body of the enemy posted with entrenchments. Heedless of a galling discharge of missiles, the Sinhalese troops advanced sword in hand, and carried the enemy's camp, in which the king of Cambodia was found among the slain. The Sinhalese general then marched on the capital and occupied it, and having made the country tributary to Parakrama, he appointed a viceroy and returned to Ceylon laden with the fruits of victory.

During this reign, also, the king of Pandia, who lived in his capital city of Madura, in the south of India, was besieged by Kulasekera, and being in dire distress, entreated Parakrama for succour. Parakrama despatched an expeditionary force to his aid under the command of a general named Lankapura. In the meantime, Kulasekera had put the king of Pandia to death and taken the city of Madura. Lankapura, landing on the Indian coast, made many Tamils captives, and despatched them to Lanka to work at the Ruanveli vihara. Ultimately, the fortress of Rejina was captured, and Kulasekera took refuge in flight. Thereupon he was dethroned from the sovereignty, and his son, Vira Pandu, was placed as king of the Pandian country, which was now made a tributary under Parakrama. Lankapura then led his army into the Choli kingdom and devastated the country; and on his return to Madura, after a successful campaign, he caused coins to be struck in the name of Parakrama Bahu, and a village called Pandi-Vijayaka was established in commemoration of the conquest of the Pandian kingdom. Finally, Lankapura returned to Ceylon with great booty and received an extensive grant of land from the king for his services.

His foreign wars being thus brought to a successful termination, Parakrama again directed his attention to religion. A golden spire was erected on the Ruanveli dagoba and costly offerings were made to the various temples. He planted large forests of fruit trees, diverted the courses of rivers in order to replenish the tanks already formed, and constructed numerous canals to bear off the water of the tanks to great distances. By means of the Godaveri canal, the waters of the Kalu Ganga were conducted to the lake called the "Sea of Parakrama," from which again ran twenty-four channels, conveying water into all the neighbouring fields. By the Kalinda canal he conducted the waters of the lake of Minneriya to the north, and by the Jaya Ganga canal he furnished the city of Anuradhapura with water from the Kala river tank.

At length, in the thirty-third year of his reign, Parakrama, who has deservedly been designated 'The Great' as much for his civil as his military qualities, expired, leaving to his nephew, Vijaya Bahu II., the heritage of his great empire. Says the chronicle: "Thus did this lord of men, Parakrama Bahu, reign three and thirty years. He was endued with excellent wisdom and might; his delight was always in the religion of the master; and he enjoyed in an exceeding great degree the reward of the many and divers acts of merit that he had wrought."

PART VIII.

THE LATER SINHALESE KINGS: 1197 A.D. TO 1215 A.D.

VIJAYA BAHU, who succeeded Parakrama Bahu the Great, was the son of the latter's sister, and is known to history as Vijaya Bahu II. He was a man of great learning and a poet of great renown, well versed in all princely accomplishments. The Raja Ratnacari gives a list of the various branches of study which formed the education of a Sinhalese prince. They were oratory, general knowledge, grammar, poetry, philology, astronomy, the art of affording wise counsel, religion, archery, knowledge of elephants, the discernment of thoughts, the occult sciences, history, jurisprudence, rhetoric, and medicine. This king was of a gentle disposition, timid and hesitating. His first act was to set at liberty those inhabitants whom Parakrama had caused to be thrown into prison, and to all of them he restored their lands and possessions. He is said to have written a letter in the Pali tongue to the king of Ramanna, "a letter of great merit," soliciting him to send to Lanka his most erudite priests to decide on some controverted points of doctrine. His was a reign of peace until its abrupt termination by his assassination at the instance of Mahinda, a prince of Kalinga. The assassination was procured by the help of an accomplice, a cowherdess named Dipani. Mahinda usurped the throne, and only ruled the kingdom for five days, for the chiefs of the army, enraged by the unlawful act, killed the usurper, and placed Kirti Nissanka, a sub-king of Vijaya, upon the throne. Nissanka was a prince of the Kalinga family from India, now known as the Northern Circars. He is known to history as Kalinga Lankesvara, and his coins bear that title. The stone lion which was his throne is to be seen at the Colombo Museum. The monuments raised to his honour describe him as a wise and able administrator, to whom was due the remarkable prosperity of the country during his reign of nine years. He is styled "the lamp by which the whole world was illumined," "protector of the earth," "fountain of renown," and such other extolling titles. He gave up a part of the royal revenues and distributed the sum among the poor, and reduced taxation for their benefit. He repaired the ancient tanks and appointed judges for every district. The religious seminaries were converted into universities, where different professors taught various branches of science. The Dambulla vihara was greatly ornamented by him, and obtained the name of Rangiri Dambulla. On his death his eldest son, Vira Bahu, was put to death by the first Adigar because he was considered unfit to assume the kingly office, and the younger son, Vikrama Bahu, was placed on the throne.

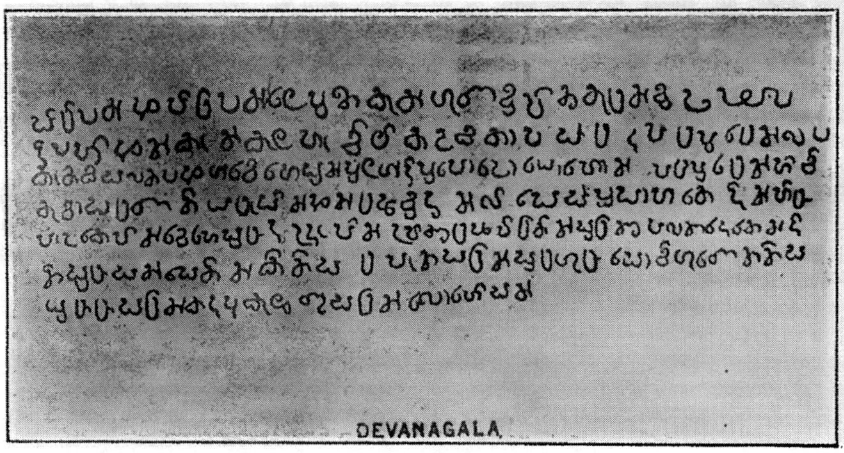

ANCIENT SINHALESE INSCRIPTION.

(Twelfth century. Cut on the face of a rock at Devanagala, in Kegalla district. The inscription refers to warlike events in the reign of Parakrama Bahu I., the most famous of Sinhalese kings.)

This was the beginning of the downfall of Lanka, of a period of internecine strife, followed by hostile invasions and the destruction of the great institutions of the country. Ceylon greatly declined from this date in opulence and in power. Vikrama Bahu only reigned for three months, at the end of which he was put to death by his cousin Chodaganga, who ruled for nine months, and was in turn deposed and mutilated by the great Adigar Kitti, who had married the widow of Parakrama Bahu the Great, Queen Lilavati. Kitti ruled for three years with his queen consort, when he was driven away by Sahasa Malla (1200 A.D.), a prince of the royal lineage. The copper coin of Sahasa Malla is found in great abundance in Lanka. History does not record the end of Sahasa Malla. It is stated that he reigned for two years and was succeeded by Ayasmanta, the chief of the army, who had married the chief queen of Kirti Nissanka. They reigned together for six years in peace, and nothing of importance is recorded except the erection by her of a temple, which she richly endowed. On her death, Dharmasoka, an infant of a few months, succeeded to the throne, and the kingdom was administered by a council of regency.

The Solians on the continent, perceiving the unsettled state of affairs in Ceylon, then invaded the country, but were obliged to retreat by Queen Lilavati, who was thus restored to the throne in 1209 A.D., to hold it for one year and to be dethroned again by the Tamil king, Lokissara, who came up from the opposite coast with a great army of Tamils, and taking possession of the island, reigned for nine months at Polonnaruwa, at the end of which time Queen Lilavati was again restored, to be again dethroned by Parakrama, the famous king of Pandia, who, landing with a great army of Pandians, deposed the queen and reigned for three years at Polonnaruwa.

The chroniclers thus describe the state of the island about this time:—

Says the Rajavaliya, "And now, as there was no more virtue to be found in the land, and wickedness had become greatly increased, and the tutelary deities had withdrawn their protection, an age of impiety followed, in which the doctrines of Buddha were no longer observed." The Ratnacari says, "With the death of the Sinhalese kings the inhabitants became so exceedingly wicked that the gods no longer protected it, and the impiety of the people became so outrageous that, as a mark of Divine wrath, the Malabar king, Magha, came from Kalinga with an army of twenty-four thousand men, which laid waste the country, destroyed the Buddhist religion, and dethroned Pandu Parakrama Bahu II. The beautiful Mahasaya of Ruanveli and many other dagobas were by these men mutilated or destroyed, and the holy abodes of the priests and the sacred depositories of the images of Buddha were converted into barracks for the Tamil soldiers, the treasures being carried off which were found in the interior of the sanctum. Virgins and honourable women were dishonoured, and the most elevated by birth and rank were reduced to the most menial and servile labour. Thus Magha and his army pursued a course of devastation, seducing to infidelity the captive inhabitants, plundering the rich of all their treasures, and cutting off the hands and legs of many. Thus, like a house filled with fire or thieves, was the island of Ceylon at this period."

The Mahavansa is even more explicit: "And it came to pass that, because of some wicked and cruel and grievous deeds that the inhabitants of Lanka had done, the gods who had been placed in different parts thereof to watch over them and to protect, cared no longer for the country, and looked not any more after their safety. Thereupon a certain wicked prince of the Kalinga race, Magha by name, invaded the country at the head of twenty thousand strong men from Kalinga, and took possession of the island of Lanka. And he was a follower of false faiths, and had a mind only to do mischief. Like unto a wild fire that consumeth the tender plants of the forests of charity, and like unto the sun when he closeth up the petals of the sacred lily of justice, and the moon when she obscureth the splendour of the lotus pond of patient endurement—even so was his mind wholly enslaved by ignorance. And this Magha, who was like unto a fierce drought, commanded an army of strong men to ransack the kingdom of Lanka, even as a wild fire doth a forest. Thereupon these mighty men, wicked disturbers of the peace of mankind, stalked about the land hither and thither, crying out boastfully, 'Lo! we are the giants of Kerala.' And they robbed the inhabitants of their garments and their jewels, and everything that they had, and violated even the chastity of families that had long been preserved inviolate. They cut off also the hands and feet of the people, and despoiled their dwellings. Their oxen and buffaloes also, and other beasts, they bound up, and carried them away forcibly. The rich men they tied up with cords and tortured, and took possession of all their wealth, and brought them to poverty. They broke down the image-houses and destroyed many Çetiyas. They took up their dwellings in the viharas and beat the pious laymen therein. They flogged children, and sorely distressed the five ranks of the religious orders. They compelled the people to carry burdens, and made them labour heavily. Many books also of great excellence did they loose from the cords that bound them, and cast them away in divers places. Even the great and lofty Çetiyas, such as the Ratanaveli, which stood like the embodiment of the glory of all the pious kings of old, they spared not, but utterly destroyed them, and caused a great many bodily relics to disappear thereby, which were unto them as their lives. Alas! alas!

"Even so did those Tamil giants, like the giants of Mara, destroy the kingdom and the religion of the land. And then they surrounded the city of Pulatthi (Polonnaruwa) on every side, and took Parakrama Pandu captive, and plucked out his eyes, and robbed all the treasures that were therein, with all the pearls and precious stones. Thereafter, Manabharana and the chief of the strong men anointed Kalinga Magha king over the glorious kingdom of Lanka. And when he had thus brought the country into subjection under him, he dwelt in the city of Pulatthi. This king caused the people to follow after false faiths, and contrived to mingle the four castes that had hitherto not mingled themselves. To the Keralites he gave fields and pastures, houses and gardens, servants and oxen and buffaloes; yes, everything that pertained to the Sinhalese. The viharas and parivenas and many sacred places also did he give as dwelling-places to his strong men, and despoiled the possessions that had been dedicated to Buddha and the Dhamma and Sangha, that so he might heap a multitude of sins to go down to hell. Even thus did Magha the king act like a tyrant, and reign twenty-one years over the kingdom of Lanka.

"And so did one king after another, moved thereto by the lust of wealth and power, murder his predecessor, though by reason of this crime none enjoyed long life, or even the sovereignty of the kingdom after they had attained unto it. Let the prudent man, therefore, abstain from taking life, and renounce the desire for wealth and power."

The reign of Magha lasted for twenty-one years. The Sinhalese, however, did not completely lose their independence during this time. A number of chieftains and princes sought the mountain districts, and building fortresses for themselves, lived in open defiance of the Tamil usurper. One of them, Vijaya Bahu, a prince of the line of Sri Sangha Bodhi, established himself in Dambadeniya and occupied himself with gathering together sufficient men and resources to win back the country. When he was ready for the enterprise, he "appeared like a flame bursting out of darkness," and at the head of his countrymen turned the tide of fortune and drove away the usurper. In the Maya and Ruhuna divisions of the island the Tamils were entirely expelled, while in the Pihiti division they continued to occupy the northern portion, as they do up to the present time. Vijaya Bahu, deeming it politic to leave them undisturbed, was content with their submission and payment of tribute.

The Tooth Relic, which in these troublous times had been hidden in the fastnesses of Kotmale, was deposited in the Beligala vihara, which the king built for its reception. The seat of government was transferred from Polonnaruwa, which had been the capital for five hundred years, to Dambadeniya. Buddhism was restored, copies of religious works which had been destroyed were brought from India and re-written, and ecclesiastical seminaries were re-established.

In this wise Vijaya reigned for four years, when he was succeeded by his son, Parakrama Bahu II., better known to history as Kalikala Pandita Parakrama Bahu. The learning of this king gave him an important position in the ranks of Eastern monarchs. He was sought after by princes of other countries as arbitrator in matters of difference amongst them, and his alliance was generally courted. He completed the reduction of the Pihiti division of the country. Says the Rajavaliya: "He harassed not the inhabitants of Lanka; recovered taxes, as his royal father had done, without oppression; imprisoned for offences worthy of death, and reigned without giving cause for sorrow to sentient beings."

In the eleventh year of his reign the island was invaded by an army of Malays, led by the Malay commander, Prince Chandra Banu. Vira Bahu, the king's nephew, met Chandra Banu and inflicted on him a severe defeat, and drove the Malays away. The remainder of this king's reign was spent in the improvement of the island and in the education of his sons. A celebrated priest, Dharmakirti, was invited from the continent, and to him was entrusted the education of the princes and the purification of the national religion. Parakrama was conspicuous as a road-maker. A road to Adam's Peak was placed under the superintendence of the first Adigar. Two bridges were erected, one over a ravine 636 feet long, the other over the Kelani Ganga, between Adam's Peak and Bentota. Polonnaruwa, Yapahu, and Kurunegala were greatly embellished. The foundations of Siriwardhanapura (the modern Kandy) were laid, and thither the Tooth Relic was removed.

While thus busy in the improvement of his country, Parakrama was again aroused by a second invasion of Malays under Chandra Banu, reinforced by large contingents of Tamils from the Pandian and Solian countries. But the valour of Parakrama once again proved too much for the invaders, and they fled in confusion from the island. During this reign the Mahavansa was continued from the reign of Maha Sen to this period, the author being the priest Dharmakirti. The king in the thirty-fifth year of his reign (1275 A.D.), foreseeing his approaching end, called together his six sons, and apportioned to each of the younger sons the government of a province under the eldest, named Vijaya, and having besought them to live in fraternal union, expired in peace.

His successor, Vijaya Bahu IV., was distinguished for his piety, and was thus known.

as Bosat Vijaya Bahu. In the second year of his reign he fell a victim to a plot laid by one of his generals named Mitta. "As this wicked man," says the Mahavansa, "lusted for the king's power, he gained over a servant in the king's household, and by means of this servant, whose heart he had deceived by bribes, he caused the king to be put to death one night." His brother, Bhuvaneka Bahu, on being apprised of the tidings of his assassination, fled from the city of Dambadeniya and took refuge in the city of Yapahu. The traitors were, however, unsuccessful in their attempt to gain over the Aryan army, the story of whose loyalty to the royal house is thus described :—

"Then Mitta, the general, entered the palace of the great king at Jambuddoni; and there, with wicked intent, he sat on the beautiful throne and showed himself to all the people, arrayed in the king's robes and ornaments. After that all the ministers who had espoused his cause gathered themselves together and supported each other, saying, 'The allegiance of the whole army, both of them that are born in the country and of the stranger, shall we secure altogether by a liberal payment of their wages.' And when they had resolved thus, they began first to give wages to the strong men of the Aryan warriors, at whose head was Thakuraka. But they refused to accept thereof, saying, 'We have always been regarded worthy of trust; and it is indeed the soldiers of the Sinhalese whose allegiance should first be bought with their pay, and whom you should satisfy by every means in your power.' Thereupon the ministers answered and said, 'Be it so'; and when they had caused all the soldiers of the Sinhalese to be paid, they asked them (the strange soldiers) to accept their wages also. But they all refused a second time, saying, 'Let our wages be given to us afterwards; we shall not take it now.' Nevertheless, the ministers continued to press them hard in every way with reasons why they should accept their wages. Whereupon all the seven hundred Aryan warriors rose up in a body, saying, 'We shall speak (all the words that we wish) in the presence of the king,' and so they went up to the king's palace. But when they saw Mitta, the general, seated on the throne there, they stood before him and did reverence to him for a moment. Then Thakuraka, a brave warrior, gave a sign to his comrades, and straightway drew out his sharp sword and cut off the head of the general in an instant and cast it on the ground.

"Thereupon there was a great uproar in the city; and all the Sinhalese soldiers who were powerful gathered themselves together, and asked the Aryan warriors wherefore they had done this unlawful thing. And they replied, saying, 'We have done this in obedience to the command of Bhuvaneka Bahu, who is now at Subha-pabbata.' Thereupon all the warriors, both Aryans and Sinhalese, joined themselves together, saying, 'Be it so.' Then they brought the chief prince, Bhuvaneka Bahu, from the city of Subhacala to the city of Jambuddoni, and anointed him king over the kingdom with great honour."

Bhuvaneka Bahu was then proclaimed sovereign, and matters again resumed their ordinary course. Bhuvaneka Bahu devoted much time to the celebration of religious ceremonies, and taking the Tooth Relic to Yapahu, made that place his capital. In the eleventh year of his reign an army of Pandians, under Arya Chakravati, marched through the country, plundering and devastating wherever they went. He laid waste the country on every side, entered the city of Yapahu, took possession of the Tooth Relic and all the wealth that he found there, and returned to the Pandian country.

On the death of Bhuvaneka Bahu, he was succeeded by Parakrama Bahu II., his nephew, and son of Bosat Vijaya Bahu (1288 A.D.). On ascending the throne he resolved to bring back the Tooth Relic to the island, and perceiving that force was unavailing for this purpose, he adopted the wiser policy of conciliation. Attended by a number of reliable nobles, he went to the Pandian country and presented himself before the king of Pandia. His agreeable address and courteous demeanour so pleased the king of Pandia, that Parakrama Bahu obtained the Tooth Relic from the king's hands, and bringing it back to Lanka, placed it in the old temple of the Tooth Relic at Polonnaruwa. On his death (1293 A.D.) he was succeeded by his cousin, Bhuvaneka Bahu II., son of Bhuvaneka Bahu I. He established himself at Hasti Sailapura—"The city of the elephant-rock"—the modern Kurunegala. His short reign of two years was only eventful in respect of the change of capital. He was succeeded by Parakrama Bahu IV. in 1295 A.D., known also as Pandita Parakrama Bahu—the "Beauclerc" of Ceylon history. He was a learned and pious prince. He built a temple for the Tooth Relic and composed a ritual for the same. He had the Jatakas, or Birth-stories of Buddha, translated into Sinhalese. He improved a number of temples, including the Dondra, Weligama, and Totagamuwa viharas. He was a poet of no mean repute, and a poem by him, the "Kausilumina" (the "Crest Jewel of Poetry"), is to this day regarded as a classic. It is descriptive of one of the lives of Buddha and is written in choice Sinhalese verse, which has been looked upon as a model by succeeding poets. In his reign was written the famous "Sidat Sangarawa," which is regarded as the standard authority on Sinhalese grammar. It was translated into English by the late Hon. Mr. James de Alwis. The chronicles do not state the length of the reign of the scholar king. He was succeeded by Bhuvaneka Bahu III. Says the Mahavansa: "After his (Parakrama Bahu I.'s) death there was a king named Wanni Bhuvaneka Bahu, and after him Jaya Bahu, a very powerful king; and after the death of these two kings there reigned a fourth ruler of men, bearing the name of Bhuvaneka Bahu, who was a man of great wisdom and faith and a mine of excellent virtues. And he dwelt in the delightful city of Ganga Siripura, near the Mahavaluka river (Gampola, near the Mahaveli Ganga)." Thus it will be seen that the capital was removed from Kurunegala to Gampola, where Bhuvaneka Bahu reigned for four years. He was succeeded by Parakrama Bahu V., who, in turn, was succeeded, in 1352 A.D., by Vikrama Bahu III.

PART IX.

THE LIFE AND TIMES OF ALAKESVARA.

THE reigns of this king and of his two successors, Bhuvaneka Bahu V. and the ill-fated Vira Bahu II., comprise in themselves the history of the rise and progress of the prime minister Alakesvara—one of the most striking historical characters, and corresponding in a way to Guy, Earl of Warwick, the "King-maker" of English history. "Now, in the time of the king Vikrama Bahu," says the Mahavansa, "there was a mighty prince of great wisdom, Alagakonara by name, of the Giriwansa, and he dwelt as viceroy in the beautiful and famous city of Peradoni (Peradeniya), which is on the banks of the river Mahoru Ganga (Mahaveli Ganga); and he was endued with majesty and faith and such-like virtues, and desired greatly to promote the welfare of the church and the kingdom. It was told by them of old time, saying, 'There is a city, Kalyani by name, that shineth with its temples and Bodhis and excellent walks; its ramparts, walls, image-houses, and çetiyas; its fine market-places and its superior gates and arches." And the great sage, moreover, visited this city of Kalyani that was so greatly praised. On the southern side thereof and nigh unto the village Darurugama, which contained a large pond and was a goodly place, wherein dwelt men of great wisdom and virtue, he built the famous city of Jaya-vaddhana-Kotta, and adorned it with rows of great ramparts and gates and towers. And this great man dwelt in that city, and being desirous of acquiring merit, he did much good, such as the advancement of religion and the like." This is all the meagre mention made in the Mahavansa of this remarkable man—illustrious equally as a warrior and as a statesman—a fact which perhaps is due to his final overthrow and assassination at the instance of a powerful Buddhist monk. It will be remembered that shortly before this time Arya Chakravati, the king of Jaffna, had devastated the country. This king, having allied himself with the Pandian ruler, made his power felt not only in the northern provinces, but even over the Tamil princes of the Wanni. The owner of a powerful fleet and the commander of a large standing army, he aimed at nothing less than being the ruler of the whole of Lanka. Vikrama Bahu, a man of peace, reigning quietly in the city of Gampola, was yet wise enough to select a man who could be a match for the king of the north. A contemporary historian has, in the Sinhalese chronicle known as the Nikaya Sangraha, made up for the silence of the Mahavansa, and from it and other contemporary works have been gathered the following facts.

Alakesvara was not a native of this island. He was a member of the princely house of the Giriwansa, a Kshattriya family from the north of India, which had established itself in the city of Kanchipura, the modern Conjeevaram. Senevirat, the minister of Parakrama Bahu V., had gone to that city for the purpose of building there shrines of Buddha. He married the sister of Alakesvara, and begot two sons, Vira Alakesvara—called after his uncle—and Vira Bahu Epa. The next we hear of Alakesvara is the information given by the Mahavansa of his appointment to the office of viceroy, or Prabhu-raja. On receiving this appointment, Alakesvara hastened to Rayigam to take measures to drive off the Tamils. It would appear that at this time the Sinhalese king of Ceylon was actually paying tribute in some parts of his kingdom to the king of Jaffna. Alakesvara's first care was to fortify the town of Rayigam. He then deemed it necessary to build a fortress near the harbour of Colombo, which, from its importance, would be the centre of an attacking fleet. And Alakesvara decided on building and garrisoning in that neighbourhood; such a fortress he erected in the town of Kotta, which, in its Sinhalese name of Jayavaddhapura ("victory-promoting city"), was destined to be the future capital of Ceylon. The Nikaya Sangraha thus describes the building of this fortress: "He issued commands through the obedient and faithful chiefs in his service, and nigh unto the haven called Çolombo he caused a mighty deep and broad ditch to be dug, dreadful to behold, like the sides of a steep rock, right round the village of Darurugama, which was situated in the midst of a lake and protected on all sides by a never-failing stream of water; and he caused to be adorned with different devices, like a creation of Visvakarma, the intervening spaces on the summit of the great rampart wall, which for the sake of stability had been built entirely out of stone, from the base of the ditch up to the coping on the wall. Thus he built a famous fortress called Abhina Jayavaddhana and well fortified. He caused to be built on the summit of the great wall of the city, for the protection of its four sides, four separate holy places dedicated to each of the four great god-kings who protect the four quarters of Lanka. And he commanded that the temple services and festivals should be maintained without intermission with every description of music, such as the music of the drum and pipe, and dancing and singing. Having filled it with all manner of riches, he peopled the city with a great multitude."

Meantime Arya Chakravati had marched down from Jaffna, and having seized the seven Sinhalese ports, had imposed a large tax on the inhabitants. Alakesvara built a walled town at Rayigam, which he equipped with men and provisions, and also another between the five villages called Kotta, and a moat and wall there drawn round it. These places, too, he provided with troops and quantities of arms, and constructed dykes round the fortresses, so as to flood the country around in the event of an invasion. He built moats and tanks to serve as reservoirs, and laid in large supplies of salt, coconuts and paddy, in anticipation of a prolonged siege. Having fortified Kotta, he returned to Rayigam, which he made the base of his operations. These preparations for the destruction of the northern power occupied Alakesvara quite twenty years. Vikrama Bahu III. had died, and Bhuvaneka Bahu V., a man of the same temperament as his predecessor, was reigning in Gampola. Alakesvara, now feeling the time had come for the crisis, initiated proceedings by hanging the tax-collectors whom Arya Chakravati had stationed in the different districts. Enraged at this act, the latter determined on a complete overthrow of the Sinhalese king by a simultaneous attack on the two great strongholds, Gampola and Kotta. A large army, whose object was the capture of Gampola, marched overland. Bhuvaneka Bahu V., hearing of its arrival at Matale, heedless of the courage of his army, fled in panic to seek the protection of his minister at Rayigam. The cowardice of the king disgusted the army of a nation which had been invariably led by their monarch in person in times of battle. Realising that defeat meant certain bondage to the Tamils, the Sinhalese forces cunningly laid their plans. Having assembled with the greatest secrecy, they made a night attack on the Tamil camp. The Tamils were surprised, and large numbers of them were speared to death, the few survivors perishing in the mountains. The force which was destined for the siege of Kotta came by sea in two divisions, one of which landed at Colombo and the other at Panadura. Alakesvara awaited the arrival of the enemy at Kotta, having with him a Sinhalese army and a force of mercenaries. When he heard of the landing of the enemy, he mounted on his elephant and led his forces to Gorakande, where, meeting with a force of five thousand Tamils, he completely routed them and cut off the retreat of the fugitives by destroying their shipping at Colombo. He then marched rapidly to Panadura, where he routed the remainder of Chakravati's forces and destroyed all the enemy's shipping in that port. He then returned in triumph to Rayigam, and was received with acclamation by the people and raised into the ranks of the five highest orders of the realm, namely, Dipadhiraja (supreme ruler of the island), Mandalikaraja (provincial ruler), Pradesaraja (ruler over a district), Antaraboghiraja (ruler of a sub-district), and Anusasakaraja (supreme counsellor). The Sinhalese bards chanted the hero's praises, some of which are still sung by the people. Chakravati's power was completely broken by the signal victories of the Sinhalese, so much so that in two reigns later Jaffna became a Sinhalese province. Bhuvaneka Bahu now returned to Gampola, but the welcome he received there was so cold by reason of his cowardice that he was compelled to return to Kotta, where he lived under the protection of his great minister, the king *de facto* of Ceylon. Having established peace, Alakesvara devoted himself to the endowment of viharas, the building of temples, and the encouragement of learning. Having established his reputation as a warrior and a statesman, he now proceeded to show himself as a man of culture and a patron of learning. On the death of Bhuvaneka Bahu V., about the year 1401 A.D., the title to the throne was disputed between the two sons of Senevirat whose names have already been mentioned. The younger brother, Vira Bahu Epa, placed himself on the throne of Kotta with the tacit, though not the direct, encouragement of his uncle Alakesvara, whose object seems to have been to see a weak sovereign on the throne. The elder brother, Vira Alakesvara, having been defeated by the younger, fled the country. About this time Colombo was besieged by a Chinese fleet, whose admiral demanded from the king of Ceylon the payment of an annual tribute. Alakesvara, resenting the insult, defeated the Chinese in an engagement and drove them back to their ships. In the meantime, Vira Alakesvara returned from India with an army given him by the king of Chola, and defeating his brother, mounted the throne at Kotta under the title of Vira Vijaya Bahu VI., whom the Mahavansa mentions as Vira Bahu II. It seems abundantly clear that Alakesvara's ambition was the throne itself, but he was only connected with the royal line by marriage; and the loyalty of the people to the royal line of Sri Sangha Bodhi was so strong and rooted that he did not think the opportunity was ripe for him to dare to assume the throne he so coveted. A few years later the emperor of China despatched his admiral, Ching Ho, to avenge the insult to the Chinese flag. Vira Bahu was at this time reigning in Kotta, and Alakesvara, settled in his native Rayigam, was meditating a *coup*, for which the arrival of the Chinese fleet afforded him opportunity. Brave as he had proved himself to be, he knew his object in this instance could only be achieved by stratagem. The king, falling a victim to a "device"—to use the word of the Sinhalese historian—was lulled into such complete security that he allowed the Chinese forces to enter his city as ambassadors bearing gifts. After their entrance they showed themselves as enemies, when it was too late to effectually resist them. The king fought with desperation, but was taken captive with a number of his nobles, and many of the princes and the nobility were slain. The Sinhalese monarch and other captives were deported to China, and the Chinese, having placed Alakesvara on the throne, acknowledged him as their tributary. After the departure of the Chinese fleet, Alakesvara assumed the sovereignty at the chief city of Kotta, and was quietly working round his people to acknowledge him as king and to assent to his coronation, when Vira Bahu II., released by the Chinese, returned with the rest of the captives to Ceylon. This was about 1413 A.D. Alakesvara received him with professions of loyalty and welcome, and bringing him into his capital, on the night of his arrival, procured his assassination, and once more resumed the government of the country. The young son of Vira Bahu, named Parakrama, was living under the protection of Vidagama, the high priest of Rayigam. So long as he lived Alakesvara could not assume the sovereignty, and he therefore sought to win over the priest. The latter, perceiving the great power of Alakesvara, decided on placing the youthful Parakrama on the throne, and having secretly obtained the sympathy of the chief nobles, who naturally resented the passing away of the dynasty into the hands of a stranger, pretended sympathy in favour of Alakesvara himself, and persuaded him to hold a ceremony for his coronation. Alakesvara, who had been dictator for three years, considerably improved the city of Kotta, and built stone baths and cisterns, spacious streets and beautiful edifices, with a view to the performance of this ceremony. "On the seventh day of the bright fortnight of the month Wesak (April—May), 1415 A.D., the old warrior, clad in all the pomp and wealth of sovereignty, sat on his throne in the city which to him owed its existence, to receive the crown which had been his supreme ambition. As he turned his face from the auspicious rite, the young prince (Parakrama) received from the high priest the sword of state, and in a few seconds the head of Alakesvara, which was to receive the crown, rolled into the tank below, and Parakrama was hailed king under the title of Sri Parakrama Bahu VI.

"Thus perished Alakesvara, like a greater figure in history, a victim to his own ambition. The manner of his death was a fitting close to a stormy career. With him passed away the age of Tamil cónquest and oppression. He left the kingdom strong and united, to revive in a measure the forgotten glories of Anuradhapura and Polonnaruwa. He rendered it possible for his successor to carry his arms into the country of Arya Chakravati, and, in fact, to be crowned king of a united Lanka. Once again under Sri Parakrama Bahu VI. the Sinhalese armies marched from the city of Alakesvara to conquer powerful kingdoms of the Deccan, as they had done in the days of the great Parakrama."

But the greatness was not to be long-lived. It was but the sunshine that heralded the clouds of internecine warfare, of Portuguese conquest, and of Dutch oppression, which were destined to follow.

Parakrama Bahu thus came to the throne in the year 1415 A.D., at the early age of sixteen, and Kotta became the seat of government. Thither the Tooth Relic was conveyed, and for its reception he caused to be built a beautiful three-storied temple. The king is described by the Mahavansa as a "temple of wisdom and courage." He did much for the cause of Buddhism during his long reign of fifty-two years, and procured learned men to write commentaries on the Buddhist scriptures. He brought into a state of subjection the Malabars of the northern districts, and the kingdom was restored to its former condition by means of an increased revenue. He loved to gather learned men around him, one of whom, the priest Sri Rahula Totagamuwa, his foster-brother, is considered to be the most celebrated of Sinhalese poets. His works were many, but he is chiefly remembered by his "Selalihni Sandesa" ("The Message of the bird Sela") and by his "Kavisekera" ("The Garland of Flowers on the Crown of Poetry"), which has not been surpassed in the whole realm of Sinhalese poesy in respect of originality, elegance, and correctness of expression. Totagamuwa was much attached to the king, and his gratitude to the royal household is manifest in his writings. The "Kavisekera" was written at the request of, and was dedicated to, the princess royal, Ulakodadevi. The following opening lines from the "Selalihni Sandesa" may be regarded, subject to the frailties of the translation, as a specimen of his poetry:—

"Hail, wondrous bird, whose wisdom pow'r elate
Yields not to that of ministers of state!
Bird of the sweet and richly varied lay,
Long mayst thou flourish 'midst thy fellows gay!
How does thy ruddy bill enchanting glow!
Not fairer blossoms can the *champak* show!
And what can match thy wing's superior hue,
Which wave wide-spreading like the lotus blue,
When beauteous as a vegetable gem,
Which winds have sever'd from its parent stem,
Thou soar'st exultant thro' the balmy air?
Have not young goddesses made thee their care,
And fixed thee fluttering in their jetty hair?
And have not bees who take their nightly rest
Within the water-lily's fragrant breast,
Around thee circled in their swift career,
In search of honey through the fields of air?
And have not Dryads, bright in charms divine,
Taught thee as pendants in their ears to shine?—
Friend of my soul! Say, hast thou e'er been prest
With pangs so fierce as those that wound my breast?
No! Happier in thy love, thy life is peace,
And rolling years but bring thy bliss increase,—
Such bliss as, searching the wide world around,
Save in thy presence, friend, is nowhere found!"

This poem is the message sent by a bird to Vibisana, presiding deity of the Kelaniya temple, invoking the blessing of a son to the princess royal, who was longing for a child.

During this reign flourished the poet Wettewa, a pupil of the celebrated Totagamuwa, best known as the author of the poem "Guttila," descriptive of one of the lives of Buddha. The hero was a musician, a player on the lute, whose pupil, ungrateful of the kindness of his master, tries to vie with him, though unsuccessfully in the end, in the practice of his art. The hero soliloquises in this wise upon the ingratitude of his pupil, who, after being educated by him, challenges him to a public competition: "He has indeed proved the truth of the old adage, 'Even if you should render assistance to a stick which is borne down by the current, render not assistance to the wicked.' As a piece of charcoal will not be white however much you may wash it in milk, so, likewise, however much benefit you may confer on the wicked, grateful they will never prove themselves to be. Without shame and fearless of sin, he has exhibited the pride of the wicked ; the knowledge which I have imparted to him has proved to be not otherwise than the milk with which the deadly venomous serpent has been fed."

On the death of Parakrama Bahu in the year 1467 A.D., he was succeeded by his grandson, Jaya Bahu. He only occupied the throne for two years, when he was put to death by Bhuvaneka Bahu VI., whom the Rajavaliya describes as a son of Parakrama Bahu VI. He reigned for seven years, and on his death was succeeded by Parakrama Bahu VII., a man of great learning. During his reign a serious insurrection broke out in the island. The king's brother quelled the insurrection and captured the leaders of the revolt. On the death of Bhuvaneka Bahu, this brother, fearing the superior claims of an adopted son of the late king, advanced to Kotta, where he found the young king had already assumed the government as Parakrama Bahu VIII. Having defeated this king, he obtained the sovereignty and ruled under the name of Vira Parakrama Bahu VIII. He occupied the throne in peace for twenty years. Two of his sons afterwards became kings of Ceylon, and the third was the grandfather of the celebrated Rajasinha.

PART X.

THE DISESTABLISHMENT OF THE SINHALESE POWER.

PARAKRAMA BAHU VIII. was succeeded by a prince of the name of Vijaya Bahu V., who in turn was succeeded by Bhuvaneka Bahu VII. The Mahavansa is very meagre in respect of these sovereigns. "These kings," says the chronicle, "advanced the prosperity of the church and the kingdom according to their faith and ability and went the way of their deeds."

While Bhuvaneka Bahu was reigning in Kotta the kingdom seems to have been subdivided into three territories, the capitals of the other two kingdoms being Kandy and Sitavaka. Vira Vikrama, a cousin of Bhuvaneka Bahu (better known in Portuguese history as Jaya Vira), was reigning in Kandy, while Mayadunna held the fortress of Sitavaka (Avisawella). It was in the period of these three kings that the Portuguese established themselves at Colombo. From this time forward and until nearly a century later the Portuguese power asserted itself in the island, and the history of Ceylon divides itself into what may be known as the Portuguese Period. The gradual decline and fall of the Sinhalese empire in the maritime provinces until only a modified independence was maintained in the hill country under the rule of the Kandyan kings, and the slow but steady acquisition of territory and colonisation by various European Powers that from time to time invaded and established themselves in Ceylon, will appear from a review of the history of the island from this stage onwards. The Portuguese were soon followed by the Dutch, and the Dutch in their turn were superseded by the English, and before three centuries had well passed, what through all the ages had been an exclusive Sinhalese sovereignty was transformed into the premier Crown Colony of the British Empire.

PART XI.

THE PORTUGUESE PERIOD.

IN the earlier pages mention has been made of the references by ancient writers to Ceylon. At this stage, before entering upon the narrative of the Portuguese occupation, it would be of interest to collate the information possessed by the geographers and travellers of the Middle Ages respecting the island. The writings of St. Ambrose, who flourished in the fourth century of the Christian era, contain references to Ceylon as described to the saint by a Theban of the name of Scholasticus, who appears to have visited the island. He describes the mode of life of the inhabitants, and he represents the king as being the chief of the kings of India. He was detained for six years by one of the Malabar sovereigns, and regained his liberty when his tributary sovereign, having rebelled against the king of Taprobane, was removed from office.

In the ninth century the commerce of Ceylon with the West seems to have been in the hands of the Arabian merchants. Abbé Renaudot in 1718 published a translation of an Arabian work of the ninth century, which gave a beautiful account of Ceylon and its people and products. He describes Ceylon as an island, and mentions the pearl fishery and Adam's Peak, and alludes to the great wealth of the country in rubies, pearls, and amethysts. "The king of the island," says the narrative, "makes laws which are the foundation of the religion and the government of the country, and there are doctors and assemblies of learned men, like those of the Hadithis among the Arabs. The Indians repair to these assemblies and write down the narratives of their prophets and the various expositions of their Lord. In this same island there is a great multitude of Jews as well as of many other sects—even Tanouis or Manichees—the king permitting the free exercise of every religion. Games are the usual diversion of the inhabitants. They play at draughts, and their principal pastime is cock-fighting. Cocks are very large in this country, and better provided with spurs than cocks usually are."

The famous traveller Marco Polo visited the island about 1284 A.D. He describes the men and women of the time. "The men," he says, "were unfit for war, and mercenaries in consequence were employed as soldiers in place of native troops. The only grains were rice and sesame, of which they made oil. Their food was milk, rice and flesh, and for drink they used wine drawn from trees (toddy). The island produced more beautiful and valuable rubies than are to be found in any other part of the world, as also sapphires, garnets, topaz, amethysts, and other precious stones. The king is said to have the finest ruby that was ever seen, as long as one's hand and as big as a man's arm, without spot, shining like fire, and not to be bought for money. Kublai Khan offered the value of a city for it, to which the king replied that he would not exchange it for the treasure of the whole world, as it had come down to him from his ancestors. There is a very high mountain in the island—the ascent to the top is only practicable by the help of iron chains —where there is to be found the tomb of Adam."

About fifty years later, Sir John Maundeville describes his visit to Ceylon. Although it is now generally believed that this writer's account of his travels is mythical and not to be relied upon, yet he seems to have hit upon a correct description of the island, especially in respect of its dimensions. He mentions particularly Adam's Peak and the trade in elephants.

The friar Odoricus visited Ceylon at the close of the thirteenth century. His account is full of the marvellous, and contains only one interesting item of information, namely, that the divers after precious stones anointed themselves with lemon-juice to keep off horse-leeches.

In 1340 A.D., the city of Venice, having obtained an authoritative Bull from the Pope, entered into a treaty of commerce with the Sultan of Egypt, and for over a century had the monopoly of the Western trade with Ceylon, until the discovery of the Cape route to India by Vasco de Gama. That the Venetians conducted their trade with Ceylon with vigour and success is proved by the number of Venetian coins found in modern times as Sinhalese treasure-trove. These coins bear on the obverse the figure of the Blessed Virgin Mary, and on the reverse that of the Pope blessing the Doge of Venice, with name and year. They are of the purest gold, being of 24 carats, and their name, "veneziano," has been corrupted and adopted into the Sinhalese language as "vilisiano," and now means pure, unalloyed gold.

The accounts of Ceylon from the fourteenth to the sixteenth century are numerous, and the information contained in them is necessarily much alike. About the end of the fourteenth century, Ludovico Barthema, citizen of Bologna, visited Ceylon. He mentions that the inhabitants were depending on the southern provinces of India for rice, the island itself not yielding sufficient for their consumption. Shortly afterwards Ceylon was visited by the Venetian Nicolo di Conte. He gives a minute description of the talipot-tree, the leaf of which, he says, was used for writing, and, when extended, as a protection against rain. He also describes the wealth of the country in pearls and precious stones, and mentions the cinnamon-tree and the method of preparing the cinnamon. Jerome di Santo Stephano, who was in Ceylon in 1499, gives a similar description of the island. The Florentine Corsalie mentions Ceylon in two letters written in 1515 and 1517. He talks of the trade in elephants, which he states to have been highly lucrative. A few years later the first Portuguese settlement was established in Colombo. Thenceforward the history of Ceylon has been laboriously detailed by European writers.

Before proceeding to detail the circumstances of the Portuguese occupation of Ceylon, it would be well to say a word or two about the causes which led to Portugal adopting the rôle of a colonising Power. To her, indeed, is due the credit of opening up the East to the beneficent influences of Western civilisation. Portugal, though at present an enfeebled and decrepit nation, can claim the privilege of being the pioneer of Christianity and Western civilisation in the Orient. The constant conflicts which the Portuguese were obliged to wage in order to keep off the Moors from the Peninsula had converted them into a race of robust soldiers, and a succession of internal troubles had made war their constant occupation. With the advent of internal peace and the foundation of the famous dynasty under John I., they began to pant for victories outside their own kingdom, and this at a time when the States of the rest of Europe were wasting their resources in internal warfare. So they pursued the adventurous Moor, whom they had driven from the Peninsula, to his home in Morocco, and their history from the time of the Crusades, in which they played an important part, was one continual struggle with the militant Mahomedans. King Alphonso V., the grandson of John I., carried on this struggle with such vigour that he obtained the surname of the "African." The Moors, however, were still rich and influential. They held in their hands the trade with the Indies; and the luxuries which civilisation had rendered popular in Europe were the monopoly of Mahomedan commerce. Venice had the foresight to meet the Mahomedan merchant half way. Her ships sailed to Alexandria and brought back to Europe the rich spices of the East, and Portugal, envying her great prosperity, resolved to obtain for herself some portion of this Eastern trade.

Prince Henry the Navigator, a son of John the Great, devoted his life to the discovery of a sea route to the continent of India. With untiring energy he sent successive expeditions to sail round the continent of Africa and thus arrive at India, but he did not live to see the fruition of his labours. It was left to King John II., surnamed the Perfect, to complete the work of his great-uncle, Prince Henry. Absorbed with the same ambition of discovering the sea route to India, he gathered round himself the most eminent mathematicians of his day, and did much to improve the art and practice of navigation.

In 1497, Vasco de Gama rounded the Cape of Good Hope, and striking the south-east coast of Africa, after many adventures, reached the port of Melinda—a place two hundred miles north of Zanzibar—in April, 1498. After a short stay there, where he was fortunate enough to obtain experienced pilots, he arrived off Calicut, on the south-west coast of India, in June, 1498. Calicut was then ruled by a powerful Hindu king who was called the Xamorin. At this period the Mahomedan power in India had not yet reached its zenith. In the north of India and the Deccan were Mahomedan States, but the south had not yet fallen under the crushing arms of Islam. The Hindu raja of Vijiyanagar was the most powerful ruler in the south, and the potentates whom the Portuguese first met were all Hindus. But the commerce of these Hindu kings was completely in the hands of Moplas, or Moorish merchants, who were therefore most inimical to the Portuguese. The Moplas objected to their monopoly of commerce falling into the hands of any European race, and the Portuguese, in turn, were only too ready to satiate their rooted hatred of the Mahomedan in the continent of India.

De Gama, having found the long-searched-for sea route, returned home in triumph in 1499, and was received with great pomp and acclamation by his king and countrymen. King John had died in the meantime, and his successor, King Emmanuel, having realised the dreams of Prince Henry the Navigator, took unto himself the title of "Lord of the Conquest, Navigation, and Commerce of Ethiopia, Arabia, Persia, and India," a title which, in 1502, was confirmed to him by a Bull of Pope Alexander VI.

It is not necessary to further follow the fortunes of the Portuguese in India. No nation that ever came to the East has been so well served by contemporary historians. The pages of De Couto, De Barros, Gaspar Corea, Ribeiro, and many others, are full of the details of the rise and downfall of a colonial empire whose greatness has only been excelled by that of Great Britain three centuries later. Suffice it to say that in the interests of their trade the Portuguese were obliged to establish and maintain factories at the chief ports of South India, as they subsequently did at Colombo. The machinations of their rivals, the Mopla merchants, compelled them to station military garrisons for the protection of these factories. As a result of the strife that gathered round their commercial operations and of the presence in India of large numbers of their nation, the Portuguese gradually transformed themselves into a colonising Power.

The missionary was not slow to follow the soldier into regions which the latter had practically made his home. First the devout Franciscan and the austere Capuchin, and then the ardent Jesuit, under the standard of the great Francis Xavier, preached that second propaganda of Christianity in the East, the results of which endure in Ceylon to the present day in spite of a century and a half of bitter persecution. To quote the words of the historian of the great Albuquerque: "At a time when the political interest in the career of the Portuguese in Asia diminishes, the religious interest increases. The new heroes of Portugal are not her soldiers or sailors, but her missionaries. These were the men who made their way into the interior of India and who penetrated the furthest East. China, Japan, and even Thibet witnessed their presence and heard their preaching. The great Emperor Akbar gave them not an unkindly welcome at his court at Agra, and they laboured among the savages of the Spice Islands as well as among the learned men of China and of India."

Don Lourenço de Almeida, son of the Viceroy of Cochin, was despatched in 1505 on a voyage to the Maldive Islands. Don Lourenço, although only eighteen years of age, was a gallant soldier, and held the appointment of chief captain of the Indian seas, and had earned for himself a great reputation at the bombardment of Quilon, in the south of India. Driven by stress of weather, he was forced to seek shelter in the harbour of Point de Galle. It is said that the king received him with great pomp and recognised the suzerainty of Don Emmanuel, King of Portugal. The truth, however, is that a chieftain of the south deceived Don Lourenço, and by personating the king of Ceylon and making promises of tribute, obtained for himself rare and costly presents from the Portuguese. This was the first visit of the Portuguese to Ceylon. The Abbé le Grand, the French editor of Ribeiro's "History of Ceylon," narrates the incident as follows: "In the same manner, Lourenço de Almeida, wishing to go to the Maldive Islands, where his father had sent him, and not knowing the right course for these islands, fell in at Point de Galle in 1505. He was made to believe that the king of Ceylon was then there, that he had heard much of the power of the Portuguese, and that from the fame of their valour and riches he was ardently desirous to know them, and to form a strict alliance with them. This assertion was too flattering not take in Lourenço de Almeida. He selected Payo de Sousa to compliment the king in his name, to offer him the friendship of the Portuguese nation, and, if possible, to form an advantageous treaty with him. Payo de Sousa landed, and was informed that the king was then at one of his country seats rather far inland. He was conducted thither through many by-ways, and was detained a long time before he received an audience, had the mortification to be obliged to go through all the weariness of Oriental ceremoniousness, and was after all deluded by an officer in some authority at Point de Galle who counterfeited the king of Ceylon. Payo only discovered on his return to the ship, after his patience had been long tried, that he had been deceived by the natives." To Albuquerque is due the honour of having established firmly the Portuguese sovereignty in India. But great as was his work, he was the victim of the jealousies of many of his own colleagues, and was in consequence recalled to Portugal. His immediate successor was Lopez Suaris de Albergaria, a powerful nobleman, son of the chancellor of Portugal. This functionary, having failed disastrously in an expedition to the Red Sea, himself incurred the displeasure of the authorities at home. In order to retrieve his reputation, he turned his attention to Ceylon, and having arrived at Colombo in the latter part of the year 1517, successfully carried on negotiations with the king, Parakrama Bahu VII., who then reigned at Kotta, or Jayawardhanapura as the city was officially called. Colombo was at this time a busy port. Ships from Arabia, Bengal, Persia, and the Red Sea crowded the harbour in search of ivory and pearls, and Albergaria was anxious to secure for Portugal too a portion of the trade in these articles, which was then in the hands of the Mopla merchants. The gentle and pacific nature of the king, and the great reputation which the Portuguese had already acquired in the neighbouring continent of India, contributed materially to help him in his negotiations. A factory was soon established in Colombo, and a fortress was built to protect it. The latter was situated at the entrance to the Colombo harbour, and occupied an almost impregnable position. Albergaria placed in it a garrison of two hundred men under the command of Juan de Silva, with a factor, a secretary, and a chaplain—the first Christian missionary who set foot on the shores of Ceylon after the lapse of several centuries. Albergaria then set sail for Cochin, leaving behind him four gunboats to protect the garrison in case of need. This fort was, however, a temporary structure. In 1520 Loupo de Britto, the successor of Juan de Silva, by a special order of King Don Emmanuel, laid the foundations of a permanent fort in Colombo.

It may not be without interest to reproduce the Sinhalese account of the arrival of the Portuguese, as given in the Sinhalese chronicle of the Rajavaliya. The record says:—

"At that time, in the year 1522 of our Lord Jesus Christ, there came a ship to the harbour of Colombo from the Portuguese settlement of Jambudwipa, having by the power of God escaped the perils of the deep. The men who saw it while lying in the harbour came and thus reported to Parakrama Bahu: 'There is in our harbour of Colombo a race of people fair of skin and comely withal. They don jackets of iron and hats of iron; they rest not a minute in one place. They walk here and there.' And with reference to their use of bread, raisins, and arrack, the informants said: 'They eat hunks of stone and drink blood; they give two or three pieces of gold and silver for one fish or one lime. The report of their guns is louder than thunder when it bursts upon the rock Yughandara. Their cannon-balls fly many a *gawwa* (league) and shatter fortresses of granite.' These and countless other details were brought to the hearing of the king. On learning this news, the king, Dharma Parakrama Bahu, summoned his four brothers to the city, and having informed them and other leading persons and wise ministers, inquired, 'Shall we live on friendly terms with them, or shall we fight?' Thereupon Prince Chakkrayuddha said: 'I will myself go, and after seeing with my own eyes what manner of men they be, advise one of the two courses.' Having so said, he disguised himself and went to Colombo harbour, watched the actions of the Portuguese, and having formed his opinion, returned to the city and addressed the king: 'To fight with these men is useless; it will be well to give them audience.' The king accordingly gave audience to one or two of the Portuguese, made them presents, and in return received presents and curiosities from them; and likewise sending many tokens of respect to the great King of Portugal, lived on very friendly terms with him. Let it be noted that from that day the Portuguese gained a footing in Colombo."

The welcome given to the Portuguese by the king of Kotta did not, however, last very long. The Moorish traders at Colombo, regarding their European rivals with jealous eyes, lost no time in misrepresenting the objects of the Portuguese to the king. Themselves a powerful political faction in the island, they approached the king and pointed out to him that his so called allies would soon procure reinforcements from India and obtain for their own king the sovereignty of the island. Convinced at length of what he thought to be the ulterior motive of the new settlers, the king gave way to their persuasion, and with his connivance a raid, headed by the Moors, was made on the new Portuguese settlement, with the result that a few of the

Portuguese were killed and wounded. The Portuguese commandant behaved with exemplary tact, and shrewdly suspecting the Moorish traders of instigating the attack, sent an embassy to the king at Kotta, which was so far successful that peace was once more established.

In the meantime the disappointed Moors invited to their assistance the powerful Moor of Calicut, whom the Portuguese historians name Baléacé. He is evidently the same as Paichi Marikar of Sinhalese history. This man set out for Colombo with four ships and an army of five hundred men, and arriving at the port of Colombo, commenced hostile operations by destroying all the shipping that lay there. He then landed in great state, and represented to the king that the Portuguese governor of India had been defeated in war by his master, the king of Calicut, and that all their men had fallen prisoners into their hands. In the name of his royal master he now demanded the surrender of the Colombo garrison, which had taken refuge within the king's citadel of Kotta. This garrison only numbered about seventy men. The king, fearing for his own kingdom, and having no reason to doubt the words of the Moorish chieftain, called the Portuguese refugees before him, and told them that he was, much against his own will, compelled, in order to maintain the safety of his own kingdom, to deliver them into the hands of the Moors. The seventy Portuguese thereupon left the city of Kotta, and fighting with the desperation caused by the prospect of certain death, succeeded eventually in driving the Moors away from Colombo and regaining their fort.

We have seen that after the death of Vijaya Bahu the kingdom was divided into three principalities, ruled over by his three sons, namely, Bhuvaneka Bahu at Kotta, Mayadunna at Sitavaka, and Rayigam Bandara at Rayigam. Peace did not prevail among them for long, owing to the intention of Bhuvaneka Bahu II. to adopt his grandson by his daughter, Dharmapala, as his successor. Mayadunna was the first to resist. In order to withstand successfully the opposition of his brothers, Bhuvaneka Bahu sought the aid of the Portuguese, and contracted an alliance, offensive and defensive, with them. In 1536, while matters were in this state and Mayadunna was making preparations for war, seven ships belonging to the Xamorin of Calicut arrived off Colombo, and sent an imperious demand for the immediate surrender of all Portuguese. With the aid of Salappu Arachchi, who led 600 men, the enemy were driven away, although a party of them managed to make their way to Sitavaka. There they persuaded Mayadunna to send a message to the Xamorin for help. The message was accordingly sent, with the result that the Xamorin despatched to Colombo a fleet of forty-five ships under the command of Ali Ibrahim Marikar, described by Ribeiro as "a bold pirate but a gallant cavalier." He arrived in Colombo at the beginning of October, and being immediately joined by Mayadunna, the two laid siege to Kotta. The king of Kotta thereupon sent an envoy to Goa and Cochin, begging for help to withstand the siege. On arriving at Cochin the king's envoy was glad to find Alphonso de Sousa with a fleet. De Sousa, realising the gravity of the situation, set sail for Colombo. The Marikar, being apprised of this fact, abandoned the siege and withdrew with his fleet, while Mayadunna made peace with his too-confiding brother. When De Sousa arrived in Colombo tranquillity had been restored. He received a hearty welcome from the king, who was thus assured of the good faith of his Portuguese allies. No sooner had Mayadunna got back to his capital, however, than he sought afresh to destroy his brother. A conspiracy was discovered to poison the king, and the conspirators were put to the torture. Mayadunna then sent another embassy to the Xamorin of Calicut, backed up with presents of great value. The Xamorin thereupon despatched a fresh fleet of fifty-one ships, with 8,000 men-at-arms, under the command of three distinguished Moors—Paichi Marikar, his brother Kundali Marikar, and Ali Ibrahim. The men carried muskets, bows, and lances, and four hundred pieces of artillery, mostly of bronze, were provided. This fleet was, however, not destined to reach Colombo. It was pursued by the Portuguese and totally defeated, and of those who encamped on land a great number were killed, two hundred guns were taken, and the camp was plundered and captured by De Sousa, who commanded the Portuguese fleet. This signal defeat of his ally did not stop Mayadunna from making further plans. The king of Rayigam happened to die about this time, and Mayadunna, entering that kingdom, took possession of it, and laid hands on the treasures of his brother, a good deal of which he sent as presents to the Xamorin, with a request for further aid. The king of Kotta simultaneously made preparations for his defence, and sent to Goa for aid. This message was received by the governor of Goa in June, 1538. The governor immediately sent for Miguel Fereira, who was particularly well acquainted with Ceylon, and placed him in charge of the proposed expedition. All preparations were completed by the beginning of the following year, when the fleet under Fereira made its way to Mannar, where he learnt that Paichi Marikar had landed and strongly established himself at the Puttalam river. The enemy's ships had been drawn ashore and secured by chains. Fereira fell on them unexpectedly, seized their boats, and after heavy fighting, the fortifications were abandoned and the Marikar's ships and artillery were all captured by the Portuguese. Fereira then sailed to Colombo with all his plunder and was warmly welcomed by the king of Kotta. Fereira now joined the king of Kotta in an expedition against Sitavaka. The allied forces entered the kingdom of Sitavaka and caused considerable damage. Fereira sent a Mudaliyar informing Mayadunna that he was determined to establish peace in the kingdom of Kotta, and demanded the unconditional surrender of the Moorish generals and their followers who had taken refuge in this court. In great alarm Mayadunna sent a humble message begging for peace, but refusing to surrender men who had sought his shelter. The king of Kotta, as usual, was inclined to make terms, but the Portuguese general insisted on the surrender of the Moors, and Mayadunna, pressed to the utmost, arranged for their surrender by means of strategy. Paichi Marikar and Kundali Marikar with their followers were advised to make their escape by night into the forests, where they were told to wait until Fereira should leave the country. While they were taking refuge in the forests they were surrounded by a force of Paduas, described by Ribeiro as the cruellest caste among the Sinhalese, were shot down, their heads cut off, and sent to Fereira. Peace was immediately made, and the king of Kotta, in great delight, distributed money and presents freely among the Portuguese, and sent 30,000 crusados to Goa, as payment for the services of the fleet.

The king of Kotta despatched ambassadors to Portugal, one of whom was Salappu Arachchi, in order to request the king, Don John of Portugal, to recognise Dharmapala, the son of Tribuli Banda by Bhuvaneka's daughter, as heir to the kingdom. The ambassadors took with them an image of the prince, as well as a golden crown set with divers precious stones. The King of Portugal received the ambassadors with great ceremony, and placed the crown upon the head of the image. An official confirmation of the event was drawn up, and the ambassadors returned to the island, together with a party of priests of the Order of St. Francis, who were welcomed by the king of Kotta and allowed full liberty to preach Christianity throughout his dominions. One of these priests, Father Pascal, with two companions, went to the kingdom of Kandy, where they were well received by Jaya Vira. They built there a church and several houses, and gained such an influence over the king that he was only prevented from becoming a Christian through the fear of displeasing his subjects. Jaya Vira thereupon sent to the governor of Goa for a captain and some soldiers for his protection. The governor, delighted with the news, promised to send a force of 200 men under the command of Antonio Barreto. Mayadunna, becoming aware of Jaya Vira's intentions, sent messengers and urged him to abandon them, pointing out that they could only result in one of two disasters—either the Portuguese would seize on his kingdom or his subjects would put him to death. Jaya Vira was so impressed with his cousin's message that he promised to kill all the Portuguese who should come into his kingdom. Barreto, unaware of the changed intentions of Jaya Vira, landed at Batticaloa, coming by way of Mannar and Galle, with 120 men and a few guns, and marched overland to Kandy. On approaching the capital city he received information, evidently from one of the priests, of the conspiracy which had been formed against him. Addressing his soldiers, he pointed out that the only course open to them was to beat a retreat ; so, burning all the baggage which he had taken and reserving only a small supply of biscuits, he made for Trincomalee. The king, apprised of Barreto's retreat, sent a large force of men to attack the Portuguese in the rear. When they came up with the Portuguese, the latter continued their retreat, all the time keeping up a continuous fight, which was only interrupted by nightfall. The morning, however, found the enemy's forces increased to about 8,000 men. The Portuguese captured one of the enemy's Mudaliyars, from whom it was ascertained that the enemy's intention was to press and surround the Portuguese at a narrow bridge. Arriving at the bridge, as a last resort, Barreto hamstrung the Mudaliyar, thus compelling the enemy to attend to the Mudaliyar, and with the delay thus obtained he was enabled to seize the bridge and cross over it in safety. He then destroyed the bridge, which prevented them from following him, and thus escaped to Trincomalee, thence making his way to Sitavaka. Says Ribeiro : "The retreat was a most magnificent piece of generalship, and can only be compared to that of Decius from before the Samnites—an incident which has been immortalised by Titus Livius." Although the retreat lasted three consecutive days, not one of the 120 men was lost. Mayadunna persuaded Barreto that all this treachery was due to the instigation of the king of Kotta, but a few days after he reached Colombo ambassadors arrived from Kandy to convey an expression of the king's great regret for what had taken place. He cast the whole blame upon Mayadunna, and as proof of his repentance he returned the guns which had been left behind, and sent 10,000 pardaos to be distributed among the soldiers.

About this time the inhabitants of the island of Mannar, hearing of the illustrious missionary, Francis Xavier, and of his preaching in India, invited him to come and preach to them. Xavier, unable to leave India at the time, sent to Mannar one of his assistants, whose preaching resulted in the conversion of the whole island to Christianity. Mannar was then a part of the kingdom of Jaffna, which was ruled by a king called Sanghili.

OLD PORTUGUESE TOMBSTONE.

(Dug up near the site of the Battenberg battery in the fort of Colombo nearly thirty years ago, when the Breakwater works were begun. It bears the following inscription : "Here lies Helena Roiz, who was wife of Fernando Roiz, whom they murdered at Berberim (Beruwala). Died on the 23rd of June in the year 1565").—Reproduced by permission from the *Journal of the Royal Asiatic Society* (Ceylon), xviii. 2, 375.

Hearing that his subjects at Mannar had embraced Christianity, the king sent an armed force to the island, and the people were asked to renounce their new religion under pain of death. On their refusing to do so they were all put to death—men, women, and children, to the number of six hundred. Francis Xavier thus alludes to the incident in a letter written to his Society, dated from Cochin, January 27, 1545 : "The island of Mannar is about 150 miles from this place. Its inhabitants sent me some of their people to beg me to go there and baptize them, as they had determined to become Christians. I was occupied on affairs of the greatest importance relating to the interests of religion, and so could not go myself, but I persuaded a certain priest to go instead of me and baptize as many as possible. He had already baptized a great number, when the Raja of Jaffnapatam, under whose dominion the island lies, most cruelly put to death a large number of the converts simply because they had become Christians. Let us give thanks to our Lord Jesus Christ that even in our time He does not let us lack martyrs, and that while He sees so few souls availing themselves of His divine mercy and indulgence to work out their salvation, He permits in the mystery of His providence that human barbarity should fill up the destined ranks and number of the blessed."

In 1548 Francis Xavier went to Kandy unattended by an escort. His name had preceded him, so that the king, Jaya Vira, received him with great respect, and allowed him liberty to preach. After having received many into Christianity, Xavier went to Goa with an ambassador of the king. Xavier subsequently got the governor of Goa to send a punitive expedition to the king of Jaffna, who finally submitted to the Portuguese and made reparation for the cruelties he practised at Mannar. In 1549 the king of Kotta was again pressed by Mayadunna, who sent ambassadors to the governor, Jorge Cabral, craving assistance against his brother and promising to pay 10,000 crusados in cash and large quantities of pepper and cinnamon. Don Jorge de Castro was selected to command this expedition, and he was put at the head of 600 men. He started at the beginning of January, 1550. On reaching Colombo, he promptly marched to Kotta, which Mayadunna was besieging. The latter retired in haste to Sitavaka, but not without leaving behind a strong garrison to oppose the Portuguese. A joint movement was arranged with the king of Kotta, and Don Jorge and the king met Mayadunna's forces somewhere in the vicinity of Mutwal. The enemy lay entrenched, but were captured in a midnight attack. The allied forces then marched until they came to a second fortified position of the enemy at Malvana, which too was carried after a sharp engagement. But the decisive battle was not fought until they got to the village of Gurubabila, which had been fortified with stout walls and bastions. There they met Mayadunna himself, and after a desperate battle, in which he was defeated, Mayadunna betook himself to the mountains, and left his capital in the hands of the allied forces, who plundered and sacked the place.

Mayadunna, finding that resistance was unavailing, once more sought a policy of conciliation. He sent ambassadors to the king of Kotta expressing his repentance and his intention to make all possible amends for his conduct. Once more was the king of Kotta deceived by his brother's protestations. Being compassionate as well as brave, he yielded to Mayadunna's request and sent him an invitation to the city for the purpose of arranging the conditions of peace. Mayadunna attended the city accompanied by his chief Mudaliyars and the king received him affectionately. Peace was made on the condition that Mayadunna should never in future make war against his brother, and that he would restore to him all the districts he had seized. He was also to pay Don Jorge de Castro 100,000 pagodas, and further to furnish all necessary supplies for the intended expedition to Kandy. Don Jorge immediately began his preparations for the expedition, though warned by the king of Kotta against the deceitfulness and treachery of the king of Kandy. The latter had in the meantime got together an army of 40,000 men, and strongly fortified his capital. On the Portuguese forces arriving within a league of Kandy, a French captain, who had been a prisoner in the city, managed to escape, and arriving at the Portuguese camp, warned De Castro of the king's intended treachery. De Castro then summoned a council, which decided that the best course would be to sound a retreat at once.

Accordingly, they began to retreat as fast as they could. The king, on realising this fact, hurriedly seized upon the defiles on the road and worried the Portuguese with shots and arrows. The Portuguese, however, struggled through, though not without the loss of 700 men, including 400 Portuguese. They then entered the territories of Mayadunna, and a Mudaliyar with 500 men met the Portuguese, and invited them on behalf of Mayadunna to Sitavaka, where all assistance would be provided. Don Jorge, suspecting the intentions of Mayadunna, suddenly withdrew by a by-road, leaving through necessity thirty wounded men in the camp, who were taken before Mayadunna and beheaded. The king of Kotta met the Portuguese forces on their retreat, and conducted them to his capital, providing them with all necessary assistance. Don Jorge then withdrew to Colombo, and left for Cochin. This was in September, 1550. In October of the following year Don Affonso de Noronha was appointed viceroy of India. On his way to Goa he was miscarried to Colombo. The king of Kotta proceeded to Colombo to welcome him, and the viceroy landed with all his nobles, and met the king at the monastery of St. Antonio. The king asked for assistance against Mayadunna, and the viceroy promising that this would be his first care on reaching Goa, asked for 200,000 pardaos at once. The king pointed out that the unfortunate expedition of Don Jorge had cost him 70,000 pardaos already, and begged to be excused. The viceroy, showing great annoyance at this refusal, went on board his ship. In order to appease him, the king sent 15,000 pardaos through the Brahman pundit, and some very valuable jewellery, including rubies and cat's-eyes, to be sent to the Queen of Portugal. Mayadunna's promises of good behaviour were not kept. He again began to make war upon his brother, and the king of Kotta sent to oppose him a force under his son-in-law, Tribuli Banda. After a few skirmishes the enemy found themselves on the other side of the Kelani river, while Tribuli Banda was encamped this side, and facing them. The king of Kotta was with his forces, and while he was looking out of the window, was unexpectedly shot through the head, and fell down dead. For some time it was doubted whether this was an act of treachery or a pure accident, until some years later a Portuguese soldier confessed on his death-bed that it was he who had fired the shot which had killed the king, though it was a pure accident, and happened when he was aiming at a dove. The death of the king naturally created much confusion at this critical time. Tribuli Banda, better known as Vidiya Raja, immediately withdrew his army into the capital, and after the obsequies were over, placed his son, Prince Dharmapala, on the throne. He himself and all the chief magistrates and nobles swore allegiance to the new king. Mayadunna, apprised of his brother's death, advanced upon Kotta, and sent a message calling upon the nobles to swear allegiance to him. They answered they had already sworn allegiance to their king, whom they were prepared to defend with their lives. Mayadunna thereupon advanced right up to the citadel of Kotta, was met by Tribuli Banda, and after a short engagement was defeated and forced to retire.

Now follows a piece of Portuguese history which tarnishes the fair fame of Portuguese rule and is stoutly condemned by the Portuguese historians themselves. In September, 1551, the new viceroy arrived at Colombo. The new king and all his nobles received him with all demonstrations of welcome. Much to their surprise, the viceroy sent his son with 500 men, who seized all the roads leading from Kotta and forcibly occupied the palace itself. The viceroy then went in person to Kotta, arrested the chief Mudaliyars, and proceeded to search for the treasures of the ancient kings. Failing to find them, he ordered some of the chief Mudaliyars to be tortured in order to gather information. The people were scandalised and stricken with horror, and within a few days 600 Sinhalese had deserted to Mayadunna. All the gold, silver, jewels, and precious stones in the palace were seized by the viceroy. The young king was forced to enter into an agreement to pay 200,000 pardaos to the viceroy for the destruction of Mayadunna's power. Of this amount 80,000 pardaos was paid at once by the sale of the royal jewels.

The viceroy now took the field with an army of 3,000 Portuguese and 4,000 Sinhalese under Tribuli Banda. Sitavaka was once more attacked, and after a desperate battle was once more taken. Mayadunna fled to Deraniyagala. The viceroy occupied the palace himself. The city was plundered and even the foundations of the palace were dug up in search of treasure. On learning that Mayadunna was at Deraniyagala, Dharmapala prayed to the viceroy to send his father, Tribuli Banda, to seize Mayadunna. The viceroy demanded 20,000 pardaos as payment for this service. The king being unable to pay this money, the viceroy pleaded want of time and at once returned to Colombo, leaving Don Joao Henriques with 400 men as a garrison for the city of Kotta. The viceroy took with him to Goa a cousin of the king of Kotta, who was there baptized with great solemnity under the name of Don Joao. This prince was subsequently sent to Portugal, where he remained for some time, receiving an allowance of 600,000 reis. It is said that he was there treated with great respect and was allowed a chair in the royal presence—a privilege only accorded to the Princes of Conde. After some time he returned to India, where he was known as the prince of Ceylon, and married a Portuguese lady, the daughter of a noble cavalier. On his death he was buried in the church of St. Francis in Goa.

The viceroy had intended to take with him Tribuli Banda, the father of the king, but the latter, suspecting his intentions, sought concealment in the forests adjoining Kotta. On leaving for Goa, the viceroy left strict instructions with Captain Henriques to arrest Tribuli. The king pointed out that this would be a most unwise step, in that his father's assistance would be of the utmost importance in the approaching campaign against Mayadunna. Tribuli returned to Kotta under a safe-conduct and made arrangements with the captain for the proposed campaign. Before they could embark upon it the captain fell ill and died on May 1, 1552, and was succeeded by Diego de Mello Coutinho, who, lacking the captain's caution, was determined to carry out the viceroy's instructions. Tribuli, relying upon the safe-conduct given by Henriques, came into Kotta, was arrested in the king's palace itself, and was taken to Colombo and kept in chains. This arrest caused considerable excitement. Tribuli's wife fled to Rayigam to arrange for her husband's release. While in prison he was influenced by some Franciscan Fathers to become a Christian, and was instructed and secretly baptized by them. The then captain of Colombo, Don Duarte Daca, hearing of this, was enraged, and forbade the priests to approach the prisoner, and made his imprisonment more rigorous. Tribuli's wife, however, was successful by means of bribery in effecting h s escape; and, getting together the men whom his wife had brought with her, Tribuli took the road to Galle, destroying and burning all the Portuguese buildings on the way, and went to Rayigam and stationed himself at Pelenda. Dharmapala was dismayed at all this. He begged the captain as well as his father to forget their private quarrels and to make common cause against Mayadunna. The captain acceded to this request, but demanded 1,000 crusados to cover the expenditure of fifty Portuguese soldiers. The king had no money to spare, and his own great chamberlain sent his girdle of gold, valued at 500 crusados, to pay for the men, but only succeeded in obtaining twenty Portuguese. Having obtained the assistance of the prince of the Seven Korales, the expedition advanced, the king's forces by one road, the prince's by another, and Tribuli Banda's by a third. The conduct of the Portuguese captain, Daca, seeming to be somewhat suspicious, the king ordered his men to retire. Tribuli Banda then determined to punish the captain for his ruthless conduct. He entered into a treaty with Mayadunna by which he was to marry Mayadunna's daughter, a widow, and her daughter to marry Dharmapala's younger brother. This, however, was prevented by the shrewdness of the aged grandmother of the king, who sought and interviewed Tribuli and persuaded him to break off the arrangement he had made. Daca was happily now succeeded by Fernao Carvalho. A new treaty was then entered into between the king and Tribuli and the prince of the Seven Korales, and the allies invaded the territories of Mayadunna so effectually that he was obliged to sue for peace. In 1553 the King of Portugal wrote to the authorities at Goa reprimanding the viceroy for his conduct towards the king of Kotta and ordering immediate restitution of all the property of the king which yet remained unsold. As a matter of fact, the king only received 20,000 pardaos, the rest being set off as arrears of tribute and as voluntary gifts to Portuguese officials.

A few years later, about the year 1555, Mayadunna again took the field. Enraged with Tribuli Banda, whom the Sinhalese chroniclers call Vidiya Raja, Mayadunna sent his fourth son, Rajasinha (the "Raju" of Portuguese historians), to take Tribuli at his fortress of Pelenda. Rajasinha succeeded in carrying the place, and Tribuli made his escape to the Seven Korales. Received there by a prince of one of the Korales, he soon turned on his benefactor, put him to death, captured the city, and made himself master of the district. This so enraged the subjects of the prince that he was forced to flee to Jaffnapatam, where he met with his death, some say by treachery, others by accident. The aged queen, her daughter-in-law and grandson, and all the treasures of Tribuli Banda, fell into the hands of the king of Jaffna.

In 1559, Don Constantino de Bragança began to prepare a fleet for the invasion of Jaffna. The following year a large force of Portuguese, led by the viceroy himself, landed in that kingdom, and were opposed by the prince of Jaffna, with 2,000 men. After a short engagement the prince was defeated and was compelled to retire. The viceroy then took possession of Jaffna, which he entered in state. The king in the meantime entrenched himself in the fort, but upon the viceroy's advancing on the fort, he abandoned it, and the fort was captured. A force was thereupon sent in pursuit of the king. The guides who accompanied the force deceived them into going the wrong way, and they were unable to effect their purpose. The king of Jaffna, seeing that all was lost, begged for peace, which was granted on the following terms: the king of Jaffna to continue in power as the vassal of the Portuguese, paying a fixed tribute; that he should give up all the treasures of Tribuli Banda, as also the mother-in-law of that prince and the wife of the king of Kotta; and finally, that he should surrender the prince of Jaffna, heir to the throne, as hostage. All this was immediately complied with. After the so-called conclusion of peace, it was found that a general conspiracy had steadily been hatching among the natives. The Portuguese army were taken unawares and were compelled to beat a retreat. Taking the prince with him, the viceroy went to Mannar and raised a fortress there, and Parawas from South India were sent for and settled in that island. From Mannar he sent to the king of Kotta his aged grandmother and the other princesses who had been surrendered to him, and to Goa he sent the prince of Jaffna.

In the meantime, by the death of Mayadunna, the succession to the throne of Sitavaka passed to his son Rajasinha, who proved to be even a more implacable enemy of the Portuguese than his father. His object was to capture both Kotta and Colombo. The lay of the country favouring stratagem, he collected a large army, well equipped with artillery, and pretending that his object was Kotta, he proceeded thither on the 5th of October, 1564. The result of this campaign was a decisive battle in the village of Mulleriyawa. Says the Rajavaliya: "King Rajasinha mounted on his horse, galloped throughout the host, and urged on the fight. The battle was like a show of fireworks, and the smoke from the discharge of the muskets resembled mists in Durutu. Blood flowed like water in the field of Mulleriyawa. The Portuguese were attacked in such wise that no chance was left them to retire on foot. There fell of the Portuguese army 1,600, besides several of the Kotta men and officers."

This signal victory of Rajasinha caused much alarm among the Portuguese in respect of the territory they still retained in the island. Help was eagerly looked for from Goa, and until such help came they confined themselves within the walls of Colombo. On the arrival of reinforcements they again advanced into the interior and erected batteries on the Kelani river, and lined both banks of the river with troops as they proceeded on their way. Rajasinha quietly awaited their advance, and on reaching a place where they had posted a detachment the Sinhalese attacked them, and the Portuguese once more found themselves back in Colombo, after the loss of a great number of men. Rajasinha now adopted the offensive, and captured Kotta and destroyed it, and while advancing with the intention of besieging the fort of Colombo, was compelled to abandon this purpose in consequence of an insurrection in the Kandyan province. His usual success followed him in the quelling of the insurrection. He seized upon Kandy, and the king fled to Jaffnapatam. Rajasinha had now placed under his dominion the whole of the Kandyan country, but suspecting that a young prince of the royal family who had settled at Peradeniya, named Wijeyesundera Banda, was intending a rebellion, sent for him under the pretext of offering him the viceroyship of that province. On his arrival he was cast into a pit and beaten to death. Konappu Bandara, a son of the prince, fled to Colombo, and sought the protection of the Portuguese. He was baptized at Goa under the title of Don John, after the Duke of Austria, brother of Philip, King of Portugal. After this nefarious act, finding that the whole of the royal family opposed his claims to the throne, Rajasinha put to death all he could lay hands on, and once more attempted to seize upon Colombo, which was the goal of his ambition. But Rajasinha's former treachery now recoiled upon him, and while he was sitting down before the fortress of Colombo in full expectation of capturing it, Don John succeeded in making his way to Kandy, and putting himself at the head of the discontented Kandyan nobles, he slowly advanced, increasing his army at every step, and found himself master of the greater part of the Kandyan kingdom. This compelled Rajasinha to abandon the siege of Colombo, and to make an advance with the whole of his army on Don John. On the approach of Rajasinha, Don John slowly retreated to the south, and then for many years followed a desultory warfare between the two forces. This was the opportunity of the Portuguese. They were again successful in seizing Sitavaka itself, and a great portion of the Seven Korales. Kandy was occupied by the Portuguese, and the new prince, Don Philip, from whom was exacted a promise that he would marry a Portuguese lady, and who was himself a convert to Christianity, was elevated to the throne of Kandy. This proceeding Don John very naturally considered to be a slight upon himself, and in his chagrin he marched to Kandy, and having succeeded in removing his rival, Don Philip, by poison, made himself master of the situation, and throwing off the mask of friendship, drove the Portuguese out of his kingdom. Rajasinha, now enraged at his new rival, once more advanced against him. A battle took place at the base of Kadugannawa. The troops of Rajasinha were unable to resist the fury of Don John's attack. The sight of his disabled force and the many dead around them seems to have unmanned the aged Rajasinha. He lingered but for a few days, his end being hastened, according to the Rajavaliya, by the treachery of his attendants. He left his young rival, Don John, to renew that contest with the Portuguese to which he had devoted the whole of his life.

The character of Rajasinha has been well summarised by Pridham: "In the character of Rajasinha I. courage and ability were strongly blended with ferocity and cunning. At the advanced age of one hundred years he maintained much of the elasticity and energy of youth. The lesson acquired under his father's reign, that Europeans were only to be repelled by an altered system of native warfare, was duly put in force, and resulted in the success it deserved. Rajasinha's merit as a ruler was, however, confined to his military virtues. His first essays in war, though rude and irregular, were successful, and it was not until he encountered the Portuguese that he learnt its varying fortune. Unable to oppose them in the open field, he engaged in petty skirmishes. Nurtured under other and different influences, Rajasinha, while equally protecting the liberties of his country, might have devoted a portion of his energies and genius to healing the wounds gaping from every part of its social and political being. Though characterised as a monster of iniquity by the priestly historians, they are not able to conceal that he had some taste for literature and patronised all men of genius. By religion a Brahman, Rajasinha was not the prince to protect, and scarcely to tolerate, the religion of Buddhism, whose sacred books he destroyed and whose priests he degraded or extirpated, while exalting those of his own community. Hence it is that the Buddhist and Christian historians, who had equal reason to hate his memory—the former in his character as a persecutor, the latter in his career as their successful opponent—have combined to traduce a monarch whom, while loathing him for his cruelty and treachery, the European cannot fail to respect for qualities and impulses in general confined in their origin to sources supposed to exist only in the bracing temperature of a northern clime."

Rajasuriya Kumaraya succeeded Rajasinha on the throne of Sitavaka, but his subjects, dissatisfied with his *régime*, declared for Konappu Bandara, and the four Korales fell away from Sitavaka. He was put to death at the instance of the queen of Vidiya Raja, assisted by Manamperuma Mohotiya. Vidiya Raja's grandson, a child of five years, was nominally chosen sovereign, but within a short while Manamperuma Mohotiya deserted to Don Juan Dharmapala, who welcomed him and gave him the title of Jayasuriya Bandara. A mixed army of Portuguese and Sinhalese under his command advanced and occupied Sitavaka, which then passed into the hands of Dharmapala. Vidiya Raja's queen and son were transported to Goa.

Says Mr. Bell, the Archæological Commissioner: "So fell Sitavaka, which from a minor principality gradually made its power felt far and wide, bringing under subjection all the neighbouring provinces, and dealing the Portuguese some of the hardest blows received in the course of their internecine wars with the Sinhalese. In its rapid rise and fall the Sitavaka kingdom presents more than one point of resemblance to Macedon. Built up by the foresight and energy of one ruler, under the government of his warlike son it carried its arms and dominions far beyond its own original narrow limits; and upon his death, when still breathing vengeance and slaughter on his enemies, fell a prey to internal dissension and inevitable decay."

Perceiving that his opportunity had arrived by the death of his only formidable rival, Rajasinha, Konappu Bandara, or Don John, who had acquired considerable influence over the natives, proclaimed his independence and assumed the sovereignty of the island under the name of Vimala Dharma. The Portuguese, of course, refused to recognise his usurpation. During the temporary stay of Pedro Lopez de Sousa in Colombo, on his passage from Malacca to Goa, the Portuguese position in Ceylon was so well explained to that general that on his arrival in Goa he did not hesitate to represent to the viceroy the necessity for active measures for the subjugation of the Kandyan territory. The viceroy and council thereupon determined to equip an expedition with this object, and selected De Sousa himself as its leader. After some hesitation, De Sousa accepted the command on condition that Donna Catherina, the daughter of Don Philip Jaya Vira, the lineal heiress to the throne of Kandy, who was then in the hands of the Portuguese, should be given in marriage to his nephew, who, with his wife, should be placed on the throne of Kandy as tributary sovereigns of the King of Portugal. This request was conceded, and it was agreed that the marriage should not take place till the expedition had achieved its purpose. De Sousa immediately set out for Mannar. There meeting with Donna Catherina, he placed her, with great ceremony, at the head of the army, and by her presence acquired considerable influence over the natives. At Negombo his army was reinforced by the adhesion of the powerful chief called by the Sinhalese Jayasuriya Bandara, with the title Maha Mudaliyar, who joined him with 20,000 native troops. De Sousa advanced against Don John of Kandy with such impetuosity that Don John was defeated and compelled to take refuge in the woods, while Donna Catherina entered Kandy in triumph. A reward of 10,000 pagodas was offered for the head of Don John, but according to the Dutch historian Valentyn, Don John was so little alarmed by this information that he is said to have entered Kandy in the disguise of a beggar, to have set fire to the town in different parts, and to have escaped in the confusion.

Don John now thought of using stratagem to destroy the alliance of the Sinhalese chief, Jayasuriya, with the Portuguese. With this purpose he indited a letter which feigned to be a reply by Jayasuriya to one from Don John himself, promising to deliver all the Portuguese into the hands of the Sinhalese on condition that Jayasuriya should be made king of the low-country as tributary to Don John. This letter was entrusted to a confidential servant, whose instructions were to fall into the hands of the Portuguese, so that the incriminating letter, of the contents of which Jayasuriya was absolutely innocent, should be intercepted by the Portuguese. The ruse succeeded. De Sousa, on reading the letter, became ungovernable in his rage, and sending for the unsuspecting Sinhalese chieftain, with his own hands plunged a dagger into his breast. The native troops, hearing of the assassination of their leader, abandoned the Portuguese and joined the army of Don John. Heedless of their defection, De Sousa sent messages for help to Colombo and continued his march, only to be surrounded by the enemy at the pass of Balana. De Sousa was mortally wounded. The Portuguese were totally routed and many officers and chieftains, together with the queen, Donna Catherina herself, were made prisoners. Don John obtained a large supply of arms and ammunition by this victory. He attacked and captured the Portuguese forts inland, and procured the submission of the small princes, and having married Donna Catherina, became paramount ruler over the whole island save the kingdom of Jaffna and the forts of Colombo and Galle, and styled himself Don John Vimala Dharmasuriya I. In the interval of tranquillity, lasting three years, the Portuguese resolved to make another attempt to capture Kandy. Another squadron was equipped and despatched to Ceylon, under the command of Don Jerome de Azevedo, and the maritime districts on the western coast were recaptured, the old military forts again occupied, and the adhesion of the petty chiefs re-obtained. Azevedo then marched to meet Don John, who was strongly posted at Balana. A sharp battle ensued, and for some time the victory hung in the balance, but at length it declared itself in favour of the Sinhalese. Azevedo, severely wounded, beat a gallant retreat, and arrived in Colombo five days after the conflict. A cruel act of the Portuguese, who put to death, with great barbarity, the Sinhalese general, named Corea, notwithstanding a solemn pledge to the contrary, was horribly avenged by Don John, who mutilated numbers of the Portuguese prisoners, and ordering them to be deprived of their eyes, sent them back to Colombo.

In May, 1597, the aged Don John Dharmapala expired, leaving a last will and testament, by which he bequeathed the empire of Ceylon to the King of Portugal. The following is the text :—

"Made this twelfth day of August, 1580, in the city and fortress of Colombo, in the dwelling of His Highness Prince Don Joam, by the grace of God king of Ceylon. Pereoa Pandar (emperor), the aforesaid king being present, states to me, Antonio Ribeiro, notary public of His Majesty the King (of Portugal), lord of this city, in the presence of witnesses, that he, the king, succeeded to this kingdom of Ceylon on the death of King Bonegabao (Bhuvaneka Bahu), his lord and grandfather, who had no children and had during his life-time adopted him as his son and made him heir, with the sanction of the King of Portugal, Don Joam III., and further states that he possessed these kingdoms in the same manner as the aforesaid Bonegabao his grandfather, having his seat in the royal city of Kotta, the capital of the kingdom, now dismantled, and that afterwards, through various causes, the Madunna Pandar (Mayadunna), king of Seita Avaca (Sitavaka) and the Raaju (Rajasinha), his son, had tyrannically occupied and taken possession of all the kingdoms, leaving him only the city and fortress of Colombo, which the Kings of Portugal through their viceroys and captains defended for a long time, in order to restore the said kingdoms to him, which restoration they had, however, been unable to carry out, in consequence of other wars the viceroys were engaged in and the impoverished state of India, and he, the king, is advanced in years and in failing health, without sons and heirs to rightfully succeed him at his death, and feeling greatly indebted to the Kings of Portugal for all their mercies and help, and especially for the comforts of religion ministered to him by their priests, whereby he was converted to the Catholic faith, he, the king, bequeaths to the King of Portugal, Dom Manuel, and his heirs, all the kingdoms and lands with the hope that he will obtain possession of those kingdoms which are now in the hands of his enemies, giving him permission to fight his enemies by sea and land until he obtain possession of the territories which he had a right to, in the same manner as the kings of Kotta, who reigned over the kingdoms in this island"; &c.

The document was signed by the king, the witnesses being Friar Sebastiao de Chaves, Manuel Luiz, Estevan Figueira, Pero Jorge, Franquo Antonio Laurenço, and Manuel de Sousa Coutinho.

When matters were in this state, the Dutch, who had already established themselves in the East, turned their attention to Ceylon. Admiral Spilbergen, bearing secret instructions from the Dutch East India Company, was entrusted with the mission in 1601 of opening up relations with the king of Kandy. Arriving off Batticaloa with three ships, he landed under the guidance of a native pilot, and sent one of his officers to open up a correspondence with the Dissawa of the district. Spilbergen was conducted, with six of his men, on an elephant to the Dissawa, by whom he was received with apparent cordiality, but not without misgivings, as the natives at first mistook the admiral for a Portuguese spy. Spilbergen, on becoming aware of this fact, succeeded in undeceiving them, and was permitted to return to his fleet, whence, procuring presents from the Dissawa and from the king himself, he returned to his camp. After some misunderstandings on both sides, an arrangement was come to, and one of the Dutch officers was sent to the king at Kandy. The envoy returned thence with presents and a gracious letter, written by Don John's own hands, inviting the admiral to Kandy. Spilbergen, overjoyed at this event, was conveyed in the king's own palanquin with every mark of distinction, and soon entered the Kandyan territory. On his arrival there he was welcomed by the Mudaliyar, who conducted him to a rest-house hung with white tapestry—a mark of the greatest honour. His entry into Bintenne, where lived one of the emperor's wives, was attended by an escort of six Mudaliyars, with musicians and a large following. Then he passed through the city of the emperor's son at Uva. On approaching within a short distance of Kandy, the king sent his own palanquin, covered with cloth of gold, together with a number of elephants for the attendants. The chief Mudaliyar, who was a Portuguese renegade, accompanied by several Portuguese officers and by several thousand soldiers ot various nationalities—Turks, Moors, Sinhalese, Kaffirs, and Malays—escorted him to his lodging, which was furnished in the European style. The very same evening Spilbergen was entertained by Don John at his palace with great pomp, and the wearisome Sinhalese ceremonies were dispensed with on the occasion. Spilbergen declared to the king that his object was not so much to trade as to form an alliance, offensive and defensive, with the Sinhalese as against the Portuguese. The idea was welcomed by the king, who offered the Dutch all the cinnamon in his store. The king made inquiries of Holland, of the European wars, of the Church of Rome, of the Dutch service, and showed Spilbergen a very high mark of favour by taking him into the queen's apartments. He found her in the midst of her children and clad in the European manner. After this success, Spilbergen took leave of the king, leaving behind him two of his musicians, and departed for the squadron, laden with presents. No sooner, however, had the admiral's fleet left the coast of Ceylon, than another Dutch expedition under De Weerd arrived, and meeting with a kind reception from the king, De Weerd concluded a treaty with Don John, engaging himself to co-operäte with the king's forces in the attack of Point de Galle. He first gave offence to the king by releasing some Portuguese vessels he had recently captured; then, subsequently, under the influence of wine, he insulted the king, which cost him his life. The king then sent the following brief note to Enchuysen, the second in command of the Dutch fleet: "He that drinks wine is good for nothing; God has executed justice; if you desire peace, let there be peace; if war, war." Enchuysen thought it prudent not to resent the death of his superior officer, and on receipt of this letter, pacified the king and laid the foundation of a perfect reconciliation. The remaining years of Don John's reign were passed in tranquillity.—He died in 1620. Pridham has thus summarised his character :—

"Without the originality of Rajasinha, he was resolute and persevering. An able general and an excellent tactician, he knew how to seize the opportunities his foresight had created. On the other hand, he was equally cruel, selfish, and tyrannical. The justice which he exercised towards his subjects is said by Valentyn to have been strict and impartial, so that few crimes were perpetrated during his reign, and great regularity and precision were to be remarked in his administration. His opposition to the Portuguese proceeded, not from patriotism, by which Rajasinha was distinguished, but from his ambition alone, and a knowledge that they were his rivals for the possession of the island. The religion of Buddha was protected by him, and its neglected rites restored by the arrival of priests from Arakan, who renewed the *upasampada* (priestly) ordination, from much the same cause. While he renounced at Goa the religion of his fathers, he appears to have only nominally assumed that of the European conqueror."

On the death of Don John, two of the nobles —the prince of Uva and Senerat (Don John's brother)—sought to obtain the regency and guardianship of Don John's children. Senerat, who was a Buddhist monk, abandoned the robe, and coming to court, succeeded in getting his rival, the prince of Uva, assassinated within the precincts of the palace itself. Donna Catherina, though displeased with this act, was fearful of further trouble, and such was the courtly grace and appearance of her brother-in-law, Senerat, that not only did he obtain the regency, but soon succeeded in winning over Donna Catherina to be his wife and then obtained the sovereignty.

In 1612 Marcellus de Boschhouer arrived at Kandy with letters from the Dutch States-General to Senerat. The visit resulted in an offensive and defensive treaty being concluded between the Hollanders and the Sinhalese monarch, and the building of a fort by the Dutch at Trincomalee. Boschhouer was appointed admiral by Senerat, created prince of Mingona, and received other great honours. The Portuguese were alarmed at these events, and despatched a force of 4,000 troops under the command of Simon Corea to reduce the fort at Kotiyar. This Corea succeeded in doing, and captured the fort and massacred every one in it. Senerat, hearing of this, marched with a body of 5,000 troops, fell on Corea, and revenged himself for the massacre of his allies. Senerat, whose great ambition was to totally expel the Portuguese from the island, sent Boschhouer to Europe to procure a force of Dutch troops for that purpose. Boschhouer departed on this mission in 1615. Arriving in Holland and finding little sympathy from the directors of the Dutch East India Company, he proceeded to Denmark and entered into a treaty with Christian IV. on behalf of Senerat. He returned to Ceylon with two Danish vessels, which were followed soon after by five other vessels despatched under the command of a Danish noble, Giedde, under the auspices of the Danish East India Company. Boschhouer died during the voyage, and Senerat, missing his favourite and distrustful of Giedde, refused to ratify the treaty that had been arranged ; and Giedde returned to Denmark without succeeding in the object of his expedition. The Portuguese in the meantime pushed through with their conquests in the maritime provinces and erected forts at Trincomalee and Batticaloa. In 1623 Constantin De Sa was appointed captain-general of Ceylon. He gave prompt proof of his energy by building a fort at Sabaragamuwa and stationing a garrison of men at Sitavaka. He set himself the task of reforming the Portuguese army. The camp at Manikkadawara, from a garrison of the Portuguese army, was transformed into a school of war, under the able superintendence of Philip de Oliveira, an experienced soldier. De Sa, in 1630, sought the overthrow of Senerat by a decisive engagement. Pressing into service every soldier whom he could obtain, whether European or native, he advanced at the head of a large force into the interior. Having forced his way through the pass of Balana, he marched into Kandy, burning or destroying everything that came within his reach. Senerat, who had taken up his residence at Hangurangetta, sought refuge among the fastnesses of Uva, and while De Sa was in occupation of Kandy, sought to divert his attention by despatching a Sinhalese force to attack the Portuguese possessions in the north. This movement compelled De Sa to retreat, but yielding to imperative orders which came through the viceroy of Goa, he again took the lead at the head of 1,500 Portuguese and 20,000 auxiliaries. He burned Kandy, which was abandoned by Senerat's son, Rajasinha. Then he marched towards Uva, only to be surrounded by thousands upon thousands of Sinhalese. Under cover of night, and with the rain making the firelocks of the Portuguese useless, De Sa and his men were attacked and totally annihilated. Senerat's army followed up this success by recapturing the forts on the Mahaveli Ganga, and by besieging Colombo itself. Assault after assault was repulsed by the brave garrison, which had to strain every nerve for the purpose. Ultimately assistance arrived from Goa and Cochin, and the siege was abandoned. Senerat died in 1634. He divided his territory between his two step-sons, Vijaya Pala and Kumara Sinha, and his own son, Rajasinha II., to whom was allotted the kingdom of Kandy. Rajasinha, however, seized upon the territories of Vijaya Pala, whose imbecility led him to seek refuge with the Portuguese, with whom he ever after remained.

Rajasinha now entered into a treaty with the Dutch, whereby he agreed to let the Dutch have all the cinnamon and pepper in his kingdom. The Portuguese, hearing of this treaty, sent ambassadors to Kandy protesting against the arrangement. To them the king replied that, having promised the same to his friends the Dutch, he would like to see the men who would dare oppose him. Nettled by this resolute answer, and resolving upon forestalling an attack by a joint movement of the Dutch and Sinhalese, the Portuguese in 1638, under Diego de Mello, marched upon Kandy, meeting with little opposition. Kandy was plundered and burned ; Rajasinha deserted his capital, but in secret arranged for means to entrap the Portuguese. On the latter endeavouring to retreat, they found the pass of Balana blocked with large trees laid across it. The Sinhalese troops, who were commanded by four Mudaliyars—Don Alexis, Don Balthazar, Don Cosmos, and Don Theodosius—deserted, and are supposed to have gone over to Rajasinha. The Portuguese endeavoured to obtain terms of peace, but could get no answer. Hemmed in on every side, without obtaining any quarter, they sold their lives dearly. The whole of the Portuguese army, together with the generals, was completely annihilated.

And now commenced the war between the Dutch and the Sinhalese on one side and the Portuguese on the other, which eventually drove the latter away from Ceylon. This war was conducted on the basis of a treaty between Rajasinha and the Dutch. How faithfully the conditions of that treaty were kept by the latter will be seen later on. The terms of the treaty are thus described by Ribeiro :—

"That prince (Rajasinha), pleased with their discourse and protestations of friendship, concluded the following treaty with the Dutch : That all forts and lands possessed by the Portuguese on the island of Ceylon should be honestly and in good faith restored to the king of Kandy and that the Dutch Company should only retain some places of safety for the reception of the forces sent to assist the king ; that the king should keep up as large an army as he possibly could as long as the war lasted ; that he should pay all the expenses of war at a fixed rate for each ship and every gun, according to the size of the vessel and the calibre of the cannon ; that in addition to these expenses it should be duly written down that he should pay a certain sum for each officer and soldier who might die in his service, according to the rank and post they filled in the Dutch army; that certain rates should be paid for wounds received, that the men might be remunerated for the loss of an arm, a leg, or an eye, and that they might receive more for the loss of a right leg than a left leg, and so forth, accordingly as the party maimed might be more or less inconvenienced; and all the payments to be made on this account were exactly defined and written down. The articles of the treaty were thus accurately agreed upon; a fair copy of them was made; and the treaty was signed. The ambassadors returned to Batavia well satisfied with their negotiations, and neither party long deferred the execution of that which had been mutually promised. And thus a war was commenced which cost the crown of Portugal the possession of the island."

In 1639 the Hollanders sent from Batavia a fleet consisting of six ships of war and a large force of troops, with orders to destroy the forts of Batticaloa and Trincomalee, and to report the same to the king of Kandy. The Dutch fleet arrived at Batticaloa and found only forty Portuguese in the fort. The landing was easily effected, and after a two days' siege the garrison capitulated, when the fort was destroyed. The fleet then proceeded to Trincomalee and laid siege to that fort, which was garrisoned by fifty Portuguese, and ill provided with arms and ammunition. After a two days' siege the fort was surrendered, not, however, before twenty-three out of the fifty men had lost their lives. After destroying Trincomalee, the fleet returned to Batavia. In 1640 war was renewed by the Dutch with increased ardour. On the 15th January twelve Dutch ships appeared suddenly before Colombo. But perceiving the strength of the garrison, or it may be with the view of taking the smaller strongholds first, they proceeded to a village within a few miles of Negombo, where they disembarked upwards of 2,000 men, who approached the fortress of Negombo and quickly took it by assault. Having taken Negombo, Lucassan, the Dutch commander, strengthened the fortress with fascines and palisades, and leaving 300 men with six cannon to guard the fort, he took with him 2,000 soldiers and made a feint of advancing upon Colombo, and quickly passing on to Galle, before any reinforcements could reach that place, captured it after a resolute defence of eighteen days. Ribeiro relates a heroic instance of female devotion which occurred at the siege of Galle. The governor, Captain Lorenço Ferreira de Brito, had but lately married a young wife, who loved him passionately. On the night of the assault she was by the captain's side, animating him and his soldiers by her presence and assuring them by her courage. The gallant captain received five wounds, one of which broke his thigh and threw him on the ground. A Dutch soldier was on the point of killing him when his beautiful wife threw herself between them and called on the soldier, as a man and a Christian, to spare her husband's life, begging him, if he was determined to refuse her request, that he should first slay her. A Dutch officer, seeing what was going on, came to her rescue, and having attended to the wounded commander with great kindness, had him and his spouse safely embarked for Batavia.

Juan de Silva Tales, having been appointed viceroy of India, arrived at Goa late in the year 1640. His arrival quickly changed the aspect of affairs in Ceylon. Don Philip Mascarenhas was at once despatched with a force of 400 men, and with a plentiful supply of provisions, to drive the Dutch from their lately acquired territories. His first enterprise was against Negombo, and was crowned with success. After a short cannonading the place was conditionally surrendered. At Galle he was not equally successful, but his attack was so vigorous and so well sustained, that the Dutch governor, Jacob Coster, thought it necessary to proceed to Candy to obtain assistance from Rajasinha. Rajasinha, however, began to perceive that the expulsion of the Portuguese would only mean the substitution of the Dutch in their stead, and Coster, seeing that his promises were not fulfilled, exclaimed loudly against the king, and openly accused some of the king's ministers by name. On his return, Coster was treacherously murdered by Sinhalese guides.

Domestic strife now increased the troubles of the Kandyan kingdom. War broke out between Rajasinha and his brother, the prince of Uva. The prince was, after a brief

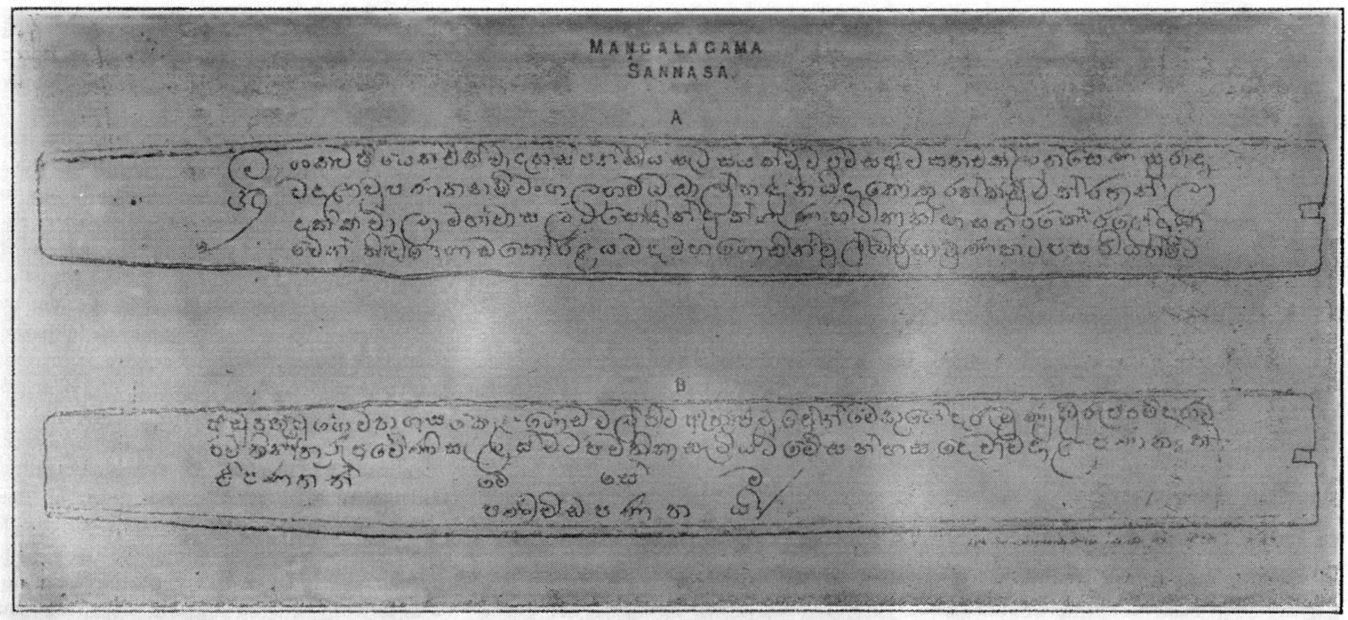

ANCIENT SANNAS (GRANT) OF THE SINHALESE KINGS.

(Dated 1644.)

war, expelled from his kingdom, and took refuge with the Portuguese. By then he was sent to Goa, where, having embraced Christianity, he lived till his death in 1654. In 1642, notwithstanding the treaty concluded between John IV., the King of Portugal, and the States-General of Holland, the basis of which was that each party should continue in the Indies in possession of what they actually held at the time, the war between the Dutch and the Portuguese continued with unabated fury in Ceylon. Rajasinha, acting on the defensive, had thrown out a chain of forts round his dominion, from the garrisons of which he obtained continuous information of the movements of the Portuguese and the Dutch alike. During the following year, 1643, several petty engagements were fought in the neighbourhood of Galle. The next year war was vigorously renewed on both sides, to the advantage of the Dutch, who, under the command of Carron, once more became masters of Negombo, which they again fortified by the erection of four earthen bastions at each corner of the fort, which formed a square. On each of these eight pieces of cannon were mounted. During the next two years nothing was attempted on either side, and after that an armistice was concluded between them, which continued in force till 1644. During this period a desultory warfare was carried on between Rajasinha and the Portuguese. Rajasinha now began to see that the Portuguese were even outmatched in rapacity by the Dutch, and accordingly he maintained an irregular struggle with both, "like a noble lion who, finding himself attacked by two tigers at once, keeps them both at bay." The last act of this long-continued tragedy was enacted in 1658. Colombo, defended by a garrison of 800 men, was besieged. It was blockaded both by land and by sea. The garrison was but ill supplied with provisions, and, in consequence, suffered severely from hunger, want, and showers of balls and shells. They were reduced to the utmost extremity, and capitulated on the one condition that they should be allowed to depart without molestation to their brethren at Jaffnapatam. This was granted, and on May 10, 1658, the Portuguese yielded the fortress of Colombo and their arms into the hands of the Dutch, who, in their turn, were in time destined to deliver it to another and stronger Power. But the refugees were not long to remain in Jaffna or Mannar. The Dutch, perceiving that the fickleness of Rajasinha might be the means of reinstating the Portuguese in their territories, advanced at once against these two strongholds, and capturing them, took the whole of the Portuguese garrison as prisoners-of-war, in which condition, the Portuguese historians bitterly complain, they and their females suffered untold injuries at the hands of their licentious conquerors. Such was the end of the Portuguese *régime* in Ceylon, the leading characteristics of which are now worthy of consideration.

The Portuguese rule in Ceylon has been criticised by many historians who wrote early in the last century. One has gone so far as to say that "in the whole of their proceedings we may look in vain for any traits of sound judgment or any justice in their conduct towards the natives of the island." Having reviewed their government at some length, we are now in a position to consider the soundness or otherwise of the criticisms which their *régime* has elicited.

In the sixteenth century the Portuguese were a great naval Power. They came to Ceylon by accident, and having discovered its commercial potentialities, determined to establish a factory at Colombo. In doing so the Portuguese had to deal with an island that was the victim of internal strife. From the inception of their government they were dragged in to share the strife. As the allies of the king of Kotta they became the enemies of Mayadunna and his successor, Rajasinha of Sitavaka, and the successive kings of Kandy, as also of the Xamorin of Calicut and his Moorish marauders. From the time of their arrival until their expulsion they were engaged in a conflict with one or more of these powers, and what they held in Ceylon they held at the point of the sword. That their intentions, from their own point of view, were good there cannot be the slightest doubt. Their missionaries, imbued with the zeal of Francis Xavier, fostered the national ambition of Christianising the whole country. It is wrong to say that they were cruel to the natives. It is true that when they fought as the allies of the Buddhist king of Kotta they destroyed the Hindu temples and *devalas* (places of worship) which the heretic Rajasinha had erected and endowed in order to make Hinduism the State religion. In such destruction the Sinhalese Buddhists were as keen as the Portuguese Christians. The King of Portugal had issued instructions to his officers that the Portuguese were not merely to settle but to colonise. An illustrious cavalier sought the hand of Donna Catherina, the rightful heiress to the throne of Kandy. Many a Portuguese nobleman intermarried with the Sinhalese aristocracy, and Sinhalese gentlemen of high rank took to themselves Portuguese wives. Among the latter may be mentioned the great general, Simon Corea Wickremasinghe. Sinhalese men of ability rose to the highest ranks. No office was too high for a native to fill, provided he was able to fill it. Don Fernando Mudaliyar rose to be captain-major of Colombo and afterwards of Goa. Pedro de Silva Mudaliyar, Peter de Abrew Mudaliyar, Belchior Butalho Mudaliyar, and others were trusted generals in the Portuguese army. Of course, warfare was not conducted in those days with that refinement to which we are accustomed at the present time; but the cruelties of the Portuguese in the treatment of their enemies were not worse than the excesses sometimes practised in European warfare three or four centuries ago.

The charge of religious bigotry which has been brought against the Portuguese is equally false. Tennent ("Christianity in Ceylon," p. 14) has asked himself the question, By what agency and expedients were effected the multitudinous conversions in Ceylon? The answer to this question can be inferred from the state of Christianity in Ceylon during the British times; while the Roman Catholic form of Christianity has survived a century and a half of Dutch persecution, and the Portuguese language, though in a corrupt form, is a living language, the number of Dutch Presbyterians is but a handful, and the language of the

OLD MURAL TABLET IN THE COLOMBO MUSEUM.

One of the few relics of the Portuguese occupation. The tablet bears this inscription: "Capella dos irmaos da confraria da santiss Rosario. Seu arco novamente feito na era de 1647 sendo prezidente Balthezar da Veiga" (Chapel of the Brethren of the Confraternity of the Most Holy Rosary. Its arch was rebuilt in the year 1647, Balthezar da Veiga being President").—Reproduced by permission from the *Journal of the Royal Asiatic Society* (Ceylon), xviii. 378.

Dutch is itself an unknown quantity. Tennent holds that Cordiner ("Description of Ceylon," London, 1807, i. 105) must have been but at least imperfectly informed when he states that the people were compelled to adopt the Roman Catholic religion without consulting their inclination, but that the Dutch, unlike the Portuguese, had refrained from the use of force for the propagation of their religious faith. "On both points," says he, "the historical evidence is at variance with these representations. I have discovered nothing in the proceedings of the Portuguese in Ceylon to justify the report of violence and restraint, but unfortunately, as regards the Dutch Presbyterians, their own records are conclusive as to the severity of their measures and to the ill-success by which they were followed."

When Ceylon was ceded to the Dutch, the Portuguese territory was full of churches and schools and convents. Says Tennent (ibid., p. 23): "In the fort of Colombo, according to Ribeiro, there were two parishes of Our Lady and St. Laurence, four religious houses of the Cordeliers, the Dominicans, the Augustines, and the Capuchins, and a Jesuits' College in which were taught the classics and philosophy. Outside the fort he says that there were seven parishes; but with the exception of those lying immediately under the walls, it is questionable whether they were provided with separate buildings. Galle contained a convent of St. Francis and a house of Mercy; Kalutara had a chapel for the small garrison in the fort; Malvana and Negombo were similarly provided, whilst to make the contrast more striking between these stations in the south and similar outposts in the Northern Province, Mannar, Mantotta, and the surrounding districts of the Wanni, had no less than fourteen churches for the accommodation of the native Roman Catholics."

The following is a list of the Portuguese captains-general who administered the government in Ceylon, to the time when they lost the fort of Colombo:—

Pedro Lopez de Sousa.
Jeronymo de Azevedo.
Francisco de Menezes.
Manuel Mascarenhas Homen.
Nunho Alvarez Pereira.
Constantin de Sa y Noronha.
Don George de Albuquerque.
Constantin de Sa y Noronha.
Don George de Almeida.
Diego de Mello.
Antonio Mascarenhas.
Philip Mascarenhas.
Manuel Mascarenhas Homen.
Francisco de Mello de Castro.
Antonio de Sousa Coutinho—under whom Colombo was lost.

The sixteenth and last captain-general was Antonio d'Amarel y Menezes, who commanded the Portuguese garrisons at Mannar and Jaffna.

PART XII.

THE DUTCH OCCUPATION.

THE history of the Dutch in Ceylon does not present the points of strong interest which mark other periods in the island's history. They came to the colony rather as merchants than as warriors. They were not "colonists" in the sense the Portuguese were; and in their dealings with the natives their attitude was uncompromisingly mercantile. On hearing of the capture of Colombo, the king promptly urged upon the Dutch its delivery into his own hands, in accordance with the treaty entered into with him. He also expressed surprise and indignation that the Dutch should have entered into a treaty with the Portuguese without his participation or sanction. The Dutch themselves had no serious intention of ratifying the treaty with Rajasinha. Instead of complying with its provisions, they retained all the fortified possessions they had seized, under the artful plea of awaiting the consent of the authorities in Europe. Enraged at this breach of faith, Rajasinha commanded his maritime subjects to lay waste the entire districts in which they dwelt, in order to deprive the Dutch of all hope of commercial gains. The latter, however, anticipated this order, and before it could be carried out or even attempted, had taken possession of the districts along their strongholds. The natives themselves do not appear to have objected to this measure; they seem to have rather welcomed it, and the ill-feeling to which it gave rise nearly caused Rajasinha his throne and life. In 1664, while the king resided at Nilambe, in the Matale district, they rose in rebellion against him, occupied the capital, and proclaimed his infant son as emperor. But their intentions were frustrated, first by the refusal of the young prince to become their leader, and then by the sudden appearance of Rajasinha himself at the head of his forces, terminating in the barbarous murder of several of the nobility, and above all of his own son.

In their desire to gain the commercial intercourse with the island, the Dutch endeavoured to keep themselves as much as possible in friendly relations with the natives. Having cajoled Rajasinha in reference to the possession of the maritime districts and addressed themselves to what they thought was Rajasinha's weakness, a love of flattery, they despatched numerous embassies to Kandy with rich presents, in treacherous insincerity, and desired peace. But the suspicions of Rajasinha, awakened by their past conduct, were not to be lulled by their present submissive demeanour. While he, in turn, received their ambassadors with similar assurances, in many cases he even detained their ministers without the shadow of an excuse for the step.

In 1659 Robert Knox, a British subject, having landed at Kotiyar, was taken to Rajasinha's court, and for twenty long years was detained a captive in the Kandyan territory. On his return from exile to England he published a work entitled "The Historical Relation of the Island of Ceylon." This work is of the utmost interest as giving an accurate and detailed description of the island in his times, and is written in a style whose elegance reminds one of De Foe. The conduct of the Dutch and the character of King Rajasinha II. were admirably and quaintly described as follows by Knox:—

"The Dutch, knowing his proud spirit, make their advantage of it by flattering him with their ambassadors, telling him that they are his majesty's humble subjects and servants, and that it is out of loyalty to him that they build forts and keep watches round about his country to prevent foreign nations and enemies from coming; and that as they are thus employed in his majesty's service, so it is for sustenance, which they want, that occasioned their coming up into his majesty's country; and thus by flattering him and ascribing to him high and honourable titles, which are things he greatly delights in, sometimes they prevail to have the country they have invaded and he to have the honour. Yet at other times, upon better consideration he will not be flattered, but falls upon them at unawares and does them great damage."

Peace seems to have followed the Dutch occupation of the Portuguese territory in all the strongholds except Jaffna. The Dutch determined to expel all the Catholic missionaries they found there, who numbered about fifty Jesuit and Dominican Fathers. They were all embarked in a small ship and sent to India, save one Jesuit priest named Caldeiro, who was unable to accompany his colleagues owing to the infirmities of age, which confined him to his bed, and who in consequence was compelled to remain at Jaffna in spite of the edict of expulsion. The native Catholics, however, did not seem to accept with cheerfulness the Dutch yoke, and a plot was formed by them to assassinate the Dutch commandant and other officials while they were at divine service on the following Sunday. The plot was discovered by Manuel de Andrado, a Sinhalese captain in the Dutch service, and on the Sunday in question Andrado arrested the conspirators and prevented them from effecting their object. They were all put to death, and the Dutch revenged themselves on the innocent Caldeiro and had him executed as well. He is said to have been dragged from his bed and beheaded in the public square.

In 1672 a new European Power attempted to settle in Ceylon. France was induced to turn her attention to Ceylon owing to the power and wealth accruing to the Dutch Republic from the island. Major Carron, formerly an officer in the Dutch service, is said to have made overtures to the court of France for the attack of Point de Galle, and M. de la Haye, viceroy of Madagascar, was despatched with a fleet of fourteen sail against that settlement. But he met with so determined a resistance at Galle that he thought it prudent to proceed to Trincomalee, and to despatch three envoys with presents to the Kandyan court. The chief of them, De Lanerolle, was so indiscreet as to refuse to comply with the strict observances of Rajasinha's court, and was consequently detained there a prisoner. Haye himself departed to the French territories on the Coromandel Coast. On his return he was met by Vanganos with a Dutch fleet, and four of his vessels were captured and the rest dispersed, and the newly raised French fort at Trincomalee, with the artillery and garrison, fell an easy prey to the Dutch admiral. In 1680 the fortress of Malvana was attacked by Rajasinha at the head of 30,000 men, but owing to the treachery of one of his generals, who went over to the Dutch with a portion of his troops, the siege had to be abandoned. Rajasinha, after a long reign of fifty years, died in 1687 at the advanced age of eighty-seven years. In person he was middle-sized and well-made, muscular and compact, rather darker in colour than the ordinary Sinhalese. Knox, who knew him intimately, says: "He bears his years well, being between seventy and eighty years of age, and though an old man, yet appears not to be like one, neither in countenance nor in dress He was temperate in his diet and chaste in his manners. Nor would he permit the slightest irregularity among his nobles in the latter respect. Many times when he hears of the misdemeanours of some of his nobles, he not only executes them, but severely punishes the women, if known; and he has so many spies that there is but little done which he knows not of. And often he gives command to expel all the women out of the city, not one to remain; but by little and little, when they thought his wrath was appeased, they did creep in again." Almost a mountebank in dress, he was fond of grandeur and magnificence, and wore splendid jewellery and precious stones on his person. Educated as he was by the Portuguese, he was thoroughly conversant with the Portuguese language, as the number of the letters he addressed in that language to the Dutch testify. But, like his uncle, Don John, while he despised the faith of his ancestors, he seems not to have regarded with any greater respect the religion he had embraced. Although vigorous and martial in his early manhood, in his old age he was slothful and inactive—a circumstance due perhaps to the state of exhaustion in which incessant civil war and foreign invasion had left his country. His son, Mahastene, succeeded him peaceably, under the title of Vimala Dharmasuriya II. Rajasinha warned him on his death-bed to remain at peace with the Dutch; and thus he reigned for twenty-two years. He was unambitious, but seems to have been devoted to the Buddhist religion. His reign was in consequence not marked by any important political event. Not an individual was put to death; war and rebellion were unknown. He endeavoured to restore Buddhism to its original splendour. During this reign, the Dutch, who in their territories were vainly, in spite of rigorous measures of persecution, endeavouring to stamp out Roman Catholicism, sought a further means for achieving their object by encouraging Buddhism, which was then decadent. With their co-operation, Vimala despatched an embassy to Siam requesting that a number of priests of the highest order might be sent to Ceylon to revive the neglected rites and ordinances of Buddhism. Twelve chief priests were accordingly procured, and the remainder of this king's reign was occupied in helping them to re-establish the church on a sounder foundation.

Vimala Dharmasuriya was succeeded by his eldest son, Kundasala, in 1707. On his accession he took the name of Sri Vira Parakrama Narendra Sinha. He followed the example of his father, and in his long reign of thirty-two years refrained from interfering with the Dutch. Narendra was a cruel king, addicted to drunkenness and regardless of any restraint upon his passions. In 1721 the queen of Kundasala died, and the Dutch, hearing of it, despatched an embassy of condolence to the king as a token of their friendship. Rumph, the Dutch governor, placed Cornelius Takel at the head of this embassy. Arriving at Kandy, the ambassadors were received by the king after they had made obeisance to him and knelt at his feet. After the usual greetings, Takel proceeded to state the principal object of his mission, which was to offer the condolences of the Dutch government on account of the death of his "late high-born, excellent, and all-accomplished queen." He prayed that the king might be long spared by the Almighty to enjoy his throne, and that the faithful and loyal Dutch might long experience the favour and protection of the king. In such wise did the Dutch flatter the man whom they were virtually confining as a sort of prisoner in the interior of his own dominions, and whose subjects they were plundering with rapacity. Though the administration of the Dutch governor Rumph was distinguished as much by ability as by humanity, yet even in his time the Sinhalese population were subjected to exactions by his subordinate officers. The death of Rumph made matters worse. Following it came the insurrection of the slaves at Colombo and the murder of some of the Hollanders. One of his successors, Vuyst, endeavoured to make himself an independent sovereign, and with this object had recourse to a system of barbarity strange in the annals of civilised nations. He employed the torture in order to extort confessions of all those who by wealth or by influence were capable of opposing his schemes. At length Vuyst was made prisoner and sent to Batavia, where he met with the fate he deserved. He was tried and sentenced to be broken alive upon the wheel, and his body to be quartered and burnt, and the ashes thrown into the sea. His successor, Versluys, heedless of the example afforded him, raised the price of rice to such a pitch as to cause a famine. He was recalled and a new governor, Doemburg, was sent to replace him. But such was the audacity of Versluys that he refused to yield his place, and actually fired on the company's vessels in the harbour. Ultimately he was compelled to submit to superior force, and was sent under arrest to Batavia.

With the arrival, in 1736, of the Dutch governor, Baron Van Imhoff, came good government, and with it the first gleam of prosperity in the Dutch settlements. Hitherto cinnamon had been the only article of commerce, but now the cultivation of pepper and cardamoms and coffee was successfully introduced. On the death, in 1734, of Narendra Sinha, he was succeeded by his brother-in-law, Sri Vijaya Rajasinha. His short reign was uninteresting and uninterrupted by civil disturbances or foreign invasion. The Kandyan provinces recovered to some extent from the state of desolation into which they had been cast. In the following reign of Kirti Sri Rajasinha (1747) hostilities broke out between the Kandyans and the Dutch, king, whereby the humiliating prostrations exacted by the proud court of Kandy from the Dutch ambassadors were dispensed with, and the forts of Puttalam and Batticaloa were given to the Dutch. In this reign the Mahavansa was compiled from the reign of Pandita Parakrama Bahu of Kurunegala by the priest Tibbotuwewa. In 1765 Falck undertook the government of Ceylon. He saw that there was no necessity to retain possession of the inland districts of Kandy, as all its products could be purchased cheaper from the Kandyans themselves. He therefore left the Kandyans alone ; and during his long administration agriculture made rapid progress, integrity and order were introduced into the several departments of government, the re-capture of the maritime provinces in 1796. Van der Graaff succeeded Falck as governor, and continued the policy of his predecessor, but his government was of too brief a duration to leave any useful results.

Towards the close of the American War in 1782, Holland made common cause with France and Spain against Great Britain. This attitude of hostility on the part of the Dutch gave the Government of Madras the long desired opportunity for the reduction of the Dutch possessions in Ceylon. A fleet under the command of Sir Edward Hughes, with troops led by Sir Hector Munro, was despatched with that object. Trincomalee was the first point of attack, and after a short resistance the place capitulated. Mr. Hugh Boyd was also despatched with an

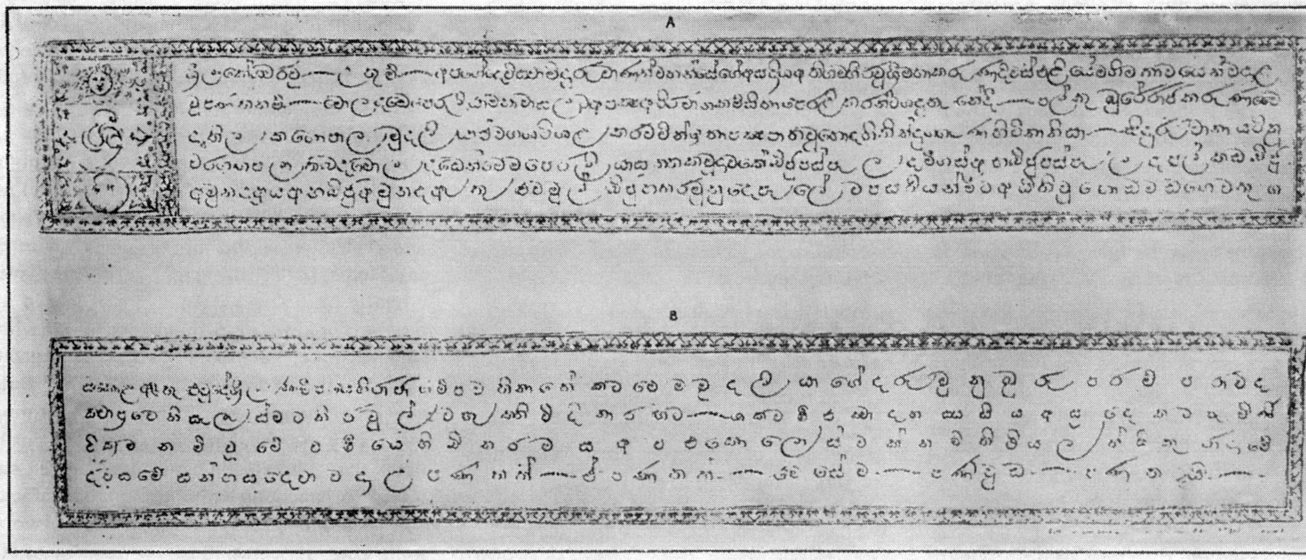

ANCIENT SANNAS (GRANT) ON A COPPER PLATE INLAID WITH GOLD.
(Dated 1760, in the reign of Kirti Sri Rajasinha.)

the king having determined upon their expulsion. But the war was not waged with any vigour on either side, and after a few successful inroads into the maritime provinces, the king was obliged to evacuate them. In 1763, encouraged by dissensions among the Kandyan chiefs, the Dutch, with an army of 8,000 men, penetrated the Kandyan territory and occupied the capital for nine months, at the end of which time their forces, harassed incessantly by the natives and thinned by disease, were compelled to abandon Kandy and to retire hastily into their own territories. Their retreat was not unattended by disaster, and but a small portion of the original army found its way back to Colombo. Governor Van Eck succeeded in beating the Kandyans back, and drove them to the mountains and forests ; but finally entered into a treaty with the venue was increased, and the Dutch were rendered independent of the Kandyans in regard to the supply of cinnamon. Kirti Sri devoted the closing years of his reign to the purification and reform of the Buddhist religion. Priests were again obtained from Siam and the ancient ceremonies revived in their purity. The king himself studied the religious books and became proficient in them. Kirti Sri died in 1768 from a fall from a spirited horse which he had received as a present from the Dutch, and was succeeded by his brother, the courtly and erudite Sri Rajadhi Rajasinha. His reign of twenty years was a peaceful one, undisturbed either by civil war or troubles with the Dutch, except on one occasion, when the latter unsuccessfully invaded Sabaragamuwa, and subsequently, when the king's forces invaded the low-country to co-operate with the British troops in the ambassador to the court of Kandy. He was empowered to enter into a treaty of peace with the king, and his mission was to remove the unfavourable opinion that the king had formed of the British. Previous to his departure from Trincomalee, Mr. Boyd addressed a letter to the king of Kandy, informing him of his mission. Mr. Boyd has given in his works a detailed account of this extraordinary embassy. Starting from Trincomalee, he did not reach Kandy till a month later, such was the inaccessible nature of the country through which he had to pass. The people generally fled from the villages on his approach, so as to escape affording the supplies which they were required to furnish, by command of the king. In one instance, where Mr. Boyd had been obliged to purchase a quantity of rice, the king, on hearing of this, ordered that the vendors should be decapitated. On his arrival at Kandy he was subjected to many tedious conferences and annoying delays. Accustomed to bad faith and unfulfilled promises of Europeans, the courtiers of Rajasinha looked upon Mr. Boyd with suspicion, and it cannot be said that his mission was a success. A French fleet under Suffrein made a surprise attack on Trincomalee, and the British garrison was forced to surrender, being allowed the honours of war and an immediate passage to Madras. Operations, however, were put a stop to by the peace of 1783. In 1795, when Holland again joined the French and began hostilities against Great Britain, Trincomalee was attacked by General Steuart, and after a determined siege, in which both sides suffered, the fortress was surrendered by the Dutch commander. After refreshing his army in Trincomalee, General Steuart commenced his advance round the north of the island, which was surrendered on the first summons. Earlier in 1796 Steuart appeared before Negombo, which also fell into the hands of the British. Steuart next turned his attention to Colombo, which, being a strong fortress and well garrisoned, promised a protracted siege. Steuart took with him three regiments of the line, three battalions of sepoys, and a detachment of Bengal Artillery, and marched towards Colombo. Arriving at the Kelani Ganga, the English troops paused, anticipating the commencement of a long struggle in view of the Dutch fort which had been erected on the other side of the river. But after two days they were surprised with the intelligence that the garrison of this fort had dismounted their guns, evacuated the fort and withdrawn to Colombo. Supposing this to be a stratagem of the enemy, the troops crossed the river with caution, while the fleet stood in readiness to assist the army. Steuart planned the operations of the siege with great precaution, which again was found to be unnecessary, as the occupants of Colombo were so demoralised that no attempt to defend it was made. The governor, Van Angelbeeck, concluded a private capitulation and surrendered without a struggle the capital of the maritime provinces of Ceylon. Galle and the other fortresses of Colombo speedily followed the example of Colombo, and the maritime provinces thus became a part of the British possessions in the East.

The following is the list of Dutch governors, with the dates of their appointments, from the date of their occupation, March, 1640, till February, 1796:—

At Galle—

Willem Jacobson Coster ...	1640
Jan Thysz	1640
Joan Matsuyker	1646
Jacob Van Kittenstein ...	1650
Adrian Van der Meyden ...	1653

At Colombo—

Adrian Van der Meyden ...	1656
Ryklof Van Goens	1660
Jacob Hustaar	1663
Ryklof Van Goens	1664
Lourens Van Peil	1680
Thomas Van Rhee	1693
Paulus De Rhoo	1695
Gerrit De Heer	1697
Cornilis Johannes Simonsz ...	1703
Hendrick Becker	1707
Isaak Augustin Rumph ...	1716
Arnold Moll	1723
Johannes Hertenberg ...	1724
Jan Paulus Schagen ...	1725
Petrus Vuyst	1726
Stephanus Versluys	1729
Gualterus Woutersz	1732
Jacob C. Pielaat	1732
Diedrick Van Domburg ...	1734
Jan Maccara	1736
Gustaff W. Baron Van Imhoff	1736
William Mauritz Bruinink ...	1740
Daniel Overkeek	1742
J. V. Stein Van Golnesse ...	1743
Gerard Van Vreeland ...	1751
Jacob De Jong	1751
Ivan Gideon Loten	1752
Jan Schreuder	1757
Subhert Jan Baron Van Eck	1762
Anthony Mooyart	1765
Imam Willem Falck ...	1765
Willem Jacob Van der Graaff	1785
Joan Gerrard Van Angelbeeck	1796

under whom Colombo, and with it the entire coast, was surrendered to the British.

We have now to consider in brief outline the characteristics of the Dutch *régime* in Ceylon. We have said that in coming to the island they came not as colonists, but as merchants. To quote the words of the Rev. Mr. Bisset, who wrote under the name of "Philalethes": "Cent. per cent. was their faith; gold was their object; and mammon was their god." The government of Ceylon was carried out altogether by the Dutchmen themselves. Only the offices corresponding to those of native headmen in the present day were available for the natives, and that only if they professed the peculiar form of Christianity which was the State religion of Holland—a policy which tended to the promotion of religious hypocrisy, the barren fruits of which are evidenced by the present position of the Dutch Presbyterians in Ceylon, who, according to the latest census, number less than three thousand. This was also the period of religious persecution. The various measures which were unavailingly adopted to extinguish the Catholic form of Christianity are detailed by Tennent, and may well be quoted. "The same fury against the Church of Rome continued at all times to inspire the policy of the Dutch in Ceylon. Their resistance to its priesthood was even more distinct and emphatic than their condemnation of the Buddhists and Brahmins. In 1658 a proclamation was issued forbidding on pain of death the harbouring or concealing of a Roman Catholic priest. But such a threat was too iniquitous to be carried into execution, and the priests continued their ministrations in defiance of the law. In 1715 a proclamation was issued prohibiting public assemblies or private conventicles of Roman Catholics under heavy fines for the first and second offences and chastisement at the discretion of the magistrate for the third. In the same year, by a *plakaat*, which was afterwards renewed from time to time, it was forbidden for a Catholic clergyman to administer baptism under any circumstances; and in 1735 the proclamation of 1658 was republished against entertaining or giving lodging to a priest, but with no better success, for twelve years later the same sanguinary order had to be repeated by a fresh *plakaat* of the governor. In 1748 it was forbidden to educate a Roman Catholic for the ministry, but within three years it was found necessary to repeat the same prohibition as well as to renew the proclamation of putting down the celebration of the Mass. Notwithstanding every persecution, however, the Roman Catholic religion retained its influence and held good its position in Ceylon. It was openly professed by the immediate descendants of the Portuguese who had remained in the island after its conquest by the Dutch, and in private it was equally adhered to by large bodies of the natives, both Sinhalese and Tamils, whom no corruption nor coercion could induce to abjure it. These measures of the Dutch, so much more stringent than any similar proceedings of their predecessors in regard to religion, had naturally the effect more of less of driving the Roman Catholics and their clergy from the maritime provinces, and Rajasinha, enraged at the deceit which had been practised upon him by the Hollanders in retaining possession of the forts on the coast, readily offered them an asylum in his dominions around Kandy. Upwards of seven hundred Portuguese families are said to have established themselves in Ruanvela, at the foot of the Kandyan hills. A colony of Tamil Christians from the coast were encouraged to settle at Galgama, and to the present day there exists in the village of Vehakota, among the mountains of Matale, a community of Roman Catholics, speaking the language and in other respects undistinguished from the Kandyans, but who are known to be the descendants of the Portuguese who had there sought concealment from the persecution of the Dutch in the low-country." [1]

[1] Tennent's "Christianity in Ceylon," p. 41, *et seq.*

No wonder that the natives of Ceylon in the maritime provinces hailed the advent of the English with delight and welcomed them with open arms; for one of their first acts was the proclamation of religious tolerance and liberty of conscience throughout their dominions, and the consequent removal of all civil disabilities created in respect of religion by the Dutch.

In order to maintain their commerce it became necessary that the Dutch should build forts all over the island, and these remain to the present day as monuments of their industry. In order to safeguard the collection of various taxes on land they kept registers of the lands in the provinces, which remain to this day as models of accurate registration. By the introduction of the Roman-Dutch law in their territory, a system based upon the great civil jurisprudence of the Roman jurists, they have given to the Ceylonese of the maritime provinces the advantages of a legal system which their British successors were only too glad to perpetuate in this colony, as they have done in the British colonies in South Africa.

We will close this chapter by once more quoting from "Philalethes": "The Portuguese were more tolerant than the Dutch, and the Dutch were less tolerant *than they ought to have been.*"

COLOMBO AS A DUTCH HARBOUR IN THE EIGHTEENTH CENTURY.
(After a Plan in the Hague)

CEYLON UNDER BRITISH RULE
1796–1906

By EDWARD W. PERERA,

Advocate of the Supreme Court of Ceylon, Member of the Royal Asiatic Society of Ceylon, Author of "The Story of the Sinhalese People."

NOT until about the middle of the eighteenth century did the British take any interest in the affairs of the island which half a century later was to fall entirely into their hands. The mission of Pybus as envoy from the Government of Madras to Kirti Sri Rajasinha (1747–1780) to draw up a treaty in 1766 against the Dutch, with whom the Sinhalese were then at war, had fallen through, though the Kandyan monarch was agreeable to the alliance. On the declaration of hostilities between Holland and Britain during the American War of Independence, Lord Macartney decided to add Ceylon to the list of conquests. For this purpose Admiral Hughes sailed from the Coromandel Coast on January 2, 1782, and by the 11th of the same month Trincomalee surrendered after a feeble resistance, the assault being made by the troops commanded by Sir Hector Munro. Sir Hugh Boyd had arrived with Admiral Hughes with instructions from Lord Macartney, who left Trincomalee and appeared before the throne of Kirti Sri Rajasinha at Kandy with a proposal of an offensive and defensive treaty to be directed against the Dutch. "Twenty years ago," said the king, "you sent an ambassador to us, when we were at war with the Dutch; your proffers of assistance were answered with guileless openness, and on the departure of your ambassador we heard no more of you and your offer, though we were subsequently attacked by the Dutch. Now that you are at war with that nation, anxious to injure them, you come to offer us your assistance to drive them from our island, and you profess to be about to yield us that assistance from the most disinterested motives." The Kandyan monarch finally refused to treat except with the King of Great Britain direct, and Boyd returned to find the French flag flying at Trincomalee. While Sir Edward Hughes returned to Madras to refit, the French admiral, Suffrein, had dashed into Trincomalee Bay, summoned the fort, and had obtained immediate surrender by the offer of the most honourable terms on August 31, 1781. On his return Sir Edward Hughes, finding the fortress in the possession of the enemy, stood out to sea, and, after an indecisive engagement with the French, sailed back to Madras. By the peace of 1783 Trincomalee was restored to the Dutch.

The design of the conquest of the Dutch possessions in Ceylon was settled at Fort St. George, Madras, on instructions from London. Hostilities had broken out between England and Holland after the Dutch had declared the Batavian Republic on the conquest of their country by the French general, Pichegru, in 1794. Letters from the Stadtholder, then an exile in England, requesting the Dutch governor of Colombo, Van Angelbeeck, to surrender the settlements to Britain to be kept in trust for him, were entrusted to Colonel J. Steuart, in command of the expedition to Ceylon.

On August 1, 1795, Colonel Steuart landed at Trincomalee, about two miles from Fort Frederick, with a considerable force, consisting of the 72nd Regiment, the flank companies of the 71st and 73rd Regiments, two battalions of sepoys, and a detachment of artillery and pioneers. As the garrison refused to surrender, operations for a siege were commenced on the 18th, and on the 26th, a considerable breach having been effected, the fortress capitulated on terms. During the siege a party of Malay soldiers, armed with *krises*, crept out of the garrison, nearly in a state of nudity, under cover of night, and advancing like snakes along the ground, got behind the batteries unobserved, and having killed or wounded nearly every person on duty in the trenches, spiked the guns and effected their retreat into the fort. Fort Ostenburgh, a fort about three miles from Fort Frederick, fell on the 31st of August. The British commander, after refreshing his wearied forces in Trincomalee, next advanced round the north of the island to Jaffna, which capitulated without a single blow being struck in its defence. On February 12, 1796, at the head of a considerable force, Colonel Steuart landed at Negombo, which surrendered in response to his summons. Three days later he appeared before Colombo by way of Grandpass, his march being only feebly opposed at the mouth of the Kelani river by a band of Malays under a French officer, whom he swept before him. This was the only attempt made by the Dutch to fight the British in defence of the dominions they had possessed for the previous hundred and fifty years. The withdrawal shortly before of the Swiss regiment of Colonel De Meuron, mercenaries in the pay of the Dutch, on the termination of their engagement, had considerably diminished the garrison. The dissensions in the Dutch camp, combined with the weakness of the defences, made Governor Van Angelbeeck open the gates of Colombo to the British invader on February 15, 1796.

In this capitulation were included "the town of Galle and the fort of Kalutara with all their dependencies, lands, domains, sovereign rights of the Honourable Dutch East India Company," for the surrender of which Van Angelbeeck undertook to issue the necessary orders.

King Rajadhi Rajasinha's expectations of at least a seaport, if not of some accession of territory, as the price of his assistance to the British in the late war were not realised, hut all political and territorial relations between the Kandyan and British Governments continued as under the Dutch.

The Dutch settlements were, in the first instance, held in trust for the Stadtholder, to whose cause a large portion of the inhabitants were attached. On February 16, 1796, commenced the administration of the Honourable the Governor in Council at Madras. The conquered settlements were associated for a time with the government of the Presidency of Madras, and the civil administration of the maritime provinces of the island was provisionally placed under a Commissioner sent from that establishment, who endeavoured to introduce the same regulations and system of collecting the public revenues which were in force on the coast of Coromandel. When the British occupied the country the Dutch possessions in the island were divided into six provinces for purposes of administration: (1) Colombo, whose dependent country under a chief, called the Dissawa, extended from the river Bentota to that of Chilaw; (2) Jaffnapatam, whose dependent country, under the chief military officer, extended along the northern parts of the island from the limits between Puttalam and Mannar to the river Kokili, the limit of Trincomalee; (3) Galle, also under a military commander (commandant), which extended from the river Bentota to the Kumbukkan river, the limit of Batticaloa; (4) Trincomalee, formerly under a civil, but latterly under a military, servant, which extended from the river Kokili, the limit of Jaffnapatam, to the border of Virgal, the limit of Batticaloa; (5) Batticaloa, under a civil servant, which extended from the Virgal to the Kumbukkan river; (6) Kalpentyn and Puttalam, which extended from the river of Chilaw, Deduru-Oya, to the limits of Mannar.

The country dependent upon Colombo was divided into eight districts called Korales, the whole being under the jurisdiction of a Sinhalese chief or Mudaliyar, who combined both civil and military jurisdiction under the designation of Korala and Mudianse. He had subordinate officers under him called Mohandirams, Arachchis and Kankanis, and was the commander of a corps of lascoreens, or local militia, who were attached to his establishment. The rule by Mudaliyar and Koralas was the ancient system of government, which, with some modification, the Dutch had preserved. The Mudaliyar's powers were defined by custom, and no officer was appointed to the post unless he professed the Dutch Reformed religion. These different Korales or districts were under the government or superintendence of a civil servant of the Dutch East India Company, called by the Sinhalese title of Dissawa, who ranked fourth in the government, of Colombo. The Dissawa collected the revenues of the country and administered justice to the inhabitants. In the Dissavoni, or the jurisdiction of the Dissawa of Colombo, were comprehended the districts of (1) Chilaw, (2) Negombo, and (3) Kalutara, whose chiefs or commandants were responsible in all civil cases to the Dissawa, administering justice in his name and referring to him all such cases as they deemed themselves incompetent to decide.

The Province of Jaffna was under the jurisdiction of a military commandant, the President of the Council, who represented the Governor and who received his commission from the Governor-General of Batavia. Jaffnapatam was divided into the three following districts: (1) District proper of that name, governed by a Dissawa who had under him the resident of Kayts and Point Pedro; (2) the Wanni, governed by a military chief, who by an agreement with Government cleared the woods and cultivated the lands while at the same time he farmed its revenues; (3) the island of Mannar, with its five opposite dependencies on the coast, under a civil servant. These three officers governed the country of Jaffna as the Dissawa administered the territory of Colombo.

In the province of Galle the civil and military authority was vested, as in Jaffna, in a military commander (commandant) and his council. It was subdivided into two districts: (1) the Galu Korale, comprehending subdivisions or pattus under the rule of Mudaliyars controlled by a civil servant, who was responsible to the commander; (2) the district or Dissavoni of Matara, which was ruled by a Dissawa, under whom Mudaliyars governed the pattus or sub-districts into which the Dissavoni was divided. Matara was dependent on the commandant of Galle for the administration of revenue, but responsible only to the Government of Colombo for the management of the other concerns of the country.

Trincomalee was under a military commander, and till 1766 had but a very small territory attached to its government. At that period the Kandyans surrendered to the Dutch the countries of Kotiyar, Tambalagama, and Kotiyar Pattu.

Batticaloa was formerly under a military chief, with the small isle of Puliantivoe at the mouth of the river. But at the peace of 1766 the Dutch had obtained in sovereignty from the Kandyans the eight provinces of Batticaloa, which at the period of the British conquest were governed by a civil servant and a Landraad.

Kalpentyn and Puttalam were under a civil chief. The Peninsula of Kalpentyn was an ancient possession of the Dutch. The very narrow district of Puttalam was ceded by the king of Kandy by the peace of 1766, together with the territory of Chilaw, which formed a part of the Dissavoni of Colombo. All the countries dependent on the six places above mentioned constituted the general division of the Dutch possessions in Ceylon. These were infinitely subdivided, and from a district to the smallest village various chiefs, under different denominations, presided. Notwithstanding that Sinhalese offices, by the company's regulations, were declared not to be hereditary, yet they almost all, except in the case of the Wanniyars or chiefs of the Wanni, in fact became so. The petty chiefs in the villages under the names of Mayarals, Patangatins, Patabendas, &c., were more numerous than the chiefs in the country, and were nominated by the commandant or Dissawa, who granted them a charter of office written upon an *ola*, or palm-leaf, the greater chiefs being employed by warrants of appointment signed by the Governor under the seal of the Dutch East India Company. The greater portion of these chiefs received no salary, but in right of their office held lands or *accomodessans*, which, added to other emoluments, enabled them to live in comparative splendour.

In 1797 Colonel De Meuron, who had transferred his allegiance to the British, was Military Administrator and Frederick Greenhill Civil Administrator of Ceylon under Lord Hobart, Governor of Madras in Council, who came over in 1798 and held a levee of Sinhalese chiefs. During this time the taxes of the country were farmed out to Dubashes or Tamil agents from the Carnatic, the Mudaliyar system was abolished, and collectors and Kachcheris, or collectors' officers, were introduced from Madras. These men ground down the people by their illegal exactions, and infuriated them by their oppressive exercise of power. Charters of appointment as headmen, or for even the high rank of Mudaliyar, were issued by them for the merest trifle to men with no claim to distinction or consideration. Eventually the prevailing discontent burst forth into flame in the rebellion of 1798. As a result the system of Dubashes was abolished, and the Mudaliyars reappointed in 1799, by the Hon. Frederick North, who assumed the government on October 12, 1798, Ceylon being declared a Crown Colony.

Soon after the Hon. Frederick North took charge of the island the laws and institutions which had existed under the government of the United Provinces were guaranteed. But the grant was subject to modification. The barbarous modes of punishment, such as torture, mutilation, and breaking on the wheel, which had hitherto prevailed, were abolished, and liberty of conscience and free exercise of religious worship were allowed to all men. These privileges were granted by proclamation in 1799. The Hon. Frederick North also established a Supreme Court of Judicature, founded the first "seminary" for the education of the Ceylonese, and commenced the publication of a *Ceylon Government Gazette.*

By the peace of Amiens, 1801, Ceylon was transferred from the rule of the East India Company to the immediate control of His Majesty's Minister for the Colonial Department, a change which dates from January 1, 1802.

In 1798 Rajadhi Rajasinha, king of Kandy, died without issue, and the first Adigar, or prime minister, Pilimi Talawwa, placed on the vacant throne a nephew of one of the queens dowager, a cadet of the royal house of Madura, called Kannasami, at the time eighteen years of age. The claims of Muttusami, brother of one of the queens dowager and heir-presumptive, were overlooked by the powerful minister, and Kannasami mounted the throne under the title of Sri Vikrama Rajasinha. Pilimi Talawwa was a chieftain of the highest rank and ability, who hated the domination of the Malabar dynasty, to which the last three Kandyan sovereigns had belonged. The prime minister for a considerable time retained an influence over the young king, whom, it is alleged, he had nominated to the throne with the object of bringing the Tamil dynasty into contempt by selecting for the throne an obscure and ignorant youth. Pilimi Palawwa, who claimed descent from a daughter of the old Sinhalese royal house, aimed at expelling the ruling Malabar Nayakkars with their troop of Tamil favourites, and founding a national dynasty in his own person on the throne. His boundless ambition and national instincts made him unscrupulous as to the means he should adopt in freeing the country from the thraldom of the Tamils. This result he expected to accomplish either by the open assistance of the British Government or by secret treason and the assassination of the king. During two occasions, in 1799, the Kandyan minister laid his scheme before Governor North, and offered to acknowledge the sovereignty of England provided the British deposed the king and placed him at the head of the government. In January, 1800, although the British Government had already saluted Sri Vikrama Rajasinha as king of Kandy, and had treated with him, Mr. Boyd, Acting Secretary of Government, on behalf of Governor North, in a conference with Pilimi Talawwa, undertook to maintain the Adigar in power provided the king of Kandy could be induced to place himself and his country under the protection of Great Britain and to admit a British garrison into his capital. Mr. Boyd at the same time intimated that he could not render him any assistance unless the king's person and the continuance of his dignity were stipulated as a preliminary to any agreement to be made, and that Rajasinha's express consent was obtained for the future connection between the two Governments. Another interview on January 21, 1800, between Mr. North and the Adigar, led to no agreement, and the British Governor decided to send General Macdowal as ambassador to Kandy to conclude a treaty, "with the proposal, should the king approve of it, that he should transport his

THE HON. FREDERICK NORTH (AFTERWARDS EARL OF GUILFORD).

(Governor, October 12, 1798—July 19, 1805.)

person and court, for greater safety, to the British territory, there to enjoy all his royal rights, and to depute to Pilimi Talawwa, the Adigar, the exercise of his power in Kandy." Considering the reception accorded to him, it is supposed that the prudent ambassador did not lay the proposal before the king. In the meantime, other interviews between the British Governor, or his agent, Mr. Boyd, and the Kandyan minister followed, but the negotiations fell through, as the contracting parties could come to no definite understanding. The negotiations at this period between the Hon. Frederick North and Pilimi Talawwa partook of the nature of a diplomatic contest in which the prize was the Kandyan kingdom. Mr. North was throughout seeking to make use of the disaffected Kandyan chieftain with the view of inducing the king to receive a British garrison into his capital. But the Governor met more than his match in the shrewd chieftain, who aimed at the removal of the Tamil king and the chiefs who stood in his way by British aid, and who, when that object was attained, intended to drive the British out of the country and crown himself the national king of a single Lanka. Had Pilimi Talawwa not been prematurely brought to the block, the course of Ceylon history might have been different. Although the designs of the two were so divergent, yet each considered that the best means of effecting his purpose would be by armed intervention by the British. Pilimi Talawwa was anxious to precipitate a war between the two Powers in the hope of vaulting into power in the anarchy that would ensue, while the Governor, discovering that he could not induce Rajasinha to receive a British garrison into Kandy, awaited an opportunity of invading the highland kingdom. The opportunity soon came in the attack on a band of Mahomedan traders whose goods, to the value of about £100, were plundered at Puttalam by some of the king's subjects, probably at the instigation of the Adigar and without the knowledge of Rajasinha. When intelligence reached Colombo, British forces were in motion for the capture of Kandy. Major-General Macdowal was in command of the army of invasion, the first division of which left Colombo on January 31st, and the second left Trincomalee, under the command of Colonel Barbut, on February 4, 1803. The British forces, without having encountered any serious resistance on the march, entered Kandy on February 21st, only to find a deserted town. Although, as stated already, Mr. North had previously acknowledged Sri Vikrama Rajasinha as king, had repeatedly pledged himself not to abandon his interest, and had despatched an ambassador to his court, Muttusami, the "pretender," was crowned king by the British amid great pomp as the rightful ruler of the Kandyans, and immediately articles of convention were drawn up between him and the Governor of the British settlements by which the new monarch agreed to receive a British auxiliary force into his capital, and absolutely surrendered to the British a portion of his dominions. This was an object at which Mr. North had long aimed, as part of his scheme for the ultimate conquest of the Kandyan provinces. Thus the Kandyan kingdom was partitioned between Muttusami and the British without the reigning sovereign having been subdued. The new king, without any adherents save his own domestics, lived in the palace at Kandy, guarded by British bayonets. Meanwhile the crafty Pilimi Talawwa, who pretended to be loyal to his king and the British, using one against the other as it suited him, persuaded the British commander to lead an expedition to the port of Hanguranketa about eighteen miles from Kandy, on a promise to deliver up the king. Batteries were erected on every eminence which commanded the paths through which the troops had to pass, and marksmen were placed in ambush in the thickest coverts of the jungle. The British lost heavily on their advance, and retreated after burning down the palace of Hanguranketa, which they found deserted. In the meantime, with their supplies almost cut off in the midst of a hostile country, the British were harassed by armed bands of Kandyans, who hovered round their outposts. Concealed in the woods and thickets, the Sinhalese fired upon the guards and sentries during the night, and the stragglers who fell into their hands were put to death. Being ill-armed and less disciplined, they knew their own weakness too well to emerge from their hiding-places during the day or to face any considerable body of troops. A reward of ten rupees was paid for the head of every European, and five for that of every other class of soldier of the invading army. While these events were passing, Major-General Macdowal, on behalf of the Governor, on the 28th of March entered into a treaty with Migastene, the second Adigar, representing his kinsman the prime minister, whereby he undertook that Pilimi Talawwa should be recognised as "great reigning prince" of Kandy, that Muttusami should be pensioned off, and Sri Vikrama Rajasinha be delivered to the British when captured, with the cession of the province of the Hat Korale to the King of England. On the conclusion of this treaty with the chief minister of the king, General Macdowal was directed to leave Kandy, which he did on the 1st of April, taking with him the 51st Regiment and the Ceylon Native regiment of 1,000 strong and a detachment of Bengal Artillery. A garrison of about 700 Malays and 300 European soldiers of the 13th and Bengal and Madras Artillery, besides a considerable number of sick, was left behind. Meanwhile, the scheme of the Adigar had so far succeeded. The Governor was anxious to seize the country, whether by treason of the Adigar or by force of arms. Pilimi Talawwa appeared at Dambadeniya by appointment, ostensibly to ratify the treaty of March 28th with Mr. North, but really to take North captive, which he was only deterred from doing by a sudden accession of strength to the Governor's escort by the Malays under Colonel Barbut from Trincomalee. General Macdowal left Kandy on the 11th of June and did not reach Colombo until the 19th, and Major Davie was left in command of the Kandy garrison, whose fate was now fast approaching. Most of the Malays and the Madras lascars deserted to the enemy. At this time the Dissawa Leuke announced to the British Government, through a confidential agent, that the first Adigar was a perfidious villain, who deceived the whole world, and that the second Adigar, Migastene, had quarrelled with him. Mr. North was as well aware of the character of his confederate as the Dissawa Leuke, but he was presumed, for the exigencies of the situation, to be the faithful friend of the British. On the 13th June, Pilimi Talawwa announced to Major Davie that he was in disgrace with the king owing to his endeavour to save the British, and requested him to undertake another expedition to Hanguranketa, which he, more prudent than General Macdowal, refused. Although the Adigar's influence was very powerful in the Kandyan councils, yet the conduct of the war was not entirely directed by him, but determined by the king in consultation with other chiefs, some of whom were Pilimi Talawwa's deadly foes. The king issued the necessary commands in the face of the national danger and took the best military measures his country afforded for expelling the invader. Soon after, the Kandyans seized the posts of Girihagama and Galagedara, about twelve miles from Kandy, garrisoned by British Malays. Before daybreak on June 24, 1803, the Kandyan army, computed at 10,000 strong, carried the British outpost on the hill overlooking the capital, making the garrison prisoners, and descended in full force on Kandy. After a brave resistance, the feeble garrison, finding it impossible to hold the town, displayed the white flag, and, after a parley, surrendered to the Adigar on terms. The conditions were not observed by the king, and the British garrison were relentlessly massacred by being clubbed to death on the Kandyan hills. One man alone, Corporal Barnsley, escaped to tell the sad tale.

Dambadeniya, in the Hat Korale, fell on the 2nd July, and in the course of ten days from the retaking of the capital not an inch of ground remained to the British beyond their original frontier. The Kandyans followed up their success by endeavouring to seduce the Sinhalese subjects of the British Government from their allegiance and to excite dissatisfaction in various parts of the maritime territory. By these means they hoped to overcome the remnant of the British army. Towards the end of July all the Kandyan frontiers were simultaneously threatened by warlike assemblies. In the months of August and September they poured down from the mountains and prevailed on many of the lowland Sinhalese to join them, the ultimate object being the expulsion of the British from the island. The Kandyan irruption extended from Hambantota on the south coast, round the whole west and north coast, to the small fort of Mullaitivu, north of Trincomalee. On the 20th of August, the enemy took the fort of Hanwella, and the next day they advanced to within fourteen or fifteen miles of Colombo, at which the Burghers in the suburbs became alarmed, and many of them took shelter in the fort. With the arrival of reinforcements from the Cape of Good Hope and Bengal, British detachments entered the Kandyan country for the express purpose of laying it waste wherever they were able to penetrate. According to the testimony of Mr. Marshall, the medical officer who accompanied the army, the orders were carried out with the utmost ruthlessness and severity. One detachment alone destroyed eight hundred Kandyan houses. With the arrival of the 65th Regiment from England it was resolved in August, 1804, to again invade the Kandyan country. The new commander, General Wemyss, after a personal inspection of the British military posts, meditated a combined attack on the enemy's capital with all the British forces in the island. The plan decided on was that six different columns should co-operate from the different stations, to effect a general junction by a given date on the heights of Kandy. Captain Johnston, in compliance with what he believed to be the general orders, but which had been countermanded, set out from Batticaloa at the head of a division on September 20, 1804. After much severe fighting and surmounting numerous obstacles in the woods and mountains of Uva, he reached Kandy on the 6th October to find no trace of the other divisions intended for the capture of Kandy. After a delay of three days he commenced his retreat. On the march back he was harassed by the Kandyans, who attacked him in front and rear and hung on his flanks. Thinned by disease and after undergoing great privations, barefooted and worn out, the remnant of the force crawled into Trincomalee on October 20, 1804. Most of the survivors died in hospital, and what was otherwise a disgraceful episode was only relieved by the gallantry and endurance of Captain Johnston. The war was conducted by both parties with savage barbarity, according to a contemporary historian, and numerous villages were burnt and large tracts of country reduced to desolation. In February, 1805, the Kandyans again invaded the British settlements, and although on the opening of the campaign the highlanders scored a few brilliant triumphs under chieftains like Dehigama and Leuke and marched to the borders of Colombo, they were ultimately driven back with severe loss. After this event there was a cessation of hostilities.

The courtly nobleman was succeeded, on July 19, 1805, by a rough and boisterous soldier, generous and autocratic, the Right Hon. Sir Thomas Maitland, who was known by the sobriquet of King Tom. Bennet, in his work on Ceylon, tells some characteristic stories of this Governor and his methods of serving his friends, such as the creation of the sinecure appointment of the Ranger of the Woods and Forests for the eccentric artist Daniells. Apparently there was no friendly intercourse between Sir Thomas, while he was Governor, and the king of Kandy, but no act of aggression was committed by either party. During his rule the severe laws against the Roman Catholics in Ceylon were relaxed. Major-General Wilson assumed the government of Ceylon on March 19, 1811. The absence of intercourse between the court of Kandy and the British Government which marked the previous governorship appears to have continued throughout his term of office. During 1811 Sir Alexander Johnston, a man of very considerable mark (who had previously been in the island as Advocate Fiscal) came to Ceylon in the capacity of Chief Justice and President of His Majesty's Council, bringing a new Charter of Justice, under which trial by jury was first introduced into Ceylon.

During this period of peace between the British and Kandyan Governments, events were moving fast in the highland kingdom. On the death of Migastene, second Adigar and Dissawa of the Hat Korale, in 1806, the district was, against all precedent and custom, divided between the two chiefs, Ehelapola and Molligoda. The people, having to pay double dues and perform double services, revolted, but the insurrection was suppressed by Pilimi Talawwa, and on his recommendation the Hat Korale was entrusted to his nephew, Ehelapola, by the king. Pilimi Talawwa's success in putting down the rebellion and his proposal to marry his son to the natural grand-daughter of King Kirti Sri aroused the king's jealousy and suspicion. Charged with a breach of duty, Pilimi Talawwa was deprived of his offices. The disappointed chieftain entered into a conspiracy to assassinate the king with the Malay Mohandiram of the royal guard. On the night appointed the king was awake when it was expected he would have been asleep, and the premature rising of the people of Udunuwara and Yatinuwara laid bare the plot. Pilimi Talawwa and his nephew were immediately beheaded.

This occurred in 1812. On the 18th March in the same year, Lieutenant-General Sir Robert Brownrigg succeeded to the government of the maritime portion of the island of Ceylon.

Meanwhile Ehelapola, who had been appointed second Adigar in 1806, succeeded his uncle, Pilimi Talawwa, as first Adigar. Ehelapola had inherited the ability, the ambition and the treachery of his uncle, but he lacked that political sagacity and shrewdness which characterised Pilimi Talawwa. Summoned to appear in court from his district of Sabaragamuwa, whither he had gone to superintend the cultivation and collect the revenue, to answer charges of extortion and injustice, Ehelapola failed to comply with the royal order, and his reply was not calculated to

GENERAL SIR ROBERT BROWNRIGG BART., G.C.B.

(Governor, March 11, 1812—February 1, 1820.)

satisfy or conciliate his sovereign. He forthwith commenced a treasonable correspondence with General Brownrigg, and assembled his adherents in Sabaragamuwa for the purpose of resisting the royal forces. His designs were made known in Kandy, and he was deprived of his offices. Meanwhile his wife and children, who were considered pledges of his loyalty, were imprisoned, and Molligoda was despatched as first Adigar and Dissawa of Sabaragamuwa to subdue the revolted province and capture the rebel chieftain. Marching over the summit of Adam's Peak, Molligoda descended on Sabaragamuwa, where Ehelapola's forces were soon scattered. Ehelapola himself fled across the border to the British in May, 1814. When tidings reached Kandy of the conduct of Ehelapola, Sri Vikrama Rajasinha, in a paroxysm of savage passion, brutally executed Ehelapola's wife and children, who were hostages in his hand, and the brother of Ehelapola, for misprision of treason. According to Marshall, they were led out from prison before the palace, and with one blow of the headsman's sword Ehelapola's eldest son, a boy of eleven years of age, was decapitated; the head was thrown into a mortar, and a pestle put into the mother's hand, with which she was ordered to pound it. The threat that she and her relations would be given over for defilement to the outcast tribe of the Rodiyas had the effect of strengthening her, and giving her courage to suffer any infliction. In her determination to face death bravely, it is said, she was encouraged by the chief who superintended the execution, a kinsman of her husband, who, at the risk of his life, reminded her of the humiliation that would be brought on her family by accepting the degrading terms. But this noble lady did not need any encouragement, she having displayed the most astonishing fortitude throughout this terrible ordeal. The wretched woman lifted the pestle and let it fall. The other children were decapitated and suffered the same awful fate. The mother and three other ladies were then led to the Bogambara tank in Kandy and there drowned. During this awful scene the crowd who had gathered to witness it wept and sobbed aloud. During two days the whole of Kandy was one house of mourning, with the exception of the court of the Tamil despot, whom treason, despair, and intemperance had developed into a maniac. Ehelapola submitted a plan of hostile operations against his native country, which, with some modifications, was carried into effect by Sir Robert Brownrigg, who had in contemplation the subjugation of the Kandyan kingdom. An attempt was made about this time, says Marshall, by General Brownrigg to induce Molligoda, first Adigar and prime minister to the king—the only general left to the Kandyans—to abandon his sovereign and join the allies, namely, the Kandyan rebels and the British invading force, but the measure did not succeed.

In 1814 ten native merchants, British subjects, who had gone into the interior for purposes of trade, were suspected by the king of being spies of Ehelapola and brutally mutilated. Three alone reached Colombo. This circumstance was considered by General Brownrigg as an act of aggression on the part of the king of Kandy which involved the honour of the British nation. A true account of the cause of the punishment of the merchants, obtained several years after the British occupation, showed that the pedlars in question were plundered by some low-caste Kandyans in the three Korales. The thieves, in order to escape justice, accused the men who had been robbed of being spies from the maritime provinces and employed by the local government. On the testimony of the men who had plundered them, the merchants were found guilty, and punished according to the common usage of the country. The king had no doubt that the men were spies of the rebel chieftain, considering that Ehelapola was well received by General Brownrigg, and it was well known that he was actively exciting rebellion against the king.[1] The principal reasons assigned for invading the country were the alleged tyranny and oppression of the Kandyan monarch, his unwillingness to enter into any terms with the representative of the British Government, the mutilation of the merchants and the irruption of the Kandyans across the boundary line of Sitavaka

[1] Marshall.

in pursuit of Ehelapola's fugitive adherents. "The irruption of the Kandyan people into our territory," continues the same authority,[1] "had, it may be presumed, very little influence in occasioning the war, all the requisite preparations having been made long before it took place." A British force accompanied by Ehelapola marched by way of Avisawella, the first division being under the command of Major Hook, for the conquest of the Kandyan country, war being declared on January 13, 1815. On the march Molligoda was won over, and he surrendered himself on the 8th of February to Mr. D'Oyley with the banner and records of his province of the Hat Korale.

On February 14, 1815, General Brownrigg, at the head of the second division, entered Kandy, which was deserted by the king and by nearly all the inhabitants. On the 18th the king was taken prisoner with two of his wives in the house of a subordinate headman, about a mile beyond Medamahanuwara. The capture was effected by the rebel chief Ekneligoda Dissawa, one of the adherents of Ehelapola, and his men. On the night of the 13th, while General Brownrigg was at dinner with a small party of officers, intelligence of the capture of the king reached him. "He stood at table," says an eyewitness, "and while the tears rolled down his cheeks, shook hands with every one present and thanked them for their assistance in furtherance of an object which seemed to be nearly accomplished, and which had been vainly attempted for nearly three centuries by three European Powers in succession —the conquest of the kingdom of Kandy." "From this day," says Knighton, "we may date the extinction of Sinhalese independence, an independence which had continued without any material interruption for 2,357 years." Sri Vikrama Rajasinha was soon after removed under a strong escort to Colombo, and in the beginning of the following year he was conveyed to the fortress of Vellore, in the Madras Presidency, where, on the afternoon of January 30, 1832, he died, aged fifty-two years, having been seventeen years a State prisoner. A son born to him in exile died without issue, and a grandson, a son of his daughter, adopted by the king, bears by the bounty of the British the empty title of Alagia Manawala Sinhala Raja, "the king of the Sinhalese."

"The king was formally dethroned by a convention held at Kandy between the Governor and the Kandyan chiefs. On this occasion the Governor was seated at the upper end of the Great Hall of Audience. The troops were drawn up in the square before the palace, where they remained while the Adigars and principal chiefs passed. Ehelapola, late Adigar, entered first and alone. He was received by General Brownrigg with great favour, and seated in a chair at his right hand. Molligoda, acting as first Adigar, next came forward, leading in the Dissawas of districts and other principal chiefs. By the treaty which was read in English by the Deputy-Secretary, and afterwards in Sinhalese by the Mudaliyar, their laws, customs, and institutions were guaranteed to the Kandyans, and the State religion, Buddhism, and its professors were declared inviolable. After the treaty was again read by the translator Mudaliyar to the headmen and others standing outside the hall, the British flag was hoisted, and a royal salute from the cannon of the city announced His Majesty George III. Sovereign of the whole island of Ceylon, March 2, 1815." The administration of the Kandyan provinces was at first conducted by a Board consisting of a president and two commissioners—one of justice, the other of revenue —together with the commanding officer of the troops in the interior. The resident was the representative of the Government, the other two members being the heads of their respective departments. The Board with the Adigars and the principal chiefs formed the Great Court of Justice, from whose sentence there was no appeal except to the Governor. Besides the Board and subordinate agents of Government at Uva, Sabaragamuwa and the Tun Korale, the civil authority of the country was exercised as before by the Sinhalese

SRI VIKRAMA RAJASINHA, THE LAST KING OF KANDY.

(Reproduced by permission of the Buddhist Theosophical Society.)

Dissawas and Ratemahatmayas. The military force, which was retained in the interior, amounted to about 1,700 or 1,800 men, who were stationed at eleven different posts. Kapuwatta was appointed second Adigar and Molligoda first Adigar, Ehelapola having declined the office. He stated that he only wished to be called the "Friend of the British," although it was well-known that he was bitterly disappointed at not being raised to the throne. Little of any importance occurred till October, 1817, when the inhabitants of the Kandyan provinces rose in rebellion and the resources of the British Government were severely taxed to suppress the outbreak. The wild district of Welassa first rose in revolt, the immediate cause being the appointment of a Moorish headman, supplanting the authority of the Sinhalese chief. Mr. Wilson, assistant resident of Badulla, in his search for a "stranger" and eight Buddhist priests, who were reported to be concealed i the forests of Welassa, was shot down, and the chief Keppitipola, who was despatched to quell the rising, joined the insurgents, though he had the chivalry to return to Mr. D'Oyley the muskets and ammunition which he had received from the Government stores. Notwithstanding the most energetic measures on the part of the British Government, the insurrection now developed into a war of independence, and spread so rapidly that by March, 1818, all the country rose in arms, except the lower part of Sabaragamuwa, and Tun Korale, and Hat Korale, Udunuwara and Yatinuwara. Eventually, with the exception of the first Adigar Molligoda, every chieftain of consequence had either joined the rebel standard or was in British custody for favouring, or being suspected of favouring, the insurrection.

On the 2nd of March Ehelapola was arrested upon suspicion of being disaffected towards the British, confined a prisoner in Colombo, and ultimately banished to Mauritius, where he died a State prisoner. For a considerable period, during May, June, and July, the issue of the contest seemed to be very doubtful. It is alleged that arrangements were in progress to withdraw the British force from the interior. There was grave apprehension that the Tun Korale and Hat Korale might join the insurgents, when communication with Colombo would be cut off. During this time the "stranger," Dura Sami, who aspired to the throne as a member of the royal family, was discovered to be a disrobed priest of inferior extraction, called Wilbawa. He was discredited by the chiefs when he sought refuge in the wilds of Bintenne, to be apprehended only in 1829. He was tried and convicted and pardoned on orders from Britain. The hostility of the people in most of the disaffected provinces abated considerably during the months of September and October. A predatory warfare had now continued for nearly a year, during which period almost the entire Kandyan

[1] Marshall.

population of men, women, and children had lived in the woods and on the tops of mountains, according to the testimony of a British officer who accompanied the forces. Their lands had been untilled for two seasons; many of their cattle were killed; their small stores of grain were exhausted. The monsoon rains were approaching, so that they had no other prospect before them, by holding out, but accumulated hardship and famine. During July and August some of the insurgents' leaders, including the chief, Ellepola Maha Nilama, were captured, and several of them were tried by court-martial. Ellepola was condemned to be hanged, a sentence which was afterwards commuted to decapitation. He met his death with the greatest firmness. His body was interred by the orders of Government, although he had himself desired that it should

LIEUT.-GEN. SIR EDWARD BARNES, K.C.B.

(Lieut.-Governor, February 1, 1820—February 2, 1822; Governor, January 18, 1824—October 13, 1831.)

be left a prey to dogs and jackals. On the 30th of October, Keppitipola and Pilimi Talawwa, son of the late Adigar, were surprised and taken by a detachment of troops under the command of Colonel Fraser in the neighbourhood of Anuradhapura. Madugalla was taken on the 1st of November, and with his capture the insurrection terminated. Keppitipola and Madugalla were tried by a court-martial and sentenced to suffer death, and both were beheaded on November 25, 1818. Several other chiefs were executed. Pilimi Talawwa was tried and condemned to death, but his sentence was commuted to banishment to Mauritius. The apprehension of future vengeance if Ehelapola attained power linked Molligoda's fortunes with those of the British and rendered him loyal. To the enmity which existed between these chiefs may in a great measure be attributed the consolidation of British power in Ceylon. Molligoda died in 1823. A considerable number of petty chiefs were banished, but on the death of the deposed king (1832), they and the other exiles were permitted to return to Ceylon, provided they engaged to reside in the maritime provinces, and not to revisit the Kandyan country. Before leaving Kandy, General Brownrigg issued a proclamation, or new constitution, for the Kandyan provinces. British officers were placed in different parts of the island to superintend the collection of the revenue and the administration of justice. The inferior headmen, instead of being yearly appointed by the chiefs, received their offices direct from Government. Early in January, 1820, another pretender to the throne of Kandy raised his standard in Bintenne as Vimala Dharma Narendra Sinha Maharaja, but a few days after he was captured and sent to Badulla. He was ultimately banished to Mauritius. General Brownrigg was a friend of Christianity, though policy made him sanction the Kandyan Convention, by which the British bound themselves to support and preserve inviolate the priests and rites of Buddhism. Under his auspices the first Auxiliary Bible Society was instituted at Colombo. During his term of office, too, commenced the operations of the oldest of Protestant Missions still existing in the island—the Baptist. It was founded in 1812. The Wesleyan missionaries followed in 1814. The establishment of the Church Mission dates from 1818.

Sir Robert Brownrigg, on his departure, handed over the government to Sir Edward Barnes as Lieutenant-Governor on February 1, 1820. This distinguished soldier, who, after brilliant service in the Peninsula, was Wellington's Adjutant-General at Waterloo, was appointed Lieutenant-Governor, as stated above, on February 1, 1820, giving place to Sir Edward Paget, who became Governor in February, 1822. After holding the office for the short period of ten months, this official proceeded to India to supersede Sir Edward Barnes as Commander-in-Chief, the latter having had a difference with the civil authorities.

Sir James Campbell held the reins as Lieutenant-Governor during 1823. During his rule a very curious case of *ex post facto* legislation produced much excitement. The Supreme Court issued a writ of *habeas corpus* for the production of a deserter, as was supposed, from the Indian Army, who was seized and held in arrest by the military authorities. Time was obtained to show cause against the writ. In the interval the Regulation No. 1 of 1824 was passed, which declared that it is and *was* lawful for the Governor to order the detention of any person, and that that order should bar the proceedings of the courts in respect of such person. Sir Hardinge Giffard, the uncle of the late Lord Chancellor (Lord Halsbury), was Chief Justice, and Mr. Matthews, father of Lord Landaff, and the author of "The Diary of an Invalid," Advocate-Fiscal. The Chief Justice, much chagrined, warned Matthews that in defending such high-handed proceedings he was preparing a bed of thorns for himself. Matthews, however, did not survive to claim the seat of Chief Justice. The brilliant humourist died of atrophy. The regulation which he drafted at the bidding of Government, though it served its purpose for the time, was subsequently revoked by an Order in Council on November 1, 1830.

Sir Edward Barnes came to the island with supreme civil and military authority in 1824, and his active and useful rule extended to nearly the close of 1831. He had been Wellington's Adjutant-General at Waterloo, and, as already stated, had laid down the bâton of Commander-in-Chief of India as his views had conflicted with the civil authorities. All this great man's energies, and the resources of money, men, and compulsory labour at his disposal, were systematically and successfully employed to open up the country by means of roads. He had, according to Major Skinner, who was one of his trusted and most useful lieutenants, the rare faculty of gaining the affections of those who served under him, and inspiring them with his own enthusiasm. The result was that within an incredibly short period the capital of the ancient kingdom of Kandy was connected with the maritime capital, first by way of Kurunegala and Galagedara, and finally by the Grand Kadugannawa Pass, by means of roads. These were marvels of engineering skill, and were valuable in a military sense, as they broke for ever the power of the highland chieftains. But their chief use was in opening up the country to industrial enterprise.

"Sir Edward Barnes, though eminent as a soldier, had a mind which reached beyond what was merely a means to an end—military security. He foresaw the great commercial possibilities of Ceylon, and laid the train of that prosperity which the island is now enjoying. Amongst the things to his credit is the fact that he did much to initiate and encourage the great coffee enterprise which his own road, the Simplon of the East, rendered possible, and which in its progress led to the supercession of the road by a railway." Barnes's statue stands at the Colombo terminus of his great work, before the gate of Government House, and the monument of Dawson, the great engineer who executed the task, looks down on the meeting of road and railway at the summit of Kadugannawa Pass. The route to Kandy before the time of Barnes was along Hanwella, Avisawella, Ambagamuwa, and Gampola. In the period of the great Governor's rule a bridge of boats was thrown across the Kelani river at Naghelagam Pass near Colombo (since replaced by an iron structure, the Victoria Bridge, in commemoration of the late Queen's Jubilee), while General Fraser spanned the Mahaveli Ganga near Kandy by the celebrated and beautiful Peradeniya satin-wood bridge which, in 1906, gave place to a more durable and less artistic iron bridge. On the road between Kurunegala and Kandy a tunnel was driven through the hill, and the Kandyan peasant called to mind the old prophecy that the sceptre would only pass away from the Sinhalese when the mountain was pierced and the national palladium, the Tooth Relic of Buddha, seized by the stranger—two events which he deemed alike impossible.

Nuwara Eliya was adopted as a military convalescent station during this rule, and "Barnes Hall," in the grounds of which Sir Edward experimented with coffee until frost came and killed his plants, stood as a memento of the great man who laid the foundation of modern progress in Ceylon. He made roads and built bridges, and he felt that enterprise and improvement would follow, though even he could scarcely have anticipated all the results of what he was able to do. The beautiful pavilion at Kandy, only a portion of the original design, which legend says the Governor sketched in claret on his table after dinner, was commenced during the time of Sir Edward Barnes. He also built the magnificent residence, Mount Lavinia, called after his wife, by the sea at Dehiwala, at a cost which Major Skinner states was moderate. Ceylon was then garrisoned by a large body of troops, whose labour the Governor utilised. He also largely resorted to that system of compulsory labour, *rajakarya*, which was abolished in the succeeding rule at the recommendation of a Royal Commission whose members, Lieutenant-Colonel Colebrooke and C. H. Cameron, arrived in Ceylon in the closing period of Sir Edward Barnes's government. It was only during the rule of Sir Edward Barnes in 1826 that the law was abolished by which capital punishment could be inflicted on women by drowning. The tragedy which surrounds the small tank at Bogambara with so terrible an interest was perhaps the last occasion of the observance of this Kandyan custom. The Colombo Friend-in-Need Society was founded during this administration by Bishop Turner, who was struck with the numerous applications for relief made to him. Bishop Heber visited the island in 1825, the year before his death, and his Journals bear testimony to the beneficent administration of Sir Edward Barnes. Major Skinner thus sums up the policy and character of Sir Edward's government: "He continued progressively to perfect the several works which in 1820 (when Lieutenant-Governor) he had commenced. Rajakariya, or the gratuitous services of the people, he availed himself of with moderation, particularly in those districts wherein the greatest efforts had been made by its means since 1820. His personal intercourse with the official headmen and chiefs and their families was frequent; his conduct towards them was kind and encouraging, evincing an interest even in their private and domestic affairs, all tending to uphold their respectability and influence, while his knowledge of every district and his frequent progresses through them induced every member of his Government, whether in the metropolitan or rural districts, to exercise the same line of conduct towards the natives, and compelled them to acquire the most intimate knowledge of the country, to prevent their appearing less informed than he was himself. He had no fears that the authority and influence of the native chiefs would be exercised prejudicially, and by protecting and upholding it, strengthened his own government and preserved order in all classes of society. His government was characterised by its decision and great energy: during the early part of it he was compelled to exact much gratuitous service from the people; still he won the affections of all classes to his person, and their attachment to his government; his name is honoured throughout the land, as well by peasant as by chief. A handsome statue has been erected at Colombo to his memory, although, owing to delays in England, it was not sent out until seventeen years after he had ceased to exercise authority in the country. On its erection, people from all districts flocked to it; during the night, offerings were so frequently left at its base that we were obliged to enclose it with a railing to prevent its being converted into an idol. I mention this fact as evidence that there is not that deficiency of gratitude and want of feeling on the part of the natives of which they are sometimes accused."

The shortest period during which a Lieutenant-Governor ruled in Ceylon was in October, 1831, when, between the departure of Sir Edward Barnes and the arrival of the Right Hon. Sir Robert Wilmot Horton, that distinguished Peninsular soldier, Sir John Wilson, K.C.B., administered the government for exactly ten days, from the 13th of October to the 23rd of October. Sir Wilmot Horton was a statesman of some mark, who had devoted considerable attention to the much-debated question of the relations between Britain and her colonies. He had filled the office of Under-Secretary of State in a Liberal Administration before being selected to govern Ceylon. His family name was Wilmot, the name of Horton being adopted when he married the beautiful heiress, Byron's cousin, and the heroine of the lines commencing :—

> "She walks in beauty, like the night
> Of cloudless climes and starry skies."

As one of Byron's executors, Sir Wilmot Horton gave his voice for the destruction by fire of that "scandalous" diary which his wife's noble kinsman had left a legacy to his friend Moore, the poet. A brother of Sir R. W. Horton, Mr. Wilmot, Government Agent of the Southern Province, was in the Ceylon Civil Service, and subsequent litigation between the brothers showed that Sir R. W. Horton had been "laying himself out for a peerage." But this ambition was never gratified, although much *éclat* accompanied his government of Ceylon, mainly in consequence of the occurrence of a series of

THE RIGHT HON. SIR ROBERT WILMOT HORTON, BART., G.C.B.

(Governor, October 31, 1831—November 7, 1837.)

wonderfully successful pearl fisheries, which, between 1828 and 1837, yielded a sum of £227,000. Sir Robert Horton, finding Sir Edward Barnes's great road made to his hand, encouraged the establishment of a royal mail coach between Colombo and Kandy, the first postal and passenger vehicle of the kind in the East Indies, according to some in Asia, superseding runners, bullocks, and palanquins. One of the great measures of Sir Robert Horton's rule was the publication of the Order of Council abolishing compulsory labour, on the advice of the Royal Commission's Report. According to this measure, Government claims to service were entirely abandoned, while the rights of private proprietors and temples were left untouched. The distinction occasioned some dissatisfaction on the part of those who felt that Government had made too great a surrender. Finally, Sir Philip Wodehouse's Road Ordinance remedied one defect in the proclamation, while the legislation during Sir Hercules Robinson's term of office provided for the gradual and equitable abolition of prædial and temple serfdom. By the Road Ordinance all males between eighteen and fifty-five years of age (except the Governor, the military, Buddhist priests, and immigrant labourers) are bound to give six days' labour or their money equivalent toward the formation and upkeep of roads and canals, a tax which in its incidence has imposed great hardship on the poorest class of the people. A new and much improved Charter of Justice superseded the previous one as the result of the labours of the Royal Commissioners. The reduction of the salaries of the civil servants and the abolition of a system of pensions, on the recommendation of the Commission of Inquiry, caused much dissatisfaction at the time.

It was only in Sir R. W. Horton's time that Moormen (the Mahomedan descendants of Arab traders and local and Indian converts) and Indian Tamils were allowed to purchase land and houses in the Fort and the Pettah of Colombo, the disability continuing from Dutch times, which probably originally arose as much from prejudice as from military considerations. Until comparatively recently, it had been an offence to sell horses to the Sinhalese of the Kandyan provinces.

The cinnamon monopoly, which was the chief source of revenue of the Dutch, and which had been continued under the British with its special departments manned by Sinhalese chiefs and labourers of a particular caste, was relinquished during this rule in 1833.

"It was in connection with the higher education of Colombo that the interest of Government in education took a practical shape," writes Mr. Harward, the Director of Ceylon Education. "The first important Government institution, the Colombo Academy, which still exists under a changed name as the Royal College, dates from 1835. It is perhaps more than a coincidence that this is the year of Lord Macaulay's famous minute, which marks the decision of the Supreme Council of India in favour of a European type of education. The question had been in the air for some time, and though the Government of Ceylon had no official connection with India, the Governor was doubtless aware of the discussions which had taken place in Calcutta. But the actual establishment of the Academy has more the appearance of a happy accident than of a deliberate act of policy. The Rev. J. Marsh, M.A., had come out to Ceylon as classical and mathematical tutor to the Kotta Christian Institution under the Church Missionary Society. He had, however, left that institution and had come to Colombo, where he acted as colonial chaplain at St. Paul's Church, and in 1835 started a private school for the sons of the upper classes among the Sinhalese. The school met a want that had been felt for some time, and the leading Sinhalese residents at once petitioned the Governor, Sir R. Wilmot Horton, to support it. The decision of Government was prompt, and was carried out with considerable liberality. In January, 1836, the new school became a Government institution under the title of the Colombo Academy, with the Rev. J. Marsh as its Principal. The experiment was watched and aided with the warmest personal interest by Sir Wilmot Horton and his immediate successor, the Right Hon. J. A. Stewart Mackenzie, who on one occasion personally conducted the school examination. The object of the school was to give to those that could afford it a good education in English, the classics, mathematics, and religious knowledge. No very advanced work was done, but the teaching was sound and thorough as far as it went, and the effect on the students was certainly good. Many of them rose rapidly to high positions in the service of Government. The main cause of the success of the school was the high personal character of its first Principal, the Rev. J. Marsh, a remarkable man who had in a very marked degree the gift of rousing and maintaining noble aims among those who worked under him."

One of the most far-reaching reforms, also introduced on the recommendation of the Royal Commissioners' Report of 1829–31, was a change in the constitution of Government. The Crown, in 1833, by an Order in Council, created an Executive Council, consisting of the Colonial Secretary, the Officer Commanding the Forces, the Attorney-General, the Treasurer and the Auditor-General, to assist the Governor when he chose to summon it, although he was not bound to follow their advice; and established a Legislative Council, to be composed of fifteen members, nine officials and six persons to be selected from and out of the chief landed proprietors and principal merchants, the officials to take precedence of the unofficial element, and the latter among themselves according to the priority of their appointments. A difficulty arose at the outset. The European members, Messrs. Joseph, Read, and Jeffery, would not accept their seats as the officials had been given precedence and Sinhalese members had been placed over some of them. A bitter controversy on the subject between the English merchants and the Government, with appeals to the Secretary of State, continued till the close of Sir R. W. Horton's rule.

Since the attempt of the pretender, "Vimala Dharma Narendra Sinha" in 1820 the Kandyan country had remained tranquil. A disturbance of a different character occurred in 1834. On information from Mahawalatenne Dissawa and other informers of a plot in the Kandyan provinces, Sir Robert Horton issued orders to seize the suspected leaders. On the night of the 19th July their houses were surrounded and twenty-three persons were arrested. Amongst them were Molligoda, first Adigar, only brother of the first Adigar Molligoda, who died in 1823, Dunuwila Dissawa, Raddegoda Lekam, two priests of the Malwatta establishment, and a Malay officer of the Ceylon regiment. On January 12, 1835, they were tried for high treason. They were charged with conspiracy to levy war against the king, to set up a pretended prince or relative of the late king of Kandy to be king of the Kandyan provinces, for endeavouring to procure assistance from Siam and from the French nation, to seduce some of the soldiers of the Ceylon Rifles from their allegiance, and to kill the soldiers and subjects of the king. The prisoners objecting to being tried by Kandyans, they were arraigned in the Supreme Court in Colombo, and after a trial of ten days were acquitted by a jury consisting of Europeans and low-country Sinhalese. Notwithstanding the acquittal, the chiefs and officers were detained, including the Adigar Molligoda. Major Skinner, who was the officer commissioned to seize the Adigar, states: "Molligoda has since died from the effects of intemperance, a vice acquired in his European intercourse. His son, a fine youth of about twenty-one years of age, has fallen a victim to the same propensity, and the name of a once high and powerful family is now extinct. My own impressions have been that the reports of this intended insurrection were wilfully exaggerated by informers, who hoped by their zeal and the importance of their information to ingratiate themselves with Government. The result of the State trials at the beginning of 1835 was seriously to impair the influence and authority of Government in the minds and affections of the people. With the exception of this supposed intended insurrectionary movement, things went on very properously. Government gave many substantial proofs of the liberality of its policy."

Sir Robert Wilmot Horton's successor was the Right Hon. James Alexander Stewart Mackenzie (November 7, 1837), who previously to his appointment sat as fellow Commissioner with Macaulay on the Indian Board. Mr. Stewart Mackenzie was an able man and a polished scholar. He worked hard himself and exacted good work from those under him in the task of administration. It was Mr. Stewart Mackenzie's misfortune to find Ceylon in a transition state; old sources of revenue collapsed, and new industries demanded expenditure of money which was not forthcoming. The pearl fishery, so prolific during the rule of his predecessor, had entered on a long period of barrenness; and cinnamon, once the mainstay of Ceylon, was, by reason of the establishments still being maintained, an additional strain rather than a source of income to the revenue. The old monopoly system and the high duties had fostered competition abroad, notably in Java. The Governor realised that the true remedies were the disposal of the Government Cinnamon Gardens, with their attendant expensive department, and the throwing open of the trade. The Crown's sanction was obtained for the measure, and matters improved, although not in his time. While the ancient cinnamon trade of Ceylon was thus in its decline, the coffee enterprise, as far as its regular and systematic cultivation was concerned, was in its very infancy. The first plantations had been opened by George Bird and Sir Edward Barnes ten years earlier; yet when Mr. Stewart Mackenzie landed in Ceylon on November 7, 1837, all the plantations in the colony did not exceed ten, and only 34,000 cwts., valued at £106,000, were exported, the coffee being almost entirely the produce of bushes grown around Sinhalese huts, as compared with over a thousand estates, with a yearly out-turn of a million cwts., worth three million sterling, thirty years later. Unfortunately for his reputation, his peace of mind, and, as it happened, unfortunately also for the interests of his family, the mania for speculation afflicted the Governor, as well as nearly all the officials, civil, judicial, military, and even ecclesiastical. To a large proportion of them the imagined El Dorado lay in the Ambagamuwa forests. The costly Ambagamuwa road was publicly denounced as being undertaken to subserve the private interests of officials, and defended as best calculated to open up what was then thought to be the best, as it was the largest, expanse of unbroken forest in Ceylon. But the warmest advocates for the road could not have anticipated what occurred. Ambagamuwa collapsed, but Kotmale, Dambulla, Dikoya, and Maskeliya were opened up, and the road was superseded by the Nawalapitiya railway. So great was the scandal that purchasers of land were permitted to select their blocks, and to obtain them at the upset price of five shillings an acre. Crown lands passed in thousands of acres into private hands, and not the least into that of the highest Government officials. The prices of labour and supplies were rapidly run up by planters, in the stress of competition to get coffee into bearing in order to make their fortunes by one or two crops before the differential duties should be abolished.

Mr. Stewart Mackenzie was able to gather round him a complete Legislative Council. The English merchants waived their objections to join the Board, where all the non-officials had precedence according to the priority of their appointment. On the death of the Tamil member in 1837, the scholarly and cultured Simon Casie Chetty, author of the "Ceylon Gazetteer," was appointed to the seat. Being in Government service at the time, he had to be pensioned off; but the then Secretary of State being opposed to the principle of pensioning off Government officers to be created councillors, Casie Chetty was soon replaced by another. It was not until the time of Sir Colin Campbell, however, that the business and debates of the Council became such as to attract public attention. Mr. Stewart Mackenzie could only, session after session, come before it with the same tale of a revenue not equal to the most economical expenditure on works in addition to establishments. The scramble for lands during this rule and that which succeeded it, and the too rapidly extended cultivation in the face of a continued depreciation in the prices of coffee, led to hasty surveys which gave much trouble in after days, and culminated in the disasters which rendered the rule of Lord Torrington so unhappily memorable.

THE RIGHT HON. JAMES ALEXANDER STEWART MACKENZIE.
(Governor, November 7, 1837—April 5, 1841.)

Mr. Stewart Mackenzie took deep interest in the moral and intellectual advancement of the people. He prepared the way for the final abolition of slavery, which his successor was able to accomplish; he made great efforts to improve lunatic asylums, prisons, and hospitals, and the then imperfect machinery for the education of the people; he sanctioned liberal grants to libraries; and it was due to his determination personally to ascertain the condition of the wild Veddahs, so as to organise measures for educating and civilising them, that he contracted the fever which ultimately forced him to leave Ceylon and accept the office of Lord High Commissioner of the Ionian Islands, the tenancy of which, there is little doubt, finally proved fatal to him. If Sir Robert Wilmot Horton's rule was memorable for the establishment of mail-coach communication between Colombo and Kandy, Mr. Stewart Mackenzie's rule was distinguished by the running of a mail coach on the Galle road. Mr. Stewart Mackenzie, as a Scotch member of Parliament and landlord—he was proprietor of the island of Lewis through his wife, the daughter of Lord Seaforth, a lady whom Scott described as "a chieftainess in every drop of her blood"—had been familiar with a system of Government bounties to fishermen, and viewed with disfavour the reverse system of the exaction of a tax of one-tenth from the fishermen of Ceylon. In the face of much opposition he abolished the tax; and its re-imposition, though often subsequently advocated on the ground that the fishermen voluntarily continued the tithes of the fish caught in favour of their churches and temples, has not been agreed to. Not the least among Mr. Stewart Mackenzie's characteristics was his piety and rigid adherence to Christian principles. In his days not infrequently the Governor presided at missionary meetings, supported by the Chief Justice and other high authorities. One of the last acts of this Governor was to enter a solemn written protest against himself or any of his successors being called upon to sign warrants of appointment for Buddhist priests, which had previously been done under the public seal in terms of the Kandyan Convention and as successors of the ancient Sinhalese sovereigns.

Sir Colin Campbell, one of the Duke of Wellington's lieutenants, was chosen to succeed Mr. Stewart Mackenzie as Governor. He assumed the government on April 5, 1841. Coffee production had increased at a rate so entirely beyond the means of communication, that it was often a greater difficulty and a matter of more time to get the produce to Colombo than to send it from Colombo to London. With the capital introduced for the cultivation of coffee and the rice imported to feed the coolies, the revenue increased until there was a sum of £100,000 per annum more available than Sir Colin's predecessor was able to command. Establishments and expenditure generally were increased in proportion. All this occurred while coffee, on which the continued prosperity of the colony depended, was not rising, but declining in price. This augmentation of establishments and the increase of expenditure, therefore, laid the foundation of an unstable edifice which came down with a crash in the time of Lord Torrington.

Lord Stanley, afterwards Earl of Derby, being then Colonial Minister, ordered the

Governor to publish in the Government *Gazette* a series of despatches in which the character of the civil service of Ceylon was assailed in terms which created intense excitement and displeasure amongst those so stringently dealt with and their friends. "There was much truth," says a contemporary, "in the description, however, many members of the service being possessed of but low general attainments, while only a very few paid attention to the native languages." The service was reconstituted, its emoluments increased, and a system of pensions revived on the principle of a deduction of 5 per cent. from salaries. This exaction was subsequently abandoned, as well as the principle of annual increases to salaries of gentlemen who did not obtain promotion. Sir Emerson Tennent, an able follower of Lord Stanley, was sent out as Colonial Secretary, the Whigs following the example and sending out Mr. C. J. MacCarthy, another able man, as Auditor-General. Both infusions of "new blood" were most unwelcome to the old members of the service, who had naturally expected to succeed to the prizes, and the feeling against Sir J. E. Tennent, especially, was intense. Mr. MacCarthy succeeded by a policy of conciliation in eventually becoming Governor, while Sir Emerson Tennent was too clever and too demonstrative in his ambition to exchange the post of Colonial Secretary for that of Governor. The change of Ministry was a disappointment to him, and his coquetting with Mr. Wodehouse for the use of his influence with Earl Kimberley, amounting to "You help me to become Governor and you'll be my Colonial Secretary, with larger fees in addition to salary," became a public scandal. Mr. Wodehouse, afterwards Sir Philip Wodehouse, had too much character and capacity to be made the tool of Sir Emerson Tennent. He adopted a strong line of opposition against Sir Emerson on several public occasions, and the feuds between the two ultimately culminated in the political ruin of Lord Torrington and the recall of themselves and the weak man whom they used as their instrument. Apart from their personal quarrels and political intrigues, both Tennent and Wodehouse were able men. The one wrote valuable reports on our system of finance, and gave the world the best account ever written of Ceylon, or perhaps of any other colony; while to Mr. Wodehouse mainly the country owes the Thoroughfares Ordinance. Both being recalled from Ceylon in disgrace, Tennent lived to be Secretary of the Board of Trade and to receive a pension and a baronetcy; Wodehouse, projected into the line of Governors, rose step by step until he became Governor of Bombay. Lord Torrington, on whose weakness each had played, never emerged from the obscurity of the ornamental Court office to which he was relegated—but we must not anticipate.

Not only was the civil service reconstituted

SIR J. EMERSON TENNENT.
(Colonial Secretary during Sir Colin Campbell's and Lord Torrington's Administrations (1841–1850). The author of the well-known "History of Ceylon.")

in the time of Sir Colin Campbell, but the whole system of the administration of justice revolutionised. Mr. Cameron's simple and well-matured system, providing for a single court of original jurisdiction in each district, with systematic rules, pleaders, assessors, &c., was deemed not to insure that summary disposal of cases which was considered almost equally important with correct and legal decisions. Minor courts were therefore established—those of commissioners of requests and police magistrates—while justices of the peace, unofficial as well as official, received commissions to take preliminary evidence in cases of serious crime. Coroners and deputy-coroners were also appointed. Slavery, which, by a series of laws enforcing registration and the payment of a tax, had been reduced to very narrow limits, was finally abolished by Ordinance, and since 1844 there has been no slavery in Ceylon. Compulsory labour due to Government had been previously abolished, and finally Sir Hercules Robinson rendered possible the emancipation of temple and village tenants, who occupy lands by tenures which involve the principle of serfdom. Mr. Arthur Buller (afterwards Sir Arthur Buller, of the Calcutta Bench) was then Queen's Advocate, and did much to enlighten the elaborate and animated discussions of those days in the Legislature, of which the late Mr. John Armitage and Mr. Edward Darley were able and industrious members. Mr. Armitage's name is also associated with the introduction of regular banking into Ceylon, and he was one of the directors of the unfortunate Bank of Ceylon—unfortunate because it departed from the leading principle of banking by advancing on "block." On its ruins, however, arose the Oriental Banking Corporation and the other financial institutions which largely aided the progress of Ceylon. Previous to the opening of the Bank of Ceylon, exchange and bill operations were conducted by the merchants, or by Government, whose drafts were eagerly competed for.

The Ceylon branch of the Asiatic Society, or rather the Royal Asiatic Society of Ceylon, was established in 1845, before the Royal Asiatic Society of Great Britain was started in England for Oriental research. It was later affiliated to the British Society.

On the departure of Sir Colin Campbell, the post of Lieutenant-Governor was assumed by Sir James Emerson Tennent, who held the office only from April 13 to May 23, 1847. On the latter date commenced the unhappy rule of Viscount Torrington. A youthful and poor member of the peerage, his only experience of public life had been obtained as a Lord of the Bedchamber and as chairman of a railway company. He had been selected to convey Prince Albert to Britain on the eve of the marriage of that Prince to Queen Victoria, and it is believed that he was not so much chosen to rule Ceylon on account of a belief in his special administrative talent as in view of a desire by certain men in power to provide for a relative. If such were the case, dire retribution followed those dispensers of patronage. For years a Select Committee of the House of Commons took evidence and reported on the affairs of Ceylon. Animated debates took place in Parliament, in which leading Liberals refused to stand by their party, and in a final division the Whig Ministry of the day was saved only by a majority of eight in a full House. Earl Grey, who was then Colonial Minister, professed that the final recall of the unfortunate Viscount was not attributable to disapproval of his political measures, but due to the fact that he was not able to preserve harmony amongst his subordinates. It is not necessary to more than recall the disgraceful episode of the production of his lordship's private letter by his "friends" Wodehouse and Tennent, followed by a flood of other private letters, until the world was ringing with the "mysteries of Ceylon," its government and its society. In the island itself there was universal anarchy and distrust. Lord Torrington's political measures were very much what his political advisers and his political chief made them. Many sweeping changes were attempted at once and by new men, while statistical queries circulated by Sir J. E. Tennent excited the suspicion and alarm of an ignorant people.[1]

[1] A. M. Ferguson.

Major Skinner, whose long residence in the island and intimate knowledge of the country and its people had rendered him an authority on all matters connected with Ceylon, in his evidence before a select committee of the House of Commons, thus summarises the causes which led up to the revolt of 1848 :—

"During the eleven years from 1838 to 1848 inclusive, a great change has occurred in the whole aspect of the affairs of the colony ; the social condition of its people has been no less affected by it than has been its commercial importance. While granting some of these changes are doubtless of a salutary nature, it is a subject of humilating regret that on the mass of society they have had a contrary and demoralising tendency. Amongst the causes which have led to this result must be enumerated the vice of intemperance, into which the people have been led, the demoralising effects of the sudden influx of enormous capital, and the encouragement to indulge in the most litigious spirit which ever affected the taste of a people. While these evils have been operating on the social condition of the people, unfortunately the authority of the Government and native executive has been exerting but very feeble counteracting influences. . . . Renters purchase from Government the monopoly of the taverns of a district. The competition for these arrack farms is so great that they are seldom sold much under their value. It is, of course, the object of the renter to sub-let as many of these taverns as possible ; they are established in every district, almost in every village of any size throughout the interior, often to the great annoyance of the inhabitants, and in opposition to the headmen. To give the people a taste for the use of spirits, it is often, at first, necessary to distribute it gratuitously, the tavern-keepers well knowing that with the use the abuse of the indulgence follows as a certainty. I have known districts, of the population of which, some years ago, not one in a hundred could be induced to taste spirits, where drunkenness now prevails to such an extent that villagers have been known to pawn their crops upon the ground to tavern-keepers for arrack. Government, by the tempting item of its revenue derivable from the arrack farms, has been induced tacitly to allow, if it has not through its agents positively encouraged, the use of spirits throughout the land. It is during the last eleven years that the influx of European capital, and the extensive cultivation of coffee, has thrown a large amount of specie into circulation in the interior—I think it is estimated at three millions sterling. As a very large portion of the money has been paid in specie for labour, it followed that temptations to, and examples of, intemperance and vice of every kind were rife ; the most profligate of the low-country Sinhalese flocked from the maritime provinces into the interior, and spread far and wide their contaminating influences over a previously sober, orderly, honest race. Robberies and bloodshed became familiar to the Kandyan, in districts where a few years before any amount of property would have been perfectly safe in the open air. While the foregoing demoralising influences have been operating on the social condition of the people, the authority and moral influence, both of European public servants and of the native chiefs, have been sadly on the decline in too many of the districts.

"With the introduction of the supposed endless stream of capital which poured into the colony, simultaneously came a number of European settlers of every grade and age, in the various capacities of capitalists, planters, superintendents, overseers, &c. Amongst these were not a few whose habits and conduct tended much to diminish the respect in which the English character had previously been held by the natives, while a most fatal error committed by Government in allowing its public servants to embark in the seductive speculation of coffee, by placing too many of them in the general category of 'planters,' weakened the moral influence and authority which they previously possessed, no less than it tended to circumscribe their pecuniary means of independence and usefulness, and finally, in too many instances, ruined their finances. It also placed their interests in rivalry with their duty, which in Ceylon (where so much depends on the individual example, influence, and energy of the public functionary) demands, and had previously received, their undivided attention and time. During the feverish excesses of this delusive speculation, little could be thought of but the wealth and prosperity to which, by its means, and the instrumentality of European capital, the colony was to be raised. As European capital was to accomplish such prodigies, it was but a natural consequence that European interests should gain the ascendancy. The natives, who had previously had comparatively little acquaintance with the precious metal, during the last ten or eleven years found it, in the coffee districts, pouring into the deep recesses of their forests with a kind of Californian superfluity, and too frequently accompanied with its attendant evils ; the cultivation of the staple article of food of the country (rice) declined ; large tracts of land were thrown out of cultivation ; while in one province alone was there to be seen any attempt to increase the means of irrigation, or to expand or improve the cultivation of native productions. Intercourse between the European public functionaries and the natives had become less frequent, while the native chiefs were placed in a position anomalous and invidious for some years past. A vague idea has prevailed that their influence and authority has been too great, and under an impression that it was necessarily subversive of the stability and efficiency of our own authority, the policy has been to allow it to decline, and without any avowed determination to destroy it, we have practically discouraged and undermined it. We have rendered them discontented, their respectability and influence for good with the mass of the people is generally impaired, and they are becoming alienated in feeling from the Government.

"Under these circumstances society in its various forms, but especially in the lower grades, has been (for the last ten or eleven years) becoming demoralised, and palpably so of late, so that it required no great power of discrimination to predict, twelve months before it manifested itself in open revolt, the anarchy to which some of the districts were approaching.

"In brief recapitulation, then, it may be said of the last thirty-one years (1818–43), that the first six were to the native population a period of trial and depression ; the next fourteen of contentment and prosperity ; the last eleven of fictitious prosperity, as transient as it was local, partial, of eventual bankruptcy to European capitalists, and as regards the natives, of demoralisation more or less in most, ending in anarchy in some districts. While the causes I have referred to were hastening the native population into various degrees of disorganisation, want of intercourse with, knowledge of, and sympathy with the people, kept many of the local European functionaries so completely in the dark as regarded the social condition of the people, that the warning I gave twelve months before the late insurrection broke out, of the state of anarchy to which the two rebellious districts, Hat Korale (Seven Korales) and Matale, were approaching, was disregarded, if not disbelieved.

"The same want of knowledge of the real state of public feeling in the country appears to me to have excited exaggerated fears in the Government when disorder overtook it, and prevented its rightly distinguishing between the feelings which prompted the people to meet in large but orderly and peaceful assemblages, to obtain information of the intentions and objects of Government (the necessity for which explanation it was the duty of the local officers to have anticipated), and those feelings which in other districts urged the disaffected to open rebellion.

"Had there existed less ignorance of the social condition of the people, the late trouble might easily have been averted, even at the eleventh hour ; while to that ignorance is to be attributed the exaggerated view taken of the nature and extent of the disaffection, and the consequent severity of the punishments inflicted on those implicated in the revolt. Although amongst the latter were to be found headmen and priests, there was that in the nature of the whole affair, and in the character of its ringleaders, to stamp it as the result of disorganisation and inefficiency in the system and machinery of our executive Government, rather than as originating from any general and serious disaffection of the people.

"But for the great sacrifice of life, liberty, and property which have resulted from the late insurrection, it might be regarded as a fortunate event, if by its means the Government has been aroused to a sense of the defective system which produced it, and which would finally have resulted in still more general anarchy, had not the state of organisation thus early developed itself."

Further, the chiefs and priests were greatly irritated at the measures taken to discontinue the connection of the British Government with Buddhism, in breach of the Kandyan Convention. The imposition of new taxes, such as the dog tax, and statistical queries by Government, excited such wide-spread suspicion and alarm that they gave rise to the wildest rumours, amongst others that a tax was to be levied which necessitated the measurement of women across the breasts. Incited by the priests and headmen, the Kandyan Sinhalese round Matale and Kurunegala rose, placing a pretender at their head. They were at once met, dispersed, and slaughtered by small bodies of troops, and, had the matter rested there, Lord Torrington would have received only credit for the promptitude and success of his measures. His fatal mistake was to insist, in opposition to the counsel of his legal adviser, Mr. H. C. Selby, on keeping the districts in which the easily suppressed risings had taken place under martial law for many months, during which a series of unnecessary executions were sanctioned. Sir Anthony Oliphant, the Chief Justice, in condemning the ringleaders of the rebellion to death for treason, felt it his duty to publicly record his opinion that justice had been already more than satisfied by the executions of persons captured. He thus rendered it impossible for Lord Torrington to act otherwise than commute the sentences of death into banishment. The judge was severely reproved for his plain speaking by the local Executive, but the position he took up was sustained by Lord John Russell. There appeared to be too much of the vindictiveness of weakness in the conduct of Lord Torrington's Government. In defence, an opinion was quoted from Forbes's work on Ceylon to the effect that, if duly severe measures had been taken on the outbreak of the rebellion of 1817, much of the evil results which followed might have been prevented. But Forbes himself came forward to support the view of those who contended that between the general rising of the then warlike Kandyan people in 1817 and the small gathering of poor, ignorant, almost unarmed peasants of 1848, who did not take a single life, there could be no possible comparison, any more than between a pitched battle and a village riot.[1] Lord Torrington took credit to himself for saving a coffee crop worth half a million sterling, but one of his misfortunes was that he succeeded to the rule of Ceylon at a period when all its interests were depressed, the great coffee interest especially, which had almost succumbed under the effects of a series of disastrous years, in which the value of produce had steadily and persistently declined. Much of the coffee property, which had cost immense sums to open between 1840 and 1845, was abandoned to weeds and ruin in the dreary period between 1849 and 1850. A railway to Kandy was suggested during the period of Lord Torrington's government, but the matter could not be seriously considered with a revenue only slightly over £400,000, the balance being on the wrong side until the last year of Lord Torrington's rule. He was recalled and left the island in October, 1850, the fact of his recall being the first item of intelligence brought from Galle by the *Observer* carrier pigeons, which henceforward seldom failed to bring budgets of exciting news, during the periods of the Crimean War and the Indian Mutiny, until, in 1858, Galle and Colombo were connected by the telegraph wire. "The continued success of this, the most prolonged and systematic experiment," writes Mr. A. M. Ferguson, an able publicist and old colonist who bore a distinguished part in the politics of the time, "in utilising the 'homing' instinct of the carrier pigeon, was due to the personal attention of the late Dr. C. Elliot, who was then the proprietor and chief conductor of the *Observer* newspaper. A warm-hearted Irishman, our late friend threw the whole energy of his nature into whatever cause he advocated, and mainly to his personal influence and efforts were due the attention which Ceylon affairs then received in the Parliament and Press of Britain, culminating in the recall of the Governor, the Colonial Secretary, Sir J. E. Tennent, and Sir Philip Wodehouse. Mr. Henry Baillie, in leading the movement, and Mr. Disraeli and others in supporting it, may have had to some extent party objects in view. But no charge of this nature could be laid against such men as Sir Robert Peel, John Bright, Joseph Hume, and other independent members. A flood of light was thrown on many social and political questions of great interest connected with Ceylon, and one great principle was decided on—that, at whatever cost, the agents of Government, through whom the people were ruled and through whom justice was administered, should be spread over the land. Although Lord Torrington took the retrograde step of again taking military possession of the 'Temple of the Tooth,' yet the whole question of the Buddhist connection was so discussed and understood that it became possible for Lord Torrington's successor to carry out an arrangement enabling the Buddhists of Ceylon to manage their own affairs without calling on the secular power to aid them, otherwise than through the duly constituted courts of justice." Lord Torrington, who several times consulted his Council as to the expediency of arresting the conductors of the *Observer*, subsequently met Dr. Elliot on terms of cordial goodwill, while Sir Emerson Tennent has acknowledged in his published works aid rendered to him by the late Mr. A. M. Ferguson, his old political opponent, in his great efforts to illustrate the history and progress of Ceylon. "In some political matters Lord Torrington displayed considerable ability, and when occasion arose he spoke clearly and well," says a contemporary. "His great and fatal faults were those of temper. He was indiscreet in his relations with the able and ambitious men who surrounded him, and was made the cat's-paw of the ambitious intrigues of Tennent and Wodehouse, Mr. (afterwards Sir Charles) MacCarthy steering a quiet and cautious course, while even in the ordinary affairs of life the young lord could not long keep out of brawls." After his enforced retirement, Lord Torrington for many many years remained in the obscurity of Court life as a lord-in-waiting.

Sir Charles MacCarthy, who, on the recall of Sir Emerson Tennent, had been appointed Colonial Secretary, held rule as Lieutenant-Governor after the departure of Lord Torrington and until the arrival of Sir George Anderson, from October 18 to November 27, 1850. By a strange combination of circumstances, indeed, Sir Charles MacCarthy continued to be the real ruler of the island for a short period, even after the arrival of Sir George Anderson. The vessel that brought Sir George Anderson from Mauritius made so good a voyage that the new Governor arrived in advance of his commission. This document reached the island by the overland mail a full week at least subsequent to the period at which Sir Charles MacCarthy had vacated Queen's House for the reception of the new Governor and his family, and ordered all honours due to a Governor to be paid to Sir George Anderson. But in the absence of the Royal Commission, Sir Charles MacCarthy felt bound to decline compliance with the demand of Sir George that he should be installed as Governor. Although Sir Charles MacCarthy was manifestly right, Sir George Anderson took

[1] A. M. Ferguson.

personal offence at a strict adherence to rule and privilege. But the man who had come to India in the same ship with Dr. Coke and the first Wesleyan missionaries to Ceylon in 1814, who had served with credit in the Bombay Civil Service until he rose to be Acting-Governor of the Presidency, who had been chosen to govern Mauritius, and governed it well through a crisis in which he had to appoint additional members to the Legislative Council to enable him to carry liberal measures against some of the elder members of the service, was now ageing and showing the first symptoms of the irritability which ended in the paralytic seizure which drove him from Ceylon.

Sir George Anderson resented Sir Charles MacCarthy's adherence to rule as a personal affront, and the relations between the Governor and his Colonial Secretary became such that at one period Sir George transacted a large portion of the business of the island through Mr. Rawden Power. Sir Charles MacCarthy was declared to be entirely in the right in a question which Sir George Anderson insisted on referring to the Secretary of State. The rule in the colony is that all official correspondence and reports, everything except despatches from the Secretary of State, are addressed to the Colonial Secretary, are opened by him, read, abridged in his office, and submitted to the Governor with all necessary information and with such draft of reply or disposal of the case as the Colonial Secretary thinks is demanded. The majority of cases is decided on precedents, and the Governor's sanction is given as a matter of course. In important cases the Governor modifies or rewrites the terms of reply or decision, and if such be his wish the disposal of a case is left entirely to his discretion. Sir George Anderson assumed the position that Sir Charles MacCarthy, in offering an opinion beforehand, was trenching on the prerogative of the Governor. Earl Grey, to whom Sir George Anderson had owed his appointment, entirely sustained the view taken by Sir Charles MacCarthy, his lordship remarking that he would consider himself ill-served if the Under-Secretaries did not bring most questions before him in a perfectly matured shape. The condition of Sir George Anderson's health prevented him from travelling and judging for himself the needs of the country. The planters felt that roads and other improvements were neglected to such an extent that decided action on their part became necessary.[1] In February, 1854, the Planters' Association, which has since developed into such a power in the State, was instituted. Under stringent orders from the Crown, Sir George Anderson addressed all his energies to the task of establishing an equilibrium in the island's finances. To effect the object expenditure was restricted to an extent which could not fail to render any Governor unpopular. Under the influence of a clever but wrong-headed and obstinate Surveyor-General, too, land sales, on which the advance of enterprise in the colony depended, were brought almost to a standstill. The economy or the parsimony of Sir George Anderson's government aided his successor, who found a handsome balance ready to hand and a revenue which the more he spent at the instance of European planters or Sinhalese cultivators the more it seemed to expand. The great political event in Sir George Anderson's rule was the settlement of the long-vexed question of the Government connection with Buddhism. Under the influence, it was believed, of an old civilian, the liberal and cultured Sir John D'Oyley, Bart., afterwards

SIR HENRY GEORGE WARD, K.C.M.G.
(Governor, May 11, 1855—July, 1860.)

Resident of Kandy, Sir Robert Brownrigg, in 1815, and again in 1818, had entered into solemn engagements with the Kandyan people to preserve the religion and rites of Buddhism inviolable. Under these engagements it was complained, in addition to other matters, that a British military guard should protect the "Temple of the Tooth," as if the Christian Government of Britain acknowledged the relic within it as the sacred palladium of Ceylon. The custody of the Tooth, the temples, and their wealth was entrusted to the Buddhist chiefs and priests, and finally a grant of land in Sir Henry Ward's time relieved the British Government from all pecuniary payments.

On the departure of Sir George Anderson, Sir Charles MacCarthy again became Lieutenant-Governor from January 18 to May 11, 1855. It was during this period that the Ceylon pearl banks, after a score of years of barrenness, again promised to yield their precious, though precarious, treasures. When Sir Henry Ward reached the island in May, 1855, the hour for a change of policy and sweeping reform had arrived, and, with it, the man under whom dawned a new era of progress in Ceylon.

"The 11th of May, 1855, will ever be memorable in the annals of Ceylon as the date on which the government of the island was assumed by Sir Henry Ward—a man, perhaps, the equal of Sir Edward Barnes in energy, his superior, certainly, in the qualities which go to make up a great statesman, and beyond all precedent fortunate, as he admitted, in the circumstances under which he found the colony whose destinies he was called to guide." His father, Robert Ward, was well known in literary circles as the author of "Tremaine," while as a politician he was highly estimated by those who knew him intimately. Pitt mentioned his name in his dying delirium, the impression created being that the expiring Minister regretted not having sufficiently appreciated Ward's claims on him. Henry Ward made himself a name as a Liberal politician when Liberalism was rather at a discount, and as a journalist he was editor of the *Weekly Chronicle* when journalism in Britain was subjected to much discouragement. He had passed through great and varied experience in statesmanship before he was summoned to exchange his troubled rule of the Ionian Republic for the more peaceful government of the "utmost Indian isle." Chosen by Canning to represent the interests of Britain in Mexico, he gave to the world one of the best descriptions extant of the Spanish-American republic, grace being added to the volumes by illustrations from the pencil of Lady Ward, a Swinburne and an aunt of the poet. On his return to Britain he entered Parliament as an advanced Liberal. He also represented Great Britain at Madrid, in a style, it is stated, of regal splendour more honourable to his country than profitable to his family. In parliamentary history Sir Henry Ward's name is associated with the "appropriation clause," by which a portion of the revenues of the Irish Church Establishment was devoted to purposes of education, part of a policy which, adopted by the Whig Ministry, led to the secession from its ranks of Lord Stanley, later Earl of Derby, the late Earl of Ripon, and the late Sir James Graham. Sir Henry Ward served for some time as an Under-Secretary of State, and he probably would have risen to a post in the Cabinet had his pecuniary position been such as to render him independent of the emoluments attached to colonial posts. In the Ionian Islands Sir Henry Ward exercised a very stringent rule over the wretched Greeks whom Britain, at great cost, "protected" but never succeeded in conciliating; and, in

[1] A. M. Ferguson.

consequence of a proclamation which he issued regarding the leaders of a political rising, obtained the sobriquet of "Dead-or-alive" Ward. He relieved the cares of protective government, however, by varying them with a good deal of devotion to out-of-door exercise in the pursuit of sport. Thus he brought to Ceylon a frame the very embodiment of physical vigour. Undeterred by the greater fervours of a tropical climate, or the malaria which haunts such scenes of ancient but abandoned splendour as the Tissamaharama and other great works, Sir Henry Ward continued his outdoor habits in Ceylon, fulfilling in the first year of his rule his promise that, whereas when he first met those associated with him in the Government and Legislature he knew less than any of them by personal inspection of Ceylon, the case would be reversed when he next formally met them. Sir Henry Ward, in meeting his first Legislative Council, considered it a matter of congratulation for himself and the colony that the average revenue of the past four years had been £415,595, while the expenditure had been reduced to the limit of £400,000. With all the difficulties and disadvantages which oppressed planters in 1854–55, the coffee enterprise was extending, and the lucrative sales of Crown land were only impeded by the policy which left the Surveyor-General with but six assistants at his disposal. The receipts of the department from 1849–54, inclusive, amounted to only £21,908, or less than a third of what has been realised in one year since then, while the expenditure was £29,840. The survey of only 34,970 acres in five years had resulted in a loss to Government of £7,932. European capitalists could not obtain land for planting purposes, while a cruel continuance of injustice was inflicted on Sinhalese holders of lots, who, on the promise of a settlement and titles for land, had deposited £8,000, and waited eleven years in vain. Thus the extension of both European and Sinhalese agriculture had been neglected by a starving policy, while as yet no real effort had been made to aid Sinhalese labour by advances of capital to restore the ancient irrigation works which had fallen into decay, or form new works where they were needed, to furnish a perennial supply of water for increasing the food resources of the country. A revision of the civil establishments of the colony had occupied much time, but had, as yet, resulted in no changes calculated to ensure good and hearty work from gentlemen desirous of being adequately recompensed in the present and of having good prospects before them. The postal facilities were few and the rates excessive, while there were no telegraphs within the island or connecting the colony with—to use President Grant's phrase—"the balance of the world." Provision had also to be made for the withdrawal of the Government paper currency, so as to afford fair scope to chartered banks, which under due restrictions should be banks of issue. To these and other important questions Sir Henry Ward applied himself diligently till the period when, with vigour sapped, and enfeebled by disease engendered by strenuous work and exposure to malarious influences, he was promoted to the government of Madras, only to give promise of further greatness and then to be struck down by the scourge of cholera.

Within two months of his arrival in Colombo, on July 4, 1855, he opened his first session of the Legislative Council in an able and comprehensive speech, in which he displayed considerable mastery of the position, resources, requirements, and prospects of the colony. That degree of ignorance of the people and localities of the country which, in his circumstances, was inevitable, he promised should not exist when he next met the Legislature. And well did he fulfil his pledge. The collected volume of his Minutes is a monument of industrious, persevering research, such as not one of his predecessors left behind. Sir Edward Barnes was personally as energetic, but the able statesman was gifted with qualities which the gallant soldier did not possess. Excepting Major Skinner, the great Ceylon road-maker, as he was called, there was scarcely a man in the island who had travelled and seen so much of the country as the Governor. He did not confine his journeys to the beaten track of the high-roads or rest in the centres of civilisation. "He bivouacked on the grassy glades and amidst the jungle knolls which distinguished the once teeming but now desolate tank region of the north and east of the island, braving in his explorations the attacks of the fever demon who haunts those scenes of silent beauty—scenes once of rich fertility; and it was but a natural and a noble wish to be the means of restoring to them fruitfulness and population." But Sir Henry Ward's mind was too practical to be seduced into attempting impossibilities. He abandoned the idea of crowding the work of generations into a few brief years, devoting himself to the really useful tasks within his reach of restoring or creating irrigation works where population was ready to enter on possession of the gifts of soil and water, and giving a legislative sanction to such local regulations as were in accordance with ancient usage and custom, for the protection and encouragement of the great staple industry of rice cultivation.[1] He stated in Council: "In dealing with a million and a half of people for whom we claim the right to legislate — whose interests are entirely in our hands, whose peaceful and orderly conduct entitles them to the highest consideration—I think we should do wisely to avoid even the appearance of neglect, if at a small additional cost we can offer them a proof of sympathy that will be most grateful to their feelings. The one thing that comes home to every Sinhalese is the improvement of those means of irrigation which the climate renders indispensable. I find upon inquiry from the most competent authorities, not only that the complaints made with regard to the neglect and abandonment of old irrigation works are just, but that it is possible, and even easy, in many cases at a very moderate cost, to substitute abundance for sterility in districts where nothing but an advance of capital is wanting to put in action the labour which invokes the aid of the Government. Surely it would be good policy and good economy to meet this demand as you are meeting others. If I have urged upon you the propriety of including some direct benefit to the native community, I have done so in the belief that you will participate in my persuasion that it is our duty to deal with a dependent people in the spirit of the religion which we profess and of the civilisation of which we are the representatives." He governed in the enlightened spirit of his words, and his name is still remembered by the Sinhalese, whose interests, in spite of opposition, he materially advanced, notably by the construction and restoration of irrigation works. Although the projected railway to Kandy could not be constructed, as the sum demanded by the railway company formed in England for the undertaking was excessive and more than the colony could bear, he realised the value of the means of communication, roads and bridges, on which more than half a million sterling was spent during the term of Sir Henry Ward's government. Among bridges five great works may be mentioned—the bridges over the Mahaveli Ganga at Katugastota and Nawalapitiya, and over the Kalu Ganga at Teldeniya, together with the Pin-Oya and Kitulgalla bridges. The Governor, while devoting his attention to increased communication, did not neglect the administration of justice or the strengthening and extension of the police force. Ambulatory courts were established to repress crime in lawless districts, an attempt was made to separate revenue and judicial duties, and new and spacious buildings were erected at a heavy cost to adequately house the District Court, Court of Requests and the Police Court in Colombo. Additions were made to the surveying department of the island, which enabled the waste lands of the country to be opened up by affording facilities to land purchase and by furnishing security of title and definiteness of boundary. His wise foresight bade him invest money on the defences

[1] A. M. Ferguson.

of the forts of Colombo and Galle to protect the interests of the colony against all emergencies. He framed and carried through Council a graduated scale of remuneration for the civil service and the higher establishments, though it was objected at the time that he did not consider it expedient to revise the scale of charges of the humbler servants of Government, the Sinhalese clerks, notwithstanding his own admission that "many of them found their wages insufficient to provide for themselves and their families the bare necessaries of life." While considering the improvements in channels of communication originated by Sir Henry Ward, it ought not to be forgotten that he restored the fine canal system opened by his Dutch predecessors. In the electric telegraph he gave the country means and facilities of communication of which his Dutch predecessors never dreamed, any more than they imagined the possibility of letters being transmitted from Galle to Jaffna and from Colombo to Trincomalee for a penny, while the periodical issues of a free Press were carried from the capital to the extremities of the island at half that cost. By the purchase of the steam vessel *Pearl*, though the outlay was heavy, he brought the northern and eastern provinces into easy and regular communication with the western and southern portions of the island. He attempted a great moral reform in the marriage customs of the Kandyans by the enactment of the Kandyan Marriage Ordinance of 1859; but it was a measure in advance of the social and moral condition of the Kandyan peasant, and though undertaken at the request of their leaders, the popular prejudice rendered it comparatively inoperative. Ten years later, owing to the objections taken to it, it was modified. Sir Henry Ward was fortunate in having the control of an overflowing treasury, the profits of the pearl fishery, the surpluses garnered by the thrift of Sir George Anderson, and the constantly increasing annual revenue which distinguished his term of office. He had the gift of obtaining the greatest benefit for the country out of his swelling exchequer, and whether he had to deal with the permanent salt monopoly, the varying returns from sales of land, or the "accident of an accident" which gave or withheld a pearl fishery, he left no measure for the improvement or development of the colony untried, and most of his enterprises and efforts eminently succeeded.

Sir Henry Ward was appointed Governor of Madras, and on June 30, 1860, he sailed for India. On the same day General Lockyer assumed the government as Lieutenant-Governor. A month later ill-health compelled him to quit the island, leaving the administration of the colony and the command of the troops in the charge of Colonel Wilkinson, R.E., till the arrival of the new Governor.

Sir Charles Justin MacCarthy, Lord Torrington's Auditor-General, was appointed Governor on the 4th of August. He arrived in the colony on October 22, 1860. During his *régime* the chief topic of public discussion was the construction of a railway to Kandy. The chief points debated were whether the work should be entrusted to a railway company and the cost of the undertaking. The subject was debated in the Legislative Council, and in 1861 a Select Committee of the Council reported in favour of the scheme. The Committee decided that the English-Ceylon Railway Company, with which the local Government had entered into a preliminary engagement, should be discharged, and the work entrusted to a contractor. This wise decision not only saved the colony from handing over what proved to be a most valuable asset into the hands of an outside syndicate for a considerable period, but enabled the work to be accomplished for a sum considerably below that demanded by the English railway company. Even a far-sighted ruler such as Sir Henry Ward was, had, in his anxiety to serve the country, urged his Council to agree to the terms of the Ceylon Railway Company. Non-officials and official civilians like the great road-maker, Major J. B. Skinner, opposed the scheme. The local public bodies, on reports of competent engineers, considered a sum of £1,500,000 sufficient to construct the line; the railway company demanded £2,214,000. It was constructed eventually at a total cost of £1,285,000.

MAJOR-GENERAL LOCKYER.
(Commander of the Forces in Ceylon during Sir Henry Ward's Governorship.)

In the same year in which the Governor arrived, intelligence reached Ceylon of the decease on board the *Ripon* of three distinguished Ceylon men on their way back to England: General Lockyer, lately commanding the forces in Ceylon, Bishop Bravi, the saintly Catholic Bishop of Colombo, and the brilliant Sinhalese naturalist, Dr. Kelart, whose investigation into the life-history of the pearl oyster was the earliest contribution to the scientific literature on the subject.

A series of important Bills was passed during Sir J. MacCarthy's term of office: a Land Registration Act, a Partition Ordinance for the division of holdings possessed in common, and a Marriage Ordinance. These measures were considered and revised by the Law Officers of the Crown in England. To this period may be traced the beginnings of the Sinhalese newspaper press, which has since become a regular institution. The first Sinhalese newspaper published in the colony, the *Lankâlokaya*, was discontinued almost as soon as it was established at Galle in 1860. Sinhalese presses were, however, soon set up at Galle and Colombo. Sinhalese periodicals, called the *Lakminipahana* and *Lakrivikirana*, under the editorship of leading pundits, were issued in 1862 and 1863 respectively.

Sir Charles MacCarthy was an accomplished scholar and a man of sound judgment, but his health broke down under the strain of government, and he went to Europe on leave in 1863, where he died at Spa in 1864. Major-General James O'Brien assumed the government in December, 1863, as Lieutenant-Governor. His tenure of office was brief, though stormy. A vote of censure on the Government with reference to the Council's reply to the Lieutenant-Governor's address was carried in the Legislative Council by the unofficial members on August 23, 1864. It was an unparalleled event in the history of the government of a Crown Colony where the Legislature was nominated and the majority Government officials. Shortly after, all the unofficial members of the Legislative Council, both European and Sinhalese, resigned in a body in November, 1864, as a protest against the heavy military charge imposed on the colony by the Government. The indignation of the colony at the inequitable exaction found expression in crowded public meetings at Kandy and Colombo, where resolutions were adopted to be forwarded to the Colonial Minister, the Right Hon. Edward Cardwell, in January, 1865, protesting against the levy. In 1864 the first special train on a Ceylon railway conveyed the Duke of Brabant, now Leopold II. of Belgium, to Ambepussa on the 27th of December. A census of Colombo, taken in March of the following year, showed the number of houses in Colombo to be 9,887, and the number of inhabitants 45,664.

Sir Hercules George Robert Robinson assumed the Government of Ceylon as Lieutenant-Governor in March, 1865, and was sworn in as Governor on the 16th of May the same year. The *impasse* that was created by the resignation of the unofficial members of the Council on the question of military expenditure continued, though their places were filled by dummy senators nominated by the Crown to secure the necessary complement of members in terms of the constitution. In no sense were the new nominees acknowledged representatives of the people. The resigned unofficial members, consisting of the most talented and distinguished Sinhalese that the colony had produced in modern times, led by an English merchant of great ability and breadth of view, Mr. George Wall, rallied the country to them in a political organisation called the "Ceylon League," formed on May 16, 1865. The different races of the island—Sinhalese, Dutch Burghers, and Tamils—whom mutual distrust had hitherto kept apart, under the inspiration of their leaders, combined as "Sinhalese" in their political campaign against the Government. By strenuous agitation and vigorous criticism of the Governor's policy, they sought to gain a remission of the disproportionate military burden imposed on the colony, a share in the administration of the Government by the election of members to the local Legislature, and a control over the finances of the island in the voting of supplies. Though representations were made to the Colonial Minister, the Right Hon. Edward Cardwell, and Mr. Watkin, M.P., moved in Parliament for a Committee of the House to inquire into the government of Ceylon, no substantial relief was obtained, owing to the uncompromising opposition of Sir Hercules Robinson, supported by his Sinhalese adviser, Queen's Advocate Sir Richard Morgan. The League agitation continued for the best period of Sir Hercules Robinson's government and rendered him unpopular with the educated classes of Sinhalese. Perhaps to the League agitation may be traced the grant, in 1865, of free municipal institutions. The grant originally was to Colombo and Kandy, but was afterwards extended to Galle. A Royal Commission, appointed at the close of 1865 to inquire into the military expenditure and establishments of Ceylon, decided that the entire cost of the force stationed in the island for local defence should be met by the colony, and the assurance of the Home Government was received that it was not to be burdened by expenses not contemplated by the Military Commissioners. The settlement of this question led to the extension to the colony of two most important financial concessions. The practice, hitherto exercised, of making appropriations of revenue under the authority of the Secretary of State, was formally surrendered, and surplus balances, within reasonable limits, were placed at the disposal of the local Legislature without previous reference to the Colonial Minister. This privilege was granted by a despatch dated July 30, 1866.

While not favouring the political aspirations of the people, Sir Hercules Robinson conferred material benefits on every province, nearly every district of the island, by the improvements he effected in new roadways, bridges, public buildings, and notably in the repair of irrigation tanks and channels and making provision for sluices.

The year 1867 witnessed the completion of the railway to Kandy. In March, 1867, the steam engine ascended the Kadugannawa incline, and a month later the first railway train rode through the long rocky tunnels, over the sharp curves and precipitous heights of the magnificent highland line on to Kandy. From Peradeniya he extended the mountain railway to Gampola and on to Nawalapitiya, a distance of nearly seventeen miles, and he laid the foundation of the scheme under which, during his successor's rule, the Colombo breakwater was commenced.

For a short period in 1868, during the absence of Sir Hercules Robinson on leave in England, Major-General Studholme Hodgson administered the government as Lieutenant-Governor, when he unveiled the statue of Sir Henry Ward at Kandy amid public rejoicing, the leaders of the Ceylon League joining in the movement as a demonstration against the policy of Sir Hercules Robinson. For the building of the new military barracks the demolition of the Colombo Dutch Fort, raised on the plans of Cohoorn, was commenced in 1869 by the blowing up of the Rotterdam bastion, and completed by the rasing of the walls and the filling up of the moat in 1871.

In 1870 the Duke of Edinburgh arrived in the colony, and was received with an outburst of spontaneous loyalty from all sections of the community. In the same year the Ceylon Medical College was opened on the recommendation of a distinguished Sinhalese Burgher, the late Dr. James Loos, sometime officiating Principal Civil Medical Officer of Colombo. He was appointed its first Principal. The institution was placed on a firm basis by its liberal endowment by two wealthy Sinhalese land-owners. By a stroke of far-sighted policy, Sir Hercules Robinson revived the ancient village councils or Gansabhawas, reorganised the Sinhalese village communities, and enabled the peasant, without expense and inconvenience, to have his disputes settled, as he had done from time immemorial under his old patriarchal system. This statute was passed in 1871. In the same year the first systematic census of the island was taken, by which the number of the inhabitants of the island was ascertained to be 2,405,287. Since then there has been a census taken once in every ten years. In the last year of the Governor's *régime* the coinage of the United Kingdom, which had been current in Ceylon since the British conquest, was withdrawn from circulation, and the decimal system of rupees and cents inaugurated on January 1, 1872.

On the departure of Sir Hercules Robinson from the island as Governor of New South Wales, Mr. Henry James Irving was sworn in as Lieutenant-Governor on January 4, 1872. The Right Hon. William Henry Gregory succeeded to the rule of the colony on March 4. He was an accomplished man, of commanding personality, far-reaching statesmanship, and high attainments. The ancient kingdom of Lanka had attractions for the polished scholar, and to quote his own words, "he turned from the West to the glowing horizon of the East, and to Ceylon, the object of my ambition and my day-dream for many a long year." A member of an old Irish family in which, as he jested, was dormant the ancient peerage of Marmion, his early years had been passed among the great *literati* and the statesmen of the Victorian era, and he came to the colony imbued with the free spirit of the British House of Commons. He combined a taste for art and literature with a kindly sympathy and an old-world courtesy and tact which won him the affections of all classes of the colony. He was the ideal of what a British Colonial Governor should be, and his memory is still affectionately cherished by the people of Ceylon. Mr. Gregory, for he was not knighted when he arrived, inaugurated his assumption of government by an extensive tour throughout the island, including the desolate and abandoned tank region of the Nuwarakalawiya, which he formed into a separate province, called the North-Central, under a civilian of high standing, Mr. Dickson, afterwards Sir Frederick Dickson, Governor of Cyprus. He proclaimed the ancient city of Anuradhapura, for centuries entombed in the forest, the capital of his new province, and the restoration of the ancient irrigation tanks formed by the old Sinhalese monarchs was undertaken. "A large number of villagers," writes Sir William Gregory, "set to work, encouraged and stimulated by Mr. Dickson, and, as well as I recollect, work was going on at some nine hundred tanks within the first year. Never was a great social experiment more speedily and entirely successful. Crops were obtained where they had failed for years. The revenue rose immensely; sickness gradually declined. An eminently listless and lazy population, being compelled to work, resumed habits of industry, and on occasions of my subsequent visits to this district, I was supplicated by various villages to inspect their tanks and see what good work they had done.". Among these restorations was the magnificent tank of Kalawewa, constructed by King Dhatusena in A.D. 459. "It was the great reservoir on which the whole water supply of that district depended. The river ran into it, and was dammed up, forming an inland sea, thirty-five miles in circumference. The bund was from sixty to eighty feet, and was several miles long. From it there used to run a canal, called the Yoda Ela, or Giant's Canal, to Anuradhapura, about sixty miles in length. This canal supplied all the great store tanks *en route*, and supplied Anuradhapura and its bathing places." He commenced with the Yoda Ela, the rough estimate for the repair of which and the tank was about £40,000. Though for lack of funds his successor did nothing to advance the work, Sir Arthur Gordon (Lord Stanmore) completed the work, and with pardonable pride Sir William Gregory writes in his autobiography: "I had the gratification of driving over the completed bund in 1890, and visiting this magnificent work, this monument of real kings, in perfect order." In September, 1872, on meeting his Legislative Council, the Governor delivered a long and exhaustive speech, in which he set forth his views on the needs of the colony. He announced the construction of a museum and a new custom house, both designed by the Government architect, Mr. Smither, a man of great taste and refinement. The same instinct of the art lover and dilettante which led the Governor to apply to Disraeli for the trusteeship of the National Gallery urged him to open a museum in Colombo. "I propose in connection with this museum," he said in his address to the Legislative Council, "to obtain reproductions of the inscriptions throughout the island, by means of photography, casts, and hand-copying. These inscriptions, varying in character and dialect, will be of deep interest to the philologist, and throw light on the ancient usages, religious customs, and early history of Ceylon. I purpose to affix a limit to our collection. They should be strictly confined to the productions of Ceylon." He took measures to reduce the liquor trade. His remarks on the question are significant. "There is one subject on which I cannot be silent, and that is the extension of drunkenness throughout the island. English rule has given to Ceylon many blessings which the inhabitants are ever ready to acknowledge—security of life and property, equality before the law, just tribunals, the abolition of serfdom, and excellent roads to promote intercourse and facilitate the conveyance of produce; but we have at the same time extended a curse throughout the island which weighs heavily in the other scale, namely, drunkenness. Some years ago a drunken Kandyan would have been disgraced in the eyes of his fellows. Now the occurrence is so common that the disgrace has passed away. I have had some remarkable petitions on this subject: . . . they say restrict the places of sale and thus discourage intoxication and diminish the great moral and social evils which flow from it. In these recommendations I warmly concurred. In restricting the sale of intoxicating liquor, some diminution of revenue was to be expected; but, in the words of the petitioners, any decrease under that head would be more than compensated by an improvement in the general well-being of the community, and in the reduced cost of establishments for the suppression and punishment of crime."

He realised the gravity of the evil, and took immediate measures to repress it by gradually reducing liquor shops throughout the country. He ordered a map to be placed in the Legislative Council on which red crosses indicated every tavern in the island and coloured marks indicated suppressions and additions throughout the island. The Ceylon breakwater was projected during the *régime* of Sir William Gregory, under the direction of Sir John Coode, Consulting Engineer to the British Government, at the estimated cost of £630,000, the scheme embracing the erection of two jetties of a thousand feet long and the dredging of the bar. The first stone of the new work was laid amid great *éclat* by His Majesty King Edward VII., when, as Prince of Wales, he visited the island in 1875. Sir William Gregory instituted the custom of an annual gathering of the Government agents, which he called the *durbar*, before the preparation of the estimates, to enable them to call the attention of the Governor to the list of works and the needs of each province. With a flourishing revenue ready to hand, he pressed on the great arterial roads to Trincomalee and Jaffna, and devoted considerable sums to the improvement of gaols, both in regard to discipline and to their sanitary condition. He built the fine convict prison at Kandy. Besides this improvement of the colonial prisons, his ample resources allowed him to expend a considerable amount on the medical department, in building, enlarging, and improving hospitals. An attempt by the Bishop of Colombo, Dr. R. S. Copleston, the present Metropolitan of India, to compel the Church missionaries in Ceylon to come under his personal control, instead of being directed by a lay committee in England, had culminated in the Bishop's withdrawal of the licenses of twelve Church missionaries. This occurred on July 11, 1876. The action of the "boy-bishop" provoked hostile comment in the colony, and roused deep resentment among the large body of Evangelical Churchmen in the island. The discontent broke out in a movement for the abolition of ecclesiastical subsidies from the public revenue. In an animated discussion in the Legislative Council, the motion in favour of subsidies was carried in October, 1876. After considerable agitation both in Ceylon and in England, Earl Kimberley, in 1881, sanctioned disestablishment and disendowment in Ceylon of the State stipends for the future Bishop of Colombo and the Episcopalian and Presbyterian chaplains. The Government was to make no more ecclesiastical appointments, but undertook to pay the existing salaries for five years after each vacancy occurred, and to transfer the church buildings in good repair to trustees.

The revenue of 1877 was the largest up to that time received, and a very considerable surplus was at the Governor's disposal. He had plenty of objects on which to expend it—the construction of the seaside railway from Colombo to Kalutara, which he intended should be ultimately extended to Matara (now an accomplished fact); increase of telegraphic communication; the establishment of fountains and pure water supply to towns; improvements at the sanatorium of Nuwara Eliya to render it attractive to all comers; forest preservation where abuses and destruction had almost denuded vast tracts of the most valuable trees—these were amongst the projects which claimed attention. He was deeply interested in the preservation of the ancient literature of the country and the scientific copying and translating of the inscriptions with which, on rocks and slabs, Ceylon abounded, and which had hitherto been neglected. "I am confident," said Sir William Gregory in his last address to his Council, in 1877, "you will agree with me that it is highly expedient to make an effort to preserve the ancient literature of Ceylon. It is a duty which we owe, not merely to the large and annually increasing number of students of Oriental history and of Oriental philology, but to the natives of the island, many of whom have already widely distinguished themselves by antiquarian research, many of whom will devote themselves to it if facilities for study be afforded. With this object for some time past the Government has annually spent a small sum in procuring copies of all books of interest which are still in existence in the temple libraries. But, in addition to this, I have thought it advisable to take immediate steps to obtain reproductions of all the other records which are to be found on rocks and detached stones, and which are gradually perishing by the action of time and weather and the ravages of man."

During the year 1877 a proposal by the Duke of Buckingham, Governor of Madras, to Governor Gregory for the construction of a railway over Adam's Bridge, connecting India with Ceylon, though favoured by Sir William, was not undertaken, owing to the opposition of the Government of India. At this period there were established local boards and village councils, institutions which Sir William Gregory deemed successful in promoting the objects contemplated—among others, of preparing the Sinhalese for a constantly expanding share of self-government. The scheme for providing Colombo with an ample supply of water was inaugurated by Governor Gregory. The works, however, were commenced only in 1882 and not completed till 1889. Among other relief measures which he proposed to the Legislative Council was the valuable boon of providing a Widows' Fund for public servants. Originally shelved by the Colonial Office to await a more comprehensive scheme contemplated by the home authorities to apply to all colonies, it was ultimately sanctioned through the persistent advocacy of the Governor. This scheme of relief, however, did not come into operation for several years after it was first proposed.

On December 1, 1875, King Edward VII., then Prince of Wales, arrived in the island and was welcomed with affectionate loyalty by all the Sinhalese people. As elsewhere stated, he laid the foundation-stone of the Colombo breakwater, and knighted the Governor at a *durbar* of Kandyan chiefs in the old audience-hall of the kings of Kandy. At the Prince's request Sir William Gregory crossed over for the festivities at Calcutta, but he was weary of the East, and after receiving the tidings of his mother's death, longed to return home. In July, 1876, he sent his letter of resignation to Lord Carnarvon, the Colonial Minister, and he sailed from Ceylon on May 3, 1877. A talented writer, surveying his career, wrote: "When the Governor left, in 1877, there were few rivers of any importance left unbridged, a large extent of previously unoccupied country had been opened up for cultivation, and an impetus given to both Sinhalese and European colonists in the extension of cultivation, especially of new products, which alone saved the island from a serious collapse in the years of commercial depression and blight on coffee which followed."

All classes united to do honour to the great Governor by setting up his statue in the grounds of the beautiful museum he had founded. This proposal was decided at a public meeting on May 8, 1877. On the following day he embarked for Europe. He returned to Ceylon three times as a visitor. In 1883 he accompanied Sir Arthur Gordon, who was coming out to undertake the government of the colony. With a chivalrous courtesy which was appreciated throughout the island the new administrator directed that his veteran predecessor should be received, and while in the country treated, with all the honours and dignity accorded to the ruling Governor. Sir William Gregory came for the last time in 1890, when "he said his farewells, feeling that it was his last look at the East and its enchanted isle."

SIR JAMES ROBERT LONGDEN, K.C.M.G.
(Governor, September 4, 1877—December 3, 1883.)

Sir James Robert Longden, who had worked his way upwards from the lowest rung of the Colonial Service ladder, succeeded Sir William Gregory. He arrived in Galle on September 2, 1877, and was sworn in as Governor on the 4th, superseding the Hon. A. N. Birch, C.M.G., Colonial Secretary, who had administered the government from the time of the departure of Sir William Gregory. During Sir James Longden's rule the colony passed through a period of great depression, consequent on the ailure of the coffee industry by fungus blight. The far-sighted, economising policy of this cautious Governor steered the island safe through the crisis, until, in the succeeding years, with the introduction of new products, such as tea, cinchona, cacao, and Liberian coffee, the colony regained its former prosperity. His policy of inactivity was the subject of much hostile criticism at the time, and it was only after he had left the country that men realised the wisdom of "Wait-a-bit Jimmy," as he was nicknamed for the persistence with which he put off demands for improvement. An extensive lunatic asylum at a cost of Rs. 600,000, and that, too, projected by his predecessor, was about the only important public work undertaken out of the revenue during the Governor's rule of six years. At the period it was considered a "white elephant," beyond the requirements of the colony, though its utility is year by year becoming more apparent.

On November 30, 1877, was published the Report of the Commission on the Incidence of the Grain Taxes which had for centuries been levied in Ceylon on home-grown rice. It recommended the abolition of the renting system and the introduction of compulsory commutation, which later entailed much distress on the peasants by causing their holdings to be sold for a pittance in seasons in which their crops failed or their lands could not be cultivated.

In December, 1877, the visit of Sir John Coode to Ceylon on his way to Australia was utilised by the colony for the examination of the harbour works and in drawing up a flood-water scheme to prevent the devastation of the country round Colombo by the periodical overflow of the Kelani river.

A Volunteer Corps, established in 1881 under Governor Longden's patronage, with the Prince of Wales, the present King, as Honorary Colonel, was the first attempt to raise a Sinhalese Militia after the disbandment of the Ceylon Native Infantry, and has proved highly successful. The most tangible advance on the path of progress during this administration was the railway extensions, the commencement of the first section of the Nawalapitiya to Nanu-Oya railway, a distance of about forty-two miles, carried through on a loan in 1880; the completion during the same year of the line to Matale; the extension of the seaside line to Kalutara, the line having been carried to Panadure and the wide river Kalu Ganga spanned by an iron girder bridge during the time Mr. Birch administered the country; and the opening of the railway extension to Hatton in 1883. An increase in the fixed expenditure of the colony in 1878, under which the Civil Service was mainly benefited, included an addition of Rs. 10,000 to the Governor's salary.

A census taken in 1881 revealed that in ten years the population of the island had increased from 2,405,576 to 2,758,529.

During this *régime* the long campaign against the Government grant of subsidies to churches terminated by the Colonial Minister, Earl Kimberley, sanctioning the prospective disestablishment of the Bishop and State-paid chaplains in Ceylon—a measure which was given effect to by a legislative enactment passed in 1881. The Act, as previously stated, provided for the discontinuance of the stipends of the State-paid clergy after five years from the occurrence of each vacancy, and the transfer thereafter of the church buildings in good repair to trustees.

In the last year of Sir James Longden's rule, 1883, came to the island Arabi Pasha and his fellow Egyptians, the leaders of the revolt of 1882. The *détenus* were guided in the choice of their place of exile by the old Arab tradition that Ceylon was the home of man's first parents. Three of the number died during their period of detention.

Sir James Longden retired in 1883, and Sir Arthur Hamilton Gordon (Baron Stanmore) followed him in the government in December of the same year, the administration being carried on in the interval by Sir John Douglas, Lieutenant-Governor. The new Governor was a son of the late Prime Minister, Lord Aberdeen, and had early served an apprenticeship to State affairs as private secretary to Mr. Gladstone. He was trained in colonial government, and had administered the affairs of Fiji. He was a man of great cultivation, sympathy with Oriental races, of large-minded toleration, but masterful to a degree, and lacking that spirit of conciliation which distinguished the career of Sir William Gregory. By his associations and instincts essentially feudal, he had a reverence for the past, and his mind was captivated by the ancient renown of the land which he was sent out to govern, with its magnificent remains, interesting people, and strange religious system. He aspired to rule the Sinhalese in the spirit of their old rulers, but failed by lacking that intimate knowledge of native institutions which free intercourse with all classes of the community alone rendered possible. He sought to maintain the pomp and circumstance of an Eastern potentate by dignified reserve and courtly ceremonial, with the result that he was charged with favouritism by being unconsciously influenced in forming judgments by intriguing headmen attached to his personal staff. His *régime* is described as a period of renewed activity, careful legislation, and material improvement. In 1887 the Governor rendered three signal services to the country. He procured a reduction of the annual military contribution from Rs. 1,000,000 to Rs. 600,000, which was fixed as the anuual charge for a period of five years from January 1, 1885. By a bold stroke of policy Sir Arthur Gordon guaranteed the notes when the country was threatened with a great financial panic on the failure of the Oriental Bank Corporation at Colombo, and he revived the issue of Government currency notes, which have since become such a financial success. His legislative acts included two acts of far-reaching reform, the Mahomedan Marriage Ordinance of 1886 and the Buddhist Temporalities Ordinance of 1889. The one removed the penal clauses for bigamy with regard to Mahomedans, and the other regulated the custody and disposal of the vast temple revenues from ancient endowments hitherto plundered by Buddhist monks and their relatives. These measures called forth vigorous protest from the advocates of intolerant orthodoxy. They opposed the association of a Christian Government with the affairs of an heathen faith, and condemned the Mahomedan Bill as a legalisation of immorality. The relation of the State with Buddhism had been complicated by a serious riot between Buddhists and Roman Catholics, which had broken out on Easter Sunday, 1883. The failure to bring these rioters to trial by the Government, who pleaded the absence of sufficient evidence, had left behind a feeling of angry resentment among the Buddhist Sinhalese population which culminated in the rise of a national religious movement. They alleged partiality of the local authorities towards the Christians, and charged the Government with breach of the covenants of religious toleration and neutrality contained in the proclamation of 1799 and the Kandyan Convention under which the country had been ceded. This was the position of affairs when Sir Arthur Gordon arrived in the colony. The Sinhalese had appealed to Lord Derby, the Secretary of State for the Colonies, for some absolute guarantee of their religious rights and privileges, for the proclamation of Buddha's birthday as a public holiday, for freedom of religious procession, for Buddhist registrars of marriages, and for legislation for vesting the vast estates of the Buddhist church in proper trustees. Sir Arthur Gordon displayed great courage, tact, and liberality in dealing with the situation. On his recommendation religious immunity was granted to Buddhists in the spirit of the old proclamations and to all other religions. Buddha's birthday and the sacred days of Hindus and Mahomedans were declared public holidays, Buddhist registrars appointed, and the Buddhist Temporalities Ordinance passed. As tolerant as he was in matters affecting the conscience of the people, he evinced a more practical sympathy for the Sinhalese by carrying forward the irrigation policy of Sir William Gregory, which had been suspended during the last rule. The magnificent Kalawewa tank was completed, besides provision being made for the restoration of numerous other tanks in the backward districts of the island. With all his considerate care for the Sinhalese cultivator, his preconceived conviction as to its necessity blinded him to the harshness of the paddy rent, an impost on home-grown rice, which, commuted for money, was depriving peasant proprietors throughout the country of their ancestral holdings by compulsory sales consequent on their inability to pay the tax. By the evictions of Walapane a whole village had been depopulated, and the homeless peasants had died of starvation on the bleak plains of Nuwara Eliya. When these facts gradually leaked out, a feeling of bitterness was aroused in the colony. The question was discussed in the public Press, by the Sinhalese political organisation, the Ceylon National Association, and representations were made to the Colonial Minister. High Government officials and experienced planters alike opposed the Governor's policy in maintaining the tax, and questions concerning the measure were asked in Parliament. Most prominent among the advocates of repeal was Mr. George Wall, one of the councillors who had resigned in 1864, and a leader of the old Ceylon League. By his whole-hearted sympathy, his convincing statements of facts, and his bold exposures in the Press, he enlisted the sympathy of public bodies and public journals in England, and it was mainly due to his generous exertions that the tax was ultimately repealed. The persistent agitation, however, stiffened the Governor's back, and the impost was still levied when he left the colony. Along with the expenditure for irrigation, large sums were voted for construction of roads—some 261 miles were opened during this administration—bridges, hospitals, and for railway extension in the low-country, the sea-line being extended to Bentota, and the mountain line from Nanu-Oya to Haputale, a distance of twenty-five to twenty-nine miles.

The ancient Sinhalese principality of Uva was separated from the Central Province in 1886, and converted into a separate province, while, in 1889, the old Dissavoni of Sabaragamuwa was reconstituted from the Western Province into a new province.

The Colombo breakwater, on Sir John Coode's admirable design, was completed and the bay and harbour have since been fully utilised as the great steamer-calling and coaling port of the East. In June, 1887, the event of the Queen's Jubilee was fittingly observed with due ceremonial in Colombo and at all provincial centres.

Sir Arthur Gordon, perhaps, took a deeper interest in Oriental research, archæology, ancient history, and antiquities than any other Governor save Sir William Gregory. The translation of the "Great Chronicle" of the island, the Mahavansa, which had helped to fix the shifting dates of Indian chronology, and a portion of which had already been rendered into English by the Hon. Mr. Geo. Turnour, was undertaken by the late Mudaliyar L. C. Wijeyasinha, on the orders of the Governor. In place of the spasmodic excavation work carried out hitherto, Sir Arthur founded an archæological department for the systematic exploration and survey of the magnificent historical remains of the island, he made contributions out of his private means to restore historic monuments, and since his departure from the colony he has not ceased to further the cause of scientific exploration in Ceylon. Important modifications in the Criminal Law were brought into operation during this *régime*. The Ceylon Penal Code and Criminal Procedure Code, based on the Indian Code, abrogated so much of the Dutch Criminal Law as prevailed in the colony, and assimilated the Criminal Jurisprudence of Ceylon with the criminal law of the neighbouring continent. This tendency to import laws wholesale from India, where hitherto legislation on original lines to suit the requirements of the colony had been pursued, with scant regard to local conditions, spoke of deterioration in the legal departments. A mosaic portion of the Indian and American codes, interspersed with local additions and rules of pleading, called the Civil Procedure Code, was issued in 1889, superseding the simple rules and orders which had previously regulated the procedure of the courts. Sir Arthur's sympathy with the Sinhalese made him constitute a subordinate branch of the Civil Service, on the representation of the Ceylon National Association, with a view to the larger employment of Sinhalese in the higher branches of the public service. In the same spirit he enlarged the Legislative Council by obtaining the Crown's sanction in 1889 to the addition of a Mahomedan and Kandyan member along with two official

SIR ARTHUR ELIBANK HAVELOCK, G.C.M.G.
(Governor, May 28, 1890—February 10, 1896.)

members. Sir Arthur Gordon quitted the colony after a vigorous rule of six years, leaving the island in the temporary charge of Mr.—afterwards Sir—Edward Noel Walker, Lieutenant-Governor.

Sir Arthur Elibank Havelock succeeded to the government in May, 1890. He had previously served in the army, and came from the rule of Natal to assume the governorship of Ceylon. He continued the beneficent policy of his predecessor in railway extension and raising of public works. One single act makes his rule memorable: He obtained the sanction of the Crown for the repeal of the paddy rent or tax which had oppressed the Sinhalese peasants for so many centuries. The agitation so long carried on at length bore fruit. The news was first transmitted to Mr. Wall by the Governor, and the gold medal of the Cobden Society soon after rewarded the services of the veteran philanthropist. This act of the new Governor inspired confidence in the minds of the people, as heralding a just, impartial, and sympathetic rule. He extended the mountain line to Bandarawela and the sea line to Katara, and opened a branch line to Kurunegala, the capital of the Hat Korale.

The administration of Sir Arthur Havelock, which gave promise of great things by such popular measures as the repeal of the paddy or rice tax, languished at the close to a weak and listless inactivity. Although men murmured at the weakness of his rule, he steered the colony clear of the quicksands of foreign speculation and extravagant expense, and set his subordinates an example of high honour and even-handed justice. The sincerity of his professions, the purity of his court and life, and his strict impartiality in dealing with the varied races of the island, were qualities the value of which were only realised long after he had left the island. Sir Arthur Havelock embarked for England, leaving his Lieutenant-Governor, Sir Edward Noel Walker, to carry on the government.

The Right Hon. Sir Joseph West Ridgeway relieved Sir Edward Noel Walker on February 10, 1896. He arrived in the colony from the government of the Isle of Man. He had served in Ireland as the lieutenant of Mr. Balfour in the days of coercion, and had served in India as Under Secretary of Foreign Affairs. He was an officer in the army and earlier in his career had been chosen to delimit the Afghan Frontier, and had gone as British envoy to the Court of Morocco. He brought with him the persevering courage, resourcefulness, firmness, and dogged resolution which enabled him successfully to lead a force of 3,000 men across the deserts of Afghanistan, and the tact and grasp of public affairs of the trained statesman. Unfortunately, he brought to bear on the affairs of Ceylon that spirit of rigid bureaucracy which characterises some phases of the Indian administration.

The outcome of this new policy was the creation of a deep spirit of resentment and dissatisfaction with the local government among the different Sinhalese races. During the years of his rule, however, Sir West Ridgeway, by his shrewdness, his beguiling eloquence, and the glamour of his forward policy in the construction of railways, irrigation and other works, lulled the people into security till they woke to the full sense of the change from the old traditional policy in the administration that followed. The rough soldier jostled with the diplomat and the statesman in the new Governor, and, although the ideals of Sir Arthur Havelock were forgotten, he rescued the country from the sluggish inactivity and despondency to which it had sunk during the long period of years he governed. One of the Governor's excellent reforms was the appointment of a Board of Education, presided over by the Director of Public Instruction, in whom lay the executive control of the department, reverting to the days when the educational affairs of the colony were managed by a "School Commission," instead of by a single literary dictator. The fear inspired by the terrible outbreak of bubonic plague in Bombay caused the Governor to take such precautionary measures that the island has been practically immune from the scourge. In January, 1896, arrived Mr. Mansergh, a leading authority on drainage schemes and the Vice-President of the Institute of Civil Engineers, with instructions from the Secretary of State to report on the sanitation of Colombo and frame a drainage scheme for the consideration of the local Government. The same year saw the adoption by the Legislative Council of a scheme for the construction of a graving dock at Colombo, at a cost of £318,000, half the cost to be borne by the Imperial Government and half by the colony. The Diamond Jubilee of Queen Victoria was celebrated with great *éclat* in all the principal towns, the Sinhalese races being foremost in furthering the loyal movement. A Jubilee address to the Queen from the Colombo Municipal Council, engraved on a gold plate and enclosed in a casket of gold of Sinhalese art-work, and also addresses from the inhabitants of Ceylon and the Ceylon Chamber of Commerce, were forwarded to London. On April 4, 1898, was laid the foundation of the North-west Breakwater without any ceremony, and on the 28th of the same month was received from the Secretary of State the sanction for the Kelani Valley Light Railway, which was to connect Colombo with the planting district of Avisawella. By the appointment of the Rev. Father Lavigne as Bishop of Trincomalee and Batticaloa, in 1888, the Order of Jesuits returned to the island for the first time since the days of the Portuguese, soon to take up the bishopric of Galle, which was entrusted to their charge. The Ocean Penny Postage was inaugurated, and the rate of postage between Ceylon and the United Kingdom declared six cents the half-ounce on December 25, 1896.

A Commission to consider an Agricultural Department for Ceylon, in 1899, resulted in the increase of the scientific staff of the colony by the appointment of a mycologist, entomologist, and advising analytical chemist. A curator was also added to the Royal Botanical Gardens, Peradeniya, and, later, a mineralogist was appointed. In January, 1899, arrived a large band of Burmese pilgrims, monks and laymen, the number including the daughters of King Theebaw and many noblemen and wealthy citizens of Rangoon. They brought with them a magnificent golden casket, studded with jewels, for which they had melted down their ornaments, to avert the doom which they believed soon threatened to overtake their country by the presentation of the casket to encase the Tooth Relic of the Buddha at the temple at Kandy.

An electric tramway service for Colombo was opened in January, 1899. In February and July returned home Toulba Pasha and Mohamed Sami, the Egyptian exiles, after receiving a pardon from the Crown, and in October, 1889, died Jacob Sami, another of the exiles at Kandy. On March 1, 1899, the Governor cut the first sod of the new graving dock in the presence of a large gathering. The offer of the Governor, when in England, to the Imperial Government of the regiment stationed in Colombo for service in South Africa was approved by the Legislative Council, and in 1900 was equipped at the expense of the colony a Ceylon European contingent of mounted infantry for service against the Boers, Ceylonese offers of service being refused on the ground that they were ineligible. In 1900 Sir West Ridgeway opened the Bacteriological Institute, which the generosity of a Sinhalese landowner, Mr. C. de Soysa, had provided in commemoration of Queen Victoria's Diamond Jubilee. This was followed by the opening of the Victoria Commemoration Buildings in Kandy, including the Ferguson Memorial Hall and George Wall Library and Tower by the Governor. 1900 saw the appointment of a Commission to report on the best way to meet the cost of improving the sanitation of Colombo, in connection with Mr. Mansergh's drainage scheme, and to inquire into the increased cost of public works. In the same year was created a special Irrigation Department for the whole island. Sir West Ridgeway, in 1900, undertook the charge of five thousand of the Boer prisoners. They were interned in the island at the Diyatalawa and Ragama camps till their repatriation in 1903.

One of the greatest monuments of Sir West Ridgeway's rule was the construction of the great northern line, from Kurunegala to Anuradhapura and to Jaffna and the port of Kankesanturai, which connected the island by rail from north to south. A measure which wrought the greatest hardship and injustice on the peasant proprietors was the Land Law of Sir West Ridgeway. The motive which inspired the Governor in framing these provisions was commendable, but their stringent and sweeping character made them bear hardly on the people. Attempts had, from time to time, been made to prevent the denudation of forests and the unauthorised sale by villagers of large tracts of Crown land in the country to speculators as their private property. In 1840 a law had been passed which declared to be Crown property all forest, waste and unoccupied land, and land cultivable after a few years, unless on proof of title or possession by the subject for a period of thirty years. An appeal to the Home Government only resulted in the proof of thirty years being reduced to five years. Subsequently the Forest Ordinance had penalised the cutting of timber and the removal of faggots from the woods adjacent to their villages—rights which the peasants had from time immemorial enjoyed. Further, special powers of summary inquiry and justice had been conferred on a special forest officer. There was a constant call from agents of Government for more stringent legislation year by year, with a view to the waiving in favour of the Crown of that strict proof of title which legal tribunals ordinarily require of a party asserting title. This demand found additional reason for support in the conduct

THE RIGHT HON. SIR J. WEST RIDGEWAY, G.C.M.G., K.C.B., K.C.S.I., P.C., LL.D., F.R.G.S.

of an ex-civil servant who had bought large native claims at low rates and was opening up the newly acquired country. Early in 1897 was framed what was called the Waste Lands Ordinance, by which a special officer was created who was charged with the duty of arranging the settlement of land claims. The measure excited keen hostility and criticism in the colony, and the agitation was taken up in England by the Cobden Club and other representative bodies. Simultaneously the measure was discussed in Parliament, and more than one deputation waited on the Colonial Secretary. A memorandum of reasons and appeal to the Crown for its repeal, signed by several past Governors of Ceylon, including Sir Arthur Gordon, gave strength to the views of the objectors, but Sir West Ridgeway held his ground, and the law is still in operation. After a period of seven years Sir West Ridgeway laid down the reins of government, and Sir Everard im Thurn was sworn in as Lieutenant-Governor.

Sir Henry Arthur Blake took charge of the colony in 1903. The publication of his farewell speech in Hong Kong, wherein he advocated principles of equal justice to all British subjects, and his liberal and sympathetic policy in that dependency, raised high hopes in the colony. The new Governor soon discovered the ultimate benefits to be derived by the country from the spread of scientific agriculture. He established an Agricultural Association in Colombo for the adoption of better methods in the cultivation of the existing products and the encouragement of the cultivation of new ones among the great mass of Sinhalese cultivators. Under this impulse, branch associations were rapidly formed throughout the island, and the scheme was eagerly taken up by the Government Agents and native chiefs in the country districts. Sir Henry Blake had scarce entered on the government ere two public questions of peculiar difficulty confronted him — the lease of the Ceylon Pearl Fisheries and the scheme for the increase of the salaries of public servants. The lease of the Pearl Fishery of Ceylon for a number of years was negotiated by the Colonial Minister in England, and the Ceylon Government supported the project. No reference, however, had been made to the Legislative Council, and no official intimation had been given to the Ceylon public. When the news leaked out in the colony the arrangements had been completed, and the Governor, at an informal gathering of members of Council, failed to convince the Ceylonese representatives of the expediency of the lease. The terms of the fishery lease were not submitted to the approval of the Legislature, and the motion for the leasing of the fisheries was carried in Council against the opposition of the majority of the Ceylonese members.

The connection of the late Governor, Sir West Ridgeway, with the leasing syndicate and the large profits of the fishery for 1905 aggravated the distrust and accentuated the sense of resentment. Questions were asked in the House of Commons, and the matter continued a source of keen controversy.

A scheme for the increase of the emoluments of the public service was passed in 1905. The appropriation of over half of the whole amount voted as increases to enhance the salaries of the civil service establishment, composed mainly of Europeans, and the distribution of the balance among the Government establishments, consisting mainly of Ceylonese, excited much criticism. At a meeting held in Colombo resolutions were passed condemning the proposal, and authorising the transmission of a memorial to the Colonial Minister. While a bitter controversy still raged in the public Press on the subject, a chance remark of the Lieutenant-Governor, Sir Alexander Ashmore, on the question of the employment of Ceylonese in the higher branches of the public service, to the effect that the Ceylonese were ordinarily lacking in that sense of duty and honour which the British Government expected, caused a wave of indignation to pass over the colony. The words were deeply resented, and a meeting of protest was held. In the midst of these events Sir Alexander Ashmore was suddenly stricken down by disease and expired within a few days. The death of the Lieutenant-Governor in the shadow of a misunderstanding lent special poignancy to the public grief, especially as he was reckoned by all classes of the people to be a firm, able, and impartial administrator.

A Bill to abolish the tolls which had so long paralysed the trade of the rural districts met with considerable opposition, owing to the proposal to impose a vehicles tax to recoup the loss to revenue, though opinion was unanimous in the colony that the tolls were "a relic of barbarism." The Bill, originally withdrawn in deference to public opinion and to enable the Government to gather the sense of the provinces in regard to the measure, was re-introduced into the Legislature in 1906, and an opportunity allowed to the public to submit any modification regarding the incidence of the new taxation. The end of 1906 was clouded by disaster. A serious slip occurred on the Jaffna line and a severe railway accident on the Hatton line by the subsidence of the railway track through a heavy rainfall on the hills. Floods in the Kelani Valley at the same time caused great distress, and there was strong criticism of the Government for not providing the necessary flood outlets. The Governor intervened at the end of the controversy to assure the public of the sympathy of Government by the appointment of a Commission and by an undertaking to carry any feasible proposal through. From the record of disasters and political strife it is a relief, both to chronicler and reader, to turn aside to consider the lines of peaceful improvement, economical progress, and the changes in society. The Sinhalese religious movement commenced during the government of Sir Arthur Gordon had developed till it had embraced a scheme for Buddhist national education, the publication of Sinhalese newspapers, and a society for the preservation of all that was characteristic of Sinhalese dress, customs, and manners, which had well-nigh disappeared under the impact of foreign disintegrating forces. Sir Henry Blake's rule also saw the beginning of a movement for the revival and preservation of Sinhalese arts and handicrafts, such as painting, carving, and metal-work, still lingering in the Kandyan districts. A great impulse was given to this movement by the sympathy of Governor and Lady Blake, and scientific guidance was lent to it by a cultured Ceylonese, Dr. A. K. Coomaraswamy, who had recently arrived from England to fill a responsible Government post. With the object of creating a taste in the public and furnishing good models to the craftsmen, a Kandyan Society of Arts and a Museum of Kandyan Art was established in Kandy under the ægis of the Ceylon Government. In spite of an enhanced duty, tea generally maintained its level in the home market, and a rubber exhibition held in Kandy proved a great success both in illustrating the potentialities of the new product and the possibilities and beauties of Kandyan Sinhalese art and architecture.

EPILOGUE.

British rule in Ceylon falls naturally into certain well-defined periods. From 1796 up to 1820 was the age of conquest. From 1820 till 1850 was the age of the consolidation of British power in Ceylon, by the opening up of communication, especially in the hitherto unknown and inaccessible mountain districts of the Kandyan provinces. The government of these earlier years was distinguished by a note of warm personal interest in the people of the country and an unaffected courtesy and kindness in their treatment. A new character in the personal relations between the British governing classes and the Ceylonese population began to spring up in the years preceding 1848. The Sinhalese, particularly the Kandyans, had by the long peace gradually become unused to arms, were losing their individuality and their ideas, and day by day were approximating more and more to the European standard of civilisation. From 1850 onwards, with slight intermissions, the island has been steadily advancing in material prosperity. Since 1860, with the progress of education, with the assimilation of new ideas and the peace and security which British rule had given the land, a new spirit was awakened in the country. The first articulate clamouring for free institutions, commenced in the days of the League, had increased with the coming year. Granted a Legislative and Executive Council before India, Ceylon was cited by John Bright as a successful example why similar Councils should be granted to the Indians. Not long after, a complete scheme of representative government, submitted by Sir Alexander Johnston, failed to become law by the mischance of the unexpected resignation of the Colonial Minister, who had favoured the reform.

Since then India has had freer institutions accorded her, and Ceylon has outgrown her political system. "The Indian Legislative Councils are more liberally constituted," says the Hon. Mr. John Ferguson, C.M.G., M.L.C., "although Ceylon has always been regarded as far in advance of her big neighbour from an educational and social as well as material point of view." An eminently loyal people, deeply sensible of the benefits of British rule, the Ceylonese are aspiring to win the full measure of British citizenship. A freer constitution, flood relief works, abolition of the poll-tax, systematic colonisation from the crowded western and southern districts to the restored tank region, a larger educational vote and a wider field for the people of the country in the higher branches of the public service, are some of the reforms which have been eagerly awaited and are urgently needed, and which alone will crown the splendid monument of administration which a century of British statesmanship has raised in Ceylon.

BRITISH GOVERNORS OF CEYLON.

The Hon. the GOVERNOR OF MADRAS in Council, February 16, 1796.

Hon. FREDERICK NORTH (afterwards Earl of Guilford), October 12, 1798.

Lieutenant-General the Right Hon. Sir THOMAS MAITLAND, G.C.B., July 19, 1805.

General Sir ROBERT BROWNRIGG, Bart., G.C.B., March 11, 1812.

Lieutenant-General the Hon. Sir EDWARD PAGET, K.C.B., February 2, 1822.

Lieutenant-General Sir EDWARD BARNES, K.C.B., January 18, 1824.

Right Hon. Sir ROBERT WILMOT HORTON, Bart., G.C.B., October 23, 1831.

Right Hon. JAMES ALEXANDER STEWART MACKENZIE, November 7, 1837.

Lieutenant-General Sir COLIN CAMPBELL, K C.B., April 5, 1841.

Right Hon. VISCOUNT TORRINGTON, May 29, 1847.

Sir GEORGE WILLIAM ANDERSON, K.C.B., November 27, 1850.

Sir HENRY GEORGE WARD, K.C.M.G., May 11, 1855.

Sir CHARLES JUSTIN MACCARTHY, Kt., October 22, 1860.

Sir HERCULES GEORGE ROBERT ROBINSON, K.C.M.G. (afterwards Lord Rosmead), May 16, 1865.

Right Hon. Sir WILLIAM HENRY GREGORY, K.C.M.G., March 4, 1872.

Sir JAMES ROBERT LONGDEN, K.C.M.G., September 4, 1877.

Hon. Sir ARTHUR HAMILTON GORDON, G.C.M.G. (now Lord Stanmore), December 3, 1883.

Sir ARTHUR ELIBANK HAVELOCK, G.C.M.G, May 28, 1890.

Right Hon. Sir J. WEST RIDGEWAY, G.C.M.G., K.C.B., K.C.S.I., February 10, 1896.

Sir HENRY ARTHUR BLAKE, G.C.M.G., December 3, 1903.

THE PRESENT DAY.

THE modern history of Ceylon might be written in one word—progress. In commerce, in education, in administration, in the material condition of the people, there has in recent years been a steady and continuous advance. Indeed, there is no other portion of the Empire which stands to-day in such a desirable position as regards the well-being of the inhabitants or in which there is a brighter promise of sustained prosperity in the future. The finances of the island are in a most healthy condition. In its early days the colony was a heavy burden on the Imperial Treasury. In 1905, the last year for which we have completed returns, there was a surplus of Rs. 4,697,256, and the total sum raised as revenue—Rs. 34,395,336—was Rs. 3,548,642 in excess of the proceeds for 1904, which up to that time was the most prosperous year in the annals of the colony. Side by side with a buoyant revenue we find an extremely light public debt: it is more than balanced by substantial assets, including a highly lucrative railway system and magnificent harbour works at Colombo, which have had and will continue to have a potent influence in promoting the trade of Ceylon. Trade is the great basis upon which this edifice of affluence rests. The island's superb geographical position and its great natural advantage in the shape of a climate well suited to tropical agriculture have been made the most of, and its products are being poured in ever increasing volume into the world's markets. An intelligent adaptability has been the mark of the operations of the great European planting community and to a lesser degree of native traders. When the collapse of the great coffee industry, through the spread of disease amongst the plants, brought widespread ruin to the island, attention was turned to tea, and with pluck and energy a new industry was created and fortune again smiled upon the country. Tea still more than holds its own as the staple product of the island—there was an increase of over 12½ millions in the export in 1905. But the planters are not content to rest on their oars. The vast potentialities of the rubber trade have attracted their attention, and a very large acreage, mainly in the low country, has been planted with rubber-trees. Nor is it in regard to this product alone that special enterprise is being shown. The leaven of the new spirit of scientific commercialism is working, and turning to account in many directions the remarkable resources of the island. The results are written large on the pages of the Customs returns. In 1905 the trade of the island reached the large figure of Rs. 224,078,800. This was Rs. 4,234,200 in excess of the amount for the previous year and about thirty millions of rupees above the return for five years previously. In fifteen years the volume of trade has about doubled.

Even outside the limits of ordinary trade, in the region of the speculative, Fortune has smiled on the island. The pearl fishery, too often a mere tantalising will-o'-the-wisp to Colonial Secretaries, last year surpassed the most sanguine expectations. The large net profit of Rs. 2,405,645 was derived from it—a sum which was over a million and one-third rupees in excess of that of 1904, which was the previous highest on record. The fact that this splendid return synchronised with the sale of the fishery to a private enterprise—the Ceylon Company of Pearl Fishers, Limited—gave rise to a considerable amount of criticism, and questions were asked on the subject in Parliament, more particularly with reference to the association of Sir West Ridgeway, a former Governor of the island, with the directorate of the company. But the case put forward by the Government in justification of the transaction seems conclusive. Certainly, in view of the precarious nature of the fishery and the difficulties in the way of development under official auspices, the terms agreed upon with the company, which are given in detail elsewhere, are good.

Passing from trade and finance to the domain of ordinary administration, we find the same evidence of progress. The number of Government vernacular schools increased from 497 in 1903 to 507 in 1904 and 529 in 1905; and of State-aided vernacular schools there were 1,386 in 1905, against 1,273 and 1,316 in the years 1903 and 1904 respectively. There are now 52,375 boys and 12,829 girls in attendance in the former class of school, and 85,436 boys and 44,144 girls in the latter. Besides these establishments, at which an exclusively native education is given, there were in 1905 221 English and Anglo-vernacular schools, attended by 26,043 boys and 5,928 girls. An Ordinance based on the recommendations of the Elementary Education Commission of 1905 was passed in 1906, introducing the principle of qualified compulsion into the educational system. In medical matters the administration of the colony keeps well abreast of scientific development, and responds fully to popular needs. During 1905 65 hospitals and asylums, 424 Government dispensaries, and 142 estate dispensaries were working. In the hospitals and asylums 68,321 patients were treated during 1905, and in the same year 1,222,790 new cases were treated at Government dispensaries. Altogether Rs. 1,809,585 was expended in 1905 on medical institutions. An important step in the direction of a systematised organisation of the medical profession was the passing, in 1905, of an Ordinance providing for the registration of medical and surgical practitioners in Ceylon on the lines adopted in the United Kingdom. It should be noted, in connection with the public institutions for the treatment of the sick, that there is no poorhouse in Ceylon. The island has been spared this dubious adjunct of modern civilisation largely owing to the benevolent principles inculcated by the prevailing creed—Buddhism.

A successful postal and telegraph administration is an almost infallible symptom of the prosperity of a community. Ceylon at the present time enjoys in full measure this advantage. In 1905 twenty-six and a half million letters, postcards, and printed packets passed through the post. The revenue was Rs. 500,000 in excess of that of 1904. Money orders of the value of Rs. 11,680,125 were dealt with, and 717,000 telegrams were sent and received. A motor mail service is the latest feature of the administration of the department. The number of depositors in the Ceylon Savings Bank in 1905 was 32,344, and the amount deposited Rs. 4,239,805. In the previous year the depositors numbered 31,507, and the sums standing to their credit aggregated Rs. 4,248,689. At the sister Government institution—the Post Office Savings Bank—in 1905 there were 63,000 depositors, and they had to their credit Rs. 1,748,127.

The Government a short time since set on foot a mineralogical survey of the colony. The expenditure in this connection has been completely justified by the results so far achieved. In 1904 Dr. Coomaraswamy, the able first director of the survey, found two new and valuable minerals—uraninite and thorium. So far only small deposits of these minerals have been brought to light, but the discovery is pregnant with interesting possibilities for the future of the mining industry. Monazite has also been discovered, and proves to be of widespread occurrence in Ceylon river sands. Small deposits of cassiterite and galena have been found, as well as molybdenite.

The survey is being continued with a view to the discovery of heavy minerals containing rare elements. These investigations relative to mining have their counterpart in the field of agriculture in a series of experiments under the auspices of the Ceylon Agricultural Society, an organisation founded in 1904 for the improvement of the great staple industry of the island. In 1905 the principal trials made by the society, with the guidance and assistance of the scientific staff at Peradeniya, were with ground nuts, new varieties of paddy, cotton, lemon-grass, rotation of crops on paddy-fields, transplantation of paddy, and English vegetables and fruit trees. Experiments in sericulture have also been made by the Government entomologists. At the end of 1905 there were some 40,000 acres under rubber, contrasted with 11,000 in 1904 and 7,500 in 1903. In 1905 the value of rubber exported was Rs. 557,945, as compared with Rs. 221,000 in 1904. Associated mainly, no doubt, with the remarkable development of the rubber industry is the large increase which has taken place during the past few years in the land sales. The following figures illustrate this phase of Ceylon administration and trade:—

Year.	Acres sold.	Price realised.
1898	16,279	£496,550
1899	21,301	728,691
1900	32,250	638,500
1901	19,585	456,089
1902	31,089	691,183
1903	23,931	681,454
1904	35,276	783,304
1905	34,383	1,062,346

Altogether there are now under cultivation 2,596,981 acres of land, or double the acreage returned in 1875.

Passing from these trade and agricultural statistics, we find in the population returns further evidence of the material prosperity of the island. When the British occupation first began the inhabitants numbered fewer than a million. By 1871 they had increased to 2,417,402; by 1881, to 2,755,558; by 1891, to 3,021,579; and by 1901 to 3,565,954. At the end of 1905 it was estimated that the population numbered 3,950,123, including immigrant coolies, of whom 166,713 arrived in excess of those who left Ceylon. In 1905 the birth-rate was 38·2 per thousand and the death-rate 27·4.

From all points of view the present-day position of Colombo provides cause for congratulation. It only remains for the Government to do its part in the great work of industrial and agricultural development by improving and extending railway communication. The evidence points to a full acceptance of this obligation. Sanction has already been obtained to the construction of a line from Colombo to Negombo, and there is a strong probability that Chilaw and Puttalam will also be linked up with the system. Other extensions which have been recommended are a line to Passara and Badulla from Bandarawela, and a branch line from Vavuniya to Mannar. The last named line is projected in connection with a scheme of direct railway communication with India. In India the South of India Railway Company is engaged in the construction of an extension to Rameswaram, and it contemplates establishing in connection with it a steam ferry to bridge the straits. The execution of the scheme in its entirety would undoubtedly give a fillip to the great and growing trade between the island and the adjacent continent; indirectly it would also have a considerable influence on the passenger traffic by diverting a portion of the stream which flows into India through Bombay.

Ceylon, with overflowing treasury, expanding trade, and a prosperous and contented people, is indeed the Happy Island. It has sometimes been called "The Pearl of the Imperial Crown," and no one will deny the appropriateness of the description. Its palm-fringed shores, its smiling valleys, its verdure-clad hills, its ancient towns with their storied past, make it a land of surpassing beauty and interest.

CONSTITUTION AND LAW

By Don ADRIAN St. V. JAYEWARDENE,

Barrister-at-Law (Inner Temple), Advocate of the Supreme Court of Ceylon,
Author of "The Roman-Dutch Law in Ceylon" and "The Law of Partition in Ceylon."

PART I.

THE CONSTITUTION.

CEYLON is a Crown Colony. It is one of those colonies where the Crown has the entire control of legislation, and the administration is carried on by public officers under the control of the Home Government. The legislative power is exercised by the Governor and a Council nominated by the Crown, the Council's authority being derived from the Crown and not from any imperial or local enactment. The Governor is appointed by His Majesty's Commission under the Royal sign-manual and signet, and his tenure lasts as a rule for about six years. Besides being supreme in the civil administration, he is also nominally Captain-General or Commander-in-Chief of His Majesty's Forces in the colony. The Governor is assisted by two Councils called—

(1) The Executive Council, and

(2) The Legislative Council.

The Executive Council was established by Letters Patent of March 19, 1833, and its constitution was directed, by Letters Patent of June 16, 1877, to be in accordance with those Letters or such other instructions as may be addressed to the Governor. At the present day the Executive Council is composed of the highest officials, civil and military, and includes the Lieutenant-Governor and Colonial Secretary, the Officer Commanding the troops, the Attorney-General, the Auditor-General, and the Colonial Treasurer.

The Governor is the President of the Council, and in the exercise and execution of the powers and authorities conferred on him by Letters Patent he is bound, as a rule, to consult with his Council. He may overrule the advice of the Executive for reasons to be recorded by him in writing. The Governor has the power to pardon offenders and convicts.

The Legislative Council was also created by the Letters Patent of March 19, 1833, and its constitution is regulated in the same way as that of the Executive Council. It is the sole repository of legislative power in the island, and the Governor can, with its advice and consent, make laws for the peace, order, and good government of the country. The Crown has reserved to itself the power to make laws with the advice and consent of Parliament, or with the advice of the Privy Council, and to veto any laws passed by the local Legislature.

The members of the Legislative Council consist of officials and non-officials. The official members are the Executive Councillors; the Government Agent, Western Province; the Government Agent, Central Province; and two other high officials whom His Majesty may from time to time appoint.

The unofficial members are all nominated by the Governor, and their number is not to exceed eight. The unofficial representation is mostly on a racial basis. Every community of importance in the island has its "representative." The representatives are selected from the low-country Sinhalese, the Tamils, the Kandyan Sinhalese, the Burgher and the European communities. The planting and mercantile interests are also represented by members on the Council Board.

The Legislative Council also sanctions the estimates of expenditure which is intended to be charged upon the colonial revenue. The Governor presides over its deliberations. The term of office of unofficial members was formerly for life. In 1889 it was reduced to three years, and afterwards extended to five years.

There is a widespread feeling of dissatisfaction with the constitution of the Executive and Legislative Councils. The Executive consists of officials, and neither in it nor in the Legislative Council have the people a voice. In some of the colonies and in India the executive body is composed of officials and unofficial or nominated members. The desirability of including non-officials becomes apparent when we find that frequently none of the Councillors have had even a year's experience in the affairs of the colony. A strong unofficial element cannot fail to be of assistance to the authorities. The Legislative Council requires complete remodelling; and the elective principle, which is now admitted in practice though not in theory, in some cases should be adopted, with safeguards and limitations. The system of appointment by nomination is effete, and does not command the confidence of the educated classes. Some selections have no doubt been happy, but the majority have been unfortunate. A body partly elected and partly nominated should supplant the present Council, and the right of sending elected representatives should

F*

be given to the provinces, and to towns having Municipal Councils and Local Boards, and to the mercantile and planting communities. Where the Crown reserves to itself the right to veto acts of the local Legislature no fears need be entertained. The present Legislative Council might, with a slight reduction in its numbers, take the place of the Executive Council.

The public service of the island may be divided into four classes or departments:—

1. The administrative department, which is manned almost wholly by members of the Civil Service, and comprises the financial and revenue departments.

2. The scientific departments, including the public works, irrigation, survey and railway departments.

3. The judicial department.

4. The general or miscellaneous department, consisting chiefly of the medical, public instruction, police, and post and telegraph departments.

The Civil Service is composed of two divisions—the higher division, recruited by competitive examination in England, and the subordinate division, to which appointments are made locally by the Governor.

For purposes of general administration the island is divided into nine provinces, each of which is under the control and management of Government Agents. "In addition to collecting the revenue these officers are responsible for the good order of their provinces, in which they make frequent circuits, and are in constant communication with the headmen and with inhabitants, whose wants and interests they bring to the notice of Government, between which and the people, through their headmen, they are the direct intermediaries" ("Ceylon Manual," 1904). The Government Agents meet in conference once a year, under the presidency of the Governor, and discuss a variety of projects and schemes, both practical and visionary. These provinces, except two, are divided into districts, each of which is under the charge of Assistant Government Agents, the Government Agent himself having the district in which the provincial Kachcheri or office is situated under his immediate charge.

Every district is again subdivided into Pattus, or Korales, and these Pattus are themselves divided into villages, hamlets, &c. The Pattus are presided over by Mudaliyars and Mohandirams in the low-country districts, by Ratemahatmayas and Koralas in the Kandyan provinces, and Maniayars and Udaiyars in the Tamil districts. The villages and hamlets are in the charge of Arachchies, peace officers, and Vidanes, who receive no salary, but who have to assist the Mudaliyars and other chief headmen in preserving peace and good order in the villages, in collecting the revenue, in protecting Government forests, and in otherwise safeguarding the interests of the Crown.

In another part of the volume the subject of local self-government is specially treated, and it is not necessary to deal at any length with the question here. The three chief towns, Colombo, Kandy, and Galle, have Municipal Councils for the management of their local affairs, and about seventeen other smaller towns have their affairs entrusted to Local Boards of Health and Improvement.

The Municipal Councils consist of elected and nominated members: the former are elected triennially by the votes of residents of the towns and the latter are selected by the Governor. The number of nominated members is generally equal to the number of those elected; and with a chairman who has two votes—one a casting vote and the other as a nominated member—and who is a Government official, the authorities are sure of a majority whenever they want to carry any measure through. The Local Boards, too, are composed of elected and nominated members, the former of whom are elected by the people. The powers and duties of these Boards resemble those of Municipal Councils. In the villages the Government has created Village Committees or Gansabhawas, under the presidency of the District Mudaliyar or chief headman, who is assisted by councillors, and has conferred on them power to frame and carry out by-laws for the regulation of education, irrigation, fishing, the construction and repair of roads and paths, and for the management of a variety of other matters connected with village life. Local self-government has not been a failure in Ceylon. Although it may be said that Municipal Councils have not fulfilled the expectations formed of them, it cannot be denied that these institutions have been to a great extent successful, and are admirably suited to carry out the objects for which they were intended. It was at one time a reproach against them that they failed to attract men of light and leading. If it ever was so, things have considerably changed within the last fifteen years, and a seat on the Council board is now a coveted position. It must, however, be admitted that the electors have not always displayed a sense of responsibility in the selection of their representatives. But that is not peculiar to Ceylon.

PART II.

THE LAW.

CEYLON occupies a unique position in the legal world. There is no other country which possesses so many legal systems within so small an area. For a population of about 3,800,000 there are about five different systems of law. The Kandyan Sinhalese is governed by the Kandyan Law, the Jaffna Tamil by the Thesayalamai, the Batticaloa Tamil by the Mukkuwar Law, the Moors by the Mahomedan Law, and the low-country Sinhalese, Burghers, Europeans, and the other inhabitants by the Roman-Dutch Law.

The Roman-Dutch Law.

It is, however, the Roman-Dutch Law moulded by Grotius, the father of international law, and Voet, the prince of commentators, which forms the Common Law of Ceylon. It is applicable all over the island, and whenever the other laws are silent on any point it is the Roman-Dutch Law which supplies the *casus omissus*. The foundation of the Roman-Dutch Law as established by the English in Ceylon is the Proclamation of the year 1799, which declared that "the administration of justice and police in the said settlements and territories in the island of Ceylon, with their dependencies, shall be henceforth, and during His Majesty's pleasure, exercised by all Courts of Judicature, civil and criminal, magistrates and ministerial officers, according to the laws and institutions that subsisted under the ancient government of the United Provinces, subject to such deviations and alterations as we shall by these presents or by any future Proclamation and in pursuance of the authorities confided to us deem it proper and beneficial for the purposes of justice to ordain and publish." It was intended to be merely a temporary measure, and by it the Roman-Dutch Law was made applicable to all the different races living in the maritime provinces—Sinhalese, Moors, Dutch, Malabars, Portuguese, and English. In the year 1801 the Sinhalese and the Moors were exempted from the operation of the Roman-Dutch Law and granted the privilege of being governed by their own laws. Five years later the Malabars, or the Tamil inhabitants of the north, or Jaffna, were declared to be subject to their laws as contained in the Thesayalamai. So that at the end of a decade of British rule the only persons who remained subject to the Roman-Dutch Law were Europeans and Burghers.

By the Kandyan Convention of the year 1815 the Kandyans had secured for themselves "civil rights and immunities according to the laws, institutions, and customs established and in force among them." But the low-country Sinhalese, or those of the maritime provinces, continued to be governed by the Roman-Dutch Law. In 1833 was published the last Charter ever published in Ceylon. It expressly repealed all the previous charters, including that of 1801, which gave the Sinhalese and the Moors the right to be governed by their own laws. The Moors and the Sinhalese should thereafter have been governed by the Roman-Dutch Law. But the courts, considering that the laws and religion of the Moors were so inextricably intertwined, and that interference with one would be interference with the other, still continued to apply the Mahomedan law when the parties were Moors. The low-country Sinhalese were, of course, all along governed by the Roman-Dutch Law, notwithstanding the privilege granted by the Charter of 1801. The Proclamation of 1799 was confirmed in the year 1835 (Ordinance No. 5 of 1835), and the Common Law was declared to be the Roman-Dutch Law—"which laws and institutions [of the United Provinces] it is hereby declared still are and shall henceforth continue to be binding and administered through the said maritime provinces and their dependencies. . . ." The Roman-Dutch Law now prevails in a very modified and amended form. Parts of it have been declared obsolete, parts have been condemned as incompatible with the refinement of modern times, and parts have been rejected on the ground that they were never introduced to Ceylon. The Legislature and the Courts have repealed and rejected considerable parts of it. The Roman-Dutch law of evidence was superseded by the English law long before the application of the latter had been sanctioned by positive enactments. The law merchant of the United Provinces has been entirely swept away. The Roman-Dutch Law relating to mercantile matters was utterly unsuited to the policy and requirements of the nineteenth century. The commercial policy of England, so broad and liberal, was entirely opposed to that of Holland, so narrow and restrictive, and the changes, when they were effected, were welcomed by all classes and communities. By Ordinance No. 5 of 1852 (§§ 1, 2) the law in respect of all contracts and questions relating to maritime matters and negotiable instruments was declared to be the same as the law in England at the corresponding period. In the year 1866 the mercantile, commercial, and insurance laws of England were introduced.

By Ordinance No. 11 of 1898 the English Sale of Goods Act [56 & 57 Vict. c. 71] was enacted in Ceylon. The privilege of *cessio bonorum* allowed by the Roman-Dutch Law to insolvent debtors was abolished, and an Ordinance embodying the English law of bankruptcy was passed in the year 1853. The Legislature and the Courts have effected very important changes in the Roman-Dutch law of persons. The Matrimonial Rights and Inheritance Ordinance, 1876, revolutionised the law of husband and wife and amended the law of inheritance. Community of property as a consequence of marriage was abolished, and with its abolition some of the most interesting and important parts of the Dutch Law were rendered inapplicable. A wife's property now belongs to her separate estate, and is not liable for the debts and engagements of the husband, but the wife has no power (except with the leave of Court) to deal with her property by an act *inter vivos* without the written consent of the husband. The law of inheritance was amended, and the Roman-Dutch Law as it prevailed in North Holland was declared to be applicable when the Ordinance is silent. The law of property underwent but few important changes. The law of prescription was superseded by a local enactment, the law of *fidei-comissum*, or trusts, and mortgage was modified, and the right to a legitimate portion was taken away.

The substantive criminal law of the Dutch remained practically untouched by the Legislature till 1883. The judges had, however, been in the practice of applying the English law of crimes long before they were empowered to do so by law. In the year 1883 the Ceylon Penal Code, based on the Indian Penal Code, passed into law, and the criminal law of the United Provinces ceased to be applicable.

The Charter of 1801 changed the course and practice of pleading, both civil and criminal. The procedure of the Civil Courts is now regulated by the Civil Procedure Code, 1889, and that of Criminal Courts by the Criminal Procedure Code, 1898, which repealed the first Criminal Procedure Code of 1883.

Trial by jury, which was unknown to the Dutch judicial system, was introduced in the very early days of British rule, and has proved a great success. A jury is allowed only in criminal trials before the Supreme Court, the highest tribunal in the island, which is empowered to try offences not cognisable either by District Courts or Police Courts. The number of jurors for a panel has been reduced from nine to seven, and a verdict by a majority of five to two is good.

The Roman-Dutch law of executors and administration of intestates' estates has been held inapplicable, and the English law as to the powers and duties of executors and administrators prevails, with the addition that the powers and duties extend to real as well as personal property. Great laxity has hitherto prevailed in the enforcement of the laws regulating the administration of deceased persons' estates, with the result that the law of administration is in a chaotic state.

Numerous other unimportant provisions of the Roman-Dutch Law have been rejected, repealed, and altered by local Ordinances and judicial decisions.

Kandyan Law.

In the Kandyan provinces (the limits of which have been defined by Ordinances) as a rule the Kandyan Law applies. This law, which is based on the ancient and established customs of the Kandyan people, is applicable only in the case of Kandyans having a Kandyan domicile. It is not applicable to Europeans, Burghers, Mahomedans, or even the Sinhalese of the maritime provinces resident in the Kandyan districts. According to Kandyan Law, marriage is divided into two kinds—*diga* marriage, where the husband conducts the wife to his own home; and *beena* marriage, where the husband comes and lives in his wife's house. In the latter case the husband loses his right to manage and control all household and family matters, and is entirely at the mercy of his wife, who can expel him and divorce him if he incurs her displeasure. In a *diga* marriage the wife comes under the control and power of the husband, and forfeits her right to her parents' property. The wife can acquire, hold, and dispose of property without the consent of her husband. She can enter into contracts independently of her husband, and may sue and be sued without his assistance. One of the grounds for divorce among the Kandyans is mutual consent of the parties, and polyandry, although penalised, still prevails among them. To judge from many of its provisions, the Kandyan law of husband and wife seems to have reached a very advanced stage in some respects.

The Thesayalamai.

This is a code of the customs of the Malabar inhabitants of the north of Ceylon. They were collected and arranged by the orders of the Dutch Governor, Simons, in 1706. It is applicable where the parties are Malabar inhabitants of the province of Jaffna or where a Malabar inhabitant of Jaffna is defendant. The Roman-Dutch Law is applicable when the Thesayalamai is silent.

Mahomedan Law.

The Moors all over the island are governed by their own laws, which were codified and proclaimed in the year 1806. The laws in the Code relate to (1) matters of succession; (2) rights of inheritance and other incidents occasioned by death; (3) matrimonial affairs. In the case of contracts and other matters to which the Code makes no allusion, the Roman-Dutch Law or the Common Law applies.

Mukkuwar Law.

The Mukkuwar Law, or the customary laws of the Tamil inhabitants in and about Batticaloa, were not interfered with by the Dutch. They have been recognised by the British Government.

Temple Land.

The inheritance and succession to lands belonging and appurtenant to Buddhist temples are regulated by the Buddhist Laws.

PART III.

THE ADMINISTRATION OF JUSTICE.

BEFORE the Charter of 1835 was published the Courts of Justice underwent frequent changes. This Charter established the Supreme Court and District Courts, and these have continued to the present day with slight modifications. In the year 1843 Courts of Requests and Police Courts were first created, and by Ordinance No. 26 of 1871 village committees and tribunals were founded throughout the island. All these courts and tribunals exist at the present time, and it is through them that the administration of justice is carried out. The powers and jurisdiction of the Supreme Court, District Courts, Courts of Requests, and Police Courts are clearly defined by the Courts Ordinance, 1889, and by the Civil and Criminal Procedure Codes.

The Supreme Court is the only superior court of record, and consists of four judges, namely, one Chief Justice, and three Puisne Judges. The Supreme Court has an original criminal jurisdiction for the inquiry into and trial of all crimes and offences committed throughout the island. As a rule, however, the criminal cases tried by it are those which are beyond the jurisdiction of Police Courts and District Courts, and are brought before it on indictments presented by the Attorney-General on behalf of the Crown. For the exercise of its criminal jurisdiction criminal sessions are held, as prescribed by the Criminal Procedure Code, principally at Colombo, Kandy, Galle, Jaffna, Matara, Batticaloa, and Trincomalee. These trials are had before a judge and a jury, and the court has the power to pass a death sentence on persons convicted of murder. The Supreme Court is the only court of appeal in the colony. Its appellate jurisdiction is ordinarily exercised at Colombo, and extends to the correction of all errors, in fact or in law, committed by a judge of the Supreme Court sitting alone or by a judge of any District Court, Court of Requests, or Police Court. In appeal the Supreme Court has very wide powers, and can make any order it thinks fit. It has also the power to revise the proceedings of the original courts, and to pass such orders as it may think fit when sitting in appeal. The Supreme Court, like the other courts of the island, is a court both of law and of equity, and has all the powers of the superior courts at Westminster. It can issue mandates in the nature of writs of *habeas corpus*, *mandamus*, *certiorari*, *procedendo*, and prohibition, and grant injunctions to restrain irremediable mischief. An appeal is allowed from the judgments and orders of the Supreme Court to His Majesty in Council in cases in which the subject-matter of the suit is over Rs. 5,000 in value. Appeals to His Majesty are also allowed in criminal cases.

The District Courts are the highest civil tribunals. For the purpose of the administration of justice the island is divided into a number of districts, each of which has its own District Court. They also possess a limited jurisdiction in criminal matters. These courts have full power and authority to hear and determine all revenue, matrimonial, insolvency, and testamentary matters, and to exercise jurisdiction over the persons and estates of lunatics, minors, wards, guardians, *cestui que trusts*, and trustees. In criminal matters their powers and duties are defined by the Criminal Procedure Code, and they cannot pass a sentence of more than two years' imprisonment or inflict a fine exceeding Rs. 1,000. All orders made by a District Court in the exercise of its civil jurisdiction are appealable. In criminal cases there is no appeal when the punishment, if imprisonment, does not exceed three months, or, if a fine, does not exceed Rs. 100, except on a point of law. The Courts of Requests, a large number of which are scattered all over the island, have a purely civil jurisdiction, and can try all suits in which the subject-matter does not exceed Rs. 300 in value. They have no jurisdiction in matrimonial matters. They have a procedure of their own which is of a summary character. In actions for the recovery of debts and demands there is no appeal except on a point of law. The Police Courts are as numerous as the Courts of Requests; they can try summarily all offences made cognisable by a Police Court, while they can only inquire into offences cognisable by District Courts or the Supreme Court. In the latter class of cases, after completion of the inquiry, the proceedings are forwarded to the Attorney-General, who performs the functions of the Grand Jury in England, and decides whether an accused should be committed for trial or be discharged. A Police Court may inflict a fine not exceeding Rs. 100 or a term of imprisonment not exceeding six months. It has the power to deal with vagrants, habitual offenders, and notorious bad livers by binding them over to keep the peace and to be of good behaviour. Except on a point of law, there is no appeal from orders of Police Courts when the imprisonment does not exceed one month or the fine is not more than Rs. 25.

The village tribunals, or committees, or Gansabhawas, are now regulated by Ordinance No. 24 of 1889, which defines their powers and jurisdiction. The President, as the judge is called, is always assisted by Councillors, and has civil and criminal jurisdiction in cases in which both parties are natives, or when the parties, if not natives, consent in writing to be tried by him. The civil jurisdiction extends to all cases in which the debt, damage, or demand does not exceed Rs. 20 or in which the property claimed does not exceed Rs. 20 in value. It may try cases when the value of the subject-matter of the suit does not exceed Rs. 100, with the written consent of the parties. The criminal jurisdiction extends to cases of petty assaults and thefts, which may adequately be punished by a fine of Rs. 20 or imprisonment for two weeks. These tribunals are also empowered to punish breaches of rules framed by the Gansabhawas. The jurisdiction, civil and criminal, conferred on village tribunals is exclusive, and cannot be exercised by any other court. They may punish by a fine not exceeding Rs. 20, and in default of payment of fine by imprisonment for any period not exceeding two weeks. There is no appeal to the Supreme Court from the decisions of these courts, but aggrieved parties may appeal to the Government Agent and from his decision to the Governor. Advocates and proctors are not allowed to appear before them. They are hampered by no codes of procedure or rules of evidence, and administer rough-and-ready justice in a fair way. In addition to these courts and tribunals, there

ADVOCATE H. A. JAYEWARDENE.
(President, Law Students' Union.)

are in Ceylon officers called Unofficial Police Magistrates.

The Governor may appoint any Justice of the Peace to be an Unofficial Police Magistrate for any district or districts. Unofficial Police Magistrates have all the powers of ordinary magistrates except the power to try and punish offenders summarily.

So far the various systems of law prevailing in the colony and the courts and judges engaged in the administration of those systems have been described. I now turn to—

The Legal Profession.

The legal profession in Ceylon is composed of two branches: advocates, having the same status as barristers, and proctors, having the same status as solicitors. The proctors are themselves divided into two classes, proctors of the Supreme Court and proctors of the District Courts; the former being entitled to practise before every court, including the Supreme Court, while the latter can do so only before the District Court and other minor courts of the district in which they are licensed to practise. The Supreme Court is vested with the power to admit, to refuse to admit, to suspend and to remove persons seeking admission or already admitted to the profession. As in England, the two branches of the profession are kept entirely distinct. The Council of Legal Education, which was incorporated a few years ago, is entrusted with the control and supervision of the education of students desiring to qualify themselves as advocates and proctors. Members of the English, Scotch, and Irish Bars and solicitors are entitled to be admitted as advocates and proctors respectively without examination, on payment of certain fees. The privilege of being called to the English Bar without examination, on payment of the usual fees and keeping three terms, has been extended to Ceylon advocates of three years' standing. Colonial King's Counsel were first created in Ceylon in the year 1903.

The Law Officers of the Crown.

The Attorney-General and the Solicitor-General are the Law Officers of the Crown. The Attorney-General, who was at one time called "Advocate Fiscal," "King's (or Queen's) Advocate," is the head of the legal department, and his office is similar to that of the Attorney-General in England. His duty is to frame Ordinances and to advise the Executive on all legal matters affecting the Government. He is also the Public Prosecutor, and all indictments are drawn up in his name. He alone can sue or be sued on behalf of the Crown. The Solicitor-General, or the Deputy Queen's Advocate as he was once called, is principally engaged in advising and directing Police Magistrates in the performance of their duties. Every Ordinance, before it is passed, is submitted to the Law Officers of the Crown for report. The Crown Counsel, for five of whom provision has been made, are chiefly engaged in conducting criminal and sometimes civil cases on behalf of the Attorney-General. The Attorney-General is also authorised to appoint in each district a proctor, called the Crown Proctor, to appear in civil and criminal cases in District Courts, Courts of Requests and Police Courts on behalf of the Crown.

The judicial system is well adapted to the present needs of the country. But the principle adopted in the appointment of judges to preside over the courts is not satisfactory. As regards the Supreme Court, the Judges, who have always been members of the Bar, have invariably proved worthy of the highest tribunal of the island. As regards appointments to the District Courts, Courts of Requests, and Police Courts, there is much room for improvement. Some of the appointments to the more important of these courts are held

H. A. LOOS.
(Senior Crown Counsel for the Island.)

by professional men and by civil servants of great experience and learning, who have spent the greater part of their lives in the service of the colony. But in the majority of cases judicial work is entrusted to Judges who have but a nodding acquaintance with the law and are very slightly familiar with the customs, habits, and language of the litigants. The officers of the Civil Service who are generally appointed to the minor judicial posts are able men with University careers. They

L. MAARTENSZ.
(Crown Counsel for the Island.)

are appointed to judicial and revenue posts according to the whims and caprices of the powers that be; and it invariably happens

CEYLON LEGAL PRACTITIONERS.

1. Advocate B. W. Bawa. 2. Advocate N. Tyagaraja. 3. Advocate M. C. Abdul Cader. 4. Advocate A. P. Savundranayagam. 5. Proctor Francis Homer
6. Advocate Louis H. S. Pieris. 7. Proctor E. R. F. de S. Wijeyeratna. 8. Proctor Arthur Alwis. 9. Advocate Donald Obeyesekere.
10. Advocate T. E. de Sampayo, K.C. 11. Proctor Charles Peiris. 12. Advocate Wm. Wadsworth. 13. Advocate F. J. de Mel.
14. Proctor Charles Perera. 15. Advocate A. St. V. Jayewardene. 16. Advocate A. C. G. Wijeyekoon. 17. Advocate J. Van Langenberg.

A FAMILY OF LEGAL MEN.

ADVOCATE E. W. JAYEWARDENE. ADVOCATE H. A. JAYEWARDENE. THE LATE ADVOCATE J. Q. JAYEWARDENE. CAPTAIN T. G. JAYEWARDENE. ADVOCATE J. S. JAYEWARDENE. ADVOCATE A. ST. V. JAYEWARDENE.

that a civilian who has been holding a judicial appointment and has begun to acquire a knowledge of law and to be interested in his work is transferred to a revenue appointment, and years elapse before he is re-appointed to a judicial post, when he has to begin his study of the law anew. This interruption and resumption of judicial functions continues, to the great detriment of the public, till the highest class of the service is reached. A separate branch of the Civil Service, called the "Judicial Branch," should be constituted, and those members of it who show an aptitude for judicial work should be drafted to that branch and debarred from holding revenue appointments. Then the administration of justice will have been placed on a satisfactory basis. Again, in many instances the combination of revenue and judicial duties is productive of much mischief. The Governor has the power to make a number of appointments to the lower branch of the Civil Service, and these appointments are usually made to judicial posts. The injustice that results from appointments of this nature is manifest. The appointment of civil servants to judicial posts within a few months of their arrival in the island is open to the same observations. Appointments of this kind might be justified if there were no suitable candidates available. There is a Bar, strong both in numbers and in intelligence, in Ceylon, and many of its members would have no objection to accept magistracies provided they were given the same opportunities of promotion in the judicial line as the members of the Civil Service. Ceylonese are by education and intelligence fitted to do judicial work, and it will not be asking too much to demand that half the judicial appointments should be confined to them. Then we shall have a judiciary possessing a knowledge of the law, familiar with the customs, habits, and language of the people, and in every way equipped to do justice between man and man.

THE LATE SIR HARRY DIAS BANDARANAYAKE, KT.

(At one time Senior Puisne Justice of Ceylon.)

HIS EXCELLENCY SIR HENRY ARTHUR BLAKE, G.C.M.G.

Sir Henry Arthur Blake comes of an old Irish family which was founded in Ireland by Richard Blake, *alias* Caddell, who accompanied Prince John to that kingdom in 1185,

A KANDYAN CHIEF.

and who, having obtained considerable grants of land in the County of Galway, settled there. A descendant of this first Richard Blake was Sir Richard Blake, Kt., of Ardfry, Member of Parliament for County Galway in 1639, and Speaker Supreme of the Council of Kilkenny in 1648. His third son was the first Peter Blake of Corbally, grandfather of another Peter Blake, who was in turn the grandfather of Peter Blake, Sir Henry Blake's father. Sir Henry's grandmother was the daughter of the Hon. John Browne, sixth son of John, the first Earl of Allamont. His descent is, therefore, Irish of the Irish. He was born at Limerick on January 18, 1840, his father, Peter Blake of Corbally Castle, County Galway, being at the time a county inspector of Irish Constabulary. Sir Henry was educated at Dr. St. John's academy, Kilkenny, and Santry College, and entered the Irish Constabulary as cadet in 1859, after the usual competitive examination. In 1876 he was appointed a Resident Magistrate, and held that position until 1882, when he was chosen as one of the five special Magistrates selected by the Government to carry out the work of pacification in the country. As the Magistrate in executive charge of County Kildare, Queen's County, Meath, Carlow, Galway East and Galway West, in this troublous period of Irish history, he greatly distinguished himself by his firm and tactful direction of affairs. Official recognition of his services came in 1884 in an offer of the governorship of the Bahamas. Sir Henry accepted this post, and so commenced his brilliant career in the colonial service. After a period of service of three years in the Bahamas, Sir Henry was transferred to Newfoundland, and filled the position of Governor of "the oldest colony" until 1888. In that year he was appointed to Queensland; but an insensate outcry having been raised by the local Irish on the ground of his connection with the special measures for the enforcement of the law in Ireland, the nomination was withdrawn. In 1889 Sir Henry was appointed Captain-General and Governor of Jamaica, and discharged the duties of that office continuously until 1897, his term of service having been extended in 1894, and again in 1896, at the request of the Legislature and public bodies. In 1897 he was transferred to Hong

AN ARACHCHI OR GOVERNOR'S PEON.

Kong, and as Governor of that dependency distinguished himself by the initiation of a policy designed to win the confidence and good-will of the natives. His efforts in this direction were highly successful, as far as the primary end was concerned. But, as was perhaps inevitable, the jealousy of the European community was aroused by the Governor's conciliatory measures and acts. The feeling vented itself in sharp criticisms in the local Press and in utterances in which the language was not always marked by that degree of restraint which is to be looked for in the public references to the representative of the Crown in a colony. Sir Henry, however, was not to be diverted from the course which he deemed to be right by popular clamour, and he continued to the end of his term of office to insist that there should be the fewest possible racial distinctions in the administration. Such was the confidence that he inspired in the ranks of the native community by his broad-minded policy, that when his period of office was approaching its close the Chinese residents of the colony forwarded a memorial to the Secretary of State praying for an extension of Sir Henry's rule. The request was not granted; but a signal proof that the Home Government appreciated His Excellency's value as an administrator was forthcoming in his appointment, in 1903, to the "blue ribbon of the colonial service"—the governorship of Ceylon. The honour was the more marked from the fact that at this time Sir Henry had entered his sixty-fourth year, and was therefore beyond the age at which colonial administrators are usually appointed. On arriving in Colombo on December 3, 1903, to take up the governorship, His Excellency met with a hearty reception from all sections of the community. The Municipal Council presented an illuminated address, inscribed on silk and enclosed in an ivory casket, mounted on a slab of ebony. Sir Henry took the oath the same day in the Legislative Council in the presence of a brilliant gathering, including, besides the heads of Government departments and principal officials, military and civil, the Maha Mudaliyar in gold and velvet, the Executive Councillors in their State uniforms, and the Kandyan Member of the Legislative Council in his picturesque attire. After the formal swearing-in ceremony the Hon. Dr. W. G. Rockwood, Member for the Tamil Community, as senior unofficial member of the Legislative Council, read an address of welcome from the members of the Council. Respectful congratulations were tendered to His Excellency on his appointment, and he was assured of the members' desire to co-operate most cordially in all measures having for their end the welfare of the people and the advancement of the interests of the colony. The high promise of a successful term of office held out by Sir Henry's earlier career has been amply realised. His great administrative skill and his ripe judgment have been manifested in all his official acts, and have given to his work in the colony a marked distinction. In its purely personal aspects His Excellency's administration has been not less successful. His kindly qualities and his strong sense of justice have been manifested in a liberal interpretation of his responsibilities to the varied native population of the colony, and the strictest impartiality has characterised all his actions in reference to them. With Lady Blake's gracious and invaluable co-operation, he has also dispensed generous hospitality and consistently helped forward all good works; while his practical knowledge and wide experience have been freely placed at the service of those promoting public movements of an educational character. In the long period of His Excellency's administration of oversea British dependencies he has ruled over no less than three-fifths of the total population of the Crown Colonies, under his governorship at different times having been included almost every race in the world.

Sir Henry Blake married first, in 1862, Jeannie, eldest daughter of Andrew Irwin, of Ballymore, County Roscommon. The issue of this marriage was a son, the late Mr. Harry Irwin Blake. Sir Henry's first wife died in 1866, and in 1874 he married Edith, eldest daughter and co-heiress of the gifted and witty M.P. of thirty years ago, Mr. Ralph Bernal Osborne. Of the second marriage there are two sons and one daughter. The elder son, born in 1877, is now Lieutenant Arthur Blake, of the 2nd Battalion East Yorkshire Regiment, and was for a time aide-de-camp to his father at Hong Kong. The other son, Maurice Bernal, resides in Ireland. Sir Henry's daughter was recently married to Captain J. B. Arbuthnot, M.V.O., of the Scots Guards, who was also for some time aide-de-camp to His Excellency. On Lady Blake's side the Osborne baronetcy goes back to Sir Richard Osborne, of Ballyntaylor and Ballylemon, County Waterford, and to the year 1629. She is a granddaughter of the eighth baronet. Sir Henry's chief recreation is riding, while he is a good swimmer and an athlete in every way. He is the owner of Raleigh House, Youghal, County Cork, which he acquired from the representatives of Sir John Pope Hennessey, who was a predecessor of his at Government House, Hong Kong. It was in its garden that Ralegh (or Raleigh) planted the first potato grown in Ireland. Associations of Edmund Spenser also cling around the famous house. The poet was often there with Raleigh, and if it is true that he was married at Youghal in 1594, he may have had his wedding breakfast there. Sir Henry has contributed from time to time articles to the *Westminster Review*, the *Fortnightly*, and the *St. James's Gazette*, and has published "Pictures from Ireland" under the *nom-de-plume* of "Terence M'Grath." Sir Henry was made a C.M.G. in 1887 and in the following year was knighted. In 1897 he received the G.C.M.G. He is a Fellow of the Royal Geographical Society and of the Royal Colonial Institute and a Knight of Justice of St. John of Jerusalem. He is a member of the Marlborough and Brooks's Clubs.

GOVERNMENT HOUSE ESTABLISHMENT.

THE GOVERNOR'S RESIDENCES.

The Governor has three official residences in Ceylon, viz., the Queen's House, Colombo, the King's Pavilion, Kandy, and the Queen's Cottage, Nuwara Eliya. Queen's House was built about 1856, taking the place of the old residence at Mount Lavinia, which has since been transformed into the Mount Lavinia Hotel. The Government House at Colombo is a handsome and spacious building, standing in beautiful gardens close to the sea, and is excellently adapted for the various social functions which from time to time take place there. Facing the General Post Office is the main entrance, and, entering this way, one passes into a commodious hall, out of which leads the broad staircase connecting with the upper portion of the building. On the right are numerous bedrooms, and on the left the Council-room, where the members of the Executive Council meet, whilst above the stairs is a large and handsomely painted portrait of Queen Victoria, presented in 1853 by her late Majesty to the colony. Proceeding upstairs, one is struck by the magnificent ball and drawing rooms, both beautifully furnished. These run parallel with each other along each side of the building. A balcony opens off the ballroom facing the General Post Office, whilst alongside the drawing-room at the opposite side runs a verandah overlooking the gardens and sea. In this room there is a portrait of His Majesty the King, which arrived about October, 1906. Between the ballroom and the drawing-room at one end is the billiard-room, and at the other end are bedrooms and a corridor leading to the north wing, wherein are situated the State bedroom and dressing-room. These are large, airy rooms, from which excellent views are obtainable. Over the north wing there is a flat roof, from which one has a comprehensive view of the whole of the harbour, and looking in the opposite direction on a clear day, the famous Adam's Peak can be seen. The gardens, which cover over eight acres, surround the house, and in most directions views of the sea are to be had. In addition to the apartments

A GROUP OF KANDYAN CHIEFS.

mentioned there are handsome reception-rooms, dining-rooms, the Governor's, private secretary's, and aide-de-camp's offices, visitors' rooms, &c. The lighting throughout is by electricity, and electric fans and punkahs are fitted in all the apartments. On the King's birthday there is a levee and ball, whilst from time to time investitures are held at Queen's House by the Governor, these functions also taking place in the ballroom. The establishment of the Queen's House includes the Governor's Private Secretary, Mr. T. L. M. Bunbury; the Aide-de-Camp, Captain H. P. Phipps; extra Aide-de-Camp, Captain G. Fraser; and a native Aide-de-Camp, Don Solomon Dias Bandaranaike, Maha Mudaliyar. The King's Pavilion at Kandy contains handsome dining, drawing, and ball rooms, a balcony, and about twenty-five acres of garden; and Queen's Cottage, Nuwara Eliya, ball, dining, and reception rooms, and about 120 acres of garden.

THE GOVERNOR'S BODYGUARD.

EXECUTIVE COUNCIL.

The Executive Council, established by Letters Patent of March 19, 1833, is a consultative body which is called together by the Governor when he considers there is business for the members to transact. It is formed of the Lieutenant-Governor, the senior military officer of the regular troops stationed in the island (if not below the rank of captain), Colonial Secretary, Attorney-General, Auditor-General, and the Colonial Treasurer, with the Governor as chairman. The Governor must in all cases where he exercises his powers as such consult the members of the Executive Council, except in cases where he considers that material prejudice would be shown by so doing or where he is of opinion that the matter is too unimportant to need, or too urgent to admit of, their being called together. In these cases he must at the earliest opportunity acquaint the members of the steps he has taken. The meetings are usually held at the Queen's House, Colombo, or at some other Government house. Minutes of the meetings are kept and sent home twice a year, and where the Governor acts in opposition to the advice of the Council the act must be recorded on the minutes, along with the reasons given by the Governor for so acting.

THE LATE LIEUTENANT-GOVERNOR.

As this work was passing through the press, the death occurred (on December 7, 1906, after an operation for appendicitis) of the Hon. Sir Alexander Murray Ashmore, K.C.M.G., who filled the office of Lieutenant-Governor of the island. In view of the high position which the late official occupied in the Government, and his distinguished services as a public servant, some reference to his career seems called for in these pages. Sir Alexander was born on February 26, 1855, and entered the Ceylon Civil Service in 1876. Arriving in Ceylon on December 6th of that year, he was appointed to the Anuradhapura Kachcheri. Subsequently, after service at Matara, Colombo, and Kandy, he was in 1878 appointed Police Magistrate at Dumbara. In November, 1882, he became Acting Office Assistant to the Government Agent, Central Province, a position which was a stepping-stone to the full appointment (in May, 1883) of Office Assistant to the Government Agent, Western Province. In April in the following year he returned as Office Assistant to the Central Province. On March 21, 1887, he was nominated Acting Second Assistant to the Colonial Secretary. Four years later, after filling various positions in the service, he served as Acting Principal Assistant to the Colonial Secretary. He left Ceylon in 1893 on leave, and instead of returning to the island, accepted an appointment as Acting Colonial Secretary on the Gold Coast. In the following year he went to Cyprus as Receiver-General, a position which he exchanged in 1896 for that of Acting Chief Secretary. Afterwards he went as British delegate to Evcaf, and in 1900–1 served on the Transvaal Concession Commission in South Africa and London. His next appointment was as Government Secretary in British Guiana. With the completion of his tenure of this post terminated his period of service outside Ceylon. On June 10, 1904, Sir Alexander returned to the island as Colonial Secretary, and held that office until his death. In September, 1905, when Sir Henry Blake went home on leave, he assumed the administration of the government, and, owing to delay in His Excellency's return, it fell to his lot to open the new session of the Legislative Council in that year. He delivered on the occasion a notable address, dealing in a masterly way with several important financial matters. Sir Alexander administered the government until December 3, 1905, when Sir Henry Blake returned to the island. In the April following the late Colonial Secretary went home on leave, and was away until August 10th. His final days were days of controversy and strenuous work, to which is probably due the grave development of the complaint which resulted in his death. A man of uncommon ability and unbounded energy and resource, he died leaving behind him a reputation which will place his name high in the ranks of successful officials of the Ceylon Civil Service. His funeral on December 8th was one of the most impressive ceremonies of the kind recorded in Ceylon annals.

BRIGADIER-GENERAL LAWRENCE (Officer Commanding Troops in Ceylon).

General Richard Charles Bernard Lawrence is the officer in command of the troops stationed in Ceylon. He is a son of the late General R. C. Lawrence, C.B., who was a brother of Henry and John Lawrence, members of a family well known in India. He was born in India in 1857, during the period of the Mutiny, but was sent to England to be educated, and was entered at Harrow. He passed into Sandhurst in February, 1876, as sub-lieutenant, unattached, and was subsequently appointed to the 5th Dragoon Guards, from which regiment, after seven years' service, he exchanged into the King's Dragoon Guards. He served in the Egyptian campaign of 1882, at the outset on special service, and later in command of the Mounted Infantry. He was awarded the brevet of Major, the Egyptian medal with clasp for Tel-el-Kebir, the Order of the Medjidie of the Fourth Class, and the Khedive's Star. He passed through the Staff College in December, 1885, and served six years in India, during which time he held various Staff appointments. He commanded the King's Dragoon Guards in England from 1894 to 1898, and was present at the Diamond Jubilee celebration of Queen Victoria in 1897 in charge of this regiment. In 1898 he was appointed Professor at the Staff College, and in 1899 was placed in the Remount Department of the War Office. In 1903 he was promoted to the Headquarters Staff at Aldershot, assuming the command of the troops in Ceylon in November, 1905. On the occasion of the Emperor Francis Joseph of Austria receiving the appointment of Colonel - in - chief of the King's Dragoon Guards, His Majesty decorated General Lawrence with the Order of the Second Class of the Iron Crown of Austria. In addition to being a member of the Legislative Council, he is *ex-officio* also a member of the Executive Council. His residence is Braybrooke Hall, Slave Island, a charming and spacious building, standing in pretty and somewhat extensive grounds, and he is also provided with an excellent house known as Bowscar at Nuwara Eliya.

THE HON. MR. G. M. FOWLER, C.M.G.

The Hon. Mr. George Merrick Fowler, the Acting Colonial Secretary, was the third son of the late Captain George Campbell Fowler, R.N., of Crookham End, Brimpton, Reading, Berks, and was born on September 21, 1852. He received his education at St. Andrew's College, Bradfield, and Cheltenham College, and entered the Ceylon Civil Service in 1874, when he was attached to the Colonial Secretary's Office. In this same year he went to the Colombo Kachcheri, and then to the Kandy Kachcheri, returning to the former in 1875. In February, 1876, he was attached to the Police Court, Colombo; in July he was Acting Assistant Collector of Customs at Jaffna. Subsequently he occupied various positions, such as Assistant Government Agent, Government Agent, District Judge, &c. In 1899 he was made Acting Government Agent, Western Province, and in 1900 Government Agent, Southern Province. In 1902 he was appointed Acting Government Agent and Fiscal, Western Province, and later was confirmed in the appointment. He received the C.M.G. decoration in 1905, and was Acting Colonial Secretary and twice Acting Auditor-General. In 1906, during the illness and on the death of Sir Alexander Ashmore, he was again appointed Acting Colonial Secretary. By virtue of his office he is a member of the Executive Council.

THE HON. MR. A. G. LASCELLES (Attorney-General).

The Hon. Mr. Arthur George Lascelles, son of the Hon, George Lascelles, was born at Harewood, Yorkshire, on October 12, 1857. He was educated at University College, Oxford, where he was second-class moderator in history. He entered the legal profession, and was called to the English Bar, Inner Temple, in 1885. After practising at the English Bar for some time, he went abroad, and on several occasions acted as President of the district courts at Cyprus and as Puisne Judge and President of the District Court at Papho in 1892. In 1893 he fulfilled similar appointments at Larnaca, and in 1895 was Acting Puisne Judge. He became Acting Queen's Advocate in February, 1896, and was President of the District Court at Nicosia in the same year. In 1898 he was appointed Queen's Advocate and to his present position as Attorney-General in 1902. During part of 1906 he also acted as Chief Justice. He takes an interest in various branches of sport, is very fond of shooting and golf, and is an active supporter of the races at Colombo, being one of the stewards of the Turf Club. His private residence is Icicle Hall, Colpetty, a charming and spacious building by the sea-shore.

THE HON. MR. H. C. NICOLLE.

The Hon. Mr H. C. Nicolle is the Colonial Treasurer of Ceylon, to which office he was appointed in September of 1904. He was born in 1855 at St. Heliers, Jersey, his father being the late Mr. J. M. Nicolle. His business career was commenced in the London and Westminster Bank in London, but in February of 1880 he entered the service of the Government, and was appointed by the Foreign Office as Assistant Auditor at Cyprus, with a special commission in regard to arrears in accounts in that island. He served three years, and was then promoted Auditor-General of that dependency. During the period 1886–89 he was the British Delegate of Evcaf in Cyprus, this being in addition to his other duties, whilst for a time he was Mayor of the town of Nicosia. From January, 1890, to February, 1904, he filled the position of Local Auditor, and in the year 1894 he assisted materially in combating the terrible scourge of plague which laid hold of the city of Victoria, Hong Kong, for which special service he was awarded a gold medal. It was in February, 1904, that he was appointed to Ceylon. He was selected by the Secretary of State to inquire into the system of public accounts in the colony, and in September of the year named he received the appointment he now fills.

THE LEGISLATIVE COUNCIL.

The laws for the government of Ceylon are made by the Governor, "with the advice and

S. N. W. HULUGALLA.
(Ex-Member, Legislative Council.)

consent of the Legislative Council." This Council consists of official and unofficial members, the official members being the principal executive officers of the colony. The meetings are held in the Legislative Council chambers in the Secretariat buildings, and a verbatim report of the proceedings appears in the newspapers, while the minutes of the Council meetings are sent home twice a year. The laws enacted by this Council are known as "ordinances," and a duplicate copy of each is forwarded to England on enactment. These come into operation immediately they receive the Governor's assent, although the Crown has power to disallow them, and where this happens such laws cease to operate immediately the disallowance is published in the colony. The annual opening of the session is a sort of State ceremony, and is attended by the Judges, heads of the civil and military departments, ecclesiastical dignitaries, foreign consuls, and representative officials in uniform or full dress. The Governor, who presides over the assembly, is met at the entrance of the chamber by the members, and is attended by his staff and received with a regimental guard of honour.

THE LEGISLATIVE COUNCIL.

1. THE HON. MR. S. C. OBEYESEKERE 2. THE HON. MR. F. A. COOPER, C.M.G. 3. THE HON. MR. J. P. LEWIS. 4. THE HON. R. C. B. LAWRENCE (Brigadier-General). 5. THE HON. MR. A. KANAGASABAI. 6. THE HON. MR. T. B. L. MOONEMALLE. 7. THE HON. MR. P. ARUNACHALAM. 8. THE HON. MR. FRANK BEVEN. 9. THE HON. MR. W. M. ABDUL RAHIMAN. 10. THE HON. MR. G. F. WALKER. 11. THE HON. MR. J. FERGUSON, C.M.G.

THE HON. MR. CHARLES THOMAS DOYNE VIGORS.

The Hon. Mr. C. T. D. Vigors is the Acting Government Agent of the Western Province. He was born on December 11, 1857, and came out to Ceylon to the Colombo Kachcheri in 1878. The same year he was moved to the Kandy Kachcheri and in 1879 was attached to the Police Court, Kurunegala. In 1880 he became extra Office Assistant to the Government Agent, North Western Province, and at a subsequent date that year was appointed Acting Police Magistrate, Kalpitiya, and Additional Police Magistrate, Puttalam. He became Acting Assistant Government Agent at Puttalam in 1883, and in 1884 assumed the post of Assistant Collector of Customs, Trincomalee. Subsequent to performing the duties of Acting Office Assistant to the Government Agent, Southern Province, he became Acting District Judge, Kegalla, and later Landing Surveyor, Customs, Colombo. He fulfilled many other offices up to 1900, when he was appointed Government Agent of Uva. In 1903 he was Acting Chairman (Municipal Council) and Mayor of Colombo. After this he was appointed Government Agent, North Central Province, and is now Acting Government Agent of the Western Province.

THE HON. MR. JOHN PENRY LEWIS.

The Hon. Mr. J. P. Lewis is the Government Agent of the Central Province. He was born in 1854, and educated at Mill Hill School, Middlesex, and Queen's University, Ireland (Bachelor of Arts, 1876; Master of Arts, 1882). After joining the Ceylon Civil Service in 1877, he served in various revenue and judicial appointments, and was Special Officer under the Waste Lands Ordinance, 1897–1901. From 1903 to 1906 he was Acting Government Agent of the Northern Province and as such was Superintendent of the Pearl Fisheries of 1904, 1905, 1906; Government Agent of the Central Province, 1906; and Chairman of the Ceylon Rubber Exhibition Committee, 1906. He held a commission in the Ceylon Light Infantry Volunteers, 1887–95. He compiled a "Manual of the Vanni Districts of the Northern Province" (1895) and has contributed papers on "Folklore from North Ceylon," to *Folklore*, vol. vi. (1895); "Dutch Architecture in Ceylon," to *Architectural Review*, vol. xii. (1902) and vol. xv. (1904); besides various papers to the *Journal* of the Ceylon branch of the Royal Asiatic Society, of which branch he is a Vice-President.

THE HON. MR. FRANCIS ALFRED COOPER.

This gentleman, a Companion of the Most Distinguished Order of St. Michael and St. George, Member of the Institution of Civil Engineers, and Fellow of the Royal Sanitary Institute, is the fourth son of the Rev. William Waldo Cooper, M.A., Rural Dean of Walshcroft, Rector of West Rasen, Lincolnshire, also Justice of the Peace of the Parts of Lindsey. The Hon. Mr. Cooper was educated at Rossall and at Loughborough Grammar School, and commenced his professional career in the office of the late Mr. James Mansergh, Past President of the Institute of Civil Engineers, Westminster, with whom he served in pupilage during the years 1879 to 1882. He subsequently became an assistant to Mr. Mansergh, which appointment he held for five years.

Mr. Cooper joined the colonial service in 1887, and proceeded to Hong Kong, where he held the Government appointments of Sanitary Surveyor, Inspector of Buildings, Assistant Surveyor-General, Acting Surveyor-General, and Resident Engineer in charge of the Water and Drainage Department. In 1891 he was appointed Director of Public Works in that colony, Member of the Executive and Legislative Councils, and four years later President of the Sanitary Board. These positions he retained till 1897, when he was appointed Director of Public Works of Ceylon.

In addition to holding that high office and being an official member of the Legislative Council of the island, Mr. Cooper is also Waterworks Engineer for the city of Colombo and a member of the Harbour Board and the Municipal Council of that city. For his services in the settlement of claims under the Tarpingsham Resumption Ordinance in 1895, as well as during the epidemic of plague in 1896, Mr. Cooper was tendered the thanks of the Hong Kong Government and the Secretary of State, and also received the Companionship of the Order of St. Michael and St. George on January 1, 1901. In 1894 Mr. Cooper married Frances Louisa, daughter of the Rev. G. T. Palmer, M.A., Honorary Canon of Rochester, Rural Dean and Rector of Newington. During Mr. Cooper's colonial career he has designed and carried out many important public works, both in Hong Kong and Ceylon.

THE HON. MR. P. ARUNACHALAM (Registrar-General).

The Hon. Mr. Ponnambalam Arunachalam, the Registrar-General, was born on September 14, 1853. He is an M.A. (Cantab.) and a barrister-at-law (Lincoln's Inn). He entered the Civil Service in 1875, when he was appointed to the Colombo Kachcheri. He was later attached to the Police Court, Kandy, and then for a time was Police Magistrate at Kalpitiya, Matara, Avisawella, and Pasyala, and then again at Matara. In 1880 he was Acting Police Magistrate at Matale and subsequently Police Magistrate, Kalutara. He acted as District Judge for various districts, and in 1887 was Acting Registrar-General and Fiscal, Western Province. In 1891 he was Acting Commissioner of Requests, Colombo, and in 1898 was appointed Registrar-General. In 1900 he was appointed Superintendent of Census, in addition to his other duties, and later he ceased to act as Registrar-General. In 1901, however, he again acted as Registrar-General, and in 1903 was District Judge, Kurunegala. He was on half-pay leave during 1904, and on return resumed the duties of Registrar-General.

THE HON. MR. GILES F. WALKER.

The Hon. Mr. G. F. Walker, the mercantile representative, was educated at Marlborough and Tonbridge. He came out to Ceylon in 1866, and from 1868 to 1896 resided at St. John del Rey, in Bogawantalawa, of which estate he is the proprietor. During that period he was several times Chairman of the Dikoya District Planters' Association, and in 1891 was elected Chairman of the Planters' Association of Ceylon, an office which he held for three years in succession. In 1894 he became the Planting Member of the Legislative Council, and remained such until 1897. From 1898 to 1902 he was General European Member, and acting member in 1903-4. For 1904 and 1905 he was a member of the Colombo Municipal Council, but resigned this appointment on taking up the duties of Mercantile Representative of the Legislative Council (acting) in 1905-6. During the period he has been in the Legislative Council Mr. Walker has served on the Silver Currency Commission, the Hospital Mortality Commission, and acted as Chairman of the Prædial Products Thefts Commission. He is a Justice of the Peace for the Western Province, and an Unofficial Police Magistrate for the Hatton and Colombo Districts. His residence at present is at Mount Lavinia.

THE HON. MR. WAPCHI MARIKAR ABDUL RAHEMAN.

This gentleman, the Mahomedan representative in the Legislative Council of Ceylon, was born at Colombo in 1868. He was educated at the Government School, Gasworks Street, and afterwards at the Wesley College, Colombo. He started his business career in 1888 in partnership with his father as building contractor, but he retired from this business in 1898. In 1900 he was appointed representative for the Mahomedan community, and is now fulfilling his second term of office. He is a member of the Agricultural Society and the Orient Club, and one of the principal members of the Ceylon Turf Club. Mr. Abdul Raheman has travelled extensively in India. He is a Vice-President of the Social Reform Society, and a keen supporter of sport among Mahomedan boys, also President of the Malay Sports Club. He is a proprietor of extensive landed property in Colombo, besides owning a large coconut estate in the North-Western Province. He has always been foremost in advocating the claims of education amongst the Mahomedans, and has spent large sums of money on schools for the community he officially represents.

THE HON. MR. S. C. OBEYESEKERE.

A full sketch of Mr. Obeyesekere's career appears in another section of the volume.

THE HON. MR. E. ROSLING.

A full sketch of the career of Mr. Rosling will be found elsewhere.

THE HON. MR. JOHN FERGUSON, C.M.G.

The Hon. Mr. John Ferguson is the oldest British editor in Asia, and one of the best known public men in the colony. For about forty-six years he has laboured in Ceylon, and his name has become familiar throughout the East as that of a writer and publicist of eminence. Mr. Ferguson was born on December 1, 1842, in Tain, Ross-shire, and was educated in the Tain Academy, winning the Sir James Matheson gold medal for mathematics at the early age of thirteen years. When the time arrived for him to put aside his lesson-books, he adopted journalism as his profession, and quickly achieved success. Proceeding to Ceylon in 1861, by dint of whole-hearted work he soon became joint editor and part proprietor of the *Ceylon Observer*, a paper which in various ways he improved and extended. He next founded the *Tropical Agriculturist*, a monthly journal which is now to be found in the library of every college of field culture in the sub-tropical world. Later he became connected with other literary productions, besides being the author of numerous manuals and handbooks. He is now editor-in-chief of the *Ceylon Observer* and the *Overland Observer*. "The Ceylon Handbook and Directory," issued annually, is edited by him, and he has compiled planting manuals on coffee, tea, coconut and other palms, cinchona, cacao, rubber, tobacco, cinnamon, nutmegs, and other spices. The "Gold, Gems, and Pearls of Ceylon" have been dealt with by him, whilst his "Illustrated Handbook of Ceylon" has passed through five editions. Mr. Ferguson has travelled a great deal—three times round the world in different directions—has written much on his journeyings, but Ceylon has ever been his chief concern since as a young man he set foot in Colombo. As a recognised expert authority he has been in great demand as a lecturer and speaker. Amongst the important assemblies he has addressed are the Royal Colonial Institute, the Society of Arts, the London Chamber of Commerce, the Royal Geographical Society in Edinburgh and Glasgow, and the Historic Society of St. Louis and Washington, U.S.A. It was doubtless in recognition of his great abilities and unique experience that in 1902 Mr. Ferguson was chosen a member of the Ceylon Legislative Council. However that may be, the Council obtained in him a valuable recruit, and one whose earnestness and zeal, used on the public behalf, have proved of inestimable value in the deliberations of the Council. In his public life Mr. Ferguson has always been a strong advocate of the proper use of public funds, the extension of the privileges of the Legislature, the promotion of education among the people, the repression and reform of the spirit monopoly, and the abolition of licensed opium shops. Amongst the offices which he holds besides the membership of the Legislative Council are: President of the Ceylon branch of the Royal Asiatic Society, President of the Christian Literature Society, of the South Ceylon Sunday School Auxiliary of the India S.S. Union, ex-President of the British and Foreign Bible Society, life member of the British Association, the Society of Arts, and the Royal Colonial Institute. He was also one of the representatives of his colony at the St. Louis Exhibition. He has made the contributions for Ceylon and its towns to the "Encyclopædia Britannica," and has for thirty-six years acted as Ceylon correspondent for the London *Times*. In recognition of his long and useful public services, he was, in June, 1903, awarded the C.M.G. decoration. He is an Evangelical Free Churchman, and a Sunday School worker of forty-three years' standing.

THE HON. MR. A. KANAGASABAI.

The career of the Hon. Mr. Kanagasabai is fully sketched elsewhere.

THE HON. MR. FRANCIS BEVEN.

The Hon. Mr. Francis Beven is the second surviving son of a family of ten sons and seven daughters of the late Mr. John Beven, who died in 1885 shortly after his retirement from the chief clerkship of the General Treasury, on the completion of fifty years' service under Government. The mother of the family, who survived her husband about sixteen and a half years, belonged to the Koertz family of Negombo, the members of which trace their descent in Ceylon as far back as 1660. The subject of this sketch was born in the Pettah of Colombo in February, 1847, and educated at St. Thomas's College and the Colombo Academy (now the Royal College). At the early age of fourteen years he won the Junior Queen's Scholarship, and two years later the Senior Queen's Scholarship which was awarded to the Ceylon student who passed highest in the First Division of the Matriculation Examination of the Calcutta University. When seventeen he won the Turner Classical Prize, and a year later passed the Calcutta First in Arts, taking a place in the first division. At nineteen years of age, when reading for his degree, he was offered a sub-editorship of the *Examiner* newspaper, and in 1871 became joint editor. A year previously he had been admitted an Advocate of the Supreme Court. Mr. Beven appeared in cases at court as frequently as his editorial duties permitted; but eventually he gave up his position on the *Examiner* and practised as an advocate in Kandy. In 1881, owing to deafness—an infirmity from which he has long suffered—he discarded the law, and took Franklands, a cinnamon and coconut estate in the Veyangoda district, about twenty-five miles from Colombo, on the Kandy railway. Shortly afterwards he again adopted the journalistic profession, rejoining the *Examiner* staff as editor. He retired in 1892, and was appointed leader-writer to one of the other evening journals, a post he occupied for a few years, giving it up in order that he might devote his time to agriculture. He was appointed a Justice of the Peace for the island, in recognition of his journalistic services, in 1892. He did not actually sever his connection with Press work until 1902. He has taken a great interest in public affairs, and was prominent in the movement to gain for the Burgher community due representation on the Legislative Council. He was elected a Vice-President of the Ceylon Agricultural Society; and during the absence of Mr. F. C. Loos, who left for England in May, 1906, he acts as Burgher representative on the Legislative Council. Mr. Beven is in his sixtieth year, and has a family of three sons and three daughters. His eldest son, Francis Lorenz, graduated with double honours at Christ's College, Cambridge, in 1895, and is now Vicar of Christ Church, Kurunegala. The second son superintends his father's estates and the third is a student at the Royal College.

THE HON. MR. T. B. L. MOONEMALLE.

The Hon. Mr. Theodore Barcroft L. Moonemalle was born on July 19, 1868, at Kurunegala. He is the son of Mr. John Marcellus L. Moonemalle, Proctor of the Supreme Court, Ceylon; grandson of Mr. John Graham Jayatileke, Proctor, Supreme Court, Ceylon, who early in his career was Ratemahatmaya of Devemedi Hatpattu, but retired from Government service, preferring the more independent life of a lawyer. He was known throughout the Kandyan provinces as "Hulugalla Dissawa." Mr. Moonemalle received his early training in letters under the Rev. H. C. Hancock, Vicar of Christ Church, Kurunegala. He then entered Trinity College, Kandy, where he served under several distinguished educationalists, principally the Rev. Thomas Dunn and the Rev. J. G. Garrett, M.A. He was enrolled a Proctor of the District Court of Kurunegala in July, 1890, taking his oath before Mr. P. Arunachalam, who was then District Judge of that station. It is a happy coincidence that the erstwhile District Judge and the new-fledged lawyer are now *confrères* at the Council, the former taking his seat as Registrar-General of Ceylon and the latter as unofficial representative of the Kandyan community. Mr. Moonemalle in 1897 presented himself for the Supreme Court examination, which he passed with distinction, securing first place among the candidates who were successful, and was sworn in as a Proctor of the Supreme Court before Sir Archibald Lawrie, who later on, when presiding at the criminal sessions of the Supreme Court, held at Kurunegala, singled out Mr. Moonemalla from amongst other practitioners for a special compliment on his able and eloquent advocacy of his client. He has from his early youth displayed a practical and loyal sympathy towards his countrymen. He has been time after time selected as their spokesman in connection with the long-continued agitation regarding the Government claims to "waste lands." A short appreciation which appeared in the *Times of Ceylon*, July 24, 1906, adequately expresses his character in the following words: "We have heard much of Mr. Moonemalle and read more of his independence, his grasp of facts and remarkable ability in presenting them, of his cool judgment and temperate speech, of his high ideals of national and political life, and of his appeals to his countrymen to forsake their obscurity and take their place among the factors of the island's progress." On July 17, 1906, Mr. Moonemalle was sworn in as the Kandyan representative on the Legislative Council on the retirement of Mr.

S. N. W. Hulugalla, who has since been appointed Adigar. We reproduce a photograph of Mr. Moonemalle in his national costume, which he wears on all public occasions, including the meetings of the Legislative Council. It may be added that Mr. Moonemalle has on several occasions acted as District Judge, Commissioner of Requests, and Police Magistrate, Kurunegala.

LEGAL AND JUDICIAL.

FOR legal and judicial purposes Ceylon is divided into four districts—the Western, Midland, Northern, and Southern Circuits as they are termed. The courts for the adminis-

THE HON. SIR J. T. HUTCHINSON.
(Chief Justice.)

tration of justice, civil and criminal, are the Supreme Court, District Courts, Courts of Requests, and Police Courts. The circuits are in turn divided into districts, each district court being presided over by a District Judge with unlimited civil jurisdiction and a criminal jurisdiction between that of the Supreme and Police Courts. Besides these courts there are the village tribunals and committees, at which offences of a minor description are dealt with. In all but these the business is transacted in English by the aid of an interpreter. Practising at the courts are advocates and proctors, corresponding to the English barristers and solicitors. Criminal sessions are held at Colombo four times a year at least, at Kandy three times, at Jaffa and Galle twice, and at such other places as are at times appointed. The Supreme Court consists of the Chief Justice and three Puisne Justices. It has an original criminal jurisdiction, besides deciding civil and criminal appeals from the lower courts. It is also a Colonial Court of Admiralty. The trials are before one judge and a jury of seven, a unanimous decision or a five to two majority being necessary to secure a conviction. The district judgeships are posts in the Civil Service, and the District Judges are Commissioners of Requests and Police Magistrates. The Courts of Requests have purely civil jurisdiction, whilst the Police Courts are on a similar footing to those at home, the Magistrates having power only to try for minor offences, the more serious ones being inquired into by them and the accused committed for trial before the Supreme or District Courts. The law of England prevails in respect of partnerships, joint-stock companies, banks and banking, maritime matters, bills of exchange, promissory notes, cheques, and other commercial matters, whilst other systems are in vogue in other particulars, these special laws including the customs of the Tamil inhabitants of Jaffna, laws and usages of the Mahomedans, the Mukkawar Law, and the Kandyan Law. The Law Officers of the Crown are the Attorney-General, the Solicitor-General, and three Crown Counsel.

THE HON. SIR J. T. HUTCHINSON, K.T., Chief Justice.

Sir J. T. Hutchinson, the Chief Justice of Ceylon, was born in 1850 in Cumberland, and educated at St. Bees Grammar School, and afterwards at Christ's College, Cambridge. At the University he took his B.A. degree in the first class of the Classical Tripos in 1873, and his M.A. in 1876. He was called to the Bar at the Middle Temple in 1879, and practised at the Chancery Bar until 1888, when he went to the Gold Coast as Queen's Advocate. He was appointed Chief Justice of the Gold Coast in 1889, and filled that position until 1894, when he was transferred to Grenada (Windward Islands) to fill the chief judicial position there. In 1898 he received the appointment of Chief Justice of Cyprus, and remained in that island until 1906, when he proceeded to Ceylon to take up the duties of his present high position, on the resignation of Sir Charles Peter Layard, who had been Chief Justice from the year 1902. Sir J. T. Hutchinson married, in 1897, Constance Mary daughter of J. Lucas, Esq., of Stapleton House, Upper Tooting. He is a member of the Reform Club, and his addresses are Colombo, Ceylon, and Braystones, Cumberland.

THE HON. MR. HENRY LORENTZ WENDT.

This Judge of the Supreme Court is the son of George Arnold Wendt, accountant, and Mary L. G. Anderson, and was born in the year 1858. He received his education at St. Thomas's College, Colombo, where he held the Gregory Scholarship, inaugurated in memory of Sir William Gregory, Governor

THE HON. MR. H. L. WENDT.
(Senior Puisne Justice of the Supreme Court.)

of Ceylon 1872-77. In 1874 he matriculated at the Calcutta University, and in 1876 passed his first examination in Arts. On leaving that scholastic establishment in 1877 he became a law student, being called to the Ceylon Bar three years later; and on a recent visit to England he was called to the English Bar, becoming a member of Gray's Inn. He commenced legal practice at the Supreme and District Courts of Colombo, and acted as Solicitor-General in 1897 and Attorney-General in 1900 and 1901. In August of 1901 he was appointed to the position of Acting Puisne Judge of the Supreme Court, and in October of the same year was confirmed in that appointment. He is now the Senior Puisne Justice. Mr. Wendt published a volume of Law Reports for the years 1882–83, while between the years 1892 and 1896 he edited the "Supreme Court Circular" Reports, and the "Ceylon Law Reports."

As a diversion from legal matters, Mr. Wendt has given some time to politics. From 1895 to 1900 he was a Member of the Legislative Council, representing the Burgher community. In addition to his judicial duties, he is a member of the Incorporated Council of Legal Education. He is also a member of the Committee of the Victoria Memorial Home for Incurables and also of the Turf Club. He fills as well the office of President of the Y.M.C.A., and is a member of the Friend-in-Need Society, also Vice-President of the local branch of the Bible Society. In 1899 he married Amelia, daughter of Mr. J. H. de Saram, C.M.G., District Judge of Kandy. His private residence is Fountain House, Union Place, Colombo, and his favourite pastime is photography, in which pursuit he is an adept.

THE HON. MR. ALEXANDER WOOD-RENTON.

The Hon. Mr. A. Wood-Renton, the third Puisne Judge, was appointed on September 3, 1905. He was born on June 24, 1861.

THE HON. MR. J. R. GRENIER.

The Greniers are descended from a well-known noble French family, some of the members of which had to leave their country at the time of the Huguenot persecution and settle in Belgium. The gentleman whose name is at the head of this sketch is a scion of that ancient family, the first member of which to arrive in Ceylon was a lieutenant in the army of the Netherlands who had taken service in the Dutch East India Company. This officer, who was born at Dinant, in South Brabant (Belgium), was the father of Jean Francois Grenier, who applied for and obtained letters of naturalisation as a British subject from Governor Sir Frederick North on June 7, 1802. Jean François Grenier, who was employed in the Maritime Customs, married Charlotta Pietersz, and resided at Jaffna One of their sons, Frederick, was secretary of the District Court of Jaffna. Joseph Richard, one of the sons of Frederick and who forms the subject of this sketch, was educated at St. Thomas's College under Warden Bacon and, like his legal *confrère*, Mr. F. Dornhorst, K.C., he became a Master of the College before entering the legal profession. He was admitted to the Ceylon Bar in 1873, and was called to the English Bar at Gray's Inn on June 27, 1906. He practised for some time at Jaffna, but returned to Colombo. He held various appointments, being in turn Police Magistrate, Commissioner of Requests, Deputy Queen's Advocate, District Judge, Solicitor-General, and Commissioner of Assize and Puisne Judge of the Supreme Court of Ceylon on several occasions. In April, 1903, he was permanently appointed District Judge of Colombo, and is now again officiating on the Bench of the Supreme Court. He is a member of the Council of Legal Education and of the Royal Societies' Club, London. His wife is the youngest daughter of the late John Drieberg, Proctor of the Supreme Court, and niece of the late Mr. C. A. Lorenz. Of his sons, the eldest, Reginald, is a civil engineer in Glasgow; the second, Jules, is preparing for the priesthood at St. Bernard's Seminary: the third, Guy Oliphant, is private secretary to Mr. Justice Middleton, and the fourth, David, is his own private secretary. The two youngest, George and Harry, are at school. He has three daughters—Gertrude, Louise, and Mary.

THE HON. MR. JOSEPH GRENIER.
(Acting Puisne Justice of the Supreme Court.)

THE HON. MR. JOHN PAGE MIDDLETON.

The Hon. Mr. J. P. Middleton, Puisne Judge, was born on June 8, 1851. He received his appointment as Puisne Justice in 1902, and was away on half-pay leave in 1905–6.

THE HON. MR. J. P. MIDDLETON.
(Puisne Judge.)

THE REGISTRAR.

Mr. **Horatio William Nelson,** B.A. Cantab., is the Registrar. He was born on June 18, 1871, and is an English solicitor and Proctor of the Supreme Court of Ceylon. In July, 1903, he became Third Deputy Registrar, and he was appointed to his present position in 1906.

FREDERICK CHRISTIAN LOOS, Jun.

Mr. F. C. Loos, jun., is the son of the Hon. F. C. Loos, Burgher representative in the Legislative Council, and was born at Colombo in 1861. He was educated at Trinity College, Kandy, and Royal College, Colombo. He read law under Messrs. Loos and Van Cuylenberg, and passed as a Proctor of the District Court in 1885. He then commenced practice in Colombo, and was afterwards for some little time at Nuwara Eliya. In 1895 he visited England, and on his return settled down at Nuwara Eliya, where he became a Notary Public and Supreme Court Proctor, Justice of the Peace, and Unofficial Police Magistrate, and finally, in 1899, Crown Proctor. Mr. Loos has repeatedly acted as Additional Police Magistrate and Commissioner of Requests, and at the present time is First Deputy Registrar. He is also a member of the Agricultural Society, and one of the most prominent members of the Ceylon Kennel and Poultry Club, being a well-known fancier, exhibitor, and prize-winner in the fox-terrier class. His private residence is Rossye Lodge, Nuwara Eliya.

Mr. **Lloyd L. Daniels** is the Second Deputy Registrar, his appointment dating from July 1, 1903. He held several appointments in the clerical service previously, and from 1901 was Third Deputy Registrar for two years. He was born on May 23, 1858.

Mr. **C. W. Goonewardene,** the Third Deputy Registrar, was appointed Itinerating Police Magistrate in January, 1905, and during the same year passed the law examination.

DISTRICT JUDGES.

COLOMBO.

JAMES RICHARD WEINMAN.

A sketch of the life of Mr. J. R. Weinman,

J. R. WEINMAN.
(District Judge.)

Acting District Judge of Colombo, appears elsewhere.

FELIX R. DIAS BANDARANAYKE.

A sketch of the life of Mr. F. R. Dias Bandaranayke, Additional District Judge of Colombo, appears elsewhere.

FELIX R. DIAS.
(Additional District Judge, Colombo.)

ANURADHAPURA.

Mr. **George Shadwell Saxton,** District Judge of Anuradhapura, was born on April 3, 1858. He entered the Ceylon Civil Service as cadet in 1879, and was attached to the Colombo Kachcheri. After working at several other Kachcheris, he was successively Acting Police Magistrate of Tangalla, Matale, and Dimbula, and in 1885 he became Police Magistrate of Matale and Dumbara. After being Acting Assistant Government Agent in several parts of the island, he became in 1902 Government Agent of the Province of Sabaragamuwa, and occupied this position until he received his present appointment, quite recently.

BADULLA.

The District Judge of Badulla is Mr. **Alexander Ransford Slater,** B.A. Cantab. He was born on November 28, 1874, and entered the Ceylon Civil Service in December, 1898, as an official at the Colombo Kachcheri. Three years later he became Acting Second Assistant Colonial Secretary, and held this position until he received his present appointment.

BATTICALOA.

The District Judge of Batticaloa is Mr. **George William Woodhouse,** B.A. Cantab. His entry to the Ceylon Civil Service dates from September, 1892, when he was attached to the Galle Kachcheri as cadet. In December, 1895, he became Assistant Collector of Customs at Trincomalee, and during the next few years he was Additional District Judge and Additional Police Magistrate in various districts. In 1905 he was appointed first as District Judge of Negombo and then of Batticaloa, and he holds the latter position at the present time.

CHILAW.

REGINALD GIBSON SAUNDERS.

Mr. R. G. Saunders is a son of Sir Frederick Richard Saunders, formerly Treasurer of Ceylon, grandson of Mr. Frederick Saunders, who occupied a similar position in 1861, and maternal grandson of Mr. W. C. Gibson, C.M.G., who held office as Auditor-General and Colonial Secretary between the years 1850 and 1860. He was born in Colombo in 1878, and educated in England at Tonbridge School and Cheltenham College. He entered the Ceylon Government service and held various minor appointments, such as Third Assistant to the Postmaster-General, Acting Assistant Collector of Customs and Police Magistrate, Trincomalee, and Office Assistant to the Government Agent, Uva Province. In

R. G. SAUNDERS.

1903 he became Police Magistrate, Matara, and in 1904 Assistant Government Agent and District Judge, Mannar, and in 1906, on his return from half-pay leave, he was appointed Commissioner of Requests and Police Magistrate, Chilaw. Later he was made Assistant Government Agent and District Judge, Chilaw. He attended the two pearl fisheries of 1904 and 1905 in his official capacity.

KANDY.

The District Judge of Kandy is Mr. **John Harvey Templer,** B.A. Cantab. He was

J. H. TEMPLER.
(District Judge, Kandy.)

born on November 11, 1847, and is a barrister-at-law of the Inner Temple. He entered the Ceylon Civil Service as Office Assistant to the Attorney-General in 1881. During 1892 and 1894 he acted as Solicitor-General, and was appointed Crown Counsel. On several occasions he has acted as District Judge of Colombo, and he was a prison visitor of the Western Province.

GALLE.

Mr. **George Algernon Baumgartner,** District Judge of Galle, was born on March 2, 1850, and entered the Ceylon Civil Service, as writer attached to the Colombo Kachcheri, in October, 1871. In 1874 he was appointed Police Magistrate of Point Pedro and Chavakachcheri, and after filling various positions he became District Judge of Negombo in 1894. In 1901 he was appointed Government Agent of the Uva Province, and his present appointment dates from April, 1903.

JAFFNA.

Mr. **William Rutherford Bogle Sanders** is the District Judge of Jaffna. He was born on October 29, 1856, and entered the Ceylon Civil Service as cadet attached to the Galle Kachcheri in December, 1879. After working in different positions all over the island, he became District Judge of Negombo in March, 1899, and of Jaffna first in 1900 and again in 1905.

KALUTARA.

Mr. **Paulus Edward Pieris,** M.A. Cantab., the District Judge of Kalutara, was born on February 16, 1874, and entered the service in 1896. He passed through various other positions, and was in 1903 appointed Acting District Judge of Matara. In 1905, on his return from the St. Louis Exhibition, he became District Judge of Kegalla, and held this position until he received his present appointment.

KEGALLA.

Mr. **H. J. V. Ekanayake,** the District Judge of Kegalla, has acted provisionally in various positions in the Ceylon Civil Service since December 16, 1901, when he became Acting Police Magistrate of Balapitiya.

KURUNEGALA.

At Kurunegala the District Judge is Mr. **Bertram Hill,** B.A. Cantab., who was born on October 16, 1864. He entered the service as a cadet in 1888, and was in that year attached to the Kurunegala Kachcheri. In 1891 he became Acting Office Assistant to the Government Agent of the Eastern Province at Batticaloa, and in 1901 Assistant Government Agent at Matara. He went to Kurunegala as Acting District Judge in September, 1905.

MANNAR.

Mr. **John Scott,** who took his B.A. degree at Cambridge, is the District Judge of Mannar. He was born on April 24, 1878, and entered the service, attached to the Kandy Kachcheri, in 1901. After filling various positions up-country he became Private Secretary to the Lieutenant-Governor, and after being Acting Police Magistrate at Jaffna, he was appointed Acting Assistant Government Agent at Mannar.

MATARA.

The District Judge at Matara is Mr. **George Frederic Plant,** B.A. Oxon., who was born on November 10, 1877, and entered the Ceylon Civil Service, attached to the Galle Kachcheri, in 1901. In 1904 he became Office Assistant to the Government Agent of the Southern Province, and in 1905 Police Magistrate at Avisawella.

MULLAITIVU.

Mr. **Charles Valentine Brayne,** B.A. Cantab., is the District Judge of Mullaitivu. He was born on August 17, 1877, and entered the Civil Service of Ceylon, attached to the Jaffna Kachcheri, in 1901. After filling various positions in different parts of the island he became Acting Assistant Government Agent at Mullaitivu in 1906.

NEGOMBO.

A. DE ALWIS SENEVERATNE.

According to the Dutch Thombo of the Kalutara district, Appolonia, widow of Alexander Alwis, had four sons, one of whom, Bastian Alwis Seneveratne, Interpreter Mohandiram of Galle Korale, had five sons. These included Floris and Izaak, who, at the time the entry was made in the Thombo, appear to have been eighteen and fifteen years old respectively. Floris became the grandfather of the late Hon. Mr. Albert de Alwis, Member of the Legislative Council, and Izaak became titular Mohandiram of Kalutara, and had an only son, Simon, the father of Mr. Alexander de Alwis Seneveratne, the subject of this sketch. He was born at Beruwela, in 1849, was educated at St. Thomas's College, and was the first scholar of that institution to pass the intermediate arts examination of the Calcutta University. After his college course he became a Master there, and occupied this position until 1878, when he commenced the study of law under Sir Charles Layard. He became an Advocate of the Supreme Court of Ceylon in 1880, and commenced practice in Colombo. In 1883 he was elected a member of the Municipal Council for Kotahena, and sat for

A. DE A. SENEVERATNE.
(District Judge.)

over seventeen years as such, whilst in 1900 he became a nominated member of the same Council. He was elected a member of the Legislative Council to represent the whole of the Sinhalese community, and sat for twelve years. During this period he served on practically all committees on important questions of the day, was instrumental in introducing the silver ten-cent piece, and made careful study of the needs of the people. In 1892 he went to England, and paid a second visit five years later as an official representative of Ceylon at the late Queen's Diamond Jubilee, when he received the Jubilee medal. He became, in 1902, District Judge of Kurunegala, and held similar positions at Colombo and Batticaloa, while since 1905 he has been District Judge of Negombo. Formerly he was a member of the Council of Legal Education and of the Royal Asiatic Society. He is the Chairman of the Negombo Local Board and president of the Negombo branch of the Agricultural Society. In 1881 he married Louisa, eldest daughter of Fred Jayatilleke, the Registrar-General, and after her death he married, in 1894, Eliza Mackenzie, second daughter of Christoffel de Saram, District Judge of Galle. His only daughter, Louisa Alexandra, married Albert Livera, district engineer of Puttalam. Mr. Seneveratne is a trustee of St. Thomas's College.

PUTTALAM.

Mr. **Robert Niemann Thane,** B.A. Cantab., is the District Judge at Puttalam. He was born on January 1, 1875, and entered the service, attached to the Galle Kachcheri, in 1898. In 1901 he became Acting Commissioner of Requests and Police Magistrate at Balapitiya, and after filling various other offices he became Landing Surveyor at Colombo in 1904.

RATNAPURA.

Mr. **Alexander Norman Galbraith,** B.A. Cantab., the District Judge of Ratnapura, was born on June 19, 1878, and entered the service, attached to the Matara Kachcheri, in 1902. In 1905, after filling various positions, he became Office Assistant to the Government Agent of the Eastern Province, and afterwards performed the same duties at Kandy.

TANGALLA.

At Tangalla the District Judge is **Louis William Conrad Schrader,** M.A. Oxon., who was born on August 18, 1873, and entered the service, attached to the Colombo Kachcheri, in 1896. In 1901 he became Assistant Government Agent at Mullaitivu, in 1903 Acting District Judge at Ratnapura, and in 1905 took up his present position.

TRINCOMALEE.

Mr. **Charles Stewart Vaughan,** M.A. Cantab., the District Judge of Trincomalee, was born on May 23, 1866, and entered the Ceylon Civil Service, attached to the Galle Kachcheri, in 1889. During the next few years he was Acting Office Assistant to several Government Agents, and became Acting District Judge at Batticaloa in 1900. His last appointment before taking up his present position was that of Assistant Government Agent at Kegalla.

COMMISSIONERS AND MAGISTRATES.

COLOMBO.

JAMES STEWART DRIEBERG.

Mr. J. S. Drieberg, the Colombo Commissioner of Requests, was born on August 4, 1846, and since he entered the service of the Ceylon Government he has occupied various posts. From 1867 to 1871 Mr. Drieberg acted as private secretary to Mr. Justice Stewart, Mr. Justice Temple, and Mr. Justice Thompson. afterwards being District Judge, &c., Negombo, Police Magistrate, &c., Point Pedro, Chavakachcheri, Kalutara, Avisawella, Pasyala, and Panadure, until 1885. He was then appointed Second Deputy Registrar of the Supreme Court. In 1890 he became Deputy Fiscal, Colombo, and two years later took over the duties of Commissioner of Requests (Acting), Colombo. In subsequent years he was Police Magistrate, Colombo; District Judge, Ratnapura, Kegalla (Acting), Kurunegala (Acting). In 1905 he was appointed to his present position.

KEITH WM. BRUCE MACLEOD.

Mr. Keith W. B. Macleod, who was born on October 30, 1865, is the Police Magistrate at Colombo, a post he was appointed to after filling various positions under Government. He entered the service in 1888, being attached to the Secretariat. He was removed in 1889 to the Galle Kachcheri and later in the same year to the Ratnapura Kachcheri. In 1890, after a few months in the Batticaloa Kachcheri, he became Acting Office Assistant, at Batticaloa, to the Government Agent, Eastern Province. In the same year he was made Commissioner of Requests and Police Magistrate, Panadure, and subsequently held appointments as Forest Settlement Officer, Acting District Judge, Acting Landing Surveyor (Customs), Colombo; District Judge, Acting Government Agent, Deputy Collector of Customs, Colombo; Acting Commissioner of Requests, Colombo. In 1905 he became Government Agent of the Province of Uva, and later District Judge, Kurunegala, whilst subsequent to a period during which he was on half-pay leave he was appointed Police Magistrate of Colombo.

ANURADHAPURA.

The Magistrate at Anuradhapura is Mr. **Wilfrid Thomas Southorn,** B.A. Oxon., who was born on August 4, 1879, and entered the Ceylon Civil Service, attached to the Colonial Secretary's Office, in 1904. During the same year he became Acting Office Assistant to the Government Agent of the Northern Province at Jaffna, and in 1905 he took up a similar position to the North Central Province Agent.

AVISAWELLA.

Thomas Richard Edward Loftus, the Magistrate of Avisawella, was born on February 11, 1876, and he has been in the Civil Service since 1896, when he was attached to the Kandy Kachcheri as cadet. Since then he has been Acting Office Assistant to the Government Agents in various provinces and Acting District Judge of Batticaloa, Ratnapura, Tangalla, and Matara, before taking up his present position.

BALAPITIYA.

At Balapitiya there is an Itinerating Police Magistrate in the person of Mr. **F. D. Pieris,** who was appointed to that position in the Southern Province in 1904. During that year he for some time fulfilled the duties of Acting Commissioner of Requests and Police Magistrate at Galle.

CHAVAKACHCHERI AND POINT PEDRO.

The Police Magistrate at Chavakachcheri is Mr. **W. G. Vallipuram.**

CHILAW.

HENRY JAMES WOUTERSZ.

A sketch of the life of Mr. H. J. Woutersz Police Magistrate of Chilaw, will be found elsewhere.

GALLE.

ROBERT LEWIS WALLER BYRDE.

Mr. R. L. W. Byrde, M.A. London, born on January 10, 1869, is the Magistrate at Galle. He entered the service of the Government in 1893, as a cadet at the Secretariat. He passed through several Kachcheris during subsequent months until appointed as Acting Office Assistant to the Government Agent of the Province of Uva. In 1895 he received an appointment as Acting Assistant Collector of Customs, Trincomalee, and the following year as Office Assistant to the Government Agent, North West Province. He filled a similar position in the office of the Agent of the Eastern Province in 1897, and of the Central Province in 1898. After acting as Police Magistrate at Galle, he became Police Magistrate at Kurunegala, but later resumed duties at Galle.

HAMBANTOTA.

JOHN O'KANE MURTY.

Mr. J. O'Kane Murty was born on April 10, 1867, and entered the Government service in 1890, commencing at the Colombo Kachcheri. In 1891 he became Acting Commissioner of Requests and Police Magistrate, Chilaw; in 1895, Acting Landing Surveyor, Customs, Galle; 1896, Acting Landing Surveyor, Colombo; 1897, Acting District Judge, Ratnapura. In 1899 Mr. Murty was Acting Police Magistrate, Colombo, and in 1900 Assistant Government Agent, Mullaitivu. He became District Judge, Tangalla, in 1901, and Assistant Government Agent, Matara, in 1902. In 1905 he was appointed to Hambantota.

JAFFNA.

G. PRINS.

Mr. G. Prins is the Magistrate at Jaffna. Previously to holding this appointment he was

GEORGE PRINS.
(Police Magistrate.)

Acting Police Magistrate, Point Pedro and Chavakachcheri, and also acted as Police Magistrate, Jaffna, from December, 1902, to March, 1903.

GAMPOLA.

The sketch of Mr. **Walter de Livera's** career appears in another portion of the volume.

KALUTARA.

J. E. DE S. GOONEWARDENE.

A sketch of the life of Mr. J. E. de S. Goonewardene, Police Magistrate of Kalutara, will be found elsewhere.

KANDY.

Mr. **Thomas Brownle Russell,** M.A. Oxon., has been Police Magistrate of Kandy since July, 1905. He was born on August 5, 1873, and entered the service as cadet, attached to the Colonial Secretary's Office, in 1897. After serving at various Kachcheris, he was Office Assistant to the Government Agents of several provinces, Acting Police Magistrate of Balapitiya, and Acting District Judge of Tangalla, Batticaloa, and Jaffna.

KAYTS.

Rasiah William Allegacoon, the Police Magistrate of Kayts, was born on September 5, 1857, but did not enter the Civil Service as cadet until 1898, although he held several appointments in the clerical service from 1878 until that date. After acting as Police Magistrate and Commissioner of Requests at various places, he became Additional District Judge as well at Chilaw in 1903, and in the following year Acting Assistant Government Agent at the same place.

MATALE.

WM. DUNUWILLE.

A sketch of the life of Mr. William Dunuwille, Police Magistrate of Matale, will be found elsewhere.

KURUNEGALA.

Mr. **Allan Beven,** who has been Commissioner of Requests and Police Magistrate at Kurunegala since March, 1905, was born on November 19, 1867, and is a barrister-at-law of the Inner Temple. He entered the Civil Service, attached to the Kandy Kachcheri, in 1892. After being Acting Police Magistrate at several places, he became Magistrate of Panadure and Additional Magistrate of Kalutara in 1898, and Acting District Judge at the latter place and at Kegalla.

MATARA.

P. B. GODAMUNE.

Mr. P. B. Godamune, the Magistrate of Matara, is acting provisionally in the Civil Service. He acted as Commissioner of Requests and Police Magistrate at Galagedara, and Additional Police Magistrate and Commissioner of Requests of Kurunegala from April to December, 1897, and in a similar position and as Deputy Fiscal and Superintendent of the Prison at Avisawella between 1898 and 1901.

TRINCOMALEE.

The Magistrate at Trincomalee is Mr. **H. A. Bell.**

PANADURE.

THOMAS WEBB ROBERTS.

Mr. T. W. Roberts is the magistrate stationed at Panadure. He was born on April 27, 1880, and entered the Ceylon Civil Service in 1902 at the Matara Kachcheri. In 1904 he was appointed Acting Office Assistant at the Kurunegala Kachcheri, and in 1905 he was made Acting Police Magistrate at Matara. Subsequently he received appointment to his present position.

HATTON.

W. H. B. CARBERY.

Mr. Walter Hugh Bertram Carbery, son of J. Carbery, M.D., Colonial Surgeon, was born at Kandy in 1869, and educated at St. Benedict's Institute, Colombo, and Stonyhurst College, Lancashire, England. In 1893 he was appointed cadet in the Civil Service, going first to the Badulla Kachcheri. In 1894 he became an Acting Police Magistrate, and two years later was made Police Magistrate of Matale. After officiating as Acting Office Assistant to the Government Agent in the North Central Province, he was, in 1900, appointed Assistant to the Government Agent of the Northern Province and Assistant Collector and Landing Surveyor at Jaffna. In 1901 he took up a similar appointment at Trincomalee, and in

W. CARBERY.

1904 became Acting Police Magistrate and Commissioner of Requests for Hatton-Nuwara Eliya, and holds that position at the present time.

ITINERATING MAGISTRATES.

PETER DE SARAM.

A sketch of the life of Mr. Peter de Saram, Itinerating Magistrate of the Western Province, will be found elsewhere.

W. N. S. ASERAPPA.

A sketch of the life of Mr. W. N. S. Aserappa, Police Magistrate of Negombo, appears elsewhere.

F. W. DE SILVA.

Mr. F. W. de Silva is at present an Acting Magistrate in the Western Province.

LAW OFFICERS OF THE CROWN.

ATTORNEY-GENERAL.

The sketch of the career of the Hon. Mr. **A. G. Lascelles,** Attorney-General, appears elsewhere.

SOLICITOR-GENERAL.

WALTER PEREIRA, K.C.

James Cecil Walter Pereira, born forty-nine years ago, is the second son of the late John Pereira, who was a Master in Queen's (now Royal) College, Colombo. His father belonged to a Sinhalese family which at one time owned nearly the whole of that part of the town of Colombo known as Kollupitiya. On his mother's side Mr. Walter Pereira comes of an old Dutch family, De Haan by name, which had settled at Point de Galle, and several members of which attained positions of great eminence at Batavia. He was educated at

J. C. W. PEREIRA, K.C.
(Solicitor-General.)

the Colombo Academy and at St. Thomas's College, and matriculated at the Calcutta University. In 1878 he was admitted as a Proctor of the District Court of Colombo, having served an apprenticeship under the Hon. Mr. F. C. Loos, one of the most methodical and successful solicitors in Ceylon, and in 1880 he was enrolled a Proctor of the Supreme Court of Ceylon. Having practised as a proctor and notary, at the end of 1885 he proceeded to England and gained admission at the Middle Temple for preparation for the English Bar. Early in 1887 he was called to the English Bar, having successfully claimed a concession as to time from the Benchers of his Inn which only English solicitors then enjoyed. On his return to Ceylon the same year he was admitted and enrolled an Advocate of the Supreme Court, but not without some opposition by the then Chief Justice of Ceylon, Sir Bruce Burnside. The Chief Justice held that Mr. Pereira could not be admitted as an Advocate, inasmuch as he had omitted to sign the Roll of Barristers at the High Court in England. The matter was mentioned by Sir (then Mr.) Henn Collins, Q.C. (now Master of the Rolls), before Lord Coleridge and Mr. Justice Denman in the Queen's Bench Division of the High Court, and their lordships overruled the decision of Sir Bruce Burnside, holding that the signing of the Roll was an obsolete and unnecessary formality. Mr. Walter Pereira soon established a sound position for himself among the best of his profession in Ceylon, and received the coveted distinction of King's Counsel in 1904. In 1901 he was admitted and enrolled an Advocate of the High Court of Judicature at Madras, and he has been for many years a member of the Ceylon Incorporated Council of Legal Education. Mr. Pereira is the author of, among other works, two volumes, covering nearly two thousand pages, on the laws of Ceylon. As at the Bar, so in official life, Mr. Pereira rose from the lowest rung of the ladder. He has acted as Commissioner of Requests and Police Magistrate, Colombo, Crown Counsel, also as Additional District Judge, Colombo. He acted three times as Solicitor-General, twice on the Supreme Court Bench as Commissioner of Assize, and twice again as a Puisne Justice of the Supreme Court, and quite recently he accepted permanent office under the Crown as Solicitor-General. He was a member of the Municipal Council of Colombo for many years. He was a prominent member of the Ceylon National Association, and had a leading hand in the organisation of the only Ceylonese social club in Ceylon—the Orient Club. In 1895 he married Helena Blanche, daughter of the late Mr. Edward McCarthy, at one time a planter in the Kelani Valley district, and whose wife was the daughter of Captain William Woodward, of Brixton, Devon. The issue of this marriage consists of one son and two daughters. Mr. Pereira's private residence is "Leafields," Barnes Place, Cinnamon Gardens, Colombo.

The accompanying illustration is from a photograph taken when Mr. Pereira was a Puisne Justice of the Supreme Court.

ASSISTANT-ATTORNEY-GENERAL.

CHARLES MATTHEW FERNANDO.

A sketch of the life of Mr. C. M. Fernando will be found elsewhere.

C. M. FERNANDO.
(Crown Counsel for the Island.)

DEPUTY FISCAL, WESTERN PROVINCE.

Mr. Ebenezer Francis Ondatje was born on December 26, 1853. He was appointed a cadet in 1898, and in the same year became Acting Deputy Fiscal, Colombo. In 1899 he was Acting Colonial Storekeeper, and in 1900 Acting Office Assistant to the Government Agent, Western Province. He was also appointed Deputy Fiscal in 1900, a position he still holds.

ADMINISTRATIVE ESTABLISHMENTS.

THE SECRETARIAT.

The Secretariat is a block of buildings adjoining the Legislative Council Chamber, and near to Queen's House, in the Fort, and comprises the chief Government offices. Here the Colonial Secretary, Auditor-General, Treasurer, &c., have their offices. It is the great office of record in the island, where are lodged the documents, or the substance of the documents, connected with every branch of the service; and it is to this office that all applications or references regarding his situation are made by every Government officer. From here also all the regulations and orders of the Government are in the first instance issued. The office is divided into the following departments: The Despatch, Councils, Correspondence and Deeds Branches, the Record Room, Library, and Petition Office. Here also those printing or publishing newspapers are required to file the declaration and deliver copies.

THE HON. MR. G. M. FOWLER.

The sketch of the career of the Acting Colonial Secretary appears under the heading Legislative Council.

CHARLES RUSSELL CUMBERLAND.

Mr. Charles Russell Cumberland is the Principal Assistant to the Colonia Secretary. He was born on August 12, 1866, and is a B.A. of Oxon. He entered the Ceylon Civil Service as cadet in 1889, and was attached to the Ratnapura Kachcheri. In 1891 he was transferred to the Colombo Kachcheri, and later to the Secretariat. He became Acting Police Magistrate at Panadure, and Additional Police Magistrate, Kalutara, in 1892, and in 1893 was Acting Fiscal, Central Province. In 1896 he was Acting Assistant Government Agent at Chilaw and in 1899 District Judge, Kegalla. He was on special duty at the camp of the Boer prisoners-of-war at Diyatalawa in 1900, and in 1902 he became Second Assistant Colonial Secretary. In 1903 he was Acting Principal Assistant Colonial Secretary and Joint Secretary to the Loan Board, and later was given the position of Second Assistant Colonial Secretary. Later in the year he acted as Assistant Government Agent, Matale, and on returning from leave in 1905 was appointed District Judge, Kalutara. He was subsequently appointed to his present post.

ARTHUR GARDNER CLAYTON.

Mr. A. G. Clayton, the Additional Assistant Colonial Secretary, was born on September 24, 1864. Previous to coming to Ceylon he was attached to the Colonial Secretary's Office, Jamaica (1886); was Chief Clerk, Colonial Secretary's Office, British Honduras, 1892; Clerk of Council, 1898; and Private Secretary to the Governor, British Honduras, 1897–98. He came out to Ceylon to the Colonial Secretary's Office in 1899.

FRANCIS JAGOE SMITH.

Mr. F. J. Smith is the Second Assistant Colonial Secretary. He was born on September 9, 1873, and is an M.A. of Oxon. He came to Ceylon as a cadet in 1896, and passed through several offices. He was appointed to the position he now holds on return from leave in 1905.

RICHARD GERALD ANTHONISZ.

Mr. R. G. Anthonisz, the Government Archivist and Librarian, was born on October 22, 1852. He held numerous appointments in the Education Department and Registrar-General's Department previous to being appointed Assistant Registrar-General in 1892. He was given his present post in 1902.

GOVERNMENT PRINTING OFFICE.

The Government Printing Office is attached to the Secretariat, and is under the charge of a Government Printer and three Assistant Government Printers. It was established in 1849, and during the subsequent years its progress has been rapid. As the colony developed and increased in importance the calls upon the Printing Office grew in proportion. The number of its employees, its expenditure, its plant, and its output of work have all been increased, and other branches of work have been added. From time to time new machines of the latest pattern have been introduced, with the result that the office is now equipped on thoroughly modern lines.

HENRY CHARLES COTTLE.

Mr. H. C. Cottle, the Government Printer, was born on November 2, 1857. He came to Ceylon in 1885 as Second Assistant to the then Government Printer, and two years later acted as Assistant Government Printer. In 1888 he was permanently appointed Assistant Government Printer, and two years later acted as Government Printer. In 1904 he acted as Controller of Government Stores. He was appointed Government Printer in 1906.

HORACE MARTIN RICHARDS.

Mr. Horace Martin Richards, the Assistant Government Printer of Ceylon, was born in 1866 at Falmouth, Cornwall, and is the son of the late Mr. R. C. Richards, for several years Mayor of that town. In 1892 he came to

H. M. RICHARDS.

Ceylon, and received his first appointment in the Government Printing Department, entering the office as Third Assistant. From this position he was promoted to Second Assistant in 1895, and to his present position of First Assistant in 1906. At the Ceylon Rubber Exhibition held at Peradeniya, Kandy, in September, 1906, Mr. Richards was awarded a gold medal for printing. At the time of writing Mr. Richards is acting as Government Printer in succession to the late Mr. George J. A. Skeen.

JOHN LAMBERT.

Mr. John Lambert, the third Assistant Government Printer, is the son of Mr. J. W. Lambert, printer and publisher, Settle, Yorkshire, England, and was born in July, 1880, in Settle. Before coming out to Ceylon he was engaged in business with his father. On November 6, 1903, Mr. Lambert was appointed superintendent of the Binding

J. LAMBERT.

Department by the Secretary of State for the Colonies. On July 10, 1906, he was promoted to the position he now holds.

THE AUDIT OFFICE.

The Auditor-General, Accountant-General, and Controller of Revenue has charge of this Department, the offices of which are situated at the Secretariat. The Auditor-General is the chief financial adviser of the Government, is *ex officio* a member of the Executive and Legislative Councils, one of the Currency Commissioners, and a Justice of the Peace for the island. His appointment ranks in Class I. of the Civil Service, and is next to that of the Colonial Secretary. His assistant also combines a number of other duties with those connected with his own particular department.

THE HON. MR. H. W. BRODHURST, C.M.G.

A sketch of the career of the Hon. Mr. H. W. Brodhurst appears under the heading Legislative Council.

EDWARD DE KRETSER, I.S.O.

Mr. E. de Kretser, the Assistant Auditor-General, was born on July 9, 1869. He never served as a cadet, being employed in the Colonial Secretary's Office from May 8, 1872, until he received the appointment he at present holds in 1901.

THE GENERAL TREASURY.

Next in rank in the Civil Service to the Auditor-General is the Treasurer, whose offices are situated at the Secretariat. This gentleman is *ex officio* a Member of the Executive and Legislative Councils, whilst he also holds the offices of Commissioner of Stamps and Treasurer of the Loan Board, is one of the Commissioners of Currency, and a Registrar of Ceylon 4 per Cent. Inscribed Stock. In his office are kept the cash book, waste book, check book of receipts, ledger, and daily balance book. He is responsible for the correctness of the Treasury books of account, and he must see that they are kept up to date and in accordance with the regulations. He takes charge of all public money accruing from the colonial revenues, or otherwise paid into the Treasury, and he must keep all accounts under their proper heads. Other invested funds are also taken charge of by him.

GOVERNMENT TREASURER.
THE HON. MR. H. C. NICOLLE.

A sketch of the career of this gentleman appears under the heading Legislative Council.

HARRY ALEXANDER MARTIN.

Mr. H. A. Martin, Financial Assistant and Accountant to the General Treasury, is the

H. A. MARTIN.

eldest son of the late Henry D. Martin, late Harbour-master of Grenada, British West Indies. He was born in the British West Indies on August 18, 1867, and received his education there. Upon leaving school he joined a mercantile firm. In 1886 he entered the Audit Department of the Government Service, Grenada, the largest of the Windward Islands and seat of the Government. In 1892 he acted for a short time as Accountant to the Treasury, St. Lucia. In 1889 he was appointed as Treasury Accountant, Grenada, British West Indies. In 1897 he was transferred to Ceylon in connection with the re-organisation of the accounts of the Public Works Department. In 1905 he received his present appointment, and during January, 1906, introduced the double-entry system of accounts in the book-keeping branches of the General Treasury. Mr. Martin is a keen cricketer, and has played much both in West India and in Ceylon.

THE GOVERNMENT AGENTS.

The island, for administrative purposes, is divided into provinces, and each province has its Government Agent. The name conveys immediately what the office is. The Government Agent is the agent of the Government, and his general duties consist of making circuits of the provinces, attending to representations and complaints of the people, and through personal communication with the headmen to acquire a knowledge of the personal character and capabilities of each. The Government Agents are the successors of the Collectors or Agents of Government in the maritime provinces and of the Revenue Commissioners of the Board of Commissioners for the Kandyan provinces, and they have vested in and imposed upon them all the powers and the duties of the latter. The Government Agents have assistants, and both classes of officers are required to submit monthly diaries to the Governor. Of recent years conferences of Agents have been held at Queen's House, Colombo, in August, the Governor presiding.

THE HON. MR. C. T. D. VIGORS.

The sketch of this gentleman appears under the heading Legislative Council.

JAMES CONROY.

Mr. James Conroy, Assistant Government Agent of the Western Province, stationed at

Kalutara, was born on August 8, 1875, and took his B.A. degree at the Royal University of Ireland. He entered the Ceylon Civil Service as cadet, attached to the Kandy Kachcheri, in November, 1899, and worked successively at Kandy, Jaffna, and Kurunegala. In 1902 he became Police Magistrate at the last-named place, and two years later Acting District Judge of Badulla. In 1905 he held the appointments of Acting Assistant Government Agent at Hambantota and Office Assistant at Galle, and his tenure of his present office dates from 1906.

CENTRAL PROVINCE.

THE HON. MR. J. P. LEWIS.

A sketch of the Hon. Mr. Lewis's career appears under the heading Legislative Council.

RICHARD ARTHUR GRINDALL FESTING.

Mr. R. A. G. Festing is the son of Major-General Festing, C.B., F.R.S. He was born in London in 1875, and was educated at Clifton and Queen's College, Oxford, taking his B.A. degree in 1898. He read for the Civil Service at Wren's, and being appointed to Ceylon in November, 1899, he was attached to the Kachcheri at Galle, moving later to the Kandy Kachcheri as Office Assistant. Since February, 1906, he has been Acting Assistant Government Agent at Nuwara Eliya, Assistant Government Agent and District Judge at Mullaitivu, and Assistant Government Agent at Matale, and a Justice of the Peace. The Assistant Government Agent's residence is the Park, Matale.

R. A. G. FESTING.

FRANK BARTLETT.

Mr. Frank Bartlett, B.A. Oxon., the Assistant Government Agent, Nuwara Eliya, was born on January 27, 1872, at Pershore, Worcestershire, being a son of the Rev. Robert E. Bartlett, who was for twelve years Fellow of Trinity College, Oxford. Mr. Bartlett came out as a cadet in December, 1895, and passing rapidly through various Civil Service appointments, he eventually became Assistant Government Agent at Nuwara Eliya in 1905. He is extremely fond of shooting, fishing, and music, and is a member of the Ceylon Fishing Club, a member of the Hill Club, and country member of the Colombo Club.

NORTHERN PROVINCE.

FERDINANDO HAMLYN PRICE.

Mr. F. H. Price, the Government Agent, Northern Province, was born on May 25, 1855, and entered the Government Service at the Colombo Kachcheri in 1878. During the first year he passed through various offices, and in 1879 was attached to the Police Court at Ratnapura. The following year he performed the duties of Police Magistrate at Point Pedro and Chavakachcheri, and later became Acting Assistant Collector of Customs, Trincomalee. After serving in these positions, he officiated as Acting Assistant Government Agent, Nuwara Eliya; Private Secretary to the Lieut.-Governor; Commissioner of Requests and Police Magistrate, Kalpitiya; Acting Assistant to the Treasurer; Acting Chairman, Municipal Council, Colombo, and Mayor of Colombo. He also held many other appointments. In 1900 he was on special service as Assistant Government Agent, Western Province, and in 1901 was appointed Government Agent of the Province of Uva. In 1905 he became Assistant Government Agent, Trincomalee, and subsequently was given his present appointment.

JOHN SCOTT.

Mr. J. Scott, the Assistant Government Agent, Northern Province, Mannar, was born on April 24, 1878, and is a B.A. (Cantab.). He has been in the Ceylon Civil Service since 1901, his first service being at the Kandy Kachcheri. In 1902 he was Extra Assistant at Nuwara Eliya to the Government Agent, Central Province, and later Acting Office Assistant at Kandy to the same official. Afterwards he was transferred to the Colonial Secretary's Office; was Acting Office Assistant to the Government Agent, Jaffna; Acting Police Magistrate, Jaffna; Extra Assistant to the Government Agent at Mannar; and Acting Assistant Government Agent at the same place. He served in the latter capacity until he was appointed to his present position.

CHARLES VALENTINE BRAYNE.

Mr. C. V. Brayne, B.A. Cantab., the Assistant Government Agent, Northern Province, Mullaitivu, was born on August 17, 1877, and entered the Ceylon Civil Service in 1901, at the Jaffna Kachcheri. In 1903 he was transferred to the Mannar Kachcheri, and later was appointed Acting Office Assistant at Anuradhapura to the Government Agent, North Central Province. In 1905 he was Assistant Collector of Customs, Trincomalee; and in 1906 he became Acting Assistant Government Agent, Mullaitivu.

SOUTHERN PROVINCE.

CHARLES MORANT LUSHINGTON.

Mr. C. M. Lushington, the Government Agent and Fiscal for the Southern Province, was born on December 26, 1854, and entered the Ceylon Civil Service in 1876. He was first attached to the Colonial Secretary's Office; then he was transferred to the Police Court, Colombo, and later acted for the Police Magistrate of Balapitimodara. In 1878 he became Acting Office Assistant to the North-Western Province Government Agent, and five years later was appointed Police Magistrate of Jaffna. He acted as Assistant Government Agent, Puttalam, in 1884, and as District Judge at the same place in 1888. In March, 1889, he was District Judge, Kegalla, and in July District Judge, Ratnapura, afterwards going on leave. On returning he acted as Assistant Government Agent, &c., Negombo. In 1890 he became Police Magistrate (Acting), Colombo; in 1892 he was Acting Assistant Government Agent at Nuwara Eliya and Hambantota respectively, and in 1893 officiated as Acting District Judge, Batticaloa. In 1894 he received the appointment of Acting Assistant Government Agent at Matara and Nuwara Eliya respectively, and in 1896 was transferred to Trincomalee as acting Assistant Government Agent. He was promoted in 1903 to Acting Government Agent, Eastern Province, in addition to his other duties; and in 1905 became Acting Government Agent, Province of Uva, and subsequently was given the post he now fills.

J. O'K. MURTY.

The sketch of the career of this gentleman appears elsewhere.

GEOFFREY MONTAGUE COOKSON.

Mr. G. M. Cookson, B.A. Oxon., the Assistant Government Agent, Matara, was born on November 14, 1867. He entered the Secretariat in 1891, and in 1892 acted as Assistant Collector of Customs, Trincomalee. He filled various appointments subsequently, such as Office Assistant to the Government Agents, Police Magistrates, Assistant Collector of Customs, Acting Government Agent, Superintendent of Police, Colombo, Police Magistrate, &c. He was appointed to his present position in 1904.

EASTERN PROVINCE.

EDWARD FRANCIS HOPKINS.

Mr. E. F. Hopkins, B.A. Dublin, the Government Agent, Fiscal, and Collector of Customs for the Eastern Province, was born on June 17, 1851. His first appointment in the Ceylon Civil Service was at the Colonial Secretary's Office in 1874, and after passing through other offices he was in 1877 made Police Magistrate of Matara and later of Avisawella. In 1883 he was Acting Office Assistant to the Government Agent, Southern Province, and in 1883 and 1884 officiated as District Judge at Kegalla and Badulla. In 1890 he was Acting Commissioner of Requests and Police Magistrate, Kandy, and the following year was appointed Assistant Government Agent, &c., Vavuniya and Mullaitivu. Returning from leave in 1892, he acted as Commissioner of Requests at Colombo, and subsequently held the position of District Judge of various districts, and in 1903 was Registrar-General. In 1904 he was appointed Acting Government Agent, Eastern Province, and subsequently the appointment was confirmed.

CHARLES STEWART VAUGHAN.

Mr. C. S. Vaughan, B.A. Cantab., the Assistant Government Agent for the Eastern Province, Trincomalee, was born on May 23, 1866. He joined the Ceylon Government Service in 1889, and since then has held various appointments in the Civil Service. He has been Acting Assistant to the Government Agents, Assistant Government Agent, Assistant Collector of Customs, District Judge, &c.

NORTH-WESTERN PROVINCE.

HERBERT RAYNER FREEMAN.

Mr. H. R. Freeman, Government Agent for the North-Western Province, was born on March 6, 1864. He came out to the Secretariat in 1885, and subsequently passed through several offices. After acting as Police Magistrate, Matara; Office Assistant to the Government Agent for Southern Province at Galle; Assistant Collector of Customs, Commissioner of Requests, and Police Magistrate, Kandy; Landing Surveyor (Customs), Colombo, &c., he was appointed, in 1902, to the position of Assistant Government Agent and District Judge, Chilaw, and the following year as Assistant Government Agent, Puttalam. Subsequently he obtained the appointment he holds at the present time.

ROBERT NIEMANN THAINE.

Mr. R. N. Thaine, B.A. Cantab., the Assistant Government Agent for the North-Western Province, Puttalam, was born on January 1, 1875. He entered the Ceylon Civil Service, at the Galle Kachcheri, in 1898. He has filled numerous Government positions, such as Acting Commissioner of Requests, Acting District Judge, Acting Police Magistrate, Landing Surveyor (Customs), Colombo, &c.

R. G. SAUNDERS.

The sketch of the career of Mr. R. G. Saunders, Assistant Government Agent, North-Western Province, appears under the heading District Judges.

NORTH CENTRAL PROVINCE.

GEORGE SHADWELL SAXTON.

Mr. G. S. Saxton, Government Agent at Anuradhapura for the North Central Province, was born on April 3, 1858. He entered the Colombo Kachcheri in 1879, and during the same year was employed at the Secretariat and in the Galle and Kandy Kachcheris. Subsequently he became Acting Police Magistrate, Police Magistrate, Acting Assistant to Government Agents, Assistant Government Agent, Acting Government Agent, &c., until, in 1902, he was appointed Government Agent for the Province of Sabaragamuwa. At a subsequent date he was transferred to Anuradhapura as Government Agent for the North Central Province.

PROVINCE OF UVA.

HERBERT WHITE.

Mr. H. White, Government Agent for the Province of Uva, was born on August 25, 1857, and was appointed by the Secretary of State to the Kandy Kachcheri in 1879. He filled various positions in different Kachcheris, was Acting Police Magistrate, Acting Office Assistant to Government Agents, Acting Commissioner of Requests, Police Magistrate, Acting District Judge, District Judge, and Acting Government Agent at different times up to 1896. In that year he become Second Assistant Colonial Secretary. He was also subsequently Acting Secretary to the Central Irrigation Board. In 1899 he was appointed Principal Assistant Colonial Secretary and Acting Secretary to both the Loan Board and the Central Irrigation Board. He held the office of Chairman of Municipal Council, Colombo, and Mayor of that town in 1900, and in 1903 and 1904 was Registrar-General. In 1905 he was on half-pay leave, and afterwards received his present appointment.

PROVINCE OF SABARAGAMUWA.

ROBERT BAILEY HELLINGS.

Mr. R. B. Hellings, the Government Agent at Ratnapura for the Province of Sabaragamuwa, was born on April 16, 1853, and entered the Ceylon Civil Service in 1885, being first attached to the Secretariat. Later he was transferred to the Treasury and afterwards to the Ratnapura Kachcheri. In 1888 he was Assistant Collector of Customs, &c., Trincomalee, and in 1889 officiated as Acting Assistant Government Agent at the same place. From Trincomalee he was transferred to Anuradhapura as Acting Office Assistant to the Government Agent. He was subsequently Acting District Judge, Acting Police Magistrate, District Judge, Commissioner of Requests, Colombo, and Assistant Government Agent, Matale. He was appointed Government Agent of the Province of Sabaragamuwa in 1906.

MALCOLM STEVENSON.

Mr. Malcolm Stevenson, the Assistant Government Agent at Kegalle, is the son of the late Mr. Alexander Stevenson. He was born on March 25, 1878, at Lisburn, and is a graduate of Trinity College, Dublin. He was appointed to the Ceylon Civil Service on November 22, 1901, and on arrival in Ceylon on December 23rd of the same year was attached to the Colombo Kachcheri. On March 18, 1902, he was appointed acting office assistant to the Government Agent, Ratnapura. On May 1, 1904, he was appointed office assistant to the Government Agent, Badulla. On January 1, 1905, he was admitted to the fourth class of the Civil Service, and on February 18, 1906, he served as Additional Assistant to the Government Agent, Northern Province, and Additional District Judge, Mannar, in connection with the pearl fishery. On the termination of the pearl fishery he was appointed Assistant Government Agent, Kegalla. Mr. Stevenson is a member of the Royal Asiatic Society of Great Britain and Ireland. His recreations are tennis and hockey.

THE CUSTOMS DEPARTMENT.

The Ceylon Customs Department differs from that of many other colonies in that it deals solely with sea Customs and has no control over the Excise or the collection of other internal revenues. The department is presided over by the Principal Collector of Customs, who also acts as Superintendent of Wrecks and Registrar of Shipping and Seamen. In 1853 the Customs was transferred to the Local Government.

THE HON. MR. L. W. BOOTH.

The Hon. Mr. L. W. Booth is acting as Principal Collector of Customs, and a sketch of his career is to be found under the Legislative Council section, of which Council he is a member *ex officio*.

WILLIAM EDWARD THORPE.

This gentleman, the Deputy Collector of

W. E. THORPE.

Customs in Ceylon, is an East Anglian by birth, his parents on both sides being natives of Norfolk. He is the son of the Rev. E. S. Thorpe, Vicar of Goring, Sussex, and was born on February 15, 1869. He was educated at St. Edmund's School, Canterbury, and at Cassel, Germany. After his school career he joined a London insurance office, and resigned his appointment in that concern after two years' service. In 1891 he entered the Ceylon Civil Service, being attached to the office of the Government Agent of the North-Western Province of Ceylon. In 1892 he became the Office Assistant to the Government Agent of the North-Central Province, and was transferred, two years later, in the same capacity, to the Northern Province. Mr. Thorpe next successively held the appointments of Police Magistrate of Matale, Office Assistant to the Government Agent of Sabaragamuwa, and of the Western Province; and in 1897 he was placed in charge of the police of the Western Province, in addition to being entrusted with the duties of Assistant to the Government Agent. In 1899 he was sent to Chilaw as Assistant Government Agent, and in the following year he was appointed District Judge of Matara, in the south of the island. This latter position he held for three years, after which period, in 1903, he went to Colombo to fill the post of Police Magistrate. Mr. Thorpe was promoted to his present position in 1905.

EDWARD BRANDIS DENHAM.

Mr. E. B. Denham, the Landing Surveyor for the Ceylon Government, was born in 1876, and educated at Malvern and at Merton College, Oxford. He came out to Ceylon in 1899, and since that time has held various positions under Government, the principal of these being Private Secretary to the Lieut.-Governor whilst the latter was Acting Governor, Secretary to the Agricultural Board, Acting Second Assistant Colonial Secretary, Secretary of the Rubber Exhibition Committee, &c. He was appointed to the position of Landing Surveyor in July, 1906, and, with Sir John Keen, he attended the coronation of the Sultan of Maldive. He was also seconded for special service with three pearl fisheries.

C. M. LUSHINGTON.

Mr. C. M. Lushington, the Collector, Southern Province, is also Government Agent, and particulars of his career are given under the heading Government Agents.

F. H. PRICE.

Mr. Price, the Northern Province Collector, is also Government Agent, and his career is sketched elsewhere.

E. F. HOPKINS.

Mr. E. F. Hopkins, Collector, Eastern Province, is Government Agent, and a notice of his career appears amongst the Government Agents.

EDUCATIONAL.

In Ceylon higher education is mainly left to local effort, though the Government entirely supports one high school, the Royal College, Colombo. The other high schools are maintained on the grant-in-aid principle. The Education Department is under the control of the Director of Public Instruction, and this official has charge of the Technical College, Colombo. The Government schools are all unsectarian. The cost of education in departmental schools is borne almost entirely by the Government, the cost of the school buildings being the only item of expenditure from which the Central Government is relieved. Teachers in departmental schools receiving salaries of Rs. 250 or over are entitled to pensions, which they may claim after they have passed the fifty-fifth year of their age.

JOHN HARWARD, M.A.

Mr. John Harward, M.A., is the Director of Public Instruction. He is the son of Mr. Arthur Harward, of Worksworth, Derbyshire, and was born in that place in 1858. He was educated at Durham School from 1869 to 1877, and at University College, Oxford, from the latter year until 1881, when he graduated B.A. From 1882 to 1892 he was an Assistant Master at Brighton College, and in the latter year he went out to Ceylon to take up an appointment as Principal of the Royal College, Colombo. He became in 1898 Acting Director of Public Instruction, and was alternately Principal of the Royal College and Acting Director of Public Instruction until 1902, when he combined the office of Acting Director with his own duties. In 1903 he was appointed permanently as Director of Public Instruction.

EDWARD ERNEST DAVIDSON.

The Assistant to the Director of Public Instruction, Mr. E. E. Davidson, is a native of Ceylon, where he was born in the year 1878. His father was Dr. J. W. Davidson, who during his lifetime enjoyed a lengthy practice in the island. Before reaching the age of fourteen years Mr. Davidson had travelled a great deal visiting several countries with his parents. Returning, he was educated at the Royal College, Colombo, and his training completed he entered the service of the Government.

STAFF OF INSTRUCTORS, CEYLON GOVERNMENT TECHNICAL COLLEGE.

For six years—1900 to 1906—he was the Inspector of the Post Office, being then appointed to his present post. Mr. Davidson is an all-round sportsman.

R. B. STRICKLAND.

Mr. R. B. Strickland, an Inspector of Schools and Acting Director of Public Instruction, is the son of the late George Strickland, and was born in Yorkshire on February 3, 1857. He was educated at Reades School in Yorkshire, and at Dublin University, where he took his Master's degree. Returning to Yorkshire, he became an assistant master in the school where he had been a pupil, and later he served in a similar capacity at Kepier's School, Durham, and at Wolverhampton. In 1894 he went to Jamaica as an Inspector of Schools, and was transferred to Ceylon eight years later.

ROYAL COLLEGE.

Mr. **Charles Hartley**, M.A., the Principal of the Royal College, Colombo, was born at Beccles, in Suffolk, in 1865. He was educated first at a private school, and at Fauconberg Grammar School, Beccles. From 1879 to 1883 he was at Marlborough, and from there he went to Magdalen College, Cambridge, and he graduated B.A. there in 1887. Whilst at Cambridge he was captain of his college boat. Upon the completion of his University course he became a schoolmaster, his first appointment being that of Classical Master at Worcester Cathedral School. He was then successively Modern Languages and Classical Master at Christ College, Brecon, and Modern Language Master at Marlborough College. In 1896 he became Lecturer in English and Modern Languages at Royal College, Colombo, and in 1903 succeeded Mr. Harward as Principal of that institution.

GOVERNMENT TRAINING COLLEGE.

Mr. **Edwin Evans**, B.Sc. Lond., is the Principal of the Government Training College, Colombo. He was born on June 27, 1869, and was appointed to his present position in 1902.

EDWIN HUMAN, A.M.I.C.E., A.I.E.E.

Mr. Edwin Human, A.M.I.C.E., A.I.E.E., the Superintendent of the Technical College, Colombo, was born on October 28, 1859, and was trained as an engineer, first at Coalbrookdale Ironworks, Shropshire. Afterwards he served at various works in London, and finally at Yarrow's shipbuilding yard. In 1893 he was appointed by the Government to organise technical education in Ceylon, and to his efforts much of the vast improvement in technical education which has been made within the last decade is due. Mr. Human has devoted a considerable portion of his leisure to volunteering, and retired with the rank of Captain from the Ceylon Light Infantry in 1906. He is a golfer, being Honorary Secretary of the Colombo Golf Club and a member of the Nuwara Eliya Golf Club.

THOMAS COCKERILL.

This gentleman, who holds the important position of Instructor in Electrical Engineering and Telegraphy at the Ceylon Technical College, Colombo, was born at Bolton, Lancashire, in 1863. He was educated at the Church Institute, Bolton, Manchester Technical School, and Owens College, Manchester; and he subsequently served with the Northern Electrical Engineering Company, Bolton. He was Lecturer in Electrical Engineering and Electro-Metallurgy at the Bolton Technical School (under the Bolton Corporation) from 1891 to 1898; and during 1897 and 1898 he filled the same post at the Halifax Technical School, Yorkshire. He was a registered teacher of the City and Guilds of London Institute. He came to Ceylon in 1898 as Instructor in Electrical Engineering and Telegraphy, on appointment by the Secretary of State. Mr. Cockerill is also the Officer Commanding the Technical College Company of the Ceylon Light Infantry. Experimental work and research form his particular hobby, and his qualifications in scientific knowledge are high. He is a silver medallist of the City and Guilds of London for electro-metallurgy; and has obtained first-class honours in electrical engineering and power distribution, besides first-class ordinary for telegraphy and telephony, and several certificates in metallurgy and chemistry from the Science and Art Department, London. In

THOMAS COCKERILL.
(Instructor in Electrical Engineering and Telegraphy, Technical College, Colombo.)

addition to his other official duties, he acted as City Analyst in Colombo, also as gas inspector, from 1900 to 1904, and as electrical adviser to the municipality of Colombo, 1899 to 1903. He is a Fellow of the Chemical Society, London, and an Associate of the Institute of Electrical Engineers, London.

ALFRED BARTLAM.

Mr. Bartlam, who holds the post of Drawing Master at the Technical College, Colombo, is a

ALFRED BARTLAM.
(Drawing Master, Technical College, Colombo.)

certificated Art Master of the Department of Education, London. He was born at Lichfield, Staffordshire, in 1869, and educated at his native town. After pursuing a course of studies at the Royal College of Art, South Kensington, London, he was selected for teaching appointments at the Londonderry School of Science and Art, also under the London and Staffordshire County Councils. To his present responsible position he was appointed by the Colonial Office, London, in May, 1900. Mr. Bartlam holds art and science certificates from the Art and Science Department, London, and technological certificates from the City and Guilds of London Institute, and is a member of the Society of Art Masters. He also holds the post of Hon. Secretary of the Ceylon Society of Arts.

SCHOOL GARDENS.

CHRISTOPHER DRIEBERG, B.A., F.H.A.S.

Mr. C. Drieberg, the Superintendent of the School Gardens, was born on December 17, 1863. He was appointed in 1889 to the position of Superintendent of the School of Agriculture and to his present post in 1902.

ST. THOMAS'S COLLEGE, COLOMBO.

St. Thomas's College, the chief establishment in Ceylon of the Society for the Propagation of the Gospel, founded and endowed by the Right Rev. James Chapman, D.D., first Bishop of Colombo, with the assistance of the above-named society, has been in active operation since March, 1851, with the Bishop of Colombo as its visitor. Beginning with seventy boys, the number has risen to over four hundred, about a hundred of whom are boarders. The Cathedral stands in the College compound, and is used as a College chapel, all boarders attending choral matins and evensong. Attached to the College is an orphan asylum, in which sixteen boys are trained as servants, receiving free board and education. St. Thomas's has always been noted for the loyalty of its old boys, and the College motto, *Esto Perpetua*, is familiar throughout the island. Low-country Sinhalese officials, especially, send their sons as boarders, appreciating the good education given, with particular attention to English, the knowledge of which tongue proves so valuable in this island in the discharge of governmental duties. Many distinguished members of the legal and medical professions are counted among Thomians, including Hon. Mr. Justice Wendt, Judge Grenier, Hon. Mr. Obeyesekere, M.L.C., Judge de Saram, C.M.G., Mr. Walter Pereira, K.C. (Solicitor-General), Don Solomon Dias Bandaranaike, C.M.G. (Maha Mudaliyar), and others hardly less well-known.

By the generosity of old boys and friends, a first-rate laboratory has been recently built and fully equipped, and students are now prepared for the London Matriculation and Intermediate, as well as Cambridge Local, examinations. The athletic side of school life is well provided for, and cricket, football, and tennis are not only popular, but also reach a high level as school games go. The cricket eleven for years past has had many fine players, and has met with great success in inter-collegiate matches. The grounds on which the College stands are spacious and cool, and the site is one of the healthiest in Ceylon, and has undoubtedly contributed much to the maintenance of the long-continued success of St. Thomas's as a boarding establishment. The Visitor of the College is the Right Rev. A. E. Copleston, D.D., in succession to the present Metropolitan of India and Ceylon.

THE LABORATORY, ST. THOMAS'S COLLEGE, COLOMBO.

WESLEY COLLEGE.

This institution is under the management of the Wesleyan Mission in Ceylon, and was opened for the purposes of higher education on March 2, 1874, in the premises still occupied in the Pettah adjoining—and, in fact, with the Girls' High School enveloping—the Pettah Church, the oldest of the Mission's churches in the island, having been built in the year 1815. The first Principal of the College was the Rev. S. R. Wilkin, now engaged in ministerial work in England. Although at first only

WESLEY COLLEGE.

able to receive a few day scholars, the College rapidly increased in numbers, and for the last ten years has had about five hundred scholars annually. With this number the limit of accommodation has been reached, and the erection of larger premises on another site has become necessary. In its educative work the College is subject to the Departmental Code of Government and annual inspection by the Government Inspector. It was, during its earlier history, affiliated with the University of Calcutta, and a respectable number of its students figure honourably in the records of that Alma Mater. When the Cambridge Local Examinations were established in Ceylon, Wesley College was among the earliest educative institutions to send pupils to undergo these tests, and for the past twenty years some of its scholars have not failed to pass both the Senior and the Junior examinations held annually, while Wesley College students have frequently gained places in the Honours Classes or other distinctions. It was not till 1896, however, that the Ceylon Government Scholarship first came to the Wesley College ; but since that date that coveted prize has twice fallen to its pupils, and the Gilchrist Scholarship, one of almost equal value, has been won once by an alumnus of this College.

In the year 1900 a determined effort was initiated to secure a more suitable locality and superior buildings for the College, and gradually a scheme was formulated, and subsequently adopted by the Governing Committee at Home, by which a great advance in the desired direction was made possible. In 1902 a new site within the municipal limits of the city, but in a more open and healthier part, was purchased. Here, during the years 1905 and 1906 a very handsome set of college buildings has been erected, having a frontage of over 300 ft., and with dormitory and other accommodation for a hundred resident pupils. The new premises are expected to be fully ready for occupation in January, 1907. To keep pace with the great advance in science study re-

quired by the affiliation with London University, chemical laboratories are included in the design of the new buildings.

ST. BENEDICT'S INSTITUTE.

ST. JOSEPH'S COLLEGE.

The Catholic Church has always been the watchful and solicitous mother of education; and she can claim to have spread over the world the light, not only of Divine, but also of human knowledge. Schools, colleges, and universities have sprung up under her fostering care wherever she has established herself, and her missionaries have ever recognised that religion and education should go hand in hand. The late Cardinal Manning once said that if he were compelled to choose between churches and schools, he would give up the churches and keep the schools. The views and work of the Church in Ceylon in regard to education are the same as elsewhere, and the work has followed the same lines. While there is no mention made of any Catholic school being in existence in the island in 1846, six years later 31 had been established, and sixteen years later there were 96 Catholic schools, with 4,208 pupils. In 1891 the number of such schools in Ceylon was 368, attended by 24,000 pupils, 9,000 of whom were girls. In 1895 an additional 4,000 Catholic children attended the schools of their own religion; and in 1903, 34,405 pupils, of whom 14,435 were girls, were receiving instruction in 379 Catholic schools.

English is not taught in all these schools, the principle adopted being that knowledge of the European tongue was not advisable where it would have had the effect of making the natives discontented with their condition and causing them to give up agricultural or other pursuits for inferior and precarious positions in the towns. But Catholic English schools have been opened where they were wanted, and where the parents could afford to pay for an education which to their children is of the nature of a luxury, or, at any rate, not an absolute necessity. At the head of these English schools in the diocese of Colombo stands St. Benedict's Institute, Kotahena, Colombo, the largest and most progressive school in the colony, which gives education to more than 1,000 boys, and is conducted by the Christian Brothers—the devoted sons of St. John Baptist de la Salle. Many ex-pupils of this institution are now filling with credit situations under Government and in business houses. For the great majority of Catholic boys requiring an English education, the tuition given at St. Benedict's is sufficient for an ordinary commercial and clerical training.

It was felt and admitted, however, that there existed a class of Catholic pupils, including those who aimed at the learned professions and the higher offices under Government, who were obliged to go further in their studies than the curriculum of St. Benedict's would carry them. For these a classical and scientific education was a necessity. Nobody recognised this want more keenly than the first Archbishop of Colombo, Dr. Bonjean, O.M.I., who had made education the study of his life; and his great talents and experience marked him out as the man to prepare the way for the foundation of the institution destined to supply this requirement. Great as were the difficulties in the way, greater still was his determination and perseverance; and to his persistence in urging the need is due the establishment in Colombo of a Catholic college. On January 6, 1892, after years of strain and suspense and striving in the pursuit of the end upon which he had set his heart, and only six months before his death, he addressed a stirring and pathetic pastoral on the subject to the

ST. JOSEPH'S COLLEGE.
(Roman Catholic.)

Catholics of the archdiocese, in which he fully expounded his views. "We shall be prepared," he said, "to offer to those Catholic youths whom their social position or their natural abilities impel to look forward towards the liberal professions or to the highest Government employments opened to natives (meaning boys born in Ceylon), a course of studies higher than what is now provided for, and which meets the requirements of the large majority of our boys—that is, a course of classical training or a collegiate education." The aged Prelate's earnest, touching, and, indeed, last appeal was liberally answered by the Catholic laity assembled in a public meeting on April 2, 1892, under a special blessing of the Holy See, and Rs. 18,500 were subscribed at its close.

At this time there was for sale at Mutwal a property of twenty-seven acres, known as Uplands. It overlooked the harbour, and was exposed to the bracing air of the open sea. It was at once decided to purchase this land as a site for the new College; and as the amount in hand was not sufficient for the purpose, it was decided to borrow the amount required. A telegram was sent to the Superior-General of the Oblates, with the result that, without any guarantee, he immediately lent 137,000 francs, and Uplands was bought. But shortly after taking possession of the property it was found that the land was required by the Government. However, after protracted negotiations, an arrangement was come to whereby the Government obtained the property, but liberally compensated the promoters of the College. The present more central site was then acquired. The plans of the College building were entrusted to Messrs. Walker, Sons & Co., the well-known contractors of Colombo, and the work of supervising the building operations was entrusted to the Oblate Fathers. The foundation-stone was laid by His Excellency the Delegate Apostolic, Mgr. Zaleski, on December 12, 1894, and the College was opened for classes on March 2, 1896, with a total of 307 pupils in the College and Preparatory School. The building, however, being unfinished, only half of it was thrown open to the students, and for several months the noise of the hammer mingled with the voices of teachers and pupils. The masons and carpenters having completed their work, St. Joseph's College was solemnly blessed by His Excellency Mgr. Zaleski, Delegate Apostolic, on November 27, 1896, and formally opened on the following day by His Excellency the Governor, Sir J. West Ridgeway.

PUPILS AT ANANDA COLLEGE.

The College is conducted by the Oblates of Mary Immaculate, and the first Rector, the Very Rev. Father C. Collin, O.M.I., is still the head of the institution. His staff is composed of priests and laymen, native and European, while lady teachers take the lower classes in the Preparatory School. The course followed in the College prepares students for the Cambridge Local and for the London University Examinations. Under what is called the "Lump-Sum Grant" System, the College first received Government aid in 1903, when that system was established in Ceylon. Speaking of this grant in his Report for 1903, the Rector said humorously: "Let, however, no one be afraid lest this new educational scheme may threaten the finances of the State. The Government has been guilty of no extravagance in this respect. Next month I shall receive from the Treasurer the first 'Lump-Sum Grant' allowed by the Government to St. Joseph's College, and I shall esteem myself fortunate if it pays the salary of one of my English masters for six months."

From the commencement the growth and success of the College were so great that within four years of its inauguration a new wing, almost equal in size to the main building, became necessary and was opened. This addition contains ten class-rooms, two lecture-halls, a library, and ten rooms for the resident Masters. Though St. Joseph's prepares for the public examinations, its proclaimed aim is the higher one of producing, not merely men of culture, but men of virtue, useful citizens, and loyal subjects. The corner-stone of the moral structure which the Rector is building is respect for and obedience to authority; and it is the conduct in after-life of those who have passed through the institution that will make manifest that St. Joseph's College has been true to its motto, *In Scientia et Virtute.*

ANANDA COLLEGE.

The Principal of the Ananda College, Colombo, the chief Buddhist institution in the island, is Don Baron Jayatilaka, B.A., the son of D. Daniel Jayatilaka, landed proprietor, of Kelaniya. He was born at Kelaniya in 1868, and educated first at the village school there and afterwards at Wesley College, Colombo. Whilst there he passed the Cambridge Local Junior and Senior Examinations with distinctions in classics, the entrance examination of the Calcutta University in the first class, and took the degree of B.A. of that University, with honours in English and classics. He also won the Hill Medal and Grenier English Prize in two successive years. Upon the completion of his college course in 1890, he went to Kandy as Principal of the Dharmaraja College, which was then known as the Buddhist High School. He occupied this position until 1898, when he became Vice-Principal of the Ananda College, and his appointment as Principal there dates from 1900.

CITY COLLEGE.

This institution—whose motto is "The truth shall make you free"—was founded by Mr. Samuel Green Lee, M.A., in 1894, and during the past twelve years nearly 1,800 pupils have been admitted. In September, 1894, the institution was recognised by the Calcutta University, and in 1897 it became the Colombo centre of the London College of Preceptors. The students of the City College have been successful in the Matriculation Examination of the University of London in the following subjects: English, Latin, logic, elementary and higher algebra, arithmetic, geometry, trigonometry and conic sections; in the Senior Local Examinations of Cambridge University: in English, Latin, logic, history, arithmetic, physical science, algebra, geography, geometry, trigonometry, conic sections, and religious knowledge; in the Junior Cambridge Local Examinations: in religious knowledge, English, history, geography, Latin, arithmetic, algebra, Euclid, trigonometry, statics, dynamics, heat, physical geography, botany, and freehand drawing. In the Senior Local Examination of 1897 one of the students obtained distinction and second place in English in the island; while in the Junior Cambridge Examination of 1900 one of the students captured the first place in "heat" in all the colonies. In the Preceptors' Examination distinctions were obtained in English, French, algebra, Euclid, arithmetic, geography, and religious knowledge; and students were also successful in other examinations, among them the Government, clerical, legal, and medical preliminary.

The students of this institution are trained to grow up as abstainers from intoxicating drinks and drugs and narcotics, according to the traditions of Oriental civilisation and religions; and in furtherance of this end it is a rule that the teachers of this College shall be abstainers and non-smokers. Wide humanitarian principles are also inculcated; and it may be mentioned in this connection that the officers and students of the College have collected and distributed sums of money to help Armenian orphans and orphans and other sufferers by the Indian famine, besides rendering similar assistance to organisations engaged in rescuing fallen women and reforming ex-convicts. They have also distributed pure literature in English and the Tamil and Sinhalese languages calculated to produce moral and spiritual regeneration in the island. The City College is an interdenominational Christian institution, and all the teachers are Christians.

S. G. LEE, M.A.

Mr. Samuel Green Lee, the founder of the College, is a Tamil gentleman and a descendant of Sri Periya Ponnambla Modaliar, a distinguished Vellala headman (chief) of Vadduk Kodai East, Jaffna, in the north of Ceylon. The late Mr. Thomas James Lee, the father of the founder, became a convert to Christianity while he was a student in the Batticotta Seminary (Jaffna) of the American Board. Consequently he lost caste with his kinsmen and was much persecuted. The son, Mr. S. G. Lee, received his education in the Jaffna College, which took the place of the former Batticotta Seminary in 1872; and he was the first to pass all the public examinations there with honours and distinctions. On graduating, in 1879, he became a member of the Faculty of the Jaffna College, and for nearly eight years subsequently he was resident instructor of that institution in astronomy and higher mathematics, English, logic, and Latin. Mr. S. C. K. Rutnam, M.A., Principal of the Central College, Colombo, Mr. W. S. John, M.A., Headmaster of the Allahabad High School, and several others holding high positions in Ceylon, India, Burma, and the Straits Settlements are among the pupils taught by Mr. Lee in the Jaffna College. He was associated with the late Dr. E. P. Hastings in missionary educational work for nearly twelve years, and Mr. Lee's ideals in educational matters were chiefly moulded by that distinguished educationist, who laboured in the northern part of the island for over fifty years. Under the leadership of Mr. Lee, a mission was organised among the students of the Jaffna College in 1882 for carrying on a Gospel school in the island of Eluvativoe, west of Kayts, Jaffna, which has proved a blessing to the people of that island. In 1887 Mr. Lee accepted the chair of mathematics and logic of Ahmednagar College, Western India, and in that post he performed useful work for three years. In 1890 he was appointed Headmaster of the Indore College, Central India, of the Canadian-Presbyterian Mission, where he was equally successful; and in 1891 he became Senior Mathematical Master of Wesley College, Colombo. Two of his pupils at this last-named seminary—Mr. R. F. Hunter and Mr. E. B. Redlech—subsequently won the University Scholarship tenable in the United Kingdom. When he severed his connection with the Wesley College Mr. Lee opened the City College, which he has carried on at a cost of nearly Rs. 75,000, without aid from Government or any mission. He has also helped nearly two hundred students, mostly Burghers, with free education in the City College. Several of those who received their tuition from Mr. Lee in that institution are now holding high positions in Ceylon, India, Burma, and the Straits Settlements. Mr. Lee visited England in 1903, and spent nearly a year in studying the various educational systems of Great Britain. He also addressed various Churches and societies, and spoke before the East India Association on behalf of the Tamil coolie education movement, which has led to compulsory vernacular education in Ceylon. In 1904 Mr. Lee visited India and Burma and acquainted himself with the educational systems of those countries.

C.M.S. LADIES' COLLEGE.

The Church Missionary Society Ladies College, Union Place, Cinnamon Gardens, is a high school for girls, of which Miss Nixon is the Principal. The College was commenced in 1900, and is under the management of the C.M.S. and not in any way a private school, though it is self-supporting, and does not receive a grant from either the Society or the Government. About 225 students attend the College, which includes, besides the ordinary school, a kindergarten department, a preparatory school for boys, and a teachers' training college. Attached to the school is a boarding establishment for students, which is under the charge of Miss Whitney. The curriculum of the College is that of the English high schools up to the London Matriculation Examination. Other examinations for which the scholars are prepared are the Cambridge Local and the Trinity College (music). The subjects taught include mathematics, English, science, modern languages, Latin, drawing and painting, music, sewing and needlework (speciality, Indian embroidery), and physical exercises, the last-named being taught by Miss Hall, who obtained a certificate for the subject. The teachers' class works for the Government certificate, and last year the only four ladies in the island who obtained this were from this College. Students at the C.M.S. College have three times taken the Government scholarship and have also obtained the Governor's science prize. In other examinations the scholars have proved equally successful, especially in the Cambridge and Trinity College examinations. Miss Nixon, the Principal, and Miss Whitney, Superintendent, were sent out by the C.M.S. to open the College, and they started with two girls. Since then, however, they have enlarged their sphere and built a large schoolroom, and also taken another bungalow for a boys' school, and at no expense to the Society. They have the assistance of Miss Brown, B.Sc., and Miss Hall, B.A., and a staff of sixteen teachers, fully qualified, most of whom were trained at the College. Miss Nixon was born in the North of Ireland and educated at Cheltenham College, and Victoria College, Ireland. At the Royal University, Ireland, she graduated with honours in modern literature. Afterwards she attended Highbury Secondary Training College and the Froebel Institute and Sesame House, London. Miss Whitney, who has charge of the drawing and painting department, was trained at an art school in America, and afterwards had charge of a department in an art school in Montreal.

BISHOPS' COLLEGE.

Bishops' College, Polwatta, is really an offshoot of the St. Margaret's School and Girls' Home—an institution under the charge of the Sisters of St. Margaret's, East Grinstead. The St. Margaret's School is a grant-in-aid institution, but the home is a purely charitable branch. The latter was founded twenty years ago, and the school has been in existence about twelve years. The St. Margaret's School is a middle-class school and Bishops' College a high school. Both places have accommodation for boarders and day scholars, and the latter is considered to be one of the best equipped colleges in the island. Sister Bertha Mary has charge of Bishops' College, and previous to holding this position taught in the St. Agnes' School of the Sisterhood at East Grinstead. The St. Margaret's School is under Sister Matilda, whilst Sister Adelaide is the Principal of the Girls' Home.

THE PRINCE OF WALES'S COLLEGE, MORATUWA.

PRINCE AND PRINCESS OF WALES'S COLLEGES.

These Colleges for Sinhalese boys and girls were founded on September 14, 1876, to commemorate the visit of His Majesty the King, then Prince of Wales, in 1875, by the late Charles Henry de Soysa, J.P. The buildings, covering five acres of ground and beautifully situated on the Lunawa Lake, about a mile from the sea, include a house for the Principal, a college hall, four large schoolrooms, numerous lecture-rooms, a gymnasium, dormitories, and other usual school premises; while the surrounding grounds, ten acres in extent, afford abundant scope for cricket and other games. In 1905 an industrial department was added for the purpose of imparting instruction in carpentry.

Besides having originally given the grounds and buildings and provided the equipment of the College, the De Soysa family still supports the institution, making good any annual deficits in the finances. The first Headmaster was Mr. W. S. Goonewardene, B.A. (Calcutta), who began his term of office with the assistance of about twenty-five male teachers and fifteen female teachers. Two of the present Masters are graduates of Calcutta University, and the other teachers hold local diplomas. From 1892 to 1896 Mr. Philip Lewis acted as Principal, and was succeeded in the latter year by Mr. John George Charles Mendis, M.A. Cam., a native of Moratuwa, born in 1865. Mr. Mendis was educated at St. Thomas's College, and afterwards at St. John's College, Cambridge. The Rev. A. W. de Mel, M.A., holds the post of Lecturer in English, while Mr. O. E. Martinus, B.A., is the general lecturer, and Miss M. C. Walbeoff is the principal lady teacher. The subjects taught in the school are English, classics, mathematics, history and geography, elementary science, senior local and London matriculation subjects, German (by the Principal), book-keeping, drawing, shorthand, and Sinhalese. Elementary education in the vernacular is also included in the syllabus; while physical training and general gymnastics are not neglected. A cadet corps of the College is attached to the cadet battalion of the Ceylon Light Infantry, of which the officer commanding is Captain F. J. Botejue. The College also has its cricket club and football club. Religious instruction is given to all students, except in the case of parental objection.

The boarding establishment has room for 25 boys, and in addition to this number there

H*

are 266 boys learning the Sinhalese language and 444 learning English; while on the girls' side 186 are learning Sinhalese and 149 English, nearly all of whom are Sinhalese. The total number of students is 1,047. The school fees range from one rupee to seven and a half rupees a month. The situation of the College is very healthy; and the institution is inspected by the Department of Public Instruction, being in receipt of an annual grant from the Government. As regards success in after-life obtained by those who have attended the College, it may be mentioned that Dr. W. H. de Silva, now a leading oculist of Ceylon, and visiting surgeon to the Victoria Eye Hospital, was educated here. For the benefit of the poorer classes, fifty scholarships for boys, covering tuition fees, were founded by Lady de Soysa, and are filled by nomination by the Principal. For girls there are three "Elsie Peiris Memorial" scholarships, tenable for three years by any girl entering for higher education These latter were founded by Mr. Charles Peiris, of Colombo.

KINGSWOOD COLLEGE, KANDY.

LOUIS EDMUND BLAZÉ.

Mr. Louis Edmund Blazé was born at Kandy in 1861, and received his education at Trinity College in that town. He adopted a scholastic career, and early in life was appointed Headmaster of the Collegiate School of Trinity College. In 1882 he went to India, where he spent eight years occupying the position of Assistant Master in James's School, Calcutta, and in the Boys' High School at Lahore. In 1884 he graduated B.A. at Calcutta University, and returned to Kandy in 1891. Here he opened a private school, which has since developed into Kingswood College, which the Wesleyan Mission took over in 1894. The College, of which Mr. Blazé is the Principal, has been from 1897 in receipt of yearly Government grants. Mr. Blazé married Miss Alice Maud Avery, daughter of Mr. W. F. Avery, a veteran planter, in 1891. He has written several elementary school books, including a history of Ceylon.

L. E. BLAZÉ, B.A.
(Kingswood College, Kandy.)

CENTRAL COLLEGE.

In 1900 a small school for boys was started in Colombo by Mr. S. C. K. Rutnam, M.A., which has steadily grown, until there are now about 180 students on the roll, 35 of whom are boarders. This school is now known as Central College. Mr. Rutnam, the Principal, is assisted in the College work by his brother, Mr. J. C. V. Rutnam, B.A. Calcutta, and ten other masters. The boys are taught up to the Cambridge Senior Local standard; and students of the College have also been successful in all the public examinations held in the island. Seven of the 25 students admitted into the Ceylon Medical College in April, 1906, were from this institution. The College is located at 26, 27, and 28, Smallpass, the central part of the most populous portion of the city; and the chief hindrance to its further development is the present limited accommodation. But the requisite enlargement of the premises at an early date is contemplated. The teaching of the history of the most progressive nations of the world is a special feature of the course of study at this scholastic establishment, and the whole work of the institution centres in the belief that the remedy for all the evils and misfortunes of a country lies in the hands of the people themselves. At more than one prize-giving of the College Mr. Rutnam has pointed out the imperative necessity for Ceylon to have its own University; and in connection with this view a large public meeting was held on January 19, 1906, with the result that the Ceylon University Association was formed, with the object of educating the public and moving the Government in the desired direction. A committee was formed of the prominent University men of Ceylonese birth, and Mr. Rutnam was appointed secretary.

Mr. Samuel Christmas Kanaga Rutnam, the Principal of the College, was born in Velanai, one of the small islands in the north of Ceylon, named by the Dutch "Leyden," on January 20, 1869. He was the third son of Rev. J. S. Christmas, a pastor of the American Mission of Jaffna, the northernmost part of Ceylon. His early education was received in the American Mission Schools of the north, until, at the age of sixteen years, he proceeded to Salem, India, where he passed the Matriculation and F.A. examinations of the Madras University. In 1889 he was successful in winning the District Scholarship for proficiency in English offered by the Madras Christian College, and at this collegiate institution he graduated two years later, having taken logic and philosophy as his optional branches of study. As a student Mr. Rutnam was noted for assiduity in study and a spirit of independence. He next became Headmaster of the London Missionary Society's High School at Belgaum, Bombay; and while filling that post the Royal Opium Commission, under Lord Brassey, came out to India to report on the opium traffic. Giving evidence before this Commission, Mr. Rutnam condemned the traffic as a morally indefensible affair. In consequence, the anti-opium societies in England invited him to proceed to England, and lecture there on the opium question. He accordingly spent about a year (1894–95) lecturing in the leading towns in England, his speeches receiving high commendation from the Press. At the instance of Lady Henry Somerset and Miss Frances Willard, he followed up the crusade in America, lecturing in many of the large cities of the United States. Having decided to undertake a post-graduate course, his predilections for theology and philosophy led him to enter Princeton University. Here he received a theological training, and obtained, in July, 1897, the degree of M.A. in logic and philosophy. While in America he met and married Miss Mary H. Irwin, M.D., a Canadian lady. In the latter part of 1897 Mr. Rutnam returned to Ceylon and engaged in evangelistic and teaching work, in which he

S. C. K. RUTNAM, M.A.

continued until he started his school—now the Central College—in Colombo, as above related.

MUSAEUS SCHOOL.

This Buddhist boarding school for girls, situated in Rosmead Place, Cinnamon Gardens, was founded by Mrs. Mary Musaeus Higgins in February, 1894. The school now consists of two two-storied buildings and several one-storied buildings, with accommodation for from seventy to eighty boarding pupils and also day pupils. It is the only school of its kind in the island of Ceylon. English, Sinhalese, and Anglo-vernacular arc taught, also needlework and housework, including cooking. In the Upper School the pupils are prepared either for the Cambridge Local Examinations (Junior and Senior), or for the Sinhalese or English Training Schools for Teachers.

ST. MARY'S BOYS' ENGLISH SCHOOL (R.C.).

This school, for the instruction of native boys of poor parents, was established by the Roman Catholic Mission in 1871, in Maliban Street, one of the thoroughfares of the native portion of Colombo, known as the Pettah. The majority of the pupils are free scholars. The school receives a grant from the Government and is annually inspected by a Government inspector. It has eight standards, in addition to an alphabet class, and the curriculum consists of religious instruction, reading, writing, arithmetic, essay writing, narrative composition, dictation, algebra, and book-keeping. The school is recognised to be doing a great amount of good among the classes of children for whose benefit it exists; for were it not for this establishment many boys now receiving useful instruction would be vagrants, and would, as their years increased, become menaces to society. There are three teachers, with an average attendance of ninety pupils, and the school is in charge of a certificated headmaster. Although the institution is conducted by the Roman Catholic Mission, it admits pupils of any religious denomination, and those who are not Roman Catholics are not compelled to be present when religious instruction is given.

THE ANAGĀRIKA (HEWAVITARNE) DHARMAPÀLA.

The Anagārika Dharmapàla, the eldest son of the late Mudaliyar Hewavitarne Don Carolis, was born at Colombo on September 17, 1864. His father was one of the best known men of his day in the Sinhalese community, a great philanthropist, and head of the well-known firm of H. Don Carolis & Sons, of Colombo. His grandfather, the late Mr. Dharmagunawardena, Mohandiram, founded the Vidyodaya Oriental College at Maligakande, Colombo, which is still flourishing under the presidency of the High Priest Sumangala, and is the most interesting of Buddhist educational institutions in the island. At six years of age Mr. Dharmapàla was sent to a Roman Catholic school (St. Mary's, Pettah) in his native city, and after a short period of tuition there, was placed at St. Benedict's Institute, Kotahena, Colombo, remaining under Catholic tutelage for four years altogether. It was the general custom in those days for Buddhist parents to send their children to Christian establishments on account of the scarcity of schools of their own faith within convenient distance. Mr. Dharmapàla next attended the Church Missionary Society's school at Kotahena, and remained there for two years, receiving instruction in Biblical subjects day by day. He then successively passed through the Royal and St. Thomas's Colleges in Colombo; and at every theological centre he attended his teachers did their utmost to bring home to him the value of the principles and practices of the Christian faith. But these efforts were in vain. What repelled him in Christianity was the deliberate destruction of innocent animal life by his Christian teachers. To his view Christianity was a religion of torture. After leaving school he apprenticed himself to a notary public of Colombo, and served his articles for some eight months. He subsequently became a clerk in the Department of Public Instruction, and was attached to the Colombo office.

About the time the young man attended St. Thomas's College, Madame Blavatsky and Colonel H. S. Olcott arrived in Ceylon, and started an ethico-religious movement, which has now come to be known universally as the Theosophical Society. Being instinctively a student of religious systems and of a meditative turn of mind, Mr. Dharmapàla's interest was aroused by the doings of this new society, and he read their journals, followed their "occult" tenets, and generally identified himself with the movement. Subsequently, however, and after patient investigation, he found reason to entirely separate himself from this association and repudiate the questionable methods of its founders. His passion for religious inquiry, nevertheless, continued unabated; and, abandoning the Government service in 1886, for which he had qualified by passing the subordinate clerical examination, he decided to devote his life to religion and the welfare of humanity. This step involved his resignation of all his interests in his father's business and estate. In September, 1893, at the invitation of the Committee of the "Parliament of Religions," he proceeded to America to attend the meeting of that body then in progress in Chicago, which was convened to discuss and examine

THE ANAGĀRIKA DHARMAPALA.

all the religious systems of the world, and had for its object the search for the highest plane of truth amongst them. At this conference of representatives of almost every known religious persuasion in the world Mr. Dhàrmapàla represented the Southern Church of Buddhism, which flourishes in Ceylon, Burma, Cambodia, and Siam, and is strictly orthodox and original in its character. Mr. Dharmapàla was specially commissioned by the High Priest for this purpose, and his mission was therefore of an official nature. In May, 1891, he started the Maha Bodhi Society, the aim and end of which is the restoration to the Buddhists of the four ancient sacred sites in middle India, the chief of which was in the possession of Hindus; and for the accomplishment of that object Mr. Dharmapàla had to institute a lawsuit against the Hindu High Priest at Buddhagaya, which became a *cause célèbre* in the history of Buddhism in India. Eventually, however, Mr. Dharmapàla was successful, and the ancient site at Buddhagaya, which had been under the control of the Hindu hierarchy for centuries past, was partially restored to the Maha Bodhi Society.

Mr. Dharmapàla has travelled three times round the world in the course of his ministry, and has at all times closely associated himself with every movement and institution that has for its purpose the revival and propagation of the Buddhist faith. He has, in accordance with the tenets of that religion, assumed the distinctive title of the "Anagārika," which means "becoming homeless"—the Buddhist religion enjoining voluntary mendicancy upon those who renounce the pleasures of the world. His headquarters are at Benares, Buddhagaya, and Colombo. He is the General Secretary of the Maha Bodhi Society, and edits both the *English Maha Bodhi Journal* and the *Sinhalese Buddhist*. The Ven. H. Sri Sumangala, High Priest in Ceylon, is the President of the society, members of which are to be found in England, France, Germany, Austria, and America, as well as in all Buddhist countries.

The Anagārika Dharmapāla is the author of the interesting article on "Buddhism Past and Present" which is published in the Ecclesiastical Section of this book.

CONVENT OF THE GOOD SHEPHERD (R.C.).

It was through the intervention of Monseigneur Sillam that four nuns of the Good Shepherd arrived in Colombo to undertake the education of the girls of the country, and also to open an orphanage for homeless children. During the first few years the work went on slowly, as the nuns were labouring under many difficulties. A church was completed in 1876, and in 1881 a spacious schoolroom, built by subscription, was opened. In 1882 the number of nuns amounted to six, while the Sisters of St. Francis Xavier, a community of native nuns, founded in 1869, numbered eight, and 56 pupils were attending the English school, 26 children being accommodated at the Orphanage. The charge of an English school for girls in the Pettah quarter, besides three native schools, was subsequently undertaken by the nuns, and the total number on the attendance registers amounted to 670. In 1887 the inmates of the convent and day-school had still further increased. The subjects taught in the school were as follows: Prayers, catechism, reading, writing, arithmetic, history, grammar, geography, and plain sewing; the more advanced pupils being also instructed in French, botany, drawing, physics, music, embroidery, and mathematics. In 1889 a branch convent of the Good Shepherd was founded at Kandy, which is now in a flourishing state, having a girls' boarding school attached, where education similar to that given in high-class convent schools is imparted. Besides the boarding school, there is also a large English day school, with 280 names on the register. In 1890 some Sisters of St. Francis Xavier were sent to Negombo, a settlement north of Colombo, to take charge of a school there, and during the last few years this institution has developed into a large and prosperous convent. Two Good Shepherd nuns were then sent to take charge of the Negombo establishment, and the novitiate for the Sisters of St. Francis Xavier has been transferred there. These sisters, numbering about sixty, have charge of several native schools in and about Negombo. There is also a branch convent at Kalutara, on the South Coast, with eight sisters in charge.

In 1891 an Industrial School was organised at Kotahena, Colombo, the children being taught dressmaking, pillow-lace making, and various kinds of embroidery and fancy work. In 1894 an Industrial School and Orphanage was added to the Kotahena convent, and other improvements were made there. In 1895 the Rev. Mother died, after spending fifteen years of her life in the Kotahena Convent in the heroic and zealous performance of her duties and most self-sacrificing devotedness. For fourteen years she had charge of the Orphanage, and was also employed in teaching in the English school. The Rev. Mother M. of St. Veronica, recalled from Bangalore, carried on the work of improvement and extended the premises. She also brought out several nuns of the Good Shepherd from Europe, received fresh recruits among the Sisters of St. Francis Xavier, and took charge of another native school. Towards the end of the year 1901 an English school was opened in Dematagoda, an eastern suburb of Colombo, and this is now conducted by one of the Good Shepherd nuns, assisted by four secular teachers—all old pupils of the Kotahena Convent. The pupils here number 153. The next step was to obtain more nuns from Europe, the staff of teachers being insufficient for the increased work. In 1902 a branch convent of the Good Shepherd was opened in Cinnamon Gardens, Colombo. The nuns of this convent also have charge of a girls' day school and boarding school. Some of the pupils of these establishments have obtained passes at the Local Cambridge Examination, while others have gained prizes for practical music, as well as a pass in theory of music. The number of pupils is 70. In 1905 another English school was taken in charge by one of the Good Shepherd nuns, and the number of pupils now attending is 150. During 1905 active measures were taken to procure funds for the erection of a new convent at the Kotahena central establishment, the old one being in a ruinous condition and held to be quite inadequate for the number now inhabiting it.

The number of Good Shepherd nuns now in Colombo is 19, of Tourier Sisters 3, and of Sisters of St. Francis Xavier 36; whilst the boarders, first and second class, number 53, the orphans 130, and the day pupils 394. The number of pupils in all the schools conducted by the Good Shepherd nuns in Colombo is 1,090, and the number of those attending the Sinhalese schools 1,121. Besides those attending school, many girl pupils are taking lessons in music, drawing, painting, and fancy work.

THE CEYLON TEACHERS' UNION.

It was on February 17, 1900, that the Ceylon Teachers' Union made its small beginning. The modest commencement may be taken as a happy augury; for here, as elsewhere, associations started with small beginnings have been more useful and longer lived than those started with a blare of trumpets. There was another element, too, which augured well for the infant institution, namely, the spirit of opposition manifested at its very first meeting. Persecution and opposition have before now proved their usefulness in making organisations of this kind hardy and permanent, and that opposition retained for the Union men whose hearts were in the cause it was formed to promote, for it bound the members together in closer union and more energetic effort. The constitution of the Union was framed on the models supplied by the National Union of Teachers and Teachers' Guild—societies of acknowledged and far-reaching power in England. But the Teachers' Union of Ceylon differs widely from those two bodies in one important particular: it is acknowledgedly aggressive. It seeks the well-being of its members and the raising of the status of the teaching profession —though not by fighting the Government or the managing bodies. It is not antagonistic in its aims to either the Department of Public Instruction or the Ceylon Educational Association, but works its way into prominence and seeks to attain its ends by fair-minded methods.

The view taken by the promoters of the Union is that members of the teaching profession in Ceylon are lacking in *esprit de corps* amongst themselves. Their ranks are torn by petty jealousies. The hard experience which falls to the lot of schoolmasters has had the effect of drying up the fountain of sympathy in their hearts. They are a class isolated, desirous of living alone, content to brood over misfortune rather than make the slightest attempt to repair it; careless and indifferent to the lot of their fellow teachers. To draw them closely together, therefore; to advance the cause of education by means of periodical meetings for the consideration of questions relating to educational aims and methods; to maintain a standard of efficiency —these are, briefly, some of the more important objects which the Ceylon Teachers' Union sets itself to accomplish. And proof that it has not failed in its purpose is afforded by the large measure of success it has met with since its establishment six years ago, as well as by the fact that it has been recognised by the educational authorities, and has come to be regarded as an institution worthy of support and encouragement. Among those whose support it has received in the past may be mentioned the present Metropolitan of India and Ceylon, Dr. Copleston; Mr. S. M. Burrows, Government Agent; Mr. J. Harward, Director of Public Instruction; Mr. R. B. Strickland, Chief Inspector of Schools; Dr. Albert Chalmers, of the Ceylon Medical School; Miss L. E. Nixon, B.A., of the C.M.S. Ladies' College; Mr. J. G. C. Mendis, M.A., of Prince of Wales's College; the Rev. Highfield, M.A., of the Wesley College; Mr. C. P. Dias, M.M.C., of the Wesley College; Mr. D. B. Jayatilleke, B.A., of the Ananda College; Miss M. F. Ledger, of Pettah Girls' High School; Miss M. Choate, of the Colpetty Girls' High School; and the Rev. A. H. Smith, of St. Thomas's College.

The membership of the Union is limited to teachers who are graduates of any British or Indian University, or have passed the first examination in Arts of any Indian University, or the Matriculation of the London University, or the Cambridge Senior Local, or hold teachers' certificates from the Ceylon Government, or have been employed in a Government grant-in-aid school for a period of not less than five years. The officers of the Union are a President, a Vice-President, a Secretary, and a Treasurer; and these, with twelve other members, form the Standing Committee.

It is felt that, in Ceylon at least, the teaching profession, which ought to rank among the learned professions, and should entitle those who practise it to the same respect as is accorded to ministers of religion, lawyers, or doctors, is, as a profession, almost non-existent. There are many teachers, but few indeed have adopted tuition as their life work. Teaching is an occupation which is looked upon by most of those engaged in it only as a stepping-stone to something better. Teachers of this sort are not likely to look upon their calling with an adequate sense of responsibility. But there are members in the Union who have devoted a great portion of their life to the teaching profession. The first President of the Union, Mr. C. P. Dias, has acted as Headmaster of one of the leading Ceylon Colleges for over twenty years, while the Secretary, Mr. C. H. Christie-David, to whom the Association owes its origin, has worked on the staff of St. Thomas's College—one of the great public schools of Colombo—for nearly fifteen years, and under no less than four Wardens in succession.

THE SHORTHAND AND TYPE-WRITING INSTITUTE.

With the growing use of the typewriter in Ceylon, and the general preference for typed matter compared with the old-style method of handwriting, a keen demand was created in the local legal and commercial world for a copying establishment where work would be undertaken and executed with all necessary precision and rapidity, and with a saving of time, trouble, and temper to the otherwise embarrassed writer and his helpless, hampered reader. This demand, however, was not supplied by local talent; and it was left to Miss

MISS MUTHUKRISHNA.

Violet Muthukrishna, who, with her sisters and brother, had gone through a course of studies in the twin arts of stenography and typewriting in Madras (India), to start, in October, 1901, the first stenotyping office in the island. The enterprise was purely experimental, and commenced in a modest way at 9, San Sebastian Hill—a central locality for business —Colombo, the whole stock-in-trade consisting of but one typewriter and a few other office requisites. Also, the custom received at first was fitful, and some measure of opposition was experienced; but, with indomitable pluck and perseverance, the business was carried on until by the excellence of the work executed, it secured the patronage and support of the leading private and professional gentlemen in Ceylon, and established for itself a wide reputation, both in the metropolis and in the out-stations of the island. With a degree of push and judicious advertising, the orders obtained were so encouraging that in a short space of time it was felt necessary to move the concern into more spacious premises adjoining. Extra machines were purchased, additional hands employed, and the general scope of operations was enlarged so as to include the undertaking of outdoor stenographic work, reporting engagements, the execution of typewriter repairs, and the supply of machine accessories.

The educational classes in shorthand and typewriting which had been started in connection with the copying business also proved successful beyond all expectations; and a large number of youths and a fair proportion of girls, noting the handsome prospects offered by this line of business, at once light and lucrative, availed themselves of the opportunity for qualifying as shorthand-typists and amanuenses. As an indication of the good work done by the Institute in this direction, it may be mentioned that over a hundred and fifty of its past students have already engaged in professional service in the various local business houses and Government offices. The business steadily expanded and flourished, and at the present time it holds the foremost position of all existing local concerns of this nature in point of equipment and patronage. Amongst its *clientèle* may be found gentlemen of the mercantile and planting communities and the commercial and professional classes, as well as every other section of official and private circles. The managers of the business hold memberships in the Incorporated Phonographic Society of London and the Association of Shorthand-writers and Typists of England, and have obtained first-class certificates from the Government of Madras, in addition to Pitman's qualifications. The status of the Institute as an educational medium, as well as an enterprising and well-conducted business establishment, is recognised; and the high appreciation of the work turned out, testified to by so large and influential a number of its constituents, speaks for the esteem in which the public hold the Shorthand and Typewriting Institute of Ceylon.

Mr. Lawrie Muthukrishna, one of the conductors of the business, typed from the manuscript a large portion of the letterpress of this book, in the form in which it was sent to the printers.

PUBLIC WORKS DEPARTMENT.

The Public Works Department is one of the professional departments, hence those who are appointed to its offices have had a distinctly scientific training, and not merely an ordinary liberal education. Originally, in the days of military administration, the construction of roads and buildings required by the Government was carried out by the Royal Engineers or other military officers, and subsequently by a small civil department which was formed, of which the present department is the offspring. The work of the department is conducted at the head office, Colombo, and at a number of provincial and district offices; and provincial and district engineers supervise work in the latter, the Assistant Director of Public Works superintending that at the head office. A Director of Public Works has charge of the whole. The annual public works include maintenance of roads and inland navigation, repairs and additions to buildings, repairs of bridges, and other miscellaneous works; and the public works extraordinary, new works and buildings, alterations, special repairs and additions to buildings, new roads and bridges, repairs of bridges, lands and buildings to be acquired, and various other works.

DIRECTOR OF PUBLIC WORKS.

THE HON. MR. F. A. COOPER.

The sketch of the Hon. Mr. Cooper's career appears under the heading Legislative Council.

CHARLES ARTHUR LOVEGROVE.

This gentleman, the Assistant Director of Public Works in Ceylon, was born in 1858 in Kent, England, and was educated at the Charterhouse School, Godalming, Surrey. In 1876 he was articled to Mr. William Wilson, civil engineer, Westminster, and followed his profession as a civil engineer in England until he attained his twenty-eighth year, when he received an appointment from the Secretary of State for the Colonies as District Engineer in the Public Works Department, Ceylon. In 1900 he was made Provincial Engineer, and in May, 1902, he was promoted to his present position.

ALFRED LEWIS.

Mr. Alfred Lewis, Financial Assistant and Accountant of the Public Works Department, is a native of Norwich. He was born in March, 1880, and was educated at the Norwich Grammar School. Arriving in Ceylon when he was seventeen years of age, he took up surveying under the auspices of the Survey Department. Subsequently he was employed for about five years as an accountant in the engineering department of Messrs. Walker, Sons & Co., Ltd. Being successful in reorganising and improving the system of engineering accounts, and having a practical general knowledge of surveying and engineering, he was given his present position. It may be mentioned that Mr. Lewis is the brother of Mr.

ALFRED LEWIS.

Frederick Lewis, F.L.S., F.O.S., Assistant Conservator of Forests.

PROVINCIAL ENGINEERS.

BADULLA.

HUGH ARTHUR GROTE GRANT.

Mr. H. A. G. Grant was born on August 21, 1851. He is now the Provincial Engineer in the Province of Uva. He entered the service of the Government in 1876 as superintending officer, and was engaged on the Manu-Oya railway extension survey. The following year he was Superintending Officer at Akuressa and Deniyaya respectively and at Hambantota in 1878. Subsequently he held positions as District Engineer in various districts and was Acting Provincial Engineer. In 1895 he became Provincial Engineer of the Northern Province, in 1898 Provincial Engineer of the Western Province, in 1901 Provincial Engineer of the Southern Province, and in 1904 he was appointed to Badulla, where he is now stationed.

HERBERT FREDERICK TOMALIN, M.I.C.E., F.R.I.B.A., &c.

Mr. Herbert Frederick Tomalin was born on February 18, 1862, at Northampton, and educated at the grammar school in that town. At the close of his school career he was articled to a well-known civil engineer in his native town. On the completion of his training he accepted a post on the London and North-Western Railway and remained in the service of that company until 1885. He engaged in private practice for some time, and in June, 1886, accepted an appointment to the Ceylon Government service from the Secretary of State. His first post was that of District Engineer, and in this capacity he was employed on architectural work, for which he was well qualified, he having passed the examination of the Association of Architects in 1883. His first professional work in this direction was in connection with buildings in Colombo, and the success he achieved induced the Government to entrust to him the designing of the Post and Telegraph Office, Colombo. The confidence reposed in him was fully justified. The structure erected from his designs is one of the finest public buildings in the island. Before being entrusted with this work, Mr. Tomalin had designed the decorations on the Galle Face on the occasion of the Jubilee celebrations of 1887. He also designed the ornate ball-room and drawing-room at Queen's Cottage, Kandy, and the dining-room at Oakley Cottage, Nuwara Eliya. He further designed the Ceylon Exhibition Building at the Chicago Exhibition, and received a medal in recognition of the excellence of the work. As an engineer he has been associated with many important public works, including the reclamation and drainage works, Colombo Harbour foreshore, and the operations in connection with the flood outlet. He also, in 1896, had charge of the works in connection with the water supply in the Northern Province. He has held many official positions in various parts of the island. His present appointment is that of Provincial

H. F. TOMALIN.

Engineer, Central Province. Mr. Tomalin is a Member of the Institute of Civil Engineers, a Fellow of the Institute of British Architects, and a Fellow of the Geological Society.

ANURADHAPURA.

PERCY MOORE BINGHAM, M.I.C.E.

Mr. P. M. Bingham, M.I.C.E., Provincial Engineer, North Central Province, was horn December 2, 1862. He was appointed a District Engineer in 1886, and subsequently held posts at Negombo, Haldummulla, Kalutara, Colombo, &c., and was Acting Provincial Engineer of the Western Province. He also acted as Provincial Engineer of the North-Western and Sabaragamuwa Provinces. His appointment as Provincial Engineer was confirmed in 1901.

COLOMBO.

WILLIAM WELLESLEY POLE FLETCHER, A.M.I.C.E.

Mr. W. W. P. Fletcher, Provincial Engineer, Western Province, was born on September 4, 1862. In 1886 he was appointed District Engineer, Anuradhapura, and in 1887 was transferred to the district of Matale. In 1892 he was the Assistant Commissioner, Chicago Exhibition, and in 1894 was on half-pay leave. In 1895 he was appointed Acting Provincial Engineer, Batticaloa, and later District Engineer at the same place. In 1896 and 1897 he was respectively District Engineer at Ambanpitiya and Kandy, and subsequently Acting Provincial Engineer, Central Province. On return from leave he resumed duty as District Engineer, Kandy, and in 1902 was acting Provincial Engineer of the Central and later of the Northern Province. In 1903 he received confirmation of his appointment as Provincial Engineer, and in 1904 was appointed to the Western Province.

KURUNEGALA.

WALTER CROMWELL PRICE.

Mr. W. C. Price, the Provincial Engineer for the North-Western Province, a B.A. (Trinity College, Dublin), was born on December 16, 1862. He became District Engineer in 1887, filling that position in various districts, and in 1896 was Acting Provincial Engineer, North Central Province. He was subsequently Acting Provincial Engineer of the Uva, Northern, and North-Western Provinces, and in 1904 was confirmed in his appointment. He was Provincial Engineer, North Central Province, in the same year, and in 1905 was appointed to his present post.

JAFFNA.

GEORGE WADDELL, A.M.I.C.E.

Mr. G. Waddell is the Provincial Engineer, Northern Province. He was born on January 21, 1861, and following service in the Survey Department from 1886, he became District Engineer in 1888 at Anuradhapura. After serving in this capacity in different districts, he was made Acting Provincial Engineer for the Northern Province in 1904, and was permanently appointed in the same year.

BATTICALOA.

THOMAS HOWARD CHAPMAN, A.M.I.C.E.

Mr. T. H. Chapman, Provincial Engineer, Eastern Province, who was born on August 6, 1866, was appointed District Engineer at Katugastota in 1888. He served in different districts until 1898, when he was detached for service in the Irrigation Branch. Resuming the following year, he was District Engineer, first at Dimbula, and later at Koslanda and Kandy. He was appointed Acting Provincial Engineer, Eastern Province, in 1904 and permanently appointed in 1905.

RATNAPURA.

CHAS. FREDERICK EMERSON.

Mr. C. F. Emerson, Provincial Engineer, Province of Sabaragamuwa, who was born on January 31, 1865, was in 1887 employed on Irrigation Surveys. In 1889 he was District Engineer at Mannar. In 1891 he served in the same capacity at Haldummulla and in 1895 at Koslanda. On return from leave in 1900, he was stationed at Kalutara, and in 1903 at Hambantota. In 1904 he was Acting Provincial Engineer of the Province of Sabaragamuwa, and in 1905 his appointment was confirmed.

EDWARD CAMPBELL DAVIES.

Mr. E. C. Davies, Factory Engineer, was born on July 11, 1849. He was appointed Factory Engineer in 1878, and has held the position since that date. He is Major Davies, V.D., and Honorary Lieut.-Colonel in the Ceylon Light Infantry.

G. H. M. HYDE, M.I.M.E.

Mr. G. H. M. Hyde, M.I.M.E., of the Government Factory at Colombo, who has supervised some of the most important public works in Ceylon during the past few years, has had a varied engineering career. Starting his pro fessional life in 1884, he served an apprenticeship with Messrs. T. Piggot & Co., Birmingham, and went through the drawing office, the pattern, smith, fitting, and erecting shops and foundry of this large firm of manufacturers of horizontal and vertical engines, boilers, refrigerating machinery, gas and water apparatus, &c. Upon the completion of this training Mr. Hyde was given a position as draughtsman by the same firm, and being promoted to be assistant to the works manager a year later, he superintended the manufacture of several large gasometers, roof girder and bridge work, &c. In 1892 Mr. Hyde undertook the superintendence of the erection of plant for a large chemical works at Lostock Gralam, Cheshire, and in the following year he went to Colombo in the capacity of Chief Engineer of the Colombo Commercial Company, which employs between 300 and 400 men. Holding this position for seven years, he designed and superintended the manufacture and erection of numerous iron factories, and the equipment of the same with machinery for the manufacture of tea, &c., the construction of several aerial wire ropeways, and large turbine installations for utilising the available water power on tea estates during this period. In the closing year of the nineteenth century Mr. Hyde obtained, at the hands of the Secretary of State for the Colonies, the responsible position of Mechanical Engineer at the Government Factory at Colombo. This branch of the Public Works Department, of which Mr. Hyde has complete control, constructs the iron work for roads and bridges, and erects all the new public buildings in Colombo.

Among the works carried out during the first year of Mr. Hyde's tenure of office were two hundred and thirty iron buildings and other general works for the accommodation of the

G. H. M. HYDE.

Boer prisoners-of-war at Diyatalawa and Ragama, two large wharf jetties, and a road bridge over the river Dandagamu. In the following two years Mr. Hyde acted as Executive Officer, superintending the following important constructions, some of which have not yet been completed: a concrete quay wall 660 ft. long, a wharf landing jetty 150 ft. long, the new Colombo Technical College, an Eye Hospital in commemoration of her late Majesty Queen Victoria, and minor harbour improvements. Some idea of the importance of the position which Mr. Hyde has filled successfully during the past few years, under Mr. E. C. Davies, Factory Engineer, and the Hon. Mr. F. A. Cooper, M.I.C.E., C.M.G., F.S.I., M.A.M.C.E., Director of Public Works, may be gathered from the fact that the public works which he has supervised have cost, or are estimated to cost, over a million and a half rupees (£100,000).

ELECTRICAL DEPARTMENT.

A Consulting Electrical Engineer is retained by the Government to inspect and report on the various public electrical installations in the island. He has under him a clerk and a typist.

ADAM SEDGWICK BARNARD, M.I.E.E., A.M.I.C.E.

Mr. A. S. Barnard is the Electrical Engineer. He was born on June 29, 1868, and was appointed by the Secretary of State in 1903. Up to 1904 he also acted as Instructor in Electrical Engineering at the Ceylon Technical College.

THE GOVERNMENT RAILWAYS.

One of the most valuable assets which is possessed by the Government is its system of railways, the profits from which in 1905 amounted to Rs. 4,483,754. From time to time these railways are extended, and in the future, perhaps not very remote, railway communication with India will be opened. Previous to the year 1896 the line, which was then about 297 miles in length, had taken about thirty years to construct, and it did not reach many districts which were thickly populated with industrious peoples. In 1905 the total mileage was 562½. The department is in charge of a general manager. The railways are owned and worked by the Government, which was responsible for the construction of the whole of the mileage with the exception of that of the section between Colombo and Kandy.

The sketch of the career of Mr. **G. P. Greene,** the General Manager, appears in connection with the special article on Railways on another page.

G. P. GREENE.
(General Manager.)

ANDREW PATON GRAY, M.I.C.E.

Mr. Andrew Paton Gray, M.I.C.E., Engineer of Ways and Works of the Ceylon Government Railway, hails from Scotland, having been born at Aberdeen in 1854. He received his education at the Aberdeen Grammar School, that well-known seat of learning which has sent so many famous men to all parts of the world. In 1872 he entered the office of Mr. P. M. Barnett, M.I.C.E., Engineer-in-Chief of the Great North of Scotland Railway, where he remained for seven years. At the expiration of that period he proceeded to Wolverton, in England, and assisted in the important work of doubling the London and North-Western Railway from Bletchley to Roade, and also was in charge of the erection of a new station for the same company at Northampton, together with the doubling of their line at Kingsthorpe, near Northampton. Returning to Scotland, Mr. Gray was appointed Resident Engineer on a section of the new line then being constructed between Portsoy and Elgin by the Great North of Scotland Railway. This section contained the largest single line span bridge in the United Kingdom. His first appointment in Ceylon dates from 1886, when he represented Mr. F. D. Mitchell in his contract for the reconstruction of four batteries at Trincomalee for the Ceylon Government. On the completion of this work Mr. Gray was appointed Assistant Engineer to the Ceylon Government Railway in 1888, and was promoted to Engineer, Ways and Works, in 1902, which position he still holds.

A. P. GRAY.

WAYS AND WORKS DEPARTMENT.

DUNCAN McMILLAN.

Mr. D. McMillan is the Assistant Engineer at Colombo. He was born in 1872 and appointed to his present position in 1902. During 1903 he was Acting Engineer, Ways and Works.

HENRY THOMAS CARTWRIGHT.

Mr. H. T. Cartwright, District Engineer, was appointed in 1905, having previously been employed on the Northern Extension.

H. T. CARTWRIGHT.
(Acting Resident Engineer, Northern Province.)

JAMES REID TODD.

Mr. J. R. Todd, Resident Engineer, Northern Extension, Jaffna, was born February 18, 1876. He was appointed District Engineer, Ways and Works, in 1901, and attained to his present position in 1905. Before holding the office named he was engaged on railway extension work.

GEORGE ERNEST HOOPER.

Mr. George Ernest Hooper, who was born on August 19, 1875, is the District Engineer, Nanu-Oya, having been appointed in 1905. Prior to this he was employed on the Northern Extension.

HERBERT GEORGE UNSWORTH.

Mr. Herbert George Unsworth, the Locomotive Engineer of the Ceylon Government Railways, was born at Derby, the headquarters of the Midland Railway, in 1857. After attending the Derby Grammar School, he was apprenticed to the Midland Railway Company. Having gone through all the various departments and drawing office, at the end of five years he joined the well-known firm of Marine Engineers, Messrs. J. J. Thompson, of Glasgow. In order to gain further experience of the marine branch of engineering he went

H. G. UNSWORTH, M.I.M.E.

to sea for three years, and upon his return he worked for several of the large engineering firms in Cardiff. This varied experience fitted him for engineering work of all kinds, and when he was twenty-seven he was appointed Assistant Works Manager of the Metropolitan Railway. He was promoted to the position of Works Manager within a few months, and he held that position for eight years. Mr. Unsworth's next move was to South Wales, where he became Locomotive Engineer and Carriage and Wagon Superintendent on the Rhondda and Swansea Bay Railway, and after filling that difficult position for six years he went to Ceylon to take up the appointment he at present holds. Mr. Unsworth has been a Member of the Institute of Mechanical Engineers for many years.

ARTHUR WORKMAN DENNIS.

Mr. A. W. Dennis, who was born on June 12, 1876, is District Locomotive Superintendent, which position he has held since November, 1902.

NEWTON JAMES PRICE.

Mr. N. J. Price, Assistant Locomotive Engineer and Works Manager, C.G.R., was born on January 30, 1864. He commenced work on the railway in 1889 as Locomotive Foreman, having had experience on the Great Western Railway, and also the railway connected with the Alexandra Dock, Newport. In 1892 he was appointed District Locomotive Superintendent, and in 1898, 1899, and 1901 he acted as Assistant Locomotive Engineer. He was permanently appointed Assistant Locomotive Engineer in 1902.

ERNEST WILFRED HEAD.

Mr. E. W. Head, District Locomotive Superintendent, was born on August 8, 1875, and received his appointment as Locomotive Foreman in 1902, and his present post in 1905.

ASHLEY CARTER.

Mr. A. Carter, District Locomotive Superintendent, Jaffna, was born on November 28, 1873. He was appointed Locomotive Foreman in 1899, in 1901 was Acting District Locomotive Superintendent, and was confirmed in his appointment in 1905.

TRAFFIC DEPARTMENT.

THOMAS ALEXANDER WYLIE.

Mr. T. A. Wylie, the Traffic Superintendent, Colombo, was born on September 7, 1866. He was appointed Assistant Traffic Superintendent in 1888, and was afterwards Acting Superintendent. In 1893 he acted as Accountant, and in 1894 was appointed Accountant. Subsequently, in 1905, he again acted as Traffic Superintendent, and in 1906 was permanently appointed to this position.

WILLIAM LUCIUS WALTER BYRDE.

Mr. W. L. W. Byrde, the Acting Traffic Superintendent of the Ceylon Government Railway, has had a wide experience of railways, having been connected with their working for thirteen years in the homeland and twelve years in Ceylon. Born in Monmouthshire, in 1866, he was brought out to Ceylon as a child, but was sent to England at the age of nine years to complete his education. He attended Monmouth Grammar School, and in 1881 commenced his business career on the Great Western Railway, filling various positions in the District Superintendent's Office at Pontypool Road, Monmouthshire. A District Traffic Superintendent being required for the Ceylon Government Railway in 1894, Mr. Byrde was selected for the post by the Secretary of State, and in addition to filling this office, he has also for ten months acted as Assistant to the Accountant and Assistant General Manager, Ceylon. He has also acted, since early in 1895, as Assistant Traffic Superintendent at intervals for over eight years, and on three occasions as Traffic Superintendent. His present fixed appointment is Assistant Traffic Superintendent. His family, it is interesting to note, has long been associated with Ceylon, his greatgranduncle having planted the first coffee bush in the island. He is also a nephew of Lieutenant Colonel Byrde, and is himself Captain in the Ceylon Light Infantry. A keen sportsman, golf and tennis find greatest favour in his eyes, whilst he has been captain of the Railway Cricket Club. Mrs. Byrde, too, is an enthusiastic tennis player, and an adept handler of the racquet.

JOHN HOWISON.

Mr. J. Howison, District Traffic Superintendent, Nawalapitiya, was born on April 21, 1867. He was appointed District Superintendent in 1895, and in 1900 became Acting Assistant Traffic Superintendent, being later placed on the permanent establishment.

CHAS. FETTIS SCOTT BLACKLAW.

Mr. C. F. S. Blacklaw is the District Traffic Superintendent, Jaffna. He was born on October 20, 1867, and received this appointment in 1906.

HENRY ASHER TAYLOR.

Mr. H. A. Taylor, Superintendent Northern Line, was born at Fochabers, in Scotland, on June 16, 1870. He was educated at the North London Collegiate School, and at St. Paul's, City of London. In 1886 he commenced work with the London and North-Western Railway Company, and in 1888 he passed the superior apprentice examination, which enabled him to obtain a thorough outdoor railway training. He was later employed in the District Superintendent's Office, Euston Station, having charge of various departments, and subsequently was appointed confidential clerk to the Superintendent, with charge of new works, accident, and special correspondence departments. He came to Ceylon in May, 1906, and after four months' service was given charge of the Northern Line, with a mileage of 200 miles. Mr. Taylor's father was Accountant of the Goods Department of the London and North-Western Railway, and on his mother's side he is related to the late Alexander Asher, K.C., M.P., twice Solicitor-General for Scotland in the late Mr. Gladstone's third and fourth Administrations.

W. ASHER TAYLOR.
(Superintendent of Northern Line)

JOHN JOSEPH POCOCK FELIX.

Mr. J. J. P. Felix was born on March 14, 1873, and was appointed District Traffic Superintendent, Colombo, a position he now holds, in 1905.

EDWARD HYDE ROBERT WYBRANTS WADE, A.M.I.C.E.

Mr. Wade, the Assistant General Manager and Accountant of the Ceylon Government Railway, is a native of Ireland, having been born at Monkstown, near Dublin, on February 14, 1867. He is the son of the late Mr. Gustavus Rochfort Wade, a Dublin solicitor, and a descendant of Field-Marshal Wade, who was Commander-in-Chief of the British Army from 1745 to 1748. After obtaining his early education at a private establishment near Liverpool, Mr. E. H. R. W. Wade passed to Reading School, and subsequently underwent a three-years' course of study at the Royal Indian Engineering College, Cooper's Hill, obtaining his diploma in 1888. Having received further technical training at the North-Eastern Railway Company's Works at Gateshead-on-Tyne, under Mr. T. W. Worsdell, then Chief Mechanical Engineer of the company, Mr. Wade was, in June, 1890, appointed Assistant-Surveyor in the Ceylon Government Survey Department. He arrived in Ceylon on July 17, 1890, and entered upon his duties. These he performed so satisfactorily that in the following year Mr. Wade was appointed a District-Surveyor. Zealous service in this position was rewarded by further promotion, and on June 7, 1894, he became Assistant-Traffic Superintendent of the Ceylon Government Railway. He acted several times temporarily as Traffic-Superintendent and as Assistant General Manager and Accountant, and was confirmed in the latter appointment on February 1, 1906.

E. H. WADE.

WILLIAM L. FRIER.

Mr. W. L. Frier, District Traffic Superintendent of the Ceylon Government Railway at Colombo, was born at Alcester, England, on November 25, 1876. He started his career as a clerk on the Great Western Railway at Evesham, in Worcestershire, and worked for the same line at many other places, principally in South Wales. He then went into the office of the District Superintendent at Pontypool Road, Monmouthshire, and afterwards was transferred to the office of the Superintendent of the line at Paddington. In 1902 he proceeded to Ceylon as District Superintendent at Colombo. Three years later he went to Jaffna in a similar capacity, and in January, 1906, he was transferred to Kandy. From March to November, 1906, he acted as Assistant Traffic Superintendent at Colombo, and on November 28 again took up duties as District Traffic Superintendent at Colombo.

WILLIAM CHARLES DYER DAVEY.

Mr. W. C. D. Davey, Assistant Accountant of the Ceylon Government Railway, is the son of Mr. William Davey. He was born at Exeter on February 18, 1876, and educated at the Grammar School in that city. He commenced his railway career in 1891, when he went into the service of the Great Western line. After occupying various positions in South Wales, he was transferred in 1894 from the Pontypool division to the Cardiff section, where he was under the District Goods Manager. For four years he was attached to the Accountant's department of the Great Western Railway at the Cardiff Head Office. In August, 1901, he became Assistant Accountant of the Ceylon Government Railway, and has during his stay in Ceylon acted on occasion as Storekeeper, as Assistant General Manager, and Accountant. He is fond of tennis, swimming, and shooting, and he is a violinist of considerable ability.

JAMES EDWARD HANCOCKS.

Mr. James Edward Hancocks, Storekeeper of the Ceylon Government Railway, is the son of Mr. John Hancocks, and has been associated with railway work all his life. He was born in July, 1876, at Crewe, which, as everybody knows, is the headquarters of the London and North-Western Railway Company. After being educated at Haslington, he entered the service of this great English company in his native town, going first into the signalling department. Three years later he was transferred to the stores department of the locomotive section, and after occupying various positions in that department, he took up his present position in Ceylon in July, 1905. For five years Mr.

J. E. HANCOCKS.
(Storekeeper, Government Railways.)

Hancocks served in a Volunteer corps in England.

MERVYN COLE-BOWEN.

Mr. Cole-Bowen is the son of Captain R. Cole-Bowen, and was born in 1875 in the County of

M. COLE-BOWEN.

Cork, Ireland. He took his B.A. and Bachelor of Engineering degrees at Dublin University, having joined the Engineering School of that University. Afterwards he accepted an appointment on the London and North-Western Railway. He was placed on the engineering construction staff, London, at a later period, and became an Associate Member of the Institute of Civil Engineers. In 1899 he came to Ceylon to take up a position on the Northern Railway Extension, and afterwards was engaged upon the Kelani Valley Extension. On the latter being completed he was given a temporary appointment under Mr. James Mansergh, the well known engineer, on the Colombo Drainage Scheme. His present position he has occupied since August, 1905.

THE FOREST DEPARTMENT.

The Forest Department, which has under its management the forests of the island and the enforcement of the forest laws, is controlled by the Conservator of Forests, who has nine Assistant Conservators, four Foresters, thirty-five Forest Rangers, and forty-six Forest Guards. The department was formed in 1883, and since then several reforms have been effected. The history of the department is traced in a special article which appears elsewhere. By means of this department the timber in the forests is protected from injury and damage, illicit felling is prevented, and the supply of timber and sale of timber and firewood properly regulated.

THOMAS JAMES ST. ALBANS CAMPBELL.

Mr. T. J. St. A. Campbell, who was born on December 21, 1856, belongs to the Imperial

T. J. CAMPBELL.
(Conservator of Forests.)

Forest Service, India, and is on furlough and deputation from that Government. He assumed the duties of Conservator of Forests in Ceylon in 1904.

ALFRED ALLEN CLARK.

Mr. A. A. Clark was born on September 8, 1853, and appointed a Forester in the Northern Province in 1875. He was promoted in 1889 to the position of Assistant Conservator, and held this post in the Western, Eastern, and Uva Provinces and the Eastern Circle. In 1901 he was Acting Conservator, and in 1904 was on special duty. He was appointed to Batticaloa in 1905.

H. F. C. FYERS.

Mr. H. F. C. Fyers is the Assistant Conservator of Forests of the Kandy Division. He is the son of the late Colonel Fyers, of the Royal Engineers, and was born in Curragh

H. F. C. FYERS.

Camp, Ireland, in March, 1859. He was educated at Bath Proprietary College, and went out to Ceylon to take up planting in 1877 in the famous coffee days. He entered the Forest Department in 1884. Five years later he became Assistant Conservator of Forests, and has acted as such in the North-west and Central Provinces and in the Hill Reserves.

HAMILTON ROBERT SPENCE.

Mr. H. R. Spence, who was born on November 29, 1853, is also an Assistant Conservator of the Kandy Division. He was made a Forester in 1888, and afterwards was Assistant Conservator in various provinces, and was several times Acting Conservator of Forests. He was transferred to the Kandy Division in 1905.

EDWARD LAMBERT BOYD MOSS.

Mr. E. L. B. Moss, born January 12, 1855, is the Assistant Conservator, Nuwara Eliya Division. He was first a Forester in the Uva Province, and after being Assistant Conservator in other divisions was appointed to Nuwara Eliya in 1905.

FREDERICK LEWIS.

Mr. F. Lewis, who was born in 1858, is the Assistant Conservator, Colombo Division. Commencing as a Forester in the Sabaragamuwa Province in 1888, he was soon promoted to the position of Assistant Conservator, and he has served in this capacity in many districts. He was appointed to the Colombo Division in 1905.

GEORGE DAWSON TEMPLER.

Mr. G. D. Templer, Assistant Conservator, Jaffna Division, was appointed to his present post in 1905. Previously he had been stationed at Trincomalee and Hambantota, after having had a year's training at the Imperial Forest School, Dehra Dun, India. He was born on March 13, 1880, and entered the Forest Department in 1902.

HARRY CHAMBERS TOLLER.

Mr. H. E. Toller was born on December 5, 1874. He is the Assistant Conservator of Forests, Matara Division, to which post he was appointed after serving in various other divisions. He has been in the Forest Department since 1905.

GEORGE THOMAS GILLAM.

Mr. G. T. Gillam, Assistant Conservator, Central Timber Depôt, Colombo, was born on August 4, 1850. Previous to his present appointment, which he has held since 1903, he was Superintendent of the railway sleeper supply and the Central Timber Depôt.

ARCHÆOLOGICAL COMMISSION.

This department is conducting an archæological survey of the island, and has a staff consisting of an Archæological Commissioner, European assistant, two clerks, three draughtsmen, native epigraphist, and two peons. In addition about two hundred hands are employed as a labour force. Work has been in progress since 1890, and that done already constitutes exploration, excavations, circuit work, epigraphical, topographical survey, and miscellaneous work.

R. S. TEMPLETON.

HARRY CHARLES PURVIS BELL.

Mr. H. C. P. Bell, the Archæological Commissioner, has been in the Ceylon Civil Service, since 1873. He was born on September 21, 1851, and since he entered the Government service he has occupied many positions. He commenced in the Kachcheris and the Colonial Secretary's Office, went from there to the office of the Government Agent, Western Province, and in 1875 was Acting Police Magistrate of Harispattu and also of Balapitimodara. Subsequently he filled a similar office at other places, was Landing and Tide Surveyor, Customs, Galle, Acting Assistant Government Agent, Acting Landing Surveyor, Colombo, District Judge at several places, and in 1890 was appointed Archæological Commissioner. In 1894 he was Acting District Judge, Kalutara, and in 1895 and again in 1903 was seconded for service as Archæological Commissioner.

THE SURVEY DEPARTMENT.

This department is directed by the Surveyor-General, who is assisted by an Assistant Surveyor-General, Superintendents and Surveyors, the Field Staff being divided into four branches, the Trigonometrical, Topographical, Block, and Application Surveys. The office of Surveyor-General was created in the year 1800, and in 1897 the department was reorganised.

PHILIP DAVID WARREN.

The Surveyor-General of Ceylon, Mr. Philip David Warren, F.R.G.S., is the son of Mr. John Neville Warren, and was born in London on February 7, 1851. He was educated at Norwich

P. D. WARREN.
(Surveyor-General.)

Grammar School, and after serving articles to surveying he did general surveying and engineering work in Swansea. In 1878 he went to Ceylon as Third Assistant Government Surveyor, and in 1904 he received his present appointment. Mr. Warren was for some time a Lieutenant in the 3rd Glamorgan Volunteers.

R. S. TEMPLETON.

Mr. R. S. Templeton, the Assistant Surveyor-General of Ceylon, is the son of Surgeon-Major R. Templeton, R.H.A., F.R.S., a native of Antrim, Ireland. Mr. Templeton was born on December 2, 1855, and first came to this colony in the year 1887, from New Zealand, where he had been engaged for several years. For the first three years after his arrival in Ceylon (October 15, 1887, to July, 1890) he was employed on the provisional staff of the Surveyor-General's Department in Colombo, and was appointed on August 1, 1890, Fifteenth District Surveyor. During his term of service he has specially distinguished himself in connection with the topographical survey of Ceylon. His father also, it may be mentioned, carried out a good deal of survey work for the Government. Mr. Templeton is a Fellow of the Royal Geographical Society and an Associate of the Institute of Civil Engineers. His favourite pastimes are shooting and riding.

HENRY OSMOND BARNARD, A.C.H., F.R.A.S., and M.S.

Mr. H. O. Barnard, A.C.H., F.R.A.S., and M.S., Superintendent of the Trigonometrical Surveys of the island, was born at Mauritius in 1869. The son of a well-known Mauritius planter, Mr. Henry Frederick Barnard, he was educated at Cooper's Hill, and in 1891 entered the Government Survey Department in Ceylon. For five years he was employed in the field section, but at the completion of that time he was transferred to the administrative department in Colombo, and in 1899 he received his present appointment.

SUPERINTENDENTS OF SURVEYS.

GALLE.

SAMUEL JOSEPH CATTLON MORE.

Mr. S. J. C. More was born on October 23, 1851. He was appointed a District Surveyor in 1877, and was promoted in subsequent years until he became Superintendent of Surveys in 1897. In 1899 he was Acting Assistant Surveyor-General.

KURUNEGALA.

JOHN LOUIS HAMPTON.

Mr. J. L. Hampton was born on May 7, 1855. He was appointed a District Surveyor in 1884. rose to Superintendent in 1897, and was Acting Assistant Surveyor-General in 1901.

KANDY.

JOHN WILLIAM VINER.

Mr. J. W. Viner was born on October 19, 1857, and was made a District Surveyor in 1886. He was promoted on later occasions, and made Superintendent in 1897.

BADULLA.

CHAS. CORNWALLIS MEADOW FYERS.

Mr. C. C. M. Fyers was born on February 13, 1854. After being a District Surveyor for about fourteen years he was, in 1897, made Superintendent.

COLOMBO (HARBOUR WORKS).

GARRET EDWARD LEEMBRUGGEN.

Mr. G. E. Leembruggen was born March 28, 1849, and appointed a District Surveyor in 1889. Having previously acted as Assistant Superintendent in 1897, he received promotion to the post of Superintendent in 1902.

ANURADHAPURA.

ARTHUR EDWARD MADDOCK.

Mr. A. E. Maddock, who was born in 1862, was appointed as a District Surveyor in 1888, and in 1897 became Assistant Superintendent. The same year he acted as Superintendent, and in 1903 was permanently appointed to this position.

COLOMBO (WASTE LANDS ORDINANCE).

JOHN BERTRAM MAIS RIDOUT.

Mr. J. B. M. Ridout was born July 17, 1866, and appointed District Surveyor in 1889. He became Assistant Superintendent in 1897, was Acting Superintendent in 1901, and finally was appointed Superintendent in 1904.

IRRIGATION DEPARTMENT.

Irrigation on a very large scale, considering the size of the island, has been carried out in Ceylon since the earliest ages, and is now under the control of a Central Irrigation Board. The policy adopted in irrigation has naturally undergone numerous changes since its introduction. The work of the department is

H. T. S. WARD.

superintended by a Director of Irrigation, who has under him an Irrigation Assistant, Irrigation Engineers, Surveyors, Inspectors, and Guardians.

H. T. S. WARD, M.I.C.E.

Mr. Henry Thomas Simpson Ward, M.I.C.E., who holds the important position of Director of Irrigation, is a native of Croydon, Surrey, where he was born in 1849. He was educated at King's College, London, and when seventeen years of age was articled to the late Mr. C. P. B. Shelley, M.I.C.E. He served as an improver with the Clyde Navigation Company, and as Assistant Superintendent of Works and Engineer of the coal mines for Mr. Thomas Jackson, Coats Iron Works, Coatbridge. In 1873 Mr. Ward went to Portugal, where he was employed by the Mina dos Monges Iron Company for two years. His first appointment in Ceylon was in 1876, when he was made Superintending Officer. From 1881 to 1883 Mr. Ward's services were lent by the Ceylon Government to the contractors of the Ceylon Government Railway, and from the latter year until 1886 the Government lent his services to the Perak Government (Straits Settlements), for the purpose of commanding a division of pioneers. In 1894 Mr. Ward was appointed Provincial Engineer of the Northern Province of Ceylon, and a year later the Chief Assistant to the Director of Public Works. His present appointment he received in 1900, when the new Department of Irrigation was formed.

RICHARD WILLIAM SMITH.

Mr. R. W. Smith is the Irrigation Assistant—the chief official under the Director of Irrigation. He was born on December 28, 1856, in

R. W. SMITH.

Dublin, and educated at Chard School, Somerset, and Trinity College, Dublin. He graduated in 1879. He held a position on harbour works in Ireland, England, and Jersey, was agent to John Dickson, of Cleopatra Needle fame, and afterwards went to the Straits Settlements. He was appointed District Engineer of Kurunegala, Ceylon, in 1892, and subsequently held various posts as District and Provincial Engineer, &c., and on various waterworks. He also built the camp for Boer prisoners in Ceylon, and was commissioned by the War Office to make all arrangements for the Boer rebels. He speaks nine languages. He is an Associate Member of the Institute of Civil Engineers.

MEDICAL DEPARTMENT.

This is now a civil department, the separation from the military service having been effected in 1858. The department is in charge of the Principal Civil Medical Officer and Inspector-General of Hospitals. Medical Officers and Apothecaries are appointed mainly from the students at the Ceylon Medical College, which was established about the year 1869.

Sir ALLAN PERRY, M.D. Durham, D.P.H. London, M.R.C.S.E., etc.

Sir Allan Perry is the head of the medical profession in Ceylon. He holds the official positions of Principal Medical Officer and Inspector-General of Hospitals and Principal of the Ceylon Medical College. Born on April 17, 1860, he adopted medicine as a profession. He holds the degrees of M.D. Durham, D.P.H. London, M.R.C.S. Eng., and L.S.A. Eng. He was for a time in the Royal Army Medical Corps, and retired with the rank of Major. He was appointed to his present position in 1897. Sir Allan has a deservedly high professional reputation in the island, and is much esteemed as a public man. His knighthood was a recognition of the good work that he has done in his official position during the period that he has been associated with Ceylon.

C. T. GRIFFIN.

Dr. Griffin is the Assistant Principal Civil Medical Officer and Inspector-General of Hospitals. He was born on April 14, 1850, and is an M.R.C.S. Eng., L.R.C.P. Edin., and L.S.A. Lond. He has been in Ceylon for a number of years, occupying various positions. His first appointment in the island was as Superintending Medical Officer, Dikoya, in 1883; later he became District Medical Officer, and in 1891 Acting Senior Medical Officer, Province of Uva. In 1892 he was appointed Government Medical Officer, in 1898 Colonial Surgeon, and in 1901 to his present position. He is a member of the Municipal Council, being a nominee of the Government.

ALBERT JOHN CHALMERS.

Mr. Albert John Chalmers, Registrar and Lecturer on Pathology, Medical College, was born on March 28, 1870, and educated at the University College, Liverpool. His degrees are M.D. Victoria and Liverpool Universities, F.R.C.S. England, and D.P.H. Camb. During his academical career he obtained several scholarships and medals, including the gold medal in M.D. examination. Previous to his appointment to Ceylon in 1901, Dr. Chalmers was employed in several posts in connection with English Medical Schools and Hospitals. In the Colonial Service he was Assistant Colonial Surgeon, Gold Coast Colony, 1897, and Acting Principal Medical Officer, Gold Coast, during the siege of Kumassi in 1900, when he was mentioned in despatches and received the medal and clasp. He is a Captain in the Ceylon Volunteer Medical Corps, and is also President of the Ceylon Branch of the British Medical Association for 1907. He is the author of "Simple Medical Directions for Officials in Ceylon," and some other small books for use in the colony, and has written several papers and reports on matters connected with tropical medicine, pathology, and hygiene.

COLONIAL SURGEONS.

GEORGE PETER SCHOKMAN.

Mr. G. P. Schokman, the Provincial Surgeon of the Central Province, was born in Colombo on January 18, 1855, and was educated at St. Thomas's and the Royal College there. In 1873 he went to Calcutta, and after making a short stay there he proceeded to Aberdeen University, where he graduated as Bachelor of Medicine and Master in Surgery, having taken honours in several subjects. Afterwards he was associated with St. Thomas's Hospital, London. In 1878 he returned to Ceylon on receiving the appointment of an Assistant Colonial Surgeon. Twelve years later he spent a holiday in England, and made a special study of skin diseases and diseases of women. In 1899 he was promoted to the rank of a Colonial Surgeon, and on his return on leave from Europe in 1903 he received his present appointment. Mr. Schokman, who is stationed at Kandy, is a member of the Municipal Council there, and also of the Board of Health of the Central Province.

H. A. MORAES.

Mr. H. A. Moraes, L.R.C.P. & S. Edinburgh, was born on October 3, 1849. He was appointed Assistant Colonial Surgeon in 1878, and acted in this capacity in several provinces subsequently. In 1897 he went to Tuticorin on plague duty, was appointed Colonial Surgeon in 1899, and in 1902 was transferred to Batticaloa as Colonial Surgeon for the Eastern Province.

J. CRAIB.

Mr. J. Craib, M.D. Aberdeen, was born on July 14, 1855. He became Superintending Medical Officer in 1886, District Medical Officer in 1888, Government Medical Officer in 1892, and Colonial Surgeon in 1898. He was appointed to the Western Province in 1903.

E. DE LIVERA.

Mr. E. de Livera, M.B., C.M. Glasgow, the Colonial Surgeon, North Western Province and Province of Sabaragamuwa, was born on April 25, 1849, and appointed an Assistant Colonial Surgeon in 1878. In 1894 he was made Senior Medical Officer, Eastern Province, Acting Colonial Surgeon in 1899, and given the appointment he now holds in 1900.

F. OORLOFF.

Mr. F. Oorloff, M.B., C.M. Aberdeen, was born on May 5, 1860. In 1881 he was appointed Deputy Assistant Colonial Surgeon, and two years later Assistant Colonial Surgeon. In 1894 he acted as Medical Superintendent, Lunatic Asylum, Colombo, and in 1896 was Medical Officer at the Police and Branch Hospital, Colombo, and Judicial Medical Officer. He became Assistant Colonial Surgeon, Kandy, in 1899, of the Eastern Province in 1900, and in 1900 was appointed to his present post.

F. G. SPITTEL.

Mr. F. G. Spittel, L.R.C.P. & S. Edinburgh, L.F.P. & L.F.S. Glasgow, Assistant Colonial Surgeon and Superintendent, Civil Medical Stores, was born January 26, 1853. He was appointed Sub-Assistant Colonial Surgeon in 1874, became Deputy Assistant Colonial Surgeon in 1885, and Assistant in 1887. He acted as Colonial Surgeon in 1902, and in 1904 was Judicial Medical Officer, Colombo, being appointed Colonial Surgeon, Northern Province, in 1905.

H. A. KEEGEL.

Mr. H. A. Keegel, L.F.P. & S. Glasgow, L.R.C.P. & S. Edinburgh, was born on December 31, 1854. He was appointed a Sub-Assistant Colonial Surgeon in 1875, Deputy Assistant in 1885, and Assistant in 1887. In 1896 he was Port Surgeon, Colombo, and in 1904 Acting Colonial Surgeon, Southern Province. He was also Acting Colonial Surgeon, Southern Province, in 1906.

GENERAL HOSPITAL STAFF.

T. F. GARVIN, Surgeon in Charge.

Mr. T. F. Garvin, M.B., C.M. Aberdeen, F.C.S. London, the Surgeon in Charge of the General Hospital, was born on December 19, 1853, and was appointed an Assistant Colonial Surgeon in 1875. In 1891 he was given the position of Physician in Charge of General Hospital and Superintendent Civil Medical Stores, whilst two years later he became Surgeon in Charge of the General Hospital. In 1900 he was appointed Chief Medical Officer, Diyatalawa Prisoners-of-War Camp, and in 1903 resumed duty as Surgeon in Charge of the General Hospital. He is the Lecturer on Surgery at the General Hospital.

W. G. ROCKWOOD.

A sketch of the life of Dr. W. G. Rockwood appears elsewhere.

H. M. FERNANDO.

A sketch of the life of Dr. H. M. Fernando, First Physician of the General Hospital, Colombo, appears elsewhere.

GEORGE THOMASZ.

A sketch of the career of Dr. G. Thomasz appears elsewhere.

S. C. PAUL.

Dr. S. C. Paul, M.D. Madras, L.R.C.P. London, and F.R.C.S. England, the Third Surgeon at the Hospital, was born on February 20, 1872. In April, 1902, he was appointed Lecturer on Anatomy of the Ceylon Medical College, with the rank of Deputy Assistant Colonial Surgeon. During a part of 1905 he was Acting Second Surgeon at the Hospital.

ALLAN DE SARAM.

Mr. A. de Saram, M.B., C.M. Aberdeen, the Second Physician at the General Hospital, was born on July 19, 1866. He was appointed Medical Officer in Charge of the Field Hospital in 1889, and Deputy Assistant Colonial Surgeon in 1893. During 1901 he was Judicial Medical Officer, Colombo, whilst he was appointed an Assistant Colonial Surgeon in 1903, and to the position he now holds in 1904. He is also the Lecturer on Skiagraphy and on Hospital Forms and Management at the Medical College.

ALDO CASTELLANI.

Dr. A. Castellani, who holds the positions of Director of the Clinic for Tropical Diseases and of the Bacteriological Institute and Lecturer on Tropical Medicine, has devoted a lifetime to the study of tropical illnesses. The son of Mr. Ettore Castellani, he was born at Florence on September 8, 1874, and studied medicine first in Germany, at the Bonn University and afterwards at Florence University and at the Lister Institute and School of Tropical Medicine in London. At Florence he took his M.D. degree, and later he took the degree of Privat-Dozent, with the title of Professor of Tropical Medicine, in the University of Naples. In 1903 he was appointed a member of the Foreign Office and Royal Society's Commission for the Investigation of Sleeping Sickness. As is well known, he was successful in discovering the germ which is the cause of this terrible disease. For this valuable work Dr. Castellani was awarded the Craig Prize for the most important discovery in the field of tropical medicine in that year. In the December following Dr. Castellani was appointed by the Secretary of State to his present position, and during his residence in Ceylon he has made further valuable medical discoveries, notably the cause of yaws, one of the most prevalent diseases in tropical countries.

M. SINNATAMBY.

Mr. M. Sinnatamby, M.D. Brux., F.R.C.S. Edin., Assistant Colonial Surgeon, Surgeon and Superintendent of De Soysa's' Lying-in Home, was born on July 4, 1859. He was appointed Supernumerary Sub-Assistant Colonial Surgeon in 1882, and later was Apothecary at the General Hospital. In 1883 he became Sub-Assistant Colonial Surgeon, in 1885 Medical Assistant, in 1893 Deputy Assistant Colonial Surgeon, and in 1899 was appointed to his present post.

MARY NONA FYSH.

Mrs. M. N. Fysh, M.B. Lond., the Medical Officer in Charge of the Lady Havelock Hospital for Women, was born on October 28, 1872, and was appointed to her present responsible position in 1899. Her Assistant is Alice de Boer, and the Matron of the Hospital M. E. Richardson, whilst Winifred Nell is the House Surgeon.

J. B. SPENCE.

Mr. J. B. Spence, M.B., C.M., M.A. Edin., the Medical Superintendent of the Lunatic Asylum, was born on November 20, 1856, and has held his present appointment since 1887. He is the Lecturer on Medical Jurisprudence and on Mental Diseases at the Medical College.

W. H. MEIER.

Mr. W. H. Meier, Honorary L.M.S. Ceylon, is the Superintendent, Leper Asylum, Hendala, to which position he was appointed in 1879.

K. C. BROWNING.

Mr. K. C. Browning, M.A. Camb., F.C.S. Lond., Professor of Chemistry, Medical College, and Public Analyst, was born on June 11, 1875, and has held his present appointment since 1904.

H. BAWA.

Mr. H. Bawa, F.R.C.S. and L.R.C.P. Edin., the Port Surgeon, Colombo, was born on July 9, 1866. He was appointed an Acting District Medical Assistant in 1888, and in 1891 became Sub-Assistant Colonial Surgeon. In 1895 he was Deputy Assistant Colonial Surgeon, and two years afterwards Medical Officer, Tuticorin, India. In 1903 he was appointed Judicial Medical Officer, and in 1904 as Port Surgeon, Colombo.

F. R. ALLES

Mr. F. R. Alles, L.R.C.P. & S. Edin., Port Surgeon, Galle, was born on September 18, 1869, and appointed to the General Hospital, Colombo, in 1893. He was Sub-Assistant Colonial Surgeon in 1894, and Acting Deputy Assistant Colonial Surgeon in 1903. In 1904 he was appointed Deputy Assistant Colonial Surgeon, and subsequently to his present position.

THE GOVERNMENT STORES.

The duties of this department consist of the supervision and direction of the Government Stores, &c., charge of the Government magazines, supply of building materials, stores, tools, and clothing; recovery and credit of value of all civil supplies, transport for civil purposes, remittances of money to all parts for expenses incurred, charge of the public furniture of the residences of the Governor, &c. Until the year 1867 the Store was known as the Commissariat Store, and the head of the department, who was then a military officer, as the Commissary-General. Now the Stores are in charge of a Controller of Government Stores and an Assistant Controller.

FREDERICK WILLIAM VANE.

Mr. F. W. Vane, I.S.O., A.I.E.E., Controller of Government Stores, was born on September 15, 1852. In 1872, after working about a year in the Post Office, he was appointed Assistant Postmaster-General, and in 1874 was Acting Secretary to the Loan Board. In 1876 he acted as Postmaster-General, and was appointed Controller of Government Stores in 1900.

WILLIAM AINSLIE TAYLOR.

This gentleman is the Storekeeper and Accountant in the Government Stores, a position he has filled since 1905, and at the present time is occupied with the work of reorganisation of the Government Stores. Born at Linlithgow in 1877, educated at Glasgow, his school career was followed by an apprenticeship in the office of the Stores Superintendent of the North British Railway, with whom he served for over fifteen years During this period he made himself fully conversant with all branches of storekeeping and the accounts in connection with the same. Consequently, from his long and varied practical experience he was thoroughly competent when appointed by the Secretary of State, through the Crown Agents, to take up the position he now ably fills.

W. A. TAYLOR.

THE LOAN BOARD.

The Loan Board in its present form was constituted by an Ordinance in 1865, and consists of three Commissioners. These Commissioners lend out at interest the moneys of court suitors, intestate estates, &c., in deposit; and rules and regulations made by the Commissioners regulate the proceedings and determine the securities on which loans are to be made, the charges payable by borrowers, the rate of interest and its distribution, the books and accounts to be kept, &c.

CHIEF COMMISSIONER.

THE HON. MR. H. C. NICOLLE.

The sketch of the Hon. Mr. Nicolle's career appears elsewhere.

CEYLON SAVINGS BANK.

The Ceylon Savings Bank was established as a Government institution in 1832, and is managed under Ordinance by a Board of Directors. During the past ten years it has made considerable progress.

The sketch of the career of Mr. **F. W. Vane,** the Secretary, appears under the heading Government Stores

WIDOWS AND ORPHANS' PENSION FUND.

In 1884 an association was formed which has for its object the providing of pensions for the widows and orphans of deceased public officers of the island. Officers holding permanent appointments in the colony which are separately provided for on the estimates, and receiving 250 rupees per annum, who have been notified as pensionable, contribute 4 per cent. of their salary to this fund. The pensions of widows cease at death or on remarriage, of boys at the age of eighteen, and of girls on marriage or at the age of twenty-one. A Board of Directors manages the fund, the moneys of which are invested with the Government, and return 6 per cent.

The Chief Director is the Hon. Mr. **H. C. Nicolle,** whose career is sketched under the heading Legislative Council.

POST AND TELEGRAPHS.

This department is under the control of the Postmaster-General. The new G.P.O. in Colombo was completed in 1895 at a cost of Rs. 372,961.65. There are 151 post offices in the island, 90 of these being also telegraph offices. There are, in addition, 164 village receiving offices and 28 railway receiving offices. The mails are conveyed by train, horse coaches, bullock coaches, and by over 290 runners. The telegraph system comprises 1,544 miles of line and 2,814 miles of wire. Submarine cable connects the island with the rest of the world. In 1896 the G.P.O. took over the telephone service from the Oriental Telephone Company, paying Rs. 42,666. There were 56 subscribers, 25 miles of posts, and 151 miles of wire. There are now 40 miles of posts, 365 miles of wire, and 274 instruments in use. There is also a Post Office Savings Bank.

HENRY LUTTRELL MOYSEY.

Mr. H. L. Moysey, I.S.O., Postmaster-General and Director of Telegraphs, was born on December 10, 1849. He entered the Government service in 1870, being attached to the Colonial Secretary's Office. In 1872 he was Police Magistrate, Kayts, and in 1873 Acting Assistant Government Agent, Kurunegala and Batticaloa respectively. Subsequently he was Acting Assistant Government Agent, Acting District Judge, Inspector of Police Courts, and Acting Principal Collector of Customs. He was appointed to his present post n 1900.

WILLIAM CHARLES MACREADY.

Mr. W. C. Macready, Acting Postmaster-General of Ceylon, was born in the island in

W. C. MACREADY.

1861, his father being Mr. W. C. Macready, of the Ceylon Civil Service. He entered the Ceylon branch of the Oriental Bank Corporation at the age of sixteen, where he served three years. In 1880 he was given a nomination in the uncovenanted branch of the Government service by His Excellency the Governor, and resigning his position at the Bank, entered the Colombo General Post Office as Second Assistant to the Postmaster-General. The inland money-order business was then in its infancy—it was opened in October, 1877—and his previous banking experience was of much service to him in managing and extending the business of this branch of the department, which was placed under his control. The Post Office Savings Bank was instituted in 1885, and was also placed under his supervision. Mr. Macready acted several times as First Assistant to the Postmaster-General, during the absence on leave of the permanent officer, between the years 1881 and 1900, and received the fixed appointment in the latter year. In addition to his duties at the Post Office, he held the appointment of Secretary of the Ceylon Savings Bank, a separate institution, from 1896 to the date of his assuming duty as Assistant Postmaster-General. Mr. Macready is one of the original members of the "A" Company of the Ceylon Infantry Volunteers, and was transferred to the Artillery Corps upon its formation. He resigned in 1896, as the exigences of the postal service prevented his devoting sufficient time to volunteering.

THEODOR HARWARD.

Mr. Theodore Harward, the Second Assistant to the Postmaster-General of Ceylon, was born in 1861 and educated at the Durham Grammar School. He came to Ceylon in 1899, and after two years' service was appointed to his present position. Previous to this he had been ten years in Queensland, and also served with the British forces in the South African campaign, afterwards being engaged in army postal work in Bloemfontein, Orange River Colony.

JOHN FOX.

Mr. J. Fox, Accountant, General Post Office, was born on August 23, 1865. He served as clerk on the establishment of the War Office, London, from 1884 to 1893, and of the General Post Office, London, from 1893 to 1900. He then came out to Ceylon to take up the duties he now performs.

H. J. LOVETT.

The Assistant Accountant of the General Post Office, Colombo, Mr. H. J. Lovett, is the son of Mr. John Lovett, of London, and was born in 1877. After receiving his education at Marlborough College he served his articles with Mr. Henry Spain, a London accountant, and became a Member of the Institute of Chartered Accountants in 1900. He obtained an appointment on the Post Office staff in Ceylon in 1901, and has acted for the Accountant during the latter's absence. He is a golf enthusiast, and in 1906 was the winner of the Governor's Cup.

DROGO MONTAGU.

Mr. Montagu has held the appointment of Superintendent of Telegraphs and Electrician in Ceylon for the past eight years. He was educated at Cheltenham College, and received his engineering training at the works of Messrs. Davey, Paxman & Co., at Colchester, and at Faraday House, the Electrical Standardising, Testing, and Training Institution, London. He worked for a short time at the Leeds and Edinburgh Electric Light Stations as an Assistant Electrical Engineer. He came out to Ceylon as the Assistant Superintendent of Telegraphs in 1896, and was promoted to his present position in January, 1899. He was born at Colchester in 1870. He is an Associate Member of the Institute of Civil Engineers, and an Associate of the Institute of Electrical Engineers.

J. ROBERTSON.

Mr. J. Robertson, the Acting Assistant Superintendent of Telegraphs, was born in the island in 1864, and entered the Post Office service in 1882 as telegraphist. He rose gradually until in 1906 he was appointed to his present position. He is the hon. secretary of the Colombo Post and Telegraph Library and Recreation Club, to which office he was elected in 1899.

PATRICK THOMAS MACNAMARA.

Mr. P. T. Macnamara, Assistant Superintendent of Telegraphs, was born on February 9, 1872. He was from 1887 in the Imperial Postal Telegraph Department until appointed to his present position in 1899. In 1900 and 1903 he acted as Superintendent of Telegraphs.

CHARLES W. LUND.

Mr. C. W. Lund, A.M.I.E.E., Assistant Superintendent of Telegraphs (Railway), was appointed to his present post in 1904.

ALFRED LESLIE COOK.

Mr. A. L. Cook, A.M.I.E.E, Assistant Superintendent of Telegraphs, who was born on September 5, 1874, was appointed to the position he now holds in 1904. He is the manager of the telephones.

HARBOUR DEPARTMENT.

The Harbour Department is under the direction of Masters Attendant, who are situated at Colombo, Galle, Batticaloa, and Trincomalee. The Master Attendant and Conservator of the Port of Colombo is also the Master Attendant of Ceylon, and is thus chief adviser to the Government in all matters nautical, as well as being the naval agent. His duties, and that of the other masters attendant, are chiefly to appoint the place of anchorage and regulate the berthing and mooring of vessels; to control the pilots; to see that the bed of the harbour is kept clear and is safe and free for navigation, and to supervise all other matters appertaining to the shipping business of the ports whereat they are stationed.

JOHN AUGUSTUS LEGGE.

Captain J. A. Legge, the Master Attendant, Colombo, is a son of the Hon. Charles G. Legge, and Mary, daughter of the Right Rev. Dean Garnier, of Lincoln. He was born on July 31, 1871, at Woodsome Hall, Farnley Tyas, Yorkshire, and educated at Bedford Grammar School and on the Thames Nautical Training College, H.M.S. *Worcester*. He sailed in Messrs. J. P. Corry & Co.'s sailing ship *Star of Austria* in September, 1887, and in January, 1892, entered the service of the P. & O. Steam Navigation Company. Whilst with this company he passed through all the ranks, rising to that of chief officer in September, 1900, and in 1902 was appointed to the position he now occupies. Captain Legge holds a master mariner's certificate of competency as "extra master." He joined the Royal Naval Reserve as a midshipman in 1889, and retired after assuming the duties of Master Attendant at Colombo.

GEORGE ARTHUR COLBERT.

Mr. G. A. Colbert, Assistant Master Attendant, Colombo, was born on October 13, 1858. He was appointed in 1902, and has acted as Master Attendant and Joint Police Magistrate.

COLOMBO HARBOUR WORKS.

With the erection of breakwaters, the south-west arm in particular, which made the harbour so much larger, Colombo became an important port of call for Eastern shipping. It was in 1875 that the building of the south-west breakwater was commenced, His Majesty the King, as Prince of Wales, placing the first block. The breakwater is 4,210 ft. in length, and shelters 400 acres of water-space, which has a depth of about 30 ft. at low water. It was completed in 1885, the cost having been £700,000. Later two other breakwaters were constructed, giving a sheltered area of 640 acres, or a square mile. There is a graving dock for the use of His Majesty's ships and the accommodation of other vessels using the port, a patent slip where smaller craft can be overhauled and repaired, and a coaling depôt. The number employed daily on these works was 2,600 free workpeople and 700 convicts. The harbour is controlled by a Harbour Board. Mr. J. H. Bostock is the Resident Engineer and Mr. J. Kyle the First Assistant Engineer.

THE POLICE.

The police force consists of Europeans, Burghers, Sinhalese, Malays, Tamils, and Moormen, the Sinhalese and Malay being the largest elements. They are under the control of the Inspector-General, though the provincial and municipal police (excepting Colombo) are under the Government Agents. The force is drilled and armed with the Martini-Henry carbine. It is maintained chiefly by means of an assessment tax. This in the majority of the towns is levied on all houses, buildings, lands, and tenements. In rural districts brought under the operation of the Police Ordinance on the application of estate proprietors, an assessment is levied on the acreage of the estates. In certain localities, other than large towns, police are maintained out of the general revenue, by which means are also defrayed the salaries of the Inspector-General and higher officers, cost of barracks, hospitals, medical attendance, and arms. All other expenses are borne by the inhabitants of the towns where police are established. In Colombo a rate is levied for police, lighting and water, and the municipality pays Rs. 60,000 annually as a contribution, whilst in the rural districts the expenses are borne in equal shares by the Government and the proprietors of estates.

CYRIL CHAPMAN LONGDEN.

Mr. C. C. Longden is the Inspector-General of Police, a position he has held since the year 1905. Previous to that he was a District Superintendent of Police, Madras Presidency. He was born on November 1, 1873.

CHAS. LANCELOT TRANCHELL.

Mr. C. L. Tranchell, who was born on January 10, 1870, is the Superintendent of Police, Central Province, Kandy. He commenced in the Police Department as Assistant Superintendent, Colombo, in 1892, and in 1893 was Acting Superintendent, Southern Province, He was subsequently attached to various districts as Assistant and Acting Superintendent, being made Superintendent, headquarters, Colombo, in 1903. He received his present appointment in 1905.

HAYMAN THORNHILL.

Born on September 11, 1876, Mr. Hayman Thornhill entered the Ceylon Police Service in July, 1895, as Acting Assistant Superintendent of Police, Colombo. On November 15, 1897, he was made Assistant Superintendent of Police, Western Province, and in September of the following year was transferred to the Southern Province. In 1901 he passed the first and second examinations in police administration, and also the examinations in elementary criminal law. On July 15, 1903, he returned to the Western Province as Assistant Superintendent. In 1904 he passed examinations in Sinhalese and Tamil, and on October 22nd in that year received the appointment of Superintendent of Police. In February, 1905, he was transferred to the headquarters staff.

EDWARD BRUCE ALEXANDER.

Mr. E. B. Alexander, B.A. Oxon., who was born on March 3, 1872, is Superintendent of Police, Southern Province. He commenced his Civil Service career in the Colonial Secretary's Office, was subsequently attached to the Audit Office and the Ratnapura Kachcheri, and in 1899 was Police Magistrate, Panadure. In 1900 he was Acting Assistant Government Agent, Matale, and in 1903 Assistant Government Agent, Kegalla. He received his present appointment in 1905.

FRANCIS GRAEME TYRRELL.

Mr. F. G. Tyrrell, B.A. Oxon., the Superintendent of Police, Kurunegala, was born September 17, 1876. He came out as a cadet to the Colonial Secretary's Office in 1900, in 1901 he was Acting Private Secretary to H.E. the Lieutenant-Governor, and was in the offices of the Government Agents of the Central Province and at Nuwara Eliya in 1903 and 1904. In 1905 he received his present appointment.

HERBERT LAYARD DOWBIGGIN.

Mr. H. L. Dowbiggin, the Superintendent of Police, Colombo, was born on December 26, 1880, and appointed Assistant Superintendent of Police in 1901. He was made Superintendent at Colombo in 1905.

THEODORE PENNYCUICK ATTYGALLE.

Mr. T. P. Attygalle, Superintendent, Criminal Investigation Department, Colombo, was born on May 3, 1876. He was appointed Assistant Superintendent in 1903 and Superintendent in 1905.

THE PRISONS.

An Inspector-General of Prisons has control and supervision of all prisons. For every prison there is a Superintendent, a Medical Officer, a jailer, and subordinate officers who are appointed by the Governor. There are twenty-one prisons, exclusive of the buildings used solely as lockups, and the penal stage prisoners of the island sentenced to over one month's imprisonment go through the prison at Welikada, Kandy, Jaffna, or Ratnapura. In these they are worked on the separate system, confined in separate cells and worked in stalls. The penal labour consists of beating coir-husk, metal breaking, and pingo carrying, whilst at the Welikada prison the treadmill is in force.

A. W. DE WILTON.

Major A. W. de Wilton, who is the Inspector-General of Prisons and Superintendent of the Convict Establishments of Ceylon, was born at Samalcotta, in India, in the year 1862. He received his early education at Brighton, and

MAJOR A. W. DE WILTON.
(Inspector-General of Prisons.)

then proceeded to Southsea Military College, where he passed out in 1880. Joining the militia in the following year, he went to Sandhurst, and after the usual course there received his commission in 1883 as an officer in the Connaught Rangers. He saw active service in the Burma Campaign, and obtained a medal and two clasps. In 1898 he was appointed Major-General of Police in Mauritius. Four years later he was transferred to Ceylon, and took up the appointment of Inspector-General of Police and Prisons. With the increase of work, however, the Major has confined himself to the supervision of the various convict establishments of the island. It may be mentioned, incidentally, that Major de Wilton is a grandson of Mr. Jacob Montefiore, the First Commissioner who went to Australia in the year 1832.

REGISTRATION.

The Registrar - General's Department is divided into two branches—the Land Registration Department and the Marriages, Births, and Deaths Registration Department. The Head Office of the Department is now in the Fort, Colombo, but formerly it was situated in Hulftsdorp, near the Law Courts. The Registrar-General has the supervision of Notaries Public amongst his duties. The Registrar-General is the Hon. Mr. P. **Arunachalam.** The sketch of his career appears under the heading Legislative Council.

LAND SETTLEMENT DEPARTMENT.

The Land Settlement Department was formed out of the Waste Lands Ordinance Department, and it is the body, as the name signifies, which settles claims to land, both cultivated and waste. Waste lands are dealt with under a Waste Land Ordinance. The department is presided over by a Land Settlement Officer, who has the powers of a Special Officer under the Waste Lands Ordinance. He has one assistant. The office of the department is at Hill House, Mutwal, Colombo.

JOHN GEORGE FRASER.

Mr. J. G. Fraser, Settlement Officer under the Waste Lands Ordinance, was born on August 5, 1864. He came out to Ceylon as a cadet to the Jaffna Kachcheri in 1887, and in 1889 was Police Magistrate, Point Pedro. He was Office Assistant in several of the Government Agents' Offices, and Acting District Judge of Badulla-Haldummulla in 1897. In 1899 he became Assistant Government Agent, Chilaw, and in 1901 Settlement Officer under the Waste Lands Ordinance, No. 1 of 1897.

HOWARD ORME FOX.

Mr. H. O. Fox, B.A. Cantab., was born on August 17, 1865. He is the Assistant Settlement Officer, and came out to Ceylon in 1889 to the Badulla Kachcheri. In 1892 he was appointed Commissioner of Requests and Police Magistrate, Point Pedro, and later in the same year was transferred to the office of the Government Agent for the Western Province. He became Acting Landing Surveyor, Customs, Colombo, and subsequently acted for the Government Agents at Kegalla, Vavuniya and Mullaitivu. He was appointed Assistant Government Agent, Matale, in 1899; District Judge, Tangalla, in 1900; and in 1903 was seconded for service as Special Officer under the Waste Lands Ordinance, No. 1 of 1897.

WALTER ERNEST WAIT.

Mr. W. E. Wait fills the position of Additional Assistant to the Land Settlement Officer. He is a son of Mr. William George Wait, a tea planter of Southern India, and was born at Coonoor, Nilgiris, in the South of India, in the year 1878. He was educated at Fettes College, Edinburgh University, and commenced service under the Government as a cadet in December, 1902. From that time he held various posts until 1905, when he was appointed to his present position. As a member of the 1st Battalion Royal Scots Volunteers he took part in the South African War, and at the present time is a member of the Ceylon Planters' Rifle Corps.

VETERINARY DEPARTMENT.

The Veterinary Surgeon, who is attached to the Secretariat, holds an office of some importance, one of his principal duties being to advise the various Government departments in the purchase of horses and cattle, and the treatment of animals which are their property. He has also to attend to the suppression of contagious and infectious diseases of animals and the improvement of native breeds of cattle and horses, besides superintending the working of the Government dairy.

GEORGE WILLIAM STURGESS.

Mr. G. W. Sturgess, M.R.C.V.S., who was born on September 4, 1871, has been Veterinary Surgeon since 1895.

IMMIGRATION.

There is a large immigration of coolies each month, but though the Government look carefully after these, there is no distinct Immigration Department. There is an observation camp at Ragama, where immigrant coolies are sent immediately on arrival, and the cost of this is voted under the Port and Marine Department (Government Agent, Western Province), whilst the cost of maintaining a Superintendent of Immigration comes under the head of Immigration (Government Agent, Northern Province). Mr. B. Paranjothy is the Superintendent.

COLOMBO DRAINAGE WORKS.

The Colombo Drainage Works Department is a temporary institution which has been in existence since 1903. In the year 1897 the Government requisitioned the services of Mr. James Mansergh to draw up a scheme for, and estimate the cost of, a system of drainage for the whole of the city of Colombo. This was prepared and submitted, but was considered too costly, and a modified scheme was suggested. This was agreed to, and work was commenced in 1904. The estimated cost is Rs. 5,000,000, and of this total about Rs. 2,000,000 have been spent. The scheme will be completed, it is anticipated, in about three years' time. There was practically no system of drainage in Colombo previous to 1897, the sewage being carried to the harbour through open drains. The system now being instituted will take away the sewage from the harbour.

R. E. TICKELL.

Mr. R. E. Tickell, Chief Resident Engineer on the Colombo Drainage Works, is a native of London, and was educated at Malvern and Hanover. He entered the engineering profession in 1887, being appointed to a position on the Stockton and Middlesbrough Waterworks, Yorkshire. In 1891 he worked on a scheme for the water supply of Birmingham, and subsequently was engaged upon the construction of the Penygareg dam, a masonry dam 600 ft. long and 140 ft. high from foundation to crest. At the present time this dam is the highest in Europe. On the completion of that work he came out to Ceylon to take over his present position.

ALEC FLEMING CHURCHILL.

Mr. A. F. Churchill, District Engineer, born April 12, 1876, was the Assistant Engineer on the Colombo Drainage Works, previous to which appointment he had been District Engineer at Ragama, Chilaw, and Kurunegala.

BOTANIC GARDENS.

ROYAL BOTANIC GARDENS, PERADENIYA.

The headquarters of the department of the Government known as the Royal Botanic Gardens are situated at Peradeniya, four miles from Kandy. The gardens cover about 143 acres, and have a general level above the sea of about 1,550 ft., the climate being warm and damp, but preferable to that of the low-country, such as Colombo. The gardens were first opened at Slave Island. Later they were removed to Kalutara, and from there, in 1813, were transferred to their present site. They are worked with great success.

JOHN CHRISTOPHER WILLIS.

Dr. J. C. Willis, Sc.D. Cantab., F.L.S., who was born on February 20, 1868, is the Director of the Royal Botanic Gardens, Peradeniya. He has held the appointment since 1896, with the exception of a brief interval in 1904, when he went on special duty to the Federated Malay States, to advise as to the appointment of a Director of Agriculture.

E. E. GREEN, F.E.S., F.Z.S.

Mr. Green occupies the position of Government Entomologist, and has his residence and laboratory at the Royal Botanic Gardens, Peradeniya. Born in 1861, he was educated at the Charterhouse School, Godalming. He came to Ceylon as a coffee planter in the year 1881, shortly before the failure of that industry. On his arrival the fatal coffee-leaf disease was at its height, and one of Mr. Green's first acquaintances in the island was Professor Marshall Ward, who had been deputed to study the disease. Mr. Green was deeply interested in natural history from boyhood, and as a planter he turned his attention specially to the study of economic entomology. When coffee, weakened by leaf disease, was attacked by an insect pest that was finally to seal its doom, Mr. Green, at the request of the Ceylon Government, made an exhaustive report on the pest, which was published in 1886. During the year 1888–89 he published a series of articles on "Insect Pests of the Tea Plant," and whilst in England on leave, the following year, he went through Professor Huxley's biological course at the Royal College of Science, South Kensington. In 1891 he was elected a Fellow of the Entomological Society of London, and was in 1897 appointed Honorary Government Entomologist. Two years later he received the appointment which he now holds. In 1901 the Royal Asiatic Society of Bengal awarded him the Barclay medal for biological work connected with India. Mr. Green has made a special study of "scale insects" (Coccidæ) a family that supplies so many serious insect pests, and he has published a monograph on "The Coccidæ of Ceylon." He was elected a Fellow of the Zoological Society in 1906.

The entomological laboratory deals with economic insects, both harmful and useful. A small silk farm has recently been opened with the object of interesting the natives in sericulture. There is also attached to the department a quarantine station in Colombo, where imported plants and fruits are subjected to fumigation to prevent the introduction of foreign insect pests.

T. PETCH.

Mr. T. Petch, B.A., B.Sc. Lond., who was born on March 11, 1870, has been the Government Mycologist since 1905.

HERBERT WRIGHT.

Mr. H. Wright, A.R.C.S., F.L.S., who was born on September 10, 1874, is the Controller, Experimental Station, Peradeniya. He was appointed Scientific Assistant to the Director, Royal Botanic Gardens, from 1900 to 1902, and in 1901, in addition to performing these duties, he was also Curator of the Peradeniya Gardens. He assumed the position he now occupies in 1902, and has since acted as Director of the Royal Botanic Gardens.

HUGH FRASER MACMILLAN.

Mr. H. F. Macmillan, F.L.S., F.R.H.S., Curator, Royal Botanic Gardens, Peradeniya, was born in June, 1869. He took up his present position in 1895, and in 1899 acted as Superintendent of the Hakgala Gardens.

HAKGALA BOTANIC GARDENS.

The site of the Hakgala Gardens was chosen in 1860, at the time cinchona plants were introduced into the island. The garden is situated on the side of Hakgala Mountain, about 5,600 ft. above sea-level, and covers about 550 acres. A large portion of the area is still covered with grass and jungle.

JOHN KNIGHTON NOCK.

Mr. J. K. Nock, born June 21, 1881, has been the Curator of the Botanic Gardens, Hakgala, since 1903.

HENERATGODA BOTANIC GARDENS.

These gardens, about 17 miles from Colombo, were opened in 1876 as experimental gardens for low-country products, and to receive the seeds and plants of the Para rubber tree. The elevation is only about 15 ft. above sea-level, and the climate is hot and steamy. The cultivated area is about thirty acres, whilst one of its features is a piece of untouched jungle. Mr. H. W. Perera is the conductor of these gardens.

COLOMBO MUSEUM.

The Colombo Museum, an excellent institution, was founded by the Right Hon. Sir Wm. Gregory, K.C.M.G., Governor of Ceylon, in 1873, and opened to the public in 1877. It contains a splendid collection of curios, &c., whilst at the rear of the building a number of Ceylonese animals are exhibited. In front of the building is a statue of the founder, handsomely executed by Boehm, which was erected by the inhabitants to commemorate the many benefits conferred by him on the colony during his administration. The Museum is under the direction of a committee of management.

ARTHUR WILLEY.

Mr. A. Willey, D.Sc. Lond., F.R.S., was born on October 9, 1867. He is the Director of the Colombo Museum, an office held by him since 1902.

GERARD ABRAHAM JOSEPH.

Mr. G. A. Joseph, the Librarian, Colombo Museum, was born on April 6, 1870. He was private secretary to Mr. Justice Clarence in 1891, and acted as Librarian, Museum, on two occasions prior to his permanent appointmen in 1893.

MINERALOGICAL SURVEY.

This department was created in 1902, to examine the occurrence of economic minerals in the island, with a view to their further development, the preparation of a descriptive report on the mineral resources and the arrangement of the geological collections in the Museum, and the accumulation of further specimens. The staff is composed of a Director and an Assistant Director, the duties of the former being carried out until recently by the well-known authority Dr. A. K. Coomaraswamy, articles by whom appear in another section of this work. Professor Parsons is the Assistant Director.

MINE INSPECTION.

THOMAS GILBERT HUNTER.

Mr. T. G. Hunter, Government Inspector of Mines, was born on September 13, 1873. He has held the position since 1900.

FOREIGN CONSULS.

The number of foreign Consuls established at Colombo is evidence of its importance as a shipping centre and port of call. All the important Powers have representatives there, whilst in addition the United States, Austro-Hungary, and Turkey have Consulates at Galle.

AUSTRIA-HUNGARY AND ITALY.

Mr. **Gustav A. Marinitsch,** proprietor of the firm of G. A. Marinitsch & Co., importers and exporters, is Imperial and Royal Consul for Austria-Hungary. Mr. Clemens Otto Pöhn, attorney of the firm, is the Acting Imperial and Royal Austro-Hungarian Consul and Royal Consul for Italy, but was only appointed to these positions in September, 1906. He is a native of Vienna and was educated at Leipzig. Before joining Messrs. Marinitsch, nine years ago, he was engaged in business in Leipzig and London. At Galle Mr. C. P. Hayley is Consul for Austria-Hungary.

BELGIUM.

The Belgian Consul at Colombo is Mr. **Arnold William Bernhard Redemann,** a partner in the firm of Messrs. Wills & Co., Ltd., shipping agents and coal proprietors, carrying on business in Colombo as the Krawehl Coal Company. He is a native of Göttingen, Hanover, and before going to Ceylon in 1889 he was in business in Antwerp. He has been Consul of Belgium at Colombo for ten years, and in 1906, for services rendered in this capacity, he was made Chevalier de l'Ordre de Leopold. He is a very keen sportsman and is an authority on most branches of sport in Ceylon.

Mr. William Frederick Diacono, manager of the Krawehl Coal Company at Colombo, is the Consular Agent for Belgium. He comes of an Italian family which emigrated to Malta, and he is a British subject, having been born in Alexandria, Egypt. He was educated at Beirut and has been with the firm of Messrs. Wills & Co., Ltd., for thirty years, first as their agent at Suez from 1879 to 1892, and since then at Colombo. He has been Deputy Consul in Ceylon for four years, and whilst he was in Egypt he was the Portuguese Consul and the agent of the Imperial Ottoman Bank.

DENMARK.

Mr. **Alfred Johnson Sawer** is the Danish Consul, and has held that position since October, 1898. He is a native of Ipswich and was educated there, and he has been connected with the shipping business all his life, at London, West Hartlepool, and Colombo. He has been at the last named place for sixteen years, with Messrs. Whittall & Co., who are the Colombo agents of the Orient Royal Mail Line of steamers, and he has charge of this department of the business.

FRANCE.

Mr. **E. Labussière,** of the Messageries Maritime Line of steamers' branch at Colombo, is the French Consular Agent at Colombo.

GERMANY.

With the exception of Mr. W. Morey, Mr. **Philipp Freudenberg** is the Senior Consul in Ceylon, and has represented Germany in that capacity since 1876. Born in Germany on February 18, 1843, he received his early commercial training at the Raubach Iron Works, which were formerly owned by the Freudenberg family. He has lived in Ceylon since 1873, and his consular appointment dates from January 18th, three years later. During his long term of office he has been the recipient of many decorations, including two from Prussia and one each from Mecklenburg, Weimar, and Oldenburg. He is the head of Messrs. Freudenberg & Co., Colombo agents for the Norddeutscher-Lloyd Company, whose operations are dealt with in another part of this volume. Mr. Freudenberg is the Vice-President of the Colombo branch of the Royal

PHILIPP FREUDENBERG
(Imperial German Consul for the Island.)

Asiatic Society, and the official Ceylon correspondent of several scientific societies in Germany. Mr. Philipp Freudenberg's son is the Vice-Consul.

JAPAN.

One of the newest Consulships in Colombo is that of Japan, which dates from September, 1898, and has been held since then by Lieutenant-Colonel **Charles Edward Hood Symons.** This gentleman comes of one of the best known county families in England, whose chief seats are in Cornwall. He is the son of General Symons, R.A., and went out to Ceylon with the Royal Artillery in 1861. He was stationed in different parts of the island from that year until 1869, when he entered commercial life in Colombo as a broker, and carries on business as such at the present time.

NETHERLANDS.

The Consul for the Netherlands is Mr. **Adalbert Theodor Schulze,** proprietor of the firm of Messrs. Schulze & Co., merchants, who has been thirty-two years in the island. He has been the Consul for two and a half years, and for twelve years previously he acted as Consul for Austria and Hungary. For his services in this capacity he was decorated with the Austrian Order of the Iron Crown. He is also the possessor of the Franz Joseph Jubilee medal.

NORWAY.

Mr. **Edward Becket Creasy,** jun., is the first Norwegian Consul in Ceylon, his appointment dating from the separation of Norway from Sweden in the early part of 1906. He was born in the island, at Galle, in 1872, but was educated in England, at Bedford Grammar School. Since 1893 he has been in business in Colombo as merchant and commission agent.

PERSIA.

Mohamed Ismail Mohamed Alie was appointed Persian Vice-Consul at Colombo about twelve years ago, and is the first Consul of Persia in Ceylon He was born in Colombo and educated privately under Mr. C. B. Nicholas, B.A., resides at Smallpass, San Sebastian Hill, and is a Justice of the Peace. He owns extensive house and shop property in Colombo and several tea estates in the Sabaragamuwa province, which he inherits from his father, who came to Ceylon from the Bombay district.

RUSSIA.

The Russian Consul at Colombo is Mr. **A. N. Bournasheff,** of the firm of Messrs. Stcherbatchoff, Tchokoff & Co., and Mr. Tchokoff is the Acting Vice-Consul.

SIAM.

Mr. **Samuel Donnaclift Young,** partner in the firm of Messrs. Clark, Young & Co., general merchants, is the Consul for Siam in Ceylon, and is the first to hold that position. He comes from Scotland, and has been in Ceylon about seven-and-twenty years, and has been Siamese Consul for ten years. In the Old Country he was in the banking business.

SPAIN AND PORTUGAL.

Mr. **M. T. Finlay,** of Messrs. Finlay, Muir & Co., is the Vice-Consul for Spain in Ceylon and the Consul for Portugal; and Mr. C. S. V. Morrison, of the same firm, is the Acting Consul for both countries.

SWEDEN.

The Consul for Sweden is Mr. **Percy Bois,** who went out to Ceylon about 1872. Although frequently acting as Consul, it is only recently that he took over the official position from Mr. F. W. Bois, who held it for a long series of years. Mr. Percy Bois is the senior partner of Messrs. Bois Bros. & Co., the Colombo agents of the British India Steamship Company. Until the separation of the two kingdoms he was Consul both for Norway and Sweden.

TURKEY.

The Turkish Vice-Consul at Colombo is **Mohamed Macan Markar,** Effendi, head of the firm of O. L. M. Macan Markar, jewellers and gem merchants. He is only twenty-eight years of age, and is said to be the youngest Consul of the East. A native of Galle, he was educated at Wesley College, Colombo, and at the completion of his course there he joined the business established by his late father, of which he is now the principal. He is a member of the Galle Municipal Council and a Mahomedan. At the time of the writing of this book he was on a pilgrimage to Mecca, his consular duties being in his absence performed by his younger brother, Macan Markar Samsideen, another member of the firm. Mr. H. A. Ebrahim Didi is Turkish Consul at Galle.

UNITED STATES.

Mr. **W. Morey,** the senior Consul in Ceylon, is the Consul for the United States, and he has held this position upwards of thirty years. For some time he has lived in semi-retirement, his son, Mr. Elmer Lake Morey, Vice and Deputy Consul, taking full charge. Mr. E. L. Morey was born in the island, and educated at the Royal College, Colombo. In 1884 he went to America and entered the University of Maine, and graduated there as a civil engineer. He then practised his profession, first in the State of New Jersey with the New Jersey Steel and Iron Company, of Trent and New Jersey, and afterwards took over the management of the American Bridge and Iron Company at Roanoake, Virginia. In 1893 he returned to Ceylon, and has since that date been the Vice and Deputy American Consul.

Mr. Jean Steiger is the American Consular Agent at Galle.

ARCHÆOLOGY

By JOHN STILL,

Assistant Archæological Commissioner of Ceylon.

PART I.

HISTORICAL SUMMARY.

CEYLON'S archæology practically dates from the time when Mahinda, the son of Asoka, the great Buddhist king, whose edicts are found widely distributed over India, landed in Ceylon and preached the religion of Buddha. No building now standing can with any accuracy be stated to have existed prior to that date, though there are several which may with some probability be conjectured to have existed even earlier than 307 B.C., the date usually given for Mahinda's arrival. But although architectural and epigraphical records of the earlier periods are wanting, Sinhalese history is by no means silent on the subject. Several of their historical books give a spirited and most interesting account of the ancestry and early youth of Vijaya, the conqueror, who landed in Ceylon with 700 followers in the middle of the sixth century B.C. The island is described as having been peopled at that time by "Yakkhus," or devils, probably merely a polite way of describing a race much darker in colour than the Sinhalese.

On his arrival Vijaya met with a serious mishap, for his followers were one by one overcome by the sorcery of a Yakkhini (female devil) and were "cast weeping into a subterraneous abode." Vijaya, however, vanquished the Yakkhini and released them. The story, as told in the Mahavansa, bears some resemblance to the tale of Ulysses and Circe in the "Odyssey." Afterwards, marrying the Yakkhini, Vijaya waged war successfully against the Yakkhus, and seems to have established himself firmly on the throne of Ceylon. It is from Vijaya's grandfather that the name Sinhalese is derived. A princess of Vanga was carried off by a lion—Sinha (probably an Eastern equivalent of our Richard *Cœur-de-Lion*), to whom she bore two children, a boy and a girl. The son established himself as king of Vanga and married his sister, who bore him Vijaya and many other children.

A still earlier record of Ceylon than the Sinhalese account of Vijaya is afforded by the Ramayana, a great epic poem by the Indian poet Valmiki, which strongly resembles the "Iliad" in its story of the long wars which ensued from the abduction of Sita. In this, too, Ceylon is described as being inhabited by demons, who were finally vanquished by an army reinforced by Hanuman and his hordes of apes. Of these early days the only tangible records that remain to us are the stones—chert and crystal—with which the "demons" pointed their arrows, skinned their game, and lit their fires. Very few of these flakes have so far been found, but prehistoric archæology is only in its extreme infancy in Ceylon.

After the death of Vijaya the capital was moved from Tambapanni to Upatissa, neither of which cities can be said to have been identified. It is possible that the Sinhalese had not yet learned to build in stone, and so have left

ANURADHAPURA—MOONSTONE AND STEPS, KING'S PALACE.

nothing sufficiently imperishable to withstand the ravages of a tropical flora and fauna. Their stone architecture shows so many signs of having been the outcome of a style learnt in building in wood, that it is certain they must have attained considerable skill in carpentry and formed a fixed convention.

SIGIRIYA.

From Upatissa the capital was moved to Anuradhapura in the reign of Pandukabhaya, who ruled from about 437 to 367 B.C., and this city was the seat of the Sinhalese kings for some 1,250 years. It is here that the oldest and finest stone mines are to be found, and this is the city which has chiefly attracted the attention of travellers, from the Chinese Buddhist pilgrims of the fifth, sixth, and seventh centuries A.D. down to our own time.

In about 307 B.C. King Devanampiya Tissa came to the throne, and very shortly afterwards becoming converted to Buddhism, started building on a large scale. In his reign were constructed the Maha Vihara, which was for centuries the centre of orthodox Buddhism; the Thuparama dagoba, which, thanks to successive restorations, still forms one of the chief attractions to Anuradhapura alike in the eyes of Buddhist pilgrims and of other visitors; the huge monastery of Mihintale, eight miles east of Anuradhapura; the Isurumuniya Vihara below the Tissa tank, even now perhaps the most picturesque of all the ruins in Anuradhapura; the adjoining Vessagiriya Vihara, with its rocky caves and old square-character inscriptions; and several other viharas, all of which he liberally endowed. He also obtained from India a branch of that bo-tree under which Buddha sat during his final great temptation, and planted it in Anuradhapura, where it (or its lineal descendant) still receives the adoration of hundreds of thousands of pilgrims. The Tissa tank was also built by and derives its name from this king.

POLONNARUWA—VISHNU DEWALA.

The next important event in Sinhalese history was the arrival, in about 237 B.C., of Sena and Guttika, invaders from the Malabar coast, who reigned for twenty-two years, after which the Sinhalese king Asela held the throne for ten years, only to be slain in his turn by Elala, a Cholian from Southern India, who reigned righteously for four-and-forty years. This was the beginning of a very long series of wars between the Sinhalese and various invaders.

When the Sinhalese were strong enough they invaded Southern India, and when they were weak were in turn overrun and ruled by Pandyan, Cholian, Kalinga or Kerala kings and adventurers. This periodical warfare continued up to the British occupation of Kandy in 1815, when a king of the Madura dynasty was on the throne; and Ceylon's history is one long tale of wars, broken occasionally by the advent of some strong-handed king who ruled with an iron rod, and forced the people to build mighty tanks and temples and to set their affairs in order generally.

Elala the Cholian was slain by Duttagamini in single combat upon elephant-back, and there was again an active period of building. Duttagamini owed his throne to his own endeavours, and the story of his long struggle against the firmly established usurper is one of the most interesting in the Mahavansa. Once fixed on the throne, however, he became as mighty in peace as he had been in war, and to him we

ANURADHAPURA—THE AVKANA BUDDHA.
(A colossal figure carved from the rock.)

ANURADHAPURA—ISURUMUNIYA.
(View from the front of the temple and rocks.)

owe Ruanveli and Mirisveti dagobas, and the Brazen Palace, three of the largest monuments in Anuradhapura. After his death, for fifty years various unimportant kings reigned, and then another great builder came to the throne, called Vatta-gamini, or Valagambahu. But before he had reigned a year he had to flee for his life from Tamil usurpers, who successfully kept him out of his throne for sixteen years. On his return he built the huge Abhayagiri Dagoba, and was responsible for many other pious acts, among which was the conversion of the great rock caves at Dambulla into a vihara.

Thirty-three more kings lived, built and restored tanks and monasteries, and died or were murdered, and then again a strong man came to the throne, about 277 A.D. Maha Sen began his career as a bitter enemy of the orthodox school of Buddhism, and even went so far as to demolish several of the most important shrines; but afterwards he more than made up by his great works of rebuilding, and new building, and of irrigation. The mightiest of all his works in Anuradhapura was the Jetavana, now clothed in forest and the most striking dagoba in Ceylon. He also formed the Minneri tank and sixteen other great irrigation works. Thus, with varying fortune, Anuradhapura remained the capital until about 846 A.D. Kasyapa I. reigned at Sigiriya towards the end of the fifth century, and three hundred years later Agrabodhi VII. made his capital at Polonnaruwa; but with these exceptions Anuradhapura was the seat of the executive.

Continually overrun by invaders of the most ruthless type, and not infrequently the scene of internecine warfare, Anuradhapura is a city of destruction and of restoration. Everywhere may be observed buildings, pavements, and walls composed of the fragments of earlier structures. For no Vandal had less compunction than a king who wished to insure comfort in the next world by extensive ecclesiastical buildings in this. Another feature of Anuradhapura is the Hindu influence as exemplified in its sculpture. This is only to be expected, for most of the kings were closely connected by marriage with the royal families of India. Besides which, the frequent domination of the country by invaders is bound to have had a strong influence, not only on the arts and crafts of the Sinhalese, but also on their religion, and even on their race. Finally, the invasions and destruction of the great religious buildings and of the irrigation works became too much to be borne, and a new capital was established at Polonnaruwa or Pulastipura. It is sometimes asked, When was Anuradhapura abandoned? It was not abandoned. No more than Winchester is abandoned because it has ceased to be the capital of England. From being capital it was reduced to the position of second city, and from that it gradually dwindled to the village found by the English. Polonnaruwa was the capital from 846 A.D. to 1277 A.D., though during that time several kings reigned at other capitals *pro tem.*

By far its greatest king was Parakrama Bahu I., 1164 to 1197 A.D. The list of his achievements is too long to be recorded here, but to show how great a king he was it will be sufficient to mention the following. He won his way to the throne after a long fight against great odds, exhibiting great personal valour as well as the attributes of a leader. He subdued several most determined rebellions in Ruhuna (the Southern Province) and elsewhere, and brought the whole country under his rule. He conquered a large part of Southern India, not only defeating the Tamils on land, but destroying their fleet in a great naval battle off the pearl banks; and he brought the king of Cambodia to sue for terms. In his own kingdom he carried out a system of irrigation so vast that only now is some idea of its extent being grasped. He practically rebuilt Polonnaruwa and caused Anuradhapura to be restored. After a stormy period of war and destruction, Polonnaruwa was again restored by Parakrama Bahu II., then a prince, while his father ruled at Dambadeniya. And in 1293 A.D. it was abandoned as the capital for Kurunegala.

POLONNARUWA—RUINED PART OF A MONASTERY.

It will be seen from this short historical summary that the main features of archæology in Ceylon are a bewildering succession of restorations and a great deal of foreign influence. Owing probably to the fact that every king held his power largely through the priesthood, the great majority of ruins are monastic or otherwise connected with religion.

For some thirty years or more the Ceylon Government has given some attention to archæological research. Photographs of many of the main buildings of Anuradhapura were taken in 1871. A survey was made in 1873, and in 1877 detailed plans and drawings were made of several of the dagobas. Between 1875 and 1879 Professors Goldsmidt and Miller collected copies of inscriptions, and a book was published. Excavation was started in 1884 by Mr. S. M. Burrows, and a good deal of exploration which he carried out in 1884–85 resulted in a great addition to the existing knowledge of the subject. Finally, in 1890 a regular archæological survey was started and has been carried on ever since. Its duties include collection of inscriptions and exploration of the whole island in search of ruins. Excavation, so far, is practically confined to Anuradhapura, Polonnaruwa, and Sigiriya, and the most important examples of restoration are at Sigiriya and Polonnaruwa. Incidentally, the department draws up reports and makes plans, surveys, photographs, &c. The archæological survey is a department of Government, and private persons are not permitted to excavate without special permission.

There is an Ordinance dealing with antiquities, and any one who wilfully damages or defaces or in any way tampers with a ruin is liable to severe penalties. This is a most necessary regulation; for not only do we hear of villagers doing a great deal of damage in their blind search for treasure, but it is to be regretted that even in Ceylon there is to be met the type of infamy-hunting idiot who fancies that his name adds to the beauty or historical interest of ancient monuments.

PART II.

ANURADHAPURA.

As stated in the historical summary, this city was the capital of Ceylon for a period of about 1,250 years. It might therefore be expected that the ruins would show striking diversities of style. But this is not the case. Owing to the conservative nature of the Sinhalese, ruins which stretch over a period of a thousand years are so much alike that without an inscription to guide one it is often impossible to even approximately fix the period of a building. This, of course, both adds to the difficulty and somewhat detracts from the interest of excavation. And despite its great historical interest, the beauty of much of its stonework, and its wonderful park-like spacious views, there is to the non-archæological visitor a certain monotony in the endless rows of great stone pillars. But this monotony is more apparent than real. When the details are looked into it is found that although similar in style, the different carvings and mouldings vary slightly one from another; and doubtless some day it will be possible to attain far more accuracy than at present.

Anuradhapura lies nearly in the centre of the wide plain of which the northernmost half of Ceylon consists. The nearest hill is Mihintale, eight miles to the east; and save for abrupt jungle-covered hills, the country is flat as far as the sea on the north, east, and west, and for twenty miles to the south, where the plain is broken by the striking mountain Ritigala. The city was thus entirely open to all invaders, and offered no sort of natural help to the defenders.

The ruins stretch roughly from Vessagiri on the south to Vijayarama on the north, and from Puliyankulam on the east to the end of the outer circle "palaces" on the west, covering approximately an area five miles long and four miles wide. It must be understood that this does not accurately represent the size of the city; for there are several ruined sites not included in these boundaries which undoubtedly form part of the ancient city or of its suburbs; while quite a large proportion of the area thus defined is composed of huge tanks or artificial lakes.

Much of the land within the city which is now under paddy-fields must have been given up to gardens, but more of it than might be suspected was built upon. Besides the very large number of monastic buildings that now show above ground there must have been an enormous area covered with the houses of the humbler people. Artists, craftsmen, tradesmen, servants, labourers, sweepers, &c., must have existed in great numbers in order to minister to the wants of those who inhabited the more pretentious buildings. So that, allowing for tanks, paddy-fields, and gardens, it is not inconceivable that the native tradition that the city covered sixteen miles each way may be more or less founded on fact. Colombo might with almost equal justice be described as stretching unbroken to Mount Lavinia. Sixteen miles each way would mean a nucleus some four or five miles square, and a straggling

POLONNARUWA—SAT-MAHAL-PRASADA, OR PALACE OF THE SEVEN STOREYS.

POLONNARUWA—FIGURE OF BUDDHA.
(Cut from the solid rock, 46 ft. in length)

connected village all along the main roads for some five or six miles further in each direction. Probably, for instance, Anuradhapura and Mihintale were thus connected. But if so, these suburbs were perishable buildings of mud with cadjan roofs, and have left no trace.

Taking the bo-tree enclosure as the centre, the ruins and ruined areas which afford most interest may be described broadly as follows :—

On the north, (1) the Brazen Palace, (2) the Ruanveli-Thuparama area, (3) the Jetavanarama area, (4) the probable site of the palace, (5) Pankuliya, (6) Vijayarama and Kiribatvihara.

On the south, (7) Elala's tomb, (8) Isurumuniya and the ruins below Tissa bund, (9) Vessagiriya.

On the east, (10) the Abahayagiri area, (11) the Tholuvila monastery, (12) the Puliyankulam monastery.

On the west, (13) the Mirisvetiya area, (14) the outer circle "palaces."

1. The Brazen Palace was built by King Duttagamini, who came to the throne about 161 B.C. It is stated in the Mahavansa to have been originally nine storeys high, to have contained one thousand rooms, and to have been roofed with brazen tiles. Later it was reduced to seven storeys, and was pulled down by Maha Sen about 300 A.D., but was again restored by the same king after he had renounced his evil ways. The present ruin covers a space some 232 ft. square, and consists of monolithic gneiss pillars, 1,600 in number. They are all plain, and most of them still rough; they must have been coated in some way which concealed their rugged outlines.

2. The Ruanveli-Thuparama area is a stretch of open park-like country, about half a mile long and half that width. At the southern end stands Ruanveli, the *magnum opus* of Duttagamini. Despite the hideous effect of modern partial restoration, there is still much to attract one in its *entourage*. On the east side, near the flight of steps, there are statues of Buddha and one of a king. This last is about 10 ft. high and is a fine piece of work. It is popularly supposed to represent Duttagamini, but this is exceedingly doubtful. At the four altars, at the four cardinal points, there are many carved stones, a large number of which show traces of having been painted, as was a great deal of the old stonework. And both on the pavements and on upright slabs there are inscriptions of dates varying from the first to the twelfth centuries A.D.

In the park, to the west of the dagoba, are two monasteries of the usual plan—that is to say, a large central building with four smaller ones arranged round it like the pips on a "five" of playing cards—but with unusually good stonework, the entrance in particular being highly ornamented, with balustrades carved in the shape of "makaras," with "Nagaraja" guard-stones, "moonstone" carved in high relief with the figures of animals, &c., and with "ganas" depicted on the steps. As these designs occur over and over again, it will be as well to explain what they are.

The makara is akin to our griffin, and is, of course, a fabulous animal. The Nagas were a snake-worshipping race of Southern India, who are always described in mythology as actually being snakes. On the guard-stones they are depicted as graceful men with from three to nine cobra heads raised as a hood behind them. Buddha is said to have converted them to his philosophy. A "moonstone" is a semicircular slab which is to be found at the foot of most flights of steps at Anuradhapura. Some "moonstones" are beautifully carved with processions of animals and geese. The ganas answer to our fairies or brownies, and are the people of Ganesh, the elephant-headed god. Of course they belong more to Hinduism than to Buddhism. In the ruins just mentioned there are delightful representations of ganas on all the pillar capitals; some singing, some playing on various musical instruments, some clashing cymbals, and all seeming as jolly a set of little men as one could wish to run across in some dark glade of the forest.

From the ruins just described the whole space north to Thuparama is covered with buildings of various sorts and sizes, ponds lined with stone, wells, &c. Several of the monasteries are of considerable size, including within their inner walls the usual set of five buildings, and within their outer premises all sorts of refectories, kitchens, bath-rooms, lavatories, &c., some of which are at least as interesting as the more pretentious structures.

At the northern end of this park stands Thuparama, which after many restorations retains its outlines much as when in the third century B.C. it was built by Devanampiya Tissa, the first Sinhalese Buddhist king. The exceedingly graceful pillars which surround it may have supported a species of cloister; they are not quite so old as the dagoba. Close beside it, on the east, is the original Dalada Maligawa—the Palace of the Tooth—into which the sacred relic of Buddha's tooth was placed when it was brought over from India in the beginning of the third century A.D. There it was in good company, for the collar-bone relic is enshrined in the Thuparama. The tooth relic is now in the Dalada Maligawa, Kandy.

The whole neighbourhood of this part of the city is studded with ruins, and not the least worthy of note is a magnificently cut monolithic cistern some one hundred yards east of Thuparama.

3. The Jetavanarama area takes its name from the huge dagoba which, towering aloft with its great brick spire on the summit, is one of the most striking features of Anuradhapura. This dagoba was built in the reign of Maha Sen, the same king who destroyed and afterwards rebuilt the Brazen Palace. But besides the dagoba itself there is plenty of interest in the forest round, which is literally full of ruins, some of them very beautiful. This area is as yet practically untouched by the archæological survey.

4. The supposed site of the palace is on the high ground, some quarter-mile north of the modern hospital. There are not many ruins there, but one brick building of the Polonnaruwan period is worthy of note.

5. Pankuliya is a complete monastery on the banks of the Malwatu-Oya, some one and a half miles north-east of Jetavanarama. There is a stone bridge in good preservation not far from it.

6. Vijayarama is a most picturesque and extensive monastery buried in the jungle a couple of miles north of Jetavanarama. It is not easy to get to, but is worth a visit.

7. Elala's tomb is south of the bo-tree enclosure; it is really a dagoba, but may mark the spot where Elala was buried.

8. Isurumuniya is a most picturesque little rock temple a mile south of the bo-tree. It was built in the reign of Devanampiya Tissa, and is one of the oldest sites of Anuradhapura. While visiting this the interesting ruins below Tissa bund and a few hundred yards north of Isurumuniya should also be seen. Like everything else in Anuradhapura, they have been restored in fairly modern times, probably in the twelfth century A.D.

9. Vessagiriya is one of the most interesting places in Anuradhapura, and will be even more worthy of a visit when the excavations now (1906) in course are carried to a close. It was founded by Devanampiya Tissa, and many of the cave inscriptions date from about that period. But the excavations now in progress show it to have been extensively rebuilt in the eighth century A.D. by Kasyapa, the parricide king, who reigned at Sigiriya.

10. The Abhayagiriya area teems with ruins, all of which have been excavated. The dagoba itself was built by King Valagambahu, who reigned in the first century B.C. Its enormous size is productive of thought. In its vicinity the most interesting ruins are the Buddhist railing to the south and a large brick building on the west.

11. The Tholuvila monastery is close to the railway station, and is noteworthy for its long street connecting the two raised areas on which stood the dagoba and the principal buildings. On either side of this street are many smaller buildings which were the dwelling-houses of the monks.

12. The Puliyankulam monastery is an extensive collection of rather plain buildings about two and a half miles from Anuradhapura town, adjoining the Jaffna road. Close to it, on the rising ground to the west of the road, are some curious shapeless brick-lined pits, which have long puzzled all endeavour to discover their use. They may have been a cemetery, or a salt store, or prisons, or wild animals' dens, or the dwellings of troglodytes. This latter I personally think most probable, but it is open to any one to theorise.

To return for a moment to the monastery, which is undoubtedly of later date than the pits. Although it is not apparent, yet when drawn out on paper it is seen that the buildings follow a regular and quite symmetrical plan, which shows some skill on the part of the designer. Most of the larger monasteries look better on paper than on the ground, as regards plan, for in their jungle-covered, ruined state the symmetry of their arrangement is often overlooked.

13. The Mirisveti area is between the Basawakkulam and Tissa tanks. The dagoba was built by Duttagamini, and has now been hideously disfigured by a fruitless attempt at restoration. The ruins which surround the dagoba are, I think, one of the comparatively modern restorations. It is noticeable that they were never finished, all the carving remaining to be done, as may be seen by the traced, unfinished designs.

14. The outer circle "palaces" are a series of sets of buildings, so called because they are on and near the outer circle road, and because they are unlike the ordinary monasteries, and are supposed to have been the houses of the nobles. They have not been excavated yet, and may yield much of interest.

15. The bo-tree itself is a living antiquity. It is not the oldest historical tree in the world, as is often stated, for even if its parent at Buddhagaya is no more, there remains the

POLONNARUWA—HIRAGE (JAIL) RUIN.
(The walls are over 8 ft. thick.)

tree planted by Confucius, who flourished about 550 B.C. But in any case this tree at Anuradhapura has been revered by millions for a period of some 2,200 years. Its enclosure, though ruined and curtailed in size, still bears witness to the accuracy of the observations of Fa Hien, the Chinese pilgrim who visited Ceylon in the beginning of the fifth century A.D.

16. Finally, a word as to the palace. There is no existing building which can be identified as such. Possibly it may have been totally destroyed; but more probably it may have been composed of a large number of different buildings, which are now supposed to be monasteries. The mere finding of images and of religious buildings in any area would not prove it not to have contained the palace; for it is almost certain that the king would have had some form of private chapel. His queens, too, would in all probability come from India, and would be of the Hindu faith. As already stated, it is supposed that the high ground north of the hospital may be the royal site; but this conjecture is only formed on negative evidence, and no certainty can be attained until some further discovery throws light on the matter.

It will be noted that gigantic stonework is a feature of Anuradhapura. Huge columns and slabs abound on every side, while the labour involved in the manufacture of some of these great cisterns and "stone canoes" is stupendous. These so-called "canoes" always provoke curiosity. They were actually to hold the boiled rice that was doled out to the priests in the various alms-halls. A splendid specimen of an alms-hall is to be seen near Ruanveli in the compound of the present rest-house.

PART III.

MIHINTALE.

EIGHT miles due east of Anuradhapura is the hill and village of Mihintale. It was on this hill that, according to the Sinhalese historians, King Devanampiya Tissa first met Prince Mahinda, the Buddhist missionary, and was, with his suite, converted on the spot. In India, Buddhism flourished as it never had before, under the protection of King Asoka. From his capital city, Pataliputra (the modern Patna), he sent envoys to all the countries he knew of, and among others his son Mahinda was deputed to visit Ceylon, where the religion of Buddha was as yet unknown.

King Tissa was hunting a sambur on the Missa mountain (Mihintale) when he came upon Mahinda and his companions, and after a very short discourse he and all his suite embraced the new faith. Helped by the royal patronage, Buddhism spread rapidly, and was soon the accepted religion of the country. One of King Tissa's earliest works was to convert the hill into a monastery, which he bestowed upon Mahinda.

The Mahavansa mentions the construction of sixty-eight rock cells, and these may still be seen in much the same state as of old, some of them still inhabited by priests and some buried in jungle. Above their entrances are cut drip ledges to carry off the rain-water, and under these there are often inscriptions dating from a time not much more modern than 300 B.C., when Mahinda still flourished. In about 259 B.C. Mahinda died and was cremated. His bodily relics were divided up and some of them enshrined at Mihintale in a dagoba there, probably the one now known as the Ambastale dagoba.

The hill itself is some 1,000 ft. high and is steep and rocky. From foot to summit it is clothed in forest, in which lie hidden numbers of caves, ponds, ruins, flights of steps, and even several dagobas. Up the eastern flank of the hill is a broad, easy flight of steps, combining a series of terraces and leading to a broad platform, where there is a fine refectory and several other ruins. From here onwards a narrower flight continues up to the present-day monastery; and then the way proceeds by other steps to the summit, where there is a small dagoba called the Et Vihara. The monks live, some in caves, and some in a long low pansala round about the Ambastale dagoba. This is supposed to stand on the actual site where Tissa and Mahinda first met, while a rocky crag just above it is said to be the spot on which Mahinda landed when he flew over from India. Although a little difficult, this crag is well worth climbing for the beautiful view that is obtained from its summit. Other items which should not be missed are Mahinda's bed, a curious rock-hewn couch on the edge of a precipitous descent to the wilderness of jungle and boulders below, and the Naga Pokuna, a rock pool with a large five-headed cobra carved on its wall.

At the foot of Mihintale there are several smaller hills, in each of which are many most interesting remains, some of them in every way well worthy of a visit. Not only do they date to a very early period and offer much of interest to the archæologist, but from their romantic situation and intrinsic beauty they must attract the admiration of all who find time to visit them. Indeed, my advice to any one, either antiquary or sightseer, is to cut short a day of the time available for Anuradhapura rather than miss Mihintale.

POLONNARUWA—JETAVANARAMA VIHARA.
(View from the north-east.)

PART IV.

SIGIRIYA.

BEYOND the last outposts of the Kandyan hills, in the borders of the wide plain that stretches north to the sea, stands Sigiriya, the cliff-crowned hill on which King Kasyapa, the parricide, built his fortress citadel in the fifth century A.D. This is by far the most striking ruined site in Ceylon. On every side Sigiriya presents an eminently attractive picture, rising high over the forest, and seeming, with its sheer ruddy-coloured cliffs, less like a hill than some huge unscalable castle.

The history of its short life as the capital of Ceylon may be briefly told. In the latter half of the fifth century A.D. King Dhatusena established himself on the throne of Anuradhapura. For nearly thirty years he had waged war on the Tamils, who overran and ruled the country, and, embittered probably by the struggle, he ruthlessly punished all who had favoured his enemies. But he ruled with a strong hand, and carried out great irrigation works. He had two sons, Moggalana, born of his consort, and Kasyapa, born of an inferior spouse; and he had a daughter, who was married to her cousin Migara, the chief of the army. In about the year 479 A.D. Migara and Kasyapa rebelled, took the king prisoner, and, after submitting him to much indignity, walled him up alive in his prison. The patience and dignity of the old king is touchingly described in the Mahavansa: "Thus," says the historian, who was a personal friend of the king, "worldly prosperity is like unto the glimmering of lightning." Moggalana, unable to make headway against his brother, fled to India, and seems there to have enjoyed some success in his quest of allies, for Kasyapa abandoned Anuradhapura, and, in the words of the Mahavansa, took himself to the Sigiri rock. that was hard for men to climb. He cleared it round about and surrounded it by a rampart, and built galleries in it ornamented with figures of lions; wherefore it took its name of Sigiri, "the lion's rock." There established, he reigned for eighteen years, and tried by good works to atone for his crime, but "he lived on in fear of the world to come and of Moggalana." At the end of eighteen years Moggalana returned from India with an army, and, driving Kasyapa away from his impregnable stronghold, defeated him in a great battle. Kasyapa committed suicide on the back of his elephant, and Moggalana established himself as king at Anuradhapura, which again became the capital.

Sigiriya was converted into a monastery and placed under the charge of Mahanama, the author of the first part of the Mahavansa. Henceforth it disappeared from history, save for one reference to it in the seventh century A.D., when King Sanga Tissa and his son were taken there and decapitated.

It is strange that a fortress so pre-eminently strong as Sigiriya should figure so shortly in the stormy history of Ceylon. But no further records have so far come to light. Possibly the great gallery may have been breached, and so the chief value of the place lost. But certainly Sigiriya, in its prime, must have been impregnable to every form of attack save starvation or treachery from within.

Its modern history dates from the time when, some sixty years ago, it began to attract the attention of English officials and others who passed through that part of the country. At that time, and for many years after, it was covered with dense jungle, save where the great cliffs towered up, hardly seeming to offer any possible means of access to the summit. And it was dreaded by the villagers as a favourite haunt of evil spirits. The first attempt in modern times to explore it systematically was made in the sixties; but for many years the ascent was a matter of great

POLONNARUWA--JETAVANARAMA VIHARA.
(View of the front, east)

difficulty, and necessitated the use of ladders for the first part, after which the climber had to trust to the narrow rock-cut grooves in which the gallery was built of old. During this period but little idea could be gained of the tremendous quantity of buildings which have since been unearthed, for the whole of the slopes below the cliffs and the whole summit were clad in forest.

The operations of the archæological survey began in 1895, and now (1906) the whole summit and several of the terraces have been completely excavated, the gallery has been repaired and has been partially restored, and the final climb up the rock face has been rendered comparatively easy by the fixing of iron ladders and railings.

The general plan of the city and citadel is as follows: Sigiriya is a steep, boulder-strewn hill, which rises abruptly for some 150 to 200 ft., and then culminates in a huge rock, some half a mile in circumference and 300 or 400 ft. high. The whole of the slopes below the rocks are terraced and were built upon. Each terrace is supported by a revetment wall of squared blocks of stone faced with brick, and they are connected and interconnected by innumerable flights of limestone steps, which finally join, and in two grand stairs lead to the lower end of the wonderful gallery which is the only means of reaching the summit. On the east and on the west the slopes are low and the cliffs proportionately high; but on the south, and more especially on the north, the terraced slopes run far higher up the rock, and in one place reach to within about 200 ft. of the summit.

ANURADHAPURA—RUANVELI DAGOBA.

The gallery commences on the western side, and running along the face of the rock, comes out on the upper terrace on the north. This is a flat space some 70 yards long and 40 wide, and on three sides of it the ground falls rapidly away. On the east is a series of precipices; on the west is a long slope which is carried into some score of terraces, only the upper three of which have been excavated; and on the north are successive precipices and terraced slopes. In the uppermost of these northern cliffs there are to be seen huge rock-cut dovetailed slots, which seem to show that there was an alternative method of approaching this upper terrace which could be used when the gallery was blocked.

ANURADHAPURA—JETAVANARAMA DAGOBA.

From this upper terrace, or platform, the gallery ran a zigzag course to the summit, ascending by the only one spot—some 4 ft. wide—in the whole circumference that does not overhang. At the present time this upper gallery has completely disappeared, but we can trace its course by the rock-cut groove which held its foundations. For this gallery, like the still existing one below, was built like a swallow's nest, right on the face of the cliff, trusting for its support solely to the cut grooves. As an engineering feat it is quite unique.

At the foot of the final gallery are to be seen the great paws of the lion which gave the rock its name. It was made of brick and plaster, and the passage ran right through it. All that remains are the mighty claws, each as big as a man, which stand on either side of the flights of steps. The summit is some 150 yards long from north to south, and half that from east to west. It is irregular in shape and in level, but the buildings with which it is closely covered, not an inch being wasted, are ingeniously planned to make the most of the site; and little flights of steps have been introduced everywhere to render intercommunication easy and rapid. Save by the gallery, nothing without wings could possibly unaided reach the top of Sigiriya; and the several large cisterns, doubtless fed from the large catchment area afforded by the roofs of so extensive a citadel, would amply provide against shortage of water.

An interesting feature is the ruined gallery on the west, which led to a small watch-cave perched high over the city on the western cliff.

At the foot of the terraced slopes is a wilderness of enormous boulders, each of which was utilised to build upon, and beneath which are caves, the inscriptions over which prove them to have existed as places of worship and the abodes of monks at about the time of Christ. Below these again is a wide space walled by a great bund, in which are several moated mounds like islands, on one of which there appears to have been a garden.

Finally, a word as to the frescoes. Some 50 ft. above the lower end of the gallery and slightly overhanging it there are two hollows—caves—in the face of the cliff. In these are a remarkable series of frescoes, representing rather handsome female figures slightly above life size. They are well executed and most spirited. From their great diversity of feature, and from their lifelikeness, it is imagined that they were actual portraits. The scene depicted seems to be part of a procession towards a dagoba, or shrine, for the ladies are followed by slaves of darker hue who bear baskets of flowers. An examination of the rock face shows that these figures only form part of a picture of the astounding dimensions of some 80 to 100 yards long and perhaps 75 ft. high. Protected by their situation in the hollow they occupy, these wonderful fifth-century frescoes have remained fresh in colour and clear in outline; while the rest of the vast picture, save for scraps remaining in holes and hollows, has been washed away by the south-west rains.

A wire-rope ladder offers a somewhat precarious means of access to this unique picture-gallery; but it is only kept in position during the working months of the Archæological Survey, usually January to April. Of these frescoes a complete full-size set of copies in oils has been completed by the Archæological Survey. These are now in the Colombo Museum.[1]

[1] A reproduction of the most perfect portions of these beautiful artistic relics, from coloured drawings specially prepared from the copies in the Colombo Museum, will be found elsewhere.

PART V

POLONNARUWA

POLONNARUWA, known of old as Pulastipura, is first mentioned in the reign of Agrabodhi III. (624–640 A.D.), and seems to have been a town of some size at that time. But it was not until the reign of Agrabodhi VII. (781–787 A.D.) that it first became the seat of government, and then only for six years. However, not long afterwards—in 846 A.D.—it was fixed upon as the capital, and it retained the honour of being premier city until about 1293 A.D., although during that period the seat of government was several times moved temporarily elsewhere.

The great builder who practically re-created the city of Polonnaruwa was Parakrama Bahu I. (1164–1197 A.D.), and it is probable that most of the existing buildings are of his period, although possibly to some considerable extent restored later. It may be said that even the area of the city of Polonnaruwa is as yet undetermined, though it is improbable that very large buildings remain undiscovered. The style is distinctly more Hindu than that found at Anuradhapura, and naturally the buildings are in much better preservation. Several are in so comparatively complete a state that the roof still remains in part.

The jungle in the neighbourhood of Polonnaruwa is of a much more open character than that round Anuradhapura, and abounds in open stretches of park country. The tank is extensive and very beautiful, showing at certain times of the year a sheet of pink lotus flowers. The principal ruins run in a line north and south, and a guide is essential if it is proposed to wander anywhere off the track. The ruins most worthy of notice are: (1) The remains of the palace, with its thickbrick walls like a castle. (2) The Thuparama (so called), a great brick building in which the roof is still *in situ*. (3) The little stone-built Siva temple, locally and erroneously known as the Dalada Maligawa. (4) The Wata-da-ge, or circular relic house, one of the finest specimens of Sinhalese architecture in Ceylon. (5) The Sat-mahal-prasada, a seven-storeyed building of the Cambodian type. (6) The Jetavanarama, an

ANURADHAPURA—THE REST-HOUSE.

VIEWS OF POLONNARUWA AND ANURADHAPURA.

POLONNARUWA.

1. The Jetavanarama (another view). 2. The Thuparama. 3. The Demala Maha Seya.

ANURADHAPURA.

4. Abhayagiri Dagoba. 5. Isurumuniya Temple. 6. Mirisvetiya Dagoba.

enormous brick structure with walls 50 or 60 ft. high. (7) The Rankot Vihara Dagoba. (8) The Kiri Vihara Dagoba. (9) The great rock-hewn images at the Gal Vihara, perhaps the most striking ruin in Polonnaruwa. (10) The Demala Maha Seya, a smaller building of the same style as the Jetavanarama, and many other buildings in the forest and park country in the vicinity. One might wander for days and yet not see all of Polonnaruwa.

Space does not allow of further description here, and the visitor is recommended to obtain from the Government Printer the Archæological Survey's Reports, in which further information will be found; while those who really wish to gain some knowledge of Sinhalese history cannot do better than study the Mahavansa, the history kept by the Buddhist priests up to the date of the British occupation of Kandy. This history was written by Mahanama in the fifth century A.D., and was afterwards at various times added to and brought up to date by various authors. It is borne out to a remarkable degree by archæological research, and gains considerable support from the accounts in the travels of Fa Hien and other Chinese travellers.

PART VI.

OTHER RUINS IN CEYLON.

After Polonnaruwa was abandoned as the capital of Ceylon no other great city arose in its place. Invaders from India overran the northern part of the island and spread down the coasts. Raids were made by expeditions of Malays and Chinese, and finally in the sixteenth century the Portuguese gained a foothold in the island. From this time onwards the Sinhalese king practically held only the Kandyan provinces, his low-country domains being gradually seized and held by foreigners, first Portuguese, then Dutch, with whom the Sinhalese maintained intermittent warfare.

In 1796 the English became possessors of the Dutch territories, and in 1815 they captured Kandy and deported the last king, who was a monster of the most cruel description. During this troublous time the following cities were successively the capital of Ceylon: Dambadeniya, Yapahu, Kurunegala, Gampola, Kotta, Sitavaka, and Kandy. At each of these there are some few remains of their former glory, Yapahu in particular possessing some fine stonework. But the more interesting ruins of Ceylon are not these decadent latter-day capitals.

Throughout the Northern, North Central, Eastern, Uva, and Southern Provinces, there are so many ruins that no forest officer, surveyor, or sportsman spends long in these wild jungle districts before he comes upon grey stone pillars standing as the sole relic of a glory which is past. At several places there are enormous monolith Buddhas, the Ankuna standing image, hewn from rock, near the Kalawewa tank, standing over 30 ft. high.

At a most inaccessible place in the Northern Province there is a buried city which has as yet not even been thoroughly explored. The tank and town go by the name of Kuruntan Kulam and Kuruntan Ur now, but their ancient name is unknown. At Kalawewa there are ruins which tradition calls Vigitapura; a city of that name was founded in the sixth century B.C., but whether these ruins are on the same site is not known. In the very wild country in the border of the Eastern Province and Uva there are scores of ruins, some of them being fortified hills which resisted the Tamil inroads in the thirteenth century A.D. The hill known

SIGIRIYA.
(The path up the hill.)

as "Westminster Abbey" is the hill which, under the name of Govinda Hela, proved almost the only city of refuge for the Sinhalese when Magha wasted the country about 1215 A.D. When cleared and excavated it may prove another Sigiriya, but as yet it has rarely even been visited. But of all these little-known cities, Tissamaharama, in the Southern Province, is the greatest, and when excavated may prove to be of great size and importance. It was founded about the fourth century B.C., and was the capital of the principality of Ruhuna. Ruhuna was sometimes a principality, sometimes an independent kingdom, and sometimes subject to and part of the dominions of the king of Anuradhapura, its condition varying according to the strength and capacity of the supreme sovereign. Any trouble which arose in the royal family usually ended in the defeated person flying to Ruhuna, there to stir up discord, which generally ended in open rebellion.

The archæology of this part of the island is little known as yet, and is expected to yield valuable results in the future. From this short account it will be seen that Ceylon affords an almost endless field for the antiquary, who may wander for months and still continue to find ruins of a great civilisation which was already decadent when we were fighting the Crusades. Although of much later date than the foregoing, and perhaps hardly ruins, mention must be made of the fine Dutch forts to be seen at many of the sea-coast towns. There are magnificent specimens at Jaffna, Galle, Matara, and many other places, and they are well worthy of a visit.

ANURADHAPURA—THE BRAZEN PALACE RUINS.

People often ask what finds are made during the prosecution of excavation in the ruined cities of Ceylon. Compared with excavations in other countries our finds have been very few, owing partly to the climate, and partly to the fact that the cities were never suddenly abandoned, but dwindled and gradually decreased in size, so that people left very little behind them which they valued sufficiently to remove. We have, however, unearthed gold necklaces and other ornaments, stones such as sapphires, rubies, spinel, tourmalines, &c., either uncut, roughly polished, or cut *en cabochon*, and numbers of beautifully cut and polished crystals. Figures of gods and animals, gongs, bells, cymbals, dishes, &c., have been found in bronze; and spear-heads, arrow-heads, knives, sickles, chisels, padlocks, hammers, adzes, ploughshares, chains, ola pens, and many other tools, implements, and weapons have been found in iron. Pottery of various kinds, beautifully moulded bricks, and ornamental tiles are not of infrequent occurrence, and we have got a fair number of coins.

Ceylon numismatics is a most interesting study, which there is not space to do more than very briefly describe here. But the following list of coins will give some idea of the large variety which have at various times been found: Punch-marked coins or "Eldlings," early Buddhist copper coins, coins of various southern Indian dynasties, Roman coins, Chinese coins, coins of the Caliphs, Venetian sequins, Portuguese coins, Dutch coins, Byzantine coins, silver fish-hook coins, or larins, and the issues of the Sinhalese kings of the twelfth and thirteenth centuries A.D. in gold, silver, and copper.

ANURADHAPURA—THE THUPARAMA.
(Doorway and arched entrance to the shrine.)

Another feature of Sinhalese antiquities is the large number of inscriptions found. These give a complete epigraphical record of the gradual change of the writing from the square character of the Asokan edicts to the present form of Sinhalese. The earliest inscriptions are on rocks, above the entrances to cave cells of the monks. These were succeeded by large rock inscriptions on levelled places; the next change was to inscribed pillars; and finally to large slabs of stone, beautifully prepared to receive the record. Almost without exception the inscriptions of every date record the granting of some gift or privilege to a monastery or to the priesthood. But many of them are long, and incidentally give much information concerning the ancestry and deeds of the king who caused them to be cut, and on contemporary history generally. The enormous majority of them are in archaic Sinhalese, though sometimes titles and honorifics are in Pali. There are a few score of Tamil and Grantua inscriptions known, and some half a dozen perhaps in Sanskrit. It must be added that it is not safe to buy antiquities unless with some knowledge of the subject. Coins, in particular, are forged freely.

A few words in conclusion on the subject of the accommodation for travellers and the means of communication. At Anuradhapura there is a rest-house, and there will shortly be a hotel for the accommodation of visitors. Guides and carriages of sorts are to be obtained for fair prices. The railway runs to within a mile of the town, and there are two trains daily. At Sigiriya there is a rest-house, with two bedrooms and four beds. No guide can as a rule be obtained further than a villager, who will speak no English. The Matale-Trincomalee coach runs within 5½ miles of Sigiriya, and passes daily. The 5½ miles from Inamaluwa are along a fairly good road. At Polonnaruwa there is at present no accommodation further than a small unfurnished bungalow, designed for the use of officials when on circuit. But there is shortly to be built a rest-house. From Habarane, on the Matale-Trincomalee coach road, a good road leads to Polonnaruwa, 26 miles away, passing on the way the great Minneriya tank. Except at Kandy, Kurunegala, and Kotta, there is no sort of accommodation at any of the other places mentioned, though in the neighbourhood of several there are official circuit bungalows. The roads all over the island are fairly good, and as a rule offer no difficulty during the dry weather.

GEOGRAPHICAL AND METEOROLOGICAL FEATURES

CEYLON occupies a commanding position in the Indian Ocean to the south of India, from which it is divided by Palk's Strait, a shallow piece of sea. Its exact geographical position is between 5° 53′ and 9° 51′ N. lat. and 79° 42′ and 81° 55′ E. long. At the narrowest part of Palk's Strait, from Point Palmyra (in the north of the Jaffna peninsula) to Point Calimere, only a distance of 40 miles separates the two countries. There are two islands in the vicinity, named Mannar and Rameswaram, and between them some sandbanks known by the name of Adam's Bridge, and across here it is proposed to construct a railway connecting Ceylon with India. Eastwards from Ceylon is Burma, the Malay Peninsula, and the islands of Sumatra and Java. To the south-east, just over 3,000 miles away, is Australia, which can be reached in a first-class steamer in about ten days. Other distances from Colombo, the principal port of call which is situated on the west coast, to the principal ports are as follow: To Madras 609 miles (two and a half days' journey), Bombay 891 miles (three days), Calcutta 1,250 miles (four days), Rangoon 1,217 miles (four days), and Singapore 1,574 miles (five days). It is a seven days' journey to Aden, 2,093 miles away; ten days to Fremantle, 3,135 miles away; seventeen days to Capetown, in South Africa, 6,154 miles off. The journey from London *viâ* Gibraltar and the Suez Canal, a distance of 7,083 miles, takes about twenty-four days. By travelling overland and embarking at Naples the voyager shortens his journey by six or seven days. Ceylon, with its islands, has an area of 25,841 square miles; its extreme length is 270 miles, its extreme breadth 140 miles, and its circumference 760 miles. The chief islands lying off the coast are Delft and Leyden, in Palk's Strait; Mannar and Karativu, off the west coast; and the Great and Little Basses off the south-east coast. The latter are two groups of rock extremely dangerous to shipping. Coming to Ceylon itself, the principal points are Point Palmyra, in the north; Kalpitiya, in the west; Dondra Head, in the south; Sangamanakanda (to the north of Komariya, in the Eastern Province), and Foul Point, south of Trincomalee Harbour. Other points are Beruwela Point, Vendeloos Point, Elephant Point, and Point Pedro. Very few of the river mouths form inlets, owing to their being blocked by sand-bars caused by the monsoons. The important inlets are Portugal Bay and Kalpitiya Gulf (now called Puttalam Lake) on the west, Weligama Bay on the south, Vendeloos Bay, Trincomalee Harbour, and Kokkilai Bay on the east.

Ceylon is very elevated in the south central portion, but round the coast there is a wide strip of low land. Of the mountains, the highest is Pidurutalagala, which rises to 8,296 ft. above the level of the sea and 2,000 ft. above the Nuwara Eliya plain. There are also Kirigalpotta, Totapala, Adam's Peak, Namanakulakanda, and Great Western, which are over 7,000 ft. above the level of the sea. Adam's Peak is sacred to Buddhist, Hindu, and Mahomedan, and was for a long period regarded as the highest point, whilst it is still the most noticeable and remarkable of the mountains, its clearly marked peak being seen far out at sea during the season of the north-east monsoon. The Horton Plains (7,000 ft. high), Nuwara Eliya Plains (6,000 ft.), and the Wilson Plains are the principal plateaus amongst these mountains. There are many rivers flowing from the hills, the largest being: Mahaveli Ganga (206 miles long), Malwatu-Oya (104 miles), Kala-Oya (97 miles), Yan-Oya (94 miles), Kelan Ganga (90 miles), Deduru-Oya (87 miles), Maduru-Oya (86 miles), Walawe Ganga (83 miles), Menik Ganga (81 miles), Maha-Oya (78 miles), Kirindi-Oya (73 miles), Kalu Ganga (70 miles), Gin Ganga (70 miles), Kumbukkan-Oya (70 miles), Mi-Oya (67 miles), and Gai-Oya (62 miles). Most of the lakes in Ceylon are made, or partially made, by damming up the lower courses of streams. Both the Kandy and Nuwara Eliya lakes are partially artificial. The chief lagoons are Puttalam, Negombo, Moratuwa, Batticaloa, Tamblegam, Mullaitivu, and Jaffna, and there are also about the island many artificial tanks for irrigation purposes. The functionary administering the government of the island is styled "Governor of Ceylon and the dependencies thereof." These "dependencies" only embrace the numerous "atolls" or groups of islets which are included in the Maldivian Archipelago. The principal of these is Malé, which is also the port of call and capital. The Sultan of the Maldives enjoys the protection of the British Government, and, by the treaty of 1883, pays annual tribute to the Government of Ceylon, which exercises certain rights in the control of the group. The islands are 400 miles distant from Ceylon, and a good many of them are hardly any more than coral-reefs. The inhabitants speak a mixed dialect of Indian and Sinhalese compounds, and engage largely in the cultivation of the coconut-palm and in the curing and preserving of fish, which is imported in large quantities into Ceylon. Cowries and coral are also exported from the Maldives.

About 270 miles to the west of Ceylon is another sandy island, Nimicoy, on which is erected a lighthouse. The island is just beginning to be inhabited, though supplies have to be drawn from Ceylon for the present.

A meteorological survey of Ceylon reveals conditions which are, practically, a combination of every degree of temperature one experiences in the East; for here Nature is not seen under one aspect, as is the case with so many other Oriental countries, but there appear to be complete transitions between the most opposite extremes which exist in the tropics. In short, it may be said that the climate of Ceylon—affected as it is by the monsoonal changes—is no less varied than its soil; and throughout the year, while no fixed seasons are remarked, variations may be found to occur from chill winter to overpowering heat. Generally speaking, the climatic conditions are mild, pleasant, and equable. Dry years, however, are not unusual; and long periods of drought often follow the failure of the monsoons. During these times the districts on the coast undergo an unpleasant change from nine months' hot weather to three months' hotter, and much anxiety is caused the heart of the poor village agriculturist by reason of the famine and hardship which ensue. At other times, again, the prodigal action of Nature in the matter of rainfall occasions him serious injury by the flooding of his fields, and not infrequently also the destruction of his homestead.

The climate of Ceylon may broadly be said to divide itself into two distinct periods. First is the dry season, which covers the months from January to May; second is a fitful period of rain and dampness extending through the succeeding portion of the year. The two principal factors in the production of these influences are the north-east and south-west monsoons, which blow across the island, the first occurring in or about May and the second in the latter portion of the year. The origin of the south-west monsoon is said to be in the union of the south-east trade winds with the circulation of the air-currents caused by heat waves as they flow across the Arabian Sea and the Bay of Bengal. In Ceylon its arrival is heralded by what is known as the "little monsoon," which, from a gentle zephyr, assumes, in a remarkably short space of time, the proportions of a furious cyclonic storm, and becomes identified with the "big" or south-west monsoon, the principal climatic feature of Ceylon. The direction of these winds determines the amount of moisture and the distribution of the rainfall, and the same influence delimits the island into its several dry and wet zones. Taking the various provinces, it may be said that while the wettest—and, consequently, the most fertile—portions of Ceylon are to be found in the mountainous country of the midlands, the districts in the north and south-east are practically arid tracts, with sparse vegetation, and the regions in the east, north-east, and around the Central Province generally are intermediate in temperature, and with a moderate rainfall. The average annual rainfall in these divisions, as will be seen from the first table below, is something like 150–200 ins. in the first case, less than a bare 50 in the next, and about 75–100 in the last.

The humidity of the atmosphere in Ceylon is reckoned at 70 per cent., while the proportion of cloud makes Trincomalee and Anuradhapura the most favoured stations, and Ratnapura, Hakgala (near Nuwara Eliya), and Puttalam the most beclouded districts. In the first quarter of the year the sky for the whole of Ceylon is fairly clear, and in the months of October and November generally overcast. Owing to certain atmospheric peculiarities, the indications of air-pressure are not of much value in weather forecasts. Barometric variations are here more or less imperceptible in the course of any given day.

Station.	Years.	Jan.	Feb.	Mar.	April.	May.	June.	July.	Aug.	Sept.	Oct.	Nov.	Dec.	Year.
Colombo ...	36	3·56	2·10	4·70	10·90	12·08	8·17	4·51	3·59	5·19	14·67	12·18	5·87	87·52
Ratnapura ...	36	5·14	4·60	7·98	13·01	18·70	20·83	12·12	12·32	15·02	18·67	14·24	8·58	151·21
Puttalam ...	36	2·43	1·45	2·92	6·08	3·72	1·72	0·45	0·84	0·94	9·21	10·47	6·58	46·81
Anuradhapura...	36	3·07	1·54	2·71	7·17	3·82	1·40	1·07	1·72	3·01	8·47	10·62	9·19	53·79
Mannar... ...	36	2·17	1·15	1·43	2·72	2·28	0·62	0·30	0·44	1·12	7·93	9·91	7·85	37·92
Jaffna	35	2·13	1·27	0·90	2·48	2·00	0·76	0·85	1·45	2·75	6·81	13·26	11·14	45·80
Trincomalee ...	36	5·75	2·22	1·51	2·20	2·40	1·36	2·05	4·14	4·66	7·83	13·94	14·91	62·97
Batticaloa ...	36	8·34	3·84	3·08	2·07	1·86	1·01	1·23	2·24	2·89	6·26	12·68	13·54	59·04
Hambantota ...	36	3·43	1·57	2·05	2·84	3·46	2·42	1·44	1·32	2·44	4·34	6·80	5·40	37·51
Galle	36	4·47	2·98	4·11	10·58	11·50	8·33	5·71	5·35	7·47	13·14	11·44	6·08	91·16
Kandy	36	4·85	2·27	3·32	7·22	6·20	9·34	6·92	5·47	5·83	11·17	10·21	8·72	81·52
Nuwara Eliya...	36	5·38	2·15	2·97	6·10	7·69	13·64	11·76	8·14	8·26	10·61	8·80	8·53	94·03
Hakgala ...	23	8·65	3·06	4·25	7·71	7·36	8·20	6·01	4·41	6·19	10·70	11·12	13·31	90·97
Badulla... ...	31	9·52	3·36	3·92	7·97	5·24	2·62	1·43	3·22	3·27	10·01	11·60	13·12	75·28
Diyatalawa ...	5	6·95	2·70	1·93	7·65	5·67	2·14	1·02	2·12	4·39	11·89	10·20	6·23	62·89
Kurunegala ...	20	5·00	1·65	4·29	11·19	7·59	8·54	3·98	0·38	4·56	16·58	10·43	7·46	81·65

Often an infinitesimal fraction of an inch may be noted before the occurrence of a severe storm.

The temperature naturally undergoes constant change with the variations of the monsoons. The following table gives the latest recorded averages in this respect:—

Station.	Years.	Jan.	Feb.	Mar.	April.	May.	June.	July.	Aug.	Sept.	Oct.	Nov.	Dec.	Year.
Colombo ...	36–37	79·1	80·2	82·1	82·5	82·4	81·0	80·6	80·8	80·8	80·2	79·9	79·2	80·7
Ratnapura ...	35–37	77·8	79·2	80·4	80·4	80·4	79·4	79·3	79·3	79·0	79·0	78·0	80·2	79·4
Puttalam ...	33–36	78·7	80·2	83·0	84·3	84·7	83·4	82·7	82·7	82·8	80·0	78·4	76·5	81·5
Anuradhapura...	33–36	76·3	78·3	81·5	82·4	82·8	80·0	82·3	82·4	82·3	80·1	78·1	76·4	80·2
Mannar... ...	34–36	78·5	79·7	82·2	84·8	85·3	84·1	82·7	82·6	82·5	81·7	79·7	78·1	81·8
Jaffna	35	78·0	79·6	86·0	85·5	84·9	83·5	82·6	82·4	83·6	81·4	79·1	77·5	82·0
Trincomalee ...	32–35	77·5	81·3	81·2	83·2	84·1	83·7	82·9	82·6	82·2	80·5	78·6	77·5	81·3
Batticaloa ...	35–38	76·4	77·6	79·7	81·9	82·7	83·0	82·6	82·5	81·5	80·0	78·1	76·5	80·6
Hambantota ...	36–38	78·1	79·1	80·5	81·6	81·0	80·3	80·2	80·1	79·8	79·8	78·9	78·4	79·8
Galle	37	78·0	79·3	81·1	81·7	81·4	80·4	79·8	80·0	80·0	79·4	79·1	78·2	79·9
Kandy	35–37	73·3	75·1	77·4	77·4	78·5	75·5	74·8	74·9	74·9	75·1	75·2	73·4	75·5
Nuwara Eliya...	35–37	56·6	57·6	60·8	60·1	60·8	58·1	57·3	57·7	58·0	58·2	57·8	57·2	58·4
Hakgala ...	22	57·4	58·5	60·9	62·3	63·2	60·7	60·1	61·8	60·8	60·4	59·3	57·4	60·2
Badulla... ...	25–32	69·3	71·0	73·1	74·8	75·4	75·2	74·7	74·8	74·4	73·7	71·9	70·5	73·4
Diyatalawa ...	4–5	63·8	65·4	67·9	68·7	70·1	69·6	69·3	70·0	68·7	67·5	65·6	64·1	67·6
Kurunegala ...	16–19	77·2	78·2	82·2	82·0	81·9	79·9	79·6	79·7	79·8	79·0	78·6	77·2	79·6

The hottest months are generally April and May, while the cold season is uniformly about January - December throughout the island. These periods mark the strength of the monsoonal winds in each instance, and are the results of the altitude of the country over which they blow. The south-west monsoon, which bursts in about May, brings with it heavy downpours and thunderstorms, showers of hail and frost, on the western extremes, and sweeps over the centres on the east in or about June in a state of burning, parching heat-waves; and the north-east monsoon, which deposits rain and moisture in its train on the eastern plains, at its height in the latter part of the year, reaches the west in the form of a cool land breeze some time about December. Thus, the temperature in the central district, protected as it is by ridges of mountains all round, is maintained in a more or less even degree throughout the year. Incidentally it may be mentioned that the climate of the midland districts is as bracing and recuperative as it can possibly be; that of the country immediately surrounding it damp and unhealthy, and, in many places, productive of malaria; while the atmospheric influences in the farther north are peculiarly suited for convalescent purposes for those affected with any tubercular disease. On the whole, however, Ceylon is wonderfully salubrious and free from the commoner pestilences which so ravage the neighbouring continent, and the disasters by flood and heat which follow the visitations of the simoon in Arabia and the typhoon in China are here conspicuous by their absence.

The worst that befalls the island is in respect of frequent erosions by sea, which sometimes cause washaways and damage bridges on the coast railway track, during the heavy tides of the monsoonal period. But, save for a slight railway accident or the breaking away of an embankment, no loss of life or property is sustained. In a similar way the flat districts on the banks of the Kelani river are laid waste by the annual swelling of the streams which are fed by the heavy volume of water rushing down the mountain region, and fields and meadows for miles around form practically one sheet of water. Some of the suburban portions of Colombo also suffer by the inundation; and despite much discussion of relief measures, nothing definite has yet been done to combat the evil. It is believed that under the ancient system of irrigation, as pursued by the Dutch in later times, the maintenance of a series of canals to drain the flood area not only secured immunity to the people who dwelt in the neighbourhood, but also served them as a means of communication with the centres on its course, and afforded them an easy method of transportation of their produce. Of recent years, however, with the keen demand for ground space and the reclamation of land wherever possible, the blocking up of the escapes for surplus water has resulted in the annual bursting of the river bounds and the devastation of surrounding property. The Soil Denudation Commission has been appointed to carry on certain investigations into the rainfall of the Kelani Valley, and a map of the catchment-basin of that river has been prepared, embodying valuable information on the contour of the ground, rainfall, floods, and cultivation within the area; and it is hoped that before long Government will take the necessary measures to mitigate the evils of the situation.

At the time of writing a scheme is in progress for the establishment of a new observatory at Colombo, and steps are being taken for its erection and equipment. All the meteorological work and records will then be transferred to the new building, and the time-ball or signal will be worked direct. The timing of chronometers will also be undertaken, and it is expected that with the amount of shipping calling at Colombo and the dry dock in use a reasonable revenue will be derived from this source.

The present Meteorological Department is merged in the Department of Surveys, and is under the control of the Surveyor-General and in immediate charge of Mr. H. C. Barnard, F.R.A.S., F.R.M.S., who contributes to the Government almanac annually the astronomical ephemeris. A small daily weather map, giving the rainfall at 9.30 a.m., the direction of the wind, and the state of the sea at the coast stations, together with a second map showing the average weather during the previous twenty-four hours, is inserted in the "Post Office Daily List," issued every morning, and the planters generally and the public at large have found these forecasts very useful.

FAUNA

BY V. A. JULIUS.

CEYLON is a paradise for the naturalist, especially as regards birds, reptiles, insects, and smaller animals, the larger being not nearly so well represented as on the continent of India. Lions, tigers, wolves, hyænas, and the wild dog, all existing in India are not found in Ceylon, the larger carnivora consisting only of the leopard, locally misnamed the cheetah, and the jackal, the reported occurrence of the fox being more than doubtful. The elephant of Ceylon differs in no respect from that of India, but a tusker is an extreme rarity in the island, though in India a large majority of the males have tusks. The largest of terrestrial animals is gradually disappearing from the island owing to the felling of large forests, formerly the favourite haunts of elephants, for the purposes of cultivation of the land. A century ago the tea-growing districts of Dikoya, Dimbula, and Maskeliya formed one huge forest, in which countless elephants roamed; and the large herds referred to in Sir Samuel Baker's books as existing around Nuwara Eliya in the hill-country are no longer to be found there. The great quadrupeds are still fairly numerous in the low-country, but their numbers seem to be decreasing, and in 1900 a Government official, who knew the jungles well, estimated the number of elephants in Ceylon at no more than two thousand. Licences are issued by the Government for the capture of elephants by noosing, and some are caught in this manner and exported to India. Another method of capture is by means of kraals. The native chiefs occasionally obtain leave to erect these enclosures, into which the elephants are driven; and the animals obtained in this way are divided amongst those organising the kraal, being then used for draught-work or for the service of the temples. A great kraal was held in 1881 at Labugama, 28 miles from Colombo, when the present Prince of Wales and his brother visited Ceylon. Very few elephants are shot by local sportsmen in the island. When a local man has been "blooded" on a herd elephant, he rarely takes up an elephant-gun again except for the destruction of a "rogue"; and the records of slaughter in the books of Sir Samuel Baker and the older pioneers of Ceylon are never repeated nowadays.

There are no wild sheep or goats in Ceylon; and the oxen are represented solely by the Indian buffalo (*Bos bubalus*), which is also common as a domesticated animal. Of deer in Ceylon there are four kinds—not including the chevrotain, known locally as the mouse-deer—namely, the sambur, miscalled the elk, the axis, or spotted deer, the hog-deer (*Cervus porcinus*), which is confined to one locality and reported to have been introduced, and the munt-jac, or barking deer. There are no antelopes in Ceylon. There is no doubt that the deer are being rapidly reduced in numbers; and the reason is not far to seek. Sportsmen who are in the habit of visiting the low-country in the drought-time for bear-shooting know that, though it is the close season, every little pool in the exhausted watercourses and tanks has its screen of branches, behind which, on moonlight nights, natives station themselves with guns to shoot the deer as they come down to drink. The meat thus obtained is dried, and cartloads of it are taken into the neighbouring towns for sale. No system of watchers could probably be organised to cope with this evil; so, as a preventive measure, the Game Protection Society is now making strenuous efforts to induce Government to forbid the traffic in dried deer-meat, or to permit it solely through licensed dealers.

The only kind of bear found in Ceylon is the sloth-bear (*Melursus ursinus*), which frequents most of the low-country. It is much dreaded by the natives, whom it frequently attacks when coming across them in the jungle, invariably striking at the head. In fact, in the bear-country you constantly come across natives with scalp wounds inflicted by these animals; and no native in these parts cares to venture into the jungle without a short axe in his hand. Apart from these occasional attacks on natives the bear does little or no harm, confining itself to feeding on roots, fruits, berries, honey, and white ants, of which last named it digs up the nests. It is shot chiefly on moonlight nights in the drought, when coming down to drink at water-holes. Monkeys are very plentiful in all the jungles, both at high elevations and in the low-country. There are four kinds of simians in Ceylon, viz., the Rilawa, a macaque or cheek-pouched monkey, and three Wanduras, or Langurs, destitute of cheek pouches. Of the Wanduras, the bear-monkey (*Semnopithecus ursinus*), which inhabits the mountains and is found in the forests round Nuwara Eliya, is peculiar to Ceylon, though some writers hold it to be but a well-marked variety of the species known as the *Semnopithecus cephalopterus*, or purple-faced monkey. Wild pigs are very common throughout the island; and as pig-sticking is not practised owing to the difficult nature of the country, the shooting of the porkers is not considered unsportsmanlike. Other denizens of the jungle are jackals, porcupines, cats, and squirrels, which are all very plentiful.

Numerous species of bats are to be found throughout the island. The largest of these (*Pteropus medius*), known as the flying fox, a large fruit-eating bat, is very common. It roosts in colonies in the daytime in high trees, one large settlement being an object of interest at the Royal Botanic Gardens at Peradeniya, near Kandy. In some places—at Barberyn, for instance, on the coast about 40 miles south of Colombo—these bats share the same trees as the crows; and, as may be imagined, the noise is very great in the evening when the birds are returning to roost and quarrelling for places and the disturbed bats are starting out, and in the morning, when the process is reversed. The small lemur (*Loris gracilis*), known as the Ceylon sloth, is not uncommon in the low-country. It is an object of superstitious horror to the natives, who subject it to great cruelty, believing that its appearance forbodes bad luck. It is peculiar to Ceylon and Southern India.

The Registrar-General has kindly furnished me with a list of deaths in the island recorded as due to injuries caused by the following creatures during the sixteen years 1890 to 1905 inclusive :—Snakes, 2,975 ; crocodiles, 174 ; buffaloes, 92 (probably largely caused by domesticated animals) ; hornets, 76 ; elephants, 70 (including, I presume, the keepers) ; leopards, 45 ; wasps, 37 ; rats, 33 ; bears, 23 ; boars, 19 ; Brahman lizards, 17 ; deer, 3 ; sambur, 2 ; monkeys, 1 (probably a tame one). I am surprised to find no deaths recorded as due to jackals, as I should have thought there would have been cases of people bitten by jackals in a rabid state, or of exposed infants attacked by these animals while the mothers were at work in the fields or gathering jungle fruits. I am still more surprised to find the Brahman lizard entered as a cause of death. This lizard is the common large skink of Ceylon (*Mabeira carinata*), called by the Sinhalese "Hikanalla." Being quite harmless, it is incapable of causing death. It is common in Colombo, where its flat-backed body is frequently seen among the pots on a verandah, and is well-known to European residents. Sometimes representations of it are met with on brass tables. Dr. Willey has dealt with the subject of its reputed poisonous bite, which he discredits, in *Spolia Zeylanica* a publication issued by the Colombo Museum.

It is a great pity Ceylon is not possessed of Zoological Gardens. An attempt was made in recent years to start a "Zoo" in Colombo ; and an exceptionally good site of over twenty-three acres was selected in the Cinnamon Gardens for the purpose. But although Governor Sir West Ridgeway and his successor in the governorship, Sir Henry Blake, and those keen naturalists, Sir Everard im Thurn and Dr. Willey, all interested themselves in the scheme, it fell through, owing to the Government being unable to guarantee a subsidy and the other promoters of the project being unwilling to start a Zoological Company or Society without financial assistance from the public exchequer. The valuable services of Mr. John Hagenbeck could have been obtained as managing director ; and owing to the geographical position of Ceylon, with so many steamer lines calling at Colombo that could have brought animals from Australia, Africa, and the Far East, together with the number of passengers annually passing through Ceylon, who would have made the local "Zoo" one of the sights to visit, the equability of the temperature (which would have obviated the necessity of heating apparatus or of winter houses), the practicability of breeding many animals for exchange, and the feasibility of keeping the higher apes in captivity, the proposed establishment at Colombo could have been made one of the finest and most frequented zoological collections in the world.

ELEPHANTS BATHING IN THE RIVER AT KATUGASTOTA.

The birds of Ceylon include nearly 400

species, of which Captain Legge, in his "Birds of Ceylon," enumerated 47 as peculiar to Ceylon alone. With one or two exceptions, the feathered inhabitants of the island are not particularly brilliant of plumage. The game-birds consist of pea-fowl, partridges, teal, snipe, jungle-fowl, and quail. Snipe are very plentiful during the north-east monsoon, the best bags being made on the east coast. A few years ago Lieutenant Rice, R.A., accounted for no less than 112½ couple with one gun at Trincomalee, which I believe to be still the Ceylon record. The jungle-fowl (*Gallus lafayettii*, or *stanleyii*) is peculiar to Ceylon, and is very common, being found at all elevations. Professor Darwin, in his "Animals and Plants under Domestication," referring to the *Gallus lafayettii*, says: "This species may in all probability be rejected as one of the primitive stocks of the domestic fowl"; and the great zoologist based this probability, *inter alia*, on experiments made by Mr. Mitford, of the Ceylon Civil Service, in crossing the jungle-fowl with the domestic fowl, when the hybrids thus produced were found to be sterile. Further experiments, however, during the last three and a half years, under the auspices of the Ceylon Poultry Club, in interbreeding with these two kinds of birds have been carried to a successful issue by Dr. J. Llewellyn Thomas. On September 3, 1906, a chicken was hatched, the offspring of a hybrid cock mated with a hybrid hen. This result tends to show that the Ceylon jungle-fowl may be classed as one of the primitive stocks of the domestic fowl.

A common bird in the low-country is the köel, or Indian cuckoo, frequently termed the "brain-fever bird," from its loud and persistent note, which mounts higher and higher. This bird lays its eggs chiefly in the nests of crows, being one of the few creatures that can score off the wily crow. The young female is nearly black, and attains its spotted lighter appearance as it grows to maturity—a strange provision, as, in general, birds of black plumage are spotted when young and attain their dark hue at maturity. The magpie-robin is one of the commonest of birds in the country, and has a very sweet song. It breeds frequently in chatties in bungalows, and is a universal favourite. At the bottom of its nest a piece of snake-skin is always to be found, evidently picked from a cast-off epidermis. The reason of this provision I do not know; but I have never examined a nest without finding it. Another feathered inhabitant of the island is the weaver bird, which builds its nests in colonies. The nest of this species is a long retort-shaped mass of woven strips of palm-bamboo or grass, suspended from the ends of the branches of the trees and with a long entrance funnel. Another pretty little nursing-home—often found in the verandahs of bungalows in Colombo—is that of the tailor bird, which is formed of the leaves of a tree or plant, drawn together and then sewn together with cotton or grass, and inside this receptacle the nest is made.

ELEPHANTS IN KRAAL.

Eagles, hawks, and owls are numerous throughout the country; and large numbers of storks, herons, and egrets are to be found in Ceylon, while the flamingo is a visitant to the island. Captain Legge was unaware that the hair-necked, or marabou, stork breeds in Ceylon; but breeding places of this bird have since been discovered in the south of the island. I took three young ones of this species from nests near Hambantota, and kept them for some years loose in my compound in Colombo. The sparrow, called by one naturalist the "avial rat," is becoming too numerous in the lowlying parts, being a mischievous little ravager. A Government official has recently called attention to the risk of damage to the paddy crops from the immense flocks of sparrows now found in the low-country. These impudent small birds also invade churches and bungalows, where they build their untidy nests and generally prove unwelcome intruders and nuisances.

The largest snake to be found in the island is the rock snake (*Python molurus*) which attains to a length of close upon 20 ft. Some of even larger size are reported; but no authentic case of one of over that length has been recorded. The python is interesting from the fact that vestiges of the hind legs are apparent, usually in the form of claw-like spurs situated on either side of the vent. The natives regard this spur with fear, referring to it as the sting of the reptile. Pythons are fairly common in the low-country, where they may be found covered with leaves waiting for their prey. I caught one over 13 ft. long near Puttalam, on the north-west coast, and brought it back to Colombo, where it lived for many months in an empty room by itself, being fed chiefly on chickens. The deadliest snake of Ceylon is the tic-polonga, or Russell's viper. It is a sluggish reptile, which does not get out of the way of passers-by, and strikes if approached too closely. The cobra is common in the jungle, and attains to a length of 6 ft. and over. It is a handsome snake as seen with its hood expanded when sitting up for attack; but, on account of its fierce nature and venomous bite, is more to be feared than admired. The Buddhists maintain that when Buddha was once exhausted with travelling in the heat, a huge cobra sat itself beside him and, by expanding its hood, protected him from the rays of the sun. Another dangerous snake is the karawala or krait. Harmless snakes are very numerous; and some of the grass snakes are very pretty. They will also thrive in confinement.

Crocodiles abound in all the lagoons and rivers, where the stream is not too strong. They lie in wait at the edges of the water for game coming to drink. Many native women have been seized, when coming to draw water, and dragged down and eaten by these saurians. Near a swamp or river-bank which man-eating crocodiles are known to infest the natives are always grateful to the passing sportsman who will shoot the reptiles. The eggs of the crocodile are laid in a big mass and covered with sand and *débris* and left to hatch. I found such a nest at Bolgoda lake, about 15 miles south of Colombo, some years ago, and took over thirty eggs from it. I then made a hole in the side of each egg, leaving the ants to clear out the contents, which they very speedily did. A crocodile over 13 ft. long has been recently caught by fishermen at Bolgoda, and its skin is now being preserved by Mr. Lazarus, taxidermist, of Colombo.

The sea, rivers, and tanks of the island swarm with fish, which form a large part of the food supply of the country. Whales, too, frequently visit the shores of Ceylon. A large dead whale was stranded on the rocks below the Mount Lavinia Hotel, 7 miles south of Colombo, two years ago, with the result that the guests fled and the hotel remained empty until the putrescent carcase could be cut up and towed out to sea or buried. The dugong, or manatee—which is supposed to have originated the idea of the fabulous mermaid—is found above Puttalam on the north-west coast, and its flesh is considered a delicacy by the natives, selling well in the bazaars. The fish known as the climbing perch (*Anabas scandens*) is found in Ceylon waters. It can travel long distances on land, and is even said to climb trees. Three of these fish were captured alive by me in Wavertree compound, in Colombo, some years ago, and were identified by the late Mr. William Ferguson, a local authority on piscatology. The sucking fishes found in the sea round the island have an adhesive disc on the upper surface of the head, by which they attach themselves to sharks or turtles or ships; and so strong is the adhesion that the fish is only detached with difficulty. I found one brought ashore in a seine at Mount Lavinia. Sharks are very numerous round the coast of Ceylon, the hammer-headed variety being particularly common. Small specimens of this species are often caught by the fishermen.

At Batticaloa, on the east coast, on moonlit nights, parties frequently go on the lake to listen to the so-called singing fish. The sounds are believed to be produced by a mollusc under the water; but I do not know that the species has been identified.

BOTANY

By J. C. WILLIS, Sc.D., F.L.S.,

Director of the Royal Botanic Gardens, Peradeniya.

THE department of the public service of Ceylon known as the Royal Botanic Gardens includes at the present time a much wider range of activity than its title would indicate to residents in Europe ; it is rather a Department of Botany and Agriculture than a Botanic Garden in the ordinary sense, though it includes a number of Botanic Gardens. In recent years especially a considerable expansion of the scope of the department, and of the work carried on by it, has taken place. In many ways the history of its gradual enlargement reflects the general history of the nineteenth century in botany and its allied sciences and arts. In the early years of the past century, when botany consisted only of the study of the external characters of plants their classification, and the investigation, naming, and cataloguing of the plants of the different regions of the world, the Royal Botanic Gardens of Ceylon were occupied principally with the collection and description of the wild flowering plants and ferns of the island, and with the gradual accumulation at Peradeniya of as many as possible of these. This branch of work is still going on, and has resulted in the formation of a great herbarium and museum of Ceylon plants, a very complete collection of living specimens in the various gardens, and the publication of a Flora of the Colony, the final volume of which was completed in 1900. A solid foundation is thus laid for the further investigation of the flora of Ceylon by agricultural and economic botanists, vegetable physiologists and pathologists, and other workers. It should, however, be noted that the work so far completed is chiefly upon the flowering plants and ferns, and that the mosses, liverworts, algæ, and fungi have yet to be worked up.

Almost simultaneously with the commencement of this systematic investigation of the wild flora, the Botanic Gardens began to be occupied, and by 1860 were mainly occupied, with the important duty of introducing into the colony all possible useful and ornamental

VIEW OF THE HAKGALA GARDEN, NUWARA ELIYA.

plants of other countries, with the view of finding out what plants would grow in the various climates which the island possesses. From 1850 to about 1890 this work of acclimatisation was carried on with vigour and with many remarkable successes. Among other things thus introduced may be mentioned cacao, cinchona, indiarubber, coca, Liberian coffee, vanilla, a vast number of plants of minor importance, new varieties of fruits, vegetables, and flowers, shade and timber trees, &c., while the spread of the cultivation of tea, cloves, nutmegs, and many other things has also been largely helped by the introduction of good kinds through the Botanic Gardens. During the latter quarter of the past century this work of acclimatisation has gradually decreased in importance, as the number of potentially valuable plants thus established in the island has become larger and larger in proportion to those still to be introduced, and as the organisation of private agencies for the supply of seeds and plants from abroad has more and more narrowed the sphere of operation of a public agency for this purpose. Plants are still being introduced into the gardens in large numbers, but the day of acclimatisation is passing, and the agricultural political outlook is changing.

CABBAGE PALMS, PERADENIYA GARDENS, KANDY.

INDIARUBBER-TREES, PERADENIYA GARDENS, KANDY.

The salient feature of the past century in Ceylon has been the occurrence of a series of "booms" in different economic products, formerly only cultivated by the native tropical races of men, or only collected from wild plants. One by one, coffee, cinchona, tea, cacao, cardamoms, indiarubber, &c., have risen into prominence. The history of the present century will almost certainly be very different. Almost all products of value are now cultivated in the tropics by European or American planters or Governments, and a period of severe competition is beginning, in which Ceylon will be to some extent handicapped by having a poor soil, much of which has been wasted by chena and by inattention to good cultivation, but in which, on the other hand, she has very great advantages in good and varied climates, almost unlimited cheap and docile labour, central position with plentiful freight to the great markets, and last, but most important of all, well-established industries with great reputations for their products, managed by experienced, enterprising, and capable men.

Acclimatisation, then, has to a large extent seen its best days here. It is now of much greater importance to attend to our existing industries, and preserve, improve, and extend them, than to devote all our attention to the comparatively minor chance of introducing something that shall take their place if they fail. We may still hope to introduce new products of value, but they are less likely to prove the commencement of large industries than has been the case in the past. It is to meet this new phase of the economic position that the constitution of the Royal Botanic Gardens has been largely changed during the past few years, and that to the old organisation for investigation of the local flora and the introduction of plants from abroad, and the trial of a few of each to see whether they can be grown in Ceylon, there has been added a staff of scientific experts for dealing with diseases and their prevention, and an experiment station—as distinguished from a botanic garden—for the study of methods of cultivation and of preparation of products for market upon a commercial scale, in the hope of thus improving our local industries to meet competition from abroad, together with laboratories and other necessary aids for the further scientific study of the vegetation of Ceylon, whether native or introduced.

It will be convenient to deal with the subject by the historical method. The present headquarters of the Royal Botanic Gardens are at Peradeniya, but this was not always the case. The Dutch had a garden in Slave Island, Colombo, but after the English conquest this was neglected and sold by the Government. The first English Governor, the Hon. F. North (afterwards Lord Guilford), had a small private garden at Peliyagoda, near Colombo, under the superintendence of Joseph Jonville, or Joinville, whom he brought out as "clerk for natural history and agriculture." In 1800 Jonville accompanied General MacDowall's embassy to Kandy, and made a collection of plants which is now in the British Museum. He also drew some of the plates in Cordiner's "Description of Ceylon." Several exchanges were made between the garden in his charge and the gardens of the East India Company at Calcutta.

In 1810 Sir Joseph Banks, then President of the Royal Society, was instrumental in causing the opening of the first English botanic garden in Ceylon, under the superintendence of W. Kerr, who was transferred from Canton, arriving in 1812. Seven acres of land were opened in Slave Island, where the site is still indicated by Kew Road, and Kerr was placed in charge of this and of the garden at King's House as "resident superintendent and chief gardener."

In 1813 the garden was moved to Kalutara, on the south-west coast, the Colombo site having been found too subject to flooding. The Government had resumed possession of an unsuccessful sugar estate of 600 acres at Ugalboda, on the left bank of the river, and upon this the garden was reopened. In the following year Kerr died, and was succeeded by Alexander Moon, who arrived in Ceylon in 1817. Under him the gardens were much improved, and in 1821, six years after the conquest of the Kandyan kingdom, were transferred to their present site at Peradeniya, four miles from the centre of Kandy, on the Colombo road. The site is almost horseshoe-shaped, occupying a peninsula round which flows the broad and rapid stream of the Mahaveli Ganga, the principal river of Ceylon. It is about one mile in length from north to south, and has an area of 143 acres, prettily undulated. The southern end is rocky, but with fairly good soil in many parts ; the northern end consists largely of old river deposits of sand and gravel. On the farther side of the river rise the hills of the experiment station, the steepest of which, to the north-east, is about 700 ft. higher than the garden, and acts as an efficient barrier against the force of the north-east monsoon. The general level of the garden is about 1,550 ft. above the sea, and the climate is warm and damp, but much pleasanter than that of the wet low-country, as exemplified in Colombo. The air has a bracing freshness that is lacking in the plains, and the nights are always cool. The climate is sufficiently warm to render possible the cultivation of all but a very few tropical plants, for which the nights are too cold in February and March and the days too dry, and sufficiently cool to allow of the cultivation of many sub-tropical plants suitable to medium elevations in the mountain zone, but not capable of cultivation in the low-country. The successful working of the Botanical Department is in no small degree due to the choice by Moon of so excellent a site as regards climate and position.

Moon transferred to Peradeniya all the plants which could be moved from Kalutara, and laid out the south-eastern part of the ground, planting especially coffee and cinnamon. He spent much time in the investigation of the flora of the colony, and collected largely in the Western Province, as well as near Kandy and in Uva. In 1824 he published at Colombo, in English and Sinhalese, his "Catalogue of the Indigenous and Exotic Plants growing in Ceylon." Of the 1,127 plants native to the colony there enumerated, 164 are new species described for the first time. He made a considerable herbarium, now mostly at Kew, and commenced the library of the department. In 1818 Harmanis de Alwis Seneviratne was appointed writer under him, and displayed such talent for drawing that Moon had him taught at his own cost and appointed as draughtsman in 1823. This was the beginning of the splendid series of coloured drawings of the Ceylon flora, and of other plants cultivated

GROUP OF PALMS, PERADENIYA GARDENS, KANDY.

GIANT BAMBOOS, PERADENIYA GARDENS, KANDY.

in the gardens, which has been steadily continued to the present time by H. de Alwis, his two sons, William and George, and his grandson Alfred, who is at present the draughtsman of the department. In May, 1825, Moon died of fever, and for some time the gardens were in charge of Andrew Walker as Acting Superintendent. He was succeeded in 1827 by James Macrae, who collected many plants, especially orchids. From this time till 1844 the department languished, being chiefly used as a Government market garden, the produce of which was sold in Kandy. Macrae died in 1830, and after another interregnum, under G. Bird, James George Watson was appointed Superintendent in 1832, and died in 1838. The rubber avenue at the entrance to the gardens was laid out by him in 1833. Another period of interregnum, under J. G. Lear, who came to Ceylon in 1837, or earlier, as collector for Messrs. Knight, of Chelsea, followed, lasting till the appointment in 1840 of H. T. Normansell, "a clever young surgeon." Lear collected and described a number of orchids, and was one of the earliest tea planters; he planted tea at Nuwara Eliya in 1837. He laid out the beautiful group of palms at the entrance of the gardens.

VIEW IN THE PERADENIYA GARDENS, KANDY.

In January, 1843, Normansell died, and W. C. Ondaatje acted as Superintendent till the arrival in May, 1844, of George Gardner, F.L.S., the well-known Brazilian traveller, who was appointed on the recommendation of Sir William Hooker. With his arrival the department started on a new career. Only one quarter of the land was then in use; the remainder was largely cleared and planted, new roads opened, and many new plants introduced from other countries. Gardner travelled almost all over the colony, and made large collections of native plants, many of which were new to science. Unfortunately for the department and for science, he died of apoplexy, at Nuwara Eliya, at the early age of thirty-seven, in March, 1849. A cenotaph, containing a brass to his memory, was erected in the gardens in 1855. His herbarium was purchased by the British Museum, and thus unfortunately lost to the colony.

From March to December, 1849, Mr. G. Fraser was Acting Superintendent of the gardens pending the arrival of the newly appointed Superintendent, George Henry Kendrick Thwaites, who was for thirty-one years to control the destinies of the department, and to do so much for scientific botany and for the planting industries of Ceylon. Born in Bristol in 1812, Thwaites was thirty-seven years old when he arrived in Ceylon, and had already won a distinguished reputation in botany.

In 1854 a vigorous attempt was made in Council to abolish the gardens. They were defended by Mr. W. Ferguson in the *Observer*, and by Dr. Lindley in the *Gardeners' Chronicle*.

In 1860 the site of the Hakgala Garden was selected by Thwaites for the reception of the cinchona plants brought from Peru by Sir Clements Markham, and was placed in charge of Mr. MacNicoll. At first planters were disinclined to try the new industry, but a few years later, as coffee ceased to flourish, cinchona was very largely taken up, finally becoming for some years the staple industry of the colony, and bridging over the period between coffee and tea. The gardens began to distribute seed of the latter about 1864, but for many years previously Thwaites had called attention to it in vain.

In the report for 1871 appears the first mention of the coffee-leaf disease, *Hemileia vastatrix*, and in all succeeding reports Thwaites deals with this, consistently rejecting the popular idea of the possible discovery of a cure. In the report for 1873 the spread of tea cultivation, in which Thwaites took a large part, is noticed, and the cultivation of cacao and cardamoms, both now important industries in Ceylon, is for the first time pressed upon public attention. In 1876, the Indian Government having obtained seeds and plants of *Hevea brasiliensis*, the Para indiarubber, from South America, it

NATIVES PICKING ARECA NUTS, PERADENIYA GARDENS.

PALMS AND FERNS IN THE HAKGALA GARDENS, NUWARA ELIYA.

VIEW IN THE HAKGALA GARDENS, NUWARA ELIYA.

was found that the climate of India was unsuitable for them, and they were sent to Ceylon, where the branch garden at Heneratgoda, 17 miles from Colombo, on the Kandy railway, was opened for their reception, and as an experimental garden for strictly low-country products.

Thwaites retired in the beginning of 1880, after a long service of thirty-one years, spent without once quitting the colony, and was succeeded by Mr. Henry Trimen, M.B., F.L.S., of the British Museum. The new Director arrived at a time of trial for the colony, for the coffee industry was rapidly sinking under the attacks of its fungus enemy. At this period the late Mr. (afterwards Professor) H. Marshall Ward came out (as Cryptogamist to Government) for two years, 1880–82, to carry out a series of researches into the life-history of the *Hemileia* with the view of endeavouring to discover preventive measures. The mission, though successful in the former object, was unsuccessful in the latter, as Thwaites and Mr. Ward himself had predicted would likely be the case.

THE "MONSTER CREEPER" IN PERADENIYA GARDENS.

The fundamental section of the present institution is the Botanic Garden of Peradeniya (143 acres), with its five branches in the different climatic regions of the island: Hakgala (opened 1861, about 40 acres cultivated, with large jungle and grass reserve); Heneratgoda (opened 1876, 39 acres, including 10 acres of jungle); Anuradhapura (opened 1883, 15 acres); Badulla (opened 1886, 11 acres); and Nuwara Eliya (opened 1902, 10 acres). The primary object of these gardens is to form as complete a collection as possible of all the native plants of the island, and of all foreign useful, ornamental, and interesting plants which can be made to grow in Ceylon. Of course, such a collection means a vast number of different kinds of plants, and each kind can only be represented by one or two specimens, or at most a little plot. The "index collection" thus formed, and continually increasing by fresh introductions from abroad, then forms the material for further work and experiment, carried out chiefly by the other divisions of the department.

In addition to forming this index collection, the Botanic Gardens are mainly occupied with horticulture and landscape gardening, with the object of forming beautiful places of resort for the pleasure and instruction of the public, and of training up gardeners, giving advice on gardening matters to residents in the colony, and trying experiments with different methods of cultivation of ornamental or minor useful plants. Until the opening of the experiment station a large amount of land and labour had to be given in the Botanic Gardens to important economic plants. This is now being altered, and special attention can be given in the future to flowers, fruits, and vegetables. It is hoped not merely to introduce further good kinds from abroad, but to undertake to some extent the breeding of good local varieties suitable to local tastes and conditions—a branch of work hitherto almost unknown in the tropics, though such marvellous results have been produced in Europe and America by its means.

Nurseries are kept up in the Botanic Gardens for the supply of the more important and interesting plants to the public, and seeds are also sold. Limitations of space and supply prevent more than very small quantities being available in this way. The chief economic plants are being gradually transferred to the experiment stations, and only minor economic plants, fruits, vegetables, and ornamental plants will in future be dealt with by the Botanic Gardens. In supplying these plants, more especially the ornamental kinds, the general principle is adopted that the gardens shall not compete with private enterprise in the district in which they lie, and that they shall cease to

ENTRANCE, PERADENIYA GARDENS.

supply plants of any kind that is really and cheaply obtainable from local nurseries. The object of the gardens is not to make money by the sale of verandah and garden plants, but to encourage horticulture and improve the variety and quality of plants in cultivation. To render the furtherance of this object more certain, it is intended in future to keep up in the nurseries small stocks of the most frequently demanded plants only, and to devote the space now given to many plants which are but seldom asked for to growing larger stocks of plants of certain kinds; to keep up these stocks for some time, publish information about them, and endeavour

THE GIANT ANTHURIUM IN PERADENIYA GARDENS.

to spread them as soon and as widely as may be possible about the island.

In the case of the more important economic products it is not enough now to know simply that such or such a plant will grow in the climate of Ceylon; it is very rarely, if ever, possible to begin a successful industry by merely introducing the necessary plants. We must know the best methods of cultivation and of preparation of the product for market. This involves cultivation and preparation on a commercial scale to test the resulting products by sale in the open market; such experiment is better suited to a scientifically equipped institution, which is not obliged to make a profit, than to private individuals, and this is the object of an experiment station, in addition to other experiments for the improvement of cultivation and preparation of crops already cultivated in Ceylon. The working of the experiment station and the actual experiments to be carried on are decided by aid of a "Committee of Agricultural Experiments," composed of members of the departmental staff and of private planters or others nominated by the Government.

The Peradeniya Station lies in the wet lower zone of the mountains and in the planting districts, and it is mainly concerned with products already established. A second experiment station has recently been started in the vast dry zone districts now being opened up by railways and irrigation in the North of Ceylon. An area of 150 acres has been reserved under Maha-iluppalama irrigation tank. The chief object in view is a thorough trial of the possibilities of cotton cultivation in Ceylon, but rubber, cacao, and other crops are also being tried under irrigation. At present there is little cultivation of any kind in this part of the island, and it is hoped that these experiments may lead to the opening up of new land.

The present staff of the institution is as follows:—

J. C. Willis, Sc.D., F.L.S., Director.
E. E. Green, F.E.S., Entomologist.
T. Petch, B.A., B.Sc., Mycologist.
M. Kelway Bamber, F.I.C., F.C.S., M.R.A.C., Chemist.
A. M. Smith, B.A., Scientific Assistant.
Herbert Wright, A.R.C.S., F.L.S., Controller, Experiment Station.
C. J. C. Mee, Superintendent, Cotton Experiments.
H. F. Macmillan, F.L.S., Curator, Peradeniya Gardens.
J. K. Nock, Curator, Hakgala Gardens.

Ceylon, though small in area, has a great variety of climates, due to differences in rainfall and in elevation, and a corresponding variety of vegetation. Its flora is very rich, comprising over 3,000 species of flowering plants and ferns (or three times as many as in the British Isles), beside a large number of mosses, liverworts, seaweeds, fungi, &c. Many of the plants are the same as, or closely related to, those of the Indian peninsula, while a large number show affinity to the Malayan

THE GIANT ORCHID IN PERADENIYA GARDENS.

flora and some to the African. The mosses, liverworts, seaweeds, and fungi have as yet been very incompletely investigated; probably they will be found to number almost as many more. A very remarkable feature of the flora is the large proportion of endemic species, *i.e.*, species confined to Ceylon. Almost 30 per cent. of our plants are endemic, a proportion usually only found in oceanic islands, far away from the continent.

The chief determinant of the climates is the position of the mountain mass of south-central Ceylon across the line of direction of the two

FLYING FOXES IN PERADENIYA GARDENS.

monsoons. The south-west monsoon (April to September) brings much rain to the western side of the hills and to the south-western plains, but little elsewhere. The north-east monsoon (October to March) brings, at first, rain to all parts, but later chiefly to the eastern side of the hills. The chief climatic zones thus are the "wet low-country" from Negombo to Matara, with rain at all times of the year (least in January to March) and a rich vegetation; the "dry low-country," comprising the rest of the plains, principally in the north and east, with rain chiefly from October to January, and the remaining months dry; and the "montane zones" of various elevations. The eastern side of the mountains is rather drier than the western, and its dry season is in the south-west monsoon, while that of the western side is in the north-east monsoon, so that the periods of flowering and fruiting of plants differ by several months in the two regions. The wet low-country was doubtless originally covered with a sheet of forest, but of this only portions now remain, *e.g.*, the Singha Raja forest to the south of Ratnapura and the lower part of the forests upon Adam's Peak. Owing to the well-distributed and abundant rainfall the vegetation is very rich. The forests are typical equatorial evergreen forests, with tall trees of very uniform height, and with a dense undergrowth of smaller trees, large woody climbers, and ground herbs. One great cause of waste of material and of land has been the destructive native practice of chena, whereby large areas of forest were annually cut and burned for the purpose of growing a few crops of grain upon the land. In a few years at most the chena is abandoned and becomes covered with a low scrub, often composed almost entirely of lantana or of a dwarf bamboo. Immense areas of land in Ceylon have been wasted in this way.

The wet low-country is one of the richest cultivated districts, and is thickly populated in the more accessible parts. The level lands and the bottoms of the valleys are chiefly occupied by rice fields, yielding two crops a year, one in each monsoon, while the higher lands between are covered with the characteristic mixed tree cultivation of the Sinhalese—jaks (often largely replaced or supplemented by breadfruit near the sea), coconuts, arecas, mangoes, plantains, limes, custard apples, kitul or toddy palms, &c., with "yams" of various kinds (especially Colocasia and Alocasia), betel, pepper, and other small plants. Large areas of ground, especially near the sea coast and along the Kandy railway, are given up entirely to coconut cultivation; the products of this palm afford many of the necessaries of life to the Sinhalese, and are also exported in vast quantity. Areca palms are cultivated for export of the nuts in special estates in certain districts, especially near Kegalla, and there are also extensive plantain estates near the railway. European cultivation is mainly found in the Kelani Valley and near Kalutara; the chief product is tea—of poor quality but large yield—but indiarubber is of late coming into prominence, and cacao, cloves, nutmegs, vanilla, and other crops are also grown besides coconuts.

THE JAK-FRUIT TREE.

At the highest levels, *e.g.*, about Nuwara Eliya and on the Horton Plains, the jungle is broken by patches of grass land, known as patanas, covered with a coarse turf of large grasses, among which are many flowers often of familiar European genera. Many plants of European genera also occur in the undergrowth of the higher forests, and such plants as brambles, buttercups, valerians, violets, teasels, skull-caps, and St. John's worts, give quite a Northern look to much of the vegetation. In many parts the forest has a very characteristic undergrowth of dwarf bamboos, or of nelu, under which name the Sinhalese include the gregarious species of Strobilanthes; these plants flower all together at the end of a period of years and then die down, to be replaced by the seedlings.

In each of the great zones of vegetation thus indicated there are of course numerous smaller areas of special interest, with peculiar floras. Thus, on the coast there is the special "coast flora" of beach jungle, shore herbs, &c. In the south this is of the almost cosmopolitan type found from Polynesia to Africa; while in the north it is of a more local Indian type. In the north, and in the south-east and elsewhere, interesting floras occur on the margins of the large salt lagoons. Mangroves are well represented in the estuarine lagoons and river mouths from Negombo to Matara and elsewhere. Water plants abound in the coast lagoons, in the paddy fields, and in the irrigation tanks of the dry country, while the peculiar family of the Podostemaceæ abound in the rapids of the mountain streams; seaweeds are plentiful on the south-west and southern coasts.

Every form of tropical vegetation, whether of wet or dry climates, of jungle, grass land, scrub, marsh, coast, water, &c., may be found represented in our flora, and owing to the small area and the convenience of travel and study, may be easily investigated in a limited time. Every facility for residence, botanical study, and scientific research is now available at the Royal Botanic Gardens of Peradeniya (close to Kandy) and the branch gardens in the wet and dry low-country and in the hills. Many scientific men from Europe have in recent years made use of these facilities, and much original research has been carried out in the Peradeniya laboratories.

IRRIGATION

By H. T. S. WARD,
Director of Irrigation.

THE history of irrigation in Ceylon goes back to such very early periods in that of the world that great uncertainty must naturally exist as to the facts. The records available are few, and not always reliable. It would appear, however, to be beyond doubt that the indigenous Sinhalese population recognised the necessity of works to assist the natural rainfall in the water supply to their lands, and it may reasonably be assumed that the chief crop—if not the only one—was rice, or "paddy," as it is now more generally spoken of locally. It may be said parenthetically that the distinction between the two exists in the condition of the grain, "rice" being only spoken of as the manufactured or husked article, and "paddy" the natural grain as coming from the threshing-floor. The term "paddy" is also invariably applied to the crop.

In the historical work known as the Mahavansa, it is stated that "tanks" (or storage reservoirs) existed at the time the invader Vijaya landed in Ceylon in 534 B.C., and it is also asserted, apparently with good authority, that most of the good irrigation works were undertaken during the period between 400 B.C. and 1200 A.D. The actual dates of the building of the original great works at Minneriya and Kalawewa (storage tanks, the word "wewa" being the Sinhalese name for a tank) are fixed as 277 A.D. and 460 A.D. respectively, and are fairly reliable. The oldest remaining masonry in connection with these works has the mark of great antiquity.

After the era of activity and construction previously mentioned succeeded another of inactivity and decay: for several centuries no great works were undertaken, and the existing works were allowed to go to ruin. Some of them are stated to have been actually destroyed by the Tamil invaders from the Indian coast, but it seems probable that the decline was as much due to depopulation as to any other cause.

This brings us down to the Portuguese occupation of Ceylon, chiefly on the coast. These new invaders are credited with even more destructive tendencies than the Tamils, who, after all, were operating under the conditions of war. After the Portuguese came the Dutch. As might have been expected from a nation with their training and business capacity, they set to work to improve the existing schemes of irrigation and inland waterways. The result is apparent to this day in many important works, amongst which may be mentioned the Urubokka dam (a masonry work) in the Matara district, and the Kalutara and Negombo canals. The Dutch occupation extended over a century and a half, and the condition of the island at that time was such as to compel them to follow more or less in the footsteps of their predecessors, the Portuguese, and confine their operations chiefly to the coast line. The result has been that their works have been found in the maritime districts.

We now come to the British occupation and the commencement of the nineteenth century. Up to this time the construction and maintenance of irrigation works had been carried on under the native Rajas, and with the assistance of old communal rules and customs which had more than the force of law as we know it. Almost the first act of the new-comers — who, like all other new-comers, thought they knew the country best—was to abolish the time-honoured customs which they found prevailing, and with them "rajakariya," or enforced labour for the service of the State. The history of our Asiatic colonies has the same tale to tell in almost every case, and the local customs which have been found to suit local and racial idiosyncrasies have to go when they are not found in line with Western prejudices.

The people were not compelled to work for their own good, and irrigation again suffered. A Commission was appointed in 1832 to inquire into the state of affairs and push forward irrigation works, and the first fruits of their deliberations was a recommendation for the abolition of "rajakariya"! So far back as the year 1847 a recommendation was made (during Sir Emerson Tennent's term of office as Colonial Secretary) for a general survey of all the tanks and irrigation works in Ceylon, and it is remarkable that only sixty years later is this work being systematically undertaken.

It is unnecessary to follow all the ups and downs of irrigation during the next ten years or so; but the arrival of Sir Henry Ward as Governor, in 1855, may be said to mark an epoch, for it was followed almost immediately by the creation of the first "irrigation fund," and by the passing in the following year of the first irrigation Ordinance, and the issue of the famous Minute on irrigation. It is remarkable and instructive to note in passing that the first and subsequent irrigation Ordinance were framed to perpetuate the old communal customs which were appropriate to the people and their surroundings. The law now existed, and it became necessary to think of the machinery to work it. But, strange to say, considering the attention which was given to the subject by successive administrators and the mass of evidence that was recorded by various officers of the Government, the institution of a regular department to organise and control the management of the whole scheme was forgotten. The first proposal for anything like systematic control came with the recommendation of Sir Hercules Robinson for the appointment of Lieutenant Woodward, R.E., as Irrigation Assistant. This cannot be said, however, to be the birth of the Irrigation Department, as matters lapsed later on into the old state, and Lieutenant (now Captain) Woodward left the island after a few years of good work. In justice to him it should be stated that some of the undertakings instituted during this period are amongst the most successful in the island, and that the capital cost compares very favourably with those of any other date.

A period now intervened when the policy of Government may be characterised as distinctly progressive. Sir William Gregory, the Governor of the day, encouraged irrigation by adopting a more generous policy in the provision of the necessary funds, generally by promoting enterprise wherever possible. To some extent the activity may be ascribed to the existence of the "paddy tax," which was in operation up to the year 1892. With this impost in force the Government of the day felt justified in incurring expenditure to foster paddy cultivation.

Sir Arthur Gordon's policy was even more progressive, not to say lavish, than that of Sir William Gregory.

Following on the period under note, the year 1887 saw the institution of the Central Irrigation Board, an executive body entrusted with the control and management of the Irrigation Fund, to which an annual contribution is made by Government amounting to Rs. 200,000 (nominally £20,000 sterling).

In addition to the Central Board (which included official and unofficial members, the Governor being President), provincial Boards were established, the Government Agent of the Province being President and the Provincial Engineer and Chief Surveyor members. These Boards were vested with advisory and executive powers. The initiation of new schemes (including the restoration of old works) generally lay with the revenue officer, the Government Agent, and a joint report on each project was made by the other two members of the Board. No very definite procedure existed in practice. Sometimes the reports of the technical members were forwarded to the Central Board, with the recommendation or otherwise (rarely otherwise) of the Chairman, and sometimes the Provincial Engineer was asked to frame a definite proposal and estimate.

The system was a bad one, and it is not surprising that the time came when it proved unworkable. The members of the Central Board had other duties and occupations, and criticism was either weak or wanting altogether. The same may be said in even stronger degree of the members of the provincial Boards. The real onus of the whole proposal lay on the local engineer, whose work represented hours, perhaps days, in comparison with the minutes spent in connection with any proposal by any other member of either Board. It was not to be wondered at that these officers in many cases took no special interest in the schemes, and that the consideration of the financial aspect was conspicuous by its absence. The engineer was a Public Works officer, with a multitude of other duties to perform, and there was no encouragement to him to give any special attention to irrigation—quite the reverse—whilst the financial aspect was supposed to be considered by the revenue officer.

TISSAWEWA TANK.

(This tank is about three miles in circumference and is supposed to have been constructed by King Devanampiya Tissa about 300 B.C.)

The maintenance of existing works of any magnitude—indeed, all but "village works"—was entrusted to the Public Works officers, not necessarily members of the Boards, and often involved travelling on inspections for very considerable distances outside their ordinary duties.

The Government Agents (*ex officio* Presidents of the provincial Boards) were supposed to collect the irrigation rates, frame lists or "specifications" of the lots of lands on which rates had to be paid, collect the dues, and take proceedings for default. In addition, they had under their control a staff of subordinate irrigation officers, who were in charge of "village" works, and responsible to these revenue officers only for the performance of their duties, entailing the details of designs for tanks, &c., and this without any technical knowledge or training.

"It is never safe to prophesy unless you know," but it required no prophetic instinct to foresee that such a state of affairs could not last for ever, and the advent of such an astute Governor as Sir West Ridgeway was the culminating point. He saw the difficulty and the necessity for a properly organised department under the control of one responsible officer who could deal with every case, and, in advising Government, secure some continuity of policy and system.

In 1900 the Irrigation Department was instituted, Mr. H. T. S. Ward, a former Public Works Department officer, being appointed Director of Irrigation, with Mr. H. Parker as the Irrigation Assistant (a title now altered to that of Assistant Director). Mr. Parker had been for many years the chief advising officer of Government for irrigation schemes, but had no general control. A staff of engineers was recruited chiefly from England, and a subordinate staff of irrigation inspectors and surveyors was engaged locally. The difficulties of organising the whole department to take over and deal with every question concerning irrigation at the particular stage when this staff took over control—or partial control—were very great. Old mistakes had to be recognised and remedied, working schemes had to be taken up for maintenance, repairs, or improvement, and proposals for new projects examined into and reported on. The difficulty of working an entirely new and locally inexperienced staff is far greater than can be appreciated to the full, except after actual experience. Climatic conditions and the necessities of irrigation work in the most out-of-the-way places play havoc with the uninitiated. Everything is different; everything seems upside down; languages have to be learned (and your average Englishman is far from being a linguist), and local prejudices studied and made allowances for. A *dolce far niente* existence suits the East, and is well typified by a quiet stream of water running down at a slow velocity in the bed of the irrigation canal, but that canal has to be surveyed and mapped and excavated first.

A word here on the class of works dealt with in Ceylon will not be out of place. It may be stated generally that the "inundation canal" so well known in India does not exist. This system requires the topographical conditions only found in the great deltas. All the important ancient channels to which the Sinhalese name of "Yoda Ela" is applied have been constructed either to lead a supply from a river source (assisted by a weir across the river) to some of the large tanks, or to convey the water from these storage basins to the fields (or minor tanks) for distribution. Some of these channels were of considerable length, and most of the principal ones have gone to ruin. The "Yoda Ela" under the great tank of "Kalawewa," in the North Central Province, is the longest at present in working order, and is 54½ miles in length.

It is a fact not generally recognised that a lake such as our Western eyes are accustomed to is almost unknown in the tropical regions of the East. The explanation is very simple. The enormous rainfall must find means of escape, and the result is that each valley presents a continuous slope towards the sea, and in wet weather the stream flows downwards without interruption.

These natural valleys afford the opportunity for throwing up dams to impound the water of the rainy season, and the necessity for irrigation water to secure the "paddy" crop has resulted in the construction of thousands of these small tanks, their number naturally increasing in proportion to the dryness of the district. The water is led from these tanks to the fields by channels, and controlled by sluices.

The system adopted in applying the water is universally that known as "flooding," and in the light of later experience and scientific observation it seems unfortunate that such a very conservative mind as that of the Asiatic should have adopted as a matter of course the particular method which gives him least trouble, which is probably the least economic and efficient, and one which tends to injure the soil in the long run. The Sinhalese villager is fond of "flooding," and carries out the principle to the extreme, not so much on any well thought out principle, but because it is easier to turn on the water and let it flow all the time until he returns some months later to reap the crops than to divert the supply or shut it off, and thereby give his corn the chance of aeration at the roots which it is longing for. The result is that Ceylon cannot, or does not, supply its population with the staple article of food, and money leaves the country which might better be in circulation at home.

I have said that irrigation in Ceylon means "paddy," and unfortunately this is not far from the truth. A word of notice must, however, be given to the alien of the north—the descendant of the Tamil invaders. I allude to the inhabitant of Jaffna, in the north end of Ceylon, which is called a peninsula, but is practically an island joined to the mainland by a causeway carrying the railway and public road. This district is all Tamil, exclusively Tamil. The local conditions as regards soil could hardly be more difficult or discouraging. Any soil there is has to be made, and nothing can grow without irrigation. The latter is all effected by "lift" from wells, averaging about 20 ft. deep, and the supply of water is universal and unlimited. The crops are varied, but tobacco is the most important, and the population may be said to live by this industry. Almost all the rice required for food has to be imported from India or the eastern coast of Ceylon.

The duties of the department involve every proceeding connected with irrigation except the actual collection of revenue. A recent Ordinance, which became law only this year, provides for a general remodelling of systems and duties, and in the case of larger works, especially proclaimed by Government, the Director of Irrigation is entrusted with almost absolute control, including the distribution of the water. The latter had been left previously entirely in the hands of the revenue officers, and it is not surprising that the system was a hopeless failure. Many schemes have got a bad name through the excessive waste of water tending not only to a failure of supply—estimated on quite different data—but also to the injuring of the lands themselves and the failure of crops. Again, the collection of dues had hardly been satisfactory in the past. The schedules or "specifications" of lands were made out by estimation and not based on actual surveys, and the generous instincts of revenue officers led them to deal leniently with the villager—perhaps more leniently than would have been the case if the holdings had appeared on their private rent-rolls! At all events, the results were evil.

BASAWAKKULAM TANK.
(One of the oldest tanks in Ceylon, called Jayawewa, constructed B.C. 500.)

Under existing regulations the initiation of the schemes or proposals for restoration of old works is left in the hands of the district revenue officers, who have to make out their case for Government, and show some estimate of a reasonable return and the probable success of each proposal. The Irrigation Department is then applied to for surveys—contour surveys of the whole area are now being made—plans, estimates, and definite concrete proposals, which must include the details of the areas to be benefited, whether in private hands or Crown property. In the latter case these lands, which would generally be valueless without irrigation, are rendered saleable, and another source of revenue appears.

When any work is sanctioned and a vote

passed in the "Supply Bill," the department undertakes its construction, and, after completion, its maintenance. The maintenance of the village works is still in the hands of the revenue officers, and they have their subordinate staff; but the latter are officers of the department, interchangeable for other duties, and properly trained.

In conclusion, a few notes are given below of some of the principal figures and statistics connected with irrigation in Ceylon. The largest "tank" is Minneriya, in the North Central Province, with a top water area of over 4,500 acres; and next in order comes the "Giant's tank" (recently restored), in the Northern Province, and "Kalawewa" in the North Central Province, with 4,425 acres each. "Kanthalai," in the Eastern Province, which was supposed to have been built in the earliest centuries of the Christian era, has an area of 3,486 acres, and so on.

The number of smaller village works is exceedingly great; for instance, the numbers of restored village tanks in the North-Western and North Central Provinces alone are respectively about 1,300 and 1,600.

The total number of principal or "major" works in charge of the Irrigation Department is 134, and the total acreage under cultivation in the island, of which any returns are available, may be taken as :—

	Acres.
Major works	132,253
Minor or village works ...	210,680
Total	342,933

The average crop secured per acre has been very variously stated, and differs very widely with the district, but it may be taken, as an average, that about two bushels of paddy are required to sow an acre, and the average return is about twenty bushels. In some places where the cultivator is careless, the return falls as low as five or six bushels per acre, whilst some of the more recent statements of returns in the Eastern Province give the crop as varying from 35 to 65 bushels per acre.

The Irrigation Staff is composed of the following officers :—

The Director of Irrigation, with an Assistant Director of Irrigation, Office Assistant, and twenty-three Irrigation Engineers in two grades. Then follow the subordinate staff, consisting of four Chief Irrigation Inspectors, one Surveyor, one Assistant Engineer, and eleven Inspectors, followed by fourteen Sub-Inspectors of the first grade and thirty-eight of the second grade, including the Superintendents of Irrigation, who are officers specially appointed to supervise distribution on only some of the larger works. Then comes the grade of Guardians (first and second class) and the clerical staff, a total of seventy-two officers of all grades.

FORESTS

CEYLON is conspicuously rich in forests. From the palm groves on the surf-washed coast to the summit of Adam's Peak in the centre of the island are to be found at many points and in varying degrees of density timber-clad land, a good proportion of which is in a primæval state. In recent decades great clearances have been made for the tea, cacao, rubber, and other thriving industries which have sprung into vigorous life under the fructifying influence of capital; but these operations, extensive as they have been, have not materially altered the character of the island. The exact area of the Ceylon forests, properly so-called, is unknown. The surveys made so far have been incomplete, and the data given, even in official publications, are often misleading. For example, in 1905, the area of "other Crown Forests"—that is to say, of the great area of forest land not brought under the direct control of the Forest Department—was given as 4,568,180 acres. But in the report of the Conservator of Forests for 1905 this figure is stated to be "hopelessly inaccurate and misleading." The actual position of affairs, as far as the Government forest land is concerned, is disclosed in a table given in the Conservator's 1905 report, which will be found below.

Proportionately these classes represent 3·56, 2·47, 7·15 per cent. of the area of the island. But it is to be noted that the table takes no account of village forests, which, in the aggregate, constitute a very large tract of country. Nor is it merely in point of area that the forests are remarkable. From time immemorial Ceylon has furnished ornamental woods for special purposes. If the identity of the Scriptural Tarshish with the port of Galle be established, as many learned writers believe it to be, it is not an impossible assumption that the Ceylon forests supplied some of the wood for the making of Solomon's temple. However that may be, ebony was undoubtedly largely exported in ancient times, and carried the fame of Ceylon as a country of rare woods into many remote parts of the world. The following list of the principal Ceylon timbers and their uses, from the "Ceylon Manual," conveys an interesting and impressive idea of the present resources of the island as a centre for the supply of useful woods :—

Sapu, S.; *Michelia nilagirica.*—Very valuable and durable timber, greenish-brown when freshly cut. Is useful for doors and windows and makes very handsome panes.

Na, S.; Nakka, T.; *Mesua ferrea.*—One of the hardest and most durable woods. Of great value for all heavy building works.

Dun, S.; *Doona zeylanica.*—Excellent timber for building purposes, beams, joints, and sleepers. Excellent for shingles, which can be easily split from it.

Halmilla, S.; Chavanadalai, T.; *Berrya Ammonilla.*—A magnificent timber. Used in boat building, for oil casks, gun carriages, and carriage shafts.

Satinwood, E.; Buruta, S.; Mutirai, T.; *Chloroxylon Swietenia.*—Most valuable wood. Unrivalled for durability. Used for furniture, especially almirahs. Largely used in Europe for brush-handles. Sleepers made of this wood have been known to last for thirty years. It is white-ant proof.

Kumbuk, S.; Marutu, T.; *Terminalia glabra.*—Hard wood. Suitable for sleepers, bridge planks, beams, and other heavy work, though sufficiently handsome to be used for ornamental work, doors, cabinets, &c.

Palu, S.; Palai, T.; *Mimusops hexandra.*—Magnificent timber, tough and durable. Excellent wood for heavy work, beams, sleepers, and posts.

Munamal, S.; Mukalai, T.; *Mimusops Elengi.*—Timber excellent for house building, beams, and other weight-supporting purposes. Durable.

Ebony, E.; Kaluwara, S.; Karunkalai, T.; *Diospyros Ebenum.*—This wood requires little description, as it is well known. It is largely exported, and in that respect is our most valuable timber, its chief use being for furniture, piano keys, inlaying and ornamental work.

Milla, S.; Kaddamanakku, T.; *Vitex altissima.*—No better wood can be found for work requiring resistance to exposure. It is therefore suitable for bridge planks, beams, posts, doorposts, shingles, and also oil casks.

Ranai, S.; *Alseodaphne semicarpifolia.*—This

Particulars.	Area on January 1, 1905.		Added during the Year.	Excluded during the Year.	Area on December 31, 1905.	
	Acres.	Square Miles.	Acres.	Acres.	Acres.	Square Miles.
I. Reserved Forests	445,657	696·34	139,000	3,001	581,656	908·84
II. Proposed Reserves notified under section 6 of the Ordinance	470,533	735·21	—	67,564	402,969	629·64
III. Proposed Reserves (not yet notified)	1,163,207	1,817·51	89,219	86,212	1,166,214	1,822·21
Total	2,079,397	3,249·06	228,219	156,777	2,150,839	3,360·69

is one of our export timbers and is suitable for building works.

Gamalu, S.; Venkai, T.; *Pterocarpus Marsupium*.—Suitable for house building, panels, &c.

Mendora, S.; *Vatica Roxburghiana*.—Excellent timber for piles or any work exposed to water.

Tumpalai, T.; *Vatica obscura*.—Affords a valuable wood; durable; suitable for sleepers, beams, and building work.

Kina, S.; *Calophyllum Walkeri*.—Applicable to all sorts of building purposes. Largely used for shingles.

Hora, S.; *Dipterocarpus zeylanicus*.—This wood is in very great demand for boat building, cask manufacture, and beams for temporary structures.

Damba, S.; *Eugenia Gardneri*. — Wood rather hard and heavy, smooth, greyish-yellow. Suitable for building purposes.

Mihiriya, S.; *Gordonia zeylanica*.—A dark red wood, hard, but easily cracked. Suitable for ceiling or flooring boards.

Mi, S.; Illupai, T.; *Bassia longifolia*.—Suitable for heavy work, such as beams, bridge planks, posts, and the like.

Lunumidella, S.; Malai vempu, T.; *Melia dubia*.—In great favour for tea boxes and dadoes, but too light to stand straining loads or exposure. Often used as outriggers for boats.

Important as the forests of Ceylon are and have always been, it was not until comparatively recent times that any steps were taken to protect and develop these great resources. In the early days of the British occupation probably no great necessity existed for supervision, as the timber export was almost a minus quantity. But towards the end of the first half of the last century a trade sprung up in timber, and great quantities of wood were exported to Europe and to China and India. "The fellings were made on the permit or licence system, under which a royalty, calculated on the local market value of the wood, or, in the case of exports, on its value at the port of clearance, less the actual cost of transport, was levied. Before the trees were felled a permit or licence had to be obtained from the district revenue officer, on which a deposit was taken, the balance not being due till the timber had been felled and a removal permit was required."[1] The system was open to serious abuse. Contractors felled more timber than their licences permitted them to do. Further, there was no check upon their operations, and they naturally selected the best trees. "In every way the old licence system was bad and ruinous. There were no means of preventing illicit felling or of protecting the standing timber from injury and damage; no thought of replanting or assisting the natural process of reproduction, whilst, in the simple matter of revenue, Government did not receive its proper share of royalty. The latter was rated first at 10 per cent., afterwards at 25 per cent.; yet when ebony was selling at £8 to £12 per ton, trees averaging 5 cwt. at least were sold at 96 cts. to Rs. 2 a tree."[1]

FOREST SCENE NEAR NUWARA ELIYA.

The evils of the system ultimately attracted official notice, and a circular was issued by the then Auditor-General (the Hon. Mr. John Douglas) calling for reports as to the levy and collection of timber revenue and the general management of the forests. The response was a unanimous condemnation of the existing arrangements. Summarising these replies in a letter to the Colonial Secretary in June, 1871, Mr. Douglas outlined a scheme for the better control of forests. He suggested that foresters should be appointed to the Eastern and Northern Provinces (those being the principal timber-producing districts), and that their duties should consist in the selection of trees for felling and the right to cut and utilise the timber marked in a certain area. Further, he proposed that nurseries should be established by guardians in charge of irrigation tanks, and that chena land should be replanted with teak, jak, and other trees on planting leases.

Mr. Douglas's suggestions were approved, and in 1873 and 1874 foresters were appointed by Sir W. Gregory for the Eastern, Northern and Southern Provinces. The forester's post in the Southern Province was abolished in 1874. On the other hand, additional appointments were made in the North Central and North-Western Provinces in 1877. In the Central Province the superintendents of minor roads were, from 1875, appointed supervisors of forests in addition to their usual duties, on salaries of about Rs. 500 a year. Later on, a forester was employed to check chena cultivation in the Kandy and Matale districts. The persons selected for the posts of foresters were, in the case of the Eastern and North-Central Provinces, officers of the Public Works Department; in the other provinces they had not previously served under Government. The foresters were placed in subordination to the Government Agents in all their work, but they maintained a somewhat distinct organisation in office work and in matters of general routine, instead of forming part of the provincial revenue administration.

The year 1882 marks an important new stage in the history of the Ceylon forest administration. In that year the Government secured from the Government of India the loan of the services of Mr. F. D'A. Vincent, an experienced forest official, to examine and report upon the forest system of the island. Mr. Vincent made an exhaustive survey of the whole field, and subsequently prepared a very able report, reviewing the history of the Ceylon forests and outlining a series of proposals for the future

[1] Mr. F. D'A. Vincent's special report on the Conservation of the Crown Forests in Ceylon (Sessional Paper XLIII. of 1882).

[1] Mr. Vincent's Report.

administration of the department. His recommendations were adopted by the Government, and Mr. A. F. Broun, of the Indian Forest Service, was appointed in 1888 to organise the new department. Mr. Broun's services were lent by the Government of India for three years, but at the expiration of that period he was transferred to the Ceylon service, being appointed Conservator of Forests. That post he retained until 1901, when he retired.

Under Mr. Broun's direction various reforms were introduced into the working of the department. The system under which the charges of the Assistant Conservators were conterminous with the Revenue Provinces, and were worked partly under the Conservators and partly under the Government Agents, was replaced by an arrangement by which Forest Circles, not coincident with any revenue divisions, were established, each being under the control of an Assistant Conservator; while definite areas were placed under the charge of the Conservator and the Government Agents respectively. There were six circles in all, these, with their headquarter stations, being :—

Northern Circle—Vavuniya.
North-Eastern Circle—Trincomalee.
Eastern Circle—Batticaloa.
South-Eastern Circle—Hambantota.
North-Western Circle—Kurunegala.
Hill Reserves Circle—Nuwara Eliya.

In a Sessional Paper (XXIX. of 1898) setting forth the details of the reorganisation scheme (which was drafted by Mr. F. C. Fisher and afterwards considered by a committee consisting of the Hon. Mr. W. T. Taylor, Mr. Fisher, and Mr. Broun), it was stated that the object in view was to divide the forest administration of the island into two parts—(*a*) general, (*b*) provincial. All reserved forests were intended to be included in the general administration, with the exception only of the reserved forests of the Western and Sabaragamuwa Provinces, which would remain for the time being under the control of the Government Agents of these provinces. The remaining tracts of forest land distributed throughout the provinces constituted the areas to come within the "provincial" administration of the Government Agents. The scheme is further outlined in this extract:—

"In the Western Province, in the Province of Sabaragamuwa, and in the Galle and Matara districts of the Southern Province, the administration of the Government Agents includes within its scope the forests already reserved and the forests which may have to be reserved. When the detached areas in these three provinces have been surveyed and proclaimed, it is contemplated that the areas finally determined as 'reserved' will be transferred to the general administration; that is, placed under the control and management of the Conservator and his staff. In the other provinces it is understood that while the areas, as defined by Mr. Fisher, are accepted as a basis of administration, the boundaries may be varied hereafter according to circumstances, the Conservator handing over to the Government Agents such portions as may be suited for cultivation and are not required to be reserved for climatic or other purposes, and the Government Agents on their part transferring to the Conservator any portions of the areas now placed in their charge that may subsequently be found to be required as reservations."

The staff is divided into (*a*) Superior or Controlling; (*b*) Executive and Protective; and (*c*) Clerical.

SUPERIOR STAFF.

1 Conservator.

1 Assistant Conservator at Rs. 6,000 to Rs. 7,000.

1 Assistant Conservator at Rs. 5,000 to Rs. 6,000.

2 Assistant Conservators at Rs. 4,500 to Rs. 5,000.

2 Assistant Conservators at Rs. 4,000 to Rs. 4,500.

2 Assistant Conservators at Rs. 3,000.

1 Assistant Conservator at Rs. 2,000 to Rs. 3,000 (special appointment).

A TYPICAL JUNGLE SCENE.

EXECUTIVE STAFF.

1 Forester at Rs. 1,250 to Rs. 1,500 by increments of Rs. 60.

3 Foresters at Rs. 900 to Rs. 1,250 by increments of Rs. 60.

6 Rangers at Rs. 720 to Rs. 900 by increments of Rs. 60.

12 Rangers at Rs. 540 to Rs. 720 by increments of Rs. 30.

12 Rangers at Rs. 360 to Rs. 540 by increments of Rs. 30.

1 Special Officer drawing Rs. 396 a year.

PROTECTIVE STAFF.

46 Guards costing Rs. 7,080.

CLERICAL STAFF.

3 Clerks (passed candidates) drawing salaries between Rs. 700 and Rs. 2,400.

3 Clerks drawing Rs. 700 each.

4 Clerks drawing Rs. 600 each.

1 Clerk drawing Rs. 484.

5 Clerks drawing Rs. 400 each.

1 Clerk drawing Rs. 330.

5 Clerks drawing Rs. 240 each.

The method of working is thus described :—

"The reserves are worked by marking and selling timber, where feasible, standing in the forests. Where this cannot be done, the timber selected is felled and removed on contract, under the supervision of the officers of the department, to certain market centres, for sale locally or for transport thence to the central depôt at Colombo.

"With reference to the working of the areas placed in charge of the Government Agents, indents for timber are met by a system of fellings under supervision on licences granted by the Government Agents. This mode of working should, however, be confined to the areas intended to be worked out and sold, and should not be applied in the case of forests which it may he considered desirable hereafter to reserve."

LIST OF DEPÔTS.

Batticaloa, timber.
Trincomalee, timber.
Talawakelle, firewood.
Nuwara Eliya, firewood (temporary).
Central Timber Depôt.
Galle, firewood.

In 1905 there were further important developments. The general and provincial distinctions of management disappeared, and all forest areas were brought under the control of the Conservator. The six circles were amalgamated with the provincial areas and converted into five forest divisions, and the arrangement into ranges and beats was partially modified. "Thus," says Mr. T. J. Campbell, the Conservator of Forests, in his Administration Report for 1905, "the dual control, so long a bone of contention, made its exit under Government orders in Proclamation No. 6,033 of February 3, 1905. The sphere for work and usefulness has consequently been considerably augmented, whilst discipline and technical control have been placed on a sounder foundation. The interest of the Government Agent has not been lost, as establishments are under his control in his own province, outside purely technical matters. Despite great misgivings, the change has developed a great success and an utter absence of friction."

The divisions as modified are represented as follows :—

(1) *Jaffna*, embracing the Northern and North-Central Provinces, exclusive of the Tamankaduwa district.

(2) *Kandy*, comprising the North-Western Province, that portion of the Central Province north of the Kadugannawa-Kandy road and west of the Mahaveli Ganga, the Tamankaduwa district of the North-Central Province, and the Trincomalee district of the Eastern Province.

(3) *Colombo*, consisting of the Western and Sabaragamuwa Provinces with the Galle and Matara districts of the Southern Province.

surplus. In 1905, the last year for which figures are available, the large profit balance of Rs. 142,541·10 figures in the year's accounts. The actual financial position was this :—

IN FAVOUR OF THE DEPARTMENT.

	Rs.	c.
Surplus	142,541	19
Outstanding due to	3,994	71
Outstanding due from	635	60
Value of stock on December 31, 1905	318,576	2
Total ... ... Rs.	465,747	52

AGAINST THE DEPARTMENT.

	Rs.	c.
Outstanding due from	127	71
Outstanding due to	10,837	64
Value of stock on January 1, 1905	106,301	66
Total ... ... Rs.	117,267	1

The surplus for 1905 was therefore Rs. 348,480·51.

The following table shows the position over a period of sixteen years :—

Year.	Revenue.	Expenditure.	Surplus.	Deficit.
	Rs.	Rs.	Rs.	Rs.
1890	510,045	421,517	88,528	—
1891	410,035	441,205	—	31,170
1892	462,427	475,491	—	13,064
1893	365,758	404,756	—	38,398
1894	384,536	456,568	—	72,032
1895	417,375	426,799	—	9,424
1896	472,980	463,375	9,605	—
1897	488,956	465,383	23,573	—
1898	510,945	496,315	14,630	—
1899	541,952	375,618	166,334	—
1900	419,621	335,515	84,106	—
1901	393,053	286,732	106,321	—
1902	360,261	268,594	91,667	—
1903	346,883	273,363	73,520	—
1904	412,846	308,337	104,508	—
1905	450,536	307,995	142,541	—

(4) *Nuwara Eliya*, including the southern portion of the Central Province, that part of the Province of Uva west of the Kumbukkan-aar and the Bibile-Bintenna road, and the Hambantota district of the Southern Province.

(5) *Batticaloa*, combining the Eastern Province, exclusive of the Trincomalee district, and the Province of Uva east of the Kumbukkan-aar and the Bibile-Bintenne road.

Turning to the financial aspects of the forest administration, we find in the statistics relating to the working of the department ample justification for the measures which have been taken to safeguard and develop the timber resources of the island. In its earliest years the department was for the most part a burden upon the revenue, but a welcome change set in in 1896, and every year since there has been a surplus.

The future work of the department will be not less important than it has been in the past. The administration has not only to check ravages committed by ignorant and interested persons, but to watch and prevent inroads upon the colony's forests for economic purposes. The dangers of laxity are well set forth by Mr. Campbell, the Conservator of Forests, in his administration report for 1905. He says :—

"The evils of soil denudation are conspicuous throughout the island. Clearances for chenas and the higher forms of cultivation are made irrespective of the physiographical characteristics of the country. A railway journey through the island is an object-lesson in this direction. The mountainous mass which seems to arrest and disburse all the elements combining for economic good, has been denuded of timber too rapidly, and it is now time to pause. Complaints are rife amongst the intellectual as well as the homely agricultural classes of the drying up of springs, reduction in the normal quantity in streams, reduced rainfall, bursts and not well distributed showers, excessive floodings of valleys, and the drying up of tanks. As the forests disappear these evils arise, and though no serious harm has been done to date, caution is necessary in the future. Government has most wisely laid down the rule that no land is to be alienated over 5,000 ft. in height, and that stream reservations are to be rigidly preserved."

Wisely directed, the forest administration cannot fail to be a substantial source of profit and at the same time to act as a guardian of the larger interests of the island by stopping clearances which would injuriously influence the meteorological conditions now existing.

Mr. **Thomas James St. Albans Campbell,** Conservator of Forests, is the son of the late Colonel Campbell, of the Royal Engineers. He was born in Manchester on December 21, 1856. He belongs to the Indian Forest Service. He served in India, where he was Conservator of Forests (second grade), from November, 1880, until August, 1904, when he took up his present appointment. Whilst in India he served principally in the Bengal Presidency and in Assam. At one time he was a keen sportsman with big game and a polo player, but of late years he has not actively participated in sport.

GEOLOGY AND MINERALOGY

By Dr. A. K. COOMARASWAMY, D.Sc., F.G.S., F.L.S., M.R.A.S.,
Director of the Mineralogical Survey of Ceylon.

THE rocks of Ceylon belong to the great group of Crystalline Schists, a term used to indicate a variety of types of foliated crystalline rocks. The Ceylon rocks can be more particularly described as *Granulites*, or, using the term in a wide sense, as Gneisses. They further belong to the local (South Indian) group known as the Charnockite series. The most conspicuous features of the rocks are their crystalline character, mineral banding (foliation), varied composition, and bedded aspect. Rocks of igneous origin form by far the greater part of the series, although it is possible that there are associated with these others of sedimentary origin, now so highly altered as to be distinguished only with difficulty. The typical charnockites include quartz rocks, leptynite, pyroxene-granulites, norites, diorites, gabbros, &c. The groups of possibly sedimentary origin include the crystalline limestones and dolomites, and the khondalites or sillimanite-bearing rocks, which, however, pass by insensible gradations into the ordinary granulites. The name "Galle Group" is applied to certain rocks with much wollastonite, in some respects intermediate between the crystalline limestones and granulites. The name "Balangoda Group" is given to a series of intrusive granitic rocks which often carry zircon and are probably the source of the minerals containing rare elements which have lately become of so much interest in Ceylon. The crystalline rocks have been thrown into a series of NNW. and SSE. folds, the direction of which has a great influence on the contour of the surface and has determined the main lines of communication. The name Taprobanian has been given to these movements. Laterite (cabook) is a typical alteration product of the granulites. So also is kaolin (china clay), but not in such extensive deposit as to be of commercial importance. Of unaltered sedimentary rocks there are river gravels, sands, and alluvial clays; and also, in some districts, marine deposits such as raised coral reefs, littoral concrete, blown sand, and marine clays with abundant fossils. "Adam's Bridge" consists of recent marine sandstones forming a series of disconnected islands. It is possible that an actual land connection once existed, of which a legendary record is preserved in the Ramayana.

Of the minerals of Ceylon, only those of special interest are here referred to.

Graphite (plumbago) is the most important of Ceylon minerals, and in some respects the most interesting. Ceylon graphite consists almost entirely of carbon, the proportion of impurity being very small. The graphite occurs as a true vein mineral, the veins generally following natural planes of division in the country rock. Usually in any single pit or series of adjacent pits there is a single main vein sending off stringers, or more often a series of parallel veins. The veins are very uncertain and rarely run for great distances, but pinch out; if followed, they may again widen, or it sometimes happens that a small vein leads to quite a large "pocket" of pure graphite; sometimes pockets are met with apparently unconnected with any vein. The graphite generally occurs as an aggregate of flakes or needles set at right angles to the wall of the vein; the veins are often, however, much slickensided and the original disposition destroyed. The minerals most often associated with the graphite are quartz and iron pyrites. It often happens that these minerals form the centre of a vein; but these details vary in different pits. The rock matrix of the veins is not much affected, and if impregnated at all with graphite it extends only a quarter of an inch from the vein. It should be mentioned that graphite in small flakes is a common mineral in many varieties of granulite and in the crystalline limestones, but its occurrence thus has no direct connection with its occurrence in veins, although a remoter genetic connection may be suspected. The origin of the vein graphite is still obscure. It is certainly not of immediate vegetable origin. The graphite appears to have been deposited by fumerole action after the cooling or solidifying of the eruptive rock in which the veins are found. It is impossible to affirm with certainty the form in which it was introduced, whether as an unsaturated carbon compound or as a saturated material which dissociated at a high temperature on the diminution of pressure due to the shrinkage and formation of cracks in the containing rocks. Emanations of carbon monoxide and of cyanogen compounds may have played a subordinate part. If the question of the origin of vein graphite is ever to be settled by reference to natural occurrences it must be in Ceylon; but it is perhaps rather a matter for laboratory experiment.

In 1896 mica to the value of Rs. 43,637 was exported from Ceylon; in 1905 the value of the export had sunk to one rupee. There has since been a revival of interest in Ceylon mica, and more than one valuable mine is being worked. The Ceylon mica belongs to the phlogopite and biotite varieties, and occurs in distinct veins which reach a width of 3 ft. or more. The colour varies from a pale yellowish-brown to dark green and deep red. The crystals rarely exceed a foot or 18 ins. in diameter.

The recently discovered mineral thorianite has attracted much attention on account of its commercial value and scientific interest. The mineral appears to occur *in situ* in feldspathic rocks belonging to the Balangoda group, but has rarely been found in its parent rock. It has, however, been lately worked in a decomposed pegmatite vein in the Hinidum Pattuwa. The principal and first discovered deposits, however, in the Bamberabotuwa district are alluvial, and it has hitherto been impossible to trace the mineral to its parent rock there. It is obtained by washing the alluvial deposits in the same way as for gems. The total quantity obtained in this district amounts to several tons, and the deposits are still being worked. The total from other localities amounts to perhaps two or three tons more. The price fetched at first was Rs. 9 per lb., but this has now fallen to Rs. 4 as a result of the action of the German syndicates. Thorianite is generally recognisable by its high specific gravity, usual cubic form, and black colour ; but all sorts of other black minerals are frequently mistaken for it.

The best qualities of thorianite contain over 70 per cent. of thorium oxide, with 12 per cent. of uranium oxide and smaller amounts of other elements. It owes its commercial value to this high proportion of thorium oxide, which is the most important element in the manufacture of incandescent gas-mantles. The world's supply of thoria was and still is obtained from monazite, a mineral containing only about 5 per cent. of thoria, and found in Brazil in large quantities ; it occurs also in the sands of Ceylon rivers, but has never been worked there. Thorianite also occurs in the river sands of Ceylon. It is possible that the sands and gravels of the beds of some Ceylon rivers would repay exploitation by dredging and the separation of the gems, thorianite, gold, monazite, &c. Gold is widely distributed in Ceylon, but has not hitherto been found in paying quantities. Cassiterite, galena, and copper are also known to occur, but very sparingly.

The reader will probably be more anxious to be informed about the famous gems of Ceylon than to hear more of the other minerals. The following is a list of the gems known to occur in Ceylon, arranged under their proper mineralogical names :—

Corundum.—Blue, sapphire ; red ruby ; star sapphire and star ruby, the same, but showing, in a favourable light and when suitably cut, a six-rayed star. White sapphires have had their original pale-blue or pale-yellow colour discharged by firing. Rubies are almost always fired in order to discharge in the same way any trace of blue. Yellow sapphires are "Oriental topaz," and violet-coloured ones are "Oriental amethyst." Pinkish-yellow stones are known as "king topaz."

Quartz.—Includes rock crystal, amethyst, cairngorm, smoky quartz, &c.

Spinel.—Green, blue, and red ; the pink and red varieties are called balas ruby ; the blue, spinel sapphire.

Chrysoberyl.—Green and yellow ; includes cat's-eye and alexandrite, the latter appearing green by daylight and red by artificial light.

Orthoclase.—Includes moonstone.

Tourmaline.—Brown and brownish-green and yellow ; often confused with zircon.

Topaz.—Colourless, erroneously known as water sapphire ; pale sea-green, known as aquamarine.

Cordierite.—The true (blue) water sapphire ; rare.

Garnet.—Red, pinkish-red and brownish-yellow (cinnamon stone).

Zircon.—Green, yellow, red ; the colourless Mātara diamonds are pale zircons bleached by firing.

All of these minerals are of igneous origin, and are derived from the crystalline rocks in which they were formed. They have been freed from the matrix in the course of its disintegration, washed into the beds of streams and rivers, and there rolled and worn, and finally deposited in the alluvial gravels in which they are now found.

The process of gemming is briefly as follows : A pit is sunk where gem-bearing gravels are known or expected to occur. A typical section would show 5 or 6 ft. of muddy alluvium, resting on a deposit of gem-bearing gravel not more than 1 or 2 ft. thick and called *illam* ; below is the decomposed country rock over which the gravel was deposited. The *illam* is removed from the pit and washed in a "gemming basket." This is basin shaped, about 2 ft. in diameter, and a foot deep. The operator stands in about 2 ft. of water, and holding the basket in the water gives it a turning movement, depressing the rim below the water once in every turn, so that the lighter stones are washed over its edge by the centrifugal movement. Fifteen or twenty basketfuls are thus washed, and the residue, consisting of the gems and other heavy minerals, carefully examined. In the same residue minerals like thorianite and thorite, if present, are to be found.

The actual gemming is done by Sinhalese, but the trade in gems is almost entirely in the hands of the Moormen. The value of the gems annually exported from Ceylon has been estimated at £300,000.

A collection of the rocks and minerals of Ceylon is shown in the Mineral Gallery of the Colombo Museum, where maps and photographs and the most important works relating to the geology of Ceylon can also be consulted.

A mineralogical survey was initiated in 1903 for a period of three years to examine and report upon the mineral resources of Ceylon. The work is now to be continued to the end of 1909. Dr. A. K. Coomaraswamy has been Director of the survey during the first four years of its work, but he shortly hands over control to Mr. Parsons, formerly Assistant Director. The minerals collected by the survey are analysed and reported on from a commercial point of view at the Imperial Institute. Reports on this work are occasionally issued, and the Survey is locally responsible for an annual Administration Report, in which the most important observations made during the year are recorded.

NATIVE ARTS AND HANDICRAFTS

By Dr. A. K. COOMARASWAMY, D.Sc., F.G.S., F.L.S., M.R.A.S.

SINHALESE.

THERE is a chapter in Ruskin's "Stones of Venice" of which it has been said that in future days it "will be considered as one of the very few necessary and inevitable utterances of the [nineteenth] century." The chapter is called "The Nature of Gothic" In it Ruskin for the first time showed that the relics of mediæval art which are treasured in European museums are not only better in quality but different in kind from modern workmanship. We all know what changes have passed over Europe since the close of the fifteenth century; her gains have been many—freedom of thought, abundance of knowledge, power over the material forces of nature, political freedom, personal comfort and security, besides all the paraphernalia of civilisation as generally understood. But there have been losses too; of these not the least is the elimination of art from the everyday lives of common people. The meaning of this fact and all it implies is rarely realised. To those who do understand the position, the survival of mediæval conditions in the East and the continued existence of even a few craftsmen of the old school—craftsmen not only understanding one craft well but practising several kindred crafts—is a matter of the utmost interest, and one the importance of which can hardly be overestimated; for it is these men and their methods that we must study if we would understand how that different order of workmanship was produced, and learn how some day to restore the popular arts to their rightful place in human life. The change which occupied four hundred years in Europe has taken place in a hundred years in India and Ceylon. But it is only complete in districts that have been long under European influence, like the low-country of Ceylon. From what has happened in these areas we are able to judge of the probable ultimate fate of all indigenous art. Unfortunately, the new knowledge of perspective, light and shade, &c., has in no wise tended to produce a more highly developed art. Without any proper training in figure drawing, the low-country artist attempts to draw in the European style, the result displaying only the perversion of his taste and the degree of his incapacity; while he is totally devoid of the very great skill in the purely decorative arts which still survives in parts of the Kandyan provinces. It is on this account that the name of Kandyan art has been generally applied to what is really a survival of old Sinhalese art, which in its turn is historically a part of Indian art, just as Ceylon is in the truest sense a part of India. Only by realising this fact, and only if we remember that the surviving decorative arts of the East belong to the same order of art as the art of mediæval Europe, can we fairly understand and sympathise with what survives of old Sinhalese art. The traditional character of the arts in Ceylon must be fully realised; the caste of craftsmen forms an hereditary guild in which traditional methods are handed down from father to son and from master-craftsman to apprentice, from generation to generation. Instructions for the making of all kinds of images are given in certain Sanskrit works (Sariputra, Vajayantaya, and Rupavaliya), which are known by heart by many of the best men, and which are taught to apprentices before they begin to draw the figures described in them. There is a regular system of teaching drawing, beginning with curves, gradually elaborated as the pupil progresses. The whole training of the apprentice is a very strict discipline in drawing. The result is a complete mastery of certain types of conventional design. Combined with this practice went thorough instruction in the theory of the crafts, in other words, learning by heart of Sanskrit works in which the traditional methods are recorded.' The accomplished craftsman is thus often a man of wide reading and real culture.

There was a time in Europe when workmen —"they who would build thy houses, win thy wheat, smooth the rugged, fill the barren, turn the bitter into sweet"—were more often than not engaged on "work worth doing, work in itself pleasant and done under such conditions as to make it neither over-wearisome nor over-anxious." Of how many workmen in England could this now be said? The time is even now passing away in the East when similar conditions prevailed. There can be no doubt that the position of the few remaining craftsmen of the old school still to be found in Ceylon is vastly superior to that of most workmen in Europe at the present day. "We cannot," says Sir George Birdwood, "overlook this serenity and dignity of his life if we would rightly understand the Indian handicraftsman's work. He knows nothing of the desperate struggle for existence which crushes the very soul of the English working man."

Let us endeavour to realise the old Sinhalese craftsmen's position in the social structure. Putting aside weaving and pottery, the work of other and lower castes, we find that the arts of building, painting, ivory-carving, jewellery, &c., are in the hands of an hereditary guild or caste of craftsmen, in social rank second to the cultivator's, but otherwise occupying a well-recognised and honourable position in the country. The craftsman's family possesses lands for which he owes a service rent, originally due to the king, but often regranted to a temple or to a local chief. It should be understood that the family relied upon the lands for food, and not upon the sale of work for money. The old Kandyan made very little use of money; the power even of chiefs lay not in money, but in men.

A POTTER AT WORK. FANCY POTTERY. CARPENTERS.

CARRIAGE BUILDERS. A BRASS WORKER.

The higher craftsmen formed a close corporation of workmen called the *pattal-hatara*, or four workshops. These men worked only for the king, or if for others, only by the king's special permission. The four workshops were respectively, the "jewel," "crown," "golden sword," and "throne" workshops. Besides these men there were a great many others forming a lower division of the craftsman caste, organised as a Public Works Department, called the *Kottalbada* department. The *Kottalbada* men in each district were under a foreman from the four workshops. So much for craftsmen serving the king directly. The *Pattal-hatara* men were liable to be continually engaged on work for the king. The *Kottalbada* men were divided into sets or relays who served in turn in Kandy for periods of two months. Besides all these regular services the king was able to command extra and more continuous service when required. In a general way, no money payment was given for these services; but it often happened that the king made presents of various kinds, particularly lands, to workmen on the completion of a fine piece of work. There was, indeed, some jealousy between chiefs and craftsmen on account of favours shown to the latter. Money payments were, however, often made in the case of the numerous viharas erected for the king. This was in order that the merit resulting from the work might be the king's, which would not be the case unless the work was done at his expense. The proportion of the public revenue spent for the execution of various works of art in this and other ways must have been very considerable, and might advantageously be regarded as a precedent for a more liberal encouragement of the indigenous arts and crafts at the present day. Besides the royal workmen there were those whose services were due to temples (viharas and dewalas) in respect of lands dedicated to them, and also those owing service to local chiefs who possessed lands held temporarily or in perpetuity from the king. Potters and also weavers belonged to inferior castes, but in just the same way held lands for which they owed a service rent.

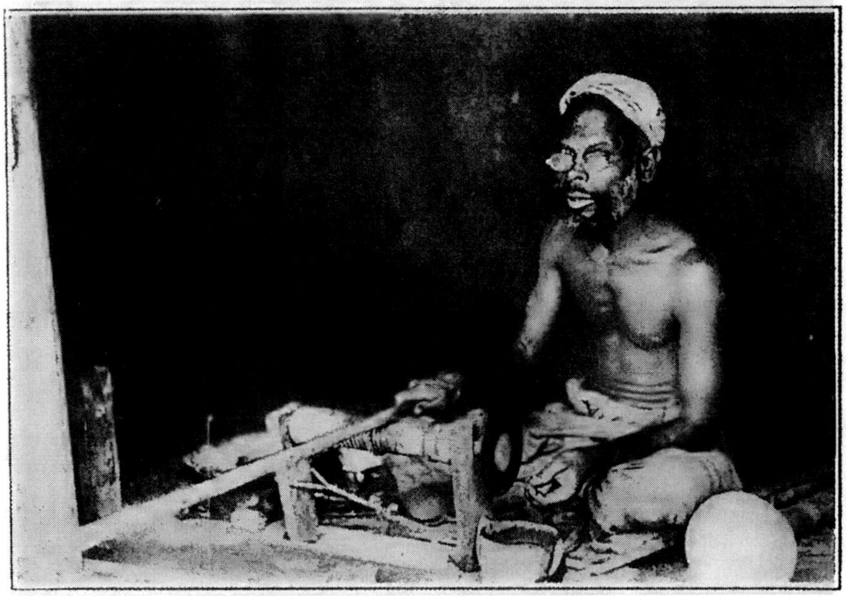

A GEM CUTTER AT WORK.

Some mention must be made of the history of Sinhalese art. Its true beginning must be traced to the time of the introduction of Buddhism by Asoka's missionaries about 300 B.C. The missionaries were accompanied by craftsmen, and a great impetus was given to the art of building and the associated decorative arts; writing was introduced at the same time. The traces of this early Buddhist style, originally in Northern India, are still clearly recognisable in modern work. The principal influence subsequently affecting this style has been the constant intercourse with Southern India. Sinhalese kings have repeatedly, up to modern times, imported craftsmen from India and settled them in villages. The amount of Tamil blood amongst the Kandyan craftsmen is very large, as is evidenced by the family names, the records of the settlements, the similarities in Sinhalese and Indian work, use of Tamil technical terms, &c. Withal, however, there has been preserved a characteristic Sinhalese style, differing from that of Southern India, not in the elements of decoration or in technical methods, but in feeling and inspiration. The reason is not far to seek; it may be found in the fact that Buddhist traditions have been preserved in Ceylon, while it is many hundred years since Buddhism died out in Southern India. It is not always easy to distinguish Sinhalese from South Indian work; but the experienced observer is often able to do so. The Sinhalese style makes a franker use of floral ornament, is less grotesque, is more evidently Aryan, and is more akin to mediæval European than the work of Southern India. But little of Sinhalese art is of indigenous origin. Part of its charm and value, however, lie in its preservation of a style older and in some respects superior to any now surviving on the Indian continent.

We may now proceed to a more detailed account of the separate crafts, in order that the reader, and especially the visitor to Ceylon, may know what to expect and as far as possible understand such specimens of new or old Sinhalese workmanship as he may meet with. It should be understood that the master-craftsman is a master of several crafts. One man, for example, may be at once a builder, painter, ivory carver, and jeweller. This will appear strange to the modern mind, accustomed to specialisation and division of labour. As a matter of fact, however, it is only under such conditions, when the craftsman understands not only one craft well but has experience of the allied crafts, and when all the crafts are united by a common bond of tradition, that the lesser arts, or even the other kind of art which is called "high art," can flourish. It may be recalled that the greatest, perhaps I should say the only great, English craftsman of the nineteenth century was a master of several crafts.

Architecture stands at the head of all the arts and crafts. The art of building in Ceylon was highly organised, *i.e.*, there existed elaborate rules to be observed in the erection of all kinds of buildings. By far the best and also most abundant remaining architecture is that of viharas and dewalas. It is a noteworthy fact that, in spite of the apparently oppressive sumptuary laws, such as those which forbade the use of tiles to any below the rank of Dissawa, the greater part of the art produced belonged really to the people. The walls of the local vihara were their picture gallery; the cloths and vessels dedicated by the king to its service were practically gifts to the whole people; and the lives even of the upper classes were so much simpler than we are apt to imagine that it was really impossible for individuals to possess and monopolise art. In other words, the system of patronage did not involve, as it would under modern conditions, a diminution in the amount of art available for all. In the same way the peasant of mediæval Europe lived in a world of art and in surroundings unspoilt by man's commercial greed—for all which a few galleries of miscellaneous pictures lacking relationship to daily life and uninspired by any common tradition are a very poor compensation. Sinhalese architecture is full of Hindu influence, but has nevertheless a distinctive character of its own. The features which most readily attract attention are the hipped roofs, carved pillars, and painted decoration. A typical Buddhist temple consists of a group of buildings, viz., the *vihara*, or image house, a *dagoba*, or dome-shaped monument enshrining relics, a *bodhi-maluwa*, or platform surrounding the *bo*-tree, and the *pansala*, or priest's residence; there may be also a *bana-maduwa*, or preaching hall, and a *poya-ge*, or confession-hall. The vihara is of course the principal building. Many of the best examples are to be found in the Kandy district; the visitor should not rely upon anything he may see in the low-country as a fair example of Sinhalese building. The vihara may be merely a rock-cave adapted to the purpose by the cutting of a drip line and the addition of a wall converting the cave into a dry chamber. In other cases the vihara is a separate building, generally of one, sometimes of two stories; the walls may be of brick, stone, or mud. The roof or upper story is supported on wood or stone pillars, octagonal and square in section and elaborately carved; the pillars in the audience hall, Kandy, are not very good examples of the style, as they are both over-elaborated and lacking in variety. The timbered roofs of many viharas and dewalas are very handsome. It may be remarked that the really national or primitive style is that of building in wood. The art of building in stone is a later importation from the neighbouring continent.

It is difficult within the limits of a short article to give a satisfactory account of Sinhalese painting. It is, next to architecture, the most important and most instructive branch of Sinhalese art. The best place to study painting is in viharas such as Degaldoruwa, Ridi Vihara, Dambulla, and Danagirigala, where there still remains good eighteenth-century work done for King Kirti Sri, who was a liberal patron of religion and the arts. Something is also to be learnt from old painted furniture, and from the few existing but very beautiful illuminated paper manuscripts of the eighteenth or early nineteenth century. Vihara paintings are executed in *tempera*, and are thus not true frescoes. The vihara subjects are, of course, religious—Jatakas, scenes from the life of Gautama Buddha, the twenty-four assurances, and the like. There are also the purely decorative paintings. Those with which the wooden ceilings are covered show great power of design and fanciful and delicate workmanship.

The old paintings are executed in a gum medium, in a very limited range of colours, chiefly red, yellow, white, and black; blue and green are very sparingly made use of, and are often absent altogether. Of these pigments the white is kaolin, *i.e.*, "Chinese white"; the red is cinnabar, *i.e.*, vermilion; the yellow is gamboge, or orpiment; the black is lamp-black; the blue is indigo. In addition to these colours, pink, grey, and light blue were made by mixture of red, black, and blue with white. The conspicuous and characteristic colours are red and yellow; the ground colour is usually red, the figures or pattern yellow, outlined in black. These limitations produced a severity and restraint suitable to the decorative character of the work required. Now, alas, the "superior" painter runs riot, and with a reckless use of the most brilliant and gaudy colours depicts pictorial designs more suitable for Christmas cards than temple walls. The visitor should beware of judging Kandyan art from degraded examples. The aforesaid pigments must be well ground; the colour improves the longer the grinding is continued—a month is not too much. The pigments are then mixed with gum of the elephant-apple tree; ordinary gum arabic is nowadays a satisfactory substitute. In the case of vihara walls, the first coat put on is one of white, the second of pink, omitting any parts which are to remain white in the final work. The figures or pattern are next inserted in yellow; then outlined in red and the background filled up with red; the last process is the outlining of the design with a fine black line.

Paintings on wood or on pottery are protected by a coat of varnish made from *dorana* oil and *dummala* resin, or covered with a thin coat of carefully strained and cleaned *keppitya* lac. The vihara wall paintings are a highly developed form of a primitive style. The method of continuous narration, where the same figures are repeated continually along a series of panels, without separation into isolated scenes, is a survival from a remote past. The figure drawing is not of a very perfected type, and yet is good enough to serve the artist's purpose very well. The full face, three-quarter face and profile are the only positions attempted; the near eye in three-quarter face and profile figures is still drawn as if seen in full face aspect. The whole style, however, is strictly decorative and appropriate, leaving the wall a wall still, not breaking it up into a series of realistic pictures.

The proportions of the larger figures and especially of images of Buddha are given in certain Sanskrit works, and are carefully followed. Plumb lines are suspended from a wooden framework above the figure, and from various points on these are measured co-ordinates, fixing the position of different features and other parts of the body. The proportions differ slightly for heroic and ordinary figures; thus the number of "heads" in a standing figure of Buddha or any of the gods is (almost) ten; the number of "heads" in an ordinary human figure is reckoned seven (male) and eight (female).

It is, however, in pattern designing that the Kandyan painter really excelled; the best examples are found in old ceiling paintings, painted furniture, &c. Very elaborate patterns

MAT WEAVERS.

are based on geometrical constructions, which, however, are not at all evident in the completed work. The best work of this kind is equal to anything that has ever been done in pattern designing.

Ivory falls into two divisions: carving and turning. The first of these is one of the higher crafts; those who are turners belong to a lower division of the craftsmen. The amount of good ivory work still remaining in Ceylon is large; the collection in the Colombo Museum is representative. The best known, perhaps, are the combs, the work on which is varied and delicate. First in importance, however, is the work applied to the decoration of buildings. The doors of viharas are decorated with strips of carved ivory along the jambs, and with carved figures at the bottom of the jamb on each side. These figures usually represent protecting spirits or guardians. Probably the finest door in the island is that at the Ridi Vihara, where, in addition to the work referred to, the lintel is elaborately ornamented with carved ivory. The old work is always done on thin plates of ivory (*i.e.*, not more than ¼–½ in. thick), so that there is no undercutting or high relief. This point is neglected in the modern caskets made in the low-country; these are wonderful in workmanship, but always fussy and over-elaborated

A NATIVE BLACKSMITH

Ivory book-covers are sometimes very handsome; the ivory handles of knives, too, are elaborately carved. One of the most interesting pieces of ivory work are the carved styles used for teaching writing in sand. The letters are traced by the teacher with the ivory style, and copied by the pupil using the middle finger, supported by the thumb and forefinger.

The ivory turner belongs to the lower section of the craftsman's caste; he makes round boxes, fan handles, book-buttons, scent-sprays, &c. All of these are beautifully decorated with incised lines and circles filled with coloured lac. Most remarkable are the scent-sprays, which are hollowed out and turned so thin as to be flexible and translucent. The ivory worker also works in horn, making very elegant pill-boxes for the doctor's use, often, like ivory, decorated with coloured lac. Horn combs are also largely used.

Old Sinhalese jewellery is of remarkable beauty and delicacy; especially noteworthy are the old chains, named after fruits and flowers, such as the "coconut-flower garland," the "aralu seed garland," and the like. The amount of work put into these delicate chains is almost incredible. Eastern taste differs, or rather used to differ, from European in preferring workmanship to weight. Another characteristic merit of Oriental jewellery is the use of so-called "uncut" stones, *i.e.*, of *unfaceted* stones. This explains the peculiar richness of colouring of Eastern jewellery, for facets on a coloured stone reflect white light, and so obscure the colour of the stone itself. The rounded (cabochon-cut) stones are usually set by a peculiar process of embedding in soft gold, a technique of Indian origin; the Indian element in old Sinhalese jewellery is very marked. The jewelled pendants of Kandyan ladies and the huge rings worn by Kandyan chiefs afford the best examples of this style of work. The European method of setting in a clawed bezel was formerly unknown. A good deal of jewellery is worn by men, but to a less extent than is the case in India. Chiefs in full dress wear, beside their rings, gold chains and richly mounted knives. Kings were accustomed to carry jewelled canes.

Gold, silver, and brass boxes and trays were extensively made, those in silver and brass now forming the staple of the passenger trade. The silver and brass trays compare favourably in design and execution with the more flimsy and rough Benares brass work which is better known to the European market. Some of the older work, too, is superior to the modern in having the ornament relieved by plain space. A certain tendency towards severity of this kind, though rare, with a greater reliance on floral forms and a smaller use of the grotesque, may perhaps be mentioned as a distinguishing character of good Sinhalese art as distinguished from much Indian work.

The appliances of the Ceylon jeweller, whether Sinhalese or Tamil, are comparatively few and simple. Seated in the verandah of his house he has around him all he needs. A charcoal fire burns in an earthen vessel, for use with which he has a rough blowpipe, crucible, and tongs; his other tools are kept in a brass-bound wooden box by his side. Seated thus on the cow-dung floor, he applies infinite patience to the turning out of the most delicate possible work.

Degeneration has perhaps proceeded further in jewellery than in other things. Kandyan ladies still treasure and preserve their old chains and pendants, but when new work is done, it is generally "improved jewellery," imitated from European trade catalogues. Low-country jewellery of the last century is mainly modelled on Dutch lines, and, though sometimes satisfactory, lacks a distinctively Sinhalese character. Of the modern work sold to passengers hardly any is distinctive, faceted stones and European designs being everywhere in evidence.

The founders and blacksmiths belong to the lower division of the craftsman's caste. They work in brass, bronze, and iron , brass is principally used for castings. The method adopted is the well-known *cire perdue* process. A wax model is first made and enclosed in clay ; then the wax is melted out and a hollow mould is ready for the molten metal. The objects made include lamps, betel-stands, spittoons, images of Buddha, &c., and nowadays also models of animals, chiefly for sale to passengers. Articles of suitable form, such as bowls, water vessels, &c., are finished on the lathe. Many of the old brass vessels are of very handsome form and are well worth collecting.

The most interesting work done by the blacksmiths is damascening, or inlaying of iron (or brass) with brass or silver. The old locks and handles on temple doors are often beautiful examples of this kind of work. Less familiar are elephant goads, areca-nut cutters, betel mortars, &c. Excellent work of this kind is still done. The method is briefly as follows : grooves are incised on the metal to be decorated, and the brass or silver wire laid into this and hammered down ; the sides of the original groove, being thus hammered together, hold the inlaid wire tightly. If a larger space is to be overlaid with metal, the space is first cut out, and undercut round the edges, so that when the plate of inlaid metal is applied the edges of the matrix can be hammered down over it. If a repoussé pattern has previously been chased on the matrix, it shows through the overlaid metal which is pressed down on to it. This technique is common in the decorated knives and swords. Some of the most delicate silversmiths' work is found on these knives and swords ; but they have a tendency to over-elaboration, and are often more ornamental than useful.

The lac industry in Ceylon is quite a small one, but of special interest on account of the curious technique. The lac is obtained from two species of the lac insect, neither indentical with the Indian. Lac is a resinous excretion from the skin of the lac insect. When the insects are abundant the branch may be completely covered with the incrustation. The lac is scraped off and enclosed in narrow bolster-shaped bags of thin cloth, which are heated over a charcoal fire until the melted lac oozes through the cloth and is thus strained. The strained lac is then drawn and redrawn, and then coloured by pounding the coloured powders (cinnabar for red, orpiment for yellow) into it while softened by heat.

The lac is now applied to wooden articles by two methods—the turning method and the finger-nail method. In the former method the lac is applied to the wood while turning on the lathe ; in this way concentric bands of colour are produced, and this decoration is suited to bed-legs, small tables, &c. The other or finger-nail process is more elaborate. It can be applied to plane surfaces, but is generally applied to various kinds of sticks. The stick, having been shaped and smoothed, is then coated with the ground colour, which is generally red. To effect this, the stick and lac are warmed over a fire, and the lac applied and smoothed out with a piece of talipot leaf while still warm. For the pattern work the lac is warmed and drawn out into thin strips. When narrow coloured bands are required, strips are applied to the stick, which is kept turning over the fire ; the strips are nipped off with the thumb-nail when a revolution is complete. For more complicated work the string lac is applied in just the same way and nipped off when required; dots are made by applying the end of a string of lac and cutting off a tiny piece with the nail ; whence the name of "finger-nail work." It will be seen that the lac work differs entirely from painting, for brushes are never used ; it has no connection, for example, with the lacquer varnish work of Japan. The work is usually limited to a small number of conventional traditional patterns adapted to the nature of the materials ; the result is appropriate and decorative.

Sinhalese embroidery is not very often seen, as it was generally applied to useful articles now out of fashion, and none of these are easily adapted to meet the taste of Europeans, whereas Indian embroideries can often be used as curtains, and so are better known. The total amount of surviving work is also limited. The embroidery is, however, particularly interesting on account of its individual character, and because there is no reason why the style of work should not now be revived and applied to modern purposes. The work was formerly done by a subordinate division of the caste of craftsmen, called *Sannali*.

The principal characteristics of the pure Sinhalese style are (1) the use only of blue, red, and white material ; (2) the use of the traditional designs common to all the crafts ; (3) the strictly decorative treatment ; (4) the application of the work to useful articles. The last three are essential features, and must be retained in any revival of the style. The limitation of colours should also as a rule be preserved, for although we do occasionally find in old work examples of the use of coloured silks and gold (obtained from India), these are likely to be used nowadays with less restraint, in addition to which must be remembered that the progress of commercial chemistry has practically put an end to the production of beautifully coloured materials.

Most of the work is done in chain-stitch ; button-hole, satin-stitch, hemstitch, and couching are also found ; successful use is also made of appliqué. There are, too, various excellent binding stitches, of which one at least, and that a very elaborate one, is peculiar to Ceylon.

The most characteristic examples of old work are the large betel bags which were used on festive occasions, especially weddings. The stitching is usually in red and white on a blue ground ; the centre is occupied with the main design, and around it are several different borders, sometimes as many as four or five. The big tassels, too, are very handsome. Nowadays, unfortunately, the fashionable thing is the making of embroidered pictures to be framed under glass, the work being often in thick gaudy wools on velvet, or, equally objectionable, in poor tinsel. Great was the outcry when the Government grant for this sort of work in schools was lately stopped.

Lace-making was probably introduced by the Portuguese in the seventeenth century, and again by missionaries at the beginning of the nineteenth century. We meet with old examples of Kandyan embroidery with lace borders and drawn thread work ; part of the lace is pillow lace. It can hardly be said positively whether any of this represents an indigenous art. Lace is principally made in the low-country—at Galle, Kotta, and near Dehiwela. The style of the lace is poor and uninteresting, because it is mainly an imitation of European torchon lace ; it is, moreover, generally made with cheap and poor materials, and so does not wash or wear well. The workers, too, are badly paid, most of the profit going to the middlemen who sell the finished product. It is unfortunate that Ceylon lace has not a distinctive style of its own, for Sinhalese art is rich in distinctive design, and were this combined with good workmanship and good materials, a characteristic type of lace might be evolved capable of holding its own with English or Maltese. The purchaser of Ceylon lace should endeavour to obtain specimens showing some originality and worked in linen or silk thread. At present the lace which is best in these respects is made by a worker at Dehiwela, whose son makes original designs for her use

The Sinhalese seem never to have made any very elaborate types of pottery, only those, in fact, required for domestic, architectural, and religious purposes. The pottery is nevertheless excellent in form, adapted to the purpose for which it is made, and when decorated the ornament is appropriate and suitable. The potters do not belong to the main caste or guild of craftsmen, occupying an inferior social position to that of the latter. The potters are found all over the country, but especially where a good supply of clay is available. Like the regular craftsmen, they held lands, either directly from the king or from a temple or the grantee of a village, *i.e.*, a Kandyan chief. At the Kandyan court one of the household departments was that of the potters, where relays of men from the villages were kept constantly at work supplying the royal requirements. The potter works in the verandah of his house or in a separate shed. His appliances are very simple. The wheel is a round board, mounted on a stone pivot embedded in the ground. The wheel is turned by a boy or by the potter himself. A lump of clay is dumped on the wheel, and the pots are moulded one by one, cut off, and laid aside to dry. The pots so made are bottomless. The under side has to be completed afterwards ; this is a very unusual feature. Ornament is added before firing, which is done in a low kiln fed with fuel from the side. The decoration referred to may consist of slip painting in concentric bands of very simple patterns, or of incised ornament, of which the best is the Greek-looking work on the pots made at Kelaniya ; or the ornament may be stamped, for which purpose small stamps of wood, horn, or ivory are used.

Painted decoration may be applied subsequently in *tempera* and varnished, but this work is done by the superior craftsmen, not by the potters themselves. Good painted pottery is nowadays rarely seen. The large painted amphoræ, exotic in form and with roughly executed ornament, are especially objectionable. Beside domestic and ecclesiastical pottery there is a good deal of interesting architectural earthenware, particularly tiles and finials. The eaves tiles, ornamented with lions or geese, are very good. The flat tiles seen on old roofs should also be noticed, as they are very characteristic and capable of arrangement into elegant patterns. They are now generally replaced by the "Mangalore" tiles, which are adopted for convenience and economy, but at the expense of comfort and appearance.

Very ancient is a knowledge of iron in the East, and throughout mediæval times iron and steel of the finest quality were made in India and exported to be made into Damascus blades. At the present day iron is still made in Sabaragamuwa, but the craft would not have survived had it not been for the smelters' obligation to pay so much iron per annum as a service rent to the local chiefs. The manufacture of steel is practically extinct, the process being only understood by one or two very old men.

The iron is smelted with charcoal in a primitive blast furnace, worked by a pair of foot-bellows ; about 6 lbs. of iron are made in one furnace in three hours, for which the labour of at least three men is required.

Steel is made in clay crucibles, into which are put a piece of iron and the due proportion of wood for carbon. These crucibles are then placed in a small blast furnace, also worked with foot-bellows, until the contents are molten, when the crucibles are removed, allowed to cool, and the steel bar removed. The steel so made is intensely hard and crystalline.

The art of weaving is almost extinct amongst the Sinhalese to-day. The craft was formerly widespread, but is now restricted to one or two families in a single village in the Central Province, and perhaps another in Uva. This is to be regretted on many grounds, both economic and artistic. Now that the real advantages of hand-made textiles are fully realised, and in view of the strength and beauty of the old cloths, it is very desirable that an effort should be made to revive the art of weaving amongst the Sinhalese ; the cloths that are now made are inferior in quality and variety to the old ones. This is mainly due to the lack of local demand. There can, indeed, be no adequate revival of any indigenous arts and crafts so long as the people of the country continue to prefer the worst and cheapest of European wares to anything locally made.

Sinhalese weaving was not a very highly developed craft, that is to say, only cotton cloths were made ; nor was there anything corresponding to the silk brocades of Tanjore, or the gold-woven kinkhabs of Benares. The cotton cloths, moreover, although very strong and handsome, included none of the fine muslins for which India is famous. Besides plain white, blue, or red materials, the Sinhalese weavers made towels, sheets, aprons, belts, chatty-covers, pillow-cases, &c. Into these were woven a great variety of handsome patterns, all, of course, traditional, and each with its own name.

The Sinhalese loom is identical in all essentials with that used throughout the East. It is established on a platform under an open shed next to the weaver's house. The technique is easy to understand, but the execution of complicated patterns requires much skill and practice. Alternate threads of the warp are separated by means of heddles, which are worked by treadles, for which there is a hole in the ground below the loom. The warp is pressed home by a suspended comb. The pattern is picked out with a weaver's sword, which is turned up sideways to hold the warp threads far enough apart for the shuttle to be thrown. Some irregular patterns, however, such as birds and bo-leaves, are tapestry-woven, the coloured threads being twisted round the warp by hand. The complete cloth is thus usually a combination of purely mechanical weaving with tapestry, the former greatly predominating.

The well-known Dumbara mats, called kalala, are made by a low-caste people named Kinnaras. The fibre used is obtained from the "bow-string" hemp (*Sanseviera zeylanica*). The round green leaves are scraped against a log with a wooden tool like a spokeshave. After the fleshy part of the leaf has been thus removed, the fibre is oiled and brushed, and is ready for use almost at once : part is used as it is without dyeing ; the remainder is dyed red, yellow, or black. The warp threads are spun like cotton, but the weft elements are not spun at all, and consist merely of the parallel fibres. The loom is a low horizontal one, more primitive than the cotton weavers use ; there is no proper shuttle, but the weft fibres are passed through the warp by means of a large wooden bodkin. The mats are worked in bold conventional designs, and are handsome enough. After two or three years, however, the colours become somewhat faded, though still pleasant. The most usual designs are quaintly conventional birds, fishes, cobras, trees, &c. As usual, even the geometrical patterns have each a separate name. The weavers have songs about their work, and trace its origin to the time of the mythical king Maha Sammata.

There is no regular practice of any organised craft of dyeing amongst the Sinhalese. *Sappan* (*Cæsalpinia Sappan*) is used for colouring palm and grass leaves red, for mat and basket weaving, also for dyeing the fibre for the Dumbara mats ; *weniwel* is used to dye the same fibres yellow ; grasses are dyed black by first boiling with a decoction of gall-nuts and then burying in rice-field mud.

The yellow dye of Buddhist priests' robes is obtained from jak (*Artocarpus integrifolius*) wood, in an extract of which the cloth to be dyed is soaked. The dye is not permanent, but is easily renewed. Cloths that have been used for years and dyed again and again are a very fine colour. It is difficult to be sure whether the Sinhalese cotton weavers ever dyed the blue and red material they used. If so, it was not a regular practice. Madder and indigo grow wild in Ceylon, but have been very little, if at all, used by the Sinhalese.

The well-known Kalutara baskets are really the best and most useful work in dyed palm leaf. There is now, unfortunately, a tendency to make use of aniline dyes, especially a crude magenta and a raw green. These the purchaser should be careful to avoid.

SHORT TABLE OF CASTES OF CRAFTSMEN.

Achari Caste. (The caste of the craftsmen.)	Higher Division.	Architects, painters goldsmiths, ivory and wood carvers armourers.
	Lower Division.	Founders, blacksmiths, turners (wood or ivory), stone carvers, lac workers, embroiderers.

Badahelayo, porters.

Yamanne, iron smelters.

Beruwayas, includes cloth weavers.

Kinnarayas, weavers of "Dumbara" mats.

Rodiyas, whips, cords, brooms, &c.

Lace-makers are not a caste. Ordinary rush mats are made by women of all castes.

TAMIL.

THE arts and crafts of the Tamils in Ceylon are similar to those of the Tamils in India, but of less interest and variety, partly owing to the isolation of the Ceylon Tamils from what is more strictly their native land, and partly because the district occupied by them has for a very long time been under European influence, and the arts and crafts have degenerated or died out as they have in the low-country Sinhalese districts. The decay, however, has not been so marked in this case as in the other, owing to the relative inaccessibility of the Jaffna and Batticaloa districts, and in some cases to the high quality of the manufactures. A case in point is supplied by Batticaloa cloth, the making of which has not been abandoned, and which is largely worn and highly valued by the wearers.

No one—certainly not the present writer—has made any detailed study of Tamil arts and crafts in Ceylon; and this is not the place to describe the arts and crafts of Southern India. It will only be possible, therefore, to give a short general account of the subject, without attempting a systematic treatment of it.

Domestic architecture may be briefly referred to. The old Tamil houses are of the regular square form, with inside courts and a verandah next the road. The old homes are commodious and cool, which the modern houses, covered with a single layer of Mangalore tiles, certainly are not. The old houses are, moreover, well and very strongly built, with solid, well-carved pillars and spacious verandahs, in the recesses of which stand large oak chests with handsome brass fittings. A garden with a well is an indispensable adjunct. Seclusion of the ladies is carried to extreme in high Jaffna society, and all gardens are protected by high cadjan walls. The gates of these are worthy of remark, being well carved in several interesting designs.

The Tamil and Sinhalese arts have naturally much in common. It will be found, for example, that the looms are almost identical. The brassfounder's methods are the same, and most of the patterns and elements of decorative design are really the same, but with a difference of style and feeling which is not difficult to recognise after some experience. This difference is partly that between Aryan and Dravidian feeling, largely due to the difference in religion, and partly to the closer connection which the Tamils have had with the rest of India. The apparent differences have been exaggerated in modern times by the dying out of crafts amongst the two races, under a process of selection which had not the same effect on both. For example, weaving still flourishes to some degree at Jaffna and Batticaloa, but is almost extinct among the Sinhalese. Weaving is, perhaps, the most important of the Tamil crafts, but it is carried on to a less extent than formerly.

TAMIL SILVERSMITHS AND JEWELLERS.

The subject of Dravidian religious architecture cannot be briefly dealt with or adequately illustrated in Ceylon, and is therefore not referred to here.

Many of the cloths woven are good, durable stuff, especially those of Batticaloa, which are in use throughout Ceylon. The material is sometimes handsome, but it must not be supposed that any weaving of special beauty or unusual interest is done. It is said that some silk weaving was carried on at one time in Jaffna, but nothing is now done except in cotton, the dyed yarns (often aniline dyed) for which are imported. The cloths made are almost entirely confined to wearing apparel, though some stout canvases are still made near Jaffna. The looms employed are of the indigenous Indian type, differing only from the Sinhalese in having extra heddles for making more complicated patterns.

Probably some yarn was generally made and dyed locally, but the only dyeing now practised is that of made-up cloth. This dyeing is a combination of the processes of dye painting and pot dyeing, and is chiefly used for decorating the cloths with narrow borders worn by men. A few decorated handkerchiefs and wearing cloths are still made for the Sinhalese market. The old Kandyan flags were no doubt of Tamil workmanship, as dye painting seems never to have become a Sinhalese craft.

Dyeing with chaya root is the principal process. The essential element in this work is the protection of part of the cloth by a coating of beeswax, which is drawn out in patterns, which appear white in the finished cloth. After the beeswax is thus applied, the whole cloth is dipped three times in hot decoctions of chaya root, the last nearly boiling. The cloth then becomes of a dull reddish-purple colour with a pattern in white. The chaya root is often, however, combined with other dyes, particularly alum and iron filings for black, and gall-nut for a redder hue. Decoctions of these are applied to the parts to be so coloured before the chaya root dyeing is begun. The chaya root industry was once very important. At the beginning of the century it was a Government monopoly, bringing in a revenue of £2,000 a year; but it declined as early as 1830, and the root is now hardly ever used, the native product having been driven out by aniline dyes.

The jewellery of Jaffna has some reputation. The old work in gold, or gold set with cabochon stones, was of the greatest delicacy and perfection of design. The special types of chains and beads were all known by name and are very constant in form. They are now out of fashion, and it is a common thing for old work to be melted down and made up again into new and worthless designs. The distinctively Jaffnese work of modern times is not much to boast of. The workmanship is still extremely fine and delicate, but is applied to trivial and unsuitable ends, often in association with tortoiseshell. The use of European designs and cut stones is perhaps less general than is elsewhere the case in Ceylon.

Brassfounding is a craft in no immediate danger of extinction. The very handsome old rice-bowls and other vessels are now out of use, but water-pots, bells, lamps, and the like are always wanted, and are found in elegant forms. The ordinary *cire perdue* process of casting is followed, as amongst the Sinhalese founders, and the cast metal is afterwards hammered or finished on a lathe.

Pottery is made for domestic purposes; but little is known of any more elaborate forms, nor have any special forms of decoration been noted, beyond the use of stamps. A certain angularity is characteristic of Tamil forms as compared with Sinhalese.

Mats and baskets woven of palmyra leaf of a superior character are in general use. The manifold uses of the palmyra have often been noticed. One of the most remarkable kinds of baskets made from the leaf are the well-baskets which are attached to the end of the long well sweeps with which water is drawn up to irrigate the fields; they are so tightly plaited as to prevent the escape of any water through the meshes.

NATIVE CEREMONIAL OBSERVANCES

By D. J. SUBASINHA.

FROM time immemorial the inhabitants of Ceylon, both Sinhalese and Tamil, have practised the ceremonies we now describe. Amongst the town population, with its divers nationalities, the observance of the rites is not rigidly followed, but among the country population the reverse is the case. It will be gathered from what follows that astrology is at the root of the system. Here, as in India and China, the influence of the planets is held to govern all human relations. To make the matter clear it is desirable to take the reader through the life of a person from the cradle to the grave.

Before the birth of the child incense is burned and milk-rice is prepared with unbroken grains of rice. A plantain leaf is spread on the ground, and the milk-rice is divided into eight parts, and offered to the deities.

On a lucky day during the waxing moon, at an hour when the position of the planets is favourable, a house is built for the confinement. If it is to take place in the same residence, a paste is made with boiled rice and mustard, over which are written the names of the nine planets, viz., (1) Sun, (2) Moon, (3) Mars, (4) Mercury, (5) Jupiter, (6) Venus (7) Saturn, (8) Carpet Draconis, (9) Canda Draconis. Incense and flowers are offered to this, and the woman is made to enter the room thus consecrated amidst the chanting of mantaras (charms).

Immediately the child is born he is shown to the father. Afterwards he is bathed, and a decoction made of gold rubbings mixed with the maternal milk, and in some instances with the juice of lunuwila—hedge hyssop (*Herpestis Monniera*)—leaves, is given to the child in drops. The object of this is to purify the blood and aid to ensure full development of the body and intellect. The infant is then handed to the father and other close relatives by the midwife, who receives presents from them. Rice is scattered over the room, and in the centre a heap of paddy is arranged, over which lotus leaves are placed. Subsequently the infant is placed on the leaves by a grandmother or aunt, his body being inclined to the right.

The day after the infant's birth an astrologer is summoned. Upon being served with milk-rice and sweets to his satisfaction, he is informed of the day and time of birth. He thereupon ascertains the position of the planets at the time, and declares whether the child is male or female. On being requested to substantiate this fact, he gives the number of males and females who were in the room at the time the child was born, and describes the number of entrances to it. If the descriptions are correct he receives presents. He then consults the ephemeris, casts the horoscope, and foretells the future career of the child.

To secure immunity from the influence of Prethas Bhuttas (evil spirits) and to conciliate the nine planets, a circular gold ornament, termed Pancha-audaya, is hung around the neck of the child with a charmed gold chain. In this are embossed the five weapons of war, namely, conch, defending rod, sword, arrow, and a short cudgel.

In the case of royalty the ceremony of naming takes place within ten days ; with Brahmans the period is twelve days, with merchants sixteen days, and others thirty days after birth. The initial letters of the name are selected in accordance with the time of birth as shown in the ephemeris, and it is considered important that this should be done at an auspicious moment. The child is named generally by a grandfather, the father, or an uncle.

In the case of a girl the ears are bored either twelve or sixteen days, or six or seven months, after the birth. This is done at an auspicious moment, either on a Monday, Thursday, or Friday.

When the infant is brought into another room from the one in which it was born, there is another ceremony like the one in naming, and it is done at an auspicious moment, care being taken that the child may not see the sun.

To insure the future prosperity of the child, he is shown the sun with no little care. Three or four months after birth a dais is prepared in the centre of the compound, above which is placed a heap of paddy. The heap is levelled in the form of a square, which is divided into eight equilateral triangles, and a seat is prepared at the point where the diagonals intersect each other. To the right of the seat is placed a pot of water, around the mouth of which is tied a threefold thread. Right over this square a canopy is hung, from the lower surface of which garlands of sweet-scented flowers and leaves of variegated hue are suspended. On the eight corners of the dais are placed eight small new pots, over the mouths of which are kept outspread coconut flowers. On these flowers are placed eight lighted lamps. Standing by this dais the parents make offerings to the nine planets. After all these preparations, priests are summoned, the child is brought to the dais and placed in the seat by the father. Holding one end of the thread which is attached to the pot of water, the other end being in the hand of the child, the priests chant Parittha, invoking blessings upon the newcomer. Thereupon a curtain is removed and the child is made to see the sun for the first time. The showing of the moon is also done in a similar manner. On these occasions offerings are made to the Brahmans and priests, and the relatives are feasted.

A month after the child's birth, at a lucky hour on an auspicious day, the child is given cow or goat milk, in case the mother's milk runs short. The weaning ceremony takes place either in six, ten, or twelve months

TAMIL FORTUNE-TELLER.

after birth, at a lucky hour, either on a Wednesday, Thursday, or Friday, on an auspicious day. The rice to be fed is cooked by a male. At first a portion of the rice is offered to the nine planets. The child is then bathed in sweet-scented water, and his body adorned with flowers. He is placed on a special dais, facing a favourable direction, with two men standing on either side intoning blessings. A plantain leaf is spread in front of him, and rice mixed with honey is placed thereon. Around the rice gold coins, gems, pearls, and garlands of flowers are placed. Either the father or the uncle, attired in clean clothes, feeds the child with rice, at the same time intoning blessings upon him. In the meantime, either the grandfather or some close relative holds a lighted lamp over the child's head. The assembled relatives now make presentations to the father, either in coin or kind. A lucky hour is always selected to insure a good future for the child. The belief is that if this is not done the child is liable to become dumb, deaf, crippled, or suffer from some other ailment.

The cutting of hair takes place in eight or twelve months, or within two, three, or five years of birth. A concoction composed of the juice extracted from jasmine and ethana flowers (a species of the panic grass—*Heteropogon Hirtus*) dissolved in water is charmed and poured into a conch. Then the mixture is poured by a fair-looking, good-sighted, and gentle-hearted man over the crown of the child's head and the hair is cut. Afterwards the child is bathed in scented water. The priests are now offered milk-rice, jaggery (unrefined sugar), and sweets, and what remains in their alms-bowls is given to the child, and as he eats the same the priests intone a blessing upon him.

Within five years of birth, on an auspicious day during the months of September, October, and November, either on a Wednesday, Thursday, or Friday, the child is taught its letters in the early morn, when the sun and moon are in combination. On these occasions he is bathed and attired in white clothes. Bearing an emblem of respect in his hand, he goes to the teacher, falls prostrate at his feet, worships him, reverently gives the present, and, facing a favourable direction, offers himself for tuition. Either the grandfather, father, or maternal uncle places a book in the child's hand and invites the teacher to perform his pleasant duty. He holds the child by the right hand, places his forefinger on the alphabet, and repeats letter after letter, which the child repeats after him. The teacher is now presented with a tray full of milk-rice, plantains, and fruits, after which the child and his well-wishers partake of the delicacies specially prepared for the occasion. In honour of the event the child receives presents from his well-wishers.

At a lucky hour the child, now a young man in his teens, is led by his father to a field. He is given a mamotie, and taught how to till the ground and the various phases of agriculture. Amongst other industries taught may be mentioned carpentry, masonry, pottery, the craft of a blacksmith, and other trades and industries.

The male is married when between twenty-five and thirty years of age, and the female between sixteen and twenty years. In the case of a son, when the time comes for contracting a marriage, the father summons an elderly, trustworthy, and well-conducted man, and commissions him to select a suitable lady, worthy of becoming the wife of his son, from a family of equal status. This man is known as the matchmaker, and it will be seen that he plays a very prominent part in this most important function. After due deliberation he visits a family on whom his choice falls, and explains the object of his mission to the chief of the family. The head of the family thus visited talks over the matter, and if the proposal is acceptable, consults his wife. Afterwards the three meet together, and the matchmaker describes the virtues of the young man and the family traditions of his parents. If the head of the family and his wife approve of the proposal, the matchmaker is informed that the girl's father will visit the young man's parents. On an appointed day the father goes there, accompanied by the matchmaker. Should he find the circumstances satisfactory, a day is appointed by the young man's father to visit the girl's parents. The return visit then follows, and if everything is satisfactory the matchmaker is requested to obtain the girl's horoscope. An astrologer afterwards calculates and finds if the position of the planets indicates prosperity, and coincides with the position of the planets in the young man's horoscope. If the astrologer's recommendations prove favourable the father gives his consent to the proposal. In like manner the matchmaker takes the young man's horoscope to the girl's parent's, who get it examined by another astrologer, and satisfy themselves. In the event of there being no bar astrologically to the union, arrangements are made for the girl's uncles, brothers, and elders to visit the young man's parents, to satisfy themselves that the circumstances of the family are acceptable to them. All being well, the young man's uncles, brothers, and elders visit the girl's parents, ascertain particulars in a similar way, and satisfy themselves. They then inquire of the girl's father how much dowry will be given in cash and what in kind. After the final settlement of this important question, they report the results to the young man's father. As a mark of acceptance of these conditions a day is appointed for the young man to visit his *fiancée*, whose face he has up to now not beheld. The young man, attired in a fashion befitting his position, and accompanied by his close relatives, visits the girl. On their arrival they are welcomed and lavishly treated. On the advent of the lucky hour, the girl, well dressed, is conducted to the hall wherein the visitors are seated. In the presence of the assembled relatives the young man gracefully steps forward, respectfully greets her, and affectionately ties a necklace round her neck, and in return she puts a ring on the forefinger of her lover, as a confirmation of the proposed marriage. The parties then repair to their respective seats, after which all the assembled relatives are feasted. On the return of the visitors the matchmaker consults the parties, and with the advice of the astrologer appoints an appropriate day for the publication of the banns. On this eventful day the bridegroom, accompanied by his parents and elders, who carry with them trays full of divers kinds of presents in the form of sweets, plantains, fruits, oil-cakes, ash-pumpkins, curds, milk-rice, and kindred things, visit the girl's house, which is decorated in honour of the event. As soon as the visitors are sighted some of the chief relatives of the girl go forward and salute them with uplifted hands, using the words, "Ayu bowan," *i.e.*, "Wish you all long life." The chief among them, always an elderly person, is the first to be conducted to the house and given the seat of honour. They are now offered trays filled with betel, areca nut, chunam (prepared lime), tobacco, cloves, ginger, and kutch. After coffee, the visitors and some relatives of the girl go to the Palliyemahatmaya (the marriage registrar) and give notice of the intended marriage. On their return the party are entertained to a sumptuous repast. In the presence of the relatives the would-be father-in-law presents to the bridegroom half the promised dowry. The happy suitor accepts the proffered present, and hands the same to the bride for safe keeping, retaining in his hands only a fraction of it, for to go away empty-handed after such an auspicious gathering is considered a bad omen. The assembled relatives then congratulate each other, and the visitors return home. An astrologer now finds out an appropriate day for the actual wedding ceremony, and the matchmaker communicates it to the interested parties. On an auspicious day the bridegroom's parents visit their relatives and friends, and tender to them betel in a tray, as an invitation to the marriage feast. The one who receives the invitation first makes a presentation to the inviter in the name of the bridegroom. A procedure similar to this is followed by the bride's parents. For the entertainment of the guests a magul maduwa (a sexagonal pavilion) thatched with coconut leaves is erected. Triumphal arches are put up near about the house, and both sides of the road which forms the approach to the house are attractively festooned. On the day prior to the ceremony those invited proceed to the respective houses and partake of the marriage feast. The relatives, as they go, carry with them pingo loads of provisions, fruits, and vegetables. In some instances they are headed by a procession. In the manner described above they are again welcomed. During the forenoon priests, generally Buddhist priests, are invited and given alms; at the termination of which incident, an atapirikara (*i.e.*, eight requisites of a Buddhist priest, namely, three robes, one alms-bowl, one girdle for the loins, one razor, one needle, and one water-strainer) is offered to them. They receive it, intone blessings by chanting Parittha, and go away. At an auspicious moment the chief among the relatives is conducted to the magul maduwa, and lavishly entertained, after which he makes a presentation to the bridegroom's father. The other relatives and friends are next feasted, and they in turn make presentations to the bridegroom's father. In the afternoon the bridegroom and his relatives, attired in the best available garb, go to the bride's house. The party is invariably accompanied by the matchmaker, the astrologer, musicians, washerman, washerwoman, and other attendants. Immediately following the bridegroom walks a low-caste (wahunpura) man carrying a talattha (a talipot leaf, used as an umbrella). This is held over the bridegroom's head when the party is going out of the house or nearing its destination. On arrival at the bride's house the matchmaker goes in advance and announces to the bride's father the approach of the party. At a signal given by the firing of a gun, the party approaches the house, the musicians in the meantime displaying their best form. The chief relatives of the bride go out to meet the visitors, accord them a welcome, and conduct them home. Attired in immaculate white, and with watchful eyes, stands the bride's brother at the entrance to the house with a vessel of water by him. As the bridegroom steps in he washes his feet, for which service he receives a gold ring. The visitors are then offered betel, and later on served with coffee. They now go to the hall wherein the bride is seated, and see the nuptial ceremony performed in the same manner as was observed by the first Aryan settlers in the island.

A special dais, termed the magul poruwa, is prepared in the centre of the hall. On the floor is spread a mat, over which is drawn an octagonal diagram divided into eight equal parts. Over this is placed a wooden board which is covered with a carpet, and this in its turn is covered with a cloth. It may be mentioned parenthetically that on all festive occasions it is customary to cover chairs, sofas, lounges, tables, and other furniture with white cloth, a duty which is always performed by the dhoby, whose services are well rewarded. Over the temporary platform described, gold and silver coins, pearls and fried paddy, and five different kinds of flowers are scattered. A canopy is suspended over the dais, at the four corners of which four pots, half filled with water and holding outspread coconut flowers, are placed. On each flower is an earthen lamp burning with coconut oil. At the auspicious moment announced by the astrologer, the bride and bridegroom are conducted to the magul poruwa, and as they mount, a coconut is split in halves with a wood chopper. Benedictory verses are now repeated, after which the bridegroom is handed a cloth, to an end of which is tied a gold coin that goes to the dhoby as a present. Spreading out the cloth, the bridegroom wraps it round the bride's waist; she in turn presents

SINHALESE DEVIL DANCERS.

him with a suit of clothes. This is called the Pilicndaweema. The maternal uncle of the bride now mounts the dais, ties together the right thumbs of the bride and bridegroom with silken threads, whilst the learned relatives of both families chant Astaka verses containing Buddha's attributes and blessings. The uncle then pours water from a ewer over the joined thumbs, and thus gives away the bride. As the wedded couple dismount a coconut is again split into halves. They are now conducted to a raised seat, termed the istharaduwa, where for the first time they sit together and receive congratulations from their well-wishers. As a form of congratulation, some sprinkle rose-water over them. The musicians, responding to the influences of the moment, now play with increased fervour. A sumptuous dinner follows, at which the relatives of both parties for the first time are entertained together. In the morning the bride is dressed with the clothes presented by the bridegroom, and her relatives are attired in festive garb. After coffee, the parties repair to the hall, where the business part of the ceremony takes place. The bridegroom presents the mother-in-law with a web of cloth, after which the father-in-law presents the bridegroom with the promised dowry. The matchmaker takes the list of wedding-presents given, reads it out for the delectation of the assembled relatives, and hands it to the bridegroom's father. Among other things, the gifts comprise household requisites of every sort. The parties now go to the Palliyemahatmaya amidst great pomp and splendour, and have the marriage registered. In some instances, where the parties can afford it, the registrar is invited to the house. After this civil ceremony the party go to the bridegroom's house, headed by the procession of musicians, where they are right royally welcomed. After a change of clothes and a wash they are served with coffee, followed a little later by a sumptuous breakfast. The rest of the day is spent in various kinds of amusements. In the evening the bride's relatives return home. On the following day the bride's father visits the son-in-law, carrying with him the presents, and later on he returns home. After dinner the new couple retire to a specially prepared room in the residence, where the honeymoon is spent. Three days later the bride's relatives come hither on a visit, bringing with them numerous presents, when they are welcomed and feasted. Amongst this party comes the bride's aunt, who reports as to the virginity of the niece, after which the bride receives the congratulations of the female relatives. At the termination of these various ceremonies the matchmaker is well rewarded by the parents of both the bridegroom and bride. For the first confinement it is customary for the bride to go to her mother's house, where every necessary attention is bestowed upon her.

KANDYAN DEVIL DANCERS.

The ceremonial observed in the case of a funeral is very elaborate. A few hours after the death of a man, the relations wash the corpse, shave it, and having clothed it in a suit of clothes which the deceased was accustomed to wear, place it on a sofa covered with white cloth under a canopy. Two lamps are lighted and placed one at the head and the other at the foot of the corpse. Those who come to see the corpse show their respect for it by sprinkling it with rose-water from a ewer placed close by. A coffin is then made, draped in white, and the body is placed in it. Before the coffin is nailed down, male and female relatives have a last look at the corpse, some kissing it and others sprinkling it with lavender-water. The male relatives carry the coffin to the grave, which, in a village, will always be dug in land belonging to the deceased. Around the grave an arch is erected, covered with a canopy. From the house of mourning to the grave the road is festooned, and white sand is scattered on its surface. The tom-tom beaters go first, followed in some instances by a chapter of Buddhist priests. This practice is, however, now dying out, for it is contrary to the teachings of Buddha. The number of priests depends upon the circumstances of the deceased, and they walk under a canopy of white cloth. The coffin is borne only by close relatives, and is followed by male relatives and friends, women in no case taking part in the funeral procession. Three times the coffin is carried round the grave, and then it is rested on two sticks placed across the mouth of the pit. The chapter of priests then come and stand in order round the grave. A web of white cloth is now spread, and one end of it is given to the priests while the other end rests on the coffin. The assembled men now kneel and invite the priests to give them Pancha Sila. After this is done, the chief among the priests delivers a sermon on the transitoriness of things material, and consoles the bereaved parties. The chapter of priests then repeat Pali stanzas. One is translated as follows by an Oriental scholar :—

> " How transient are all component things
> Their nature is to be born and die ;
> Coming, they go ; and then is best,
> When each has ceased, and all is past."

After the repetition of this stanza three times, the priests set aside the cloth. A ewer and a cup are then placed on a plate, and the close relatives pour water, as an invitation to the deceased to partake of the meritorious actions they have performed in his name. In the meantime the priests chant Pali stanzas, of which the following is the meaning :-

> " As rivers, when they fill, must flow,
> And reach, and fill the distant main;
> So surely what is given here
> Will reach and bless the spirits there.
>
> " If you on earth will gladly give,
> Departed ghosts will gladly live ;
> As water poured on mountain tops
> Must soon descend and reach the plain,
> So surely what is given here
> Will reach and bless the spirits there."

The relations then place the coffin in the grave, and each throws in a handful of earth. At this juncture the priests leave with the offerings made to them. The grave is filled in, and over it a mound of earth is raised in the shape of a coffin. Two lights, one at the head and the other at the foot of the grave, are left burning. Three or seven days after the burial a priest is invited to the house in which the deceased died, and his visit is usually paid by night, when he explains the doctrines of Lord Buddha. He illustrates his subject with a great many examples, and points out that man, being born subject to change, must die, and that it behoves every one throughout his life to make the best use of his time and perform meritorious deeds. In the morning he receives an offering of cloth and alms. A day later, a number of priests, not less than seven, are invited and given alms. The practice of burial is of comparatively recent origin. Three centuries since, cremation was general. Even at present, when a man of some means or a priest dies, the body is placed on a pyre of wood about 18 ft. high and cremated.

Pirith is the Sinhalese term for the Pali word Parittham, which literally signifies "protection." When we speak of going to hear Pirith, it means to listen to the chanting by priests of the nine Suttas, or discourses, entitled Mangala, Rathana, Mettha, Khanda, Mora, Dhajagga, Bhojjanga, Angulimala, and Atanatiya. To trace its origin we have to turn to the religious history of India. About 2,400 years ago a plague called Ahivatthaka prevailed in Vesali, known in modern geography as Allahabad. During this time there was a protracted drought, vegetation was dried up, and famine prevailed, as the result of which large numbers of people were carried off by the plague. This disease is supposed to have been first contracted by flies, then by rats and other small animals, and then by human beings. Owing to the extraordinary number of deaths, corpses were left rotting in the open, and the putrid matter emanating therefrom attracted evil spirits, and thus aggravated the gravity of the pestilence. Being subjected to the threefold dreadful calamities mentioned, the people complained to the king, who, together with some of his subjects, deliberated as to the best means of warding off these misfortunes. After due deliberation, Lord Buddha, who was then living at Rajagaha (modern Rajagiri, Behar, India), in the territory of Bimbisara Raja, was invited to visit the city and afford relief. Upon Buddha's arrival within the precincts of the city, peals of thunder burst forth, and the lightning flashed out, vapour-laden clouds darkened the air, and torrents of rain fell, cleansing the town of all impurities. Buddha requested Ananda Thero to take an alms-bowl filled with water, thread, and flowers, and along with the Lichchavi Rajas perambulate the city, repeating the discourse entitled Ratana Sutta. This was done, and the wonderful efficacy of it was immediately felt by the famine and terror stricken people. From this circumstance it will be seen that the object of chanting pirith was to ward off fever in any form. Chanting of pirith is done either by one, five, seven, sixteen, or twenty-one priests, the number varying according to the occasion. The larger the number the greater the efficacy. The site selected for the ceremony is well cleaned. A mandappa or enclosed space, either in a square, hexagonal, or octagonal form, is prepared. Above it is fixed a canopy attractively decorated with leaves and flowers. Seats covered with white cloth are prepared in it for five or more ordained priests, as the novitiates (Samaneras) do not partake in this function. In the centre is placed a small table at which two priests sit and chant pirith from an ola book during all times of the day, though the Maha Piritha is chanted during early morn, afternoon, and close on midnight. On the table is kept a pot of strained water, with its mouth covered with a white cloth, on which is placed an areca nut flower. At the four corners of the enclosure are disposed four pots bearing outspread coconut flowers. Coconut-oil lamps are lit and placed over these. Around the mouth of the pot, over the draped part, runs a reel of thread, one end of which is held by the priests as they chant the stanzas. Around the enclosure mats are spread on the floor, on which both males and females, clad in white, squat and attentively listen to the chanting. The attractive part of the ceremony is the time at which the Maha Piritha is chanted, and it is at that time that people congregate in large numbers. When pirith is chanted to a sick person, one end of the pirith nula, or the enchanted thread, is held by the priests and the other by the patient. The idea is to join the chanter and the chantee and fix their concentrated thoughts on the ceremony. The action exercises a magnetic influence on the mind of the patient and relieves his mental pains. It is also considered that a current of good wishes from the chanters flows towards the patient and the listeners, as the stanzas are repeated in a melodious and soothing manner. At the termination of the Maha Piritha, water is taken from the pot on the table into smaller vessels, and first distributed among the priests, who either drink it or wet their heads and faces with it. The enchanted water is then given into the hands of the listeners, but if there is a large number of them, it is sprinkled over them by an elderly man. As a specimen of the verses constituting the pirith, a free translation of four is given below :—

"If there be any spirits assembled here belonging to the earth or living in the sky, let all such spirits be of good mind ; let them moreover listen attentively to what is said. If the sage of the Sakya race, of a tranquil mind, has attained any state of extinction, which is passionless, immortal and excellent, there is nothing equal to that law. And this excellent jewel is found in the law. May there be happiness from this truth ! If the supreme Buddha has extolled pure meditation, if he or others have spoken of any unceasing meditation, there is nothing equal to that meditation. And this excellent jewel is found in the law. May there be happiness from this truth !" (Ratana Sutta).

"Whatever living beings there be, all these, without exception, be they movable or immovable, long or great, middle-sized or short, minute or vast, visible or invisible, living far or near, already born or about to be born, let them all be happy minded" (Metta Sutta).

"Bhikkus, I declare, if any fear or consternation or shuddering were to arise in you, who proceed to the forest, to the root of a tree, or to a solitary spot, meditate of me in this wise, that Bhagawa is sanctified, allwise, endowed with knowledge and conduct, happy, knowing, pre-eminent, a guide of men whose passions have to be quelled, the teacher of Devas and men. When you meditate on me any fear, or stupor, or shuddering will cease" (Dhajagga Sutta).

The pirith ceremony is first known to have been performed in Ceylon about A.D. 680, during the reign of the saintly king Akbo Sirisangabo. It is again described as a private ceremony in the 31st chapter of the Mahavansa during the reign of Sena, about A.D. 880, and Kasub V., about A.D. 935. About A.D. 1260 Parakrama Bahu, of Dambadeniya, resorted to it publicly, during a season of great drought. In the reign of Upatissa, about A.D. 400, there was a great drought and pestilence, and the pious king formed a stately procession, as described in the Mahavansa, and caused the priests to perambulate the city all night, repeating the Ratana Sutta. The next day dawned in torrents of rain, and the grateful king ordered the like ceremonies to be performed in future on occasions of great distress.

WATERFALL BETWEEN AMBAWELA AND NANU-OYA. BETWEEN GALBODA AND WATAWALA.
"DUKE'S NOSE," BETWEEN HATTON AND KOTAGALA.
"LION'S MOUTH," KADUGANNAWA INCLINE. VIEW FROM SUMMIT OF THE TUNNEL OVER UVA.

RAILWAYS

THE Ceylon Railway system supplies perhaps the most notable example of successful State ownership and direction of railways that the Empire affords. Planned carefully with regard to the great commercial needs of the country and efficiently managed, it earns a revenue sufficient, after paying working expenses and debt and sinking fund charges, to allow of a substantial contribution being made to the general revenue of the colony. In 1905 the profit on the year's working (receipts amounting to Rs. 9,690,653 and expenditure to Rs. 5,206,899) was no less than Rs. 4,483,754, an amount which showed an increase of Rs. 633,201 on the profits of the previous year. Taking the whole of the outlay on the lines from their inception, the surplus of 1905 represents a return of 6·3 per cent.

The history of Ceylon railways dates back some sixty years, to the period following the railway mania in England, when promoters were turning their minds to the great possibilities of profitable railway development offered by India and the colonies. A project for the construction of a line from Colombo to Kandy was the first proposal framed. This scheme for connecting the modern with the ancient capital of the island had much to recommend it on the score of commercial advantage as well as of administrative utility. But it was brought forward in advance of its time. Railways then, as far as the East was concerned, were experiments, and the financial risks were considered too great to be undertaken. Not until the late fifties, during the administration of Sir Henry Ward, was the scheme seriously taken in hand. The work was one of enormous difficulty. Kandy lies 1,727 ft. above the sea-level, and the route which had to be traversed by the line was through a mountainous region covered for the most part with jungle.

After many delays and disappointments the private company which originated the venture started operations with Mr. (now Sir) G. L. Molesworth as chief engineer and the late Mr. W. F. Faviell as contractor. The section from Colombo to Ambepussa (a distance of 34½ miles 45 chains) was opened in two portions, the first on October 2, 1865, and the second on January 1, 1866. A further section of 10·69 chains, to Polgahawela, was completed by November in the same year, and the entire line to Kandy was made available for traffic by August 1, 1867. While the work was in progress the Government bought out the company and assumed the financial responsibility for the scheme. The burden was a heavy one. From first to last the 47½ miles of line cost no less than Rs. 17,384,831. But though money was no doubt frittered away in some directions, there was never any serious question that the Government had obtained good value for their money. At the present day, more than forty years after the first sod was turned, the Colombo-Kandy Railway remains amongst the great railway engineering feats of the world—a solid and enduring testimony to British engineering skill and ingenuity. Substantially constructed on the broad Indian 5 ft. 6 in. gauge, with lofty viaducts and a series of tunnels, and rising by a gradient of 1 in 45 in places, the line is a marvel of adaptability. The grandeur of the scenery through which the railway passes enhances its impressiveness. If Ceylon had no other spectacle to offer than this line, the visitor from afar would be well repaid the trouble and expense of the long sea voyage.

From the time when the first length of railway referred to above was opened in Ceylon, the extension has continued until at the end of 1905 (the date up to which the latest returns available bring us) the total mileage stood at 562. But the rate of extension has been by no means regular. When Kandy had been connected with the sea it seems to have been thought that, for a time at least, sufficient had been done in the way of railway construction in the island. In 1873, however, a further step forward was taken in extending the railway inland into the up-country planting districts by carrying the iron road from Peradeniya, a point on the line from Colombo to Kandy some 4 miles short of the latter centre, to Gampola, a distance of 7¾ miles; and in the following year a further extension of 9 miles 4 chains brought the rail-head to Nawalapitiya, the foot of the Ghât section of the line. In 1874, also, short sections in Colombo were opened. The years 1875 and 1876 saw no expansion of the system; and the next important addition was in a southern direction along the coast from the capital. In 1877 the South Coast line was opened from the Fort to Moratuwa, and six months later from Moratuwa on to Panadure, a distance of 16¼ miles in all; but 1878 was practically a blank year, witnessing only the completion of the local line to the Colombo Wharf. In 1879 the South Coast line reached Kalutara, thus adding 9¾ miles to its length, and in 1880 the railway from Kandy to Matale, 17¾ miles, was opened, bringing the total mileage in the island up to 139¼. During the ensuing decade, the period of the deepest depression following upon the collapse of coffee cultivation in Ceylon, only some 52 miles were added to the existing system. The main extension was of the Ghât section, which was carried southwards to Hatton from Nawalapitiya, and then in a zig-zag route east to Talawakelle (28½ miles additional), being completed to the latter point in 1884. It was opened to Nanu-Oya, another 12¾ miles eastward, in the following year. Five years then elapsed without further additions; and in 1890 the South Coast line was opened to Alutgama, this addition of some 11 miles bringing the total mileage of railway up to 191½. Both 1891 and 1892 were also blank years. But in 1893 the Ghât section was extended in a south-easterly direction from Nanu-Oya to Haputale (25 miles 37 chains), and in 1894 it was carried north from Haputale 7 miles on to Bandarawela, its present terminus, 161 miles from Colombo. In the latter year, also, the South Coast line was opened to Galle, the principal southern centre and seaport of the island, 72 miles from the capital. In 1894, too, a line was completed running some 13¼ miles north from Polgahawela (45½ miles from Colombo) on the main line to Kurunegala, the centre of a low-country coconut-planting and plumbago-mining district. This was the beginning of the line which now connects Colombo with Jaffna and the north of the island. In 1895 the South Coast line was opened to its present terminus at Matara, at the extreme south of the island and 26¼ miles beyond Galle. During the three years then ended over one hundred miles altogether had been added to the system, the total railway mileage of Ceylon on December 31, 1895, standing at 297.

The up-country planting districts inland being provided for by the Main line *viâ* Kandy, Nawalapitiya, Hatton, Nanu-Oya, and Haputale to Bandarawela, and the south of the island being served by the Coast line to Galle and Matara, the only large extension of the railway system remaining in immediate prospect in 1895 was a line to connect Colombo with the north-central districts and the northern peninsula. This was accordingly the next work of importance to be undertaken. But from 1895 to the end of 1901 no additional railway facilities were afforded in Ceylon. It was not until September, 1902, that the Northern line, the construction of which had been started at Kankesanturai, a small port at the northernmost part of the island, passing southward through Jaffna, was opened to Pallai, in the southern portion of the Jaffna peninsula, the distance between the terminal points being 34½ miles.

Meanwhile a light line of 2 ft. 6 in. gauge was being carried inland from Colombo by way of the Kelani Valley, for the benefit of the planters in the tea country directly east of the capital. This railway was opened to Avisawella, 36¾ miles, in 1902, and completed to its present terminus, Yatiyantota, a further distance of 11 miles, in the following year. In 1903, also, a Ghât line of similar gauge to the Kelani Valley line was opened, connecting Nanu-Oya (on the Main line to Bandarawela) with Nuwara Eliya, the principal health resort of the island, 6½ miles from Nanu-Oya and 134½ miles from Colombo; and this section—known as the Udapussellawa branch—was completed to Kandapola, a further 6 miles in a north-easterly direction, in the same year. It was opened to its present terminus at Ragalla in 1904, the total length of the branch being 19¼ miles. The steepest gradient in this section is 1 ft. in 24, while there are numerous curves of 80 ft.

At the end of 1903 and 1904 the total mileage of railway in full working order in Ceylon was 368¼ and 391¾ respectively. But the two following years were to witness enormous strides in the extension of the system, entirely owing to the successive completion of long

J. H. BOSTOCK.
(Resident Engineer.)

sections of the Northern line. The level character of the north-western, north-central and northern parts of the island and the general absence of engineering difficulties enabled the construction of this trunk line to be pushed on rapidly. It was completed from Kurunegala to Anuradhapura (68 miles) on November 1, 1904, and from Anuradhapura to the junction with the peninsular line, already mentioned as finished in 1902, at Pallai (95½ miles) in the following year. On August 1, 1905, the populous town of Jaffna, 245¾ miles from Colombo, with Kankesanturai, the northernmost port of Ceylon, 256½ miles from the capital, were thus brought into railway communication with the central and southern parts of the island. The completion of the Northern line raised the railway mileage of the colony to a total of 562 miles, at which figure it now stands. (There has been no addition to the mileage up to the time of writing—November, 1906.)

And now let us see what it has cost to provide Ceylon with this system of railway—which has given the premier Crown Colony the modern means of rapid transport and communication along its total length and between the inland centres of its staple industry and the ports whence the products of the plantations are exported to all parts of the world. As a producing country and a progressive part of the British Empire, it was necessary for Ceylon to have an efficient railway system serving the various parts of the island, which could not hope for due development of their natural resources without intercommunication by this means. The question that next suggests itself is—What has the fulfilment of this indispensable requirement cost? The original capital outlay on the whole system up to the end of 1905 has amounted altogether to a little over 71 millions of rupees, and, taking the rupee at the standard rate of 1s. 4d. in British currency (equal to fifteen rupees to the pound sterling), this outlay amounts to just about 4¾ millions of pounds sterling, in round figures, that is, say, £8,450 per mile. This may seem rather a high cost for a single-track railway system. But, on the other hand, the enormous engineering difficulties met with in constructing the Ghât section, with its tremendously steep gradients (the ruling grade is 1 ft. in 44 ft.), its sharp curves (very many of 5 chains radius), the heavy nature of its earthwork both in cuttings and embankments, the large number of bridges and culverts, many of the former being from 50 ft. to 100 ft. above river bed, its many tunnels, of which there are thirty-eight in all on the line, eight of these being grouped on one mile of the Ghât section, must be taken into consideration. It must also be borne in mind that the gauge of the main trunk lines is 5 ft. 6 ins. throughout, a width that necessitates a heavy permanent way as well as heavy rolling-stock; also that the original cost includes full equipment with rolling-stock, signals, station buildings and residences—in fact, all requisites for working the traffic. An examination of the accounts shows that the cost of constructing the 74¼ miles of main line from Colombo to Kandy, notwithstanding that the route is practically level for 52 miles of the distance, cost no less than Rs. 17,384,831, or, in round figures, £1,160,000. In the 13 miles, however, from Rambukkana to Kadugannawa, the line rises 1,400 ft., and on the incline in this section the ruling gradient is 1 ft. in 45 ft., besides twelve tunnels. The speed over this section of the line is restricted to 15 miles an hour, owing to the gradients and curves, and the trains are all run with two engines. These facts indicate the costly nature of the Main line, owing to the mountainous character of the country traversed above Rambukkana. In the 56 miles of line winding southwards and eastwards from Ulapane to Pattipola, the line rises again from a height of 1,846 ft. at the former point to its greatest altitude at the latter of no less than 6,224 ft. above sea-level. From Pattipola for the remaining 21½ miles to the present end of this section at Bandarawela, the line drops down to 4,036 ft. at the latter point. Along the whole length of this mountain railway of 108 miles, from the beginning of the climb at Rambukkana to Bandarawela, there is hardly a mile without costly construction works of one kind or another. No wonder, then, that this part of the system is found to be responsible for so great a portion of the total capital outlay, and that each mile of the Up-country line has cost many times as much to construct as each mile on the flat coast and northern trunk routes.

In addition to the original capital outlay of 71 millions of rupees in building and equipping the railways, over 5 millions more have been expended on additional accommodation and improvements, including deviations at dangerous spots on the Ghat section. The total capital expenditure has thus been brought up to 76½ millions of rupees. But supplementary to this total, some 4½ millions of rupees have, during the past nine years, been expended out of revenue on new works and rolling-stock. The grand total, therefore, of outlay, taking together capital and revenue expenditure, has amounted to 81 millions of rupees, equal to 5⅖ millions sterling in English currency. This figure is certainly high for a single line of 562½ miles. It is equal, roundly, to £9,600 per mile. But so successfully has the railway, as a whole, been worked that only the first two years (1865 and 1866) after the first line was built have shown a loss on working. Ever since then an annual surplus of receipts over working expenditure has been returned; and since (and including) the year 1868 that surplus has not only sufficed to pay the yearly interest on the capital outlay, but has also provided, in every year with the single exception of 1894, for contributions to the sinking fund, besides leaving a substantial nett balance over for supplementing the general funds of the colony. Take 1905, for instance. The profit on working was Rs. 4,483,753. Out of that amount the interest charges, totalling Rs. 1,472,763, were paid, and Rs. 418,815 went to the sinking fund. Thus a net balance of Rs. 2,592,175 remained as the railway contribution to the general funds of the colony, or, in other words, as dividend on the capital invested in the railways. The automatic operation of the sinking fund, added to the direct repayment of some small temporary local loans in bygone years, has resulted in a reduction of the capital raised for construction and equipment by nearly half. In the latest annual Railway Administration Report (that for 1905) the General Manager says: "On January 1, 1905, the capital outstanding on loans was Rs. 39,521,626, or Rs. 872,863 less than on January 1, 1904." This continual annual reduction of the loan capital is not only eminently satisfactory in itself, but also means, of course, a correspondingly lessening annual charge for interest. Such a satisfactory state of things as this may well be set off against the initial high cost of the system. In short, as far as existing lines are concerned, the railway of Ceylon is freeing itself at an appreciably rapid rate from the debt originally incurred for construction and equipment, while at the same time making liberal contributions to the general colonial fund, though the last railway extension that has been sanctioned—that from Ragama to Negombo—is to be constructed from the surplus proceeds of the Pearl Fishery. For future extensions, as they become necessary, further loans will probably have to be raised. But it is obvious that so long as the proposed lines promise such handsome returns as the existing lines are giving, the prospect of increasing the loan capital need in no way be feared. The new obligations will only be created to be gradually extinguished by contributions to the sinking fund from the profits derived from working such extensions.

Turning from the capital to the revenue account, the latter is found to be in an equally satisfactory condition, bearing evidence not only of a continually swelling annual income, but also of what is of equal importance in connection with a great State business, namely, economy of working. The gross railway receipts for the year 1905 (the latest for which full particulars are available at time of writing) amounted to Rs. 9,690,653 (remember that fifteen rupees go to the English pound sterling), an increase of no less than Rs. 799,067 over the gross income of the previous year. That is a completely satisfactory proof of progress. On the other side of the account, the working expenditure for the year stated, totalling Rs. 5,206,899, shows an increase of only Rs. 165,866 over that for the previous year. Thus there was a net gain of Rs. 633,201 in 1905 compared with 1904. Deducting the amount of the expenditure from the receipts, the profit on working for the year under review is found to amount to the substantial sum of Rs. 4,483,754 (as against Rs. 3,850,553 for 1904). Out of this surplus, as explained above in dealing with the capital account, interest on the loan capital absorbed Rs. 1,472,763, and the contribution to the sinking fund amounted to Rs. 418,815. This left a nett balance over and above all charges of Rs. 2,592,175 available for general colonial purposes, an increase of Rs. 589,374 compared with the balance under this head for the previous year (1904). These figures afford full warrant for the General Manager's statement in the annual

FORT RAILWAY STATION.

(Decorated by J. V. Atapattu, Mudaliyar, Station Master, when the Duke of Connaught visited Colombo.)

Administration Report that "the result of the year's working is most satisfactory."

It is somewhat of a curious coincidence that of the increase of Rs. 799,067 in the gross railway income for 1905, the passenger and the goods traffic are each responsible for, roughly, one half, the increase from fares being Rs. 397,073, and from goods traffic Rs. 392,169. The increase in passenger traffic was general throughout the system, with the single exception of the short branch from Kandy to Matale, in regard to which there was a falling-off in receipts of Rs. 3,468. A satisfactory increase in receipts from season tickets on the Colombo suburban sections points to progress, coupled with permanency, as regards this class of traffic; while the non-local and non-special nature of the increase in the total passenger traffic may be taken as an indication of general advancement throughout the system. Not including holders of periodical tickets, the number of passengers carried during the year under review, taking all the lines together, was 6,281,537 (an increase of 253,777 over 1904). Of this total some three millions travelled on the South Coast line, including the suburban section, and over one and a half millions on the Main line between Colombo and Nawalapitiya, *viâ* Kandy. The passenger receipts for ordinary and periodical tickets together totalled Rs. 3,597,897; and the average sum received for carrying one ordinary passenger one mile was 2·47 cents.

Following are the passenger rates in force:

CENTS PER MILE.

	Single.			Return.		
	1st.	2nd.	3rd.	1st.	2nd.	3rd.
Ghât Section above Nawalapitiya (exclusive of Udapussellawa line)	12	8	2⅔	18	12	4
All lines below Nawalapitiya	8	5⅓	2⅔	12	8	4

The higher charge for the portion of the line above Nawalapitiya is rendered necessary by the higher working expenses of this mountainous section to Bandarawela. On the small Udapussellawa branch of 19 miles on the 2 ft. 6 in. gauge — from Nanu-Oya through Nuwara Eliya to Ragalla—still higher rates are charged, owing to the very heavy working expenses. Return tickets for all classes on all lines are issued at the price of one single fare and a half, except on the Udapussellawa branch, on which no reduction is made for return tickets. Season tickets are issued at reduced rates. It will be noticed that the cost of a first-class return ticket over the line below Nawalapitiya works out at 6 cents, or about a penny, a mile—the third-class Parliamentary fare on English railways. The third-class return fare is equal to one-third of a penny a mile over the same sections.

The goods traffic is classified under six headings, or classes, numbered 1 to 6, the charges in No. 1 (for explosives, otherwise dangerous and fragile goods) being the heaviest, and in No. 6 (for rough materials) the lowest. The rate in each case is calculated in cents per ton per mile, and a terminal charge of 25 cents per ton is added to cover the service of loading and unloading the goods at the forwarding and receiving stations. Following are the rates :—

CENTS PER TON PER MILE.

	1st Class.	2nd Class.	3rd Class.	4th Class.	5th Class.	6th Class.
Main Ghât line above Nawalapitiya	46½	31	25	20	20	16
Main line below Nawalapitiya, also Matale, Kurunegala and Kelani Valley lines	37½	25	17	12½	10	8
South Coast line and Northern line (north of Kurunegala)	24	16	12½	12½	10	8

A specially reduced rate for goods traffic for consignments of not less than four tons is in force over the Northern line north of Kurunegala into the Jaffna peninsula. Over the Udapussellawa branch line 44 cents per ton per mile is charged on all goods traffic, this high rate being necessary owing to the exceedingly heavy working expenses of this mountain railway.

The total tonnage of goods conveyed in 1905 was 580,120, and the receipts for this freightage amounted to Rs. 5,664,897, the average earnings per ton per mile working out to 13·65 cents, or approximately 2¼d. in English currency. The principal articles of commerce conveyed on the railway in Ceylon are, as would naturally be expected, rice and tea. The latter, the staple product of the island, is brought down from the plantations all along and about the whole length of the section to Colombo for shipment; and the quantity carried by the railway during 1905 was 88,112 tons, the receipts from this source amounting to Rs. 1,116,059. But rice figures even more prominently in the goods traffic list. Although a good deal of rice is grown on small plots in Ceylon for personal consumption, not nearly sufficient is produced in the island to meet the demand of the army of coolies employed on the estates and the native population generally for this their staple article of food. Consequently enormous quantities of the grain are imported from India, and have to be distributed throughout the island. The trains that bring the tea down to Colombo take the rice up for the coolies on the plantations and the villagers inland. The total quantity of rice carried over the various lines during 1905 was 134,289 tons, or considerably more than one-fourth of the whole volume of the merchandise traffic; and the receipts under this head amounted to no less than Rs. 1,929,890, or more than one-third of the whole amount received for the conveyance of articles of commerce. The item of next importance on the goods traffic list is the produce of the coconut-palm tree—the standby of Ceylon. Were all the other productive industries in the island to fail, the cultivation of this tree, which

AMBALANGODA STATION.

grows everywhere throughout the low-lying country, with its varied marketable products —copra, fibre, coconut-oil, poonac, &c.— would suffice to save the colony from complete collapse. This item on the list accounts for 37,823 tonnage and Rs. 296,859 in receipts for carriage. The conveyance of manure, which article is imported in large quantities as well as manufactured locally, mainly for use on the tea plantations (generally termed "estates" by the people of Ceylon) is accountable for 45,402 tons of the traffic, and added Rs. 259,137 to the receipts. The principal articles carried, and their relative importance from the railway point of view, are shown in the following list of the goods traffic for 1905, taken from the official report :—

	1905.	
	Tonnage.	Receipts.
	Tons.	Rs.
Rice	134,289	1,929,890
Tea...	88,112	1,116,059
Coffee	244	3,561
Cacao	3,864	39,743
Cinnamon...	553	3,710
Cardamoms	441	6,566
Rubber	12	158
Coconut Produce, including Poonac	37,823	296,859
Fruit, Vegetables, and other 5th Class Goods...	15,052	107,266
Plumbago...	17,143	73,919
Tea-packing Materials ...	17,563	150,341
Tobacco	2,478	41,267
Timber, including Staves	5,052	40,245
Manure	45,402	259,137
Sundry Goods	135,800	1,563,462
Total Merchandise ...	503,828	5,632,183
Railway Materials and Free Goods	58,084	20,550
Stone Traffic conveyed in Harbour Works Wagons	18,208	12,164
Grand Total ...	580,120	5,664,897

The above list is interesting as affording a general insight into the position of the leading industries of the colony and showing the way in which their development affects the railway traffic. The pre-eminence of tea as a staple product, for instance, is immediately evident. It is not only accountable for a large tonnage and consequently an appreciable proportion of the total goods receipts, but is also responsible, in the way already explained, for a large portion of the traffic in the carriage of rice—the principal item in the schedule—as well as for that in the conveyance of tea-packing materials and manures to the plantations. In contrast, the low position to which the production of coffee—once the staple product of the planting industry—has fallen is as conspicuously demonstrated. It will be noticed that rubber, the product upon which the hopes of so many of the planters in the island—as, indeed, in other parts of the world as well—are fixed, does not, as yet, burden the railway department to any appreciable extent. But, in view of the area of land now being planted with the tree from which this substance is obtained, "it will be interesting"—to quote the Report from which the information in this article is mainly derived—"to watch the growth of this new and valuable product of the island."

The earnings from live-stock traffic during 1905 amounted to Rs. 18,664; while, among minor receipts, under the head of Coaching Traffic, Rs. 217,445 were earned for parcels conveyed, Rs. 65,076 for mails, Rs. 15,799 for horses, Rs. 11,201 for carriages, Rs. 6,594 for dogs, Rs. 10,249 for bicycles, and Rs. 1,214 for private special trains. Miscellaneous receipts for warehouse, platform and refreshment-car rents, sleeping-car tickets, sale of old materials and unclaimed goods, rent of buildings and sundries, amounting in all to Rs. 81,615, make up the balance of the grand total of Rs. 9,690,653 forming the year's revenue. The income side of the revenue account may be summarised as follows :—

	Rs. Cts.
Coaching (Passengers, Parcels, Mails, etc.)	3,925,477 16
Goods Traffic	5,664,896 63
Live Stock conveyed	18,664 02
Miscellaneous Receipts (Rents, etc.)	81,615 23
Total Receipts	9,690,653 04

Before leaving the earning side of the revenue account, it should be mentioned that free transport to the value of over Rs. 25,000 was afforded in 1905 in connection with the annual volunteer encampment held at Diyatalawa, near the end of the Ghât section; also that exhibits were conveyed free of charge to and from agricultural shows and public exhibitions in various centres. Concessions of this nature are made in accordance with the aim of the Government to promote and assist the development of agricultural industries and cognate trades, encourage intercommunication, and further mutual knowledge between the various parts of the colony with the view of engendering public spirit and unity of sentiment throughout the land.

Having explained how the annual income of the most important branch of the Government service of the colony of Ceylon is raised and demonstrated by official figures the flourishing condition of the railway revenue, it remains to examine the expenditure side of the account. The total of the working expenses for the year under review (1905) was, as has already been stated, Rs. 5,206,899; and the items, as summarised in the official report, are given in the accompanying table.

This total expenditure for 1905 works out to the satisfactorily low percentage of 53·7 of the gross earnings (Rs. 9,690,653), being also a reduction of 3 per cent. as against the proportion of working expenses to revenue in 1904. The principal saving was effected in the Locomotive and Carriage and Wagon Charges, which show a reduction of 2·2 in percentage to gross receipts as compared with the preceding year, despite the fact that 174,062 additional traffic train-miles were run; and this result is singled out by the General Manager for special remark in his annual report as "a striking testimony to the increased efficiency of the department under the care of Mr. Unsworth, the present Locomotive Engineer." From the detailed accounts, it appears that the expenditure of the Locomotive Department has not increased anything like in ratio to the measured mileage, but has rather decreased. This decrease is principally in connection with the Running Department, and is due to economy in coal, oils, &c. The expenditure of the Locomotive Department amounted to Rs. 2,157,692, a little more than two-fifths of the total working expenses. "Exchange Compensation," which figures several times in the above table, and altogether represents a total of Rs. 15,195, stands for an allowance which is granted to a certain proportion of the railway officials (in common with other Government servants) to compensate for the depreciation of the value of the rupee, which, though nominally worth 2s., is at the present time worth only 1s. 4d.

It will be noticed that Maintenance of Way and Works necessarily absorbed a large figure, of which approximately one-tenth was expended in new works, the total representing

WORKING EXPENSES.

	Rs. Cts.
Maintenance of Way and Works	1,368,463 3
Exchange Compensation ...	1,360 83
Locomotive Charges :—	
General Superintendence ...	32,562 23
Locomotive Power	1,685,880 74
Exchange Compensation ...	7,084 53
Carriages and Wagons ...	393,746 96
Exchange Compensation ...	453 90
Plant and Machinery... ...	37,963 32
Traffic Charges :—	
General Superintendence ...	96,011 66
Exchange Compensation ...	1,081 7
Traffic Charges	613,336 7
Running Staff	229,078 47
Exchange Compensation ...	3,122 72
Telegraph Charges	79,925 36
General Charges :—	
General Manager's Department	25,288 44
Exchange Compensation ...	1,125 0
Accountant's Department ...	111,642 82
Exchange Compensation ...	798 31
Auditor - General's Department	5,694 61
Stores Department	34,624 1
Exchange Compensation ...	168 84
Crown Agents' Allowance ...	1,035 0
Salary of Consulting Engineers	7,500 0
Charges incurred in England	14,594 0
New Works	454,356 52
Total Expenses	5,206,899 44

a little more than one-fourth of the whole expenditure. The chief items of ordinary expenditure under this head are general superintendence (Rs. 54,400), maintenance of permanent way (Rs. 714,107), relaying of lines (Rs. 332,664), repairs to bridges and tunnels (Rs. 41,504), repairs to stations and buildings (Rs. 70,757), and maintenance of signals and interlocking gear (Rs. 14,481); while the special expenditure on new works and renewals and repairs, including those rendered necessary by slips of land and washaways, amounted to Rs. 134,453. The friable nature of the soil along the route of the Ghât section, coupled with the precipitous character of the country, renders this line peculiarly liable to landslips and washaways under the deluges of rain which descend upon the heights during the changes of the monsoon seasons. Between October 27 and November 13, 1905, as the result of a tremendous storm from the south-west, followed by the break of the north-east monsoon, no less than 127 slips, subsidences, washings and floods were recorded, a large proportion of these taking place in a single night (October 27th). As a result, the traffic over a large section of the line was totally interrupted. One station (Gampola) was submerged to a depth of 5 ft. 9 in. Travellers on railways in England can scarcely realise the destruction that can be wrought by the "burst" of a monsoon. Huge rocks, loosened by the rains, also sometimes fall upon the line from the heights above, forming a further source of damage and danger; and consequent disaster to the trains is only prevented by unremitting vigilance. Washaways also occur in the low-country sections of the system during the wet seasons, at which times the traffic on one part or the other is sometimes thus seriously dislocated for days at a time. The Engineer of Way and Works and his assistants are continually watching the whole length of the line with a view to anticipating and taking measures for preventing slips and washings.

The Traffic Charges, as enumerated in the above table, form just under one-fifth of the total expenditure. Under this head are comprised the usual expenses connected with the running of the trains, exclusive of the locomotive charges. The total expenditure incurred by the Traffic Department in 1905 was Rs. 1,022,555. As against the earning of Rs. 5.58 per train-mile run in 1905, the expenditure amounted to Rs. 3, leaving a profit of Rs. 2.58 per train-mile, an increase on the corresponding figure for 1904 of 11 cents. The total number of traffic train-miles run during 1905 was 1,737,300, as compared with 1,563,238 in the preceding year.

REFRESHMENT CAR.

In the Locomotive and Carriage Department the work necessary for bringing the railway service up to the highest possible standard of efficiency is being vigorously prosecuted. The construction and repairing shops at Colombo are being enlarged and equipped with plant and machinery of the latest labour-saving type, in order to meet the ever-increasing traffic demands for rolling-stock. In the past there has indubitably existed cause for complaint by the travelling public on the Ceylon railways on account of the uncomfortable nature of the older patterns of passenger carriages. But these are now being replaced by new vehicles, constructed in accordance with modern requirements, including refreshment cars and carriages fitted with lavatories for the long journeys, and comfortable sleeping-cars for night travelling. A gratifying point worthy of mention in connection with this development is that the new rolling-stock is being constructed in the departmental workshops at a cost far below that formerly paid for imported carriages. The 130 locomotives in use have come from well-known manufacturers in Great Britain: Messrs. R. Stephenson & Co., Beyer and Peacock, Kitson & Co., John Fowler & Co. Vulcan Foundry Company, Messrs. Dubs & Co., Neilson & Co., Hawthorne, Leslie & Co., the Hunslet Engine Company, Messrs. Sharp, Stewart & Co., and the North British Locomotive Company. Different kinds of engines are provided for the different kinds of traffic; and, as may be imagined, an exceptionally powerful class of locomotive is required for negotiating the steep gradients on the Ghât section. Most of the trains in this route have to be assisted up the gradients by a bank-engine. The engines for incline work have six wheels coupled, with diameters of 4 ft. 5 ins. The diameter of the driving wheels of the fast passenger bogie engines (four wheels coupled) is 6 ft., and their weight, in steam, is from 35 to 39 tons each, without tender. But the majority of the locomotives for the mixed trains (which are the rule on the Ceylon railway system) on the Up-country and South Coast lines, have four wheels coupled, of 5 ft. and 4 ft. 5 ins. diameter, some of these engines weighing, in steam, as much as 50 tons each, without tender. On the Northern section, with its lighter traffic and generally level road, a less heavy type of locomotive (28½ tons), with six wheels coupled; 3 ft. 6 ins. in diameter, is employed; while the narrow-gauge (2 ft. 6 ins.) line of the Kelani Valley is served by still lighter Hunslet engines with four wheels coupled, of a diameter of 3 ft. each; and radial-wheel tank engines, with four wheels coupled (2 ft. 2 ins. in diameter), weighing 19 tons, haul the small trains on the steeply mountainous Udapussellawa branch. Other types of tank-engines are employed in local and shunting work. Both coal and wood are used for fuel for the locomotives. The total weight of fuel consumed during the year 1905 —computing the wood at its equivalent in steam-production with the coal—was over 50,000 tons.

In regard to the permanent way of the line the rails in use are of the flat-bottom tee

SENSATION ROCK, KADUGANNAWA INCLINE. SATINWOOD BRIDGE, PERADENIYA.
SENSATION ROCK AND KADUGANNAWA INCLINE (ANOTHER VIEW).
VIEW FROM RAILWAY LOOKING TOWARDS NAWALAPITIYA. GAMPOLA STATION.

section, fastened with spikes directly to the wooden sleepers. On the Main line between Colombo and Nanu-Oya the section of rail adopted at present weighs 88 lbs. per lineal yard, the lengths varying from 21 ft. to 30 ft. On the Coast line, as also on the Nanu-Oya-Bandarawela section—the type of rail used weighs 72 lbs. per lineal yard. On the Northern line, and also on the narrow-gauge sections, a lighter rail of 46½ lbs. per lineal yard is used. The number of sleepers under each pair of rails varies from eight to eleven, according to the length of rail.

The sleepers hitherto in use have consisted principally of creosoted pine from England, and jarrah and blackbutt from Australia; now, however, sleepers are being obtained locally in satinwood, milla, and palu from the native woods of the island, thus rendering the Railway Department independent for the present of imported supplies, while at the same time effecting a saving in cost.

A difficulty met with on the long stretch of the Northern line is the lack of a supply of suitable water for the locomotives, and various works for removing this obstacle have been initiated and are now being carried out. In some places on this section the water has to be conveyed considerable distances to the line-side, the supply from the wells along the route containing a deposit injurious to the engine boilers. All the other sections are fairly free from this disability; indeed, they suffer from too much rather than too little water, the damage to the permanent way in various parts, particularly on the Up-country line, caused by floods, being, as has already been pointed out, a recurring and serious trouble to the Railway Department in the rainy seasons.

Taking the results of the traffic per section as given in the official report for 1905, it is found that the Main line from Colombo to Kandy (74½ miles) and thence south to Nawalapitiya, some 13 miles farther along the Up-country route, gave the largest return. The receipts on this section, which were much larger than those for all the rest of the lines together, showed an increase over 1904 of Rs. 342,924, while the expenditure only grew to the extent of Rs. 86,610, the increase in profit on working consequently amounting to Rs. 256,314, or over two-fifths of the total increase for all the lines. The rest of the Up-country line, from Nawalapitiya to Bandarawela, a distance of 73½ miles, however, gave a proportionately better result; for this section not only showed an increase in receipts of Rs. 103,509, but also a decrease of Rs. 84,570 in expenditure, the increase in profit thus amounting to Rs. 188,079. The returns for the South Coast line—from Colombo to Galle (72 miles) and Matara (98½ miles)—were not so satisfactory. A decrease of Rs. 2,972 in receipts on this section was, however, far more than met by a decrease of Rs. 53,780 in expenditure, the resultant increase in profit being Rs. 50,808. The branch from Kandy to Matale (17½ miles) showed the small net improvement, compared with the preceding year, of Rs. 740. But this was obtained, as in the case of the South Coast line, by a saving in expenditure of Rs. 4,017, against a falling off in receipts of Rs. 3,277. On the Kelani Valley line (47½ miles) the increased profit for 1905 was Rs. 48,276, due to both an increase in receipts and a decrease in expenditure; while the Udapussellawa narrow-gauge mountain railway, of 19½ miles, from Nanu-Oya through Nuwara Eliya to Ragalla, returned a profit of Rs. 36,145, or an advance of Rs. 27,865 on the net balance for the preceding year. Some half of the Northern line having been opened for traffic five months before the end of 1905, and nearly the other half at the end of the preceding year, no proper comparison of the results for the two periods on the whole of this line is possible.

As this line, south of the Jaffna peninsula, passes for the most part through jungle and waste country, it is dependent for results upon through traffic. When, however, in course of time, the suitable tracts of land along this route shall have been brought under cultivation—and the provision of the railway should hasten, as it must facilitate, the desired development of these parts—this long arm of the railway system will greatly benefit by the intermediate traffic that will thus be created. Thus the Jaffna peninsula line was the only section of the whole railway system which returned a loss on working for 1905; and this deficiency was considerably less than half of that for the preceding year. The satisfactory feature regarding this section was an increase of Rs. 29,632, equal to nearly 50 per cent., in receipts as against an increase of only Rs. 5,496 in expenditure. At this rate the earnings on this line (Rs. 90,558 for 1905) will soon overtake and pass the outgo (Rs. 107,065 for 1905) and return a substantial balance to the good.

A few words as to the *personnel* of the Railway Service. At the head of the staff is the General Manager, who, under the Governor and Colonial Secretary, is in control of the whole business and is responsible to the representative of the Crown for the administration of the Railway Department. The present occupant of the managerial position is Mr. G. P. Greene, of whom a biographical sketch, with accompanying portrait, is given at the end of this article. As policy, control, and management require long and careful expert training, the higher positions are usually filled by experts in their several lines of service, who are "recruited from Europe," as the colonial phrase runs: men who have received a training on the staff of one or the other of the great English railways. But, in accordance with the policy so eloquently proclaimed by Mr. Morley in his last Indian Budget speech as governing the attitude of the ruling race towards the subject population in the great dependency, the educated natives of Ceylon are freely admitted to such posts in the railway service of the colony as their ability and training justify. The Sinhalese, Tamil, or Eurasian stationmaster is as much a feature of the colonial service as is the Babu who delights in displaying his dignity and authority on the railway platforms in India; while office and booking-clerks and all the subordinate railway staff are natives. A number of the engine-drivers and guards are drawn from the European class, they being obtained under engagement from England for a certain term of service. But in many cases natives will be found in charge on the foot-plate as well as in the guard's van. With a staff thus composed of diverse elements, it is evident that a responsibility far beyond that which rests upon the shoulders of the headquarters officials of an English railway is ever pressing upon the Manager and directing officers of the Ceylon Government Railway, and that unceasing vigilance has to be exercised in the control of every branch of the service.

As regards speed, the trains on the Ceylon railways cannot, of course, compare with the expresses on the European or American systems. The frequent and heavy curves and gradients on the Up-country section militate against fast running on that route, and the 74½ miles on the Main line between Colombo and Kandy are not covered by the speediest trains under 3¾ hours. But the somewhat slow rate of progress gives the traveller on the Up-country line, if journeying by day, full opportunity of enjoying the magnificent scenery all along the route; and if he is travelling by the night train, he can slumber restfully. It can be truly said that no part of the country traversed by the railway throughout the whole island is without its interesting aspects; and the views to be obtained from the carriage windows as the train winds round and about the mountains of the interior highlands, passing along the edge of sheer precipices and among towering heights rising abruptly thousands of feet from undulating valleys, form a gigantic and continuous panorama of natural grandeur and beauty hardly to be equalled anywhere else in the world. In view of the interesting relics of ancient days in Ceylon, at Anuradhapura and elsewhere, now accessible by a railway journey of a few hours from Colombo, and the scenic attractions along the various routes, particularly on the Ghât section, it is no wonder that the tourist traffic forms an appreciable portion of the railway revenue. There is also a considerable traffic in excursions in connection with the various native pilgrimages common among Eastern peoples, at certain seasons of the year, to religious festivals at various sacred centres on the Northern line and other parts of the railway. Another noteworthy feature of the railway business is the carriage of the Indian coolies who are the workers on the estates of the island, between the ports and the planting districts.

Every care is taken to ensure the safety and comfort of passengers on the Ceylon railway system. All the trains have been or are being fitted with the vacuum brake ; and the adoption of the Tyer's tablet system of working traffic on a single line obviates danger of collisions and accelerates the handling of the traffic. Lavatories are attached to most of the first-class carriages. Sleeping cars are run on the night trains and refreshment cars are run on the principal up-country day trains and up night mail; while, by order beforehand, refreshment baskets are supplied for any train. There are also refreshment-rooms at certain of the principal stations, and hotels or Government rest-houses (which are really hotels) at the main stopping-places.

An important work rendered necessary by the increase in the railway business generally, and with which a beginning has been made, is the rearrangement and enlargement of the railway stations in Colombo. When this work is completed, the principal Main-line passenger trains will start from and arrive at either the Fort or the Slave Island station, which will have to be considerably altered and enlarged to serve as the terminus. The single track will also be doubled through Colombo and as far as Mount Lavinia, the end of the southern suburban section (7 miles from the city). Maradana Junction, from which the Kelani Valley narrow-gauge line starts, will also be freely enlarged, and the adjacent goods yard will be extended.

With the opening in August, 1905, of the last section of the Northern line, from Anuradhapura to Pallai, bringing the Jaffna peninsula and the intermediate northern and north-western country into railway communication with Colombo and the south of the island, the last of the railway extensions in Ceylon sanctioned by the Secretary of State up to the end of 1905 was completed. But further expansion of the system in general directions is contemplated in the near future. The principal extension proposed is a line about 50 miles in length from a point north of Anuradhapura on the Northern railway to Mannar on the north-east coast, where connection would be made by sea with the South Indian railway system, and probably at some future date by the bridging of the intervening strip of sea by way of the islands of Mannar and Rameswaram and the connecting sand-banks. This undertaking would not only provide for all the Indian coolie traffic to and from Ceylon, but would also be fraught with immense future importance as giving railway communication between the great Asiatic dependency of Britain and the premier Crown Colony. At the time of writing the advisability of the construction of this branch line was being laid before the Secretary of State by the Government of the colony, and the official sanction was hoped for. As the line would pass through level country all the way, the cost of construction should not be great, and the work could be carried out expeditiously.

Other proposed extensions in the immediate future are : (1) A narrow gauge (2 ft. 6 ins.) line to run in a south-easterly direction from Avisawella, on the Kelani Valley railway, to Ratnapura, the centre of the gem-producing districts ; (2) the extension of the Up-country line (about 36 miles) from Bandarawela north to Badulla, near the easternmost extremity of the hill country, to traverse the Passara planting district in the Province of Uva ; and (3) a line 14½ miles long from Ragama station on the Main line near Colombo to the town of Negombo. This last project has been sanctioned by the Home authorities and will be built out of general colonial revenue. For the construction of the other contemplated additions loan capital will probably have to be provided. But as the colony is now in a most flourishing state generally and possesses an overflowing exchequer, no reasonable objection can be raised to these undertakings in the face of the estimates formed of the additional traffic they will create proving immediately profitable, and the desirableness of their construction for the purpose of developing the country.

Looking at the map of Ceylon, it will be seen that while Colombo, as the main centre, the capital and chief seaport, is connected by railway with the north and south of the island as well as with the tea-planting districts in the hill-country, the whole of the extensive eastern and south-eastern portions of the colony are without this means of communication. They remain for the major part in the grip of primitive Nature, the forests and jungle with which they are covered being inhabited by wild beasts and a few representatives of the Veddah tribe, a primitive native race whose origin is lost in the mists of antiquity. But this will not always be the case. The progressive development of Ceylon will in time gradually dispossess the elephant, the bear, the leopard, and the other denizens of the jungle of the territories over which they have held sway and roamed unmolested from time immemorial, and the virgin lands of these parts will be brought within the sphere of civilised effort. In that future time the pioneer here, as everywhere else, will be followed by the railway, and the present primeval conditions will disappear. The first extension of the iron road to the east coast would probably be a line from the junction of the proposed Mannar connection with the Northern line to Trincomalee. When this is effected the magnificent natural harbour at the latter place, now practically unused, may become a centre of ocean traffic on the east side of the island. A railway across the jungle from the hill-country to Batticaloa, further south on the east coast, may also be a dream to be realised within the course of a generation ; for who will venture to fix an absolute limit to railway extension in so prosperous, progressive, and populous a country as Ceylon?

GEOFFREY PHILIP GREENE, General Manager.

This gentleman was born on May 25, 1868, in Dublin, and was educated at private schools in that city and Yorkshire, and subsequently at Clifton College. In July, 1886, at the age of eighteen, he joined the London and North-Western Railway as a clerk in the passenger department of the office of the District Superintendent, Southern Division. Subsequently he was engaged in outdoor work in that district, until promoted to be outdoor assistant on the staff of the Superintendent of the line. This position he occupied for some years, being stationed first in London and afterwards at Crewe. Mr. Greene's last appointment in England was to that of Assistant District Superintendent of the North Wales (Chester and Holyhead) section of the London and North-Western Railway. On October 11, 1901, while holding that post, he was appointed General Manager of the Ceylon Government Railway by the Secretary of State. He arrived in Ceylon and took up his present duties on November 4, 1901.

INFORMATION FOR TOURISTS

By H. B. SMITH.

CEYLON is becoming more widely known, year by year, as a winter resort, as a charming island to visit in conjunction with a trip to India, or as a convenient point at which to break an ocean journey, thus relieving the monotony of a long steamer trip.

The stranger arriving at Colombo is at once struck with the bright colours everywhere prevailing. The trees seem to have many brilliant shades of green, while their flowers, crimson and yellow, are a constant delight to the eye of the visitor—a fact at once noticed by the crowd of beggar urchins in the streets, who eagerly press flowers upon strangers in European dress, suggesting in return money from their "father" or "mother"—terms of relationship they bestow on all and sundry. The pleasant roads, bordered with trees and flowers, are in themselves sufficient to repay time spent in driving round Colombo ; and to this pleasure is added the interest arising from the fact that each of the several races of people whose members are met with has its own distinctive dress—some certainly rather scanty, all together forming the most extraordinary diversity of colouring.

Mount Lavinia, on the seashore, seven miles south from the Colombo General Post Office, and the Buddhist Temple near the Kelaniya River, about five miles north-east from the same centre, are points to which visitors frequently drive out from the town, thus enjoying the opportunity for obtaining a good general idea of the city and its environs. Longer excursions, also, in all directions will well repay the new-comer, the roads in and about the city being nearly all in excellent condition.

To leave for up-country by the Ceylon Government Railway, the visitor takes the train at the Colombo Terminus Station, and for about 45 miles travels through almost flat country, the cultivation of rice in various stages and coconut-palms appearing to form the principal business of the people in this part. The railway then begins to ascend the Kadugannawa incline, and the visitor, from his seat in the train, views mile after mile of splendid scenery. The constructors of the line should certainly be thanked by the man in a hurry—the view from the railway track being much better than that from the road. There are no enormous mountains in Ceylon, though some of the hills reach an elevation of several thousands of feet above sea-level, the highest—Pidurutalagala (commonly "Pedro"), at Nuwara Eliya, being 8,296 ft. above the surface of the ocean. But the effect of the abrupt rocks, the winding valleys, waterfalls, and jungle of all sorts, displayed in profusion, is worthy of appreciation by even the most jaded traveller, "tired of temples and tombs." As the hill-country is reached and traversed, tea estates are seen on all sides, and the stranger naturally becomes interested in the leading industry of Ceylon, and all its peculiarities and details. A word of warning must be given to the unsuspecting new-comer to beware of the invitation of the planter, who—a sportsman and the best of good fellows—is in perfect training and has long stretches of estate roads and "near-cuts" that he wants you to "walk with him," each mile of which would, for its length, put any mile in Ireland to shame. Any one suggesting a "short-cut" from one estate to another should be avoided as the average tenant avoids the man "come for the rent."

From the top of the Kadugannawa Pass onwards to Peradeniya is a distance of only a few miles ; and at this place, with the entrance quite near the railway station, is the Government Botanical Garden, only four miles from Kandy by road or rail, and especially well worth a visit. Kandy, a fairy hollow, charms the eye ; and here visits to the lake and "bund" (both the work of the last Kandyan king), drives along the winding roads, a pilgrimage to the Temple of the Sacred Tooth (of Buddha), the drive to and from the Peradeniya Gardens—all should be undertaken, and will be enjoyed.

Continuing the tour across the hill-country by railway, the traveller passes through an almost unbroken line of tea plantations—or tea "estates," as it is the fashion in Ceylon to designate these properties—covering the slopes and undulations on the route. Hatton Station is reached in 3½ hours from Kandy, and this is the point from which should be made the trip to Adam's Peak, the most famous mountain in the island, on the summit of which, 7,300 ft. above sea-level, Buddha (or our first father Adam, as some have it) has left his footprint. The coach takes the traveller 16 miles to the Laxapana rest-house, where he dines and sleeps. He is roused at about 3 a.m., and starts to climb the mountain, following the local guide's lantern. This bit of hard work, but healthy exercise, is amply repaid by the view at sunrise from the Peak. The mountain is held sacred by the Buddhists, who have a temple on the summit. But, according to the other tradition, it was from this spot that Adam took his farewell look on Eden. Returning to Hatton, and continuing the journey eastward by rail—still passing through tea plantations—Nanu-Oya is reached in two hours. Nanu-Oya is the point of departure of the branch narrow-guage (2 ft. 6 ins.) railway for Nuwara Eliya, Ceylon's chief sanatorium and pleasure resort. A cool climate, bracing mountain air, and beautiful surroundings make walking, riding, and driving round and about Nuwara Eliya to the various points of interest, including Pedro, the highest elevation of Ceylon, charming to the visitor, who soon realises how Colombo residents enjoy an occasional "pick-me-up" in the form of a flying visit to this spot.

Returning to Nanu-Oya Junction, the visitor should continue his railway journey, by Pattipola, Ohiya (where the railway line is over

6,000 ft. above sea-level), and Haputale—all centres of the great tea-growing industry—to Diyatalawa and Bandarawela. Diyatalawa is famous as having been the camp in Ceylon of the Boer prisoners-of-war; and some of the buildings erected for the temporary accommodation of the captives are now used in connection with the permanent camp for health recuperation established here for the navy, military, and volunteers. The situation is eminently suitable for the purpose. Jungle is conspicuous by its absence; the rolling country reminded the Boers of the scenery of their own land, and the long grassy slopes afford a splendid training-ground for the sailors and soldiers. Bandarawela, the terminus of the hills line, is only two miles distant from the camp; and from that point trips by coach or motor-car can be made to Badulla and into the Uva Province generally, also—though at present not with very great comfort—as far as Batticaloa, on the eastern coast. If from Bandarawela the return journey is made by road to Colombo, delightful scenery is met with in passing through Balangoda and Ratnapura, the latter the centre of the district where the famous Ceylon gems are found.

If the visitor returns by rail from Bandarawela, he should travel to Kandy, stay there at least for the night, and leave by the morning train, *viâ* the Kadugannawa incline, to Polgahawela, the junction for the northern main line to Jaffna, in the extreme north of the island. Travelling 80 miles in this direction, he will arrive at Anuradhapura, the most famous of the ancient "buried cities" of Ceylon—and the neighbouring historic town of Mihintale is only six miles distant. These ruins show plainly how beautiful these cities must have been in the time of their glory, over two thousand years ago. But in 540 B.C.—according to the Mahavansa, the ancient Sinhalese chronicle, which has been carefully preserved—the conquering Tamil from India descended upon them from the north in hordes, and destroyed all he could not steal. Then Nature kindly covered the ruins with jungle for about two thousand years. But in recent times many of the buried remains of the "City of the Ninety Kings" (the meaning of the word "Anuradhapura") have been excavated; and as explained in the Archæological section in another part of this book, wherein the ruins of Anuradhapura and other ancient cities are described in detail, the Government is still prosecuting researches on this site.

If a visit to Jaffna is included in the itinerary, the railway offers an easy trip to this northernmost town of Ceylon; and it should be said that the contrast between this mode of travel and the journey by the bullock cart—which was the only means of conveyance from Anuradhapura to Jaffna until the northernmost railway was completed between these points three years ago—must have been experienced to be appreciated. The roads in all directions from Anuradhapura are excellent, and the surrounding jungle scenery and life most interesting. If time permits, one or other of the following routes from Anuradhapura to Colombo is suggested: (1) By road to Trincomalee on the eastern coast, where there is a magnificent natural harbour, then back by road *viâ* Dambulla to Matale, where the train can be taken to Colombo *viâ* Kandy; (2) by road direct to Dambulla, *viâ* Kekerawa, and thence to Matale and so back to Colombo by rail; (3) by road to Puttalam, on the west coast, thence southwards down the coast *viâ* Chilaw and Negombo to Colombo, all the way by road. A glance at the map of the island will show these several routes clearly defined.

Trincomalee, with its magnificent bay and harbour, Dambulla, with its rock temples, Sigiriya, the rock fortress near Dambulla, where there are some famous ancient inscriptions and pictorial representations on the rock surface, and Matale, with its rock temple, should all be visited if possible.

The sea-coast railway, south from Colombo to Galle (72 miles) and Matara, the terminus and the southernmost town of the island (98 miles from the capital), offers an easily made visit to Galle, the former chief sea-port of Ceylon, and still surrounded with the old fortifications. Before Colombo became the chief business centre, Galle was the main port of call of the island, and a place of considerable importance. But now the town's chief claim to attention is its extremely picturesque appearance with the great walls, gateways, escarpments, bastions, and sea-front fortifications practically unaltered since the days of the Dutch occupation of Ceylon.

The passenger carriages on the Ceylon Government Railway are frequently criticised and blamed by persons more or less competent to give an opinion. But in relation to these criticisms and complaints, the effect on the rolling-stock of the heat of the plains, the cold of the up-country and the torrential rains should be taken into consideration. Practically all the cars are locally constructed; and some of them, especially the sleeping cars of the up-country night-mail, would be a credit to any colonial railway. Refreshment cars are run on the principal trains on the main hills line, usually between Colombo and Hatton. On the Northern line between Polgahawela Junction and Jaffna refreshment cars are not at present provided; but the Refreshment Car Company at Colombo, if instructed beforehand, will furnish lunch-baskets.

Travelling in Ceylon by railway costs very little. For example, the visitor may take a first-class ticket from Colombo to Kandy, Nuwara Eliya, Bandarawela, back to Kandy, thence, *viâ* Polgahawela Junction, to Anuradhapura and Jaffna and back to Colombo for Rs.53.88 (£3 12s.). On the seaside line the fare first class from Colombo to Galle and return is Rs. 8.71 (11s. 9d.).

As regards hotels in the island, Colombo, of course, stands first in the number and size of its hostelries. They provide interesting experiences even for residents, and present novelties to the stranger who walks their verandahs, possibly meeting friends from all parts of the world, and bargaining with the wily "Tamby" (Moorman merchant)—who, by the by, invariably succeeds in effecting a sale, notwithstanding the resolutions the visitor may have formed to avoid Ceylon jewellery, curios, and Oriental drapery, with all their charms.

Kandy, Nuwara Eliya, Hatton, and Galle all possess spacious and comfortable hotels, ready to welcome the stranger. At Nuwara Eliya the competition between the four different hostelries established there is very keen, and the visitor begins to realise how much he is sought after when representatives of each establishment appear determined to bear him off *vi et armis*.

In other places the Government has established at intervals of, say, about 14 miles along most of the principal roads, rest-houses, which are, in fact, miniature hotels. This provision is ostensibly made for the accommodation of officials on circuit. But the existence of these places of accommodation enables non-official persons to travel practically all over the island without risk of finding themselves houseless and foodless. The rest-houses, as also the meals and refreshments supplied in them, vary greatly in quality, as is only natural; but, generally speaking, neither the Government nor the customers have reason to be dissatisfied with this system of wayside provision for travellers. The Government levies a small charge for occupation of rooms, which is carefully noted in the rest-house book, while the meals and other refreshments are supplied by the keeper of the establishment on his own account, but at a tariff fixed by official authority.

Motor-touring is very popular and enjoyable in Ceylon, especially in the low-country of the maritime provinces and in the north of Ceylon, where there are no steep or high hills to climb. Cars can be hired in Colombo from Messrs. Walker & Sons, or in Kandy from the Kandy Motor Car Syndicate, by the day or at mileage rates; or if the visitor brings his own car, he will find the Ceylon roads suitable for practically any make of automobile, though large cars of 30 horse-power or over are not recommended. The bridges, curves, corners, and ways generally were all designed for slow traffic, and in some cases the roads are somewhat narrow and difficult, though the experienced motorist will rejoice at the opportunities presented by these conditions for testing his nerves and skill.

THOS. COOK & SON.

The world-renowned firm of Messrs. Thos. Cook & Son, Tourist and General Passenger Agents, has a branch office in the Victoria Arcade Buildings, York Street, Colombo, under the popular and able management of Mr. H. B. Smith, where inquiries concerning all matters relating to travelling are satisfied. Tickets are supplied for any journey, baggage can be shipped—and insured if required—circular notes and letters of credit are issued, which are payable at any of the agencies of the firm in all parts of the world, and itineraries are prepared for any trip to the beauty spots and interesting localities in Ceylon, or across to India and through any part of that country, the port of Colombo being a very convenient point for through passengers by steamship to break their journey and visit the great dependency.

The firm was founded by the late Mr. Thomas Cook in 1841, and the business has since grown to enormous proportions. The present partners, Messrs. F. H., E. E., and T. A. Cook, are grandsons of the founder. The head office is in Ludgate Circus, London, and there are branch establishments or agencies in almost every place of importance throughout the world. Besides owning the well-known funicular railway on Mount Vesuvius, Messrs. Thos. Cook & Son maintain a large staff in Palestine, with horses and all camp equipment necessary for tours of any length always in readiness, while in Egypt they have a fleet of twenty-seven passenger boats on the Nile,

POST AND TELEGRAPHS

A HIGHLY efficient and complete system of postal and telegraphic communication exists in Ceylon. The department is controlled by the Postmaster-General, who has under him two assistants and a Superintendent and Assistant Superintendent of Telegraphs to advise on technical matters connected with the telegraph and telephone branches; an Accountant and Assistant Accountant for financial work; two Inspectors of Post Offices, whose duty is to examine the accounts of out-station offices; a Resident Postmaster, who supervises the mail arrangements at the General Post Office; and a Telegraph Master to supervise the Telegraph and Signalling Department. The General Post Office is one of the finest buildings in Colombo. It was erected from the plans of Mr. H. F. Tomalin, of the Public Works Department, at a cost of Rs. 372,961·65, and was opened in July, 1895. There is every accommodation in the building for the work of the department, and in the spacious main hall the members of the general public find the best arrangements for the prompt despatch of business. In connection with the establishment is a good Library and Recreation Club for the use of the staff.

The postal work of the colony is carried on under varying conditions as regards methods of transit. The railway carries the mails to those parts of the island which are served by the system, but these constitute only a comparatively limited portion of the total area. The service has to be supplemented by horse coaches, bullock coaches, and in the last resort by runners, of whom over 200 are employed by the department. Since 1886, when village receiving offices were established, the rural districts have been well looked after. Now there are few parts of the island, however remote, which are without a regular service. An intimate postal connection exists between Ceylon and Southern India, mainly owing to the fact that a large number of Tamil coolies from the Madras Presidency are employed on the various tea and other estates. For many years this portion of the service was carried on between Kankesanturai, on the coast of Ceylon, and Point Calimere, on the coast of India. The distance of 29 miles was covered by catamarans, perhaps the most remarkable vessels ever employed in any country for the sea transit of mails. These craft received a subsidy of Rs. 110 per month, and did their work very efficiently, having regard to the difficulties of the crossing. But when the regular daily service of steamers was established between Colombo and Tuticorin in 1892 a new system

POST OFFICE PEON.
(Sergeant.)

was introduced, and finally, in January, 1899, the catamaran service was completely suspended as a precaution against plague.

At all post offices money order, savings bank and postal business is transacted. Letters are addressed in many languages, but the great bulk of the addresses are in English, Sinhalese, or Tamil. The various periods at which the different features in the system were introduced are as follows: inland money order system, 1877; savings bank, 1885; exchange of money orders with the United Kingdom, 1873.

The Telegraph Department dates back to 1857, in which year the Ceylon Government took the preliminary steps for establishing communication between various parts of the island. The first line actually constructed was between Colombo and Galle, a distance of 74 miles. Coconut-trees were used as posts, and instead of insulators wooden brackets nailed to the trees were employed. Owing to the line being exposed to the full force of the monsoon there was frequent interruption of communication. Eventually posts and porcelain insulators were substituted for the improvisations first used. The next section of line constructed was from Colombo to Kandy, this work being executed in June, 1858. In October of the same year a more ambitious enterprise was carried through in the form of a line 250 miles long, connecting Colombo with Mannar and Talaimannar, and so providing direct telegraphic communication with India. At that time the interior of Ceylon was very little developed, and considerable difficulty was experienced in maintaining communication. Herds of wild elephants roaming the countryside knocked down the posts and broke the wires, and there were other mishaps due to the unsettled conditions then prevailing. Ultimately, in 1882, the whole of the line was reconstructed and an additional wire provided to meet the increasing traffic. It was an excellent piece of work and made possible direct communication between Colombo and Madras, over 600 miles of wire. Another important work was the carrying of a telegraph line from Kandy *viâ* Dambulla to Trincomalee. The same difficulties from wild elephants were encountered on this line, and such were the drawbacks of the route that in 1881 the line was abandoned and a fresh one constructed *viâ* Anuradhapura, over a country which presented fewer drawbacks. Some time before the execution of this work—in July, 1880—the whole of the lines in the island were transferred from the Government of India, which had hitherto controlled them, to the local Government, which has ever since had charge of them. The system now comprises 1,653 miles of posts and 3,366 miles of wire. All the greater towns and many of the lesser ones are connected. Lines cross from the west to the east coast, passing over the mountain ranges which constitute the backbone of the island. In places where the country is rough the wires cross great ravines, several of the spans being as much as 800 yards in length. From the extreme south to the extreme north of the island, a distance of 400 miles, there are lines which on one portion of the route—the section beyond Matale—pass through dense forests and a sparsely peopled country. Telegraph money orders were introduced on May 1, 1893, and four years later a system of 25-cent telegrams was established.

MAIL COACH PREPARING TO START.

Associated with the postal telegraph administration is the control of the telephone system. Originally established by the Oriental Telephone Company, the system was acquired from that company by the Government at a cost of Rs. 42,666. At the time of the transfer of the system, January 1, 1896, there were 56 subscribers, 25 miles of posts, and 151 miles of wire. At the present time there are 150 subscribers, 44 miles of posts, and 490 miles of wire. The number of calls on the Exchange in 1905 was 358,000.

Some facts and figures taken from the latest Administration Report—that for 1905—may be given to illustrate the work of the department as a whole. In the year under report 26,586,540 articles passed through the post, an increase on the year 1904 of 2,530,242. In 1901 the number of articles handled was 21,021,820. The number of registered letters dealt with increased from 170,949 in 1904 to 179,871 in 1905. In the ten years from 1896 the weight of letters and postcards despatched to the United Kingdom increased from 9,427 lbs. to 18,436 lbs., and the weight of "other articles" grew from 27,774 lbs. to 63,379 lbs. in the same period. During the year 1905 414,203 parcels were dealt with, or 3,032 less than in the preceding year. In the period under report 422,843 money orders were issued for an aggregate sum of Rs. 11,680,125; in 1896 the number was 209,425 and the amount Rs. 6,386,160. The savings bank business shows a similar high rate of progress. On December 31, 1905, the amount standing to the credit of depositors was Rs. 1,748,127, an increase of Rs. 57,912 on the previous year. In 1896 the amount at the credit of depositors was Rs. 1,026,471. In regard to telegraphs, the total number of telegrams sent during the year was 717,564, an increase on the previous year of 55,182 sent from offices in Ceylon and 2,422 received from abroad. The total revenue of the department in 1905 was Rs. 1,241,810 and the expenditure Rs. 1,362,026. In 1896 the figures were: revenue, Rs. 768,373; expenditure, Rs. 914,739. The total number of employees in the Postal and Telegraph Department, exclusive of runners and contractors' agents, was 1,317 in 1905 against 1,280 in the previous year.

COLOMBO POST AND TELEGRAPH LIBRARY AND RECREATION CLUB.

Largely owing to the energy and enthusiasm of Mr. F. W. Vane, who was then Assistant Postmaster-General, a Library and Recreation Club for members of the Post Office staff was established as long ago as the year 1883, and from small beginnings it has grown until in 1906 it had a membership of 400 and a library of no fewer than 1,535 well-selected volumes. Various kinds of recreation are provided under the auspices of the club, including tennis and cricket: and at its well-appointed reading-room a large number of newspapers, magazines, and other periodicals are supplied.

Mr. Robertson was appointed Honorary Secretary of the club in the year 1899, and has held that office ever since. He was born in the island in 1864, entered the Post Office service in 1882 as telegraphist, and rose gradually until in 1906 he was promoted to be Acting Assistant Superintendent of Telegraphs.

THE POST OFFICE.

LOCAL GOVERNMENT

FROM time immemorial the inhabitants of Ceylon have been familiar with the principal of local government in its primitive form. When the island first emerges from the mists of antiquity into the light of European knowledge, we find existing, side by side with an Oriental despotism in its most naked form, a system of local popular control of the completest kind. Every village and every hamlet had its Gansabhawa, or village council, and side by side with this body was the Ratasabhawa, or district council, which had the oversight of the wider affairs of the district. Sir Emerson Tennent, in his work on Ceylon,[1] refers to the Gansabhawa as "merely a miniature council of the peasants, in which they settled all disputes about descent and proprietorship, and maintained the organisation essential to their peculiar tillage, facilitating at the same time the payment of dues to the Crown, both in taxes and labour." Elsewhere this distinguished writer contrasts the Gansabhawa with the Punchayet, or village tribunal, of India, and points out the identity of aims of the two. Subsequent writers have gone further, and sought with much show of reason to establish a connection between these village bodies and the free institutions which were the common heritage of the earlier races touched by Aryan influence. On this point some interesting remarks were made in a report issued by the Ceylon Government when the village councils were reconstituted in 1871. "It has been ascertained," says the writer, "that the mark and tything of the Gothic races, the Sclavonian Commune and the Indian village present points of resemblance too numerous and too well defined to be the result of mere accident. It may be assumed that a thousand years ago social relations and duties in the English village were regulated, if not by the same system, yet by principles having a common origin and very similar development, and that while in England the system with the lapse of centuries became profoundly modified, it retained, as the Gansabhawas, most of its original features in the Kandyan country to the date when the British Government replaced the last native king." How the system worked is vividly described in Major Forbes's "Eleven Years in Ceylon." "The village council," the author says, "was composed of the head of every family residing within its limits, however low his rank or small his property. From this tribunal there was an appeal to the district council, which consisted of intelligent delegates from each village to the Pattu, or subdivision of a district."

[1] Vol. i. p. 497

The village court met under the shade of some convenient tree, and it was open to all. Trial by ordeal, dipping the hands in boiling oil or heated cowdung, were in use for deciding cases prior to the advent of the British. But generally speaking, the efforts of the councils were directed to securing an amicable adjustment of disputes. The system lingered on after the British occupation, and in the Charter of 1833 a special proviso appears safeguarding the jurisdiction of the Gansabhawas. In the absence, however, of direct official sanction and patronage, the interesting institution fell more and more into desuetude. In connection with the irrigation schemes undertaken during Sir Henry Ward's government, measures were resorted to to revive the principle of personal service and responsibility at the root of these councils. But it remained for the administration of Sir Hercules Robinson (afterwards Lord Rosmead) to infuse new life into the old bones of Sinhalese civilisation. In this period the village communities were reconstituted and definite authority was conferred upon them. Afterwards, other ordinances were passed strengthening and extending the system. The operative law on the subject is that embodied in Ordinance No. 24 of 1889. By the provisions of section 6 of this edict the inhabitants of subdivisions proclaimed under the Ordinance "may either make rules or delegate that function to committees elected by themselves." The subjects with which such rules may deal comprise a variety of purposes of local interest and importance, such as the construction, maintenance, regulation and protection of village paths, bridges, wells, water and bathing-places, ferries, markets, grounds for the burial or burning of the dead, and for the conservancy of springs or watercourses. The councils also may have the control of the construction and repair of schoolrooms, the regulation of fisheries, the care of waste and common lands, the encouragement of the cultivation of industrial products, the prevention of nuisances, the prevention of the use of abusive language, the prevention of accidents, the prevention of gambling and cock-fighting, the collection of tolls, the construction and maintenance of village roads, and the repair, protection, and maintenance of village canals and tanks. Associated with these powers is the right of imposing an annual tax payable in labour in respect of the duties of the council which call for the use of labour. The maximum amount of labour which may be demanded in any one year is ten days, and power is given to a council to allot such labour as it deems necessary. Finally, the councils are endowed with power to make regulations prohibiting the sale of intoxicants to females. The rules framed by the councils are transmitted through the Government Agent of the Province to the Governor for approval or disallowance, and if His Excellency's approval is given the rules are published in the Government *Gazette*, and thenceforward have the force of law.

In connection with the village councils are village tribunals, which are empowered to try breaches of the rules framed by the councils, as well as petty civil and criminal cases. These courts of petty jurisdiction are presided over by a paid president, who is assisted in his duties by three village officers.

On the whole, this system of local self-government has worked well. On the one hand, the inhabitants have received valuable lessons in self-reliance and public spirit; on the other, the country has benefited by the improvements which have been carried out through the agency of the village organisations. The liabilities imposed under the law are cheerfully borne. Labour, or its equivalent—a monetary contribution at the rate of 25 cents per head for each day of labour exacted—is freely rendered, and there are actually instances mentioned in the reports of the volunteering of labour beyond the amount which could be legally exacted. In the last Administration Report for the Western Province—that for 1903—(Acting) Government Agent, the Hon. Mr. H. L. Crawford, makes some interesting remarks on the spirit animating the village communities. Speaking of one of the bodies, he says: "The honesty of the administration is testified to by the fact that, though accounts in the vernacular, giving to the minutest detail a full statement of the revenue and expenditure of the committees, both in money and labour, and a full description of all works carried out, were printed and scattered broadcast throughout the district, there was not a single representation calling in question the accuracy of or suggesting malfeasance in any item. . . .

"The extent and importance of the work may be judged from the fact that the total cash revenue of the committees in 1905 was Rs. 23,356·78, which, with a balance of Rs. 11,019·84 from 1904, placed Rs. 34,376·62 at the disposal of the committees, of which they expended Rs. 28,421·63 in carrying out the duties imposed on them by the Ordinance. I have no hesitation in saying that no other public body in the island could have spent that sum to better advantage, or even made it go so far in the carrying out of useful works, and this was done by local self-government in its most absolute form."

Working on these lines, the village communities may be expected to become a permanent and valuable feature of the local governing system of the colony.

The general organisation of local government, apart from these interesting bodies, embraces a mixed system of Local Boards, Boards of Health, Provincial and District Road Committees, and, for the towns of Colombo, Kandy and Galle, Municipal Councils. The Local Boards were brought into existence in 1876, to supply the machinery of local administration in places which were not deemed sufficiently large or important to be endowed with full municipal powers. There are eighteen of such boards at the present time, and in 1905 their total revenue was Rs. 272,985·18, while their total expenditure was Rs. 321,757·31, and their aggregate indebtedness Rs. 317,316·48. The principal Ordinance regulating the constitution and working of these authorities is No. 13 of 1898. Boards are established by proclamation. They consist of three official and three unofficial members. The official members are the Government or Assistant Government Agent, the Public Works Officer, and the Civil Medical Officer. The qualification for unofficial membership is the possession of property of not less value than Rs. 1,000; but the person appointed must not hold any office of emolument under Government, and must not have been convicted of any infamous crime. The constituency which elects the unofficial members is made up of householders who, as either owners or tenants, occupy houses of not less value than Rs. 50 per annum. The boards are entrusted with the making, repairing, cleaning, watering and lighting of the streets, and the construction and upkeep of roads, canals and bridges of the town, the supervision of weights and measures, the establishment of public markets, and the supervision of private markets, bakeries, dairies, laundries, washing places, common lodging-houses and latrines. Other duties are the establishment and regulation of slaughter-houses, the regulation of dangerous or offensive trades, the suppression of cruelty to animals, the care of waste or public lands, the setting apart and regulation of bathing places, and the destruction of ownerless dogs. The boards also have power to determine the amount to be paid in commutation of the labour due from the inhabitants, the calling out and enforcement of such labour, and the infliction of penalties amounting to double labour or increased or double commutation, in event of default. Further, various powers relating to sanitation and the abatement of nuisances are vested in the authorities. The financial resources of the boards are drawn partly from fines imposed under the Ordinance, partly from duties on boat, cart and coach licences and fees and duties relating to opium, firearms, butchers, poisons, petroleum, explosives, &c. A further source of revenue are the proceeds of moderate taxes which the boards have power to levy on vehicles, horses, cattle and dogs.

The following is a list of local board towns:—

Western Province.
Kalutara.
Negombo.
Minuwangoda.

Central Province.
Gampola.
Matale.
Nawalapitiya.
Hatton.
Dikoya.

Southern Province.
Matara.

Eastern Province.
Batticaloa.
Trincomalee.

North Western Province.
Kurunegala.
Puttalam.
Chilaw.

North Central Province.
Anuradhapura.

Province of Uva.
Badulla.

Province of Sabaragamuwa.
Ratnapura.
Kegalla.

Supporting and reinforcing the work of the local boards is a group of bodies known as Provincial and District Road Committees, whose special function it is to see to the maintenance of the roads of the colony. The main point of difference between the two classes of committees is that the first-named is a purely nominated body while the last-named consists of partly nominated and partly elected members. The district committees have a good deal in common with the local boards in the two systems—that while for the local boards the members are drawn indifferently from those of the inhabitants who possess the requisite qualification, for the District Road Committees there is a special representation of each of the three sections of the population, European, Burgher, and native. The elections for the district committees are triennial, and the arrangements for the elections are controlled by the provincial committees. Financially, the backbone of the system is the road tax of six days' labour annually, which was first imposed in 1848. The operative section of the Ordinance is the following: "Section 49—Every male inhabitant between the ages of eighteen and fifty-five years shall be liable to perform six consecutive days' labour in each year upon the thoroughfares in this colony, or on works necessary for the formation, repair, or improvement thereof, or in the collection and preparation of materials required for any such purpose, or any work sanctioned by the Legislative Council under this Ordinance." Persons liable to labour who fail to attend when called upon are liable to be required to perform double labour. If the delinquent still continues recalcitrant he may be sentenced to one month's imprisonment. The labour tax, however, may be commuted by a money payment. The total receipts of the road committees in 1905 were Rs. 1,526,666, and the total expenditure amounted to Rs. 1,524,651.

Coming now to the three municipalities, in which local government is seen in its most advanced form, it is to be noted that all are governed by the principle of partly nominated, partly elected members which is seen in operation in the local boards and the district committees. The constitution of all is practically the same, but while the chairman of the Colombo municipality is a civil servant, appointed by the Governor and holding no other office, the chairmen of the councils of Kandy and Galle are the respective Government Agents. The Ordinances regulating the working of the three municipalities provide that at least one half of the members must be elected, and that the councillors not elected shall be nominated by the Governor. The qualifications of elected councillors are that they must be males who have completed their twenty-sixth year, who are acquainted with the English language, who reside within the municipal area, and who either possess property of the value of not less than Rs. 5,000 or occupy a house the annual rental value of which is not less than Rs. 500. No Government or municipal servant, except the chairman, can be a member of the councils. The chief voting qualification is the occupation of a house of a monthly rental value of not less than Rs. 15 or the possession of property to the extent of not less than Rs. 180. Graduates of universities in the United Kingdom or the British Colonies or India are entitled to vote by reason of their academic distinction.

The purposes for which municipal councils are authorised to expend funds are as follows:

(*a*) Lighting public streets, places, and buildings; control, supervision, and removal of dangerous places, buildings, trades, and practices; regulation of traffic; and prevention and removal of obstructions in public streets or places.

(*b*) Construction, maintenance, supervision, and control of public markets and slaughter-houses; latrines, privies, urinals; drains, sewers, drainage works, tramways, and other works for the removal of sewage; waterworks, drinking fountains, tanks, and wells; parks and gardens; acquisition of land necessary for any of these purposes; reclamation of unhealthy localities; and other sanitary measures of a like nature.

Cleansing and watering of streets and sewers; scavenging; removal of excessive or noxious vegetation; and, generally, the abatement of all nuisances.

(*c*) Maintenance of schools in which the English language is taught in accordance with the provisions of Ordinance No. 33 of 1884.

(*d*) Construction, maintenance, and alteration of streets, bridges, causeways, culverts, and the like, and acquisition of land necessary for any of these purposes; regulations of buildings; removal of undue projections; naming streets and numbering houses; and planting trees in public streets and places.

Construction, purchase, and maintenance of all buildings required in order to give effect to the purposes of this Ordinance. Survey of houses and lands.

(*e*) All matters necessary for, or conducive to, public safety, health, or convenience.

(*f*) Contributing, with the previous sanction in writing of the Governor in Executive Council, towards the cost incurred on the occasion of any public ceremony, or for purposes of public recreation or entertainment in the municipality.

Under the separate headings will be found particulars of the three municipalities; but we may usefully reproduce here the following statement from the Report in the Ceylon Blue Book of 1905 showing the financial position of the bodies as a whole:—

COMPARATIVE STATEMENT OF THE TOTAL REVENUE AND EXPENDITURE OF MUNICIPALITIES FOR THE FIVE YEARS ENDED DECEMBER 31, 1905.

Name of Municipality.	Revenue or Expenditure.	1901.	1902.	1903.	1904.	1905.
		Rs. c.	Rs. c.	Rs. c.	Rs. c.	Rs. c.
Colombo	Revenue	1,230,005 20	1,405,838 88	1,337,344 8	1,567,907 46	1,591,742 10
	Expenditure ...	1,306,278 56	1,175,727 7	1,494,429 40	1,656,127 70	1,387,277 98
Kandy	Revenue	181,107 91	173,202 85	199,303 84	192,150 47	188,553 17
	Expenditure ...	186,728 3	185,364 63	196,217 71	179,583 10	207,938 78
Galle	Revenue	86,222 74	91,652 67	92,886 64	95,911 93	104,899 28
	Expenditure ...	94,009 28	92,535 45	88,115 81	86,563 57	110,473 50

It will have been gathered from the foregoing that though in some directions satisfactory progress has been made in recent years, the system of local government, using that term in the sense in which it is understood in the more advanced communities of the Empire, is still in its infancy. The difficulty of grafting Western institutions upon an Eastern stock is notoriously great, but in no direction, perhaps, are more serious obstacles to be encountered than in the domain of local administration. Racial, religious, and caste prejudices have to be overcome; immemorial usages penetrating deep into the life of the people have to be combated; above all, that ingrained conservatism which is the most characteristic phase of the Oriental mind stands in the way of the introduction of representative municipal institutions, with all that they imply in sound and efficient administration. Mr. C. M. Lushington, Government Agent for the Southern Province, has some instructive remarks on this subject in his Administration Report for the Southern Province for 1905. "I am afraid," he says, "that Ceylon is not yet ripe for anything of the nature of representative government. It is very seldom that candidates come forward for election from purely public-spirited motives, and it is certainly not with the object of securing the best candidate or the man who will best look after the interests of the people that voters are induced to come forward and record their votes. The Ordinance provides for preliminary lists of persons entitled to sit as councillors and persons entitled to vote, and some months later revised and corrected lists are published and should be final; but the public show no interest in getting the lists corrected, and it is only when an election is imminent that the candidates begin to hunt up the lists and raise objections to those who may be rival candidates or likely to vote for rival candidates.

"The election is therefore held on technical lines. Proxies are frequently given by the same voters for *both* the candidates, and when the time for the election comes the presiding officer is called upon to decide objections to the candidates, objections to the voters, and to decide whether the proxies are genuine, and perhaps on the priority of the proxies. The whole business assumes a technical character.

"A meeting was held in the first week of December for elections of Unofficial Members of the Galle Municipality, and there were contested elections for two of the wards. After much wrangling one candidate for one ward was declared disqualified and in the other ward six of the voters were declared disqualified. In both cases applications have been made to the Supreme Court to set the election aside.

"In one case the elected member has been unseated, and the candidate who was declared disqualified is given the chance of contesting the election again. The second case is still pending. As regards the working of the Council I am not able to form an opinion after so short an experience. One department, however, and that the most important one—viz., that dealing with the sanitary arrangements of the town and called the "Health Department"—has been found to be rotten to the core. The disclosures made to the Committee were horrible and disgusting. A radical change is imperative. The "manager" of the department has been given notice to quit, and a thorough reorganisation of the service is being set on foot. If other departments are equally bad, I fear there is not much to be said for the interior working of the municipality."

This picture of Ceylon municipal government as it is to-day refers only to one town But it is to be feared that the strong remarks made by Mr. Lushington as to the apathy of the inhabitants of Galle have a general application. Often it has been found that the people of a district or town have deliberately declined to avail themselves of the machinery of self-administration offered in the Local Board Ordinances, preferring to remain in the state of disorganised squalor and confusion which is their lot to accepting the responsibilities of a duly constituted authority. A case in point is supplied by the Hon. Mr. H. L. Crawford, Government Agent for the Western Province, in his Administration Report for 1905. Mr. Crawford says :—

"Towns like Moratuwa and Panadure have had plenty of opportunities of electing self-government in the form of a Local Board, but the majority of the inhabitants have objected to its introduction because it involves the payment of an assessment rate. The only alternative is the inclusion of such places under the Small Towns Sanitary Ordinance, in which case the inhabitants of the locality have no voice in the administration of the funds collected, which rests with the Board of Health, a body composed exclusively of officials. In the ordinary villages the village committee is the sanitary authority, but in the Moratuwa division the inhabitants declined to avail themselves of the machinery of this Ordinance, and at the present moment there is no authority of any kind to govern the sanitation of this populous division. It is impossible that such a state of things should be allowed to continue, for it is bound, as population increases, to become a menace to the health of the whole neighbourhood. The leading men of Moratuwa have fully recognised the position, but the uneducated majority have so far successfully resisted the introduction of any sanitary authority."

The Small Towns Ordinance to which Mr. Crawford refers was passed in 1892, and its provisions were strengthened by an amending Ordinance which received sanction in 1900. The object of the original Ordinance was "to make provision for the imposition of a sanitary rate in certain localities." But the powers conferred by the instrument go a good deal beyond the imposition of taxation. Power is vested in Provincial Boards of Health, of which the Government Agent of the Province is *ex-officio* chairman and treasurer. Extensive authority is given to the boards to improve sanitation by removing huts or buildings crowded together, by preventing overcrowding in other buildings, by limewashing houses, by supervising drains, and by scavenging operations. Under the later Ordinance the powers of the boards were considerably enlarged. In addition to the rate of 4 per cent. on the assessment which the boards were authorised to levy under the original Ordinance, the boards had placed at their disposal the proceeds of stamp duties for licences of carts, carriages, boats, and coaches, and other fees of a similar character. They were also empowered to levy a water rate up to 6 per cent. of the annual value of premises, and to borrow on the security of the rates and taxes for public works likely to improve the sanitary condition of any town or village or to add to the comfort of the inhabitants thereof

These Ordinances supply the Government, as Mr. Crawford suggests in the extract given above, with a powerful lever by which to push backward communities into line with their more progressive brethren elsewhere. With the adoption of such means, and with the spread of enlightened ideas amongst the masses of the people, the principles of self-administration will, without doubt, find wider scope in the immediate future. It is too much to hope, however, that anything approaching the free popular system of the United Kingdom and the self-governing colonies can be introduced for many years to come.

FINANCIAL

THE COLONIAL TREASURY.

By Hon. Mr. H. C. NICOLLE.

THE Colonial Treasurer is in charge of the financial and accounting operations of the colony, subject to the control of the Governor through the Colonial Secretary. Formerly the Auditor-General was also the Accountant-General, but from January 1, 1906, the accounting work was handed over to the Treasurer. The Colonial Treasurer, in addition to his other duties, is also Commissioner of Stamps, a Commissioner of Currency, Chief Commissioner of the Loan Board, and a Director of the Widows and Orphans' Pension Fund.

The staff of the Treasury consists of a financial assistant and accountant, who is responsible for the accounting work and general supervision; of an office assistant, whose main duties are in connection with the currency and stamp work; of a Shroff, or cashier, who deals with all pure cash transactions; and of a number of clerks. The Government Agents, Assistant Government Agents, and a large number of heads of departments are sub-accountants to the Treasurer both for receipts and payments, but eventually all the accounts are focussed in the Treasury, where the balance-sheet of the colony is prepared. The transactions are of considerable magnitude, and amount to some Rs. 130,000,000 on either side of the account annually.

The revenue of the colony for 1905 was Rs. 34,395,336, the largest on record. It included an amount of Rs. 2,626,175, the result of an abnormal pearl fishery. For the year 1906 it is hoped that the revenue will be over Rs. 33,750,000, and this without the assistance given by the results of the pearl fishery mentioned above.

The principal sources of revenue are the Government railway, customs, arrack rents, salt monopoly, revenue stamps, postage, telegraphs, interest, pearl fishery, land sales, licensing, and harbour dues. For details of the revenue, reference must be made to the annual Blue Books, but for those who are interested in figures, and to show the progressive state of the colony's revenue, a statement is appended giving the gross revenue for each of the ten years from 1896 to 1905.

The expenditure of the colony in 1905 was Rs. 29,739,900, and the estimated expenditure for 1906 is Rs. 31,500,000. It is impossible in an article of this nature to go into the details of the expenditure. One or two points may, however, be of interest. The personal emoluments are about 25 per cent. of the whole expenditure, which it is believed will compare favourably with other colonies. The charges on account of the public debt, which will be referred to later, constitute a heavy item, as also does the military contribution of 9½ per cent. paid to the Imperial Government on the gross revenue of the colony other than railway revenue, where only the net revenue is liable. On land sales no contribution is paid. The military contribution for 1905 was Rs. 2,439,800. Very large sums are spent on public works. In dealing with the expenditure, only expenditure on account of items chargeable to the revenue of the colony has been considered. Loan expenditure will be dealt with later. A statement showing the expenditure of the colony for each of the years from 1896 to 1905, exclusive of loan expenditure, is appended.

It is a well-known fact that in Government accounts no capital account is kept, including as assets the value of the properties of Government, such as railways, docks, buildings, &c., as is usually done by public companies; nor do the fixed loans constituting the public debt appear as liabilities. Practically only cash items are dealt with as assets and liabilities in considering the financial position so far as Government accounts are concerned. The balance of assets over liabilities of the colony on this basis on January 1, 1906, was Rs. 3,419,068, to which must be added sums amounting to Rs. 4,610,397, advanced from revenue on account of works to be eventually charged to loans; so that, including money expended in this manner, the colony had a balance of Rs. 8,029,465 on January 1, 1906. A loan has been authorised, and when it is raised the Rs. 4,610,397 can be repaid to revenue account; but so long as the colony is in a position to finance works chargeable to loans, it appears better to save the interest payable on the loan, and so far further sums amounting to some Rs. 2,380,000 have been advanced in 1906. It is estimated that on January 1, 1907, the balance of assets, including advances on account of loans, will be at the least Rs. 10,000,000.

The public debt of the colony on January 1, 1906, was in all, after deducting sinking funds invested and available for repayment of debt, Rs. 65,790,585, or a little less than double one year's revenue. A further loan of £1,000,000, or Rs. 15,000,000, has been authorised, and the necessary Ordinance for raising it passed, but up to now the loan has not been put on the market. The particulars of the existing loans will be found in the annual Blue Book, the interest paid being at rates varying from 3 to 4½ per cent. The 3 per cent. sterling loans stand to-day in the London market at £94, and the 4 per cent. rupee loan in the local market at 109. The greater portion of the debt, both sterling and rupee, is repayable by means of sinking funds, and the annual charges on

O*

the revenues of the colony for interest are Rs. 2,693,694, and sinking fund Rs. 959,668.

As has been stated previously, the properties of the colony are not included as assets and the public debt is not included as a liability; but it may be of interest to point out here that the greater part of the loans raised have been utilised on two great works, viz., the railways and the harbour. The capital cost of the railways to January 1, 1906, was in round figures Rs. 81,000,000, yielding about 5·60 per cent. interest. The capital cost of the harbour on the same date was Rs. 35,000,000, and after paying interest and sinking fund on loans, there is a small net revenue. From the above it follows that as against the colony's loans it has railways of the capital cost of Rs. 81,000,000, yielding about 7½ per cent. interest against a borrowing cost of 4 to 5 per cent. interest and sinking fund, and a harbour of the capital cost of Rs. 35,000,000, the returns from which just pay the interest and sinking fund on the cost of construction.

In considering the finances of the colony, all municipal and other revenues and expenditure of the various local authorities have been omitted. These will be dealt with in their proper place, but it may be mentioned that at the present time the colonial accounts show that some Rs. 2,000,000 have been lent by Government to local authorities. The loans are for the most part being repaid by means of annual payments to sinking funds.

The standard coin of Ceylon is the rupee of India, and the subsidiary coins are its decimal subdivisions, viz., the Ceylon silver fifty, twenty-five, and ten cent pieces, and the Ceylon copper five, one, half, and quarter cent pieces. Rupees are legal tender to any amount, the subsidiary silver coins to an amount not exceeding five rupees, and the copper coins to an amount not exceeding one-half a rupee. The Indian eight-anna or half-rupee, and four-anna or quarter-rupee pieces are legal tender as single coins. In 1906 the sovereign was made a legal tender for any amount at the rate of one sovereign for fifteen rupees. The half-sovereign, although it circulates to a very limited extent, is not a legal tender.

The only note issue is that of the Ceylon Government, and it consists of notes of Rs. 1,000, Rs. 100, Rs. 50, Rs. 10, and Rs. 5. It is managed by three Commissioners of Currency, viz., the Colonial Secretary, the Treasurer, and the Auditor-General, and is regulated by law. A reserve equal to the circulation has to be maintained, of which half must be in specie, the balance being invested in approved securities, provided, however, that should the specie reserve fall below one-half the circulation, the Commissioners are not bound to sell securities until it drops to one-third, when it is compulsory to sell securities to bring it up to one-half. The present circulation is about Rs. 18,000,000. There is a depreciation fund, which now stands at nearly Rs. 1,000,000, to cover any loss by depreciation in the value of investments.

When the sovereign was first made a legal tender large quantities were imported and exchanged for notes, the latter being subsequently changed for rupees, and to stop the drainage of rupees from the reserve, special legislation was introduced to limit the amount of the gold reserve. At present it is limited to £200,000, so that practically when the gold reserve reaches that amount the sovereign ceases to be a legal tender.

The Commissioners have the option of redeeming notes in gold or silver. There are some interesting forgeries of notes. The execution as a rule is not very good, and one of the best is made with two pieces of paper pasted together, the watermark being formed by means of strips of tissue paper cut out and inserted between the two main pieces.

All stamps in use in the colony, whether postage, telegraph, revenue, or judicial, are issued in the first instance from the Stamp Office. Revenue and judicial stamps can be sold only by the Commissioner of Stamps, a Government Agent, or Assistant Government Agent, and licensed vendors. The system of keeping a check on stamps sold is most complete, as every vendor has to place his initials, together with the true date of sale, on each revenue or judicial stamp sold, in addition to which each stamp of each value has to be numbered in consecutive order for each month, and a true record kept of the persons to whom stamps are sold, with the date of sale and the numbers appearing in each stamp. The result is that if a document has not been properly stamped and it comes into the hands of any court official or other Government officer, the stamps on it can be traced, and so it is very difficult to fraudulently stamp a document which has not been properly stamped at time of execution. A discount of 5 per cent. is allowed to licensed vendors on all stamps sold to them, and there is never any difficulty in finding vendors willing to take out a licence, the cost of which is Rs. 10 a year.

The Loan Board is administered by three Commissioners, generally the Colonial Treasurer, the Postmaster-General, and the Solicitor-General. The Financial Assistant to the Treasurer is Secretary to the Board.

The functions of the Board are to invest the moneys of suitors in the supreme and district courts of the colony, and from time to time to declare dividends out of the interest earned, which are paid to the credit of the various suits in the courts. The moneys at present under the control of the Board amount to about Rs. 1,850,000, and an average annual dividend of 4⅔ per cent. has been declared for the past ten years, which is satisfactory, seeing that one-third of all interest earned is paid to Government before the dividends are calculated. The moneys are as far as possible invested in good mortgages. Except the clerks in the office, none of the Government officers who deal with Loan Board affairs draw any salary, but the duties in connection with the management give a very fair amount of work to a number of officers in the courts and kachcheries, as well as to the Commissioners and the Secretary.

Although the Widows and Orphans' Pension Fund has nothing to do with the general finances of the colony, it is administered by the Treasurer and other Directors appointed by the Government from time to time, and therefore may be worthy of a passing notice. The fund has been formed by a deduction of 4 per cent. from the salaries of all pensionable officers who draw salaries of Rs. 250 per annum or over, and it provides pensions, according to actuarial tables, for the widows and orphans of contributors. The fund at the present time amounts to some Rs. 4,300,000, and is invested with the Government, who allow 6 per cent. on it. The fund will gradually cease to exist, as, by a recent Ordinance, contributions from new members of the Government Service are to be credited to revenue, and the Government guarantees the pensions to widows and orphans of such contributors in accordance with tables at present in force.

It is not within the scope of an article of this nature to deal fully with figures giving in detail the financial position of a colony; for, as has been said, full information can be obtained by those interested from the Blue Books, but it will be patent to every one who reads this paper that, at least from a financial point of view, the colony is in a flourishing condition, and that there are no signs that this prosperity is not likely to continue.

The following table, showing the revenue and expenditure of the colony, exclusive of loan expenditure, for the decade 1896–1905 supplies, in a succinct form, a record of the finances of the colony during that period:—

Year.	Revenue.	Expenditure.
	Rs.	Rs.
1896	21,974,573	21,274,955
1897	24,006,521	21,639,470
1898	25,138,669	22,845,521
1899	25,913,142	24,952,460
1900	27,325,930	28,948,927
1901	26,437,102	29,216,747
1902	28,435,157	28,042,105
1903	29,423,308	27,078,759
1904	30,846,694	32,019,392
1905	34,395,336	29,739,899

REVENUE AND EXPENDITURE.

THE Ceylon Government derives its revenue from the following sources: (1) Customs; (2) Port, harbour, wharf, and lighthouse dues; (3) Licences, excise and internal revenue not otherwise classified; (4) Fees of court or office, payment for specific services, and reimbursements in aid; (5) Post and telegraphs; (6) Government railway; (7) Rent of Government property; (8) Interest; (9) Miscellaneous receipts; (10) Sale of Government property; (11) Land sales. Roughly, about one-fourth of the total revenue is furnished by the Customs duties, rather more than one-fourth by the Government railway, and a little less than one-fifth by "licences, excise and internal revenue not otherwise classified." The following statement, giving the actual revenue collected in 1905, shows the exact proportions in which payments are made under the several heads to the Exchequer:—

	Revenue of 1905. Rs. c.
1. Customs	8,183,728 22
2. Port, Harbour, Wharf, and Lighthouse Dues	1,428,973 39
3. Licences, Excise, and Internal Revenue not otherwise classified	6,860,293 93
4. Fees of Court or Office, Payment for Specific Services, and Reimbursements in Aid	1,985,101 35
5. Post and Telegraphs ...	1,235,706 17
6. Government Railway ...	9,648,651 33
7. Rent of Government Property	206,164 51
8. Interest	462,411 93
9. Miscellaneous Receipts ...	261,821 24
10. Sale of Government Property	2,988,915 81
11. Land Sales	1,133,568 23

Analysing the various items of revenue, we find the following facts:—

(1) Customs.

Imports.—The sub-heads are: Grain, cotton manufactures, spirits and cordials, sugar, kerosene oil, other goods, undervalued goods, sundries. The grain duty is 50 cents per cwt. on all grain. Nearly the whole of the revenue under this sub-head is derived from the import duty on rice.

Exports.—The sub-heads are: Plumbago, royalty of 25 cents per cwt.; elephants, royalty of Rs. 200 per head; chanks; horns and hides of spotted deer and sambur; and arrack, Rs. 1·25 per gallon.

(2) Port, Harbour, Wharf, and Lighthouse Dues.

The sub-heads are: Colombo Harbour dues, port dues at outports, pilotage at Colombo and outports, and sundries.

(3) Licences, Excise and Internal Revenue not otherwise Classified.

Excise.—Salt: all salt in the island is collected and manufactured on account of Government, which from time to time fixes the retail price. Arrack, rum, and toddy: this is in general the price of the exclusive privilege of retailing spirits derived from the palm-tree and the sugar-cane, commonly called "arrack rent."

Licences.—Opium: the price of the privilege of possessing and selling opium.

Land Revenue.—Paddy, royalty on cabook, incidental.

Rents, exclusive of Lands.—Road tolls, bridge tolls, ferry tolls, canal tolls. These are usually farmed. The farm is called "toll rent," and the farmer "toll renter."

Stamps.—Revenue (various services). Composition duty on bank cheques.

Fines and Forfeitures.—Supreme Court, District Courts, Courts of Requests, Police Courts, Government Agents, other departments. forest offences.

(4) Fees of Court and Office, Payment for Specific Services, and Reimbursements in Aid.

The sub-headings are numerous. They embrace a wide variety of matters, ranging from judicial stamps and survey fees to value of tools lost and hire of anchors.

(5) Post and Telegraphs.

The sub-heads are: Postage stamps, commission on money orders, postage on unpaid letters, other collections, telegraph receipts, telephone receipts, transit conveyance of foreign mails.

(6) Government Railways.

The sub-heads are: Goods, passengers, miscellaneous.

(7) Rents on Government Property.

The sub-heads are: Government buildings and houses, garden rents, rent of reclamation grounds, rent of lands.

(8) Interest.

On public funds invested, on bank balances, on suitors' fund and intestate estates, on arrears of revenue, on loans to corporations.

(9) Miscellaneous Receipts.

The sub-heads are: Sale of old stores, overpayments recovered, unclaimed deposits, value of salved coal, profits on new coins, sundries.

(10) Sale of Government Property.

The sub-heads are: Produce of Botanic Gardens, timber and firewood, crops and Crown lands, sale of sand and stone, other forest produce, pearl fishery, sale of Delft horses, sundries.

(11) Land Sales.

The sub-heads are: Lands, premium on leases. In regard to these items paragraph 13 of the financial instructions states that the proceeds of the sale of Government lands and premium on leases is not strictly revenue, and though it should appear in the estimates, it should be kept distinct from the total revenue from other sources, and this is accordingly done.

Turning to expenditure, the following statement for 1905 shows the apportionment of the revenue to public purposes:—

Heads of Service.	1905. Rs. c.
1. Charges on account of Public Debt...	3,647,878 54
2. Pensions	1,392,614 3
3. His Excellency the Governor	139,300 85
3a. Civil Service	683,041 55
4. Secretariat	312,231 39
5. Audit Office	64,582 32
6. Treasury	50,974 14
7. Provincial Administration ...	1,257,612 53
8. Survey Department	780,133 50
9. Customs Department ...	135,537 86
10. Port and Marine Department, Colombo	413,189 57
11. Port and Marine Department other than Colombo ...	40,454 87
12. Botanic Gardens	131,114 35
13. Colombo Museum	26,473 93
14. Legal Departments:—	
Supreme Court	159,192 58
Attorney-General	64,905 63
Solicitor-General	11,002 25
District Courts	166,031 97
Courts of Requests and Police Courts	136,339 31
Registration of Lands ...	107,499 65
Registration of Marriages, Births, and Deaths ...	123,182 65
Fiscals	234,091 16
Loan Board	4,079 83

Heads of Service.	1905. Rs.	c.
15. Police	809,593	86
16. Prisons...	527,232	87
17. Medical Department... ...	443,998	8
18. Hospitals and Dispensaries...	1,323,673	62
19. Ecclesiastical...	9,260	0
20. Education	1,098,793	17
21. Transport	18,595	8
22. Exchange	216,050	16
23. Military Expenditure ...	2,504,390	38
24. Miscellaneous Services ...	869,825	77
25. Government Stores	82,232	23
26. Crown Agents, London ...	2,715	0
27. Forests	310,554	92
28. Post Office and Telegraphs...	1,401,899	15
29. Railway Department, Open Lines	5,196,895	43
Railway Construction Account	—	
30. Settlement Officer, Waste Lands Department ...	76,391	49
31. Veterinary Department ...	17,729	38
32. Consulting Electrical Engineer...	14,283	98
33. Irrigation Department ...	547,398	6
34. Immigration Department ...	42,334	4
35. Public Works Department...	410,287	39
36. Public Works Annually Recurrent	2,040,985	59
37. Public Works Extraordinary	1,693,315	17
Total Expenditure chargeable to General Revenue ...	29,736,899	28
38. Public Works Extraordinary, chargeable to Loan Funds	2,350,592	37
Grand Total ...	32,087,491	65

Taking the position as it is left by the figures quoted, it is one of great financial prosperity. The estimated revenue for the year was Rs. 29,698,080, while the actual revenue came to Rs. 34,395,336, an increase over the estimate of Rs. 4,697,256 and over the revenue of 1904, the highest previously obtained, of Rs. 3,548,642.

BANKS.

IN 1845 the Oriental Banking Corporation started operations in Ceylon, taking over the business of the Bank of Ceylon and the Bank of Western India, which had been established a year or two earlier. It was not until 1858 that the Chartered Mercantile Bank of India, London, and China commenced business in Ceylon. The Oriental Bank failed in 1884, when the New Oriental Banking Corporation was formed and remained in existence till 1892, when it also stopped payment. The Chartered Mercantile Bank of India, London, and China was reconstructed in the year 1892, when the name was changed to Mercantile Bank of India, Limited.

The banks at present doing business in Ceylon are the four Eastern Exchange Banks, viz.: The National Bank of India, Limited, established 1862—Head Office, London; the Chartered Bank of India, Australia, and China, established 1853—Head Office, London; the Hong Kong and Shanghai Banking Corporation, established 1865—Head Office, Hong Kong; the Mercantile Bank of India, Limited, established 1892—Head Office, London. Besides the above-mentioned "Exchange" Banks we have a branch of one of the Indian Presidency Banks, the Bank of Madras, which has its headquarters in Madras.

The chief business of an "exchange" bank, as the name denotes, is the purchase and sale of bills of exchange. Had the merchant who ships his produce to Europe, Australia, America, or whatever country it may be, to wait until such shipments were realised and the proceeds remitted back to him, trade would be hampered to such an extent as to become well-nigh impossible, but here the exchange bank steps in and purchases the bills of exchange drawn against such shipments, so that the merchant has not to remain without his money. The banks, however, have to get their money back to the island, and this is done in several ways, the most direct being by sale of their own drafts and telegraphic transfers on London at such a rate of exchange as leaves a narrow margin of profit on their purchasing rate. Other means are the purchases in London of the Secretary of State's drafts on India, known as "Council Bills," shipments of sovereigns from Australia to India (gold not being accepted by the Ceylon Government beyond a limit of £200,000 in the Treasury), and the sale of the banks' bills by their branches in India. These latter are indirect means, as the funds have again to be transferred from India to Ceylon, and the only ways open are the importation of rupees from India, and the sale of the banks' drafts on India.

As regards local business, this is conducted on very similar lines to those adopted by the English banks. Funds are employed in local trade discounts, cash credits, and advances against approved security, the ruling rates of interest being somewhat higher than those obtaining in England. It may strike a stranger to one of the local banks that cheques are not cashed over the counter as promptly as in the great London institutions, but the circumstances are so very different in Ceylon, that the banks must not be blamed for taking extra precautions for the protection of both themselves and the public. Time must be allowed for the posting of the cheque to the customer's debit in the ledger, and for the careful scrutiny of signature and endorsements by one of the European assistants before it can be passed on to the "shroff," or paying cashier, who in turn has to assure himself that he is dealing with the proper party before he pays over the cash. Forgeries, unfortunately, are not unknown in Ceylon, whilst other devices have also been resorted to for obtaining money under false pretences from the banks.

As in other centres, the Colombo banks have their "clearing house," which meets daily at 2 p.m. During the year ended February 28, 1906, the value of cheques cleared amounted to Rs. 261,328,192, as against Rs. 51,740,748 for the year ended February 28, 1886, when the "clearing house" was first started.

In connection with the exchange value of the rupee it is interesting to note the effect of the closing of the Indian mints to the free coinage of silver, which measure was adopted by Government in the year 1897. Previous to that date the value of the rupee was measured by the intrinsic value of the silver it contained; when silver rose in price the rupee advanced, and when silver fell the rupee declined. There are old colonists in the island now who can remember the days when they remitted to England at a fraction over two shillings for every rupee, whilst a resident of twelve years' standing will recollect the sterling value of the rupee being one shilling and a halfpenny.

This serious depreciation meant a very heavy loss to the Indian Government, which has large sterling obligations to meet annually, and so exercised the minds of the authorities that a Currency Commission was appointed in London to inquire thoroughly into the question and devise some means of getting out of the difficulty. As a result of this Commission's deliberations, the Indian mints which had hitherto been open to the free coinage of silver were closed to the public, Government at the same time undertaking to receive sovereigns and give in exchange fifteen rupees for each sovereign, or, in other words, putting a value of one shilling and fourpence on the rupee. The measure at the time was considered a drastic one, and there were many who doubted its efficiency, but the ten years during which it has been in force have proved its thorough success, the fluctuations of the rupee during that period being of little moment, and due solely to temporary variations in the money markets of London and India.

NATIONAL BANK OF INDIA, LIMITED.

The headquarters of the National Bank of India are in London—at 17, Bishopsgate Street Within, about a stone's-throw from the famous "Old Lady's" establishment where the music of money is everlastingly to be heard. The famous institution has its Home agencies in Edinburgh, Glasgow, and Manchester as well; and the branches in India and the Near East are at Calcutta, Bombay, Madras, Karachi, Rangoon, Chittagong, Amritsar, Cawnpore, Lahore, Tuticorin, Aden Steamer Point (Aden), Zanzibar, Mombassa, Nairobi, Entebbe, Mandalay, and the historic Delhi; while in Ceylon, besides the head office in York Street, Colombo, there are branches at Kandy and Nuwara Eliya. The net profit on the bank's business for 1905 amounted to the comfortable figure of £162,266, on a paid-up capital of £600,000, and the shareholders received the satisfactory dividend of 10 per cent., together with a bonus of 2 per cent. The Scottish caution, joined with equally Scottish acumen and enterprise, which characterises the management is manifest in the maintenance of a substantial reserve fund, now amounting to £575,000; and a glance at the balance-sheet for the year mentioned is sufficient to show that the financial business is conducted on thoroughly sound lines. The gross profits for the year to December 31, 1905, after providing for bad and doubtful debts, amounted to £310,172. The Ceylon business is not shown separately on the balance-sheet; but this branch of the institution no doubt contributes in no small degree to the satisfactory results which, year by year, make such pleasant reading for the shareholders.

Mr. **D. R. Marshall**, the Manager in Ceylon of this great financial institution, was born in Edinburgh in the year 1862—just one year previous to the establishment of the bank in Calcutta. He was educated at the Royal High School in "Auld Reekie," and joined the head office of the bank in London in 1880. In 1884 he went out to the Calcutta branch. He also served two years in the bank's employ in Bombay and Madras. Mr. Marshall came to Ceylon in the year 1886 as Acting Accountant, and was appointed Manager in 1894. He is a member of the Committee of the Chamber of Commerce, at the meetings of which body his sound, shrewd counsel is much valued.

D. R. MARSHALL.

BANK OF MADRAS.

This institution was founded in the capital of the Madras Presidency on July 1, 1843, and was subsequently constituted and regulated by the Presidency Banks Act of India (No. XI. of 1876). The total capital amounts to 60 lakhs of rupees, and there is a reserve fund of 32 lakhs. The affairs of this important financial institution—the head office of which is in Madras—are in a most flourishing condition; and the Ceylon branch transacts a large volume of ordinary banking business. The office of the bank in Colombo is in Baillie Street, in the Fort—or European—quarter.

HONG KONG AND SHANGHAI BANKING CORPORATION.

The Ceylon branch of this great Eastern financial institution was founded on July 3, 1892.

The half-yearly reports of the bank (which was established in Hong Kong in 1867) do not disclose the Ceylon business apart from the general operations of the institution. On the principle, however, that the whole not only includes the part, but that the part is also reflected in the whole, it may be assumed that the Ceylon branch is in a highly flourishing condition; for the report of all operations for the half-year ended December 31, 1905, revealed a very satisfactory state of affairs. The profits for the half-year provided for a bonus of £1 per share in addition to a dividend of £1 15s. sterling on the shares of £28 2s. 6d. each. Besides this handsome return to the shareholders, the staff generally received a bonus of 15 per cent. on their salaries.

The headquarters of the Colombo branch are located in a central part of Queen Street, and here all the usual business of a leading exchange bank is transacted.

Mr. **W. Reid** is the present local Manager. Born in Ireland in the year 1866, and educated in that island, he joined the bank over twenty years ago, and subsequently served in many of its branches in China. He came to Ceylon only a few months ago to fill the position of Manager in the island. He is a keen sportsman, and in his younger days exhibited prowess in the football field.

W. REID.

CHARTERED BANK OF INDIA, AUSTRALIA, AND CHINA.

The Ceylon branch of this great financial institution—the headquarters of which are in Hatton Court, Threadneedle Street, London, and which has branches or agencies in every important trading centre in the Middle and Far East, and correspondents practically all over the world—was established in 1892, and the Colombo offices are conveniently situated in Queen Street, nearly opposite the Queen's House and close to the General Post Office. Here the usual business of a bank is carried on, and the volume of transactions is commensurate with the growth and prosperity of the colony. The directors' report, with statement of accounts, presented at the fifty-second ordinary general meeting held on April 18, 1906 (the latest details with which we have been furnished), discloses a most flourishing state of affairs as regards the total business of the bank. The figures show a net profit for the year 1905 of over £342,000, including the balance brought forward from the previous year, amounting to over £80,000.

After giving a bonus of 10 per cent. on the salaries of the staff, this surplus provided for a dividend to the shareholders of 13 per cent. for the year, also for an addition of £100,000 to the reserve fund (already standing at £975,000) and of £10,000 to the officers' superannuation fund, besides writing £25,000 off the premises account and carrying forward a balance of £86,000. The capital of the bank, which is paid up in full, is £800,000, consisting of 40,000 shares of £20 each. The Manager of the Ceylon branch is Mr. William Dickson.

MERCANTILE BANK OF INDIA, LIMITED.

This institution—formerly the Chartered Mercantile Bank of India, London, and China—was established forty-nine years ago, and was reconstructed in 1893, since which time the usual exchange and banking business has been carried on with great success. The staff of the Ceylon branches consists of seven Europeans and fifty-five natives; and the headquarters in the island are located in Queen Street, Colombo, with sub-agencies at Kandy and Galle. In the capital city the bank owns fine premises close to Queen's House, containing on the ground floor the public office; strong-rooms, and the managerial departments.

It may be mentioned that the Mercantile Bank of India, which has an authorised capital of 1½ millions sterling and a subscribed capital of 1¼ millions (of which £562,500 is paid up), has just taken over the Bank of Calcutta, with the result that the main operations of the thus enlarged institution have been greatly increased. Mr. F. H. Yeats is Acting Manager of the Ceylon branch. The head office of the bank is at 40, Threadneedle Street, London, E.C.

NATIVE SYSTEMS OF FINANCE.

ASSOCIATED with the banking system described above, and an invaluable and almost indispensable feature of the commercial life of the island, is the financial system maintained and directed by the Chettys. The Chettys—or, to give them their full caste designation, the Nattu Kotle Chettys—are an influential and highly intelligent class of native merchants who are engaged largely in financial operations. They are spread all over Southern India, where for generations they have played an important part in the operations of trade. In recent times they have found scope for their energies in a wider field, and to-day are to be met with outside Madras, in centres as widely apart as Calcutta, Rangoon, Colombo, and Singapore, and other towns of the Straits Settlements. At Colombo they constitute quite a considerable community, and a large proportion of the purely native financing business is in their hands. The Chettys advance money to traders on bills which run from one to four months, and such bills are brought to the bank with their endorsements and discounted. In addition to the endorsement of the Chetty who makes the loan, the signatures of other Chettys appear on the document. These are in the nature of an additional safeguard against loss, but the standing of the Chetty who is primarily responsible is usually sufficiently high to make the transaction a perfectly safe one. Apart from bills there is a business done in demand notes, called "loans." These are signed by two or more Chettys, and the banks advance money upon them. The amounts so advanced are regulated by the standing of the Chettys who sign the notes. In appraising the credit of a particular Chetty the bank seldom errs. But as an additional precaution some institutions insist on a personal guarantee from their own "shroff," or head cashier, himself a Chetty. The transactions carried through annually under the Chetty system represent in the aggregate a considerable sum. For instance, a leading Chetty estimates that the total business done in Colombo alone in 1906 was from fifty to seventy lakhs of rupees. So elaborate are the precautions taken, and so great is the business aptitude and reputation of the Chettys, that the losses incurred by the banks are relatively small.

On an entirely different plane exists another system of native finance which calls for brief description here. Located in the island, principally in Colombo, is a rather numerous body of Afghans, who prosecute a combined system of trading and money-lending somewhat on the lines of the packmen who haunt back doors at home. They sell at extravagant rates cloth and other goods on the instalment system of payment, and at the same time give accommodation loans at usurious rates of interest. When the purchasers or borrowers as the case may be, are in default with their payments, the screw is mercilessly put on, and the arts of intimidation reinforce the arm of the law. Indeed, it is said that the fear of physical force is largely accountable for the success which these men have in exacting payment of their oftentimes monstrous claims. However that may be, the truculent-looking Afghan in his picturesque turban and robes, and bearing as an indispensable part of his equipment a heavy staff, is a sinister and familiar figure in the highways and byways of the capital of Ceylon.

EDUCATION

FROM the very earliest times there has been some system of education in operation among the people of Ceylon. The oldest form was that given in the Pansala schools, which are attached to Buddhist temples, and even at the present day a few of these and some seminaries for Buddhist priests are to be found in districts where the pupils study the Buddhist scriptures from ola or palm-leaf manuscripts, as they have done for centuries. The present system of education, which is under the control of the Department of Public Instruction, dates from the formation of that department thirty-seven years ago; but for a century and a half before the British occupation of Ceylon, in 1796, our predecessors, the Dutch, had founded an educational system which they placed under the control of a body called the Scholarchal Commission, consisting of about eight members, clerical and lay. During the whole of the eighteenth century there were not only Dutch schools in the principal towns, but also vernacular schools in all the most important parts of the country held by the Dutch, and in the latter part of the century the number of children at school in the Dutch territory averaged about 70,000. Mr. J. Harward, M.A., the present Director of Public Instruction in Ceylon, in an admirable and authoritative article on education in the "Ceylon Handbook" prepared for the St. Louis Exhibition in 1904, writing of this Dutch system, says:—

"Registers were kept in every school, and compulsory attendance was enforced by a system of fines. . . . Even those who had left school were obliged to attend at intervals for a further period of four years and show that they had not forgotten what they had learnt. The subjects of instruction were mainly religious, and the whole system formed a part of the policy by which the Dutch attempted to bring about the conversion of the entire population of their territories in Ceylon. Political machinery was utilised to carry out this policy, and a motive for conformity was provided by confining all offices, ranks, and titles to professing Christians. The motives of the Dutch Government in Holland seem to have been perfectly sincere, and many of their clergy in Ceylon showed real missionary zeal. But the Dutch Reformed Church of that date was not a type likely to be attractive to the Oriental mind, and it is probably not unfair to say that the efforts of its clergy produced very little in the way of real conviction. The schools, however, must have had beneficial effects, and tended to give orderly habits to a people who really required paternal government. The system certainly deserved most respectful treatment from the British when they took over the government of the country. Organised educational effort was not a familiar idea to the English in the eighteenth century; in England itself it was not felt to be any part of the duty of the State to maintain and direct a system of national education. It is therefore hardly a matter for surprise that no real effort was made to carry on this part of the work of the Dutch in Ceylon. The Rev. J. Cordiner, the Anglican chaplain to the first English Governor, was appointed Principal of all the schools in Ceylon, but no system was created for making his supervision operative. The Dutch Church was left intact and its ministers allowed to continue their work on reduced pay provided by the British Government. But the amount of the public funds available for education was reduced to a fixed total of £1,500 annually, and the compulsory attendance which had been the keystone of the Dutch system was abolished. Schools under clerical supervision continued to be maintained in the towns, but in the course of a few years rural education had ceased to exist. The loss was recognised and deplored by Government, but no step was taken to remedy it beyond reporting to the Home Government the lamentable lack of clergy in Ceylon. It looks almost as if the Governors of the period cherished the hope that, if only a sufficient number of clergy could be imported, the necessary minimum of education would go on of its own accord in Ceylon as it did in England. And in the course of time missionary effort did actually do a great deal towards supplying what the country wanted. During the earlier years of the British rule mission work was confined almost entirely to the Roman Catholics; but in 1812 some Baptist missionaries from England established themselves, and were followed in the course of the next six years by the Wesleyans, the American Mission, and the Church of England. All these bodies, English, Roman, and American, have made schools a prominent part of their work, and to their efforts the country owes a substantial part of such privileges in the way of education as it has enjoyed."

The difficulties which these missionaries had to contend with in their early efforts to educate native children were very great. When a schoolhouse was erected the wildest conjectures were formed as to its design. Some thought the children were to be enslaved, others that the boys were to be sent into the interior of the island or to some foreign country as soldiers; none could understand why men of another nation should come to them and, from mere benevolence, offer to feed, clothe, and educate their children gratis. With regard to the girls, the obstacles in the way were even greater. "It is not our custom," was the invariable answer given when the parents were asked to send their girls to boarding schools. It was considered a disgrace for a woman to be able to read and write, and at the present time it is officially estimated that only about 25 per cent. of the girls of school-going age are attending school.

In 1830 a Royal Commission of Inquiry visited the island, and, as a result of their Report, issued four years later, a Commission was appointed for the supervision and control of the Government schools that then existed, but no account was taken of the Mission schools, which were at that time seven times as numerous as the Government schools.

PHYSICAL DRILL AT A VILLAGE SCHOOL.

To quote again from Mr. Harward's article: "It was in connection with the higher education of Colombo that the interest of the Government in education first took a practical shape. The most important Government institution, the Colombo Academy, which still exists under a changed name as the Royal College, dates from 1835. It is perhaps more than a coincidence that this is the year of Lord Macaulay's famous Minute, which marks the decision of the Supreme Council of India in favour of a European type of education. The question had been in the air for some time, and though the Government of Ceylon had no official connection with India, the Governor was doubtless aware of the discussions which had taken place in Calcutta. But the actual establishment of the Academy has more the appearance of a happy accident than of a deliberate act of policy. The Rev. J. Marsh, M.A., had gone out to Ceylon as classical and mathematical tutor to the Kotta Christian Institution under the Church Missionary Society. He had, however, left that institution and had come to Colombo, where he acted as Colonial Chaplain at St. Paul's Church. and in 1835 started a private school for the sons of the upper classes among the Ceylonese. The school met a want that had been felt for some time, and the leading Ceylonese residents at once petitioned the Governor, Sir R. Wilmot Horton, to support it. The decision of Government was prompt, and was carried out with considerable liberality. In January, 1836, the new school became a Government institution under the title of the Colombo Academy, with the Rev. J. Marsh as its Principal. . . . No very advanced work was done, but the teaching was sound and thorough as far as it went, and the effect on the students was certainly good, and many of them rose rapidly to high positions in the service of the Government. The main cause of the success of the school was the high personal character of its first Principal, the Rev. J. Marsh, a remarkable man who had in a very marked degree the gift of rousing and maintaining noble aims among those who worked under him.

"The policy into which, after forty years of inaction, Government tumbled in this somewhat accidental fashion has much to be said for it. In the order of natural development the higher education of the few has usually preceded the elementary education of the many, and if a new education is to be artificially introduced, the best course, perhaps, is to begin by training a small section of the population very carefully under the best personal influences that can be brought to bear upon them."

In 1841 the Commission of 1834 was dissolved, and a board called the "Central School Commission for the instruction of the population of Ceylon" was established in its stead. This Commission was composed of four laymen and three clerical members, and as private educational efforts were recognised, considerable progress was made. But the labour of this body was essentially volunteer and the results spasmodic; and the conviction began to gain ground that the efficient control of the education of the country could not longer be assured at the hands of such a Board. In 1865, therefore, a special Commission of Inquiry was appointed, and its Report led to the abolition of the Central Commission, and in 1869 the administration of education was centralised in a department entitled the Department of

A SCHOOL GARDEN.

Public Instruction, with a Director at its head responsible only to the Governor. This is the system which obtains at the present day.

THE CADET BATTALION AT A CEYLON SCHOOL.

The first Director of Public Instruction was Mr. J. S. Laurie, who was succeeded almost immediately by Mr. W. H. Sendall, afterwards Sir Walter Sendall, G.C.M.G., who must be regarded as the originator of all the best work that has been done in Government elementary schools. His first step was to get Government to establish a normal school in which teachers could be trained both for English and vernacular schools. As teachers became available Government schools were established. In 1869 there were only 64 of them; in 1889 there were 431, with 27,677 children attending them; and in 1905 there were 554, with 70,715 children attending them. The policy of this new department was essentially unsectarian, and the system of payment by results in all schools for secular instruction only has been strictly adhered to, though it is worthy of note that the present Director of Public Instruction, in his Report for 1905, "regrets that no further steps have been taken towards the introduction of definite moral teaching in schools."

Unfortunately, the policy which established the normal school was not adhered to. At the time of the coffee disease, when the revenue was in danger, some expenditure had to be cut down. The English schools were among the first interests to suffer, and the normal school soon followed, and not until 1902 was this serious error of policy rectified.

To quote again from Mr. Harward's article: "The establishment of Government schools was only a small part of the work of the new department. The system of grants in aid was put on to a new footing, all sectarian regulations were abolished, and, provided that a certain number of hours were devoted daily to secular work, the Mission bodies were left free to give what religious instruction they wished during the remainder of the school hours. The result has been that side by side with the new Government schools in which religious instruction is not permitted, there has been a much more rapid growth of aided schools. This growth has been accelerated by the fact that the non-sectarian policy of the Government left it open to non-Christian bodies to enter into competition with the Christian organisation."

The following table, in which the figures include all registered schools, higher as well as elementary, shows the educational progress made during the last three decennial periods:

	Government.		Aided.	
Year.	Schools.	Scholars.	Schools.	Scholars.
1875	296	12,856	654	41,343
1885	429	26,624	856	58,918
1895	477	44,252	1,096	90,229
1905	554	70,715	1,582	156,040

Under the heading of elementary education Mr. Harward in the article afore-mentioned says: "Two questions suggest themselves—Does it include the whole population of school-going age? Is it good of its kind? The first question is easily answered. The number of children of school-going age depends, of course, on the duration assigned to the school-going period. In Ceylon six years may perhaps be assumed as a desirable average. The census for 1901 shows that if every child attended school for an average of six years there would be about 520,000 children at school. The total number of those attending schools of all kinds

A PANSALA SCHOOL

was 218,479. It would be a mistake to suppose that by subtraction we should get the number who are receiving no education at all. The fact is that many of those attending school do so for very short periods, and it is doubtful if the actual average of school life at all exceeds four years. Adopting this figure, it has been estimated that at the present time about three-fifths of the children are getting something in the way of education and the remainder nothing. But there are still some large but sparsely inhabited districts that are almost entirely destitute of schools. Those who have read the earlier part of this article will have inferred that the quality of the education is of the most varied description. It may be granted at once that a large number of the unregistered schools are as bad as they can be. In Government and in aided schools the work is of a totally different description. In both there are strong inducements to efficiency. They are examined annually by Government inspectors, and on the results of the examination depend the grant of the aided school and the prospects of the teacher in the Government schools. . . . The Government schools had until quite recently one great advantage in most of the areas in which they exist: compulsory attendance enforced by means of the Gansabhawa, or village tribunal."

In 1905 a Commission on Elementary Education was appointed and its principal conclusions were: "That it is desirable that the male population as a whole should receive some elementary education; that in places where schools exist attendance should be made compulsory in aided schools as well as in Government schools; that a conscience clause should be adopted as a guarantee that religious instruction is not given to those whose parents disapprove of it; that in all parts of the island where the population is sufficiently dense the establishment of schools for boys should be made compulsory, and that improved local organisation should be in introduced for the purpose."

These recommendations refer to rural districts, and an Ordinance which will give effect to them is now under consideration in the Legislative Council. But the principle of compulsory attendance has already been adopted in the case of municipalities and small towns, and an Ordinance was passed in 1906 giving the necessary powers to the local authorities in such places.

A CLASS AT THE VEDYALANKARA BUDDHIST COLLEGE.

During the last few years a successful attempt has been made to make gardening a part of the work in Government vernacular schools. In each province schools have been selected in which the conditions necessary for successful gardening are present, seeds are supplied by the department, and the produce is divided between masters and boys. There are at the present time 106 garden schools.

Allusion has already been made to the first steps taken by Government and by Mission bodies for the establishment of institutions devoted to higher education. Since that time much progress has been made. In 1853 the Church of England founded, in close connection with the Cathedral, St. Thomas's College, which now has an honourable history of half a century of good work. Other Mission bodies have followed suit, and there are now four large institutions in Colombo, while Kandy, Galle, and Jaffna each have two or three colleges and high schools. Government has given a great impetus to the work of these colleges by providing annually a scholarship of £200 a year for four years, with outfit allowance and free passage to and from England. The scholar selected continues his education at an English University, Medical College, or Engineering College.

The biographical sketches of many of the prominent doctors, lawyers, and civil servants which are given in another part of this work bear testimony to the soundness of the education given in some of the Ceylon schools.

A further step in advance has recently been taken—two scholarships are to be given annually instead of one, and they are to be awarded on the results of the intermediate examination of the University of London in arts and sciences. All the larger colleges will thus be encouraged to carry on the instruction in arts and sciences in accordance with the regulations of the London University, at any rate as far as the intermediate examination. The University of London has aided this scheme by allowing the necessary examinations to be held in Colombo.

While the best of the secondary scnools are certainly good, it must be acknowledged that there are many so-called English schools which reach a depth of badness not easy to describe. The growth of English schools has been too rapid, and the supply of qualified teachers has not kept pace with it. The salaries offered in the large majority of cases have not been sufficient to tempt young men of ability to enter the teaching profession, and there has been no institution for training teachers for English schools. The result is that in a large number of the 159 English schools much of the instruction is given by persons who are not properly qualified for such work. This serious state of things the Government is now attempting to remedy by the establishment of a training college for English teachers, which was opened in January, 1903.

In their out-of-school life the colleges have attempted with some success to follow the model of English public schools. Cricket is played with enthusiasm, and some of the school teams can hold their own against the best English clubs. Football and athletic sports are being generally introduced, and in the elementary schools physical drill is a regular feature. A very promising cadet battalion was organised in 1902 by the late Director of Public Instruction, Mr. S. M. Burrows. It consists of seven companies, one from each of seven of the leading schools, and has acquitted itself most creditably in the annual volunteer camps.

In 1893 the Colombo Technical College was established, with twenty-five students, and three years later it was organised in four departments: civil engineering, surveying and levelling, telegraphy, and electrical and mechanical engineering. In 1901 an art department was added, and it now consists of the five departments named, and at the present time there are over two hundred students on its rolls. Permanent buildings on a large scale were erected in 1904, and opened in the following year.

In 1905 the total expenditure of the Public Instruction Department was Rs. 1,099,057·61 (£73,270), and the nett cost to the Government, after deducting sums credited to revenue on account of school fees and sale of books and stationery, was Rs. 1,058,998·52 (£70,600). The average cost to revenue of each pupil in Government schools in 1905 was Rs. 5·20 (6s. 11d.), while the average grant paid to each pupil in grant-in-aid schools was Rs. 3·65 (4s. 9½d.). In Government schools the cost of education is borne almost entirely by the Government. The only item of expenditure from which the Central Government is relieved is the cost of school buildings. These the village authorities have to provide and maintain as a condition precedent to the establishment of the school. No fees are levied in Government vernacular schools. In Government Anglo-vernacular schools a uniform fee is charged. In the first two standards the monthly payment is 25 cents per head of the boys learning English; in the fourth and fifth standards, 50 cents; and in the sixth, seventh, and eighth standards, R. 1.

In the Royal College the monthly fees are Rs. 5 in the lower school and Rs. 10 in the higher school. In the aided English schools the fees vary largely: some approximate to those charged at the Royal College, others to those charged in the Government Anglo-vernacular schools.

THE WELLAWATTE BOYS' INDUSTRIAL HOME AND ORPHANAGE.

This institution, which has been in existence about sixteen years, represents a very practical and necessary form of education. Its object is to teach useful trades to boys, whilst at the same time giving them an education suitable to the trade they learn. Half of each day the boys spend in the educational section of the school, and the other half in the industrial department. It is the largest school of its kind in Ceylon, having nearly 150 boys who are wholly maintained within its premises. They are admitted in their early years, and taught and trained until they are sixteen or seventeen years of age, when they are able to earn their own living at the trade they have followed in the school. The school is specially meant to help destitute boys, and to give them a good opportunity of growing into useful and honourable men. It is open to boys of any nationality or creed, the only condition of admittance being that it be a case of proved need. The home is a philanthropic enterprise rather than a charity, since it aims at teaching that a needy boy is not so much dependent upon the gifts of others as upon his own brains and hands. With this important principle in view the industries of the school are conducted on strict business lines. The work done is not mere sample work, but work that has to bear the criticism and competition of the market. The boys could receive no better apprenticeship than the Home gives them. The workshops are large, possess many machines run by power, and are always full of work, while the men under whom the boys learn are all skilled workmen. The business spirit dominates the whole institution, and there is therefore in the boy's environment everything that tends to make him smart and skilful. In the school boys learn their own vernacular, and English by means of the vernacular. There is a competent staff of teachers, and the school is subject to an annual Government examination and shows increasingly satisfactory results. The Home is under the general supervision of a Wesleyan missionary, and has an English manager and a large and capable general staff. It costs about £1,000 (Rs. 15,000) per year to finance the home. This sum is partly earned by the increasing trades of the school, but a large margin has to be provided for in other ways. The Wesleyan Missionary Society, which is responsible for the Home, subsidises it. Further, there is a Government grant on the educational results, and a generous local public subscribes to its funds year by year. These sources of income liquidate the yearly cost of the school. The trades taught are printing and bookbinding, carpentry and furniture-making, boot and shoe making, tailoring, rattan work, &c. The press is the largest vernacular press in Ceylon. The school holds the Government contracts for furniture.

The verdict of H.E. Sir Henry Blake, the Governor of the island, is that "the Home is doing an excellent work," and all who, like His Excellency, have seen the school for themselves bear similar testimony.

BUDDHIST EDUCATION.

BUDDHIST education on Western lines dates practically from the year 1880. In olden times, when this island was under its own kings, education seems to have been general and well patronised by the Government. The Buddhist temples served as schools for the young, and the work of teaching was carried on for the most part by the Bhikshus (monks). But with the occupation of the country by the English this system of temple education has gradually fallen into disuse, the change of circumstances demanding a knowledge of subjects not usually taught in the Pansala (temple) schools. Consequently until 1880 the education of the country remained almost entirely in the hands of the Government and the Christian missionaries. The children of Buddhist parents flocked to Christian schools for the sake of that secular education which had become necessary for their success in life. But, the main purpose of the missionary schools being conversion, a very large number of Buddhist children who attended them were induced to give up their ancestral faith. In fact, the Christian school became the most effective means of undermining the position which Buddhism held in this island. Matters were in this condition when, in 1880, Colonel H. S. Olcott, President-Founder of the Theosophical Society, arrived in Ceylon, and, as an avowed Buddhist, received an enthusiastic welcome from the Buddhist community. He had not been long in the island before he saw the peril that threatened the national faith from the side of education, and he at once pointed out to the Buddhists the supreme importance of educating their children under Buddhist influences. He proposed a scheme of Buddhist education which received the approval of the leading Theras (chief monks), and was readily accepted by the Buddhist public. That scheme has been in operation for the past quarter of a century, with results that must be described as eminently satisfactory from the Buddhist point of view. The Registrar-General, Mr. P. Arunachalam, M.A., C.C.S., in the last Census Report (1901) bears the following testimony to the vast change in the condition of the people brought about by the work inaugurated by Colonel Olcott: "The Buddhist has advanced at the same rate as the Sinhalese population (14 per cent.), but faster than in the previous decade (10·5), the result of increased Buddhistic zeal and propagandism in the decade, brought about mainly by the efforts of the Theosophical Society, founded by Colonel Olcott and Madame Blavatsky. Previously it was considered among Sinhalese rather fashionable to be thought Christians; and I have, in my judicial experience, known Buddhists taking their oath on the Bible as a matter of course. This is no longer the case. They are rather proud of their religion, and have even become aggressive to Christianity. . . . The Buddhists, too, show a considerable increase in the number of literates. In every hundred Buddhist males there were, in 1901, six literates more than in 1891 and eleven more than in 1881, while the proportion of Buddhist female literates (5·2) is twice the proportion of 1891 and nearly four times that of 1881. Of late years, thanks to Colonel Olcott, the Buddhist community has awakened from its lethargy and made great advance in the spread of instruction. There are now Buddhist schools throughout the island, under the management of the Theosophical Society founded by him, and really good work is done by them."

The number of Buddhist schools in Ceylon is at present about three hundred, of which no less than two hundred are under the management of the Buddhist Theosophical Society of Colombo. The total number of children attending the schools of the Society is 24,927, made up of 16,497 boys and 8,430 girls. A large majority of Buddhist schools are situate in country districts, and the teaching imparted in them is confined to the vernacular. But in the important towns there are English schools, chief among which are the Ananda College (Principal: Mr. D. B. Jayatilaka, B.A.) and the Musaeus School for Girls (Mrs. M. M. Higgins) in Colombo, Mahinda College (Mr. F. L. Woodward, M.A.) in Galle, and the Dharmaraja College (Mr. K. F. Bilimoria, B.A.) in Kandy. Students are prepared in these institutions for University and other public examinations. In 1904 the Government University Scholarship of the value of £200 a year and tenable for four years in a British University was won by a student of Ananda College. In all these schools, both English and Sinhalese, Buddhism is regularly taught to the children of that faith, and every possible effort is made to inspire all with a love for their country and a pride in the glorious traditions of its past.

No account of Buddhist educational work in Ceylon can be complete without a reference to the Pirivenas, or Oriental colleges, conducted more or less on the system in vogue in olden times. In these institutions, of which there are now quite a number, Sinhalese, Pali, and Sanskrit, as well as allied subjects, are taught. The majority of students are young Bhikshus, who also go through a special course in Buddhism and Buddhist philosophy. The best known Pirivenas are the Vidyodaya College, Colombo, and the Vidyalankara College, Kelaniyà, presided over respectively by the Ven. H. Sri Sumangala, Nayaka Thera, and the Ven. Dharmakirtti Sri Dharmarama, Nayaka Thera—the two foremost Oriental scholars in the island. These colleges are doing a great work, and are mainly responsible for the revival of interest in Orient scholarship which is in evidence at the present time.

THE MEDICAL DEPARTMENT

By Sir ALLAN PERRY, M.D.

THE earliest history of systematic medical practice in Ceylon dates from the third century B.C., when Asoka, the great Buddhist sovereign who promulgated the famous decrees, reigned in India. Many monasteries and hospitals were established by this monarch, and the priests of the day were also the physicians. The Buddhist doctrines, which according to tradition were first reduced to writing in Ceylon, specifically enjoin the wealthy to establish refuges for the blind, the destitute, and the sick and wounded of both man and beast, and these injunctions have ever been carefully observed by followers of Buddha. At the present day there are Buddhist priests who enjoy great reputation in the treatment of several diseases, notably dysentery and hydrophobia. Presumably there have always been native doctors in addition to the priests. We find them to-day, at all events, in great numbers, for the native doctor's profession is a popular one and attracts to itself many recruits. There are members of it who understand diseases common to the country, and their remedies, but the majority of the fraternity are charlatans.

The Portuguese occupation of the island contributed little to the local medical history. A brief description of the diseases which prevailed in Ceylon, written in 1865 by Juan Ribeiro, is, indeed, the only piece of literature bearing on the subject which has survived. The Portuguese priests and captains of companies appear to have had the medical charge of the garrisons of Colombo, Kalutara, Negombo, Batticaloa, Trincomalee, Jaffna, and Mannar. From this circumstance it may be pretty safely inferred that a regular medical department was not a part of the Portuguese establishment.

The Dutch records in regard to medical science are even more barren than those of the Portuguese. The sole reminder we have of the fight against disease in the period of their occupation is the site, sixteen acres in extent, on which the existing leper asylum is built. Tradition affirms that the original establishment on this spot was erected at the cost of a philanthropic Dutch lady—the daughter of a Dutch Governor—who was a victim to this disease, and who left her property to the Government in trust for the pauper lepers of the colony. There is no authentic record of the foundation of the asylum, but there is a stone on the premises inscribed with the word "Anno" and the year 1708. In a memorandum left by the Dutch Governor, Van Imhoff, he commends this institution to the care of his successor. Though, as has been stated, no certain information is available as to the state of medical practice during the Dutch occupation of the island (which extended from 1656 to 1795), we know that there were Dutch medical men in the island, because a Dr. Danielsz and his apprentice were summoned to the court of Kandy in 1739 to treat King Raja Singha for a bad leg. The result of the treatment is said to have been unsatisfactory.

The more authentic medical records date from the British occupation of the island. For half a century or more the military medical officers were responsible for both the military and the civil medical wants. This arrangement as regards the civil side was found unsatisfactory, and in the year 1858 the civil medical department was established independent of the military. The civil medical staff then consisted of 1 principal civil medical officer and 38 medical officers. Its strength at the present time is 1 principal civil medical officer, 140 medical officers, 247 apothecaries, 152 nurses, 114 vaccinators, 46 clerks, and 8 stewards. During the year 1905, 65 hospitals, 424 Government dispensaries and 142 estate dispensaries were in operation. 68,321 in-patients were admitted to the hospitals, with a death-rate of 9·80 per cent. 1,849,544 visits were registered at the Government dispensaries, and 2,497 serious operations were performed, with 88 deaths. The hospitals include a lunatic asylum, a leper asylum, a lying-in home, a women's hospital, and the ophthalmic hospital which is Ceylon's memorial to the late Queen Victoria. In addition, this year a clinic for tropical diseases has been established in a separate building in Colombo. Furthermore, there is a bacteriological institute and a medical college.

The gross expenditure of the Ceylon Medical Department in 1905 was:—

	Rs.	Cts.
Civil Branch...	1,449,264	90
Estates Branch	576,043	53
Total ...	2,025,308	43

The nett expenditure was:—

	Rs.	Cts.
Civil Branch...	1,187,897	43
Estates Branch	168,617	17
Total ...	1,356,514	60

The Ceylon Medical College was opened in the year 1870, but the establishment of such an institution was advocated as far back as

1852, during the governorship of Sir George W. Anderson, K.C.B. In the year 1887 the Ceylon Medical College was recognised by the General Medical Council of Great Britain, at a meeting of the Privy Council held at Osborne House, Isle of Wight. This recognition of the Ceylon Medical College by the General Medical Council confers on its licentiates the advantage of being registered as medical men under the English Medical Act of 1886. The course of study is for five years, at the end of which time, and after satisfactory examinations have been passed, the student is granted a diploma to practise medicine and surgery. Nearly all the officers of the Ceylon Medical Department have been students at the Medical College, and they pay from Rs. 800 to Rs. 1,000 for their medical education. There are 118 medical and apothecary students at present undergoing their course of training. The College contains lecture-rooms for male and female students, dissecting-rooms, laboratories, and two libraries. The Ceylon Technical College is in affiliation with the Medical College for giving instruction in physics and chemistry.

The teaching staff consists of the visiting medical and surgical staff of the General Hospital, Colombo, and lecturers specially appointed from Home for such subjects as practical anatomy, chemistry, physiology, physics, biology, pathology, and bacteriology. Recently the Council of the London University has recognised the lectures of this College in the subjects constituting Part II. of the preliminary scientific examination of that University, which examination is held locally.

In the year 1905 the Ceylon Medical College was incorporated by an Ordinance enacted by the Governor of Ceylon with the advice and consent of the Legislative Council of the island, and a Council of the Ceylon Medical College was created. In the same year an Ordinance for the registration of medical practitioners in Ceylon was enacted.

THE PEARL FISHERY

By JAMES HORNELL,

Late Marine Biologist to the Ceylon Government.

OF the world's great fisheries, none can compare either in point of antiquity or in the continuity of their prosecution with the Pearl Fishery of the Gulf of Mannar, whereof the portion belonging to Ceylon is now by far the more lucrative and famous. Three thousand years ago the Tamil kings of Southern India reckoned this fishery one of the principal sources of their large revenues, so much so that the chief of the pearling centres was second only to Madura, the capital, and was the residence of the heir apparent.

The pearl banks of Ceylon came into historic ken rather later—not, indeed, till the sixth century before Christ, a fact due rather to the absence of all historical data prior to the Aryan conquest of the island about 550 B.C. than to their non-existence. A gift of pearls by Vijaya, the leader of the invaders and first Sinhalese king of Ceylon, to his father-in-law, the Pandyan king of Madura, is duly set down with a list of other essentially Ceylon products in the Mahavansa, the Royal Chronicle of the Sinhalese. Such a gift bespeaks a settled fishery for pearls on the coast of his dominions, undoubtedly carried on by men of Tamil race, even as is the case to-day in large part; the Sinhalese themselves have never taken to this industry, their instincts being largely, if not exclusively, agricultural.

From the dawn of our own era historic references become frequent. In Rome, in the days of Pliny, pearls from the Gulf of Mannar were valued at a high price, and Pliny himself refers to this fishery as the most productive of pearls in all the world. Ptolemy and the author of the "Periplus of the Erythræan Sea" both knew its location well, and the latter gave definite sailing directions for the use of mariners navigating the gulf.

But it would take too long to recount all that adventurous Greeks, Barbary Moors, Venetians, and Genoese have jotted down of the wonders of the pearl harvest of these seas, in the centuries immediately preceding the arrival of Vasco da Gama off the Indian coast. Within a quarter of a century from this date the Portuguese, with a daring never excelled by any race, were in possession of the chief ports on the west coast of India and a goodly part of the seaboard of Ceylon. Sooner or later the great wealth of the pearl fisheries was bound to attract them, and so it was that in 1524, taking advantage of the hostility existing between the caste of sea-faring Hindu Tamils called Parawas, who from time immemorial had the conduct of the pearl fisheries under the king of Madura, and the energetic coast Mahomedans ("Moormen"), who had largely adopted pearl diving as their profession, the Portuguese entered into a pact with the Parawas by which this tribe agreed to work the pearl fisheries under their new masters in return for protection against the aggressive Moormen. An interesting sidelight on the character of the Portuguese is that an article of the treaty stipulated for their new subjects to become converts to Roman Catholicism. The Parawas kept most zealously to the faith so strangely adopted. Rome has no more faithful adherents to-day than this Indian community, which in part still remains under the Portuguese Mission, and remembers with traditional veneration the holy zeal of that prince of missionaries, St. Francis Xavier.

It is unfortunate that no official records exist

MEN CARRYING THE SHELLS INTO THE KOTTUS.

DIVERS AT WORK.

of the revenue derived from the pearl fishery under Portuguese rule. So far as we know, all such were destroyed by the Dutch when they ousted the Portuguese from Ceylon. Still, from stray scraps of information casually noted in diaries kept by several Portuguese soldiers of fortune—the great author of the "Lusiad" served in Ceylon—we have reason to infer that the revenue system adopted was to lease the fishing rights to local speculators, and that during their first century of power the fisheries were highly productive. From about 1600 matters appear to have been on the whole unsatisfactory. Corruption was rife in all departments of the administration; the flashes of chivalric action that illumined the rise of Portuguese power in the East were seldom seen; signs of decadence were increasingly apparent; as a result merchants kept away from fear of exactions of the officials, while the divers were impoverished by the exactions alike of Church and State. The fisheries languished, and when the Dutch expelled the Portuguese from their last holds in Ceylon, Mannar, and Jaffna, no pearl fisheries had taken place for several years.

In full possession of Ceylon, the new power set itself with characteristic thoroughness and method to develop the commercial resources of the island. One direction to which attention was turned was the pearl fishery, and in 1666 and 1667 fisheries were held off the Ceylon coast, conducted directly on behalf of the Government and resulting in fair profits. From this time forward the records were kept with exactitude, and formal regulations were drawn up to ensure both the regular and methodical examination of the pearl banks and a business-like conduct of any fisheries that occurred.

Compared with the facilities which the present day offers for the conduct of the fishery, such efforts were of necessity crude and imperfect, especially as in the early Dutch days prospecting arrangements were largely in the hands of the native headmen. Lengthy intervals between fisheries alarmed the authorities and led the great Dutch statesman, Baron Van Imhoff, then Governor of Ceylon, to the conclusion—paralleled by the decision of our Government this last year (1905)—that the revenue would gain greatly, and the management of the pearl banks be improved, if the fishery were not carried on directly by Government but rented out to a single individual. Accordingly the fishery in 1746 was conducted under the new system, and it was found so satisfactory by the Dutch Government that all subsequent fisheries were held in the same fashion.

So far as we can learn, the following fisheries were held during Dutch rule in Ceylon, producing the revenue shown, namely :—

In 1796, English rule replaced Dutch, and, as in the case with both the Portuguese and the Dutch, the early years of the new Government were characterised by rich pearl harvests. Fishery succeeded fishery with few breaks indeed from 1796 to 1809. From 1809 the fishery, although receiving more intelligent and careful attention than ever before, and in spite of better appliances and the aid afforded by more reliable charts, did not till recent years show the improvement that was expected. Spite of every care on the part of the inspectors, long series of recurring failures took place, cycles of good years alternating with longer cycles of blank years. Many reasons, some fanciful, others approximating more or less to the truth, were adduced from time to time; Governors repeatedly called for reports, and twice over, in 1857 and in 1865, a scientific inquiry was attempted, but with no practical result in the betterment of the industry. Finally, in 1900, after a continued failure of the fishery for ten years, the enlightened Governor of Ceylon, the Rigbt Hon. Sir West Ridgeway, decided again to appeal to science for aid, and upon the advice of Professor E. Ray Lankester, Professor Herdman, F.R.S., was asked to advise. Eventually he, in company with the writer as his assistant, arrived in Ceylon in 1902 to carry out investigations on the spot. Even at this recent date no exact data existed. Nothing was known of the habits of the pearl-oyster; the causes of its erratic appearanees and disappearances were obscure, and the origin of Ceylon pearls bad never received satisfactory study. The influence of varying conditions of environment were quite unknown. Even the question of whether the sexes were separate or united in each individual was open. To-day nearly all these problems have been solved, and the results of tbe researches appear in five bulky volumes published by the Royal Society.

PARTICULARS OF PEARL FISHERIES UNDER THE DUTCH FROM 1666 TO 1796.

Year of Fishery.	Government Proceeds.	Remarks.
	£ s. d.	
1666	4,913 15 11	Fished on Government account, giving net profit as shown.
1667	6,160 7 5	Ditto.
1694	5,264 16 1	Ditto.
1695	6,177 3 9	Ditto.
1696	6,331 18 4	Ditto.
1697	6,453 0 0	Ditto.
1708	8,848 0 0	Ditto.
1732	Not ascertainable.	An unproductive fishery.
1746	4,766 13 4[1]	Fishery rented out to adventurers.
1747	21,400 0 0	Ditto.
1748	38,580 0 0	Ditto.
1749	68,375 0 0	Ditto.
1750	5,940 0 0	Fishery of six days only.
1753	6,360 0 0	Fishery rented out.
1754	1,469 0 0	Ditto.
1768	Not ascertainable.	Very unsuccessful on account of bad weather.

[1] According to Schrender; £12,000 according to Lee.

We now know the chief causes which have prevented annual fisheries, and the general life-history of the pearl-oyster has been worked out in detail. As a consequence, measures can now be taken to counteract many of the adverse influences at work, and to decrease the number of naturally barren years. To attain such results large expenditure and a complete reorganisation of the methods and system was, however, necessary. The Ceylon Government was unwilling to face this, and accordingly decided to revert to the lease system recommended a hundred and sixty years ago by the most capable Governor which the Netherlands ever gave to Ceylon. The fishery of 1906 was the last under old auspices; the fishery is now leased to the Ceylon Company of Pearl Fishers, Limited, for a term of twenty years from the beginning of 1906, under conditions which bind the lessees to carry out a great cultural programme and costly permanent improvements. The rental to be paid is £20,666, or Rs. 310,000 per annum.

Scientific development and management will now have their opportunity. A huge scheme for the transplantation annually of many millions of young oysters from sections of the banks which are naturally unsuitable to others where the conditions are satisfactory, is to be carried out, while hard bottom is to be made over great areas where sand predominates. From the success that for years past has attended similar operations in Home waters when applied to the cultivation of the edible oyster, we need scarcely doubt that with good management eventual success will be attained. But progress does not only consist in the adoption of up-to-date cultural methods. The vast extent of the ground whereon new beds of pearl-oysters may naturally develop requires elaborate and thorough inspection if the risk of missing a valuable deposit is to be avoided, and in this section of the fishery most notable progress has been made during the past three years.

A scientific system—more exact, and utilising apparatus and knowledge undreamed of by the marine officers who till 1903 were entrusted with this vitally important duty—has been adopted, and already has afforded large additional revenue by the improvement thus effected on the old methods. It was inspection on scientific lines that endowed the colony with the fishery of 1904, resulting in a net profit of over £60,000 to the Government, a sum which would have been entirely lost had not scientific methods been requisitioned. And if we have one undoubted instance in respect of this fishery of 1904, how many of the blank years of the past might not have been converted into years of great profit had the present system been in operation! Apart, then, from the question of culture, times of increased prosperity are in store for the Ceylon Pearl Fishery by this enlistment of biological science in conduct of that great prospecting search for oyster-beds which is known locally as the annual "Inspection of the Pearl Banks," an operation as exciting in its possibilities as any hunt for a gold reef upon land—from day to day the quartering of sea-bottom, exceeding in the aggregate three hundred square miles in extent, may yield knowledge of an oyster deposit worth £100,000 of clear profit to be earned by a month's fishing! The responsibility upon the shoulders of the officer in charge is indeed a heavy one.

The following table gives the particulars of all fisheries held under British rule to the present date:—

PARTICULARS OF PEARL FISHERIES UNDER THE ENGLISH FROM 1796 TO 1906.

Year of Fishery.	Government Proceeds.	Remarks.
1796	£37,096 15 0	Fishery rented out.
1797	£123,982 10 0	Do.
1798	£142,780 10 0	Do.
1799	£23,319 7 6	Net proceeds, fished on Government account.
1801	Rs. 150,227	Gross proceeds, fished on Government account.
1803	163,154	Ditto.
1804	720,202	Gross proceeds.
1806	412,842	Do.
1808	842,577	Do.
1809	Rs. 272,463	Gross Proceeds.
1814	1,051,876	Do.
1815	5,842	Do.
1816	9,266	Do.
1820	30,410	Do.
1828	305,234	Do.
1829	382,737	Do.
1830	222,564	Do.
1831	293,366	Do.
1832	45,810	Do.
1833	320,896	Do.
1835	403,460	Do.
1836	254,395	Do.
1837	106,312	Do.
1855	109,220	Do.
1857	203,633	Do.
1858	241,200	Do.
1859	482,159	Do.
1860	366,816	Do.
1863	510,178	Do.
1874	101,199	Do.
1877	189,011	Do.
1879	95,694	Do.
1880	200,152	Do.
1881	599,533	Do.
1884	17,153	Do.
1887	396,094	Do.
1888	804,247	Do.
1889	498,377	Do.
1890	313,177	Do.
1891	963,748	Do.
1903	829,348	Do.
1904	1,065,772	Do.
1905	2,461,679	Do.
1906	1,376,744	Do.

The pearl banks appertaining to Ceylon are all situated off the north-west coast. They consist mainly of more or less level rocky outcrops from the surface of the wide and shallow submarine plateau occupying the Ceylon side of the upper end of the Gulf of Mannar. They stretch from the Island of Mannar to as

THE PEARL FISHING FLEET RETURNING.

THE STOCK OF OYSTERS AFTER THE FISHERY.

far south as the sea between Chilaw and Negombo. Most of the banks—párs or paars (a Tamil word meaning rocky bottom)—are in depths ranging from 5 to 10 fathoms. The shallow plateau over which they occur varies from some 20 miles in breadth in the part opposite Arippoo to some 4 miles wide in the southern section. On the western edge of this area there is a steep declivity, the sea deepening within a few miles from 9 to over 100 fathoms, which again leads abruptly into greater depths.

Each bank, and there are fully fifty in all, is known by a distinctive name, the majority of Tamil origin and going back beyond historic records. The most productive are the Cheval and Moderagam Párs ; until 1889 these yielded all the important fisheries of the past century. Since that year more exact inspection has brought other párs into economic importance, notably the great Muttuvaratu Pár, lying off Karativu Island, and the still newer fishery section named Kutiramalai Pár to the north-west of the point of the same name. The great fisheries of 1889, 1890, 1891, and 1906 were upon the former, that of 1905—by far the greatest in yield of which we have record—in large part upon the latter. From this and from various biological and physical evidence the conclusion has been come to that practically the whole of the area of the submarine plateau comprised within the 5 and 12 fathom lines between Arippoo and Chilaw is potential pearl-oyster bearing ground ; that almost anywhere oysters may occasionally appear and grow to maturity. But we recognise that the probabilities are greater in certain sections than in others ; the reasons are various and complex. Chief of all is the determining play of the water flowing over the banks at the times when the oysters spat, because the young oysters enjoy some days of a free swimming existence before settling down to a prosaic sedentary life on the bottom, and during this early stage are at the entire mercy of the current and drift. Again, some of the banks which appear well suited to bear oysters seldom or never bring them to maturity ; currents may deposit spat upon them, but when the ground is close to the edge of the submarine cliff that marks the 20-fathom line, the sea-turbulence of the south-west monsoon period sweeps them all to destruction by reason of their peculiarly exposed situation.

Oyster deposits in shallow waters have their own special enemies to contend with. On banks close to the 5-fathom line, as on the Kutiramalai and Moderagam Párs, hordes of greedy starfishes abound, destroying myriads. Other enemies comprise boring sponges, which tunnel the substance of the mother-of-pearl in a complex network of tiny chambers ; carnivorous molluscs that bore circular holes in the shell and suck out the contents ; octopods that first smother their prey before devouring it, and above all, hard-toothed fishes of several kinds—rock-fish (*Vellamin* in Tamil) and trigger-fish (*Balistes*) work havoc among beds of young oysters, while stony-mouthed rays or skate (*Rhinoptera javanica*) crush the thickest-shelled adults with perfect ease.

These latter fishes are gregarious, and consorting, as they do, in shoals, the damage they do has at times been sufficient to cripple a fishery. Fortunately such wholesale depredations are rare, and here comes in an unexpected consideration — source of continual anxiety to the pearl-oyster culturist as they are, these great rays are indispensable to the pearl industry; without them no pearls of the glorious "water" for which the Ceylon pearl is famous would be produced—none save those of misshapen and irregular form would be yielded, and the fishery would sink into insignificance.

During the investigation carried out by Professor Herdman and the writer into pearl causation, we found that the kernel of the great majority of "fine" pearls that we decalcified consisted of the dead body of a little globular tape-worm larva. Further inquiry showed that living facsimiles of this tiny parasite—smaller than the head of the tiniest pin—abound in a large proportion of adult pearl oysters. Eventually we demonstrated beyond the slightest shadow of doubt that the principal exciting cause in the production of an "Orient" pearl is the irritation caused in the mantle of the oyster by the death therein of one of these little parasites. How exceedingly rare an occurrence this is, is difficult to realise. I have dissected hundreds of oysters and counted thousands of living larvæ in their tissues—in the gills and liver they may swarm without apparent ill-effects upon the oyster's health—and in the whole lot I might find but a solitary cyst-pearl, as we name the pearls produced by this particular irritation. The ratio is probably not 1 in 1,000. It is on this rare occurrence, however, that the prosperity of the Ceylon fishery depends.

Another long and tedious investigation had next to be entered upon to make out the life-history of this exceedingly valuable parasite, and Professor Herdman and myself have little doubt that certain tapeworms living in the intestine of the oyster-eating ray (***Rhinoptera javanica***) are the adults of our pearl-inducing larva. Hence it is clear that any large reduction in the numbers of this fish will influence adversely the production of pearls and greatly decrease the value of the industry. At the same time a shifting of the balance in an opposite direction is equally dangerous, and when it occurs it may result in the wholesale depletion of a promising bed of oysters.

Until the present year, when the control passes into the hands of a private company, the system prevailing was for the preparations and actual fishery to be carried on directly by Government. Twice a year the banks were systematically examined, formerly by the Inspector of Pearl Banks, who was usually the Master-Attendant of Colombo, but since 1903 by a scientific officer termed the Marine Biologist. The chief object is to locate fishable beds of oysters, ascertain their condition, and estimate approximately the numbers available for fishing. Samples of from 10,000 to 20,000 are collected by the inspection staff of divers, and the pearl produce of these oysters ascertained. If found to average Rs. 10 or over per 1,000 oysters, the Government usually decide to proclaim a fishery in the ensuing February, March, and April—the usual fishery months. Advertisements are published broadcast throughout the East, in the chief languages in use by the divers and pearl merchants whose presence is desired. Details are given in these advertisements of the estimated size and duration of the fishery, the value of the pearl samples, and the names of the banks to be fished—the last a matter of infinite importance, for to buyers and divers the respective merits of the different banks have been the subject of practical attention for generations.

Till 1889 the fishery headquarters were at Silavatturai—the "port of the Pearl Fishery"—but since 1890, a new site, Marichchukadde, a mean and fever-stricken village on the desolate coast a couple of miles northwards of Kutiramalai Point, has been used whereon to build the fishery camp, on account of the better facilities it affords to the fishing fleet in its goings and comings.

In December this village waste is given over to a couple of hundred poverty-stricken villagers and to herds of half-wild buffaloes. Big game wanders freely on the confines of the village, spoor of elephant, bear, wild pig and deer meet the eye in the damp places of the jungle, while the cry of the jackal and the hum of the mosquito bear the restless company during the long watches of the night.

In January bungalows for the officials and storage sheds for the daily catch of oysters begin to rise, roofed and walled with the indispensable "cadjan"—the plaited leaf of the coconut. Rafters, beams, supports, all come from the jungle adjoining, a trade which, under the watchful superintendence of the Forest Department, becomes a source of considerable revenue to Government. Another month and a miracle is wrought. Steamers and innumerable sailing craft arrive daily from India and Colombo, disgorging a motley crowd of pearl merchants, oyster buyers, divers, petty traders, and coolies by the thousand. Every man brings his own cooking utensils, but no dwelling awaits his arrival. Each, in his own way, has to run up a cadjan dwelling before he can sleep in any comfort. By the magic of the cadjan and of bitter necessity a town arises within a night, and at the end of the week this pearl metropolis of the world boasts a population of from forty to fifty thousand—a city inhabited by workers only, without schools, but in other respects fully organised, with an ample police force, a sanitary corps, spick and span hospitals with a medical staff ready for every emergency, a magistracy, postal and telegraphic services, a Custom House, and even a Harbour Master's office.

The divers and boat owners who attend and work the fishery in conjunction with the Government do so on the share system. In return for permission to fish on the banks, the divers and boat owners agree to render to Government two-thirds of the entire catch, the remaining third being the remuneration given to the divers and boat owners.

Usually the fishing fleet sets sail for the

MAIN STREET OF THE FISHERY ENCAMPMENT.

banks at midnight, at which time a signal gun is fired. By sunrise the fleet, numbering sometimes nearly 250 boats, is at anchor round the old barque which serves as headquarters to the Marine Biologist and as mark vessel on the centre of the fishing ground.

The area over which diving is permitted is marked off prior to the fishery by means of flag buoys along boundaries, and the occurrence of the oyster patches is indicated to the divers by others of different colour.

Diving begins an hour after sunrise, when the mounting sun has dispelled the chilly vapours of the early morning. A gun fired from the inspection ship gives the signal to commence, and the reverberation has not died away before the low hum of thousands of voices rises from the boats, followed after a scarcely perceptible interval by the sound of a great splashing as a full half of the divers drop into the sea.

Of the men who attend as divers four types stand out distinct in race and characteristics—Christian Tamils from the little ports from Cape Comorin northwards to Tondi and Ammapatam, Mahomedan Lebbais or Moormen from the same locality, Malabars (Malayalim people) from Travancore and Cochin, and, lastly, a heterogeneous collection of Persian Gulf mongrels, exhibiting every gradation and blend from a full-blooded negro to men of clear-cut, handsome Arab features. All save the Malayalim divers, who plunge head foremost from a spring-board, descend to the bottom in an upright position, carried swiftly down by a weight on which they place their feet—a stone of forty to fifty pounds in the case of the local divers, a lead of not more than ten pounds in that of the Arabs. Each diver is tended by "manduk," whose duty consists in the care of two ropes slung over a rude rail above the side of the ship, and which are attached respectively to the diving stone and the oyster basket. When ready to descend, the diver, if he be a Tamil, adjusts the basket on the top of the diving stone and secures it in position by placing one foot upon it. He draws a long breath, closes his nostrils with the fingers of one hand, raises his body as high as possible above water to give force to his descent, and then suddenly releasing the loop that supports the stone, is carried swiftly to the bottom. An Arab diver closes the nostrils with a horn clip suspended from a cord slung round the neck. His descent is slightly less rapid than that of the Tamil, and this tends to lessen the danger to which the drum of the ear is subjected if insufficient time be allowed for adjustment to the heightened pressure on the sea bottom.

On reaching the bottom the diver steps off the sinker, slips the noose of the bag or basket round his neck and swims slowly over the bottom, transferring to his bag all the oysters he can see. Meanwhile his manduk has hoisted up the stone and adjusted its rope in position on the rail ready for the next dive. Almost as soon as this is done the diver below is ready to come to the surface, indicating this by a signal twitch on the basket rope. Instantly two munduks (the divers work usually in pairs, one in and the other out of the water) haul in the rope with the utmost despatch, the diver being drawn up with it. The bag is lifted over the boat's side, the contents emptied, and the bag returned to the diver, who after a few minutes' rest is ready to descend again. When a man has been in the water half an hour, and has made perhaps seven or eight descents, he is glad to get a rest and let his comrade take his place. It may be noted that by this system a single set of gear serves two men; in the old days a boat's capacity was stated as so many "stones," and when this is known the number of the divers is ascertained at once by merely doubling the number of these stones. In the Dutch days a tax or licence was placed on each stone employed at a fishery.

The weakest divers are the Malayalim men; 40 seconds is their average below water. The Christian Tamils are better by 5 seconds, and the Moormen excel this by another 5 seconds, 50 seconds being their average. The Arabs do much better and think nothing of 70 to 80 seconds in depths of 7 to 8 fathoms. The Arabs will go much greater depths than the others; whereas the Malayalim divers do not care to go beyond 7 fathoms, and the Tamils and Moors will work down to 9 fathoms. The Arabs find no difficulty in prosecuting diving at 14 and 15 fathoms, and even go down to 20 fathoms on occasion.

About mid-day, signal is made from the mark boat to cease work, and as this signal usually coincides with the onset of a brisk sea-breeze, the boats of the fleet lose no time in weighing anchor and starting shorewards. With favourable weather the foremost boats reach the shore by three o'clock, but occasionally head winds and rough sea scatter the fleet and make headway so difficult that many do not reach port till the following day.

Arrived at Marichchuikadde, the little port which forms the fishery headquarters, the boats line up in front of a huge palisaded enclosure—the Government kottu or oyster store. Into this the divers carry their individual catches, and, in a numbered section of one of the long sheds filling the interior of the kottu, throw down their oysters, dividing each lot into three heaps of approximately equal size. Soon a native clerk comes round and indicates the one which he allots to the diver as his share. The diver gathers up his oysters and moves towards a gate, here perhaps to have himself and his belongings subjected to an inefficient search for pearls stolen from the oysters when *en route* for the shore. Safely past this danger with his share of oysters and cleverly secreted pearls, the diver may either open the oysters himself, or more usually may dispose of them to petty merchants. Meanwhile the Government share of the various boatloads is heaped and counted; as soon as the approximate total is ascertained the figures are handed to the Government official in charge of the camp—who for many years past has been the Government Agent of the Northern Province. At 6 p.m. this official begins to auction off the day's total of oysters in lots at the option of the buyers, custom being not to put up a definite number of oysters, but to put up the rate per 1,000 oysters to bidding. If the oysters be of good quality bids may begin at about Rs. 50 per 1,000, and gradually creep up to say Rs. 70 per 1,000, beyond which no offer may be made. Then the auctioneer declares he will book a quantity of oysters at this price, and the names of a dozen may be accepted as buyers at this price, each naming the quantity of oysters he desires to purchase. If much eagerness be shown, the booking of purchases is stopped, and the rate put up again, when, if there is a general fear that there are not enough of oysters to go round, a considerable advance may be recorded. So the sale goes on till the total is exhausted.

Next morning the buyers pay into the Treasury the value of their purchases—it is a purely cash business—and receive orders upon the Government storekeeper in exchange.

The oysters received, coolies carry them into little enclosures close to the sea, which their employers have leased from the Government for the duration only of the fishery. Here the precious bivalves are thrown in heaps on mats and guarded with zealous care by the owners during the period of seven to ten days that must elapse ere they be ready to wash for the pearls contained. This preparatory process is a malodorous one, but it is not, as is commonly supposed, a process of rotting. Fly maggots are the active agents; the greater the plague of flies the more the maggots and the more rapid the "rotting" process. At the end of a week the oysters are usually mere empty shells, clean and free from smell. The owner now has them placed in a dug-out canoe filled with water. Coolies under close supervision pick out, separate, and rinse the valves till nothing is left at the bottom but a débris of sand, shell fragments, and pearls. This débris is gathered with religious care, spread in the sun to dry, and then carefully picked over for pearls—if possible by the owner's relations, for none others can be trusted! Picked out, the pearls are graded according to size and colour, and according to rules that have existed for centuries.

The bulk of Ceylon pearls find their way, in the first instance, to Bombay, where the majority are perforated and strung into ropes, in which condition they find their way to brokers and wholesale dealers throughout the world, more especially to London and Paris.

To-day we are on the threshold of what may prove great alterations and improvements in the conduct of the Ceylon Pearl Fishery, and much of what has been written above may prove of quaint historical interest to readers ten years hence.

A well-considered experiment in oyster cultivation on an immense scale is about to be tried ; all the suggestions that biological science can make are to be carried out, and we may face the future in the full assurance that if judicious management be linked to vigorous development on modern scientific lines, the venture of the Ceylon Company of Pearl Fishers, at whose head stands the man who of all living has done most for the advancement of Ceylon, will eventuate in such an improvement of the Ceylon Pearl Fishery as will double and even treble its value to the people of Ceylon.

JOHN I. SOLOMON, B.Sc.

Towards the close of 1906 Mr. John I. Solomon, an American inventor, arrived in Ceylon from the United States for the purpose of conducting experiments which, if successful, will revolutionise the pearl-fishing industry. Mr. Solomon's idea is to apply to living oysters Röntgen ray photography by a process which he has devised, whereby, without injury to the oysters, it can be discovered whether they contain pearls or not. The value of such a process developed on a commercial scale is clearly apparent, and the advantages over present methods are manifold. One of the most valuable results to be obtained by the successful working of this system will be the possibility of keeping alive, and the cultivation to a larger size, of oysters in which seed pearls are found, because the process will reveal not only which oysters contain pearls, but also the size of the pearls. In this way theft can be prevented, those oysters in which pearls are found can be used for propagation purposes, and the existing disagreeable and disease-breeding method of extracting the pearls will be abolished. At present, of course, these are more or less "castles in the air," but at the time of writing the experiments give every promise of success. Naturally a great deal of interest and curiosity has been aroused by Mr. Solomon's experiments, and their results will doubtless attract almost world-wide interest. The experiments are being financed by an American syndicate, of which Mr. Solomon is the head.

JOHN I. SOLOMON.

Mr. Solomon was born in New York in 1871, and educated at a public school, and at the City of New York College. After passing through the latter he entered the Massachusetts Institute of Technology, the great engineering school of the United States, and there, in 1893, he graduated as Bachelor of Science in the course of electrical engineering. He then actively followed the electrical profession, being employed by several large electrical corporations, and his last position before going to Ceylon was that of electrical expert to the General Electric Company. He has already patented several of his inventions, but his experiments in Ceylon are the most important he has yet undertaken.

RUBBER

By HERBERT WRIGHT, A.R.C.S., F.L.S.

GENERAL.

THE development of the rubber industry of Ceylon has attracted the attention of almost every one interested in tropical economic botany, and the prospects of its future have aroused the investing public to a degree which is described as being unparalleled in the histories of other products which have had their day. Planters are eager to experiment with soils in districts which have hitherto been disregarded. Efforts have been made to grow rubber-yielding plants in the north, south, east and west of the island at altitudes ranging from sea-level to over 5,000 ft. Already it is possible to say that certain species will only thrive under certain climatic conditions, and a centralisation of individual species over large areas having similar climates is now manifest.

At the present time but few Ceylon estates have large acreages of rubber-trees in bearing, and it is with surprise that one realises how keenly and thoroughly the methods of collecting, purifying, coagulating, drying, smoking, and forms of preparation have been already taken up in the island.

The amount of rubber annually exported from Ceylon is small, but the knowledge which has been so eagerly gained concerning its preparation, and the freedom with which it has been circulated, will materially help the industry and assist all to place it on a sound basis long before the large acreages are in bearing.

Rubber consists of the dried milk or latex of certain plants. In the temperate and subtropical zones several species possess laticiferous systems: the number of these in the tropical zone is very often considerable.

Plants possessing latex are distributed in various parts of both hemispheres, where they grow under a variety of conditions, sometimes on hilly land, sometimes on alluvial plains, and also in swamps and desert areas. Some of the rubber plants are shrubby in character, notably the Guayule (*Parthenium argentatum*); others have a climbing habit, such as *Landolphias* and *Willughbeias*; but most of those which are of considerable importance form large trees, often measuring nearly a hundred feet in height, and frequently over 9 ft. in circumference. To the last group belong the *Funtumia* trees of Africa, the *Castilloa*, Para, and Ceara rubber-trees of tropical America, Gutta Rambong and species of *Sapium* and *Palaquum* in the Indo-Malayan region.

In Ceylon a large number of plants are known which yield rubber of commerce. There are several species of *Ficus*, *Sapium*, *Bassia*, *Palaquum*, and *Willughbeia* which yield latices possessing high percentages of resin, and there are also several introduced species, such as *Palaquum Gutta*, *Payena Leerii*, *Sapium biglandulosum*, &c., which, though they yield varying quantities of caoutchouc, have not yet taken a place in the rubber industry of Ceylon.

The sources of rubber in Ceylon are mainly *Hevea brasiliensis*, Mull.-Arg., which yields the Para rubber of commerce; *Castilloa elastica*, Cerv., or Panama rubber; *Manihot Glaziovii*, Mull.-Arg., which gives the Ceara rubber of commerce; *Ficus elastica*, L., the source of Gutta Rambong, and the Landolphia vines. It is interesting to note that the three most promising forms of rubber in Ceylon—Para, Ceara, and Castilloa—have all been introduced from other tropical countries, and that at the present time not a single native or indigenous species is known in this island which promises to produce rubber in quantity and quality sufficient to make it a commercial success.

Though rubber-trees had been known for many years, it was not until about 1875 that they were seriously considered suitable for *experimental cultivation in Ceylon*. Various expeditions were sent out to tropical America by several countries, and this island ultimately obtained Castilloa, Ceara, and Para rubber plants in 1876 and 1877.

In the early days the planters appeared to have more confidence in their quick-growing Ceara rubber plants, but finding that they did not give profitable yields after a few years' waiting, they were either left to grow in the wild state or were cut down to make room for other products. Ceara rubber-trees grow well in many climates, and have been successfully reared in the dry, arid, northern parts as well as in the damp, cooler parts of the south of the island. This species grows from sea-level to over 4,000 ft., and has, at the present time, a wider distribution in Ceylon than any other introduced rubber-yielding species.

Castilloa rubber cultivation appears to have been taken up seriously at a later date, but at the present time, owing to difficulties in obtaining a free flow of latex and a sufficiently large quantity of rubber therefrom, is showing signs of being neglected, and on several estates is being cut down to make room for Para rubber-trees. Castilloa rubber-trees grow best where the temperature never falls below 60° F. and in districts with a well-distributed rainfall of at least 70 ins. They have been tried in the Kalutara, Matale, Dumbara, Peradeniya, and Passara districts, and, though they grow very rapidly in the first three years, do not appear

A PLANTATION OF "CASTILLOA ELASTICA" RUBBER-TREES.

(This is the rubber-tree of Central America, and is not such a favourite in Ceylon as the *Hevea brasiliensis*. The plantation shown is four years old, and the trees are 20 ins. in circumference. It is a handsome tree, but has a curious habit of shedding its lower branches as it grows, leaving a tall, bare stem. The rubber cannot be obtained till the tree is eight to ten years old, as in young trees the rubber contains too much resin, &c.)

to give as favourable results as those of Para rubber.

Para rubber-trees are being successfully cultivated in districts with a rainfall of 60 to 120 ins., and encouraging results have even been obtained in relatively dry districts, and in some with a high rainfall.

The Para rubber districts of Ceylon range from sea-level to over 3,000 ft., though the best results have been obtained below 2,000 ft., where the average annual mean temperature varies from 75° to 81° F. and the rainfall from 70 to 120 ins. Para rubber to-day appears to be the favourite, and the extension of its cultivation has been influenced or determined by the results obtained during many years of patient waiting and working. The opinions of many persons vitally concerned in the Ceylon rubber industry is that, where Para rubber-trees will grow, they can be cultivated as the mainstay of the estate.

The rate of growth and present immunity from pests of *Hevea brasiliensis* put it, in Ceylon, above *Funtumia*; its yielding capacity places it on an equal or even higher plane than the best *Castilloas*, and its hardy characteristics and response to the extensive use of the ordinary tapping knife appear to render it superior to Ceara and other rubbers. Para rubber-trees, as far as can be judged—in growth, hardiness, and yielding capacity—are superior to many other rubber-trees. The confidence in this species is not confined to Ceylon, but has spread to many islands and territories throughout the tropical zone.

Planters in the Indo-Malayan region are unanimous in their opinion, and trees of Ceara, Castilloa, and Gutta Rambong are often felled in order that Para rubber-trees may be planted or their growth encouraged. Africa, or at least the West Coast of that vast continent, will take as many seeds of *Hevea brasiliensis* as we can give, because it has been found to be superior to others native in that area. Even during this year thousands of seeds, for planting purposes, have been sent to Brazil—the country whence all our Hevea rubber seeds were obtained in 1876.

The cultivation of Gutta Rambong and *Landolphia* is in a backward state in this island, and it is not likely to develop at a rapid rate if considerable improvements are not evolved. Trees of Gutta Rambong are somewhat difficult to establish, and owing to the enormous size which they attain, are planted at very wide distances from one another, thus allowing only a small number of trees to each acre. A few estates at a high elevation possess a small number of trees.

The *Landolphias* are creeping plants, and must be grown among other trees if success is to be attained; they appear to thrive at Heneratgoda. Gutta Rambong trees and *Landolphia* vines do not yield good rubber until they are many years old, and do not appear to be regarded in Ceylon with as much favour as is even *Ceara* and *Castilloa*, and for the purposes of this article they may be disregarded.

The development of the rubber industry in Ceylon should not be associated exclusively with the fact that excellent rubber-yielding trees have been acclimatised.

The impetus to the planting of rubber-trees is partly due to the discovery of improved methods of tapping, of new paring and pricking knives, to information regarding the best frequency for tapping, and to the invention of machinery for smoking, coagulating, drying, and blocking of rubber. Simultaneously with these general improvements there has been a rise in price to over 6s. a pound for some samples of plantation rubber, and this alone has been responsible for much of the activity during the last few years. In 1892, when the price of some samples of plantation rubber was 2s. 10d. per pound, the planted area in Ceylon was only 400 acres. In 1903, when the price was 5s. a pound, 7,500 acres were planted in Ceylon; in 1905, when the price rose to 6s., the planted acreage rose to 40,000 acres; and now, at the end of 1906, when prices range from 5s. 3d. to 5s. 11d. per pound, Ceylon alone can claim over 100,000 acres of planted rubber, and promises in the near future to far exceed its already large acreage.

Rubber-trees are sometimes cultivated as a single product, and frequently very large blocks of land are planted with one kind only. On several estates the Para rubber-trees are interplanted with tea and cacao, and appear to give profitable results, especially with the latter product. Where the rubber is first planted alone it is customary, on a few properties, to plant catch crops in the form of chillies, cassava, lemon grass, cotton, and other products which may give a return during the first or second years. Where such catch crops are not used it is customary to regularly weed the whole of the estate, or to interplant herbaceous green manures (*Crotalaria* and *Vigna* species) or leguminous trees such as *Albizzia moluccana* and *Erythrina lithosperma.*

Before planting operations are commenced it is usual to cut down and burn the vegetation on the forest or chena land; the clearing is then lined and holed, and when suitable weather arrives the seeds or young rubber plants are put out. Ceara plants may be easily propagated from cuttings, but most species are in Ceylon grown from seed only.

Ceara, Castilloa, and Para rubber-trees are planted at distances varying from 10 ft. to 30 ft. apart, according to the local conditions prevailing. They require approximately the same distances in similar stages of their development. Each species regularly sheds the whole of its foliage after it is three to five years old, during the hot and dry part of the year. The Ceara rubber-trees remain leafless for several weeks or months, while the Para and Castilloa trees are leafless for only a few days or a couple of weeks each year.

Thirty-year-old trees of Para rubber often grow to an enormous size, producing stems 90 ft. in height and 109 ins. in circumference. They tend to produce taller trees, for a given age, than either Ceara or Castilloa. The Ceara rubber-trees, though they do not produce such tall stems as either Para or Castilloa, are characterised by a low and spreading branch system, and rarely grow to a height much above 40 ft. Castilloa rubber-trees are considered to require shade, and species of *Erythrina* and *Albizzia* have been used for such a purpose.

The methods adopted in tapping, collecting, coagulating, washing, and general preparation of rubber are somewhat similar for each of the three species. The latex is extracted from the trees by making incisions in the cortex or bark of the trunk and branches, this being done in such a manner as not to injure the trees. With Para and Castilloa rubber-trees the outer rough bark is simply cleaned by hand, but with Ceara rubber-trees it is often necessary to remove the thin, hard outer bark before tapping operations can be commenced. The incisions in the trees may take the form of a V,

A RUBBER NURSERY AND YOUNG PLANTATION IN THE SOUTHERN PROVINCE.
The trees are seventeen years old, and 20 ft. and upwards in height.)

a single oblique cut, V's joined by a vertical line to form a herring-bone arrangement, or long spiral lines. This operation is usually carried out on the trunk from the base to a

"HEVEA BRASILIENSIS," OR PARA RUBBER-TREE.
(A tree in the Royal Botanic Gardens, showing the fruiting branches and foliage.)

height of 6 ft.; occasionally the first branches and the higher parts of the trunk up to a height of 20 ft. are tapped. In each case the incision is made carefully, to avoid damaging the cambium, and the line is made on a gradient to allow a flow of latex along the lower surface of the line of excision from above downwards. Water, either from bottles or drip-tins, is allowed to flow along the cut in order to accelerate the flow of latex and to prevent coagulation from taking place in the cut.

In most of the systems of tapping the operator commences at the highest point and repeatedly pares off the surface of the lower edge of the bark (cortex) until he has completely stripped it to the base of the tree. At each paring or shaving operation only a small piece of the dried corky tissue is removed so as to reopen the latex tubes; on certain days, instead of paring the lower surface, a rotatory or comb pricker is used, the teeth of which penetrate the inner cortex and cut or prick the latex tubes. The tapping operation is performed at intervals varying from twice per day to once per month on individual trees. It is therefore obvious that by the method of extraction of latex at present employed the laticiferous system is temporarily depleted, cut and torn, and a large quantity of the bark or cortex is cut away. The latex tubes of Para and Ceara rubber-trees do not arise from internal tissues and push themselves into the cortex, but by a process of decomposition of the partition walls of the cortical cells. The bark or cortex, which is thus the mother of the future laticiferous system is, during paring operations, either partially or entirely removed from the tree at a time when the component cells possess reserve food material intended for the future use of the plants. The latex, as it issues from the tree, has a milky appearance, and in very dry weather is apt to coagulate at the point of issue or in the cuts.

When large quantities of latex have been obtained in the liquid condition, they are removed to a central factory. On arrival at the factory the latex often contains a large proportion of foreign matter, such as sand and pieces of bark. These mechanical impurities are removed by filtering the latex through thin porous cloth or by means of a centrifugal machine made to revolve at the rate of about 3,000 revolutions per minute. The latex thus freed from some of its impurities is then either accumulated in settling tanks or placed in coagulating receptacles. Sometimes it is smoked by being passed through an apparatus charged with the smoke from smouldering logs of wood which have been soaked in creosote; this operation is often considered advisable in order to prevent subsequent softening of the rubber.

In coagulating the latex different methods are adopted. In the first method it is poured into a barrel-like receptacle; acetic acid is added, and the apparatus made to revolve. The coagulated latex accumulates in the centre and the watery portion on the outside. When the latter is no longer turbid the coagulation of the latex is considered perfect and the rubber removed. In the second method acetic acid is added to the latex which has accumulated in large settling tanks and the rubber allowed to accumulate on the surface. The third method—often spoken of as the natural one—consists in allowing the latex to undergo ordinary putrefaction. If the latex is allowed to stand in any receptacle some of its constituents decompose and give rise to acidity; this is followed by coagulation, when the rubber rises to the surface.

The freshly coagulated rubber is soft, pliable, and spongy, and while in this condition is subjected to much stretching and washing. The washing machines in use in Ceylon consist essentially of pairs of metal rollers running at uneven rates. They are supplied with a pipe which delivers cold or hot water between the rollers. The rollers are usually fluted horizontally or spirally, and when the rubber is placed between them it is thoroughly pressed, stretched, and washed. The rubber, after it has gone through the rollers, is usually free from all mechanical impurities; the superficial or soluble ingredients are considerably reduced in quantity; it is often much torn and irregular in outline, and is subsequently passed through smooth rollers, there to be finished off as crêpe rubber.

Where the freshly coagulated rubber is not passed through a washing machine it is generally allowed to set in circular or rectangular receptacles, and is turned out in the shape of biscuits and sheets. In other cases the freshly coagulated rubber is cut up into thin strips or "worms," and at other times converted into a lace-like mass of thin rubber. But whether in the form of crêpe, biscuit, sheet, worm, or lace rubber, the prepared material possesses a large percentage of water, and hitherto the Ceylon planters have generally tried to remove this moisture in order to be able to ship the rubber in a dry state. The drying is usually done in hot-air chambers, supplied with the minimum amount of light and a good current of hot, dry air. The wet rubber is either arranged on shelves or hung up on strings, and is allowed to stay in this condition for a few days or weeks until the moisture content is less than 1 per cent. The time taken in the hot-air drying process is a great disadvantage, and a few estates are contemplating the introduction of vacuum dryers, which, by means of high temperatures and low pressures, enable the operator to

TAPPING AN OLD RUBBER-TREE ON THE FULL HERRING-BONE SYSTEM.
(The coolie using the "pricker." The small cups at the top of the cuts are full of water, which drips into the cut and keeps the milk flowing steadily into the pan until the bark is drained.)

sufficiently dry the rubber in a few hours instead of days. It is not unlikely that several planters will to a large extent dispense with the drying process and ship their rubber in large rectangular blocks containing as much moisture as the rubber which is exported at the present time from tropical America and Africa. Rubber possessing 20 per cent. of water may be sent over long distances without deteriorating, providing it has been properly treated with antiseptics.

The biscuit, sheet, crêpe, worm, lace, and scrap rubber is usually sent from Ceylon in rectangular boxes made to hold one or two hundredweight. Some of these, especially the biscuits, are difficult to pack, and in all cases a very large surface of rubber, per unit of weight, is exposed to the air. In order to overcome the disadvantages associated with the original and more recent forms in which plantation rubber is exported, several planters have adopted the "block" rubber devised by Mr. Pears, of Lanadron Estate, Johore. Each block of rubber is rectangular in form, and may weigh from 25 to 30 lbs. or even more. The block is made from partially dried crêpe rubber, but there is no reason why it should not be made from lumps of freshly coagulated latex, if the presence of moisture and antiseptics is not objected to by the Home manufacturers. Block rubber has also been made in Ceylon by pressing biscuits which had been kept in a dry state for several weeks, and though the immense pressure obtained by a large screw-press made a satisfactory block, the lines separating some of the biscuits could be distinguished. The great reduction in area exposed to light and air by turning out the rubber in block form is manifest from the fact that 100 biscuits, each measuring 8 to 10 ins. in diameter, and $\frac{1}{8}$ to $\frac{1}{4}$ in. in thickness, were pressed into one block measuring 12 × 12 × 5 ins. The weight of the block was approximately 26 lbs., and several such samples could be packed easily in one box for shipment. At the present time block rubber prepared from well-washed and partially dry crêpe rubber is in favour among Ceylon planters, though it may yet be necessary to make the blocks not quite so thick, but of larger area than those recently placed on the market.

HIGH TAPPING OF HEVEA OR PARA RUBBER ON THE HERRING-BONE SYSTEM.

(This method is adopted on some old trees. A light scaffolding of "giant bamboo" poles is fixed against the tree, and on this the coolie mounts and taps the bark.)

AN OLD PARA RUBBER-TREE TAPPED ON THE FULL SPIRAL SYSTEM.

(The bark is cut away in long spirals, encircling the trunk corkscrew fashion. To tap it the coolie pares away a thin shaving of bark, thus inducing the latex, or rubber milk, to flow.)

It cannot be doubted that the features on which the prosperity of the rubber industry depend are the yields of rubber obtainable and the period over which they can be guaranteed. Old trees of Ceara rubber have given from 65 to 169 grams of dry rubber each in a period of three to four months, whilst others have given an annual average yield of $\frac{1}{2}$ to 1 lb. of rubber per tree for a few years in succession. Trees of Castilloa have given somewhat similar yields, and it is generally conceded that an average annual yield of 1 lb. of dry rubber per tree is rarely exceeded by either of these species. Para rubber-trees, on the other hand, have given far more promising yields, and much information has been published showing the results obtained on private and public properties in various parts of the island. A yield of 1½ lbs. of dry rubber per tree per year for nine years has been obtained from a few old Para rubber-trees at Heneratgoda. Estates in the Matale and Kalutara districts have given an annual yield of ¾ lb. to 3 lbs. per tree, and during 1905 a known 138,655 trees yielded 189,743 lbs. of rubber Individual trees at Heneratgoda have given 2, 3, 8, 10, 11, 12, and 15 lbs. of dry rubber each in eleven months, when tapped on certain systems, and it would not be an exaggeration to say that thirty-year-old trees of Para rubber could be made to yield as much as 50 lbs. of rubber each in one year, at the sacrifice of the tree. The manner in which trees of Para rubber have yielded to the use of paring and pricking knives has occasioned much surprise, and though it is perhaps too early to make any definite statement as to the ultimate effects, the results have admittedly exceeded expectations.

OLD PARA RUBBER-TREES IN THE HENARATGODA BOTANIC GARDENS.

(This is one of the oldest plantations in the East, and the trees were raised from the first seeds harvested in Ceylon. The trees are the subjects of various experiments, and those tapped on the spiral system are seen.)

One of the most serious troubles to the rubber planter in Ceylon is the liability of the prepared rubber to become soft and sticky during the course of drying or in the packing-cases during transit. The rubber first becomes sticky or tacky in local areas. These sticky patches spread, and the whole biscuit or sheet may rapidly soften and become almost liquid. The change is supposed to be due to the development of bacteria which live on the sugary, proteid, or foreign impurities in the rubber or latex. Rubber obtained from the first tappings of young and old trees appears to be specially liable to become tacky, but the change is due to a disease which may appear on the best rubber prepared without smoking, and be spread by contact. Its appearance may often be associated with the use of impure water, or insufficient washing. In one case rubber from thirty-year-old trees developed tackiness along the lines where the rubber, when drying, had been in contact with strings of fibre. In order to keep this disease in check it is advisable to store and dry the rubber in dark rooms, and to effectively wash the freshly coagulated material. Any pieces of tacky rubber should be isolated, and the affected area either cut away or treated with formalin. Smoking the rubber and making it into blocks is also said to reduce its liability to become tacky.

The latex of most of the rubber is, as it issues from the tree, of a creamy white colour, faintly alkaline or neutral, and rapidly turns acid and coagulates on exposure to the air. By the addition of ammonia or formalin it may be kept in a liquid state indefinitely. The composition varies according to the age, season, and section of the stem from which it is obtained, but as a general average that from *Hevea brasiliensis* possesses 50 to 55 per cent. of water, 30 to 40 per cent. of caoutchouc, 2 to 3 per cent. of proteid matter, 2 to 4 per cent. of resins, and varying proportions of other constituents. The proportions of resins and proteids appear to be higher in the latices from Ceara and Castilloa rubber-trees. In the same tree the percentage of caoutchouc often shows a decrease in young trees, branches of old trees, or when obtained from the renewed bark of tapped areas.

During the coagulating and drying processes it is obvious that the main loss is water and ingredients of the latex which remain in solution in the mother liquor. When the rubber is subjected to washing

THE CEYLON RUBBER "BISCUIT."

(The Ceylon rubber "biscuit" is well known through the factories of the world. The "milk" is left overnight in enamelled pans, and in the morning the cake of fresh white spongy rubber is rolled out flat, and then dried in the factory.)

and rolling, superficial and soluble ingredients are also largely removed, so that the proportionate composition of the final dry product may be slightly different from that of the original latex. Samples of dried Ceylon rubber possess from 76 (Ceara) to 86 (Castilloa) and 95 (Para) per cent. of caoutchouc, from 2 to 12 per cent. of resin, 0·8 to 8 per cent. of proteids and other ingredients. By a change in methods of coagulation and preparation it is possible to considerably change the percentages of the caoutchouc and other constituents. The elasticity, resiliency, colour, and odour of Ceylon rubber vary according to the species, age of trees, and methods of preparation. Ordinary rubber reacts with chlorine, bromine, acids, alkalies, sulphur, &c.; it rapidly swells when immersed in water, and becomes sticky when subjected to high temperatures. Quite recently the desirability of colouring and sulphurising the latex before coagulation, and coating or mixing it with various mineral and fibrous substances, has been publicly discussed, but as yet no definite commercial importance has been associated with such changes in preparation and manufacture.

In connection with other products, especially coffee, cacao, and also tea and coconuts, the planting community have realised that pests of some kind or other usually make their appearance when large acreages of the same species are planted, that it pays to keep a sharp look-out for parasitic fungi and insect pests, and to attack them while their numbers are small. The rubber plants in Ceylon suffer from the attacks of root, stem, and fruit pests, but by isolating, spraying, excising, or destroying affected specimens the injurious insects and fungi are easily controlled. The list of insects and fungi known to attack the various parts of rubber plants from the nursery to maturity is a very long one, but up to the present none have been recorded which are incapable of being effectively dealt with.

In the early days of the Ceylon rubber industry, most of the rubber-producing species—Para, Castilloa, and Landolphias—were considered suitable only for places at or near sea-level, and even Ceara rubber-trees were tried mainly below 2,000 ft. altitude. Para rubber-trees were, whenever possible, planted along the banks of rivers, where, owing to occasional floods, the conditions in the Amazon Valley—the home of the *Hevea brasiliensis*—might be as nearly as possible imitated. Experience has shown that this species can be successfully grown not only on alluvial banks, but on poor cabooky and even swampy land, when the latter has been well drained. The climate and soil conditions under which it has been proved that our introduced rubber-trees and vines can be grown have aroused the interest of all persons and institutions concerned with tropical cultivations, and it would be difficult to forecast the ultimate effect which the publication of the results of our experience will have. Certainly every one now knows that there are thousands of acres which can be made to grow rubber-producing plants, not only in parts of Ceylon at present under forest and chena, but in the Malay Archipelago, West Indies, Africa, and South and Central America. Ceylon is under a disadvantage when compared with many parts of Africa and tropical America, as it does not possess any endemic or indigenous rubber-trees of value, and the whole of the forest has to be cleared and four to six and seven years allowed to lapse before any returns are obtained from the rubber plantations; whereas, in the forests of many other countries an immediate return is obtained from the rubber-trees already in the forest at a time when the price paid for rubber is very high.

DRYING PARA RUBBER "BISCUITS" AND "SCRAP" RUBBER.
(The drying is done on wire-netting shelves in the factory.)

The future of the Ceylon rubber industry is intimately associated with that of the countries just enumerated, and the developments in all parts of the tropics will require constant and close study. Rubber cultivation in other countries is rapidly developing into a science, and the areas possessing indigenous rubber vines and trees are being surveyed, exploited, planted, and controlled by men of high scientific ability. In these circumstances it becomes necessary for Ceylon to carry out its land selection and planting operations in the best possible manner, to continue exercising every care to eradicate pests as soon as they appear, and for all planters to use the latest results of research in their attempts to place on the world's markets the best specimens of rubber they can. The Indo-Malayan region alone may, in a few years, be able to turn out rubber from one quarter million acres, and by that time must be prepared to meet competition from all parts of the world.

Of the many introduced rubber-trees which have been tried in Ceylon, but few can authoritatively be said to give less favourable results than in their native homes. Certainly *Funtumia elastica* trees are annually defoliated by an insect pest, the Castilloa trees do not quite give the yields which were originally expected, and Ceara rubber-trees have, in Ceylon, to be tapped with care. Para rubber-trees, on the other hand, appear to be exceedingly hardy. Trees may be blown over and give off shoots which subsequently form upright stems capable of being tapped. Many can be made to yield several pounds of rubber, though their root systems are nearly all under water. The bark may be occasionally completely stripped without killing the tree ; and fungi and insect pests have hitherto not proved unsurmountable. The trees of *Hevea brasiliensis* readily produce large and paying quantities of latex of high quality, and the future difficulty will probably lie in supplying the labour necessary to take full advantage of the trees which have already been planted. Even to-day, on estates which have a few hundred acres in bearing, labour difficulties are experienced, and should it ultimately be proved that the trees will stand tapping every alternate day throughout the greater part of the year, the question of labour may become serious. The best results appear to be obtainable when the trees are tapped in a definite manner, and according to a certain frequency, and if it is necessary to continue such, it may possibly result in only a part of each estate being tapped during particular seasons. In any case, it appears very probable that the tapping operations will ultimately be limited to the first 5 ft. or 6 ft. of the trunk, and that the collecting of latex from above this height, involving a much increased labour force, will not be practicable.

It must be admitted that our experience of the effect of tapping, repeatedly extracting the latex, and excising the bark or cortex is still young. It is, however, well known that the extraction of the latex, and nothing more, means the removal of a liquid which contains the minimum of reserve food, and essentially belongs to what are described as waste products. The laticiferous system is not of vital importance to plants, and, indeed, most of the native species in the island thrive luxuriantly without any vestige of such a system. In those plants where latex tubes occur, the latter are not vitally associated with the more important structures of the cortex, though, in periods of drought, they may serve some useful purpose. Trees of Para rubber which have given 10 lbs. to 25 lbs. of rubber annually, or the equivalent of about 20 lbs. to 50 lbs. of latex per year, appear to be almost as healthy as others which have never been tapped. The bad effect of tapping cannot, at present, be solely associated with the removal of latex, but with injury done to the cambium or healing layer and the mutilation and excision of the cortex while in a living condition. At the present time the methods of tapping involve the gradual paring away of the cortex from above downwards, and, though systematic and satisfactory as far as we have gone, may be subject to much modification in the near future. From results which have already been published, it is probable that the extraction of the latex may be done by incising instead of excising the latex tubes ; the more frequent use of pricking knives and slower rate of bark paring. The rapid paring away of the bark is an unnatural process analogous to the treatment meted out to cinchona in the past.

An important question arises regarding the susceptibility of the renewed bark to atmospheric conditions and various pests. The renewed bark is not at first protected by a hard, corky layer, similar to that which covers the original tissue ; immediately following the removal of the bark in the paring operation a comparatively soft inner cortical tissue is exposed, which may prove to be less resistant than the original covering.

TAPPING PARA RUBBER.

(The scene is a low-country plantation with Sinhalese coolies.)

CACAO

BY HERBERT WRIGHT, A.R.C.S., F.L.S.

CACAO, often termed cocoa or chocolate, has been known for many years in Ceylon. At the present time it is cultivated in various parts of the island. It is essentially a seed product, and in this respect somewhat resembles coconuts, arecanuts, crotons, and other articles of export, and essentially differs from leaf products such as tea, or stem products such as rubber, cinchona, and cinnamon.

Cacao was cultivated previous to the sixteenth century by the Mexicans, but does not appear to have been known in Europe until about 1519. The seeds were first used in association with powdered maize, sugar, and various flavouring bodies, but are now manufactured into cocoa, chocolate, &c. The cacao-tree has been distributed to various parts of South and Central America, Africa, the West Indies, Samoa, Philippines, Java, Madagascar, Ceylon, and other countries.

There are several species of plants which yield the cacaos of commerce, the more notable being *Theobroma cacao, L.; T. bicolor, Humb. et Bonpl.; T. pentagona, Bern.; T. angustifolia, Moc. et Sessé;* and *Herrania balaënsis, Preuss;* but, as far as this island is concerned, only one species represented by many varieties —*T. cacao*—is largely cultivated.

The cacao plant is one which in its native habitat, in the forests of tropical America, is accustomed to the protection of large trees, under whose shade it flourishes. It is not what might be termed a hardy plant, being easily torn and uprooted by strong winds, and subject to many diseases. When in the young state, and often when mature, the cacao plants are usually grown under the shade of trees of *Erythrina lithosperma, Bl.*; (*Dadap*), *Albizzia moluccana, Miq.*, or in conjunction with trees of *Hevea brasiliensis, Mull. Arg.* (Para rubber); *Castilloa elastica, Cerv.* (Panama rubber); *Manihot Glaziovii, Mull. Arg.* (Ceara rubber), or in association with *Musa paradisiaca, L.* (banana), and other plants. When grown under very favourable conditions the plants may produce their first blossoms when only three years old, and on most estates yield a crop of fruit of value in their fourth or fifth years. Once the trees have produced fruit they usually continue to do so for many years, many of the best yields being given by trees which are twenty to twenty-five years old.

The relatively delicate nature of the cacao plant is against its profitable cultivation in all parts of Ceylon, though some varieties, owing to their hardier constitution, appear to be capable of being successfully grown in districts subject to drought or heavy rainfall. The cacao zone in Ceylon is practically limited to districts in the southern half of the island, especially those having a rainfall varying from 55 to 120 ins. per year and a mean annual average temperature of 75° to 80° F. Generally speaking, Para rubber-trees can be grown in all the cacao districts, and it is the recognition of this fact that has led to such a large increase in the acreage of cacao and Para rubber, as a combined cultivation, in the Polgahawela, Kurunegala, Dumbara, Kandy, Matale, and Passara districts.

It is curious to note that cacao, though first established in the Kalutara Botanic Gardens in 1819, has never been taken up on a large scale by planters in districts much below 500 ft.

CURING THE CACAO SEEDS.

(After the fermented seeds are washed they are spread in the sun to cure and thoroughly dry. During the few days they are exposed to the sun they must be repeatedly turned over to insure a good colour and even curing. Sun drying insures a good colour of a rich red-brown or chocolate.)

altitude. Nevertheless, in various parts of Central and South America, the West Indies, and Samoa, the best yields are often obtained in districts near or a little above sea-level. Most of the cacao in Ceylon is grown between 500 and 1,600 ft. above sea-level; but some large cacao estates are known to give good results up to 2,000 ft. altitude, and a few even still higher than this.

Notwithstanding the limited range within which cacao can be cultivated in Ceylon, it is surprising to notice that this industry has steadily developed, and is now represented by a total of about 34,000 acres. During the next few years there is every prospect of an increase in the acreage of cacao. At the present time the total of 34,000 acres is represented by 20,291 acres of cacao alone, 7,852 acres in rubber, 817 acres in tea, 2,056 acres in coconuts, and 578 acres of cacao and coffee. The importance of this industry, mainly managed by Europeans, is manifest from the fact that during the last ten years the value of the cacao exported from Ceylon was no less than Rs. 19,590,000, the year 1905 being responsible for nearly two and a half million rupees' worth of dried cacao.

A cacao estate, unlike one of coconuts, tea, or cinnamon, usually consists of a mixture of different species of plants growing on the same soil, some of which protect the cacao against excessive exposure to light and wind; others supply large quantities of food to the growing cacao, and many yield vegetable products of economic importance. It is generally accepted that when cacao-trees are grown alone from the beginning they produce their first crops earlier, but also degenerate earlier than when planted in conjunction with other tree forms.

THE YOUNG CACAO-TREE (NICARAGUAN VARIETY).

(Showing its appearance and vigour when it commences to bear, in its fourth year.)

A CACAO GROVE OR WALK.

The main feature which strikes the visitor to a good cacao estate is the shaded character of the plantation and the diversity in form and colour of the immature and ripe fruits. A heap of ripe cacao fruits is a pretty sight, with its colours ranging from yellow to red and green, its forms varying from that of a smooth melon to the long, attenuate Forastero, and rugged, stumpy Caracas. Sections through the fruits reveal pure white and also coloured seeds, mixed in various proportions.

The history of the cacao plant from seed to maturity is not without interest. Trinidad and parts of tropical America appear to have been the homes of most of the cacao grown now in Ceylon, seedlings usually being sent carefully packed in Wardian cases and despatched through Kew to the Botanic Department in this island. In some cases ripe fruits have been sent from various countries, but on arrival in Ceylon the seeds have more often than not been dead. From time to time interchanges of cacao seedlings have been made between Ceylon and other tropical countries, and various consignments have been sent to Trinidad, Queensland, Cameroons, Samoa, British Central Africa, &c. When trees have been established the planters select the seed supplies for planting from their own stock. The ripe fruits are taken from the heavy yielding and mature trees and broken; the fresh seeds, surrounded by a conspicuous white pulpy mass, are rolled in earth and exposed to the sun for a few hours at a time, until sufficiently dry, the exposure not destroying their vitality. They are then either planted out direct or placed in nursery baskets and reared until planting weather arrives. The seeds or seedlings are planted in areas the soil of which has been thoroughly overturned, and exposed to the sun for several weeks. The original holes are made at a distance of 9, 10, 12, and even 15 ft. apart. Between each couple of plants seedlings of Erythrinas, Albizzias, rubber-trees, or bananas are planted in order to shade the cacao plants in their young stages, and perhaps give a profitable return. Under such conditions the cacao plants thrive, and at the end of three or four years have a height of about 6 ft., a branch system measuring about 5 ft. in diameter, and a root area in relation to the latter. When of such dimensions flowers begin to appear, from which the fruits are subsequently developed.

During the first three or four years all parts of the plant show successive vegetative development, but once the flowers begin to appear certain changes are obvious in the periodicities of the various members. Prior to the cacao-trees yielding flowers and fruits, the foliar and root systems regularly increase, but after this stage has been arrived at the foliage is developed more during two special periods in the year, separated by an interval of about six months. The flowers and fruits appear abundantly during one or more periods, and the root development shows periodic activity in association with the above. Though all parts of the plant tend to show a definite periodicity after the sexually reproductive stage has been attained, there are also minor and irregular periods of activity during most months of the year.

When the cacao has reached maturity various operations become necessary, and seed selection, harvesting, shelling, washing, curing, regulating shade, manuring, sanitary measures, vegetative propagation, and collecting of by-

COLLECTING THE RIPE FRUIT FROM A "CARACAS" CACAO-TREE IN FULL BEARING.

(The high-grown pods are reached by a long-handled knife, or on some estates a light portable ladder is used.)

products become essential. Cacao, unlike many other tropical plants, lends itself to improvement in many ways, and the more important factors which are at present borne in mind by the Ceylon cultivators may be briefly described.

Seed selection, or the selection of the parents for the future plantations, must always rank of the first importance. The varieties at present cultivated in Ceylon vary in their rate of growth, yield, and quality of cacao, and may each be improved by careful seed selection. The varieties are all capable of being grouped under one species—*Theobroma cacao*—and may be very roughly classified as the (1) Caracas, Criollo or old Ceylon Red; (2) the Forastero; and (3) the Amenolado.

Caracas or Criollo cacao has long been known in Ceylon, and was among the more important varieties introduced many years ago. Trees of this variety are relatively small, and do not produce a large number of fruits, though the seeds usually fetch a higher price than those from the more prolific varieties. During the last ten years this variety appears to have been supplanted by the Forastero kind, but it is again coming into prominence on account of the high quality of the produce obtainable therefrom. The fruits are red when young, reddish-yellow when ripe, and have a rough surface divided by deep furrows; the base is usually wide and the apex short and blunt. The seeds of this variety are popularly believed to have been wholly white in colour when originally introduced, though at the present time there are purple and white seeds in the same fruit. Some fruits possess white seeds only (about 58 per cent.), others purple and white, but none have yet been observed to possess purple seeds only. Among a large number of fruits examined, Lock found 84 per cent. of the seeds were white and 14 per cent. purple, the rest being intermediate in colour. The seeds are usually plump and round in shape, possess thin skins or testas, and weigh on an average about 1·27 grams.

A form of cacao known as the Nicaraguan-Criollo cacao, capable of being brought to the productive stage in the fourth year, and possessing the largest seeds and yielding the best quality of cacao at present known, is being considered, and may play an important part in the future of the cacao industry.

The Forastero cacao, divisible into numerous sub-varieties, according to the shape and colour of the fruits and seeds, has been largely planted, especially in the last ten years. It is characterised by a quicker rate of growth, a more massive tree, and a larger yielding capacity than the Caracas, though its seeds or beans are not as highly valued as those of the latter. The most valuable form of this group is possibly that known as the Cundeamor, characterised by fruits possessing reddish-green walls and seeds of mixed colours. The fruits of Cundeamor never possess wholly white seeds, and thus differ from the Caracas group; about 61 per cent. of the seeds are purple and 37 per cent. white.

The Amenolado variety, probably the most cosmopolitan form at present cultivated in the tropics, is remarkable for the rapidity of its growth on soils of superior and inferior quality and its early and copious yielding capacity, but the quality of its seeds is very inferior. In Ceylon the fruits are green when young and yellow when ripe. In shape they resemble a melon. Each fruit possesses a constricted base, a blunt apex, and smooth wall with shallow furrows. The seeds are very flat and of a deep purple colour. This variety, analogous to the Calabacillo of Trinidad and other countries, is the only one which in Ceylon possesses 100 per cent. of purple seeds. Fruits of this variety having white seeds have not yet been recorded.

Cacao plants are not easily propagated from cuttings, but are capable of being grafted or budded on to one another. In this way a considerable improvement can be effected by grafting or budding the high quality Caracas and Nicaraguan-Criollo on to the quick-growing Forastero types. The latter have a much better developed root system than the Criollo, and would therefore provide a better food supply for the Criollo shoots. These practices are, however, not frequently carried out in Ceylon.

The harvesting of cacao or collecting of the fruits is carried out during almost every month in the year, and is especially interesting during those months when large numbers of fruits take on the colour indicative of ripeness. The fruits when ripe change colour, the green fruits becoming yellow and the red ones reddish-yellow. On tapping the wall of a healthy mature fruit a hollow sound is emitted, and by this test many coolies are able to detect internal ripeness of the seeds when the change in colour of the fruit wall is not complete. The fruits are obtained by cutting the peduncles or stalks with knives. Those on low branches are cut with an ordinary pruning knife, whilst those on the higher parts are cut by means of hooked or wedge-shaped knives supported on long wooden handles. In addition to ripe fruits, there are many others which are removed, among which may be mentioned the shrivelled or dried pods, those attacked by parasitic fungi or squirrels, and others which have been damaged by the fall of branches or excised

HARVESTING THE FRUIT.

(Tamil women coolies collecting the fruit on a cacao estate. A typical "Amenolado" tree.)

in the carrying out of sanitary operations. These are sorted into separate groups, and the seeds from each transported in separate baskets. The fruits are opened by means of a hand knife or by impinging them against a knife lodged in a piece of wood; the seeds are removed by hand, accumulated in baskets, and finally taken to the fermenting house.

The fermenting process is either carried out in heaps covered with layers of banana leaves, sacking, and earth, or in closed cement receptacles. The fresh seeds are surrounded with a sugary white pulp, and in section vary in colour from white to deep purple. In taste there is much variation, the flat purple seeds from the Amenolado fruits being very bitter, whilst the white seeds from Caracas and Cundeamor fruits, though astringent, are less markedly so. The object in fermenting the cacao seeds is to obtain a friable bean with a cinnamon or chocolate colour, pleasant taste and flavour, and to remove the superficial pulp. These physical changes are effected by allowing the fresh seeds to "sweat" or ferment in large quantities, with occasional stirring, for periods of one to twelve days, and are accompanied by various chemical changes involving the production of alcohol, acetic and butyric acids.

The time taken to effect a complete fermentation varies according to the condition of the fresh seeds, their quantity and quality. Those seeds which are white are fermented in twenty-four to thirty-six hours, but the purple seeds may require from three to twelve days; and for this reason the fruits, before being shelled, are grouped according to their variety, and the seeds therefrom fermented in separate heaps. During fermentation there is considerable loss in weight, more especially with the Forastero and Amenolado varieties, and the temperature often rises to over 40° C. When fermentation is complete, the seeds are removed and usually washed. In the washing process the residual stringy or pulpy material is removed, and subsequent drying is consequently more easily effected. Washing does, however, remove a large quantity of material, the estimated loss being on an average about 15 per cent., and for this reason is dispensed with by some Ceylon planters.

The fermented seeds, whether washed or not, are then dried in the sun, or in curing houses. Drying in the sun gives very good results, but cannot always be relied on. Any delay in drying the fermented seeds, especially when they have not been washed, may result in disaster, and for this reason each planter is usually provided with some form of drying apparatus.

The ordinary cacao curing house generally consists of a two-storeyed building, the floor of the upper storey being covered with coir matting on which the fermented seeds are placed. The hot air enters into the lower chamber, passes through the wet cacao, and the moisture-laden air is then drawn off by means of a fan. By this means the cacao is thoroughly dried, the cotyledons or substance of the beans become brittle and of a cinnamon colour, the change being effected in about three to five days, when the temperature is maintained at 90° to 100° F. The seeds thus fermented, washed and dried will not germinate, and after a little sorting they are packed in gunny bags, made to hold about 100 lbs., and shipped.

The Ceylon cacao is mainly shipped to the United Kingdom, though Germany, Straits Settlements, Australia, and France take large quantities each year. The cacao sells fairly well, prices ranging from forty to eighty shillings per cwt. according to the quality. The round, plump beans with a good colour and fracture, derived from fruits of the Caracas and Cundeamor types, realise the highest prices; the flat and purple beans from the Amenolado fruits have the minimum value.

The yield obtainable on Ceylon estates varies according to the age and variety of the cacao and the manner in which sanitary and manurial operations are carried out. A yield of half to three-quarters of a pound of dry cacao per tree is all that may be expected when the trees are beginning to produce regular crops. Later, a yield of one to three or more pounds of cacao per tree may be annually obtained.

A CACAO GROVE.
(A typical view of a cacao grove in a mixed low-country plantation of cacao and coconuts, and, along the roads, areca nuts.)

From a series of estates the yields per acre per year for each of the last few years have been 1·18, 2·07, 3·57, and even up to 5 and 6 cwts., a yield of 2 to 3 cwts. being usually considered satisfactory. It may be said that a cacao-tree yielding 2 lbs. of dry cacao per year brings in approximately the equivalent of about one shilling (gross).

HARVESTING AND SHELLING THE CACAO.

(The harvest time is always a very busy season on the cacao estate, for the pods or fruit must be collected at once when ripe. The collecting is done by men and women, who bring the different coloured pods, red, yellow and green, to a central place in the plantation and pile them in heaps. The pods are then split open with a knife, or cut on a knife-edge fixed in a board, as shown with the woman on the left, and then passed to another woman, who empties the seeds with their surrounding white pulp into baskets to be carried off to the factory.)

On most estates in Ceylon there are, besides the main product, others which give profitable returns. When the estate is young, bananas, chillies, cotton, cassava, lemon grass, &c., are often grown to give a return during the first or second years; in other cases the land is either regularly clean weeded every month or the seeds of herbaceous green manure plants, such as *Crotolaria striata* and *Vigna* species, are broadcasted and allowed to grow and cover the soil. Once the cacao estate has attained to the productive state, it is usually impossible to cultivate the catch crops just enumerated on account of the absence of sufficient light and root space. Cacao estates in bearing do, however, often possess large quantities of pepper (which has been allowed to climb along the stems of the shade trees), and also rubber from the Hevea, Castilloa and Ceara rubber-trees with which cacao has been interplanted.

The extent to which cacao and rubber-trees have been combined in various parts of the island is remarkable, and already good reports, from estates where both products have reached the bearing stage, have been published.

During the life of the cacao-tree the soil is continually drawn upon, and when the trees are in bearing the exhaustion is further increased by the complete removal of the crop of cacao from the land. On most Ceylon estates the fruit walls and prunings are returned to the soil, so that the actual amount of ingredients removed is mainly determined by a study of the incremental growth of all parts and the seeds removed. The seeds are very rich in potash and phosphoric acid; they also contain quantities of nitrogen, lime, magnesia, and other constituents in varying proportions. Though several estates have not yet taken up the practice of manuring their cacao-trees, there are several others which have, and the use of the requisite quantities of cattle manure, green manure, and various artificial manures has been attended with good results. At the same time it should be borne in mind that cacao-trees in Ceylon usually form a part of a mixed forest vegetation, intermingled with various leguminous and rubber-trees, and under these conditions the necessity for manures is modified.

Whenever the leguminous trees—***Erythrina*** and *Albizzia*—are grown in association with cacao, it is generally admitted that the artificial manures applied need not contain as much nitrogen as when the cacao-trees are grown alone, as they do, by means of their root nodules, absorb nitrogen directly from the air in the soil. The leaves of herbaceous and arborescent green manures are valuable as food supplies to the cacao-trees, especially when used in conjunction with lime, basic slag, and various concentrated mineral manures.

This brings us to the possibilities with the trees which are used to protect the cacao-trees from excessive exposure to light or wind. Experience has taught most Ceylon planters that the necessity of wind-belts and shade trees is dependent upon local conditions, and while both may be dispensed with under certain environments, the cultivation of shade trees in the cacao can always be advantageously carried out. Most products in Ceylon, especially those at low altitudes, appear to thrive better when grown under partial or temporary

HARVESTED CACAO FRUITS.

(The seed is gathered in baskets and the emptied pods or husks are collected and buried with quicklime in pits in the plantation.)

shade, the intermittent light being quite sufficient to enable the green leaves to carry on their work. The species most frequently used for this purpose are *Erythrina umbrosa, H. B. K.; E. indica, L.; E. velutina, Willd.; E. lithosperma, Bl.; Albizzia moluccana, Miq.; Pithecolobium Saman, Benth.; Gliricidia maculata*, and others.

Until quite recently it was customary to allow these shade trees to grow into very large trees, but during the past few years planters have regularly lopped, rung, and re-supplied trees previously used for shade purposes only. The branches are generally lopped at the beginning of the wet dull season—June—and allowed to throw out their branches right throughout the hot season, thus ensuring that the trees offer least shade when light is not intense, and the maximum shade during the hot dry season. The old trees are rung when from three to seven years old, so that only the cacao-trees are allowed to permanently occupy the soil. Such treatment assists the cacao plants, much organic matter is obtained, the soil is broken up by the roots, and diseases are better controlled. There are, however, a few estates where the old methods are still carried on.

In most countries where cacao has long been grown, parasitic fungi and injurious insect pests abound. Ceylon is no exception, and at the present time pests are known which attack (1) the stems and branches, (2) fruits, (3) leaves, (4) roots, (5) stems and leaves, and (6) the leaves and fruits. It is satisfactory to know, however, that when pests are taken in hand at the right time and in the improved manner, they can be successfully fought; the success which has attended the efforts made during recent years has led to the adoption of systematic sanitary operations being carried out on all good estates. The sanitary operations consist in excising and burning the diseased stem and branch tissues which have been penetrated by the canker fungus (*Nectria*) or borers, &c., the removal and burning of all dead branches which show signs of fungus or the attacks of insects, the isolation of cacao-trees whose roots are badly affected, and the frequent collecting and periodic spraying of fruits in order to reduce the ravages of the fungi which produce discolouration and rotting of the pods in all their stages. The excision and burning of diseased vegetative tissues are usually carried out during the dry hot season from January to April, and the spraying of the fruits during August to October, when the young pods begin to set. Almost every estate can claim to have effected great improvement by adopting curative measures, the crop gradually increasing with decrease in the ravages of various pests. As a good example may be quoted one property which in 1902 possessed 90 per cent. of diseased cacao-trees and harvested a crop composed of 35·5 per cent. of fungus fruits; sanitary measures—excision, burning, and spraying—were carried out, and in 1903 only about 6 to 10 per cent. of the trees were diseased, and the crop possessed only 2·3 per cent. of fungus pods; with this reduction in disease a remarkable increase in crop occurred, the yield during 1902, 1903, 1904, and 1905 being respectively 0·83, 1·18, 2·07 and 3·57 cwts. of cured cacao per acre. It is now fully recognised that all varieties of cacao growing in Ceylon are liable to diseases, and that only by repeatedly inspecting, excising, burning and spraying can the industry be maintained in a profitable condition.

At the present time cacao does not appeal to capitalists as much as many other products, and but few appear to be planting it alone. The discovery that cacao can be successfully cultivated in association with Para, Ceara and Castilloa rubber-trees has led to a great increase in its acreage, and it is mainly with Para rubber-trees (*Hevea brasiliensis*) that immediate future extensions of importance will probably lie.

In matters of cacao diseases and plant sanitation operations Ceylon stands in a satisfactory position, owing to the keenness and thoroughness with which the planting community pursue their work. In fact, it may be said that the Ceylon cacao planters, in associating rubber-trees with their product, and in successfully combating diseases, occupy a unique and enviable position in the eyes of cacao growers in other parts of the tropics. On the other hand, cacao growers in Ceylon do not appear to have adopted the practices of pruning and intercropping which are found to be so beneficial in other countries; neither does the same amount of attention appear to be given to the fermenting of their produce as in the West Indies and tropical America. Much improvement is likely to be effected by the distribution of varieties of superior value, by grafting and budding and by changes in manurial methods, as well as in the proper and more frequent use of leguminous plants.

WASHING THE CACAO BEANS.

(After fermentation the cacao seeds are washed in running water to rid the seeds or beans of the sugary pulp which surrounds them. The seeds are taken from the heaps of fermenting cacao, placed in baskets, and then washed by hand. The illustration shows the process, and the baskets of fermented seeds ready to be washed.)

THE TEA INDUSTRY

By M. KELWAY BAMBER, M.R.A.C., M.R.A.S., F.C.S.

TEA is not indigenous to Ceylon, but was first introduced in December, 1839, from India. In that year Dr. Wallich sent seeds of the then newly discovered Assam tea to the Peradeniya Gardens, and he followed up the consignment in 1840 by despatching about two hundred plants. It was represented to Government that tea was likely to prove a new and profitable speculation and a valuable source of revenue, and some of the plants were sent to Nuwara Eliya, and are supposed to be still in existence on Naseby Estate. In 1841–42 one or two planters imported plants from China and Assam, the former being planted on Rothschild Estate, Pussellawa, and the latter on Pen-y-lan, Dolosbage. The first tea was apparently manufactured in Pussellawa by Messrs. Worms, but the cost was prohibitive. The plants throve well, however, on Kondegalla, on the Ramboda Pass, at about 4,000 ft. elevation, and in 1865 the Ceylon Company, Ltd., took over the properties of Messrs. Worms, including the small extent of tea on Kondegalla. Attempts were made at the time to manufacture the tea by experienced Indian planters and Bengali coolies, but so little success was achieved that Ceylon planters generally did not take up the cultivation.

An exception to the rule was Mr. Taylor, of Loolecondura Estate, Hewaheta, who collected seeds from Peradeniya and planted them along roadsides in 1866. An experienced Ceylon coffee planter, Mr. Arthur Morice, was then sent to report on the Assam Tea Districts, a valuable report by him being subsequently published by Government. A consignment of Assam hybrid tea seed was then imported, and planted on Loole Condera, in a forest clearing of 20 acres. Although the cultivation of this tea met with a fair measure of success, it was not until Mr. William Cameron, an ex-Indian planter, so improved the local system of pruning and plucking tea as to show a wonderful difference in increased crop returns, that Ceylon planters saw sufficient inducement to cultivate tea on a large scale.

During 1873 and 1874 many plants of both the Assam hybrid and the China variety were distributed from the Peradeniya and Hakgala Botanical Gardens, and then large quantities of Assam seed were imported from Calcutta, but the comparative scarcity and dearness of tea seed helped to restrict the industry up to 1883, when seed became available from some of the older local plantations.

The prevalence of leaf disease, and afterwards of green bug, on coffee, and later the overproduction of cinchona, now caused planters to look to the new product in earnest, and a rush into tea took place, increasing rapidly from 1884 onwards.

The progress of tea cultivation in Ceylon is indicated by the following table :—

Year.	Acres.	Year.	Acres.
1867	10	1888	183,000
1868	200	1889	205,000
1869	250	1890	220,000
1872	260	1891	250,000
1873	280	1892	262,000
1874	350	1893	273,000
1875	1,080	1894	289,000
1876	750	1895	305,000
1877	2,720	1896	330,000
1878	4,700	1897	350,000
1879	6,500	1898	364,000
1880	9,274	1899	378,000
1881	11,350	1900	384,000
1882	22,000	1901	387,000
1883	32,000	1902	383,000
1884	37,000	1903	384,000
1885	102,000	1904	386,000
1886	150,000	1905	390,000
1887	170,000	1906	386,000

There are also about 3,000 acres of tea in native gardens. Owing to the large amount of rubber now planted amongst tea in the low-country, the total yielding tea area may now be looked upon as 380,000 acres.

The bulk of the area under tea lies at an elevation of over 3,000 ft., but it is planted at all elevations from almost sea-level to nearly 7,000 ft., on Excelsior Estate, Kandapola, this probably being the highest cultivated tea in the world. There is a great difference between the tea grown at low and high elevations, partly owing to diversity of soil, but more to climatic influences. Low-country teas are strong, without a distinct flavour, while high grown teas are remarkable for their good quality and usually fine flavour.

The soils of Ceylon on which tea is grown are very variable, ranging from the poorest quartz, containing less than 0·05 per cent. of nitrogen, to rich forest loams containing up to 0·5 per cent. of nitrogen. Almost all have been derived from the decomposition of gneiss and similar rocks *in situ*, there being practically no alluvial soils, as in Assam and other tea-growing countries. Chemically the average Ceylon soil is poorer than the rich volcanic soils of Java, or those of Southern India, and is also physically different to these and the soils of Assam; but although Ceylon teas have not the strength of some Assam teas, or the combined strength of Darjeelings, they hold their own as regards general fine quality, especially the teas grown in high elevations.

The climate of the various hill districts and low-country districts in which tea is grown is very variable with mean temperatures ranging from 65° F. to 85° or higher, and a rainfall of from 80 ins. to over 250 ins. To the south-west of the mountain ranges the climate is more uniform throughout the year than on the north-east, where there are more marked differences between the dry and wet periods and the tea is more subject to prolonged droughts. There are two seasons, the one during the south-west monsoon, when rain is more or less continuous, from June to September, on the hills facing south-west, while it is dry on the other side, the drought being often accentuated by high winds. The second season is during the north-east monsoon, from October to January, which is usually characterised, after the first burst, by fine mornings with heavy rain later in the day.

The effect of climate on the flavour of tea is very marked, the colder, less forcing conditions in the hills tending to check the actual rate of growth and allow of the fuller development of the essential flavouring constituents. During the months in which growth is more active, viz., March to May, and again to a less extent in October and November, quality decreases even in the highest estates, to reappear when the rate of growth is checked by less favourable weather. In the Uva district a few days of dry, windy weather will completely change the character of the teas, giving a flavour that enhances the value of the tea immediately.

Much of the tea in Ceylon was planted on the old coffee and cinchona estates, as the latter products died out or decreased in value, and of recent years it has been found necessary to manure artificially in order to maintain the yield. This is accompanied in most cases with very systematic cultivation of the soil, and careful and more scientific treatment of the bushes with regard to pruning and plucking, with the result that the bushes are now as strong and vigorous as ever, and show every indication of permanent improvement. It might be thought that quality would deteriorate when manuring became necessary, but experience has shown that this is not the case, provided the manure employed is not of too forcing a character, and the general aim now is to improve the physical conditions of the soil by green manuring and cultivation, and to manure sufficiently to give healthy frames to the bushes, and so make them capable of maintaining the best average yields before any manure was employed. A continuance of this policy will certainly make for the permanence of the industry, the most important in Ceylon.

The yields of tea per acre vary in every field of an estate, depending largely on the soil, jat, original planting, and subsequent treatment. It ranges from 300 to 1,200 lbs., but 500 to 600 lbs. would be a good yield, the average for Ceylon being about 450 lbs.

The planting up of shade and wind-belt trees through the tea, from about 1889 onwards, no doubt did much to improve the tea and probably minimised the risk of fungus pests to some extent. The trees employed for this purpose were chiefly the Australian *Grevillea robusta*, and at high elevations (*Acacia dealbata*) *Cedrella Toona*, and *Albizzia stipulata*, the growth of which must have considerably improved the appearance of the hill districts of Ceylon. Recently, *Albizzia Molucanna* and *Dadaps Erythrina* have been more widely planted throughout the tea, where the elevation is suitable, and kept pollarded to supply material for green manuring purposes, as the gain of nitrogen from these leguminous trees is very considerable, and the humus is particularly valuable for improving the soil.

Crotolaria striata is another native plant now much employed for the same purpose, and has the advantage of giving three or four crops before the trees yield anything.

The life of a tea bush is unknown, but in China there are many of great age, and in Java China jat bushes of sixty to eighty years are still flourishing. The same may be said in Ceylon, as the oldest field of tea on Loole Condera, now thirty-eight years of age, is still looking remarkably well, and continues to yield its 400 or 500 lbs. of tea per acre per annum without manure. Many fields of higher jat, such as "Assam indigenous," now over twenty years of age, are still as vigorous as ever, though cultivation has had to be given to maintain this condition ; but from the freedom with which they respond to careful treatment or resting, there is no reason why they should not be as permanent as the hardier China variety first imported into Ceylon.

The manufacture of the tea is less simple than it looks to any one passing casually through a well-organised factory, for to get the full advantage of the leaf every care has to be taken that the best conditions are obtained at each stage of the manufacture. To begin with, the carefully-plucked leaf is sent to the factory two or three times during the day, to prevent heating in the coolie baskets. It is then spread on the withering tats, in the lofts above the rolling and drying-rooms, in a way to insure a succession of leaf becoming withered to suit the roller accommodation. If this were not carefully arranged much of the leaf would be over withered or dried, and a less valuable tea would result. The loss in weight in withering varies from 30 to 45 per cent., or even more. The amount depends on the weather conditions when the leaf is plucked, wet leaf often containing 12 to 15 per cent. of rain water adhering to it. To remove this and promote more even withering, the lofts in most factories are filled with fans, by which the warm air from the drying-rooms below is circulated through the withering-rooms, enabling a good wither in from eighteen to twenty-four hours, the period in which the active enzyme, causing the later oxidation assumes its maximum development.

When withered the leaf is sent to the rolling-room in masses of 200 to 300 lbs., the product being emptied from the rollers several times to allow of the sifting out and removal of the finer grades, which do not require so much rolling as the larger leaves Every precaution is taken to keep the leaf from becoming unduly heated by friction, which would produce an undesirable dull soft liquor.

After rolling, the finer grades are put to oxidise in layers one or more inches thick, while the rolling of the larger leaves is continued. In the best factories every care is taken to insure cleanliness and almost sterile conditions for this process, special tables being employed. The oxidising enzyme now produces the well-known coppery colour of the leaf, at the expense of some of the free tannin compounds, and the soluble matter assumes the rich colour seen in an infusion of black tea.

During this process a peculiar aroma is also developed, which gives some indication as to when the oxidation is sufficiently far advanced for the leaf to have the remainder of its moisture removed in the drying or firing machines. Different conditions under which the leaf is plucked, wet or dry, the rate of growth, and the extent of the wither, all have a marked influence on this oxidation process, which requires modifications to meet them to obtain satisfactory results.

Modern machinery has superseded the old-fashioned chula system of firing, which was too slow for present-day requirements, though probably its effect on the teas was better than any system now employed. In the present machinery the leaf is dried on trays or travelling webs, through which a current of hot air is drawn by the aid of fans, or a natural draught. Here the leaf assumes the black appearance as it becomes desiccated, the change being chiefly due to the removal of the water, but partly also to increased oxidation and consequent darkening of the tannin and other products in the leaf before it becomes dry. The temperature employed in the various machines and factories ranges from 180° to 240° F. or even more, but about 210° F. is the most common, and the average time of drying from 25 to 35 minutes.

The grading of the dried teas is the next process, and is one of the most important, as the fact of being "true to grade" or the reverse may considerably affect the price. Machine grading is chiefly employed for the sake of time and economy, but it is sometimes supplemented by hand sieving with advantage.

The tea is then packed with the aid of a rapidly vibrating packing machine, which shakes the tea down compactly into the chests, so that pressing with the hands or feet is unknown; in fact, at every stage of the manufacture machinery has as far as possible replaced hand labour, with greater economy and cleanliness.

The work of a tea estate in the field and factory is done almost entirely by Tamil coolies from Southern India, under the direct superintendence of Europeans. About 400,000 coolies are employed, or rather more than one coolie per acre of tea. They are good workers, and are well looked after, medical assistance being rendered free. Their conditions of living and their power to earn money are far superior to those prevailing in their native villages, and most of them are able to save and acquire land out of their pay.

The serious diseases affecting tea are very few, and are now so well recognised that any new outbreak could probably be checked at the beginning without serious expenditure or loss. In some districts serious diseases such as Borea Xyloborus Cornicalus have now been prevalent for some years, and it has become a difficult matter to eradicate it, owing largely to the want of concerted action on the part of every estate affected. In order to try and effect a check on the spread of these or other diseases, a Plant Pest Ordinance will, it is hoped, be shortly passed, which would make it compulsory for immediate steps to be taken to eradicate disease whenever or wherever it appears.

There is a Government entomologist and mycologist in the Botanical Department at Peredeniya, whose duty it is to give advice on any insect or fungus pests, and point out the methods of prevention and cure, and their work has done much to produce the healthy condition of tea generally at the present time.

The exports of tea from Ceylon every fifth year from 1875, according to the Customs accounts, have been as follows :—

Year.	Lbs.	Value.	Average Price in London.	Average Price, Colombo
1873	23	58	Nil.	Nil.
1875	1,438	2,402	"	"
1880	162,575	150,641	"	"
1885	4,372,722	2,842,269	1s. 2½d.	"
1890	45,799,519	22,899,759	11d.	43½ cts.
1895	98,581,061	49,290,530	8·62d.	47 "
1900	149,264,602	53,735,257	7·20d.	34½ "
1905	170,183,558	59,564,250	7d.	34 "
1906	165,000,000 (estimated)			

The lowest average price in 1901 was 6·86d. in London and 33 cents in Colombo.

A tea cess of 30 cents on every 100 lbs. of tea exported is levied under special Ordinances, and is employed for the opening up and pushing of teas in the various markets of the island.

The chief markets to which Ceylon teas are distributed are :—

Country.	Distribution, 1905.
United Kingdom	112,620,026
Australasia	24,643,360
Russia	11,134,768
America	12,522,490
India	2,070,385
Africa	905,720
China	5,662,011
Other Countries	3,071,200

The area under tea has practically remained stationary since 1899, and although there is still some suitable land available, it is not likely to be opened up to any extent in the near future. No further forest land is available above 5,000 ft. for planting in tea, as it is reserved by Government for climatic reasons, and to insure a water supply to the low-country cultivators. In the low-country rubber planting is extending rapidly both in virgin forest and on many tea estates. The growth of the rubber in the latter, especially when closely planted, will in a few years considerably affect the yield of such estates, but to counterbalance this many up-country estates are considerably increasing in yield as the result of the more scientific cultivation now being conducted, and far more attention is likely to be paid to this in the near future than to the planting up of fresh areas in tea.

The custom of taking pupils or "creepers" on estates to learn tea planting in a practical manner still continues, and seems to be on the increase. No doubt this is largely due to the new rubber industry, which affords good openings to men of experience on tea estates who are good at the management of coolies. How long this demand is likely to last is uncertain, but judging from the careful supervision that is required when rubber comes into bearing, more Europeans will probably be required than is at present supposed.

COCONUT CULTIVATION

"IT is, perhaps, not surprising that new products should not greatly attract the native cultivator so long as he can plant coconuts. Tea and rubber, ground nuts and cotton, he looks on in the light of speculative investments, but planting coconuts in this province is to him what buying Consols is to the English investor." Thus wrote the Hon. Mr. H. L. Crawford in his Administration Report for the Western Province for 1905. The remarks are profoundly true if we substitute "was" for "is" in the last sentence, for the faith of the Sinhalese in coconuts is much deeper than is the confidence of the Home investor in Consols in these days of depressed markets. Certainly there is nothing which figures so largely in the native imagination when he is sketching his ideals of material happiness as a coconut plantation. And from his point of view he is right. Most products of the soil are affected by vicissitudes of season and by caprice of taste or fashion. But the coconut knows little or nothing of these. Year in, year out, it produces its fruit in regular quantity to satisfy an apparently inexhaustible demand. The trees take something like ten years to come into bearing after planting, but to compensate for this they live long and give little or no trouble during their existence. But their greatest virtue is their extraordinary range of utility. Practically no part of the tree or its products is unmarketable. Before the tree comes into bearing its leaves are plaited and used as partitions or roofs of houses, and the thin central stalk is used in the construction of serviceable household brooms. When the plant reaches the flowering stage it can be tapped for toddy, and toddy in its turn can be made to yield *jaggery* (a coarse sugar) or *arrack* (a potent spirit). Later on the fruit comes into consideration. When quite young the nut is full of a delicious, watery juice which is most refreshing in the torrid heat of a tropical day. With the beverage is associated a soft, pulpy lining which may be scooped out with a spoon and eaten with relish by the fruit-lover. In about twelve months the nut reaches maturity, and then the most important commercial stage is reached. The fresh nuts are vended in every village and in every street of the towns of the island. They constitute an important element in the local *cuisine*. The grated nut is indispensable in curries, and the milk is a favourite flavouring essence. On a larger commercial stage the nut figures in not less important *rôles*. The dried kernel, known in the produce markets as *copra*, is pressed and yields an abundance of oil, and the residuals, called *poonac*, constitute an excellent fattening material for animals. Large quantities of the nut are exported for use in the manufacture of soap, the vegetable fats it contains making an admirable emollient material. Latterly considerable consignments of the coconut products have gone to the margarine manufacturers of Belgium and Holland, who, like the soap-factors, have been glad to find a substitute for the increasingly costly animal fats upon which they once relied. The hard shell of the nut has little commercial value outside the island; but locally it is useful as fuel and for manufacture into spoons and other kitchen implements. The fibrous outer husk supplies the coir of commerce. Mats, brushes, and rope are made from it. Indeed, there are few materials which have a wider range of usefulness or are more extensively distributed throughout the countries of the world. Finally, there is the trunk of the tree. The coconut-tree is too valuable as a fruit pro-

THE PRODUCTS OF THE COCONUT-TREE.

ducer to be grown for timber ; but it produces a wood with a beautiful grain which works up well in ornamental furniture. Consequently, when a tree is blown down or has to be cut down for any purpose, the wood has a good marketable value in most districts. In any event it can be turned to good use for posts, the jambs of doors, and other kindred purposes on an estate.

In all these various ways the coconut-tree justifies its reputation as the most reliable wealth-producer the tropical agricultural world knows.

Although the coconut grows in such lavish profusion in Ceylon and bulks so largely in her commercial outlook, the coconut-palm is not an indigenous growth of the island. The tree is traditionally supposed to have been introduced from the Eastern Archipelago ; when and how it was brought to Ceylon can only be conjectured, but the history of the palm in Ceylon goes back to very ancient times. The Mahavansa, the great Sinhalese record, alludes to the establishment by a king who reigned in the sixth century of coconut plantations 36 miles in extent in the south of the island. There are also other references which point to the fact that in succeeding centuries the tree assumed an important place in the life of Ceylon.

GATHERING THE FRUIT.
(The start.)

No doubt the salubrity of the climate and the suitability of the soil greatly aided its diffusion. The tree grows readily on a wide belt of country fringing the coast, and once established, it needs little attention, though experiments made in recent years have shown that careful and systematic manuring is essential if the best results are to be obtained. Low-lying land, where the tree derives benefit from seepage, is hest adapted to its growth ; but it is thought that it might be introduced successfully in favoured positions on high ground if the proper degree of care were taken in the cultivation. Quite recently a plot of elevated land near Talawa, in the North Central Province, was opened up as the nucleus, if successful, of a large coconut estate which would depend on rainfall and not irrigation. The experiment, however, had to be abandoned owing to labour difficulties. Meanwhile, the area under the coconut-palm in districts known to be favourable to its cultivation is receiving wide extension. Both European and native planters are finding that the coconut, though slow, is sure, and with the prospect of increasing demands from Europe for the products of the tree, they are putting more and more of their capital into this branch of agricultural enterprise. The industry, however, is already one of very large proportions. It is estimated that not less than 700,000 acres are at the present time planted with the coconut-palm.

The produce of this area must be immense. Some conception of it may be formed from a calculation which is made by Mr. Edward F. Hopkins, Government Agent, Eastern Province, in his Report on the administration of the district for 1905. He says: "The exports by sea during 1905 amounted to 131,251 nuts and 36,022 cwt. of copra. Taking 200 nuts to 1 cwt. of copra, the nuts exported by sea amounted, in round numbers, to 7,300,000. Yet this number is but an insignificant portion of the annual crop. If we take 80 trees to the acre, and 20 nuts to the tree, the produce of the 31,308 acres planted with coconuts amounts to the prodigious number of 50,092,800 nuts. Assuming 50 nuts a year per head of population are consumed as food, the number for 153,522 people is 7,676,100. Thus something more than 15 million nuts are accounted for, leaving a balance of 35 million nuts to be exported by land, converted into coconut oil, and otherwise consumed. I am quite unable to account for this large balance." If we accept Mr. Hopkins's calculation of the number of nuts produced in the Eastern Province, we have a record of considerably over a thousand million nuts as the annual produce of the coconut trees of the entire island. Passing from the region of speculation to actual fact, we have in the official returns of exports interesting figures showing the enormous magnitude of the coconut industry and the important place it occupies in the world's markets. Taking the various products as they are classified in the Government Blue Book, we have the following statistics :—

DESICCATED COCONUT.

Quantity. Cwt.	Value. Rs.
184,039.	3,301,491.

PRINCIPAL COUNTRIES TO WHICH EXPORTED.

	Quantity. Cwt.	Value. Rs.
United Kingdom	98,204	1,735,993
New South Wales	2,074	53,543
New Zealand	1,711	32,943
Victoria	2,669	49,069
Austria	2,692	50,245
Belgium	4,931	93,733
Germany	26,026	451,968
Holland	4,285	71,629
Spain...	1,417	24,899
United States	35,918	658,634

FRESH COCONUT.

Quantity. Cwt.	Value. Rs.
18,115,165	945,894

PRINCIPAL COUNTRIES TO WHICH EXPORTED.

	Quantity. Cwt.	Value. Rs.
United Kingdom	12,536,630	655,807
British India...	131,407	5,235
Belgium	877,445	45,191
Egypt	3,065,539	162,489
Germany	1,309,026	65,810

COPRA.

Quantity. Cwt.	Value. Rs.
391,438	4,904,209

	Quantity. Cwt.	Value. Rs.
United Kingdom	6,865	77,111
Austria...	118,976	1,226,490
Belgium	14,799	149,196
Denmark	13,003	157,950
France...	44,725	999,038
Germany	150,824	1,833,234
Russia ...	40,786	446,265

COCONUT SHELLS.

Quantity. Cwt.	Value. Rs.
1,474	53,535

PRINCIPAL COUNTRY TO WHICH THE MATERIAL IS EXPORTED.

	Quantity. Cwt.	Value. Rs.
British India	1,473	53,515

The following table shows the total value of the exports in each case :—

	Rs.
Desiccated Coconut ...	3,301,491
Fresh Coconut	945,894
Copperah	4,904,209
Poonac	1,038,236
Coconut Oil ...	9,815,992
Coir Matting ...	5,615
Coir Rope	213,460
Coir Yarn	1,177,161
Coir (other) ...	3,555
Coir Fibre	927,672
Coconut Shells	53,515
Grand Total ...	22,186,800

COCONUT OIL.

Quantity. Cwt.	Value. Rs.
587,428	9,815,992

PRINCIPAL COUNTRIES TO WHICH EXPORTED.

	Quantity. Cwt.	Value. Rs.
United Kingdom	312,530	5,222,376
British India ...	40,125	670,489
Straits Settlements	1,294	21,622
Austria...	91,096	1,522,214
Belgium	9,784	163,491
Germany	8,842	147,750
Holland	5,038	84,185
Sweden	1,934	32,318
United States ...	114,091	1,906,460

COIR FIBRE.

Quantity. Cwt.	Value. Rs.
150,841	927,672

PRINCIPAL COUNTRIES TO WHICH EXPORTED.

	Quantity. Cwt.	Value. Rs
United Kingdom...	61,091	375,709
New South Wales	7,392	45,460
Queensland	2,476	15,228
Belgium ...	31,364	192,889
France ...	2,561	15,750
Germany ...	32,403	199,278
Holland ...	3,074	18,905
United States	4,160	25,621

GATHERING THE FRUIT.
(The climber at the top.)

COIR.

	Quantity.		Value.
	Packages.		Rs.
Matting	394	...	5,615
	Cwt.		
Rope	21,346	...	213,460
Yarn	107,700	...	1,177,161
Other	156	...	3,555

POONAC.

Quantity. Cwt.	Value. Rs.
265,993	1,038,236

PRINCIPAL COUNTRIES TO WHICH EXPORTED.

	Quantity. Cwt.		Value. Rs.
Belgium	99,619	...	388,866
France	4,003	...	16,000
Germany	162,317	...	632,953

It is noteworthy that during 1905 the United Kingdom only imported 1 cwt. of poonac, the value of which is given as Rs. 15.

In this list no account is taken of arrack, a considerable quantity of which is manufactured from toddy drawn from the coconut-trees, and the export of which in 1905 amounted in value to Rs. 115,829. Taking the figures as they stand in the list, we have the striking fact that the coconut exports very nearly reach one and a half million pounds annually. It is proverbially unsafe to prophesy, and the risk is especially great in the domain of tropical agriculture. Nevertheless, it may be confidently said that the returns will be still larger in the coming years. The virtues of the coconut are daily being more widely recognised. The soap, candle, and margarine manufacturers, and also the confectioners and biscuit-makers of Europe, the United States, and our colonies are making ever-growing demands upon the industry for a share of its products; and, meanwhile, the indispensable coir is finding extended fields for its utilisation. In this way a justification is being given to the shrewd business instinct of the natives of Ceylon, who cling tenaciously to their coconut plantations, and are ever seeking to extend their boundaries.

LABOUR ON ESTATES

BY EDGAR TURNER, SECRETARY OF THE PLANTERS' ASSOCIATION OF CEYLON.

AMONGST the most important problems with which the Government and the commercial community in Ceylon have to leal is the provision of labour for the cultivation of tea, cacao, rubber, cardamoms, &c. On most of the estates which grow these products the bulk of the work is done by Tamils from South India. The Sinhalese do a certain amount of felling and clearing work, and in some districts help to pluck the tea-leaf at certain seasons of the year, but they are uncertain and do not work regularly right through the year.

Trichinopoly, Madura, and Tanjore are the great recruiting centres in Southern India for the Tamils employed on the Ceylon estates. The service is a very popular one with the natives. High wages and constant work with good treatment are advantages which appeal powerfully to the South Indian native, to whom seasons of scarcity and consequent impoverishment are a recurring phenomenon. The consequence is that the Tamil villagers are flocking to Ceylon in ever-increasing numbers annually. They are a splendid labour force and give very little trouble.

The system of recruiting labour is peculiar, and may be described at some length. On every estate there are Kanganies who are in charge of the coolies, and they are in touch with their village in South India and keep the estate on which they are working supplied with labour. When labour is required Kanganies go over to South India with money to recruit, money being given to the relatives of those coming over to provide for their maintenance during the absence of their people in Ceylon. The coolie on arrival on the estate is entered in the register and becomes a monthly labourer. There is a special Ordinance in Ceylon designed to regulate the various questions of wages, &c. On the whole it has worked satisfactorily. To assist the immigration the Ceylon Government a few years ago inaugurated a system of tin tickets. Every estate using them has a registered number and letter, and a Kangany when going to the coast is given as many as he thinks he will require; and on the arrival of a Kangany with the coolies he has recruited in South India at Tataparai—a special camp about ten miles from Tuticorin, the port from which a steamer runs daily to Colombo, making the passage in about twelve hours—the Kangany shows his tin tickets, and they are registered. The coolies are then fed and medically examined and seen off by Government peons to the steamer. On arrival in Colombo they are again taken charge of by representatives of the Ceylon Government and conveyed by train to Ragama —a station nine miles from Colombo—where they are again registered, fed, and looked after, and the estate to which they are going is then advised by telegram of the train they are leaving by.

To further assist the immigration of Tamils, the Planters' Association of Ceylon in 1904 started a Coast Agency, with headquarters at Trichinopoly, in South India. The head of the Agency is Mr. Norman Rowsell, a Ceylon planter, who is called the Labour Commissioner. The estates making use of the Agency, instead of giving money direct to the Kanganies, keep the Labour Commissioner supplied with funds, and give the Kangany a form on which appears his name, village in South India, and caste and other particulars. This the Kangany in turn hands to the Central Agency at Trichinopoly, at which the Kangany is registered and given a certain amount of money to travel to his village. On his advising that he is able to recruit labour, money is sent to the nearest sub-agency to his village, and every assistance is given to him. On arrival at Tataparai he produces the necessary tin tickets, and he and his gang are then taken charge of by the representatives of the Ceylon Government as mentioned above. There is no indentured labour in Ceylon, and the coolie is free to come and go and move about at a month's notice, but before leaving any estate he must pay up the amount he owes either to his Kangany or to the estate. The daily wage of a Tamil man on estates is from 33 cents to 40 cents. The women get 25 cents to 30 cents. The women always make the best pluckers, the work being light. On most estates there is a head Kangany, who is in charge of all the labourers working on the estate, with sub-Kanganies under him, and the labourers work under the sub-Kangany. On some estates there are several Kanganies without a head Kangany. The sub-Kanganies draw from 2 to 4 cents from the estate for every labourer daily who turns out to work, and the head Kangany 2 cents daily for every labourer who turns out.

The estate finds the coolies in lodgings, which consist of rooms 12 ft. by 12 ft., called "lines." On an average three coolies live in each line or room. These rooms are very much better than their lodgings in their native villages in South India. In addition, all medical attendance is paid for by the estates.

SPORT

BY H. WOOSNAM MILLS,

CO-EDITOR "TIMES OF CEYLON" (AUTHOR OF "THE PATHAN REVOLT" AND "THE TIRAH CAMPAIGN").

"No game was ever yet worth a rap
For a rational man to play,
Into which no accident, no mishap
Could possibly find its way."

ADAM LINDSAY GORDON wrote these lines before golf had become a cult, and it is open to doubt whether he would have qualified them had he lived in these days, when the Royal and Ancient holds such an important place among the pastimes of the British people. So far as Ceylon is concerned, golf is the newest of all games, and its popularity dates from the English rather than the Scotch invasion of the island; for in the early days of Ceylon's planting and commercial interests, when Scotsmen were more numerous than Englishmen as settlers, the national game of Scotland had not been introduced, whereas horse-racing flourished and cricket was by no means unknown nor unpopular. When we find that the history of horse-racing in England is "wropt in mystery," it is not to be wondered at perhaps that there is no certain knowledge of the date of its introduction into Ceylon. It is a popular and easy assumption that horse-racing in England first originated at the precise moment when two energetic men found themselves side by side on high-couraged horses, which takes us back to the dawn of things in the nation's history; and we may safely conjecture, therefore, that the sport of kings as we know it in England had its commencement in Ceylon when the soldiers of King George definitely settled down to keep and to hold this outpost of Empire. There are no records of this that I have been able to discover, but we may be perfectly sure that in those early days, when men of our race commenced to write the British pages of the history of an ancient and civilised island, there were horse-races on the esplanade facing the sea. We have seen British soldiers hold a race-meet in the valley of Maidan after having lifted the *purdah* from this delectable retreat of the fierce Afridis; we have seen them organising a pagal gymkhana on the plains of Omdurman on the *lendemain* of a bloody fight; and from what we know of the sporting instincts of our ancestors it is anything but rash to assume that the officers of the British garrison in Ceylon were racing their horses one against the other in Colombo the whiles the Corsican was fluttering the dovecots of Europe and dipping his sword deeper into carmine than even the bloody revolutionaries had done in his vain, ambitious struggle to recolour the map of three continents. It may well be pointed out, however, that sport in Ceylon could not have begun with the British, and that an article dealing even briefly with the past history of the island should have something to say of the games and pastimes of the Dutch, the Portuguese, the Tamils, and the Sinhalese. There is ample literature, well authenticated, on the subject, but the briefest of references must suffice here. Chariot racing was well known in Ceylon from the earliest days, and fighting was done on elephants. Hunting was the royal sport, *vide* the chapter in the Mahavansa on the introduction of Buddhism by Mahinda, son of Asoka. The king, Devanampiya Tissa, was out hunting at the time. Cock-fighting was a favourite pastime with the Sinhalese. The Portuguese introduced the Carnival on Shrove Tuesday, and even at this date in Catholic villages in Ceylon rotten eggs and mud are thrown at people in jest. I cannot find that the Dutch, who contributed so much towards the industrial development of the island, introduced any sport of their own; and this is confirmed by a student of their times, who writes to me, not in the most complimentary terms, it must be conceded, that "the Dutch were too fat and too sleek to go in for games or pastimes." Of the Malays we know that they were the pioneers of football into Ceylon, although it did not resemble in any way either of the British games which are now in the very forefront of the sports of the island. So much for sport in Ceylon before the days of the British Raj.

Mr. M. H. Thomas, of Gallahena, Ceylon, the much respected proprietary planter, was one of the committee of the Ceylon Turf Club in the late sixties and early seventies, and in response to an application for some recollections of sport in those early days of which we have no written records, he writes me as follows:—

"Racing has been an annual institution in Ceylon from some time in the forties, but I think it was the Bakers, or rather John Baker, as thorough an all-round sportsman as ever lived, who first imported English thoroughbreds for racing and breeding purposes. He cut out a small circular training course round a hill close to his house near Nuwara Eliya, where he used to train his own horses and, what was more, generally ride them himself at the Colombo and Kandy races. He left Ceylon in 1856, but returned to the island with Mrs. Baker some years later, resuming residence at Magastotte, where he built a new bungalow. He was to be seen occasionally riding his own horses up to within a few years of his death, and must have been over sixty years old when he rode his last race on the old 'Galle Face' racecourse. And a nasty course it was—hard in dry weather and sometimes very heavy going in wet, with a couple of hundred yards of steep up and down at one end, and the dangerous turn near the garrison cemetery, which it was always a relief to get safely round, at the other. In the period from '55 to '65 the military and one or two planters were the chief contributors to such sport as we had; but more than one member of the Civil Service and of the mercantile community occasionally showed their colours. Sometimes, too, Indian stables were represented; indeed, some of the best horses we ever had in those days were sent down by the Arbuthnots and others. The planters' and military horses were for the most part Arabs, and were trained and ridden by their owners—but 'weight for age and class' races formed a part of every year's programme, and it was not considered then, as it is now, impossible to bring Australians and Arabs together, probably because Australians were far inferior and Arabs very much better than the class of horses running now. One instance at any rate may be recalled of an Arab beating three Australians—one of them, to the best of my recollection, a horse that had run that year for the Viceroy's Cup in Calcutta. The Raja of Ramnad presented a hundred-guinea cup—no rupees then—to be run for at the C.T.C. meet in Colombo, and sent his own horse, a milk-white Arab of 14.2, by name Nuseeb, to compete for it. The distance was three miles. The horses started at a common canter, and continued to keep that pace for half a mile, when the Australians all began to draw away, leaving the Arab more and more behind. After a mile had been covered, and when Nuseeb was quite a hundred yards in the rear, the Australians again increased their pace, and were soon racing together in earnest, with the result that, as far as they were concerned, the race was over a good mile from home and the Arab quite 400 yards from them. The latter had by this time been set going, however, and steadily decreased the space between them till, with nearly half a mile still to go, he challenged the leading horse and had him beaten a few hundred yards further on, cantering in an easy winner by eight or nine lengths.

FOOTPRINT.
(The winner of the Governor's Cup, 1906.)

"I was at the Colombo races a few years ago and was struck with the very little interest taken in them, notwithstanding the fine racecourse, the big fields entered, the number of events, and the much larger amount of added money given. Is it because there is less of the sporting element than there used to be in Ceylon men, or that the sport itself has become too costly for any but a few to participate in? Probably both causes have had some effect; but it seems at least doubtful if those who have made racing so expensive a pastime, by importing such valuable horses and such costly men to ride them, have done as much for real sport as distinguished from money-making as they have been credited with. We miss now the bright young regimental subaltern or the junior civil servant, both of whom had possibly ridden on the flat, or at any rate were good cross-country riders, at Home; whilst Heaven help the planter whom his V.A. finds indulging such propensities in the more work and less pay days we now live in. The polo ground is not without its share in the change, but this is not a rival which any one would dream of discouraging. It is a question if it might not be made an ally by devoting more funds to polo pony races. Arab racing could probably never be revived, but there is no prettier sport than three-quarter-mile heat races for Arabs, if there were plenty of them, as there used to be."

What an admirable picture the above is, giving us a comprehensive glimpse of those distant days when "that gentleman Coffee" held real court in this island, and before tea and the strenuous life had made their advent! Mr. Thomas speaks of the forties, but 1866 would appear to be the first year when the Ceylon Turf Club began to keep records. It appears curious that newspaper files should not have enabled information of earlier days to be collected, particularly as Colombo had an English newspaper so far back as 1834; but it seems beyond doubt that racing and sport of all kinds were viewed with disfavour by the conductors of that newspaper, and all hospitality was refused. The tyranny of the Nonconformist conscience is no new manifestation, therefore, in the life of the Empire, but it is noteworthy that probably a unique instance of its ravages should have occurred in the sporting history of Ceylon. This is all a thing of the past now, as Colombo, with its two evening and three morning daily newspapers, gives the fullest possible welcome to sport in all forms. The hostility, however, died hard, and not so many years ago the old tradition still so far prevailed in one office that it not only did not publish any news of local racing, but rigidly censorised Reuter's telegrams which gave the results of the Derby, the Oaks, and the St. Leger; whilst in this year of grace 1906 a Colombo daily newspaper still refuses to give the betting in Ceylon races, although it has relented so far as to publish it in English, Indian, and Australian races. To a newspaper editor and proprietor, however, very properly belongs the credit of redeeming past neglect which besmirched Ceylon's newspaper fame. Mr. Herbert H. Capper—whose lamented death at Home in 1905, at an early age, removed one of the best sportsmen as also one of the truest friends of Ceylon—set himself the task of collating past records, and it is to his efforts very largely that we know as much as we do of racing forty years ago. There appears to have been the greatest enthusiasm over racing in the sixties, and the big meet in September always extended over a week, with five days' racing.

NORTH BRITISH.
LEAH.
MERLOOLAS.

COMEWELL.
JACK O'LANTERN.

There is a vast deal that is entertaining and informative about the sport in those days; but I must only dwell on a few of the purple patches, and note but a few of the more important finger-posts which help to realise the conditions under which racing in past years existed. No times were kept until the year 1874, and in passing it may be permissible to observe that too much attention need not be paid to the times that have since been kept. The value of times is always very disputable; for how few are the timekeepers at small race-meets who know the rudiments of time-keeping, or who have a watch which is capable of clocking a race even approximately accurately! Those who dispute this can test the matter for themselves at the next race-meet they attend by comparing the times kept by, say, half a dozen of their friends whom they see with watches out when a race is about to be run. I see a soldier, Lieutenant Lawrie, was the first winner of the Crusaders' Cup, the blue riband of the C.T.C. meet, which, owing to its hampering conditions, became a terrible white elephant, resulting in a walk-over for many years, until it was finally painlessly extinguished by arrangement. The present American Consul won the cup in 1869, which reminds me of the fact that Mr. Morey had some time previous to that been landed off a ship in Colombo and taken to the hospital "to die"! The veteran is still with us, although he does not quite so regularly as of yore dispense cake and wine to the many who call at the Consulate to offer congratulations on July 4th.

Looking over the names of the members of the C.T.C. in 1871, there are few who are still with us in Ceylon, and few, indeed, who are alive. The first name on the list, however, is that of the veteran Walter Agar, still in Ceylon, the head of a brave and distinguished family. Of those still in the island we can only recognise F. J. de Saram, George John, Hon. Mr. F. C. Loos, Sir W. W. Mitchell, W. Mitchell, W. Morey, W. T. Saunders, Lieutenant-Colonel C. E. H. Symons, J. H. de Saram, C.M.G., M. H. Thomas, and J. Wickwar. Other well-known persons, some of whom are still alive to be honoured, are the Hon. Mr. H. H. Cameron, L. St. G. Carey, R. B. Carson, G. W. Carlyon, Henry Dias, Sir John F. Dickson, T. S. Dobree, A. and Charles Fetherstonhaugh, Sir John J. Grinlinton, James Gibson, J. A. Hayley, J. R. Hedges, L. F. Kelly, C. Layard, R. H. Morgan, E. H. Prins, G. W. Rudd, John Rogers, C. Harcourt Skrine, Duncan W. Skrine, H. S. Saunders, Sir F. R. Saunders, Charles Strachan, C. H. de Soysa, G. H. Vane, P. Vanderstraaten, J. Van Langenberg, and E. Wale.

I must find space for the first leaf of the C.T.C. rules of 1871:—

PATRON AND PRESIDENT.

His Excellency Sir Hercules Robinson, Kt., K.C.M.G.

VICE-PRESIDENTS.

Major-General H. Renny, C.S.I.
The Hon. Mr. H. T. Irving, Colonial Secretary.

COMMITTEE.

Armitage, H., Esq.
Barnes, J. W., Major, 73rd Regiment.
Bell, J. A., Esq.
Chapman, G. H. J. M., Captain, A.D.C
Charsley, W. P., Dr., P.C.M.O.
Crowe, R., Esq.
Douglas, the Hon. W. J., Auditor-General.
Drewe, F. E., Colonel, D.A.G.
Ferdinands, C. L., Esq.
Hook, Major, C. R. Regiment.
Saunders, F. R., Esq., C.C.S.
Thomas, M. H., Esq.
Trotter, H., Esq., P.M.G.
Vane, the Hon. Mr. G., Treasurer.
Watson, R. C., Captain, C. R. Regiment.

HONORARY SECRETARY AND TREASURER.

G. V. Lambe, Esq., at Colombo.
R. B. Donnall, Esq., at Kandy.
Turf Club Office, Colombo.
10 February, 1871.

The fields were almost always large in these days, and there was a good deal of speculation, which came to a climax in 1872, and threatened at one time to extinguish racing altogether. F. D. Mitchell ("Wild Dayrell" of the *Times of Ceylon*, who died last year at Home) came to the island in 1872, and he says of the crisis: "A few sparks were anxious to ramp the public by pulling old Cyclops for one race in the hope of winning another; but the sparks got ramped and there was a general break up of the Club. There had been a thorough good gamble this year under the wing of Captain Lambe, but the general result was so disastrous that many thought racing in Ceylon was doomed. Not so, however, as with judicious prudence it was resolved that racing should be on a milder scale; and for the years 1873 and 1874 no jockeys were allowed, and merely Sky Meetings were held in Colombo." Let the dead past bury its dead. I will only quote what a native said to me of racing at that time: "Those were the great days, sir, when all the gentlemens went to the races and all the ladies too. Long tail coats and white tall hats were worn by every gentleman, and coaches and four drove to the racecourse. The stakes, in golden sovereigns, were handed over to the winners in brass pots, and with my own eyes I have seen one man carry off seven pots. [Can this be the origin of the expression 'pots'?] But in 1872 the cat got amongst the pigeons, sir; there was bad work with jockeys and owners, and there were bankruptcies. One jockey, who was suspected of robbing his owner by selling races, fell down dead when going to England with his bad-earned money!" I wonder how much of this was true, and how much of it the *gup* of the bazaar.

I am unable to say when racing first commenced at Nuwara Eliya, where there is to-day one of the prettiest racecourses in the East. An interesting photograph in the *Times of Ceylon* Christmas number fixes the date of the first Gymkhana Meet at 1874, when the grand-stand was a cadjan shed; but I have a note of "Wild Dayrell's" by me which states "the Nuwara Eliya Gymkhana had been revived in 1873, probably on account of the decadence of Colombo," so that it would appear there was racing at Nuwara Eliya earlier than the seventies. There undoubtedly was racing of a kind in the hills at Darrawella and elsewhere in the early seventies, and probably before, although I have been unable to unearth any records of them. Before finally closing with the black year 1872, let me give a brightly written picture of the scene at the races in that year, which I take from the file of the *Times of Ceylon*:—

"A large and fashionable assemblage of spectators began rapidly to fill the grand-stand very soon after four o'clock, whilst the usual motley crowd thronged the course—a crowd composed of non-members of the Turf Club, who did not care to pay ten shillings for admittance to the sacred precincts of the ring—soldiers of the 73rd in scarlet tunics, artillery-men in blue, riflemen in green, sailors, Buddhist priests in their yellow robes Burghers on foot, Burghers conveyed in every description of [Ceylon] vehicle, from the comfortable palanquin to the less imposing bullock hackery; swell Moormen willing to take the current 'odds'; Tambies from the Pettah, Tambies in reduced circumstances, native gentlemen in gorgeous apparel, native ladies in still more startling colours, filthy horse-keepers, innumerable coolies in rags—altogether forming a collection drawn from all classes in Ceylon."

There was a meet in Colombo in 1873, but it was not much of a success, and the Governor's disapproval of the work of 1872 was shown by the fact that there was no Governor's Cup, whilst the Ladies' Purse was also remarkable by its absence. In 1874, however, there was a reorganisation of the Turf Club, and some excellent racing was the result. A mare called Clochette distinguished herself tremendously, winning a punishing race of 1⅜ miles over six flights of hurdles and a 1¼ mile flat race in the course of the same afternoon. All the riders were gentlemen, and in one race I see such a well-known list as this: Skrine, Graeme, Darley, Carlyon, Dobree, Bacon, and "Hampden." The weights were 11 stone and upwards. What would we not give for such a field of G.R.'s in these decadent days, when there is such difficulty in finding gentlemen to ride for the famous trophy of the Horse Club! There was a strong plea, however, in 1874, for the restoration, in part at least, of the old conditions regarding professional jockeys and first-class horses; and 1875 saw the old conditions revived, when, we read, "there was not the faintest breath of scandal or ill-feeling to mar the general harmony." Mr. Duncan Skrine was mainly instrumental in the revival of racing, and the name of Mr. Dodwell Browne appears first among the Committee in the 1874 meet. "Mr. Hampden" (poor Mr. Waller, whose tragic end at Darrawella course is still remembered and regretted) made his first appearance as a rider in 1874. The next year saw "Wild Dayrell" among the Committee, with Mr. G. C. Walker secretary at Colombo, and Mr. R. B. Donnall (afterwards Planting Member in Council for several years) still doing secretary's duties at the planting capital, Kandy. The drawback to the 1875 meet was the handicapping of Sir William Gregory, which, apparently, was weird in the extreme. In 1876 we find Mr. Ronald J. Farquharson riding a loser—an inglorious commencement to the most successful owner-trainer-rider career we have ever had in Ceylon. Besides "R. J." there was his brother Eric, who had a most successful career and was a splendid rider. The Farquharsons formed a confederacy which met with great success for years, and one of their horses, Ramrod, wrote his name largely in the records of the Governor's Cup.

THE RACE-COURSE, COLOMBO.

In 1877 there was a strong movement to change the date of the meet from September to August, and this was done with great success and the foundations laid of the present August week. In 1878 we see the name of Mr. G. D. Alston as one of the clerks of the course, and we find Mr. Joseph Wickwar receiving hearty congratulations on the successful way in which he had performed the duties of secretary. This position Mr. Wickwar first filled in 1877, and he was a great success in that position for several years. Mr. Wickwar is still to the fore in racing matters in Ceylon, and besides being secretary of the Nuwara Eliya Race Committee, his valuable experience of racing, both as a rider and official, is always at the disposal of the Turf Club. In 1879 we see Mr. George J. Jameson, the popular Fort merchant, among the officials, and in the same year Mr. Dick Lauder appears for the first time among winning owners and Mr. Ronald Farquharson on the Committee of Management. Bad times were now looming on the horizon for Ceylon. The great tragedy of the death of coffee was to be enacted, with all its lamentable accompaniments, and there was to be much grief and lamentation before tea was to spring into success out of the ashes of the old staple. The year 1880 saw the disappearance of the tall white hats and the long dust-coats of the Ascot and Goodwood types, which gave way to billycocks and sober tweeds. In 1882 we see F. D. Mitchell, Sydney Vowler, J. M. Robertson, and J. G. Baker

THE OLD RACE-COURSE, GALLE FACE.

among the stewards, but the great depression interfered with the entries and the betting. In 1884 we notice Dr. Tothill, Major Knollys, A. A. Delmege, and A. H. Murray Menzies among the stewards, with L. H. Kelly as judge and G. J. Jameson clerk of the scales. The silver lining on the cloud of adversity had so far failed to put in an appearance, and there was serious talk of abandoning the races altogether. Luckily this was not done, and 1886 saw a revival, with large fields, good racing, and an abundance of G.R.'s—there being no less than eight amateur riders in one race. The handicapping was done by "Wild Dayrell," and was a splendid factor in the success of the meet. So considerable was the enthusiasm engendered by the meet that a syndicate was formed to import horses, and a great argument took place over the rival merits of Arabs and English griffins. "Wild Dayrell" was the leader of those who wanted English griffins, from which attitude he never swerved. How it would have rejoiced his sporting heart if he had been asked to assist in the selection of the thirteen English griffins imported at the back end of 1906! but his untimely death prevented this, and Mr. Ronald Farquharson did not have the benefit of his expert opinion. In 1886 a *pari mutuel* was started by Mr. C. E. H. Symons—Lieutenant-Colonel Symons, of Colombo—and it is a useful argument in favour of the replacement of bookies by a *pari mutuel* that in 1886, out of the seventeen races on which the *pari mutuel* did business, an odds on price was only returned in one race, and then the return was 10 to 9. Compare this with the August meet of 1906, and it will be seen that those who attack the bookmaker monopoly system have sound reason on their side.

One of the most important steps forward ever taken in Ceylon racing was the acquisition by the Turf Club, in the early nineties, of the land in the Cinnamon Gardens which forms the present racecourse. It was high time that the Turf Club had a proper home of its own, with a course that it could fence in, and from which it could exclude the ordinary traffic, which it frequently failed to do on the Galle Face, for we read of such curious accidents as a cart containing beer barrels being run into by the field in an actual race. With the removal of the races to the beautiful turf track in the Cinnamon Gardens—opened on June 22, 1893—Ceylon racing began a prosperous and uneventful career, with plenty of popular support which made good stakes possible. Below is a list of the winners of the Governor's Cup for the past twenty years, together with names of owners, jockeys, &c.

The following shows who were the principal winning owners during the past half a dozen years :—

THE WINNING OWNERS.

			Rs.
1901	...	Mr. de Soysa	7,450
1902	...	Captain Lewin	7,500
1903	...	Mr. R. Farquharson (11 firsts)	8,700
1903	...	Mr. D. Williams	5,900
1904	...	Mr. Farquharson (9 firsts) ...	8,180
1904	...	Mr. C. C. Herbert	5,101
1905	...	Mr. Farquharson (11 firsts) ...	11,622
1905	...	Mr. de Soysa	2,109
1906	...	Mr. James	8,057
1906	...	Mr. de Soysa	4,000

The Turf Club stands to-day in a fine and healthy condition. Its stewards are capable men, and desirous to promote the best interests of sport, and have shown that they are prepared to consider suggestions for improvement even when they are made outside. They have just carried through successfully an English griffin scheme, thirteen carefully selected young horses having been sent out from England under the eye of Mr. Ronald Farquharson, and delivered over to the subscribers for considerably less than £100 each. If this scheme is repeated every two or three years there should be no dearth of horses for racing. Appended is a list of the present officials of the club.

THE GOVERNOR'S CUP.

Year.	Owner.	Winner.	Weight.	Distance.	Rider.	Time.
			st. lb.			m. s.
1886	Mr. A. Murray Menzies	Ramrod				
1887	„ A. W. Jackson ...	Zerlina	9 3	1 m.	Mr. Farquharson	1 55
1888	„ Le Mesurier ...	Lady Durham ...	9 4	„	Cavanagh ...	—
1889	„ A. W. Jackson ...	Giddy Girl ...	10 1	„	Wall	1 46
1890	Do.	Do.	10 1	„	Do.	—
1891	Do.	Do.	11 2	„	Do.	1 47⅘
1892	„ R. Jackson ...	Smash	10 6	1¼ m.	Thompson* ...	—
1893	Do.	Do.	10 6	„	Trahan ...	2 18⅘
1894	Colpetty Confederacy	Master Walter ...	10 8	1 m.	Wall	1 45
1895	Mr. H. Lubbert ...	Norbert	10 3	„	Kaye	1 48
1896	„ E. L. F. de Soysa	Jack O'Lantern ...	10 5	„	Trahan ...	1 46⅘
1897	Do.	Do.	10 0	„	Do.	1 47
1898	„ Tom Walker ...	Redavni	9 10	„	Ramshaw ...	1 45
1899	„ E. L. F. de Soysa	North British ...	8 10	„	Gibbs	1 45⅘
1900	Do.	Merloolas	9 0	1¼ m.	Ramshaw ...	2 17
1901	„ Bonaparte Wyse ...	Devoted	9 0	„	Mirza	2 20
1902	Captain R. S. Lewin	Do.	9 0	„	Ramshaw ...	2 17
1903	Mr. H. D. Williams ...	Gabelle	8 12	„	Lansdown ...	2 17½
1904	Mr. R. J. Farquharson	Prince Lyon ...	9 3	„	Fisher ...	2 17
1905	Do.	Do.	9 3	„	Firth	2 18⅘
1906	„ E. L. F. de Soysa	Footprint	9 3	„	O'Neill ...	2 14⅘

PRESIDENT.—His Excellency Sir Henry A. Blake, G.C.M.G.

VICE-PRESIDENT.—Brigadier-General R. C. B. Lawrence.

STEWARDS.—The Hon. Mr. A. G. Lascelles, K.C. (Attorney-General); the Hon. Mr. G. M. Fowler, C.M.G. (Acting Colonial Secretary); the Hon. Mr. W. H. Figg; Messrs. G. E. Woodman, F. C. Allen, L. Bayly, and S. Payne Gallwey.

COMMITTEE.—The Hon. Mr. A. G. Lascelles, K.C. (Chairman); the Hon. Mr. G. M. Fowler, C.M.G.; the Hon. Mr. H. L. Crawford, C.M.G.; the Hon. Mr. W. H. Figg; Messrs. S. D. Bandaranaike, C.M.G., F. C. Allen, J. Wickwar, G. E. Woodman, L. Bayly, W. B. Barkleh, E. J. Weatherall, H. S. K. Marrell, L. F. de Soysa, B. W. Bawa, C. M. Fernando and W. P. D. Vanderstraaten.

SECRETARY.—Mr. J. Lochore.

GOLF.

Though it is now nearly the most popular pastime in Ceylon, golf was only started here about a quarter of a century ago. The game was at first played on Galle Face, but on December 10, 1896, the present links in Borella were opened, and styled the Ridgeway Links, after the Governor, Sir Joseph West Ridgeway who took a keen interest in the game and gave the club its home. The Colombo Golf Club was established in 1880 by Messrs. William Law, William Somerville, R. Webster, F. A. Fairlie, E. Aitken, and R. L. M. Brown, who formed the first committee, Mr. Brown being the hon. sec. About 1890 the Nuwara Eliya Golf Club was founded, and possesses now, perhaps, the most beautiful and the best full course in the East. The Ridgeway Links have also been considerably improved, and the Colombo Golf Club now boasts of a most handsome pavilion, completed in 1905 at a cost of Rs. 32,000, raised by debentures among the members, of which a considerable number are redeemed each year out of the handsome profits. Names prominently associated with the earliest history of golf in the island are those of Mr. F. A. Fairlie, a Lindula planter, and Mr. W. Somerville, the veteran Fort merchant. The former was the crack golfer of the period, and the first player to win a competition. This was the club gold medal for one round of eighteen holes, won by Mr. Fairlie, in 1884, with a score of 87. Mr. Fairlie won this twice after, and then left the island. In 1888 the Hon. Mr. J. N. Campbell won the gold medal, and he and Mr. W. Somerville are, it is believed, the only two original members of the Colombo Golf Club still associated with the game. The former won the championship of Ceylon in 1897, and is still a very consistent player. Golf in Colombo made rapid strides during the latter eighties, thanks to the fillip given to it by the officers of the 1st Gordon Highlanders, from Colonel Boyes downward. In fact, to the military was due to a great extent the sustained interest in a pastime that took some years to gain in popular favour; and there is still one competition played for annually in Colombo which is connected with a past Major-General, namely, the Lady McLeod Vase, instituted in 1887. Major Craufurd, of the Gordons, was the first military player to win this or any other competition. He won the silver medal too that year; and the following year Colonel Boyes carried off the gold medal. The latter was also the first to win the club aggregate medal, while the Calcutta medal was won by four other officers before it came into the possession of a civilian in the person of W. E. Mitchell.

CHAMPIONSHIP.

The championship of the island was instituted in 1891, and till 1905 was played for twice annually, in Nuwara Eliya and Colombo. The first to gain the honour of champion was J. W. Gowan, a player of exceptional merit. He was the same year defeated by J. N. Campbell in Colombo, but carried off the cup twice again in 1892. This was the period of guttie balls, but a fairly high standard of play had nevertheless been reached, and 1893 saw the advent of one of the finest golfers Ceylon knew, namely, H. C. Rose, a banker, who, between 1896 and 1897, won the championship thrice in succession. He was also a winner of the Calcutta medal, the Lady McLeod Vase, the club gold medal, the aggregate gold medal, and the winner of the gold medal at Nuwara Eliya in 1896 and 1897, soon after which he left the island. In 1899 the championship fell to two military officers—Colonel Quill, of the R.A.M.C., at Nuwara Eliya, and Lieutenant P. Balfour, of the Highland Light Infantry, at Colombo, who beat C. W. Mackie, the previous year's winner in Colombo, and holder of the Colombo Golf Club gold and silver medals. In 1900 C. B. Elliott won the championship both at Nuwara Eliya and Colombo, while he secured the honour again in 1903, beating J. G. Melrose by 2 up and 1. This was one of the most remarkable championship games on record. In the second round Melrose was 8 down at the seventh hole, when he began to play a wonderfully fine uphill game. He reduced Elliott's lead to 2 up and 2 to play, but missing a 15-in. putt at the seventeenth hole, was only able to halve it in 5, which gave Elliott the match.

A GREAT GOLFER.

Though not able to win the championship till 1904, Melrose was regarded as one of the finest golfers Ceylon has ever known. He holds the record for the best scores on the Ridgeway Links—72 in the President's Cup in 1903, and 69 when the Haskell ball was first introduced. Besides winning the championship twice, Mr. Melrose carried away four aggregate gold medals, three gold medals, two president's cups, three captain's cups, one Calcutta medal, two quarterly silver medals, and other valuable trophies, including the handsome Coronation Cup presented by Mr. A. Lampard, and the Kenna Hotel Cup, Nuwara Eliya. Mr. Melrose left Colombo for Calcutta in 1905. Though Ceylon has been the poorer for his departure, the island has yet two fine golfers in the brothers Ogilvie and D. W. Watson.

In Colombo, while competitions are spread over a long period, they are in Nuwara Eliya nearly always confined to a week, the principal meet being held during Easter. The record score for the new course at Nuwara Eliya is held by Mr. C. M. Hutchinson, a scientist attached to the Assam Planters' Association, who, while on a visit, went round in 73. In fact, several fine records have been put up by visitors to Nuwara Eliya, one of the most notable being in Easter, 1906, by a military visitor from India, Captain Hunt-Grubbe, who won nearly everything at the week. Ceylon golfers heard with great regret of his demise a few months later, in India, from cholera.

THE LADIES' CHAMPIONSHIP.

A name prominently associated with the early history of ladies' golf in Ceylon is that of Mrs. Fanshawe, wife of Colonel Fanshawe, of the R.A., a daughter of Sir Frederick Saunders. The ladies' championship was instituted in 1895, and was won for the first two years by Miss Saunders, in 1897 by Miss N. Saunders, and in 1898 by Miss Saunders again. Miss R. Elliott was the winner in 1899, and after holding her own twice in one year—and on five different occasions—she had to give up the title of Ceylon lady golf champion in 1905 to Mrs. F. A. Saunders, the holder of the gold bangle in 1903 and 1904. Up to 1904 the championship competition was held in Colombo. It was put on a firmer footing with the competition which took place at Nuwara

Eliya in April of the same year, and now takes place annually at the Sanitarium, where in 1906 Mrs. F. S. Mitchell wrested the championship from Mrs. Saunders.

It has been said that golf has ruined European cricket in Ceylon, and that racing in Colombo will never be what it should as long as the Ridgeway Golf Links last. This, of course, is an extreme view, but it is apparent that the game is making great headway in Ceylon. An indication of this is in a proposal under consideration to secure the services of a golf professional.

In recent years the Ceylonese have also taken enthusiastically to golf, and count a number of good players. The Victoria Golf Club have their links on the Victoria Park, and the Havelock Golf Club in the southern suburbs is another rising institution.

FOOTBALL.

Football in Ceylon was started about the year 1879, but there is very little on record to show what progress the game made twenty years ago. The Colombo Football Club was instituted in 1880, the committee of management being Messrs. E. Cave-Browne, G. Plaxton, H. W. Bradhurst (now Government Agent of the Western Province), E. C. Davies (the Factory Engineer), and the late Mr. Ralph Tatham, who was captain and hon. sec. In spite of the disadvantages as regards climate, Rugby football was always more popular than the Association game. The principal matches were between Colombo and Up-country, and in view of the great interest centred in this annual fixture at the present time it seems a pity that a record of the earlier results is not available. In the later eighties the Colombo Football Club was in very nearly a dormant condition, but, thanks to the interest which Mr. V. A. Julius, a keen sportsman, continued to take in the club, the annual contest with Up-country was not allowed to drop. In 1890 the club was put on a firmer footing, and with the late Mr. H. H. Capper as President, Surgeon-Captain Pike as Captain, Mr. H. S. Jeafferson as hon. sec., and Messrs. J. Macdonald, Black, Bremner, Kirkpatrick, and Neave on the committee, the club made excellent progress. About 1896–97 hockey was introduced into Ceylon, and, the interest in Association football being revived, the present Colombo Hockey and Football Club was inaugurated to govern the three games. Since then both "Rugger" and "Soccer" have made great strides in Colombo, and the increasing popularity of the Association game has led to an annual fixture between Colombo and Up-country since 1898. The "Rugger season," both in Colombo and Up-country, is confined to the wet period between May and September. The Colombo Hockey and Football Club have the advantage of more regular practice as compared with their rivals Up-country; but since 1892 Colombo have only been able to win twice, the conditions of life Up-country enabling the planters to come down to the field of play invariably the "fitter" team, and thus to hold their own in the great struggle for supremacy. In spite of Colombo's repeated failures, the annual "Rugger" match continues to be the most attractive feature of the August Carnival in Colombo. Year after year new hope is given to Colombo by the infusion of new blood from among the ranks of the Army and Navy, but it is worthy of note that since 1892 Colombo have been only able to cross the Up-country line five times, and have in all scored only 21 points against 178 scored by Up-country up to August, 1906. Colombo's best effort since 1894 was when they drew with Up-country in 1904, this being the only occasion when the metropolis had a well-trained fifteen in the field, led by Mr. L. H. Combe, a sterling forward.

Besides the Colombo–Up-country match, the season is kept very much alive by a series of interdistrict matches, the four districts taking part being Colombo, Kandy, Dikoya, and Dimbula. In recent years Colombo has nearly always been able to hold its own in these matches; but Dikoya, while scoring many wins against the Colombo Hockey and Football Club, has a fair claim to be regarded as the premier "Rugger" district Up-country.

Ceylon has not played any matches against outside teams, but the belief has often been expressed that the standard of "Rugger" in the island compares favourably with that of any ordinary English county. The departure to the Federated Malay States of B. C. N. Knight and W. R. F. Brock has been a great loss to Up-country and the colony, for Ceylon has never known a finer half-back or three-quarter respectively. In J. E. Biddell, C. R. Mudie, F. R. Dakeyne, C. H. Williams, H. B. Bremner, W. E. M. Patterson, D. M. Murray, W. Lockman, J. Tilly, S. P. Bell, A. E. Ogilvy, H. G. Moir, R. M. Ash, D. Robertson, A. F. West, J. H. Cantrell, J. H. L. Dowbiggin, F. H. Tatham, W. Moir, and others, however, the island has still a fine lot of players, and the game bids fair to continue to arouse the interest it always has done. It is not a game which suits the Ceylonese, who lack the necessary *vim* and weight; but it has been sportingly taken up by them, and the Ceylonese Hockey and Football Union and the Kandy Rovers have an annual match in which the greatest interest is centred. In earlier years three Ceylonese played for Colombo, two of them, W. Van Langenberg and E. H. Joseph, having had an English training.

Previous to 1897, when the C.H. & F.C. was founded, Association football in Colombo was seldom played, and the class of play was very different to what it is now. The various regiments that have been stationed in Colombo have done much to make the game popular, and in 1902 it is estimated that between 5,000 and 6,000 spectators were present to witness a match during the Coronation festivities between civilians and the military. Some of the most prominent exponents of the game at the present time are C. W. Mackie, J. A. Symons, W. A. Cole, W. E. M. Paterson, A. G. G. Hyde, W. H. M. Davies, R. H. Williams, A. F. West, A. Warden, A. J. Lintott, J. Moir, and F. C. Doyle. The game has not yet thoroughly "caught on" Up-country, but since 1903 the planters have sportingly brought down a team to play Colombo annually. Among the Ceylonese the game has made rapid strides, and there are few towns where it is not assiduously indulged in by the youth of the country. In Colombo the number of Association clubs is legion, the principal ones being the Chums, the Bloomfield Club, the Colombo Rovers, and the Ramblers.

CRICKET.

Cricket in Ceylon dates back to the early sixties, but it was not till 1900 that Mr. P. L. Bartholomeusz, a Ceylonese member of the staff of the *Times of Ceylon*, first rescued from oblivion the most salient records connected with the game during the last quarter of the nineteenth century. The defective nature of old records and the difficulty of getting at most of them rendered the compilation no easy matter; but in gathering together the scattered fragments of the history of local cricket Mr. Bartholomeusz has done a public service. The principal cricket clubs in Ceylon now are the Colombo Cricket Club, the Colombo Colts, the Colombo Nondescripts, the Colombo Sports Club, the Colombo Bloomfield and Athletic Club, the Sinhalese Sports Club, the Colombo Malay Club, the Kandy Sports Club, the Dikoya and Maskeliya Cricket Club, and the Dimbula Athletic and Cricket Club. But none of these clubs can claim an existence of forty years, unless the Colombo Cricket Club had its origin in the Colombo XI., of which, with the Union Club, the Smallpass Club, the Slave Island Club, the Juvenile Graduates, the Hultsdorf Club, the Fort Club, and the Military Club, we first find mention made in 1869. The Colombo Cricket Club was probably established about

1876, the office-bearers at the time being as follows :—

PRESIDENT.—Mr. B. Pauncefort.

HON. SECRETARY.—Mr. G. L. Taylor.

HON. TREASURER.—Mr. G. J. Jameson.

COMMITTEE.—Messrs. J. M. Robertson, E. P. Willisford, W. G. Inglis, W. Somerville, and Captain Morewood.

Mr. Pauncefort was a quondam captain of Oxford, and is said to have been one of the very best batsmen that played for the C.C.C. Of the then office-bearers, Mr. W. Somerville, whose connection with Ceylon cricket dates from 1861, is still resident in Ceylon. The original headquarters of the C.C.C. were the Rifle Green in Slave Island, which was given up after a few years in favour of the present Sports Club pitch on the Galle Face, the venue of some of the most historical contests on local record. The C.C.C. stayed here till 1894, when their present excellent ground adjoining the racecourse was opened. The principal test match in the early sixties was between Colombo and Up-country, but though traced so far back as 1875, it has not been possible to compile the results of these matches since that time. It is interesting, however, to recall the names of those who took part in the match of 1875. Those who played for Up-country were T. Dobree, W. Saunders, French, A. Mercer, W. H. Anderson, L. H. Kelly, H. H. Carfe, H. Wickens, D. Drake, H. W. Ridley, and A. G. Scovell. Colombo was represented by Captain Budgeon, G. L. Taylor, H. P. Dawson, S. M. Munro, G. J. Jameson, P. A. Templer, W. G. Inglis, H. C. P. Bell, E. T. Noyes, C. V. B. Kuper, and R. Tatham. Only one innings a side was played, and Colombo won, the scores being Colombo 99, and Up-country 43. For Colombo Captain Budgeon scored 48. Ridley and French trundled for Up-country, and the bowling was presumably very weak, as it is recorded that four wides and a bye were registered before Taylor scored a single. Ridley and French bowled seventeen wides between them, and Inglis and Taylor three.

The match of the following year was played on three afternoons, and was more of a first-class character, as we notice that both sides were well represented, W. Vanderspar, Humphreys, and Halliley being among the Up-country eleven ; while the Colombo team included F. S. Shand (a splendid left-handed bowler), Pauncefort, and W. Somerville. The scores were : Colombo 100 and 29 for five wickets ; Up-country 77 and 94, the result being a draw. Halliley and Shand trundled with equal success.

Since 1890, 28 matches have been played, Colombo being credited with 15 victories against 8 belonging to Up-country. The majority of Colombo's victories were scored in the metropolis, due to Up-country's inability to bring down their best teams.

Some of the heroes of these past matches were : B. Pauncefort, G. Vanderspar, G. H. Alston, Ashley Walker, F. Stephens, H. C. P. Bell, W. H. Jackson, E. Cave-Brown, H. Goodwyn, G. L. Taylor, M. H. Paine, and Colonel Churchill for Colombo ; and A. Tabor, P. F. Hadow, F. A. Fairlie, C. Inglis, A. J. Denison, W. P. Halliley, A. C. W. Clarke, R. H. S. Scott, J. G. Fort, J. Ingall, F. F. Mackenzie, and A. O. Whiting for Up-country. In late years J. A. Symons, E. R. Waldock, T. Leese, E. T. Etlinger, F. Balkwill, A. J. G. Field have been Colombo's mainstay, assisted from time to time by military cricketers, amongst the best being Lieutenants C. Bowen (of the Lancashires), Ames (of the Madras Infantry), E. H. Rooke (of the Royal Engineers), and Farrell (of the Worcesters), the latter being the finest all-round military cricketer that Ceylon has known since the departure of Colonel Churchill, at one time D.A.A.G. of Ceylon. For Up-country, P. J. Gaisford, G. F. Cornish, T. Y. Wright, P. H. Papillon, G. H. and D. L. Gibson, G. C. Fraser, N. Mansergh, F. C. Smith, P. Healing, and E. Cowen have in the last decade done yeoman service. The first century in these matches was scored hy M. H. Paine (for Colombo) in 1891, T. Y. Wright (for Up-country), J. A. Symons (for Colombo), and A. L. Gibson (for Up-country) being the only other batsmen to have reached the coveted three figures, A. L. Gibson having five to his credit. T. Y. Wright scored 92 in a match played Up-country in 1892, Halliley

J. C., J. T., AND L. O. WEINMAN.
(Sons of Mr. J. R. Weinman, District Judge of Colombo—a notable sporting trio.)

scored 96 in 1895, and W. H. Howorth scored 97 in 1900. 941 runs for 32 wickets at Nuwara Eliya in 1906 is the highest aggregate in these matches. The longest stand for the first wicket in these matches was made by W. H. Howorth (97) and J. A. Symons (77) at Colombo in 1900. H. B. T. Boucher and C. Tarrant scored 80 runs for the last wicket for Up-country at Colombo in 1903.

A HISTORIC FIXTURE—UP-COUNTRY.

In 1872 the annual Dimbula-Dikoya matches were started, and are the principal Up-country fixtures, two matches being played annually, alternately at Rodella, the home of the D.A.C.C., a splendid cricket pitch situated in an amphitheatre of hills, and at Darrawella, also a picturesque ground. Between 1872 and 1906 the two rival districts have engaged in 69 matches, Dimbula being credited with 35 wins and Dikoya with 29. Five matches were drawn. The 69 matches have yielded an aggregate of 33,869 runs, an average of 130 runs an innings. The aggregate standing to Dimbula's credit is 17,035 runs for 129 innings, an average of 132, and to Dikoya 16,834 runs for 130 innings, an average of 129. Dimbula holds the record for the biggest innings in these matches, namely, 437 for seven wickets in 1895. Dikoya were twice out for 32, in 1878 and 1882. The latter occasion furnished the most exciting finish on record, Dimbula winning by a run. The match at Darrawella in 1903 produced the highest aggregate of runs, namely, 869. A. L. Gibson, a Wykehamist, holds the record for the highest individual score, 218, for Dimbula at Rodella in 1902. In 1874 W. P. Halliley, for Dimbula, took 9 wickets (all clean bowled) for 7 runs, a record for the island. Between 1872 and 1903 his analysis in these matches was 1,708 overs, 674 maidens, 2,945 runs, 366 wickets, average 8. In his day the finest bowler in Ceylon, Halliley is known to have placed a rupee between wickets and to have bowled on it five times in succession. In the 1903 matches A. O. Whiting, an old Oxford blue, who was a capital wicket-keeper, in addition to being a sterling bat, stumped three and caught seven batsmen, and only gave 16 byes out of a total of 777 runs. Thirteen centuries in all have been scored in these matches, and of this number A. O. Whiting and A. L. Gibson each claim three. Mr. W. S. T. Saunders made the highest score in the first of these historical fixtures. For Dikoya in 1884 he scored 52.

In connection with Up-country cricket the names may be recalled of P. F. Hadow, the old Harrovian, A. J. Denison, F. A. Fairlie, A. Tabor, C. G. Inglis, A. L. Ingall, and A. C. W. Clarke, who in the eighties were very prominent cricketers. Hadow was probably the pick of the batch as a batsman, and scored three centuries for the Kandapolla C.C. in three consecutive matches between February 24 and March 13, 1888. Later came O. Marks, P. H. Papillon, P. Gaisford, C. Philcox, A. A. Pillaus, G. F. Cornish, C. Fraser, G. H. Gibson, and A. L. Gibson, the latter being the best batsman in Ceylon at the present time.

THE COLOMBO COLTS.

The Colombo Colts, the premier Ceylonese cricket club in the island, was started in 1873 and reorganised in 1886, since when the club have had a phenomenal run of success. Their record up to 1900 was 170 matches played, of which only 14 were lost. They have since 1888 played eleven picked European teams representative of the island, being defeated on only one occasion, by the narrow margin of 36 runs. One of the best feats of the Colts was in dismissing a team captained by Mr. L. H. Gay, the English wicket-keeper, for 13 runs; but the Colts had previously got the A.B.C.D. Club out for 9 runs in a match at Kandy on June 28, 1887; while in 1891 the Colts dismissed the Nondescripts for 11 runs. One of the most notable defeats of the Colts was in the year 1890, when the A.B.C.D., practically represented by a picked European team, defeated them by one run. In 1892 the Colts played a match against Lord Hawke's team of English cricketers, which included the Hon. F. S. Jackson. The English eleven were dismissed for 81 in their first innings—the lowest score in their whole tour in the East, and victory for the Colts was not thought unlikely; but 24 runs were all they could put together! In their second innings the visitors were again dismissed for a poor score, namely, 107, which left the Colts with 165 runs to make to win, but F. S. Jackson was largely responsible for the dismissal of the Colts for 44 runs. The Colts' strength about this time chiefly lay in their bowling, C. Kelaart, D. Robertson, E. Christoffelsz, W. de Fransz, T. Kelaart, and A. Raffel being trundlers of exceptional merit. Kelaart and Raffel were in a class by themselves, one of the latter's best achievements being in capturing 14 wickets for 87 runs against Mr. Stoddart's team of 1894, which passed through Ceylon. He clean bowled ten batsmen, including the famous English captain in both innings.

But to T. Kelaart must be given the credit of being the finest bowler Ceylon has known, an average of 5 runs a wicket for sixteen years being his record. Between 1899 and 1905 Kelaart bowled in 275 innings and captured 1,284 wickets for 7,596 runs; while for the Colts he has bowled in 253 innings and captured 1,245 wickets for 7,118 runs, an average in both instances of 5 runs a wicket. The headquarters of the Colts is the Racquet Court in the Pettah, popularly known as "the cradle of Ceylonese cricket."

NONDESCRIPTS CRICKET CLUB.

The Nondescript Cricket Club, the members of which are drawn from the Colombo colleges, was started in 1891, and also counts among its members several excellent cricketers, notably Mr. Douglas de Saram, who has scored more centuries than any other Ceylonese batsman, while his success as a bowler has won for him the distinction of being one of the best all-round cricketers in the island. In recent years the Nondescripts have proved formidable rivals to the Colts.

This club, which has its venue in Colombo, is open to all nationalities—hence its non-definitive title. It is now in its nineteenth year, having been founded on March 19, 1888, at a meeting held for the purpose at Sea View, Colpetty, at which Mr. Advocate H. L. Wendt, now the Senior Puisne Justice of the island, occupied the chair. It was originally decided to have tennis courts adjoining the cricket field, and accordingly the club was first styled the Nondescripts Cricket and Tennis Club. But this idea of including both games was subsequently dropped, and the club exists for cricketing purposes only. The late Sir Samuel Grenier, one time Attorney-General of Ceylon, was the first President; so it is seen that the law was well represented in the foundation of the club. It has, in fact, always attracted members of that profession. The first match on record was a contest with the Garrison, which took place on July 25, 1888, and was doubtless played on the Barrack Square, as the club had not then selected a site for its grounds. It was not till later in the same year that the Colombo Municipality, under the mistaken belief that they owned the land in question, permitted the club to take on lease the plot of land adjoining Victoria Park, which, until a rude awakening at the end of 1905, was the site of the club grounds. The Government, not the municipality, has been proved to be the real owner of this land; and the erection by the former of the Telephone Exchange on this spot has rendered the grounds unsuitable for match play, though practice at the nets is still possible thereon. The club has, however, been promised by Government the use of a block of land adjoining the Colombo Cricket Club grounds, where it hopes to be even more comfortably settled by the end of 1907.

The fixture card of the club is usually a very full one, and not the least attractive event is the annual up-country tour, when matches are played with the hospitable tea-planters of Ceylon. The colours of the Nondescripts are dark blue, maroon, and gold, and Mr. Jas. van Langenberg, Advocate, is the present popular President of the club.

The Ceylonese Sports Club and the Bloomfield Cricket Club are closely allied to the Nondescripts and Colts respectively.

CEYLON TEAMS IN INDIA AND THE STRAITS.

Cricket in Ceylon is at present under a cloud which does not seem to be lifting. There is not the same enthusiasm for the game, due very largely to the fact that men have not the time they used to have to spare for cricket matches. It is long since we have seen an Australian or an English team playing a match in Colombo; yet in the old days this was a regular occurrence. The greater interest taken years ago in the game is clear from the representative character of the teams that went out from Ceylon to India and the Straits. Since 1884 eight European cricket teams have gone from Ceylon, seven visiting India and one the Straits Settlements. Out of a total number of 29 matches played, 10 have been won by Ceylon, 10 lost, and 9 drawn. The most successful tour was that of 1886 to Bombay, when Ceylon had the great satisfaction of not only beating the Bombay Gymkhana, but also the Parsees—by 16 runs. The scalps of the North-West Province cricketers were also brought back to Ceylon. The Ceylon team on that occasion was Ashley Walker (Captain), P. F. Hadow, F. A. Fairlie, F. L. Shand, A. J. Denison, F. F. Mackenzie, J. G. Fort, G. Vanderspar, G. H. Alston, F. Stephens, and G. L. Taylor—probably the strongest team that ever went out of Ceylon. Ceylon twice scored 400 runs in an innings against the Terai Hockey Club in Calcutta in 1884, and against Bangalore in 1885, H. J. Meaden and J. G. Fort being credited with centuries on each of these occasions, Fort and Walker establishing a stand of over 200 in the latter match. On the occasion of the last two visits of the Ceylon team to Madras the island was very poorly represented, but on the occasion of the 1901 tour Ceylon made a very good draw against Madras, having scored 333 runs in their first innings against 107 runs put up by Madras. On this occasion, however, Ceylon were badly beaten by the Madras Presidency by an innings and 332 runs, the Presidency scoring 537 runs, of which Captain Challonor was responsible for 216. In the 1905 tour the Ceylon team was a very poor one and was badly beaten. In the first match Madras scored 560 for 7 wickets, against 265 and 292 for 7 wickets by Ceylon. Ceylon were very lucky indeed in drawing this match, but they were beaten by the Moffusil by an innings and 65 runs, and by the Presidency by an innings and 147 runs, the latter scoring 451 runs for 5 wickets in their only innings. There were five centuries made against Ceylon! Mr. George Vanderspar's team which visited the Straits in 1890 included two Colts, E. Christofelsz and T. Kelaart, the former of whom trundled with success.

For the first time in the history of Ceylon cricket a purely Ceylonese team visited Bombay in 1906. The team was severely crippled by the inability of T. Kelaart and J. Ludovici, the two Ceylonese crack bowlers, to make the trip. Of 6 matches played, Ceylon won 3 and drew 3. Their victories were against Elphinstone College Past and Present, the Islam Gymkhana, and the Parsee Gymkhana. The matches drawn against the Bombay Gymkhana and Elphinstone Club were moral victories for Ceylon. Where Ceylon perhaps fell short of Indian cricket was in the bowling, but D. Joseph's 55 wickets for 12 runs apiece was a splendid achievement.

Two Madras teams and one Straits team have visited Ceylon. In 1892 Ceylon had the better of the Madras visitors.

VISITS OF THE ENGLISH AND AUSTRALIAN TEAMS TO CEYLON.

Besides Lord Hawke's team referred to above, Ceylon has had the privilege of seeing four Australian teams and two English teams playing in Colombo. In the case of the Australians the Ceylon XI. shaped very creditably against Mr. J. J. Lyons's team of 1890. Kelaart and Christofelsz, the Ceylonese bowlers, were mainly responsible for the disposal of the visitors for 187 runs. The Hon. Ivo Bligh's team of English cricketers is said to have played Ceylon while passing through, but there is no record of the visit. In 1891 Lord Sheffield's team played a Ceylon eighteen. The English team were disposed of for 143 runs, of which Mr. Stoddart was responsible for 70. Ceylon scored 70 for 10 wickets. The team included A. O. Whiting, P. F. Hadow, F. Stephens, C. Inglis, A. J. Denison, W. Sevier, M. Thomasz, Captain Block, Colonel Churchill, T. Kelaart, G. S. Saxton, R. Gatehouse, G. Vanderspar (captain), Colonel Skinner, Ffinch C. Wilkins, and F. L. Shand. The public had the opportunity of seeing Lohmann bowl on this occasion, but Briggs proved the most effective bowler. In 1894 Mr. Stoddart's team scored 76 and 81 for 8 wickets (13 men), and Ceylon 58. Briggs's analysis was 14 overs, 9 maidens, 6 runs, 6 wickets.

COLOMBO ROWING CLUB.

By V. A. Julius.

The Colombo Rowing Club was started in 1864 or in the beginning of 1865, but I am unable to give the actual date or the names of the first committee, as the earlier minute books of the club have been mislaid, and I have been unable to get hold of any records previous to February, 1892.

The formation of the club was decided on at a tiffin party at Tom Hudson's house at Polwatta. Sir Edward Creasy was the first President of the club, and two of the first members of the first committee are still in Colombo, viz., Colonel C. E. H. Symons, then a subaltern in the gunners, and F. W. Bois, the first secretary of the club. The boat-house then was at the mouth of the old sally port of the Fort, near the present Fort Railway Station. The present boat-house was built in 1900 at a cost of Rs. 6,000. The present stock of boats numbers 24, including two sliding-seat and two fixed-seat racing fours and two carvel-built racing pairs, besides several racing single-sculling boats, tub pairs, and pleasure boats. The racing course on the Beira Lake is a very fine one. It is a mile and a quarter long on still water, is almost straight, and there is room for five boats at least abreast. The starting post is from just below the Fort Station, and the finishing post is at the Travellers' Palm-trees in the Bishop's compound. The course for the shorter races is from the tail of Dhoby's Island, finishing at Travellers' Palms. The first racing against a foreign crew was at Calcutta in January, 1882, when a crew composed of W. E. Davidson, stroke (now the Governor of the Seychelles Islands), V. A. Julius, three, J. G. Fort, two, and R. H. Leslie, bow (probably the prettiest bow the club has ever seen), and J. Murray Robertson, cox, challenged for the Hoogly Challenge Cup. They were opposed by a Calcutta crew composed of Lyall, stroke, Daniel three, Collins, two (now high in the Indian Civil Service), and Smith, bow. Smith had rowed on the Thames in the race between the Atlanta crew, U.S.A., and the London Rowing Club. That fine oar J. M. Boustead, who rowed for Oxford three times in the Inter-varsity race, including the memorable dead-heat year, was eligible to row for Colombo, but was unable to get away, and kindly coached the crew. The race was held on the Barrackpore course, the practice of the crews being held in Garden Reach, now long unavailable for rowing owing to the influx of ocean-going steamers. The fours were won by Colombo, and the pairs were won by Davidson and Julius for Colombo, Julius being beaten by Garbett, a Kingston Rowing Club man, in the single sculls.

In December, 1894, when a cricket team from Colombo visited Rangoon, a rowing team composed of Captain Poole (Royal Warwickshire Regiment), stroke, V. A. Julius, three, E. R. Williams, two, H. M. Bremner, bow, and F. M. Simpson, cox, went to Rangoon to try conclusions with the Rangoon Rowing Club, but were beaten after a good race.

The next foreign race was in August, 1898, when a crew composed of H. E. Holmes, stroke, R. B. Hadland (who had rowed in the Lady Margaret boat), three, A. A. Hankey, two, C. Massy Dawson, bow, and F. M. Simpson, cox, were beaten on the Colombo Lake by 1½ lengths by a Madras crew consisting of C. G. Todhunter, stroke, C. R. S. Walker, three, C. R. Taylor, two, E. Edwards, bow, and R. Molesworth, cox. Hadland and Holmes, for Colombo, beat Todhunter and Walker for the pairs, and Hanna won the challenge sculls from Edwards amongst others. In August, 1901, Madras again sent a crew to compete at our regatta, composed of Captain Poole (formerly of Colombo), stroke, W. Ferrier, three, N. M. Murray, two, A. H. Welman, bow, and R. Molesworth, cox, but they were beaten by about four lengths by a Colombo crew made up of F. G. Tyrrel, stroke, A. D. Michie, three, H. S. Dix, two, R. Freudenberg, bow, and C. Massy Dawson, cox. The pair oars were won by the Madras pair, Welman and Murray, against the Colombo pair, Michie and Tyrrel, by three lengths.

On Christmas Day, 1902, a crew composed of A. D. Skrine, stroke, F. G. Tyrrel, three, J. Scott, two, and R. Freudenberg, bow, steered by Colonel Forbes, of the Royal Warwickshire Regiment, rowed a race on the Long Tank at Madras against the following crew representing Madras: G. A. D. Stuart, stroke, W. S. Adie (an old blue), three, H. M. Gibson, two, W. W. Paul, bow, and G. K. Gillon, cox, and the Colombo crew won by 2½ lengths. The pair-oared race was won by the Madras pair.

At Christmas, 1903, a Colombo four composed of J. Scott, stroke, L. C. Larmour, R.A., three, W. Freudenberg, two, W. A. Cave, bow, and C. Massy Dawson, cox, won on the Colombo Lake from a Madras crew consisting of J. B. Cunliffe, stroke, H. H. Goddard, three, R. C. M. Strouts, two, K. Kay, bow, and W. G. Molesworth, cox. This was a very good race for about a mile, when a slide came off in the Madras boat, and the Colombo crew finished alone. In the pair-oared race the Colombo pair, J. Scott, stroke, L. C. Larmour, bow, and C. Massy Dawson, cox, beat the Madras pair, J. B. Cunliffe, stroke, K. Kay, bow, and W. G. Molesworth, cox, by two lengths.

THE MORATUWA CYCLISTS' UNION.

The club had a challenge sculling cup for many years, which was to become the property of the first sculler who won it on three occasions. This provided a great deal of sport, and was finally won by H. J. Starey in 1879. A new cup was then offered on the same terms and was won by V. A. Julius in the years 1880, 1881, and 1882. The terms for the next cup were then altered and the cup was never to be won outright, the winner in each year receiving a presentation cup. The challenge cup is now held by D. M. Hanna.

At present it is impossible to take racing boats on the lake owing to the weeds, and no regatta has been rowed for some time, nor is there any immediate chance of one being held. The weeds seem to grow worse each year, but periodically die down and allow rowing for a few months. They were very bad in February, 1902, when a committee meeting was held to consider the question of moving the boats to the harbour, but the weeds dying down shortly afterwards, the project was abandoned. More recently there has been a suggestion to move the boat-house to the Kelani river, but the distance and the liability of the banks of the river to floods are against the scheme. The members of the club number nearly 100, and the club colours are blue and white.

COLOMBO GARDEN CLUB.

This high-class club was founded in the year 1879 "for the social amusement and recreation of a limited circle of friends, and for the making and maintenance, for their use, of lawn tennis and other recreation grounds." It consists of proprietary, annual, and honorary members, and the President is His Excellency the Governor (Sir Henry Arthur Blake), while Mr. F. W. Bois fills the office of Vice-President and Mr. Sutherland Ross officiates as hon. sec. and treasurer. The club maintains four croquet courts and sixteen tennis courts, covering in all ten acres of land, the grounds being situated in a central part of Cinnamon Gardens. The spacious club-house contains, on the upper floor, a large ball-room, measuring about 60 ft. by 30 ft., where during the season select dances are held. On this floor also there is a handsome withdrawing-room for ladies. Members' card-rooms, smoking, reading and dressing rooms are also provided in the club-house. A spacious verandah affords shade and shelter both at the front and the back of the building. The grounds are invitingly laid out, the playing courts are carefully tended and maintained, and altogether the institution forms a charming rendezvous for the residents in the surrounding chief residential quarter of Colombo. There are about 300 active members on the list of the club, including most of the leading constituents of the local social world. Provision is also made for the admission to the privileges of the club of visitors to Colombo who are duly accredited and introduced.

THE FORT TENNIS CLUB.

This club, the name of which sufficiently indicates its location and its purpose, was founded in 1887, the number of members being limited to thirty. There are three playing courts, which are situated just outside the old Fort walls of Colombo and behind the present Fort police station. During the years of its existence the club has always been well supported by those for whose benefit it was established. The club holds an annual meet of members in August, when its challenge cup is played for; also a half-yearly tournament in February. Mr. W. A. Cave is the hon. sec.

THE SINHALESE SPORTS CLUB.

This club was inaugurated in 1899. The objects for the formation of such an institution were twofold, namely, to encourage sports—not only among the townsfolk, but throughout the country—so as to introduce some diversion into the lives of the people and keep them from pernicious amusements; and, secondly, to create a common ground on which all classes of the Sinhalese community could meet together with an ultimate view of facilitating a removal of distinctions which divide the community. The first President of the club was Sir Harry Dias, K.T., and its first secretary Mr. H. J. V. Ekanayake, to whose energy is due to a large extent the founding of the club. On the death of the first President, the Hon. Mr. S. C. Obeyesekera, M.L.C., was elected to the office, and he continues to hold that position. There are eight Vice-Presidents, and eleven members of the committee. The captain of cricket is Mr. D. L. de Saram, while Mr. Henry M. Gunasekera is the hon. treasurer and secretary. The number of members of the club is 125, including honorary, non-resident, and playing members. Cricket matches are played with all the leading clubs in Colombo, and the Sinhalese Club is considered to be sufficiently powerful to hold its own against any local club. The club ground is situated at Victoria Park, alongside the Colombo Museum.

THE CEYLON FISHING CLUB.

The numerous streams in the beautiful Nuwara Eliya district—the part of the hill-country of Ceylon most favoured by those in quest of a pleasant climate, scenic attractions, and healthful outdoor recreation—abound with fish, especially in their valley courses; and here the angler finds good sport. This centre is the headquarters of the Ceylon Fishing Club, which was founded in 1896, not only for the actual prosecution of the art immortalised by old Isaak Walton, but also for the organisation of efforts in the direction of acclimatising and breeding fish for sport. A beginning was made, however, some time anterior to the existence of the club, experiments in trout-breeding having been initiated in 1880 by the late Mr. Hugh L. Hubbard, who was assisted in his endeavours by Mr. C. J. R. le Mesurier and Mr. Hearn. In 1882 about twenty fish were turned into the Nuwara Eliya stream by Mr. Hubbard; and in 1886 his efforts were successfully followed up by Mr. le Mesurier, then Assistant Government Agent of Nuwara Eliya. As Chairman of the Local Board, Mr. le Mesurier invited public support for these efforts, and, meeting with favourable response, began operations on a larger scale, with the result that in 1886 and 1888 the public subscribed liberally to the breeding operations, while an equal amount was contributed by the Local Board. Originally the ova imported were those of the brown trout; but in 1899 the ova of the rainbow-trout were imported for the first time, and as this species stand the climate better than the brown trout, this experiment has proved very successful, and the rainbow variety is now breeding freely. All the waters in the island above the level of 4,000 ft. have been leased to the club by Government, and every year efforts are made to increase the stock of trout. The fishing season of the year extends from April to October and the close season from November to March.

The club consists of 141 members, and has His Excellency the Governor, Sir Henry Arthur Blake, for its patron, with Brigadier-General R. C. B. Lawrence, the officer commanding the forces in the island, as President; while the Vice-Presidents are the Government Agents for the Central and the Sabaragamuwa Provinces. The committee consists of twenty members, ten of whom form the managing committee. The joint secretaries are Messrs. F. Bartlett, Assistant Government Agent, Nuwara Eliya, and J. Wickwar. The club is in a flourishing condition, and affords a means of pursuing the fascinating pursuit of angling in most congenial circumstances and pleasant surroundings.

THE COLOMBO CROQUET CLUB.

Having to commend it both qualities of mildness as well as of fascination, the pastime of croquet has been firmly rooted in the scope of this island's outdoor recreations. For upwards of thirty years the game has found votaries in almost every section of the Ceylon community, though, naturally, it has come to be considered as a first favourite with ladies more than with the sterner sex. With a view to bringing the game into greater popularity, and in order to provide a venue for those who indulge in it, the Colombo Croquet Club was established in 1881 in Kotahena, an important residential quarter of the town, by Mr. C. H. Christie-David, who remains its active secretary. The grounds are at St. James's Lawn, Kotahena.

It is an interesting fact that this club is about the oldest-established sporting institution in Ceylon; and though it is still more or less in a transitional stage of its existence, it promises to develop into larger dimensions in the near future. In spite of constant change of the habitat of the club's members, a fair number of supporters remain on the roll, an annual tournament being held for the purpose of bringing the members together for play and social intercourse. The club offers a cup as a championship award, the conditions attaching to its possession being that the competitor shall score three successive wins. This coveted trophy, together with the Challenge Shield, is now held by the secretary, who won it in the tournament of 1895 in a field of over fifteen entries.

CHRISTIE-DAVID.
(Secretary, Colombo Croquet Club.)

The President of the club is the Rev. W. Armstrong Buck, the late Warden of St. Thomas's College, who, although at present away in England, interests himself in the affairs of the institution, and, with the energetic secretary, has contributed mainly towards its establishment. The motto of the club, appropriately enough, is *Fide et Fiducia*; for while its inception was attended with not over-propitious circumstances, the maxim has justified itself in this case by the fact that the institution has outlived all rivals, and is achieving strength and status by its survival.

ECCLESIASTICAL

THE CHURCH OF ENGLAND.

BY THE REV. W. HENLY, PRIEST-IN-CHARGE, CHURCH OF ST. MICHAEL AND ALL ANGELS, POLWATTA, COLOMBO.

WHEN, at the beginning of the last century, the maritime provinces of Ceylon came into the possession of the British nation, the State religion was at one stroke transformed from Dutch Presbyterianism to Anglican Episcopacy, as it had before been changed, a century and a half earlier, from Roman Catholicism to Dutch Presbyterianism. According to computation, based on such records as are available, the change affected some 300,000 natives, who were, at the time, baptized members of the Dutch Church. But by far the greater majority of these were Dutch Presbyterians only in name. Many in heart were Roman Catholics; still more Buddhists or Hindus.

The Church, as distinguished from the State, was not at that time sufficiently awakened to make use of the opportunity thus afforded of effectually Christianising this large body of half-hearted adherents. The new Government very rightly did not continue the efforts of their predecessors to induce their subjects to profess any particular religion. Accordingly, though for some time the Dutch system of catechists and proponents (lay preachers) was continued, the number of Government Christians, as they were called, very rapidly decreased, and has now long passed beyond vanishing point.

What the British Government did do for the Church was to provide clergy for the places where its own officials were stationed, and in some cases for the planting districts. These clergy, known as colonial chaplains, were at first under the episcopal control of the Bishop of Calcutta. Later, Ceylon became part of the diocese of Madras. In 1845 it was constituted a separate diocese, James Chapman being the first Bishop. He was paid by the State, and was, officially, the head of the ecclesiastical department, which consisted of the State-provided clergy, though by his letters-patent he had also the control of all Church of England clergy working in his diocese. This system of Government aid to the Church continued till 1881, when the local Legislature determined that no further State appointments should be made to any ecclesiastical office. An Ordinance was passed giving power to the members of the Church of England in Ceylon to establish a Synod to regulate their affairs, and to elect incorporated trustees to hold their Church property.

The cessation of State aid, though gradual, would have been far more severely felt if the Government chaplains had been the only clergy ministering in the diocese. But this was not the case. Soon after 1815 the Church Missionary Society had begun work in Ceylon. The aim of this Society is rather to evangelise the heathen than to minister to those already within the Church. But success in the work of conversion necessitates the assumption of the pastoral charge of the converts. So that, besides the European missionaries, the Society had many native pastors labouring in various places where settled congregations had been built up. There were, indeed, few parts of Ceylon where its influence was not felt; and everywhere the Church Missionary Society's clergy showed themselves ready to assist in supplying those ministrations, the loss of which seemed threatened, alike to native and European Christians.

The sister Society—the Society for the Propagation of the Gospel in Foreign Parts—was also active in the diocese, and took a large part in the foundation of many institutions which still exist, notably St. Thomas's College, Colombo. This Society still contributes an annual sum to the work of the diocese, the distribution of which is in the hands of a local committee, of which the Bishop is chairman. This contribution is used to foster and encourage local efforts. Thus it was that, when the withdrawal of State aid was determined on, there was a very considerable part of the Church which was in no way affected. Consequently there was no panic, and little, if any, discouragement. Steps were at once taken to meet the emergency, the most important of which was the starting of the Bishopric Endowment Fund. This was largely helped by Church societies in England; and when, two years ago, the then Bishop, Dr. R. S. Copleston, was translated to Calcutta, an income of £1,000 per annum was available from this source for his successor. A Central Clergy Endowment Fund was also started, which is still slowly growing, and now amounts to Rs. 37,000. Many local endowment funds were also initiated, the total amount invested with the incorporated trustees being Rs. 137,451.

These endowments, with the exception of the Bishopric Endowment, are obviously only adequate to assist the efforts of the present generation to provide clerical ministrations. The bulk of the clergy are supported by the voluntary contributions of their individual flocks. One only of the colonial chaplains now survives—the Rev. C. A. Koch; but the number of clergy ministering in the diocese has risen from about 60 in 1881 to 84 in 1906, and most certainly the standard of work has been greatly raised. Much educational work is being carried on, not only in large central institutions like St. Thomas's College, Colombo, and Trinity College, Kandy, but in the school, or schools, established in nearly every parish, many of which have attained to a high standard of efficiency. Other means of Christianising the people are also exercised, in connection with all of which the clergy receive valuable aid from the laity.

In 1887 a branch of the Sisterhood of St. Margaret's, East Grinstead, was established in Colombo, which is carrying on most useful educational work in Bishop's College, St. Margaret's School, and the Girls' Home in the city, besides rendering valuable assistance among the poor of many of the Colombo parishes.

The present Bishop of Colombo—the diocese covering the whole of Ceylon — Dr. E. A. Copleston, has known the island for many years, and had wide experience of work among all classes of the population. He is the younger brother of Bishop Copleston of Calcutta, who formerly administered the diocese of Colombo, and is now the Metropolitan of India and Ceylon. These two brothers have presided over the fortunes of the Church in the island in a time of great difficulty. The present Bishop of Colombo was selected by the authority of the Synod of the Diocese; and as he has the experience to direct and stimulate the efforts of the Church with wisdom and knowledge, so it is certain that he will find himself amply seconded by the loyal co-operation of all, whether clergy or laity, over whom he is called upon to preside.

In conclusion, it is not too much to say that the Church of England in Ceylon is to-day a strong and vigorous body, which has at least held its own in the past, and is looking forward hopefully to increased usefulness and activity in the future.

ROMAN CATHOLIC CHURCH.

THE earliest reliable notice of the existence of Christianity in Ceylon comes from Cosmas Judicopleustes (fifth century), an Egyptian merchant, afterwards a monk, who states that there existed in Ceylon at that time a community of believers with an episcopal form of discipline, priests, deacons, and a liturgy; but he adds that the members of that Church were Persians and mere sojourners (perhaps traders). The ten following centuries are silent with regard to any form of Christianity in the island, though some travellers mention Jews and Mahomedans as resident there. Marco Polo, in 1290, expressly says that the inhabitants of Ceylon were idolaters. It was only with the advent of the Portuguese, in 1505, that Christianity first became rooted in the island.

Portuguese Period: 1505 to 1658.

The Portuguese openly professed that the exaltation of the faith was the main object of their conquests. Nothing that missionary labour could effect for the conversion of the natives was left undone; and whenever the Portuguese formed an alliance with any of the Sinhalese princes, they always stipulated for liberty to preach Christianity. In 1518 the first Catholic missionaries, consisting of a few Franciscan friars, arrived in Ceylon. In spite of obstacles raised by the Buddhist bonzes and persecution resulting from the bad conduct of some of the Portuguese, the native Sinhalese Buddhists soon entered the Church by thousands. After the construction of the fort of Colombo the adjoining districts were erected into a bishopric, and placed under the jurisdiction of Don Juan de Monteiro, the first Catholic prelate in Ceylon, whose tomb was discovered in 1836. Under his direction Christianity was speedily proclaimed throughout the Sinhalese districts. In 1540 the Portuguese established themselves at Puttalam, on the north-west coast, and built a large church there, which became the centre and headquarters of missionary enterprise. Among the converts of that time was Dharmapala, grandson of Bhuvaneka Bahu VII., who was crowned king in the palace of Lisbon under the name of Don Juan in 1541. After his return to Ceylon he, with many of his followers, received baptism, and he ruled as a Christian monarch from 1542 to 1597. In a special treaty of alliance with this ruler the Portuguese had stipulated that the Franciscan missionaries should be allowed to preach the Gospel throughout his dominions, and conversions to Christianity consequently became more and more numerous along the coast.

The missionaries, who so far were only able to work among the Sinhalese population on the west coast, in 1554 extended their sphere to the Tamils in the north. The Paravas, or fisher caste, of Mannar, in the kingdom of Jaffna, hearing of the preaching and miracles of St. Francis Xavier on the Coromandel coast, sent some messengers to him with the request that he should visit their island. At that moment unable to come to Ceylon himself, St. Francis sent some other priests, who in a short time baptized from 600 to 700 Tamils. These neophytes were destined to become the pro-martyrs of the island of Ceylon. Sanghili, the Raja of Jaffna, in whose dominion Mannar was situated, was greatly enraged at the conversion of his subjects, and he confiscated the property of the neophytes, imprisoned, branded, and maimed them. But, finding that all these oppressive measures to extirpate Christianity from his dominions were utterly futile and unavailing, he ordered 600 of the converts to be put to death, and issued a decree prohibiting the landing of Christian missionaries. Nevertheless, Christianity made such progress among the Tamils in Jaffna that two sons of the Raja, besides a brother, a sister and her son, embraced the Christian religion, placing themselves under the protection of the Portuguese Viceroy at Goa.

Thus masters of the whole western coast of Ceylon from Colombo to Jaffna, and of the interior as far as Kandy, the Catholic missionaries turned their attention to the Sinhalese and Buddhists in the south, west, and centre of the island, and the Tamils in the northern extremity; and the whole extent of the island was thus brought by them under the influence and authority of the Church. In 1548 the Catholics in Colombo numbered 12,000 souls. Ceylon was divided into parishes, each of which was provided with a church or chapel, a school, and, where required, a glebe for the residence of the priests and missionaries. By this time the latter, representing variously the Franciscan, Dominican, Jesuit, and Augustinian orders, had greatly increased. In Jaffna itself a college of Jesuits, a church and convent of Dominicans, and a convent of Franciscans were coexistent; and in 1658 there were in that town altogether 50 priests of these three orders. In Colombo there were two parishes—those of Our Lady and St. Lawrence—four religious houses—of the Cordeliers, Dominicans, Augustinians, and Capuchins—and a college of the Jesuits with seven parishes outside.

There is no proof that compulsion was resorted to by the Portuguese for the extension of the Catholic faith, or violence employed for the extinction of the national superstitions; and the probability is that the priests and missionaries of the Portuguese were contented to pursue in Ceylon the same line of policy and to adopt the same expedients for conversion which had already been found successful by their fellow-labourers on the opposite continent of India. When King Don Juan Dharmapala died at Colombo in 1597, he made over his dominions to Philip II. of Spain and Henry of Portugal conjointly, and liberty was granted to Catholic missionaries to preach the Gospel where they pleased throughout the island.

Dutch Period : 1658 to 1796.

The Dutch made their first appearance in Ceylon in May, 1602 ; and their struggle with the Portuguese for possession of the island lasted till 1658, when the latter lost their last footing in Mannar and Jaffna. The conquerors, in their policy towards the Catholic Church, showed that their main object was to banish the religion from the island. The Reformed Church of Holland was established as the religion of the colony in 1642, and the Catholic priests who were found in Colombo and Jaffna were banished to India. Father Caldeiro, S.J., whom sickness prevented from following his colleagues, was beheaded at Jaffna. A proclamation was issued on September 19, 1658, forbidding, on pain of death, the harbouring or concealing of Catholic priests ; and this decree was successively renewed on March 25, 1733, on August 10, 1734, and on February 25, 1745. Other proclamations—of January 11, 1715, and July 31, 1751—forbade Catholic assemblies, whether public or private ; of August 8, 1715, and February 25, 1745, the celebration of Mass and the administration of baptism, and of August 10, 1751, the education of any Catholic for the ministry. At the same time the Dutch proceeded steadily and systematically with their work of proselytising the Tamils in the north, and took possession of the Catholic churches in the Jaffna peninsula.

Yet, in spite of all these efforts, the influence of the Dutch form of Christianity declined, while that of the Catholic clergy continued to increase. Among the most distinguished Catholic missionaries was Joseph Vaz, of Goa, whose journeys and imprisonments have gained a great veneration for his name among the Ceylon Catholics. For five years he went about through the swamps and jungles of the island, making converts among the heathen by the austerity of his life and the warmth of his zeal. He visited Vanny, Puttalam, and Kandy in 1692. In Kandy he was imprisoned for two years, and during his incarceration he applied himself to the study of the Sinhalese language. In 1694 he was set free ; and, a deadly pestilence happening to be raging, he followed the sick into the jungles, performed for them the most menial services, and opened hospitals to shelter them. These devoted services gained for him the confidence of the Kandyan king, Vimala Dharma II. (1688–1707), who allowed him to rebuild some of the old churches in his kingdom. Father Vaz then undertook a second journey through the island. In 1696 he was made Vicar-General of Ceylon, under the Bishop of Cochin, and new priests were sent to help him, foremost among them being Father Gonzalvez. Father Vaz died in Kandy in 1711, after a laborious, eventful, and fruitful life of twenty-four years' work. Though the Dutch persecution lessened the number of Catholic adherents among the natives of Ceylon, yet, owing to the zeal of the companions and successors of Father Vaz, the Church maintained a firm footing in the island, and many of her children remained true to their faith.

English Period : from 1796.

When, in 1795, war broke out between England and Holland, a small English force landed at Trincomalee, and this town surrendered after a siege of three weeks. Jaffna was taken by the British in September of that year, and Colombo on February 16, 1796. But the conquest of the whole island was not completed until 1815. The English had scarcely begun the administration of their new conquest when they perceived that Ceylon could not be governed on the Dutch plan of persecuting the Catholics, "as the Catholic natives had shown that they could neither be bribed nor terrified." One of the first acts of the new conquerors after they had taken possession of the island and brought it into a settled position was to grant the Catholic Church in the island full liberty and freedom of action. On May 27, 1806, all the laws of the Dutch against the Catholics were repealed by Governor Sir Thomas Maitland (1805–12), on the urgent representations of the Chief Justice, Sir Alexander Johnston. The Catholics, "who are a numerous and peaceable body of His Majesty's subjects" (words of Sir Thomas Maitland in 1806), were allowed the unmolested exercise of their religion in every part of Ceylon, and were relieved from all civil disqualifications. They were admitted to all civil privileges and capacities, and their marriages were declared valid, notwithstanding the laws to the contrary which had been enacted by the Dutch. The Catholic natives of Ceylon were thus confirmed in the faith to which they had adhered with remarkable tenacity for 300 years ; while of the enforced converts of the Dutch Government—called "Government Christians"—few remained.

The Catholic population of the island, which in 1796 amounted to 50,000, was in 1806 calculated at 66,830, according to the official returns presented to the Government ; whilst the census of 1809 gave the number as 83,595. That the religious professions of the natives and the conversions from paganism were not merely nominal is proved by the testimony borne to the character of the Catholics of Ceylon by Sir Alexander Johnston, Chief Justice of the colony, who in 1807 wrote to the Archbishop of Goa : "The propriety of their [the Catholics'] conduct reflects great honour upon the priests of the Order of St. Philip Neri who have the charge of their instruction. In a circuit which I lately made round the island, I was much pleased to find that there was not a single Catholic brought before me for trial, and not a single individual of your religion was even accused of the smallest misdemeanour."

When the Emancipation Act, which removed from Catholics all civil disabilities, was extended to Ceylon, the Catholics of the island were released by Propaganda from the jurisdiction of the diocese of Cochin, to which they had been subjected since the erection of that see in 1592, with the object of withdrawing them from the pernicious influence of the Goanese schism, and providing for their better spiritual assistance. Pope Gregory XVI. issued, in 1834, the brief "Ex munere pastorali," by which Ceylon was erected into an independent vicariate-apostolic, with Father Francis Xavier as the first Bishop. This brief, however, owing to Father Francis Xavier's death in the following year without having been consecrated as Bishop, was not put into execution. In 1836 the same brief was re-enacted, and Mgr. Vincent de Rosario, Titular-Bishop of Tamacene, was appointed Vicar-Apostolic. Some Catholics, dissatisfied with this nomination, sent a memorial to the Holy Father asking for a bishop and some priests of English or Irish origin. They remained, however, under the jurisdiction of Bishop Rosario till his death in 1842. But they repudiated his successor, Bishop Caetano Antonio, and, withdrawing from submission to his authority, placed themselves under the jurisdiction of the Archbishop of Goa. Thus commenced a schism in Ceylon.

As the number of Catholics was year by year increasing, Propaganda in 1845 divided the island into two vicariates-apostolic, namely, Colombo for the Sinhalese population in the south, under Mgr. Caetano Antonio (who died in 1857) and Jaffna for the Tamils in the north. In 1847 the latter division was placed under the jurisdiction of Mgr. Bettachini, who had been coadjutor to Bishop Rosario since 1845. In that year new auxiliaries had arrived in the promising field of the "Gem of the East," under the leadership of their Superior, Father Bravi, O.S.B., who brought with him priests of the Benedictine Congregation of the Sylvestrines. The Church establishment was further strengthened in 1847 by the arrival of Father Semeria with some priests of the Congregation of the Oblates of Mary Immaculate, an order which was destined to play an important part in the history of the Catholic Church and her development in the island.

In spite of the harm done by the Goanese schism to the success of the Church in Ceylon, the Catholic faith continued to spread in the island. The census, as returned by Bishop Caetano Antonio in 1849, enumerates two vicariates-apostolic, 33 priests, 500 native catechists, 300 churches, 46 schools, 2,000 pupils, and some 116,000 Catholics—consisting of 83,561 Sinhalese, 31,952 Tamils, and 1,141 Europeans and others. Bishop Caetano Antonio, as already stated, died in 1857, after having entrusted his vicariate (of Colombo) to the Benedictines of the Sylvestrine Congregation in 1855, and was succeeded by Bishop Bravi, O.S.B., 1857–60; Valerga of Quilon (as Apostolic Administrator), 1860–63; Sillani, O.S.B., 1863–1879; and Pagnani, O.S.B., from 1879. After the death of Mgr. Bettachini in 1857 the vicariate of Jaffna, embracing the northern part of the island, was handed over to the Congregation of the Oblates, by whom it has been administered ever since, under Bishops Semeria, O.M.I., 1857–68; Bonjean, O.M.I., 1868–83; Melizan, O.M.I., 1883–92; and Joulain, O.M.I., since 1892. In the year 1857 a concordat was concluded between the Holy See and Portugal to regulate the exercise of the Portuguese patronage in the East; but as Portugal was not able or not willing to comply with the conditions laid down, the concordat was of little effect, and was abrogated and replaced by another thirty years later. As the work of the mission grew heavier every year and the missionary districts became over-extended, the vicariate of Colombo was, on April 27, 1883, and at the request of Bishop Pagnani, O.S.B., divided into two separate vicariates, of Colombo and Kandy respectively. There were in 1883 in Ceylon 195,000 Catholics—Colomho vicariate having 115,000 Catholics, with 27 priests, and Jaffna 80,000 Catholics, with 36 priests—and 103 Catholic schools, attended by 7,730 pupils, had been established in the island.

Colombo was entrusted to the Oblates, and Bishop Bonjean was transferred from Jaffna to Colombo, while the new vicariate of Kandy was handed over to the Sylvestrines, with Mgr. Pagnani, O.S.B., as first Vicar-Apostolic of that centre. In order to improve the schools in his new vicariate, Bishop Bonjean left nothing untried. He appealed to Europe for help, matured the plans for the foundation of a college for the higher education of Catholics, and built a number of elementary schools, both English and Tamil. The progressive number of schools in the island is conclusive evidence of the zeal and energy displayed by the Catholics of Ceylon within fifty years. In 1849 there were 46 schools with 2,000 pupils; in 1862, 96 schools with 4,208 pupils; in 1891, 368 schools with 24,000 pupils; in 1904, 570 schools with 45,549 pupils.

In 1886 Pope Leo XIII. made a new concordat with Portugal, by which the patronage of the latter, with all the rights hitherto exercised over the Church in the East, was abolished. In consequence of this concordat the Pope obtained a free hand to establish the hierarchy in Ceylon. Colombo was accordingly raised to the rank of an archbishopric, with Jaffna and Kandy as suffragan sees. Towards the end of December, 1886, Mgr. Agliardi, Archbishop of Cæsaræa, was sent to Ceylon as Delegate-Apostolic; and on the Feast of the Epiphany, January 6, 1887, he held a Synod in the Cathedral of St. Lucia, Colombo, when Mgr. Bonjean, of Colombo, was raised to the dignity of Archbishop of Colombo, whilst Mgr. Melizan, O.M.I., and Mgr. Pagnani, O.S.B., were appointed Bishops of Jaffna and

RT. REV. DR. ANTHONY COUDERT, O.M.I.
(Roman Catholic Archbishop of Colombo.)

Kandy respectively. In April, 1887, Mgr. Agliardi was called away to Europe, and was succeeded as Papal Delegate of the East Indies by Mgr. Aiuti, 1887–92, and then by Mgr. Zaleski. This latter has fixed his residence in Kandy; and there, by the munificence of Pope Leo XIII., the General Seminary for training native youth in the East for the priesthood was established in 1893. It was entrusted to the care of the Fathers of the Society of Jesus. This seminary had, in 1905, 88 students, representing 21 dioceses of India and Ceylon. In the same year (1893) Ceylon saw a further development in its ecclesiastical hierarchy, when the two new dioceses of Galle and Trincomalee were formed from the existing divisions of Colombo and Jaffna, and entrusted by the Holy See to the Society of Jesus. Mgr. Van Reeth, S.J., was appointed Bishop of Galle in 1896, and Mgr. Lavigne, S.J., Bishop of Trincomalee in 1898.

That the Catholic Church is still progressing in the island is made plain by the following figures:—

		No. of Catholics.		No. of Priests.
1873	...	182,610	...	83
1883	...	195,000	...	76
1893	...	246,000	...	117
1904	...	293,929	...	171

Archdiocese of Colombo.

The archdiocese of Colombo comprises two out of the nine provinces into which the island of Ceylon is divided, viz., the Western Province (chief town, Colombo) and the North-Western Province (chief town, Kurunegala). On September 1, 1886, Colombo was erected into an archiepiscopal see; and by a brief of His Holiness Leo XIII., dated August 26, 1893—at the time the two new dioceses of Trincomalee and Galle were created—the number of suffragan sees under the metropolitan see of Colombo was raised to four, namely, Jaffna, Kandy, Trincomalee, and Galle.

His Grace the Most Rev. Anthony Coudert, D.D., O.M.I., consecrated at Colombo on November 30, 1898, as coadjutor (with right of succession) to the Most Rev. Dr. Melizan, O.M.I., succeeded to the metropolitan see of Colombo on June 27, 1905. Under his zealous, able, and paternal care and direction the Catholic community and Catholic interests cannot but increase and prosper. His Grace is aided in the task by his Vicar-General, the Right Rev. Father I. Bell, O.M.I., and by the Archiepiscopal Court, consisting of eight Oblate Fathers, mostly superiors of missions and all possessing a wide experience in administrative work. There are in the archdiocese about 97 missionaries, including 90 Oblate Fathers, of whom 10 are native, 2 secular European, and 5 secular native priests. The number of churches is almost 300; and the Catholic population, out of a total population of 1,300,000, amounts to 206,000 souls. The Sinhalese form the majority of the Catholic population.

Mission Work.

The work of the Fathers in their respective missions is chiefly parochial and educational. The administration of education is entirely in their hands, the total number of the schools in the interior being 366. The parochial branch includes the building or repairing of the churches, the conferring of Sacraments, the visitation of the sick, and the usual parish duties. As a rule the Catholics are kind and obedient to their pastors, whose influence with them is often paramount, especially when disputes—inevitable in a country of so many racial and religious differences—arise. On more than one occasion the Government Agent and officials have been able to test, use, and admire that influence when they themselves were powerless in the face of perhaps 4,000 or 5,000 rioters. Here may be mentioned the friendly, sometimes cordial, relations subsisting between the Fathers and the Government Agents, as well as between the Fathers and the European planters in the up-country parts. The Government has placed on record that the most loyal of its subjects are the Catholic missionaries; and more than one Governor of the island has been struck by, and has expressed admiration for, their spirit of organisation. Meanwhile, on their side, the Catholic clergy and laity recognise appreciatively that in Ceylon, as in all other colonies, England wishes her flag to protect every religion.

Religious Communities and Education.

The strongest religious community in the archdiocese of Colombo is that of the Oblates of Mary Immaculate. In 1883 the late Archbishop Bonjean, O.M.I., founded, at Borella, Colombo, St. Bernard's Ecclesiastical Seminary, where, under the able direction of two European Fathers, 25 young native students prepare themselves for the mission work and the priesthood. His Excellency the Apostolic Delegate, Mgr. Zaleski, never comes to Colombo without visiting the seminary and expressing his utmost satisfaction at the working of this institution, which he holds to be the pattern for all the dioceses of India.

In 1893 Archbishop Melizan founded St. Aloysius's Preparatory Seminary at Union Place, Slave Island, Colombo, for younger students. The 20 boys here follow the classes or lectures at St. Joseph's College, and often shine on the prize-distribution day. A European Father, O.M.I., is in charge. Besides the Oblate community, there are two other religious orders of men, namely, the Christian Brothers, or Brothers of the Christian Schools, and the native Brothers of St. Vincent de Paul. The former number about 50, divided between their two houses, the Noviciate at Mutwal and their flourishing Institute at Kotahena, Colombo. The native Brothers of St. Vincent de Paul, founded in 1892, number from 15 to 20, and are employed in teaching native children in the vernacular language, and supervising the orphanage and industrial schools at Maggona, about 32 miles south from Colombo, and the schools at Wennapuwa and Chilaw, two other centres in the archdiocese, situated north of Colombo.

The same educational work as that performed for the Catholic boys by the Oblate Fathers and by the Brothers is done for the girls, with equal earnestness, care, and success by several female religious communities. The Nuns of the Good Shepherd, numbering 23, have their most important community at Kotahena, Colombo, and are employed in teaching in five high schools for girls in Colombo itself. The principal one of these schools is at Kotahena, where the English school is attended by 396 girls, of whom 32 are boarders. This institution has on more than one occasion been praised by the Government examiners; and in 1906 the girls' scholarship went to Kotahena Sacred Heart High School. The second of the institutions conducted by the Nuns of the Good Shepherd is St. Mary's High School, Pettah, which has a roll of 95 children; while the third is St. Bridget's School, Colpetty, in the part of Colombo known as the Cinnamon Gardens, where 96 children are in attendance. The Nuns of St. Francis Xavier, a native order, are also under the direction of the Nuns of the Good Shepherd. They number 82, have a Novitiate, and their central house is at Negombo. They conduct no less than 20 vernacular schools in different parts of the archdiocese, the number of children under their care being 3,000. Then there are the Nuns of the Holy Family, numbering 23, who conduct three important schools—one at Bambalapitiya, with 105 children; one at Wennapuwa, and one at Kurunegala, the total number of children attending the two latter being 135. This order also controls the native Nuns of St. Peter, who number 120, and have the conduct of no less than 28 vernacular schools, the number of children under their care being about 3,205. In addition, the Franciscan Nuns, Missionaries of Mary, conduct a growing and already flourishing institution at Moratuwa, called the School of our Lady of Victories, and attended by 160 children.

These various religious orders do not, however, entirely confine themselves to educational work, but have won the admiration of Catholics, Protestants, Mahomedans, and Buddhists alike for their almost superhuman devotedness in charitable work.

Religious Orders and Charitable Institutions.

The Nuns of the Holy Family conduct at Kurunegala an orphanage for girls, the number of inmates being 42. Seven of the Sisters are also selected for special work at the Government hospital. The Nuns of the Good Shepherd educate in their orphanage at Negombo 55 girls, in that at Kalamulla 16 girls, and in that at Kotahena 134 orphans. At Kotahena, besides, they conduct an industrial school in which a great number of girls are taught lace-work, embroidery, and other useful accomplishments. The Franciscan Nuns, Missionaries of Mary, are at the head of a flourishing orphanage of 125 girls at Moratuwa, where they also conduct a largely attended industrial school. Their principal sphere of labour, however, is the nursing department of the General Hospital, Colombo, which has been entrusted to them by the Ceylon Government. In this hospital work 32 European Sisters spend their youth with zeal and disinterested devotedness; and, considering the nature of the diseases and the increasing number of sick people they have to look after, it is not to be wondered that the medical authorities and the Government—as well as the people at large—highly prize their assistance as nurses. Their care extends equally to all, heathen and Christians, rich and poor. Then there are the Little Sisters of the Poor, whose work is known all the world over; and in Colombo, as elsewhere, their special care is the management of a home for the aged. About 20 Sisters are engaged in this labour of love, and the inmates of the home, men and women, number nearly 200. His Excellency the Governor frequently visits this institution, in which he takes a warm interest.

Industrial School and Reformatory.

Perhaps the most interesting (although the least known) of all the Catholic institutions in the archdiocese of Colombo, if not in the whole of the island, is St. Vincent's home, situated at Maggona, 32 miles south of Colombo, on the main railway line to Galle. It is an estate of 332 acres, planted mostly with coconut and cinnamon; and scattered over that area stand a number of bungalows, each quite a separate institution, the whole forming a little village of about 350 persons. The principal bungalow shelters two European Fathers, Oblates of Mary, and six European lay brothers, also Oblates, who together hold the direction and management of the whole settlement. The principal branch is a boys' orphanage, in which about 115 children of the poorer classes receive food, clothing, and instruction. Attached to the orphanage and conducted by the native Brothers of St. Vincent de Paul is a Sinhalese school, which is attended in the morning by the orphans. These bereft boys are taught printing, binding, carpentry, tailoring, and gardening under European and native Brothers, and are thus fitted for earning their own livelihood. St. Vincent's Home also includes the Boys' Reformatory. For a great many years the Wesleyans of Ceylon had been entrusted with this reformatory work. In 1898 the Government asked Archbishop Melizan to undertake the maintenance and management of a penitentiary for boys of all denominations—Protestants, Buddhists, heathens, Mahomedans, and Catholics. Accordingly, buildings for the purpose were erected or enlarged; and at the present day the reformatory thus established at Maggona contains nearly 200 boys, under the surveillance of two European Brothers and a dozen native watchmen. This establishment is registered by the

Government as a certified industrial school, and is used for the detention of juvenile offenders up to the age of eighteen years. These youngsters under detention attend the Brothers conduct, in another bungalow, a normal or training school for Sinhalese Catholic schoolmasters, which is attended by some 30 students.

towards the building on the condition that the ground floor should be set apart for the use of the College. The Catholics of Colombo and of other parts of the island also subscribed

LACE MAKING IN THE CONVENT.

GALLE CONVENT.

THE CONVENT PUPILS.

industrial school above mentioned—but not at the same time as the boys from the orphanage—and also have a school of their own. It is worthy of particular remark that this school has been very successful. In 1903 it gave the best results of all the native schools in the island, the mark awarded to it by the Director of Public Instruction being 99 per cent. And in the same year the two schools—orphanage and reformatory—sent in 225 boys for examination, with the result that the whole number passed. When ex-Governor Sir West Ridgeway paid an official visit to Maggona, he expressed his admiration at the spirit of organisation displayed in connection with this institution. The founder of the Maggona settlement was the Rev. Father Charles Conrard, O.M.I., who conducted the institutions here for ten years, under the guidance and direction of the late Archbishops Bonjean and Melizan. Close to the bungalow of the Fathers is what is styled the "Home," in other words the Mother House, of the native order of the Brothers of St. Vincent, whose members are engaged in the work of the settlement. Three of these

Catholic Union and other Institutions.

St. Joseph's College—an account of which Catholic institution is given in the Educational Section of this book—has up to now lent part of its fine premises to the Catholic Union of Ceylon. This is an association of all the Catholics of the island, and its general purpose is to serve Catholic interests on all questions, social and political. The particular object of the club is to enable Catholics to meet together in a Catholic atmosphere for recreation and social enjoyment. Besides the usual attractions of a social club, the members are provided with all kinds of Catholic literature, in the shape of reviews, papers, magazines, periodicals, and other publications unobtainable elsewhere in the island.

Another noticeable institution, on the grounds of St. Joseph's College, is the Bonjean Memorial Hall, erected to perpetuate the memory and the life-work of Dr. Christopher Bonjean, O.M.I., the first Archbishop of Colombo. His immediate successor, the late Most Rev. Dr. T. A. Melizan, O.M.I. (who died in 1905), contributed Rs. 20,000 generously to the fund for the erection of the building. The hall is a two-storeyed building, 120 ft. in length and 30 ft. in width, not counting the verandahs, which are 10 ft. wide. The foundation-stone was laid on March 19, 1902, by His Eminence Cardinal Moran, Archbishop of Sydney, Australia, in the presence of an unprecedentedly large and enthusiastic gathering. The building is designed to continue and develop the three great purposes of Archbishop Bonjean's life, which are specifically defined as education, the uplifting and strengthening of Catholics, and the bringing them together in a Catholic atmosphere. The educative work is carried on in the lower portion of the building, the second line of effort in the upper portion, which is the home of the Catholic Union above mentioned, and the third purpose is served by the Catholic Club, a new two-storey structure built to the north of, and at right angles to, the Bonjean Memorial Hall.

The Catholic Mission of Colombo possesses a printing establishment, situated near Archbishop's House, Borella. From this press,

ST. LUCIA CATHEDRAL—VIEWS OF INTERIOR, EXTERIOR, AND PLAYGROUND.

besides religious works in English and Sinhalese, two bi-weekly newspapers—the *Catholic Messenger*, in English, and the *Nanartha Pradipaya*, in Sinhalese—are issued.

The above particulars suffice to show the general position and activities of the Roman Catholic Church in its archdiocese of Colombo.

Following is a summary of the Church's educational establishments in the archdiocese and in Ceylon generally: (1) St. Joseph's College, Colombo, with nearly 800 boys; (2) St. Benedict's Institute, Colombo, with nearly 1,100 boys—both separately noticed elsewhere; (3) in the archdiocese 379 schools with 35,600 pupils, 30 of these schools being English and the rest vernacular schools, (4) of 30 prominent boarding schools in the whole of Ceylon 9 are Catholic; (5) of 36 industrial schools in the island 22 are Catholic; (6) of 120 English schools in Ceylon 40 are Catholic; (7) although only two Catholic institutions of the 13 normal or training schools in the island are registered under this head, the number of passes at the examinations of these two schools is superior to that of all the others.

ST. LUCIA'S CATHEDRAL, COLOMBO.

This cathedral, the Roman Catholic Metropolitan Church of Ceylon, is a landmark for miles around Colombo on every side, standing as it does in a commanding position on an elevated part of Colombo. This edifice is undoubtedly one of the most magnificent buildings in the island. Its length is 250 ft., the breadth being 140 ft., while the cupola by which it is surmounted reaches a height of 180 ft. from the ground. The architecture is that of the Venetian Renascence, and under the sanctuary there is a crypt. The interior can easily accommodate 6,500 persons. The building of this great monument has occupied thirty-four years, and the finishing touch was not put to it until 1906.

THE SOUTHERN PROVINCE.

The diocese of Galle, which comprises the political portions known as the Southern and Sabaragamuwa Provinces, was formed by an edict of Pope Leo XIII., in 1893, which was carried into effect by the Belgian Jesuit Fathers in the year 1895. At the end of that year Dr. Joseph Van Reeth, with three priests and one lay brother, arrived in Ceylon and devoted themselves mainly to education. A few comparisons will show the great progress made in consequence of their efforts. Whereas in 1896 only 10 Catholic schools existed in the new diocese, with an attendance of 350 boys and 360 girls, a total of 710 scholars, in 1906 there were 36 schools, with a total attendance of 2,877 scholars. And whereas in the year 1896 the number of Catholics in the diocese amounted to 5,466, in 1906 the number had increased to 9,063. While in 1896 there were 13 churches and 7 chapels in the diocese, in 1906 there were 19 churches and 21 chapels. The staff, which in 1896 consisted of 3 priests and 1 lay brother, in 1906 consisted of the Bishop, 17 European and 2 native clergy, and 3 European lay-brothers.

A convent was established at Galle in 1896 by 5 European sisters, which number had increased by 1906 to 15 European and 3 native sisters. The convent accommodates about 70 boarders and considerably more than that number of day scholars, as well as providing a home for some 50 little orphan children. The education imparted at the convent is of the highest standard; and in connection with this establishment there is an industrial school, attended by the daughters of the poorer classes. Here is made the

THE INTERIOR. THE ROMAN CATHOLIC CHURCH, GALLE.

beautiful Galle lace, for which the convent received the gold medal at the St. Louis Exhibition, U.S.A., in 1904.

The large and beautiful church of Our Lady of the Rosary at Galle was built in 1874, with the aid of funds collected at Manilla, in the Philippine Islands, by the Rev. Father Martin, a Spanish Benedictine.

St. Aloysius's College, which was erected next to the church and the Bishop's house in 1902, was formerly an episcopal institution. It was taken over by the Jesuit Fathers in 1905, and has now on the roll nearly 300 boys, who are in the charge of a staff of 5 European Fathers, assisted by 8 native teachers. The school teaches up to the local Cambridge Senior Examination, and being subject to Government inspection, receives a grant in aid from the Government Treasury. Within the diocese of Galle there are also English schools at Matara, Tangalla, Hambantota, Ratnapura, Balangoda, and Kegalla.

CEYLON INDEPENDENT CATHOLIC MISSION.

The Ceylon Independent Catholic Mission is a body which dissociates itself from the influence of Rome. The formal establishment of the Mission only dates from 1888, but forty-five years previously the predecessors of the Independent Catholics, under the leadership of Dr. John Boniface Misso, who was the Portuguese Consul-General in Ceylon at the time, banded themselves together in vigorously opposing papal authority. These pioneers, who were known as "Padroadists," were publicly branded as heretics and schismatics by the Roman Catholic clergy of the island, and the Roman Catholics were forbidden to have any intercommunication with them. But this was not sufficient to break down the Independent body, and for some years there was a truce between the combatants. In 1886, however, a papal document, under the title of "Brief Studio et Vigilantia," was published. It declared the Padroadist Mission extinct, and gave over all the churches to the Roman Catholics. This work naturally caused a furore in Independent Catholic circles, and on legal advice all their churches were closed against Roman Catholic encroachments on January 2, 1887. At this juncture the Rev. A. F. X. Alvares and Dr. Lisboa Pinto came from India to assist the Independents, and after lengthy negotiations with the Patriarch of Antioch, through his representative Mar Dionysius, Syrian Metropolitan of Malabar, the Mission was eventually placed in the patriarchate of Antioch, and the Rev. A. F. X. Alvares was elected first as Prefect-Apostolic and afterwards as the first Archbishop of Independent Catholicism. Mgr. Vilatte, coming to Ceylon from America, was consecrated a Bishop by Archbishop Alvares and two other Syrian Bishops, and he spread the faith of Independent Catholicism in America and Europe, ordaining, amongst others, the Rev. Father Ignatius, of Lanthony Abbey.

At the present time the Mission, on account of constant litigation, is at a standstill, and its temporalities are administered by three trustees elected annually under the local law

THE WESLEYAN METHODIST MISSION.

SOUTH CEYLON.

BY REV. ROBERT TEBB (CHAIRMAN).

THE Wesleyan Methodist Church has always, from its commencement, been a missionary Church. Dr. Coke, a gentleman commoner of Jesus College, Oxford, an ordained clergyman of the Church of England, when he joined Mr. Wesley in his evangelistic mission, became largely responsible for establishing and superintending Wesleyan Methodist missions. He was, like Mr. Wesley, a lover of mankind on the most extensive scale, and after his conversion ever considered "the world his parish." Dr. Coke's theatre of missionary operations included the four quarters of the globe. In three of them he was the actual founder of missions, for whose support, after spending two ample fortunes of his own (by patrimony and marriage), he went about begging from door to door throughout the United Kingdom; and that not once or twice, but regularly for several years, until the close of his life. Having established missions in America in 1769, among the enslaved Africans in the West Indies in 1778, in Western Africa in 1792, and in various parts of Europe, he had long been impressed that he should preach the Gospel in Asia also. He engaged in correspondence on the subject as early as 1784, but many difficulties necessitated delay in carrying out his purpose. In 1809 the way seemed opening for commencing a mission in Ceylon, which, being under the care of the Colonial Office, enjoyed far more liberty for carrying on evangelistic work than was possible in India under the despotic rule of the East India Company. The story of the establishment of the Ceylon Missions is briefly this :—

In the year 1809 the Hon. Sir Alexander Johnston, the Chief Justice of Ceylon, while on a visit to England, desirous of bringing to the people of the island the blessings of Christianity, on the advice of Mr. Wilberforce, the great philanthropist, and an intimate friend of Dr. Coke, applied to the Wesleyan Methodist Church to undertake a mission to Ceylon. Some temporary difficulties occurred to prevent its immediate adoption, but an application from such an influential official, supported by a cordial promise of help, was thankfully hailed by Dr. Coke as an advance of no small importance towards the attainment of his cherished plan of an Oriental mission. The difficulties, largely financial, and partly relating to the superintendence of the work, were overcome by the Doctor generously proposing to guarantee the sum necessary for the outfit of the mission, and also offering personally to conduct the mission. At the Conference of 1813, held in Liverpool, the scheme was finally sanctioned, and the ministers appointed to accompany the Doctor—viz., Messrs. Ault, Lynch, Erskine, Harvard, Squance, and Clough —left London for Portsmouth on December 10, 1813, and embarked there on the 30th of that month. Dr. Coke, as is well known, did not survive the voyage: he died suddenly on May 3rd, and was buried at sea. His bereaved companions landed at Bombay on May 21st, and after receiving remarkable kindness there, landed in Ceylon on June 29, 1814.

The special attention shown to the missionaries in India was repeated in Ceylon. They were enabled under encouraging auspices to make arrangements for commencing the work. At the first synod held in Galle it was determined, for purposes of missionary administration, to divide the island into two districts—viz., the Northern District, where, the mass of the population being Tamils, the missionaries would use the Tamil language, and the Southern District, where, the great majority of the people being Sinhalese, the missionaries would use the Sinhalese language. This division into two districts still remains, and it is to the Southern District alone that the following remarks apply. To accomplish the aims of the mission in the most effectual manner, suitable centres were selected, and from the places thus selected villages within comparatively easy distance were regularly visited for evangelistic purposes. Soon suitable persons who had been converted were selected as helpers, and thus the nucleus of a native ministry was formed. This enabled additional centres to be occupied and the surrounding villages to be evangelised in a similar manner. By these simple but efficient measures an effort has been made to cover the district with a network of evangelising agencies. Among the means used for this end we may mention preaching the word of God. As there were no places provided for regular worship, the open-air preaching, which is still one of our most useful means of reaching the unconverted, was an absolute necessity. The missionaries and their native helpers, where they could gather a congregation in the streets, compounds, or private houses, made known their message. When a few had received the Gospel, an effort was made to erect a building of some kind for regular worship and instruction. The converts were urged to become workers. Thus a band of lay helpers was under constant training. Another effort has been made by opening schools. At the commencement of the mission the possibility of doing good through establishing schools was pressed on the missionaries by the Government. In response to this appeal an English school was opened in every station where a missionary lived. Naturally, as the work extended to the surrounding villages, the children of the converts and the children of non-Christians whose parents desired their instruction became a claim upon the missionaries. Schools for teaching in the vernacular were opened as opportunity offered.

The press has ever been an auxiliary to preaching and educational efforts. Among the first missionaries appointed to Ceylon two were practical printers, and since that time, with rare exceptions, there has been at least one printer among the missionaries. Dr. Coke included a printing press and other necessary requisites as part of his missionary equipment. The press thus established has been continued, improved, and enlarged, and is still in active and beneficent operation at the Industrial Home, Wellawatte. Thousands of publications have issued from the press. Early in the missionary history the Bible Society placed its printing under our care, and nearly all the vernacular Scriptures from that time to the present have been issued by us. Books also have been regularly circulated through the Book-room, which continues its useful ministry at Colpetty.

Women's work has ever been kept to the front in the operations of the Mission.

Medical, industrial, temperance, and orphanage work has also not been overlooked.

A few statistics taken from the last available report give the following information as to the present position of the Mission so far as figures can instruct us. Only a very few illustrations can be selected.

For support of the ministry there was given last year	Rs. 18,335
Extension Fund, to send the Gospel to spiritually destitute localities	Rs. 2,933
Auxiliary Fund, to assist aged ministers and widows	Rs. 943
Churches and other preaching places	171
Missionaries and ministers	42
District agents	16
Local preachers	164
Day schools	213
Class-leaders	191
Members in full communion	3,613
" on trial	1,045
" Junior	1,848
Christian Community	12,776
School teachers: Male	281
Female	299
Scholars: Boys	11,329
Girls	5,466
Sunday schools	188
Teachers	690
Scholars	9,247
Total children under instruction: Boys	12,198
Girls	6,511

A few sentences may be added as to the organisation of the Church and the efforts which are being put forth to make it self-supporting, self-governing, and self-propagating. All the central stations above mentioned are called "circuits." Each circuit has its own quarterly meeting, more or less efficient, for the management of its own local affairs. The whole work in South Ceylon is under the supervision of the District Synod, which meets annually. The work in the circuits is in various stages of development, and may be summarised under three heads. The first class is entirely self-supporting. The money needed for the support of the ministry and other agents is raised in the circuit and distributed under the directions of its quarterly meeting, the Mission being in no way financially responsible. There are now six self-supporting, self-governing circuits, viz., Colombo English, Colombo Jampettah Street Tamil, Moratuwa-Rawatawatte, Moratumulle, Kurana, and Seeduwa. This pleasing development of self-support has greatly lessened the work of oversight, as the ministers appointed to them are the superintendents, and manage their own affairs, under the general care of the chairman of the district. These circuits have the privilege of sending at least two representatives each to the General Synod.

A second class of circuit is called *aided*, and is only placed in this class when the circuit raises a substantial sum towards the support of the ministry, and gives promise of steady approach to the standard of the above-mentioned six circuits, both as regards self-support and the administration of affairs. The aided circuits are Colombo Sinhalese, Kollupitiya and Wellawatte, Panadure, Kalutara, Kandy, Negombo, Katana, Galle Fort, Galle Richmond Hill, and Matara. A grant in aid for the support of these circuits is made by the local committee, which is allotted under the direction of the Synod to the several circuits. The principle of distribution is by a regularly diminishing subsidy of not less than 2½ per cent. per annum. Each of the grant-in-aid circuits is privileged to send one representative to the Synod.

The third class are called *mission* circuits, and are under the direct financial administration of the local committee, and except for purposes of report and information their concerns do not come into the District Synod. Every effort is of course made to develop the local income and call out the abilities of all willing to help in administration, so as to bring the mission circuits into the class of aided circuits, which will thus bring them into the care of, and give them a direct representation in, the District Synod. There are 21 mission circuits.

The District Synod has ever sought to extend the work and open up new stations. In 1873 a fund for the purpose was instituted, and has since, with more or less energy and success, been maintained. An influential Extension Fund Committee has recently been appointed by the Synod. It is expected that under improved administration more funds will soon be available and that places now entirely neglected and spiritually destitute will be provided with Gospel ministrations.

NORTH CEYLON.

By Rev. G. J. Trimmer (Chairman).

Under this division is included the Wesleyan Mission work in the Tamil country of Ceylon. It embraces the Northern and Eastern Provinces. There are five principal stations, which are the headquarters of English missionaries, and fourteen sub-stations or circuits. Wesleyan Methodist Missions in the East began in 1814. As has been related in the companion article, they owe their origin to the quenchless zeal and ardent advocacy of Dr. Coke, who, in 1813, sailed for India with a party of missionaries chosen by the British Conference and died on the voyage out.

It is difficult to summarise the growth of nearly a century in the space which can be allotted to us. The following table shows the progress in members, schools, and school-children by decades :—

Decade.	Members.	Schools.	Boys.	Girls.	Total Children.
1814–25	92	26	—	—	795
1826–35	144	30	975	174	1,149
1836–45	277	—	814	200	1,014
1846–55	288	16	761	123	884
1856–65	406	30	960	234	1,194
1866–75	829	83	4,083	909	4,992
1876–85	1,329	129	6,343	1,849	8,192
1886–95	1,799	137	7,740	2,370	10,110
1896–05	2,439	160	8,984	2,904	11,888

Two things are evident from the above table. First, as regards membership the growth has been continuous; there has never been a decrease in any decade. Second, school work fluctuated more or less during the first fifty years. But between the years 1866–75 the grant-in-aid system was introduced by the Government. At the earnest request of the Governor then in Ceylon, Sir William Gregory, the Mission threw itself heartily into the work of extending education—especially in the vernacular—with the result that in 1905 we return ten times as many scholars as we did in 1865.

A few other salient features of our progress may be noted. In all the principal and sub-centres property has been acquired, houses, churches, and schools built, and thus the needs of the Mission in regard to plant are met. Continuous expansion and growth leave us invariably a little in arrears in this matter. But our principle, always to own our land and buildings, has, on the whole, been fairly well adhered to.

Education, up to the limit of our resources, has always had a prominent place in our work. In 1833 the Jaffna Central School, forerunner of the present Jaffna Central College, was founded. In 1837 the Jaffna Girls' Boarding School was opened.

Tamil workers have been sought out, trained, and entrusted with responsible work as soon and as widely as possible. The first Tamil minister was received into the ministry in 1825. He was the first of a number of devoted and able men who have served and still serve our Church. The period from 1845 to 1855 was a time of great stress and difficulty, but it seems to have been but the "wintering" of our work. Since 1856 progress has been rapid and continuous. To write in detail of growths, developments, re-organisation, and so forth of the forty years would need a volume. The following are some of the chief points to be noted: 1866–75 was a period of great activity in providing buildings and extending our work. The number of schools grew from 30 to 83. Large sums were raised locally to supplement grants from England. In the period 1886–95 a Provincial Synod was established to review the work of the island. Thus the two districts, divided since 1819, were brought into touch again, though retaining their own status and authority. To this period belongs the commencement of Home Missionary Societies by the various Churches of the district. In these societies the Mission Church, the fruit of British missionary effort, becomes in its turn missionary. During this decade medical work for women and children began at Batticaloa. The last decade has seen the extension of this work to Kalmunai and Puttur, where a Deaconess Home has been established and two Wesleyan deaconesses have been appointed to work.

The first place in our methods is given to preaching. Besides the regular services in our churches (which are principally for our own Christian people), regular preaching services are conducted weekly in our school bungalows. These are attended by non-Christians. In bazaars and streets open-air services are held which excite considerable interest and not a few inquiries. We are also often allowed to hold a meeting in the compound or verandah of a house, and our host then invites his neighbours and friends to be present. In all these meetings we make use of music, pictures, and the magic lantern as aids and attractions.

Our educational work occupies a prominent place among our agencies. We have schools of all kinds. For the most part they are vernacular day schools, in which the education is of the simplest, and is in Tamil. But we have a complete chain, and the student may pass through our schools from the alphabet to the First in Arts (intermediate) examination of the Madras University. We have, in addition to our day schools, boarding schools in which some 500 children (of whom the greater part are girls) are educated. Three schools have been established for the training of teachers, two for boys and one for girls. We have also two industrial schools, in which carpentry, black, and tin smithing, printing, and book-binding are taught.

Reference has been made to our medical work for women and children. Two deaconess sisters at Puttur, and one at Batticaloa, and a lady at Kalmunai are engaged in this branch of our operations. Their duties consist principally of outdoor dispensary work and visits to the homes of patients. But each centre has a small ward in which urgent cases can be received for more personal attention.

The district has a press at Batticaloa which supplies the Mission with much of its literature, besides doing a great deal of work for the general public. At Trincomalee a well-equipped Soldiers' Home was established about ten years ago. This is for the use of the men of both arms of His Majesty's service, and has proved a great boon to them.

For the work very briefly outlined above we have the following staff of workers: 9 missionaries, 6 missionaries' wives, 8 lady missionaries, 18 Tamil ministers (3 on the retired list), 22 catechists, 20 Biblewomen, 311 male and 135 female teachers. These are the staff of paid workers. We have in addition, as unpaid workers, 69 lay preachers, a large number of other lay helpers, and 343 Sunday-school teachers. Many of the latter are also day-school teachers. We have 18 churches, 160 schools, and 126 school-chapels and other preaching places.

No estimate of the position and outlook of our labours can be formed without some reference to the extent to which our people support the work. In 1905 they raised Rs. 7,076 for the support of the Tamil ministry, Rs. 970 for the upkeep of their churches, and Rs. 2,777 for home mission work. The central churches on all the five chief stations are self-supporting and self-governing. We may say, therefore, that the Mission is firmly rooted in the soil. In educational work also a considerable sum is raised locally by means of fees and Government grants in aid. In 1905 the fees amounted to Rs. 16,610 and the Government grant in aid for the year to Rs. 41,662. The Government grant is a "result grant." An examination in all secular subjects is held in each school annually. On the results of this examination the grant is paid. Every rupee paid out of the Treasury represents full value received by the Government in the shape of secular education. It is now proposed to introduce a system of compulsory education throughout the island. This should lead to a large extension of educational work. There seems a possibility, however, that the provisions of the new system may be unacceptable to mission managers. If so, we shall take no part in the further extension, and may even retire from some part of the work we are at present doing.

That mission work has profoundly influenced the faith and ideals of the people cannot be doubted. The old, crude forms of superstition are passing away, discredited in the eyes of the present generation, which may be called an educated one. The revival of Vedantic Hinduism and the race aspirations of the people is also, indirectly, a result of mission work. Missionaries of experience look forward with great confidence. The Tamils are a conservative race, and move somewhat slowly. But the current of modern thought, aspiration and ideal, if it does not yet reach the goal we aim at, moves in that direction. We may therefore wait with patience the development of the forces—educational, social, and religious—which missions have introduced into North Ceylon.

DUTCH REFORMED CHURCH

(INCLUDING THE SCOTCH PRESBYTERIAN CHURCH).

ALTHOUGH the Dutch had not finally expelled the Portuguese from Ceylon until 1658, the Reformed Church of Holland was formally established as the religion of the colony in 1642, and the first Protestant clergyman commenced his ministrations at Galle in October of that year, in the building which is still used as the Dutch church by the descendants of the original colonists. From Galle southward to Matara and northward to Jaffna, as the Portuguese were ousted their churches and religious buildings were taken possession of by the Dutch, but it was not until they became sole masters of the maritime provinces that anything like a Church organisation was attempted. During the early period of their rule in Ceylon it is admitted even by the warmest partisans of the Dutch that they displayed a spirit of intolerance in painful contrast with the advanced liberalism of the national character; but it was an intolerance inspired by fears of political intrigue, and all the edicts issued on the subject were directed against the clergy, while the lay Catholics were left comparatively unmolested. Catholic worship was certainly discouraged, but no Catholics were persecuted to death on account of their religion, and the disabilities imposed upon them were with a view to inducing them to join the Reformed Church. The system adopted by the Dutch Church was to utilise the village school as the nucleus of the future Church. Here children received instruction and adults were taught the leading truths of Christianity. But the measures adopted by the Dutch Government for converting the heathen were hardly calculated to secure that end. The fact is that the Dutch were never a proselytising nation. More conservative than expansive in their religious aspirations, their first care was to provide for the religious wants of their own people and their descendants. This is the case to the present time, as is shown by the fact that, of their membership of about 3,000, 99 per cent. are Burghers descended from the Dutch settlers in the island. This primary duty provided for, they considered it of far more importance to impose the laws of Holland rather than its religion upon their newly made subjects. It is certainly true that the Dutch failed, and signally failed, in their efforts at converting the heathen, and the Dutch Reformed Church of the present day can hardly be reckoned as one of the missionary forces of the island. Indeed, it would scarcely be too much to say that the Church has "progressed backward." In the seventeenth century there were usually four European ministers at Colombo, four at Jaffna, and four at Galle; now there are two ministers in Colombo (Rev. D. Tweed and Rev. J. Rowland), at Galle there is one and at Matara one, while the old Dutch church at Jaffna is no longer used as a place of worship.

The Wolfendahl Church, Colombo, is at once the monument and the nursery of the Church. It is a noble structure, built in the shape of St. Andrew's Cross on Wolfendahl Hill, the highest eminence within the city limits. Built in the year 1749 with all the solidity of Dutch architecture, it has withstood wind and weather in a remarkable degree; and though the storms of a century and a half have beaten on its sides, it still survives as one of the most durable structures erected by the Dutch, the only portion that has undergone repairs of any consequence being the dome. It is interesting to note that the belfry of this place of worship is situated half a mile from the church, as it was erected near the worshippers' residences. In former days the bell was rung as a sort of curfew bell at 9 o'clock every night, and it is still used to call people to service. The other Dutch Reformed churches in Colombo are those at Bambalapitiya and Milagakande, which have been erected to meet the needs of those who have gone to live in those suburban districts. The Church membership in Colombo is about 1,000.

The Wolfendahl Church and the Dutch churches at Galle, Matara, and Jaffna are kept in repair at Government cost, and the British Government has also undertaken the maintenance of the clergy of those churches ever since the cession of the island by the Dutch in 1796. In this connection it is a curious fact that a previous minister of the Dutch Church in Ceylon retired on account of ill-health in 1864, and is still living in retirement with his wife in the Isle of Wight. They are both over ninety years of age, and during the last forty odd years they have drawn over £10,000 in pensions from the Government.

The Dutch Church is governed by a Consistory composed of the ministers, four elders, and six deacons, and this body has legal standing, having been incorporated by an Ordinance.

In the early eighties the Scotch Presbyterian Church was amalgamated with the Dutch Church, but the Scotch Presbyterians form but a very small proportion of the total membership of the Dutch Church. A large Scotch church, to be known as St. Andrew's, is in course of erection near the Galle Face, and the Rev. A. Dunn is the minister in charge.

BAPTIST MISSIONARY SOCIETY, CEYLON.

THE Baptist Missionary Society, which has been longer established in Ceylon than any other now working there, commenced operations in the island close upon a century ago. Its first missionary was James Chater, the pioneer Protestant missionary in Ceylon, who landed at Colombo in the year 1812, and commenced to work among the Sinhalese and Burghers of the Western Province. His first convert was a Buddhist priest, named Theophilus, who died soon after baptism, but was an unshaken Christian to the end. Five years after his arrival, Mr. Chater settled at Grandpass, and built a residence and a chapel there. The Church which was formed here was probably the first native self-supporting Church in the island. After seventeen years of uphill work, Mr. Chater was obliged to leave for England to recuperate his health, but he never saw the old country again, as he died on the homeward voyage in 1829. In the following year (1830) Mr. Chater was succeeded by Ebenezer Daniel, who was accompanied by his wife and three daughters. He found that consequent on Mr. Chater's departure the work which he had started and carried on single-handed for so long was languishing. But Mr. Daniel's apostolic fervour soon revived the Mission, and his manifold activities during fourteen years are recalled with thankfulness by many to this day. He pressed every form of missionary activity into service, and by continually making difficult journeys to distant villages, preaching the Gospel from house to house and hut to hut, he earned the name of "the Apostolic Daniel." In 1835, Mrs. Daniel and her three daughters, who had been ceaseless in school work and missionary work among the native women and girls, had to leave the island on account of broken health, and Mrs. Daniel died a fortnight before the boat reached England. In 1836 the formation of new village stations and the opening of fresh schools necessitated a request for another missionary from England, and Mr. Harris was appointed and arrived at the end of 1838. The number of members at this time was 135. There were six stations supplied by two European and five native missionaries, and 17 schools containing about 450 children. In 1839 the rapid extension of missionary labours and their encouraging results necessitated still more help, and a printing press was urgently applied for. This was taken out by Mr. Dawson, who arrived in 1841. He set to work at Kandy, and in a very short time tracts and school-books in Sinhalese, from type cast in the island, as well as in English and Portuguese, were being distributed in large quantities. In 1844 Mr. Daniel died. Nothing could bear better testimony to his worth and excellence than the feverish suspense in which the whole community was placed during the short period of his illness. Persons of all ranks, classes, and persuasions, Protestants of every denomination, Roman Catholics (against whom he had written uncompromisingly), and even Buddhists, either visited his sick-chamber or made anxious inquiry after his state; while an immense concourse attended the funeral. In the same year Jacob Davies with his wife arrived to take up the work in Colombo, and in 1846 Mr. and Mrs. Allen and Mr. and Mrs. Lewis came out, but the latter removed to Calcutta in the following year. In 1849 the grants from the Home Society were reduced, and retrenchment necessitated giving up the work in the Matara district, Kandy and Colombo being retained as the only two centres of work. In this year (1849) Mr. Jacob Davies died at the residence of Dr. Elliott in Colombo, and a year later Mr. Dawson was lost in a shipwreck with his wife and three children while on the way to England. In 1853 Charles Carter arrived from England. In this year the baptized membership of the Churches had reached 500. In 1858 Mr. Carter began the translation of the New Testament into Sinhalese direct from the Greek text, and the first edition of the work was issued five years later. In 1862 Henry Robert Piggot and Frederick D. Walcock went to Ceylon. The former did good work in Colombo and Ratnapura for twenty-nine years, and the latter—excluding intervals spent in England—has been at work in the island for thirty-eight years, and has left his mark as the architect of many beautiful chapels and mission buildings in the island, including the fine Cinnamon Gardens Church. In 1864 the Grandpass Church became self-supporting, and in 1866 James Allen died. In 1873 work was started in the Province of Sabaragamuwa, and in 1877 the Cinnamon Gardens Church was built and opened, and the society published the Old Testament, translated by Mr. Carter from the Hebrew, in Sinhalese. Between 1880 and the present time a number of missionaries have spent varying periods in the island, including H. H. Lapham, who spent twenty-two strenuous years here, H. Sims, G. Gray, W. Thomson, J. A. McCallum, G. T. Wood, W. D. Hankinson, B. Etherington, B.A., J. A. Ewing, H. J. Chanter, B.A., B.D., and S. F. Pearce; and the last four, with Mrs. Etherington, Mrs. Ewing, and Miss Robinson, Principal of the Colombo Girls' Boarding School Mission, constitute the present European staff. The method of the early missionaries of devoting their main strength to the evangelisation of the heathen by the preaching of the Gospel in the vernacular from village to village has been continuously maintained by succeeding missionaries, and the work of the Baptists being still mostly in the vernacular, the proportion of native to European adherents is probably higher than in most other Missions. But the rapid spread of the knowledge of English, which is so marked a feature in educational development in Ceylon, is being met by a new forward movement inaugurated in 1906, which provides for a large increase in the number of European missionaries and the setting apart of two of them, who have been specially trained for the purpose, for educational work. Adjoining the Cinnamon Gardens Church is the Ferguson Memorial Hall, erected by near relatives to the memory of Mr. and Mrs. A. M. Ferguson, who for many years were prominent members of the Church. In this building is conducted the Sunday school, with which the Hon. Mr. J. Ferguson, C.M.G., has been connected for forty years. He has been Superintendent for over thirty years, and still holds that office.

THE SALVATION ARMY.

The work of the Salvation Army in Ceylon was started in the year 1883 by Commissioner Booth-Tucker, who, prior to his connection with this organisation, was a civil servant under the Indian Government. The work was first started in Colombo, and in course of time it has extended its borders and has developed itself into the social and spiritual branches. The work of the latter is divided among six chief territorial divisions, namely, (1) Kegalla and Kurunegala; (2) Colombo division; (3) Heneratgoda district; (4) Kandy district; (5) Madampe and Chilaw division; and (6) Jaffna district. These divisions altogether comprise 60 corps and 127 outposts. The social operations are represented by a prison-gate home for the reclamation of the ex-criminals and a rescue home for the uplifting of the fallen women. In connection with the prison-gate home a dairy is maintained, which is recognised officially by the municipality of Colombo, and also a grass farm. Meetings are held in the jail every Sunday, and prisoners are met at the prison gate daily on their discharge. In the rescue home, needlework and lace-making are the chief industries carried on by the inmates. Three village banks have also been established by the Army for the purpose of relieving the less fortunate classes and to prevent them from falling into the clutches of the exorbitant money-lenders, who are so great a curse to the island. Stranded Europeans are also received and cared for when funds for the purpose are available.

A naval and military home is another distinct feature of the work. Here board and lodging for a few soldiers and sailors is provided, also a refreshment bar. This home is situated at De Soysa's Buildings, Slave Island, and meetings are held at this centre every night. The educational work of the Army is also making considerable progress. There are 25 day schools and a boarding school under the control of the Army's officers. The present position of the Army in Ceylon is officially recorded as follows: Number of members, about 1,500; officers, 143; number of services or indoor meetings held monthly, about 1,000; number of hours spent in visiting the people monthly, about 9,000.

THE AMERICAN MISSION.

THE American Board of Commissioners for Foreign Missions, organised in 1810, early determined to open work in Ceylon. The Rev. S. Newell, one of its earliest missionaries, was refused admittance to India and visited Ceylon in 1813. When Mr. Newell reached North Ceylon there were no missionaries on the field, the London Missionary Society having just withdrawn. Two Protestants only, a Burgher woman and a Tamil man from Travancore, were attempting to give religious instruction. The opening seemed peculiarly inviting. Acting on the recommendations of Mr. Newell, the American Board began its work in Ceylon. The first missionaries from America were the Rev. Mr. Poor, the Rev. Mr. Meigs and the Rev. Mr. Richards with their wives, and the Rev. E. Warren. They were warmly welcomed by Governor Brownrigg and other officials, and, proceeding to Jaffna, they took possession of the old Dutch house at Tillypally Lands, and the remains of the large Dutch churches at several stations were generously turned over by Government to the infant Mission. Work began with great zeal and interest. The first plan of operations was to visit and receive visitors, to explain the object of the Mission, to gather the people into meetings when possible, to preach, to open schools, and to dispense medicines—by any and all means to commend the Gospel of Christ. From the first the people took kindly to the idea of education for their sons, and, as early as 1817, a small beginning was made in teaching even girls to read. Day schools were opened, and were followed by small boarding schools at each of the five stations first occupied. Soon a few little girls were gathered into the missionaries' families to be taught. In 1823 a central seminary for boys was opened at Batticotta, and the next year one for girls at Uduville, all the station boarding schools being closed. In 1820 reinforcements arrived from America. They were just in time, for in that same year began, on the part of the Ceylon Government, a policy of bare toleration towards the missionaries. The Mission printer was refused admittance, and Government officials frankly said that they proposed to let the enterprise die out, and that they would not allow any other Americans to join the Mission. It is a curious fact that from the announcement of this programme till its withdrawal in 1832 the American Mission lost only one man by death and suffered little from sickness. Two members of that company lived and worked fifty years in Jaffna.

From 1824 on the work of the Mission was greatly strengthened and the workers cheered by a series of very marked revivals. The Rev. L. Spaulding went in 1834 to India and found there was an opening for missionary work among the Tamils of the Madura district. Mr. Woodward secured the permission of the Madras Governor, and the Revs. Messrs. Hoisington and Todd were sent with some native helpers to begin the work of the American Madura Mission. Two years later the Revs. Messrs. Winslow and Scudder opened a similar work in Madras. The former became widely known throughout India as the author of the standard Tamil-English dictionary, and the latter was the founder of a notable missionary family, of which in the second and third generations, several members are still at work in the American Arcot Mission. Meanwhile the work in North Ceylon grew apace. In 1850 there were eight organised Churches with 200 members and nearly 100 free schools with more than 4,000 pupils under Christian instruction.

A printing establishment was opened at Manipay in 1834, and proved a most useful agency in the spread of Christian truth. During the twenty years that it was under the charge of an American printer, 172,000,000 pages of Christian literature were printed and distributed. The *Morning Star* was begun in 1841—a Christian newspaper which has had at times a great influence for good.

A deputation sent from America in 1855 freely revised the plans used by the Mission, and determined a new policy. Schools were to be cut down to 20 for Christians and 20 for non-Christians. Government grants were to be respectfully declined. English educational work at Mission expense was to be stopped. The female seminary at Uduville was to have no more than 35 pupils, all supported by the Mission. The Batticotta seminary likewise was to be much reduced in numbers, and the teaching designed solely for the training of Mission helpers.

These drastic changes were never fully carried out, though an attempt was made to meet the views of the American Board.

The Batticotta seminary, so long a powerful evangelising force, was closed, and a few years later a Tamil Training and Theological Institute was begun to supply the pressing need for trained assistants. In 1872 the leading Tamil Christians organised the Jaffna College, under a separate charter. This college was meant to be wholly independent and interdenominational. Circumstances, however, have brought about a close, though not an organic, connection between the Jaffna College and the American Mission, in whose field it is located.

The medical work of this Mission was begun in a very simple way by two of the first band of missionaries, and was taken up more formally by Dr. Scudder, afterwards of the Arcot Mission. He was followed by Dr. Nathan Ward, who for twelve years carried on a small medical establishment at Batticotta. Dr. S. F. Green, who succeeded him, set about developing a strong medical department, not only to cure the sick who might come, but to send out into the villages Tamil physicians thoroughly trained and equipped. In addition to the care of the hospital of the Friend-in-Need Society, Dr. Green had his own hospital and dispensary, trained 60 Tamil young men as doctors, translated or compiled eight medical text-books, wrote numerous tracts, and was, as well, an earnest and faithful preacher of the Gospel. The American Mission Medical School antedated that carried on by the Government in Colombo, and was largely subsidised by the Government.

From 1873 to 1893 the work was under the care of the men trained in the Medical School. Then the Rev. T. B. Scott, M.D., and Mrs. Scott, M.D., joined the Mission, and in 1896 Miss Curr, L.R.C.P.S., came for special work among women and children. The Mission has now two fine medical establishments, the General Hospital at Manipay and the McLeod Hospital for Women at Inuvil. Both are eminently successful.

So far from "respectfully declining" the Government grants for schools, the American Mission may be said to have operated its educational system in later years almost wholly from funds received from the Ceylon Government. This connection can never be entirely satisfactory from a missionary point of view, and there are not wanting those who would still carry out, if possible, the old programme of 40 schools and no grant.

The number of village vernacular schools and of English schools varies slightly from year to year. In 1905 there were 129 schools of all kinds, having 10,739 pupils, of whom 3,129 were girls. This number includes the students of the Tellippallai Training School for Teachers and the Uduville and Udupiddi Girls' Boarding Schools.

These boarding schools, which grew out of the female seminary, have long been one of the most potent evangelising forces of the Mission. Hundreds of Hindu girls have professed Christianity while in the schools, and more than a thousand Christian homes are witness to the reality of the work done there. The printing establishment was sold in 1855 to Messrs. Strong and Asbury, Tamil gentlemen long associated with it. The business was bought back by the Mission in 1902 and located at Tellippallai in connection with the industrial school. A large printing and publishing business is now being carried on, chiefly Christian text-books and periodicals.

One great object of this Mission, to plant self-sustaining Churches, is being accomplished. Eighteen Churches have been organised, with a membership of about 2,000. The Tamil members pay 95 per cent. of the cost of maintaining the work of these Churches. A native pastorate, begun in 1855, has developed, not indeed in sufficient numbers to occupy all the churches, but honest and able and devoted enough to form a great encouragement to the cause of missions. The activities of the native Church are multiplying. For sixty years the native Evangelical Society has supported schools and catechists on the neighbouring islands. The Christian Endeavour Society has 14 societies and 400 members. The first C.E. Society in Asia was organised in the Uduville school in 1885, and the first Y.M.C.A. begun on missionary soil is connected with the Jaffna College. A students' mission and a women's mission, organised in 1899, unite to send workers and funds to Tondi, an unevangelised district nearly opposite Jaffna on the Indian coast. The Churches of the American Mission have formed recently a united Congregational Church for the development of local evangelistic work and the aid of weak Churches.

In all, including eight now on the field, 104 missionaries have spent a longer or shorter time in this work, only 38 of them being ordained ministers. Of all these, ten served over thirty years each, six of them more than forty years, and two a full half-century. Among the chief and permanent influences of this Mission must be counted these great lives spent in its service—great in purpose, in character, in length of days, in eternal results: Dr. Poor, "Father and Mother" Spaulding, Miss Agnew, "Father and Mother" Howlands, Dr. and Mrs. Hastings, Dr. Green—these and many others can never be forgotten by the Tamil people.

YOUNG MEN'S CHRISTIAN ASSOCIATION.

THE Young Men's Christian Association at Colombo is the most cosmopolitan institution in Ceylon. Its membership includes all the races and religions in the island—Sinhalese, Tamils, Malays, Moormen, Parsees, Europeans, and Burghers; Christians, Buddhists, Hindus, Mahomedans, and Zoroastrians. Like the Y.M.C.A. movement all over the world, the Colombo branch of this world-wide institution has grown from small beginnings. It was inaugurated in 1882 by Mr. W. Chapman, of Glasgow, who was then an employee of Messrs. Cargills, Ltd., and a few young men of the place, among whom were Messrs. J. A. Rode and J. A. Jansz, who are still connected with the Association. It took its present form in 1894, and in 1897 the first permanent General Secretary, in the person of Mr. Louis Hieb, was appointed, his expenses being wholly provided by the International Committee of Y.M.C.A.'s, New York. This was the commencement of a great development in the work of the Association. Beginning with a membership of about 50, there has been a continual increase during the last eight years, until at the present time its membership numbers 330 and the daily average attendance at the rooms is over a hundred. The present home of the Association at the Racquet Court, a handsome three-storeyed building, has recently been erected at a cost of Rs. 80,000 (£5,333). The provision of the establishment has been made possible by generous friends in America, Ceylon, and Great Britain, and it stands as a monument to the untiring zeal, energy, and faithfulness of Mr. Louis Hieb, the first General Secretary. The site of the building has been leased to the Association by the Government, with the approval of the military authorities. It is pleasantly situated, and contains a reading-room and library, reception and recreation rooms, bath and locker room, restaurant, secretaries' office, small lecture and class rooms; hostel to accommodate recent arrivals at the port, students, and other young men who have not permanent residences in Colombo; and a large gymnasium, which is one of the finest in the island, and is well equipped with the latest apparatus.

Y.M.C.A. BUILDING, COLOMBO.

The religious work of the Association is not only its *raison d'être*, but is also its motive force, and the Y.M.C.A. is the only organisation which tries to break down the racial prejudice that exists in Ceylon and unite all classes into one common brotherhood, and thus help them to work in mutual kindness. On this account it has the sympathy and support of almost all the British merchants, and its board of directors includes the best men in mercantile and other circles—men who are held in the highest esteem and regard by the general public. The membership is of two classes—active members and associates. The latter class of membership is open to all men of good moral character, without regard to race, rank, or religion. Active members must give evidence of faith in the principles of Christianity, acknowledge their willingness to work for the cause, and be in full communion with a Protestant Christian Church.

Aiming, as does the Y.M.C.A. everywhere, at the spiritual, social, intellectual, and physical welfare of young men, there is activity under all these heads: Bible-classes, Gospel meetings, &c., social hours and "At Homes," gymnastics, cricket, football, rambling, and camera clubs, educational classes, lectures, &c. The Y.M.C.A. throughout the island has been directed since 1900 by the Ceylon Central Committee, which is affiliated with the World's Committee. Affiliated to the Central Committee are 18 associations with a total membership of nearly 1,200. The most important branches are at Colombo, Galle, Kandy, Jaffna, and Batticaloa. Quite recently a bungalow at Bambalapitiya, a residential suburb of Colombo, has been adapted and opened as a branch of the central Y.M.C.A. There are also branches at Galle, Kandy, Jaffna, and Batticaloa. The President of the Colombo Association is the Hon. Mr. Justice H. L. Wendt, of the Supreme Court, who has occupied this position for ten years, and the Vice-President the Hon. Mr. J. Ferguson, C.M.G. (General European Member of the Legislative Council). Mr. Chauncey A. Adams, B.A., a Canadian, is the General Secretary and Secretary of the Central Committee, and has held this position since 1905.

YOUNG WOMEN'S CHRISTIAN ASSOCIATION.

IN the year 1882 a weekly Bible-class for young women was started in Colombo, which in 1884 was established as a Young Women's Christian Association Class. Shortly afterwards a second and a third class were formed in different parts of the city, and important mission work was undertaken by some of the members. In 1890 the Association was organised more fully, a President and a Secretary being appointed and Y.W.C.A. literature introduced. By the year 1895 there was need of a secretary who could devote her whole time to the work, and application was made to the Y.W.C.A. headquarters in London for such a worker. Since that time the Association in Colombo has seldom been without a General Secretary.

The management of the Association is vested in a general committee of ladies representing the various Churches, thus ensuring an interdenominational basis for the work. The number of committee members elected annually does not exceed twelve; but the fourteen branch secretaries also are *ex-officio* members of the committee. The General Secretary is the executive officer of the committee. The number of branches in the Colombo Association has increased to 14, and the total membership is approximately 400. Of these branches 12 are English-speaking, 1 is Sinhalese, and 1 Portuguese.

The conditions of membership are the same as prevail elsewhere. Any young woman is eligible for active membership who is a communicant member of a Protestant Christian Church, and who wishes to be known as distinctly and avowedly on the side of Christ, while any young woman of good character, who is suitably recommended, may become an associate member. Active members alone have the right to vote and hold office. A small annual membership fee is levied. Meetings for Bible study are held in the different branches weekly or fortnightly; and evangelistic meetings, in which the members of all branches unite, are held monthly, while the annual meeting of the Association is held in the first quarter of the year. The World's Y.W.C.A. Week of Prayer is also observed annually in the month of November. Social gatherings are held frequently, and occasional courses of lectures or classes in practical secular subjects have been instituted. A circulating library is maintained for the use of all members, and "Y.W.C.A. Bible Notes for Daily Reading," in English and in Sinhalese, are distributed to the members each month. Each member also receives a yearly almanac and motto card; and among the publications taken in by members are *Our Own Gazette*, *Our Onward Way*, *Go Forward*, the English *Y.W.C.A. Magazine*, and the *Young Women of India and Ceylon*, published monthly.

The port city of Colombo affords numerous opportunities to the Association for helping young women who are travelling alone. In the early nineties travellers' aid work was begun by the Association, girl passengers being met on the boats and suitable lodgings secured for them by a Travellers' Aid Secretary. Later, a new wing was added to the house occupied by the General Secretary for the accommodation of such travellers; and finally the Y.W.C.A. Boarding Home was opened. In 1901 the committee took a house on Kanatta Road, in the Borella division of the city, which is now occupied as headquarters for the general work as well as a boarding home. The house provides room for about ten persons at one time, including the General Secretary and the Home Superintendent. Teachers, students, nurses, governesses, up-country members visiting the city, and others from many parts of the world, are here welcomed; and more than fifty persons have been accommodated each year. The home, which is easy of access by tram, borders on Cinnamon Gardens, one of the favourite residential districts. The charges are made proportionate to the income of the boarder and the scale of the accommodation, varying from Rs. 40 per month upwards. By special arrangement, in cases of need, the minimum charge is made still lower. Passing visitors usually pay Rs. 3 per day. With capacity so limited and prices so moderate, the home, even when filled with boarders, cannot be self-supporting, and friends subscribe towards the payment of rent and other expenses. A fund has therefore been started for the provision of a larger and more central building. The total volume of the Association's business in 1905 amounted to about Rs. 3,500.

A flourishing branch of the Young Women's Christian Association exists at Kandy, with groups of members also at Gampola, Nawalapitiya, Kadugannawa, and Matale, in the surrounding districts, the total membership being about 250. A beautiful little hall has been erected by the Kandy Y.W.C.A. at the cost of Rs. 8,000, which was opened in December, 1905, by Lady Blake, the wife of the Governor. Kandy is the headquarters of the Y.W.C.A. Travelling Secretary for Ceylon. At Badulla, in the far hill-country, where a branch was started about three years ago, there are 35 members, at Galle 41, at Nuwara Eliya and Nanu-Oya 30, and at Heneratgoda 10.

Colombo is the working centre of a "scattered" branch established in 1894, and now composed of about 200 members, who, while living in isolated stations throughout the island, wish to be identified with the Association and keep in touch with its work by correspondence and by receiving the Association literature. The Secretary of this branch sends to its members each month the "Y.W.C.A. Bible Notes" and a printed letter from the Y.W.C.A. headquarters in London, written by different ladies. When a sufficient number of "scattered" members live in one place to hold meetings, they form what is known as a

"Scattered Circle." Such "circles" exist at Negombo, Trincomalee, and Veyangoda.

Early in January, 1906, a separate "student" branch was organised in the Church Missionary Society Ladies' College, with 29 members, and the membership has since increased. This branch is affiliated with the National Student Department of India, Burma, and Ceylon.

All the Y.W.C.A. branches in India, Burma, and Ceylon are united under the name of the "National Young Women's Christian Association of India, Burma, and Ceylon," the headquarters of which are in Bombay. This Association is affiliated with the "World's Young Women's Christian Association," which has its headquarters in London and numbers over 370,000 members. The total membership in Ceylon, in 1906, was about 1,000.

A Y.W.C.A. Camp Conference was held at Mount Lavinia from January 3 to 10, 1906, and fifty young women from Ceylon and South India enjoyed a week of Bible study, prayer, and Christian fellowship together at this pleasant seaside resort. The object of the Y.W.C.A. is to promote the spiritual, intellectual, physical, and social welfare of young women ; and wide opportunity exists for the growth and development of the Association in the island of Ceylon.

BUDDHISM, PAST AND PRESENT

By the ANAGARIKA DHARMAPALA, General Secretary of the Maha Bodhi Society.

BUDDHISM has been the national religion of Ceylon from almost the earliest times of which reliable records are preserved. To the ancients generally Ceylon was known under several different names. According to the Mahavansa, the ancient Sinhalese chronicle, it was called Tambapanni, Taprobane, Lanka, Ratnadwipa, Sihaladwipa, Serendib, Zeylan, and Ceylon. In the time of the Buddha Kasyapa (the Buddha previous to the Buddha of our age) the island was called Mandadwipa, and in the prehistoric ages it was known as Ojadwipa and Varadwipa. Prior to the advent of the Sinhalese from India the island was inhabited by a non-Aryân tribe allied to the Dravidian race, who were called Yakkhus. The new race came from Bengal as invaders and conquerors. The Mahavansa states that Prince Vijaya with 700 men, who were banished from India 2,450 years ago on account of their lawless habits, landed in the "division Tambapanni of this land Lanka." As Vijaya was a scion of the Kalinga royal race, whose ancestral habitation was at Vanga, the present Bengal, the origin of the Sinhalese race may be traced to the Aryan stock. After he had made himself master of Ceylon, Vijaya sent a message to the king of Madura, soliciting the hand of his daughter. The king sent his daughter, together with 699 noble virgins, to Ceylon. King Pandava of Madura was also of Aryan origin, and from the union of two Aryan families there sprang up the Sinhalese race. In habits, manners, customs, features, and language, the Sinhalese are more allied to the Aryans of Bengal than to any other Indian people.

The Introduction of Buddhism.

After the death of Vijaya the crown passed on to another Bengal prince named Panduvasadeva, who married the Princess Bhadda Kaccana, daughter of the Sakya prince Pandu, son of Amitodana, of the royal family of the Sakyas of Kapilavastu. It was by this union that the royal family of Ceylon became related to the Buddha, whose religion was introduced to the island 236 years after his Parinirvana—that is, the absolute consummation of charity, love, and wisdom, a condition indescribable by mortal man and only fully realised by the Arhats (saints). Anterior to the introduction of Buddhism the religion of the Sinhalese was a form of Saivism, the worship of Siva. The grandson of Panduvasadeva, by name Pandukabhaya, became king in the year B.C. 437 ; and this king founded the city of Anuradhapura, which subsequently became so famous as the chief seat of Buddhism in Ceylon. In the reign of Pandukabhaya's grandson, Devanampiya Tissa, the religion of the Buddha was introduced by the great Arhat (saint) Mahinda, son of Asoka, the famous ruler of Maghada, in Northern India, and was made the State religion of the island.

From the earliest times Ceylon was noted for its pearls, gems, and precious stones ; and when Asoka was reigning in India-near-by, King Devanampiya Tissa sent very valuable gems and pearls as presents to the Indian emperor, who, in return, sent costly gifts to the king of the island, as well as a message in this wise : "I have taken refuge in Buddha, his religion, and his priesthood ; I have avowed myself a devotee in the religion of the descendant of Sakya, ruler of men. Imbuing thy mind with the conviction of the truth of these supreme blessings, with unfeigned faith, do thou also take refuge in this salvation." It followed that in the month of Jeshta, in the 236th year of Buddha, the Arhat Mahinda converted the king of Ceylon to the religion of the Buddha. Thus, the Sinhalese, banished from their own home in Northern India, founded a colony in Ceylon, and, without foreign intervention, established in the island a purely religious civilisation, which has in part survived the terrible shocks which it has received at the hands of different successive invaders, namely, Tamils, Cholians, Keralas, Maghas, Javanese, Portuguese, Hollanders, and—last, but not least—the British ; while other civilisations, contemporaneous at one time or the other with the original Sinhalese dispensation, have all disappeared, leaving little but literary trace of their past greatness. The Hellenes, the Egyptians, the Persians, Babylonians, Carthaginians, Romans, Etruscans, shed lustre on the world for a time, and then vanished. Their glory has departed, and only the record of it remains embalmed in the ancient writings. Modern races, having accepted new theological ideas, acknowledge no debt to all these bygone civilisations. Buddhism remains—but has suffered similarly. India, the birthplace of Buddhism, has no living witness of its forgotten greatness. The ruins of archaic temples abound in various parts of that great country ; but no man who has had a training in a purely native school has acquired knowledge of the great heroes who lived when Buddhism was a vitalising power in the land. A thousand years ago the Mahomedan invasion swept like a hurricane over the greater part of India, destroying all the old institutions ; and on the sites of the destroyed ancient greatness were built new creeds and alien faiths. But the glorious inheritance of Aryan ancestors, uncontaminated by Semitic and savage ideas, though lost to India, has been preserved by the Aryan Sinhalese in the luxuriant isle of Ceylon.

The Mahavansa tells us that "the lord of Lanka (Buddha) knowing by divine inspiration the inestimable blessings vouchsafed to Lanka, the all-bountiful luminary visited this most favoured land thrice. From this circumstance this island became venerated by righteous men. Hence, it shone forth the light itself of religion." Since the conversion of King Devanampiya Tissa and his court by the Arhat

Mahinda, the religion began to spread rapidly over Ceylon. Not only were men admitted to the priestly order, but also women, chief of the latter being the queen-consort. To admit her into the order of Bhikkhunis (nuns) a message had to be sent to the saintly Sanghamitta, daughter of the Indian emperor, and sister to the Arhat Mahinda. It is unique in religious history that a son and a daughter of a reigning emperor should be chosen for the conversion of a people. The Sinhalese people, as a whole, have for 2,214 years remained loyal to the saintly apostles of Buddhism and to the noble teaching that gave them an individuality so full of vitalising power that they have been able so far to withstand the sledge-hammer attacks levelled at their faith by persistent propagandists of other religions since the year 1505 of Christ.

The first colony of Sinhalese, although in faith Sivite, yet had the tolerant principle prominent in them; for the first lord of the land built for the sectarians different temples for their respective worships. The royal apostle first preached an appropriate sermon showing the supremacy of the Tathagata (the "Great Teacher," *i.e.*, Buddha) as the divine authority, who taught the doctrine of peace and immortality; and the foundations of the faith were by his strenuous advocacy so well laid that for fully 1,899 years this teaching held supreme sway. The first paralysing blow it received was from the parricide Rajasinha, who reigned in Ceylon about the year of Christ 1552. Having killed his father, he embraced the Sivite faith, and "after that," so we are told in chapter 13 of the Mahavansa, "he began to destroy the religion of the conqueror by slaying its priests and burning its sacred books and breaking down its temples; and thus did he bar the way that leadeth to heaven."

During the long period of Buddhist sway temporary outbreaks of this nature occasionally suspended for the time being the religious continuity and prosperity of the people. But it was a common saying with the ancients that "Lanka remaineth not under the rule of kings that are followers of false creeds."

An Anti-Buddhistic Invasion.

In the year 237 B.C. the Tamil invader, Elala, usurped the Sinhalese throne. But for several years anterior to that event there had been a suspension of religious activities in the northern part of the island. The Tamils, fiercely antagonistic to Buddhism, committed acts of vandalism in the sacred city of Anuradhapura, and—for a time—there was none to deter them. At this crisis there arose a wonderful prince, whose father was then reigning in Southern Ceylon. He was in his previous birth a young Bhikkhu (Buddhist monk), who, when dying, was solicited by the queen to be re-born in her womb. Particulars of this phenomenal birth are given in the Mahavansa, chap. 22. This young prince, Gamini Abhaya, after he had reached maturity, made war upon the usurper, Elala. After a series of pitched battles, the Sinhalese prince defeated Elala in single combat and slew him on the battlefield. Then began the building of magnificent temples, dagobas (monuments), by the conqueror, who, reducing Lanka (Ceylon) under one rule, became king. From the world-renowned ruins of these dagobas at Anuradhapura an idea of their original splendour may be obtained. The war that Gamini Abhaya waged with Elala was of a religious character, and he made it known by a solemn proclamation that "this enterprise of mine is not for the purpose of acquiring the pomp and advantages of royalty. This undertaking has always had for its object the re-establishment of the religion of the supreme Buddha. By the truth of this declaration may the arms and equipments of my army in the hour of battle flash, as if emitting the rays of the sun" (Mahavansa, chap. 25). It is said that one day when, after his victorious conquest, the king was reflecting with dismay on the recollection of innumerable lives sacrificed in the attainment of his end, eight holy saints (termed Arhats) came to him miraculously and administered spiritual comfort. And the king said, "Lords! what peace of mind can there be left to me, when I have been the means of destroying great armies?" And the saints answered, "Supreme of men! From the commission of that act there will be no impediment in the road to salvation. Herein no more than two human beings have been sacrificed; the rest are heretics and sinners,

TEMPLE SCENE, MATARA.

who are on a par with wild beasts. And as thou wilt cause the religion of Buddha to shine forth in great splendour, on that account, O ruler of men, subdue thy mental affliction!" (Mahavansa, chap. 25). Thus was the king consoled. It was always a custom with the Sinhalese kings when engaged in wars to take with them the "sons of Buddha," evidently to show that the wars were conducted in a spirit of religion. To these rulers nothing appeared more supreme than this religion, which was called the "religion of the conqueror," and was thus completely identified with the racial individuality of the people.

The Zenith of Buddhism.

Impelled by the supreme force of the truth of the Dhamma (as Buddhism is termed in the Pali tongue), the youthful race of Ceylon, in the vigour of renewed vitality, engaged under the new king, in making themselves serviceable to their country and religion—a religion that suggested disinterested activity in the performance of benevolent deeds for the good of man and beast. Under King Gamini Abhaya, who had driven out the Tamil usurper, and as if by the waving of a magic wand, temples, tanks, parks, gardens, public baths, resting-houses for man and beast, hospitals—also for man and beast—free almonries, schools, colleges for Bhikkhus and nuns, gymnasiums, and public halls were erected throughout the land. Free from foreign influences, untainted by alien customs, with the word of Buddha as their guiding light, the Sinhalese people lived a joyously cheerful life in those bygone times. Biographical sketches of men and women, descriptions of gorgeous processions circumambulating the city of Anuradhapura, are given in the Mahavansa and the Saddhammalankara records. There was dazzling magnificence within the sacred city, which contained nine-storeyed houses; and the streets were crowded day and night by throngs of pilgrims and also traders from all parts of the then known world. The atmosphere was saturated with the fragrance of sweet-smelling flowers and delicate perfumes. Elephants, superbly caparisoned and with gilded howdahs on their backs, and chariots drawn by prancing steeds, paraded the wide ways of the city. The glittering spears, burnished helmets, and coats of iron of the cavalrymen, and foot soldiers armed with bows and arrows, were seen in the thoroughfares; and the air reverberated with joyous shouts of "Sadhu! sadhu!" ("Hail! hail!"). Such was the glorious period of Buddhism in Ceylon in the days when the foreigner was not in the land. Afterwards he was to come with his licensed opium dens, arrack taverns, whisky saloons, and butcher stalls for slaughtering animals. Under the Buddhist sovereignty there was no shedding of blood, and the killing of cattle was prohibited. But fish and game could be obtained and eaten, except on the "poiya" days, which fell four times a month, coming with the changes of the moon. On these "poiya" days the whole city presented a marvellous spectacle. The garb of religion was seen everywhere, and the whole population observed these holy days with fraternal rejoicings. The king himself wore the

INTERIOR OF DAMBOOL TEMPLE.

white robe of the ordinary Upasaka (novice) and ate the same food with the rest, thus exhibiting the spirit of brotherhood so much emphasised in the Buddhist doctrine as requisite. On all festive days the king, "ever mindful of the welfare of the people," provided, at the four gates of the city, "numerous bath attendants, barbers, dressers, clothing, garlands of fragrant flowers, and savoury provisions," for the free use of his subjects. The dogs and other beasts were fed, and even rice for the ravens was provided. In the Mahavansa mention is made of several kings who gave bulls for the carrying of cripples; while lands were provided for the halt and the blind and the "well-born women who were widows," and "hospitals for the treatment of pestilential diseases, and dispensaries were also built" (Mahavansa, chap. 41). These and many other things for the "welfare of the people of the land" the kings of old did for the acquisition of that "enviable body of glory that will endure for ever."

BUDDHIST PRIEST AND YOUNG PUPILS.

In the eleventh century after Christ the Sinhalese had a regular navy, a fleet of sailing vessels which was used for fighting purposes, and all the country round about the coast seemed "like one great workshop busied with the constant building of ships." In those days the Sinhalese were famous for their knowledge of things that went to make a nation great. Their fleet that went forth to conquer Lower Burma—a most memorable expedition and achievement of bygone days—had a well-fitted hospital ship, and there were "physicians and nurses also." Whatever the Sinhalese accomplished in their days of glory was done by the impelling force of the religion of Buddha, whose fundamental principles, to this day subscribed to by nearly five hundred millions of people in Asia (most of them in the Chinese Empire), may be summed up in these words: "Avoid all evil; accomplish all that is good; purify the heart." In its primitive purity, however, it is generally acknowledged that this religion is only to be found in the Southern Church of Buddhism, which is identified with Ceylon.

Definition of Buddhism.

A more comprehensive definition of this wonderful Eastern doctrine is that it is a transcendentalism enunciating a refined code of evolutionary ethics and a metaphysical psychology. The promulgator of this religion is known as the Buddha Bhaghava, the Tathagata, the Sakya Muni. To quote Sir Edwin Arnold's description in his great poem, "The Light of Asia":—

> "He is the Saviour of the world,
> Lord Buddha—Prince Siddhartha styled on earth—
> In earth and heaven and hells incomparable,
> All-honoured, wisest, best, most pitiful;
> The Teacher of Nirvana and the law."

In the Dhamma or Dharma (*i.e.*, Buddhism) is embodied all that is useful for the salvation of all beings. It has "one taste—the taste of emancipation." The essential principle that the Lord Buddha emphasised is ceaseless activity—activity in destroying evil; activity in generating good thoughts, good words, good deeds—thereby achieving the peace and happiness of Nirvana. Buddhism teaches that ignorance of the scientific law of evolution and of the law of causes and effects, that the desire to enjoy purely an egoistic happiness, that hatred, ill-will, pride, stubbornness, covetousness, envy, lust, and all selfish passions, produce misery, and that this misery is visible in the several planes wherever the individualised consciousness operates. The living being, so runs the doctrine, is a compound of five skhandas (physical states in which sensations, perceptions, karma-producing thoughts, and totalising consciousness are experienced), and these skandhas are in a state of perpetual change. Birth and death is the law of the "seven states of existence." An individualised consciousness may last for a moment and die, or it may last for 84,000 kalpas—a kalpa is an æon of a million million years—as in the case of those horn in the Nevasannanasanna Arupa state—the fourth of the formless heavens where consciousness operates—and then die, and are re-individualised again according to karma—*i.e.*, the law regulating the future state of each person according to his deserts.

The above are the basic principles; and—if the uninitiated can follow the terms of the exposition—the elaborate superstructure of Buddhism is made up as follows. First come the twelve Nidanas, the bases of evolutionary life, which collectively constitute the most subtle phase of Buddhist psychology, namely: (1) Avijja—ignorance of the laws of Nirvanic enlightenment, the comprehension of which is possible only for him who understands the twenty-four physical categories; (2) Sankharas—thoughts of threefold kind that produce karmic variations and operate in the realms of good and evil; (3) Vinnana—consciousness

A BUDDHIST HIGH PRIEST.

operating through the six senses subjectively and objectively; (4) Nama-rupa—"name-and-form," the former including sensations, perceptions, and thoughts, while the latter includes the physical organism; (5) Salayatana—the six seats of sense-consciousness, viz., eye, ear, nose, tongue, body, and mind ; (6) Phasoo—contact caused by the coalition of one of the six senses with an object and the operating consciousness of the subjective sense organ; (7) Vedana—the three states of experiencing sensations either pleasant, unpleasant, or indifferent; (8) Tanha—the three egoistic desires, to live, to die, or to enjoy ; (9) Upadana—the fourfold basis of re-incarnation caused by clinging to base physical pleasures, to undue metaphysical speculations, to morbid ascetic habits, to an egoistic personality; (10) Bhavo—ninefold realms where consciousness takes birth according to the sum-totality of thoughts ; (11) Jati—birth either in a high or low state ; and (12) Jara-marana—decay, disease, and all forms of physical deterioration. Next we tration, and equal-mindedness ; the eight attributes of Nirvana—right comprehension of the foregoing principles, right aspirations after love and renunciation, right, gentle, truthful speech, right action in abstaining from the five evils, right livelihood (that is, abstinence from slavery, selling liquor, poisons, flesh, and destructive weapons), right exertion to do good and avoid evil, right analysis, right concentrations of the four Jhanas (defined below) ; the six Ayatanas—seats of consciousness ; the six Dhatus—elements of evolution, namely, matter, liquids, heat, air, ether or space, and consciousness ; the four Jhanas—the spiritual conditions that may be realised by the spiritual student who follows the virtuous life as pointed out by the Lord Buddha as well as by the Brahmans ; and the twelve Vimokkhas—successive states of psychical emancipation through eight spiritualising stages.

ELEPHANT CARRYING TRIBUTE TO THE TEMPLE.

have, in order, the four Satipatthanas—analysis of body from a biological basis, analysis of experiencing sensations, analysis of volition, and analysis of the five obstacles to spiritual development; the four Sammappadhanas—unceasing exertion to cast off existing evil, unceasing exertion not to create fresh evil, unceasing exertion to create good, and unceasing exertion to increase the good ; the four Iddhippadas—desire to progress, strenuous ceaseless exertion, analysis of thoughts, and investigation ; the five Indriyas—physical bases, including faith, attentiveness, exertion, concentration, wisdom, and such-like; the five Balas—physical powers such as faith, presence of mind, energy, concentration, and knowledge of "the four noble truths"; the seven Bajjhangas—presence of mind, analysis of mind, exertion, joyfulness, serenity, concen-

With cosmic theories of an animistic or ghostly ego or "soul" that inhabits the body and which at death goes to the gods, Buddhism has no kinship. It transcends the knowledge of Aryan pantheists, Semitic prophets, and Arabian reformers. It ignores a Creator and ridicules the existence of great celestial spirits, counting such theories as pretences and impositions upon the credulity of the ignorant. It argues the uselessness of prayer, maintaining, by means of the parable of a body of men who, having thrown a rock into the depths of water, foolishly began praying for the stone to come up, that every man must work out his own salvation. It holds that his own evil deeds bring suffering on the doer, while, correlatively, his good deeds promote his own happiness and so far secure for him the delights of heaven according to his deserts. Ordinary good deeds, such as giving alms to the poor, observing the five precepts—abstinence from destruction of life, from dishonest gain, from committing adultery, from narcotic drugs and from intoxicating drinks—belong to the domain of good karma, the reward of which is birth in one of the four Maharajikkas (lower celestial spheres) or in one of the six kama heavens. The higher Bramachari life, that of saintly celibacy, is rewarded by elevation to one of the Rupa Brahmalokas (higher heavens). Those who spend their time in sober asceticism, purifying celibacy, and higher forms of psychical emancipation (the Vimokkhas, mentioned above) are elevated to the Arupa Brahmalokas, or formless heavens. To be raised to any one of these states, the doctrine, as taught by the Brahman Rishis, indicates the spiritualising process. These heavens are not eternal. They belong to the pantheism of the Brahmans ; and as they are within the circle of cosmic evolution, they are included in the Buddhist cosmogony. But, being within the limitations of karma, they are consequently repudiated by the Tathagata, as they do not give the highest unchanging happiness. His was the unique discovery of the "Middle Path," the only way to the eternal happiness of Nirvana. The Middle Path condemns ascetic and painful practices, as well as sensual, vulgar, profitless and ignoble pleasures. The Nirvana doctrine ennobles and sublimates both body and mind, and produces the calm, cheerful, energetic, analytical life of equal-mindedness which is the ideal that the Lord Buddha held out as the best to those who are inclined to lead a religious life of eternal peace and rest. Death, decay, and disease are, in this way, for ever destroyed ; also lust, anger, and ignorance.

In Buddhism there are five unpardonable sins, called the Anantariya, the commission of any one of which sends the doer after death to Avichi—the lowest sphere of torment. All other sins may be atoned for by good karma ; and the highest and best way to atone for the past is to become a Bhikkhu (monk). This is the "new birth" that is spoken of in the Angulimala-sutta, a discourse preached to Angulimala, and recorded in the Majjhimanikaya portion of the Sutta Pitaka, a collection of sacred Buddhist writings. Every good act done with an unselfish motive and without the association of the ego consciousness is helpful to realise the Nirvanic ideal. The ego aspects of consciousness, with all their speculations, are relegated to the limbo of silence. Do good, and no devil can send you to hell ; do evil, and neither prayer nor any one of the gods can send you to heaven. That is the essence of the Buddhist doctrine. Each individual enjoys the reward of his own good deeds, suffers according to his evil deeds. A Buddhist is expected not to believe any revelation, but to judge of the results before accepting any theory. He accepts the principle of evolution and its complex changes—the birth of the cell and its developmental changes, its maturity in the human organism, and its dissolution and re-evolution in an unending chain of consciousness. The myth of creation was ridiculed by the Buddha, who held that its acceptance retards the spiritual growth of the individual. Similarly, predetermined fatalism and a nihilistic materialism are condemned by the religion he established. The Buddha taught that nothing exists in a permanent condition ; and this teaching involves necessarily the elaborate scheme of changes of condition in every individual life which is sketched above. Buddha enunciated the eight cosmic principles of gain and loss, prosperity and adversity, blame and praise, happiness and misery, as the ruling conditions of life. Every individual's experience must fall within this category.

The Western Invasion and Decline of Buddhism.

The Sinhalese people for the first time came face to face with a Western race four hundred years ago ; and their ancient glory, so closely associated with Buddhism, began to decline simultaneously with the appearance of the invaders. Thenceforth, for nearly three hundred years, Ceylon became the hunting-ground of the Portuguese and Dutch, and both these Powers carried out vandalistic work. They destroyed the ancient Buddhist monuments, and forced a Semitic religion down the throats of the Sinhalese. The Mahavansa chronicler (chap. 95) writes: "These men were called Parangis [foreigners] and were all of them wicked unbelievers, cruel and hard of heart. And they entered into fruitful provinces and laid waste fields and gardens, and burned houses and villages, and ravished women of rank, and sorely troubled the Sinhalese in this manner. They broke into towns and temples and image-houses, and destroyed Bodhi-trees and images of Buddha, and such-like sacred things."

Narendra Singh, who died in 1734 after Christ, was the last of the Sinhalese line of kings. Thenceforward the country passed into the hands of the Tamil princes who came from Southern India. In consequence of these foreign invasions and conquests, the Sinhalese of the maritime provinces became alienated, and a new race of Sinhalese, with foreign traditions, customs, laws, and religion, came into existence. The weakening process was consummated by the surrender of the Kandyan territory to the British in 1815. The "law of change," acknowledged as inevitable by the Buddhist doctrine, was thus verified ; and the "brave and lion-hearted Sinhalese," who had enjoyed the spirit of independence for fully 2,359 years, ceased to exist as an individualised race.

The British have built roads, extended railways, and generally introduced the blessings of their materialistic civilisation into the land ; and with this inception of the modern era the Aryan Sinhalese has lost his true identity and become a hybrid. Practices which were an abomination to the ancient noble Sinhalese have to-day become tolerated under the influence of Semitic sociology. The Buddhists complain that opium, alcohol, arrack, bhang, ganja, and other poisons are distributed in the villages by men holding licences, without regard to the degenerating effects they produce in the human organism. In the days of the Sinhalese kings and under the Buddhist rule no liquor was sold, no animals were slaughtered ; land was not sold. The people held the land in common, there being no landlords except the "Rajabhogis," who received certain grants of property for having rendered special service to the country and king. Now the Sinhalese, once the lord of the soil, is but a stranger in his land. It is sold to him—his own land—and his future is indeed dark.

BUDDHIST TEMPLE, COLOMBO.

The Present Position.

The present spiritual condition of the Buddhist population in Ceylon is causing anxiety to the orthodox followers of Buddha. There is very little inclination shown by either the clericals or the laity to observe strictly the precepts of the "Noble Eightfold Path." As regards materialistic development, however, the Buddhist community in the island has, since 1862, been showing its ability to march with the times. Printing presses, newspapers, and journals devoted to the religion have been established, and colleges for teaching Pali, Sanskrit, classical Sinhalese, Ayurvedic medicine, astrological mathematics, and kindred subjects have been founded. The Vidyodaya College at Colombo was founded in 1873.

The present generation of Buddhists in the maritime provinces of the island are showing remarkable activity in opening elementary schools for children. Several English colleges and about 400 Buddhist vernacular schools under Buddhist management have been established, while about 7,900 Bhikkhus (monks) are keeping up the ancient traditions, and new temples are being built in various parts of the island. Ancient historic dagobas (monuments) in the ruined sacred city of Anuradhapura, in the North-Central Province of Ceylon, and in Magama, in the hill-country, another of the ancient capitals of Lanka (Ceylon), are being restored by Buddhist contributions. Pilgrims from Japan, China, Cambodia, Burma, Siam, Tibet, and even from distant Siberia, still visit Ceylon in large numbers to worship at the ancient shrines, to adore the Sacred Tooth of Buddha at Kandy, and to ascend the sacred mountain of Samana-Kuta (Adam's Peak), a conspicuous elevation of 7,353 ft. in the south-central portion, whereon Buddha left his footprint.

But in spite of the activity of the leaders of the 1,700,000 Sinhalese Buddhists to conserve their ancient religion, the flower of the land, the rising generation of Sinhalese youth, has come under the influence of Christian propagandists. Supported in their efforts by the 120 millions of Christians in England and America, the Christian missionaries are striving to uproot this "noble and æsthetic religion of righteousness."

An Appeal for Official Countenance.

But it is in the power of the British Government, which now rules the land with absolute sway, to protect the Sinhalese race from further losing its ancient religion by following the ennobling instructions laid down by the Tathagata. Let the Buddhists be given a form of local self-government according to the ancient traditions, based on the beneficent teachings of their Saviour. By nature the Sinhalese Buddhists "are polite, kind to their children, and fond of learning." Let the noble British nation, so eager to do good, prevent the sale of opium, arrack, and other intoxicating drugs to the Buddhists. Let industrial and technical schools be started in populous towns and villages. Let the methods adopted in the ancient days by the good kings of old, like Gamini, Buddhadasa, Parakrama Bahu, and other rulers, be repeated. Let the Mahavansa be a guide, and let the learned elderly Maha Theros (high priests) of the different parts of the island be asked to advise the Government as to the best means to be adopted for promoting the material and moral welfare of the Sinhalese Buddhists. That both the British and the Buddhists may thus thrive side by side in Ceylon is the sincere wish and prayer of the Anagārika Dharmapala.

BUDDHIST SECTS.

By H. SUMANGALA, M.R.A.S., High Priest.

THOUGH the Buddha visited Ceylon three times, Buddhism was not introduced into Ceylon till 236 years after the demise of the Great Teacher, during the reign of Asoka (B.C. 307) by Mahinda, Ittiya, Uttiya, Sambala, and Bhadda, the great Arhats, and Sanghamitta, the great priestess, who brought with her a branch of the sacred Bo-tree from Buddhagaya. At this time the reigning king in Ceylon was Devanampiya Tissa. The religion spread very fast, and temples sprang up all over the island. In the royal garden, Maha Megha, situated to the south of his capital, Anuradhapura, the king built the Maha Vihara (great temple), Thuparama and Isurumuni temples, and enshrined the relics of Buddha at the shrine of Thuparama. He offered land to the priesthood, which they consecrated as Mahasuna (the place for conducting priestly ceremonials).

In the year of Buddha 296[1] (B.C. 247) King Suratissa built 500 temples in the different parts of the kingdom. In the year 382 (B.C. 361) King Duttagamini built the Mirisaweliya dagoba, the Brazen Palace, Ruanveli dagoba, and further spread the religion. At this time there were many Parivenas or educational institutes for the priesthood. In A.B. 406 (B.C. 137) King Saddhatissa built temples at every yojana.

BUDDHIST TEMPLE, KELANI.

[1] The Buddhist era is reckoned from the Parinirvana (death) of Buddha, which took place 543 B.C. A.B. stands for Anno Buddha.

In A.B. 454 (B.C. 89) King Vattagamini Abhaya built the Abhayagiri vihara and many educational establishments. The sacred books (Tripitakas) were written in book form for the first time. Up to this time the priesthood was united in one fraternity, known as the Maha Vihara fraternity. It was guided by rules and regulations which had been handed down from the time of Mahinda, the great Apostle. But about this time two secessions of the priesthood took place, forming the Abhayagiri fraternity and the Dakkhina fraternity. The unorthodox Dakkhina Vihara fraternity later became the Jelavana fraternity.

In A.B. 953 (410 A.D.) in the reign of King Mahanama the Great, Buddhaghosa arrived in Ceylon from India, and translated the Commentaries (Atthakathas of the Tripitaka) from Sinhalese to Pali, according to Maha Vihara traditions.

In A.B. 1600 (A.D. 1057) King Vijayabahu the Great sent an embassy to Anuruddha, the king of Ramanna, and brought down priests and increased the number of ordained priests. The priesthood may be said to belong to the Ramanna fraternity from this time downwards, although it was considered to be a section of the Maha Vihara fraternity.

In A.B. 1698 (A.D. 1155) Parakrama Bahu the Great united the priesthood in one sect and did away with all dissensions. Many commentaries were also made and educational institutions established. The Tamil invasions, which had done great damage to the Buddhist faith, nearly destroyed Buddhism about the year 1760 (A.D. 1217), in the reign of Magha. So in A.B. 1785 (A.D. 1242) Parakrama Bahu II. invited many learned priests from the Soli country in Southern India, who brought with them many sacred books that were non-existent in Ceylon, and established the religion and priesthood on a firm basis. A medical book, "Bhesajja Manjusa," was made by a Brahman priest for the treatment of the Buddhist priest-

CREMATION OF A BUDDHIST PRIEST.
(Before the firing of the pyre.)

hood. Five Parivenas were also established by him, and the united priesthood flourished under the Maha Vihara rules, although the priesthood was composed of the Ramanna and the Soli fraternities.

In A.B. 1953 (A.D. 1410) King Sri Parakrama Bahu established the Vijayabahu Parivena in the Wellaboda Pattu of the Galle district, Sunetra Parivena in Salpiti Korale, Padmavoti Parivena and the Uttaramula Parivena in Siyane Korale, and Irugaltilaka Parivena in Matara district. At these Parivenas an education corresponding to a college and university education was given.

In A.B. 2007 (A.D. 1410) King Bhuvaneka Bahu of Kotta sent ordination (upasampada) to the country of Ramanna (Lower Burma). The priests were of the Ramanna-Soli fraternity, but were considered by that king of the Maha Vihara fraternity. In A.B. 2100 (A.D. 1503) King Rajasinha I. adopted Hinduism and destroyed the priesthood and most of the sacred books. At this time, owing to the invasion of Ceylon by the Portuguese, Buddhism was in a very backward state.

In A.B. 2135 (A.D. 1592) Vimala Dharma I. brought ordained priests from Rakkanga (Arakan), and attempted the work of reconstruction with limited success. In A.B. 2227 (A.D. 1684) Vimala Dharma II. made a further attempt with priests brought from Arakan. In A.D. 1753 Kirti Sri Rajasinha invited thirteen ordained priests with the aid of Parama Dhammika, king of Siam, and ordained the Sâmaneras (novices) of the Ceylon priesthood. Ten of these Siamese priests stayed for six years at Kandy, and helped to consolidate the priesthood. The Siamese sect of the Ceylon priesthood (Siam Nikaya) owes its origin to these priests. From the head priest, Upali, of the thirteen Siamese priests, the Siamese sect is known as Upalivansa (Upali dynasty). As the ordination ceremonies were held at the Malwatta Temple and Asgiri Temple at Kandy, the Siamese sect is further divided into Malwatta and Asgiri sub-sects. According to old rayal traditions the ordination was conferred on the novitiates after due inquiry into their family and caste.

In 1803 a party of Samanera priests of the Siamese sects from the temples of Welitara and Ambagohapitiya started for Siam. Afterwards another party, consisting of Kapugama Dhammakkandha and several other priests who had received ordination in a manner different from that usual at the hands of Wagegoda, who had left Kandy some time previous to this, contrary to the wishes of the king and the clergy, also started for Siam to be ordained. But at Madras, hearing of the Burmese ordination, these two parties went to Amarapura in Burma, which was then an independent country, and received their ordination at

Amarapura at the hands of the Burmese Sangha Raja.

These two parties, together with a third from Deundara, who also received their ordination at Amarapura, constituted the Amarapura sect.

In 1853, owing to some controversy, the Amarapura sect split into two sections, the Deundara Amarapura sect also separating as a third sub-section. There is, besides, a fourth sect of the Amarapura priests, known as the Matara Nikaya.

In 1856 some of the priests of Siamese Nikaya, of the Malwatta Vihara section, together with other priests under the high priests of the Western Province then living at Kotta, and some others favouring Rev. Atthadassi of Bentota, owing to some controversy, formed into a sect known as the Kalayna sect.

In 1864 several Samanera priests of the Amarapura sect received ordination from the Sangharaja at Mandalay, and became known as the Ramanna sect.

Such is the brief history of the formation of the different sects of the priesthood in Ceylon. The growth of these different sects is not due to any difference in their beliefs or doctrines, but to some controversial points with regard to the functions of the priesthood. There is no doctrinal dissimilarity, as there is between the Northern and Southern Buddhists, nor is there any real dissension among them, all the different sects working and co-operating harmoniously in important matters. The priests of one sect often receive education from priests of another sect.

At the present time, according to the last census, there are 7,331 Buddhist priests. Approximately, there are about 3,000 temples. Of the different sects, 3,200 belong to the Siamese sect of the Malwatta Vihara; 750 belong to the Asgiri sect. There are 1,330 in the Amarapura sect, 150 in the Matara sect, 150 in the Deundara sect, and 600 in the Kalyana branch of the Siamese sect. The Ramanna sect contains nearly 1,070 priests.

After the Portuguese invasion both the educational and religious works of the Buddhist priesthood suffered heavily, and the intellectual desolation was so great that learned Brahmans had to come from India to teach in Ceylon. But about the year 1780 the Malwatta and Asgiri Vihara became the centre for the spread of religious and secular education both for the up and low countries. Since 1873 there have been established about 20 Parivenas. Elementary education for the children of the laity was given in the temples till the Government took up the task of education.

The Parivenas are the university colleges of the Buddhist priesthood. At these are taught Oriental literature in all its aspects, the curriculum including logic, prosody, rhetoric, medicine and astronomy, and the Buddhist sacred books. Both the priests and the laity are here educated. The Parivenas, besides, exercise great moral influence on those who come in contact with them. The Buddhist temples, to which more than 2,500,000 flock every year, exercise great influence on the village population. But the increased sale of intoxicants, which daily become more and more accessible to the poor, largely interferes with the good works of the priesthood. There has been within the last fifty years a revival of Buddhism, and the prospects for the future of Buddhism, both in Ceylon and abroad, are distinctly good.

CREMATION OF A BUDDHIST PRIEST.

(After the pyre had been fired.)

KANDY AND THE KANDYANS

By Major FRANK MODDER, F.R.G.S.

ENCIRCLED by an amphitheatre of hills, clad in Orient verdure and decked with tropical flowers of varied hue, lies nestled the Queen of Lanka's imperial cities, the last of her historical capitals — Kandy, whose charming beauty is reflected on the rippling waters of a picturesque lake at the base of the surrounding acclivities.

To use the quaint language of Knox, who spent his twenty years of captivity in the Kandyan country, "The first is the city of Candy, so called from *Condi*, which in the Chingulays language signifies 'hills,' for among them it is situated; but by the inhabitants Hingodagul-neure." Kandy is called in the books *Senkhanda, Saila, Nuyara.* In the Mahavansa it is referred to as *Senkhanda Sela Siriwaddhana*, to distinguish it from Siriwaddhana of Dambadeniya. By dropping the *Sen* and *Sel* you get *khanda*, which the Tamils designate *kandi*, and the Europeans *kandy*. There is a rock, in the modern town, which is still known as *Sengada Gala*, "The Rock of Sengada," and a tradition about the building of the ancient city and palace is attached to it. Kandy we owe, of course, to the Portuguese, but when the name first appears in Portuguese relations of the island is not ascertained. The "Kandyan provinces," as distinguished from the maritime provinces, was a general appellation assigned to such districts in the interior of Ceylon as were formerly under the dominion of the kings of Kandy. Extending from about 6° 20′ to 8° 45′ North, they lay, according to Davy, between 80° 8′ and 81° 45′ East longitude. As an approximation, their superficial contents may be stated at 12,360 square miles—nearly five-eighths of the whole island. They occupied the whole middle of the island and a great portion of its southern extremity, and were bounded by a belt of maritime district irregularly varying in width from 8 to 30 miles, and at the northern extremity amounting to nearly 80 miles. The maritime district formed a belt round the island, extending in some places more than 6, in others 30, and on the northern side 60 miles into the interior.

The inland provinces, cut off from all communication with the sea and occupying the greater part of the island, were still retained by the Kandyan monarch.

The Kandyan kingdom consisted of twenty-one chief divisions, of which the first principal ones were called *Dissawaniers* (signifying literally *side*, says Davy, perhaps from their situation) and the majority of the rest *rataval;* or to use Knox's antique phraseology, "It is convenient that we first understand that this land (the inland country being that which is now under the king of Candy) is divided into greater or less shares or parts. The greater part, give me leave to call provinces, and the less, counties, as resembling ours in England, though not altogether so big."

Dissawani was a division presided over by a chief or governor called *Dissawa*, and a *Rate*, which may be properly denominated a district, usually by an officer who was distinguished by the name of *atemahatmaya*, equivalent to a lord-lieutenant of Ireland. These divisions, established by long custom, were occasionally, though rarely, altered by the reigning monarch.

The *Dissawanies* were eleven in number and the districts nine. The cession of the Kandyan provinces to the British took place on February 15, 1815—the day from which, says Knighton, "we date the extinction of Sinhalese independence, and the independence which had continued without material interruption for 2,359 years"—so far as the Kandyan Sinhalese were concerned. The Union Jack was for the first time hoisted and the establishment of the British dominion in the interior announced by a royal salute from the cannon of the city of Kandy. All the troops were under arms on the occasion of this important event.

After the British occupation detailed reference to the Kandyan provinces is for the first time made in the Proclamation of November 21, 1818. In order to give effect to the plan for the administration of justice, to collect the public revenue, and to insure the execution of public duties, the provinces were assigned to the immediate control and exercise of jurisdiction of a Board of Commissioners and, under their superintendence, of resident agents of Government. The chiefs and inferior headmen were to perform their duty to Government under the orders of the Board and British agents, and not otherwise.

The Board of Commissioners was abolished in 1833, in which year the island was divided into six provinces, the *Dissawanies* and *districts* being distributed among them. On the creation of the *North-Western Province* in 1845 two districts were included in it. The area covered by the Kandyan provinces was defined in Schedule B of Ordinance No. 3 of 1870. In order to improve the condition of the neglected Kandyan districts it was determined to create them into a new province. The North-Central Province was accordingly formed in 1873.

The district of Badulla was severed from the Central Province and created into the Province of Uva on February 1, 1886. In 1817 the district was the focus of a formidable rebellion against British rule, in the suppression of which many valuable lives were lost, chiefly owing to the insalubrity of the climate, the operations being mostly confined to the unhealthy and low-lying portions of the district. In the course of the military operations villages were burnt, crops and fruit-trees laid low and devastated, and it is doubtful whether even to this day the portions in question have wholly recovered.

For some time petty garrisons were maintained at different posts, but they were all gradually withdrawn, and the administration of the district, which from 1821 to 1845 had been entrusted to military officers, was again placed entirely in the hands of civil servants of the Crown. When the Kandyan Board of Commissioners was abolished, Badulla was the seat of an assistant agent, and this arrangement was continued until the district was formed into a separate province.

The Province of Sabaragamuwa was constituted and proclaimed as a separate province on January 4, 1889, a change which has certainly been appreciated by the people, who are now saved the delays and vexations consequent on repeated references to Colombo for decision on matters affecting their interest, and who now find at their own Kachcheri in Ratnapura the facilities for settlement which previously necessitated long and expensive journeys to the metropolis.

"Three hundred years ago," wrote Davy in 1820, "there is good reason to believe that the Sinhalese were one people, without any points of difference, excepting such trifling ones as might result from the peculiarities of climate and of other physical circumstances of the lowlands and highlands. But since that period—since the maritime provinces have been in the possession of Europeans, a change has been taking place in the lowland Sinhalese, which, though very slow, gradual, and imperceptible in progress, is now obvious in effect and easily discernible in certain alterations and innovations in their language, manners and customs—varying in degree of change, more or less, according to proximity to our settlements."

The Kandyans, who are commonly known as the *uda-rata* people—that is, highlanders—are distinguished from the Sinhalese of the maritime portions of the island, who are termed *pata-rata* people—that is, lowlanders—in various ways, more especially with regard to dress, habits, institutions, laws, manners, customs, and usages. The former, by reason of their secluded and exclusive position in the inaccessible rocky fastnesses of the interior, and through not having been affected by the influence of successive European conquests, were estranged from and had very little in common with their sea-board brethren for several decades past. From the little intercourse that subsisted with the maritime provinces, the habits and institutions of the people were of the most simple and primitive kind, exhibiting curious memorials of their social condition in remote ages. So that while the low-country Sinhalese materially changed with the tide of each successive European administration, and adapted themselves to Western modes, manners, and habits, the Kandyans remained *in statu quo*.

No corresponding change that we know of has occurred among the highland Sinhalese. The probability is that they are much the same now as they were three hundred years ago, and that they were then very similar to what they were in ages preceding. Supposing this view to be correct, no small interest is imparted to the study of such a people by the consideration that they are the living examples of a remote antiquity, and that they are almost as fresh and original to us as the inhabitants of the coast of the island were to the early invaders; and this feeling of interest is surely not diminished by the reflection that this people, for ages the same, have in their turn arrived at an eventful period of change, so that the next generation probably will no longer be the exact likeness of that past, and a good deal of that which is still in practice or fresh in remembrance in a few years will be altered or forgotten, and if not recorded now, lost perhaps for ever.

It will not be strictly within the legitimate scope of this sketch to enter into a disquisition on all the peculiar customs and habits, the traits and characteristics, of an interesting people such as the Kandyans are, although there are ample and varied information and material sufficient to form

"A quaint and curious volume of forgotten lore."

There are, however, some points which call for remark and criticism, and which may be briefly dealt with.

Are the Kandyans excessively hairy? "Nature has given the Kandyans a liberal supply of hair, which they universally allow to grow on their face as well as head to a considerable length, being of opinion that the beard does not deform but improves the face; and certainly, in many instances, I have seen it have the effect of giving to the countenance an air of dignity that would have disappeared with the use of the razor." So wrote Davy, whose knowledge and experience of the interior of the island, and chiefly of the Kandyan districts, come next in point of accuracy and extensiveness to Knox's. "But," says Sir John Budd Phear, writing on the same subject, "their most striking peculiarity, perhaps, is the excessive hairiness of both male and female. The chest of the man often resembles a doormat, and the hair of his head reaches low down his back, a feature which attracted the notice of the earliest Greek geographers." This extraordinary capillary development is certainly the reverse of what we see in those Mongolian peoples with whom we are best acquainted It seems, however, that the Ainos, a Turanian race on the extreme coast of Asia, possess it even to a greater extent than the Sinhalese, and that they at an early historical period were widely spread over the islands and tracts of country now covered by the Japanese, Chinese, and Malays. "Can it be," asks Sir John Phear, "that the Sinhalese are by blood, in a large measure, traceable to an Aino or cognate origin, and that they owe little more than the language, literature, and religion to the invasion of Aryans from Upper Bengal of which history tells us?"

Sir John Phear unfortunately does not mention the source of his information on this point, and his startling conclusion is not based on any data. There are to be met with among the Kandyans, as in every other race, typical representatives of Esau, but they are more the exception than the rule, and the suggested theory that, on the ground of this "extraordinary capillary development," the Kandyans may be traceable to an Aino or cognate origin cannot be accepted in the total absence of material in its support.

A feature common to both the low-country and the Kandyan Sinhalese is that the hair of his head reaches low down his back. The exceptions to the rule among the males are when the flowing locks give place to the "regulation crop" *à la mode*, or to the still shorter dressing insisted on by prison discipline.

Seventeen hundred years ago Ptolemy and Agathemerus spoke of this peculiarity. According to the former, the men who inhabit Ceylon allow their hair an unlimited growth, and bind it on the crown of their heads after the manner of women.

Tennent, commenting on this passage, observes that these writers had doubtless been told of the custom by some Grecian seamen returning from Galle, for this fashion of dressing the hair is confined to the south-west coast of the island, and prevails neither in the interior nor amongst the people of the north and east.

The fashion does not obtain in any part of the island among the natives. Both the up-country and low-country Sinhalese, men and women, roll up their hair into a coil called *konde*, which is located, not on the crown, but at the back of the head. Some of the illustrations in Knox's book show that the natives fix their *kondes* on the crown, but this is as much a mistake, evidently of the artist, as the pictorial representation given hy Tennent is a faithful delineation of how a low-country Sinhalese wears his hair, and belies the author's own description of it in the letterpress. There is a difference, however, in the style in which the two classes make up their hair, and in the use of head ornaments. The men of the low-country comb up their hair, without parting it in the middle, and coil it into a knot at the back of the head, whilst, as Tennent puts it, "the hair is drawn back from the forehead *à la impératrice* and secured on the crown of the head by a circular comb," known as the *nevi* or abbreviated *pepanava* (bent or "crooked" comb). It also helps to keep the front hair in trim. The official native or villager of position or status, on ceremonial occasions, wears, in addition to the circular comb, a high comb (*kelin panava*), which is stuck into the back knot at its point of formation. The women wear no combs. They tie up their back hair into a knot like the men, but the chignon is invariably larger, and rendered so by extraneous hirsute contributions (*havariya*), of which a stock is an indispensable article of every lady's toilette. The short hair over the ears is gathered up in front, waxed and turned up into a circle or concentric circles called *tupa*, and pasted on the temples. This is a highly prized adornment, and is considered one of the most ornamental items of the *coiffure*, and the woman who puts it on carefully and tastefully is sure to be an object of attraction among both sexes. Hairpins (*kuru*), with large heads set with precious stones, are stuck into the back knot.

The Kandyans, male and female, part their hair in the middle. The *konde* is made up in the same way as in the low-country, but it is fixed and hangs lower down at the back of the head. The men wear no combs. The women wear hairpins and other head ornaments.

Kandyans living in villages immediately adjoining the maritime districts ape their low-country neighbours in various details of dress and costume. In the *Pitigal Korale*, Kurunegala district, which borders the Negombo and Chilaw divisions, some of the Kandyans have adopted combs, and affect other articles of dress which are foreign to them. To carry this inquiry further, and to show the extent to which the system of imitation is pushed, it may be mentioned that—

"Living among the Tamils, the Sinhalese of the Vanni have to some extent begun to copy their customs. They have adopted the Tamil system of proper names: thus, a man has his father's name prefixed to his own, and does not take his own from the village or family he belongs to, or the land he owns, as is the common Sinhalese custom elsewhere. Many of their names, too, are Tamil in a Sinhalese shape; *e.g.*, Vellatte, Kathira-Vellatte, Kathiratte Sinatte, Kandappu, Udayase, Kandate. The older generations have taken to wearing earrings, but this practice has been discouraged by the present Sinhalese headmen. The Sinhalese have as much faith in the Hindu god, Pillaiyar (Ganesa), as have the Tamil villagers. As far as morality is concerned, the two races are on a par. A Sinhalese girl generally has a "succession" of husbands, from the beginning of her married life. The Sinhalese registrar of marriages has not much to do. As regards dress the Sinhalese keep generally to their own customs, but they often wear the Jaffna cloth (*chaya-veddi*), and fasten the handkerchief on their heads after the Tamil manner. The koralas and arachchis on duty wear the round cloth hat with a flat top (obtained from Matale) which is a badge of office in all Kandyan districts, and are thus conspicuous at all official assemblies among the turbaned Tamil Udaiyars and Vidanes." [1]

But it is really pitiful to behold a transformation scene which is of frequent occurrence in the Kandyan districts. At one moment there appears a highlander in all the panoply of Kandyan state—in the finest embroidered muslin, swelled out by a number of *tuppoti*, put on one over the other; his shoulders widened in appearance by a jacket stuffed and puffed out into gigot sleeves; the whole surmounted by a large pincushion hat, which Tennent likens to a goffred Vandyke; the *tout ensemble* comprising a striking national costume. Five minutes elapse, and in steps an apologetic-looking individual in a doubtful array of miscellaneous European clothes, shorn of his dignified muslin circumference, his pincushion hat, his radiant jacket, and his state jewels, his face hidden by the depressed brim of an ancient Elwood—a veritable jackdaw without his plumes—in this case *not* borrowed! Some officials refuse to give audience to such ill-clad Kandyans, while others are indifferent, with the result that the bad example set by those who ought to know better is widely followed by all ranks of society. In this way slovenliness is bred, and a disregard of elegance of dress and the donning of the national costume on necessary occasions, a circumstance which is much to be regretted.

It may not be quite germane to the subject to trace out when the first settlement of the Kandyan Sinhalese in the villages in the Vanni took place, although evidence is not wanting of the steady increase of the colony since the British occupation. Suffice it to say that the adoption by the settlers of the customs and even the names of the original inhabitants forcibly reminds the writer of a remarkable coincidence with regard to the Moorish residents in the Kurunegala district. Although they adhere to the Mahomedan faith, they have by long residence among the Kandyans so habituated themselves to the ways and manners of the latter that it is a common experience to hear of the patronymic given by a Moorman, for instance, as "Tambi Lebbe Aracci *lage*," &c., not to speak of their marrying out their children in *diga* or settling them in *bina*—terms peculiar only to the Kandyans, whose laws and usages have, by express statutory provision, been declared not to apply to the Moors.

The Proclamation of 1818 enacted that no Kandyan chiefs should exercise jurisdiction over the Moormen, and that the Mohandirams over the various Madige (bullock-transport) departments should receive their appointments direct from the several Agents of Government. This was in acknowledgment of the fidelity of the Moormen during the rebellion of 1817–18. The appointment is often confined to a family, descending from father to son, and a curious circumstance in connection with Madige families in the Kurunegala district is that the officiating member allows the hair of his head to grow long, and wears it in a *konde* like the Kandyans—a custom contrary to the habits of the Moors, who shave their heads.

Ramhukkandana is a Moorish village, twelve miles from Kurunegala, which has been registered under the Service Tenures Commission as subject to services to the Ridi Vihara, a celebrated temple in the Kurunegala district. The case of the tenants of this village is cited by the Commissioners as a remarkable instance of religious toleration which has become known in the course of the Service Tenures Inquiry. The tenants are all Mahomedans. "The service which they render to that establishment (Ridi Vihara) is confined to the payment of dues and the transport of produce, &c., and has no connection with the services of the Buddhist vihara, and their own *lebbe* or priest is supported by a farm set apart by the Buddhist landlords for the purpose. There are thus Mahomedan tenants performing without reluctance services to a Buddhist monastery, which is freely supporting a priest for its Mahomedan tenants." [1]

Writers on Ceylon display a variety of opinion as to the general character of the Kandyans, and oftener than not their verdict has been unfavourable. Knox, who viewed them through the spectacles of a captive, was naturally prejudiced against them; but it is not generally known that the worst diatribe that could have been levelled at them emanated from the pen of De Quincey. He described the Kandyans as "a desperate variety of the tiger-man, agile and fierce, but smooth,

[1] "Manual of Vanni Districts (Vavoniya and Mullaitiva) of the North Central Province," by S. P. Lewis, C.C.S., Colombo, 1895, pp. 102–3.

[1] Administration Reports, 1870, p. 285.

insinuating, and full of subtlety as a snake." As compared with the low-country Sinhalese, whom he painted as "soft and passive," the Kandyan was represented as "a ferocious little bloody coward, full of mischief as a monkey, grinning with desperation, and laughing like a hyæna." [1] The extreme exaggeration and inaccuracy of these passages, as pointed out by Sir J. Emerson Tennent, "are accounted for by the personal inexperience of the author, De Quincey having applied to the normal condition of a race epithets merited by rare barbarities, such as the massacre of Major Davies's companions."[2]

Similarly, it would be the height of injustice if we were to judge of the character of the Kandyans in general by the cruelties and oppressions which disgraced the reign of the last Sinhalese ruler, and led to his deposition and exile and to the overthrow of the Kandyan dynasty.

Dr. Conan Doyle, in his account of the last Boer campaign, appositely points out the unwisdom of running down a whole race owing to the faults of a few units who are unfortunately included in it. "In every race there are individual ruffians, and it would be a political mistake to allow our action to be influenced or our feelings permanently embittered by their crimes. It is from the man himself, and not from his country, that an account should be exacted.[3]

As in the Aryan family, to which the Kandyan belongs, exclusiveness is his marked characteristic. In the earliest beginnings to which we can get back, to use the words of a recent historian of Greece,[4] "the house of each man was to him what the den is to the wild beast which dwells in it—something, namely, to which he only has a right, and which he allows his mate and his offspring to share, but which no other living thing may enter except at the risk of his life." Every hut or cottage is carefully shaded from the view of its neighbour, fairly established on its own account, so much so that it would appear as though the inmates had written up in barbarous Sinhalese characters, "No connection with the house next door." It may or may not be a superstition among native hut-builders as to the variation in the aspect of their domiciles, but certain it is that no two dwellings face precisely the same points of the compass. You may box your compass round the village, but in vain.[5]

With the Kandyan "a little learning is a dangerous thing," and the hankering after Government employment a positive disgrace.

[1] De Quincey's Works, vol. xli., p. 14.
[2] Tennent's "Ceylon," 223, *in notis.*
[3] "The Great Boer War," 1900, pp. 410–11.
[4] Cox's "Greece," p. 13.
[5] Capper's "Old Ceylon," 1877.

A boy whose education has been carried beyond a certain point becomes conceited, and will not be content to move as his forefathers. Instead of working in the ancestral paddy fields, he prefers to lounge about the courts, taxing his family for his support, till he can get some minor Government post, the demand for which is now far in excess of the supply. Moreover, this results in the abandonment of extensive tracts of uncultivated lands, and has given the Government the opportunity of enforcing the very exacting provisions of the Waste Lands Ordinance in all their rigorous severity.

The Kandyan has a rooted aversion to migrate under the strongest inducement. Tissamaharama, in Hambantota, may be taken as an example. There were hundreds of families on the Uva border living within twenty miles of this splendid work who were without any regular cultivation, and suffered from periodic famine, and yet preferred to cling to their squalid homes, supporting life when they had consumed their last grain of paddy or kurrakan by eating the berries, leaves, and roots of wild plants. The Horaborawewa, in the same district, another colossal irrigation work restored in 1869, was equally unattractive. The Kandyan is held to his birthplace by an attachment that scarcely any allurement can overcome.

A distinguishing feature is their feudal subserviency to the conventional authority of their chiefs and the unreasonable devotion with which they worship rank. Although all real power for oppression or coercion has been abolished under the mild rule of the British, this form of traditionary subjection remains unaltered and apparently indelible in the national instincts of the peasantry.[1]

Prior to 1859, there being no written law to regulate the subject of matrimonial alliance in the Kandyan provinces, loose and casual connection and fitful cohabitation of the sexes—with the paternity of the offspring resulting from such pernicious intercourse ever enveloped in a cloud of doubt and uncertainty—were of common occurrence. Even the simple taking and receiving a woman was sufficient to constitute a union, and the fact of the parties of the same class living as husband and wife was looked upon as evidence of such union.

> "They called it marriage, by that specious name,
> To veil the crime and sanctify the shame."

There was no law against concubinage, if the woman was of equal caste with the man; but, in fact, such connections, if not stigmatised by some decisive acts on the part of the man's family or by the man himself, were considered as marriages, and the issue of such connections had all the privileges of legitimate children. In short, nothing but a direct declaration disinheriting such issue would have cut them off from the privileges of legitimate offspring.

[1] Sir J. Emerson Tennent's "Ceylon," vol. ii., p. 233.

In order to constitute a regular marriage in the older days, the customs of the country demanded the observance of certain formalities and ceremonies known as *Magul-paha*, or the "Five Feasts": (1) First feast, on solicitation of bride and approval of suit by parents; (2) second feast, on the day the horoscopes of the contracting parties are examined and found accordant, on which occasion coconuts are split and muskets are discharged to appease the God of Wisdom; (3) third feast, on the day of the presentation of apparel; (4) fourth feast, on the day of the ceremony of the ligature, which consists of the two little fingers of the right hands of the pair being tied with a gold thread or chain; (5) fifth feast, on the day of the ceremony of bathing.

As the formalities and ceremonies already described could only be observed by the higher, more influential, and affluent classes, a compliance with them was not insisted on as a condition precedent to a lawful marriage, nor was it demanded that they should in every case precede the espousal. Although the five feasts, except first perhaps the marriage feasts, are rarely held nowadays even by the most orthodox of the Kandyans, yet traces of some of the ancient marriage customs survive. The tendency is to conform with Western ideas and ways and modern instances—witness the exchange of rings taking the place of the ceremony of the ligature, and the introduction of the wedding cake *à la mode* doing service for the sweetmeats.

Registration, as will be seen hereafter, being the chief requirement to the validity of a marriage nowadays, the ceremonial occasions on which friends and relations meet to rejoice with and offer their congratulations to the contracting parties are restricted to the day on which the notice of marriage is given to the registrar, being generally followed by the conducting of the bride to the house of her husband, or the installation of the bridegroom, as the case may be, on the day on which the marriage is registered. Moreover, Christianity to some extent has abolished such heathen observances as the splitting of coconuts, &c.

Polygamy and polyandry were of common occurrence, and prevailed in Ceylon from early times, but received their death-blow in 1859, when the Legislature declared the custom illegal. It is as yet by no means extinct, and still enters as a curious factor in the law of inheritance which has to be administered by the Civil Court. No infamy appears to have attached to the result of such union, and the offspring were regarded as equally legitimate with those born in wedlock.

As regards civil immunities, the conventional law of the country divides marriage into two kinds : (1) Marriage in *diga*, by which the woman is conducted from the parents' abode and is settled in the house of the husband. A plurality of daughters in a family necessitates this mode of marriage with regard to the majority of them, the common property being too limited in extent to be enjoyed by a numerous family. The marriage of the daughters and their departure from the parental house generally involve a forfeiture of the inheritance, and thereby reduce the number of the shareholders. (2) Marriage in *bina*, by which the bridegroom is received into the house of the bride and abides therein permanently. This occurs only in cases where the bride is an heiress or the daughter of a wealthy family in which there are few sons. The bridegroom does not by such a union acquire any right to his wife's property, which remains her own and subject to her sole control. He is, besides, bound to obey her, and is subject to all her whims and caprices. She may even order him out of the house at any time that he happens to incur either the displeasure of her parent or, what is more frequent, the jealousy of herself. This right of expulsion was also exercised by the brothers, and at times by the children of the wife by a former bed. The position of a *bina* husband was under all circumstances a precarious one, whence has arisen the old Kandyan adage that a husband settling in *bina* should always have ready at the doorway his walking-stick, a torch and a talipot, articles of travel indispensable in an emergency, for he might be unceremoniously turned out at any moment, no matter at what time of the day and in what weather, and he would have to depart and find his way. On the death of the wife intestate, her children, and, failing them, her collaterals or their heirs, or her descendants, succeed to her property in preference to her *bina* husband. The only way in which a *bina* husband may acquire a right to his wife's estate is by gift or by prescriptive possession. A marriage in *bina* is especially interesting because of the disclosure of it which is given us in the book of Genesis. The law does not recognise community of property between the spouses, the estate of each remaining separate and distinct from that of the other.

As in the case of marriages, divorces took place on the mere whim and fancy of either of the parties to a union who felt dissatisfied with the other, and the wife might dismiss her husband and take unto herself another man as she pleased. The matrimonial tie was contracted and dissolved with such consummate recklessness and facility that it almost passed into a proverb that a marriage among the Kandyans "was contracted with a wink and dissolved by a kick." The Kandyan law, vague as it was, provided for compensation to be made to the woman, who, however, had no reason to complain on being sent away by the husband, for marriage was dissoluble at the will of either party. The compensation was small, sometimes only the cloth she wore and a brass pot, but then there *was* compensation.[1]

The courts of law had, in case of inheritance, and consequently legitimacy, to inquire into innumerable unpleasant details, and the difficulty was rendered greater owing to the prevalence among the Kandyans of polygamy and polyandry. The most trying task was not simply ascertaining how many wives a man had, but how many husbands a woman was wife of ! In face of the precise terms of the Convention, it was a delicate matter for the Government to interfere in. In this aspect of affairs Lord Lytton, Secretary of State for the Colonies in 1858, gladly seized the opportunity of a representation made to him by certain Kandyan chiefs for the suppression of these odious customs, and as the result of his interference Ordinance No. 13 of 1859 was passed, disallowing polygamy and establishing registration as a legal requisite to a marriage. The law, which does not seem to have worked satisfactorily, was amended by Ordinance No. 3 of 1870, which obtains at the present day. Its main provisions are : (1) To validate the unions contracted before and after the Ordinance of 1859 came into operation ; (2) to legitimise the issue of such unions ; (3) to dispense with the necessity of judicial intervention in case of divorce ; (4) to enable parties to obtain a divorce by mutual consent, amongst other grounds ; (5) by petitioning the Government Agent or his assistant.

The Kandyans are governed by their own legal code. The Convention of 1815, entered into between the British and the Kandyan chiefs, secured "to all classes of the people the safety of their persons and property, with their civil rights and immunities, according to the laws, institutions, and customs established and in force among them." To no customs or usages which have from long observance in any state or country acquired the force of law can be more fittingly applied, than to what is known as the Kandyan law, the lines of Tennyson :

> "A lawless science,
> A myriad of precedents,
> A wilderness of single instances."

With the numerous encroachments which the English law has made upon it, the Kandyan law as it obtains in the present day is restricted in its application to the following subjects : (1) Marriage, considerably modified and regulated by local statutes ; (2) the rights of inheritance and succession, including adoption, and the right of acquest, mainly on deeds of gift.[1] But these in themselves present an interesting field of research and afford sufficient scope for the devotion of a special study to him who desires to master their intricacies.

The Kandyans were not numbered separately from the low-country Sinhalese in any of the censuses of 1871, 1881, or 1891. Governor Sir Edward Barnes in 1824 directed a return to be framed, and it was published in 1827, giving the population of the Kandyan provinces according to the provincial divisions then existing.[2] In 1901 a census was taken of the Kandyans as distinguished from their low-country brethren. According to this report the Kandyans numbered 873,580, nearly four times the population as ascertained by the return of 1827. Of this population the Central Province, which continues yet to be the stronghold of the highlanders, contained 28·2 per cent. ; the Province of Sabaragamuwa 25·8 per cent. ; the North-Western Province 24 per cent. ; the Province of Uva 12·9 per cent. ; and all the other provinces 9·1 per cent. 1,368 Kandyans were enumerated in the Colombo municipality and 3,129 in the rest of Colombo.

From this statement it would seem that the vast and rapid changes which progress and civilisation have effected since British rule, and the facilities of travel afforded by railway extension, have had the tendency of fostering and encouraging the spirit of unrest which is manifesting itself in the most populous parts of the Kandyan provinces, so much so that it requires, as aptly remarked by a local writer, no prophetic faculty to be able to picture that in a not too remote future there will be found, among the grim ruins of a bygone age, happy colonies emulating the industry and

[1] Mark the close resemblance between the Kandyan customs and those of the Romans under the Empire. Cf. Juv. vi. 145 :—

> "Fiant obscuri dentes oculique minor
> 'Collige sarcinulas' dicet libertas 'exegi
> Iam gravis es nobis et sape emungeris, exi
> Ocius et properti, sicco venit altera naso.'"

Sarcinulæ may well stand for the cloth and brass pot

[1] "Manual of Kandyan Law," by Frank Modder, Proctor Supreme Court and Notary Public. Albion Press, Galle, 1901.

[2] Owing to the fact that more than a half of the Sinhalese community was composed of Kandyans, Governor Sir Arthur Gordon (now Lord Stanmore) considered it necessary that the latter should have their own representative in the Legislative Council, and on his recommendation the Home Government duly sanctioned the appointment in 1889.

prosperity of the generations whose monuments overshadow them.[1]

Very nearly a century has elapsed since the cession of the Kandyan provinces to the British, and manifold though the changes are which have come over the spirit of the Kandyans in general, and particularly in such as have had intercourse with the more enlightened settlers of the maritime borders, yet while conceding the innumerable benefits these have reaped from the civilising leaven, we cannot go the length of asserting that such contact has leavened the whole of the Kandyan population. True to its national characteristics, it has clung most tenaciously to its ancient traditions, from which it will be many an age, if ever, before it is successfully weaned.

Another important factor of conversion and change from the old order of things to the new may be traceable to the settlement in the Kandyan provinces of colonies of low-country Sinhalese, of the trading class generally, who have migrated thither with a view of laying out profitable investments and reaping the fruits of their industry and labour, supported by ingenious tact, clever device, and hard dealing—traits which the indigenous population lack—against the results of which they are, unfortunately for them, not sufficiently careful to guard.

As a striking contrast to this state of things, there are certain other parts of the Kandyan provinces whose remoteness and the inaccessibility of their situation from the disturbing action of foreign influence of any kind may safely be taken, even at this day, to furnish us with an actual living specimen, typical of an agricultural economy and civilisation which probably characterised the Ceylon of early times.[1] Such is the case with the North-Central Province, whose political condition differs from that of the rest of the island. Here the original Oriental village remains in a pure and simple type, while in the rest of Ceylon it has generally disappeared under the influence of foreign government and the jurisdiction of English courts. If these districts have failed to share in the general progress which has been going forward around them, they have at least this compensation—that that have retained, almost in its pristine purity, the ancient village system of the Aryan races.[1]

But the blessings of peaceful order, the beneficent influence of religion and education, the gradual influx of wealth, and the inestimable benefits of railway extension have not failed to produce their accustomed results; and it is beyond all doubt that the pride of a fabled splendour of a descent from the Sun, and a kindred relation to the Lion, is fast vanishing into the true glory, the real prosperity, and the solid advantages—commercial, moral, and intellectual—which the Kandyan provinces have derived from their connection with the British Empire.

[1] "Census of Ceylon," 1891, vol. i., p. 22

[1] Phear's "Aryan Village in India and Ceylon," p. 176.

[1] Admin. Repts. N. C. Prov., 1878.

LAND SURVEY

ONE of the oldest and most important of the sections of the Ceylon administration is the Survey Department. Established just as the nineteenth century dawned, with a Dutchman as the first Surveyor-General, this organisation supplies an interesting link between the British and the Dutch occupations. Its earliest operations were of limited scope and conducted on unscientific lines. But as the narrative will show, its importance increased with the agricultural and industrial development of the island. Now, under the able direction of Mr. P. D. Warren, F.R.G.S., who has held the position of Surveyor-General since 1904, it is one of the best equipped and most valuable departments of the kind in the colonies.

The foundations of the department were laid by a Proclamation dated August 2, 1800. By this instrument the special office of Surveyor-General was created and the island was divided into its several jurisdictions under five assistant officers, called Principal Surveyors. The circuits then described comprehended respectively the districts between the river of Chilaw and the Kelani Ganga; between the Kelani Ganga and the river of Galle; between the river of Galle and the north-easterly extremity of the Mahagampattu; between the north-easterly extremity of the Mahagampattu and the northern extremity of the district of Mullaitivu; and the remaining one, between the northern extremity of Mullaitivu and the river of Chilaw. The officers in charge of these circuits were severally distinguished as the Surveyors of Negombo, of Colombo, of Matara, of Trincomalee, and of Jaffna, and had under them assistant and sub-assistant surveyors. The first Surveyor-General was Captain G. Schneider, who assumed office in the year of proclamation; but it was not until half a century later that anything in the direction of a proper scientific survey of the island was attempted. With the appointment of Captain Gossett, R.E., in 1855, marked advances were made in the several departments, and the triangulation of the Negombo district was taken in hand. The work of the department for the next three or four decades was mainly confined to surveys in connection with the settlement of encroachments and the sale of building sites and cultivation plots. But under Mr. F. H. Grinlinton's administration (1897–1904) the department was entirely reorganised, and the more systematic methods which were adopted resulted in an adjustment of the existing state of affairs, and it was left to his successor, Mr. P. D. Warren, F.R.G.S., the present Surveyor-General, to continue a forward policy.

Meanwhile, the machinery of the department was considerably augmented from a bare 8 field and 15 controlling officers in 1856 to 132 and 87, respectively, in 1902, and further increases have since been made in both departments of the staff. Entrance to the subordinate grades of the department is possible by passing the departmental examinations or by securing a diploma in Civil Engineering from the local Technical College, which has a course arranged for this purpose of three years' duration. Vacancies in the senior grades of the service, however, are filled up alternately from the department and from Cooper's Hill College. Appointments to the office staff are made from the ranks of "volunteers," who enter the department on probation and qualify themselves for inclusion in the fixed or substantive staff by the aptitude they show in the execution of the work of the department. The field staff of the Surveyor-General consists of four branches—Trigonometrical, Topographical, Application and Block Surveys. The Superintendent of Application Surveys, the Superintendent of Trigonometrical Surveys and Meteorology, and the Superintendent of Surveys, Western Province, have their headquarters in Colombo, where also is the office of the Surveyor-General, while the work of the studio maintained in connection with the department is under the supervision of a European assistant.

The primary triangulation of the island has been now completed, and according to the latest Report of the Surveyor-General, that for 1905, all that remains to be done is the computation and scoring of points for the purpose of connecting up the old work.

The following table shows the progress of field work since the year 1897:—

	1897.	1898.	1899.	1900.	1901.	1902.	1903.	1904.	1905.
	Acres.	Acres.	Acres.	Acres.	Acres.	Acres.	Acres.	Acres.	Acres.
Block	128,471	231,108	210,862	235,040	168,885	212,858	282,149	198,383	157,348
Topographical	64,000	985,600	2,127,360	2,628,487	1,871,360	1,961,600	897,920	536,320	217,600 41,600
Applications, &c. ...	104,016	38,297	34,228	22,318	41,659	34,293	47,195	33,864	39,030
	296,487	1,255,005	2,372,450	2,885,845	2,081,904	2,208,751	1,227,264	768,567	455,578
	Rs.	Rs.	Rs.	Rs.	Rs.	Rs.	Rs.	Rs.	Rs. c.
Expenditure	480,280	567,613	608,757	639,798	656,489	646,632	651,455	664,137	785,830 98

Further details for the last year under review are furnished below, and will be found of interest.

Nature of Work.	Province.	Number of Lots.	Area in Acres.	Cost.	
				Rs.	c.
Block	Southern, North-western, Uva, and North-central	—	157,348	110,640	30
Applications from the Public and Special Questions ...	All Provinces	8,094	39,030	117,045	53½
Topographical	—	—	259,200	38,991	82
Triangulation	—	—	—	18,622	29
	Total		455,578	285,299	94½

At the office in Bambalapitiya, a suburb of Colombo, is housed an important branch of the Record Map Department, the institution being located in this comparatively remote portion owing to the lack of accommodation for its maintenance at headquarters. At this office the topographical record maps are prepared on a scale of 2 ins. to the mile for reduction to 1 mile; and the 1 mile maps are specially

Province.	Europeans. Lots.	Extent.			Amount and Fees.		Average Rate per Acre.		Natives. Lots.	Extent.			Amount and Fees.		Average Rate per Acre.	
		A.	R.	P.	Rs.	c.	Rs.	c.		A.	R.	P.	Rs.	c.	Rs.	c.
Western	156	2,649	3	15	150,794	90	56	90	4,563	8,629	1	4·39	320,925	79	33	75
Central	25	404	3	8·25	16,079	40	39	70	140	536	1	29·35	18,671	9	34	83
Northern	7	266	0	3·15	3,331	50	12	52	446	1,609	3	19·50	32,002	80	19	89
Southern	12	30	0	35	1,499	50	49	62	1,616	3,865	3	37	129,040	32	33	38
Eastern	14	73	0	13·50	1,001	0	13	71	250	807	3	27·50	13,357	92	16	53
North-western	4	22	1	12	679	50	30	89	528	4,238	0	21	95,104	24	22	44
North-central	—	—			—		—		351	1,646	1	6	20,302	40	12	33
Uva...	37	609	2	25	11,366	12	18	66	163	702	0	5	7,867	85	11	20
Sabaragamuwa	146	3,481	0	37	146,730	99	42	15	288	4,810	2	0	93,590	90	19	45
Total	401	7,537	0	28·90	331,482	91	43	98	8,345	26,846	1	29·74	730,863	31	27	22

drawn up to be photographed down to the 4, 8, or 12 mile scales. According to the latest returns the number of title plans issued by the department runs into something like 10,543 sets in triplicate, covering an area of 51,446 acres.

With the boom in rubber, applications for surveys were received on all hands, and special arrangements and exertions had to be made to meet the demand, and the preliminary plans were issued on an average of under two months, which is a result that was never achieved before. In fact, in every branch of this important department increased efficiency is revealed in the operations of the survey. As to the work as a whole, the Surveyor-General reports a more than usually brisk and satisfactory year. "I have several times," he writes, "both as head of the department and as Assistant Surveyor-General, drawn attention to the manner in which some or all previous records have been broken, and pointed out that such an event could not possibly occur every year; the top limit must be reached shortly, if, indeed, it has not already been arrived at. But as greater out-turns have become imperative, new devices for the simplification of processes or the modification of detail have been devised; besides, greater experience in studio and lithographic work, and therefore increased out-turns, have all assisted to combine with an extended system of payment by results in supplying the figures for the remarkable returns during 1905." The results of land sales for that year are given below, set forth in respect of their purchase by (*a*) Europeans and (*b*) natives in the several provinces of the island.

The Surveyor-General makes some noteworthy comments on the above statistics. "The amount," he says, "realised by the sale is the most gratifying item; and here we find only two years on record with larger credits, *i.e.*, 1877 and 1878"—during the period of the coffee boom—"while it is about Rs. 420,000 over last year's takings. This result is, of course, due to the demand for land for planting rubber, and though much has been said about high 'upset prices,' the handsome returns to Government have, no doubt, been arrived at through the keen competition of those fortune-hunters who, looking upon the price paid for land as really a very small item in comparison to the income to be derived from it, with rubber over 6s. per lb., have run the prices up at the Crown sales. . . . Government is clearly not responsible for long prices being paid under such circumstances, except by exposing lands for sale that several people are determined to have, and thus creating competition." From the figures given it will be seen that the average rate paid by Europeans during 1905 was Rs. 43·98 an acre, while lands acquired by natives were alienated by the Crown at only Rs. 27·22 an acre.

With the development of the country and the maintenance of commercial enterprise at its present high pitch, the work of the Department of Surveys will necessarily be enlarged in the next few years, and will involve further and considerable additions to the controlling staff and to the equipment needed for the more complete and comprehensive demarcation and survey of the island. Whatever the future may bring, the department, we may confidently anticipate, will maintain the great reputation it has secured for efficient and thorough-going work.

The Surveyor-General of Ceylon, Mr. **Philip David Warren**, F.R.G.S., is the son of the late Mr. John Neville Warren, C.E., and was born in London on February 7, 1851. He was educated at Norwich Grammar School, &c., and after serving articles to a borough engineer he did general surveying and engineering work in South Wales for six years, being employed by the Swansea Corporation engineer, the Landore Siemens Steel Works, the engineers for the Swansea and Neath Tramways Companies, &c. In 1878 he went to Ceylon as Third Assistant Surveyor in the Survey Department. At the reorganisation in 1897 he became Assistant Surveyor-General, and in 1904 received his present appointment. Mr. Warren was for some time a Lieutenant in the 3rd Glamorgan Rifle Volunteers.

THE PRESS

INTRODUCTORY.

By the Hon. Mr. FRANCIS BEVEN, M.L.C.

THERE is no record of the existence of newspapers in Ceylon before the British occupation. Though adventurous Englishmen found themselves in Kandy about the middle of the seventeenth century, a special mission being necessary for their release from the captivity which rewarded their enterprise, it was not until a century later that any attempt was made by the British to secure a footing in Ceylon. Two centuries elapsed after their appearance on the adjoining continent before the idea of acquiring Ceylon entered into the minds of the East India Company; and after the British had assumed control of the island, in the last decade of the eighteenth century and the beginning of the nineteenth, there was a considerable interval before the need of newspapers disclosed itself to the colonists. Indeed, it was the local Government which first recognised, in a practical way, that the absence of means for the circulation of information was a hindrance to the progress of the country. The explanation is that for several years after the island had been acquired it was little more than a military station. The revenue it yielded was derived mainly from certain monopolies of products, such as cinnamon, for instance, and fell considerably short of the expenditure.

Immediately after the surrender to the British of Colombo by the Dutch in 1796, the administration of the maritime provinces was at first vested in the Governor of Madras in Council; and this arrangement was continued until October, 1798, when the Hon. Frederick North (afterwards Earl of Guilford) was appointed Governor by the British Government, which then acquired the Company's rights. Governor North was succeeded by four military men in sequence; and it was during the rule of the sixth Governor, a trained English statesman, the Right Hon. Sir Robert Wilmot Horton, Bart., whose appointment dated from October, 1831, that the need of a newspaper was specially recognised. The result was the publication of the *Colombo Journal*, in 1832, issued from the Government press, and this was the first newspaper in Ceylon. The Governor himself wielded a facile pen, and he had in his private secretary, Mr. Tuffnell, who was also his own son-in-law and who afterwards became a Lord of the Admiralty, an assistant of considerable literary gifts. Among the civilian officers, too, were men with a taste for letters, notably George Turnour, who rose to be Treasurer of Ceylon, and whose name is still perpetuated by a classical prize attached to the Royal College, Colombo; and George Lee, who became Postmaster-General, the translator of Rebeiro's "Ceylon" from the Portuguese and other works. But the Home authorities did not approve of the development of newspaper enterprise under official auspices, and requested their representatives to confine their energies to the Government *Gazette*, which still continues to be the ponderous official organ, the receptacle for information which scarcely tempts private subscriptions. The taste for journalistic pabulum, however, having been created, the enterprise of the Colombo merchants speedily manifested itself in the foundation of the *Observer*. This journal was started in 1834, under the control, and for some time the editorship, of Mr. E. J. Darley, whose name is still perpetuated in the well-known local firm of Darley, Butler & Co., the present partners of which maintain the old traditions of independence and energy. Subsequently, Mr. George Winter (whose name is perpetuated in the firm of Messrs. Winter in Baddegama) was appointed editor by the merchants.

After the maritime districts came under British rule, the cession of the Kandyan kingdom followed in 1815, as the result of military operations which gave the seal to the gradual extension of British power throughout the island. Between 1820 and 1832 Sir Edward Barnes carried out a series of military roads between Colombo and Kandy, Badulla, Trincomalee, &c. The door was thus opened to commercial and agricultural enterprise in the newly acquired hill territory, under less hazardous conditions than had existed previously, when the country was without means of communication and in an unsettled state owing to successive treacherous outbreaks in the Kandyan territory. Coffee, which had been introduced by the Dutch into the low-country in 1740, began to attract attention, and the suitability of the uplands for the cultivation of the plant was discovered. In 1825 the Governor himself (Sir Edward Barnes) embarked in the new industry, and had a plantation laid out near Sinnapitiya, in Gampola. The advance of this promising agricultural industry coincided with the initiation of the newspaper enterprise which it justified. After the short period during which George Winter was editor, the proprietorship of the *Colombo Observer*, then a small weekly broadsheet, passed from the merchants into the hands of Dr. Christopher Elliot, who relinquished his connection with the Colonial Medical Service in order to become the editor and proprietor of the first newspaper in Ceylon unconnected with the Government; and this he conducted as a small weekly, and then bi-weekly, sheet, with marked ability and independence, for about twelve years, at the same time practising as physician. Indeed, the tone of the journal was of too outspoken and independent a type to please the Government, and by way of counterpoise the *Colombo Chronicle* was launched under private auspices, but as an official organ. Thus, it may be said, the behests of Downing Street were obeyed in the letter while violated in the spirit. After Mr. Stewart Mackenzie became Governor, in 1837, the name of the Government organ was changed to the *Herald*, but the change failed to prolong the life of this venture, and the *Colombo Observer* remained sole possessor of the field. In 1840 a monthly, afterwards a fortnightly, and more recently a weekly edition for Europe, called the *Overland Observer*, was started.

This brief retrospect of the first establishment of unofficial journalism is both interesting and instructive, as exemplifying the British dislike of autocratic and bureaucratic methods of interference with the conduct of the Press. Alike in the Mother Country and the colonies, a hired or inspired press runs counter to national instincts. During the more tolerant *régime* of the Right Hon. Mr. Stewart Mackenzie there was less friction between the Government and the unofficial Press; and, curiously enough, Mr. Alastair Mackenzie Ferguson, who came to Ceylon originally under the auspices of this Governor in 1837 (after nine years of varied experience as planter, man of business, Customs officer, and magistrate, all this time being a frequent contributor to the *Colombo Observer*), was, in 1846, invited by Dr. Elliot to become his co-editor. Subsequently, in 1859, when Dr. Elliot was appointed Principal Civil Medical Officer of the colony, and had to sever his connection with the Press, Mr. Ferguson became sole proprietor as well as editor. Thus Mr. A. M. Ferguson, as the editor who first gave his whole time to the work, may be truly described as the Father of Ceylon Journalism.

A Facsimile of the First Number of

THE CEYLON GOVERNMENT GAZETTE.

Nº 1 MONDAY *March* 15th 1802

GOVERNMENT ADVERTISEMENT

His Excellency the Governour being of Opinion that great convenience would arise to the Publick if all Government Orders & Notifications were made known and Circulated, through the Medium of a News-Paper, has been pleased to direct that a Prospectus of such a Paper should be prepared, & Published, as follows, Viz:

COLOMBO 27th February 1802.
By Order of the GOVERNOUR
Signed Robt Arbuthnot,
Chief Secy to Govt

AT a Council held at COLOMBO on Friday the 25th February 1802.
Present HIS EXCELLENCY THE GOVERNOUR.

TO HIS EXCELLENCY
The Honourable FREDERIC NORTH

MAY IT PLEASE YOUR EXCELLENCY

MAHA MODELIARS, MOHANDIRAMS, CHIEFS, & NATIVE HEADMEN of the ISLAND

DEPARTURES ARRIVALS

Printed by FRANS DE BRUIN, at the Government Press.

A FACSIMILE OF THE FIRST NUMBER OF THE "CEYLON GOVERNMENT GAZETTE."

Naturally, neither the syndicate of merchants who started the *Colombo Observer* as a small sheet in the early thirties, nor the versatile and capable physician and surgeon who purchased the paper for the magnificent sum of Rs. 1,200 (a sum equivalent, at the then value of the rupee, to about £120) devoted themselves or himself entirely to journalism. To do so would not have paid either, and the interests and tastes of both pointed in other directions. The paper was merely designed to form a lever to move the Government in the path of progress, by compelling the recognition of the needs and claims of commerce and agriculture, as well as those of the people of the country generally, whose rights were too often trampled upon by an inexperienced and unsympathetic bureaucracy. Necessarily, Mr. Ferguson's duties and responsibilities extended far beyond those suggested by the title of colleague or assistant, as the proprietor-editor's energies were chiefly devoted to his profession, in which he was an enthusiast, and the calls of which on his time increased as his deep sympathy with suffering and his medical skill became more and more widely known. When, in 1859, the Government invited into the official ranks this merciless critic of Government measures—the arch-rebel (so regarded) of 1848, whom the then Governor, Lord Torrington, would gladly have had tried by court-martial and shot for fomenting the so-called "rebellion" of that year, when the Sinhalese met in thousands along the Kotta road to march to Queen's House and protest against the new taxes then proclaimed, but were turned back by his influence, lest they should be shot down on approaching the Fort—when Dr. Elliot assumed charge of the newly-constituted Civil Medical Department as its first Principal Officer, his connection with the Press had to cease, and he sold the paper to his colleague, who had much in common with his predecessor and chief in fearless independence and a hearty interest in the people of the country.

Born in Wester Ross, Scotland, in 1816, Mr. Ferguson had enjoyed no special educational advantages when he arrived in the island, at the age of twenty-one. But he had early shown a taste for writing, in poetical as well as prose contributions to the *Inverness Courier*, and these had attracted the attention of the influential family after one of whose members he was named. Thus it came to pass that he was introduced into the "gorgeous East" by the first of the Seaforths, who had been sent out as the representative of royalty to administer Ceylon. What Mr. Ferguson was able to achieve with the weekly and bi-weekly sheet which had changed hands in the thirties for £120, the influence he personally wielded for a full generation as citizen and editor, the services which his paper rendered in promoting the material and moral advancement of the country—these all testify to his possession of exceptional powers, unselfishly devoted to the public good. Like all strong men, he had the faults of his virtues; and his strong nature and ardent convictions at times betrayed him into action and language which alienated sympathy and even sundered friendships. But, this trait notwithstanding, he was esteemed by all as an honest man and a true friend of the colony; and, while his associates rejoiced with him when his services as the Commissioner for Ceylon at the Melbourne Exhibition in 1881 secured for him from his Sovereign the Companionship of the Distinguished Order of St. Michael and St. George, the general public joined them in testifying to their regard by a testimonial of Rs. 10,000, a gold watch, and a service of plate. Friend and foe alike felt, when his end came, rather suddenly, on December 26, 1892, that a good and great man, strong in religious as in political convictions, free from guile, and fearless in the pursuit of what he conceived to be his duty, had passed away.

The story of the *Observer*—the *Colombo Observer* till 1867, and since then the *Ceylon Observer*—would be wholly incomplete without mention of his nephew and successor, whom Mr. A. M. Ferguson called to his aid within two years of his assuming the sole editorship and proprietorship of the paper. Arriving in the island in November, 1861, at the age of nineteen (all but a month), Mr. John Ferguson (though with a brief Press training in Inverness and London) may be said to have started with even less of an equipment for a Ceylon journalistic career than his uncle, who had nine years' experience of the island before becoming editor. But editor never found a safer, a more painstaking, or more loyal fellow-worker than his relative, the youthful assistant-editor, proved. In addition to maintaining the traditions of the paper for courage and principle, and as the chief exponent of public opinion, especially on questions relating to the all-important industry of planting—for coffee filled even a larger place in the sixties and seventies in the affairs of the island than tea has occupied during the last twenty years, or rubber up to and at the present time, the berry being then not merely one among many great staple products, but practically the sole mainstay of the island's prosperity—the nephew helped to strengthen the influence of the paper by extending its scope, enlarging its sheets, and increasing the frequency of issue, thus generally promoting its usefulness in a way which came as a revelation to its numerous readers. Being, further, of a tactful and conciliatory disposition, he was able, while holding his own, to achieve his ends with a minimum of friction, and generally without giving offence to those from whom he differed. The measure of the confidence felt in him by the public, as estimated by his chief, was perhaps best indicated by the fact that the editor (only sixteen months after his nephew's arrival in the island, and before the latter had attained his majority) decided on taking his first holiday in Europe after a quarter of a century's strenuous work, and left the control of the paper in the hands of his youthful nephew without any misgivings concerning the latter's fitness to assume the full charge of what had become the leading organ of public opinion in Ceylon. The history of the *Ceylon Observer* during the editor's absence, and, indeed, ever since, proves how well placed was the confidence felt in the capacity, the principles, and the resourcefulness of the young recruit from Scotland. From the position of assistant-editor, Mr. John Ferguson rose to be joint-editor in 1870, and afterwards in 1875 to be a partner, not only in the ownership of the paper but also in the expanding business, as printers and publishers, of the firm of A. M. & J. Ferguson. The *Tropical Agriculturist*, a monthly periodical which gradually acquired a world-wide celebrity, was started by Mr. John Ferguson during his uncle's absence in Australia in 1881, and from 1863 onwards he became responsible for the annual production of the "Ceylon Handbook and Directory," a work which Governor Sir Arthur Gordon said was unique in the whole range of British dependencies. Mr. A. M. Ferguson never attended the *Observer* office after 1879, so that he had thirteen years of retirement before his death in 1892. Mr. John Ferguson has now practically retired from the active conduct of the *Observer*, having installed his elder son, Mr. Ronald Haddon Ferguson, B.A. (Lond.), whom he has admitted into partnership, as editor of the paper; and the latter is supported by two nephews of Mr. John Ferguson (Messrs. Donald—"Hansard" and chief reporter—and Ian Shioch Ferguson, manager), thus forming the third generation of a journalistic family whose name is a household word in the island, and who are proving themselves worthy of its traditions. Meanwhile, Mr. Ferguson, sen., as a member of the Legislative Council, representing the general European interests, is very far from being idle, either in his own interests or in those of his adopted country. As a lecturer in the United Kingdom and the United States, as a speaker on influential platforms, as a member of learned societies, (including the Presidency of the Ceylon Branch of the Royal Asiatic Society and Christian Literature Society), as the author of illustrated books on Ceylon issued in several editions, and of many Planting Manuals, as writer of the articles on Ceylon in the "Encyclopædia Britannica," as correspondent for over thirty years for the London *Times*, and in other ways, he continues to further the interests of Ceylon, and to make its beauties and its resources known throughout the world.

Passing reference must be made to Mr. Donald Ferguson, second son of Mr. A. M. Ferguson, who was a member of his father's editorial staff for several years, taking his full share of the work in the office, and at times having charge of the *Ceylon Observer* in the occasional absences of his cousin. But neither the climate of Colombo nor the rough-and-tumble experiences of colonial journalism suited his health and literary and antiquarian tastes. He finally left the island soon after his father's death at the end of 1892, and he retired from partnership in the firm a few years later. He now devotes himself to literary work in England, which affords him abundant opportunity for indulging his love of languages and of historical research.

Mention should also be made, in connection with the *Observer*, of Mr. Wm. Digby, C.I.E., who came out as its chief reporter and sub-editor in 1871, and after six years' good work passed to be editor of the *Madras Times*, in which capacity and for help in connection with a famine relief fund the Viceroy, Lord Lytton, made him C.I.E. Mr. Digby died in London in 1905.

Nor should reference be omitted to the growth of the *Observer* from a weekly print, first to a publication issued twice a week, and then to a daily journal, the original single sheet having, during this process, expanded to its present dimensions of an eight-paged full-sized newspaper of forty-eight columns, with frequent supplements. The *Overland Observer*, started in 1840 in connection with the original paper for Home subscribers, has grown proportionately, and is now issued weekly to catch the homeward-bound mail steamers of the Peninsular and Oriental and the Orient Shipping Companies; and that other notable publication issued by Messrs. Ferguson, the *Tropical Agriculturist*, which is perhaps the finest monthly magazine published in connection with tropical products, commands a circulation in every part of the tropical world, being now incorporated with official agricultural publications, as well as being the organ of the Ceylon Agricultural Society. The "Ceylon Handbook and Directory" has already been referred to. These are a few of the publications which issue from the *Ceylon Observer* Press, which, by the by, has the unique distinction of occupying the same premises in the centre of "the Fort," in Baillie Street, though greatly enlarged and improved, from which the original print first emerged. It should here be added that, on the recommendation of His Excellency Sir West Ridgeway, in 1903, His Majesty King Edward conferred the Companionship of St. Michael and St. George on Mr. John Ferguson, in acknowledgment of public services, more particularly through the "Ceylon Handbook and Directory," the value of which for over forty years—to the local Government as well as to the Colonial Office—had been repeatedly acknowledged by successive Governors and the staff of the Secretary of State.

The thirties seem to have been fruitful in the birth (and death) of newspapers. Besides the *Colombo Journal*, started by the local Government in January, 1832, and discontinued "by order" in December, 1833, the *Ceylon Chronicle*, also an official organ, appeared in 1837, only to be discontinued during the following year. The revival of the latter was attempted at the end of 1838, with some success; but its existence, together with that of an overland edition added in 1843, terminated in 1846. That was the last attempt at the establishment in Ceylon of official journalism; and the comparative success that attended it for a few years was probably due more to the dissensions among officials than to the paper having supplied any special need. The dissolution, impending and attained, of the official journal was the signal for the birth of other unofficial newspapers. In a varied community it could not be expected that one public organ could reflect every phase of thought, or promote diverse and often antagonistic interests. The *Ceylon Advertiser and General Intelligencer* enjoyed but a brief existence, from September, 1845, to April, 1846, despite its elaborate title. The *Examiner*, started in Colombo in January, 1846, and the *Times*, which made its bow on July 1st in the same year, both lived considerably longer, and did excellent service to the public and the country.

The *Examiner* was intended to be a mercantile organ, and was first owned by a few Colombo merchants. It evidently had to battle against difficulties from the outset. The first authentic information available in regard to this journal is that in 1848 it passed into the hands of Mr. R. E. Lewis, of the firm of Parlett, O'Halloran & Co., who had arrived in the island in 1841 as a young man of twenty-four. He advanced his savings on the security of the paper, and was obliged to take it over in satisfaction of the debt. He edited and conducted it himself for five years in the mercantile interest, with a special feature in the advocacy of Free Trade, then a new platform. In 1853 he sold the paper to three friends—two of whom were Mr. Cuffe, Registrar of the Supreme Court, and Mr. John Selby—and left for England in November of that year. Returning to Ceylon in 1855, Mr. Lewis joined the firm of Darley, Butler & Co. After many vicissitudes, he finally left the island in 1870. He was hale and hearty in England to the end of 1899, but died at Anerley in March, 1900, at the age of eighty-two. Mr. Lewis's successor as editor of the *Examiner* was Mr. John Selby, an advocate of the Supreme Court, and brother of Mr. Henry Collingwood Selby, at that time Queen's Advocate (or Attorney-General) of the island. The subscription list, however, continued to be limited, though the paper commanded considerable influence. Early in 1859 it passed from the hands of Mr. Selby, on his appointment to the District Judgeship of Colombo, to those of a syndicate of lawyers, at the head of which was Mr. C. A. Lorenz, then a brilliant young lawyer of thirty, with a leading practice in the Colombo Courts and a seat in the Legislative Council as Burgher Member. The other holders of shares were Mr. (afterwards Sir) Henry Dias; Mr. C. L. Ferdinands, who died while District Judge of Colombo; Mr. Advocate James de Alwis, the great Oriental scholar; and Mr. J. A. Dunuwille, the distinguished Kandyan advocate.

After a short period during which Mr. Louis Nell, his brother-in-law, acted as editor, Mr. Lorenz himself assumed the editorship, with Mr. (afterwards Sir Samuel) Grenier as sub-editor. On Mr. Grenier's appointment in 1866 to the secretaryship of the Colombo Municipality, just established, Messrs. Leopold Ludovici and Francis Beven—presently acting as Burgher Member in the Legislative Council—succeeded him, dividing the duties of sub-editorship; and they remained in office until 1871, when, on Mr. Lorenz's death, they succeeded to his shares in the *Examiner* under the special terms of his will, and thenceforth for a time conducted the paper jointly as editors. When Mr. Beven moved to Kandy in 1873 to practise his profession there, he transferred his interest in the paper to Mr. Ludovici, who thus became sole editor and proprietor. The paper fell on evil times in the later seventies, towards which the financial depression caused by the collapse of the coffee industry mainly contributed; and after Mr. Ludovici's death it was acquired by a joint-stock company, which included the leading members of the Burgher, Sinhalese, and Tamil communities. Mr. Beven, who retired from the legal profession owing to deafness, then accepted the editorship once more. In 1893 he finally relinquished the position, and was succeeded by Mr. J. T. Blaze, who continued as editor for seven years. But the capital of the company proved insufficient to meet the increasing competition in the journalistic field, and the paper, which scarcely ever had been conducted on business lines, having only existed as a political force, stopped publication on December 31, 1900. Ever since its acquisition by the Lorenz syndicate, in 1859, the *Examiner*, afterwards styled the *Ceylon Examiner*, was conducted with conspicuous ability, under its successive editors, in the special interests of the Ceylonese (*i.e.*, all the locally-born inhabitants of Ceylon, without distinction of race or colour). It was recognised as the Ceylonese organ, and wielded considerable influence with the Government and in official circles. Its discontinuance was regretted even by the communities outside those it specially represented.

The *Ceylon Times*, which was started in 1846, a few months after the first appearance of the *Examiner*, will ever be associated with the name of Capper, as the *Observer* is connected with that of Ferguson. Like the *Examiner*, the *Times* seems to have been established exclusively for the furtherance of sectional mercantile interests, and consequently failed to command a large *clientèle*. When Mr. John Capper acquired the paper in 1858 it was, as he himself described it, "on its last legs." Mr. Capper was then forty-four years of age, with considerable journalistic and mercantile experience, gained in Ceylon and elsewhere. He had been sub-editor in London of the *Mining and Steam Navigation Gazette*, before he came to Ceylon in 1837 as an assistant in the firm of Acland & Boyd, whose cinnamon cultivation and coconut oil mill business he successfully conducted. In 1851 he was sent to England as the representative of the island in the poor show it made at the Great Exhibition; and while there he added to his income by contributing to *Household Words*, Charles Dickens's new venture of the day, also by sub-editing the *Globe* and by other literary work. From London Mr. Capper went to Calcutta, and he set in motion the first jute-weaving machinery started there. But the outbreak of the great Mutiny upset all his dreams of prosperity in India, and he returned to Ceylon, in the hope—alas! not to be realised—of finding success in the island. The *Ceylon Times* was then in the market, the nominal owners being Messrs. Wilson, Ritchie & Co., a large and influential firm which, among other properties, owned the extensive coconut oil mills at Hultsdorf, Colombo, now in the hands of Messrs. Freudenberg & Co. That Mr. Capper had no capital, as he confessed, made no difference. He had abundant credit, owing to the keen competition for business between the local banks; and with the varied experience of the world he had gained in many climes and many pursuits, it is not wonderful that he was full of hope that the exceptional literary gifts and training he was bringing into Ceylon journalism would lead to success. But this expectation, so far as pecuniary results were concerned, was not realised, though the editor worked as hard as he could, and the quiet humour of Dickens's disciple was well set off in his editorials in polished phrases. The *Times* brought no wealth to its new proprietor; it merely jogged along; and Mr. Capper, after acting as Mercantile Member of the Legislative Council in the early sixties—resigning that position with his unofficial colleagues in 1864 as a protest against the disposal of the revenue by the Government in accordance with the behests of Downing Street—was glad a few years afterwards to accept the paid secretaryship of the Cattle Commission appointed by Sir Hercules Robinson, then Governor of Ceylon. Mr. Keppel Jones, a nephew of Mr. Capper, came out opportunely at that time and assumed charge of the paper, with the result that it put on a spurt for a time in his younger and more energetic hands. In 1874, however, the property, when very low, passed into the hands of a limited company, backed by a local bank, and Mr. Allardyce was specially imported from Bombay to undertake the editorship, with Mr. Willoughby (afterwards editor of the *Melbourne Argus*) as sub-editor of what was now called the *Times of Ceylon*. The fates still proving unpropitious, the paper collapsed in 1882, when Mr. Capper, still struggling against adversity, secured the plant, and starting with a single-page print, and with the assistance of his sons, Herbert and Frank, gave new life to the *Times of Ceylon*, which has since proved a marked success.

The era of the *Ceylon Times* corresponded with the period when the three principal papers shared the week between them—the *Observer* appearing on Monday and Thursday, the *Times* on Tuesday and Friday, and the *Examiner* on Wednesday and Saturday. This arrangement was not only well suited to the day of comparatively small things, but also contributed to the comfort of the reader, who was thus not compelled, in his daily perusal of the local newspapers, either to gulp down incompatible dishes or merely skim over the surface of questions demanding close attention. But before Mr. Capper finally quitted the island, in 1884, the era of daily newspapers had begun, and soon after he left the *Times of Ceylon* had fairly turned the corner on the path of prosperity, under the businesslike and energetic control of his two sons, in whose hands it continued to grow in a fashion that must have cheered the heart of the father in the last years of his chequered life. The founder died in England in 1898, at the ripe old age of eighty-five.

A still further advance in the field of journalism was made when, from the publication of daily evening papers in the capital, a step was taken which gave Ceylon the first morning paper for the people, the price being 5 cents (four-fifths of a penny) a copy. The originators of this enterprise in 1888 did not live or remain in the island to witness its success. One of them, Mr. Heath, of Reuter's Agency, died after a stroke of paralysis a few months after the new venture, the *Ceylon Independent*, was started, in 1888, and Messrs. Tiller (of the *Observer* office) and William Maitland, the other promoters, left the island. The paper and plant then passed into the hands of Mr. Hector Van Cuylenburg, who was fortunate enough soon after to secure for the post of editor the services of Mr. George Wall, a colonist of consummate ability, who, as planter and merchant and public man, had occupied a position among the foremost in Ceylon for more than a generation. The collapse of the coffee industry had ruined Mr. Wall's business—that of one of the leading agency firms in Colombo and Kandy—and, while his restless energy, only partially subdued by failing eyesight, found abundant and congenial scope for its exercise in the editorship of a daily paper, sympathy with him in his misfortunes, and the memory of his valuable services to the country, insured ready support from both Europeans and Ceylonese for the journal with which he identified himself in his old age. Mr. F. Crosbie Roles, now a joint proprietor and editor of the *Times of Ceylon* (ably assisted by Mr. H. Woosnam Mills, formerly of the *Pioneer*, India), was associated with Mr. Wall when he gave tone to the first "penny" paper in the island, and secured prominence for it. Mr. J. Scott Coates, a forcible writer with an immense capacity for work, is now editor of the *Ceylon Independent* jointly with the proprietor (Mr. Hector Van Cuylenburg).

In 1898 the *Ceylon Standard* was started under the auspices of a limited company as the second morning paper, in the proprietorship of which wealthy Sinhalese residents in, or connected with, Moratuwa held a prominent place. Mr. Windus was procured from England as editor, but died shortly after his arrival. The sub-editor, Mr. F. J. Wayman, who had come out from Home with Mr. Windus, succeeded to the editorial chair, but left the island in 1904, joining the staff of the *West Australian* later on, without having been able to make the venture a financial success. The *Standard* is now owned by a few Sinhalese gentlemen and edited by Mr. Gardiner-Brown. A yet further step in journalism was taken when Messrs. H. and F. Capper, F. C. Roles, and A. L. Hutchison, the owners of the *Times of Ceylon*, started the issue of a morning edition of their paper at a cheap figure—5 cents—with features which appeal to a wider class than that which subscribed to the evening edition. Mr. Herbert Capper, with whom the idea originated, happily lived long enough to see his bantling fairly established, but died, much regretted, in 1906 in England. This completes the record of regular daily newspapers published in English in Colombo since 1834.

A Roman Catholic press was established in Colombo in 1843, and the first issue of the *Catholic Messenger* appeared in 1869. Since 1873 this leading journal of that Church has been published twice a week. Although its scope as a medium of news is exclusively insular, no English or foreign telegrams appearing in its columns, the *Messenger* has been conducted with considerable ability by the Roman priesthood, or by laymen under their direction. As the title implies, this journal specially appeals to those who pay allegiance to the Roman Church. Of newspapers in English published outside Colombo, the oldest was perhaps the *Ceylon Freeman*, founded in Jaffna in 1862, which became extinct soon afterwards. But its successor, the *Ceylon Patriot*, founded in 1863, and published weekly in Jaffna, the northernmost town of the island, still survives. In that busy place, practically an Indian centre, inhabited mostly by "Island Tamils," who originally came centuries ago from the mainland close by, the *Catholic Guardian* (in English, weekly) established in 1876, the Hindu organ (in English, weekly) and the *Morning Star*, a Protestant organ (in English and Tamil, fortnightly) are also issued; while at Batticaloa, on the eastern coast of the island, an acceptable Wesleyan sheet, entitled *The Lamp*, periodically sheds its rays abroad.

An account of the extra-metropolitan press of Ceylon would be incomplete without mention of the *Kandy Herald*, which played a prominent part in the local world of politics during its brief existence. From the time of the united resignation of their seats in the Legislative Council by the unofficial members in 1864, until 1868, the newspapers, despite their disagreements and bickerings over every conceivable subject, were agreed on the need of legislative reform and loyally supported the Ceylon League, formed to secure that end. Both Europeans and Ceylonese were practically of one mind regarding the main objects for which the League was labouring, save a small remnant of Queen's House favourites and men who were in business or personal antagonism to the leaders of the movement. Appeals to the Home Government during two or three years having failed to effect the desired reform, a more moderate platform was, as the result of official suggestion, being considered in February, 1868, when the *Herald* was started in Kandy under the editorship of Dr. Bayliss, a learned but erratic planting doctor, and Arthur Jones, the blind nephew of Mr. Capper, a well-informed and accomplished writer. An early number contained the trenchant confidential despatch of Sir Hercules Robinson (afterwards Lord Rosmead), written in 1866, on the League petition, and the publication of this document came as a bolt from the blue. Pacification, then in the air, was thus rendered impossible, as much owing to the aspersion in the paper that factiousness had inspired the resignation of the unofficial members as to the manner of the publication of the despatch, which was ascribed to official connivance, and believed to have been effected through the agency of a Kandy firm whose senior had accepted the planting seat in the Legislative Council at a time when most planters and Colombo merchants refused to serve on that body. The storm of indignation which the incident raised cannot be appreciated at this distance of time; but it was expressed in the rest of the Press and in fiery speeches delivered at a public meeting, and many friendships were sundered in consequence. But the officials were soon dissatisfied with the tone and principles of the weekly organ of which they had thus made use, and the *Kandy Herald* ceased to exist in December, 1869, without having added to the reputation of any of those directly or indirectly connected with its existence, notwithstanding influential support and well-written articles. The *Ceylon Native Opinion*, first published in 1892 and since discontinued, had a spasmodic, but scarcely creditable, career, as its editor made acquaintance with the inside of the jail more than once for criminal libel.

The first paper published in Sinhalese was the *Lakminipahana*, which made its bow in Colombo in 1862, and is published weekly. And the number of vernacular newspapers since started, from the appearance of the *Gnanartha Pradipaya* in 1867, and including the *Dinakaraprakasa*, started in 1885, and the *Sihala Samaya* in 1904, all three published in the capital, testifies to the spread of education among the Sinhalese, as well as to the growth of a healthy public spirit. Most of the educated Sinhalese read the English newspapers; but the majority of the subscribers to the vernacular papers include the great mass of the native population, who either cannot read English or whose knowledge of that language is limited. A similar remark applies to the Tamil people and the Tamil Press, the first newspaper published in that language having been the *Morning Star* above mentioned, which was founded in Jaffna in 1841 and is still flourishing.

THE "CEYLON OBSERVER" AND THE "TROPICAL AGRICULTURIST."

The *Ceylon Observer*, the oldest Ceylon newspaper, which was established in 1834 under the motto *Fiat Justitia*, which has guided its conductors continually, is issued daily at from 5.30 to 6 o'clock p.m., with a morning edition on Mondays only at 6 a.m.; and the annual subscription in advance is Rs. 32, without postage, or Rs. 36 with local postage, including all regular extra supplements, the price of single copies being 10 cents each (1½d.) The *Observer* is the only Ceylon newspaper which has continually supplied its readers with European news by telegraph since the Indian cable was first laid. Its foreign cable service has very largely increased, and now includes not only Reuter's complete service, but also a variety of special cablegrams daily, comprising a supply from its London office (52, Gracechurch Street, E.C.), which covers all news of interest to Ceylon merchants and planters—such as relates to company dividends, flotations, and so forth — and the general public, also special telegrams from Calcutta (including special London cables re-telegraphed), Madras, Bombay, Singapore, Hong Kong, and other

R. H. FERGUSON.
(Assistant Editor.)

Eastern centres, and a very large local telegraphic service from accredited correspondents in every out-station of any importance in Ceylon. The paper devotes particular attention to political and planting affairs, and is specially up to date with all news of the Port

J. S. FERGUSON.
(Manager.)

of Colombo shipping traffic, also all that interests business circles, including Chamber of Commerce information, produce market reports, complete lists of prices at local tea sales, as well as Customs and other commercial statistics. As regards planting intelligence, the *Observer* is recognised as the foremost journal of the island. Up-to-date interviews and articles dealing with all tropical products of local interest are published at frequent intervals, and are acknowledged to be of the highest practical value. Another special feature of the paper is the accurate and careful reports of cases in the Colombo law-courts and those of the various provincial tribunals, according to their importance. It provides daily a complete and officially numbered list of cases decided in the Supreme Court of Appeal, with details of the decisions in each, including the full text of every judgment of importance or peculiar interest.

Every up-country and Colombo sporting or social meeting of any size is fully and brightly described, and every form of sport receives attention; while specially written articles on interesting topics are supplied by well-qualified correspondents, occasional and regular, in different parts of the world, including a weekly London letter, a monthly "Tea Letter" from the City (London), and a "Ladies' Letter." Subscribers to the *Ceylon Observer* receive gratis numerous special supplements, including half-tone block illustrations, connected with leading public events, and an annual sheet almanac replete with useful information, besides reduced rates for the yearly "Ceylon Handbook and Directory," an essential book of reference on the colony, and numerous standard

IVOR ETHERINGTON.
(Sub-Editor, *Tropical Agriculturist.*)

planting works on the staple, as well as the minor products of the island. The *Weekly Observer*, published at the same office on mail days (Thursdays almost invariably), two hours before the mail closes for England by alternate P. and O. and Orient steamers, contains a complete epitome of all the week's local news. The subscription for this weekly issue is—Ceylon or India (with postage), Rs. 16 in advance; elsewhere, Rs. 20 in advance; and without postage, Rs. 14 in advance; while the price for single copies is 35 cents (about 5½d.).

The *Tropical Agriculturist*, also published by the *Observer* Press, is a monthly illustrated magazine dealing with all branches of tropical agriculture and planting matters, and the subscription price with postage to any part of the world is £1 sterling per annum, post free. This publication was founded in 1881 by the Hon. Mr. John Ferguson, C.M.G., who realised that there was scope for such a periodical apart from the daily *Observer*, and since that date the successive volumes have formed a yearly history of the progress of agriculture in the tropics throughout the world. It may be said, without any exaggeration, that no other periodical published includes so wide a range of tropical and sub-tropical topics. During the past twenty-five years the following are among the subjects very fully dealt with in its pages: Coffee, cinnamon, tea, cacao, rubber, sugar-cane, cotton, areca, palmyra, and other palm products, coconut, spices of every kind, fibres of all varieties, tobacco, drugs, and medicinal plants, forestry and timbers, horticulture, poultry-rearing, and stock-raising. The *Tropical Agriculturist* has been always filed, by order of the Government, at every revenue office and agricultural and normal school in Ceylon; the Indian Government place it in their agricultural colleges and schools, model farms, museums, libraries, and other such-like institutions, and it is supplied to their agricultural schools and departments by the Governments of New South Wales, the West Indies, the Philippines, the United States of America, and other countries. It has always been recognised as the authority on such large industries as coffee, cacao, tea, and rubber growing. It may be mentioned that the *Tropical Agriculturist* has, since its first volume, steadily advocated rubher planting as a profitable industry. The regular publication of the market prices of tropical products, the Ceylon exports returns, the share lists and annual reports of tropical planting companies, has made the paper a valuable one for reference to merchants, traders, and others interested in business concerns in the tropics. When, in 1904, the Ceylon Agricultural Society was founded by His Excellency Sir Henry A. Blake, the publication of an organ of the society was regarded as essential; and the society approached Messrs. A. M. and J. Ferguson, the proprietors of the *Tropical Agriculturist*, with a view to supplying the want. The result was an arrangement whereby the proprietors agreed to give the magazine in trust to the Agricultural Society, the publication to remain the property of Messrs. Ferguson, and be printed and published by them, but to be edited by the Director of the Royal Botanic Gardens.

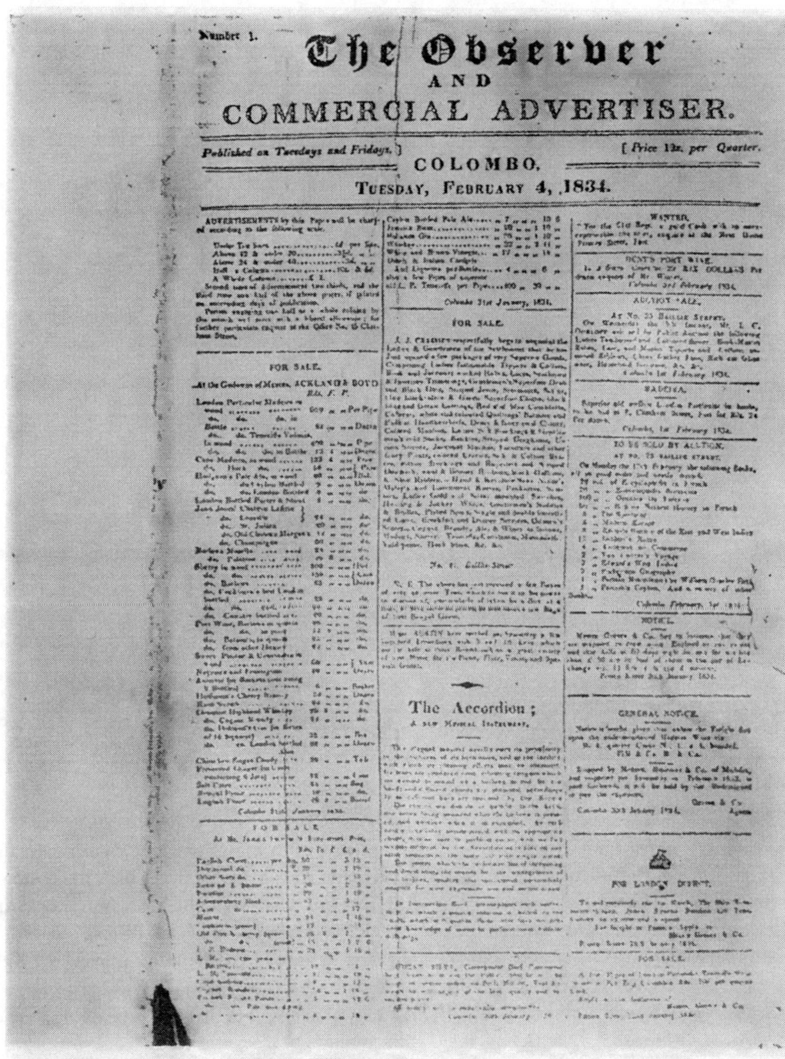

Number 1.

The Observer
AND
COMMERCIAL ADVERTISER.

Published on Tuesdays and Fridays. COLOMBO, [*Price 12s. per Quarter.*

TUESDAY, FEBRUARY 4, 1834.

FOR SALE.

The Accordion;

"OBSERVER" FIRST ISSUE, 1834.

This led to the periodical being sent to every member of the Agricultural Society, which includes—apart from a large number of planters and merchants (European and native)—a host of leading natives, low-country proprietors, farmers, and garden cultivators. The magazine is therefore now seen and read very freely and filed in every district throughout the island. It has, besides, a large circulation in India, the Straits Settlements, Java, Borneo, and all round the sub-tropical world. The foreign subscriptions and advertising department the publishers retain in their own hands, while subscription to the Agricultural Society covers a free copy of the local issue. Several changes and improvements were then made in the magazine, though it continues to cater for all tropical agricultural industries as previously.

The "Ceylon Handbook and Directory," published annually in July, now thoroughly established as the recognised statistical and directory authority on Ceylon, was begun by the late Mr. A. M. Ferguson, C.M.G., as the "Ceylon Commonplace Book" in 1859. In 1862 the Ceylon Government was induced to give up the publication of its "Ceylon Government Calendar and Directory" volume and confine itself to an annual Civil List and Blue Book. In 1863 Mr. J. Ferguson took charge of the compilation, and soon after changed the title to its present form. The book, forty years ago, seldom exceeded 450 pages. Year by year it has grown until it often comprises 1,600 to 1,800 pages, filled with information on every possible subject connected with the colony, with complete lists of all plantations and full statistics of the planting enterprise. Successive Governors have given high praise to the volume, as also Colonial Secretaries and the officials of the Colonial Office. Sir Arthur Gordon (now Lord Stanmore) and Sir West Ridgeway, both of whom had a very extended service, declared that in no British dependency did they know of so valuable a handbook and directory, or such full statistics, unless in Victoria, where a paid public officer is at the head of a Statistical Department. It was mainly on account of his forty years' labour on this annual volume, and his twenty-one years' labour for tropical agriculture through the monthly *Tropical Agriculturist*, that Mr. John Ferguson received from His Majesty the King the honour of C.M.G. on the recommendation of Sir West Ridgeway in 1903. The latest volume of the "Ceylon Handbook and Directory" is for 1906–7, and covers 1,551 pages. Its price is £1 per copy, and it is procurable at the *Observer* office, Colombo.

THE HON. MR. JOHN FERGUSON, C.M.G.

THE "TIMES OF CEYLON."

The *Ceylon Times*, the forerunner of the present *Times of Ceylon*, was started in Colombo in July, 1846, and the *Ceylon Overland Times* in 1860. Mr. John Capper, a Colombo merchant, who had been one of the two sub-editors of the London *Globe*, as well as a contributor to Dickens's *Household Words*, was the editor and proprietor; but in 1874 he sold the paper to a company and returned to England. The venture did not prosper under the company, which soon went into liquidation. Mr. Capper, who had meanwhile returned to Ceylon, resumed control of the paper; and Mr. Frank Capper, one of two sons of the founder who had shortly before begun life in the hills as coffee-planters, came down to Colombo to help his father. The elder son, Mr. H. H. Capper, joined them soon afterwards. Great energy was then infused into the business, and the paper, the name of which had been changed to the *Times of Ceylon*, soon flourished exceedingly, rapidly taking first place in point of circulation amongst the planters and other European residents. In the eighties Mr. Capper, sen., retired to England, but continued his journalistic work as London correspondent of the paper, a position which he filled until his eighty-third year. The title of the firm is still Capper & Sons.

In 1894 Messrs. H. H. & F. Capper, who had become sole proprietors of the business, built on a prominent site their own newspaper offices, an enterprising example in connection with journalism not even yet copied in Ceylon. A view of the *Times* buildings is given in an accompanying illustration. In 1905 Mr. H. H. Capper unexpectedly died while in London; but in 1904, during the Russo-Japanese war, he had started the *Morning Times*, which, combining several novel features, including illustrations of local current events, a magazine page, copyright serial and short stories, with accurate and up-to-date news service, has already carved out for itself a position which makes it as indispensable to the Ceylonese as the evening paper is to Europeans. No other newspaper house in Ceylon publishes two daily papers. To this firm belongs the credit of introducing illustrated journalism into Ceylon, and important developments are contemplated in this direction.

The *Times of Ceylon* is an eight-page paper, and besides being in its ordinary form larger than any other of its local contemporaries—the *Morning Times* is the same size—it gives ten pages once and sometimes twice a week. The price of the *Times of Ceylon* is 10 cents ($1\frac{1}{2}$d.) and of the *Morning Times* 5 cents ($\frac{3}{4}$d.).

The complete service of special telegrams from their own correspondents has always been a special feature, besides a special London service. They have correspondents at Calcutta, Department of Agriculture by the Government. It took a leading part in initiating the first World's Rubber Exhibition of 1906, and made a special feature of it in a variety of ways.

The Christmas number of the *Times of Ceylon*, which claims to be the best art publication produced east of Suez (price R.1, or 1s. 4d.), Two printing presses, fourteen printing machines, four cutting, three stitching, two perforating, two ruling, one routing, one blocking, one stamping, one punching, one eyeletting, two numbering, and one stereo machines. The firm are printers to, among other corporations, the Planters' Association of Ceylon and the Ceylon Chamber of Commerce.

"TIMES OF CEYLON" BUILDING.

Bombay, Madras, Rangoon, Singapore, Hong Kong, and Melbourne, who keep them thoroughly posted by cable with news of importance. Agriculture being the mainstay of the country, the *Times of Ceylon* has always paid special attention to this subject in its varied phases, and a large planting circulation —three-fourths of the entire community are its regular subscribers—enables it to keep thoroughly abreast of developments. It is a vigorous advocate of the creation of a separate

was also started in 1904. In the two preceding years the issue was quickly exhausted; and out of 7,000 copies of the 1906 Christmas number it was expected 2,000 would be sold outside of the island—among Ceylon people and their friends in the United Kingdom, as well as among residents in India, Malaya, and elsewhere in Asia.

Combined with the production of these various publications is a general printing office, with the following machine equipment:

The whole establishment employs over 220 hands.

The chief members of the staff are recruited in Europe; and, besides Mr. F. Capper, there are Mr. Francis Crosbie Roles, F.J.I., who has been editor for eight years and partner for six; Mr. H. Woosnam Mills, who is now co-editor and holds the firm's power of attorney; Mr. Alfred Scanes, M.J.I., manager; Mr. Tom Jones, sub-editor; Mr. D. Arklay, chief reporter; and Mr. S. R. Thornely, manager of the printing department. There is also a full staff of Ceylonese reporters, with Mr. F. F. Martinus as sub-editor of the *Morning Times*. The *Times of Ceylon* has always been a recognised organ of sport of all kinds, of the games and athletic pursuits which figure so prominently in Anglo-Indian life, and the popularity of which explains why English people in the tropics maintain their activity and health longer published more cabled news of the great Boer War than any other newspaper in Asia; and Ceylon enjoys what India does not possess, namely, a foreign press-message copyright, lasting for forty-eight hours after first publication.

The *Times of Ceylon* is well represented in London, having as manager, at its office at 27, Mincing Lane, E.C., Mr. A. L. Hutchison, sulted, and other detailed information about Great Britain's leading Crown Colony obtained at any time.

Frank A. Capper arrived in Ceylon in September, 1875, and was engaged in coffee planting on the Haputale, Kahagalla and Sherwood estates in the Haputale district till November, 1881, when he came to Colombo to

THE "TIMES OF CEYLON" STAFF.

than tropical colonists of other nationalities. Among the book publications issued from the *Times* office is the annual "Ceylon Handbook of Sport," edited by Mr. P. L. Bartholomeusz, of the literary staff.

India, Ceylon's huge neighbour, recognises the enterprise and ability of the island press, and in establishing this reputation the *Times of Ceylon* has taken a leading part. It is, for example, its well-authenticated boast that it

who has been associated with Ceylon since his youth, while Mr. Alexander Bethune, J.P., a recognised planting and business authority, whose contributions and exclusive cablegrams are regularly reproduced by Calcutta and South Indian journals, is London correspondent. At the London office is kept a register of addresses of people connected with Ceylon; and there files of the various *Times of Ceylon* publications can be con-

assist his father, the late Mr. John Capper, in restarting the moribund *Ceylon Times* as the *Times of Ceylon*, in which they were joined in 1882 by the late Mr. H. H. Capper. The firm of Capper & Sons was then started, and in 1903 that of Capper Bros., to carry on the London work of the firm at 27, Mincing Lane. Mr. F. Capper worked as sub-editor and manager of the *Times of Ceylon* till 1886, when, on the retirement of Mr. John Capper, with his brother he assumed the joint editorship and control of the *Times of Ceylon* and allied publications, till the death of Mr. H. H. Capper in 1905 left him sole proprietor.

FRANK CAPPER.

Francis Crosbie Roles, born in 1867, was articled to journalism in England, and went to Colombo when twenty-one years of age as chief reporter of the *Ceylon Independent*, then edited and managed respectively by the late Mr. George Wall and Mr. C. J. Higgs, now of Madras. Mr. Roles returned to England in 1893, but went back to Colombo in 1895 as sub-editor of the *Times of Ceylon*. Appointed leader-writer in 1897 and partner in 1900, Mr. Roles has had joint charge of the *Times of Ceylon* establishment ever since. He was Treasurer of the Ceylon branch of the Royal Asiatic Society for eleven years, and is a life member of that body. A member of the old national Association of Journalists of Great Britain and Ireland, Mr. Roles became an original member of the Institute of Journalists on its formation in 1889, and was elected a fellow in 1901. He is also a life-fellow of the Royal Colonial Institute. He represents the Central News (London). In 1896 he married, in New York, the only daughter of the late Mr. John A. Nichols, a lawyer of that city, and has twice since visited America. On one of these occasions, in 1904, he was an Official Visitor for Ceylon at the St. Louis World's Fair. Mr. Roles drafted the original of the Foreign Press-Messages Copyright Ordinance of 1898, which affords forty-eight hours' protection, and he is in favour of the extension of other copyright laws to Ceylon. He has drafted and may shortly publish a "Ceylon Chairman's Handbook." He contributed to the second edition of "The Law and the Press." He has specially studied the subject of rubber cultivation, and has published a *brôchure* on this industry. He is a director of the Indo-Malay Estates, Ltd., and of the Bharu Selangor Rubber Syndicate, Ltd., as well as of the Nuwara Eliya Hotels Company, Ltd. The Indo-Malay Estates, Ltd., was established by Mr. Roles at the request and with the approval of a number of public officers who can own rubber properties in Malaya and South India, but cannot own any Ceylon property. Ceylon public officers were thus at liberty to take shares, and their applications were treated preferentially. This company has the further distinction of being the lowest capitalised limited liability company yet formed. Mr. Roles is a member of the Automobile Club of Ceylon (owning a "Rover" car). His telegraphic address is Roles, Colombo.

F. CROSBIE ROLES, F.J.I.
(Editor.)

Harry Woosnam Mills—born in 1873—the son of a newspaper proprietor. On leaving school he was sent to the *Warrington Guardian* to learn his profession in the "Mackie School," Dr. Mackie having very definite ideas of what a journalist's training should be. In 1894 Mr. Mills left the *Guardian*, being offered the sub-editorship of the *Stockport Evening Chronicle* and *Cheshire County News*. Six months of the smoke of Stockport proved sufficient, and when Mr. Mills was invited to start a paper for Mr. Cripps and others at Maidenhead, he did so. An opportunity which came to him in 1895 was too tempting to be missed, however, even for the attractions of the river, and in the winter of that year he accepted the invitation of the late Sir George Allen and Mr. George Chesney to join the staff of the *Pioneer* and *Civil and Military Gazette*. Mr. Mills spent three years in India, succeeding, by the way, to the chair which Mr. Rudyard Kipling formerly occupied at Lahore. The frontier troubles of the late nineties gave him the subject-matter for a couple of books, "The Pathan Revolt in North-West India" and "The Tirah Campaign," both of which are still in constant demand for text-book purposes. Returning to Europe, Mr. Mills settled down in the Quartier Latin of Paris, where he spent nearly two years as a student of the language and literature of France. When the desire to return East of Suez came along, Mr. Frank Capper opportunely asked him to join the staff of the *Times of Ceylon*. Before leaving England, in April, 1901, he was married to Kathleen, the second daughter of George Nagington, of Comberley Hall, Staffordshire. In 1903 Mr. Mills became sub-editor of the *Times of Ceylon*, and he was made assistant-editor before going Home on furlough in 1905. He was associated with the late Mr. H. H. Capper in the inauguration of the Christmas number of the *Times of Ceylon* and the *Morning Times*,

H. WOOSNAM MILLS
(Co-Editor.)

both of which have been highly successful departures. Mr. Mills is a member of the London Press Club.

Alfred Scanes was born in 1877. He has been a member of the Institute of Journalists since 1897. In 1892 he started journalistic work on the staff of the *Devon and Exeter Daily Gazette*, conducted by Major G. F. Gratwicke (President of the Institute of Journalists, 1905–6). He also filled the position of foreign sub-editor of the *Western Daily Mercury*, Plymouth. He arrived in Ceylon in March, 1899, and joined the staff of the *Times of Ceylon* as chief reporter. He became sub-editor after two years, and, later, was appointed manager and chief sub-editor.

THE "CEYLON STANDARD."

The *Ceylon Standard* was started in January of the year 1898 as a daily morning paper of eight pages, each consisting of seven 20-in. columns, and soon achieved the popularity which it has since enjoyed. This is not surprising when it is remembered that the paper has followed, throughout the whole of its existence, the policy best explained by a quotation from its first issue, which runs: "With the first issue of the *Ceylon Standard* the public will naturally expect some statement as to the policy of the new morning journal. To make a brief statement upon this point is,

GARDINER BROWN.

therefore, our first duty. The *Standard* has been inaugurated with a view to giving full and fearless expression to honest, well-meant public opinion with reference to the government of the island, legislative and municipal, and supporting the efforts of all who are in any

"CEYLON STANDARD" BUILDINGS.

way endeavouring to develop the resources of this country. In dealing with matters affecting the representation of the people, the policy of this journal will be broadly progressive, seeking always to voice genuine popular feeling, and to secure the greatest good for the greatest number. At the same time there will be every desire to treat public affairs in a spirit of true loyalty, and with due respect to those in authority. Each of the many important interests of Ceylon—social, official, educational, and industrial—will be carefully studied, but no preference will be given to any of these to the detriment of the others. Finance, commerce, and agriculture will alike receive constant attention, and any assistance which may be given to the paper in this work will be heartily welcomed. In short, the object of the *Standard* will be to work for the general well-being of the entire island. In the pursuit of this policy, it is hoped that this journal may receive from the public of all classes appreciative and cordial support. By devoting itself to the service of the public, by striving to promote healthy progress, and by avoiding petty personalities, the *Standard* expects to secure a permanent and influential position amongst the journals of Ceylon." A high ideal, truly, but one which the *Standard* has consistently aimed at.

The *Standard* is thoroughly up to date, receiving, as it does Reuter's full telegraphic service and holding its columns open till the last moment for the important telegrams, which leave London just when the newspaper world there is most busy and arrive in Ceylon in the middle of the night. As many keen followers among its readers of Home and foreign events know, the *Standard* has often been the first to give them important news—such as the result of a big race meeting—by reason of the fact that its favourable position in the Fort gives it a great advantage in this direction. No pains are spared to insure that its readers shall have the very latest, both of local and foreign intelligence. Its leading articles on current topics may be regarded as expressions of sound, sober opinion, and their influence has been undoubted in furthering the general weal. Ample reports of all local functions are given; the paragraphing work is attended to with thoroughness and accuracy, whilst every precaution possible is taken to eliminate anything in the contributions submitted which seems to be inspired by malice. The result is that the sales of the *Standard* go on steadily improving.

The offices were originally situated in Chatham Street, Colombo; but a move was made during 1905 to the present site, No. 6, Canal Row. A more suitable building for the purpose it would be difficult to devise. It is conveniently situated, and compact, yet each department has spacious accommodation, with plenty of light and air. The machinery is of the best kind procurable, one machine having only recently arrived from the makers, the type is new, and the paper is as well turned out as any in the island. In addition to the plant for producing the paper, there is an extensive jobbing plant, a large amount of general printing being dealt with. It speaks well for the excellence of the work done in this department that repeat orders are constantly being received. The proprietors of the whole business are Messrs. J. G. C. Mendis, J. W. Charles de Soysa, and F. J. Mendis, who took over the concern in August, 1904, from the limited liability company which previously owned the paper.

A word as to some of those who have been connected with the *Standard*. Mr. Maurice Windus was the first occupant of the editorial chair. A London journalist, his career in Ceylon, which opened with promise of great things to be done, was ultimately brought to a sad close some six months after he landed. He was succeeded by Mr. Francis J. Wayman, who came out to take up sub-editorial duties soon after the paper was started. For seven years Mr. Wayman conducted the journal, doing much by his writing to enhance its popularity, more especially during the South African War, of which he made a careful study. His "Topics of the Hour" attracted a good deal of attention, and for some years were quite a feature of the paper. A successor was appointed in the person of the present editor, Mr. William Smith, who for private reasons was unable to occupy the position at the time, and in the interim Mr. F. Gardiner Brown, who early in 1905 had joined the staff as chief reporter, was induced to accept the acting post *pro tem*. Previous to his coming to Ceylon Mr. Brown was chief reporter of the *Leamington Spa Courier*. The present editor is well and favourably known in Ceylon, where he has

W. SMITH.
(Editor.)

resided since the early seventies, having been until some three and a half years ago proprietor and manager of Queen's College, one of the leading schools for girls in the island. The first manager was Mr. William Mackenzie, who afterwards found his way to Australia. The present manager, Mr. W. H. Taffs, has been for many years a resident in the island, and has been connected with the *Standard*, with but one brief break, since 1899.

W. H. TAFFS.
(Manager.)

The *Standard* claims to be the only paper in Ceylon which cannot be said to cater for any specified community. Its sympathies can be enlisted in no cause whatsoever unless it can be conclusively shown that that cause is a right one. Its columns are kept free from the baneful influence of local prejudices; hence its popularity with its growing circle of patrons.

THE "CEYLON INDEPENDENT."

The *Ceylon Independent* was the pioneer of the cheap newspaper in the East; and this, the first "penny" newspaper in Ceylon, was started by Mr. Hector Van Cuylenburg and Mr. William Maitland. The venture was an immediate success from the first, and can claim to have "never looked back." The first number was issued on July 4, 1888, when the evening papers were being sold for 15 or 12½ cents. The drop to 5 cents was rather a startling innovation; and not long after, the *Observer* and *Times*, the evening "dailies" of Colombo, perceived the advantage of reducing their price to the uniform rate of 10 cents a copy. The necessity of placing a newspaper within the reach of the people was generally acknowledged. The *Ceylon Times* Press Company, Ltd., which had been floated locally by some wealthy merchants, planters, and influential bankers of the island for the purpose of opposing the *Ceylon Observer*, the oldest of the Colombo journals, had come to grief. The plant and machinery were sold by public auction, and thus practically dispersed. But, by a peculiar irony of fate, a great portion of the type, together with a famous quad-crown Wharfedale machine, eventually came into the possession of Mr. William Maitland, who was associated with Mr. Van Cuylenburg in the early days of the *Independent*. With the equipment thus acquired, a job-printing establishment was started in Chatham Street, Colombo, on the site of the premises now tenanted by Messrs. E. Cahill & Co., and Mr. W. H. Tiller, late of the *Observer* staff, was appointed manager.

The *Independent* made its bow with a subscription list of over 1,500 supporters. Mr. Tiller soon afterwards left for South Africa, and was succeeded in the managership by Mr. C. J. Higgs, now a partner in Messrs. Higginbotham & Co., Madras. Later, Mr. E. H. Joseph succeeded Mr. Higgs as manager, and has retained the position since 1892. The first editor was Mr. Heath, who had formerly been Reuter's Agent in Colombo. He died shortly after his appointment; and, chiefly through the good offices of Mr. F. H. M. Corbet, the services of the late Mr. George Wall were secured as editor in 1889. Mr. Wall was a well-known public man, possessing an experience of the public affairs of Ceylon which was probably unrivalled. He had been Chairman of the Planters' Association of Ceylon, Chairman of the Chamber of Commerce, also Planting Representative in the Legislative Council; and what he wrote men read gladly, all classes acknowledging his authority, from the Governor—first, Sir Arthur Gordon (now Lord Stanmore) and, later, Sir Arthur E. Havelock—downwards. So well did the paper flourish under the editorship of Mr. Wall that it became necessary to enlarge the editorial staff, and another recruit in the person of Mr. Francis Crosbie Roles, now one of the editors of the *Times of Ceylon*, was brought out from England to assist, and rendered good service as chief reporter. Mr. Wall's connection with the paper lasted until his death, which occurred in December, 1894. At that time Mr. Roles had also left the staff, and Mr. J. Scott Coates was brought out, in March, 1895, to assist Mr. Hector Van Cuylenburg and Mr. C. W. Gray ("Saxon") in the conduct of the paper. Mr. Van Cuylenburg remained editor-in-chief till 1898, when he relinquished the active duties of the post to Mr. J. Scott Coates, the present editor, always, however, retaining in his hands the control of the paper and guiding its policy.

The chief feature of the *Ceylon Independent* is its outspokenness; and it bases its main claim to popular support on the fearless ventilation of public questions and the bold exposure of public evils. Following this course, it espouses the cause of no one section of the community, but addresses itself impartially to the necessities of each. One of the greatest achievements of this paper was the agitation which led to the repeal of the paddy tax in 1890, when Mr. George Wall was at the helm. In 1899 Mr. Hector Van Cuylenburg, as editor and proprietor, had to defend an action for damages brought against him by Mr. C. J. R. Le Mesurier, an ex-Ceylon civil servant, in the High Court of Justice, England. At the first trial, in June, 1902, before Mr. Justice Grantham and a special jury, a verdict in favour of the plaintiff for £1,500 and costs was returned by the jury. Mr. Van Cuylenburg, nothing daunted, filed an appeal, contrary, it is said, to the advice of many eminent lawyers, who advised him "not to throw good money after bad." The appeal was successful, the present Master of the Rolls being emphatic in his ruling that there had been a miscarriage of justice, and a second trial was ordered. This second trial took place before Lord Alverstone, the Lord Chief Justice, and a special jury, and ended in a verdict for the *Independent* after a three days' trial. Sir Arthur Collins, late Chief Justice of Madras, and Mr. Quinton Hogg appeared for the plaintiff, and the late Mr. Macaskie, K.C., and Messrs. Storry, Dean, and F. H. M. Corbet appeared for the defendant, the successful appellant. The average daily circulation of the *Independent*, as certified by Mr. H. P. Church, incorporated

"INDEPENDENT" PRINTING WORKS.

accountant, is 3,270. A notice of the proprietor, Lieutenant-Colonel Hector Van Cuy-

LT.-COL. HECTOR VAN CUYLENBURG.
(Proprietor.)

lenburg, appears in the Military Section of this book.

JOHN SCOTT COATES (Editor).

This gentleman, son of Mr. W. H. Coates, of Tunbridge Wells, Kent, is the third of four sons who have all found their living abroad—one under the Egyptian Government (since retired), two in South Africa, and one in Ceylon. Mr. J. Scott Coates's journalistic experience dates back to 1882, when, after completing his education at the Brighton Grammar School, he joined the *Sussex Daily News* in Brighton as an apprentice in the editorial department. In 1888 he was appointed district reporter for the same paper, having his headquarters in Horsham, North-west Sussex. Eighteen months later he

J. SCOTT COATES.
(Editor.)

resigned this position to take charge of an Eastbourne edition of the *Sussex Express*. Owing to the unpopular attitude which this paper assumed on the Salvation Army riots question, Mr. Coates resigned his position, and was next appointed chief reporter of the *Brighton and Hove Gazette*, which position he vacated, in March, 1895, to come out to Ceylon, where he joined the editorial staff of the *Ceylon Independent* in the capacity of chief reporter. From that position he was successively promoted to be sub-editor, assistant-editor, and finally, in 1898, editor. Mr. Coates has been, for the last fifteen years, a member of the Institute of Journalists, and was formerly hon. secretary of that body for the Sussex district. He is an expert shorthand writer, and has frequently been commissioned by the Government to take the shorthand notes of the Annual Conference of Government Agents and various commissions. He is also the President of the Ceylon Shorthand Writers' Association. Under his charge the *Independent* has witnessed expansion, not only in size, but in circulation, the limit of which has not been reached. Mr. Coates was born on January 27, 1867, and married in Colombo, on November 24, 1898, Miss Kathleen Cooper, elder daughter of the late Mr. R. Cooper, artist, of Preston Park, Brighton.

ERNEST HENLEY JOSEPH (Manager).

Mr. Ernest Henley Joseph, the eldest son of the late A. O. Joseph, Proctor of the Supreme Court of Ceylon, was born in Colombo in 1868. In 1880 he left for England to receive his education, and entered Bath College, Somerset, where he pursued his studies for three years. He also previously received private tuition at Clifton. During his stay in England he scored success both in football and cricket. He returned to Ceylon in April, 1886, and two years later joined the *Independent* staff as general assistant, rising afterwards, in 1892, to the position of manager of that organ, which office he has retained ever since. During his leisure hours, sports claim him as a devotee, especially football and cricket. As a member of the Colombo Hockey and Football Club, he played at both games in the annual matches Colombo *versus* Up-country for eight consecutive years, viz., 1892 to 1899. As the best football forward for the year 1895 he received a presentation cap. In October, 1894, he played for Mr. George Vanderspar's eighteen of Ceylon against the English eleven which Mr. Stoddart was taking out to Australia; and in April, 1896, playing for eighteen of Ceylon against the Australian team captained by George Trott, and which visited England that year, the subject of this notice made the highest score (23) for Ceylon. In 1899 he headed the batting averages for the island in cricket.

Volunteer work also occupies some of his time. He joined the Ceylon Artillery Volunteers in 1900, and two years later he was made Lieutenant, receiving the appointment of

E. H. JOSEPH.
(Manager.)

Captain in 1905. His private residence is "Stockton," Maitland Crescent.

LLOYD'S GREATER BRITAIN PUBLISHING CO., LTD.

Into this section seems to appropriately fall a description of the organisation which has been responsible for the production of "Twentieth Century Impressions of Ceylon." The company itself has only a temporary foot-hold on the island, but its work here as elsewhere has been essentially of a local character, and its influence in Ceylon, it may be reasonably anticipated, will be far from transient. Established in Australia in 1900 by Mr. Reginald Lloyd, in association with Mr. P. W. H. Thiel, the company has passed through various stages of development, until to-day it is revealed as a flourishing concern, with a business domicile in Durban, Natal, and world-wide activities. But though changes have marked the machinery of the organisation, there has been no departure from the principles originally adopted by the founders as their rule of action. The root idea of the system which they established was the widening of public knowledge of the great self-governing colonies—the "free nations" of Kipling's poem—and the vast dependencies which together give such impressiveness to the British Empire. At the time they embarked upon their task there was much talk of the necessity of the diffusion of full and accurate information regarding the component parts of the Empire. Mr. Chamberlain had stirred the dry bones of the Colonial Office by his vigorous action, and had evoked interest, and even enthusiasm, in "the Britains beyond the sea" by his eloquent dissertations on the importance of knowledge as a factor in the furtherance of Imperial ideals. The promoters took their cue from the greatest of Colonial Secretaries and the best business man who has ever figured in the Imperial Government. They adopted as their ideal a publication which should deal exhaustively with every phase of the life of a colony or dependency, and which should be attractive as well as informing. They went upon the assumption that there was a public which would welcome a work of this class where it would turn with indifference, if not aversion, from a Blue Book or a volume in which facts and figures were set out without the graces of illustration and the lighter features which are possible in a work of a popular type. Events have justified to the full the soundness of their views. In Western Australia, in Natal, in the Orange River Colony, and lastly and most decidedly in Ceylon, it has been shown by the successful production of volumes in each case that a compilation on the lines indicated is a thoroughly acceptable, and even invaluable, addition to local literature. The magnitude of the literary scheme and the sumptuousness of the artistic features have been appreciated as belonging to a class of enterprise which ordinarily lies apart from Colonial publications ; while the thoroughness and comprehensiveness of the operations as a whole have appealed to the business instincts of communities which are above all things commercial. In fine, the company has carved out for itself a distinct position in the publishing world, and in doing so has performed no small public service by adding to the sum of public knowledge of the outlying portions of the Empire.

In Ceylon the company started its operations in May, 1906. Mr. Somerset Playne, the manager, who had been to England to see the Natal and Orange River Colony volumes through the press, established the headquarters in the Victoria Arcade, Colombo, and gathered about him there a staff of workers. Mr. Reginald Lloyd, the general manager, was detained in South Africa until August, and on his arrival in that month the staff was complete. Thenceforward the work proceeded steadily all along the line. The various districts of the island were mapped out and visited by members of the staff, and a mass of information dealing with the multifarious phases of Ceylon life was garnered for future use. Meanwhile the services of many able local writers—experts in various lines—were enlisted to make special contributions on subjects of importance in the scheme of the work. This assistance was freely and generously rendered, with the ultimate result that the pages of the book are adorned with monographs, some of which have a permanent interest because of the light they throw on the history and interests of the island, and all of which are of value as authoritative pronouncements on the subjects treated. This aid notwithstanding, the work of the regular literary staff has been very onerous. The task of compiling such a publication as this would be no light one in England or Australia, where every facility is at hand for the purpose. But in a tropical land, where literary work can only be done under many disadvantages, owing to the lack of conveniences, and where the climate is inimical to the constitution, the operations are doubly difficult. This truth forced itself into prominence as the work of compilation proceeded. Eventually, owing to the depletion of the staff through illness, new blood had to be infused from Home. The services of a new editor and two assistants were secured early in November, and with their arrival at the end of that month the work of the office once more dropped into a normal groove. Thereafter, until the final stage was reached early in March, no serious difficulty was experienced. But a constant and vigilant supervision had to be exercised to insure that faith was kept with the public. In particular the photography necessitated continuous watchfulness and unremitting energy. A glance through the pages of the volume will reveal even to the uninstructed the reason for this. The many hundreds of reproductions of photographs which appear there represent the work of months of several firms, whose assistants had to travel in some instances scores of miles to obtain the many beautiful and interesting sun pictures which appear in the work. The duty of registering, classifying, and arranging these productions was no light one. Errors had to be guarded against by an elaborate system of checks ; the best use had to be made of the material at hand : so from first to last the photographic work was a source of anxiety and occasionally embarrassment. But the result more than compensates for all the troubles that have been experienced. It will be generally admitted, we think, that the illustrations in point of vivid, living interest and artistic excellence surpass any that have ever appeared in a work of this character relating to the colonies. It may be added that without the backing of a powerful organisation assisted by local goodwill they would not have been possible.

LLOYD'S REPRESENTATIVE UP-COUNTRY COLLECTING INFORMATION AT NATANDIYA, IN THE NORTH-WESTERN PROVINCE.

Of the work as a whole it can be truthfully said that throughout it has been received with the most cordial sympathy. His Excellency Sir Henry Blake, the Governor, extended to it his patronage, and showed an interest in the working out of the scheme which was highly encouraging. His Excellency's example was widely followed. From many and diverse sources and in various shapes the staff received encouragement and oftentimes active assistance in the prosecution of their labours. In this way the compilation derived an aspect which differentiates it from publications of an ordinary character, in which the author or editor has to work with no other force behind him than his own enthusiasm and material interest.

One of the characteristic features of the organisation of Lloyd's Publishing Company is that its work knows no break. Long before one volume is completed another is sketched out, and ere the editor has set his seal to the last pages a portion of the staff is commencing work upon a new enterprise elsewhere. So it happened that the early days of December saw Mr. Somerset Playne thoroughly equipped in the field at Singapore, laying the foundations of a volume dealing with the Straits Settlements and the Federated Malay States. It is too early yet to speak of this enterprise fully, but it may be said generally that the book will be a worthy successor of the existing volume, embodying all its salient features and its manifold points of interest and attractiveness. After the publication of the work on the Straits Settlements a volume will appear dealing with Hong Kong, and this in turn will be succeeded by Twentieth Century Impressions of other important centres. In this way a library will ultimately be formed which will go far to meet that demand for a comprehensive survey of British possessions beyond the sea which Mr. Chamberlain made in his historic speech.

J. ELLIS BROWN, J.P.
(Chairman of Directors.)

The directorate of Lloyd's Greater Britain Company, Ltd., includes some of the best known and most substantial business men and financiers in South Africa. Mr. J. Ellis Brown, the chairman of the company, who was Mayor of Durban for many years, is a director of the Natal Trust and Finance Company, Ltd., as is also the deputy-chairman, Sir Benjamin Greenacre, head of the great Durban firm of Harvey, Greenacre & Co., and deputy-chairman of the Natal Bank, Ltd., while the chairman of the Natal Trust and Finance Company, Ltd., Mr. Maurice Evans, C.M.G., M.L.A., is also a member of the Board. The other two directors are the Hon. Mr. Marshall Campbell, M.L.C., managing director of the Natal Sugar Estates, Ltd., the largest concern of its kind in South Africa, and Mr. Alexander Harvey Rennie, resident partner (in Natal) of the "Rennie" Steamship Company, both gentlemen being also on the directorate of the Natal Trust and Finance Company, Ltd. The secretary of the company is Mr. Henry Ernest Mattinson, F.I.A.N., Club Arcade, Durban, and the auditor is Mr. George Mackeurtan, of that town.

THE "SANDARESA."

A quarter of a century ago vernacular journalism in Ceylon was in the hands of one

LLOYD'S PRESS.

1. J. W. DENNY. 2. ARNOLD WRIGHT. (Editor.) 3. J. ADDY. 4. LAWRIE MUTHUKRISHNA.
5. MISS EDITH ASHLEY. 6. REGINALD LLOYD. (General Manager.) 7. SOMERSET PLAYNE. (Manager.)
8. E. MANNHEIMER. (Field Representative.) 10. S. G. SAMUEL. 12. J. HOLDSWORTH.

or two private individuals of very conservative ideas, with the result that punctuality, precision, and promptitude, which are essential in this as in other lines of business, were more honoured in the breach than in the observance. Thirty years ago Ceylon possessed the notoriety of schisms unknown during the reigns of the Sinhalese kings, for each of the various sects attempted to gain predominance over the others. This was a source of hindrance to united action, and the Buddhists felt the situation more keenly than the other religious denominations. This state of affairs was aggravated by the introduction, later, of other sects of Buddhist monks, who vied with each other to raise their respective schools of thought into prominence. The result was that the laity, who were barricaded by differences, were still more hindered. This trouble naturally affected the journalists, who were under the obligation of taking some side or other. They were thus placed in an awkward position, as they were few in number and had to satisfy the particular needs of their supporters.

With the advent of the Theosophical pioneers in 1880, the position of the Buddhists particularly was thoroughly reviewed, and an organisation called the Buddhist Section of the Theosophical Society was started in Colombo on the 17th of June of the same year, with the following objects :—

(1) The promotion of Buddhism by guarding it from the attacks of those who profess other religions ; (2) the strengthening of Buddhists in their faith and in the practice of Buddhist morals ; (3) the dissemination of Buddhist doctrines. A large number of prominent Buddhists joined the movement, and then was recognised the absolute necessity for establishing a first-class vernacular newspaper under the auspices of the Theosophical Society of Colombo. The paper was started in December, 1880, as a weekly (published every Friday), and consisted of four pages. But the demand for the journal was so great that in May, 1887, it was converted into a bi-weekly (published on Fridays and Tuesdays). The employment of able pundits on the editorial staff popularised the venture to such an extent that it grew into a leading vernacular organ, and gave an impetus to the study of Sinhalese by the natives. The progress of the paper became manifest in May, 1901, when the Friday issue assumed the dimensions of eight pages ; and in January, 1902, the Tuesday issue followed suit.

The remarkable change effected by this Sinhalese paper, with its national aims, in bringing about a healthy union, is attributable to the firmness with which the society which owns the *Sarasavi Sandaresa* has conducted its business in conformity with the objects originally laid down. As regards commercial success, the paper claims to be a recommendable medium for advertisers, the weekly circulation being 8,000 copies ; while, in reference to its propaganda, closely watches, on behalf of the Buddhist community, the legislation of the day, and advocates the cause of Buddhism irrespective of caste and sect. It also aims at bringing before the public, as well as the Government, all needs pertaining to the amelioration of the condition of the Sinhalese population generally. The English weekly edition of the *Sandaresa* is an addition to journalism started in June, 1905, which has, in the view of its promoters, supplied a great want in bringing before the governing body particular grievances of the Buddhists in a fashion and with a completeness not to be expected from other journals. This English edition is published every Friday, and has a large and growing circulation. The printing establishment is being brought up to date, to cope with the development of the business. The primitive hand-presses with which the *Sarasavi Sandaresa* started in the eighties have given place to improved machines driven by gas-power, and a large expenditure has been incurred in fully manning the composing staff and the management. Any surplus of income over expenditure is devoted to the furtherance of Buddhist education undertaken by the Colombo Buddhist Theosophical Society. This society has under its management over 200 schools, with an attendance of over 30,000 boys and girls. Thus the *Sarasavi Sandaresa* claims not only to be the mouthpiece of the two millions of Buddhists of Ceylon, but also to have contributed largely to the education of the masses on Buddhist lines. There being no means of obtaining an income from foreign countries, this work of education would have been seriously hampered had it not been for the support rendered by the *Sarasavi Sandaresa*. The paper is conducted by Mr. H. S. Perera, as editor-in-chief, and Mr. T. Karunaratne, Pundit, assisted by an able staff, the manager being Mr. G. H. de Soysa.

MALAY NEWSPAPERS.

The *Alamat Lankapuri*, or "News of the Island of Lanka," was the first newspaper printed in the Malay vernacular, a language written in Arabic characters with the addition of six letters from other alphabets, and it existed nine years, from 1869 to 1878. In 1895 the *Wajah Selong*, or "Light of Ceylon," was published, its fortnightly issues circulating largely amongst the Malay-speaking races in Ceylon, the Straits Settlements, Java, Batavia, Holland, &c. These were the only papers of the kind that ever existed in Ceylon, and

B. O. SALDIN.
(Editor.)

the latter was published until disease incapacitated the editor. The lithographer, editor, and publisher was the late Mr. Baba Ounoos Saldin, who was a prominent figure among the Malays ; and in Mr. Skeen's pictures of Ceylon races

MALAY PAPER PUBLISHED FORTNIGHTLY SINCE 1869.

Mr. Saldin's portrait stands for his kinsfolk as a representative of the Malay. He died in 1906, in his seventy-sixth year

HEMENDRA SEPPALE PERERA.

This gentleman was born at Kandy in 1868, and was educated at the Kandy Central High School and St. Paul's College, Kandy. The Theosophical Society made him manager of their press in 1890, and in 1903 he was appointed chief editor of the *Sandaresa* newspaper (of which an account is given elsewhere in this section).

H. S. PERERA.

THE "SIHALA SAMAYA."

The above bi-weekly journal (the *Sinhalese Times*) was established about the year 1902 by Mr. Stephen de Silva, who still continues to conduct it. The paper is an eight-paged one, and is printed in clear type in the Sinhalese vernacular. Supplements are frequently issued with the sheet, a feature of the paper being its illustrated journalism. Cartoons and caricatures of local interest may be often noted in its columns, while cablegrams are taken over from the evening English papers under the usual copyright provisions. The circulation is estimated at about 3,000, copies being posted to out-station centres in the island as well as to foreign parts where Sinhalese-speaking residents are to be found. In the latter business Reuter's Telegram Company act as distributing agents for the paper. The journal is now in the sixth year of its existence, and seems to be well in demand. At the time of writing arrangements are in hand for its further development and the extension of its scope of usefulness, and the sheet promises to grow into twelve pages before long. The price of the paper is 5 cents for a single copy (about five-sixths of a penny). The publishing offices are at 3, Canal Row, in the Fort of Colombo.

THE "DINAPATHA-PRAVRUTTI."

Established in 1895, the *Dinapatha-Pravrutti* (the Sinhalese *Daily News*) has constituted itself an eagerly sought for paper by the masses, who may find in its columns the latest news relative to the welfare and interests of the island in general and the Sinhalese community in particular. The paper claims to be entirely non-sectarian, and works mainly in the cause of the betterment of the colony's peoples. The founder and present editor of the journal is Mr. C. Don Bastian, and the publishing offices are at Malibam Street, in the Pettah of Colombo. The native branches of the trade avail themselves readily of its columns for purposes of advertisement, and recognise in it a medium of far-reaching usefulness. The paper is a large folio sheet of four pages in extent, and sells at 5 cents. With the awakening of the Sinhalese people and the growing disposition to support every description of native enterprise, there is reason to believe that the future conduct of the paper is well assured and that developments will rapidly follow At the present time it commands a good circulation, and has the distinction of being the only daily vernacular paper in the island.

THE "MUSLIM FRIEND."

Although the mass of Mahomedans generally speak the Hindustani language, or dialects related to it, the usual medium of communication amongst the Moors and Mahomedan settlers in Ceylon is Tamil, which, in the case of a good many of the more illiterate classes, is the only tongue they know. A newspaper in the interests of the Mahomedan community has therefore necessarily to be published in the Tamil language if it is to command their attention at all, or in any way cater for their needs. The *Muslim Friend*, with which is incorporated the *Ceylon Mohammedhan*, was founded a few years ago by the exertions of prominent members of the community, and is at present conducted by Mr. A. T. Shamsudeen, the publishing offices being at 51, Malibam Street, in the Pettah of Colombo. The *Muslim Friend* is an exclusively Tamil publication, while the *Ceylon Mohammedhan* is printed in English and forms a kind of supplement to it. Both sheets are issued bi-weekly, and the subscription is practically the same. The journal is essentially established in the interests of all professors of the Islamic faith, who, in Ceylon, comprise the Mahomedans proper, the Moors (both descendants of the ancient Arab traders and those who have settled down in the coast districts of South India), Malays, Javanese, Afghans, and other minor sections of Mahomedans. The paper aims at conserving the interests and safe-guarding the rights of Mahomedans throughout Ceylon, and its news service is therefore responsible and representative. It is the only Mahomedan paper in the island, and its circulation is consequently well maintained.

SPICES AND OTHER PRODUCTS

THE "spicy breezes" of Ceylon are proverbial—and mythical—but spices no longer monopolise the field as a mercantile asset. The old order in this matter as in others has changed. Gone are the cinnamon gardens which once spread over a considerable portion of what is to-day the chief residential centre of Colombo, and departed are the conditions of the period of Dutch ascendancy, when a considerable portion of the revenue of the Government was derived from a cinnamon monopoly, and when it was death for a native to even pluck a branch of a cinnamon tree. The name of the reserve survives, and with it a few isolated trees which carry forward the old tradition, but the Government long since washed its hands of the business, and the commodity now, under the overshadowing influence of larger interests, has lost much of the trade importance which belonged to it. Still, it remains a respectable industry. The exports in 1905 amounted to 46,925 cwts., and they contributed Rs. 2,312,464 to the total sum of the island's exports. The United Kingdom took about one-eighth of the whole, Germany about one-third, and the United States and South America each about one-ninth. The area under cultivation is some 44,000 acres. Much of it is on the west coast about Colombo and Negombo, but there are also estates at Kalutara, Galle, Matara, and Kegalla. The tree does not flourish inland. It likes a white sandy soil, such as is to be found about the estuaries and lagoons of Western Ceylon. In the halcyon days of the monopoly era the price of the bark reached as high a figure as 8s. a pound; now the rate of the best kinds is less than a shilling, and inferior qualities fetch little more than half that rate. The great drop in price was brought about by competition. An inferior quality was imported into Europe from the Malabar Coast, and China also entered the lists. Gradually the rates were forced down to the existing level, and the probability is that the old prices will never be reached again. It should be mentioned before passing from the subject that cinnamon is exported in two forms—as "quills" and "chips." The "quills" are the ordinary cinnamon of commerce, the "chips" are the cuttings from the imperfectly grown cinnamon branches. The latter are chiefly used in the manufacture of cattle food and the distillation of cinnamon oil.

Cardamoms, "the seed of Paradise," are another spice which figures largely in the trade returns. This spice was not grown to any extent until about thirty or forty years ago, but the trade has now assumed considerable dimensions. As against an export in 1878 of 124 cwts., there was in 1905 one of 7,888 cwts. Though prices have fallen considerably in late years, the value of the produce exported reaches Rs. 583,072. British India took 3,900 cwts. and the United Kingdom 2,641 cwts. Germany was the next largest buyer, with 1,010 cwts. to her account. Cloves and mace are grown to a small extent, and also ginger and nutmegs. Pepper is a larger interest, with an export of 769 cwts. valued at Rs. 29,642; while vanilla to the amount of 56 cwts. and of a value of Rs. 37,465 was exported in 1905, almost exclusively to the United Kingdom.

In the list of "other products" included in the heading of this article comes the important item of essential oils. During 1905 cinnamon oil worth Rs. 15,397 and cinnamon leaf oil of the value of Rs. 5,982 were sent out of the country. But the most conspicuous product of this class was citronella oil, the exports of which in the year mentioned aggregated in value Rs. 1,041,256. Concerning the citronella oil industry, Mr. B. Samaweera, of Weligama, who is an extensive planter and exporter, wrote an interesting paper which was read before the Ceylon Agricultural Society on April 2, 1906. From this we gather that some 40,000 acres of land in the Southern Province are occupied with citronella plantations. Some idea of the magnitude of the industry, as well as its steady advancement, may be gathered from the export figures for the years given below. There are no available figures before 1887.

EXPORTS OF CITRONELLA OIL.

		lbs.			lbs.
1887	...	551,706	1896	...	1,132,141
1888	...	659,967	1897	...	1,182,867
1889	...	641,465	1898	...	1,365,917
1890	...	909,942	1899	...	1,478,756
1891	...	603,974	1900	...	1,409,058
1892	...	844,502	1901	...	1,430,168
1893	...	668,520	1902	...	1,294,750
1894	...	908,471	1903	...	1,062,594
1895	...	1,182,255	1904	...	1,156,646

The history of the citronella plant at present cultivated is shrouded in mystery. It is thought by some to be an indigenous plant which has been improved by cultivation; by others it is considered to have been introduced into Ceylon from India. There is, Mr. Samaweera thinks, an element of truth in either view. Further, he is inclined to believe that the four different varieties of the plant now existing and classified under the Mahapangeri and Lenabatu groups are the degenerate products of the exotic variety, or the product of a cross-fertilisation between the indigenous and exotic varieties. Or even it may be that the indigenous variety has been improved as a result of cultivation. The citronella plant is the ***Andropogon Nardus***, ***Linnæus***, of the family Graminæ, and is extensively grown for the distillation of oil in the Southern Province, on the declivities of hills where the soil is not by any means considered to be rich. There are four different varieties of the plant met with in plantations. They are grouped under two classes, the

Mahapangeri and the Lenabatu. Each group has its advantages and disadvantages. The Mahapangeri gives a larger yield of oil, and a higher percentage of the aromatic constituents which go to increase the value of the oil from this group of plants. On the other hand, its chief disadvantages are that it requires a comparatively rich soil, is not able to withstand prolonged drought, and requires greater attention. Further, it has to be frequently re-planted. The Lenabatu, though giving a smaller yield of oil, is a more hardy plant, thrives in poor soil, requires very little attention, and does not necessitate re-planting. The oil it yields contains fewer aromatic constituents, and always obtains a lower value than the oil from the other variety. Since the bulk of the oil in Ceylon is that obtained from the Lenabatu variety of citronella, it is, Mr. Samaweera thinks, on account of its poor quality that Ceylon citronella oil obtains a lower market price than the oil from Java and Singapore. But he is of the view that if greater care is exercised in cultivation there is no reason why Ceylon oil should not command as good a price as that from the Straits. The popular belief that all Ceylon citronella oil is adulterated is discredited by Mr. Samaweera. That there is adulteration in this as in many another trade, he says, is beyond dispute. But he asserts that there does not exist the wholesale adulteration which is generally represented. The poor quality of the oil is due to the bad variety of plants cultivated, and still more to over-production. However that may be, the question of the purity of the Ceylon citronella oil is receiving increasing attention, and no doubt, as a result of the attention given, as well as of efforts to improve the cultivation on the lines suggested by Mr. Samaweera, the exports of this commodity will be largely augmented in the next few years. Meanwhile, considerable attention is being given to the cultivation of lemon grass as an adjunct of citronella, and the industry offers promising possibilities.

The products of the coconut-palm have been dealt with in a special article, but no reference has so far been made to the areca-palm, which bulks very largely in the social and industrial life of Ceylon. No luxury is more esteemed by the natives of India as well as of Ceylon than the areca nut. Wrapped in a leaf of the betel-tree, and with the addition of a little lime to give increased pungency to the whole, it is chewed by all sorts and conditions of men and women. At every street corner almost are to be seen vendors of the nut, and no row of boutiques, as the smaller shops are called, is complete without an establishment at which the article is sold. The local consumption must be enormous, but that it is only a part of the whole is demonstrated by the Customs returns. In 1905 the exports reached 125,565 cwts., and their total value was Rs. 1,525,916. All but about 10,000 cwts. went to British India. The areca-palm grows all over the low-country, and has been introduced with success in some hilly districts up to 3,000 ft. elevation. In some cases the tree has been planted to mark the boundary between estates, and the step has proved financially successful. The total area under the tree is estimated at 70,000 acres.

To other products which are included within the scope of this article, such as croton seed, palm and jaggery sugar, only passing allusion can be made. Nor is it necessary to do more than note briefly that cinchona, which once filled a big place in the planters' horizon, has receded into the background until the exports in 1905 were only 152,397 lbs., against 15,892,078 lbs. in 1887, when the industry was at high-water mark; and to record further that tobacco is steadily forging ahead as a crop, though it must be confessed that the "Jaffna cigars," made of local tobacco, do not find much favour outside native circles in the island.

A SINHALESE GIRL OF THE RODIYA CASTE.

POPULATION:

THE ISLAND'S RACES, RELIGIONS, LANGUAGES, CASTES, AND CUSTOMS

BY THE HON. MR. P. ARUNACHALAM, M.A. (CANTAB.);

CEYLON CIVIL SERVICE; MEMBER OF THE LEGISLATIVE COUNCIL OF CEYLON; BARRISTER-AT-LAW, LINCOLN'S INN.

THE total population of Ceylon returned at the last decennial census (March 31, 1901) was 3,578,333. Excluding the military, the shipping, and the 4,914 South African prisoners-of-war then in the island, the population was 3,565,954. The estimated population at the middle of 1906 was 3,968,541, or close on four millions. The increase of population in the decade 1891–1901 was at the rate of 18·6 per cent., or double the increase in the United Kingdom of Great Britain and Ireland in the period.

The population at the last census was distributed over 28 towns, 12,870 villages, 598,076 houses, and 664,311 families. The area of Ceylon (25,400 square miles) is about the same as Greece, or as Belgium and Holland together, about one-fifth less than Scotland or Ireland, and about one-half the size of England and Wales. The average density of the population of Ceylon at the census was 141 persons to a square mile, each person occupying an average area of 4·5 acres, and the average distance separating him from his nearest neighbour being 159 yards. The conditions of the island in this respect are about the same as those of Scotland or Ireland.

The provinces of Ceylon greatly vary as well in area as in the proportion of the population which they contribute to the island's total. The table annexed (Table A) gives information on this head.

TABLE A.

THE PROVINCES OF CEYLON, THEIR AREA, DENSITY OF POPULATION, AND PERCENTAGE OF TOTAL AREA AND TOTAL POPULATION—CENSUS 1901.

Province.	Area in Square Miles.	Persons.	Persons per Square Mile.	Percentage of Total Area.	Percentage of Total Population.
CEYLON	25,332	3,565,954	141	—	—
Western Province	1,432	920,683	643	5·65	25·82
Central Province	2,299½	622,832	271	9·08	17·47
Northern Province	3,363¼	340,936	101	13·28	9·56
Southern Province	2,146¼	566,736	264	8·47	15·89
Eastern Province	4,036½	173,602	43	15·93	4·87
North-Western Province	2,996⅞	353,626	118	11·83	9·92
North-Central Province	4,002¼	79,110	20	15·8	2·22
Province of Uva	3,154½	186,674	59	12·46	5·23
Province of Sabaragamuwa	1,901⅛	321,755	169	7·5	9·02

The average size of a province is 2,815 square miles, and the average population 396,217. The bulk of the island population is settled along the coast. The province with the smallest area, the Western Province (in which the capital, Colombo, is situated), has the largest population. With about 6 per cent. of the total area of the island, it holds more than one-fourth of the total population. The Southern Province, with 8½ per cent. of the total area, contains 16 per cent. of the total population. The Central Province, with 9 per cent. of the total area, has 17½ per cent. of the total population, a percentage which must be reduced by half if the Tamil immigrant population, which is the creation, as it is the basis, of the tea industry, and which exceeds the indigenous Sinhalese population, be excluded. The Eastern and North-Central Provinces, the largest provinces in the island, which between them cover nearly one-third of the whole area of the island, hold only 7 per cent. (5 and 2 per cent. respectively) of the population.

The unequal distribution of the population in the island is chiefly due to the presence or absence of large towns or centres of industry—which, again, are mainly the result, direct or indirect, of European enterprise—and to the proportion of mountainous area. The Western Province, which contains the metropolis and four other important towns, has the high average of 643 persons to the square mile, and is more than twice as densely populated as any other province. The only other provinces which contain over 200 persons per square mile are the Central (271) and Southern (264). From 100 to 200 persons per square mile are contained by the Northern (101), North-Western (118), and Sabaragamuwa (169) Provinces; while in the Uva, Eastern, and North-Central Provinces the density dwindles to 59, 43, and 20 persons, respectively, per square mile.

The population, area, and density of population of the various districts are shown in Table B:—

TABLE B.

DISTRICTS OF CEYLON, THEIR POPULATION, AREA, AND DENSITY—CENSUS 1901.

District.	Population.	Area in Square Miles.	Number of Persons per Square Mile.
Western Province.			
Colombo Municipality	154,691	10	15,469
Colombo District (exclusive of the Municipality)	387,886	550¾	704
Negombo District	148,249	247½	599
Kalutara District	229,857	623¾	369
Central Province.			
Kandy District	377,591	911	414
Matale District	92,203	925⅝	100
Nuwara Eliya District	153,038	462⅞	331
Northern Province.			
Jaffna District	300,851	1,265	238
Mannar District	24,926	943¼	26
Mullaitivu District	15,159	1,154¾	13
Southern Province.			
Galle District	258,116	652¼	396
Matara District	203,750	481¼	423
Hambantota District	104,870	1,012¾	104
Eastern Province.			
Batticaloa District	145,161	2,871½	51
Trincomalee District	28,441	1,165	24
North-Western Province.			
Kurunegala District	249,429	1,844⅞	135
Puttalam District	29,779	889¾	33
Chilaw District	74,418	262¼	284
North-Central Province.			
Anuradhapura District	79,110	4,002¼	20
Province of Uva.			
Badulla District	186,674	3,154⅝	59
Province of Sabaragamuwa.			
Ratnapura District	132,964	1,259	106
Kegalla District	188,791	642	294

Annexed is a map illustrating the comparative density of the population in the different districts of Ceylon. It should be borne in mind, however, that the districts are "hatched" according to the average struck between the densities of their constituent divisions, and that these densities show great variation. The Jaffna district, for instance, is "hatched" to represent an average density of between 100 and 250 persons per square mile. But the density ranges in its thirteen divisions from one person per square mile in Tunukkai to 2,469 in Jaffna division, while two divisions (Valikamam north and west) hold each between 1,000 and 2,000 persons, three divisions (Vadamaradchi west, Valikamam east, and the islands) each between 500 and 1,000, one between 400 and 500, two between 100 and 250, and three between 1 and 100. Then, as regards the North-Central Province or Anuradhapura district, the average shown of 20 persons to the square mile is apt to mislead, unless it is remembered that the population of 79,110 persons is far from equally distributed over the 4,000 square miles which constitute the area of the district, but is chiefly fixed in a compact space within the outlying forests, which are of vast extent and uninhabited.

It is interesting to compare the present distribution of population with that recorded under the native rulers 600 years ago. Of the three great divisions of the island, *Pihiti* or *Raja rata*, so called from its containing the ancient seats of royalty, embraced all that part of the island north of the Mahaveli Ganga; the *Ruhunurata* (of which the name still lingers in Ranna or Rohana in Tangalla district) embraced the mountainous zone and the region which rose up to it ladder-wise (rohana) from the western, southern, and eastern seas, and was bounded on the north by the rivers Mahaveli Ganga and Kalu Ganga; the *Mayarata* lay between these two rivers, the mountain zone, and the western coast, and was bounded on the north by the river Dedu-ru-Oya. The Pihiti or Raja rata corresponds, roughly, with the present Northern and North-Central Provinces, the Puttalam district of the North-Western Province, part of the Central Province, and the Trincomalee district north of the Mahaveli Ganga; the Ruhunurata corresponds with the rest of the Central and Eastern Provinces, the Sabaragamuwa and Uva Provinces, and the Southern Province; the Mayarata with the Western and North-Western Provinces, exclusive of the Puttalam district.

The Sinhalese chronicle, Rajavaliya, relates that in 1301 A.D. King Parakrama Bahu III., on the eve of his death, reminded his sons that, having conquered the Tamils, he had united under one rule the three kingdoms of the island, the Pihitirata with 450,000 villages, Ruhunurata with 770,000, and Mayarata with 250,000, or a total of 1,470,000 villages. Taking only a million villages, and allowing two houses to a village and five persons to a house, the population would be ten millions.

This can hardly be deemed an extravagant estimate. As Sir Emerson Tennent observes in his work on Ceylon (1859): "The labour necessary to construct one of these gigantic irrigation works" (with the ruins of which the island is strewn) "is in itself an evidence of local density of population; but their multiplication by successive kings, and the constantly recurring record of district after district brought under civilisation in each successive reign, demonstrate the steady increase of inhabitants and the multitude of husbandmen whose combined and sustained toil was indispensable to keep these prodigious structures in productive activity. . . . No one who has visited the regions, now silent and deserted, once the homes of millions, can hesitate to believe that when the island was in the zenith of its prosperity the population of Ceylon must of necessity have been at least ten times as great as it is at the present day." The decline was due to the troublous times of foreign war and internecine strife that preceded the establishment of the British dominion. How rapidly a population may decline was illustrated by Germany during the Thirty Years' War (1618–48 A.D.). The population fell from twenty to less than ten millions in that period.

At the beginning of the fourteenth century, then (according to King Parakrama Bahu's death-bed address to his sons) the population was distributed in the three regions in the proportion of 31 per cent. in Pihitirata, 52 per cent. in Ruhunurata, and 17 per cent. in Mayarata. At present the proportion stands, roughly, as 19, 46, and 35. The most striking change is the advance, by over 100 per cent., of the last region, the western sea coast and its vicinity, and the decline by almost as much in the population of the ancient kingdoms—a decline more marked still, if, excluding the Jaffna peninsula, we consider the true "royal" country the Anuradhapura, the Mullaitivu, and Mannar districts, which, embracing about one-fourth of the total area of the island, hold less than 3 per cent. of the total population.

The change indicates clearly the difference caused in the condition of the island by the disorganisation of its great irrigation system and the consequent decay of the national industry, rice cultivation, and by the advent of Europeans. Population and wealth have faded away from their ancient seats and gathered towards the west coast. The island, no longer self-sufficient or self-centred, is dependent for its prosperity mainly on foreign enterprise, on the European capitalist and planter, and the South Indian labourer and tradesman. The wealth that trickles from this source, circulating through the country, maintains among the native population an air of prosperity, which will hardly long survive the stoppage by any cause of the fountain, unless new sources of wealth are created and maintained by indigenous labour and energy.

England in the fourteenth century was, in respect of population and prosperity, hardly better off than Ceylon. A writer in the "Encyclopædia Britannica" (edition 1902, vol. 26, p. 675) says: "The population of England from the Conquest to the fourteenth century is estimated at between 1½ and 2½ millions. London, it is believed, had a population of about 40,000. Other towns were small. Two or three of the larger had four or five thousand inhabitants. The only substantial building in a village, apart perhaps from the manor-house, was the church, used for many secular as well as religious purposes. In the towns the mud or wood paved huts sheltered a people who, accepting a common poverty, traded in little more than the necessaries of life (Green, 'Town Life in the Fifteenth Century,' i. 13). The population was stationary. Famine and pestilence were of frequent occurrence (Creighton, 'Epidemics in Britain,' p. 19), and for the careless there was waste at harvest time and want in winter. Hunger was the drill sergeant of society." What a change to a population of 32½ millions, a public revenue of 140 millions sterling, and the sovereignty of a world-wide empire! Not by "flying with others' wings" was this high place won. Only by ceaseless energy and the strenuous pursuit of high ideals has England been able to raise herself and "soar triumphant through the lips of men."

"Town" and "village" are ordinarily words of somewhat vague application in Ceylon, and are not easily defined and distinguished. Size, compactness, and certain architectural or industrial features enter into the definition of a town. There are also certain social characteristics to be considered. A most marked feature of a village is the close bond uniting all its inhabitants. The relations subsisting between them subsisted between their fathers, grandfathers, and remoter ancestors. The farmer holds the land his father held, and his ploughmen are the descendants of his father's. The simple wants

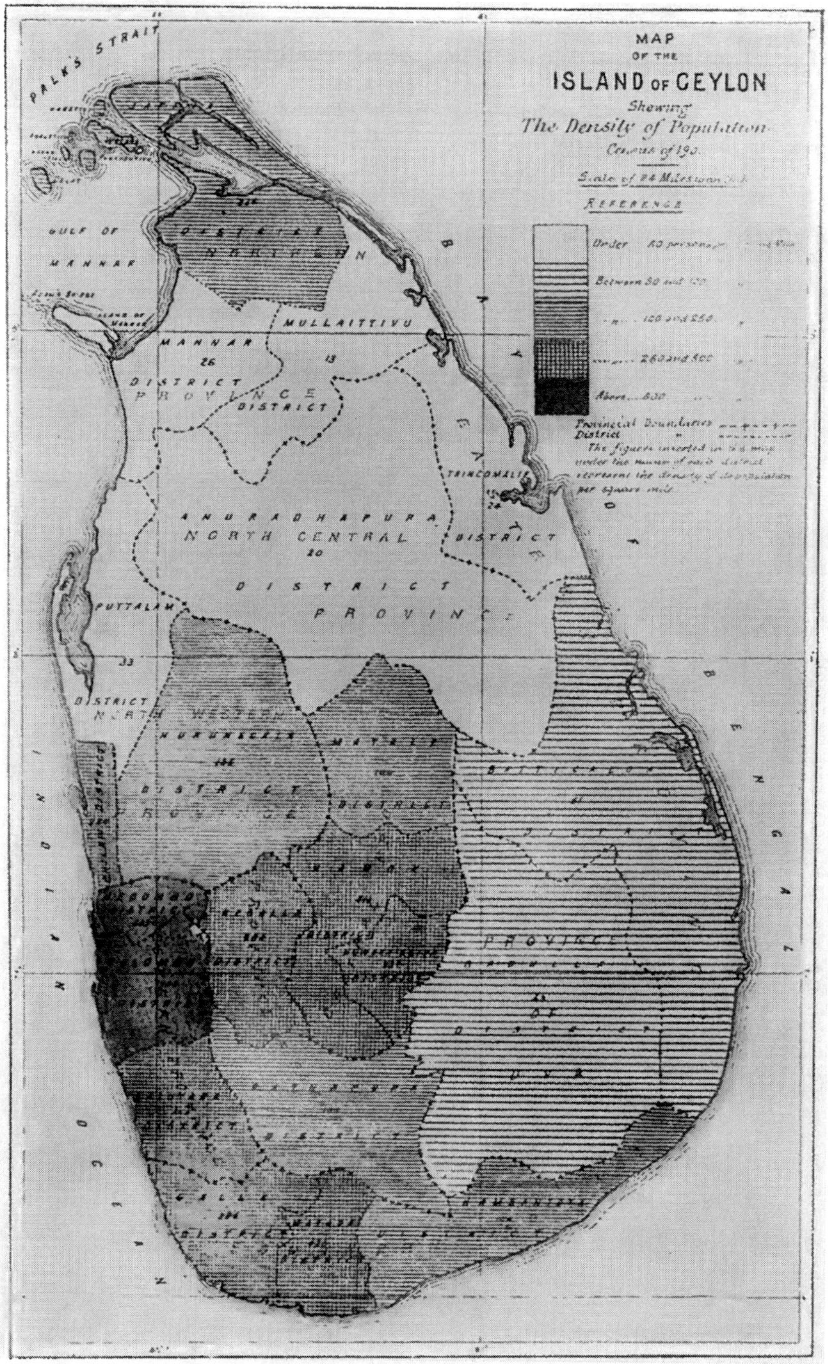

of the village are supplied by the village artisans. The inhabitants are washed for by the village dhoby and shaved by the village barber. As the village increases in size, the hereditary artisans are no longer capable of supplying all its requirements. Strangers enter and settle in the village. New influences arise, and the social constitution of the community is radically changed. The village headman is overshadowed by the comparatively wealthy shopkeeper and the sharp lawyer. The authority of the old heads of the community is weakened, the depressed classes assert their independence, their old masters no longer take a paternal interest in them. The transition is sometimes slow and sometimes rapid. The construction of a new public work or the opening of a new railway station may bring about the change in a year or two, while at times a village may go on increasing in size without ceasing to be an aggregation of hamlets and acquiring an urban character.

Villages sometimes disappear, especially in those outlying parts of the island where villages shift from year to year, or have been abandoned in the people's search for water for cultivation, or in their fear of the *genius loci* suddenly turning malignant and visiting them, their cattle or poultry, with sickness and death. The mode of life and the system of exploiting the soil in these regions are not unlike that of Horace's "rigidi Getæ":—

> "Immetata quibus jugera liberas
> Fruges et Cererem ferunt,
> Nec cultura placet longior annua."

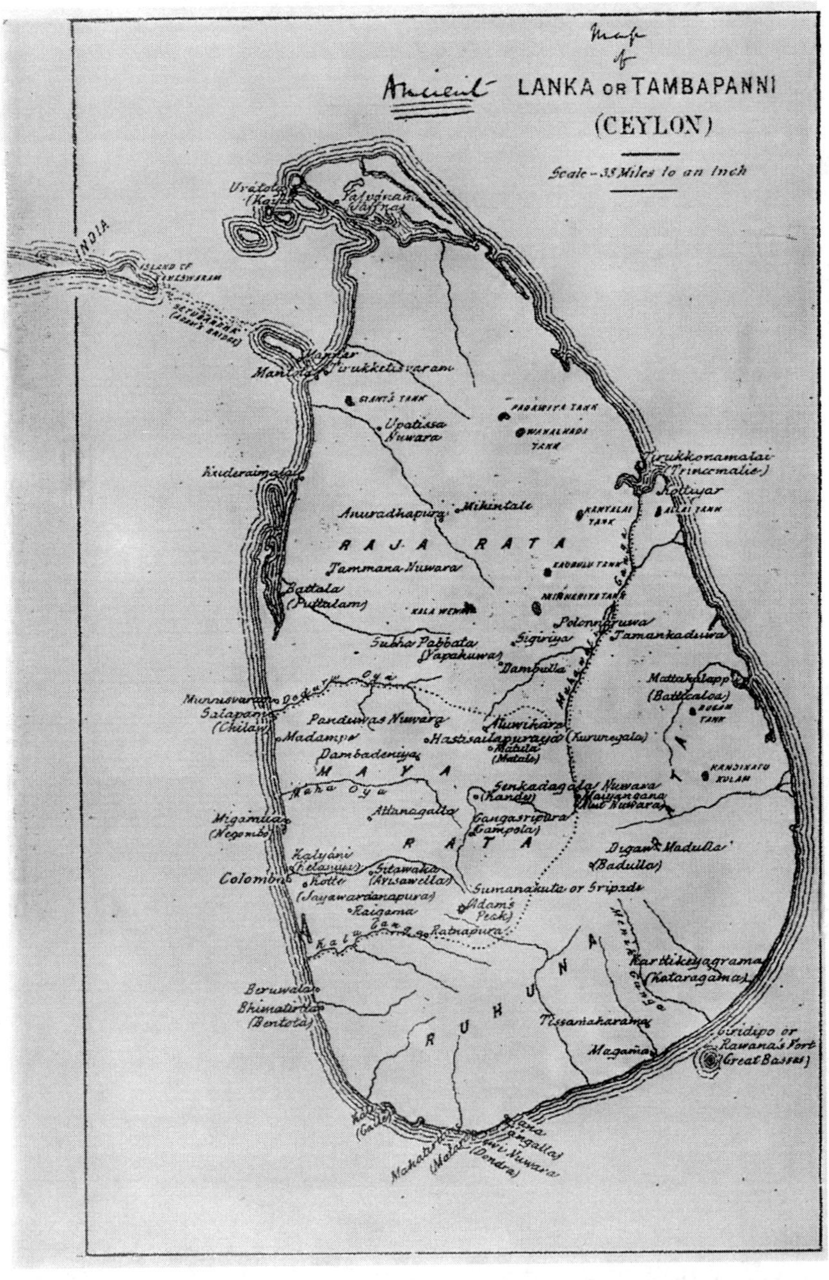

Robert Knox, who in the seventeenth century spent twenty years of captivity in the island, says in his very interesting "Relation of the Island of Ceylon" (published in London in 1681): "And, as I said before of their cities so I must of their towns, that there are many of them here and there lie desolate, occasioned by their voluntary forsaking them, which they often do in case many of them fall sick and two or three die soon after one another; for this they conclude to happen from the hand of the devil: whereupon they all leave their town and go to another, thinking thereby to avoid him: thus relinquishing both their houses and lands too. Yet afterwards, when they think the devil hath departed the place, some will some time come back and resume their lands again."

At the census of 1901 there were 28 towns and 12,870 villages. The urban population numbered 418,970 and the rural population 3,146,984. The urban population constituted 11·8 per cent. of the total population, and the rural 88·2 per cent.: a great contrast to England, where the proportions are 77 and 23 per cent. respectively.

The population of the 28 towns, their area, and density are shown in the following table. The population varies from over 150,000 in the town of Colombo to less than 1,000 in Vavuniya.

Colombo, which at the census of 1901 had a population of 155,000 and probably has now close on 200,000, is the "Clapham Junction" of ships voyaging in the East. It has been an important city for at least 600 years. Ibn Batuta, a Moorish traveller from Tangiers, who visited Ceylon, 1347 A.D., on a pilgrimage to Adam's Peak, speaks of "Kolamba" as "the finest and largest city in Serendib."

The trade of the island was exceedingly valuable, and embraced not only (as now) pearls, gems, spices, and elephants, for which the island was celebrated from remote times, but the products of Eastern and Southern Asia, brought here by the Chinese to be exchanged for the wares brought by the Arabs from the countries beyond the Euphrates. The Arabs were masters of the Indian seas and trade from the tenth to the fifteenth centuries, when they were ousted by the Portuguese.

Among the exports of the island, cinnamon was the most prized. It was a luxury so rare as to be a suitable gift for a king, so costly that a crown of cinnamon tipped with gold was a becoming offering to the gods. It is believed to have been originally obtained by the Arabs from Eastern Africa, and to have gained a footing in India and afterwards in Ceylon, where, favoured by natural conditions of climate and soil, the Ceylon variety became the most perfect sample, and grew wild in the woods. Strangely enough there is no reference to Ceylon cinnamon in the account of the travels of Marco Polo, who, towards the end of the thirteenth century, visited Ceylon on his homeward route to Venice from China, where he had for seventeen years resided at the court of the Emperor Kubla Khan.

"And the king of this island," says Marco Polo, "possesses a ruby which is the finest and biggest in the world. . . . You must know the great khan sent an embassy and begged the king, as a favour greatly desired, to sell him this ruby, offering to give him for it the ransom of a city, or in fact what the king would. But the king replied that on no account whatever would he sell it, for it had come to him from his ancestors. Furthermore you must know that in the land of Seilan there is an exceeding high mountain. . . . Now it befel that the great khan heard how on that mountain there was the sepulchre of our first father Adam, and that some of his hair and of his teeth and the dish from which he used to eat were still preserved there. So he thought he would get hold of them somehow or another, and despatched a great embassy for the purpose in the year of Christ 1284. The ambassadors with a great company travelled on by sea and by land until they arrived at the island of Seilan and presented themselves before the king, and they were so urgent with the king that they succeeded in getting two of his grinder teeth, which were passing great and thick, and they also got some of the hair and the dish from which the great personage used to eat, which is of a very beautiful green porphyry."[1]

The earliest reference to Ceylon cinnamon is by Ibn Batuta, the Moorish traveller. He landed at Puttalam and found the shore "covered with cinnamon wood, which the merchants of Malabar transport without any other price than a few articles of clothing which are given as presents to the king. This may be attributed to the circumstance that it is brought down by the mountain torrents and left in great heaps upon the shore." He found the greatest king in the island to be the Tamil king of Jaffna, Arya Chakravati, who had a powerful fleet commanding the western coast, and under whose protection he accomplished the pilgrimage to Adam's Peak *viâ* Chilaw and "Konakar" (? Kurunegala), extending his journey to the temple at "Dinaur" (Devinuwara, the Dondra Head of English maps) and returning by way of "Kale" (Galle) and "Kolamba" (Colombo), "the finest and largest city in Serendib."

Galle and Jaffna are still the second and third towns in Ceylon. Far older than these or Colombo is the "buried city" of Anuradhapura, the "Anuro-Grammum" of Ptolemy. It was founded about 500 B.C., and became the capital about 437 B.C., with a fairly complete municipal organisation and excellent sanitary and administrative arrangements, which are described in the ancient Sinhalese chronicle, the Mahavansa. Its glory increased when the kings of Ceylon embraced Buddhism (about 300 B.C.), and a branch of the sacred Bo-tree, under which Buddha had attained wisdom, was

[1] Colonel Yule's "Travels of Marco Polo," vol. ii., p. 295.

TABLE C.

TOWNS IN CEYLON, THEIR POPULATION, AREA, AND DENSITY.

Name of Town.	Population, 1901.	Area in Square Miles.	Number of Persons per Square Mile.
Western Province.			
Colombo	154,691	10	15,469
Moratuwa	29,600	8 1/5	3,610
Negombo	19,819	7 1/4	2,734
Kalutara	11,500	1 2/3	6,900
Panadure...	3,845	1	3,845
Central Province.			
Kandy	26,386	11	2,399
Matale	4,951	1/4	19,804
Nuwara Eliya	5,026	4 7/8	1,031
Gampola	3,791	2/3	5,686
Nawalapitiya	2,454	9/32	8,502
Northern Province.			
Jaffna	33,879	7 1/2	4,517
Mannar	5,332	1	5,332
Mullaitivu	1,308	3	436
Vavuniya...	566	2 1/4	252
Southern Province.			
Galle	37,165	6 1/2	5,718
Matara	11,848	1 1/2	7,899
Weligama	7,583	2 1/2	3,033
Hambantota	2,843	1 1/2	1,895
Tangalla	2,333	1/6	13,998
Eastern Province.			
Batticaloa	9,969	1 1/4	7,975
Trincomalee	11,295	1	11,295
North-Western Province.			
Kurunegala	6,483	1 1/2	4,322
Puttalam	5,115	8 5/8	593
Chilaw	4,168	3/4	5,557
North-Central Province.			
Anuradhapura	3,672	5 3/8	683
Province of Uva.			
Badulla	5,924	3 1/32	1,954
Province of Sabaragamuwa.			
Ratnapura	4,084	2 1/4	1,815
Kegalla	2,340	7/8	2 674

brought here from Northern India. The tree still flourishes at Anuradhapura, the oldest historical tree in the world and the object of profound veneration to millions of Buddhists throughout the world. The Chinese traveller, Fa Hian, who visited Anuradhapura about 412 A.D. and remained there two years engaged in transcribing the sacred books, describes vividly the splendour and magnificence of the city and of the national religion and the prosperity of the island. Anuradhapura remained the capital continuously till 850 A.D., and occasionally afterwards till the end of the eleventh century. The subsequent centuries of neglect made it a scene of wildest desolation, till thirty years ago the British Government turned its attention to the town and district, restoring the ancient tanks, reviving agriculture, establishing hospitals and dispensaries. The population of the town in 1881 was 1,301, and by 1901 had slowly risen to 3,672.

The sacred tree attracts crowds of pilgrims, especially at the full moons of May, June, and July. About twenty or thirty thousand pilgrims come on these occasions. There are no houses for their reception, but under the grand umbrageous trees of the park-like environs of the city they erect their little booths and picnic in the open air. As the height of the festival approaches, the place becomes instinct with life. Men, women, and children revel in the luxury of the copious streams of water that course by the sides of the streets from the stupendous tanks. The town resounds all day with shouts of "Sadhu! sadhu!" from relays of pilgrims, as they walk through the ancient streets or bow before the sacred tree reverently with offerings of fragrant flowers. The tree has its trunk enveloped in cloth and its branches decorated with flags, while at night countless lamps illuminate the square in which it stands. In a few days the pilgrims are gone, and the city reverts to its normal condition of peaceful solitude.

Of the 3,565,954 persons returned at the census of 1901, 1,458,320, or 4·09 per cent., were low-country Sinhalese; 872,487, or 24·4 per cent., were Kandyan Sinhalese; or, in all, 2,330,807, or 65·3 per cent., were Sinhalese; 951,740, or 26·7 per cent., were Tamils; 228,034, or 6·4 per cent., were Moors; 23,482, or 0·7 per cent., were Burghers and Eurasians; 11,902, or 0·3 per cent., were Malays; 6,300, or 0·2 per cent., were Europeans; 3,971, or 0·1 per cent., were Veddahs; and 9,718, or 0·3 per cent., were "others."

The numbers of the various races, and the proportion of each to 1,000 of the total population at the census of 1901, and as estimated for the middle of 1906, are shown below.

It will be seen that since the census of 1901 the proportion of the various races has decreased, except the Tamils, who show an increase of 17·3 per 1,000, a result due mainly to the excess of arrivals over departures of Indian Tamil coolies.

A TAMBY (MOORMAN).

The Sinhalese and Tamils are the most numerous races of the island, and together constitute 92 per cent. of the population. They have lived here for over 2,000 years, whether in friendly intercourse and the harmonious development of the country or in the fierce conflict of war and devastation. In course of time they have settled in distinct parts of the island, except in and near the larger towns and the tea districts, where they are intermixed, and where the Tamil element is chiefly an immigrant population from India, and sometimes (as in the Central Province) exceeds the Sinhalese. Speaking generally, the Sinhalese inhabit the hilly zone and the fertile and wet Western and Southern Provinces (where they attain their greatest density), in the greater part of the North-Western Province, and in the sparsely populated regions of the North-Central Province and Lower Uva. The indigenous Tamils occupy the northern and eastern coasts, and their real centre is the densely populated peninsula of Jaffna, which is nearest to India, and where they live almost to the exclusion of every other race. Mannar and Puttalam are Tamil districts, and there is a large admixture of Tamil blood and speech in the Sinhalese districts of Chilaw and Negombo.

A broad belt of forest separates the purely Sinhalese from the purely Tamil zone. This belt, almost uninhabited, and in many parts completely so, begins to the east of Sabaragamuwa. It is about 20 miles broad near Lower Uva, and expands to 40 miles in Anuradhapura district and 60 miles in the north of the island. This forest and the open park country adjoining it on the east is the abode of the Veddahs, a race which, from the low order of its intellectual development, from the defects in its physical organisation, and from its primitive habits, which long isolation in the woods has tended to preserve in a remarkable manner, presents a most interesting subject for the study of ethnography.

TABLE D.

RACE DISTRIBUTION OF THE POPULATION.

Race.	Census, 1901.	Middle of 1906.	Proportion to 1,000.	
			Census, 1901.	Middle of 1906.
Europeans	6,300	6,484	1·8	1·6
Burghers	23,482	24,588	6·6	6·2
Sinhalese	2,330,807	2,547,355	653·7	641·9
Tamils	951,740	1,127,978	266 9	284·2
Moors	228,034	237,221	63·9	59·8
Malays	11,902	12,003	3·3	3·0
Others	13,689	12,912	3·8	3·3
All Races	3,565,954	3,968,541	1,000·0	1,000·0

The Veddahs represent the aboriginal population of Ceylon, and are generally supposed to be the posterity of the Yakkhus and Nagas whom, according to the ancient Sinhalese, chronicles, the first Sinhalese king, Vijaya, found on his arrival in Ceylon (*circa* 540 B.C.). Very little is known of these aboriginal tribes. They were a branch of a prehistoric, probably Dravidian, race which colonised South India and Ceylon. The term "Yaksha," which is the Sanskrit original of "Yakkhu," is in the Indian epic, the Ramayana, and other Indian traditions, applied to a race of spirits whose chief was Kuvera, king of Lanka, who was dispossessed by his half-brother, the famous Ravana, and is now regarded as the regent of the Northern quarter of the world and as the god of wealth. The Yakshas were akin to, if not identical with, the Nagas, the Dragon race. They appear to have attained a high state of civilisation, and the names of Nagapatam in the Madras Presidency, of Nagpore, in the Central Provinces of India, and of the Naga hills, the north-easterly offshoot of the Himalayas, attest the wide extent of the ancient Naga dominion. Long before the Vijayan invasion Mahayangama (now called Alutnuwara), in the Bintenne division of Uva, had been one of their chief cities, and Gautama Buddha, on his first visit to Ceylon, is said to have descended on "the agreeable Mahanaga garden, in the assembling place of the Yakkhus," a site marked by the ruins of a great dagoba built about 300 B.C., and still a great place of Buddhist pilgrimage. It was the "Maagrammum" of Ptolemy, who describes it as "the metropolis of Taprobane beside the great river" (Mahaveli Ganga). The modern representatives of this ancient race are the fast dwindling Veddahs of Ceylon and the Bhils, Santals, and other wild tribes of India.

Vijaya, on his arrival, married (under circumstances[1] which recall the meeting of Ulysses and Circe in the "Odyssey") Kuveni, a Yakkhu princess of great beauty and much influence among her countrymen. With her aid he suppressed the Yakkhus and established his power, fixing his capital at Tambapanna, also called Tammana Nuwara. He then basely discarded her for a Tamil princess of South India. Kuveni, seeking refuge among her own people, whom she had betrayed, was killed by them. Another tradition says that the deserted queen flung herself, with curses on her husband, from a rock called after her Yakdessagala ("The Rock of the Yakkha's Curse"), one of the hills that give picturesqueness to the town of Kurunegala. Tonigala ("The Rock of Lamentations"), and Vilakatupota ("The Vale of Tears"), both in the Kurunegala district, are also associated with her sorrows.

[1] Mahavansa, i., pp. 32, 33; and "Odyssey," x., 274 *et seq.*

Kuveni Asna, which relates the story of her love and sorrows, says that in agonising shrieks she wailed: "When shipwrecked and forlorn, I found thee and thy men food and home. I helped thee to rout the Yakkhus and raised thee to be king. Pledging me thy troth, thou madest me thy spouse. Didst not thou know *then* that I was of the Yakkhu race? Loving thee with unquenchable love and living in such love, I bore thee children. How canst thou leave me and love another? The gentle rays of the rising full moon are now to me the blaze of a red-hot ball of iron; the cool, spicy breezes of the sandal groves are hot and unwelcome; the cuckoo's sweet song pierces my ears as with a spear. Alas! how shall I soothe my bleeding heart?"

Her children, a son and a daughter, whom she bore to Vijaya, escaped the fate of their mother by the intervention of their uncle, who fled with them into the forest near Adam's Peak. There the brother and sister are said to have intermarried and founded a wild race, who kept aloof from their neighbours, and from whom the region was called Sabaragamuwa, the land of the barbarian (*habara* or *sabara*). As this tract became colonised by the Sinhalese the Yakkhus retreated into the forests of Wėlassa and Batticaloa, and became the Veddahs or "hunters" of Ceylon.

There are other legends, curious and extravagant, which assign a different origin. According to one of these, King Vijaya's nephew and successor, Panduvasa, was, as the result of the perjury committed by Vijaya in repudiating his marriage with Kuveni and of her curses, afflicted, like him, with a dire

NATU KOTTE CHETTIES.

disease called the *divi dosa.*[1] The gods consulted on the means of restoring him to health, and found that it could be effected only by one not born of woman. Rahu was commissioned by Sakra, the king of the gods, to find out such a person, and discovered Mala Raja, king of Malawadesa, who had sprung from a flower. Rahu thereupon concerted a plan for bringing him to Ceylon. He proceeded to India, and, assuming the form of a boar, laid waste the gardens of Mala Raja, to the consternation of the gardeners, who fled to the palace and informed the king of what was passing. The king, who was a keen sportsman, ordered his men to surround the garden and drive the boar towards him. Thus pressed, the boar made directly towards the place where the king stood. The king shot his arrow, but the boar received not the smallest injury, and continued his flight. The king, with his attendants, gave pursuit. The boar leaped into the sea and landed in Ceylon at Uratota ("Hog-ferry"), the chief port of the north,[1] and, traversing the forests and hills, made a breach in the Kurunegala chain of rocks at Uru-pa-kada. The king came up with the beast on the hill at Hantane, near Kandy, attacked it sword in hand, and with the first blow inflicted a deep gash. On receiving this wound, the boar became transformed into a rock, now called Uragala ("Hog-rock"), which is said to retain the mark of the wound. Mala Raja, who was unable to comprehend the meaning of the marvels he had just witnessed, received a visit from Sakra and other gods, who explained the mystery, and that the object of drawing him to Ceylon was to break the charm under which Panduvasa laboured. Mala Raja complied with the wishes of the gods, and ordered the Kohomba Yak dance to be performed. This drove the sickness out of the king into a rock to the north of Kandy, still called Divi-dos-gala, or "The Rock of the *Divi* Sickness." The king thereafter returned to Malawadesa, leaving most of his attendants in Ceylon, at the desire of the grateful Panduvasa, who allotted them the forests as their exclusive possession, so that they might enjoy their favourite diversion of hunting. The Veddahs are said to be their descendants.

A MALAY.

Another legend says that a young king of the island was very cruel and addicted to many vices; that he even killed and ate men, a crime held in the utmost abhorrence; that he was taken by his subjects and condemned, together with his ministers, either to lose their lives or to remain so closely immured in the forest as never more to be seen. The second alternative was chosen, and the king and his ministers, in obedience to the sentence, never came forth from the woods, and founded the race now known as Veddahs.

The term "Veddah" means "hunter," and is indicative of their mode of life. There are two classes of Veddahs at the present day, viz., the *Gan* (village) Veddahs, who have been domesticated and brought under humanising influences, and the *Kele* (forest) Veddahs, otherwise called *Dada* (game) Veddahs, who dwell in the recesses of the woods and subsist upon the fruits of the chase.

The "forest Veddahs" are squalid in appearance, of moderate stature, and of active habits. They are good marksmen, using as weapons bows and arrows, with which they kill the wild boar, stag, and elk abounding in their forests. They eat meat, either dried in the sun or preserved in honey. They live in rude huts covered with leaves or grass, prefer caves in the rainy season, and change their residence frequently in the year. Their dress is a string tied round the loins with a thick belt of leaves. With other races they hold no intercourse, and they speak a dialect of their own which is not understood by their Sinhalese and Tamil neighbours, though it contains an admixture of Sinhalese and Tamil words.

They rarely venture out of their boundaries.

[1] Variously translated as "the affliction caused by the gods" (*deva*) or "by the tiger" (*divi*, Skt. *dvipin*), which form Kuveni is said to have assumed to wreak vengeance on him, or "the affliction (resulting from) the (false) oath" (Skt. *divya*, oath, the root of which occurs in Sin. *divuruma*). The disease is said to have been a compound of cough, asthma, fever, diabetes, and consumption.

[1] Called in the English maps by its Dutch name Kayts, and usually called by the Tamils *Uraturai*, *turai* being the Tamil for ferry. Tamil scholars write the name as *Ur-kavatturai*=the ferry which guards the country; rather a forced derivation.

and then only for the purpose of exchanging honey, wax, skins, ivory, or venison for axes, arrow-points, &c. Their mode of trade retains somewhat of the mysteriousness recorded of old by Pliny from the mouths of the Sinhalese ambassadors to the Roman Emperor Claudius: these native tribes "go to the further side of some river, where wares and commodities are laid down by the strangers, and if the natives list to make exchange, they have them taken away and leave other merchandise in lieu thereof to content the foreign merchant." This singular characteristic is mentioned by the Arab geographer of the eleventh century, Albyrouni (who adds that the people who held these mysterious dealings were regarded as demons or savages), by the Portuguese historian Ribeiro, by the Dutch historian Valentyn, and by Knox, the English captive of King Raja Sinha.

Though a wild people, the habits of the Veddahs are thoroughly peaceable, not only among themselves, but also towards others. Conjugal fidelity, monogamy, and love for their children are said to be matters of course among them, though, strange to say, polygamy and even polyandry were till recently prevalent among their more enlightened neighbours, the Kandyans, to such an extent as to call for special legislation to prevent it.

Of the 3,971 Veddahs enumerated at the census of 1901, the great majority (2,859) were in the Eastern Province (2,345 in Batticaloa district, and 514 in Trincomalee district). There were 529 in Uva, 402 in Anuradhapura, 124 in Mullaitivu, 53 in Kurunegala. The purest Veddahs are to be found in the Nilgala and Bintenne divisions of Uva and in the Eastern Province, near the Maha-Oya and the Friar's Hood range. Notwithstanding their degraded condition they are held in high esteem by the Sinhalese. A report of 1820, published in the *Journal of the Ceylon Royal Asiatic Society*, says of the Uva Veddahs: "Both the wild and village Veddahs rank with the Vellalas (who claim to be the highest caste). When the more civilised Veddahs go to the house of a district chief of the Vellala caste, they receive water out of an earthen pot with a spout to it, a privilege that belongs only to the Vellalas." "While the Sinhalese," says Mr. Nevill ("Taprobanian," vol. i., p. 193), "held and hold the Veddah race to be most honourable, and had no reluctance to give their daughters to a Veddah (by Sinhalese I here mean the Goyiyas, *i.e.*, Vellalas), and were ready, and often eager, to marry Veddah girls, yet the Veddahs, as a rule, look down upon descendants of these mixed marriages, if sons, because they are not of pure blood."

The number of the Veddahs, the real wild race, is rapidly diminishing. Civilising influences are being brought to bear upon them, and they will soon be absorbed into the ranks of the Sinhalese and Tamils, and cease to exist as a distinct race. In fact many Veddahs, who have settled down to agricultural habits and live in the villages, already call themselves Tamils or Sinhalese, according to the nationality of the people amongst whom they dwell and with whom they intermarry. A praiseworthy attempt has been made under the auspices of the Wesleyan Mission to make the Veddahs of the Batticaloa district abandon their wandering habits and to raise them to a higher culture. A number of Veddahs have been brought together and a settlement formed, where they are fed and clothed at the Mission expense. Arrangements have also been made to teach carpentry to such of the younger men and boys as are not wedded to nomadic life, but show an aptitude for industrial education.

The name and origin of the Sinhalese have exercised the ingenuity of historians and antiquaries, and the very etymology of the term "Sinhala" is still uncertain, and has been variously explained. The explanation suggested by the Portuguese historians is as far-fetched and fanciful as it is ingenious. According to them, "The Chinese having been, at a very remote period, the masters of Oriental commerce, some of their vessels were driven upon the coast near the district which they subsequently termed Chilaw; the marines and passengers saved themselves upon the rocks, and, finding the island fertile and prolific, soon established themselves upon it. Shortly afterwards the Malabars (*i.e.*, the Tamils), having discovered it, sent hither their exiles, whom they denominated 'Galas.' The exiles were not long in mixing with the Chinese, and from

A COLOMBO CHETTY.

the two names was formed at first Chingalas, and afterwards Chingalais" (Lee's Ribeiro's "History of Ceylon," p. 6).

The old Sinhalese chronicle, Mahavansa, explains it thus : "By reason of the King Sinhabahu having slain the *siha* (lion), his sons and descendants are called *Sihala* (the lion-slayers). This Lanka having been conquered by a Sihala, from the circumstance also of its having been colonised by a Sihala, it obtained the name Sihala." Another explanation is that Vijaya's father, Sinhababu, having sprung from a lion, his descendants received the distinctive appellation of Sinhala. The allusion is to the following legend. The king of Wanga, a principality of Maghada, had a beautiful daughter, whose union with a lion, when she came of age, was predicted by soothsayers, and who, notwithstanding the strict confinement in which she was therefore kept, contrived to elude the vigilance of her watchers and to run away from home. While passing through a wilderness she was carried away by a lion, and the prophecy was fulfilled. To the lion she bore a son and a daughter (twins), Sinhababu and Sinhawalli. The son in course of time grew ashamed of his sire, and in the end killed him. Sinhababu and Sinhawalli intermarried and begot a numerous offspring, of whom the first-born was Vijaya, the founder of the Sinhalese.

The term "Sinhalese" is said to mean lion-slayer, a meaning derived from the story in the Mahavansa. But nations have often derived their names from some accidental circumstance, and too much importance should not be attached to ingenious derivations. It is generally believed that the progenitors of the Sinhalese race were Aryan settlers from Maghada (the modern Behar), in North India. "According to tradition, both Indian and local," says Dr. Copleston, late Bishop of Colombo, and now the Metropolitan of India and Ceylon, "the Sinhalese are of Aryan race, and connected with the north of India; and this is borne out by language, customs, and subsequent history. The ancient North India poem Ramayana (dating from 500 B.C. at least) and the inscriptions of Asoka (230 B.C.) prove early intercourse between North India and the island, and the chronicles compiled in Pali in the fourth and fifth centuries A.D. out of the archives of the great Buddhist monastery at Anuradhapura (it is the peculiar distinction of the Sinhalese among Indian people to possess such histories) describe the establishment of the Buddhist religion in the island by Aryan influences in the third century B.C. These same chronicles ascribe, and with all probability, the previous civilisation of the island to Aryan immigration."

"The Sinhalese language is closely akin to the Sanskrit; that is, it is one of that group of Indo-Aryan languages of which Sanskrit is the literary type. It comes nearer, probably, to the Bengali than to any other of the present forms of this group. In its modern form its true characteristics are disguised by the abundance of words which it has borrowed in later times from the Sanskrit, just as the old English stock of words akin to Latin, but not borrowed from it, is overlaid by a later borrowing. For instance, 'man,' 'name,' and 'draw' correspond to the older and truer Sinhalese; 'human,' 'nomenclature,' 'attract,' to the modern element in it. But the Sinhalese is much nearer to the Sanskrit than the old elements of English are to the Latin. This old Sinhalese, or Elu,[1] is characterised, in comparison with Sanskrit, by lightness and brevity, avoiding long vowels, compound consonants, and long words. 'Raksha' is in Sinhalese 'raka,' 'manushya' is 'miniha,' 'kshira' is 'kiri,' &c. The pronouns, as 'ma,' 'me'; the numbers, all radically identical with our own; the verbal terminations 'mi,' 'si,' 'ti'; and not a few common words, which, in the course of change, have rested in a form like the English—such as dora, 'door,' band, 'bind,' &c.—show us that the Sinhalese language belongs to our own Aryan stock.

"It is probably a mistake to call Sinhalese a derivative of Pali, though this, being the sacred language of Buddhism, has greatly influenced Sinhalese. Like Pali, Sinhalese avoids all compounds of *r*, but, unlike Pali, it rejects double letters, and allows short diphthongs. Hence, the usual sequence of the three languages is represented by the series marga, magga, maga; or sreshta, settha, seta.

"During nearly the whole of its history Ceylon has been in close relations, sometimes hostile through invasions and occupations, sometimes friendly through alliance and settlements, with the Dravidian races of South India, especially the Tamil; and the Sinhalese language has been greatly affected, especially in the later three or four centuries, by the influence of Tamil, from which it has borrowed not only words but grammatical forms and inflections of verbs and nouns. The most usual form of plural in the modern Sinhalese is probably an imitation of the Tamil plural.[2] But there is no fundamental Dravidian element in the language.

"Many Portuguese words, names of things which the Portuguese introduced, have become naturalised in Sinhalese, and not only the words for 'table' (mese), 'bread' (pan), and 'carriage' (karatte), but that of the now characteristic 'hackery,' are of this origin. The Dutch language, coming afterwards, left far less trace, though a 'verandah' (itself a word which the English climate obliged us to borrow from the East) is still called an 'istoppuwa' ('stoep' at the Cape). The present prevalence of English in the maritime provinces is producing rather a jumble of both languages than a legitimate modification of the vernacular."

No definite conclusions are possible, however, as to the true ethnic origin of the Sinhalese and their relation to the Veddahs and the Tamils without a more searching investigation than the subject has yet received. The Sinhalese language, especially in its earlier, the Elu, form, has hardly been studied by philologists, much less the language of the Veddahs or of that interesting tribe of Rodiyas, the outcasts of the Ceylon highlands, who hold among the Sinhalese much the same position as the Parias of Tamil-land or the Cagots and Caqueux of the Pyrenees Valley. More important than the scientific study of the language is careful observation by anthropologists of the crania, facial features, bodily structure and proportion, microscopic structure of the hair, colour of the skin, &c., of the Veddahs, Rodiyas, Sinhalese, and Tamils. Studies have been conducted in this direction by Professor Virchow and by Drs. G. F. and P. B. Sarasin. But much remains to be done. Professor Virchow himself never visited Ceylon. The brothers Sarasin spent but a few months here, and only incidentally engaged in this inquiry. Better results would be obtained if these investigations, which demand abundance of local material and of time and labour, were systematically conducted by residents of the island, European as well as Sinhalese, and the recorded observations submitted for the opinion of scientists of the eminence of Professor Virchow. In the present state of knowledge it is possible to express only a reserved opinion that there is a greater affinity of the Veddahs with the Dravidian Tamils than with the Sinhalese; that the Sinhalese are a mixed race combining Aryan, Dravidian, Veddah, Mongolian, and Malay elements; and that the negritic element suggested by the French anthropologists is wanting, whether in the Veddah, the Tamil, or the Sinhalese.

The Veddah himself belongs probably to a proto-Dravidian or pre-Dravidian stream of invaders, who colonised Ceylon from India and attained a high state of civilisation, from which they have retrograded. Evidence of this is furnished by the reported greatness and splendour of their cities at the time of the arrival of the first batch of Sinhalese under Vijaya (*circa* 540 B.C.), by the high social status still accorded by the Sinhalese to the Veddahs, by their strict practice of monogamy, and by their use of costly jewels and even golden cooking pots till within recent times.

Speaking of their household equipments,

[1] The name Elu is derived from Sinhala rather than from the Tamil Ilam. The process of change was probably as follows: Sinhala, Sihala, Helu, Elu.

[2] For a long list of Tamil words adopted into the Sinhalese language, see pages 356–368 of Mudaliyar A. Mendis Gunasekara's "Comprehensive Grammar of the Sinhalese Language."

the late Mr. Nevill, of the Ceylon Civil Service, a distinguished antiquary and zoologist, writes ("Taprobanian," i., p. 188): "The wilder people will have a few earthen crocks or a copper one, a few bits of cord, some dried skins, and some empty gourds for honey. . . . Sinhalese who are old and intelligent, and who have lived among Veddahs. all agree that in ancient times Veddahs had no more furniture than this, but that they were often very rich and powerful. In such cases their wealth was put into golden cooking vessels and strings of gems, &c., for their women. The last of these gold vessels were lost by them during the long guerilla wars between the Kandyans of Welassa and Dumbura and Europeans, especially the English. The tradition is positive and seems reliable. Nilgala Banda, a splendid old Kandyan chief, now Ratemahatmaya of Lower Bintenne, whose ancestors have lived among the Veddahs of Nilgala from time immemorial, assures me there is no mistake in this, but their former use of gold cooking vessels is clearly true, and that people nowadays have no idea how proud and powerful they were until the Maha Kerella (the long war with the English)."

King Duttagamini (*circa* 200 B.C.) appointed Veddahs (more probably restored them to an ancient office) as guardians of the oldest shrine in Ceylon, the shrine at Kataragama of the god Skanda, who, according to tradition, headed the first army of invaders to Ceylon and married at Kataragama a Veddah chieftain's daughter, Walli, a name not uncommon among Veddah girls. Both the Skanda purana and the Ramayana represent the then inhabitants of Ceylon as enjoying a high degree of civilisation, with every luxury and refinement. They were worshippers of Siva, but "enemies of gods," and subjected the latter to grievous hardships, the relief of which was the object of the invasions of both Skanda and Rama. It is not clear how a votary of Śiva, admittedly the primal and supreme god, could be an "enemy of the gods." The explanation probably is that these were the tribal gods whom the Aryan Brahmans of the Rig-Veda used of old to invoke "to slay the Dasyus [the non-Aryan aborigines] and protect the Aryan colour" (*varna, i.e.*, caste), much as the Israelites called on their tribal god Jahveh against their foes, and that the authority of the Brahmans and their tribal gods was repudiated by the islanders. The Brahmans have taken their revenge by gibbeting the audacious dissenters for all time as wicked savages and monsters.

The Ramayana, which records the second invasion, relates that after the slaughter of Ravana, his brother Vihisana was installed in his place as king of Ceylon by the victorious Rama. Lakshmana or Samana, brother of Rama, still holds an important place in the worship of the Sinhalese, and their sacred peak is called after him Samana-kuta. In the long interval which separates these epochs from the Vijayan invasion the aboriginal inhabitants no doubt passed through many vicissitudes, but they remained the ruling race, and retained somewhat of their old culture and civilisation until, too proud to submit to or live with the Sinhalese invaders, they retired into the forests and, gradually losing all trace of refinement, sank into their present condition.

AN AFGHAN.

Whether the Sinhalese language is a language with an Aryan structure and an Aryan glossary, or is a language with a Dravidian structure and an Aryan glossary, is a question which has divided scholars, and must await a thorough philological investigation. This is a question independent of the origin of the race. "That language does not depend upon race," says Whitney, "is demonstrated by the facts most numerous and various. The African, whose purity of descent is attested by every feature, is found all over the world speaking just that language or jargon into which the fates of present or former slavery have brought his parents. Every civilised community contains elements of various lineage combined into one by unity of speech ; and instances are frequent enough where whole nations speak a tongue of which their ancestors knew nothing. For example, the Celtic Gauls and the Germanic Normans of France speak the dialect of a geographically insignificant district in Central Italy, while we ourselves can hardly utter a sentence or write a line without more or less of the same dialect." As to the contact and mixture of races and languages, Whitney adds: "Mixture of race and mixture of speech are coincident and connected processes; the latter never takes place without something of the former, but the one is not at all a measure of the other, because circumstances may give to the speech of the one element of population a greatly disproportionate preponderance. Thus there is left in France only an insignificant trace of the Celtic dialects of the predominant race-constituent of the French people. French is the speech of the Latin conquerors of Gaul mixed perceptibly with that of its later Frankish conquerors; it was adopted in its integrity by the Norse conquerors of a part of the land, then brought into Britain by the same Norsemen in the course of their further conquests, this time only as an element of mixture, and thence carried with English speech to America to be the language of a still further mixed community. . . . In strictness, language is never a proof of race either in an individual or in a community; it is only a probable indication of race in the absence of more authoritative opposing indications." These more authoritative indications are of an anthropological character, such as I have referred to above.

The extant literature of the Sinhalese is of comparatively recent date, the earlier works having, it is said, perished during the troublous times of the Tamil incursions. It includes the Sidat Sangara, the standard grammar of the language, and some poems of considerable literary merit, such as the Kavyasekara, Selalihini Sandesa, Paravi Sandesa, Guttila, Kusajatakaya, Gira Sandesa, and Hansa Sandesa. Their most valuable literature, however, is in Pali, one of the Prakrits of ancient India, and the language in which Buddha preached. Most of this literature has been translated into Sinhalese. It consists of the Buddhist scriptures called the Tripitakas, estimated to be about eleven times the extent of the English Bible, and dating from 300 B.C.; the commentaries of Buddhaghosa, the ultimate court of appeal on all doctrinal matters; historical, grammatical, and other works, of which the most important are the chronicles called Dipavansa and Mahavansa, the only authentic sources of the history of India prior to the Christian era and of Ceylon up to the arrival of the Europeans. The ancient Sinhalese works were written in the Asoka or old Pali characters About 1,200 years ago the grantha characters of South India were adopted, and, in a modified form, have been in use ever since.

A SINHALESE OLD WOMAN (HIGH CASTE).

There are material differences of custom and law between the Sinhalese of the low-country and those of the highland districts, who have the distinctive name of "Kandyans." "Seaports," said Aristotle, "are most quickly affected by new doctrines;" and the lowland Sinhalese, being on or near the coast, were the first to come under foreign influences, and by long intercourse with foreigners have lost some of their native characteristics. But the Kandyans, who till 1815 were ruled by their own princes, and jealously kept themselves aloof from the foreigner, are very conservative, and have retained in larger measure the purity of the race and ancient customs.

The low-country Sinhalese occupy the sea-coast of the Western and Southern Provinces. They are a handsome and well-made race, and their appearance and character are gentle rather than bold or hardy. Nature has been bountiful to them, and their wants are readily supplied. This very bounty, however, has been unfavourable to the development of active habits and enterprise. The cultivation of the soil is the favourite pursuit of the Sinhalese, and it is in landed property that they best love to invest their money. They are by no means deficient in quickness or talent, and when educated make good scholars. The turn of their minds is metaphysical and speculative. They have naturally a great aptitude for figures, and readily acquire a knowledge of mathematics. Their national religion is Buddhism, though there are many converts to Christianity among them. The ordinary dress of the men is a white or coloured cloth called a "comboy," folded round the lower part of the body, and depending below the knee more or less, according to the caste of the wearer. The hair is allowed to grow, and is tied in a knot at the back of the head, where it is secured by a large tortoiseshell comb, similar to that worn by European ladies some fifty years ago; a small semicircular comb in front of the large one completes their head-dress. The better orders assume the European coat, either of modern cut or of the old Dutch pattern, with gold huttons and gold-worked button-holes, and sometimes the comboy over the trousers. But many of them have adopted the European costume *in toto*.

The highest rank among them is that of Mudaliyar. It is either borne *ex-officio* or is conferred by the Governor as an honorary distinction. On State occasions the Mudaliyars attend Government House in full costume, when they wear handsomely ornamented curved dirks, suspended from the shoulder by richly worked gold belts. Some of them wear round their necks golden medals of considerable size, bearing an inscription commemorative of the services rendered to Government by the wearers or their ancestors on account of which the medal was presented to them.

Many of the Sinhalese have Portuguese names, such as De Zylva, De Livera, De Saram, Gomez, Fonseka, Dias, &c. These names were assumed by their ancestors at their baptism, with the sanction of their Portuguese godfathers. The manners of the Sinhalese are gentlemanly and polished in the extreme, and many of them are highly informed and agreeable in conversation. The houses and tables of the higher classes are furnished in English style, and on festive occasions are decorated most tastefully by means of garlands and the young leaves of the coconut, and by transplanting plantain and other trees, which retain their verdure sufficiently long to produce a very beautiful effect when lighted by lamps symmetrically arranged among them.

The Buddhist monks invariably wear a yellow robe, and have their heads closely shorn, in whatever part of the island they may be. They are held in high esteem, and it is deemed meritorious to provide for their subsistence and comfort. Some of the leading monks, such as Sri Sumangala, Abbot of Adam's Peak, are men of saintly character and great learning. In the maritime districts, where they have hardly any endowments, the monks still observe the custom which requires them to go out every morning to beg their meals. It enshrines the ancient ideal of mutual obligation between them and the laity—the monks to give spiritual and intellectual food to the laity and receive from them physical sustenance.

The Sinhalese women generally wear a short jacket and a comboy, and secure their long and glossy hair with gold or silver pins, and sometimes a small prettily worked comb. No covering for the head is used. The wealthier wear European costume and a profusion of jewellery when they go abroad.

The Kandyans are, as a body, hardier and more robust than their brethren of the low-country, though of the same race. Breathing the bracing air of the hills, which they are constantly ascending and descending, their limbs are wiry and their habits active. Their ordinary dress is a cloth round the loins. They never wear the comb, and their beards are allowed to grow. Their chiefs envelop themselves in an immense quantity of muslin, wound again and again around the waist and allowed to fall in folds to the ankle. When in full dress they wear a jacket with wide gigot sleeves, a ruff, and a peculiarly shaped hat, somewhat resembling two saucers laid one on the other, with the rims meeting, made either of white or black cloth, and ornamented with silver or gold. The dress of the women consists of a cloth, which they fold, after the fashion of Hindu women, gracefully about them; their hair is tied in a knot hanging down rather low at the back of the head, and they are fond of jewellery.

The homesteads of the Kandyans are often substantial buildings, forming a quadrangle, which faces inwards, whitewashed and thatched with straw, sheltered by umbrageous trees in a nook of the valley, and surrounded by tracts of rice land, terraced up the neighbouring hills, and irrigated by streams which flow into them, while their herds of small black cattle and buffaloes graze on the slopes. In some districts, especially in Badulla, which is comparatively a dry one, water is led in channels for miles along the sides of the hills to irrigate the fields which are remote from streams.

The spirit of independence is strongly developed in the Kandyans, and was exhibited in the heroic struggle they sustained against the Portuguese and Dutch invaders for three centuries. Their submission to British rule in 1814 was voluntary. Their attachment to their hereditary lands is extraordinary. Nothing will induce a Kandyan to sell his patrimony; and he will spend pounds willingly in lawsuits to secure a slip worth a few pence. This characteristic is not to be lost sight of in forming an opinion of the people. It is one strongly developed in most Asiatics, but peculiarly so in the Kandyans. They are averse to servile employment, and though they might secure high wages on the European tea estates, they prefer earning a subsistence by cultivating their own patches of land. The only occupation they will undertake is felling forest trees, at which they are very expert. The tea estates are consequently worked by Tamil coolies from South India, who numbered at the last census nearly half a million. The Kandyans have no little artistic instinct and skill, but their arts and crafts have been in large measure crushed out by the relentless competition of cheap machine-made goods from Europe. There lingers in the villages enough knowledge to supply their domestic and agricultural needs But European articles are cheaper and are readily bought.

The Kandyans are fond of burying valuables under the earth in pots. The spot is often known only to the head of the house, and there are instances where he has come to an untimely end and the secret has died with him. Education has not made the same progress among the Kandyans that it has in the maritime districts. The villagers are consequently very superstitious and very credulous. A state of feudal tenure still prevails among them resembling in some respects that which existed in Europe of old. There are chiefs who own tracts of country and whole villages, the inhabitants of which are hound to do certain services for their tenures. In the neighbourhood of Kandy and in the town itself the influences of European civilisation extend to the natives, and there are Kandyan gentlemen whose manners and habits are entirely English.

There are two kinds of marriages according to Kandyan custom: (1) *Diga*, by which a girl is given away (*di*, root *da*, to give)[1] to her husband with a dowry and passes into his family and loses all claim upon her ancestral property, except for maintenance in case she becomes destitute; (2) *Bini*, where the husband enters the wife's family and is dependent on her and her parents, and is liable to be turned out at short notice, and the wife may take another husband more agreeable to her or to the rest of the family. Hence the Kandyan saying that a bini husband should not take to his wife's house any property save a torch and a walking-stick. With these he may at any time depart and find his way. The bini marriage is generally contracted by heiresses, and the name *bini* seems to be derived from the fact of the husband coming or entering into (*ba*,[2] to come or descend) the wife's family.

The bini marriage is a relic of the primitive family system of mankind, which was based on "mother-right." In it the mother belonged to her tribe and lived amongst them, regarding not her father but her brothers and the brothers of her mother as her nearest kith and kin; and her child belonged not to her, and even less to her husband, but to her family. The husband remained unknown outside the family—sometimes he entered it as a sort of slave, performing menial work, sometimes not living in the house, but only paying

[1] According to some scholars, *diga* is a derivative of *dirga*, "long," the bride being sent away to a distance, *i.e.*, to her husband's family.

[2] Other derivations make *bini* a contraction of *bihini*, which, again, is derived from *bhagini* (root *bhag*, to divide, to take to oneself, possess, enjoy carnally); or make it equivalent to *bhinna*, broken, split, merged, united.

occasional visits, and never regarded by his children as their father.

The conducting of the wife to, and the living in, the husband's house or in any family residence of his—or if he does not own a house and lands, the taking her as his wife and the conducting her away from her family to a place of lodging—constitutes a diga marriage.

For a marriage to be in accordance with the proper customs of the country the following five customary festivities should be observed, and for persons of rank the marriage ceremonies are as follows:—

(1) When a wife is sought for a man the parents or a chief relation of the bridegroom will inform a chief relation of the family of a woman of equal caste that they are desirous of forming an alliance. If the proposed match is approved of by the parents of the bride and her family relations, intimation thereof is given to the bridegroom's family, whereupon his friends visit the bride, and, having determined on the marriage, partake of food and betel. A relation of the bridegroom's family then goes with a "pingo" to the bride's house and obtains her horoscope, which is then compared with the bridegroom's in its good and bad aspects, a lucky hour for the marriage is determined on, and information thereof is sent to the parents or the guardians of the bride, by whom the necessary arrangements are made.

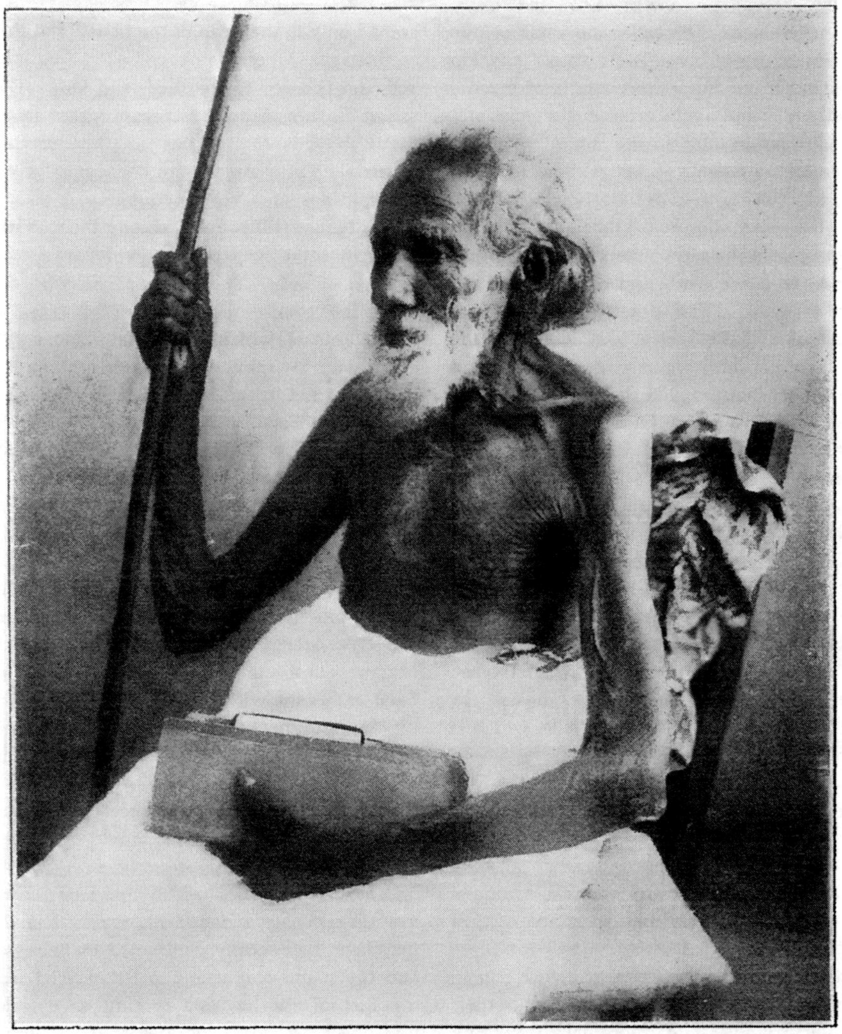

A SINHALESE CENTENARIAN.
(Reputed to be 116 years old when the photograph was taken.)

(2) The bridegroom then, preceded by presents, starts with his relations and attendants to conduct the bride. When close to the bride's house some of her relations, coming out to meet the party, conduct it with due respect to the house. Before the arrival of the lucky hour the mother, or some other fit relation of the bridegroom, presents the mother of the bride with a *kiri-kada-halaya* (white cloth) and a suit of apparel, while the father of the bride gives the bridegroom a suit of clothes. The lucky hour having come, the bridegroom, after giving a *halaya* (cloth) to the bride, throws a chain over her neck and presents her with a set of female apparel. Arrayed in this, she steps on to the *magul-poruwa* (a raised seat) together with the bridegroom. A maternal uncle of the bride or some other principal member of her family then, with a chain, joins together the little fingers of the right hands of the bride and bridegroom, who thereupon turn three times round to the right. The chain is then taken off and the bridegroom takes a seat prepared for him on the magul-poruwa. Some balls of the cakes, rice, milk, &c., kept on the *magul-pata* (festal-dish) are then made by some chief member of the family and handed to the bride and bridegroom, who thereupon exchange them. After the assembled guests have been fed, and the betel and sandalwood paste distributed amongst them, on the bride and bridegroom leaving the bride's house a close male relation of the bride's family accompanies them; and this relation, on the approach of the party to the bridegroom's residence, is met by an elderly kinsman of the bridegroom and greeted with due respect. At the lucky hour the bride and bridegroom enter the room prepared for them.

(3) The person who came from the bride's house having been hospitably entertained, on the seventh day after, the ceremony of pouring water on the head takes place: a maternal aunt and uncle of the bride together, or some other two chief persons of the bride's family, come to the bridegroom's house, and at the lucky hour the uncle pours water on the heads of the married couple and goes away.

(4) A few days after this the bride's parents or her principal guardian relations pay the husband and wife a visit, according to their means present a dowry of movables and lands, and depart.

(5) After this the husband and wife visit the wife's parents.

Either the diga or bini marriage is dissolvable by mutual consent, or on the ground of the wife's adultery, the husband's adultery coupled with incest or gross cruelty, complete and continued desertion for two years, or inability to live happily together. No wonder that divorces are very common among the Kandyans, the proportion of divorces to marriages in the decade 1891-1901 being 4·46 per cent.

Polygamy and polyandry were till lately not uncommon among the Kandyans. The latter practice is the relic of a primitive culture, of which traces have been found in many nations. In the Indian epic, the Mahabharata, one of the heroines, Draupadi, was the wife of five brothers, who had each also a separate wife. It was an exceptional practice at that period, and needed an elaborate apology, which the Brahmans had no difficulty in making. Herodotus says of the Agathyrsi, a Scythian people : "They have their women in common, that they may all be brothers of each other" (iv. 104). The custom prevailed, according to him, also among the Nasamones (iv. 172) and Massagetæ (l. 216). According to Aristotle ("Pol.," ii. 3–9), the Libyans had their women in common, and distributed the children by their likeness to the men. The custom prevailed among the inhabitants of Britain at the time of Julius Cæsar's invasion. He says : "Ten or twelve men have wives in common, and chiefly brothers share with brothers and fathers with children. If any children are born, they are deemed children of those who first conducted the maidens" ("De Bello Gall.," v., c. 14). The fraternal arrangement was, according to Polybius, not unknown among the Spartans. It prevails still in many parts of the world. It is "the rule of life among thirty millions of respectable people" in Tibet (Wilson's "Abode of Snow") and among the Nairs of Travancore, among whom it has given rise to complicated rules of succession through the female. Of these rules traces are seen in the Mukkuwar Law of Batticaloa, in the Eastern Province of Ceylon. So far from degrading woman's status, polyandry is reported in Tibet to have "resulted in the assignment to the wife of a paramount position, which in the north-east and east of the country has grown among certain tribes into a real sovereignty."

This primitive practice was incompatible with the high civilisation attained by the Kandyan Sinhalese, and was maintained chiefly owing to the necessities of feudal tenure. Each landholder had to render personal service to his lord at great distance, it may be, from home. The duty was specially obligatory on the nobles, and necessitated their attendance on the king for considerable periods. During their absence from home their family and lands would have been unprotected and exposed to danger, unless the duty of protecting them and cultivating the lands devolved on a brother or near male relation, and was fortified by the bond of interest and affection. The custom also served as a check on the excessive subdivision of land which naturally occurs in Ceylon, where law and custom favour the transmission of parents' property in equal shares to their children. The British Government, who became masters of the Kandyan provinces upon the deposition of the last king, Sri Vikrama Raja Sinha, in 1815, were bound by treaty to protect "all classes of the people, the safety of their persons and property, with their civil rights and immunities according to the laws, institutions, and customs established and in force among them," and were hardly, therefore, at liberty to interfere with their marriage customs. But with the abolition of personal service and the introduction of settled Government by the British the Kandyan chiefs applied to the Government to prohibit the practices of polyandry and polygamy, which were the frequent causes of litigation and crime ; and they were accordingly declared illegal, and punishable with three years' rigorous imprisonment.

Polyandry, though illegal, continues to exist among the Kandyan peasantry, especially in the case of brothers. The law against polyandry is evaded by not registering the union at all or by registering it as with one brother only. In all cases the ceremonies of marriage are performed with one brother only. The association of other husbands, follows by consent of parties, but when once established, becomes matter of public notoriety, and no disgrace attaches to it. The progeny of the woman is deemed the progeny of each husband individually, and collectively, and the property is thus conserved in the family. The husbands do not call themselves husbands, but say they "live in one house," while the wife speaks of herself as "cooking rice" for all of them. It is true now as in Knox's time that "the children do acknowledge and care for both fathers.

SINHALESE MAN.
(Bullock driver.)

Children born from marriages of this sort call each brother by the common name of father and have no idea of their being more nearly related to one father than another." The elder father is called "great father" and the younger is called "little father," and if there was an intermediate father, he would be called "middle father."

By the same statute (Ordinance No. 13 of 1859, now replaced by Ordinance No. 3 of 1870) which made penal polyandry and polygamy, registration was made essential to the validity of a Kandyan marriage. This requirement, now fifty-eight years old, is still in advance of the wishes and sentiments of the Kandyan Sinhalese, nor is any other community subject to such a provision, an enactment made in 1886 and 1895 to enforce it on others having been disallowed by the Secretary of State. Despite the fact that the law makes the issue of their unregistered unions bastards, the Kandyans are indifferent to registration, and are content to contract marriages according to custom. Under the pressure of the Government Agents there is occasionally a sudden rise in the registration, to be followed, when the pressure is relaxed, by the normal state of indifference and an increased number of applications for divorce. The Kandyan marriage is thus a very uncertain and disturbing factor in the marriage-rate of the island, and renders trustworthy conclusions difficult.

The low-country Sinhalese, like the Tamils, the Burghers, and Europeans, are subject to the general law, which is now contained in Ordinance No. 2 of 1895 (as amended by Ordinance No. 19 of 1900). Registration is not indispensable to the validity of a marriage, but is usually availed of by the well-to-do classes, and universally by the Europeans and Burghers. The solemnisation of Christian marriages is usually performed by a minister in church upon a registrar's certificate that all preliminary conditions required by law have been complied with. Non-Christian marriages are solemnised by the registrar himself. Among Buddhists a ceremony similar to that among the Kandyans is usually added at home. The bride and bridegroom, seated on a dais covered with a white cloth, strewn with rice, have the thumbs of their right hands tied together by a maternal uncle of the bride, and water is poured on the tie as a sign of giving the bride over to the bridegroom; and finally the uncle wraps a cloth round them as an additional symbol of their union. Recitation of benedictory verses brings the ceremony to a close. With these ceremonies the Buddhist priest, or rather monk, true to his ascetic ideals and traditions, has nothing to do. But he is indispensable at funerals, perhaps because his testimony to the vanity of the world has a better chance there of making some impression.

A third division of the Sinhalese must be added, viz., the outcast *Rodiyas*, whom the Sinhalese hardly regard as fellow-countrymen. For centuries treated worse than beasts and regarded with loathing, their touch, nay, their shadow, being deemed pollution, the Rodiyas have sunk to the lowest depth of degradation and have become hardened and shameless, their hand against every man and every man's hand against them. They number now about 1,500 persons, and are scattered mainly in the Sabaragamuwa, North-Western, Uva, and Central Provinces.

Knox, who was a captive among the Kandyans for nearly twenty years in the seventeenth century, says that they were persons whose duty it was to supply the king with game; and that on one occasion they produced human flesh, which his majesty enjoyed so much that he directed them to procure more of what he supposed was part

A FAKIR OR HOLY MAN.

of a wild animal. The deception became known, however, to the royal barber, who acquainted the king with it. The rage of the king may be imagined; and as the direst punishment he could inflict on the offenders, he decreed that henceforth they, as well as all their tribe, should be outcasts from other society; that they should not be allowed to pursue any calling, but beg their bread from door to door, and be shunned by all others. This order of things being once established, it became no unusual practice for the king to punish noblemen and women who incurred his displeasure by condemning them to join the Rodiyas with their whole families—a sentence worse than death. This fact may account for the beauty of form peculiar to this class, in spite of the abject demeanour which their degraded position superinduces. It is thought by some that they were originally a separate race, in fact, the aborigines. Knox, who must no doubt have had many opportunities of learning about them, gives in his truthful and quaint way the traditions common in his time. He says that they were originally "Dodda Veddahs, which signifies hunters." Now "dodda" is probably Knox's mode of pronouncing the Sinhalese name for game; they were called "Game Veddahs." If, then, a branch of the Veddah tribe, most probably they were the descendants of the aborigines; and whereas the other Veddahs, occupying the feverish jungles of Bintenne, and carrying on a hard struggle with privation and hunger, have become more squalid in appearance, these, being recruited by noble families, and living in a healthier part of the island, have improved rather than deteriorated in form.

The Rodiyas live in villages of their own, and obtain their subsistence by begging, their importunity and the aversion with which they are regarded being in their favour, for people are glad to purchase their departure by a gratuity. They have the credit, moreover, of being expert thieves, and on that account, too, the fact of a Rodiya locating himself near a Sinhalese village, which under the present Government there is nothing to prevent his doing, occasions considerable excitement and indignation, something akin to the feeling excited in an English village by a gipsy encampment. Having formerly been debarred from tilling the soil, they have learnt to make articles of handicraft, such as grass ropes, baskets, and mats. They also make strong hide ropes for securing cattle and wild elephants. This was a service they were obliged to render the Kandyan kings; consequently they claimed the carcases of all the cattle that died, and it is said that this is their favourite food, especially when in a high condition. From the fibre of a species of aloe they also manufactured whips, which are carried before the great in processions, and cracked with a noise like the report of a pistol. It is rather curious that rope-making is also the occupation of the outcast Cagots and Caqueux of the Pyrenees valley, and hide-making of the outcast Paria population of South India.

The women are expert at such feats as spinning brass plates on one finger, tossing balls in the air and catching them, &c. At the great festivals in Badulla, when thousands of persons, both men and women, are assembled, the Rodiyas, who come as spectators, can always be distinguished at a glance. The Sinhalese women on these occasions go hand in hand, some four or five being thus strung together; and the reason assigned is that they are afraid of being kidnapped by the Rodiyas. Their habits of life are said to be unnatural and immoral. In former days the women were only allowed to cover the lower part of the person, but this prohibition no longer exists, and they generally wear a coloured silk handkerchief tied round the neck and waist. Their figures are erect as arrows. One can hardly view a race so fine in a physical point of view, so degraded in a moral aspect, without pity, and a desire to see them raised. A Commission was not long ago appointed by Government to consider the question, and made suggestions for the amelioration of their condition. The headman of a Rodiya settlement used a striking Oriental illustration to convey to the Commission the hopelessness of their position ; he said it was as hard for them to better their position as for a tortoise to insert its neck in the hole of a yoke rolling in a storm-tossed sea. It will be long before the Kandyans learn to regard them with any other than their present feelings. The men might find employment on the public roads, but they are averse to labour. There are words in use among them not spoken by the Sinhalese generally. Mr. Simon Casie Chetty, in an interesting article on these people in the Asiatic Society's *Journal*, gives upwards of a hundred words peculiar to them.

The Tamils, who next to the Sinhalese are the most numerous race in Ceylon, are an old Dravidian race, who, before the dawn of history, preceded the Aryans in the colonisation of India, and who, though in later times they adopted Aryan civilisation, have modified it and retained their individuality. As in the case of Sanskrit, it is not possible to say when Tamil became a literary language. But while Sanskrit is a dead language and spoken only by scholars, Tamil, which is so old that its words have passed into the Old Testament of the Hebrews,[1] continues to be the vigorous living speech of eighteen millions of people. From a very early period they have cultivated their language with such earnestness and assiduity that (in the opinion of Bishop Caldwell, the grammarian of the Dravidian languages) "it is impossible for any European who has acquired a competent knowledge of Tamil to regard otherwise than with respect the intellectual capacity of a people amongst whom so wonderful an organ of thought has been developed." Its literature is in its best periods characterised by "enthusiasm for Tamilic purity and literary independence," and "is the only vernacular literature in India which has not been content with imitating Sanskrit, but has honourably attempted to emulate and outshine it."

The language and literature were under the Pandyan kings of South India the special charge of an academy of poets and *savants* analogous to the Académie Française, and the three epochs of that academy are the great landmarks in ancient Tamil history. The literature of the first two epochs has perished, save one work, a grammar called *Tolkappiam*, which is to Tamil what *Paniniyam* (Ashtadhyahi) is to Sanskrit. The loss of the literature is attributed to the destruction by the sea, at successive periods, of the two earliest Pandyan capitals, old Madura and Kapadapuram. Of the works of the third epoch which have survived, the best known is the "Kural" of Tiruvalluvar, a poem of singular literary and ethical value, which has been translated into most European languages.

Of the later literature, the most interesting to Ceylon is the epic called the *Chilappadikaram*, one of "the five poems" *par excellence* of Tamil literature. In it a contemporary poet, a prince-monk of the ruling Jain family, sings of the life and death of Kannakai, the faithful wife, who received the honours of canonisation immediately on her death, and is better known in Ceylon as the goddess Pattini Amman. Gaja Bahu, king of Ceylon (*circa* 100 A.D.), was, according to the poem, present at the ceremonies of canonisation. He introduced her

TAMIL GIRLS.

[1] The Hebrew word used for peacock (*tuki*) is unmistakably the Tamil word *tokei*, while the word for apes (*kapi*) is the Sanskrit and Tamil *kapi*, and the word for ivory (*shen habbim*, the tooth of the *habb*) is the Sanskrit *ibham* and Tamil *ibam*.

worship into Ceylon, where it flourishes to this day. The symbols of her worship are copies of her golden anklet, which he is said to have brought from India. Oaths are not infrequently taken on them in courts of justice. No oath is more dreaded by the Sinhalese peasant. At the annual *perahera* festival at the Temple of the Tooth Relic at Kandy, a festival which has come down from the time of Gaja Bahu, the goddess Pattini holds a high place, Buddha's Tooth Relic, which now heads the procession, being a later addition made a hundred and fifty years ago. In her honour Gaja Bahu established also the great Sinhalese national game of the *an-keliya*[1] or horn-pulling, held especially on the occasion of epidemics, and conducted on a scale of magnificence and in the presence of thousands of spectators. It concludes with a torchlight procession through the infected villages, which recalls the "need-fires" lighted by farmers in England on the occasion of epidemics among cattle. Many a Sinhalese family traces a hereditary connection with one or other of the rival factions which in times past celebrated this festival with boisterous merriment, and not infrequently with such excess that the king had to intervene and forbid the celebration.

The chief contribution of the Tamils to philosophy and religion is the Saiva Siddhanta system, which the learned Dr. Pope regards as the "most influential and undoubtedly the most intrinsically valuable of the religions of India." This attempt to solve the problems of God, the soul, humanity, nature, evil, suffering, and the unseen world has never been fully expounded in a European language except in some measure by Dr. Pope himself, and is little known to Western scholars and divines. There is an extensive literature of esoteric philosophy attributed to an ancient brotherhood of adepts, of whom the saint Agastya is the reputed chief, and whose seat is the mountain of Agastya Kutum in Tinnevelli district. "So great and extensive has been their influence that the Tamil literature is permeated with esoteric truths in all its ramifications, and a vast mass of proverbs and popular songs circulating among the Tamils to-day conceals under frivolous guise profound truths." The grammar, too, is linked to the occult philosophy of the people. A large number of works on astrology, magic, and other black arts exist, which have a great vogue among certain classes of the population. These works have extended their baneful influence to Ceylon, and are among the chief authorities for the practices of demonism among the Sinhalese.

The Ceylon Tamils are the descendants of the bands of Tamils who came over, upon the invitation of the first Sinhalese king, Vijaya, and his successors, to develop the country, and later bands, by whom Ceylon was frequently overrun, and who on several occasions acquired the supreme power. The indigenous Tamils inhabit for the most part the Northern and Eastern Provinces. The Jaffna district, which is the chief centre of the population, is (says Sir Emerson Tennent) "almost the only place in Ceylon of which it might be said that no one is idle or unprofitably employed. . . . There is a satisfaction experienced in no other part of Ceylon in visiting their villages and farms, and in witnessing the industrious habits and improved processes of the peasantry." The indigenous Tamils receive yearly large accessions from the Tamils on the continent, and together with them are among the principal factors of the island's prosperity. At the census of 1901 the immigrant Tamil coolie population on the tea estates numbered nearly half a million, and in some districts, such as Nuwara Eliya, was greatly in excess of the indigenous population.

Bishop Caldwell writes: "All throughout Ceylon the coolies in the coffee [now tea] plantations are Tamilians; the majority of the money-making classes even in Colombo are Tamilians. . . . The majority of the domestic servants of Europeans and of the camp followers in every part of the Presidency of Madras being Tamil people, Tamil is the prevailing language in all the military cantonments in Southern India, whatever be the vernacular language of the district. The majority of the Klings (Kalingas) or Hindus who are found in the further East are Tamilians; a large proportion of the coolies who have emigrated in such numbers to the Mauritius and to the West Indian colonies [South Africa might now be added] are Tamilians. In short, wherever money is to be made, wherever a more apathetic people is waiting to be pushed aside, thither swarm the Tamilians, the Greeks or the Scotch of the East, the least superstitious and the most enterprising and persevering race of Hindus."

TAMIL COOLIE WOMAN.

The chief Tamil settlement, which is at Jaffna, is said by tradition to have been founded by a blind minstrel from the Choli country of South India. Being blind, he depended for his subsistence on the earnings of his wife. One day he quarrelled with her and left home, saying he was going to Lanka (Ceylon). "Ah, you are going to Lanka," she said sneeringly, "to obtain a tusked elephant and a fertile land." On his arrival at the king's court he was refused admittance to his presence, as it was deemed inauspicious for a king to see a blind man. It was, however, arranged that the king should stand behind a curtain and hear the minstrel's song. Unknown to him, the king exchanged his royal robes for an archer's dress, and stood bow in hand. The minstrel, divining the disguise, improvised this stanza, comparing him to Rama, the hero of the Ramayana.

"O Aditya (meaning Rama), whose mighty arms stemmed the sea waves, why have thy hands assumed the bow? For prosperous Lanka has neither her king (meaning Rama) nor the stag (meaning that which decoyed Rama away from Sita and left her alone to be carried off by Ravana) nor the seven *mara* trees (meaning those which Rama shot through with a single arrow) for thee to shoot."

The king immediately laid aside the archer's garb and successively wore his queen's robes and his own. The minstrel composed *extempore* a lyric in ten stanzas to suit the different guises, and sang it to the accompaniment of his lute. The king was greatly pleased with the minstrel, and bestowed on him a tusked elephant and the peninsula of Jaffna, thus making true the ironical remark of his wife. The land was mostly uninhabited and covered with jungle, which he cleared with the aid of colonists imported from South India and converted into a rich country. From his professional name (*Yal-panar*, the lute-minstrel), the land was called *Yal panam*, the Minstrel's Land. The Sinhalese changed the name into *Yapane*, which the British anglicised to Jaffna.

The minstrel invited from the continent a son of the Choli king, and installed him as king under the name Sing Arya Chakravati. The installation is said in the *Kailasa Malai* to have occurred in the year 3,000 of the *Kali Yuga*, equal to 101 B.C. If this date be correct, the Ceylon king who patronised the minstrel was

[1] For a description of the game see the Royal Asiatic Society's *Journal*, Ceylon, vol. viii., pp. 368 *et seq.*

probably Pulattya, the Tamil who expelled Valagambahu and ruled in his place at Anuradhapura. The capital of the kingdom of Jaffna was fixed at Nallur ("the good city"), and the kings, known under the title of Arya Chakravatis, soon became powerful rivals of the kings of Anuradhapura and Polonnaruwa. It was a scion of this line of "Arya Chakravatis" that Ibn Batuta, the Moorish traveller, found to be the chief king of the island in the fourteenth century.

The north-western ports of Mantotta and Kudurumala (the *Hippuros* of Pliny), which from ancient times had been the ports of call of Greek, Roman, Arab, Indian and Chinese ships, served as the basis of a naval force which often gave the kings of Jaffna the command of the Ceylon seas and a predominant influence in the island. The Hindus, who constitute the vast majority among the Tamils, attach great importance to the ceremony of marriage, which they regard as a sacrament. The ceremony is performed at an auspicious hour by a Brahman priest before an altar of fire. The bride and bridegroom sit on a dais opposite it, while the purificatory and other rites prescribed in the sacred books are gone through. Often in the course of these rites the couple, with the little bridesmaids and men, and attended by married ladies, walk in picturesque procession round the altar. The bride and bridegroom having signified their consent, the father, or, if he is dead, the nearest male relation, solemnly delivers the bride to the bridegroom with an oblation of water, the bridegroom ties a necklace called *tali* round her neck, and the fire, the sun, moon, and stars, and all present are called upon to witness that the couple accept each other as man and wife for this world and the next and for eternity. The bridegroom with his hands places the right foot of the bride on a mill-stone. The bride is shown the star Arundati, the perfect wife translated to the skies as a pattern to all women. The priests and elders and all married ladies (no widow may take part) strew rice, symbol of prosperity and fertility, over the heads of the couple and bless them. The *tali* or necklace above-mentioned is the sign of a married woman, and is never removed till her husband's death. Among the poor who cannot afford this ceremony, or among those living far from Hindu centres (as in parts of the Eastern Province), a valid marriage is constituted by the acceptance of the bridegroom by the bride's parents, by his presenting her with a trousseau, which consists of a cloth some yards long, and being served by her with food at a feast to which the relations are invited.

No divorce is permitted by religion to either party, though it is allowed by the local statute. Re-marriage of widows is not usual among the better classes of Hindus, and is not regarded with favour.

The Moors are the next most numerous race in Ceylon, and at the census of 1901 numbered 228,034, or about one-fourth of the Tamil and one-tenth of the Sinhalese population. According to its strict interpretation, the term "Moor," which means an inhabitant of Morocco, is misleading when applied to the people of Ceylon who go by that name, and who do not lay claim to an African origin. In Ceylon the term is a relic of the rule of the Portuguese, who gave to the Ceylon Mahomedan the name of his co-religionist of Morocco, and is used to designate all Mahomedans (other than Malays) born in Ceylon or Southern India and speaking Tamil as their mother-tongue. From the tenth to the fifteenth century the Arabs were undisputed masters of the Eastern seas and trade, and exercised great influence in Ceylon till ousted by the Portuguese. During this period they settled on the Indian and Ceylon coasts, and intermarried largely with the natives, especially the Tamils. Their first settlement in India was Kailpatnam (east of Cape Comorin), which is still regarded as the fatherland of the Moors. According to one of their traditions, their progenitors fled from the tyranny of the Caliph Abu al Melek ben Merivan in the eighth century. According to another they were expelled from Arabia by the founder of their religion, Mahomed, for cowardice at the battle of Ohod. A later colony is said to have arrived at Beruwela (in Kalutara district) 1024 A.D.

Whatever may have been their place of origin,[1] the Moors have now lost connection with it, and have permanently settled in this country. They call themselves *Sonahar*,[2] as distinguished from the *Sammankarar*, the later arrivals from India. They are an enterprising and speculative race. Their chief occupation is petty trade, and as traders it is difficult to surpass them. They are ubiquitous and active in the metropolis as in the remotest village. They are an exclusive and conservative race. Even in the case of solitary Moorish villages planted for generations in Sinhalese districts, the Sinhalese language has not been adopted, but Tamil is invariably spoken by the Moors. They seldom mix with other races, except the Malays, with whom they intermarry, and Moorish women do not appear in public unless very poor. Though the Moors are by no means deficient in intelligence, they care little for education, especially education on Western lines. The presence of Arabi Pasha and his fellow Egyptian exiles in Ceylon during the latter part of the nineteenth century has had the effect of stirring up the Moorish community, but this has shown itself mostly in externals, the adoption of the dress of European Turks, &c. There is little sign as yet that they realise, or desire to make themselves worthy of, their great heritage from Islam, whose votaries during the darkness of the Middle Ages kept the lamp of learning and civilisation trimmed and burning throughout the greater part of Europe and Asia.

[1] See an interesting paper on "The Moors of Ceylon" by Mr. P. Ramanathan, C.M.G., in the *R.A.S. Journal*, vol. x., No. 36.

[2] *Sonaha* is derived from *Yavana*, originally applied in India to the Ionian Greeks, and afterwards to any people who came from the north and brought in new rites, and finally to the Mahomedans. *Sammankara* is probably from the Malay *sampan*, a boat, and apparently meant a boatman, the idea retained in the ordinary Sinhalese and Tamil title for Moors, *Maraikkar* or *Marakkalaha*, the Tamil for "ship" being *marakkalam*, a wooden vessel.

The Malays, whose numbers are very small, were originally imported to Ceylon from Java by the Dutch for military service, and some were Javanese princes and their attendants deported here for political reasons. When the Dutch rule in Ceylon ended, some of the Malay soldiers, with their wives and children, were sent to Java at the expense of the British Government. Those who chose to remain in the island entered into the service of the British Government, and were formed, with Kaffirs and sepoys, into the Ceylon Rifle Regiment, the last of which was disbanded in 1873. They are Mahomedans in religion, in habits less exclusive than the Moors, and are characterised by a military spirit. On the disbandment of the Ceylon Rifle Regiment a great many joined the Ceylon Police Force, of which they are among the most efficient members. One of their race carried off the Government English University Scholarship in open competition with youths of other races, and had a distinguished career at Cambridge, an achievement of which this small community may well be proud.

The Mahomedans of Ceylon are governed in matrimonial matters by laws and customs of their own. Only a small part of them have been reduced to writing in the Code of Mahomedan Law of 1806, a meagre document, which has to be interpreted and supplemented by the light of the unwritten custom of the community. Under no system of law does woman enjoy more rights and safeguards than under the Mahomedan—an advantage she probably owes to the high regard of the prophet and lawgiver, Mahomed, for his noble and devoted wife, Kadija. But in practice his good intentions have been defeated by man's selfishness. On the day of the marriage the terms of the contract (with special reference to the amount of dowry and to the *magar*, or compensation, to be given to the wife by the husband in case of divorce) are entered by the priest, in the presence of witnesses, in a register called the *kaduttam* (apparently a corruption of the

Tamil *kaditam*, a document). The consent of the parties to the union is signified by the bridegroom, and on behalf of the bride by her father or guardian, who signs the register for her. The priest's benediction concludes this ceremony, which is followed, according to Tamil custom, by the bridegroom tying the *tali* round the bride's neck.

The marriage may be dissolved by the husband delivering to the wife letters of divorce or addressing her three times "I divorce thee." The right of divorce is equally open to the wife. The divorce is entered in the *kaduttam*, and can only take effect if the husband returns the *magar* agreed upon at marriage. The Mahomedan law permits a man to marry four wives, but coupled with the almost impossible condition that all are treated by him with strict impartiality. The custom of polygamy was found by the prophet Mahomed to be too strongly established among the Arabs to be rooted out, and he did his best to moderate and reform it.

In Ceylon polygamy and divorce are opposed to the sentiment and practice of the majority of the Mahomedans, but are deplorably prevalent among certain classes in the Batticaloa district, and inflict cruel hardships on the women. The largest proportion (160 per 1,000) of widowed (which includes divorced) females in the island is among the Moors of Batticaloa district; also the smallest proportion (17 per 1,000) of widowed males. Gross frauds having been found prevalent in connection with the *kaduttams* or registers kept by the priests, the Ordinance No. 8 of 1886 was passed, on the recommendation of the then District Judge of Batticaloa (Mr. Worthington), giving the Mahomedans the opportunity of registering their marriages in registers kept by officially appointed Mahomedan registrars. In some districts, Puttalam and Galle, the Mahomedans have readily availed themselves of the opportunity, but in most districts the operation of the law is impeded by religious prejudice.

A KANDYAN GIRL.

The term "Burgher" in Ceylon properly belongs to the legitimate descendants of the Dutch and of the Portuguese who elected to remain in the island after the fall of their respective Governments, and of whom a considerable number eventually took employment under the British. At the time of the capitulation of Colombo in 1796, the Dutch community in Ceylon, which consisted of the European residents and the descendants of the earlier settlers of Dutch, German, and other European nationalities who came out in the Dutch service, had been broadly divided into two classes: "company's servants" and "Burghers." The former were the civil and military employees of all grades of the Netherlands East India Company, and the latter included (1) those (also called Vryburgers) who, having obtained their discharge from the company's service, were permitted to reside and carry on trades and occupations on their own account in the different towns; and (2) the train-band or militiamen of the towns, whose ranks were composed to a great extent of men of mixed Portuguese descent, who practised for their livelihood various handicrafts, and came in later times to be known as mechanics. With this class the Dutch Burghers had little or no connection.

When Ceylon came under the British Government, the distinction between "company's servants" and "Burghers" lost its significance, and the Dutch community in Ceylon began to be designated the "Dutch and Burgher inhabitants" without any distinction between the elements. But in course of time, with the death of the men who first took the oath of allegiance to King George III., or were permitted to remain in Ceylon on passports, the appellation resolved itself to "Burghers." Yet it was always recognised as applicable only to the legitimate descendants of the Dutch and of the Portuguese and other Europeans who had taken service under the Dutch company. Sir Richard Ottley, Chief Justice of Ceylon, in his replies to a series of questions proposed by a Commission of Inquiry in 1830, thus defines the term "Burgher":—

"The name Burgher belongs to the descendants of the Dutch and Portuguese and other Europeans born in Ceylon; the right to this distinction must be decided by the country from which the father or paternal ancestors came. Whatever the number of generations through which the family has passed in this island, if the male ancestor were Dutch, Portuguese, or other European, whoever may have been the female parents, if the parents were married, the offspring would be Burghers. If the parents were not married, the country of the mother would decide the question. If the right to be denominated Burgher be once lost by the legitimate father being a Sinhalese or other Indian, it cannot be recovered."

Bishop Copleston has thus described the Burghers: "The descendants of Portuguese who occupied parts of the island from near 1500 to about 1650 A.D., and of the Dutch who succeeded them and handed it over to the English a little before 1800, are alike called 'Burghers,' though the title must have belonged originally to the Dutch. Few of these Burghers are now of unmixed European descent, but most are of unblemished and some of noble origin. The term 'Eurasian' is not applied to them." The Burghers of Ceylon have thus had an origin quite different from that of the Eurasians of India or of the rapidly increasing half-caste population of Ceylon, although, owing to imperfect knowledge of their history and antecedents, it has become common to speak of these classes together, and to use the words "Burgher" and "Eurasian" as synonymous terms. The language now used by the Burghers is English. Dutch has been altogether forgotten, except by the antiquarian. A corrupt Portuguese *patois* is occasionally used, but is fast dying out.

There are practical difficulties in the way of an enumeration of the "Burgher" population according to the correct and proper acceptation of that term. Many persons called themselves Burghers, and returned themselves as such in census schedules, who had no right to that appellation. As a Burgher gentleman has observed, "It is not an uncommon experience for every nondescript who affects a pair of trousers and cannot with any right be classed under any particular category to call himself a 'Burgher,' and to take refuge under that very convenient term."

Though numerically an insignificant element of the population (about 9 per cent.), the Burghers represent a considerable proportion of the talent of the country. They do not readily take to agricultural or industrial work. But in the learned professions they have done their part with distinction to themselves and with credit to the colony. They form the backbone of the clerical service, and until recently held practically a monopoly of the highest posts in that service.

HIGH CASTE TAMIL GIRL.

According to the numbers of their adherents at the census of 1901, the several religious faiths of Ceylon rank in the following order:—

Buddhists	2,141,404
Hindus	826,826
Christians	349,239
Mahomedans	246,118
Others	2,367

In other words, out of every 10,000 of the entire population 6,005 are Buddhists, 2,319 Hindus, 979 Christians, 690 Mahomedans, and 7 "others."

Of the "others" the great majority are the Veddahs. Their religion, as the religion of most of the forest tribes of India, is what in the science of religion is known as Animism. This is the distinctive philosophy of primitive culture. Every brook and well, every rock and glade, heaven and earth, sun and moon, rain, wind, and thunder are believed to be peopled by spirits, who directly influence the lives of men, whether as guardian spirits or hurtful demons, and have to be propitiated. They appear to men either of their own accord or conjured by some spell, and afflict them with diseases, especially convulsions, delirium, madness. The phantom souls of the departed live on as hovering ghosts, continuing a life more or less similar to the present, and able to help or injure the survivors of their kindred or tribe.

There are traces in the Veddah worship of a more highly developed religion, inherited probably from earlier Indian colonists. The kings of Lanka (Ceylon), whose fortunes are told with poetical embellishments in the Skanda purana and the Ramayana, were devoted worshippers of Siva. The oldest shrine in the island, Kataragama, was, as it still is, sacred to his son, Kartikeya or Skanda, god of war and wisdom, and its priests have from time immemorial been Veddahs. Hardly less old is the shrine of Siva on Sami Rock, Trincomalee, on whose summit, since the Portuguese in the seventeenth century destroyed its "temple of a thousand columns," a picturesque open-air worship is celebrated, and the offerings cast into the deep blue sea beneath. Munisvaram (near the town of Chilaw) was, even in the time of the hero of the Ramayana, an ancient temple dedicated to Siva. Near Mannar there stood another celebrated temple of Siva called Tirukketisvara, which, according to an ancient tradition, was destroyed by an earthquake or sandstorm, and of which the ruins are still traceable at great depths from the surface.

The most widely professed faith in Ceylon, and that which is most characteristic of the country, is Buddhism. It is the national religion of the Sinhalese, and surpasses in the number of its followers all other forms of belief prevalent in the island together.

The essential doctrines of Buddha are known as "The Four Noble Truths." Life, he taught, is sorrow; desire is the cause of sorrow; sorrow ceases with the removal of desire; this is effected by a certain course of conduct called the Eightfold Path. This consisted of right belief, right aim, right speech, right conduct, right living, right endeavour, right recollection, right meditation. Desire is the seed of life, and is itself the product of past thoughts and acts, according to the inexorable law of cause and effect, called *Karma*. What a man sows, he must reap. To use George Eliot's words: "Our children may be strangled, but our deeds never; they live and act apart from our will." Neither priest nor God can prevent each act bearing its own consequence; nor are the inequalities of this life to be compensated by rewards in the next. Our condition in this life is the result of our acts in past lives, and our future condition is shaped by our conduct in this life. But all component things are impermanent. The conviction of the impermanence and vanity of the world is the beginning of spiritual life. When in the evolution of countless births and by the strenuous pursuit of the Eightfold Path desire ceases, its effect, life, ceases, and perfected being enters upon the final emancipation, called *Nirvana*, the extinction of conscious life and of sorrow. This goal Gautama attained unaided, and so may all others if they will, like him, persevere. He could not keep this knowledge to himself. For love of humanity, and to release it from sorrow, he "set in motion the wheel of the law as a king the triumphant wheel of his kingdom."

His teaching thus contained in it, as the author of the "Light of Asia" has said, "the eternity of a universal hope, the immortality of a boundless love, an indestructible element of faith in final good, and the proudest assertion ever made of human freedom. The extravagances which disfigure the record and practice of Buddhism are to be referred to that inevitable degradation which priesthoods always inflict upon great ideas committed to their charge. The power and sublimity of Gautama's teachings should be estimated by their influence and not by their interpreters, nor by that lazy and ceremonious church which has arisen on the foundations of the priesthood or Sangha.'

The teaching was not in its essence new to India. He himself declared that it had been taught by numerous Buddhas before him. Professor Wilson was of opinion that it was merely the Sankhya philosophy of the Hindus turned into a national religion. In earlier works, the Upanishads of the Vedas, these doctrines appear, even the denial of a personal God. "The purpose of the Upanishads was," says Professor Max Müller, "to show the utter uselessness—nay, the mischievousness—of all ritual performances; to condemn every sacrificial act which has for its motive a desire or hope of reward; to deny, if not the existence, at least the exceptional and exalted character of the Devas, and to teach that there is no hope of salvation and deliverance except by the individual self recognising the true and universal self, and finding rest there, where alone rest can be found." Often in the history of India such teaching was suppressed by the priests, bent on keeping the people in the fetters of ignorance and of a rigid system of caste and an elaborate lifeless ritual; and often there were popular revolts against the despotism.

The times were now ripe for a revolt, and Gautama headed it. Every reformer in India has to reassert in some form the brotherhood of man. Gautama addressed himself not to select disciples, but to all the people, and proclaimed a deliverance from the sins and sorrows of life by self-conquest and universal love, and to his message he added the magnetism of his personality and the undying influence of a noble life. That was the secret of his marvellous success. While denying the existence of any external being or god who could interfere with the immutable law of cause and effect, his teaching linked together mankind as parts of one universal whole, and denounced the isolated self-seeking of the human heart as the heresy of individuality. Its mission was to make men more moral, kinder to others and happier themselves, not to propitiate imaginary deities. It accordingly founded its teaching on man's duty to his neighbour instead of on his obligations to gods, and constructed its ritual on a basis of relic worship, or the commemoration of good men, instead of on sacrifice. Its sacred buildings were not temples to the god, but monasteries (*viharas*) for the religious orders with their bells and rosaries, or memorial shrines (*dagobas, stupas*) reared over a tooth or bone of the founder of the faith.

With a zeal that has never been surpassed the heralds of the "Great Doctrine" went in search of the remotest barbarous or civilised peoples, everywhere proclaiming the good tidings of equality, self-abnegation, justice, and brotherly love. Crossing the Hindu Kush, the Pamir, and Himalayas, they undertook the moral conquest of the regions stretching from these lofty ranges to the Pacific seaboard. Their faith subdued the peoples of Tibet, Mongolia, China, Japan, while their influence was felt, under the form of Shamanism, amongst the Chukches, Tunguses, Samoyedes, and other tribes dwelling along the shores of the Frozen Ocean. Buddhism brought with it the moral and legal discipline of mankind, softening their rugged character, polishing their rough edges, and introducing arts, sciences, and literature to the nations. What Buddhism has done for Mongolian culture cannot be too highly appreciated. Till the middle of the nineteenth century, before the great convulsions in China and the enormous increase of the white race in Europe and the New World, the followers of Buddha were still far more numerous than those of all the Christian sects combined.

At the present day it prevails in Ceylon, Tibet, Nepaul, China, Burma, Siam, Japan, Siberia, &c., and counts probably about 500 millions of votaries. While in other countries Buddhism is more or less subordinate to the national religion or philosophy—Confucianism or Taoism in China, Shintoism in Japan, &c.—in Ceylon it holds a more commanding place, is of a purer form, and has a longer continuous history. The Buddhism of this island was derived from the original stem at a time when it was still but little altered from its primitive form. Centuries afterwards the religion, with the wide divergences that had then arisen, passed into China, Japan, and Tibet, constituting what is sometimes called the "Northern" school.

The introduction of Buddhism into Ceylon occurred, according to the Sinhalese chronicles, about 300 B.C., in the reign of Devanampiya Tissa, to whom the monk Mahinda was sent by his father, the Emperor Asoka, as an apostle of Buddhism. The Sinhalese king, who was, like his predecessor, of the Hindu faith, became an enthusiastic convert, and the religion spread rapidly. In the work of propagandism Mahinda was aided by his sister, Sanghamitta, who followed him to Ceylon for the purpose of initiating the women of the island. She brought with her a branch of the tree (*Ficus religiosa*) under which Buddha had sat at the time he attained supreme knowledge, and which is accordingly known among the Buddhists as the Tree of Knowledge, *Bodhi* or *Bo*. This branch was planted at Anuradhapura, and the tree that sprang up still stands, the oldest and most venerated tree in the world.

In Ceylon Buddhism has become intermixed with popular Hinduism. "The historical causes of this," says Dr. Copleston in his work on Buddhism, "are obvious. A large proportion of Hindus from Southern India became mingled with the population of the island. Tamil soldiers were employed as mercenaries by the native kings; alliances in marriage were repeatedly, almost regularly, made with the royal families of the continent. A succession of Tamil conquerors invaded the island and usurped its thrones. All these things, as well as the ordinary intercourse of commerce between neighbouring countries, familiarised the Sinhalese with the Hinduism of the time. Nor was it altogether an alien influence, for it was on a Hindu foundation, we must remember, that all the social system of the Sinhalese had been built, and this Buddhism had not destroyed."

It has thus happened that to every Buddhist temple (*vihara*) is attached (though not officially recognised by the Buddhist priests) a Hindu temple (*dewale*), where the cult of Hindu deities under the names of Natha, Vishnu, &c., flourishes, and shares with Buddhism imposing festivals, the chief of which is the yearly festival and procession held in the month of July at the Dalada Maligawa, Kandy, the temple of the Sacred Tooth Relic of Buddha. "Buddha for the soul, the gods for this world," was, according to Knox (the captive of King Rajasinha), the rule of action of the masses of the people in his time (1660–1680), and it is still true. Demonism and astrology also play an important part in the popular religion.[1] A better day appears to have dawned for Ceylon Buddhism. Thanks to Colonel Olcott and Madame Blavatsky, the founders of the Theosophical Society established in Ceylon in 1880, truer ideas of Buddha's teaching have been spread, and a remarkable revival has occurred under leaders of high character.

The ordinary profession of faith of a Buddhist declares that he seeks refuge in Buddha, in his law or doctrine, and in the community of his monks. Of Buddha and his law I have spoken. The community, during the long course of the island's history, has undergone numerous vicissitudes. Whenever the kings were unable or unwilling to support the community, its members rapidly fell off, till (as frequently recorded in the chronicles) there were no longer enough members to form a chapter; and it even happened that there

SINHALESE GIRL.
(Carrying water vessel on head.)

was not a single qualified monk left. The community had then to be renewed by the king importing monks from abroad. The three ancient orders of monks, the fraternities of Maha Vihara, the Abhayagiri, and the Jetavana, which date respectively from about 300 B.C., 100 B.C., and 300 A.D., no longer exist. Their place is taken by fraternities of quite recent origin—the Siamese, the Burmese or Amarapura, and the Ramanna.

The first named is the oldest of the three, and dates its origin from about 1750 A.D., when Kirti Sri Rajasinha obtained twenty monks from Siam to revive the succession. The Amarapura sect, which was founded about 1800 A.D., comes next, while the Ramanna sect is the youngest, as it is the smallest. The home of the Siamese sect is the Kandyan country; but it is largely represented in the low-country or maritime provinces, where about 20 per cent. of the monks belong to it. The Amarapura and Ramanna predominate in the low-country, but are little by little gaining ground in the Kandyan, where they amount together to 10 per cent. of the whole. It is roughly computed that of the total number of Buddhist priests about half belong to the Siamese sect, 34 per cent. to the Amarapura sect, and 16 per cent. to the Ramanna. This division into sects, however, does not affect the laity to any great extent. All Buddhists, to whatever sect they may belong, attend the principal places of worship, and a layman gives alms to Buddhist priests without regard to their sect.

There are many points of difference between the three fraternities, but to an outsider only two or three seem to be important. The Siamese sect admits to the priesthood none but members of the Vellala caste, the other sects admit members of most other castes. At the present time the Amarapura sect includes a member of the royal family of Siam. Another point of difference is that the Amarapura and Ramanna sects recognise and use, while the Siamese disallow, the chief formula for giving to the priests: "To the Buddha, to the monks, and to the nuns I give." The reason given for disallowing it is that Buddha is no longer alive and in a position to receive gifts. The sects which use the formula contend that the absent or deceased Buddha may be represented by his relics, and a casket of them is made to do duty as his representative. The Ramanna monks aim at a more genuine poverty, possess no lands, use no smart robes or silk umbrellas, but carry only the native palm-leaf umbrella; they avoid all association with Hindu rites and temples of Siva, Vishnu, &c., and denounce the worship of all those lower deities which occupy in practice so large a part of the field of popular Buddhism. It is not perhaps surprising that this sect, being so radical, is not influential.

Hinduism is the religion which, next to Buddhism, has the largest number of followers in Ceylon—826,826 at the last census (1901), or 2,319 in every 10,000 persons of the population. "Hindu" is a very comprehensive and elastic designation, and embraces great varieties of religious belief and philosophy. The term is in fact a foreign one, and does not exist in the Indian languages. It is used by the Indian Government to mean the large residuum that is not Sikh or Jain or Buddhist or professedly Animistic, or included in one of the foreign religions, such as the Christian, Jew, Mahomedan, or Parsee. "Thus limited," says Mr. Baines, the Indian Census Commissioner of 1891, "a more applicable title for it would be

[1] See an interesting article on "Demonology and Witchcraft in Ceylon," in the Ceylon Royal Asiatic Society's *Journal*, vol. iv., by Dandris de Silva Gunaratna, Mudaliyar.

Brahmanism, which connotes its two chief characteristics in the present day, the recognition of inherited social status and the authority of a hereditary sacerdotalism." Another chief characteristic which ought to have been added is the recognition of the authority of the Vedas, the sacred lore of the Brahmans.

There is a countless multitude of Hindu sects, old and new, but the main divisions are the Saivas, Vaishnavas, and Saktas. The two former are worshippers of Siva or Vishnu, the principal members of the Hindu trinity. The Saktas are worshippers of the female personification of the divine energy (Sakti):

"Mother of millions of world-clusters, yet Virgin
by the Vedas called."

Few Hindus of learning will acknowledge themselves to belong to any of the popular divisions of the faith, although, as a matter of simple preference, they more especially worship some individual deity as their chosen or *Ishta devata*. They refer also to the Vedas, the books of law, the Puranas, and the Tantras as the only ritual they recognise, and regard all practices not derived from those sources as irregular and profane. On the other hand, many of the sects seem to have originated in a great measure out of opposition to the Brahmanical order. Teachers and disciples are chosen from any class, and the distinction of caste is in a great measure sunk in the new one of similarity of schism.

A fundamental distinction must be noted, even among the most orthodox, between the ritual priest—who is always of a hereditary high caste, a Brahman, and in Tamil-land may be a Vellala—and the spiritual priest, who may be of any caste. This is one of those transcendent things which puzzle the student of Indian life, who is accustomed to associate with it, and in great measure truly, the immutable and depressing barriers of caste. But high spiritual culture is held to overleap these barriers, which are intended, say the Hindu masters, not to cramp and crush, but to safeguard and develop the soul, as a plant is protected by an enclosure, which may be dispensed with as soon as the plant grows out of the reach of cattle. Among the saints of the Hindu calendar worshipped in the temples are men of the lowest castes and even outcasts, and to this day members of the highest castes do not scruple to pay divine honours to living men whom they regard as saints, however low their caste.

Hinduism undoubtedly sought, like all other religions, to conquer the world. It reached the Caspian Sea on one side, and on the other the island of Java. Mighty ruins of temples attest its former predominance, and its influence still survives in the dialects, traditions, manners, arts, and political institutions of the people. All the languages of Eastern Asia preserve, at least, the traces of the myths and heroic legends disseminated by the Hindu missionaries. Even among the pagan communities of the Malay islands and of the Indo-Chinese forests ceremonies are still observed which here and there recall the rites formerly practised in the Punjab.

The extraordinary vitality of Hinduism and its power of adapting itself to new circumstances have been often remarked. "Among all the kindred conceptions that we meet with," says Mons. Barth, "there is not another which has shown itself so vigorous, so flexible, so apt as this to assume the most diverse forms, and so dexterous in reconciling all extremes, from the most refined idealism to the grossest idolatry; none has succeeded so well in repairing its losses, no one has possessed in such a high degree the power of producing and reproducing new sects, even great religions, and of resisting by way of perpetual regenesis in this way from itself all the causes that might destroy it, at once those due to internal waste and those due to external opposition." Buddhism is perhaps the most conspicuous instance of a great religion and philosophy which arose out of Hinduism, and which has become absorbed in it so completely that no Buddhists are now left on the Indian peninsula, where once their faith reigned triumphant from Nepaul and Cashmere to Cape Comorin. Evidence of this vitality and elasticity is still furnished, on the one hand, by the process now going on of absorption by Brahmanism of the forest tribes of India and Ceylon with their tribal gods and spirits, and, on the other, by the way in which the religion is meeting the forces of modern science and civilisation.

The explanation is to be found in the absence of dogma. The fundamental idea of the religion is thus stated in the Bhagavad Gita: "However men approach me, even so do I accept them, for the path men take from every side is mine" (iv. 11). "They who worship other gods with devotion, full of faith, they also worship me. I am indeed the enjoyer of all sacrifices and also the lord. But they know not me in essence" (ix. 23). The knowledge of God is the goal set before every human being, and God is not far off, but is "seated in the hearts of all beings, like fire in wood, ghee in milk," waiting to be manifested. All religions are ways, short or long, to the goal; none is false.

The Hindu sages claim to have organised a system providing for the needs and capacities of persons in every stage of intellectual and spiritual growth, and significantly called the *Sopana Marga*, or the Ladder-way. "Each soul," it has been said, "is potentially divine. The goal is to manifest the divinity within by controlling nature, external and internal. Do this either by work or worship or psychic control or philosophy, by one or more or all of these, and be free. This is the whole of religion. Doctrines or dogmas or rituals or books or temples or forms are but secondary details." In this process of evolution, which is not limited to one life, but may extend over many lives, the pilgrim soul passes step by step from animism, polydæmonism, idolatry, therianthropic and anthropomorphic polytheism, henotheism, monotheism, to the most absolute monism. *Ekam sat* is the last word, "*All that is, is One.*"

"What is here is that there, what is there is that here,
By the mind this must be grasped: there is not here many, no, not at all.
From death to death he goes who sees here many.
Who sees but One in the changing manifoldness of this universe,
Unto him belongeth Eternal Truth, unto none else, unto none else."

Numerically, the Christians occupy the third place among the religions of Ceylon. The earliest reference to Christianity in Ceylon is made by Cosmas Judicopleustes, a Nestorian, who lived in the reign of the Emperor Justinian, and who alludes to a colony of Christians, who were probably followers of the Patriarch of Constantinople, as sojourning in the island for purposes of trade. But no systematic attempt at propagating Christianity seems to have been made in Ceylon until the Portuguese established themselves.

The Roman Catholics were the first in the field. One of the earliest and the greatest of their missionaries was St. Francis Xavier, a native of Navarre, who was one of the seven original members of the celebrated "Company of Jesus," and has been called "the Apostle of the Indies." He arrived in the island in 1542 and commenced a mission among the Tamils of the district of Mannar. It is a remarkable testimony to the success of his ministrations that Mannar contains, out of a total Christian population of 12,367, as many as 11,245 Roman Catholics, and is one of the two districts in the island in which Christianity is the predominant religion, the other district being the almost adjoining district of Chilaw, in which more than half the population are Christians. The Portuguese Government never neglected an opportunity of propagating their faith. The Portuguese navigator Cabral, in the sixteenth century, was instructed by royal commission to conquer territory and to propagate Christianity, beginning the latter task "with preaching, and, if that failed, proceeding to the sharp determination of the sword." Fortunately for the cause of Roman Catholicism the Portuguese rule ceased, and with it the policy of forcible conversion. The self-sacrificing zeal and devotion of the missionaries has proved a far more potent instrument for the spread of the religion. The result is seen in the fact that of Christians those of the Roman Catholic sect are far the most numerous in the island.

The Dutch, who succeeded the Portuguese in the occupation of the seaboard of Ceylon, were not less ardent in establishing their own religious denomination. They made public offices the monopoly of the Protestant Christians, and withheld other civil privileges from all who had not been so baptized. Proclamation was publicly made (*circa* 1640) that no native could aspire to the rank of Mudaliyar, or even be permitted to farm land or hold office under Government, who had not first undergone the ceremony of baptism. In 1692 Buddhist ceremonies were prohibited at the Kelani temple, near Colombo, and the priests ordered to withdraw from the temple. A marriage could not be registered unless the parties were Christians, nor a child's birth registered unless baptized. Very many who were Buddhists at heart made a formal profession of Christianity in order to secure the privilege of duly registered baptism and marriage. These disqualifications remained in force till removed by the English Government. On the cession to the British Crown of the possessions of the Dutch East India Company in 1796, the maintenance of their religious establishments was by treaty secured to the Dutch, their ministers being paid by the British Government. The Church of England then became a department of the State, and so continued until the connection between Church and State was severed in 1878.

Of the Protestant Missions now in the island the earliest was the Baptist Mission. The London Missionary Society seems to have sent out to Ceylon in 1804 three Germans to found a mission, but that body has no footing here now. In 1812 a deputation arrived from the Baptist Mission at Serampur, near Calcutta, for mission work in Colombo. The Wesleyans founded a mission in Ceylon in 1814. The American missionaries (Congregationalists), whose operations have been confined to the Northern Province, were the next to arrive (1815), followed by the Church Missionary Society in 1818, and the Society for the Propagation of the Gospel in 1840. The Salvation Army was first introduced into Ceylon in 1883.

Mahomedanism is professed in Ceylon by Moors and Malays. They are of the Sunni sect—the Shia sect being hardly represented except among Indian Mahomedans—and, though strict in the observance of their faith, are less bigoted than their co-religionists in India. The main difference between the Shias and Sunnis is that the former specially venerate Ali, "the Lion of God," son-in-law of the Prophet and the fourth Caliph. They consider that part of the divine inspiration descended on him, and refuse to recognise the first three Caliphs. The sons of Ali, Hassan and Hussein, were murdered, one by poison and the other on the field of Kerbela. "O death," cries the bandit-minstrel of Persia in his last song before his execution, "O death, whom didst thou spare? Were even Hassan and Hussein, those footstools of the throne of God on the seventh heaven, spared by thee? No, thou madest them martyrs at Kerbela." The martyrdom of these heroes is annually celebrated by the Shias during the Moharrum festival by most affecting passion plays[1] (*tazias*), at which at frequent intervals all the multitude cry with the actors, "Ya Hassan! Ya Hussein!" ("O Hassan! O Hussein!"). At the conclusion, stately structures, representing the tombs of the martyrs and crowned with burning candles, circles of light, to show that they have entered into glory, are carried round in procession with the same cries. Hence the Anglo-Indian word "Hobson-Jobson" and the Ceylon word "Jausan" for this festival. The Sunnis are said not to observe the Moharrum except on the tenth day (when they believe Adam and Eve to have been created) and to abhor the *tazias*. But most of the Ceylon Mahomedans observe it in spite of their being nominally Sunnis.

A SINHALESE FAMILY.

The following table gives the numbers of the population deriving their livelihood from each class of occupation, with the proportion it bears to the total population :—

[1] See an interesting account of them in Matthew Arnold's "Essays on Criticism," First Series, vii., "A Persian Passion Play."

TABLE E.

NUMBER OF PERSONS OF EACH SEX SUBSISTING BY EACH CLASS OF OCCUPATION AND THE PROPORTION OF SUCH PERSONS TO 1,000 OF THE TOTAL POPULATION, 1901.

Occupation.	Persons.	Males.	Females.	Proportion to 1,000 Persons of the Total Population.		
				Persons.	Males.	Females.
Government	60,883	34,617	26,266	17·07	18·3	15·7
Agriculture	2,359,570	1,259,231	1,100,339	661·70	664·1	659·0
Personal Services	134,706	70,764	63,942	37·80	37·3	38·3
Preparation and Supply of Material Substances	613,689	296,858	316,831	172·10	156·5	189·8
Commerce, Transport, and Storage ...	185,761	111,059	74,702	52·09	58·6	44·7
Professions	71,431	44,384	27,047	20·03	23·4	16·2
Unskilled Labour, not Agricultural ..	125,606	72,035	53,571	35·20	38·0	32·1
Means of Subsistence Independent of Occupation	14,308	7,264	7,044	4·01	3·8	4·2

It will be seen that the largest proportion of the population—nearly two-thirds—falls under the agricultural class. Ceylon is an agricultural country *par excellence*. Land here is not the luxury of a few, but the business and concern of the vast majority of the inhabitants. Custom and tradition have assigned an honourable place in society to landholders, and the equal division of property, whether by the operation of the law in the case of intestates or by the force of public opinion and custom, to which, in the few cases where wills are made, testators as a rule conform, has led to a very extensive distribution of property. Not to own land is deemed in the rural parts almost to argue one a vagabond, while the tenacity with which the people cling to infinitesimal interests in land, and the bitterness with which their disputes about land are contested, have passed into a proverb. While those who are thus interested in land are probably more numerous than in any other country in the world, the great majority of the labourers in the island, whether native or immigrant, are agricultural labourers.

SINHALESE FAMILY GROUP.

It is well known that in Ceylon, as in India, occupation has, by inheritance and endogamy, been developed into the peculiar institution called "caste." The subject is an exceedingly interesting one, but too large to be adequately treated here. Among all civilised communities there are certain inevitable and natural divisions of society, by whatever name they may be called. A large number of the population must be employed in the production of food, clothing, shelter, and other physical necessaries of the community. This is the productive class. Then, there is the distributing class, which gathers the products of the former and scatters them through the community and makes them accessible to all. These two classes carry on their functions in peace and safety under the protection of what may be called a guardian class. It includes the soldiers and sailors who protect the people from foreign attack, and the civil officers who preserve internal order, governors, judges, lawyers, &c. Another class is indispensable for the healthy progress of the nation, a teaching class—teachers of science, philosophy, and religion.

The principal divisions of the Indian caste-system corresponded to those four great classes. The *Sudras* were the producers, the *Vaisyas* were the distributors, the *Kshattriyas* were the guardians, and the *Brahmans* the teachers. In course of time these four divisions differentiated into countless subdivisions, each calling itself a caste, and keeping itself exclusive by restrictions on marriage and on eating with other castes, and by rules of ceremonial observance and purity. Inherited occupation, which was the original bond of connection between the members of a caste and generally gave it its name, gradually ceased to be of primary importance, and the caste name was retained by members who had abandoned the original caste occupation for other occupations.

Inherited status has prevailed in many countries, ancient and modern. In many European countries sovereignty and nobility still pass solely by right of birth. By right of birth, kings and nobles rule, make laws, take titles. The eldest son of a duke or earl becomes duke or earl on his father's death, and the moment he gets his title, if of age, he goes into the House of Lords and makes laws for the people. The whole British Empire is ruled by that House, in conjunction with the Crown and the Commons, and the order of peers is filled, except in the case of the first generation, not by right of knowledge, wisdom, age, or capacity, but of birth. In an early period of English history the great middle class, which grew up slowly under the shadow of the nobility, devoting itself o commerce and agriculture, and whose achievements are the main burden of English history, formed themselves in the towns into guilds, corresponding to the *collegia* of ancient Rome, for different kinds of trade and handicraft for commercial and technical education, for the maintenance of the tradition of each calling, for protection against the aggression of other classes, and for the kindly charity of mutual help, purposes which Indian castes still fulfil. Below the middle class was the mass of the cultivators and producers tied to the soil, with duties of what are called feudal tenure, bound to discharge these duties in exchange for protection, ever bound so strictly to the soil that even to-day in England, if a man is starving, the first question that is asked is, "What parish does he belong to?" which means, "Where was he born?" "Which is the place that is responsible for his maintenance?"

Nor are the restrictions on the right of intermarriage and on the right of eating together features peculiar to India or Ceylon. These phenomena have long been known to historians and jurists, and received distinctive technical names : *connubium* and *commensality*. The connubium was the cause of a long and determined struggle between the patricians and plebeians of Rome. Evidence has been accumulating as to the existence of both kinds of restriction among other Aryan tribes, Greeks, Germans, Russians, &c. In fact, rules of endogamy and exogamy, privileges restricted to certain classes of eating together, are not only Indian or Aryan, but world-wide phenomena. Both the spirit and, to a large degree, the actual details of modern Indian caste usages are identical with these ancient and no doubt universal customs.[1]

"Public opinion still insists, in considerable circles even in Europe, on restrictions of a more or less defined kind, both as to marriage and as to eating together." [2]

Aristotle showed in his "Politics," a work which has been called "the statesman's manual" and "the greatest work in political science," that unless the purpose of a civil and social life is carefully considered and clearly realised by those who desire to improve its condition, no change for the better can result from individual or associated action. The special characteristic of the Indian caste system is that it sought to organise the four indispensable functions of civilised society on a definite plan, so that the nation shall be orderly, not anarchical, contented, and not continually at struggle and strife. The system has lasted in India longer than elsewhere for this reason, and because the particular group that worked its way to the top based its claims on spiritual culture, not on political power nor wealth.

The underlying ideal was that humanity is a brotherhood in which every one holds his power for the common good, and uses his faculties for the common service. If he is strong, he is strong not to injure and bully the younger mambers of the family, but to defend and guard them, and so to serve the whole. The greater the strength, the greater the duty ; the greater the power, the greater the responsibility to discharge. The burden laid on each must be in proportion to his strength, knowledge, and capacity.

For the lowest of the four castes, the *Sudras*, the great mass of manual workers and the least equipped with knowledge and capacity, the duties prescribed were, as for children, the duties of subordination, obedience, and service. The discipline, too, was light. They might do almost anything in the way of occupation, and eat, drink, and travel almost as they would. On the *Vaisya* was the heavy responsibility of wealth, hand in hand with severe restrictions put upon him. His duty was to be a faithful steward in the national household. By him labour and trade were to be organised, and everything else done that was necessary for the production of national wealth. This wealth he was to distribute in such manner that plenty, not poverty, shall become permanent, and learning and virtue find an abiding home in the land. The poor and destitute were to be fed and clothed, learning and religion supported, temples, schools, and pilgrim-houses maintained.

A RODIYA FAMILY.

Heavier still was the demand on the *Kshattriya*. He held his life for the national service and the national welfare. If there was danger, it must not strike the Sudra, the Vaisya, or the Brahman. It was the Kshattriya's privilege to go out for their defence and give his life as sacrifice for the people, who looked to him as ruler and protector. Then there came the fourth class, that of teacher, the *Brahman*. Hedged about with hard restrictions, cut away from the enjoyment of life, bidden to have no worldly wealth, for wealth belonged to the Vaisya ; bidden to have no right to struggle for liberty, for that belonged to the Kshattriya ; bidden not to eat and drink and travel about as he liked, for these were the privileges of the Sudra; but he had the hard life of self-denial, which cut him off from the enjoyment and luxuries of life and marked him to be kept pure in his magnetism, guarding his magnetism for the welfare of his people, not for selfish pride and conceit, not for personal arrogance or for personal domination, but in order that the gods might have a mouth to speak through to the people, and that the lips of the Brahman might be the lips that should teach the law.

This was the basis of caste, the idea of the ancient order. No doubt through the many centuries of India's life these ideals were often lost sight of, often outraged, and perhaps never more so than in the present age, when caste no longer stands for settled obligation and unrelenting duty, but rather for the assertion and grasping of rights. But even in its embers the ideal is there. It lingers in every village community, the primitive, self-centred, self-governing institution, which, despite domestic anarchy and foreign conquest, has through countless generations preserved its simple customs written only on the imperishable tablets of tradition. Lord Metcalfe said to a Select Committee of the House of Commons in 1832 : "The village communities are little republics, having nearly everything they can want within themselves and almost independent of any foreign relations. They seem to last when nothing else lasts. Dynasty follows dynasty, revolution succeeds to revolution; Hindu, Patan, Mogul, Marhatta, Sikh, English, are all masters in turn ; but the village community remains the same." It has been truly said that the caste

[1] Compare, *e.g.*, Daniel's objection to "defile himself with the portion of (Nebuchadnezzar) the king's meat, nor with the wine which he drank" (Book of Daniel, i. 8).

[2] "Encyclopædia Britannica," vol. xxvi., ed. 1902, p. 433.

system of the village communities alone has saved the civilisation of India from shipwreck and enabled her to witness the rise and fall of many empires and civilisations.

The evolution of caste has not proceeded on the same lines in Ceylon as in India. The Sinhalese, the vast majority of whom are Buddhists, do not assign to their priests the highest place in their social system. They have, in fact, no priest caste, but only fraternities of monks, which any qualified person may enter and leave at will. Theoretically, at least, birth is not a qualification, but in practice only the higher castes are admitted. Among the Hindus a priest must be by birth of the Brahman caste, and among the Tamils he may also be of the Vellala caste ; and he must be a married householder. The status and dignity of a Brahman or Vellala attach to every member of the priest's family. The priest is indispensable to the Hindu social system, for he alone can conduct public worship in temples and can perform the domestic ceremonies which mark every stage of a Hindu's life from the womb to the grave.

Though these ceremonies are designed to develop spiritual life in the laity, the Brahman is to be regarded mainly as a ritual priest, and must be distinguished from the true spiritual priest, who sows his seed in the soil prepared by the other, and is more highly revered. The relationship of the spiritual priest to his disciple is a purely personal one, and no caste, race, or sex qualification is necessary either for teacher or pupil, for the spirit has no caste, race, or sex. A person of a low caste or even outcast may be a spiritual teacher. This rule has lightened the burden of the Sudra's lot, for it throws open to genius the highest of positions. The best known of modern Hindu sages, Ramakrishna Swami, of Bengal, who died in 1886, and whose life was written by Professor Max Müller, had for his teacher a woman, who was for him what Diotima was to Socrates, and who inspired in him the same devotion, love, and gratitude.

It is related of Sankaracharya, the great Hindu apostle, to whose philosophic expositions and zeal as itinerant preacher is attributed the overthrow of Buddhism in India, and whose successor at the abbey of Sringeri in Mysore is the spiritual head, if there be one, of the Hindus, that on one occasion, while travelling with the pomp suitable to his dignity, he suddenly met on the road a Paria bearing a load of beef fresh slaughtered and dripping with blood. Shrinking from the sight with a holy Brahman's horror, he called out imperiously to the outcast to move out of sight. "Whom dost thou order," answered the Paria with amazing boldness, "to move out of sight, the spirit or the flesh ?" Sankaracharya, remembering that the flesh of his own body did not differ from that of the Paria or the beef, and realising that the all-pervading Spirit of God was equally in Paria and Brahman, recognised in this outcast his long-waited-for spiritual teacher, and descending from his palanquin, prostrated himself at the Paria's feet. The Paria, who was (it is said) no other than the lord Siva, vanished. Sankaracharya's conversion dates from this incident, and to him Hinduism owes more than to any other man.

That the Brahmans were in the early times confined to ceremonial and sacrifice appears from a remarkable passage in the Chandogya Upanishad of the Sáma Veda which has escaped the revising hands of the Brahmans, who have for centuries been the sole repositories of the sacred books. A Brahman there sought instruction in the mysteries of spiritual knowledge from a king. The latter "was afflicted" by the request, and after deliberation reluctantly assented, saying, "As to what you have thus inquired, no Brahman ever knew it before, hence of all people in the world the Kshattriyas alone have the right of imparting this instruction" (Chand. Upanish., v., iii., 7). The commentator, the celebrated Sankaracharya above-mentioned, explains : "It is a well-known fact that heretofore Brahmans knew nothing of this subject ; now were they guided by this knowledge. The Kshattriya race alone are its possessors. Hitherto it has been preserved among them from generation to generation. I shall now relate it unto you, and henceforward it will remain with the Brahmans."

Another difference between the North Indian and Ceylon caste systems is that the former had an ethnological origin. The term "caste" (which is the Portuguese *casta* and French *caste*, from Latin *castus*, pure) means breed or race, and was first used by the Portuguese for the social divisions of the Hindus. The Sanskrit term is *varna*, colour, this having been the original ground of caste distinction. The old Aryan invaders of India belonged to the same stock that founded the nations of Persia, Greece, and Rome, and which produced the forefathers of the Celts, Teutons, Goths, and Slavs, who people the English, German, Latin, and Slavonic countries of modern Europe. The invaders were of a fair complexion, and with a noble self-confidence, which is a great aid to national success, called themselves Aryas, "noble." They found in India a dark, squat-faced race, probably of Mongol origin, with whom the newcomers long waged war, and whom they finally drove back before them into the mountains, or (according to the custom of primitive times) reduced to slavery, branding them with the name of *Dasyus* (slaves or devils) and *Sudras* (vile). The Aryan poets praised in the Rig Veda (as in like circumstances the Hebrews praised Yahveh) their bright gods, who, "slaying the Dasyus, protected the Aryan colour" (*varna*), who "subjected the black skin to the Aryan man." The sacrificer gave thanks to his gods for "dispersing the slave bands of black descent" and for "sweeping away the vile Dasya colour." The aborigines are described as "noseless," and his own gods are described as "beautiful-nosed" gods.

At this period there was among the invaders little differentiation of occupation. Each father of a family was the priest of his own household as well as warrior. The chieftain acted as father and priest to the tribe, but at the greater festivals he chose some one specially learned in holy offerings to conduct the sacrifice in the name of the people. Domestic duties were left to the women ; disagreeable or low occupations were assigned to the aborigines. The English word "daughter" (which is the Sanskrit *duhitri*, Greek θύγατηρ, Scotch *dochter*, German *tochter*, and is derived from the Sanskrit root *du*, to milk, a root which is traceable in the Hindustani *dudh*, milk, and English *dug*, a teat of a cow or other animal) preserves the memory of the time when the daughter was the little milkmaid in the primitive Aryan household.

In course of time, as the Aryans spread and settled in the country, they were themselves obliged to engage in some of the lower occupations. But they did not deem themselves thereby lowered to the level of the aborigines. Here the feeling of race came in, and an Aryan who became, say, an agriculturist or artizan, though not equal to those of his class who remained warriors and priests, was separated by a gulf from the Sudra who engaged in agriculture or handicraft. At a later period a split occurred between the priests and warriors, and a fierce contest for supremacy arose, which ended, strangely enough, in the all but extermination of the warriors, and the reduction of the survivors to the second position. The priests then manipulated the scriptures to still further establish their predominance. They made codes of laws, imposing on the lower castes (who had by this time become very numerous by differentiation of occupation and by intermixture of blood of separate castes and races) heavy disabilities, and often breathing somewhat of the fierce malignity which characterises the relations of the whites to the blacks in some American States.

These Brahmanical laws and institutions were the outcome of race arrogance. But even in these fierce codes the noble ideals of the sages, which I have referred to, and which alone can make caste a useful and beneficent institution, were not ignored. Specially for the Brahman was a severe life of discipline laid down in four clearly defined stages of student, householder, forest recluse, and ascetic.

"It may be objected," says Sir W. Hunter, "that so severe a life of discipline could never be led by any large class of men. And no doubt there have been at all times worldly Brahmans; and the struggle for existence in modern times has compelled the great majority of the Brahmans to betake themselves to more practical pursuits. But the whole body of Sanskrit literature bears witness to the fact that this ideal life was constantly before their eyes, and that it served to the whole caste as a high standard in its two really essential features of self-culture and self-restraint. Incidents in the history of Buddha, in the sixth century before Christ, show that numbers of Brahmans at that time lived according to its rule; and three hundred years later the Greek ambassador, Megasthenes, found the Brahmans discoursing in their groves, chiefly on life and death. The Chinese travellers, down to the tenth century A.D., attest the survival of the Brahmanical pattern of the religious life. The whole monastic system of India, and those vast religious revivals which have given birth to the modern sects of Hinduism, are based on the same withdrawal from worldly affairs. At this day Brahman colleges, called *tols*, are carried on without fees, on the old model at Nadiya in Bengal, and elsewhere. I can testify from personal visits to the stringent self-discipline, and to the devotion to learning for its own sake, often protracted till past middle life, and sometimes by grey-haired students, in these retreats.

"The Brahmans, therefore, were a body of men who, in an early stage of this world's history, bound themselves by a rule of life, the essential precepts of which were self-culture and self-restraint. As they married within their own caste, begat children only during their prime, and were not liable to lose the finest of their youth in war, they transmitted their best qualities in an ever-increasing measure to their descendants. The Brahmans of the present day are the result of three thousand years of hereditary education and self-restraint; and they have evolved a type of mankind quite distinct from the surrounding population. Even the passing traveller in India marks them out, alike from the bronze-cheeked, large-limbed, leisure-loving Rajput, or warrior caste of Aryan descent, and from the dark-skinned, flat-nosed, thick-lipped, low castes of non-Aryan origin, with their short bodies and bullet heads. The Brahman stands apart from both, tall and slim, with finely modelled lips and nose, fair complexion, high forehead, and slightly coconut-shaped skull—the man of self-centred refinement. He is an example of a class becoming the ruling power in a country, not by force of arms, but by vigour of hereditary culture and temperance. One race has swept across India after another, dynasties have risen and fallen, religions have spread themselves over the land and disappeared. But since the dawn of history the Brahman has calmly ruled, swaying the minds and receiving the homage of the people, and accepted by foreign nations as the highest type of Indian mankind."

Among the Dravidians of South India and Ceylon the caste system was rather different in origin and character. This race appeared in India before the Aryans or the Dasyus, whom they subdued, and belong to a widely distributed stock, which is sometimes called the Ural-Altaic, Scythian, or Turanian family. It founded the ancient civilisation of Babylonia, and colonised Europe long before the Aryans. Among its descendants are the Lapps and Finns of Northern Europe, the Basques of the Pyrenees, the Magyars of Hungary, the Ottoman Turks, the Ostiaks and other Ugrians of Siberia. Linguistic and other affinities seem to indicate that the inhabitants of some of the islands of the Pacific Ocean and the aboriginal tribes of South and West Australia were derived from Dravidian settlements in India, or from an earlier common source. The Dravidians

NATIVE CHILDREN.

probably once occupied the greater part of Northern India, where traces of their blood and speech are still found, but their seat from the dawn of history has been South India. They are also called the Tamilian race, because the Tamils are the oldest and most influential representatives of the race.

On their arrival in South India they found in possession of the land, and reduced to subjection, a people of whom the modern *Parias*, the outcasts of Tamil-land, are the representatives. This tribe forms the most numerous section of the population of the Tamil country and derives its name from the use of the drum (Tamil *parai*, Sinhalese *bera*)—they are the drummers at funerals. Curious vestiges of their ancient power survive in the shape of certain privileges, shadows of long departed supremacy, which are jealously cherished. In the great and ancient temple of Tiruvarur, near Negapatam, at the annual festival, the procession is headed by the headman of the Paria caste mounted on an elephant in front of the image of the god. At the Mailapore temple in the city of Madras, when the annual marriage ceremony of the goddess is celebrated and a *tali* (the symbol of marriage) is tied round the neck of the image in the name of the entire community, a Paria represents the community. In many villages of the Madras Presidency the lower village officers are Parias. Their ancient connection with the soil has made them the guardians of the boundaries. Whenever there is a dispute about the boundaries of a field, the Paria walks the boundaries with a pot of water on his head and settles the dispute.

The Paria, as Bishop Caldwell mentions, is, in spite of centuries of cruel servitude, filled, not less than the higher castes, with that compound of pride of birth, exclusiveness, and jealousy called caste - feeling. They have waged a long and bitter contest for precedence with the *Palla* caste, and they deal to inferior castes, such as the shoemakers and the lowest caste of washermen, the same unjust treatment they receive from the higher castes. They are a hardworking, honest, and simple people, and compare favourably with "the submerged tenth" of any other land. There is apparently a good deal of capacity in them. More than one has risen to be a saint of the Hindu calendar—proof, as creditable to the Paria as to the higher castes, of the impotence of caste barriers in the presence of genius. Under the influence of education, thanks to Christian missionary zeal, some have of late raised themselves to honourable positions in life, and earned the respect of the classes who previously oppressed and trod on them. To Ceylon the Parias and other inferior tribes owe much. They constitute the bulk of the immigrant labourers on tea estates, and of the grooms, rickshaw pullers, and scavengers of Ceylon. Here they are able to earn enough to supply their simple wants and even to send savings home, and they are subjected to valuable educational and civilising influences. From the Ceylon planter they learn the habit of methodical, honest work and discipline, and from the Ceylon laws they acquire a sense of justice, humanity, and equality, of self-respect and independence. These are not the least valuable of the acquisitions they carry home, and should prove important factors in the amelioration of the condition of their tribesmen.

The next most numerous section of the Tamil population of India and Ceylon is the *Vellalas*, or caste of cultivators, who hold a high social position, next only to the Brahman, in the Tamil country. There was no special priest-caste among the Tamils, and the Brahman appears to have been imported from the north when they adopted the Aryan civilisation. When the Tamils are spoken of in South India, the Vellalas are meant, as being the Tamils *par excellence*, both the Brahmans at the top of the modern social system and the aborigines at the bottom being excluded. This seems to indicate that these two are regarded as heterogeneous elements not reduced to the national type. The Aryanisation of the Tamils was carried out, not as in Northern India by conquest, but by the peaceable process of colonisation and progressive civilisation. All existing traditions and the names by which the Brahmans are designated in Tamil—*Aiyar* (fathers, instructors), *parppar* (overseers, the "episkopoi" of Arrian), *anthanar* (the gracious ones)—tend to show that the Brahmans acquired their ascendancy by high spiritual character, intelligence, and administrative skill. But the Tamils, while adopting Aryan civilisation, have left on it the impress of their own ancient civilisation and of their individuality. Their earliest recorded sage is called Akattiya, whom the Brahmans claim as one of themselves but whose name and history point rather to Accad, the ancient capital of Babylonia.

The Tamils were, like the Romans of old, "a nation of yeomen," and like them held agriculture in the highest esteem. "Of all pursuits from which profit accrues," says Cicero, "nothing is superior to agriculture, nothing more productive, nothing more enjoyable, nothing more worthy of a free man." "The world wheels behind the plough," says the Tamil sage, Tiruvalluvar; "of all work, therefore, ploughing is chief." "The ploughman is the lynch-pin of society: all others are maintained by him." "Those who live by the plough alone live: all others eat the bread of service." In this race of farmers three families appear to have early attained to a predominant position, and they founded the famous Pandya,[1] Choli, and Chera dynasties. They were by their Brahmanical preceptors dignified with the Aryan title of Kshattriya (a caste which did not exist in South India), and taught to trace their origin from the lunar race of the Aryans.

In the oldest extant of Tamil works, the *Tolkappiyam*, which is at least three thousand years old, and is attributed to a pupil of Akattiya, the Vellalas are described as "standing at the side of the king," and as being employed as generals, governors, ambassadors, &c. Among the ten virtues assigned by tradition and the books to the Vellalas, the first is loyalty to the king. The other qualities are the raising up of the fallen, payment of debts, compassionateness, support of relations, undaunted perseverance, peaceful living, hospitality, and unblemished conduct. The Portuguese historian of India, Faria y Souza, writing of the social divisions of his time (the seventeenth century), says: "The most renowned families are the Rajas, an ingenious people, who would rather lose their lives than their arms in battle; and the Brahmans, who contend with the Rajas for precedence. The Chetties[2] are the richest merchants. The Vellalas, or the country people, are held in such esteem that kings marry their daughters to Vellalas, saying they are the public substance."

There are two main divisions of the Vellalas from early times: those who themselves cultivated lands and those who had them cultivated by others. There was another division into merchants, chiefs, titled Vellalas and other Vellalas. Together with the priests and the kings they constituted the aristocracy of the land. The order assigned to the merchant indicates the advance of commerce or of Aryan ideas, according to which the Vaisya held the third place. Under the protection of the head of each family lived "in dependent freedom," analogous to the relation of client to patrician in ancient Rome or of vassal to lord in the feudal times in Europe, classes who performed personal and domestic services and laboured for their chief in industrial and other occupations and were called *kudi makkal*. The chief was entitled to the service of the feudatory whenever required, and the latter to a share of the produce of the land cultivated, to perquisites at weddings, funerals, &c. These classes were the washerman, barber, potter, gold or silver smith, brazier, mason, blacksmith, carpenter,

[1] A king of the Pandyan line was the first who sent an embassy from the East to Europe (*circa* 20 B.C.) to the Emperor Augustus. The second embassy to Rome was from the king of Ceylon to the Emperor Claudius (*circa* 50 A.D.).

[2] Not the Natu Kotte Chetties of the present day (who have within the last fifty or sixty years risen from a humble place in the social system), but the old merchant caste.

oilmonger, salt dealer, betel seller, garland maker, grave digger, chank blower, fisher, tailor, &c.

After the Aryanisation of the Dravidians was completed, the chieftains, merchants, and titled Vellalas were often called *Vaisyas* and the untitled Vellalas *Sudras*, both titles quite inappropriate, as Bishop Caldwell points out. "While it is evident that the entire mass of the Dravidians were regarded by Manu (the Aryan lawgiver) and the authors of the Mahabharata (the Aryan epic) and the Puranas (the Aryan legends) as Kshattriyas by birth, the Brahmans who settled amongst the Dravidians and formed them into castes, in imitation of the castes of the north, seem never at any time to have given the Dravidians, with the exception perhaps of the royal houses, a higher title than that of Sudra. They might have styled the agricultural classes Vaisyas, and reserved the name of Sudra for the village servants and the unenslaved low castes, but acting apparently on the principle that none ought to be called either Kshattriyas or Vaisyas but Aryans and that the Dravidians were not Aryans, they seem always to have called them Sudras, however respectable their position.

"In consequence of this the title Sudra conveys a higher meaning in Southern than in Northern India. The primitive Sudras of Northern India seem to have been slaves to the Aryans, or in a condition but little superior to that of slaves. They seem to have had no property of their own, and can scarcely be said to have had any civil rights. In Southern India, on the contrary, it was upon the middle and higher classes of the Dravidians that the title of Sudra was conferred ; and the classes that appeared to be analogous to the servile Sudras of Northern India were not called Sudras, but Pallas, Pareiyas, &c., names which they still retain. The application of the term Sudra to the ancient Dravidian chieftains, soldiers, and cultivators does not prove that they had ever been reduced by the Brahmans to a dependent position, or that they ever were slaves, as the northern Sudras appear to have been, to any class of Aryans. The Brahmans, who came in 'peaceably and obtained the kingdom by flatteries,' may probably have persuaded the Dravidians that in calling them Sudras they were conferring upon them a title of honour. If so, their policy was perfectly successful, for the title of Sudra has never been resented by the Dravidian castes ; and hence, whilst in Northern India the Sudra is supposed to be a low-caste man, in Southern India he generally ranks next to the Brahman. The term Sudra, however, is really, as we have seen, as inappropriate to any class of Dravidians as the term Kshattriya or Vaisya. It is better to designate each Dravidian caste simply by its own name, as Vellalas, Nayakkas, &c., in accordance with the usage prevailing amongst the people themselves in each locality, without attempting to classify the various castes according to Manu's principles of classification, which in reality are quite inapplicable to them, if not, indeed, equally inapplicable to the castes now existing in the North."

It was the Dravidian, not the Aryan caste system that found its way into Ceylon. Vijaya, the founder of the Sinhalese dynasty, is, it is true, described as a scion of a royal race of Northern India. But what is recorded of him, his parents and grandparents in the Mahavansa shows that they could hardly have been within the pale of the Brahmanical caste system. His parents had intermarried, although they were brother and sister, a heinous crime against the Brahmanical law, and they were themselves the issue of a princess who, under the influence of a degrading passion, ran away from her parents' protection, joined a caravan, was carried off by a lion (whom I take to be a bandit of the woods, called a lion from his fierce courage) and bore him two children, who became the parents of Vijaya. It is perhaps not surprising that with such antecedents he became such "a lawless character" as to necessitate his banishment from the country with 700 of his comrades. Arriving in Ceylon, he formed a temporary alliance with an aboriginal princess, and with her aid mercilessly slaughtered the aborigines or drove them into the mountains, and when he had established himself, discarded her and obtained wives for himself and his comrades from the court of Pandya, the chief Tamil king of Southern India. Far from his northern home, and separated by an impassable gulf from the aborigines, he and his successors were forced to depend more and more on the Tamil alliance and to employ Tamil colonists in developing the resources of the island by irrigation and agriculture and in establishing the civil and military administration. The introduction of Buddhism from the north made no difference in the social institutions of the court and of the people. No doubt the influence and prestige of the hereditary Brahman priest was reduced, but this was not repugnant to the Tamil ideals and traditions. The system was perpetuated during centuries by the close intercourse maintained with South India by alliances of marriage almost regularly made with its royal families, by the continuous employment of its soldiers and civilians by the kings, by a succession of Tamil kings who invaded and usurped its thrones, and by the ordinary intercourse of commerce.

VEDDAHS.

Thus arose the social importance in Ceylon of the Vellala, or *Goyi-gama*, as the caste is called, in the ancient Sinhalese polity. The order of castes was *Bamunu* (the Brahman), *Raja* (the king), and *Grahapati*, a term which became *Goviya*. Later, with the development of commerce, the *Velenda* or merchant was added. The first two castes were of course limited in numbers, and their relative precedence fluctuated : sometimes

Raja, *Bamunu*, and sometimes *Bamunu*, *Raja*. The *grahapati* or *goviya* class, like the Tamil Vellalas, consisted of the *radala* or *mudali peruwa*, chiefs; the *sitano*, persons nominated by the king as *sitano* or nobles (Sanskrit *sreshthi*), titled Vellalas; and the rest of the goviyas. Dependent on them was the class of artizans, &c., corresponding to the *kudi makkal* of Tamil-land. The manufacturers of cloth were a later importation from India. They were brought in the thirteenth century by Arab merchants and presented to the king of Ceylon, and were treated with distinction till their numbers and power excited jealousy. For an alleged offence against the king's authority they were deported to the south-west coast and employed in the packing and preparation of cinnamon, which then grew luxuriantly.

With the decline and fall of the native dynasties, the disorganisation of the irrigation system of the island and the consequent decay of the national industry, rice cultivation, with the advent of Europeans and the openings created by them for foreign trade and new industries, a change has come over the scene. Population, power, and wealth have been transferred from their ancient seats to the seaboard, new ideals and forces have arisen, and the daring seamen of the coast, and other castes, quickened into vigorous life by contact with Western influences, naturally contest the precedence of the Vellala, who hardly realises the importance of the struggle.

Both the Vellala and the castes which dispute his precedence are often very unjust and arrogant to the castes below them, and are open to the retort which Iphikrates made when upbraided by a young aristocrat for his low birth: "My family begins with me, yours ends with you." It is compatible with "high caste" in Ceylon to seek not only to exclude members of the other castes, however worthy, from public offices, but in the rural districts to prevent them from adopting modes of dress, living, or locomotion hitherto used by the higher castes. Serious breaches of the peace and riots have occurred from these causes, to such a level of fatuity has caste been reduced; and they constitute one of the difficulties of administration in Ceylon.

"Political disturbances," said Aristotle, "may arise out of small matters, but are not therefore about small matters." Caste cannot be abolished; it is too much ingrained in human nature and in the Oriental nature. It is not an affair of religion. The adoption of Christianity makes little difference: Christians in Ceylon are among the greatest sticklers for caste. Its badges of *connubium* (intermarriage) and *commensality* (eating together) are matters of private concern with which a Government cannot interfere. But in public matters, as in selection for public office, treatment at public places, &c., it has been the policy of the British Government to disregard caste as much as possible,[1] and too much firmness cannot be shown in adhering to the policy. The true ideal of caste should be impressed on the people, and they should be made to see that the *raison d'être* of a high caste is that it has higher ideals, higher spiritual and intellectual culture, higher devotion to duty than other castes, and that the doom of a privileged caste is not far off when it is no longer able to adapt itself to changing circumstances, and loses the resolution

> "To build, not boast, a glorious race,
> No tenth transmitter of a foolish face."

Neither Buddhists nor Hindus can complain of such a policy. Of the Hindu ideal I have spoken. The Buddhist ideal is contained in the celebrated saying of Buddha:

> "Na jachcha vasalo hoti,
> Na jachcha hoti brahmano.
> Kammana vasalo hoti,
> Kammana hoti brahmano"—

"Not by birth does one become a vasala (outcast), not by birth does he become a Brahman. By deed does one become a vasala, by deed does he become a Brahman."[2]

A KANDYAN CHIEF.

[1] On the introduction of trial by jury into Ceylon in 1811, jurors were empanelled according to caste, and Chief Justice Ottley in 1830, in his answers to the Royal Commission, deplores the inability of the Supreme Court to override the strong objection of the higher castes to sit with the lower. It was only in 1843 this practice was abolished by the Legislature. See Digby's "Life of Sir Richard Morgan" (vol. i. p. 120 *et seq.*) for an account of the discussion in Council on the Bill.

[2] *Vasala Sutta*. This idea is also expressed in the *Kural* of the Tamil sage, Tiruvalluvar (chap. 68, v., 2): "By birth are all men equal, by difference of deed unequal."

AGRICULTURE

AGRICULTURE is the staple industry of Ceylon. It employs the great mass of the population, and upon its prosperity depends the general welfare of the island. The soil is generally speaking poor and shallow, but Nature has compensated for its drawbacks in this particular by endowing the country with a fine climate. Droughts are rare, and in the moisture-laden air nearly all products known to the tropical zone flourish. Under the favouring conditions which obtain, tea, cacao, cinnamon, rubber, and other products are yielded in yearly increasing quantities under European supervision and management, and in accordance with the latest scientific principles. But the purely native agriculture is mainly constructed on primitive methods. The system chiefly favoured is that known as chena cultivation. Land tilled under this system is never fertilised. Seeds are sown and Nature is left to do her work without assistance. When, as happens in due course, all the plant food is extracted from the soil, the land is abandoned and the cultivator takes up new ground, there to repeat his shortsighted and objectionable practices. Meanwhile, the abandoned land is given over to jungle, and remains in its wild condition until it is once more required. Then it is cleared and the old process renewed. And so the work of native agriculture proceeds in a vicious circle. Some time since an organisation known as the Ceylon Agricultural Society was formed to educate the natives to better methods. The society has set itself particularly to combat this evil of chena. It is attempting to impress the cultivating community with the value of manure and the advantage and necessity of introducing the principle of rotation of crops. Already its lessons are bearing fruit, and there is reason to hope that within a short period a considerable improvement will be visible in the general agricultural conditions of the island.

The native villagers all cultivate such products as are necessary for their sustenance. Paddy, their staple item, is grown in the fields, whilst on the highlands grow trees and plants of varying kinds. The most important of the former is the coconut-palm (or in Tamil districts now, the Palmyra palm), from which they obtain oil, fibre, thatch, food, and some necessaries of life ; and amongst the fruit trees are plantains or bananas, breadfruits, mangoes, pomeloes, pineapples, pomegranates, jaks, oranges, and limes. The vegetables grown are principally yams, sweet potatoes, cassava, peas beans, brinjal or egg-fruit, and bandakai or okra, and of spices there are chiefly pepper, gourds and squashes, and chillies. There are also the areca-nut palm and betel pepper, and in some districts tobacco. The villagers, however, will not make the best use of their opportunities. They might, with the great assistance afforded by Nature in this climate, become extremely prosperous agriculturists, but in the majority of cases they will only produce sufficient for their own private use. To be fair. however, this is in many cases due to inability to risk the outlay rather than to any feeling of obstinacy.

To turn to agriculture as worked by Europeans, the principal agriculturists are the planters, cultivating mainly at the present time tea and rubber, though in the western districts there are also the wheat and fruit industries. The larger part of the export trade of Ceylon—and a great portion of the revenue —is dependent on the planting industry, and every improvement in machinery and method is welcomed and adopted, new markets are exploited, and experiments made with new cultivations. When planting was first introduced, such Indian products as sugar, indigo, &c., were vainly tried. Then came the coffee boom, and in the year 1841 78,685 acres of land were sold to planters. The industry succeeded, wavered in its prosperity, recovered, and was from about 1855 to 1882 the principal export industry. It reached its zenith when in 1875 almost one million hundredweights were exported. But the plants had then been attacked by leaf disease, which, spreading rapidly, throttled the industry. Cinchona followed, and then came the tea industry, which has grown phenomenally and is still progressing. With the collapse of the coffee and cinchona industry came the introduction of many other products besides tea, chief amongst these being cacao or chocolate and cardamoms, and a little later Ceara rubber. The last-named, however, has since given place to Para rubber, which promises to become one of the most important of the exports. Nutmegs, cloves, cinnamon, pepper, vanilla, drugs, various dry grains, dyes and tanning substances, oils, camphor, gums and resins are also produced in the island in a smaller way. The agricultural industries are assisted by the Ceylon Government, which maintains an Irrigation Department, and, in addition, a Scientific Department, in which a scientific study is made of the botany, entomology, agriculture, and horticulture of the colony. These departments are dealt with specially elsewhere. There are also the Royal Botanic Gardens, a Government department, which provides a bureau of technical scientific information and advice. Another useful organisation, under the Department of Public Instruction, is the school gardens, established for the improvement of village agriculture and gardening. In another portion of this work will be found articles on the tea, rubber, and other industries, and it is therefore not necessary to deal with them here at length. The island comprises 16,200,000 acres, of which about 3,500,000 are at present cultivated. The chief products and the acreage devoted to them are : Rice, 610,000 acres ;

dry grain, 120,000 acres; coconuts, 660,000 acres; other palms, 110,000 acres; fruits, 250,000 acres; vegetables, 150,000 acres; cinnamon, 40,000 acres; citronella, 35,000 acres; tobacco, 25,000 acres; tea, 385,000 acres; cacao, 35,000 acres; rubber, 11,000 acres; cardamoms, 10,000 acres; other spices, 4,000 acres; coffee, 4,000 acres; and cinchona, 3,500 acres. The first eight represent mainly native industry, and the eight last-named European. In 1905 the export of tea amounted to about 170,183,512 lbs., coffee and cacao 6,686,848 lbs., and rubber 1,401 cwts. The yield of rice is now about 8,500,000 cwts. There are many products of the coconut-palm, and the export trade is large. The figures are given in a special article which appears elsewhere. The coconut-palm flourishes best in the west coast regions, though it will grow for a considerable distance inland, and also amongst the hills. Every part of it is put to some profitable use; for instance, the leaves are made into baskets, mats, &c.; the stalks into fences, brooms, yokes; the trunk into rafters, beams, canoes, furniture, and the like; the bud at the apex of the stem makes an excellent vegetable. When flowering it is tapped and a "toddy" is obtained from which sugar may be made. The toddy fermented makes a strong alcoholic liquor, and distilled produces a spirit known as arrack. Further fermentation forms vinegar. The kernel of the nut is eaten, and the liquid inside makes a refreshing drink, whilst oil is also derived by boiling the nut. Elsewhere appear articles treating of spices and other products which figure largely in the list of exports, and it is unnecessary to refer to those articles in detail. Generally it may be said of Ceylon agriculture that it is in a most flourishing condition, and offers a rich promise of future prosperity to the island.

NATIVE AGRICULTURE AND ITS IMPROVEMENT.

By C. DRIEBERG, Superintendent of School Gardens.

An account of native agriculture or village cultivation must of necessity leave out of consideration all estate products—the special concern of the planting industry—viz., tea, cacao, rubber, cardamoms, coconuts, cinnamon and citronella; though a good deal of the land planted with the last three is in the hands of the wealthier natives. The cultivation of cereals consists of paddy growing on the one hand and the raising of chena (prepared jungle land) crops or dry grains on the other.

A PADDY FIELD.

Paddy is more or less an irrigation product, though the variety known as hill-paddy is practically independent of irrigation. There are two sowing seasons for the long-lived varieties, which grow for six and seven months, known respectively as the Yala and the Maha season, the former occurring about March–April and the latter in July–August. In the case of paddy crops of shorter duration, the sowing takes place later, so as to bring the harvest in about the same period, viz., August–September for Yala and January–February for Maha. Of so-called varieties there is legion (roughly between three and four hundred), but in most cases the differences are merely the result of local conditions of soil and climate. The variety known as ma-vi ("great paddy") may be said to rank first in importance. The total yield of the island—some 8,000,000 bushels—is only about half the quantity required for local consumption, so that a great deal of rice has to be imported, most of it coming from India.

The dry grains referred to depend entirely on seasonal rains, and comprise the following:—kurakkan, the ragi of India (*Eleusine coracana*), amu (*Paspalum scorbiculatum*), meneri (*Panicum militare* and *Panicum miliaceum*), tana-hal (*Setaria italica*), and kumbu (*Pennisetum typhoideum*), the bajri of India. None of these is of very high feeding-value; but in the poorer districts they are the only available cereal food. Dry grains are easily grown, and yield an early harvest; but the system of cultivation in vogue is wasteful, inasmuch as little tillage and no manuring is carried out, the practice being to work new areas and depend on natural fertility till exhaustion of soil suggests abandonment and the seeking of fresh fields, or a return to those that have become renovated by long fallowing. Maize, or Indian corn, is pretty common as a dry-grain crop in some parts of the island; but this useful cereal has never had fair treatment under the rough-and-ready system of chena cultivation. With the cereals referred to above are generally sown, as a mixed crop, such legumes as mun-eta (*Phaseolus maximus*) or kollu (*Dolichos biflorus*) and species of amaranthus, the fine seeds of which are utilised.

Of the fruits chiefly cultivated for sale, coconuts deserve first mention, particularly the golden-coloured variety known as the "king coconut," grown, not for its commercial products (copra, fibre, etc.), but for use in the half-mature stage, when it is called a "young coconut," which furnishes a soft jelly-like substance, found lining the interior of the shell (endocarp), and a refreshing liquid in the central hollow. This liquid is coconut-water, erroneously called the milk of the coconut, which is the expressed juice of the fresh mature kernel so largely used in Eastern cookery. Other common fruit found in the village fruit-garden are oranges, with a firm skin that cannot be peeled off (sweet limes, they are sometimes called), loose-skinned mandarins or "king oranges," and other smaller forms of citrus fruits. The mango (*Mangifera indica*), which may be considered, *par excellence*, the fruit of the East, is represented by typical varieties called the Jaffna, parrot, dampara, heart, and rupee mango. These are all of good flavour, and, when well grown, are free from fibre, the last-mentioned reaching almost to the size of a husked coconut. Plantains are common enough, including both the so-called banana or dessert variety and that which is cooked and used as a vegetable. The best kinds are known by the native names of kolikuttu, suwandel, and puwalu. The pine-apple (*Ananas sativa*) is much cultivated in the Western and Central Provinces, the favourite varieties being the "Mauritius" and "Kew"; while the papaw (*Carica papaya*) flourishes in all parts of the island. Other less common fruits are the mangosteen (*Garcinia mangostana*), durian (*Durio zebithinus*), sapodilla (*Acras sapota*), custard-apple (*Anona squamosa*), rambutan (*Nephelium lappaceum*), limes, lemons, and a large number of inferior fruits that do not deserve special mention. The bread-fruit (*Artocarpus incisa*) and jak-fruit (*Artocarpus integrifolia*), though they must be considered as fruits, are both eaten only in the cooked condition, the latter being of the greatest importance in many outlying districts, where it is the mainstay of the people. There is practically no export trade in fruits, though there is a large demand for plantains and papaws for the passenger steamships calling at Colombo port.

Vegetable cultivation is chiefly confined to the vicinity of towns. Native vegetables comprise beans of sorts (species of phaseolus and vigna); various gourds, such as the bottle-gourd (*Lagenaria vulgaris*), bitter-gourd (*Momordica charantia*), snake-gourd (*Trichosanthes anguina*), loofa (*Luffa acutangula* and species), ash-pumpkin (*Benincasa cerifera*), sweet-pumpkin (*Cucurbita maxima*), the okra or bandakka (*Hibiscus esculentus*) and—perhaps the two most commonly cultivated—the brinjal or egg-plant (*Solanum melongena*) and the chilli (*Capsicum frutescens* and species). The chief "root crops" are varieties of yams (*dioscorea*), which are largely cultivated and constitute an important article of native diet, besides the cassava (*manihot*) and the tania of the West Indies (*colocasia*). There is much room for extending the cultivation of a class of vegetable products much used in Eastern cookery, to wit, onions, ginger, turmeric, chilli (for drying), coriander and other so-called "curry-stuffs," a large quantity of which come over every year from Southern India.

SOWING SEED.

The extension and improvement of vegetable cultivation generally is receiving special attention in the gardens of Government village schools, which, distributed as they are all over the country, offer special facilities for this work. At higher elevations the natives are beginning to cultivate with success the commoner English vegetables. Such crops as are included in native agriculture, but have not been referred to above, may be grouped together as miscellaneous (mostly non-edible) products. Of these tobacco is one of the most important, especially in the north and east of the island. Its cultivation is confined to the drier parts, and is mostly in the hands of the Tamils. The plant has undoubtedly taken very kindly to the country; but it has yet to be proved whether the finer varieties of Cuba and Sumatra will thrive as well as the coarser kinds now raised in the country. The manufactured products, which are almost entirely consumed locally, consist of chewing-tobacco and cheap rank cigars, as a rule not much larger than cigarettes, made up in bundles of ten, and priced at a penny the bundle. It is generally thought that much can be done in the way of better "curing" of the leaf, and that this—at least for the present—is the direction in which to improve the tobacco industry of the island. Good manufactured articles in the shape of cigars will most probably find a ready sale in the same way that locally manufactured cocoa and chocolate are now doing. It may here be mentioned that the cultivation of cotton is also likely to become a native industry of some importance.

REAPING PADDY.

The kitul palm (*Caryota urens*) deserves mention as the tree which takes the place of the coconut at higher elevations where the latter will not thrive. One of the many products of these palms is the sap, or "toddy," got by "tapping" the unexpanded inflorescence, while still within the spathe. In the unfermented condition (in which it is kept by the addition of certain vegetable anti-ferments) the juice is boiled down to form a crude sugar, called "jaggery," which is most useful in the preparation of native sweetmeats. The fermented juice, on the other hand, is the bane of the villager; it is intoxicating in itself, and when distilled forms a most potent alcoholic liquor. Old kitul trees are cut down for the "sago" found in the pith region (hence the name "bastard sago") as well as for their valuable timber; but the palm is best known outside Ceylon as producing a fibre used in brush-making.

The areca-nut is perhaps the most graceful of the palms of Ceylon, and has been likened by the Hindus to "an arrow shot from heaven." The nut is exported and chiefly employed for the manufacture of catechu. In the north of the island the Palmyra palm (*Borassus flabilifer*) is of the greatest utility to the inhabitants, every part of it being put to some use, while the timber is the best of all the palm tribe. Both the kitul (as already stated) and Palmyra produce a commercial fibre; and it is interesting to note that while the fibre of the coconut is extracted from the husk (mesocarp) of the nut, that of the kitul and the Palmyra is got from the base of the leaf-stalk (petiole). There are a great many other miscellaneous economic products of Ceylon plants falling under the classes of fibres, tanning-stuffs, dyeing-materials, &c., which, however, are not cultivated and therefore cannot be reckoned as agricultural crops. The gingelly plant (*Sesamum indicum*) is, however, grown to some extent in the northern parts of the island for its seed, which yields a valuable oil used for culinary and medicinal purposes. There is one other plant which should not be omitted in this list of miscellaneous crops, and that is the betel vine (*Piper betel*), a species closely allied to common pepper (*Piper nigrum*), also found growing in a semi-wild condition near villages. Betel, however, is systematically grown on trellises or pergolas and most carefully tended. The leaves are gathered as they become fit and are sold at good prices, being used as a masticatory in combination with sliced areca-nut (hence called betel-nut), a little slaked lime, a piece of chewing-tobacco, and a fragment of catechu. This compound is chewed to a pulp and produces an expectoration of a sanguineous hue, which when projected promiscuously is apt, especially on white walls, to produce a gruesome effect. But the practice is said to preserve the teeth and promote digestion, so that on hygienic grounds, at least, it may have a claim for toleration, though the practice of "betel-chewing" is prohibited in public places, such as courts of law.

The improvement of native implements of husbandry is necessarily slow and gradual. The native plough, made of wood, which has no mould-board, and is more of the nature of a cultivator, is practically only used in paddy cultivation. The points to be considered in seeking to improve this implement are that it should be suitable for use in soft land, easily reparable by a village smith, light enough to be carried to and from the field on a man's shoulder, and capable of being drawn with facility by the ploughing animal of Ceylon, viz., the water-buffalo (*Bubalus bubalis*). Thrashing is effected by the treading of cattle made to walk round and round a thrashing-floor, winnowing is performed by means of a hand-winnow, while hulling is the result of manual labour with mortar and pestle. Such are the primitive methods of the Ceylon paddy-cultivator. In all other forms of land preparation the stock implement is the mammoty, which is the equivalent of the English spade and is very deftly used by the Sinhalese husbandman. Another handy instrument is the cattie, which is indispensable to rural life. A very light mould-board plough, designed by the Superintendent of School Gardens and made by local blacksmiths, has already won approval. Light wheeled labour-saving hand implements of the Planet Junior type are also likely to find favour if they can be cheaply produced locally; while a simple form of drill that can be adapted both for wet and dry cultivation will be of great service when the advantages of regular planting come to be recognised. But, as already stated, drastic reforms are to be strongly deprecated, and improvements and innovations must be gradual, because, firstly, local conditions and requirements almost exclusively understood by the natives have to be fully and carefully taken into account, and secondly, local prejudices demand due consideration. Undoubtedly there is much to admire in the methods of the village agriculturist, however antiquated those methods may be. His skill in terrace-cultivation, seen in the Kandyan districts, and his ingenuity in well-irrigation, as shown in the north of the island, are, considering his opportunities and resources, nothing short of marvellous.

The initiation of local work connected with agricultural education and the improvement of native agriculture must be credited to the late Mr. H. W. Green, who, while Director of Public Instruction in the island, established, under the patronage of His Excellency Sir Arthur Gordon (now Lord Stanmore), then Governor of Ceylon, a School of Agriculture, with a view, as one of its chief objects, to train and send out agricultural instructors to various parts of the island. In spite of a want of popular sympathy and support, Mr. Green, entirely by his own personal efforts and influence, carried out the objects he set before him with considerable success from an administrative point of view, and also to a great extent succeeded in drawing the attention of the more intelligent native cultivators, as well as of low-country planters, to the need for a better knowledge of soil and plant in the ordinary practice of agriculture. Perhaps one of the chief defects in this pioneer movement was its too special application to the improvement of paddy cultivation and the rather premature and persistent effort that was made to replace the native digger with an iron plough —an innovation which, if it was to come, should have begun rather with improvement and modification of the implement which had the sanction of the usage of centuries. With the removal of Mr. Green from the head of affairs and a change of Government, the temporary prosperity of the School of Agriculture began to wane, for the want of proper support from the authorities above, and, as a natural sequence, from the students below ; since the class from which the latter were originally drawn, to wit, the youth of the land-owning families, failed to supply vacancies as they occurred. Though it was the intention of the founder of the school that the native "headmen" (or chiefs of degree) should be recruited from among the men trained in the Government agricultural school—a most excellent idea that might with advantage have been carried into effect in a modified form—this intention never reached practical realisation.

In 1901 it was decided—ill-advisedly, as some thought at the time—to close the central educational institution and substitute for it an organisation for carrying agricultural teaching to the doors of the cultivator, particularly the rising generation in cultivating communities. With this end in view, a few schools were first selected which offered special facilities for starting school gardens, and here the *raison d'être* of the new scheme was demonstrated. The main idea, stated shortly, is to induce school children, through the medium of the school garden, to take an intelligent interest in Nature around them, and, at the same time, to train them in cultural methods and give them a grounding in the elementary principles of agriculture. The scheme has so far progressed that at present 125 school gardens have been established, the majority of which are operating satisfactorily. Indirectly, through the medium of the gardens, new products are introduced into the villages, and better varieties of existing products are brought within the reach of cultivators. Altogether the scheme has proved itself suitable to local conditions, and is bound to materially benefit rural life. Of late its activities have been strengthened by the co-operation of the newly formed Ceylon Agricultural Society, as well as by the staff of the Royal Botanic Gardens at Peradeniya. Indeed, agriculture in Ceylon, as a whole, is receiving the hearty support of Government under the present *régime;* and it is devoutly to be hoped, for the welfare of the agricultural community, upon which so largely depends the prosperity of the whole colony, that the same policy will be maintained under future rulers.

The Government Stock Garden, which is situated in the south end of Colombo, was established in 1901 as a central depôt where plants could be grown and distributed in the most convenient way, as seeds, cuttings, &c., to school gardens, where experiments with new varieties of plants could be carried on, and where teachers could see cultural work on the most approved lines. The garden consists of two sections, and illustrates the cultivation of flowers, vegetables, and fruits, the laying out of grounds, the fertilising of crops, and, in short, all that pertains to the pursuit of agriculture. The office of the Superintendent of School Gardens stands within the grounds, and here either that officer (except when absent on inspection duty) or one or other of his two assistants is always to be found. There are also on the staff a clerk and a foreman-cum-seedsman, while the operatives consist of a head gardener and six coolies. The stock garden is a rendezvous for village teachers, who visit it with the object of carrying away, in the abstract, ideas and information, and, in the concrete, plants and seeds. Minor industries—such as apiculture and sericulture—likely to be of benefit to the village population are also fostered and practically demonstrated.

An important line of work which is occupying the attention of the Superintendent of School Gardens and his staff is the trial of fertilising agents, with a view to convincing the native agriculturist of the necessity for manuring his crops, the true object of which is at present little understood by the mass of cultivators. A haphazard system of selection and errors in method of application have, separately and together, done much to make the use of recognised artificial fertilisers unpopular. The adoption of rational manuring as a detail of cultivation may, however, be expected to ultimately prevail, as the result of experiment and demonstration, and a consequent better comprehension of the possibilities of artificial fertilisation.

The present general policy of the Government is directed to concentration and the combination of allied interests, and it may be expected that before long a central Department of Agriculture will be established. The Agricultural Society, which may be looked upon as the nucleus, or at least the forerunner, of such a department, lately decided to appoint a number of agricultural instructors, who receive part of their training at the Government stock garden. Altogether, the agricultural education of the natives of Ceylon may be said to be well in hand.

SINHALESE PLOUGHING PADDY FIELDS.

The staff of the School Gardens Division

(which is administered by Dr. Willis, chief of the Botanic Department) consists of Mr. C. Drieberg, B.A., F.H.A.S., Superintendent, Mr. H. D. Lewis Wijeyesinghe, first assistant, Mr. Alexander Perera, second assistant and manager of the stock garden, Mr. M. J. Fernando, foreman and seedsman, and Mr. T. D. S. Dharmasena, clerk.

CEYLON AGRICULTURAL SOCIETY.

Necessarily in a country which depends for its prosperity mainly on the products of the soil, especial attention is paid in Ceylon to the promotion and extension of agricultural operations; and in these directions the Government is quick to supply every incentive and give all possible assistance. With the view of developing the agricultural industries of the island the Ceylon Agricultural Society was founded on November, 1, 1904, following on an inaugural public meeting held on 18th October, which was presided over by the Governor of the colony, Sir Henry Blake. His Excellency, on whose personal initiative it was inaugurated, is President of the society, while the Hon. the Lieutenant-Governor and the Hon. the Colonial Treasurer are *ex-officio* Vice-Presidents, with the Hon. Messrs. John Ferguson, S. C. Obeyesekere, F. Beven, and Dr. W. G. Rockwood, M.D., Sir William Twynam, Mr. H. T. S. Ward (Director of Irrigation), Mr. W. Forsythe (Chairman of the Planters' Association of Ceylon), Mr. W. D. Gibbon and Mr. C. P. Hayley, as additional Vice-Presidents. The affairs of the society are conducted by the board, which includes, in addition to the officers above-named, the following *ex-officio* members :—Members of the Executive and Legislative Councils, Government Agents of Provinces, the Director of the Royal Botanic Gardens, Peradeniya ; the Controller of the Experiment Station, Peradeniya ; the Superintendent of the Experiment Station, Maha Iluppalama ; the Government Entomologist, the Government Mycologist, the Director of the Museum, the Director of Public Instruction, the Government Veterinary Surgeon, the Superintendent of School Gardens, and the Conservator of Forests. The nominated members for each province of the island are : Central Province, Messrs. T. B. Rambukwelle, R.M., Daniel Joseph, W. Dunuwille, and Dr. Valentine de S. Duke ; Eastern Province, Messrs. Varitambi Kurunathapillai and C. A. Lienard ; Northern Province, Messrs. V. Casipillai, V. Vraspillai, Adigar and J.P., K. U. Tampaiya, District Mudaliyar ; North-Central Province, Messrs. C. J. C. Mee, S. Sampander, L. B. Nikawewa, Dissawa, G. W. Jayawardene, Mudaliyar and J.P., and C. Taldena, R.M.; North-Western Province, J. Clovis de Silva, G. W. Dodanwela, and E. Scott ; Province of Sabaragamuwa, Messrs. W. Forsythe, Dan J. Jayatileke, and J. H. Meedeniya, R.M.; Southern Province, Messrs. C. G. Simmonds, E. R. Gooneratne, Gate Mudaliyar, D. A. Gooneratne, Gate Mudaliyar, and B. T. Doole, Gate Mudaliyar ; Province of Uva, Messrs. A. T. Rettie, James Duncan, H. O. Hoseason, J.P., and T. B. Katugaha, R.M.; Western Province, Messrs. R. Morison, M. Kelway Bamber, Solomon Seneviratne, Atapattu Mudaliyar and J.P., Don Solomon Dias Bandaranaike, C.M.G., Maha Mudaliyar, Dr. H. M. Fernando, M., and Messrs. W. N. S. Aserappa, W. Jardine, and E. B. Denham, C.C.S., late Secretary of the society; while the Secretary is Mr. A. N. Galbraith, C.C.S.

BUFFALOES TREADING OUT PADDY.

The society has a membership of over 1,100, with forty-six affiliated branches, covering the whole of the island and situated in the following centres : Anuradhapura, Badulla, Balangoda, Batticaloa, Chilaw, Colombo (Agri-Horticultural), Delft Gansabhawa, Dumbara, Galle District, Gampola, Gangaboda Pattu, Hambantota, Harispattu, Jaffna, Kalutara, Kandaboda Pattu, Kandy, Katana, Katunayake, Kegalla, Kudagama, Kurunegala, Kuruwita, Mannar, Matale, Matara, Matugama, Minuwangoda, Mullaitivu, Nattandiya, Negombo, Nuwara Eliya, Panadure, Passara, Puttalam, Ratnapura, Talangama, Tangalla, Telijjawila, Three Korales and Lower Bulatgama, Trincomalee, Vavuniya, Welimada, Wellaboda Pattu (Galle), Wellaboda Pattu (Matara).

The objects and scope of operations of the society are officially stated as follows : (*a*) To obtain for members the latest information on matters affecting the agricultural interests of the island, *e.g.*, directions for the cultivation of new products, hints as to the best soil, the best manures, and the best markets, the results of experiments in farm products, improvements in live stock, &c. ; (*b*) efforts in pioneer cultivation will be generally assisted by the officers of the Government Botanic Garden at Peradeniya; and, in cases favourably reported upon, Government assistance may be given ; (*c*) suggestions as to improvements in cultivation, &c., will be fully considered, and will obtain the benefit of full publication and discussion at meetings of the board and through the *Tropical Agriculturist*, the magazine of the society ; the latter will enable agriculturists to impart and obtain information and offer facilities for exchange and disposal of farm produce ; (*d*) members will be taking part in a scheme for the general improvement of agriculture throughout Ceylon.

The following are the rules of the society :—

1. The society shall be called the Agricultural Society of Ceylon.

2. The business of the General Society shall be conducted through the Board of Agriculture of Ceylon.

3. The board shall meet for despatch of business on the first Monday of each month at 2.30 p.m. Seven members shall form a quorum.

4. Notices of motions or questions shall be sent to the Secretary at least one week before the meeting of the board.

5. All motions will require to be seconded, and will be circulated before the board meets.

6. A general meeting of the society may be called by the President at any time, and may be held at any place to be fixed by him.

7. All members of the board will be nominated by the President.

8. Candidates for membership of the society must be proposed by a member of the board for the district in which the candidate resides or owns landed property.

9. Members of the society shall pay a subscription of Rs. 5 per annum.

10. Payment of the subscription in advance will entitle a member to receive all publications of the society. All subscriptions shall be paid to the Secretary of the board.

11. Lists of members will be published annually in the Government *Gazette* and in the *Journal* of the society.

12. Local societies may be formed with a membership of not less than twelve members.

13. Each local society should be represented by a secretary, through whom correspondence with the board can be conducted.

14. All local societies will be registered at the local Kachcheri and by the Secretary of the board.

15. The revenue officers of the province and district shall be *ex-officio* members of local societies within the province.

16. Local societies are empowered to make their own rules.

17. All local societies will be entitled to receive all publications of the society on payment of an individual subscription.

18. The funds of the Agricultural Society will be lodged in the Bank of Madras in the name of the Agricultural Society of Ceylon. The Secretary will be responsible for the accounts, and all cheques will be signed by him and the President or Vice-President of the Board of Agriculture.

19. A statement of expenditure incurred, &c., shall be tabled at each meeting of the board.

20. All grants in aid of local societies or special experiment must be approved by the board.

21. All accounts will be audited annually.

COLOMBO AGRI-HORTICULTURAL SOCIETY.

This important organisation, of which the Governor of the colony (Sir Henry Blake) is patron, was established in 1870 with the general object of promoting agriculture and horticulture in the Western—the principal—Province of the island; and with this view shows of soil products and all that is connected with the rural and gardening industries, including the rearing of live stock, are held in Colombo, which are always well attended and form useful and instructive exhibitions. The Hon. G. M. Fowler, C.M.G., is (1906) the President of the society; while the Government Agent of the Western Province is ex-officio Vice-President and chairman of committees. The executive committee consists of the Hon. Messrs. H. L. Crawford, C.M.G. (Acting Colonial Secretary) and S. C. Obeyesekere, M.L.C. with Messrs. B. Horsburgh, C.C.S., Mayor and Chairman of the Municipal Council of Colombo, E. B. Denham, C.C.S., C. Drieberg, B.A., F.H.A.S., J. W. Chas. de Soysa, J.P., Solomon Seneviratne, J.P., Atapattu Mudaliyar, James Peiris, J.P., M.A., LL.B., S. P. Jeffery, Jacob de Mel and P. D. Seibel. There are now one hundred active members, among the names on the roll being those of most of the leading landed proprietors in the western district and professional men in Colombo. The rules provide that shows shall be held under the auspices of the society at such centres in the Western Province as shall be determined by the committee; also that at least one-tenth of the funds of the society shall be annually expended in the purchase and free distribution of seeds and plants to the members. Mr. W. A. de Silva, J.P., of Darley Gardens, Colombo, is the Hon. Secretary and Treasurer.

THE CEYLON POULTRY CLUB.

Poultry-raising is an important industry in the colony, and the Ceylon Poultry Club was formed in the Coronation year, 1902. The post of President has been held by the successive Governors, Sir Joseph West Ridgeway and Sir Henry Blake, the latter being the present holder of the office. The club is affiliated with the Poultry Club of Great Britain, and is managed by two vice-presidents, a committee, hon. secretary and hon. editorial secretary. The objects of the club are the promotion of the breeding and exhibition of poultry, the encouragement of the importation of pure-bred fowls into the island, and the arrangement and management of poultry shows. The club issues to members a monthly *Poultry Club Magazine*, which is greatly appreciated, and the members number some 140. A chief annual show is held by the club in Colombo every August, when many special handsome prizes are offered by the club in addition to ordinary class prizes; and smaller shows in other centres on the island are conducted under the Poultry Club Rules, which are assisted financially and in other ways by the club. The impetus given to the rearing of fancy poultry since the formation of the club has been very great. The number of importations of pure-bred stock is increasing every year, coming mostly from Great Britain and in a lesser degree from Australia. The work of the club also in improving the poultry in the island is very marked in those districts in which its members mostly reside. Suggestions have been made by the club to the Ceylon Agricultural Society for the formation of a central poultry farm for the purpose of improving generally the poultry stock of the island, and these proposals are expected to bear good fruit.

SALT

THE salt industry of the island deserves special prominence in a review of the economic resources of the country, by reason of the fact that it has been pursued from time immemorial and has ever played an important part in the trade of the island. Authentic information as to whether the industry received a due share of administrative control in times past, or was looked upon in the light of a royal monopoly, is not available, but it is reasonable to assume that it has at all times contributed largely to the revenue of the country. It was only at the beginning of the last century, however, that systematic measures were adopted for the regulation of the working of the industry and a firmer supervision exercised to prevent illicit operations. Government claimed it as its exclusive right to regulate and dispose of the areas of formation and manufacture; and the beds were farmed out on special licences, the lessees in each case stipulating to sell to Government their entire output and agreeing to receive as remuneration such rate per hundredweight as the latter might deem it just to allow them. This arrangement still holds good in the North-Western and Eastern Provinces, where the salterns are practically private property and worked by private enterprise, though the out-turn may only be disposed of to Government; but in the Southern and Northern Provinces the system has been superseded by a method of exclusive Government control. In the former of these provinces the collections are of manufactured salt, in the Southern Province of naturally formed salt, and in the Northern Province of salt of both descriptions. Naturally formed salt is collected from shallow salt water "lewayas," or marshy lagoons, while "manufactured" salt is secured by leading the salt water into brine-pits and allowing it to evaporate. The lewayas are in all instances the property of the Crown, but the brine-pits are under private ownership. The areas of salt collection are principally in the four following districts: (1) Hambantota, in the Southern Province; (2) Puttalam, in the North-Western Province; (3) Jaffna, in the Northern Province; (4) Trincomalee, in the Eastern Province. The usual stock of salt held by Government is something like 980,000 cwts., or very nearly a quantity equal to two and a half years' consumption, to which the provinces contribute as below:—

	Cwts.
North-Western	620,762
Southern	186,804
Northern	129,325
Eastern	43,109
	980,000

It will thus be seen that the North-Western Province gives the greatest yield, though the retailing price of Government, since the year 1887, has been here fixed at Rs. 2·46 per cwt., being 10 cents in excess of that claimed for in the other provinces. The salt area of the North-Western Province comprises seven salterns, each of which is again composed of a number of waikkals, or manufacturing beds. These are severally held on title-deeds, certificates against the right of the Crown, or on Crown grants; and the jurisdiction is vested in a Salt Department, under the control of a chief Salt Inspector, who draws an aggregate salary and allowance of Rs. 3,560 per annum, and is *ex-officio* police magistrate for the district under his charge. Under him are supervisors, who are paid salaries ranging from Rs. 360 to Rs. 650 a year, and under the supervisors first and second class constables, on salaries of Rs. 330 and Rs. 180 respectively, while the actual care of the pits devolves on patrols, about six of whom are allotted to every saltern and receive wages from about Rs. 150 to Rs. 180 a year. The storage work is carried out partly under the direction of the saltern staff and partly under the control of special storekeepers, who, again, have under them constables and patrols for the stricter surveillance against theft and illicit disposal. In the Northern Province the privilege of retailing salt is disposed of in much the same way as the farming out of arrack revenues, and is annually put up for sale and purchased by the highest bidder. The renter pays his instalments of purchase money in exactly the same way as the arrack farmer, and is allowed a certain number of stores and retail shops all over the district, the retailers being in each instance licensed by Government. In the Southern and Eastern Provinces a greatly modified system of supervision prevails, and is administered by the revenue officers of the district, with the aid of special checkers and constables.

Having briefly outlined the measures taken by Government to regulate and supervise the sources of supply, it will be interesting to observe the methods adopted in the various processes of collection and manufacture in the different provinces. Naturally the seasonal tides of the monsoons, as they set in on the west or on the east, have much to do with the collection, and the rains which follow determine, in a degree, the quantity available. The usual method is to throw across a shallow portion of the lagoon an embankment, constructed of sticks and plastered clay, so as to make the enclosed area undisturbed by the waves and violences from without. The water contained within the bund then forms a sort of reservoir for providing the necessary supply to the salterns, and is from time to time replenished by the admission into it of supplies from the lake, generally by apertures cut in it during the rising of the tides. From this reservoir the salt water is conducted by means of canals to the salterns, from which, again, smaller conduits carry the brine to warming-pans or "condensers," and thence to the scores of crystallisers, where, eventually, evaporation occurs. The bottoms of the crystallising beds are generally prepared a few days in advance by trampling, drying, and excavating the soft mud which is to he found on them, and spreading over the denuded surface a few layers of clean sand to form a base for the process of evaporation. Salt crystals usually appear within forty-eight or sixty hours of the reception of water, but the formation is not complete until thirty to forty days after that date. The formation is then scooped out—an iron fork, a stick with nails studded across, or, sometimes, even the hand being used for the purpose—and fresh brine is introduced for a second collection, the ripening stage being reached a week or so in advance every time the process is repeated. At the end of the third collection, however, water is introduced direct from the canal to swamp the beds before a formation is allowed to take place, in order to prevent the production of bitter and deleterious salt, which may easily be detected by the appearance of needle-shaped crystals in the course of evaporation. In areas where the salt is "naturally" formed, the brine is collected in the lagoons and preserved by enclosure, this being effected by blocking the passage of communication at the "modara" or mouth of the backwater. The bed of these lagoons is said to be old sea bottom, and the salt in the water is supposed to be obtained from the saline mud and by infiltration from the sea. The rest of the process is similar to what occurs in the course of manufacture, except that, while in the former case the production is entirely by means of solar evaporation, in manufacturing tracts Nature is aided and hastened in her work by a resort to artificially made pans, brine-pits, and crystallising beds. There is a distinction and a difference between naturally formed and artificially made salt; the former is undoubtedly purer and safer in use, while the quality of the latter is affected and influenced by the temperature of the warming-pans and other contrivances. In the first case, also, the salt produced is often of beautiful shades of pink and lilac, while that obtained by the use of beds is generally of a snow-white colour. The presence or admixture of iodine or other forms of saline chemicals and constituents must doubtless account for this variety of tints.

The salt manufactured in the Puttalam district is purchased by Government at the rate of 25 cents (about 4d.) per hundredweight, while the renter of Jaffna is allowed salt from the stores at 40 cents the hundredweight. In the latest (1905) Administration Report for the Northern Province, however, it is notified that after the year 1906 the system of renting will be abolished, and Government will sell salt to local retailers at the rate of Rs. 3·50 per cwt., with leave to them to sell it at their own price to the public. It may be added that the old system carried with it many undesirable features and gave room for the commission of irregularities of a serious description, one of which was the illegal overdraw by the renter at the close of his rent in order to interfere with the incoming renter. For the year 1905 the revenue derived by the sale of the salt rent in the Northern Province amounted to Rs. 60,551. For the same year the figures for the North-Western Province show a nett revenue to Government of Rs. 801,920; those for the Eastern Province, Rs. 435,436; and those for the Southern, Rs. 151,186.

So far, the chief difficulties that have been brought to light in the working of the industry are the shortage of labour and the extreme arduousness of transport. The supply has at no time been in proportion to the demand; and even the scanty number that may be obtained has to be secured from great distances, rendering the timely collection of the product more or less impossible. Where salt is manufactured, of course, a sufficient supply of labour is always maintained; but in areas where it is self-formed and has to be gathered under the direct oversight of Government executive officers, the conditions are hardly inducive enough to draw the necessary force. In the lewayas of the Southern Province, in especial, the salt gatherers have to walk up to distances of four or five hundred yards on the hard surface of the ridges, with the constant fear of having their feet cut by the rough crystals, and after they have filled their baskets with whatever quantity they can carry, make their way back to the storing point, slowly and painfully. This primitive method of collection has been strongly condemned, and the erection of wire shoots has been projected on the more extensive areas. The transportation of the collected material is also receiving attention, owing to the dearth of bulls in certain districts and the difficulty of obtaining them, where available, at the present unattractive rates. The construction of a mono rail has been discussed, but it is not supposed that it will be sanctioned. The proposal for the establishment of a tramway by bullock traction seems to be in favour, and it is believed that its adoption will prove of great utility to all concerned. In the Administration Report for the year 1905 by the Assistant Government Agent of the Southern Province the subject is dealt with exhaustively, and some very pertinent remarks may be found. "The construction of a tramway for salt transport by bullock-traction," it is said, "would enable salt to be removed to store in at least half the time now taken, would save a large sum of money now paid by Government to salt watchers at the lewayas, and would reduce by at least half the expenditure now necessary to keep the roads in a proper state of repair."

When salt is issued from one province to another, the province into which it is imported has to bear all expenses connected with its weighing and transport, but no further charge is allowable. Under contract with the Government, the vessels of the Ceylon Steam Navigation Company's service transport salt from and to the different collecting and receiving centres at a uniform freight value of Rs. 7·50 (10s.) per ton. All charges in regard to the weighing of salt at the time of issue and of removing it to the places of sale are debited to the retailer's account; but some recoupment is afforded by an allowance made them for cart hire, and a commission of 5 per cent. is added on the nett quantity purchased; they are also paid a rebate of 12 cents per cwt. to compensate them for selling to the public at Rs. 2·24, instead of Rs. 2·36 the cwt. By this latter arrangement the purchasing price of the public is fixed at 2 cents a pound, and they are, in some measure, protected against the fluctuations of the market and the raising by the retailers of the rate to any prohibitive pitch. The contemplated action of Government to do away with the renting system and to fix the sale price at Rs. 3·50 the cwt. uniformly throughout the larger number of provinces, with sanction to its customers to retail the article at any price they desire, would appear to tend to the harassing of the poorer classes of consumers, who will suffer under the arrangement. But it is suggested that competition amongst the retailers would prevent the exaction of exorbitant selling prices; and if that did not secure redress, as a last resource Government stores might be opened in competition with the retailers. There is no doubt, however, that a better system might be devised, which might lead to results less conflicting and effect a complete standardisation of purchasing and retailing rates, thus preventing the constant fluctuations of price of a commodity which subserves so many useful purposes. In fact, it is considered that the present methods as pursued in the various departments of the industry are far too antiquated, and must sooner or later be superseded by modern equipment and conveniences.

The work of storage at the present time is carried out by collecting the salt into heaps on the banks of the lagoons or in close proximity to the salterns, and covering it with cadjans, or plaited coconut leaves, until its removal to the depôts or the Government stores. In some cases Government constructs raised platforms of earthwork, and supplies timber free of charge for the erection, at the manufacturer's own expense, of kottus, or sheds, for the temporary reception of the collected material. The protection offered by these coverings is of a meagre character, and much wastage is noted as a consequence. The authorised limit of wastage is 2 per cent. in transit and in store for the first eleven months, and about three and a half pounds for every cwt. thereafter for forty-four months. Wastage also occurs in another form by the destruction by Government every year of naturally formed salt in or about areas where manufacture obtains. This is primarily to prevent the illicit sale or appropriation of the product by people in the district, though it is also acknowledged that most of these self-formations do not repay the cost of collection. Experiments are being carried out with a view to checking these formations by placing coconut-husks along the marshes where the crystals usually appear. It is not clearly established whether it is the fibre in the husks or some intrinsic property in the produce of the coconut-palm which causes the absence of crystallisation, but, so far, the results have proved eminently successful. The stumps of the ingini tree are also effective in this respect, and such are the strong chemical properties of the tree that a root of it, it is said, placed in a brackish well, will sweeten the water. But, however this may be, the prevention of formation will eventually cost less than its subsequent surveillance and destruction by patrols and cattle, and means to this end will, therefore, be adopted shortly.

The financial results of the industry have proved most satisfactory, and it is expected that, with increased efficiency in the different processes of manufacture and collection, the salt department will soon prove one of the most lucrative sources of revenue to the colony. Hitherto, apart from the consumption for local culinary purposes—the native palate requires very strong piquancy, pungency and seasoning to tickle it—there has hardly been any demand for the article in dependent industries, except for a small call for fish curing, which is carried on on the western coast of the island. The export trade in the article is not great, and there appear to be no immediate prospects of any circumstance occurring which might contribute to raise its present market value. But with the establishment, as proposed, of extensive curing and tinning works for the preparation and export of this country's food products, there is the possibility of a keen demand being created for the commodity and greater attention being devoted to improved and economic methods of cultivation. At the present time the one great unfavourable factor is the sudden change of atmosphere over the producing districts, this causing the laboured collection of weeks to be washed away in a day and resulting in absolute ruin to the capitalists. The effect of such vicissitudes is to damp enterprise and check further cultivation, while eventually Government is under the necessity of offering more favourable terms to manufacturers to induce them to continue their efforts. The rates now ruling are considered by the manufacturers to be wholly inadequate, and an association has been formed under the presidentship of Mr. A. P. Savundranayagam, M.A., for the conservation of their interests, and Government is to be approached with a view to securing an increase of purchasing prices. There is every hope that with individual effort on the part of the manufacturers, a better system of collection, transport, and storage, more modern methods of cultivation, the adoption of more economic and scientific measures generally, the sympathetic co-operation of Government with the manufacturers' endeavours, and the establishment of kindred operations and industries, wherein scope may be found for its use and more extensive appropriation, the salt industry of Ceylon, which already thrives so well, will be susceptible of the greatest possible development, and will yield benefits in incalculable proportion to the care and labour expended on it.

CHAMBER OF COMMERCE

As in the case of other flourishing institutions in the island, the Ceylon Chamber of Commerce started in a very modest way. When the Chamber came into existence sixty-seven years ago—to be precise on March 25, 1839—it had a roll of only ten subscribing firms as against the seventy-eight who to-day are associated with it. It says much for the transitoriness of things that not one of these firms figures in connection with the Chamber to-day. The first chairman, Mr. Joseph Read, too, has long since passed away. The initial work of the Chamber appears to have been the tabulation of rates of commission and charges then usual for the conduct of business and the preparation of returns of imports and exports. At that time the principal exports were coffee, cinnamon, and coconut oil, and business generally was in a very undeveloped state. The exact position of affairs is strikingly illustrated by a comparison of the figures of the imports and exports for the first year of the Chamber's life with those for 1905, the last year for which returns are available. In 1840 the total imports only reached £368,380, while the exports stood at the lower figure of £308,871. In 1905 goods to the value of no less than £7,221,621 were imported, and the exports totalled £6,812,647. Thus, the trade has increased twenty-fold since the Chamber's birth.

The records of the Chamber from 1840 to 1855, unfortunately, are missing, and it is therefore impossible to see what was its attitude to the total abolition of slavery in Ceylon, which took place in 1844. In 1855 the membership was about eighteen firms, and the Chamber recorded its opinion that the proposed railway to the interior should preferably be constructed by Government and not by a private company under guarantee, and seven years later this suggestion was adopted by the Government. Little of importance occurred in the annals of the Chamber until 1870, when an address of congratulation was presented to the Duke of Edinburgh on the occasion of his visit to the island in that year. During the next few years the Chamber was principally occupied in agitating for increased shipping accommodation, and even at the present time the question of wharf and harbour improvements bulks largely in the attentions of the Chamber. In 1872 the Chamber presented to the Right Hon. W. H. Gregory (afterwards Sir William H. Gregory), upon his arrival to take up his appointment as Governor and Commander-in-Chief, an address of welcome, in which emphasis was laid "upon the great importance in Ceylon commerce of increased and improved harbour accommodation at Colombo," and in the year it is recorded that, as a result of steam vessels to a great extent taking the place of sailing ships, the resources of the port were strained to the utmost limit, and representations were made to the Government with a view to securing the better working of Customs. In the same year the currency of the island was changed from pounds, shillings, and pence to rupees and cents, and the committee of the Chamber of Commerce reported "That the distasteful change that has been effected was found attended with great inconvenience, and the committee is of opinion that if the rupee must be the unit its Indian subdivisions should have been introduced." Curiously enough, mercantile opinion with regard to this step changed entirely shortly afterwards, and although it was effected in face of the strongest opposition, the change has long been admitted to be a wise and statesmanlike measure.

In 1875 the want of increased shipping accommodation became more and more felt, and Mr. W. W. Mitchell (now Sir W. W. Mitchell), who first became connected with the Chamber in 1867, on representations being made by the Chamber, was nominated as the first Mercantile Member of the Legislative Council. Two years later the Chamber presented an address to Sir James Longden, K.C.M.G., who became Governor of the colony in that year.

The following year marks an epoch in the history of the Chamber and of the trade of the island. In the report of the Chamber of Commerce for the first half of the year appears the first reference to tea, now the staple export of the island. The committee requested the Collector of Customs to add a fresh column to the export list published by him in the Government *Gazette*, to include tea, adding the prophecy, which has since been fully amplified, that "the export of this article is likely to assume considerable importance ere long." Later in the same year a special meeting of the Chamber was held in order to deprecate statements made in England to the effect that the leaf disease, *Hemileia vastatrix*, had practically brought the cultivation of coffee in Ceylon to an end. At this meeting a resolution was passed vouching for the fact that plantations which had been attacked had completely recovered, and since produced large crops of unimpaired quality, and whilst admitting that serious injury had been effected, the resolution continued: "That the Chamber feels assured by the experience of the last seven years that the coffee enterprise in Ceylon still exists on a sound basis and is in no danger of being brought to an end by the agency of the Hemileia." In the light of present knowledge, one sees how the Chamber, in common with all interested in the industry, were hoping against hope in wording such a resolution.

In 1880 the Chamber passed a resolution representing to the directors of the P. & O. and Messageries Maritimes Companies the advantages to the Ceylon community, as well as to themselves of the removal of their headquarters from Galle to Colombo, and this transference was made early in 1882. Proposals were also made to the Government in that year requesting consideration of the necessity of appointing a Harbour Committee, composed of officers and mercantile men, to consider the general arrangements of all harbour works. Eventually this led to the appointment of the present Harbour Board, and the chairman of the Chamber at that time (Sir William Mitchell) was invited to sit thereon.

In the year 1884 there was a crisis in Ceylon's commercial history. On the 3rd of May the Oriental Bank Corporation, the largest banking institution in the island, suspended payment. The consequent discrediting of some Rs. 3,200,000 (£200,000) worth of notes would have caused serious distress, had not the Government, at the instance of the banks and the Chamber of Commerce, promptly guaranteed the notes and thus averted the threatened crisis.

Very little of importance appears in the reports during the next few years, but in 1890 as a result of representations from the Chamber, a reduction of from 25 to 28 cents for postage to the United Kingdom was effected and the parcels post system was introduced. The next important step in the history of the Chamber was taken in 1894, when under its auspices was formed the Tea Traders' Association, and the site of the building still occupied by the Chamber was acquired from Government. In the following year it was noted at one of the meetings that the membership had reached the record total of 78, being an increase of 27 in ten years, and that number has never been surpassed in the succeeding years. It was agreed that the necessary funds (Rs. 20,000) for the erection of the new building should be raised by means of 7 per cent. debentures, and a special Ordinance was made incorporating the Chamber. The erection of the new building was completed towards the end of 1897 and the Chamber took possession of it early in the following year. In it provision is made for the offices of the Chamber and other offices which are let off, a reading-room for members, and a sale-room, in which auction sales of tea are held weekly by the Tea Traders' Association. As much as a million to a million and a half pounds of tea are sold here weekly, the prices obtained being accepted as the current market rates. In 1905 and the first half of 1906 the average price obtained was 33 cents a pound as against 36 cents in 1904, 38 cents in 1903, 33·07 cents in 1902, and 33·55 cents in 1901.

In the latter half of 1900 the Chamber of Mines became associated with the Chamber of Commerce, but is now defunct, its functions being performed by the older Chamber as occasion requires.

During 1901 the question of the over-production of tea presented itself in an urgent manner, and an attempt was made to arrive at some arrangement for a reduction of the output, but it was unsuccessful. The encouragement of green tea manufacture presented itself as an alternative and the most beneficial measure. The most important decision of the Chamber of Commerce in the following year was that in which the Planters' Association concurred against the proposal to abolish the duty on tea entering Ceylon.

In the following year a signal honour was paid to the Chamber in the selection of its chairman (Sir Stanley Bois) by the Government as Ceylon Commissioner to the St. Louis Exhibition. The members of the Chamber made a fitting presentation to Sir Stanley upon his return from St. Louis.

PROMINENT MEMBERS OF THE COLOMBO CHAMBER OF COMMERCE.

F. C. ALLEN. F. M. SIMPSON. C. W. SUHREN. SIR WILLIAM MITCHELL. J. C. NORMAN.
W. SHAKESPEARE. ALEXANDER FAIRLIE. G. H. ALSTON.

MEMBERS OF THE COLOMBO BROKERS' ASSOCIATION.

1. F. N. Sudlow. 2. W. Seale. 3. C. E. Haslop. 4. P. J. Parsons. 5. L. O. Leefe. 6. Wilton Bartleet. 7. H. B. Philips. 8. William Somerville, Sen. 9. W. E. Drury. 10. R. W. Forbes. 11. A. H. Barber. 12. W. Somerville, Jun. 13. W. E. Keell. 14. H. E. Guimaraens. 15. C. H. Wellard. 16. D. M. Hanna. 17. R. M. Meaden (Secretary.) 18. A. F. West. 19. W. B. Cooke. 20. G. R. Bacot. 21. E. Masters.

The Budget of 1904, increasing the duty on tea entering the United Kingdom by twopence a pound, was received with great indignation by the Chamber, which has for some years actively associated itself with the agitation of the Anti-Tea-Duty League in England for the abolition of the duty. Two members of the Chamher were in the same year appointed to attend a conference of Indian Chambers of Commerce in Bengal.

In 1905 H.M.S. *Sealark*, in response to petitions from the Chamber, was detailed by the Government to commence a re-survey of part of the coast of the island.

His Excellency the Governor (Sir H. A. Blake) intimated in 1906 that he had no objection to the formation of a Port Trust, and in consequence the committee of the Chamber is now formulating a working scheme to be laid before the Government. The most recent important step taken by the Chamber was to send a cable to the Colonial Secretary expressing disapproval of the policy of "marking time" which the Colonial Office had intimated was to be observed in Ceylon. Mr. A. Fairlie is the President of the Chamber at the present time and Mr. F. M. Simpson is the Secretary.

Here this outline of the history of the Chamber of Commerce can be fittingly closed. It will be seen that since its formation it has caused or accelerated every important decision for the development of the commerce of the isle, and its value to the community in this way can scarcely be overestimated.

THE BROKERS' ASSOCIATION, COLOMBO.

This institution was founded in 1896—the first title being "The Sharebrokers' Association"—to cope with the large and increasing business in share-dealing in Colombo, principally in the shares of tea companies. The following firms engaged in this line of business combined to form the original association, namely, Messrs. E. John & Co., Forbes & Walker, E. Benham & Co., Somerville & Co., A. M. Gepp, George Armitage & Co., W. Moir, and C. E. H. Symons. In 1904 the Sharebrokers' Association was dissolved, and the members formed themselves into "The Brokers' Association," consisting of the following firms: Messrs. E. John & Co., Forbes & Walker, Somerville & Co., Gordon & Wilson, C. E. H. Symons, and Keell & Waldock; while in 1906 Messrs. George White, Bartleet & Co. joined the membership.

The meetings of the association are held at the Chamber of Commerce usually twice, and sometimes three times a week, to record share quotations. Although the bulk of the business transacted is in the shares of tea, rubber, and general commercial companies, the members of the association have their other departments, confined entirely to the sale of the principal products of the island, such as tea, coconut oil, cocoa, copra, rubber, plumbago, and so forth, as well as the negotiation of bills. With the exception of tea, which is sold by public auction, all sales of produce are conducted privately. The weekly sales of tea—the principal product—range from 1,000,000 to 2,000,000 lbs. The transactions in tea form the stand-by of the brokers, though the bulk of business in rubber and tea shares runs that of the tea market very close. The tea sales are held at the Chamber of Commerce weekly. The first Secretary of the association was Mr. W. Moir, while the present Secretary is Mr. R. Meaden, of Messrs. E. John & Co., the committee being composed of a member of each firm.

H. M. WALDOCK.

SHIPPING, COMMERCE, AND CUSTOMS

COLOMBO has sometimes been called "the Clapham Junction of the ocean." The designation is not inappropriate, for as most of the trains which enter or leave London from the South pass through the well-known station, so the bulk of the steam shipping going to or from the Far East and Australia puts in at the capital of Ceylon. Colombo owes her preeminence as a port more to her geographical position than to her natural advantages. She has a splendid harbour, but it is largely the product of human skill. What man did not confer upon her was her great strategical position, almost athwart the route which all ships coming through the Suez Canal and proceeding to Eastern India, Burma, the Straits Settlements, Malaysia, China, Japan, and Australasia ordinarily take. Coal in these days is the breath of the nostrils of shipping, and the principal points where the commodity can be taken on board are marked out in unmistakable letters on the map. Colombo is one of these. Most vessels bound for the Far East run as far as Port Said without coaling, and then replenish their bunkers to a sufficient extent to carry them to Colombo, where special facilities for rapid and economical coaling exist. It was as a coaling port that the centre first attracted the patronage of the long distance ocean traffic. But more and more the port is now becoming a popular place of call for long distance tourists who are either visiting the East or are passing through on their way to China, Japan, and Australasia. Furthermore, a traffic to and from India, and especially Southern India, is being developed by way of Tuticorin (for which port a British India Steam Navigation Company's vessel leaves Colombo

CEYLON STEAM NAVIGATION COMPANY'S STEAMER.

RECAPITULATION OF HARBOUR DUES SINCE FIRST COLLECTED IN 1883.

Year.	Entering Dues.	Over-hour Dues.	Tonnage Dues.	Live Stock Dues.	Wharfage Dues.	Total.
	Rs. c.	Rs. c.	Rs. c.	Rs. c.	Rs. c.	Rs. c.
1883	99,075 0	8,738 75	108,450 16	—	162,754 32	379,018 23
1884	100,862 50	8,092 50	104,717 83	—	162,349 53	376,022 36
1885	103,465 0	8,982 50	114,132 10	7,385 80	160,417 7	394,382 47
1886	109,412 50	8,826 25	106,706 98	9,198 20	163,735 7	397,879 0
1887	119,645 0	9,172 50	117,682 81	11,384 80	185,241 37	443,126 48
1888	132,610 0	10,952 50	142,810 86	14.019 20	200,012 87	500,405 43
1889	140,542 50	11,505 0	153,018 79	14,150 60	203,684 82	522,901 71
1890	149 065 0	11,417 50	171,151 66	16,352 90	226,345 53	574,332 59
1891	158,967 50	11,196 25	179.325 98	21.973 0	248,219 98	619,682 71
1892	159,410 0	12,343 75	190,947 32	28.310 60	277,071 98	668,083 65
1893	166,512 50	10,958 75	190,380 56	27,919 60	278,912 7	674,683 48
1894	179,612 50	12,046 25	209.621 1	24.847 17	280,596 3	706,722 96
1895	189,207 50	14,005 0	228,874 27	30,083 80	317,206 90	779,377 47
1896	202,707 50	13,985 0	233,215 29	38,115 0	348,517 82	836,540 61
1897	191,255 0	17,162 50	260,297 21	36,145 60	365,816 56	870,676 87
1898	219,490 0	16,471 25	291,582 77	35,923 20	401,880 14	965,347 36
1899	230,617 50	15,375 0	307,713 74	46,799 80	407,707 21	1,008,213 25
1900	247,907 50	20,769 50	368,913 41	51,721 25	457,457 60	1,146,769 26
1901	249,418 50	18,108 0	366,296 99	49,581 90	440,022 99	1,123,428 38
1902	258,727 50	16,342 50	343,111 75	55,196 35	430,635 16	1,104,013 26
1903	255.675 0	17,063 75	354,677 99	55,812 90	464,961 11	1,148,190 75
1904	273,040 0	15,548 50	391,050 77	49,101 60	470,385 97	1,199,126 84
1905	274,502 50	21,435 0	387,625 95	51,779 45	451,599 62	1,186,942 52
Total ...	4,211,728 50	310,498 50	5.322,306 20	675,802 72	7,105,531 72	17,625,867 64

at six o'clock every evening); and when the long talked of railway connection between the island and the peninsula is established, there can be little question that the route to India *viâ* Colombo will be a very popular one.

The lines whose steamers regularly call at the port are the P. and O. Company, the Orient Company, the British India Steam Navigation Company, the North German Lloyd's, the Bibby Company, the Messageries Maritimes, the Austro-Hungarian Lloyd's, the "Nippon Yusen Kaisha" (Japan Mail Steamship Company), the Brocklebank Company, the Natal Direct Steamship Company, the Asiatic Steam Navigation Company, the Compania Transatlantica (Spanish mail), the Clan, the Anchor, the Glen, the Star, the Milburn, the Shire, the Harrison, the Shell, the Ben, the City, the Ocean, the Ducal, Holt's, and the Rafaelle-Rubattino lines. The vessels of the Russian Volunteer Fleet also make periodical calls, and the port, further, is visited by many purely cargo steamers, while there is a constant coming and going of picturesque native sailing craft engaged in the coasting trade of Ceylon and India. War ships of all nations, too, are frequent visitors, and contribute their share to the volume of trade by their coaling and victualling operations. In 1905 no fewer than 2,000 steamers, aggregating 5,129,235 tons, and 465 sailing vessels, aggregating 49,810 tons, entered the port, and the dues paid in respect of these ships amounted to the large sum of Rs. 1,186,942·52. The figures in both cases show a falling off compared with those for the previous year—in tonnage of 168,808 and in dues of Rs. 12 184·32. But the check is probably only a temporary one, due mainly to trade disturbance caused by the Russo-Japanese war. However that may be, the growth of Colombo as a port has been phenomenal. In 1883, when the harbour revenue was first established, the receipts were only Rs. 379,018·23. In other words, the income of the port has increased by about 300 per cent. in twenty-three years. The above table, showing the dues paid in each year, illustrates the progressive growth of income.

The commanding position of Colombo is revealed even more impressively when we examine the figures for the shipping trade of the island as a whole. The total tonnage of vessels arriving at all the colony's ports during the year was 5,605,664 tons. Consequently, Colombo's share was about eleven-twelfths. Galle, which once threatened to be a powerful rival of Colombo in the competition for the ocean-going trade, could only claim in the year under report 151 steamers, aggregating 328,509 tons, and 8 sailing vessels of a total tonnage of 611 tons.

The nationality of vessels inwards and outwards during the year 1905 for the island is thus made up:—

	ENTERED INWARDS.		CLEARED OUTWARDS.	
	No	Tons.	No.	Tons.
British ...	1,756	4,040,723	1,749	3.998,158
Colonial ...	1,382	97,900	1,393	99,990
American ...	—	—	—	—
Austrian ...	51	166,182	51	166,182
French ...	139	419,172	136	412,290
German ...	198	751,405	197	746,445
Japanese ...	—	—	—	—
Maldivian ...	83	10,047	82	9,620
Russian ...	3	7,201	3	7,201
Danish ...	3	7,332	3	7,332
Spanish ...	26	65,594	26	65,594
Norwegian .	10	9,801	9	9,142
Italian ...	11	26,771	11	26,771
Dutch ...	2	3,536	2	3,536

There can be no doubt that the decrease in the number and tonnage is mainly due to the Russo-Japanese war. Not a single Japanese vessel entered during 1905, and only three Russian.

Compared with the years 1901, 1902, 1903, and 1904, the result inwards and outwards is as follows:—

INWARDS.

Year.		Vessels.		Tons.
1901 ...	An increase of	297	...	1,048,057
1902 ...	An increase of	246	...	624,080
1903 ...	An increase of	212	...	420,974
1904 ...	A decrease of	55	...	40,352

OUTWARDS.

1901 ...	An increase of	226	...	1,081,298
1902 ...	An increase of	233	...	578,589
1903 ...	An increase of	205	...	420,213
1904 ...	A decrease of	63	...	28,322

If we turn to the statistics of trade we find in the figures a striking reflex of the prosperity which is shown in the shipping returns. In 1905 the value of the imports, including specie to the extent of Rs. 6,912,907, amounted to Rs. 115,237,235·27, and that of the exports, inclusive of Rs. 300,350 in specie, amounted to Rs. 116,054,839, a balance thus being shown in favour of exports of Rs. 817,603·73. The imports (omitting specie) showed an increase of Rs. 2,999,608·90 as compared with 1904, and of Rs. 7,434,955·47 as compared with 1903. The exports (omitting specie and the value of coal) were Rs. 1,080,833 in excess of the returns for 1904, but as compared with 1903 there is a decrease of Rs. 38,014. In the following table showing the trade of the colony (omitting specie) in each year since 1894 we have a clear view of commercial development :—

	Rs.
1894	147,621,610
1895	161,040,346
1896	162,436,216
1897	168,959,460
1898	181,326,925
1899	213,007,870
1900	220,550,716
1901	204,232,206
1902	208,614,933
1903	214,410,335
1904	219,834.335
1905	224,078,817

Supplementing this table in a useful direction is Table C, showing the countries which export the largest number of articles to Ceylon in order.

In regard to tea the export of 1905 was 170,183,572 lbs. against 157,929,342 lbs. in 1904, the average value being 35 cents per lb. as against 39 cents in 1903. Of the total export

TABLE A.

Year.	United Kingdom.		British Possessions Abroad.		Foreign Countries.	
	Imports from	Exports to	Imports from	Exports to	Imports from	Exports to
1901	301	501	628¼	164	110½	207½
1902	268¼	536½	599¾	161½	110¾	284¼
1903	257¾	541¼	633¾	166	117¼	315
1904	260½	511¾	665¾	183	127	316¼
1905	251¾	539¾	705¼	190	126¼	292¼

TABLE B.

	Imports from—					
	United Kingdom.		British Possessions Abroad.		Foreign Countries.	
	1904.	1905.	1904.	1905.	1904.	1905.
Cotton Piece Goods—	Rs.	Rs.	Rs.	Rs.	Rs.	Rs.
(1) Bleached	1,640,000	1,675,500	215,500	157,500	24,500	13,000
(2) Dyed	416,500	718,000	1,380,500	1,535,500	608,500	724,500
(3) Grey	685,500	1,163,000	10,000	28,000	79,500	107,000
(4) Muslin	37,000	26,500	4,000	7,000	1,500	600
(5) Printed	758,000	972,500	26,000	20,500	22,500	13,500
(6) Other	244,500	407,500	117,500	118,500	42,500	153,500
Apparel made up	245,500	203,500	31,500	33,000	138,000	293,000
Flannel	83,000	54,000	9,500	12,200	36,000	60,000
Silk and Satin, broad stuffs	85,850	52,700	62,800	41,700	154,000	178,000
Haberdashery	745,200	852,000	663,000	816,000	111,500	130,200
Hardware	791,500	894,750	23,500	16,000	128,000	141,000
Cement	96,000	110,000	—	—	88,000	123,000
Galvanised Iron	532,000	597,000	500	4,000	65,000	122,000
Hoop Iron	69,500	88,000	18,000	14,000	105,500	146,500
Cast Steel	65,500	72,250	3,700	2,000	62,000	127,500
Manures (manufactured)	180,000	213,000	1,094,500	1,126,000	591,500	555,500
Biscuits	201,000	232,500	9,500	9,000	85,000	55,000
Milk (preserved)	7,500	9,500	1,330	2,760	266,400	265,800
Refined Sugar	67,500	59,500	1,287,000	1,605,600	693,000	1,051,300
Potatoes	3,800	3,700	174,100	173,500	167,100	189,500

In regard to the distribution of trade, Table A, showing in lakhs of rupees the imports and exports during the past five years, is instructive.

From this it will be seen that of the total imports—

65·1 came from British Possessions as against 63·2 in 1904.

23·3 came from the United Kingdom as against 24·7 in 1904.

11·6 came from Foreign Countries as against 12·1 in 1904.

Of the total exports—

52·8 went to the United Kingdom as against 50·6 in 1904.

28·6 went to Foreign Countries as against 31·3 in 1904.

18·6 went to British Possessions abroad as against 18·1 in 1904.

Another interesting official statement is given in Table B, which shows the comparative values in round numbers of some of the chief imports.

TABLE C.

	Imports from Foreign Countries.			Difference Compared with	
	1903.	1904.	1905.	1903.	1904.
	Rs.	Rs.	Rs.	Rs.	Rs.
1. Germany	2,061,008	2,452,637	2,692,913	+631,905	+240,276
2. Japan	1,583,483	1,757,074	1,623,854	+ 40,371	−133,220
3. Russia	897,421	1,445,802	983,291	+ 85,870	−462,511
4. Austria	985,006	841,819	878,261	−106,745	+ 36,442
5. United States of America	721,887	725,963	801,157	+ 79,270	+ 75,194
6. France	744,550	750,635	755,239	+ 10,689	+ 4,604
7. Holland	488,582	653,938	677,506	+188,924	+ 23,568
8. Belgium	469,883	377,162	544,566	+ 74,683	+167,404
9. Switzerland	370,762	438,662	431,801	+ 61,039	− 6,861
10. Italy	369,440	270,540	322,936	− 46,504	+ 52,396
11. Sweden	250,442	184,864	182,330	− 68,112	− 2,534
Total of all Foreign Countries omitting Specie...	11,726,139	12,700,007	12,624,888	+898,749	− 75,119

A companion table (D) relating to exports may be also given.

Finally may be cited a statement (Table E) showing the value in round numbers of the staple exports of the colony, excluding tea,

112 million pounds went to the United Kingdom, or 7·7 millions in excess of the amount exported in 1904; 11·2 million pounds to Russia (an increase of 0·6); 9·25 to New South Wales (a decrease of 0·12); 8 to Victoria (increase of 0·3);

TABLE D.

	Exports to Foreign Countries.			Difference Compared with	
	1903.	1904.	1905.	1903.	1904.
	Rs.	Rs.	Rs.	Rs.	Rs.
1. United States of America	8,545,632	8,193,536	8,151,821	− 393,811	− 41,715
2. Germany	7,069,284	8,666,251	6,568,464	− 500,820	−2,097,787
3. British India	3,656,483	4,708,931	5,071,733	+1,415,250	+ 362,802
4. Russia	6,018,743	4,992,282	4,415,455	−1,603,288	− 576,827
5. New South Wales ...	2,875,004	3,566,907	3,465,672	+ 590,668	− 101,235
6. Victoria	2,653,019	3,046,823	2,996,746	+ 343,727	− 50,077
7. Austria	1,163,376	1,975,232	2,962,389	+1,799,013	+ 987,157
8. Belgium	2,662,663	2,834,307	1,995,701	− 666,962	− 838,606
9. China, excluding Hong Kong	1,886,766	688,096	1,526,360	− 360,406	+ 838,264
10. France	1,754,506	1,840,939	1,367,542	− 386,964	− 473,397

TABLE E.

	To United Kingdom.		To British Possessions Abroad.		Foreign Countries.	
	1904.	1905.	1904.	1905.	1904.	1905.
	Rs.	Rs.	Rs.	Rs.	Rs.	Rs.
Products of Coconut Palm	7,883,500	8,963,000	1,096,000	1,439,000	15,429,500	12,046,000
Plumbago ...	1,800,000	1,929,500	40,500	33,500	4,660,000	5,207,500
Cinnamon ...	328,000	296,000	66,500	81,000	1,877,500	1,935,000
Cacao ...	1,559,000	1,611,000	225,000	333,500	663,500	489,000

and 2 to South and West Australia. The total value of the tea exported in 1905 was Rs. 59,564,245 as against Rs. 56,854,563.

A large proportion, nearly one-fourth, of the total revenue of the Government of Ceylon is derived from Customs duties. In 1905 the amount so raised was Rs. 8,183,728·22. This was Rs. 318,553·64 more than was paid into the Treasury in 1904, and Rs. 609,922·44 in excess of the sum obtained in 1903. The following table of gross Customs revenue for the twelve years ended 1905 shows that the Customs revenue has more than kept pace with the development of trade :—

	Rs.	c.
1894	4,931,967	42
1895	5,770,241	2
1896	5,550,971	65
1897	6,278,787	49
1898	6,714,625	82
1899	7,101,851	73
1900	7,620,432	29
1901	7,446,807	26
1902	7,630,175	62
1903	8,043,062	94
1904	8,334,431	74
1905	8,652,985	38

A general import tariff and certain export duties are the sources of the Customs revenue. A duty on rice imported is the basis of the whole system. In 1905 the amount secured from this one source alone was Rs. 2,963,077·43. "Other grain" accounted for Rs. 367,093·05, so that no less than Rs. 3,330,170·48 was raised from foodstuffs during the year under report. The policy of taxing so heavily the food of the people has often been severely criticised. But there can be no question that in a country like Ceylon indirect taxation is best suited to the needs and habits of the population, and that being so, there is a good deal to be said for a system of grain duties. Next to these imports the most productive sources of revenue are :—

	Rs.	c.
Spirits	1,101,328	21
Sugar	626,294	0
Cotton Manufactures	321,737	0
Tobacco	265,096	5
Fish Dried and Salted	173,854	72
Earthenware and China ...	106,455	42
Kerosene Oil	783,594	0

In addition to the amounts raised on account of imports, a considerable revenue is derived from duties on certain exports. In 1905 the total sum collected in this connection was Rs. 913,615·68, distributed under the following heads :—

	Rs.	c.
Medical Aid Duty on Tea	151,944	6
Do. Coffee	532	15
Do. Cacao	6,944	31
Do. Cinchona ...	68	16
Government Cess on Tea	509,472	32
Government Cess on Cardamoms	3,052	24
Royalty on Elephants	400	0
Royalty on Plumbago	153,216	22
Duty on Arrack	68,158	33
Duty on Chanks	5,202	44
Duty on Deer and Sambur Horns	14,625	45
Total	913,615	68

The duties on tea, coffee, cacao, and cinchona are levied in order to provide funds for furnishing medical aid to immigrant estate coolies. Besides the tea cess under the Medical Ordinance there is a further duty imposed, with the assent of the planters' organisations, "in order that the proceeds of such duty may be devoted to increasing the consumption of Ceylon tea in foreign lands." The amount raised in 1905 on this account was Rs. 509,472·32. From 1st October last a sum of Rs. 3,052·24 was recovered as export duty on cardamoms, the produce of the colony, to be devoted to a like purpose as regards cardamons.

The duties on plumbago and arrack are imposed for revenue purposes. The impost in respect of elephants, which amounts to Rs. 200 per head, is levied for the purpose of protecting these valuable beasts, of which large numbers still exist in the wilder parts of the interior. A similar explanation may be given of the duty on deer and sambur horns. Without the assistance that the duty affords there would be a danger of the deer of the island being exterminated for purposes of gain.

It is to be noted that the Ceylon Customs Department is exclusively concerned with the collection of sea Customs. The modern history of the department dates from January 6, 1853, when the Customs were transferred to the local governments. At that time four districts were formed, the first consisting of the ports in the Western and North-Western Provinces, the second of the ports in the Southern Province, the third of the ports in the Northern Province, and the fourth of the ports in the Eastern Province. The whole department is controlled by a Principal Collector of Customs, who is also Superintendent of Wrecks and Registrar of Shipping and Seamen.

CEYLON HARBOURS.

By Captain J. A. Legge, Master Attendant.

THE artificial harbour of Colombo, a magnificent monument of engineering constructive skill, may be termed the "hub" of the island of Ceylon's prosperity. Without a suitable and safe anchorage, the trade of Ceylon would have been hampered and retarded until it could not have approached its present prosperity and magnitude by a degree that it is, perhaps, even now not possible to estimate. Without a convenient outlet to the sea, the present highly remunerative railway system would not have, perhaps, done more than pay its way; and in many other ways too numerous to mention trade and prosperity would have been restricted.

When Ceylon was first colonised by the Portuguese in 1505, the open roadstead of Colombo was used by their shipping; and in 1518 they established a trading depôt and fort on the rocky spit of land that forms the base of the south-west breakwater. In 1656, after a siege of seven months, Colombo fell into the hands of the Dutch, and the shipping enterprise of the sturdy Hollanders, too famous to require more than passing comment, supplanted that of their precursors on the coasts of Colombo. In 1796, the Dutch, in their turn, were ousted, and Colombo fell into the hands of the British. From that date the harbour and port of Galle became the principal port of call in Ceylon for shipping, being a natural, though not very safe, harbour, its bottom being studded with submerged rocks and its entrance masked more or less by rocky reefs, besides being exposed to the full force of the south-west monsoon gales.

In the year 1864 what appears to have been the first proposal to construct an artificial port at Colombo, either by a breakwater or docks, or both, was put forward, and for the next few years rival plans for the protection of Galle or Colombo were designed. For some time Galle seems to have been the more favoured. What seems to have clinched the matter, and turned local opinion finally in favour of the more northern port, was the completion of the railway between Colombo and Kandy. The last Commission on the protection of Galle harbour sat in 1869; and previous to that, from the year 1866, some nineteen papers and reports of the first importance passed between the Secretary of State, the local Government, and the different local authorities on the subject. In the sessional papers of the local Legislature it was recorded, as an argument in favour of a harbour being constructed at Colombo as against Galle, that the former was 30 miles only off the course of steamers from Aden to the Far East, or Calcutta, and only 18 miles off the course of steamers from Bombay, both of which would, in the ordinary course, call at Galle.

In 1871 Mr. Townshend, the engineer of Plymouth breakwater, was appointed to report on the practicability of constructing protective works at Colombo. He reported favourably,

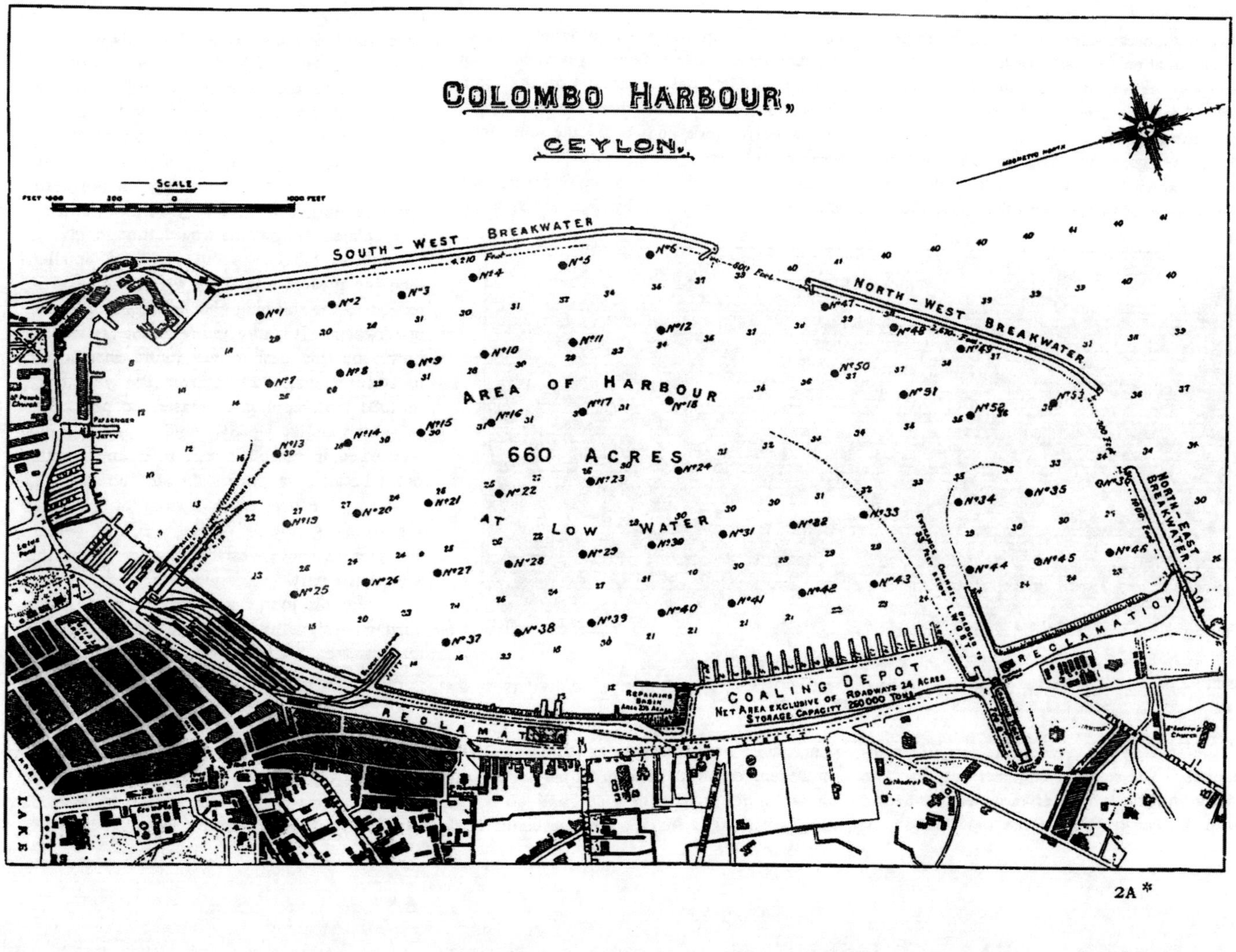

and framed estimates and designed plans for effecting the desired object. In 1872 the late Sir John Coode, the eminent harbour engineer, was consulted, and he submitted his first plan, embracing a breakwater with jetties combined, and reclamation of the foreshore. To Lord Carnarvon, as Secretary for the Colonies, in 1866, and to two successive Governors of Ceylon —Sir Hercules Robinson, in 1870, and Sir William Gregory, in 1872, both advised by Captain James Donnan, the Master Attendant, Colombo—belongs the credit for the initiation of the great works now on the verge of completion. The resident engineer was the late Mr. John Kyle, who afterwards was connected with the construction of the new harbour at Dover, and died while carrying on that great undertaking; and no greater monument of that engineer's skill exists than the magnificent Colombo breakwater, erected as it was under most adverse conditions, and in what is probably the record time of nine years, with an average working period actually on the main breakwater of only about three months a year. This massive work, known as "the south-west breakwater," was commenced from a reclamation of four and a half acres, and the first block was set by His Majesty the King when visiting Ceylon as Prince of Wales in December, 1875. The great barrier is 50 ft. in width for 1,350 lineal ft., and 40 ft. for the remaining 2,862 ft., the top being 9 ft. above high water, while the total length is 4,212 ft. The reasons for the extra width are explained by the accompanying plan, which shows that the original design was to moor ships to the breakwater and to two breakwater piers. To any one, however, who has seen Colombo harbour in June, the impossibility of carrying this idea into practice will have been ocularly demonstrated. The breakwater is constructed of concrete blocks, weighing about 21 tons each, and resting on a rubble mound. These blocks are sloped, bonded and joggled together, the root, or base, being a solid mass of concrete weighing no less than 437 tons in one block.

COLOMBO HARBOUR FROM THE P. AND O. OFFICE.
(The Diamond Jubilee Statue of the late Queen Victoria is seen in the foreground.)

THE ARTIFICIAL HARBOUR.
(Built for the shelter of the native fishing population. The celebrated Ceylon outrigger canoes are seen on the foreshore.)

This magnificent structure was finished in 1883-84. But even from its commencement trade was attracted to the port of Colombo, and began to develop. In June, 1882, this development may be said to have reached the point of full justification; for in that month the Peninsular and Oriental Company's Royal Mail steamships abandoned Galle and commenced using Colombo as the port of call of Ceylon. Their first vessel to use Colombo was the old *Rome* (now the pleasure yacht *Vectis*); and the advent of this vessel was made the occasion of a commemorative trip to Galle on her by some of the leading men of the colony.

Sir John Coode's design "B," dated September 30, 1878—which was formulated to coincide with the estimate of cost when the then Chamber of Commerce limited the money to be spent on harbour protection to a maximum of £800,000, being in favour of a small close harbour of some 400 acres—shows a northern arm enclosing a harbour of 502 acres; and as a completed design this would, though giving Colombo a harbour about one-third smaller than the present one, have given entire protection to the shipping and lighters within the breakwaters. It is interesting to note, however, how soon this design was found insufficient in scale of magnitude. From the year 1883 to 1889 the shipping increased 60 per cent. in value; and a steady, though perhaps not so marked, increase has continued almost without a break ever since. To Sir John Coode, however, the port owes a debt of gratitude for adhering to his design "B," of which the present south-west breakwater forms the completed part.

In 1891 Sir John Coode was asked to frame further designs and estimate for a northern breakwater. He died very soon afterwards, and the present Consulting Engineer of the Ceylon Government, Sir William Matthews, then took the matter in hand, and formulated the present north-east and north-west breakwaters. The latter is similar in construction to the south-west barrier, but is 23 ft. wide and 2,655 ft. long, the top being 8 ft. 6 ins.

SUNSET IN COLOMBO HARBOUR. THE COLOMBO BREAKWATER DURING THE SOUTH-WEST MONSOON.

FISHING CANOE.

THE WESTERN HEAD OF THE NORTH-WEST BREAKWATER.
(Just before completion. The lighthouse is built of steel. Two British warships will be noticed at the moorings.)

LOADING TEA FROM LIGHTERS IN COLOMBO HARBOUR.

above high water. These works have been executed by Mr. J. H. Bostock, Resident Engineer, assisted by Mr. John Kyle, jun.

In the year 1897 the Legislative Council voted £318,000 towards the construction of a graving-dock in the harbour, half this cost to be borne by the colony and half by the Admiralty; and in the following year £33,000 was provided for a patent slipway. On March 1, 1899, Sir West Ridgeway, the then Governor of the colony, cut the first sod of the graving-dock, since officially opened by Sir Henry Blake, the present Governor. It should be mentioned that the patent slipway has reaped a fair revenue since 1903.

COLOMBO GRAVING DOCK FROM THE HARBOUR.

S.S. "MONKSEATON."

(Length, 325 ft.; breadth, 40 ft.; depth, 26 ft. 4 ins.; tonnage, 2,772. The first ship to enter Colombo Graving Dock on October 31, 1906. The photo shows the dock from the inner end and also the entrance to the harbour.)

The Colombo harbour, as it now appears, is an artificial haven of 640 nett acreage, enclosed by three breakwaters: the first, or south-west breakwater, 4,212 ft. long; the centre, or north-west breakwater, a detached or island work, 2,655 ft. long; and the northern arm, a rubble work, running out 1,000 ft. from the shore. The entrance between the south-west and north-west works is 800 ft. wide, a concrete lighthouse showing a red second-order light at night on the extremity of the south-west breakwater, and a steel lighthouse showing a green fourth-order light on the western extremity of the north-west breakwater. The minimum depth of water in this entrance is 40 ft. The northern entrance, between the north-west breakwater and the northern arm, is 700 ft. wide, with a depth of 34 ft. of water, and is marked by a steel lighthouse recently completed, standing on the eastern end of the north-west breakwater, which shows a fourth-order red light. A steel lighthouse is (at time of writing) to be erected on the western end of the northern arm, which will show a fourth-order light, having a green sector from north through west to south, and a red sector from north through east to south. Two red lights in line lead through the southern entrance, and show the way clear of buoys to the eastern tier of moorings. A red light over a green in line leads through the western channel, and a green light over a red through the eastern channel. This latter beacon, though showing rather to the eastward of the centre, may be used as leading lights through the northern entrance. The harbour is dredged to a minimum depth of 30 ft., which is being increased to 33 ft.; and it can accommodate 46 of the largest sized vessels during the south-west monsoon, and 42 during the north-east monsoon.

In the harbour service there are two twin-screw tugs of 500 horse-power on each engine, capable of towing the largest vessel afloat. These tugs are also fitted with hydrants to which six hoses can be attached, with a

GALLE HARBOUR. BATTICALOA OPEN ROADSTEAD.

JAFFNA ROADSTEAD. TRINCOMALEE HARBOUR.

working pressure of 80 lbs. to the inch, for extinguishing fire, one of the tugs carrying a Clayton disinfecting machine as well. Eight small landing-jetties are provided for cargo-lighters, one excellent jetty for passengers, and eighteen for coal-lighters. It is much to be regretted that as yet no ocean steamer jetties for enabling passengers and cargo to land direct without the inconvenience, cost, and delay of boat carriage have been constructed. Among the machinery equipment are three steam-cranes of 2 tons capacity each, one of 5 tons, one "Fair Brane" of 15 tons, five electric cranes of 2 tons, two of 4 tons, eight Grafton hand-cranes of 3 tons, three Gibbins of 4 tons, one Stoddart and Pitts of 3 tons, four ordinary of 1 ton, and one steam Titan of 40 tons. The landing and shipping arrangements are very contracted in space as regards the foreshore, and serious congestion is a not infrequent consequence. But with the completion of the sheltering work the landing facilities will be largely increased by the removal of all the coal-sheds, stocks, and depôts now occupying this part of the foreshore to a new site farther north in the harbour, thus affording an additional frontage of 2,235 ft. for ordinary wharfage purposes. The graving dock, of 700 ft. on the floor, with a depth of 32 ft. over all at high water and a breadth at the entrance of 85 ft., recently completed and opened, is designed and fitted on the most modern and approved lines, with hydraulic capstans and other up-to-date appliances.

The patent slip, completed three years ago, is capable of accommodating vessels up to 1,200 tons displacement. A sheltered basin for the repair of lighters and small craft was completed at the same time. Altogether 133 acres have been reclaimed from the sea on the foreshore, of which 24 acres are allotted to the new coal depôts. A fishery harbour has been constructed to the north of the main harbour, sheltered by a rubble breakwater 800 ft. in length.

To complete the present works it is proposed to construct an outside sheltering arm (suggested by the present Master Attendant) from the curve of the south-west breakwater, of 2,000 ft. in length in a northerly direction, to mask the southern entrance from the heavy westerly sea that still finds its way into the harbour at that spot, and has the effect at times of stopping work at the 18 new coaling jetties as well as at several of the steamer moorings in this vicinity. A survey having the construction of a wet dock of 115 acres as its object has also been carried out. But the cost of such proposed work has been considered so great as to postpone its consideration indefinitely. Such a dock would accommodate 25 of the largest vessels, and have 13,200 ft. of quayage. The maximum rise and fall of tide in the harbour is about 2 ft., and is therefore practically negligible. A scheme for jetties alongside which large steamers may be moored is also under consideration, the adoption of which will insure a most welcome and greatly needed addition to the facilities for embarking on or disembarking from the ocean liners.

In conclusion, it is desirable to lay stress on the fact that had Sir John Coode in the first instance been commissioned to design a harbour of 646 acres, the protective arm referred to would not have had to be considered. His design "B" is as near perfect as it is humanly possible for an artificial design to be, and Sir William Matthews has had to labour under the disadvantage of what may be termed altering a coat after it has once been cut to order, with the natural result that its first excellence of fit can never again be attained.

HIS MAJESTY'S SURVEY YACHT "SEALARK."
(On the patent slip, from the harbour end. The slip will take vessels up to 1,200 tons.)

COLOMBO GRAVING DOCK.
(Looking towards the harbour. Dimensions: Length, 700 ft.; width, 85 ft. at the entrance and 32 ft. on the sill.)

OTHER HARBOURS.

There are two other harbours of Ceylon and two roadsteads on the coast-line deserving mention. The first of the former is Galle, which is a circular-shaped harbour with deep water all round its foreshore and a steep sloping beach of rock and sand. Beautiful from a scenic aspect, the harbour is sheltered in every direction by elevated land, except to the south. In this direction the entrance is open to the wind and sea, especially during the south-west monsoon months. But in this haven there are some twenty-two dangerous submerged rocks; and in consequence of those sources of danger, coupled with its exposed entrance, this harbour is not popular with mariners. The trade of Galle has been stagnant since the shipping was diverted to Colombo, and now hardly three ships a week on the average throughout the year call at the southern port. The exports from Galle are chiefly citronella oil, fibre, cocoanut oil, and copra, and there is a coaling depôt on the foreshore. Owing to its geographical position and its configuration, had it been possible to remove the rocks and build a sheltering breakwater at the entrance at a cost Ceylon could have afforded, Galle harbour could have been converted into a fine anchorage, with deep-water wharfs round its extensive shore-line for steamers to lie at, and other advantages and accommodation.

Batticaloa, on the mid-eastern coast of the island, is an open roadstead off the bar at the outfall of a series of lakes fed, among other rivers, by the Mandeniya Aru. Batticaloa exports much the same produce as Galle; and its shipping consists of two weekly calls of the Ceylon Steam Navigation Company's steamers, besides the native sailing craft, the whole, however, not amounting to any quantity.

COLOMBO HARBOUR FROM THE GRAND ORIENTAL HOTEL.
(Showing the landing jetty and a portion of the Customs premises. There were a Bibby liner and a British cruiser in the port at the time.)

Trincomalee, on the north-eastern coast, is a magnificent harbour, nearly landlocked, and capable of sheltering a very large number of vessels in a safe, snug, and deep-water anchorage. This port, until last year, was the head-quarter harbour of the Navy's East Indian station, and large numbers of workpeople were employed in the shipping yard here. It has since been abandoned, and the splendid residences provided for the Naval Commander-in-Chief of the station and the officials connected with the naval yard have been handed over to the tender mercies of caretakers. The impregnable fortifications have been dismantled, the garrison has been withdrawn, and Trincomalee has dwindled into insignificance, being now nothing more than a veritable "sleepy hollow." The value of this harbour as a naval station was fully appreciated by combatants on both sides during the French wars of the eighteenth and the early part of the nineteenth centuries, and the place changed hands more than once during the struggles between the French Admiral Suffren and the British Naval Commander-in-Chief of that period, it being the only safe harbour in which to refit the sailing ships of war on two long coast-lines. The nature of the trade of Trincomalee is much the same as that of Galle and Batticaloa, and the shipping consists of the steamers that also call at Batticaloa, farther south, and native craft. As a naval port Trincomalee stocked coal and was visited by steam colliers from time to time. This business has now passed away with the official abandonment — possibly only for a time, possibly for ever; and the visitor to either Trincomalee or Galle cannot contemplate without a pang of regret the effacement of their glory and importance in the inexorable march of progress.

Jaffna, the northern port of Ceylon, is a shallow roadstead, only used by shipping during the north-east monsoon. In the south-west monsoon season Kankesanturai, the extreme northern gate of the island, is the port of call on this coast-line. The outgoing trade from Jaffna is mostly concerned with coconuts, fibre, tobacco, and other local products, and the nature of the shipping is the same as at Batticaloa. With the completion of the northern railway connecting Jaffna with Colombo, the produce of the Northern Province, for which Jaffna was previously the main outlet, has been diverted from sea to land transport to a considerable degree.

P. & O. STEAM NAVIGATION COMPANY.

Ever since the Peninsular and Oriental Steam Navigation Company commenced to carry English mails to China and Australia the company's boats have called at ports in Ceylon both ways for the receipt and despatch of mails, and a big business has been built up with the island. Previous to 1880 Point de Galle was the port of call, but in that year the P. & O. Company, together with other lines, transferred their business to Colombo, the magnificent breakwater erected about that time making it a secure harbour. The company has had a remarkable history. Its first ship was built in 1829—the *William Fawcett*, of 206 gross tonnage—but its regular career dates from the year of Queen Victoria's accession, when mail-packets were run from London to Lisbon and Gibraltar under contract with Her Majesty's Government. In the course of two or three years the line was extended to Malta and Alexandria, and the company was incorporated under Royal Charter in 1840. The first P. & O. steamer from England to India was the *Hindostan*, of 1,800 tons, which left England in September, 1842, and sailed *viâ* the Cape of Good Hope. Towards the end of 1844 the company was in a position to undertake a mail service from England to Alexandria, and from Suez to Ceylon, Madras, and Calcutta, with a further extension from Ceylon to Penang, Singapore, Hong Kong, and Shanghai. In those days passengers, goods, and mails were conveyed overland from Alexandria to Suez, and previous to the construction of the railway from Alexandria to Suez this had to be done in a very primitive manner, affording a striking contrast to present-day modes of travel. Caravans numbering no less than 3,000 camels had to be employed to convey a single steamer's load from Cairo (whence it came by rail from Alexandria) to Suez. This system was in operation for nearly twenty years, but it was not until 1888, seventeen years after the opening of the Suez Canal, that the conveyance of mails was made by the canal route. The P. & O. Company now carry the English mails to India, Ceylon, China, and Australia. To India there is a weekly service, and to China and Australia a fortnightly service, and some faint idea of the importance of this postal work may be gathered from the fact that the mails from Brindisi for conveyance by the Indian and Australian steamers usually amount to some 4,000 bags and boxes. The company's fleet at the present time consists of steamers aggregating 300,000 tons, and the original cost of these ships amounted to seven millions sterling. Ever since the first English mails were carried by P. & O.

COALING JETTIES.

THE COLOMBO COALING JETTIES

(Built from reclaimed ground. The P. & O. R.M.S. *Macedonia* is conspicuous in the harbour, with His Majesty's Survey Yacht *Sealark* away over at the breakwater.)

THE LANDING FACILITIES IN COLOMBO HARBOUR FROM THE SEA.

DINING SALOON.

PROMENADE DECK.

THE S.S. "PUNDUA."

boats the company has had two objects in view ; the reduction of the time taken on the voyage and a decrease in the cost to the Government. That these have been attained is attested by the facts that the P. & O. have held the Government contract continuously, though it is always open for public tender, and that the price paid by the Government is a quarter of a million sterling less than it was twenty-five years ago.

BRITISH INDIA STEAM NAVIGATION COMPANY, LTD.

The British India Steam Navigation Company, which runs some of the most important ocean services in the East, naturally plays a conspicuous part in the shipping trade of Ceylon. Registered over half a century ago, the company now has a fleet of about 120 vessels afloat. Of the services to and from Colombo, perhaps the most important are the daily service between Tuticorin and Colombo and the bi-weekly service between Tondi, Amnapatam, and Paumban and Colombo, as these are the means of bringing most of the Tamil labour, upon which the industries of the island are so dependent, into Ceylon. Some years ago the Tuticorin service enjoyed the unenviable reputation of being the most uncomfortable of cross-channel services, and the Tuticorin boats were nicknamed "the mosquito fleet." A glance at the accompanying photograph of the *Pundua*, which crosses to Tuticorin, will, however, show that the old order has passed away, and that the new state of things would be hard to beat for comfort. The *Pundua* (Captain J. C. Kirkham, R.N.R.) is 3,305 tons gross, and the *Purnea* (Captain C. Willis) 3,306 tons gross, and the horse-power (nominal) of both is 400. During the pearl fisheries the *Aska* and *Bhadra*, which are the boats on the Pass run, sail between Paumban and Marichchukadde and Colombo and Marichchukadde. On the Tuticorin–Colombo boats the Calcutta mails for Ceylon are carried, and the company's boats also carry the mails on their four-weekly service between Ceylon and Mauritius. In addition to the services already mentioned, the others which the British India Company provides to and from Colombo are: fortnightly to and from Aden, Marseilles, and London ; fortnightly to Mombasa, Zanzibar, Delagoa Bay, and Durban *viâ* Bombay and Aden ; fortnightly to Madras, Coromandel Coast ports, and Calcutta ; weekly to Rangoon *viâ* Madras, and weekly to Rangoon and Moulmein *viâ* Calcutta ; fortnightly to Malabar Coast ports and Bombay ; weekly to Arakan, Burma, and the Straits Settlements *viâ* Calcutta ; fortnightly to Karachi, Persian Gulf ports, and Baghdad *viâ* Bombay ; and frequent sailings to Java and Queensland direct as inducement offers.

THE NORTH GERMAN LLOYD'S SERVICE.

Progress, steady and continuous, marks the record of the great marine companies of Germany, and from a position of comparative insignificance they have in the last few decades taken a leading place in the front rank of the world's shipping. In no direction has this advance been more marked than in the Eastern and Australian trade. The North German Lloyd's Company's steamers have become favourites with the travelling public, with British *voyageurs* in particular, and deservedly so, for the company has shown itself enterprising in the truest and best sense of the

THE S.S. "BULOW" UNDER STEAM ON THE RIVER WESER.

FIRST-CLASS DINING SALOON ON THE S.S. "BULOW."

LADIES' SALOON ON THE S.S. "PRINZ HEINRICH."

FIRST-CLASS CONCERT-ROOM ON THE S.S. "PRINZ LUDWIG."

THE S.S. "PRINZ LUDWIG" UNDER STEAM.

THE "GROSSER KURFURST" ENTERING BREMERHAVEN. GYMNASIUM ON THE "PRINZ EITEL FRIEDRICH."

FIRST-CLASS SMOKING-ROOM ON THE S.S. "KAISER WILHELM II."

DRAWING-ROOM ON THE S.S. "GROSSER KURFURST." THE S.S. "KAISER WILHELM II." UNDER STEAM.

word. Its boats are not only "well found" in the ordinary sense, but they represent the last word in comfort, sea-going qualities, and all that goes to make up the mammoth floating hotel of twentieth-century civilisation.

The Far Eastern and Australian run of the company was commenced in 1886, about twenty-eight years after the formation of the company. The German Government, recognising the national importance of the service, gave to the company a contract for the conveyance of mails, and this support was not only valuable directly, but indirectly helped the company materially by conferring a prestige upon the service which it would not otherwise have enjoyed. The service is maintained by a main and branch lines to Eastern Asia, two lines to Australia, one Australia–Japan line, and sixteen branch lines in the coast and island service of the East. The route was commenced with a monthly service of old English-built vessels of the *Hohenstauffen* class, of about 3,000 tons, but since the institution of the line the vessels and their tonnage have been continually increased, and to-day steamers of the *Barbarossa* type, up to 13,000 tons, are running fortnightly. The ships engaged on this line call at Colombo, and the improvements which the company have carried out on these liners have considerably increased both the passenger and cargo traffic to and from Ceylon. A large share of the transport of goods is done by the vessels of the Norddeutscher Lloyd Company, whilst their attention to the comfort of passengers has induced many persons going from India to journey to Ceylon and book by their line instead of sailing from Bombay. It has been decided to accelerate the service to Eastern Asia and Australia from January, 1907.

The history of the company is interesting. The Norddeutscher Lloyd, Bremen, was formed in 1857, and now runs steamers to all parts of the world. The backbone of the business is constituted by the Bremen–New York line, on which are engaged the best vessels of the company in a weekly service.

These vessels are amongst the largest and fastest in the world. Besides these there are many twin-screw mail steamers which run to America, five running to North and two to South America, and one to Cuba. Then there is the Far Eastern service to which reference has already been made. Better vessels have been put on this run, others have been materially improved, and a great improvement has been made in the working out of the time-tables. The company has paid particular care to the Mediterranean lines, of which five are now worked, amongst these being one in direct connection between Genoa and New York, this being an immensely popular route. The lines of the N.D.L. are particularly adapted to tours around the world, and tickets for excellently arranged trips are issued. The vessels of the company are well fitted up with every convenience, and, as an instance of the company's desire to obtain every comfort for the passengers, it may be mentioned that this company was the first to place electric fans in the cabins free of charge. Appended are the names and tonnage of the vessels of the company calling at Colombo on the Eastern and Australia circuit: *Grosser Kurfürst* (13,182 tons), *Bremen* (11,570), *Barbarossa* (10,915), *Prinzess Alice* (10,911), *Prinzess Irene* (10,881), *Königin Luise* (10,711), *Friedrich der Grosse* (10,695), *König Albert* (10,643), *Prinz Eitel Friedrich* (8,865), *Scharnhorst* (8,131), *Gneisenau* (8,081), *Zieten* (8,043), *Roon* (8,022), *Seydlitz* (7,942), *Prinz Regent Luitpold* (6,288), *Prinz Heinrich* (6,263), *Sigmaringen* (5,710), *Preussen* (5,295), *Schwaben* (5,102), *Hessen* (5,100), *Westfalen* (5,100), *Lothringen* (5,100), *Karlsruhe* (5,057), *Stuttgart* (5,048), *Bayern* (5,034), *Sachsen* (5,026), *Darmstadt* (5,012), *Oldenburg* (5,006), *Gera* (5,005), and *Weimar* (4,996).

The agents for the company at Colombo are Messrs. Freudenberg & Co., Chatham Street.

THE NIPPON YUSEN KAISHA

(*Colombo Agents, Carson & Co.*).

Considering that Japan is an island empire, and that therefore her communications with foreign countries are entirely maritime, it is not surprising to find a first-class steamship line controlled by a Japanese company calling at Ceylon. This line, the Nippon Yusen Kaisha, or Japan Mail S.S. Company, Ltd., was created in the year 1885 by the amalgamation of two existing companies, the Mitsubishi Kaisha (Three Diamonds Company) and the Kyodo Unyo Kaisha (Union Transportation Company), the present name being then given to the undertaking. The Mitsubishi Kaisha was practically the pioneer of modern Japanese steamship enterprise. Before its organisation, in 1871, there had been some tentative efforts to establish steamship communication, but the year named is generally regarded in Japan as the actual starting-point of Japanese maritime development on Western lines. For some time the Mitsubishi had as its rival an official organisation known as the Yubin Kisen Kaisha, but ultimately, in 1876, the Government deemed it advisable to withdraw from the arena, and the officially owned vessels were handed over to the Mitsubishi Kaisha. The Mitsubishi Kaisha thus came virtually into complete occupation of the maritime highways of Japan. It enjoyed its supremacy until 1882, when the Government, deeming it desirable to increase the mercantile marine of the country, encouraged the formation of a new company under the designation of Kyodo Nnyn Kaisha, or Minor Transportation Company. But a trial of three years demonstrated the inexpediency of having two rival companies in the field, both receiving a measure of State aid, and the amalgamation was carried out as mentioned. A large measure of success awaited the new combination. During the first nine years of its life the bulk of the coastwise carrying trade was worked by means of its fleet, whilst regular services were maintained between Kobe and Vladivostock, Kobe and Tientsin *viâ* Korean ports, and Yokohama and Shanghai. When, in 1892, the rapid development of the cotton-spinning industry in Japan made it necessary to obtain a regular supply of raw cotton, a line of steamers was established to run between Japan and Bombay, and in addition to this emigrant ships under the company's flag made frequent voyages to Australia and Hawaii. A yearly sum of money was received from the Treasury, in return for which the company was pledged to maintain several mail routes to carry mails between the ports to which its steamers plied, and, should occasion arise, to place its fleet at the disposal of the Government for transport purposes. In 1894, when China and Japan were at war, most of the company's large steamers were required by the Government, and had to be detached from public service. As a consequence it became necessary to purchase many vessels, and the capital of the company was increased to twenty-two million yen, and steamship services to Europe, America, and Australia were established. Twelve twin-screw steamers of over 6,000 tons were built for the European service, and three, ranging from 3,800 to 5,500 tons, for the Australian line. The company's fleet now totalled 78 steamers, aggregating 260,000 tons gross. Most of these were new vessels, fitted in an up-to-date manner, everything being provided with a view to promoting the comfort of the passengers and to providing facilities for trade. In addition to its lines between the principal Japanese ports, the company maintains regular services with China, Korea, Formosa, Asiatic Russia, the Straits Settlements, India, the Red Sea and Mediterranean, Europe, Canada, America, and Australasia. Subsidies were granted in 1899 by the Japanese Diet to the company's European and American lines, and thus, with but a few exceptions, the whole of the foreign and home lines are run under mail contract with the Imperial Government. The head office of the company is situate in Tokyo, and at every port of call and some other important points there is an agency. Besides being

PROMENADE DECK. PROMENADE.

FIRST CLASS SALOON LOOKING AFT.

THE DECK AND THE SMOKING ROOM.

a comfortable line to travel by, the Nippon Yusen Kaisha is noted for its cheapness. The employees of the company, exclusive of about 4,800 representing crews, firemen, &c., number about 1,380. The late Baron M. Morioka was the first president of the company, he being nominated by the Government in 1885. On his death, in 1894, he was succeeded by Mr. T. Yoshikawa. This gentleman occupied the position for a year, when his death necessitated a further appointment, and the present president, Mr. R. Kondo, was elected. This gentleman's term expired in 1902, but he was re-elected.

Messrs. Carson & Co. are the Colombo agents of the company.

THE CARGO BOAT DESPATCH CO.

Among the principal firms engaged in the heavy cargo work in Colombo harbour is the above company, which was established in 1866 by Ana Ghose Mahamadu, who started business as a landing and shipping agent at the wharf. The present proprietor is Baron de Livera, the manager being Mr. James Gibson, with Mr. James de Livera as first assistant. In all, the company employs some 700 hands, and has a fleet of 120 boats of various tonnages, the average being 20 tons capacity each, the boats ranging from 10 to 50 tons each. The company has its own boat-building yard at Matakuliya, near the mouth of the Kelani river, and repairing yard at Kochchikade. Ten water boats, of a total capacity of 113,400 gallons, belong to this company, also an 80-horse-power steam launch, built in 1898 at Stoney Stratford, England, by E. Hayes. The company contract for the landing of cargo for the Hansa Line of steamships, the Hamburg-Amerika Line, the Well line, the Campania-Transatlantica Barcelona (Spanish Mail) line, the Austrian-Lloyd steamers, the Indian-American (Bucknall's) line, the Animal line, and others; and it ships cargo to every line of steamers calling at the port of Colombo. There is also a forwarding branch attached to the business, and the company are special landing contractors for Messrs. Darley, Buller & Co., who are Colombo agents for F. W. Heilgers & Co., of Calcutta, coal merchants. The office premises occupied by the firm are leased from the Government, and all the gear and hoisting used is Government property. The principal local articles shipped are plumbago, coconut oil, tea, copra, desiccated coconut, poonac, coconuts in bags, rubber, hides, and fibres of every description; while on the import side, large quantities of rice are landed by the firm weekly. The manager, Mr. James Gibson, arrived in Ceylon as early as 1872, and previous to taking his present position, in 1892, had an extensive planting experience in Dikoya, Maskeliya, and the Knuckles districts, having been one of the pioneers in opening up the district of the Kelani Valley.

THE CEYLON WHARFAGE CO., LTD.

The Ceylon Wharfage Company, Ltd., was formed in 1899 for the purpose of taking over and extending the old-established business of the Wharf and Warehouse Company, Ltd., which came into being in January, 1875. The company at its inception leased from Government a large part of the Customs premises, and has since made extensive improvements to these, both as regards facilities for landing and delivering cargo, and also in the matter of increased warehouse accommodation. In 1899 all rice and bag cargo was landed at an extensive sandy beach by coolies wading into the water and bringing the bags to shore on their heads

All this has now been changed, and quay walls having been built, the former sandy beach has been transformed into a miniature wet-dock, well supplied with steam travelling cranes and all appliances for the rapid handling of cargo. Extensive additions have also been made to the company's fleet of cargo, coal, and water lighters, no less than 48 steel or composite barges, aggregating in all some 3,770 tons, having been built at the company's boat-building yard on the Kelani river since 1901, while additional 24 similar barges, equalling in all 1,000 tons, are now in hand. The total tonnage of the fleet of lighters is already close on 8,000 tons, with every prospect of a large increase in the near future. For the rapid movement of this fleet the company owns four handy tugs of the latest design. The tonnage of the water fleet amounts to an aggregate of 750 tons, with six steam-pumps and boilers. For the upkeep of this fleet there are two yards, one—the building yard—on the Kelani river, and the other—the repairing yard—on the north-east side of the harbour. At the latter point the company has laid down a small patent slip for convenience in the repair of its tugs and large 100-ton barges.

The company lands and ships all coal for the P. & O. Company, the British-India

BARON DE LIVERA. (Proprietor.) JAMES GIBSON.

LOADING TEA FOR EXPORT.

Steam Navigation Company, and the Messageries Maritimes Cie.; and during 1905 it handled no less than 380,000 tons, of which, on more than one occasion, over 20,000 tons were boated during one week. The company is also the cargo-landing and boating contractor for the P. & O., British India, Orient Royal Mail, Bibby Line, Harrison Line, Messageries Maritimes, Asiatic S.N. Company, Nippon Yusen Kaisha, Clan Line, City Line, Holt Line, Anchor Line, and others; and it ships cargo to every steamer line entering Colombo. The number of packages of cargo boated during 1905 reached the enormous total of 8,146,808, equal, at ten packages to the ton, to 814,680 tons. The quantity of fresh water supplied to steamers during the same period aggregated 80,000 tons. To carry out these great undertakings a large labour force is naturally required, and it is estimated that the company's average check roll would show a daily staff of close on 5,000 men. One feature of the company is the successful employment of Parsees for exercising immediate supervision over the labour, eight specially selected men having been engaged in Bombay and sent to Colombo.

The head office of the company is at 9, Throgmorton Avenue, London, E.C., the chairman of directors being Sir James L. Mackay, G.C.M.G., K.C.I.E., a member of the India Council and of the Suez Canal Board, managing director of the British-India Steam Navigation Company, &c., and a member of the British Commission sent to China to negotiate the commercial treaties after the outbreak in that country. The chairman of the local consultative committee is the Hon. Sir S. Bois, M.L.C., the other members being Messrs. W. Buckland, agent for the P. & O. Company; E. C. Skrine, of Messrs. Skrine & Co.; W. Shakspeare, of Messrs. Carson & Co.; E. Labussiere, agent for the Messageries Maritimes Cie., and A. P. Waldock, of Messrs. Aitken, Spence & Co. Mr. J. A. Ridge has charge of the local business as manager, the assistant manager being Mr. W. Y. Fleming, the superintendent afloat Mr. R. G. MacIver, the accountant Mr. J. F. Sibbald, C.A., while Mr. E. E. Powell is in charge of the bonding and clearing and forwarding departments.

CEYLON WHARFAGE COMPANY, LTD.

IMPORT WAREHOUSES. PLAN OF PREMISES. PATENT SLIP. BONDED WAREHOUSE. EXPORT WAREHOUSES.

THE BIBBY LINE.

Of steamship lines running directly to Ceylon, there is none which enjoys a larger measure of popularity than that owned by Messrs. Bibby, of Liverpool, and familiarly known by the designation which heads this article. The line is synonymous for comfort and expedition, combined with moderate charges.

The steamers take only one class of passenger, and those who travel by them profit by the fact, inasmuch as they have the undivided attention of officers, and, what is highly acceptable to the peripatetic traveller, the run of the ship. The founder of the line was Mr. John Bibby, the grandfather of the present representatives, who, in 1807, commenced business as a shipowner in Liverpool. Those were days, of course, of sailing vessels, and for many years the firm's transactions oversea were carried through by means of a fleet of vessels which were puny indeed compared with the splendid craft which now fly the company's flag. Steam propulsion was not introduced until 1851, and it was forty years later before the existing service was instituted. Comparatively young as the system is, it has become thoroughly established. The Bibby boats are amongst

THE BIBBY LINE.

THE "WARWICKSHIRE."
DINING SALOON

FIRE DRILL.

AT PORT SAID.

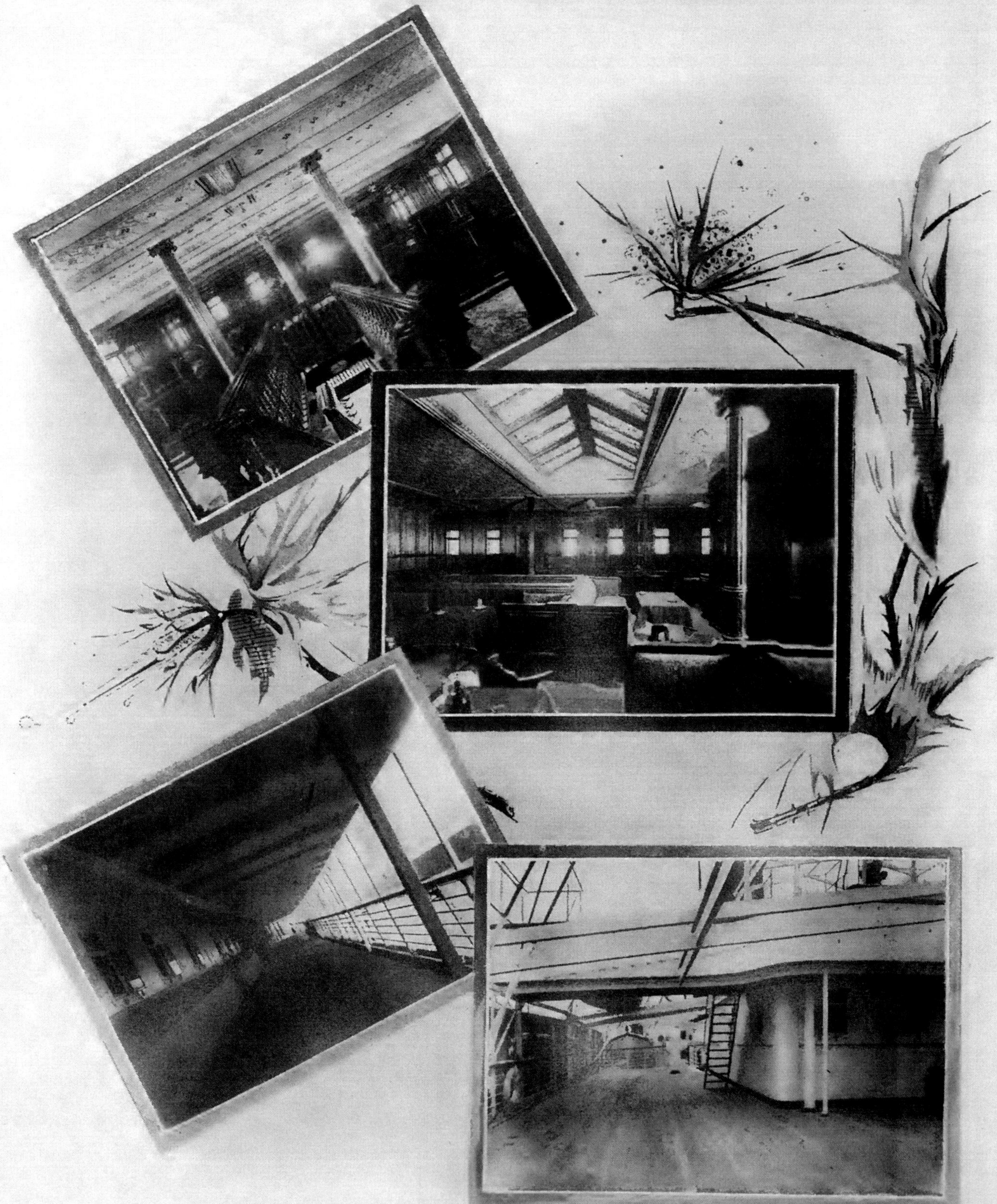

THE BIBBY LINE.

Drawing-Room.
Lower Promenade Deck

Smoking-Room.
Upper Promenade Deck.

the best known "greyhounds of the Indian Ocean." The company's run is outward from Liverpool to Marseilles, and thence to Colombo and Rangoon; and homeward from Rangoon and Colombo, and thence to Marseilles and London. A regular fortnightly service is maintained both ways throughout the year by a fleet of twin-screw steamers of the highest class, and specially designed for the Eastern passenger service. There are seven of these vessels, each named after an English county, the septette being the *Cheshire* (5,775 registered tonnage, 4,500 h.p.), the *Shropshire* (5,785 registered tonnage, 4,500 h.p.), the *Staffordshire* (6,005 registered tonnage, 4,500 h.p.), the *Derbyshire* (6,636 registered tonnage, 5,000 h.p.), the *Worcestershire* (7,160 registered tonnage, 5,500 h.p.), the *Herefordshire* (7,182 registered tonnage, 5,500 h.p.), and the *Warwickshire* (7,966 registered tonnage, 5,500 h.p.). All the units of the fleet hold the highest class at Lloyd's, and are built and equipped far in excess of the official rules, while they comply with all the requirements of the British Admiralty. They are modelled on identical lines, though they differ somewhat in internal details. All are fitted with watertight bulkheads, and have a double bottom throughout their entire length, an arrangement which reduces to a minimum the dangers of accident, whether from collision or stranding. The risk of fire is provided against by the provision, in the case of every hold, of a powerful injector (controlled from above deck), by which a supply of steam sufficient to choke and extinguish any fire can at once be turned on from the main boilers, without involving the usually dangerous expedient of removing the hatches. Regarded from the point of view of comfort, the vessels leave nothing to be desired. The state rooms are so arranged that each has a port or window giving free access to the outside open air. The method employed to secure this highly valuable, and in the tropics indispensable, condition to perfect comfort is the system of "tandem cabins," which, first introduced on the Bibby boats, is now being adopted in the case of practically all up-to-date steamers. Under the system the inner cabin of the two which constitute the tandem has a port-hole at the end of a narrow way which runs at the side of the outer room; and as it is also in most cases provided with a skylight, which can be opened in all weathers, it is oftentimes preferred by travellers to the outside accommodation. Wardrobes are fitted in most of the cabins, and all are equipped with electric fans, which are maintained for constant use east of Suez. The state rooms are on the main or promenade decks, and so have the advantage of the freest possible circulation of air. As regards the supply of material needs, the ships are splendidly equipped. Each steamer has powerful freezing machinery and ample cold storage, by the aid of which English meat, game, poultry, vegetables, &c., are available throughout the voyage, while a plentiful supply of pure ice is forthcoming for each day's use. Apart from the inherent excellence of the boats, the service is recommended to the intending traveller by the facilities offered by the company for breaking the journey in Egypt and at ports *en route*, and by the specially favourable terms extended to families. Officials are able to journey by the line, since the Government, recognising the superior character of the service, has placed the company's boats on the list of those available for officers returning from leave. Another testimony to the high position of the line is the fact that the steamers carry French and Egyptian mails between Marseilles and Egypt and between Suez and Colombo, and also carry supplementary English mails between Rangoon and Colombo and England. Messrs. Carson & Co., it may be added, are the Ceylon agents of the company.

HEWADEWAGEY PALIS FERNANDO VIMALA GOONEWARDENE, Mohandiram.

This gentleman, the son of Simon Fernando, a merchant of Colombo, was born at Mount Lavinia in the year 1853, and was educated privately in different schools. When he was fifteen years of age he joined his uncle in business, trading as H. A. Fernando, ship chandlers and contractors. After Mr. H. A. Fernando's death, in 1886, the nephew carried on the business—to which is added that of naval contractor and stevedore. His head office is at No. 39, Chatham Street, Fort, Colombo. The firm have been contractors to the Royal Navy for thirty-six years for the supply of stores, water, provisions, and other requisites. They also contract for the Glen, Orient-Pacific, Shire, and Clan Lines of steamers, as well as other shipping companies and privately owned vessels. They employ 25 lighters and barges, 6 water boats and gigs, and close upon 500 men. Mr. Fernando was made Mohandiram (Lieutenant) by Governor Sir West Ridgeway in recognition of services rendered by his firm to the Admiralty, as well as to the local shipping community in general.

He owns various estates planted in coconuts and cinnamon, of which Welikelle, in the Kurunegala district, and Boralesgamuwe are the most important. He also owns large tracts of paddy lands in the Western Province. He is a proprietor of land in Colombo, owning such well-known city properties as the Lord Nelson Hotel in Chatham Street, and "Conniston" and "Glenfield" in Cinnamon Gardens, besides various business blocks in the Pettah. He is a Buddhist by religion, and holds the post of treasurer and committee member of the Theosophical Society, being also trustee of the Vidya Lankara Pirivena at the Buddhist temple at Palinagoda. He is also a member of the Agricultural Society. He owns the Factory Clothing Company, which is a large gentlemen's outfitting establishment in Chatham Street, Colombo, and is the principal partner in the firm of Messrs. Mirando & Co., plumbago and cinnamon merchants. His chief assistant is Mr. T. R. Fernando.

H. P. FERNANDO, MOHANDIRAM.
HEAD OFFICE.

OPIUM

THE import of opium, which is annually increasing in volume, and now amounts to over 10 tons a year, is chiefly derived from the neighbouring continent, where the white poppy is extensively cultivated and furnishes a lucrative source of revenue. The customs duty is as much as Rs. 2 (2s. 8d.) per lb., but even under this rate it is found advantageous, from a commercial point of view, to import the drug. The right to expose opium for sale is reserved by Government, and is disposed of under conditions similar to those obtaining in the farming out of arrack rents.

Special regulations are in force for the prevention of any adulteration in the article; and, under the ordinance, the drug may not be sold to any person apparently under the age of fifteen years, or allowed to be consumed on the premises. A curious provision in this regard is that the premises licensed to retail opium shall be restricted to the sale of cigars, and shall close at eight punctually at night. The maximum quantity allowed to any individual buyer at any one time is 180 grains; and the possession of the drug in excess of this amount is considered illegal. Such are the stringent measures adopted to prevent any illicit traffic in this article, that few irregularities are found to occur; and where their occurrence is noted, dire penalties are imposed upon the offenders.

Opium forms one of the principal constituents in the native pharmacopœia; and owing to the absence of any surgical practice, its narcotic properties afford a helpful anæsthetic in cases of difficult treatment. But apart from the demand for the drug for medicinal purposes there does not appear to be any circumstance to lead to the supposition that the people of the island are addicted to opium in the sense that the Chinese are. In fact, the only section of the population which resorts to the drug freely is the Malay or Javanese element, as also a good proportion of the Pathans and Afghans who visit the island from time to time or temporarily settle in it. The abstinence from every form of intoxicants and narcotics enjoined by the local religious systems is responsible for the small demand that exists for the drug among the Sinhalese and Tamils; but, as pointed out, among the foreign peoples resident in the island, opium, both in its unprepared form and in the form of pastilles, known as "layîgium," is much in request. Bhang—the dried leaves and small stalks of hemp (*Cannabis indica*)—and ganja—its flowering shoots, so much in demand in Persia and other parts of the Mahomedan world as "hashish"—are also included in the provisions governing the sale and possession of opium. At the time of writing a suggestion has been made in the Legislative Council to introduce the system of selling opium as it obtains in the Philippines and other places, where the drug may only be sold by Government officers. It is asserted that by the disposal of licences to private individuals the habit is being fostered, and the retailer does his best to further it. On the other hand, if the right of sale were vested in the hands of specially appointed controlling officers, only registered consumers would be supplied, and then under the strictest supervision of Government. An increase in the import duty of the drug has also been proposed, and every measure will be adopted to check the use of the narcotic.

COLOMBO

THIS, the capital city of Ceylon, the seat of Government and the principal centre of the colony's commerce and trade, is situated on the west coast of the island, the exact geographical position being 6 degrees 56 minutes latitude North, and 79 degrees 49 minutes longitude East. The magnificent artificial harbour on the Indian Ocean which constitutes the main feature of Colombo from the point of view of the outside world and has made it a port of call of the first magnitude and importance in the East, is fully described elsewhere in these pages. Confining the present description of the city to the land side, we find it situated on a plain, practically at sea-level, but dotted with knolls or small elevations through which, to the immediate north of the city, the Kelani river finds a sluggish outlet to the sea.

The most prominent feature of the city is a large lake or lagoon, covering an area of 416 acres, and almost surrounded by buildings, but with open spaces of slightly elevated ground on the side fronting the Indian Ocean. It seems probable that in days gone by an arm of the Kelani river meandered across this flat to the sea, spreading itself slumberously over the site of the present lagoon. But having now neither proper inlet nor outlet, this imprisoned water, although picturesque in appearance, has the disadvantage of being both shallow and stagnant. It is used as the common wash-tub of Colombo ; and as the result of the laving in this water of all the dirty clothes, the carts, the draught-bullocks, and the bodies of the natives for generations past, the surface is, for the most part, covered with an evil-looking, thick scum. The existence of the lake in its present condition is therefore recognised to be detrimental to the health of the city—a fact properly estimated to outweigh the consideration of its ornamental aspect, and plans have been prepared by the municipal authorities for extensive improvements, which embrace the reclamation of the more objectionable portions of the lake, the land thus reclaimed to be converted into a public park.

Within the municipal limits the city contains an area of ten square miles, on which is settled a total population—according to the latest returns—of 171,549 souls. Of this number only a very few, comparatively, are Europeans, the rest being principally Sinhalese, Tamils, and Moormen, in about the same relative proportions as are maintained in regard to the whole of the inhabitants of the island, as given in another section of this book dealing with the population of Ceylon. There is also a considerable leaven of Eurasians — or "Burghers," as they are locally termed—occupying an intermediate position between the pure whites and the coloured people proper. Among the Europeans are the principal officials in the Government service and the heads of the large business houses, besides the officers and men of the English army stationed for the time being at Colombo on garrison duty. One feature of interest to the observant visitor to the city from overseas is the heterogeneous mixture of races to be seen on all sides in the streets, the difference between the coloured people of one race and another being generally discernible by some

CHATHAM STREET.

distinguishing peculiarity of attire or appearance. The Sinhalese, the true son of Ceylon, will be seen wearing his hair long, and held back from the forehead by a high semicircular comb, his nether limbs enveloped in a "camboy," a wrapper resembling a petticoat; the Tamil, from India — the race next most numerously represented—more scantily clothed, and, if still professing the Hindu religion of his forefathers, with his head shaven in fantastic fashion; the sedate Moorman, wearing a high and coloured brimless head-covering—either a tarboosh, or a fez, or what is locally known as a "tile" cap; the Buddhist priest, man or boy, with clean-shaven poll, and a long yellow toga for his only covering; the chetty (peripatetic money-lender) also with close-shaven head and who does not advertise his lucrative trade by wearing a superabundance of clothing; the Malay, generally in a policeman's uniform; the Parsee, in his distinctive dress and dignified of mien; and other varieties of coloured folk in various attire, besides an occasional Roman Catholic priest or Protestant clergyman, whose generally sombre attire contrasts conspicuously with the white and coloured costumes of the rest of the perambulating population.

The present name of the city appears to have been suggested to the Portuguese by the ancient title of Kalambu, meaning "good harbour," given to the spot by the Moors who settled on the shore here in the twelfth and thirteenth centuries; and a writer of a somewhat later period alludes to Kalambu as "the finest and largest city in Serendib" (*i.e.*, Ceylon). Kalambu became Kolambu, which was converted by the Portuguese, when they subsequently took possession of the island, into Colombo. Before the advent of the Moors the place was known as Kalan-totta—that is, "the ferry of the Kelani river"—under which designation it figures in the Rajavaliya, the chronicle of the ancient Sinhalese kings. But although settlement on the site of the present city dates back to a sufficiently early period, it cannot be said that Colombo possesses any charm of antiquity, any more than it can boast of scenic attractions. The little native township, or outer suburb, of Kotta, some six miles to the north-east of the city, is of older origin as an administrative centre, having been at one time, in the pre-European days, the capital of Ceylon. At Kotta some ruins which provided evidences of an interesting past existed up to modern times.

But to-day no traces of ancient or even mediæval ruins are to be found in or around Colombo. The only venerable object of special note in the city, and which forms a connecting link with the past era when Buddhism was the dominating religion of the island, is the sacred Bo-tree (or Bodhi-tree, *i.e.*, tree of Buddha), a species of fig (*Ficus religiosa*). This tree, by no means of imposing appearance, which stands at the junction of three principal streets of the Pettah, is believed to have sprung from a transplanted branch of the original Bo-tree at Buddhagaya, in India; and under its not overabundant shade the principal gatherings of the

NORRIS ROAD.

Buddhist natives of Colombo, for either religious or secular purposes, are held. Other Bo-trees of minor importance are also scattered about in the native quarters of the city. Who would. however, see the most famous relics of the ancient days of Ceylon *in situ* must journey to Anuradhapura, in the North Central Province, or the other "buried cities" in the island, where he can contemplate ruined dagobas—huge bell-shaped structures in which were deposited the sacred relics of the Buddhist era—and other interesting antiquities, of which descriptions are given elsewhere in this book. Colombo is comparatively a modern city, and, it may be added, a city still in the making. At the time of its capitulation by the Dutch to the British (February 16, 1796), the city is thus described in Walsh's "Military Reminiscences": "Colombo, the capital of the Dutch in Ceylon, is a place of considerable consequence and strength from its natural position, as well as from its works, which were numerous and in good condition. The fort, which is extensive, contained many capital dwelling-houses, including the Governor's palace, which is a most superb building. The Pettah had also several good houses, churches, &c., in it; and in the place, altogether, were many respectable inhabitants. . . . Colombo is also a place of great traffic by sea, the roadstead being extremely safe and commodious, particularly during the north-eastern monsoons."

Thus early, in modern times, was recognised the value of Colombo as a port; and since, under British rule, the city has gradually grown in size and importance, mainly on account of its being the most convenient sea-gate of the island on its western and more frequented side. This advantage of situation led to the construction of the fine harbour which has elevated Colombo to the position of one of the principal ports of call of the world—"the Clapham Junction of the East," as it has been aptly dubbed—as well as made it the head centre of the railway system of the island.

STREET SCENE.

CHRIST CHURCH, GALLE FACE.

But within recent years the appearance of the city has completely changed from its aspect in the days when the Dutch held sway and it was a fortified position with both seaward and landward defences. A few big guns, in charge of the garrison artillery force, are to be found mounted in positions commanding the approach to the harbour. But the landward fortifications have altogether disappeared and the term "Fort" only serves to-day to distinguish the division of the now wide-spread city which occupies the site of the former circumvallated town, and which, still the main part of the city, is the quarter wherein the Government establishment and offices, together with the banking houses and the principal European places of business, are situated. The "Fort" forms one of the nine wards into which Colombo is divided for municipal purposes, the area of this division being 220 acres.

Adjoining the Fort on the northern side is the Pettah quarter, the most densely populated part of the town and inhabited almost entirely by "natives," the coloured people of whatever race being indiscriminately included in ordinary parlance under this designation. Here are the principal business establishments of the native merchants, a few of these buildings being of large dimensions and imposing appearance. The Pettah, too, has been almost entirely rebuilt since the days of the Dutch occupation, few of the congested blocks of small buildings in this quarter being more than fifty years old. Only the old disused cemetery, filled with crumbling tomb-

THE BEIRA LAKE.

stones, and the old belfry at Kayman's Gate, the centre of the main street, remain to tell of the past sway of the ousted Hollander. The only public building of importance in this division of the city is the Town Hall, which includes the municipal offices and court, and is situated in the centre of the native dwellings, produce stores, large warehouses and multitudinous boutiques (booths or small shops) which constitute the Pettah. This civic building, of quite modern construction, being designed with an eye to use rather than ornament, presents no architectural features worthy of note, and the same must be said of the central municipal market across the Main Street. In fact, unless having business in this part, or curious to see, for once in his life, how Mid-Eastern natives live and move and have their being, the visitor to Colombo will find little to attract him in the Pettah. The tram line from the Fort to the northern suburbs passes along the main thoroughfare which traverses the centre of the quarter, and on either hand branch off narrow and tortuous cross streets and lanes, which, as well as Main Street, are crowded from earliest morn until far into the night with a teeming mass of coloured humanity, proffering and purchasing wares of all descriptions, to the usual Eastern accompaniment of incessant jabbering and gesticulation. Here, in the heart of the native part of Colombo, is never lack of bustle and life, and, it may be added, never lack of smell. Formerly the Pettah was specifically known as the "Black Town," and from the earliest times of the city this part has been the principal centre of the coloured population. At one time the houses extended from this side right up to the walls of the Fort, but the last Dutch Governor caused a space to be cleared between the cemetery and the fortifications as a preventive measure against attack from the land side, and this precaution was subsequently maintained by the British commanders until modern times, with the result that to this day these, the two main business divisions of Colombo, the European and the native, remain distinctly separated. The word Pettah is derived from "pettai," in the Tamil language, which signifies an extramural part of a town. Although the Pettah ward comprises an area of only 92 acres, it contains about 8,000 inhabitants.

Adjoining the Pettah to the northward is the large and populous Kotahena division of the city, with an area of 1,649 acres and over 33,000 inhabitants. Another large ward of the municipality in an easterly direction from the "Fort" is Maradanà, comprising 1,297 acres and with a population almost equal to that of Kotahena. The north and north-eastern spread of the city, taking the Fort quarter as the point of radiation, also includes the wards of St. Sebastian (area 116 acres, population about 10,000), St. Paul's (area 143 acres, population over 20,000), and New Bazaar (area 289 acres, population about 18,000). The lake, with its irregular shoreline and various winding arms, intervenes between the sea-coast and these several divisions of the native part of the city.

Leaving the Fort quarter southwards by

way of Queen Street, after passing on the left the extensive group of buildings (enclosing on three sides a spacious recreation ground) erected as barracks for the British troops forming the garrison, the visitor finds himself on the fine open military reservation bearing the world-famed name of the Galle Face. This is a delightful stretch of grass land sloping gradually upwards from the ocean beach on the right hand and falling again on the left to the west shore of the lake. On the summit of the gentle elevation thus separating the two waters, and with its front to the sea, stands the building of the Colombo Club, with uninterrupted outlook towards the ocean; while at the far or southern end the grassy expanse is bounded by the huge pile of the Galle Face Hotel, a description of which hostelry appears elsewhere in this book. Along the sea-wall is the Galle Face Walk, a broad carriage-way and promenade some three-quarters of a mile in length, running southwards direct from the end of Queen Street to the hotel. A memorial tablet by the side of the roadway states that the Walk was commenced by Sir Henry Ward (a former Governor of Ceylon) in 1856 and completed three years later, being "recommended to his successors in the interests of the ladies and children of Colombo." This is the Corso of Colombo, along which of an afternoon the principal residents of the city are to be seen driving, or being driven, up and down in well-appointed carriages of all descriptions and smart motor-cars, or being drawn in the all-pervading rickshaw; while the equestrians enjoy a gallop on the grass alongside and the pedestrians lounge leisurely along the promenade which flanks the roadway on the sea-side and is conveniently provided with seats at intervals. The Galle Face, continually swept as it is by the ocean breezes, forms a splendid "lung" for a tropical city like Colombo, with its generally oppressive, warm and humid climate, and is thûs somewhat of a set off against the insalubrious influences arising from the stagnant shallows of the lake. Round and across this extensive open space are other roadways affording opportunities for pleasant drives, and the national games of cricket and football are played on the intervening stretches of grass. The esplanade on the sea front is brilliantly lighted at night, so that a drive or a stroll may be enjoyed here in the cool of the evening by the side of the murmuring waves.

South-eastward from the Fort boundary and bordering the lake on the western side lies the quarter of the city known as Slave Island. This ugly and un-British appellation perpetuates the memory of the days when, under Dutch rule, household slavery prevailed, and the native menials were confined at night to this part of the city, their presence within the houses of their masters in the Fort during the hours of darkness constituting a source of danger to the white inmates. It is on record that the whole of a Dutch family in the Fort was murdered one night by the coloured bondmen of the household. As a warning to the subject population, the Dutchmen erected a high gibbet on what is known as "Captain's Island" in the lake, where it could be seen from all sides. All such relics of those "good old days" have long ago disappeared from the neighbourhood, only the name of the district remaining to preserve from well-merited oblivion the memories of a benighted past. Slave Island is now both a residential and business quarter, with a small but thickly populated native section on the borders of the ubiquitous lake. This latter congeries of small and miserable tenements and narrow and winding malodorous streets and lanes is marked for extensive improvements by the civic authorities, which, according to the plans prepared, will take the form of new, wider, and straighter streets, the removal of the worst class of native habitations, the erection of a better type of dwellings for the lower classes, and the provision of proper drainage. The sooner these, together with similar improvements in the other native quarters, are effected, the sooner will a serious reproach be removed from the city. Slave Island belies its name in not being an island, but an irregularly shaped tongue of land, almost surrounded by the waters of the lake. It has an area of about 313 acres, with a population numbering some 17,000 persons, nearly all of whom are coloured. A main thoroughfare, Union Place, traverses the ward in a south-easterly direction, and on each side of this road, as well as in the streets and lanes which branch off on either hand, are to be found substantial residences

THE LIGHTHOUSE AND CLOCK TOWER, CHATHAM STREET.

surrounded by gardens side by side with large tea factories and packing stores, engineering works, plumbago yards and other business premises. As the eastern extremity of the peninsula is approached the private residences come more into evidence, and at the point where it touches Victoria Park the commercial part of Colombo may be said to be left behind, the extensive tea-packing stores of Lipton, Ltd., at the top of Union Place, being the last commercial establishment in this direction. On emerging into the park at this corner several public buildings will be found clustered together or within a few minutes' walk of one another, including the Victoria Memorial Eye Hospital (a description of which appears in following pages), the Public Hall, the General Hospital, the Medical College, and the Government Medical Department's storehouse, from which last-named institution the out-station and village dispensaries throughout the island are supplied.

Victoria Park is an extensive grassed pleasaunce of 100 acres, oval in form and open for the most part, but with trees singly and in groups scattered over its surface; while it is surrounded by the residential quarter bearing the far-famed name of Cinnamon Gardens—somewhat of a misnomer now that only a few cinnamon bushes are to be found in the neighbourhood. This part is the pleasantest, and may be termed the most aristocratic, portion of Colombo, where the houses of many of the wealthiest and most notable of the citizens are situated. Numbers of these residences—most of which are owned and occupied by high-class "natives" or "Burghers"—are of palatial proportions, and all are surrounded by well-kept lawns or carefully tended gardens. The annual shows of the Ceylon Agricultural Society are held in Victoria Park, on a site immediately to the rear of the Museum, which institution (described in detail in following pages) occupies a fine position at the eastern extremity of this demesne. On this side of the park, too, are the houses and grounds of several of the leading recreation clubs of Colombo, also described elsewhere in this volume. The park is intersected in various directions by well-made roadways, while the thoroughfares in and about Cinnamon Gardens are for the most part avenues shaded by trees, constituting a labyrinth of pleasing leafy vistas flanked by imposing and charming dwellings. Beyond Cinnamon Gardens, on the further side from the city, lies the Havelock racecourse, the chief centre of the Ceylon Turf Club, where, during the "August fortnight" of festivities which constitutes the Colombo annual carnival, the great race meeting of the year in Ceylon is held, the principal event of which is the race for the Governor's Cup. Polo is also played on the racecourse when the ground is not being used for its primary purpose, while Victoria Park affords a field for cricket and football and recreation generally. The avidity and adaptability shown by the Sinhalese in relation to the English national games is a remarkable feature in connection with British rule in Ceylon.

KELANI TEMPLE.

But Cinnamon Gardens, although the most prominent and best known, is not the only residential quarter of Colombo. The portion of the Maradana Ward adjoining this premier locality on the north side and known as Borella possesses the same characteristics of shady thoroughfares and handsome dwellings standing in their own gardens, while on the other side—that is, between Cinnamon Gardens and the sea—stretches the populous Colpetty suburb, reaching southwards from the Galle Face to the southern boundary of the municipality. The Colpetty Ward, which embraces the residential suburb of Bambalapitiya, comprises an area of nearly 2,000 acres, on which is settled a population of about 19,000 persons. Possessing the advantage of direct and frequent railway communication with the Fort and the chief railway depôt at Maradana, by means of the south-coast line which runs close by the sea—along the very edge in places—to the southernmost points of Ceylon, Colpetty and Bambalapitiya contain the homes of a large number of the people engaged in business in the central parts of the city during the day-time, and the morning and evening trains to and from the Fort Station are always crowded. This suburban traffic, indeed, extends beyond the southern municipal boundary at Wellawatte, and does not entirely exhaust itself until the popular sea-side resort of Mount Lavinia, seven miles from the Fort, is reached. From the Galle Face south this coastal fringe is one succession of bungalows, standing in their own compounds and nestling in the groves of lofty coconut-palms which cover all the maritime country on this side of the island. Southwards, the houses become gradually fewer after Colpetty is passed, until approaching Mount Lavinia they are only found at intervals. Most of these residences are of comfortable appearance, and not a few are of large dimensions, with stables and grounds—including lawn-tennis courts—attached. Substantial dwellings standing in their own grounds also line each side of the portion of the main road to the south of the island—which traverses Colpetty and Bambalapitiya parallel with the railway—as well as the thoroughfares which branch off to the northwards from this main artery of traffic and lead to Cinnamon Gardens and the adjoining small residential quarter named Havelock Town. Colpetty possesses also in its centre a native settlement of its own, with a line of boutiques on each side of the Galle Road, a small but always busy municipal market, one or two private medical dispensaries, and the inevitable police-station.

The sea-side suburb of Mutwal, the northernmost portion of the city, also includes a few of the more imposing residences of the richer class of "native" citizens, conspicuous among which is the famous Whist Bungalow, described elsewhere in this book; while a less pretentious type of dwelling, occupied by what in European communities is termed the middle class, is prevalent throughout the rest of the extensive northern and north-eastern divisions of the city, which comprise the section of the Kotahena Ward known as Grandpass, also the St. Sebastian, St. Paul's, and Maradana Wards. As regards the racial distribution of the coloured lower classes, while the Sinhalese—with the exception of the class exclusively engaged in fishing; whose special habitat is the Mutwal suburb—are resident in all parts of the city indiscriminately, the Tamils of the Hindu religion are mostly found clustered around their numerous temples in the heart of the Pettah, the Moormen more particularly favour certain streets in the same quarter which are in the neighbourhood of the mosque, and the Malays chiefly reside in Slave Island, principally in Malay Street and Kew Street. It should be mentioned that most of the private land within the municipality of Colombo, if not nearly all, is owned by natives and Burghers, some of whom are proprietors of real estate on a very extensive scale and are consequently men of large and independent means, holding high social positions and maintaining liberal establishments.

Besides the Galle Face, Victoria Park, and the Havelock Town Park, Colombo possesses minor "lungs" and pleasure-grounds of varying extent. Notable among these are the Gordon Gardens, an expanse of nearly three acres, which, with gravelled walks under shady silver-leaf trees, raised terraces, and a miniature cascade, forms a pleasing attraction. These gardens adjoin the grounds of the Governor's residence in the Fort, and were given to the people in 1890 by Sir Arthur Gordon (now Lord Stanmore), then Governor of Ceylon, as his personal contribution to Colombo in honour of Queen Victoria's Diamond Jubilee. Then there is the Racquet Court, an open space of nine and a half acres on the land reclaimed from the lake between the Fort and the Pettah, where cricket and football matches are played. This is also the favourite site of circuses and other travelling shows, as well as the mustering ground of the processions, religious and otherwise, so dear to the Eastern heart. Other public recreation grounds are Campbell's Park, in the centre of the Maradana Ward, the Price Park in the heart of the Pettah, wherein a recently built Tamil theatre stands, and the Rifle Green, at the Fort end of Slave Island, which is used for drilling purposes by the native regiments forming part of the garrison, and where the annual police gymkhana is held. The band of the local volunteers plays occasionally at all the public grounds in turn.

SKINNER'S ROAD, KOTAHENA.

Colombo being situated on the flat coastal land, with no elevation of the dignity of a hill in the surrounding neighbourhood, there is no point from which a clear panoramic view of the city as a whole, with its leading features and principal buildings standing out in relief, can be obtained. The voyager approaching the harbour from the west will first sight

THE NATIVE QUARTER.

the spire of All Saints' Anglican (Sinhalese) Church, which stands on the highest part of the town, namely, the northern portion. He will next perhaps catch a glimpse of the dome of St. Lucia's Roman Catholic Cathedral in the Kotahena division, also northward. And other prominent buildings will gradually come into view, rising above the dense vegetation which surrounds the city. But the most conspicuous object as the breakwater is neared is the whitewashed lighthouse, standing on the most elevated part of the Fort division, which was erected in the year 1857. The revolving dioptric white light at the summit, standing at a height of 132 ft. above the sea-level, and showing at night a triple flash at intervals of thirty seconds, is a safe beacon for ships at sea, being visible at a distance of 17 miles in clear weather. A closer view of the shore will disclose the line of coconut-palms, which extends as far as the eye can see along the coast on both sides of the town.

On landing at the passenger jetty the visitor to Colombo will find himself at the termination of York Street, a principal thoroughfare of the Fort, the upper portion of which is shaded by a double row of ingosaman trees, whose branches, stretching overhead across the roadway, afford a welcome shade. A fine white marble statue of Queen Victoria, the work of Mr. G. E. Wade, of London, and erected by the colony as a memorial of the late sovereign's Diamond Jubilee in 1897, occupies a space immediately on the left-hand side, while opposite, and directly fronting the harbour, rises the imposing façade of the Grand Oriental Hotel (more particularly described in following pages), and on the left, a little way further up the street, is the Bristol Hotel, the other leading hostelry in the Fort. The rest of York Street comprises many of the principal business emporia of the city and the island. The Arcade Buildings, an extensive modern pile opposite the Grand Oriental Hotel, contain on the upper floor an extensive range of offices—including those of Lloyd's Greater Britain Publishing Company, Ltd.—while the premises of the National Bank of India occupy the eastern extremity. Two other large and lofty new blocks, further up the street on the other side and opposite the Bristol Hotel, house several of the leading wholesale and retail establishments of Ceylon, detailed descriptions of which, with accompanying illustrations, will be found in subsequent pages. In this street also are the attractive establishments of the dealers in jewellery, the precious stones for which Ceylon is famous, art work of all kinds, and the Oriental draperies and wares generally which form so conspicuously picturesque a feature of all Eastern cities. Immediately to the east of the Bristol Hotel is a large block of Government buildings, in which are lodged the Public Works Department and the establishment of the Registrar-General; while in the lower part of Chatham Street, which intersects York Street at right angles at this point and leads to the Fort station, is the extensive building of the Government Survey Office on one side, confronted, on the other, by a block divided in occupation between the Chamber of Commerce, the Government Land Registry, and the Ceylon Savings Bank. The continuation of York Street eastward, after its intersection with Chatham Street, leads to Slave Island, and in this winding section of the thoroughfare the only notable building is a block on the left containing the offices of the Government Irrigation Department, while the back walls of the garrison barracks—the front entrance to which is in Queen Street—abut on the right.

Queen Street, which runs parallel to York Street, on the left-hand side coming from the jetty, contains the chief buildings of the Governmental establishment. Proceeding up this street from the Customs and shipping offices and the wharves, the Gordon Gardens lie to the right, and next adjoining is Queen's House, the stately and commodious Colombo residence of the Governor, the erection of which was completed in 1856. The house and grounds occupy some four acres. Outside the northern gate stands a fine bronze statue of Sir Edward Barnes, one of the worthiest of the early Governors of Ceylon (from 1820 to 1822 and from 1824 to 1831), a distinguished administrator and celebrated as a road-maker. Opposite Queen's House is the General Post Office, an extensive modern pile in the style of what is known as the English classical renaissance, and constructed with due regard to the convenience of the public as well as of the officials engaged at the headquarters of the postal and telegraphic business of the colony; while opposite the Gordon Gardens is the long, continuous two-storeyed block in which are housed the Legislative Council Chamber, the Secretariat, and other principal administrative departments of the Government. On the sea-front, between the end of this block and the Grand Oriental Hotel, stands the Anglican church of St. Peter, which is used by the military. Occupying the most elevated part of Queen Street and in the centre of the roadway stands the light-tower, already mentioned, not many yards distant from Queen's House. On either side of the continuation of this thoroughfare as it trends from this point towards the Galle Face, as well as in the part of the street intervening between the lighthouse and Queen's House on one side and the lighthouse and the Post Office on the other, are some of the principal banks and business houses and mercantile offices; while at the southern end of the street the military establishment comes into evidence, the garrison barracks, situated on the left-hand side, forming three sides of a huge square, enclosing a spacious parade and recreation ground, occupying altogether an area of several acres. Erected on the site of part of the old fortifications and facing the sea, this handsome range of buildings occupies an unequalled position as regards the enjoyment of the healthy ocean breezes. On the right-hand side of the roadway and extending some way back towards the sea verge are the quarters of the married officers, both commissioned and non-commissioned. On the rocky sea-shore immediately behind Queen's House is located the flagstaff battery, the guns of which, with those of the larger battery at Mutwal on the other side of the harbour, command the approaches to the roadstead. On this spot also is a look-out and signalling station, with flagstaff. A branch railway line from the Fort station runs round the barracks to this spot and to the wharves beyond.

Almost opposite the northern gate of Queen's House, Prince Street connects Queen Street with York Street; and in this short thoroughfare on the one side, in a building adjoining and forming the top of the block of Government offices in Queen Street, are the departments of the Auditor-General and the Director of Public Instruction, the rest of the street being occupied by large commercial establishments. Two other short cross streets further east connect Queen Street with York Street, namely, Baillie Street and the main section of Chatham Street. In the former of these are the premises of two banks and the offices of a number of mercantile firms, while Chatham Street is for the most part lined with small shops and restaurants. The continuation of Prince Street after its intersection with York Street forms the Main Street leading to and through the heart of the Pettah quarter, passing on the left, first the large engineering establishment and general stores of Messrs. Walker, Sons, & Co., Ltd., and then a succession of harbour coal sheds, while on the right-hand side, after leaving York Street, is the site of the town drainage works and the Racquet Court recreation ground.

Among the more notable buildings of Colombo outside the Fort division—in addition to the Government medical establishments previously mentioned—are the Public Hall, in Slave Island, used for theatrical performances, concerts, lectures, and public meetings; the fine Roman Catholic Cathedral of St. Lucia, in the Kotahena Ward; the Anglican Cathedral (Christ Church), in the same division; All Saints' Anglican Church in the Hultsdorf district, immediately north-east of the Pettah, in which fane services in Sinhalese are held; the church of the Dutch Reformed denomination (a form of Presbyterianism) on an eminence at Wolfendahl, in St. Paul's Ward, a fine cruciform building in the Doric style, and one of the oldest edifices in Colombo, having been erected in 1749 as the place of worship of the Dutch Governors, and where many of them were buried; Holy Trinity Anglican Church, on St. Sebastian Hill, where the State services are held; the Buddhist temples, the principal of which, with sacred museum adjoining, is in the Kotahena Ward, while three others are to be found respectively in the Kelaniya, Maligakande, and Maradana districts of the town; the numerous Hindu temples in the Pettah and Kotahena division; the Central Mosque, situated in the Maradana Ward, with a school attached, and two other Mahomedan places of worship—one in the Pettah, the other in Cinnamon Gardens; the Colombo Museum, with the fine statue of Sir William Gregory in front, in Victoria Park (fully described in a

IN THE PETTAH.

following section of this book); the Tamil theatre in the Pettah; the Sinhalese theatre in Maradana; the military headquarters, a series of massive buildings in Slave Island, with tectural excellence, but occupying a central and commanding position on the slight eminence dignified by the name of Sebastian Hill; the Training College, an unpretentious edifice of the Anglican Cathedral in the Kotahena division; St. Benedict's Institute, a college forming an important part of the Roman Catholic head establishment in Kotahena; and

MAIN STREET, THE PETTAH.

Braybrooke Hall, the official residence of the officer-commanding, hard by; the police headquarters in Maradana, an extensive range of buildings in the form of a quadrangle; the police training school in the Pettah, a large building in the Corinthian style; and—last, but certainly not least—the fine range of the new Law Courts buildings at Hultsdorf.

As may be gathered from the separate description given in subsequent pages of the various colleges and schools, Colombo is well provided with educational establishments of all kinds, and conducted by various religious denominations, the buildings of some of which rank among the architectural features of the city. Among the Government institutions are the Royal College (formerly the Colombo Academy), a group of old single-storey buildings with no particular pretensions to architectural excellence, but occupying a central and commanding position on the slight eminence dignified by the name of Sebastian Hill; the Training College, an unpretentious edifice in Cinnamon Gardens, appropriately remote from the city's din; the Technical College, a new building and one of the most imposing and attractive structures in the city, situated on an elevation in the St. Sebastian Ward; and the Medical College in Regent Street, Maradana Ward, opposite to the General Hospital, an important branch of the Government Medical Department and the chief school of medicine and surgery in Ceylon. Among the denominational colleges, those deserving special mention, owing either to their educational importance or their claims of structural design, are St. Joseph's Roman Catholic College, a fine building, or rather group of buildings, occupying a conspicuous position on the eastern shore of the lake; St. Thomas's College (English Church), a group of single-storey buildings in the grounds of the Anglican Cathedral in the Kotahena division; St. Benedict's Institute, a college forming an important part of the Roman Catholic head establishment in Kotahena; and the new Wesley College, a large and handsome new edifice on Karlsruhe Grounds, in the Borella residential district of the Maradana Ward. The non-governmental public institutions of note in Colombo include a general library in the Fort, temporarily lodged in the lower floor of the Government buildings in Prince Street, with admission by membership, there being no free libraries in the city; the Pettah library, occupying a two-storeyed building standing in the Racquet Court ground; and the Young Men's Christian Association building, a large three-storeyed brick structure also situated in the same enclosure. Near by, in Norris Road, Pettah, is the large brick building of the Soldiers' and Sailors' Home, conducted by the Wesleyan Mission. The principal charitable institutions of the city are a Home for the Aged, located in the

Borella district, and maintained by the Roman Catholic religious order of the Little Sisters of the Poor; the Victoria Institute for Incurables, in Base Line Road, Borella, supported by public contributions; and a Prison Gate Brigade Home, founded and conducted by the Salvation Army, and consisting of a number of small tenements situated opposite the general cemetery, in the Borella quarter. The necessary detention and punitive establishments of the Government located in Colombo comprise a lunatic asylum, appropriately occupying a secluded spot near Havelock Town, and two gaols, the main convict establishment being at Welikada, in the Borella district, while on the northernmost shore of the harbour at Mutwal is a prison for the convicts employed at hard labour on the breakwaters.

MAIN STREET, THE PETTAH.

In Gasworks Street, in the Pettah quarter, the Government maintains a large engineering establishment, including an ironfoundry, where all the heavy ironwork—for bridges, public buildings and other works—for the Public Works Department, as well as woodwork, is moulded, put together, and finished. Occupying an extensive yard close by are the gasworks of the city and the premises of Messrs. Boustead Bros., which latter include the power station of the Electric Tramways Company. This station also supplies the current for electric lighting to the principal hotels, leading business establishments, and the residential districts of the city. In Norris Road, not far distant, are the extensive yard and stores of the Eastern Produce and Estates Company, Ltd. Out eastwards, towards Havelock Town, the Government maintains a model farm and stock-garden for agricultural and horticultural experiments in connection with the school gardens scheme which forms part of the public educational system of the colony, and the purpose of which is to instruct the sons of village cultivators how best to utilise the soil from which they will have to gain their living. The principal place of interment in the city is the general cemetery in the Borella district; while a crematorium—which is in general use with the Hindu and Buddhist communities for the disposal of their dead—is provided at Madampitiya, in the Kotahena Ward. The Parsees have their own burial ground in the Bambalapitiya suburb. A fountain of Doulton ware, standing in a triangular plot off Union Place, Slave Island, and erected to the memory of a well-known and highly esteemed citizen of the name of George Wall, who died in 1894, deserves mention as one of the few memorials to its departed worthies to be found in Colombo. The tablet affixed to the fountain bears the simple inscription; "George Wall, Philanthropist." But this gentleman is elsewhere described as having been a pioneer, planter, merchant, politician, and journalist as well, and "a man justly esteemed in his day for his nobility of character, unselfish devotion to the interests of the public, and the manly independence which distinguished all his actions." Truly a fine record, and one constituting an example for the rising generation of the island of Ceylon.

COLOMBO MUNICIPALITY.

Colombo shares with the principal Indian cities the possession of a municipal constitution differing widely from that of the cities and towns of the United Kingdom and of the principal colonies. In its broad aspects, the system follows the lines of the general administration of the colony. It may be described as one of representation tinctured with nomination. Every three years the nine wards into which the city is divided elect by popular vote representatives to the Municipal Council, and the Governor in Council, at the same time, nominates an equal number of citizens. His Excellency also appoints the Mayor, who, as Chairman of the Council, possesses a casting vote, and so holds the balance of power. But there is no such thing as an official majority. A member, whether elected by popular vote or nominated, is perfectly independent and votes exactly as he pleases, quite irrespective of the method of his election. Furthermore, the Colombo municipality, though controlled by Government, has a distinct existence of its own. It has its own executive, its own departments, and possesses the power of the purse within well defined limits. Prior to 1865 Colombo had no regular system of municipal government. In that year an Ordinance was passed providing for an administration on specific lines. The existing constitution of the municipality is governed by an Ordinance passed in 1887, which conferred a wider measure of local government upon the capital, in common with the towns of Kandy and Galle. Under this law no person can be an elected councillor who does not understand the English language and who has not property to the extent of Rs. 5,000 or, in the alternative, does not occupy a house of a rental value of Rs. 500 a year and upwards.

With an area of 10·09 square miles and an estimated population, at the end of 1905, of 171,549, the affairs of the capital city of the island are necessarily of considerable magnitude. The municipal revenue of Colombo for the year given amounted to Rs. 1,591,742 (£106,116), the principal items contributing to this figure being the consolidated rate—which provided some 40 per cent. of the total—licences, market rents, tolls, fines, sale of water and amounts collected for the sanitary work. The total receipts exceeded those for the preceding year by Rs. 23,834, while the total expenditure under the various municipal heads amounted to Rs. 1,387,278, leaving a substantial balance on the right side of Rs. 204,464 (£13,631). The addition of this amount brought up the total of accumulated surpluses to the credit of the municipality

PETTAH STREET SCENE.

to Rs. 936,191 (£62,418). The principal item on the expenditure list for 1905 was Rs. 417,648 for general public works in the city, such as the construction and maintenance of roads, pathways, culverts, drains, and sewers; while the acquisition of land for recreation and for drainage works was responsible for nearly half of Rs. 195,000 expended under the head of miscellaneous charges. An annual contribution of Rs. 130,000 is made by the municipality in repayment of part of the cost of the original construction of the waterworks. The charge for police maintenance totalled Rs. 60,000, street lighting absorbed Rs. 161,743, salaries and allowances amounted to Rs. 155,381, the work of the public health conservancy department cost Rs. 147,135 and Rs. 78,564 were expended on scavenging.

The sum paid during 1905 as interest on the money raised for carrying out the comprehensive scheme of deep drainage and sewerage designed by the late Mr. James Mansergh, the eminent English sanitary engineer, and adopted by the Council, amounted to Rs. 9,841. This indispensable undertaking was carried on during the year under an arrangement with the Government of the colony whereby the latter advanced the necessary funds at a charge of 4 per cent. to the Council, pending the raising of a municipal loan for the whole work. At the end of the year seven miles of the deep system had been completed, 1,300 men having been employed on the works. In consequence of the death of Mr. James Mansergh in June, 1905, some delay was caused in the revision of the original estimates (Rs. 3,000,000) for the first part of the work, rendered necessary by the discovery of unexpected unfavourable conditions in the sub-soil along the various routes. At the end of the year under review the nett expenditure on the drainage works amounted to just under Rs. 1,000,000; and it is anticipated that, in consequence of the difficulty mentioned, the original estimate will be considerably exceeded before the whole undertaking, the cost of which will ultimately have to be provided for by a loan, is completed. The work is still under the supervision of the firm of Messrs. Mansergh & Sons. The nature of the constructive operations being carried out, and of the difficulties met with, as well as the progress being made, may be gathered from the following quotation from the Municipal Report for the year 1905:—"On June 1, 1904, the street sewers were commenced in the Fort and the Pettah. The work proved to be more difficult than had been expected, owing to the presence of quicksands in the neighbourhood of the lake and Lotus Pond, and of rock all through the centre of the Fort. These trenches run to 17 ft. in depth and are only 1 ft. 9 ins. wide between timbers. Work has been carried on in this confined space at the rate of nearly half a mile a month, in close proximity to defective foundations of houses, under tram lines, and beneath a network of gas and water pipes, electric mains and old sewers, the positions of which were in some cases unknown beforehand. In the Fort nearly 3,000 tons of rock was blasted out of some of the busiest streets without any serious accident, although the notes of the blasting horn were said to have been the cause of much moral and intellectual damage."

In addition to the general scheme for the adequate drainage of the city, a much needed improvement is contemplated in connection with the Colombo lake, which, on account of its stagnant nature and its reception, under present conditions, of the greater portion of the town sewage, forms a serious menace to the health of the inhabitants, and is doubtless largely responsible for the high death-rate of the city—31·12 per 1,000. It has been decided to effect as speedily as possible the diversion from this broad sheet of water of the sewage from the thickly-populated native quarters on its shores; and the cost of this portion alone of the main drainage scheme is expected to amount to some Rs. 2,000,000, while an expenditure of Rs. 5,000,000 is estimated in connection with the harbour sections of the work. Although the undertaking of generally providing Colombo with an efficient and complete sewerage system is being carried on persistently, some years must elapse before it can be wholly finished. Meanwhile the residents must perforce put up with the present primitive sanitary system of removal of house refuse by night carts and burial of the same in a depôt without the city boundary.

During last year nearly Rs. 11,000 were expended in dredging the Colombo lake. But this work will not do all that is necessary in removing the unhealthy and obnoxious conditions arising from the presence in the midst of the city of a wide stretch of polluted and stagnant water, and plans have been prepared for the canalisation of the lagoon and the reclamation of the most objectionable portions on the north-western side. By the adoption of this scheme the upper reaches to the south-east would be purified, while the reclaimed land at the other end, off the Fort, would be converted into a fine open space to serve as a public park. A canal carried through the Fort quarter to the harbour would give water connection between the chief railway goods station at Maradana and the ships, and a western branch would connect this waterway with the factories at Slave Island. This project—which has not yet emerged from the chrysalis stage—would be to the advantage of Colombo in every way. It would immensely improve the general health of the city, besides adding an element of beauty in an extensive public park and serving most desirable utilitarian ends in providing for water conveyance between the Maradana railway depôt and the Slave Island business establishments and the shipping in the harbour.

NEGOMBO CANAL, NEAR COLOMBO.

In regard to water supply, Colombo is better provided than in respect to drainage, mains having been laid down to bring water for domestic purposes into the city from a reservoir at Labugama, and two service reservoirs having been constructed at Maligakande and Elie House, within the municipality, with which the distribution pipes within the city are connected. This undertaking was carried out by the Government at a total cost of Rs. 6,770,000. The waterworks were constructed by the Government, and are maintained, and the supply regulated, under the provisions of Ordinance 7 of 1886, the Director of Public Works being appointed as the Colombo waterworks engineer. The annual cost of the maintenance of the waterworks is about Rs. 5,000, which is borne by the Government. The average daily supply furnished by the Colombo waterworks during 1905 was four million gallons, some three hundred thousand gallons in excess of the average daily consumption. Samples of water from various parts of the town are taken monthly and subjected to chemical analysis, the analysts' reports certifying that the water is good and wholesome. The average rainfall at Labugama is 161 ins. annually, whilst in 1905 it reached 162·81 ins., and the collecting area of the reservoir is 2,385 acres, consequently the yield of this area is amply sufficient to meet present requirements and probably those of the future for some considerable time. The sale of water contributed Rs. 158,848 to the municipal revenue for 1905, a slight increase on the figure for the preceding year.

From January 1, 1905, the scavenging work has been performed by the municipality departmentally instead of by contract, as was the method up to that date, the chief advantages of the new system being control over the disposal of street garbage, more systematic cleansing of the roadways, and retention of the sweepings as a valuable asset in the hands of the Council. The change added some Rs. 33,000 to the cost of scavenging for the year; but this additional expenditure is considered justified by the better results obtained. Under the head of "Lighting" there was an increased expenditure of Rs. 11,000 in 1905 compared with the preceding year's figure, due to the extension of the gas mains, and in his annual report the Mayor states that "the town lighting system may now be looked upon as sufficient for present requirements."

NEGOMBO CANAL—ANOTHER VIEW.

The municipality pays an annual contribution of Rs. 8,000 to the Government towards the cost of the Victoria Bridge over the Kelani river at the northern boundary of the city, and among the items of miscellaneous expenditure for 1905 are Rs. 4,500 as annual contribution to the Volunteer band (in return for which the band plays periodically in the public gardens and parks), Rs. 65,120 for purchase of land for road improvement and for the main sewer, and Rs. 30,000 for land for extension of Havelock Town park, in the southern portion of the municipality. It is satisfactory to find that the municipality is evidently not prone to litigation, the total expenditure in law costs during 1905 amounting to only a trifle over Rs. 1,000, while on the other side the fines recovered for breaches of the civic ordinances totalled over Rs. 32,000. The watering of the streets, a very necessary provision for the abatement of the dust nuisance in the hot climate of Colombo, cost some Rs. 10,700 for the year. But this service is as yet far from meeting requirements, particularly in the suburbs, and it is being extended by means of water-posts, placed at distances of 500 yards apart along the principal suburban thoroughfares, at which the sprinkling carts can readily be supplied.

Although Colombo can boast of one or two fine streets in the Fort division of the city, lined for the most part by buildings, public and private, that would disgrace no city, the thoroughfares in the various native districts of the metropolis are for the most part both narrow and tortuous, in addition to being flanked by hovels. Large improvements will have to be carried out in the future in the direction of widening and straightening the streets and abolishing the native rookeries in these congested quarters, where whole blocks of crazy, squalid, and crowded tenements await demolition. In connection with the need for widening the streets in the populous portions of the town outside the main thoroughfares in the premier ward, the Mayor makes the following important pronouncement in his official report for 1905: "Had this important question received in the past the careful and continuous attention that it deserves, I venture to say that the Colombo of to-day would be a different place in the matter of 'streets' to what it now is. Simple legislation, say ten years ago, empowering the Council to fix the line of streets and to prevent encroachment thereon, paying due compensation for private rights invaded, would have, at small cost, secured to the public an ever-improving road system, and have saved thousands of rupees in buying up buildings the erection of which ought never to have been allowed. Once started, the system would work automatically without effort or expense to the Council. At the present day small and inexpensive buildings within what should be the line of street are being replaced all over the town by large and valuable structures which the Council will some day have to purchase at enormous cost. Speedy legislation in this direction should be pressed for as a matter of highest importance."

COAST SCENE, COLOMBO.

ANOTHER COAST SCENE, COLOMBO.

In regard to open spaces and recreation grounds, the native wards of the city are also sadly deficient, though the European and chief residential quarters are well provided. The want of more "lungs" in the congested portions of the city is emphasised in the annual report referred to, wherein it is pointed out that "there is no time like the present" for acquiring the necessary lands. Including the 52 acres of the grand expanse of the Galle Face and the 92 acres of the fine Victoria Park, the total area of the public parks and gardens and recreation grounds within the ten square miles of the municipality amounts to only something over 200 acres. The upkeep of these in 1905 amounted in round figures to Rs. 12,000, not including Rs. 23,477 expended on the rebuilding of the sea-wall of the Galle Face promenade. The care of the two general cemeteries—at Kanatte and Madampitiya—also lies with the municipality, and the maintenance of these burial grounds involved an expenditure of some Rs. 4,400 during the year under review.

A WAYSIDE BOUTIQUE (STORE).

The annual revenue from the markets in the different quarters of the city, which establishments are all under municipal control, amounted to Rs. 50,000, as against an expenditure of some Rs. 8,000; but this source of revenue showed a slight decline of Rs. 1,400 from the figure for 1904. Larger, more airy and generally more suitable premises, as well as improved methods in connection with the retail of provisions in Colombo, will have to be provided before long, the present market buildings and arrangements not being in accordance with civilised requirements. The same opinion may be more emphatically asserted in regard to the slaughter-houses of the city, also under municipal control, the operations at the two abattoirs—at Dematagoda and Madampitiya respectively—being conducted in a primitive, not to say barbaric fashion. A site has been selected near the former slaughter-house for a central cattle quarantine station and market. The total number of cattle, sheep, goats and pigs killed for consumption at the establishments named during 1905 was 86,956. The revenue for the year from the slaughter-houses—comprising charges for feeding and killing, sale of offal and fees for inspection of frozen meat—amounted to Rs. 46,614, as against an expenditure of Rs. 8,450 in connection with these establishments, of which sum something less than half was represented by feeding charges. The quantity of frozen meat imported into Colombo during the year and inspected by the municipal officers was 227,206 lbs., as against 226,448 lbs. in 1904.

A NATIVE BOUTIQUE.

In connection also with the care of the public health of the city is the supervision of the dairies, bakeries, public bathing-places, and laundries exercised by the civic authority. In the native quarters of the city continued vigilance is necessary to maintain a civilised standard of living. In the past, for example, considerable difficulty has been experienced with numbers of owners of dairies within the city bounds who would not keep their premises clean. But the adoption of stringent measures is having the desired effect upon these delinquents, and material improvement has taken place in the sanitary condition of these establishments. In connection with the 41 dairies in the city supervised during 1905, prosecutions for breaches of the sanitary regulations were instituted in 71 cases, of which 68 resulted in convictions. Samples of milk are also collected with a view to the standardisation of this article of diet. Laundry-men, locally known as "dhobies," are not allowed to carry on their business within the city unless registered and so brought under municipal control, and the number on the register at the end of 1905 was 444, against 517 a year previously. During 1905, 21 convictions were obtained against owners of unregistered laundries, and three against owners of laundries for having filthy premises. In the year under review there were 64 registered bakeries in Colombo, and in 32 cases it was found necessary to prosecute offenders against the by-laws regulating the methods of business in these establishments, 31 convictions being obtained. Colombo is as yet unprovided with public baths and wash-houses, so necessary in any large and populous city, and particularly requisite under a tropical climate. The natives use the lake both for bathing and as a general wash-tub, as well as for cleaning carts and draught animals, with the result that the shallow and stagnant water, already sufficiently polluted with the sewage which, under present arrangements, is permitted to run into it, is converted into a liquid abomination exhaling pestilential vapours. But, as the Mayor remarks in his annual report for 1905, now that a sufficient supply of fresh water is being obtained from the hills, there should be no further delay in providing proper and sanitary public baths and wash-houses in the city. Other operations being carried on by the municipality in the interests of the public health of the city are the destruction of rats, as possible disseminators of bubonic plague (over 42,000 of the rodents being accounted for in 1905), and the prevention of grass lands from being manured from objectionable refuse—an insanitary practice which breeds flies and is fraught with pestilential possibilities; while the employment of six midwives for work among the poorer classes, with a view to the reduction of the excessive infant mortality, and the appointment of a female sanitary inspector in connection with the prevention of infectious diseases among the Moorish community, are further means instituted for combating the conditions among the natives which favour disease and would, if uncontrolled, decimate the population. An Eastern city, owing to the climatic conditions, the density of the population and the native ignorance and neglect of sanitation, is peculiarly liable to epidemics; and in Colombo special precautions are taken by the municipal authorities against the outbreak and spread of infectious diseases. In June, 1905, an outbreak of small-pox, general in all the wards, occurred in the city, the total number of cases being 54, of which 16 resulted fatally. But the prompt and vigorous efforts of the medical officer and his staff in isolating the contacts and the stricken stamped out an infliction which might have been very serious for the city. Other zymotic diseases caused 144 deaths during the year, of which enteric fever accounted for 126 and measles 16. To deal with outbreaks of contagious diseases in future, the City Council, in co-operation with the Government, has decided upon the institution outside the municipal limits of a permanent hospital for infectious cases and a separate establishment for contacts. A vote on account in respect of this scheme has been taken in the 1907 Budget. The Council has also in view the installation of a modern refuse destructor for the incineration of street rubbish.

A growing need of the city is a new Town Hall to replace the present municipal headquarters building in the Pettah quarter, which, despite continuous enlargements, does not afford sufficient accommodation for the office work, and is, moreover, unworthy, from the architectural standpoint, of the dignity of the metropolis of Ceylon. A suitable situation is likely to be provided by the proposed removal of a leading educational establishment from the centre of the city to the suburbs, and this site will probably be secured for the purpose. A material work of improvement already effected is the removal of the municipal workshops and stores from a confined area in the congested native quarter of the Pettah to a more commodious site on waste land that has been reclaimed from the Suduwella swamp. The renumbering of the houses was another useful work begun in 1905. The town was divided into 128 blocks, the houses in each block being consecutively numbered.

In consequence of the long immunity of the city from serious conflagration, attention has not been vigorously directed in Colombo to

THE MOSQUE, CINNAMON GARDENS.

HINDU TEMPLE, PETTAH.

FISHING CANOES, COLOMBO.

fire-prevention ; and the Mayor, in his annual report for 1905, insists upon the inadequacy of the local Fire Brigade, a municipal institution, to cope with an outbreak of large proportions ; and in this expression of opinion the chief of the municipality is supported by the superintendent of the brigade. The 1905 equipment consisted of only one horsed steam-engine, manned by an engineer and six firemen, one hand-transport fire-escape, with three attendants, and two manuals for use in small fires. None of the twenty-four outbreaks attended by the brigade during 1905 was of serious dimensions, though two fatalities were caused. The cost of the Fire Brigade for 1905 was just over Rs. 15,000 (£1,000).

The system of electric tramways in Colombo, which traverses the city in two main directions from the centre of the Fort, is not a municipal enterprise, but the property of a private company. The City Council, however, is invested with powers in regard to the undertaking, which are exercised in the public interest and to insure an efficient service. There were no extensions of the tramway lines during 1905, and there was a slight decrease in the number of passengers carried in the cars as compared with the total for 1904, the figures being 6,555,338 and 6,599,059 respectively, the total mileage run during 1905 having been 814,725. The minimum fare is 5 cents (⅞d. in English money) for a distance of a mile and a half.

The municipality has a court of its own, presided over by a special magistrate, who sits daily at the Town Hall to deal with prosecutions for offences against the municipal by-laws. The number of cases disposed of before this tribunal during 1905 was 17,123, and fines were recovered to the aggregate amount of Rs. 32,256. The Council also licenses and controls the vehicles plying for hire in the city, an annual tax being collected from each vehicle according to its nature, hackeries and bullock-carts paying Rs. 4 each and jinrickshas Rs. 2·50 each. The total revenue under this head for 1905 amounted to Rs. 13,651, the number of hackeries (two-wheeled vehicles drawn by trotting bullocks) being 256, jinrickshas 2,369, and freight carts drawn by bullocks, under double and single yoke, 1,676 There were also 191 horsed carriages for hire on the streets. Both the vehicles and the draught animals are inspected, and licences

COLOMBO MUNICIPAL COUNCIL.

ALEXANDER FAIRLIE. W. SHAKSPEARE. B. HORSBURGH (Mayor). DR. T. C. GRIFFEN. H. A. JAYEWARDENE.
HON. P. D. WARREN. M. L. M. ZAINUDDEEN. JAMES PEIRIS. CHARLES PERERA. CHAS. P. DIAS. M. F. KHAN. H. TIRUVILANGAM. DR. C. W. VAN GEYZEL.
HON. F. A. COOPER. R. R. DUNUWILLE (Secretary). L. B. FERNANDO.

(The names on the left run towards, and those on the right from, the head of the table.)

BUDDHIST TEMPLE (INTERIOR).

are suspended in cases of either being found unfit. Dogs, too, are subject to municipal taxation, the impost for 1905 being fixed at one rupee per head, with the result that Rs. 5,382 were collected. As cases of rabies occasionally occur in Colombo—five were reported in 1905—the necessity for exercising control over the canine inhabitants and destroying the pariahs is obvious. The number of wandering dogs seized during the year was 2,072, of which 689 only were redeemed. Of the rest, 1,374 were destroyed, 19 died in captivity, and 21 were sold. It may also be mentioned that the municipality has its own printing department, the cost of which for 1905 amounted to Rs. 7,416.

The receipts from licences to sell opium in the city amounted during the year 1905 to the large total of Rs. 51,457, while permits to sell intoxicating liquors realised Rs. 17,200. The revenue from tolls totalled Rs. 138,000, of which amount Rs. 92,676 was collected at the Victoria Bridge over the Kelani river, a main inlet and outlet of the city on the north-eastern boundary, and Rs. 43,294 at Bambalapitiya, at the southern extremity. The collections on account of the consolidated rate, the largest item of the annual municipal revenue, amounting in 1905 to Rs. 637,500, including arrears due for previous years, were made at a cost of Rs. 15,000, and no large balance remained for subsequent recovery.

B. HORSBURGH.
(Mayor.)

With the charge of so large a city as Colombo in their hands, a city, too, in which so many improvements are under consideration and great extensions of the residential quarters are annually taking place, the Municipal Council and its officers are continually occupied with important business of various kinds. The ordinary meetings of the Council are held monthly in the Town Hall, the Mayor presiding in his capacity as Chairman; and on these occasions the discussions are often long and animated, civic feeling being keen, and often running high, in the capital of Ceylon. The present Mayor (at time of writing) is Mr. B. Horsburgh, who, since his occupancy of the responsible position, has particularly distinguished himself by energetic efforts to improve the sanitary conditions of the city. During the year 1905 there were fifteen

THE LANDING JETTY.

THE COLOMBO CLUB.

THE GORDON GARDENS.

IN COLOMBO GARDENS.

VICTORIA MASONIC TEMPLE.

meetings of the Council, and all the members have a high record of attendances. In addition to the meetings of the full board, the Standing Committee on Law and General Subjects held ten meetings, that on Markets and Sanitation eleven meetings, that on Finance and Assessment eighteen meetings, and that on Works ten meetings ; while twelve special committees of the Council appointed to report on various matters requiring particular consideration sat at various times during the year.

BENJAMIN HORSBURGH.

Mr. Benjamin Horsburgh, the Acting Mayor, was born on April 10, 1868, and is an M.A. of Edinburgh University. He entered the Ceylon Civil Service in 1889, being attached to the Jaffna Kachcheri, whence he was transferred to Galle in 1893 as Acting Office Assistant to the Government Agent of the Southern Province. From 1895 he served in various districts of the island as Assistant Government Agent, and also on special duty at the Pearl Fisheries. In 1905 he became an officer of Class II., and was appointed to act as Mayor in March, 1906.

COLOMBO VIEWED FROM MUTWAL.

THE COLOMBO MUSEUM.

BY GERARD A. JOSEPH, ACTING DIRECTOR.

The Colombo Museum, as seen from the accompanying illustration, is a strikingly handsome building of admirable structural proportion and elegant elevation. Designed in the Italian style of architecture, and possessing a fine façade, it is one of the most attractive edifices in Ceylon, reflecting in its appearance the highest credit on the architect, Mr. James Smither, F.R.I.B.A. The Museum was founded by Sir William Gregory, Governor of Ceylon, in 1873, and was opened to the public on January 1, 1877. There is a handsome statue of the founder, by Boehm, in front of the building, which was erected by the inhabitants of Ceylon to commemorate the many benefits conferred on the colony by Sir William Gregory during his administration of the government from 1872 to 1877.

The collections of objects exhibited are of a varied nature, consisting of specimens of the old-time famous handicraftsmanship of Ceylon

COLOMBO MUSEUM.

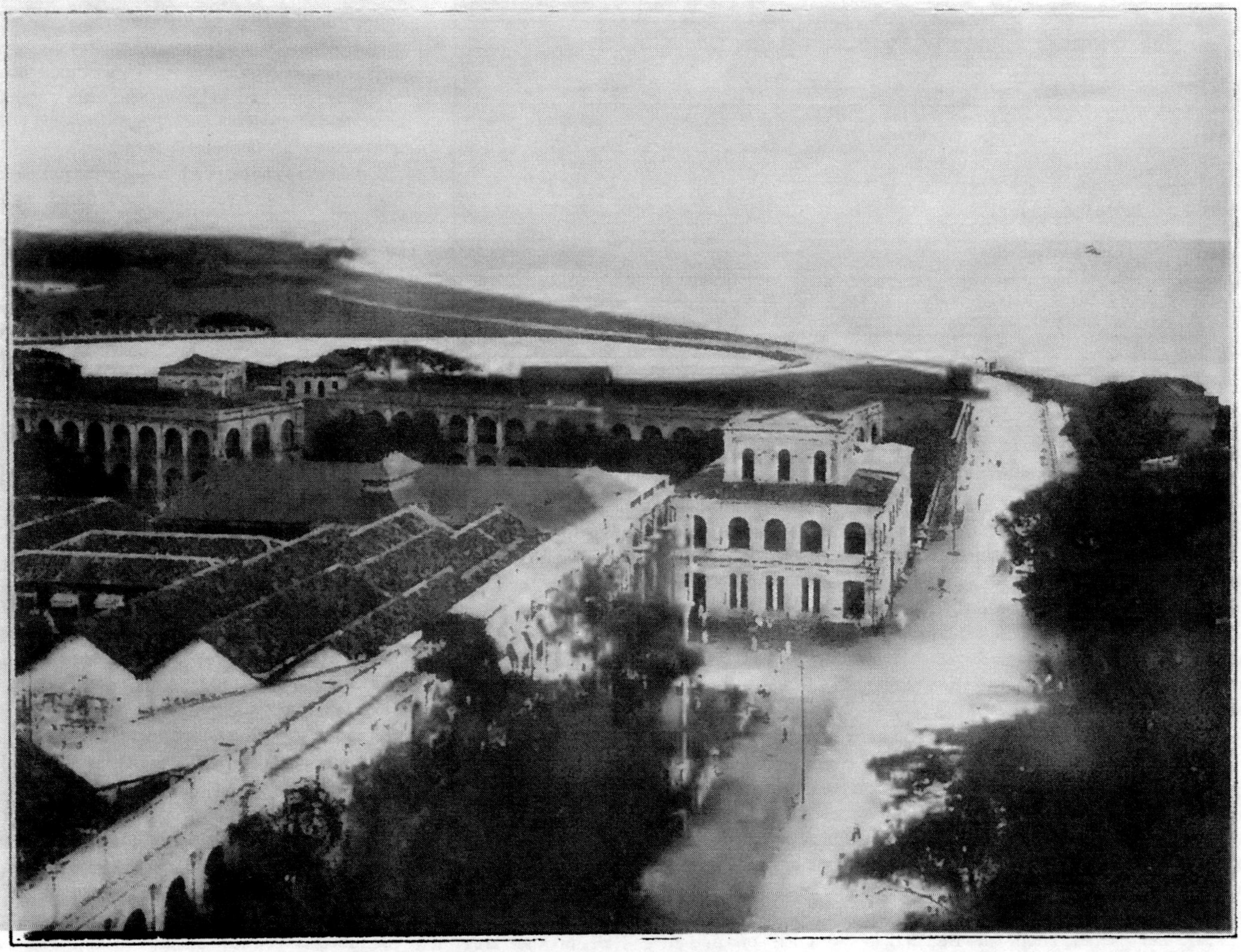

THE GALLEFACE PROMENADE.

and of the works of Nature in the island and its dependencies. Additions are continually being made to the collections, and they have quite outgrown the space accommodation which the building affords. The urgent need for extension is recognised, and it is expected that shortly the building will be enlarged to satisfy the daily increasing demand for space in all the departments of the institution. Various publications are issued by the Museum authorities, dealing with the collections; and a well illustrated guide-book gives a description of the general contents of the building.

In the central hall are to be found images of Buddha in various attitudes, executed in metal, wood, and ivory, also a selection of the peculiar Sinhalese jewellery of the Matara district. The Palmyra and coconut palms have a case each, containing a selection of objects illustrating the uses of the two distinct kinds of palm: and a collection of articles from the Maldive Islands, which pay annual tribute to Ceylon, is shown. Among these exhibits some beautiful lacquer-work is displayed. The grotesque masks shown here also attract attention, and prove of interest especially to non-resident visitors. Some of these disguises represent various diseases, and are still employed by the devil-dancers to exorcise the demons who occasion the disorders.

The Mediæval Room contains, in a large case, a varied and valuable collection of ivory-work, including fan-handles, combs, panels, miniature dagobas, and other articles. A model of the "Dalada," the Sacred Tooth of Buddha, is exhibited in this room, the reputed original of which famous relic is preserved in Kandy. The original is said to have been brought to Ceylon about 310–313 A.D. Numerous Kandyan swords, with carved hilts and scabbards, and Kandyan knives of curious workmanship are shown, many of which articles are characterised by elaborate damascening and highly ornate and bejewelled hilts. The collection of coins is most valuable, and over this display the numismatist will be tempted to linger longingly. First he will notice the ancient Sinhalese currency, comprising the coins of the kings of Ceylon from Parakrama Bahu, 1153 A.D., to Bhuvaneka Bahu, 1296 A.D. Then he will be interested in the display of foreign coins, chronologically arranged, which were introduced in succession into the island by traders of all nationalities from the time of the Roman Emperors down to the beginning of British rule. Among the host of interesting articles in the mediæval division, the tortoise-shell work, Kandyan pottery, a large series of boxes and implements used for areca-nut and tobacco, examples of Kandyan, Chetty, and Jaffna jewellery, will command especial attention.

THE MUSEUM STAFF.

In the Stone Gallery the visitor will find the most notable objects in the museum, including remains and traces of the architecture and civilisation of two thousand years ago. Statues, pillars, friezes, and slabs, carved out of the gneiss which forms the country rock of Ceylon, and some of crystalline limestone, will arrest notice. The lion which formerly stood in the Council or Audience Hall of the king at Polonnaruwa is a wonderful and exceptionally valuable and interesting relic of the past. An inscription discloses that this piece of stonework formed the base of the throne of King Nissanka Malla during the years 1187–1196 A.D. Facing the lion is a beautifully carved stone window, which lighted the hall of the royal palace at Yapahu in the thirteenth and fourteenth centuries. It consists of a single block of gneiss, cut into the semblance of a frame, which surrounds a composition hieroglyph consisting of forty-five circles in five vertical rows, joined together in a moniliform pattern, each circle containing an emblematic figure repeated on both sides of the stone. The matrix of the slab between the carved portions was removed by the artist who designed and executed this unique triumph of tracery.

A pillar which formerly stood in the Pattini Dewala (temple) at Medegoda is to be seen in one of the accompanying illustrations. It is a beautifully carved monolith, octagonal in shape, rising from the back of a broad-faced couchant lion with frilled mane and raised tail.

The south verandah contains an important relic of the Portuguese occupation of the country in the form of a large copper cannon with embossed coat-of-arms, which was dredged up in the Colombo harbour. This cannon most probably belonged to the Portuguese warship commanded by Francisco Pereira which was wrecked in this harbour in 1613.

The inscribed pillars which form the principal feature of the west verandah show the changes which have taken place in the character and language of the Sinhalese since the end of the first century after Christ. Firstly, the Ruanveli slab relates to the restoration of certain temples during the reign of Gaja Bahu, who was king of Ceylon from 113 to 125 A.D. The Tissamaharama slab, which comes next, is the finest known specimen of inscription of the fourth century A.D.; while the Dondra slab records the granting of land to the temple of Vishnu in the fourteenth century. The ethnological casts which are shown in the Stone Room include a Ratemahatmaya (Kandyan chief) in national dress, a Sinhalese bride, and a Buddhist priest, the latter dressed in his toga-like yellow robes, forming one of the characteristic elements of the picturesque scenes of Ceylon. There are also figures of a Veddah man and woman, members of the aboriginal hunting caste or hill tribe of the island. These exhibits are especially interesting in view of the fact that this primitive race, which is now only found in the remote eastern parts of Ceylon, is fast disappearing, owing to the inroad of civilisation into their secluded fastnesses, while those that still survive are being gradually reclaimed from the state of their pristine savagery. These hunting nomads are identified with the Yakkus, the aborigines of the island, who, after the conquest (B.C. 543)

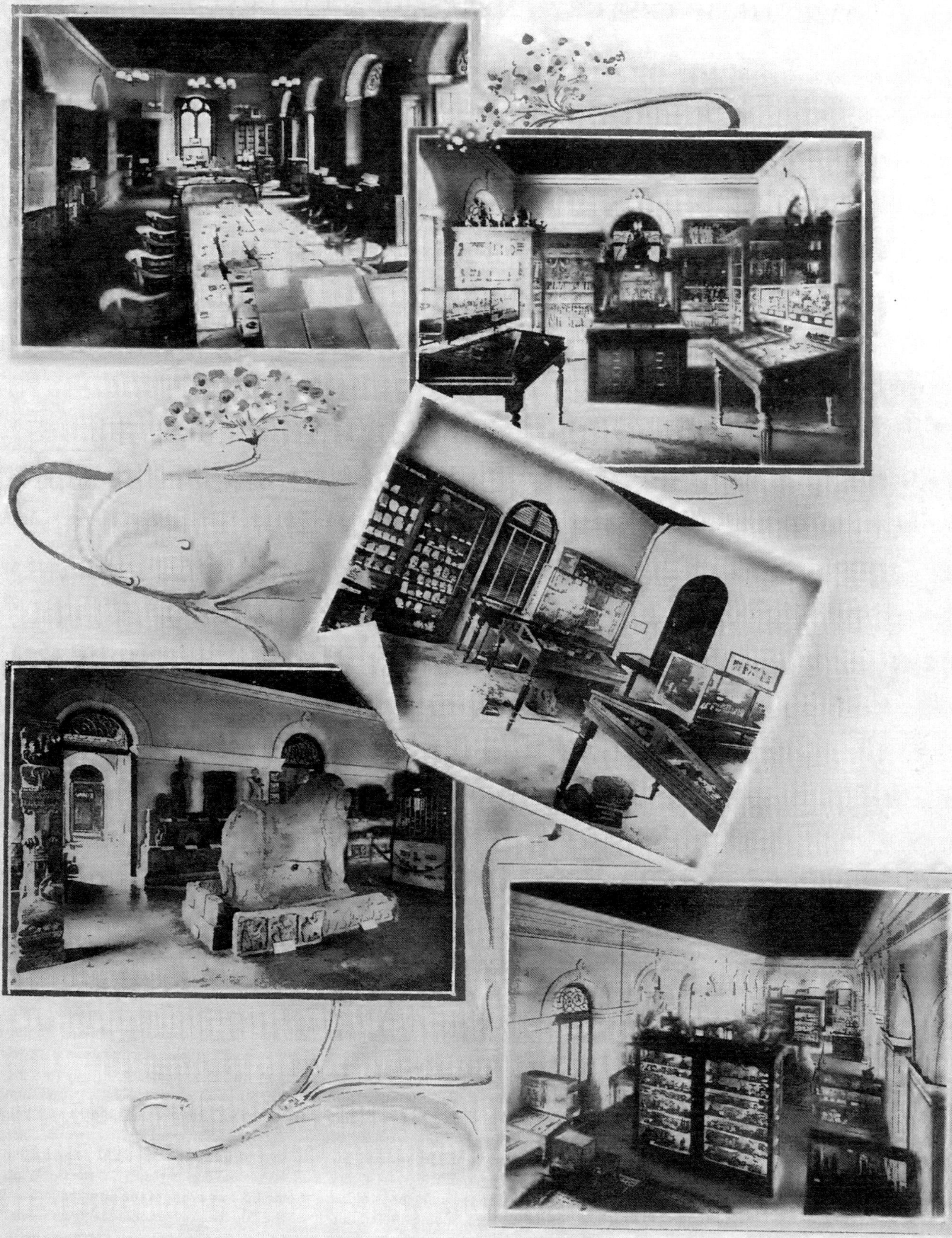

THE COLOMBO MUSEUM.

The Reading-Room. The Mineral Gallery. The Medieval Room.
The Stone Gallery. The Natural History Gallery.

of Vijaya, the founder of the Sinhalese dynasty, retired before the invaders into the wilds. In the north verandah, at the back of the building, are tombstones, capitals, inscriptions, and such-like relics.

Copies of the celebrated Sigiriya paintings will be found flanking the main staircase. The originals are in a cave of the ancient fortress of Sigiriya, near Dambulla, one of the Buddhist centres in Ceylon of old. These paintings were executed upon stucco plastered upon the smooth surface of the walls in 475 A.D. They are still to be seen in a remarkable state of preservation. The pictures are said to be the portraits of the wives of the Sinhalese parricide, King Kasyapa, who fled to Sigiriya after the unnatural crime perpetrated on his father, King Dhatusena.

At the back of the Museum is a palm-thatched structure, called the "Buddha shed," which houses, among other stone figures, a large sedent figure of Gautama Sakya Muni (the Buddha), which was dug out of the ruins of the sacred city of Anuradhapura, and is held to be the finest yet brought to light by the excavations of that ancient city. In this shed, also, will be found a beautiful floral moonstone of unique and admirable design, embossed with wreaths, festoons, and garlands, with a pair of fabulous monsters ("makaras") at the sides, and at the base a pair of twofold representations of the Sri Patula, or sacred footprint of Buddha.

The Museum stands in charming grounds of its own, traversed with shady walks lined with seats for visitors. In covered cages a small zoological collection, consisting of a few live animals, such as leopards, bears, porcupines, and other mammals, besides birds, is maintained. In another shed may be seen the skeletons of a sperm whale (*Physeter macrocephalus*) and whalebone whale (*Balænoptera indica*) whose carcases were washed ashore on the western coast of the island. These huge specimens are awaiting the extension of the Museum to receive due exhibition within the permanent building.

The Mineral Gallery, situated behind the main building, contains a representative collection of marine fossils, rocks, minerals, and gems of Ceylon, arranged by the Director of the Mineralogical Survey of Ceylon and his staff. The rooms facing the Mineral Gallery and the one adjoining are the workshops of the taxidermist, and an accompanying illustration shows this important member of the Museum staff and his assistants at work.

The natural history collections are housed in the upper storey, and consist of an exhibition of vertebrate and invertebrate animals included in the fauna of Ceylon. Here are to be found representatives of the fishes, amphibia, reptiles, birds, mammals, insects, crustacea and mollusca occurring within the zoological province of the island. The guide-book gives full particulars about the natural history of these specimens.

In a building of two storeys detached from the main structure a duplicate collection of specimens, known as the Student Collection, is kept, and is available for examination on application to the Director of the Museum. This department includes, besides other selected specimens, the Pole collection of Lepidoptera, the Swayne collection of snakes, and the valuable Collett collection of land mollusca. In this building also a laboratory is provided for the use of students.

The Museum is visited by a large number of travelling scientists, some of whom remain in the island for short periods while engaged in special study and research. The institution is also a favourite resort of the residents of Colombo, and is one of the principal attractions of the city for non-resident sightseers—visitors from up-country, and passengers by the ocean steamers. On the occasion of festivals such as the *Wesak* (the Buddhist New Year) and the *Hadji Perunal* (the Mahomedan New Year),

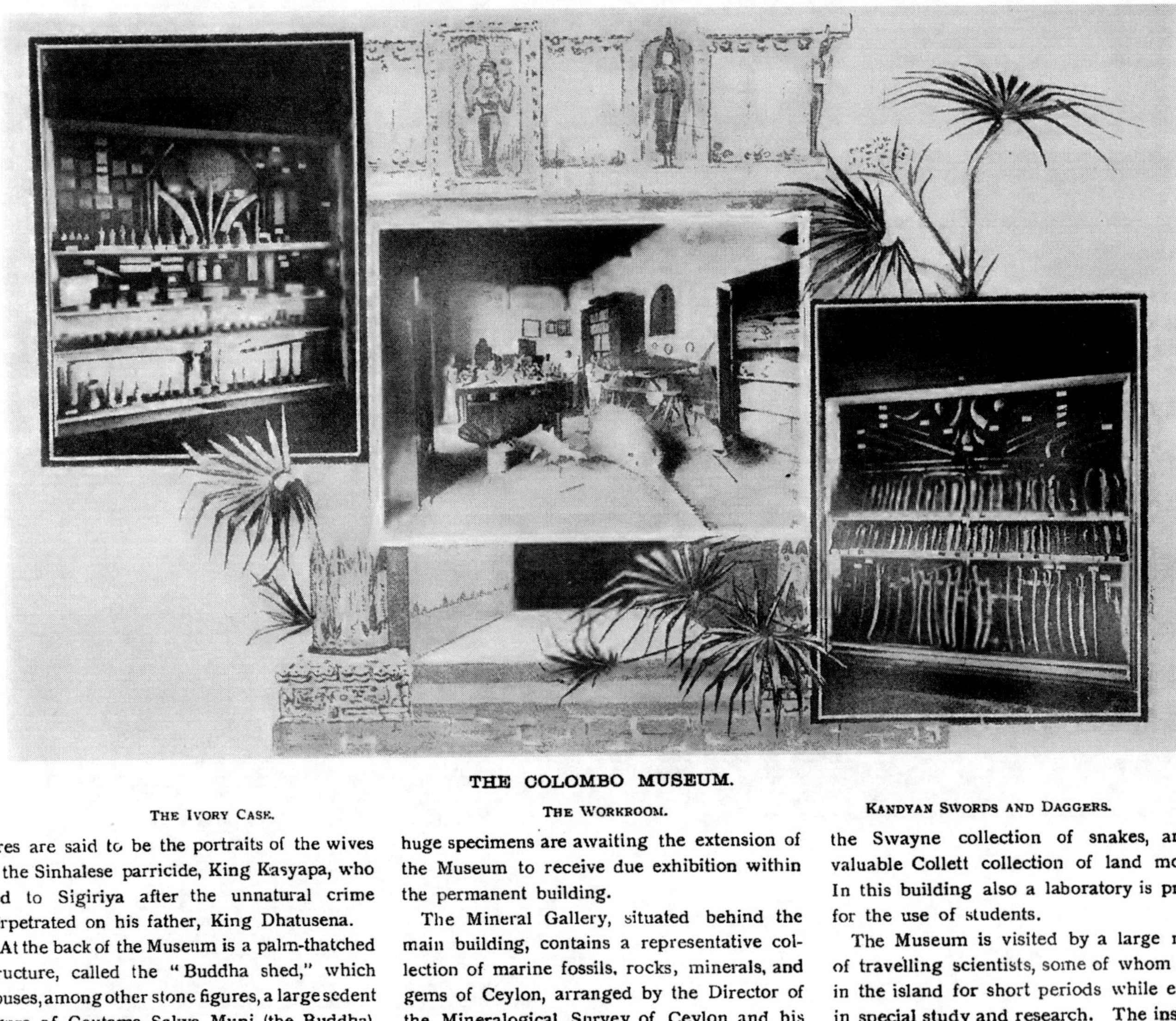

THE COLOMBO MUSEUM.

THE IVORY CASE. THE WORKROOM. KANDYAN SWORDS AND DAGGERS.

which are proclaimed public holidays, the grounds, filled by swarms of natives in gay festival attire, present the appearance of a fair. Of all days, naturally, Sunday—a *dies non* with all classes and communities—is the one which sees the largest number of visitors to the Museum. The labouring classes, taking advantage of their hebdomadal rest from toil, flock to this institution to spend their Sunday afternoon in profitable sightseeing. It is computed that, in the course of a year, the Museum is visited by some 150,000 persons.

In the accompanying photograph of the staff, it was, unfortunately, impossible to include the Director of the Museum, Dr. A. Willey, D.Sc. (London), Honorary M.A. (Camb.), F.R.S., as that gentleman was absent from Ceylon at the time the photograph was taken.

Museum Library.

The library of the Colombo Museum, occupying the rooms to the right of the entrance hall, is the only free public library in the colony. Founded at the same time as the Museum (1876), it contains a valuable assortment of books of material assistance in the work of the Museum in illustrating, indexing, and identifying the collections. Apart from fulfilling this institutional purpose, the library affords to students and all classes of readers the opportunity for perusing historical (local), biological, and Oriental literature. Useful works of reference are numerous, and altogether the Museum contains one of the best—if not absolutely the best—collections of books on Ceylon. Since 1885 a copy of every work published in the colony has been sent to the Museum library.

A most valuable collection of Buddhist palm-leaf manuscripts, commonly called *ola* manuscripts, is a prominent feature of the Oriental section of the library, some of them presented by the King of Burma. Much of the important Sinhalese literature of Ceylon—which is of the remotest antiquity, and dates back to several centuries before the Christian Era—is enshrined in the *ola* manuscripts. This valuable section of the library contains nearly 500 manuscripts in Sinhalese, Burmese, and Cambodian characters. These documents have been written with a stylus upon the prepared slips of palm-leaves called *olas*, and chiefly consist of works on the Buddhist religion—the island of Ceylon possessing special interest as the chief seat from the earliest times of Southern Buddhism—but include, besides, some historical, medical, poetical, and other works. It has been well said that "though the production of a comparatively small nation, the historical works of the Sinhalese far surpass in value any produced in India"; and Ceylon possesses, in the Mahavansa, a metrical chronicle in the Pali language, containing a dynastic history of the island for twenty-three centuries—from 543 B.C. to 1758 A.D. This well-known historical work is to be found in manuscript in the Oriental section of the library.

The policy of the library has been to acquire works of reference on natural science and Oriental literature as affecting Ceylon, also all other books relating to the island; and numerous and costly works of these kinds have been from time to time added to the shelves. To the student the general collections of books and leading scientific and other periodicals to be found in this institution offer invaluable facilities for study and research. Persons desiring to be admitted as readers are required to forward to the committee of the Museum an application supported by the recommendations of two persons of respectability. If the application be approved by the committee of the Museum, a reader's ticket is issued to the applicant. The Museum and the library are open to the public on Monday, Tuesday, Wednesday, Thursday, and Saturday in each week from 10 a.m. to 6 p.m., and on Sunday, Christmas Day, and New Year's Day from 3 p.m. to 6 p.m.

THE COLOMBO CLUB.

This institution, which occupies a splendid position with an extensive lawn frontage to the wide green expanse of the Galle Face and overlooking the sea, was founded in 1871 "for the promotion of social intercourse among gentlemen residing in Ceylon," and the list of the twenty-three original members includes names prominently associated with the progress of the island—among them that of Sir Hercules Robinson (afterwards Lord Rosmead), then Governor of Ceylon. These foundation members were: T. Berwick, H. Cross Buchanan, G. W. R. Campbell, W. J. Carver, J. W. M. Coghill, Colonel J. F. Drew, J. Duncan, J. L. Gordon, G. B. D. Harrison, Thomas Helmer, W. W. Hume, Hon. H. T. Wright, Colonel J. G. Jervois, W. M. Leake, G. B. Leechman, W. C. Leechman, Sir Hercules Robinson, Hon. F. R. Saunders, C.M.G., H. S. Saunders, W. Bowden Smith, J. G. Smither, C. E. H. Symons, and Thos. Wright. For many years Colonel C. E. H. Symons (now Consul for Japan) acted as secretary—an honorary position—and to his zealous efforts and devoted service in that capacity much of the success of the club may be ascribed. The present number of members is about 700, including the leading representatives of the official, commercial, and social circles of Ceylon. The institution is, in fact, the premier club of the island, the post of Patron and President being practically always filled by the Governor of Ceylon for the time being, while the general management is in the hands of a committee of influential local gentlemen. Under certain conditions, officers of the Army or Navy serving in or calling at Ceylon are admitted to honorary membership, and distinguished visitors to the island are enrolled by invitation on the honorary list. The club house is open to members from 5.30 a.m. until 2 a.m.; but the institution also partakes largely of the character of a residential club, bedrooms being procurable by members in adjacent club chambers, a separate building belonging to the institution.

The club house is the old Assembly Rooms, formerly a popular public and society rendezvous in Colombo. Perhaps with equal zest the pursuit of social enjoyment is still continued here under the auspices of the club at fitting times and seasons. *Dulce est desipere in loco.* The spacious apartments on the first-floor afford every facility for festive gatherings, and the club assemblies held here are very popular, while the Turf Club ball is one of the events of the Colombo festive season every August. But to the true clubman it is sufficient to say that, under a European steward and with a competent *chef*, the cuisine is excellent, and that the fine dining-hall, among the pleasantest of surroundings, and the smoking, billiard and reading rooms are all that can be desired.

FREEMASONS.

Until 1901 the Masons of Colombo did not possess a proper home, but in 1899 the influential members of the craft met together to discuss the possibility of erecting a suitable temple in the capital of the island. With much effort the necessary funds were raised by subscriptions and debentures, and plans were made and approved, a site in Galle Face being obtained from the authorities. On November 27, 1900, at 7.15 a.m., the foundation stone was laid by W. Bro. the Hon. J. N. Campbell, in the presence of a few Masons connected with the undertaking. The building was erected to plans designed in England and adapted to local requirements by Bro. E. Skinner, A.R.I.B.A. The work of construction was carried out, under contract, by the Colombo Commercial Company, Ltd. The temple was completed in August, 1901, and formally opened on the 1st of September in that year. An opening ceremony and dedication on a big scale was planned, and Grand officers from India were to have come to Colombo for the occasion; but owing to the plague and consequent restrictions on travelling, this programme had to be abandoned. The trustees of the debenture holders were W. Bros. J. N. Campbell, H. J. Scott, and E. J. Hayward. Of these, W. Bro. Scott has passed away, and the trust is now in the hands of the remaining two appointees.

All the Lodges, Chapters and connections in the island are associated in the Temple and are represented by a committee, the latter body being composed of the following: W. Bros. G. H. Alston, 18°, P.M., E. J. Hayward, P.M., J. W. S. Attygalle, P.M., M. Burge, P.M., J. N. Campbell, 32°, P.M., Lieut.-Colonel F. McCarthy, P.M., and T. C. Huxley, 30°.

In Colombo there are five Craft Lodges, viz., St. George's Lodge, No. 2,170, E.C., W. Sutherland Ross, W.M.; Connaught Lodge, No. 2,940, E.C., J. Crowe, W.M.; Sphinx Lodge, No. 107, I.C., A. C. Edwards, W.M.; Leinster Lodge, No. 115, I.C, M. Wilson, W.M.; and Bonnie Doon Lodge, No. 611, S.C., C. Viney, W.M.; two Craft Chapters, viz., Hercules Royal Arch, No. 2,170, E.C., C. Henly (Z.), E. J. Hayward (H.), E. E. Powell (J.), and Lanka Royal Arch, G. W. R. Willicott (Z.), A. C. Edwards (H.), H. Wilson (J.); two Mark Lodges, viz., St. George of Colombo, No. 464, E.C., C. Henly, W.M., and Lanka Mark Lodge, No. 107, I.C., G. W. R. Willicott, W.M.; two Preceptories, viz., Colombo Preceptory, John Walker, E.P., and Ceylon Preceptory, C. Henly, E.P.; also a Provincial Priory, H. Byrde, P.P., the Lanka Conclave, Red Cross of Constantine and K. H. S., No. 156, W. H. Figg, M.W.S., and the Allied and Cryptic Councils, G. H. Alston, W.M. In other parts of the island there are the following Congregations: Grant Lodge, Galle; St. John's Lodge and Henry Byrde Mark Lodge, Kandy; Adam's Peak Lodge, Dimbula Lodge, Adam's Peak Chapter, Rose Croix, Campbell Royal Arch Chapter, Hatton, and the Nuwara Eliya Lodge, at that centre. Councils of T. and K. S. and Secret Monitor are being formed, and a dispensation is being sought for the establishment in Ceylon of a District Grand Lodge of England. The Hon. Secretary to the Grand Committee of the island is W. Bro. E. J. Hayward, P.M. At one time there existed in Colombo a Provincial Grand Lodge of Ceylon, working under the Irish Constitution. It was formed in 1877, and went into abeyance in 1890.

GERMAN CLUB.

Those excellent colonists, the Germans, know well how to make themselves comfortable, and wherever they have established themselves in any part of the world their natural clubbable instinct has led to the institution of meeting-places for pleasant social intercourse. In Colombo, as elsewhere, the German Club—or "Deutscher Verein," to call it by its national name—is a prominent feature of the social life of the community, occupying as it does a most charming situation in Cinnamon Gardens, fronting the Colombo Museum. The club was founded on December 7, 1900, and the handsome buildings it occupies were inaugurated on November 13, 1903, by H.R.H. Prince Adalbert, the German Emperor's third son. Mr. Philipp Freudenberg, the Imperial German Consul for Ceylon, is the club's patron; while Mr. A. Schulze, of the well-known Colombo firm of Messrs. Schulze Bros. & Co., is the President, and Mr. H. Behring the Hon. Secretary. The club buildings include a handsome billiard-room, a large and beautifully furnished drawing-room, a reading-room, retiring-rooms, refreshment-rooms, bath-rooms, and—most important departments of all with many—a well-appointed bar and well-equipped kitchen. There are also stables for members' horses and a garage for motor-cars. A principal attraction of the club is formed by two spacious tennis-courts in well laid out grounds covering some two acres of land. The number of resident members is about forty, but the club is largely patronised also by hundreds of visitors from all parts of the island, as well as by over-sea travellers passing through Colombo. It is, in short, an ideal rendezvous at which to spend one's leisure hours—those hours that often lag so drearily in a tropical country.

THE GERMAN CLUB.

THE CEYLON SOCIETY OF ARTS.

This society was founded about sixteen years ago as an amateur art club. The object of the society was then, as it is mainly now, the encouragement of pictorial art in Ceylon; and for this purpose annual exhibitions of amateur productions have been held from almost the first year of the foundation of the society, with, on the whole, encouraging results. The original displays were held in a small store on the site of the present *Times of Ceylon* buildings in Main Street, Fort; but the space there proving quite inadequate to house the number of exhibits, which increased year by year, the Public Hall and the School of Agriculture were successively tried. In recent years the exhibition has been held in the Chamber of the Legislative Council. Consequently, every year the Parliament Chamber blossoms out into a miniature Burlington House. Mr. E. O. Walker, a former Director of Telegraphs, and Mr. C. Drieberg, B.A., Superintendent of School Gardens, have successively acted as hon. secretaries of the society. But on the arrival of Mr. A. Bartlam in the island in 1902 as instructor in drawing at the Technical College, Colombo, that gentleman undertook the by no means invidious duties of the unpaid post, which he still fills. Being, however, an ardent votary of pictorial art beyond his own special branch of lineal representation, Mr. Bartlam has laboured earnestly and zealously for the local Society of Arts, which, under the guidance of its president, vice-president, and committee, has endeavoured, whenever possible, to recognise deserving productions, and thus assist the tyro. The quality of the exhibits shown at the 1906 exhibition, as compared with that of those sent in on previous occasions, testifies that improvement has been effected in the period of the society's existence in Ceylon; and Mr. Bartlam is of opinion that, with proper encouragement and the co-operation of the Government in establishing a picture gallery in the island, where aspirants might study works of art by leading masters and derive practical help in the pursuit of their ideals, the artistic instinct in the Ceylonese, so long dormant and neglected, is susceptible of cultivation. What has hitherto been wanting is the incentive to high aspiration that can only arise from knowledge of what is really good and sound art. At present the knowledge of technique even is generally rudimentary.

In order, therefore, to help the society in the accomplishment of its object, a number of prominent European and Ceylonese ladies and gentlemen have volunteered to offer prizes for the best work; and this has persuaded many amateur artists to take to their studies with greater zest and keenness. The society is also receiving very satisfactory general support, about a hundred members being on its list, while fresh members are being continually enrolled. The patron of the society has always been the officer administering the government of the colony, and the committee is composed of several well-known local artists, including ladies. The one great difficulty the society has to cope with at present is the want of a proper habitat, and its present efforts are directed towards supplying this want and establishing an art gallery containing a small diversified collection of standard works to serve as an educative influence and provide models for imitation. In spite of present disabilities, however, the committee of the society has never failed to make the art exhibition one of the most interesting events of the annual August festivities in Colombo. An attractive feature of these exhibitions is a nne display of photographic views of the interesting scenery of Ceylon by local photographers, which are always of a highly artistic order.

THE VICTORIA MEMORIAL EYE HOSPITAL.

Although the idea of establishing an eye hospital in Ceylon had been mooted for a number of years, it was due chiefly to Her Excellency Lady Ridgeway that the memorial to the late Queen Victoria took the form of this institution as it exists at present in Colombo. On the suggestion of Lady Ridgeway, Dr. (now Sir Allan) Perry and Dr. W. H. de Silva sent out a joint circular, stating the need that existed for the establishment of an ophthalmic institution, and suggested that the proposed hospital should be associated with the name of her late Majesty. The then existing eye infirmary, built in memory of Sir Samuel Grenier (late Attorney-General) only provided for out-patients. As the result of the appeal made by Drs. Perry and De Silva, promises of contributions were received from prominent citizens of Ceylon, among them the late Mohandiram N. S. Fernando, who a few years previously had offered Government the sum of Rs. 5,000 as a nucleus for a fund for the establishment of a hospital for diseases of the eye. Other handsome donations, given by some of the more prominent Ceylonese gentlemen, assisted to carry the idea into proper execution. On February 15, 1902, Lady Ridgeway addressed a letter to the Press of Ceylon, in which she stated: "If it is still proposed to have a local memorial to our great Queen, surely it could take no better form, or one that would be more acceptable to her kind heart, than this" (the eye hospital). The idea was warmly supported in the Press, and being accepted with ready enthusiasm by the community in general, a public meeting was held in the Legislative Council chambers, under the presidency of Sir West Ridgeway, then Governor of the colony, on March 18, 1902, at which almost all the leading official and unofficial sections of Colombo were represented. Thenceforth the scheme never lacked popularity. More than Rs. 30,000 were collected up to the date of the meeting, and the Governor generously pledged the Government to double whatever sum the public might subscribe. Thus the amount promised was at once raised to over Rs. 60,000, the contributions continuing afterwards until they reached a total of Rs. 100,000. It was little anticipated then that the estimate would need to be more than doubled to meet the generous response of the public. It may be mentioned that the benevolence of the public had been severely taxed only a short time earlier by contributions for the relief of the famine-stricken population in India, also that urgent appeals were still being made on behalf of the various war funds, and more especially for the Ceylon Contingent Memorial Fund. But the revered name of Queen Victoria proved one to conjure with, and the committee of the Eye Hospital Memorial carried on their work of initiation with vigour. Every source of public generosity was systematically tapped, and the aid of every public body—official, commercial, religious, and social—was enlisted. Mr. (now Sir) Stanley Bois approached the heads of the various commercial and mercantile houses in the Fort, and won a large measure of unstinted and large-hearted help. Every other community was thoroughly exploited, the very Natu Kotte Chetties being infected with the enthusiasm, their donation of Rs. 4,000 odd constituting one of the most unique and memorable features of the campaign. The ladies of Ceylon also employed persuasive eloquence with effect. Mrs. James Peiris alone collected over Rs. 5,000. There never had been so popular a movement in Ceylon before, never a public subscription of such magnitude. An executive committee was appointed, consisting of the Lieutenant-Governor, Mr. (now Sir) Everard im Thurn, Mr. (now Sir) Stanley Bois, Messrs. A. S. Pagden, the Hon. Mr. F. A. Cooper, the Hon. Mr. S. C. Obeyesekere, Messrs. F. Dornhorst, K.C., James Peiris, S. M. Burrows, P. Coomaraswamy, and Dr. Chalmers, with Mr. D. R. Marshall as treasurer, and Sir Allan Perry and Dr. W. H. de Silva as hon. secretaries. On the two last-named fell most of the burden of organising the subscriptions, which continued to flow in until the highest anticipations were surpassed. Then arose the question of a site for the building, which, it was recognised, must be in a central part of the city, also within easy reach of the General Hospital, so as to answer the object of training medical students and of attending to any cases that might be transferred from the General Hospital. Sir West Ridgeway particularly pointed out in his speech at the inaugural meeting of the movement that the hospital was intended, not only to deal directly with eye diseases, but also to equip medical men for ophthalmic work in other places. It was necessary, therefore, that the institution should be within easy reach of the Medical College. The selection of a site, therefore, involved anxious and careful deliberation. It had to be borne in mind that the hospital was not to be a private institution, nor even an official establishment, but a public memorial of the great name it bore.

Lady Ridgeway laid the foundation stone of the hospital on August 6, 1903. By that time the estimates of the cost had undergone many changes, and the original modest computation of Rs. 50,000 had become a jest. The further extended estimate of Rs. 100,000 had also been discarded, the total of the subscriptions having surpassed that amount by several thousands. Among the largest subscribers were Mr. N. S. Fernando, who gave Rs. 7,500; Mr. Charles Peiris, who gave Rs. 7,500, in memory of his late only daughter Elsie, to establish a children's ward; Mr. H. J. Peiris, who gave Rs. 5,000; the Municipal Council of Colombo, who subscribed Rs. 2,000; Mr. Tyagaraja, Rs. 1,500; and the family of the late Mr. D. S. Cargill, Rs. 1,500.

A suitable site having been obtained, the preparation of the plans was entrusted to Mr. Edward Skinner, Associate of the Royal Institute of British Architects, a well-known Colombo architect. The style of architecture is that known as the Hindu-Saracenic, and according to Mr. Skinner's preliminary estimate

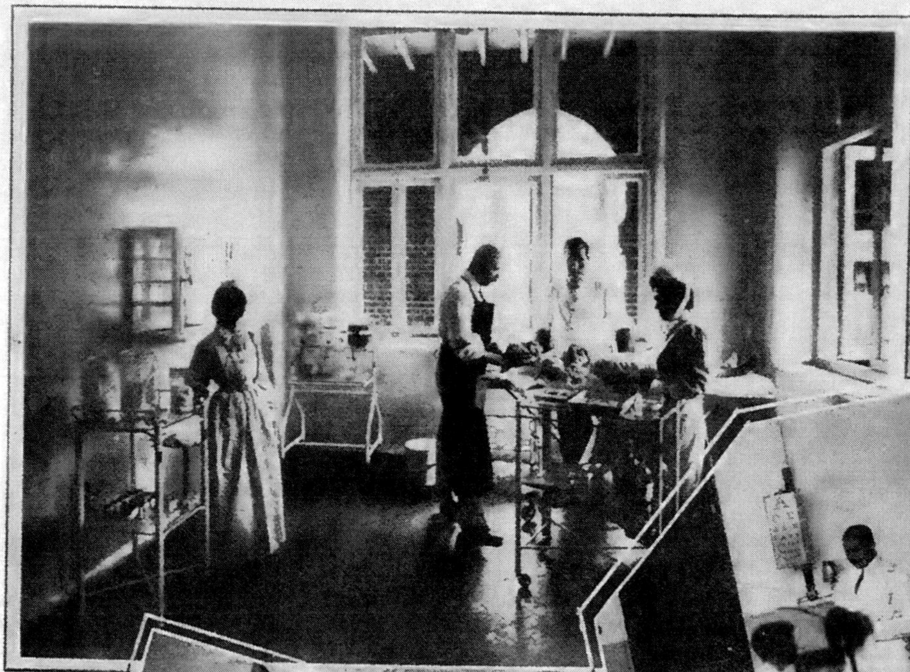
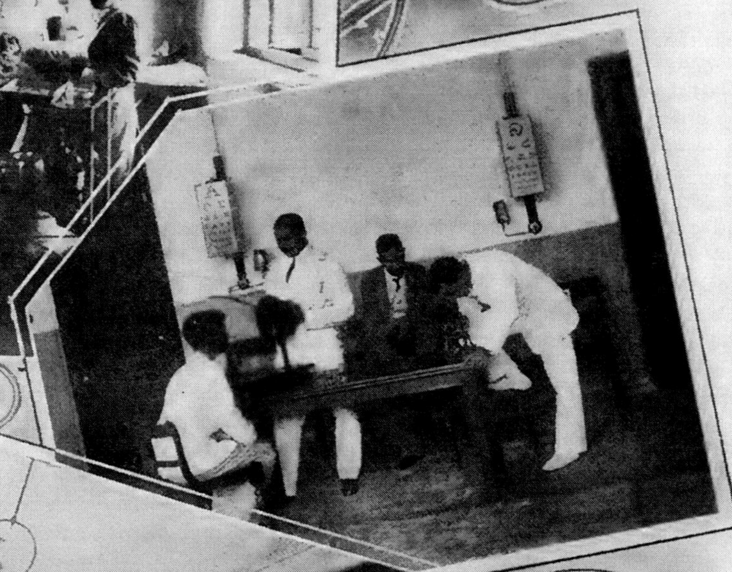

THE VICTORIA MEMORIAL EYE HOSPITAL.

THE OPERATING ROOM. THE TESTING ROOM

THE MALE WARD. THE VICTORIA EYE HOSPITAL.

the work was reckoned to cost not less than Rs. 168,000. The Department of Public Works was instructed by Government, at the request of the committee, to undertake the work; and the officers more prominently associated with the building were the Director of Public Works, Hon. Mr. F. A. Cooper, C.M.G., Mr. E. C. Davies, Mr. G. H. M. Hyde, and Messrs. Ohlmus and De Saram. In design the building is a copy, with modifications, of the central portion of the public building at Kuala Lumpur, in the Federated Malay States. In equipment and appliances and in the arrangement of light and air, and in all its aspects, the Victoria Memorial Eye Hospital of Ceylon is hardly equalled in the colonies, and only surpassed by a few institutions of the kind in England. The building has a frontage of 200 ft., with a depth of 97 ft. from wall to wall, and 38 ft. at the façade, the inside height of the wards being 14 ft. Accommodation is provided for 45 patients.

The handsome entrance hall is adorned with a large painting of her late Majesty Queen Victoria, specially presented by the Hon. Alexander Yorke, Equerry to her late Majesty, and below is a miniature marble bust of Her Majesty enclosed in brass railings. On one side wall is a large portrait of Lady Ridgeway, presented by Mr. Simon Fernando Sri Chandrasakara Mudaliyar. The walls of this hall as well as of all the rooms are enamelled, and tiles of a special type of glass and enamel arranged in pretty patterns cover the floors. Branching from the entrance hall on either side are two corridors, the one on the left leading to the house-surgeon's rooms and the preparation and operating rooms, that on the right giving access to the office of the surgeon-in-charge, the matron's rooms, the nurses' dining-room, and the hall porter's room. Next to these is the surgical operation room, with walls of white enamel and a blaze of light which can be regulated with accuracy, according to the requirements of each case dealt with. This apartment is fitted with electric light, and a variety of electric and other appliances, forming the most modern equipment for eye-work, including electric sterilisers and boilers. Having no angles or corners, every square inch of the ceilings, walls, and floor of the operating room can be sprayed and washed with the hose, and thus thoroughly cleansed and disinfected. From the main hall a broad staircase takes the visitor to the paying patients' ward, and on one side of the staircase hangs a portrait of the late Mohandiram N. S. Fernando, who, as already stated, initiated the fund for the Eye Hospital with a large donation, afterwards substantially increased. Accommodation is provided upstairs for six paying patients, the rooms being fitted up luxuriously with all manner of appliances and accessories for the comfort of their occupants, the equipment including electric fans and electric light and bells. There is also a well-furnished sitting-room for patients. The nurses' sleeping rooms are also located upstairs.

In the block forming the left wing of the building is the men's department, which consists of two wards with ten beds each, and two other wards of two beds each. These apartments are equipped in keeping with the rest of the building, and furnished with a dining-room as well as a room for the nursing attendants, the windows of which enable them to overlook all the wards. Ample provision in the way of bathrooms and lavatories is provided in these quarters. Another range of buildings, which forms the base of a triangular space, contains the kitchen, storerooms, attendants' rooms, and other offices. This part of the hospital terminates in the Grenier Memorial out-patient infirmary, which has been transferred to the institution. This auxiliary department of the institution is furnished with a dispensary and waiting hall for out-patients, an operating room and a dark-room. The right wing of the main building contains the women's ward and children's Elsie Peiris ward above referred to, which are, in general arrangements, similar to the male wards opposite. There are ten beds for women patients and six cots for children, a dining-room, nurses' room, scullery, and minor offices.

In the centre of a beautifully laid out garden, enclosed by the inner verandah, is to be fitted a fountain, which has recently been presented by Mr. Peter de Abrew in memory of his father.

The total cost of the hospital, with site and equipment, will represent about two and a half lakhs (250,000) of rupees to the public and the Government of the colony. The hospital is now in full working order, only a few additional ornaments and appliances, ordered from England, being required to complete the equipment. A pathological room for investigation of eye diseases in Ceylon is to be established, and a clock in the tower is a desirable addition. Up to the time of the establishment of this hospital most of the eye cases were treated by native curative methods. The number of blind persons in Ceylon is about 8,000; yet, according to the statistics of civilised countries, the total ought not to be more than 2,000. It is therefor econfidently hoped that the establishment of the Victoria Memorial Eye Hospital in Colombo, with the far-reaching effects of its establishment throughout the island, will substantially reduce, if not altogether abolish, this enormous difference. The hospital is always crowded, and numbers of sufferers requiring attention are frequently kept waiting for want of room. The number of out-patients has increased by about 25 per cent., and a large number of operations are always being performed. The following constitute the staff of the hospital: Consulting Surgeons and Physicians, Sir Allan Perry, M.D., M.R.C.S.; T. F. Garvin, M.B., C.M.; A. J. Chalmers, M.D., F.R.C.S.; H. M. Fernando, M.D., B.Sc.; Surgeon-in-charge, W. H. de Silva, M.B., C.M., F.R.C.S. (Edin.); House Surgeon, A. Nell, M.R.C.S.; Matron, Miss Fraser; Apothecary, Miss Siebel. As a centre of teaching the hospital is fulfilling a great purpose. Medical students attend the lectures given here and study the curative work as part of a regular course, thus becoming specially trained in the treatment of ordinary eye affections.

THE CEYLON BRANCH OF THE ROYAL ASIATIC SOCIETY.

By Gerard A. Joseph, Hon. Sec.

The Ceylon Branch of the Royal Asiatic Society was started in 1845, and in 1846 was incorporated as a branch of the Royal Asiatic Society of Great Britain and Ireland. The society has its office and library in the Colombo Museum. Under the Museum Ordinance No. 11 of 1873, a special room is provided in that institution for the use of the society to hold its meetings and to house its books. Indeed, the Museum chiefly owes its existence to this society's having advocated the founding of the institution. When the Colombo Museum was opened in 1877, it started with the nucleus of exhibits belonging to the society's museum, and with a large number of books presented by the society to form the museum library. The society played a particularly important part in the formation of the colony's natural history collections. Before the different scientific departments of the Ceylon public service had been fully developed the society anticipated their work, and drew attention to the necessity of their establishment. It has been laid down that the design of the society is to institute and promote inquiries into the history, religions, languages, literature, arts, and social condition of the present and former inhabitants of the island, with its geology and mineralogy, its climate and meteorology, its botany and zoology.

The society has issued fifty-five numbers of its *Journal*, forming eighteen volumes and containing papers on a variety of subjects, many of which display much learning and research. An elaborate index accompanies these publications up to the year 1890. The society's *Journal* is highly prized by students and scientific workers, and the older issues are considered to be of special value, being difficult to obtain, in spite of the reprints that have been issued from time to time. The value placed on the society's publications is shown from the frequent applications from learned societies all

BOIS BROS. & CO.'S ESTABLISHMENT—OFFICES, TEA-PACKING DEPARTMENT, GREEN-TEA MACHINERY, MANUFACTURING TEA TINS.

over the world to be placed on the exchange list. Many of these applications the society is obliged to refuse, owing to the large number of such requests received.

The library of the society contains, besides many valuable books on Ceylon, works on archæology and Oriental literature, also a large collection of the publications of learned societies with which the institution exchanges publications. It is rich in its records of voyages, which consists of those of Hakluyt, Churchill, Pinkerton, and others. India and Indian subjects are also well represented in the collection of books.

In short, the Ceylon branch of the Royal Asiatic Society can claim to have played a considerable part in the development of the colony by the circulation of interesting and instructive literary information regarding both its past and present history. The accumulated results are to be found in the society's journals, which contain learned contributions from competent authorities in various departments of scientific and general knowledge.

COLOMBO COMMERCIAL: FORT SECTION.

BOIS BROS. & CO.

This well-known and leading Ceylon firm of general merchants, exporters, and estate and commission agents was founded in Colombo in 1891, in succession to the firm of Messrs. Alstons, Scott & Co., which at that time ceased to carry on business. Mr. Percy Bois, the senior partner of the present house, came out from England to Ceylon in 1873, and entered the service of Alstons, Scott & Co., wherein he rose to the position of senior assistant. Those were the halcyon days of the coffee-growing industry in Ceylon, and the plantation agencies formed a principal part of the business. The other head of the firm, now Sir Stanley Bois, followed his elder brother out from the Homeland in 1882—the year in which Colombo became the port of call for the ocean mail steamers instead of Galle—and also became an assistant in the same establishment. In taking over the general business of Messrs. Alstons, Scott & Co., the brothers Bois also acquired the local agency of the British India Steam Navigation Company, which is now the main branch of their business, having expanded, with the growth of the port of Colombo, to very large proportions. This shipping trade includes a daily service between Ceylon and Tuticorin (south of India), a service twice weekly between Ceylon and the South Indian ports of Tondi, Pamban, Ammapatam; a fortnightly service between Colombo and London, Madras and Calcutta; steamers to and from Mauritius monthly and a ten-daily service in connection with Coromandel and the Malabar Coast ports. As many as 6,000 coolies per week are conveyed each way by the British India steamers plying between Ceylon and the ports of Southern India; while on the London fortnightly service a high class of vessel is employed in the conveyance of both passengers and cargo, among them the *Rewa* and the *Rohilla*, two fine new ships, each of 7,000 tons burden.

Besides being agents for the Roeberry Tea Company, Vellekelle Tea Company, Patiagama Cinchona Company, Ltd., Tyspane Tea Company, Ltd., St. Heliers Tea Company, Ltd., Lindoola Tea Company, Ltd., Craighead Tea Company, Ltd., Palmerston Tea Company, Ltd., Macaldehiya Tea and Rubber Company, and the Rubber Plantations of Kalutara, Ltd., Messrs. Bois Bros. own the Hunupitiya Mills, Colombo, where they carry on a large business as tea-packers and shippers, while their head office is at 11, Queen Street, Fort, Colombo. They are also agents for the Standard Life Assurance Company, Wm. Younger & Co, Ltd., Chas. Kacinlay & Co., Canadian Pacific Railway Company, Imperial Fire Insurance Company, Royal Exchange Assurance Corporation, the Petroleum and General Storage Company, Drexel, Morgan & Co., and the Ceylon Company of Pearl Fisheries, Ltd. The European assistants of the firm are Messrs. E. John (chief assistant), T. H. Tatham, Neville White, O. Spain, and A. G. T. Hyde.

The senior member of the firm and his brother, Sir Stanley Bois, take it in turns to visit England. The firm originally consisted of the two brothers only, but Mr. J. E. Alston was subsequently admitted to partnership. He, however, died during 1906, and on January 1, 1907, Mr. W. Sutherland Ross, a brother-in-law of Sir Stanley Bois, joined the firm.

In addition to his connection with this leading house of business, Sir Stanley Bois is an influential man in the public life of Ceylon, having filled many high positions with credit. He was for many years a member of the committee of the Ceylon Chamber of Commerce, becoming vice-chairman and ultimately filling the post of chairman for three consecutive years (1891–92–93). He was a member of the Colombo Municipal Council in 1899, and acted as Mercantile Member of the Legislative Council in 1903 and European Member during 1906. His knighthood was conferred upon him for his special work as Commissioner-General for Ceylon at the St. Louis Exhibition of 1904, as well as for his public services generally. He is a member of all the leading clubs of the island. He divides his leisure hours between music and motoring. His private residences are Hunupitiya Cottage, Colombo, and Silha, Nuwara Eliya, in the hill country.

FINLAY, MUIR & CO.

The firm of Finlay, Muir & Co., carrying on an extensive business as general exporters and importers, produce merchants, and estate agents, was originally founded in Glasgow, under the style of James Finlay & Co., with offices in London and Liverpool. With the rapid development of the business, branches were opened in Calcutta, Bombay, and Karachi, in India, and a Ceylon house was established in 1893 at 10, Queen Street, Colombo, which still constitutes the head office of the business in the island. The Glasgow house was founded over a century ago, and the prosperous continuance of the business to the present time speaks for its solid nature, and the importance and standing of the firm in the mercantile world. The local "go-downs" and factory of the firm are situated in Vauxhall Street, Slave Island, Colombo; and there the tea, coconut, rubber, and other produce brought from the estates under the firm's control are stored, and the processes are carried on of blending and packing black tea and of finishing green tea for export to the markets of the world. Finlay, Muir & Co. also represent in Colombo the Clan Line of fifty steamers trading between Great Britain and Eastern and South African ports, and Archibald Currie & Co.'s steamers, which ply between Australia and India.

The director-in-chief of the firm's operations is Sir A. K. Muir, Bart., of Deanston House, Perthshire, Scotland; while the manager of the local business is Mr. Alexander Fairlie, who came to the island some twelve years ago and is an eminently qualified business man. He is at the present time Chairman of the Ceylon Chamber of Commerce and connected institutions. Mr. Fairlie is a

FINLAY, MUIR & CO.'S ESTABLISHMENT.

THE OFFICES. THE STORES.
THE GREEN TEA FACTORY. TEA AND RUBBER PACKING.

UNLOADING COPRA AT FREUDENBERG'S MILLS.

HULTSDORP MILLS.
(From Skinner's Road.)

HULTSDORP MILLS.
(From the Law Courts.)

ENTRANCE, HULTSDORP MILLS.
(As seen from the oil mill.)

MAIN ENGINE, FREUDENBERG & CO.'S OIL MILLS.

OIL YARD AND OIL MILLS.
(From the entrance of the Hultsdorp Mills.)

member of the Golf, Tennis, and other local Clubs. His private residence is Calton Lodge, Turret Road, Colombo.

FREUDENBERG & CO.

The firm of Freudenberg & Co. was founded on July 1, 1873, by Philipp Freudenberg, the present senior partner. He came to Ceylon to buy coffee and to develop direct trade between the island and the Continent of Europe, the opening of the Suez Canal suggesting the diversion of Colombo shipments from London to other ports. As coffee went down the firm gradually took up other lines, and it is now carrying on business in banking, exports and imports, owns the "Hultsdorf" Oil Mills and Manure Works and the "Kotahena" stores, has the agency of the Norddeutscher Lloyd, the Deutsche-Australische Dampfschiffs-Gesellschaft, the Deutsche Ost-Africa Linie Steamship Companies, represents the Kali-Syndicate, Stassfurt, the Aachen-Munchen and Magdeburg Fire Insurance Companies, the Deutscher Lloyd, and is the correspondent of the leading German Banks.

Mr. Philipp Freudenberg was nominated German Consul in 1876, and is the senior Consul in the island. His son Reinhart (German Vice-Consul) is his partner. The office and superintendence staff numbers 22 Europeans and 70 Ceylonese clerks.

The "Hultsdorf" Mills are the oldest industrial establishment in the island, having been founded in 1835 by the late Mr. Wilson in connection with Price's Patent Candle Company, Battersea, London. They were worked by Freudenberg & Co., on behalf of the then owners, Messrs. Antony Gibbs & Sons, London, from 1886 to 1895, when Mr. Philipp Freudenberg bought the concern. In 1898 the old oil mills were burned down. A new, enlarged and quite modern plant has since been erected. The mills are 13 acres in extent within the walls. One part forms the oil-crushing department with its adjuncts, such as copra stores, oil yard, cooperage, &c. Another is devoted to extensive manufacture of artificial manures. Early in the nineties experiments with Freudenberg & Co.'s artificial manures for tea were first made on a scientific basis, and from that time onward the demand has steadily increased. About 800 hands are employed in the Hultsdorf mills.

WHITTALL & CO.

This important business house was started in Ceylon in 1880 by the late Mr. James Whittall, who came to the island from China to look after the affairs of Messrs. Matheson & Co., then largely interested in the coffee growing trade. On the founder's death in 1903, the business came under the control of Messrs. A. Thomson and G. W. Carlyon. Messrs. G. H. Alston and the Hon. Mr. W. H. Figg joined the firm in 1896, and Mr. T. C. Huxley became a partner in 1906, in which year Mr. Carlyon retired. Messrs. Thomson, Alston, Figg, and Huxley, therefore, constitute the firm at present. Besides being exporters of all kinds of Ceylon products, and importers of all requisites for the work on planting estates as well as of various other articles of commerce, Whittall & Co. act as agents and secretaries for a large number of planting companies which they have floated. Many of these concerns have made very handsome returns to the shareholders. The firm has also lately floated several companies for the cultivation of rubber, which product promises to show a good profit on the capital thus invested. It is thus seen that the firm's operations embrace financial as well as commercial business in connection with the principal productive industries of the island. All the local operations of the house are directed from the head offices on the storey above the Mercantile Bank of India's premises in Queen Street, Colombo, where a staff of seven Europeans, in addition to the partners, is employed, with about 25 Burghers and native clerks. There is also a branch of the business at 135, Front Street, New York, U.S.A., while the firm's London agents are Messrs. Matheson & Co., Lyall, Anderson & Co., Thomson, Alston & Co., and J. Whittall & Co., Ltd.

The factory premises of the firm are situated at Mortlake, Slave Island, at a distance of about a mile from the head offices in the Fort. They consist of sixteen separate buildings standing in a compound of about seven acres. The principal branch of this establishment is the tea factory, where the tea purchased at public auction and sent down from the estates undergoes the various processes of preparation for shipment, being fired, when necessary, bulked, weighed, and packed in succession. The work of the several departments of the factory is carried on with the regularity of clockwork, the tea passing from hand to hand swiftly, and with due regard for absolute cleanliness, affording to the visitor a most interesting insight into the methods of preparing this staple product for the world's markets. In a wood-working shop attached to the factory the boxes in which the tea is to be packed can be viewed in course of rapid manufacture, three circular saws being constantly at work in this subsidiary department. Especial attention is paid to the weighing of the product and the labelling of the packages. The labels are printed in colours on the premises, a complete plant for the purpose—consisting of six presses, three ruling machines, two guillotines, and a bronzing machine, all driven by a Crossley gas engine of 16 horse-power—having been installed. The printing equipment also includes a stereotyping outfit, many founts of type, and all necessary appliances for impressing the firm's stationery.

An important branch of the business conducted at the Mortlake establishment is the preparation of cardamoms for the market. The spice, which is handled in large quantities, passes through several processes in order to obtain the requisite bleached appearance. A great number of women and children are employed in the work of clipping off the ends of the capsules containing the seeds, and they are sorted into sizes by a large revolving cylindrical separator. Another division of the business which is growing with the rapid development of the rubber industry in the island is that devoted to the preparation of this product for shipment. It is first sorted, then cleaned, and finally packed for export. Altogether some 300 to 400 coloured labourers, with two Europeans, are employed in the factory establishment, which is under the control of Mr. J. S. Collet.

Among the numerous agencies held by Whittall & Co. should be specially mentioned that of the well-known Orient-Pacific Royal Mail Line between London and Australia, owned conjointly by the Orient Steam Navigation Company, Ltd., and the Royal Mail Steam Packet Company. The steamers of this line, which maintain a fortnightly service between London and Australia, calling at Colombo, are the *Ormah* (twin-screw), 8,291 registered tonnage; *Ophir* (twin-screw), 6,910; *Orient*, 5,385; *Ormuz*, 6,387; *Ortona* (twin-screw), 7,945; *Oroya*, 6,297; *Oruba*, 5,887; *Orontes* (twin-screw), 9,000; and *Oratava*, 5,857. The firm is agent also for the Glen Line of steamers, for tea, coffee, and rubber estates, too numerous to specify, and for a number of leading insurance companies.

CARSON & CO.

One of the most important mercantile companies in Ceylon is that of Messrs. Carson & Co., and they have an enviable record of fifty years' standing, having been established in 1857. The house was founded by Mr. R. B. Carson, and is an illustration of the gradual development, under vigorous and efficient management, of a small business into one of large proportions. It is now one of the leading and most substantial business houses in Ceylon. The senior partner, Mr. Geo. J. Jameson, represents the firm's interests in London at Leadenhall House, E.C.; while the resident partners in Ceylon are Messrs. W. Shakspeare,

LAKE VIEW TEA STORES.

LAKE VIEW TEA STORES.
(Another view.)

LAKE VIEW TIMBER STORES.

E. R. Waldock, and H. C. Bibby. The offices are in the Australian Buildings, Colombo, and Messrs. E. J. Weatherall, Alfred Warden, J. W. Mitchell, A. Pelly Fry, and H. Tindall are the European assistants. The firm is intimately connected with shipping interests, being agents for the well-known Bibby Line, also for the Nippon Yusen Kaisha (Japan Mail Steamship Company). Both these lines of steamships are favourites with Ceylon shippers, owing to the regularity of their respective services, and they annually convey a very large proportion of the island's produce to the foreign marts. With all other branches of the island's trade the firm is also closely identified, it being one of the largest importers of Manchester piece-goods in the colony, and holding a very considerable tea-estate agency. Messrs. Carson & Co. are also importers of Welsh and Indian coal for supplying ocean-going steamships.

The firm's Lake View Stores are situated at Kew Lane, Slave Island, Colombo, where extensive packeting and blending of Ceylon tea is carried on for export to all parts of the world, and this business is under the supervision of two tea-experts. Here also is the depôt of Messrs. Millar's Karri and Jarrah Company's well-known Westralian hardwoods, for which Messrs. Carson & Co. are agents. Messrs. Carson & Co. are also agents for, besides several others, the three largest rubber companies in Ceylon, which together have a total of over 12,000 acres of plantations. Following are the principal shipping and mercantile agents and correspondents of the firm: Bibby Bros. & Co. (the Bibby Line), Liverpool; Nippon Yusen Kaisha (Japan Mail Steamship Company), Tokio; Ismay, Imrie & Co. (the White Star Line), Liverpool; the Cunard Line, Liverpool; Alexander Howden & Co., London; Arakan Company, Ltd., Rangoon; Macleod Company, Calcutta; Horrockses, Crewdson & Co., Ltd., Preston and Manchester; James Burton & Sons, Manchester; F. Steiner & Co., Ltd., Church, Lancashire; Beith, Stevenson and Co., Manchester; Alexander Drew & Sons, Manchester; Lomitz & Duxbury, Manchester. Messrs. Carson & Co. also hold the local agencies for the London Assurance Corporation; Fire, Life, and Marine, London; Phœnix Assurance Company, Ltd., London; Union Marine Insurance Company, Ltd., and Tokio Marine Insurance Company, Ltd., Tokio. They are, further, agents in Ceylon for Messrs. W. H. Tindall & Co., London; Rowe, White & Co., London; J. A. Bell & Co., London; General Ceylon Tea Estates, Ltd., London; Gona Adike Tea Company, Ltd., Manchester; the Kelani Tea Gardens Company, Ltd.; the Kandyan Hills Company, Ltd.; the Donnybrook Tea Company, Ltd.; Messrs. Millar's Karri and Jarrah Company; the Raneegunee Coal Association, Ltd., Calcutta; the Gourepore Company, Ltd., Calcutta; the Grand Central Rubber Company, Ltd.; the Durampitiya Rubber Company, Ltd.; the Hinwerelle Rubber Company, Ltd.; the Weyganga Rubber Company, Ltd.; and the Weniwella Rubber Company, Ltd.

COLOMBO COMMERCIAL COMPANY, LIMITED.

It was in 1876, the year following that during which the export of coffee from the island reached its greatest volume, that this company was founded, in London, with the purpose of acquiring estates in Ceylon for the production of the berry and carrying on the business of curing and exporting this product. On the decline of this then staple industry of the colony, in the succeeding years, owing to the spread of the coffee-leaf disease (*Hemileia vastatrix*), the Colombo Commercial Company, in common with the rest of the firms and corporations engaged in the planting business in Ceylon, found their salvation, in the nick of time, in the growth of tea for export. The phenomenal rise of the tea industry from the time, in the early "eighties," it assumed the premier place among the products of the island has been reflected in the growth of the company's business, which now ranks among the largest and most important, as well as most varied, in the colony. The company is not only concerned with the production of tea on its own estates, but, as the list given below shows, acts as agent for a number of other owners of tea estates in the colony, and also purchases largely for its export trade from the teas offered on the local market. In addition, the company holds agencies for shipping, insurance, and engineering firms and companies, and, besides, carries on a very large engineering business in manufacturing machinery for the complete equipment of tea factories, both on its own estates and on other properties. A speciality in the engineering branch is the manufacture of tea desiccators, rollers, and sifters; and large numbers of these machines are turned out, not only for use in the island, but also for export to the tea planters of India and Java. So great is the demand for the patent machinery manufactured by the company for treating the all-important leaf, that the workshops find difficulty in keeping pace with it, even by running overtime and although the engineering shops and plant have continually been largely increased.

The scene of the company's operations at Slave Island, about a mile and a half from the centre of the city, is a veritable hive of industry. Altogether the premises cover an area of some 13 acres; and even a casual tour through the series of large buildings in which the different branches of the business are carried on is sufficient to give an insight into the manner in which the premier productive industries of the colony are prosecuted, as well as a good idea of the wide scope, immense volume, and up-to-date methods of the company's business. The administrative offices are located on the ground floor of a palatial two-storeyed bungalow, one of the largest in Colombo, substantially built of cabook, and containing spacious and lofty apartments. Here a clerical staff of 50 persons is busily employed; while the upper storey is occupied by the manager as a residence. This building, known as "Adland House," was purchased from the Ceylon Company. It was originally the mess-house of the Ceylon Rifle Regiment, consisting of Malays, and since disbanded, and stands in the centre of park-like grounds, extending over seven acres.

As may be imagined from the number of important agencies held, the financial business of the company is very considerable, and requires highly skilled ability in the managerial department. The present manager, Mr. John G. Wardrop, has occupied his responsible position for thirty years past. Being also a member of the London board of directors, he spends six months of each year in England. The other members of the directorate are Mr. Alfred Brown, the chairman (son of Mr. John Brown, the founder of the company), and Messrs. P. C. Oswald and J. Alec Roberts. The latter gentleman also occupies the post of secretary, the head offices being at 5, Dowgate Hill, London. As indicating the prosperity of the company, it may be mentioned that the profits for the year ended September 30, 1905, as certified on the annual balance-sheet, returned a dividend of 6 per cent. on the preference capital of £18,185 (paid-up), and 8 per cent. on the ordinary capital of £70,000 (paid-up), while a substantial contribution was also made to the reserve fund.

In addition to the other lines of business in which the company is operating so successfully earnest attention is being given to the cultivation of the rubber-tree, and the treatment of the product which is (at time of writing) advancing by leaps and bounds to a foremost place among the staple products of Ceylon.

The mills and stores, with spacious yards intervening, which form the manufacturing division of the business, are situated on a block of land adjoining that on which the administrative building stands, and cover an area of six or seven acres. Of the mills, the engineering shop is the most important, and here may be seen, in process of construction, the various machines for the tea factories, also other work in iron; while in the adjoining carpentry shop huge balks of teak-wood, principally from Burma, are cut to required sizes in planks by

PREMISES OF THE COLOMBO COMMERCIAL COMPANY, LTD.—TEA PACKING, LOADING TEA, ERECTING YARD, AND ENGINEERING DEPARTMENT.

powerful steam-driven frame saws, and then worked up by hand. Besides manufacturing machinery for tea treatment, the engineering branch carries out important contracts for building and structural work. In this department the dredger for the lake was constructed for the Colombo Municipality, being the largest piece of work of the kind ever turned out in Ceylon by a private firm. Harbour barges and lighters have also been built by the company, the cast-iron in the rough being imported from Scotland. Structural works of this nature form a special feature of the business, and all the shops in the yard were built on the spot. In the carpentry shop woodwork of all descriptions for offices, bungalows, and other buildings is turned out, and among the large contracts carried out in the construction departments, the rebuilding of the Chartered Bank and the building of St. Paul's Church and the Wesley College, all three in Colombo, deserve special mention. The last is an extensive and highly finished edifice, the work on which occupied nine months. A brass foundry for small work is also included in this branch of the establishment. The driving power for the workshops is mainly derived from a Marshall's high-speed horizontal engine, of 150 horse-power, served by a Babcock's watertube boiler; while a smaller engine of 95 horse-power is ready for emergencies, and there are two spare boilers. A pneumatic plant is used for riveting, drilling, and caulking. Altogether some 350 to 400 hands are employed in the engineering and carpentry shops and yards, including seven Europeans in controlling positions, two of the latter being engaged in erecting machinery and fittings at the factories up country. The bulk of the men are Sinhalese machine men and Malabar coolies. Two cranes, respectively of 5-ton and 4-ton lifting capacity, are used in the yards for lifting the balks of teak, timber, and other heavy articles. The company also carries large stocks of machine parts, pulleys, shaftings, and all other engineering requisites for the factory.

Another important branch of the company's business is the tea-buying department, which occupies separate offices, situated in Queen Street, Fort, in the centre of the tea market. The business transacted in this department is quite distinct from that of the estates agency. Orders are received from Australasia, America, Africa, and various other quarters of the globe, and are filled from the teas which are put up for sale at the weekly public auctions in Colombo. Three expert tasters are engaged in this work. In many instances the teas are blended and repacked into lead packets, fancy tins and boxes, and only those who are familiar with the tea trade can appreciate the care and expert knowledge necessary in order to carry out this work satisfactorily. The volume of the trade controlled by the purchase department is now very considerable, and is steadily increasing.

Coming to the storage department, in one very long building will be found rows upon rows of tea chests piled high upon one another, ready packed for shipment to all parts of the world. The product is thus brought down by rail and boat from the estates inland where the leaf has been grown and prepared for consumption. Immense stocks of all requisites for tea packing, including momi-wood boxes from Japan, and the more lightly constructed Venesta boxes from Russia, jute and lead lining, are also stored in different buildings on the premises. A large business is done in supplying artificial manures to the planters. In a fully equipped laboratory, occupying a part of the premises which in earlier days was the site of the barbecues for coffee, the various fertilisers are tested for their suitableness for the different classes of up-country soil. Castor poonac, ground-nut cake and rape cake from Southern India, the refuse after the extraction of the different oils, form the bases of the manures. Special manures are also imported from Europe, and guano and nitrate of soda from the west coast of South America. The refuse cakes from India are crushed small by huge revolving wheels in large mortars on the premises. The stuff is then bagged and stored ready for despatch. About 60 coolies are employed in the storage departments, while the extensive transport business of the company necessitates the employment of some 35 carters and 30 pairs of bulls.

On adjoining premises the Colombo Lead Mills roll imported pig-lead into sheets, from which the linings of the tea chests are cut. This business is worked by some 70 Sinhalese machine men and 30 to 50 Indian coolies, under two European superintendents. A branch office is maintained in Queen Street, Fort, for shipping and tea valuing purposes.

The following are the principal members of the staff: Manager, Mr. John G. Wardrop; sub-manager, Mr. A. A. Prideaux; assistants, Messrs. C. E. Stevenson, J. W. R. Still, M. J. Cary, G. R. Marnoch, Wm. Simmons, and G. A. Rettie; accountant, Mr. A. Young, C.A.; analyst, Mr. J. O. Ferrier, F.C.S.; tea department, Messrs. F. N. Mackie, O. M. Ash, and J. W. Cock; engineering department, Messrs. H. J. W. Oxlade, J. G. Benzie, C. P. Hall, D. W. Waddell, R. F. Browne, H. A. Dixon, and G. W. Johnson, C.E.; agent at Bandarawella, Mr. C. J. Donald; visiting agent, Mr. Joseph Fraser (reckoned the first authority on manuring in Ceylon).

WEBSTER AUTOMATIC PACKETING FACTORY, CO-OPERATIVE TEA GADRENS COMPANY, and MARAVILLA CEYLON TEA COMPANY.

The origin of this extensive tea-growing and shipping business, or combination of businesses, is traceable to the fact that the proprietor, Mr. Roland Valentine Webster, sent in his resignation as superintendent of the Opagalla and Nargalla Tea Estates on April 1, 1889, and, with a capital of only £50, started business under the name of the Co-operative Tea Gardens Company. Having appointed a local firm as agent for his new venture, Mr. Webster sailed for Africa, and there planted the first seeds of his new enterprise, which grew by leaps and bounds until the Co-operative Tea Gardens Company became known not only in Africa, but even in remote corners of the globe. The now famous "Bee" brand of teas were the first thus introduced to the world, followed by the Ugalla, Voonia, Temple, Wigwam, Rajah, Tusker, Queen Bee, Jaya, and Quaker brands, the different qualities being obtained by careful expert blending of various Ceylon teas. In 1894 Mr. Webster purchased the Maravilla, Ancoombra, Ugalla, and Jaya tea estates, starting at the same time a second business under the title of the Maravilla Ceylon Tea Company. The shipments during the first twelve months of the new venture totalled only 60,000 lbs., as at that time Ceylon teas were little known outside Great Britain, and it was only with the greatest difficulty Home firms could be persuaded to take small experimental shipments. By perseverance and judicious advertising, however, the exports of the various brands enumerated above soon ran into millions of pounds weight. In 1898, having completed his twelfth tour round the world, and having arrived in Cairo from Turkey in Asia, Mr. Webster took his first holiday, and, being asked to organise the civil transport from Cairo to Berber, joined the Sudan Expedition under Lord Kitchener —then Sirdar Sir Herbert Kitchener. Mr. Webster was present at the Battle of Atbara, where he acted as assistant to the officer commanding the Army Service Corps, and also as special war correspondent for the London *Morning Post*, receiving the Sudan medal and clasp, British-Egyptian medal, and Royal Humane bronze medal. In 1900 Mr. Webster was in Paris, where he acted as Assistant Tea Commissioner at the Paris Exposition of that year. At the close of the Exposition Mr. Webster formed the Ceylon Tea Pavilion, Ltd., and Tea Planters, Ltd., with the object of developing the sale of Ceylon teas on the Continent, more especially packet teas exported by the Co-operative Tea Gardens Company

WEBSTER AUTOMATIC PACKETING FACTORY—MAIN BUILDING, MACHINE-ROOM, WEBSTER'S PATENT PACKER, PACKETING-ROOM, OFFICE, AND CARPENTERS' SHED.

and the Maravilla Ceylon Tea Company—the businesses of his own creation.

In 1901 Mr. Webster started for the Boer War in South Africa as special war correspondent for the London *Daily Express*; but shortly after his arrival on the field he accepted a commission as lieutenant in the Cape mounted troops. Two months later Lieutenant Webster went to Pretoria as Organising Secretary to the Transvaal Land Settlement Board; and within three months he was appointed Financial Adviser for this Board, under Lord Milner. In January, 1902, Lieutenant Webster was promoted to a captaincy and given command of General Barton's scouts, the duties of which position he performed in addition to his civil duties on the Land Settlement Board. In September, 1902, Captain Webster was invalided to England on board the transport *Avoca*, as the result of his attempt to save life during a hurricane at Port Elizabeth, for which act of bravery he was awarded the Queen's medal and five clasps, also the Royal Humane Society's silver medal. When convalescent, he was transferred to the City of London (Rough Riders) Imperial Yeomanry, with the rank of captain.

In January, 1905, finding his business growing to very large dimensions, and having decided to build a tea-factory in Colombo on the latest improved American labour-saving lines, Captain Webster sailed for Ceylon in the *Ophir*, arriving in Colombo on February 6th. Within twenty-four hours of his arrival, and before any one had the least idea of his intention, he had purchased a valuable piece of ground known as the Staples property, situated within a mile of the landing jetty at Colombo, and in the midst of the largest tea warehouses of Ceylon. Without disturbing the historical bungalow and garden on the site, Captain Webster laid out the ground plan for what is now among the first and largest tea-factories in the East, if not in the world. Two months later contractors in Colombo were flashing cables to England for the massive steel columns and girders required for the building, to Germany for the corrugated iron, to America for machinery, and to Burma for teak joists and flooring. Nine months later the Webster Automatic Packeting Factory was complete, and hundreds of busy hands were employed there executing orders for tea from various parts of the world.

The main building of the factory, in which tea only is treated, is 390 ft. long and four storeys high; while running at right angles is a second building, 200 ft. long, where the boxes for holding the packets are made. At the further end are the coffee department, the rubber department, and the spice department. The box-making department is equipped with a 30-horse-power gas engine, circular saws, panel-plaining machines, dovetailing machines, and other apparatus. On the ground floor of the main building is the engine-room, which is equipped with a 20-horse-power gas-engine (fed by a suction gas-generating plant), a dynamo, switch-board, and fitters' bench. Adjoining is the electric-storage room, containing cells capable of storing 30 electrical horse-power; also a lift, capable of raising 2 tons, and numerous automatic weighing and packeting machines, including Davidson's bulk packer. On the second floor are the store-rooms and the office, fitted with a tea-tasters' counter 60 ft. long, electric fans, and all the most modern improvements. The third floor contains one of Bartlett & Sons' largest tea bulkers; also tea-cutters, sifters, green tea polishing machines, and a full-size down-draft sirocco. The top floor, especially arranged for storing tea, at times contains over 1,000,000 lbs. of the leaf. Some idea of the capital required to run this gigantic concern may be gathered from a glance through the store-rooms, in which are a reserve stock of labels amounting to over 30,000,000 in number, decorated tins numbering 1,000,000, lead to the extent of 200 tons, paper and tin-foil for packing weighing 100 tons, besides hoop-iron, nails, and advertising matter; and timber to the extent of some 200,000 ft. is stacked in the surrounding compound. This great factory in Colombo, together with the gardens up-country yielding tea, coffee, spices, cocoa, and rubber (the latter planted on 900 acres), and in addition to considerable interests in Europe, represent the result of Mr. Webster's efforts since he started in the tea business on his own account eighteen years ago, with a capital of only £50.

ALFRED CHARLES CRAMER.
(Manager.)

The Webster Automatic Packeting Factory, Colombo, act as estate agents as well as buyers, packers, and exporters of tea; and they also effect insurances at special rates. Mr. O. C. Cramer is the superintendent of the business, with Mr. P. J. Farrin as assistant-superintendent, both of whom are expert tea-tasters, having served for many years with the English and Scottish Wholesale Co-operative Societies, Ltd., of London.

Correspondence is maintained by the firm with business houses in all parts of the world which are either already engaged in trade with Ceylon or are seeking commercial intercourse with the island, particularly in connection with its principal product, namely, tea.

BOSANQUET & CO.

The well-known house of Bosanquet & Co., merchants, estate and general commission agents, was founded in Colombo in 1879, at which time it took over the business of the famous old firm of George Wall & Co., in their day the largest agency house in the island. Messrs. Bosanquet & Co. are exporters of tea, cocoa, coffee, cardamoms, and other lines of Ceylon produce, and are largely interested in the import of cotton piece-goods of all descriptions, while as sole agents for Nobel's Explosives Company, Ltd., they control the main share of the dynamite trade in Ceylon, besides holding other valuable connections. They are also agents in Ceylon for the Australian Timber Export Company, Ltd., of Sydney. The firm consists of Messrs. R. A. Bosanquet, Gilbert F. Traill, H. W. Unwin, and D. W. Watson. At their extensive "Blomendahl" Mills, comprising a ground area of over 14 acres and located in Mutwal, the northern suburb of Colombo, a room 300 ft. long is devoted to turning out tea in packets for all parts of the world; and in their capacity of estate agents, as well as merchants, the firm deals with over ten million pounds weight of tea on their premises annually, exclusive of other produce. At this establishment, also, cocoa is prepared for the market, and cardamoms are bleached, cured, and sorted by experienced hands, though these processes are necessarily of minor importance compared with the handling of the staple—tea. The aggregate area of the estates for which Bosanquet & Co. are agents amounts to 33,445 acres, comprising many of the finest tea properties in the island; and the visiting agents are the Hon. Mr. Edward Rosling, M.L.C., and Mr. W. D. Bosanquet.

The head office of the business is at 17, Chatham Street, Colombo, and the office staff consists of five Europeans, together with 30 clerks and assistants, while a large number of labourers are constantly employed at the mills. The London house of the business is Messrs.

MESSRS. BOSANQUET & CO.'S GENERAL OFFICE, DYNAMITE MAGAZINE, AND GENERAL VIEWS.

R. A. Bosanquet & Co., of 2, Fenchurch Avenue, E.C., and the firm have, in addition, correspondents in all parts of the world.

AITKEN, SPENCE & CO.

This firm of general merchants, exporters, importers, agents for shipping companies and representatives for various other concerns—notably Lloyd's—was founded early in 1870. The general executive offices are situated in Prince Street, in the Fort of Colombo; and branch houses and connected establishments are maintained at Galle, under the style of Clark, Spence & Co., and in London in the name of Spence, Wallis & Co., while the New York agents of the house are Messrs. Chevalier Bros. The partners of the firm are Messrs. E. Aitken, P. G. Spence, A. S. Berwick, and A. P. Waldock; while the principal European assistants are Messrs. C. S. Burns, R. Fowke, B. F. H. Armitage, H. S. Jeaffreson, and W. E. M. Paterson. This firm are the largest plumbago exporters in Ceylon, shipments of the mineral being made regularly to almost every part of the world. The house is in the front rank of European mercantile enterprises of Ceylon.

J. M. ROBERTSON & CO.

This, one of the leading businesses of the colony, was founded in 1845 by the great house of Baring Brothers, London, and originally embarked in the business of coffee cultivation, the mainstay of Ceylon agriculture from 1840 to 1880. The first partners were Messrs. J. M. Robertson and George Christian. On the retirement of these two gentlemen, Mr. J. T. White assumed the control of the business, he being later joined in partnership by Mr. H. Bois, father of Messrs. H. G. and Herbert Bois. Thus the family which now owns the business was brought into connection with it, the partners being Messrs. Henry Bois, F. W. Bois, H. G. Bois, and Herbert Bois.

Ever since its foundation the firm has been identified with the principal industries of the colony. With the decline in the production of coffee, the firm embraced dealings in tea, cocoa, and rubber in its sphere of operations; and the principal business at the present day is the management and superintendence, on behalf of owners who are absent in England and elsewhere, of estates in the island on which these three latter products are cultivated. All kinds of requisites for tea estates are also imported by this house. The business of tea-packing is not carried on to any large extent by the firm; but cocoa is prepared for shipment, the useless beans being picked out by hand and the rest of the product re-dried. In handling rubber the firm expect that the Sinhalese, although useless for tea cultivation, will prove expert, and extensive developments in this new and important line of planting business, promising to give employment on an extensive scale for native labour, are being projected.

Another branch of the business is the importation of teak wood in logs from Siam, for building purposes. The firm also acts as agents for Baring Bros. & Co., Ltd., the Caledonian Tea Estates, Ltd., Herries, Farquhar & Co., Glyn Mills, Currie & Co., London; P. J. Landry; the Hague United States Mortgage and Trust Company, New York; Hope & Co., Amsterdam; Lanka Plantations Company, Ltd., Pundaluoya Tea Company of Ceylon, Ltd., the Bogawantalaga District Tea Company, Ltd., New Dimbula Company, Ltd., Templestone Estate Company, Ltd., Wm. McEwan & Co., Ltd., Fountain Brewery, Edinburgh; Sun Insurance Office, North British and Mercantile Insurance Company (in which is now merged the Universal Life Assurance Society), China Mutual Steam Navigation Company, Ltd., the Eila Tea Company of Ceylon, Ltd., Great Western Tea Company, Ltd., Uvakelle Tea Company of Ceylon, Ltd., Doomoo Tea Company of Ceylon, Ltd., Kotmallie Valley Company, Ltd., Galkandewatte Tea Company, Ltd., Monerakella Estates Company, Ltd., and Lunugalla Tea and Rubber Company, Ltd.

Appropriately, in view of the old standing of the firm, the business premises (No. 6, Prince Street, Fort) comprise one of the oldest buildings in Colombo. The accompanying illustration gives a view of this interesting relic and reminder of bygone days and other rulership. Although the title-deeds of this property only date from 1805, it is established that the house was in the occupation of the Burgomaster a good many years previous to that time.

AN OLD COLOMBO BUILDING.

WALKER, SONS & CO., LTD.

In essaying to give a comprehensive description of the business of this prominent Ceylon firm, of Colombo and Kandy, it is difficult to decide with which branch of the subject a start should be made—so numerous and varied are the operations of Walker, Sons & Co. in engineering, contracting, and general commercial directions. More than half a century has elapsed since this now extensive business was founded in Ceylon by John Walker, a native of Perthshire, Scotland, who came to the island in 1842. An engineer and inventor of superior attainment, he commenced business in 1854 as a manufacturer of coffee-treating machinery at Kandy, a main centre of the then staple industry. To John Walker and to his brother William, who joined him in partnership in 1862, the planting industry of the colony owes a deep debt of gratitude, for to their efforts much of the prosperity it has enjoyed, and is enjoying, is due. To keep pace with the rapid extension of coffee planting in the fat year of 1870, Messrs. Walker opened branches in Badulla and Haldummulla, and subsequently, in 1873, at Dikoya and Dimbula; and when Colombo began to attain supreme importance as the sea-gate and capital of the island, the brothers decided to remove their headquarters from Kandy to the port city. In 1880 the transfer was effected, and premises were acquired in a central position. From these beginnings the business of the house has expanded with the industrial development of the colony, and despite the temporary but severe check caused by the collapse in coffee production, to its present enormous dimensions. When the business was started in Kandy, the total number of employees did not exceed 50. To-day, besides a staff of 35 Europeans, no less than 1,300 Eurasians and natives are employed in the different departments at Colombo and Kandy, the other up-country branches having been separated from the parent house.

In 1891 the firm was converted into a limited liability company, under the title of Walker, Sons & Co.; and with the continuous growth of the business, additional area has been repeatedly acquired, on which new buildings have been from time to time erected. The general offices, engineering works, and retail store in the Fort section of Colombo occupy a large extent of ground, of which the machinery department alone covers two acres. Being fully equipped with the latest and most approved machinery, the engineering shop is equal to dealing with work of the heaviest type. Two massive steam-hammers and other iron-working plant—including lathes, drilling, and planing machines, and all the ingenious apparatus for cutting, turning, and shaping iron—are located on the ground floor; while the upper storey comprises large showrooms, where various types of tea, coffee, and fibre machines, steam and oil engines of different patterns, turbines and other machinery are on exhibition. The well-found draughtsmen's office adjoins the showroom; while the foundry, saw-mills, and carpenter's shop occupy a site on the Reclamation Ground, about a quarter of a mile away. In the retail store, housed in a handsome three-storeyed building recently erected on the west end of the main block at Colombo, are displayed large stocks of furniture, tools, arms, and ammunition, and general ironmongery for up-country estates, as well as the household; and adjoining is a building entirely devoted to the exhibition of motor-cars of different makes, a branch for the supply of these vehicles, as well as all motoring accessories, having been established to meet the growing demand in the island. Bicycles of every description are also on view. Conspicuous among the various types are the famous "Rover" and the "Serendib," the latter being manufactured on the premises. Walker, Sons & Co. have been appointed suppliers to the Automobile Club of Ceylon, which already numbers 200 members; and to cope with the growing requirements in this department of the business a commodious garage has been provided in the main establishment, as well as supplementary accommodation of the same kind at the company's large store in Darley Road. A special product of the engineering shop is the pneumatic rickshaw manufactured by the company, the principal feature of which is the adaptation of bicycle-wheels to the ordinary carriage body, for which conception Mr. Gnapp, the engineer in charge of the motor department, holds patents in Ceylon and other colonies.

At the foundry, castings up to 10 tons weight are turned out; and the carpenter's shop and sawmills are equipped with up-to-date machinery capable of executing any class of woodwork, including the manufacture of highly finished furniture. In the adjoining timber yard, large stocks of teak, pine, Johore, and other timbers are maintained. On the premises at the Reclamation Ground also salvage pumps are always in immediate readiness to meet any cases of accident and damage to vessels, and a slip for taking up small craft is located here; while the marine department of the engineering branch is always prepared to despatch a staff of skilled hands to cope with any emergency work in connection with repairs to ships. In this line of work the company has carried out most important operations, including some of the heaviest repairs executed in the East, with the most complete success. Launches for the harbour and lakes are also built in the engineering shops; and all machinery used in connection with the tea industry, together with factories ready for erection, is turned out here and kept in stock; also coffee pulpers, peelers, and sifters, either for home use or export to India, America, Java, Africa, or other parts of the world.

An important and growing department of the business is the building branch. Besides erecting their own stores and workshops, the company have put up some of the largest and most important edifices in Colombo, among them the handsome and colossal Galle Face Hotel, the Australia Buildings, the Fort Land Arcade, the National Bank of India, the Bristol Hotel, and Cargills' Emporium. The Kandy branch of the company consists of fully equipped workshops and a retail store on the same lines as the warehouse at Colombo, but on a smaller scale. The general management of all the Ceylon business is centred in the hands of Mr. E. J. Hayward, at the head office in Colombo, Mr. D. K. Michie controlling the engineering department and Mr. Hunter the retail store in the capital; while at the Kandy branch, Mr. W. A. Goodman is in charge of the engineering business and Mr. R. Wilson of the retail stores. The registered office of the company is at 36, Basinghall Street, London, where Mr. Frank Walker, the chairman, controls the affairs of the corporation. Among the fifty important businesses for which the firm act as agents, the following may be specified: Marshall, Sons & Co., Ltd., William Jackson, Campbell Oil Engine Company, North British and Mercantile Insurance Company, Equitable Life Assurance Society of the United States of America, and "Locomobile" Company.

The company are also agents for the Ceylon Steamship Company, which was founded in 1889 to furnish an up-to-date service of steamers round the island. The round trip is performed in eight or nine days, and the vessels maintained are continually travelling—one in each direction—calling *en route* at all the ports of the island.

LEECHMAN & CO.

This firm was established in the year 1866 by Mr. George Barclay Leechman, who was subsequently joined in partnership by Mr. Christopher Anderson Leechman; and it has since been continuously engaged in business in connection with estates, as proprietors or agents, and in buying and exporting tea and other articles—the produce of the island and of the adjacent coast of South India—to England and to the Continent of Europe, as well as to Australian and American ports. On the failure of coffee, owing to the leaf disease, the firm were among the pioneers who introduced cinchona cultivation and the cultivation of tea. Similarly, they are now among the first to interest themselves in rubber both in Ceylon and in the Federated Malay States. Mr. C. A. Leechman retired in 1898, since which time Mr. Robert Farquhar Spottiswood Hardie has joined the firm, being still a partner. The firm are agents for the Carolina Tea Company of Ceylon, Ltd. the Nuwara Eliya Tea Estates Company, Ltd., and other estates privately owned; also for the Norwich Union Fire Insurance Society, the New Zealand Insurance Company, Ltd., the London and Lancashire Life Assurance Company, the Batavia Sea and Fire Insurance Company, the Norwich and London Accident Insurance Association, and the Beverlac (Selangor) Rubber Company, Ltd. Their principal correspondents and friends in London are Messrs. Frith, Sands & Co. and Messrs. Grindlay & Co.

The firm of G. & W. Leechman was likewise formed in 1866 by Mr. George Barclay Leech-

PREMISES OF WALKER, SONS & CO., LTD., SHOWING MOTOR DEPÔT, FOUNDRY, AND TIMBER YARD, EXTERIOR, CYCLE DEPÔT, AND ENGINEERING SHOP.

man and Mr. William Carey Leechman, to lease and work the Hultsdorf (Coconut Oil) Mills in Colombo, which business they carried on for about twenty years. Since 1888 Messrs. Leechman have been the agents of the Colombo (Coconut) Oil Mills Company, Colombo. Mr. W. C. Leechman retired from the firm of G. & W. Leechman at the end of 1899. The two firms have their offices together at 13, Queen Street, Fort, Colombo, and their principal European assistants are Mr. W. A. Jones, Mr. G. A. Ginn, and Mr. Barclay Leechman.

MESSRS. LIPTON & CO., LTD.

Familiar as a household word in the United Kingdom, the name of Lipton in Ceylon enjoys a distinction of another kind. In the island the firm is very little of a retailer, and very much a producer and exporter. It is the proprietor of great estates, the grower of vast quantities of tèa, and the operator in produce on an extensive scale. The thousands of passengers who drop in at Colombo *en route* for the Far East or Australia catch a fleeting impression of the importance of the company's business as they saunter through the Fort and note the extensive premises in Prince Street which constitute the Colombo headquarters of the firm. If curiosity prompts them to enter the building they find it a great hive of industry, in which a considerable staff is engaged in the preliminary operations associated with the provision for the home market of the supplies of Ceylon tea, which perhaps more than any other article has contributed to the remarkable success of the great business of which Sir Thomas Lipton is the head. But it is, of course, in the interior—far removed from the eye of the globe-trotter or the casual visitor—that the real strength of the firm centres. A good many years have now elapsed since Sir Thomas Lipton, with that business prescience which is his most distinguishing trait, gave practical force in Ceylon to the principle upon which the firm's tea business is conducted of furnishing the consumer with the leaf direct from the estate, and one property has been added to another until the company possesses a very considerable area of tea land. This land is of the best, and that is tantamount to saying that it is situated at a high elevation, for the most part removed from the beaten track of tourists. The company's principal estates are in the Haputale district, in the province of Uva—a glorious upland country with a dry, invigorating air, which is not only peculiarly health-giving, but is exceptionally favourable for the production of tea of the highest quality. Here is situated the famous Dambatenne group of estates, which contribute so largely to the company's supply of tea. The group consists of Dambatenne, Maha Dambatenne, Bandara Eliya, and Sunny Peak. It has a total acreage of 1,099, and of this 944 acres are under tea. Another and even more extensive property in Haputale is the Monarakande group, including Leymastotte, Nahakettia, and Upper Lyegrove. This group has an acreage of 2,101, and of that area 1,389½ acres are under tea. Also in the Haputale district are Messrs. Lipton's Keenapitiya estate, with a total acreage of 187, of which 145 acres are under tea, and the Oakfield

PLUCKING TEA ON LIPTON'S MAHA DAMBATENNE ESTATE.

DESPATCHING TEA FROM THE FACTORY ON THE ESTATE. BULLOCK CARTS ON THE ESTATE.
COOLIES MUSTERING FOR MORNING WORK ON LIPTON'S DAMBATENNE ESTATE.

LOADING TEA INTO CARTS AT LIPTON'S LEYMASTOTTE FACTORY, HAPUTALE.

estate, with an area of 452 acres, 242 of which are under tea. Other estates owned by the firm are the Pooprassie group in Pussellawa, with an acreage of 1,365, of which 866 acres are under tea; the Karandagalla estate in Dumbara (160 acres); and the Panilkanda estate, in the Morawak Korale, with an area of 852 acres, of which 663 acres are under tea. All the estates are under the supervision of experienced planters, and the cultivation is conducted on the most approved scientific principles. It follows that the equipment is of the most up-to-date description. At Dambatenne the bulk of the tea land is on the upper slopes of lofty hills, upon which there is no room for buildings. The difficulty of preparing the tea on the spot has been overcome by the provision of an aërial tramway, which transmits the produce as gathered from the gardens to the factory in the valley below. The baskets, as filled, are put upon the wire, and whizz through space until they are brought to a standstill at the factory building, which is situated 2,000 ft. below. On arrival the tea is subjected to the usual drying and other processes, and, when duly prepared, is packed in wooden cases for shipment. In the transport of the produce from the estate a large number of the bullock carts which are a characteristic feature of the Ceylon roads are employed. The labour force on the Lipton estates, as on other similar properties, is mainly composed of Tamil coolies. They are comfortably housed upon the estates, and their medical and other needs are attended to under arrangements carefully devised with a view to the preservation of health. A happy and contented body they for the most part are. Many of the pickers are women and children, and a very picturesque sight is presented by the tea gardens in early morning when work is in full swing. The coolie muster at commencement and close of the day's labours is an indispensable part of the routine of an estate. In one of the accompanying illustrations we have a representation of a muster on the Dambatenne estate, and the reader may obtain from this a very fair idea of the appearance of the body of industrious labourers who perform the initial operation in the preparation of the leaf for the market.

Lipton's teas have carried the name and fame of Ceylon into the remotest villages of the three kingdoms and to the furthest corners of the Empire. It is a moot question, indeed, whether it is not the splendid advertisement Messrs. Lipton have given the Ceylon leaf that is mainly responsible for the present flourishing condition of the trade. However that may be, it is certain that no other undertaking has more popularised Ceylon tea or has won for it a higher reputation in the world's markets.

REUTER'S TELEGRAM COMPANY, LTD.

The ramifications of the wonderful system of telegraphic intercommunication instituted by Baron de Reuter, and by means of which all parts of the world are brought within speaking distance of one another, of necessity embrace so important a ganglionic centre of Eastern commerce and travel as Colombo. At this port large steamers as well as smaller craft call on their way East and West, North and South ; and the movements of all the more important vessels are flashed over the earth in several directions. Some forty years ago a branch of Reuter's famous telegraphic agency was established in Galle, on the southern coast, then the principal port of Ceylon. On the removal of this outpost of the business to Colombo, some ten years ago, the material progress being made by the colony was naturally reflected in a large increase in the volume of messages received and despatched over the far-reaching wires converging at this centre ; and the business has grown, until at the present time the number of cable messages handled in the Colombo office of Reuter's Telegram Company, situated in the Victoria Arcade, amounts to the enormous figure of 50,000 annually, while the company's cablegraphic code for the use of the public embraces no less than a quarter of a million words.

The present manager of the Colombo branch is Mr. Percy A. Griffiths, who came from the London headquarters on his appointment to this post six years ago, after serving a short term of six months in the Calcutta office of the company ; and the staff under Mr. Griffiths' control consists of ten hands. Besides supplying all the Ceylon newspapers with the cablegrams which form generally the most attractive feature of the daily print, and in connection with which information the name of Reuter is deservedly celebrated all over the world, the company carries on an extensive business in the remittance of money to any part of the globe at specially low rates, thus providing a much-appreciated convenience for the travelling public and the commercial community generally. Their system of registered addresses for the use of the public, whereby many pounds per annum may be saved in the cost of cablegrams, is also a boon of which those for whose benefit it has been instituted are not slow to avail themselves. Any two addresses may be registered free of charge, thus establishing a means of intercommunication at reduced rates between cable correspondents. Yet another advantage in lessening the cost of messages is provided by the company's method of issuing passenger tickets, by means of which persons travelling homewards may announce by cable their safe arrival at their destination.

The company includes in its scope of operations the agency for all Home and colonial newspapers for the advertisement branch ; also the local agency for the Oriental Bank of New York for the remittance branch of the business.

THE KRAWEHL COAL COMPANY, LTD.

(The Ceylon Branch of Wills & Co., Ltd.)

This important company was founded in Liverpool in the early sixties, and a depôt was established in Egypt in 1865, a considerable while before the opening of the Suez Canal. The head office is still in the great Lancastrian seaport, while the London offices are at 50 and 51, Lime Street, E.C. A local branch was formed in Colombo in the year 1889, and the Ceylon offices are located in the Victoria Arcade, where Mr. A. Redemann, conjointly with Mr. W. F. Diacono, directs the operations of the firm, the two alternately controlling the business, each during the other's absence from the island. The principal line of business done is in the import of Cardiff steam coal in large quantities for the purpose of bunkering ships calling at Colombo, and the firm has standing contracts with the Norddeutscher-Lloyd, the Hamburg-Amerika, the East Asiatic Company of Copenhagen, the Austrian-Lloyd, and other steamship companies for the supply of coal to all vessels of these respective lines touching at the port. They are also contractors to the Governments of France and Italy for supplying coal to the warships of these two nations. The firm employ some 300 hands in the coaling department of their business, and have a storage capacity in their coal-yards for over 60,000 tons. The firm also contract for lightering work, maintaining, for this purpose, two steam tugs and other small craft of their own. In addition to their other duties, Messrs. Redemann and Diacono represent the Belgian Government as Consuls for Ceylon.

The firm also publish the well-known journal *Out and Home*, which has a large circulation throughout the East, and gives detailed information of great importance to the mercantile, shipping, and commercial world. Distributed daily on the Suez Canal and in monthly form throughout Egypt and the ports of the East, as far as Japan, and including the vast field of Australasia, the *Out and Home* has a wide scope, which makes it a valuable medium for the dissemination of commercial and general intelligence. The matter published is well selected with a view to the requirements of traders and the travelling public, and is presented in crisp paragraphs written in eminently readable style.

The important department of the business, however, is comprised in the Ceylon agency for the great house of Wills & Co., Ltd., of Liverpool and London, which supplies Australian frozen meat and other colonial produce, besides travelling outfits and requisites of all kinds, and has extensive refrigerating stores at Port Said, Gibraltar, and Malta, also coaling depôts at Port Said and Suez.

CROSFIELD, LAMPARD & CO.

A century has elapsed since this mercantile house was founded in Liverpool, England, by Daniel Harrison, whose youngest son, Charles, is one of the present partners, and has been connected with the firm for over fifty years. The founder was subsequently joined in partnership by Messrs. Joseph Crosfield and Smith Harrison ; and two sons of the former of these two gentlemen, namely, Mr. J. B. Crosfield and Mr. G. T. Crosfield, are also included in the firm as at present constituted. Messrs. Charles Heath Clark and C. A. Lampard joined the house fifteen years ago. In 1840 the headquarters of the business were removed to London, and a few years later the present premises in that city, at 3, Tower Street, E.C., were built. The London branch trades under the style of Harrisons & Crosfield, while the branch at Calcutta is Lampard, Clark & Co., and those at New York, Montreal, and Chicago are entitled Crosfield, Lampard, Clark & Co. During the present year (1906) the firm has opened a branch in the Straits Settlements, where it holds large interests in rubber estates. The Ceylon business was established twelve years ago ; and Mr. George Croll, who became a member of the firm in 1903, is the managing partner, the offices being at 21, Baillie Street, Colombo. The tea and other products dealt in are treated and warehoused at the firm's Victoria Mills, Hyde Park Corner, Colombo. The principal department of the business is the export of tea, and the firm has agencies all over the world in connection with the supply of this staple article of consumption. Rubber and other products of the Malay States, India, and Ceylon are also exported to different parts of the globe.

The Victoria Mills consist of four main buildings, the premises occupying a spacious site of eight acres, surrounded by a wall. This was formerly the scene of coffee treatment, and the old barbecues are still to be seen. The establishment is a large one, some 200 to 300 coolies being employed, the number varying according to the press of work. But the machinery is always in full operation. In one of the two principal buildings the black tea is treated and stored, in the other the green variety. On these premises there is also a branch office with a staff of Burgher clerks, the whole establishment being in the charge of two Europeans. Large consignments of the well-known "Nectar" blend of tea, both in bulk form and in packets, are shipped by the firm. On the upper floor of the black-tea warehouse at the mills the packeting is performed, in which class of operations numbers of women and boys are employed, besides the men engaged in the heavier work. The packets of this company are hermetically sealed, so as to prevent admission of air or moisture to the contents.

The principal machinery is installed on the upper floor of the green-tea warehouse, this variety of leaf requiring more treatment than black kinds. As they come to the mills in the unfinished state the different kinds of green teas are sorted into sizes, and undergo a finishing process before being put up separately for the market. Besides the mechanical screens, hand-sifters of various meshes are in use in this department; and if special small sizes of tea are required, the leaf is cut accordingly by machinery. The whole of the machinery in this factory is driven by a Robey engine of 15 horse-power, which has, on occasions, worked continuously night and day for three months without failing. In this way the different kinds of gunpowders, hysons, and other green teas are differentiated for the market, in classes varying from coarse to very fine, from the leaves plucked from the same bush, the size of the leaf being the determining factor. In a small room on the floor of the factory the various kinds are tasted before being blended; and here all the variations in form, size, and colour of the treated article are open for inspection, the pale yellow appearance of the green tea in the cup being conspicuous. A feature of the factory is a hydraulic machine, from Middleton & Co., for compressing the tea into brick form for the Russian market. This machine is driven by a Marshall horizontal engine of superior type.

In one of the two one-storeyed buildings on the premises is the carpentry shop, where the various tea boxes are fitted together from the different kinds of woods used; and here the resiliency of the three-ply Venesta tops and sides may be tested. In an adjoining department the lead-foil cases for the packets are made up by the aid of a hot iron applied with great manual dexterity. The other one-storeyed building is used as a general store; while in the cartage department fifteen bulls are maintained. Crosfield, Lampard & Co. are agents for the Manchester Assurance Company, the Commercial Union Assurance Company (Marine Department), the English and Scottish Co-operative Wholesale Societies, and the Bambrakelly Tea Estates of Ceylon, Ltd., in addition to their branch houses mentioned above.

CLARK, YOUNG & CO.

This firm was established in Ceylon in 1894 by Messrs. T. S. Clark, S. D. Young, and E. S. Clark, who continue to be the present partners of the business. The importation of coal from Bengal and Cardiff, for bunkering purposes, is the principal line of the business, and the firm usually carries a stock of about 15,000 tons of this fuel, which is stored at their coal-grounds at Kochchikade Island, Colombo. These grounds cover an area of nearly one and a half acres, and here some 300 coolies, under European supervision, are busily engaged in storing and shipping coal for steamers' bunkers. The firm is staffed by five Europeans,

CLARK, YOUNG & CO.'S COAL WHARVES. PLUMBAGO YARDS.
THE STORES.

CROSFIELD, LAMPARD & CO.'S ESTABLISHMENT.

GENERAL VIEW OF VICTORIA MILLS. BLACK TEA FACTORY, VICTORIA MILLS.

TEA TASTING ROOM. PACKING STORE, INTERIOR.

who conduct the business in the city offices at 15, Baillie Street, in the Fort of Colombo, where a staff of twenty assistants is maintained. The managing partner at present is Mr. Young, who came out to Ceylon in 1879, after an experience of six years in Burma; and the business, under his direction, has grown considerably. Among the large number of well-known businesses for which the firm acts as agent are the Bengal Coal Company, Ltd., and the Colombo Coaling Company, besides life, fire, marine and accident insurance companies. The business operations of the firm also embrace the export of plumbago, tea, citronella oil, oyster and tortoise shells, while the chief article of import is teak logs for building purposes. The oyster-shells are exported mainly to Hamburg, where they are manufactured into the well-known mother-o'-pearl buttons, and a considerable business is done in this line. The manufacture of citronella oil, in which the firm deals largely, is carried on at Galle, where the oil is extracted from the citronella grass, distilled, and bought by the firm in bulk, being subsequently filtered and packed in drums and cases for shipment to, practically, all parts of the world. The firm also handles the milk of the papaw-fruit (*Carica papaya*), for export, in dried form, to America and London, where a large demand exists for this medicinal product in the manufacture of papain and pepsin. In the export of tortoise-shell a great deal of care has to be exercised in sorting, sizing, and classifying the article for shipment, and the firm gives special attention to these necessary operations. The supply of plumbago for export is obtained principally through native firms and producers. It may be mentioned that the firm was one of the first in the island to make shipments of indiarubber —a product which has come into so much notice of late and promises to become one of the staple articles of the commerce of Ceylon.

THE ORIENT COMPANY, LTD.

The Orient Company, Ltd., was originally launched by a London syndicate in 1889. The venture proved successful beyond all anticipations, and the business was converted into a limited liability company, with head offices at 7, East India Avenue, London, while a local branch was established in the Chamber of Commerce Buildings at Colombo. The firm is engaged principally in the curing and export of desiccated coconut, copra, and fibre of every description; but other articles of produce are also handled and shipped to order. The company's principal desiccating mills are situated at Veyangoda, on the main line of railway, some 22 miles from Colombo, where heavy machinery has been installed, and a small army of about 800 hands are engaged in dealing with the products from the moment they enter the factory in their raw condition to the final stages of treatment, packing, baling, and transportation to Colombo for shipment to all parts of the world. The factory is furnished with its own electric-lighting plant and dynamos, which equipment contributes considerably to the despatch with which the articles treated are handled; while the stores and yards are spacious, covering an area of about 6 acres. The whole of the operations are under the direct control of Mr. F. Maxfield, who is resident manager of the mills. The company also owns the Horrekelly Mills at Madampe, where 200 hands are employed, under the superintendence of Mr. Van Dort. Mr. J. C. Norman, who was connected with the London office for five years and came out to the island in 1896, is manager of the Ceylon branches.

TARRANT & CO.

Founded in 1895 as general exporters and importers, produce merchants and shipping agents, this firm has rapidly expanded its business operations, until, at the present time, it ranks amongst the foremost of Colombo mercantile and commercial houses and is fast establishing a reputation throughout the world for the excellence of its exports, which include all the staple articles of the island. Like so many other Ceylon business houses, this firm is chiefly occupied with the blending, packing, and export of tea to the United Kingdom, Australia, United States of America, Canada, and various other parts of the globe; and for these purposes they maintain a well-equipped factory, supplied with all the latest machinery, at Union Place, Slave Island, Colombo, where the leaf is blended to suit the various markets abroad. In the carpenter's shop on the premises any description of package can be made, either chests, half-chests, cases, or boxes; and adjoining this branch is a spacious packeting-room, where the tea is put up in packets, either by hand or machinery, under immediate European supervision.

One of the principal lines of articles imported by the firm is cotton piece-goods from Manchester and other places, specially manufactured for local requirements. The head office of the business is located at Slave Island, while the piece-goods business is carried on in the Fort at No. 2, Baillie Street. The partners of the concern are Mr. Herbert Tarrant, who came out to the island over twenty years ago and is an eminently experienced business man, and Mr. A. Odell Figg, who has been connected with the firm since its formation, and was admitted into the partnership in 1903. Mr. Figg undertakes the buying of general produce, while Mr. S. F. O. Lovell, who was for many years on the London tea market, has full control of the tea department. The firm has also a London house, which operates under the style of Herbert Tarrant & Co. The local establishment holds agencies in Ceylon for the following: The Western Assurance Company, of Toronto; the China Mutual Life Insurance Company, Ltd.; the National Guarantee and Suretyship Association, Ltd.: Foucar & Co., Ltd., Rangoon (Burma); and Rowbotham & Co.

RIPLEY & MARSHALL.

The firm of Messrs. Ripley & Marshall, general merchants in all products of Ceylon, importers and exporters, is of recent foundation. The offices are situated at 3, Baillie Street, Fort, Colombo, and the firm's large mills at Maradana, Colombo, where the Ceylon produce is prepared for export. The over-seas trade is a very large one, the exports being carried to all parts of the world, principally the United Kingdom, and various parts of Europe, America, and South Africa. Messrs. Ripley & Marshall are the sole agents for the Ammonial Explosives Company, and for a valuable anti-fungus stain called "Solignum," which is manufactured by Messrs. Major & Co., of Hull, England. This stain is a preservative of wood, stone, and brickwork, and protects against decay, fungus, dry rot, the ravages of insects and vermin, as well as the action of the weather. "Solignum" is especially adapted to the climate of Ceylon, where the ravages of the white ant in woodwork are particularly destructive. The firm also hold the local agencies for J. G. Thompson & Co.'s well-known brand of whiskies, the marine insurance department at Lloyd's, and the South British Fire and Marine Insurance Company. The firm's corresponding houses are Ripley & Co., Bimlipatam; Ripley & Hartley, Cochin & Alleppy, Southern India; and Sydenham & Pound, London. Mr. A. H. Marshall is the managing partner of the Colombo business.

SCHULZE BROS. & CO.

This firm of general produce and import merchants was founded in the year 1887 at Colombo by Mr. Adalbert Theodor Schulze. The firm does an extensive business in the export of Ceylon products and import of Manchester and continental goods, and is represented by agents all over Europe, Japan, Australia, Canada, and the United States of America. Among these agents the chief are Messrs. Kaltenbach & Schmitz, London, Liverpool, and Hamburg; Messrs. Smith, Smith & Co.,

TARRANT & CO.'S ESTABLISHMENT.

THE STORES. LAKE SIDE STORES
TEA ROOM. THE OFFICE.
INTERIOR.

Glasgow; Messrs. James Williamson & Son, Lancaster; Messrs. L. Permezel & Co., Lyons; the Portland Cement Fabrik & Ziegelei Actien

A. SCHULZE'S RESIDENCE.

Gesellschaft, Pahlhude; and the Red Star Glass Works Company. Ltd., Marchienne-au-Pont. Messrs. Schulze are also experts in marine insurance, and represent the Board of Hamburg Underwriters and the Joint Underwriters' Union of Amsterdam, being agents as well for the Federal Marine Insurance Company, Ltd, Zurich, the Norddeutsche Insurance Company, Hamburg, and the Manchester Assurance Company. The firms also are average commissioners for the Universal Underwriting Association, London; the Patriotische Assecuranz Compagnie, Hamburg; the Mit- und Ruck Versicherungs Gesellschaft Kosmos, Hamburg; the Allgemeine Seeversicherungs Gesellschaft, Hamburg; the Badische Schiffahrts Assecuranz Gesellschaft, Mannheim; the Fonciere Pester Versicherungs Anstalt, Buda-Pest; the Providentia Allgemeine Versicherungs Gesellschaft, Vienna; the Salamandra Insurance Company, St. Petersburg; the Société d'Orient, St. Petersburg, the "Rhenania" Versicherungs Actien Gesellschaft in Köln on Rhine; the Frankfort Marine Insurance Company, of Frankfort-on-Maine; the "Fortuna" Allgemeine Versicherungs Actien Gesellschaft, Berlin; the "Deutscher Lloyd" Transport Versicherungs Actien Gesellschaft, Berlin; the Eastern Carrying Insurance, Storing and Warrant Company, St. Petersburg; the Internationaler Lloyd Versicherungs Actien Gesellschaft, Berlin; the Bayerischer Lloyd Transport Versicherungs Actien Gesellschaft, Munich; the "Schweiz' Allgemeine Versicherungs Actien Gesellschaft, Zurich; the "Alianz" Versicherungs Gesellschaft, Abtheilung Transport Versicherung, Berlin; the Versicherung Gesellschaft "Jakor," Moscow; the Forsakrings Aktiebolaget "Hansa," Stockholm; the Comitato delle Compagnie d'Assicurazioni Marittima di Genoa, Genoa; the Dusseldorfer Allgemeine Versicherungs Gesellschaft, of Dusseldorf, and others.

Mr. A. Schulze, the head of the firm, who has resided in Ceylon for over thirty years, is the local Consul for the Netherlands, and is a gentleman held in high esteem in local commercial and mercantile circles. The principal European assistants employed in the Colombo business are Messrs. Hans Behring and A. B. Sawer. The head offices are at 25, Upper Chatham Street, Fort, while the stores for the treating and packing of the articles dealt in are situated at No. 2, Sutherland Lane, Captain's Gardens, Colombo. The firm has been operating in Colombo for nearly twenty years, and has successfully established itself on a substantial and permanent basis, being in the front rank of local commercial enterprises.

C. M. WRIGHT & CO.

In connection with the development of the tea industry in Ceylon, this business was established in 1902 by Mr. C. M. Wright. The firm are buyers and shippers of tea, and represent Messrs. Nelson, Moate & Co., Ltd., in Colombo, who are by far the largest importers of tea in New Zealand. They have offices, packing and blending stores at Ambewatta, whence they export over 1,500,000 lbs. of tea every year, principally to Australia, New Zealand, and America. Having found the buying of whole crops on estates unsatisfactory, they now purchase almost entirely in the local auction market. They employ some 50 hands, and their packing stores cover an area of 6,000 square ft. In the stores the tea purchased is blended and put up in packets and boxes for shipment. Mr. Wright had five years' experience as a tea-broker in Mincing Lane; and on arrival in Ceylon, in 1893, became a planter for some time in order to get an insight into the growing of tea before embarking in the export business. He is a member of the Chamber of Commerce and Tea Traders' Association. His firm are also importers of Clement-Talbot motor-cars and the well-known Continental tyres, for both of which lines of goods they are sole agents in Ceylon.

HAROLD MONTGOMERY MOORE.

Mr. Harold Montgomery Moore, son of James Moore, was born in 1880 at Belfast, Ireland. He was educated in the Royal Belfast Academical Institution (of which he was elected a Governor in 1902), and also at the Polytechnical College, Zurich, &c. He commenced a business career in 1895, serving

HAROLD M. MOORE.

his time under his father, a leading printer and publisher, &c., in Belfast. During the six years he was in the Belfast business he gained considerable experience in mechanical matters, and subsequently he laid the foundation of a good commercial training in the firm of Marcus Ward & Co., Ltd., the well-known London publishers. He entered the firm of Davidson & Co., Ltd., "Sirocco" Engineering Works, Belfast, in 1903, and came out almost immediately to Ceylon to manage the Colombo depôt of the firm, who cater on an extensive scale for tea estates both in Ceylon and India, supplying "Sirocco" machinery and all engineering requisites. His chief pastime is sailing, and he has been an active member of the Colombo Sailing Club since his arrival in the island, has sailed in the majority of their races, and been successful in winning a number of "firsts." Clubs—Colombo Sailing Club, Ulster Reform, Belfast, Royal Ulster Yacht Club.

W. S. KING.

This firm of tea-buyers was established in Colombo about four years ago, and it acts as agent in Ceylon for the firm of S. W. Litvinoff & Co., Hankow and Kiukiang, also for King, Son & Ramsay, of Hankow, Shanghai and Foochow. The firm's head offices are in Shanghai, where a staff of 17 Europeans is maintained. Tea of every grade and description is handled at the Colombo business house, and exported to all parts of the world. The Colombo business is under the management of Mr. Stanley H. Dyer, who came to the island in the beginning of 1892, and was a tea-planter for nine years before taking up his present position. Mr. Dyer was born in London, and partly educated on the Continent, and has been

STANLEY H. DYER.

connected with the tea industry for the last fourteen years. Under his direction the Colombo business is steadily developing, import and supply of estate requisites also being included in its operations at the present time. The headquarters of the firm are at the *Times of Ceylon* buildings, Fort, Colombo.

E. B. CREASY.

The business of E. B. Creasy, general merchant and importer, was established in Colombo, Ceylon, in 1882, by Mr. E. B. Creasy, sen., who is still the proprietor, the office being at 12, Baillie Street, Fort, Colombo. The London and Colombo forwarding agency was subsequently formed in connection with the main business. Mr. E. B. Creasy, jun., is now managing the whole business, which includes that of shipping, clearing, general express agents, general commission agents and merchants, as well as estate agents. A principal line is the importation of tea boxes from Japan, and the firm are agents for Messrs. Okura & Co., of Tokio, in this branch of trade. They have corresponding agents in their general business in every port in Europe, the United States of America, and South Africa. In Colombo they employ two Europeans and 20 Burgher and native hands, the latter mostly at their stores at St. Sebastian Hill. Mr. E. B. Creasy, junior, who has recently been appointed Consul for Norway, is a member of most of the principal clubs in the island. The firm is always ready to answer queries regarding Ceylon on any subject, from any one in any part of the world. Mr. E. B. Creasy, sen..

E. B. CREASY, SEN.

SAN SEBASTIAN STORES.

is a member of the Ceylon Chamber of Commerce.

C. A. HUTSON & CO.

Founded in 1886, this firm, who own the Ceylon Engineering Works, Colombo, with a branch at Kandapola, have recently erected new and commodious premises at Mutwal, immediately facing the entrance to the harbour, having outgrown their old premises on the seashore. This well-known landmark had to be removed owing to the harbour improvements. The firm's new engineering shop is fitted with the latest machinery, also with the electric lights for the nightwork rendered continually necessary owing to the large amount of ship repairs undertaken. The firm engage in engineering work of all kinds. They have built the large oil tanks seen from the harbour, also several of the launches and tugs for use in the harbour and many of the factories of the island. They are agents for Messrs. Ruston, Proctor & Co., of Lincoln, England, and Messrs. Crossley Bros., Ltd., of Manchester. Their fine new foundry has a moulding floor of 4,500 sq. ft., and contains three cupolas as well as three brass furnaces, and can turn out castings up to 10 tons each in weight. A full set of propeller blades, each weighing 2¼ tons, for the s.s. *Istria*, may be specified as a typical piece of work turned out here. There is also a smithy, with forges, steam-hammers, and bending-rolls, and a carpenter's shop, thus enabling the firm to take up any construction work. The business is under the direction of Mr. C. A. Hutson and his manager, Mr. W. R. Burnett, assisted by five European engineers and about 350 native employees. The firm are on the Army and Admiralty lists as capable of undertaking contracts for those great departments of State.

COLOMBO APOTHECARIE ' COMPANY, LIMITED.

This important mercantile company, with its present extensive premises in Prince Street, Colombo, had its origin in the chemist's shop instituted by Mr. W. M. Smith and Mr. James Smith Finlay in the De Soysa Buildings, Slave Island, Colombo, in 1883. Four years later the two founders moved into a small store at the junction of York and Prince Streets; and from these small beginnings the business has grown commensurately with the rapid progress of the capital of the colony. Although still retaining the title of "apothecaries," the conductors of the business decided to extend the scope of operations so as to embrace other branches of retail trade. Accordingly, an oilman's store and wine and spirit departments were added in 1889, and subsequently stationery, china, fancy goods, photography and photographic supplies, electro-plated ware, boots and shoes. A further extension took in drapery, outfitting, hardware, toys, games, and athletic goods. In connection with the dispensary an optical department, in charge of trained experts, was established. The company, under its present designation, was founded in 1892, and this step led to further extension of premises and business. The photographic studio was moved to more suitable quarters at Kandy, where climatic influences are more propitious for high-class photographic work than in Colombo. At this studio views are turned out by thousands and sent to all parts of the world. They include representations of the famous Buried Cities of Ceylon, concerning which the company publishes a very interesting catalogue; while at the Colombo store is a dark-room, where all conveniences are provided for the use of amateurs, passengers, and others, and a large stock of photographic materials is kept. A

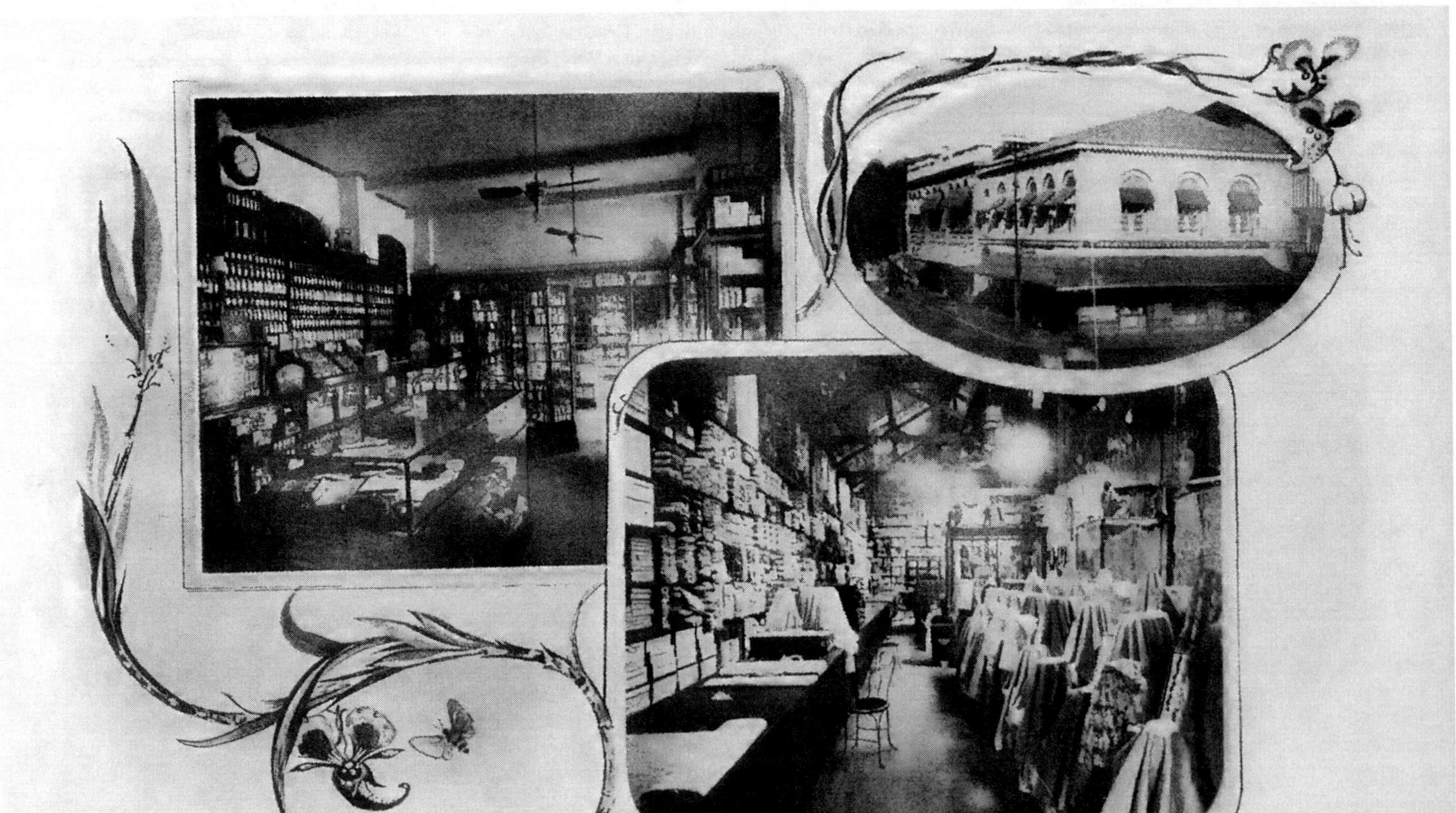

THE COLOMBO APOTHECARIES' COMPANY.

THE PHARMACY. DRAPERY DEPARTMENT.

F. SKEEN & CO.'S PREMISES.

F. SKEEN.

completely fitted job-printing department has also been added, having electricity for its motive power.

In the Baillie Street branch the company carries on a large business as outfitters and tailors, as well as manufacturing saddlers and shoemakers, employing some 300 hands in this department alone. Again, this many-sided company exports tea to China—which sounds something like carrying coals to Newcastle!—and as wholesale and retail chemists and druggists it ranks among the largest houses in the East. The present chairman is Sir W. W. Mitchell, C.M.G., Mr. C. Davidson being the general manager of the company.

F. SKEEN & CO.

The business of Messrs. F. Skeen & Co., who are in the front rank of Colomho photographers, and have taken large numbers of the photographs reproduced in this volume, was established by Mr. Parting in the early sixties, and was purchased by Mr. W. Skeen, then the Government printer, for his son, Mr. W. H. Skeen about ten years later. In those days the only system of photography was the daguerreotype, by which the photograph was taken upon a silver sensitised plate, and developed by being fumed in ammonia. Customers had to pay as much as two guineas for the single photograph, as there was no system of printing or reproduction. Mr. W. H. Skeen continued to manage the business until his death in 1903, and it increased greatly during that time. The particular forte of the deceased gentleman was landscape photography, and the firm still has a large connection in this class of work, and possesses one of the finest collections of landscape photographs in Ceylon. In the course of the years every form of photography has been added, and now the business done includes indoor and outdoor, landscape, architectural, enlarging, lantern slide-making work, and picture framing, whilst an important feature is the process work carried on by the firm. For this work the firm has its own plant, and it practically leads the way in this department in the island. Until the Surveyor-General's Department undertook their own process work recently, Messrs. Skeen made a large proportion of the blocks for Government publications. It is intended shortly to inaugurate a new system of block-making, and a European is to join the firm in order to superintend this department. Mr. F. Skeen, the present head of the firm, joined the business first in 1878, and assisted his brother for nine years. He then went to Burma, and established a large business at Rangoon, and returned to take charge of the Colombo concern in 1903.

BRODIE & CO.

Under the name of Messrs. Brodie, Bogue & Co., this business was established in Colombo, as far back as 1846, by the late Mr. W. C. Brodie. In 1867 the name of the firm was changed to Brodie & Co.; the present partners are Messrs. C. B. Brodie and W. C. Brodie, junior. The firm's premises at 26, Chatham Street have been occupied by Brodie & Co. since 1880. The firm deals only in imports—as wholesale wine and spirit merchants and suppliers of estate requirements. The premises comprise cool cellars and stores, covering several hundred feet, and bottling is performed on the premises. The house carries on a large trade, having business connections all over Ceylon. For thirty-five years Messrs. Brodie & Co. have acted as sole agents for W. & A. Gilbey, Ltd., and they have been members of the Ceylon Chamber of Commerce since the foundation of that institution in the island. They are agents for Cutler, Palmer & Co., London; Jas. Aitken & Co., Falkirk; Robert Porter & Co., London; Jas. Saunders & Co., London; Morgan Bros. & Co., Oporto; Robert

Brown, Ltd., Glasgow; George Younger & Son, Ltd., Alloa; Jules Mumm Company, Reims; Justerini & Brooks, London; and the Bremen Brewery, Bremen. They correspond with leading houses in Great Britain, Australia, the Straits Settlements, the United States of America, and China.

E. CAHILL & SONS.

The firm now trading under the above title as gentlemen's complete outfitters and manufacturing tailors, at 44 and 45, Chatham Street, Colombo, was first established in October, 1887, at Galle Face Cottages, by Mr. Edward Cahill, sen., an Irishman, who received his training in London. In January, 1891, Mr. Cahill removed his business to the Bristol Hotel, where he remained for eleven years. He then assumed occupation of the present premises in Chatham Street, where the firm own large showrooms, consisting of two floors, and containing woollen, cotton, and silk materials for suits, as well as hats, shirts, under-wear, hosiery, boots and shoes, and, in fact, every requisite in the gentlemen's outfitting line. The present proprietors of the firm are Messrs. Edward Cahill, sen., Patrick Cahill, Edward Cahill, jun., and John Cahill; while the number of hands employed is 30. They supply all descriptions of tropical wear, and have a large staff of workmen on the premises, all the work being under European supervision, and the cutting itself being in the trained hands of Mr. Edward Cahill, sen. The firm also undertakes to supply outfits at the shortest notice with the best style and fit. Besides being direct importers from England, India, and the United States of America, Cahill & Sons carry on a large local trade. A special feature of this firm is that visitors can rely on receiving every attention at their establishment, the reputation of which extends all over the island.

THREE VIEWS OF MESSRS. CAHILL'S ESTABLISHMENT.

GRAND ORIENTAL HOTEL.

The "G.O H.," as it is familiarly known far and wide, was the first of the modern type of imposing hotels erected in the East. With its towering front facing the harbour and the shipping and its main portico separated by only a few yards from the principal landing-stage, it occupies both a commanding and convenient position; and passengers by the mail steamers who are passing through the port are specially catered for at this establishment in the very best style. The hotel is also largely used by visitors to Colombo from various parts of the island, while it is a favourite place of resort with the residents of the city. An exceedingly pleasing feature of the establishment is the tropical garden, where the guests may rest in charming surroundings while listening to the hotel band. Of an evening the grounds are illuminated by electricity. Here also various kinds of musical and theatrical entertainments are given. The building contains 154 bedrooms; and special arrangements can be made as regards board and apartments by those making a stay of over a few days in the city. The hotel is lighted throughout by electricity, and all the public rooms and bedrooms are kept cool by means of electric fans. A lift gives easy access to the upper floors, and the telephone connection is a convenience that meets with high appreciation. On the ground floor of the large building are the entrance hall, with the manager's and the inquiry offices, spacious lounge verandahs, a billiard-room (with four first-rate tables by Burroughs & Watts), the palm court, and the grand dining-room. The latter is recognised as one of the largest, best appointed and coolest in the East. It is fitted with electric lights and fans, and is capable of seating 300 persons; while the cuisine is under the control of an experienced

THE GRAND ORIENTAL HOTEL—THE DINING HALL, EXTERIOR, AND GARDEN, TOGETHER WITH A PORTRAIT OF THE MANAGER (G. LOOSEN).

chef. The palm court is another special feature of the establishment. Here visitors may receive their friends and enjoy their afternoon tea in surroundings of Oriental luxury, or pass out into the hotel garden, with its wealth of tropical plants. Upstairs there are numerous suites of private apartments, commanding fine views of the coast and sea. On the first floor also is the ladies' drawing-room, which opens on to a charming fernery: while writing, reading, and

W. T. S. SAUNDERS
(Managing Director.)

music rooms, as well as private dining-rooms, overlooking the harbour, with its interesting spectacle of stately ships ever passing in and out, are provided for the use of visitors and their guests. The tariff for meals and apartments is comprehensive and carefully varied so as to suit all classes of travellers, whether voyagers by land or sea; and special arrangements are made for the accommodation of parties, families, children, and servants. Mr. G. Loosen, the present manager of the hotel, took charge in October, 1904, and he was immediately struck with the promising and great possibilities there existed for developing the business into one of the largest of its kind in the East. Mr. Loosen's long and varied experience in the hotel world stood him in good stead in this work of development, he having conducted the management, successively, of some of the leading catering institutions in London during the past twenty-five years, including the Hotel Belgravia, the R.A.M.C. College in connection with St. Ermyn's Hotel, the Gaiety Restaurant, and the Savage Club. With this experience, and with the assistance of his wife, a very capable and accomplished lady, as manageress, Mr. Loosen lost no time in availing himself of the resources of the Grand Oriental Hotel, with the result that it now occupies a premier position among the hotels of the East. The secretary of the company which owns the hotel is Mr. R. E. Pineo.

The managing director is Mr. Wm. Tudor Stephen Saunders, who was born in London in 1848, and was educated at Blackheath School. He arrived in Ceylon in 1868, and started coffee-planting in the Morawak Korale. Mr. Saunders continued his planting career until the coffee collapse ruined that industry. He then purchased the Hornsey and Aberlerney tea estates in the Dikoya district; and these properties he subsequently sold to the Hornsey Tea Estates Company, of which he is the managing director. Shortly afterwards he settled down in Colombo, and was instrumental in starting the Bristol Hotel, of which he was the first managing director. Leaving the Bristol Hotel in the year 1901, he became the managing director of the Grand Oriental Hotel, which position he has held ever since. Mr. Saunders is also the managing director of the Ceylon Railway Refreshment Car Company, the Hatton Hotel, and the Grand Hotel at Nuwara Eliya, as well as a director of numerous other companies. In 1901, during the visit of the Prince of Wales, Mr. Saunders was appointed comptroller of Government House. He is one of the keenest sportsmen in the island, having in his early days been an ardent cricket, football, and tennis player, and is patron of the Dimbula and Maskeliya Cricket Club, of which he was active captain and president for eighteen years. Mr. Saunders is a Justice of the Peace for the island.

GEO. STEUART & CO.

This prominent Colombo firm of private attorneys and estate, commission, and banking agents, whose offices are at 14, Queen Street, Fort, was founded in 1844 by George Steuart. The business is carried on at the present time by Messrs. William Anderson, Thomas S. Grigson, Edward S. Grigson, John Paterson, C. M. Gordon, and T. L. Villiers. The principal line of the business is the Colombo agency for a very large number of plantations both in the tea and rubber growing districts of Ceylon. The firm has also connections with leading business houses in different parts of the world.

G. H. ALSTON.

Mr. G. H. Alston is a member of a Scotch family, and was born at Uddingstone, Lanarkshire, in the year 1859. He passed his collegiate career at Marlborough College, Wilts, where he was a member of the cricket eleven in 1877. His business career was commenced in London, and having received a training with several firms there, he, in 1880, joined the family firm of Alstons, Scott & Co. in Ceylon. After serving here for a period, he spent a few years in business in Southern India. Returning to Ceylon, he became connected, in 1894, with Messrs. Whittall & Co., of which firm he has been a partner since July 1, 1896. It was in 1903 that he was first nominated a member of the Municipal Council, whilst in 1906 he was elected as the Fort Ward representative of the same body. He is a member of the Thirty Committee for the distribution of the tea cess, of the Chamber of Commerce Committee, and of all the principal clubs. Mr. Alston is also a Freemason (Eighteenth Degree), and has passed through all the chairs but one. He has always been a keen sportsman, though, perhaps, with the exception of shooting and fishing and golf, he does not now take an active interest in any branch of sport.

H. W. CAVE & CO.

Mr. H. W. Cave, M.A., F.R.G.S., who has obtained wide fame by his well-written and

H. W. CAVE.

finely illustrated works on Ceylon, came out to the colony from England as secretary to the Anglican Bishop, and started literary work by editing the *Ceylon Diocesan Gazette*, the first Church paper in Ceylon. In 1876 he opened business in Chatham Street as an importer of religious books, and subsequently moved to his present premises, a spacious double-storeyed

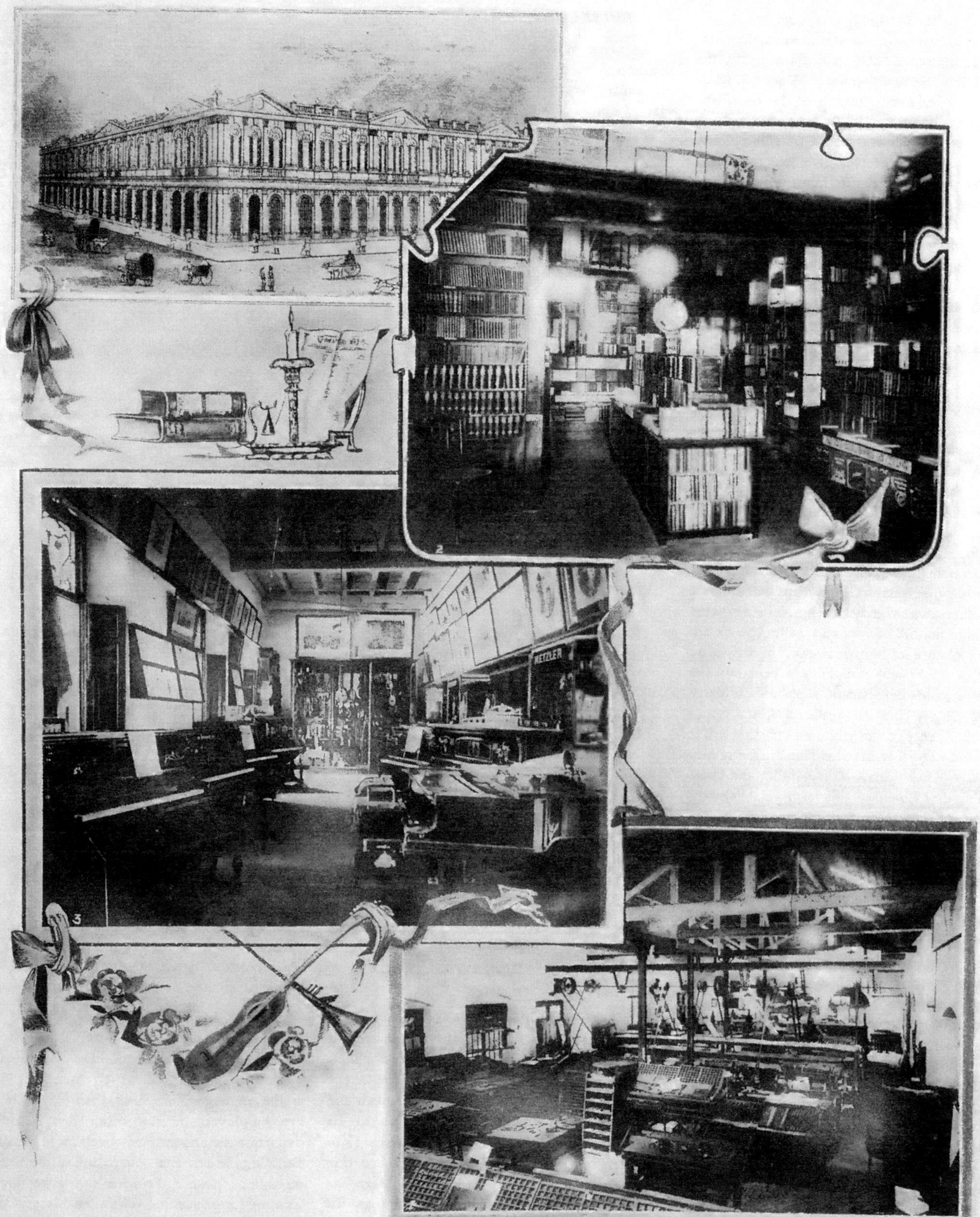

H. W. CAVE & CO.'S BUILDINGS.
MUSIC DEPARTMENT

BOOK DEPOT.
PRINTING WORKS.

building, with a frontage of 400 ft. H. W. Cave & Co. are booksellers, stationers, printers, and publishers, and also stock sporting goods; in addition, they are agents for Henry S. King & Co., and the total strength of the establishment is 350 hands.

After writing several books on the Colony, which were well received at Home and have become standard works in their line, Mr. Cave started photography in order to illustrate his works. Undertaken first as a hobby, this line of work has proved very useful to him in the illustration of his books and as an aid to his lectures. In his youth Mr. H. W. Cave was at Oxford, and after fourteen years of successful business life in Ceylon he returned to England and took his degree, his college being Queen's, Oxford. The partners in the present firm are Mr. H. W. Cave, the founder and senior; Messrs. A. E. and S. Cave, his brothers; and Mr. Walter A. Cave, his nephew. Mr. C. A. Cave, who joined the founder in 1878, remained in the firm until his death, in April, 1906.

The firm have large stocks of pianos and American organs of various makes; and they have a fancy goods department, where perfumery, smokers' requisites, and all the usual articles in this line can be obtained. Cave & Co. pride themselves on their up-to-date stock of pictures, which may be framed in any style on the premises. Silver and leather goods are also a feature of the business; and a large stock of books and stationery is kept. In the sporting goods department, rickshaws, billiard-tables, Singer and Alldays' cycles, and appliances for every sort of game and pastime are to be found. The firm have held the Singer agency for twenty-five years. The printing and bookbinding department of this large establishment is also very extensive, the equipment including six cylinder and four platen machines, besides ruling and cutting machines. A minor branch of this department is half-tone block-making; while cycle repairs, racquet stringing, and cabinet work are executed on the premises.

In connection with Mr. H. W. Cave's literary career his book "Golden Tips," a brightly written description of Ceylon in especial connection with its staple industry of tea-production, and containing numerous interesting illustrations, deserves particular mention. This literary work, which passed through four editions, received high encomiums from the leading journals of England. Reviewing the book, the London *Athenæum* says: "Mr. Cave seems to hold a brief for the whole island of Ceylon, with its varied attractions. . . . The charm of Sinhalese life and nature is depicted with glowing colours and interesting details. . . . The simple, peaceful village life, and the more stirring existence of the townspeople, with their varied avocations, are equally well described."

WHITEAWAY, LAIDLAW & CO.

The name Whiteaway, Laidlaw & Co. is a household word throughout the East. In the domain of retail business there is no firm east of Suez which has wider ramifications or a more extensive *clientèle*. Establishments in connection with the firm are to be found at Colombo, Calcutta, Bombay, Madras, Rangoon, Lucknow, Karachi, Mandalay, Darjeeling, Poona, Moulmein, Simla, Murroe, Prome, Naini Tal, Mussorie, Lahore, and Singapore. The Colombo business is housed in a fine building in the best part of the Fort, and there a very considerable business is done in all classes of goods which are customarily to be obtained at a first-class general store. Such headway has been made by the firm in the last few years, that it has outgrown even the ample accommodation which it has at its command in Australia Buildings. A magnificent new building is now under construction for the firm in Prince Street, and there the business will be transferred as soon as the building operations are completed.

WHITEAWAY, LAIDLAW & CO.'S NEW PREMISES.

MILLER & CO.

Among the principal firms of general importers in Ceylon is the well-known one of Miller & Co., founded over forty years ago in Kandy by the late William Crammond Miller, and still carried on by members of the deceased gentleman's family. Messrs. Miller & Co. import all kinds of merchandise (with the exception of soft goods), wines—the firm doing a large business in Australian wines—spirits, and oilmen's stores being the leading lines in which they deal; and they are the local representatives of the Distillers' Company, Ltd., of Edinburgh, and the St. Pauli Brewery Company, Ltd. At the Colombo headquarters of the business in York Street, Fort, of which Mr. W. Philps is the manager, no less than 42 assistants are employed in the retail and household departments, and extensive cellars in Australia Buildings are in the occupation of the firm for storage purposes. To meet the large demand existing for household requisites, Messrs. Miller & Co. find it necessary to carry large stocks of china, glass, and electro-plated goods, as well as of every description of household sundries. In cutlery and silver goods none but articles of the best English manufacture can be found on the premises.

The branch establishment at Kandy, where the business originated, is under the management of Mr. R. Gordon.

CARGILLS, LTD.

Messrs. Cargills, Ltd.—whose name, as practically "universal providers," is a household word throughout Ceylon and a synonym for quality—is a development of the firm of Milne, Cargill & Co., which started business in Kandy in 1844. When Colombo became a port of call, that firm followed the trend of business thitherward, and steadily grew in importance in the city, retaining, however, the Kandy establishment, which is still extant. Later the designation of the firm became "Cargill & Co.," and it continued to prosper through the halcyon days of the coffee industry. With the failure of coffee, in common with practically every other Ceylon firm, it underwent severe vicissitudes. One of the few enterprises which weathered the storm attendant upon the collapse of the then staple industry of the island, with the rise and progress of tea the firm eventually became the leading distributors in the island. In 1896 it was converted into a private limited liability company, under its present title. The principal departments, wholesale and retail, are ladies' drapery, dressmaking, millinery, household furnishing, wines and spirits, groceries, horse-feed, gentlemen's tailoring and outfitting, and drugs and dispensary.

The magnificent block of buildings which Messrs. Cargills, Ltd., now occupy in York Street, Colombo, was commenced in 1902 and was completed in 1906. These premises are deservedly considered the finest of their kind east of Suez, and possess an extensive installation of hydraulic lifts and electric fans. Since the firm became a limited company they have absorbed the businesses of Messrs. James McLaren & Co., of Nuwara Eliya, and Messrs. Neil S. Campbell & Co., of Cinnamon Gardens, Colombo, and they have established thriving branches at these respective places. Altogether, in their four establishments, Messrs. Cargills have an executive staff of 32 Europeans, and in Ceylon the firm employs 600 hands. The registered office of the company is in Glasgow; and the founder of the business was the late Mr. D. S. Cargill, for many years chairman of the Burma Oil Company, Ltd. The present managing director is Mr. W. Jenkins, and the general manager for Ceylon is Mr. James Mathieson.

MILLER & CO.'S COLOMBO PREMISES, INTERIOR AND EXTERIOR, AND VIEW OF THEIR KANDY BRANCH.

"COLOMBO ADVERTISER AND SHIPPING GAZETTE"—H. C. HITCHINGS & CO., PRINTERS AND PUBLISHERS.

Mr. H. C. Hitchings, the principal of the firm, came to Ceylon in 1899 for Messrs. Capper & Sons. After being manager of their printing office for about four years, he paid the firm liquidated damages as agreed and commenced a new general printing business in the Victoria Arcade Buildings, putting down an entirely new and most modern plant for the purpose. In 1904 the *Colombo Advertiser and Shipping Gazette* was undertaken—a weekly journal devoted to shipping and commercial interests, and observing a strict line of impartiality in its editorials and notes. It possesses a guaranteed circulation of 2,500 copies a week, which are distributed in a manner calculated to attract the tourist and passenger and benefit the trade of the port. The *Colombo Advertiser* is edited by a European journalist

PRINTING ESTABLISHMENT (INTERIOR).
TRAM ADVERTISEMENTS.

of long standing in the island, and the generous support accorded the enterprise of the proprietor by all classes of advertisers is the best proof of the popularity of Colombo's first English weekly paper and the recognition that it fills a needed place. The photograph shows a portion of the works. These have the advantage of being under one roof-span, an arrangement which enables more efficient supervision to be exercised. The motive power in the works is gas, and the printing machinery, guillotine, punkah, and fans are all driven by this means from one engine. The staff consists of over 50 hands, with Mr. J. Hitchings as assistant manager. An adjunct of the business is the carrying out of the contract for advertisements on the Colombo tramcars. It will be seen from the illustration that the contractors enjoy the support of the leading firms in England.

THE ROYAL PHARMACY.

By the enterprise of Mr. F. A. Palewandrem, a local medical practitioner, the Royal Pharmacy was established in 1901 at 14, Chatham Street, within easy reach of the business places of the Fort. The Pharmacy has, in its short existence of five years, earned for itself a reputation for businesslike methods and considerate treatment and attention to all callers; and its central position makes it possible for the working classes and others engaged in the Fort to procure their medicines here without any inconvenience to themselves. Prescriptions are dispensed at all hours of the day, and a special feature of the establishment is the supply of drugs and medicinal requirements to the shipping. As a pharmaceutical chemist's establishment it carries on an extensive business and has a large and appreciative number of patrons. Mr. Palewandrem is helped in business by his brother and five other assistants.

C. MATHEW & CO.

Necessarily in connection with the shipping of so important a port as Colombo there is a large field for the business of ship chandlers and stevedores; and Messrs. C. Mathew & Co., the leading local firm in this line, conduct operations on an extensive scale. This business was established nearly a hundred years ago on the present site, near the British India Hotel, in the Fort of Colombo, by a Mr. Bastian. It came into the possession of the Mathew family some fifty years ago; and Mr. C. Mathew, the father of the present owner, died in 1892. His son, Mr. C. J. Mathew, who was born in 1875, at Galle, and educated at the Royal College at Colombo, in 1892 took over his father's business in Canal Row, where the present fine buildings of the firm were erected in 1896. Mr. Mathew employs about 600 hands, and stevedores for the Peninsular and Oriental Steam Navigation

THE ROYAL PHARMACY.

TOPUNSING MOTOOMULL & CO.'S ESTABLISHMENT—VIEWS OF EXTERIOR AND INTERIORS.

Company, Messrs. Delmege, Reid & Co., Delmege, Forsyth & Co., Skrine & Co., Clark, Young & Co., and several other steamship lines.

Mr. Mathew also owns coconut estates in the Kalutara district and landed property in Colombo. His private residence is "Glendale," Barnes Place, Cinnamon Gardens, Colombo, and his favourite recreations are sailing and billiards.

C. J. MATHEW.

TOPUNSING MOTOOMULL & CO.

This firm, founded in Ceylon in 1864, was the first house in the island to engage largely in the import and sale of Eastern ware and curios, and it continues to maintain, after nearly half a century's existence, a premier position among similar enterprises in the colony. The firm's general executive offices are at Hyderabad, Sindh (India), while the head offices and principal showrooms of the Ceylon business are located in the Australia Buildings, in the Fort of Colombo. Branch establishments are to be found in Yokohama, Japan, and in Bombay, India. In Ceylon the firm has also a branch in Nuwara Eliya, and two others in Kandy—in Trincomalee Street and at the Queen's Hotel—besides a number of showrooms in various parts of the capital city, namely, at 5, Grand Oriental Hotel and Verandah, 5 and 6, Victoria Arcade, Fort, and 82 and 83, Main Street, Pettah. The business comprises, chiefly, the import of Indian, Japanese, and Chinese art-ware and curios, Burmese carvings, Persian rugs, and Kashmir embroideries ; and these, together with Ceylon-made articles, of tortoiseshell, ivory, ebony, silver, and gold, are to be seen displayed in Oriental fashion in the showrooms of the firm. Silks and fabrics, set jewellery and precious stones, ornamental and antique ware, and bric-a-brac generally, are dealt in ; and at all the firm's establishments brisk business is carried on. Orders for any of these wares are executed by rail or steamer to suit the convenience of patrons, and the firm has gained a wide reputation for strictly honest and business-like dealings. Distinguished visitors who pass through Colombo make it a point to visit the magnificent showrooms of the firm ; and on the occasion of the recent visit to Colombo of the Prince and Princess of Wales the firm received a large order from the royal visitors, who expressed satisfaction at their purchases, through their private secretary. The following is a sample of the testimonials received by the firm : "This is to certify that Their Royal Highnesses the Duke and Duchess of Cornwall and York inspected and made purchases from the curiosities, embroideries, and silverware exhibited by Messrs. Topunsing Motoomull, of Colombo, and were much pleased with the same."

Mr. Topunsing Motoomull, who founded the firm and continues to direct its operations in

Colombo, is assisted in the business by a large number of hands, in addition to his partners. Mr. Topunsing Motoomull and his colleagues and staff are all Hindus by persuasion and are liberal supporters of local charities and charitable institutions. A little more than ten years ago the business was converted into a company, but the lines on which it is conducted remain the same, and under the new style the old traditions of the business continue to be upheld.

M. ATMARAM.

One of the largest and best fitted Oriental shops in Colombo is that of Mr. M. Atmaram, tailor, outfitter, silk merchant, jeweller, and dealer in curios, brass, copper, bronze and china ware, also Indian and Kandyan work in gold and silver. Mr. Atmaram commenced business in the capital as a Bombay merchant eighteen years ago, first establishing himself in Chatham Street. Thence he moved to the Galle Face Hotel, where he conducted his increasing business for eight years; and in January, 1906, he took possession of his present premises in Cargills' Building, York Street. The showrooms here are lofty and capacious. A conspicuous feature is a wide staircase in the centre of the lower floor leading to the upper storey. The premises are kept cool by electric fans. They are also artistically adorned in approved Oriental style with a display of magnificent silks and fabrics of varied colours, while large show-cases filled with curios and other attractive articles of all sorts arrest the visitor's attention, and beautiful vases are met with at every turn. The profusion of splendid silks, shawls, rugs, and carpets from India, Assam, Bokhara, China, and Japan are alone well worth a visit of inspection. But besides these are to be seen a remarkable collection of precious stones of India and Ceylon, fine work in gold, silver, copper, brass, and bronze, carved work in ivory and sandalwood, exquisite inlaid and enamelled ware, also Ceylon hand-made lace and the old embroidery. In addition to the wholesale and retail dealing in jewellery and set and unset stones, gem-cutting and goldsmith's work to specification and in any design is carried out by the firm. Household furniture of all kinds is also supplied from this emporium; while in the tailoring department a special feature is the prompt execution of orders for costumes suitable for the tropical climate for travellers and others, of both sexes. To accommodate travellers, foreign money is exchanged on the premises at moderate rates. Mr. Atmaram employs a dozen assistants in his fine establishment.

N. D. H. ABDOOL CAFFOOR.

Mr. Caffoor is a pearl and diamond merchant and dealer in precious stones, and also a manufacturing gold and silver smith. He gained a gold medal for precious stones exhibited at the St. Louis Exhibition of 1904. His showrooms, attractive with glittering jewellery, are at 9 and 10, Bristol Buildings, York Street, Colombo, and form one of the chief attractions for tourists and visitors to Colombo. The business is represented in London by Messrs. Neresheimer & Co., 27, Holborn Viaduct, and Mr. Benjamin Warwick, King William Street, City. Mr. Caffoor also has correspondents in every part of the world. Although this establishment was only started in 1893 by its present proprietor, he has by businesslike acumen and enterprise brought it to the forefront of similar establishments in Colombo. The precious stones displayed are all found in Ceylon, coming from the chief gem-mining districts of Ratnapura, Morawak Korale, and Rakwana. By special command, this firm was allowed the privilege of exhibiting its precious stones and art-ware to the Prince and Princess of Wales at the Pavilion, Kandy, in 1901, during their royal visit, and large sales to the royal visitors and their suite resulted. Regardless of expense and trouble, the proprietor, Mr. Caffoor, has secured a superb collection of antique Kandyan jewellery, one that any of the museums in the world would be proud of, and it forms a gorgeous display, truly Oriental in design. A noticeable article of this collection is the headpiece of a crown lavishly set with diamonds, rubies, and emeralds.

M. ATMARAM'S ESTABLISHMENT—EXTERIOR, TWO VIEWS OF INTERIOR, AND TWO VASES.

ABDOOL CAFFOOR. THE SHOWROOM. AN EXHIBIT OF PRECIOUS STONES.

O. L. M. MACAN MARKAR.

EXTERIOR.

INTERIOR.

JEWEL EXHIBIT.

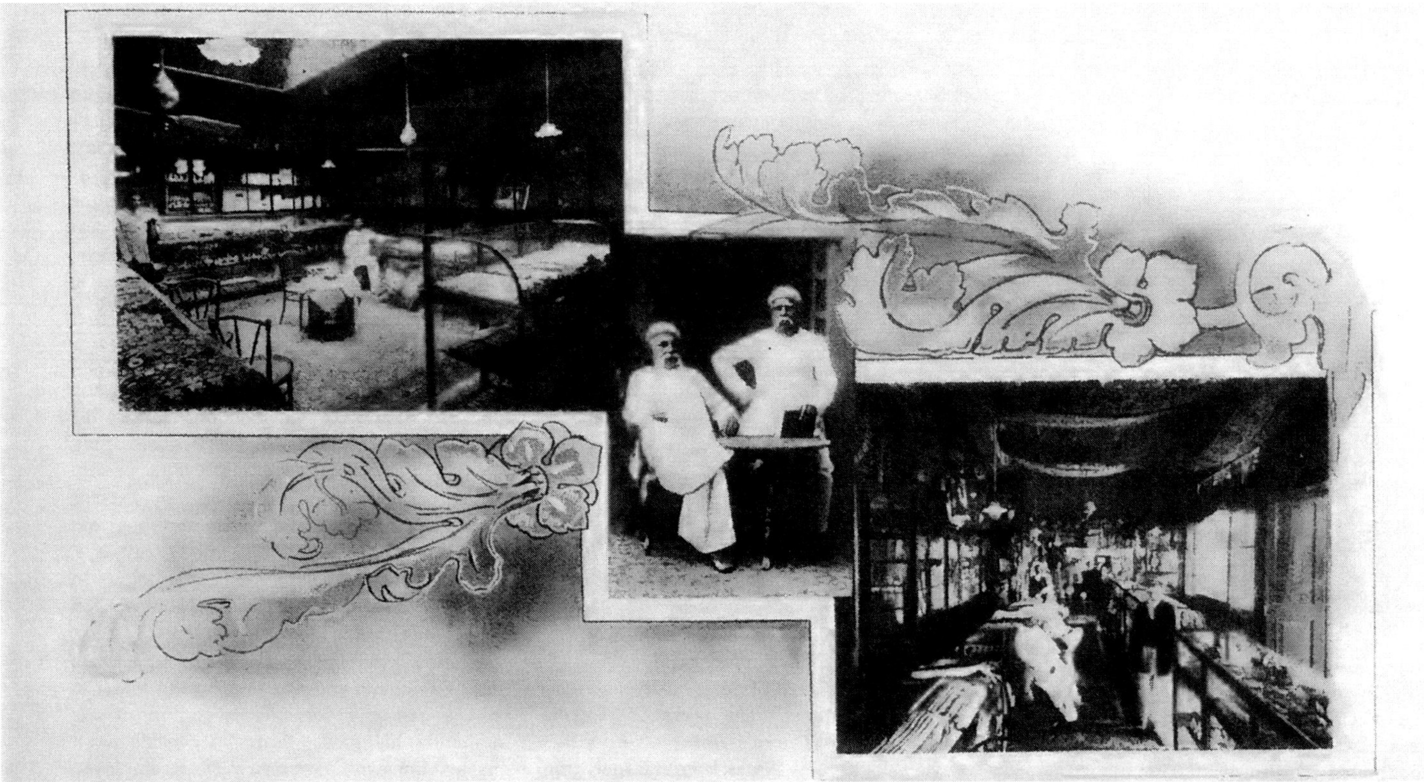

J. N. RAMSAMMY & BROS.—INTERIORS OF THE GALLE FACE HOTEL AND THE FORT ESTABLISHMENTS.

Another valuable work of art is an elephant richly carved in ivory, with gold trappings and a howdah crusted with Ceylonese precious stones. Among the large precious stones exhibited by the firm the following are particularly noticeable : a magnificent Ceylon ruby, rich in colour and weighing 20 carats, considered to be the best stone of its kind ever found, having no defect whatever, and valued at £5,000 ; an alexandrite, a stone peculiar to Ceylon, whose colour is a fine green by day and a bright red by night, also a perfect specimen of its kind, and valued at £1,500 ; a cat's-eye weighing 57 carats, egg-shaped, and of the rich colour of honey and milk, with a silver centre line and beautifully marked ; a fine blue sapphire of 25 carats ; also some excellent king topazes, and a beautiful star sapphire of 170 carats.

Another feature which arrests the eye of the visitor to this establishment is the immense variety of sterling silver and electro-plate ware in rich, rare, and artistic designs. Art-ware and curios from India, Burma, China, and other important centres are also given prominence in the show. The workshop of the establishment is replete with every accessory for smiths, lapidarists, and other craftsmen in the jewellery and art-work trades.

J. N. RAMSAMMY & BROS.

Messrs. J. N. Ramsammy & Bros., silk, silver and gold, and general merchants, dealers in precious stones, manufacturing outfitters for ladies and gentlemen, of Nos. 7 and 8, Bristol Hotel Buildings, Fort, Colombo, started business in Karachi Camp, India, about 1850. In 1880 they opened in Chatham Street, Colombo, and eighteen years ago the firm removed to their present quarters. Here they carry on an extensive import trade with India, China, Afghanistan, and the United Kingdom ; while a large export trade is done with Egypt, China, Australia, and the United Kingdom. All kinds of tropical outfits are made by the firm on their own premises, the local population being extensively catered for. The proprietor of the business, Naroomal Dharamandas, was born at Hyderabad in 1859, and educated in India. He received his business training at Karachi, and subsequently he came to Ceylon and founded the Colombo firm. By persuasion, Mr. Naroomal Dharamandas is a Hindu, and his private residence is No. 7, Hospital Street, Colombo.

This important firm has branches at the Galle Face Hotel, the Galle Face Hotel Verandah, and at 9 and 10, Victoria Arcade, Colombo ; and at the branch establishments the same class of goods is supplied as at the headquarters in the Fort. They also own large workshops and factories in Colombo, employing in all about 75 hands. The firm has the privilege of boarding all incoming and outgoing steamers to supply goods of every description to the passengers. Their goods, which were exhibited at the St. Louis Exhibition (1904) by Sir Stanley Bois, C.M.G., of Ceylon, were greatly admired. Queen's House and King's Pavilion were supplied by this firm with some exquisite carpets of Eastern manufacture for the occasion of the Prince of Wales's visit to the island. The royal visitor also purchased many of the beautiful goods stocked by this well-known firm.

OTHMAN LEBBE MARKAR MACAN MARKAR.

Dealing in jewels and precious stones is a much favoured line of business in Ceylon, and this is the trade carried on by the firm of O. L. M. Macan Markar, whose establishment, with its glittering contents, is conveniently situated on the Grand Oriental Hotel premises, York Street, Colombo. This is the oldest established jewellery business in the island, it having been founded at Galle in 1860 by the late Othman Lebbe Macan Markar, the father of the present proprietors. He started as a gem-trader in a small way, buying and selling single stones. Finding that the results were satisfactory, he removed to Colombo ; and when the latter place became the port of call for the island, he began to reap the rewards of

THE BUNGALOW.

his enterprise. He started in Colombo, at 1, Grand Oriental Hotel Arcade, and by 1870 his business had attained large dimensions, being patronised by British and foreign visitors of distinction, the Duke of Manchester and other peers among them. The present King, too, when staying at Queen's House on his visit to Ceylon as Prince of Wales, bought largely from the firm, members of the suite, Lords Carrington and Suffield prominent among them, following suit. Likewise, on the occasion of the visit of the present Prince and Princess of Wales in 1901, the firm's representative attended by special request at the King's Pavilion, Kandy, where several special articles were bought by the royal visitors ; and a letter certifying to the great satisfaction afforded them by these purchases was subsequently received by the firm. The Duke of Roxburgh and other members of the suite also gave the firm their patronage on this occasion.

The firm claims to do more than any other in Ceylon in the way of exporting cut and polished stones to the London market, the monthly sales in that great centre averaging thousands of pounds sterling. The present large premises and splendid showrooms have been occupied since October, 1905, and here may be seen a world-famed cat's-eye, one of the largest and best ever found in Ceylon, weighing 105 carats, of green sheen with white centre-line, and valued at £3,000. This stone was found by a coolie on a tea estate near Ratnapura, and was sold by the finder to a boutique-keeper for only Rs. 10 ; and it was not until it had passed through six hands that it reached the firm. Some 50 men are employed

DON THEODORIS & CO.

D. N. SINHO HAMY. — THE SHOWROOM. — R. D. ALWIS. — D. E. WEERASIRIE. — E. D. H. WEERASIRIE.

D. J. DE SILVA. W. D. PROLIS. THE SHOWROOM. THE LATE D. F. DE SILVA.

in the factories of the firm, the senior partner being Mahomed Macan Markar Effendi, Consul for Turkey, whose private residences are at Colpetty, Colombo, and Sea-view House, Galle.

Mr. Markar has founded a school for Arabic at Galle, which the firm maintains. He is a keen cricketer, and a member of the Galle Municipal Council. In connection with the business, the firm owns lands in the gem district of Ratnapura. A special feature of the showroom in Colombo is the magnificent display of antique Kandyan jewellery, consisting of the most delicate specimens of the goldsmith's art, thickly crusted with magnificent jewels of all descriptions. These heirlooms of former Kandyan chiefs have been in the possession of the Markar family for about three generations, and are of inestimable value. For the excellence of specimens of fine jewellery shown the firm obtained medals at the Colonial, Indian, Chicago, and St. Louis Exhibitions.

DON THEODORIS & CO.

Like so many other of the now flourishing business houses of Colombo, this of Don Theodoris & Co. has grown to its present eminence from small beginnings. It was founded at Galle, then the chief entrepôt of the island, in 1865, by Mr. D. T. Weerasirie, who started in business as a dealer in tortoiseshell, curios, and jewellery. The headquarters of the business were removed to Colombo when that city became the port of call for Ceylon, though the establishment at Galle was retained; and with the new progress of the city rapid expansion proceeded, until at this day Messrs. Don Theodoris & Co. rank among the very first of local jewellers and dealers in precious stones, articles in tortoiseshell, ivory, sandalwood, and ebony, carved curiosities, bric-à-brac, articles of vertu, and ornamental ware of all kinds. There are at present five members of the firm, the managing partner being Don Hendrick Weerasirie; and at Galle and Colombo about 70 men are employed, all the workmen being trained by the firm. For their exhibits at the Paris Exhibition of 1900 the firm received a prize medal and diploma; and at the St. Louis Exhibition (United States) in 1904 they won silver medals, besides a diploma for ivory carving, a special feature of the exhibit being a huge elephant carved in ebony covered with beautiful hand-chiselled silver trappings and bearing a silver howdah containing a reproduction of the Sacred Tooth of Buddha. In 1901 the Prince of Wales and Prince Waldemar of Denmark, when visiting Ceylon, made large purchases of the firm, who received signed photographs from the royal visitors. The firm carries on a large business as working jewellers, cutting and polishing stones obtained by their own agents direct from the mines. They also export gems to England, Germany, and France, and import silver-ware from India, Burma, and China, and jewellery from England. A special branch of the trade of this house is dealing in Kandyan and Indian antiques, arms, coins, and other curios. The members of the firm are all followers of Buddha.

D. F. DE SILVA & CO.

Conspicuous among the attractive jewellery establishments of Colombo are the showrooms at 7, Chatham Street, and 2, Grand Oriental Hotel Arcade, of D. F. de Silva & Co., jewellers and dealers in precious stones, working gold and silver smiths, tortoiseshell, ivory and ebony carvers. The business, which has, in the course of years, attained a forefront position, was started in a small way in Colombo in 1870 by the late Devendera Frederick de Silva (who died in October, 1904), in partnership with Messrs. P. L. Don Juanis de Silva and W. A. Don Prolis, the present managing partners; and the firm employs about 75 hands. They have supplied jewellery to Queen's House, Colombo, from the commencement of their business; and when the Prince and Princess of Wales visited Ceylon in 1901, the firm attended at King's Pavilion, Kandy by special order, and the royal visitors bought largely from them. The articles which mainly form the glittering display in the showrooms are manufactured from gold and silver. The firm also cuts and polishes stones bought by their own agents at the mines direct, and exports them, mostly to London. Amongst the articles they showed at the St. Louis Exhibition of 1904 was a beautifully carved ivory casket, mounted in gold, which was specially commended. They recently sold for a large amount a sapphire weighing 122 carats, 1 in. by 1½ ins., and reckoned one of the best stones of its kind. Among the fine samples of manufactured work executed by the firm are a Jubilee (1887) presentation casket, presented to Queen Victoria by the Ceylon Government; a Jubilee (1897) casket in carved ivory, also presented to the late Queen, which was mounted in gold and set with jewels, and made to the order of the Ceylon Government; a Coronation casket for the present King, supplied to the Government of the Straits Settlements; and a magnificent casket presented by the Planters' Association of Ceylon to the present Prince of Wales in 1901. This last article was made of carved ivory and gold, set with pearls and all the different Ceylon gems, numbering about 384. The firm has also manufactured many ornamental silver trowels for use in the ceremony of laying foundation stones for public buildings. Specimens of Messrs. D. F. de Silva & Co.'s work have been awarded many prize medals at exhibitions in different parts of the world, including the following: Melbourne International Exhibition, 1880; Agri-Horticultural Society, Ceylon, 1883, for precious stones, pearls, ebony, and carved works; Colonial and Indian Exhibition, 1886; Agri-Horticultural Society, 1887; diploma for gold medal, Earl's Court, London, 1896, for jewellery; République Française Exposition Internationale, 1900, and gold, silver, and bronze medals at the United States Universal Exposition, St. Louis, 1904.

COLOMBO COMMERCIAL: GENERAL.

GALLE FACE HOTEL.

This superb and extensive establishment, with its magnificent position, lavish decorations and equipment, and high-class accommodation, is renowned, not only throughout the Orient, but also wherever travellers who have passed through Colombo are to be found. It occupies the whole of the southern side of the famous Galle Face Promenade, which runs along the sea-front, with its adjoining open expanse so aptly termed the "lungs of Colombo," and thus rounds off and fitly completes a pleasure-ground and fashionable resort that is only equalled in the East by the Maidan of Calcutta or the Esplanade of Bombay. Here is ample provision for equestrian, carriage and pedestrian exercise, and here the leading inhabitants of Colombo, European and native, are wont to ride and drive, and, in the old-fashioned phrase, "take the air." It is the sea air undiluted; for the waves wash the wall of the Promenade along its whole length of nearly a mile, and the spray will, under a strong wind, sprinkle the roadway. Occupying so delightful and so health-giving a site, and one which is the centre of fashionable resort, it is no wonder that the Galle Face Hotel is so popular a place of entertainment, and has the world-wide reputation it possesses.

The architecture of the huge building is in the Renaissance style, and the interior arrangements are on a scale befitting the imposing exterior. The lofty reception hall leads into the various wide verandahs which abut upon the spacious ground-floor apartments; and through this hall the principal dining-room is reached, which has a verandah facing the sea and is fitted with electric fans. This is the largest hall in the island, the dimensions being 76 by 39 ft. and 30 ft. high. It accommodates 350 diners. There is also a smaller dining-room, with a verandah facing the Galle Face Esplanade, which is used for private dinner parties and banquets, the dimensions of which are 54 by 25 ft. and 17 ft. high. Of the same size is the ball-room, also provided with a verandah facing the Galle Face Esplanade, where weekly dances are usually held. During the "August week," the annual festive season of Colombo, this finely proportioned apartment is the main scene of the leading festivities and lavish entertainments which mark the gay period of Ceylon's capital. The reading-room and library, which faces the sea, is the finest situated room in the hotel, and is provided liberally with English and foreign newspapers. The drawing-room, also with a verandah facing Galle Face Esplanade, is handsomely furnished, and contains a Bechstein Grand piano; while the public billiard-room is equipped with four Burroughs and Watts tables and all the usual appointments in the best style. The dimensions of this room are 60 by 39 ft. and 30 ft. high; and there is also a small private billiard-room for the use of ladies and parties. The saloon bar has a length of 52 ft. and breadth of 36 ft., and is well equipped and stocked with specially imported wines, spirits, and cigars—with all, in fact, that a thirsty yet fastidious man may require.

The hotel possesses exterior attractions of a high order in an extensive lawn facing the sea and electrically illuminated, where a band performs twice a week, and in a swimming bath—the only one in Ceylon—which is 50 ft. long and 20 ft. broad, and laid with alabaster tiles. Here fresh-water showers are provided, also an American bar.

That very important branch of a hotel business, the culinary department, is in charge of a French *chef*, assisted by a large staff, and the kitchen is the largest in the island. Carriages and riding-horses may be engaged from the stables, and motor-cars can be obtained at short notice. The electric light is installed throughout the whole of the premises, and a lift gives convenient access to the different floors of the huge four-storeyed building. Suites of rooms with private bathrooms attached and elaborately furnished apartments are provided on every floor, while over 200 bedrooms are included in the sleeping accommodation, also bathrooms for ladies and gentlemen on each floor. The management is entirely European. Established over twenty years ago, the hotel was entirely rebuilt on an enlarged scale in 1894, and now it can claim to be provided with every comfort and convenience. The hotel porters meet all steamers on arrival as well as the principal trains arriving in Colombo.

CONRAD PETER.

Mr. Peter, the manager of the Galle Face Hotel, Colombo (of which establishment a description is given elsewhere in this section), was born in the year 1877 at Salzbrunn, near Breslau, Germany. He was educated at the principal town school in Breslau, and at the

GALLE FACE HOTEL—EXTERIOR, DINING HALL, GARDENS, AND SWIMMING BATH.

age of sixteen left his native land and went to London. In that great centre he obtained large experience in the management of hotels, and for three years he held the position of head reception clerk at the Charing Cross Hotel, in the Strand. He was then appointed to a responsible post in a leading hotel in Scotland. Mr. Peter s next move was to New York, where he accepted a similar position. After sojourning for a period in the United States, he received a hotel engagement in France. Eventually he came to Colombo as assistant-manager of the Galle Face Hotel, in the year 1902. On May 1, 1906, Mr. Peter was promoted to the position of acting head-manager of that well-known establishment, and on January 1, 1907, the appointment of manager was confirmed.

THE MANAGER, GALLE FACE HOTEL.

FAIRFIELD IRONWORKS.

Owing to the interdependent and conjoint nature of the larger commercial businesses carried on in Ceylon, several of the leading houses are found operating in more than one field of industry, and it therefore becomes impossible to classify them definitely and exclusively according to the branches of trade with which they are concerned. A case in point is the Fairfield Ironworks, a concern which, in addition to its engineering undertakings, carries on the business of general merchants and exporters of products of the island. This engineering business was first established in Colombo in 1867, and was taken over by Mr. Charles W. H. Duckworth, the present sole proprietor, in January, 1904. Mr. Duckworth was born in Liverpool in 1880, was educated in that city, and, later, obtained his training in mechanical engineering with Messrs. John H. Wilson & Co., engineering contractors to the British Government. He came to Ceylon in August, 1903, for his health, and joined his present business in the capacity of manager, afterwards taking the concern over on his own account. About a hundred hands are employed at the works; and a great deal of work is done in the manufacture of estate and tea machinery, pumping and mining gear, as well as other branches of civil engineering, the machinery used on the premises being mainly of English and American manufacture. During 1903 bulk oil (petroleum) was used as motive power for the constructing machinery; but since 1905 liquid fuel, used with Hornsby-Akroyd oil engines, has supplied the necessary power. Machinery of all descriptions is manufactured on the premises, and the firm send their own engineers as required to any place in the island to examine and report on machinery, and to erect plant and structural works generally. A speciality of the business at Colombo is the packing and baling of fibre of every description by means of a very powerful hydraulic baling-press, manufactured by Mills, Huddersfield. The firm exports tea, fibre, coir, plumbago, and all other local produce, the principal markets being Great Britain and Germany, and acts as local agent for John Birch & Co., London Wall, E.C., engineers; also for De Grelle, Houdrit & Co., London Wall, E.C., general merchants and exporters, and G. D. Jennings & Co., London. The Fairfield Ironworks are situated in Union Place, Slave Island, Colombo.

PLÂTÉ & CO.

This well-known firm of photographic artists was originally established in 1890, under the title of A. W. A. Plâté, in a small studio at the Bristol Hotel, Mr. and Mrs. Plâté then representing the whole staff. From the very outset the business progressed rapidly, and in 1892 the proprietors moved into more commodious

FAIRFIELD IRONWORKS.

W. H. Duckworth.
Baling Department.

Portion of Heavy Machine Shop
Small Machine Shop.

PLÂTÉ AND CO.—THE STUDIO (EXTERIOR AND INTERIOR).

premises at Colpetty. Soon after this Mr. Heinemann joined the firm as managing partner, and the business continued to steadily expand, with the result that the present staff of the establishment comprises ten Europeans and over 60 natives. Besides their Colpetty studio and several others in Colombo, Messrs. Plâté have a branch establishment at Nuwara Eliya, in the hill-country, and, in addition, hook-stalls at the Queen's Hotel, Kandy, and the Galle Face Hotel, Colombo. The Colpetty studio and office practically represent the head-quarters of the firm, and here are located extensive work-rooms, dark-rooms, show-rooms and other adjuncts to a photographic establishment, in addition to the spacious studio, reckoned one of the finest in the East. On these premises almost all the printing and finishing work of the firm is carried out, and thence pictures are despatched to all parts of the world.

The firm is now styled Plâté & Co., and is the property of a small private company, the alteration from the original style having been effected in 1900. In connection with this change the scope of the business was considerably enlarged, and the firm embarked in dealing largely (both wholesale and retail) in all kinds of photographic supplies and apparatus. A little later, when picture postcards came so universally into vogue, the firm again extended its trade to embrace this new line of business, being the first in the island to supply the demand for this novelty. Messrs. Plâté & Co.'s output of picture post-cards now reaches half a million each year. Their numerous series of views of Ceylon are well known, and are ever in increasing demand. The portrait work of this firm has gained a wide reputation, and they have, during the past sixteen years, photographed many celebrities (including members of the Royal Family) from all parts of the globe. The variety and high quality of the photographic pictures make the galleries at the different studios well worth a visit.

KEARLEY & TONGE, LTD.

This well-known house of tea-shippers and importers of food produce, whose head office is in Mitre Square, London, E.C., and who have an Indian branch at 2, Mangoe Lane, Calcutta, carry on a large business in Ceylon in buying and shipping tea to their London house direct, also to all parts of the world, their Colombo depôt being at Stratford House, Union Place. Kearley & Tonge are the proprietors of the popular "Ceylindo" brand of tea. The manager of the Colombo branch is Mr. A. Hudson, and the nature of the main operations carried on at the Ceylon establishment is the blending and packing of teas of all sorts for export.

THE CEYLON MANURE WORKS.

This business was originally established in Cramer's Lane, Pettah, Colombo, by Mr. A. Baur, the present proprietor, in 1897. Owing to the inadequacy of the premises there for the extensive operations rendered necessary by the steady growth of the business, the works were moved to Kelaniya, the first station of the Up-country railway line after leaving Colombo, where the working plant has been erected on a spacious ground of four acres, adjoining the Kelaniya railway station. The storage floor measures 60,000 square feet, and all the buildings are constructed of brick and iron. The firm has its own private railway sidings for the more convenient and speedy loading and unloading of the trucks, which are run over the firm's weighbridge. The imported manures are loaded into trucks at the wharf and run straight into the firm's premises; and the manures for the various planting districts are sent to their destination direct from this private siding, where the material is loaded under the direct supervision of railway officers. The machinery used for the manipulation and manufacture of the manure is thoroughly up to date. It consists of four powerful disintegrators, with mechanical sifters attached, two small disintegrators, two large side-rollers with mechanical sifters, one bone-breaking machine, five large bone-steaming boilers with a powerful drying apparatus, two fish-drying machines, and other apparatus. The motive power is derived from a 200-horse-power steam engine, manufactured by Gebruder Sulzer, of Winterthur, Switzerland In addition to the mechanical appliances used, the firm employs over 300 hands.

The firm is the only one in Ceylon exclusively concerned with the manure industry, and it possesses by far the largest manure works in Ceylon. The rapid development of Mr. A. Baur's business speaks to the popularity of, and the demand that exists for, the manures sold by the firm. Among the more widely used kinds of manure sold are castor-cake, ground-nut cake, rape cake, fish, steamed and unsteamed bone meal, burnt coral lime, basic slag, sulphate and muriate of potash, superphosphate and concentrated superphosphate, sulphate of ammonia, nitrate of potash, blood-meal, nitrate of soda, kainit, and precipitated phosphate of lime. In addition to these manures, Mr. Baur makes a speciality of special fertilisers for tea, rubber, cacao, coconuts, and other Ceylon-grown products, which are in great demand. He has been making the preparation of these fertilisers a close and special study for years past. Among the firm's constituents are most of the Colombo estate agencies and the majority of the planting companies of Ceylon. Large stocks of manure are always kept on hand to meet any possible demand that may be made beyond the average quantity taken. A chemical laboratory is attached to the works, where soils are analysed and suitable manure mixtures recommended.

Mr. A. Baur, who is a native of Switzerland, is the sole proprietor of the concern, while the local manager is Mr. J. Haemmig, who is assisted by Mr. T. Wagner and a large staff of native employees. The head offices are at Prince Street, in the Fort of Colombo.

THE GALAHA CEYLON TEA ESTATES AND AGENCY COMPANY, LTD.

The head office of this business, which is extensively engaged in the cultivation, preparation, and export of tea and produce of all kinds, as well as in acting as shipping and general agents, is at 4, Lloyd's Avenue, Fenchurch Street, London, with Messrs. Rowe, White & Co. as secretaries, while the Ceylon offices and stores are in Union Place, Slave Island, Colombo. The managing director in England is Mr. C. E. Strachan, and the manager in Ceylon is Mr. G. Hathorn. The largest tea factory in Ceylon, namely, that at Galaha, in the Kandy district, is owned by the company, and here just under 2,000,000 lbs. weight of tea is turned out per annum. Besides Galaha, a large number of tea and rubber estates belong to the company, including Kitoolamoola, Maousakelle, Vedehette, Goorookelle and Kirrawana and Dunally, all belonging to the Galaha group, of which Mr. L. Carey is the resident manager. The company are also agents for the Ragalla and Halgranoya estates, which belong to the Ragalla Tea Estates Company, Ltd., and manage the Campion, Cottaganga, Freshwater, Hauteville, St. George, and Katoolooya estates, personally owned by Mr. C. E. Strachan. They are agents for the Associated Tea Company, who own the Horagoda, Chesterford, Doragalla group, and Silverkandy estates; for the Dimbula Valley Tea Company, who own the Eladuwa, Bearwell, Belgravia, Elgin, Langdale, Lippakelle, Mousa Ella, and Tillicoultry estates; for the Matale Ceylon Rubber Company, who own the Ambaganga group, comprising Ambaganga, Arolsen, and Waradaminie; and they are also the shipping agents for the Ceylon Tea Plantations Company, which is the premier planting company in Ceylon. Further, they are the agents for the rubber, cacao, and tea properties of the Rubber Estates of Ceylon, Ltd., which are situated in the Kegalla and Kurunegala districts, and comprise Morankande, Maousava, Muwakande, Udahena, Kalugalla, and Debatagama. They are agents for numerous other individual estates as well as for the Goomera Estates Company, and the Maturata Estates Company, and are local agents for the

ÇEYLON MANURE WORKS, SHOWING THE VARIOUS DEPARTMENTS OF THE BUSINESS.

Imperial Tea Chest Company, and co-agents for the Guardian Assurance Company, while their London correspondents are Messrs. Rowe, White & Co., 4, Lloyd's Avenue, and Messrs. M. P. Evans & Co., 30, Mincing Lane. The Galaha Company was originally established in London in June, 1896, both the estates property and the Colombo business being owned at that time by Mr. C. E. Strachan, with Mr. Hathorn as manager of the company.

All tea and other products from these numerous estates pass through the Colombo stores of the company; and practically every kind and class of tea manufactured finds its way to the various markets through the channels of the company. In the Colombo stores 70 to 80 hands are employed. The buildings, covering nearly three acres of ground, afford a flooring storage of 350 ft. by 38 ft. The tea is packed in the factories on the estates, and then brought to the Colombo stores ready for shipment. Cardamoms are also cured locally, and exported to the United Kingdom. All the tea estates are supplied with their stores, foodstuffs, and other requirements through the Colombo office. The European assistants at the Colombo establishment are Mr. W. E. Gildea and Mr. H. W. Crabbe, and 15 clerks are also employed there. The codes used by the company are the A B C, Western Union, and Lieber's.

THE GALAHA CEYLON TEA ESTATES AND AGENCY COMPANY'S FACTORY.

GEORGE ROBSON & CO.

This firm of merchants and engineers was founded in the year 1903 on its present site, at 5 and 6, New Moor Street, Pettah, Colombo. The business done on these premises embraces the baling of coir and fibre by hydraulic presses, the installation of factory and pumping machinery, the import of dynamite, hardware, and estate requisites, and the shipment of all kinds of Ceylon produce. The premises, which include the general offices, baling and engineering departments and stores, have a ground area of 20,000 sq. ft.; and the plant and appliances used are of the finest British make. Messrs. Robson & Co. are agents for Thomas Firth & Sons, Ltd., engineers, of Sheffield; William Bennett, Sons & Co. (safety fuse makers), of Camborne; the Actien-Gesellschaft Siegener Dynamit-Fabrik, of Cologne.

GEORGE ROBSON.

Mr. George Robson, who was born at Aberdeen in 1864 and trained in various technical schools in Scotland, came out to Ceylon in 1892 as manager of Messrs. W. H. Davies & Co.'s business (mentioned elsewhere in this section of the book). After ten years' connection with that house, Mr. Robson started business on his own account, and the present flourishing firm bearing his name is solely controlled by him. His private residence is Augusta Cottage, Ward Place, Cinnamon Gardens, Colombo.

FRANCIS F. STREET.

This firm, engaged in the tea industry, was established in Colombo in 1885 by Mr. Francis F. Street, who was the first tea-buyer in Ceylon. The firm now carries on a large export in tea, their packing and storing offices being situated at Ambawatte Mills, in Slave Island, Colombo. The firm also makes a speciality of reporting on and valuing tea, while other kinds of Ceylon produce are shipped to order. The boxes used for packing tea are manufactured on the premises, sapu-wood being employed for the 5-lb. and 10-lb. boxes in preference to any other, for its light weight, whiteness, and absence of any disagreeable smell.

LOUIS SIEDLE.

Mr. Louis Siedle, who came to Ceylon some thirty-five years ago, was born at Woolwich in the year 1852, and started his business career at an early age, apprenticing himself to the well-known firm of Siemens Bros., engineers, Charlton, Kent. With strong inclinations for travel and adventure, he left England in 1872, and settled himself in Ceylon, where he has been engaged in the gemming industry and in the purchase and export of precious stones and pearls. With his long experience he may be considered an expert in this special line of business. So comprehensive is his knowledge of everything connected with precious stones that he is often consulted by intending purchasers for purposes of valuation and advice. On the occasion of the Prince and Princess of Wales's visit to Ceylon, Mr. Louis Siedle met the royal visitors by special request, and was commissioned to value and select precious stones for them. His operations in the gem business include mining, polishing, and the export of precious stones to London and the Continent, and the import of stone-set jewellery for local requirements. He has been connected with the pearl fisheries of Ceylon from almost the time of his arrival, and visits the annual pearling station for personal inspection and selection of specimens.

Mr. Siedle's chief recreation is shooting, and he is an exceptionally good marksman. He has great musical talent, and takes part in local concerts and the performances of amateur orchestral societies. He was Bugle-major of the Ceylon Light Infantry from 1881 to 1889. Subsequently he joined the Ceylon Planters'

LOUIS SIEDLE

Rifle Corps, and has since been placed on the reserve. His private residence is Egerton House, Kollupitiya, Colombo.

W. H. DAVIES & CO.

This house was established in Colombo twenty-seven years ago by the present head of the firm (Mr. W. H. Davies) for import business; but since that time an export trade as well has grown up and developed, until now the firm ships Ceylon products to all parts of the world. Dealing first with the original side of the business, the chief among the articles imported are machinery, galvanised and other iron, metals, general hardware, cement, lubricating oils, materials for light railways, momi-wood tea-chests, and lead for lining the tea-cases, the firm dealing largely in the last-named commodity. W. H. Davies & Co. also hold the Ceylon agency for Australian produce from the State of Victoria, conceded to them ten years ago, the import consisting principally of compressed forage. Other cattle foods are also handled, among which "Cattleloid" is imported in large quantities for use at the various Government dairies and throughout the island. The firm has also been entrusted with extensive Government contracts, including one for railway sleepers, and another, now in course of completion, for telegraph and telephone poles. Explosives form another class of imports, and these are stored in the firm's four large magazines, having a capacity of from 3,000 to 4,000 cases. The well-known Cooppal brand of sporting powders is also stocked. The firm also holds the sole agency in the island for many kinds of special machinery used in up-to-date tea treatment, including Parnall's cutters and Barber's sifters; and the engines and boilers of Messrs. E. R. & F. Turner, the well-known English engineers, are also stocked.

In connection with the supply of requisites to tea estates, the firm established large engineering works at Fairfield, Slave Island, Colombo, some fifteen years ago, and has since erected and equipped many tea and other produce factories in the low-country, while nearly all the owners of plumbago mines have been supplied from the same source with pumping plant and other mining machinery.

The export business of the house is extensive, embracing trade in all the principal products of Ceylon. Besides owning several tea estates, the firm is agent for numerous others. The green varieties of the leaf, in request for the American markets, receive special attention, one of the firm's estates being entirely devoted to this class of the staple product. Copra and fibres in large quantities are cured and baled for shipment at the firm's own stores at Panchikawatte, where every facility exists for these processes, as well as for manipulating tea-fluff, cardamoms, kapok, cowries, and other products. Messrs. Davies & Co. also control the output of two mills turning out desiccated coconut, the brand of the firm being well known in the English and Continental markets. To cope with the increasing demand for this article the mills are now being enlarged. The firm exports sapu-wood, satinwood, and ebony, and is sole shipping agent for the only "prepared" cocoa in the island, which is turned out from the factory established in 1901 by Messrs. C. C. Barber & Co. on their "Grove" cacao estate, Ukuwella. Messrs. Davies & Co. have their own establishment at Kanatta for curing plumbago, and large quantities of the mineral are here prepared and put up for shipment to England, America, and the Continent of Europe.

Besides the line of operations above specified, the firm—whose offices are in Baillie Street Colombo—has been for eleven years in succession sole agent for advertisements on the Ceylon Government Railway, and also represents the following firms: The Yorkshire Fire Insurance Company, Messrs. E. R. & F. Turner's engines, the Imperial Jarrah Timber Company, the Globe Oil Engine Company, Messrs. McLean & Co., "Coronet" cement, the "Blickensderfer" Typewriter Company, Messrs. Phillips & Sons (safes), Messrs. Wm. Edward & Sons (edge tools), the Challenge Air Propeller Company, the Midland Gun Company, Sir William Burnett & Co., and Gould's Manufacturing Company (pumps).

HENDERSON & CO.

Mr. J. A. Henderson is at the head of this Colombo firm. He received his early training in the tea trade with Messrs. Lloyd, Matheson & Carritt, the well-known London brokers, and counts nearly twenty years' experience in this particular line. The export to all parts of the world of tea, cinnamon, desiccated coconut, fibres, and other Ceylon produce constitutes the principal business in which the firm of Henderson & Co. are engaged; while they also import cotton goods and other commodities falling within the category of general merchandise. As regards the exportation of tea, the packet business forms a special feature in which this firm are particularly interested. They have their own proprietary brands of tea labels, chief among which, and very attractively got up, are the "Corona," "Elixa," "Pearlana," and "Vittana."

The firm's Nilwatte tea factory is located in the suburb of Colpetty and is fully fitted with all the latest machinery, this equipment insuring rapid, though regular and well-executed work. Packets of tea are here turned out in great numbers, in different sizes and description, labelled with variegated designs of wrappers, and cased for shipment, the cases being put together in a woodworking shop on the premises. In other departments of the factory cinnamon, cocoa, and other articles of produce raised in the island are prepared for the market with due attention to obtaining the best results. The firm have published a handy little pamphlet on "Tea Cultivation and Manufacture in Ceylon," descriptive of the growth and manufacture of tea in the island. Messrs. Henderson & Co. are agents in Ceylon for a number of important firms in Great Britain and elsewhere.

HARRY ERNEST BROCK.

Mr. Harry Ernest Brock was born in 1882 at Newport, Isle of Wight, and educated at Margate College. On leaving school he was apprenticed to Messrs. Walker Bros., and served his time at their engineering works,

H. E. BROCK.

Bouverie Street, Fleet Street, London. After his apprenticeship he received a practical training in the mechanism and working of motor-cars in connection with the well-known Kingston Motor Works, the Flight Motor Company, of Hornsey, London, and the Beaufort Motor Company, of London and Germany. In 1905 he came to Ceylon, and occupied the position of chief engineer of the Ceylon Motor Company, Ltd., Colombo, until that corporation was wound up in the first half of 1906. Mr. Brock then proceeded on a visit to England. Football and cycling claim the greater part of his leisure. He was a member of the Hornsey Park Football Club—the holders of the North London Football Cup and winners of the North London Football League continuously since 1901.

A. RANDEL.

This business, of the European Cycle and Motor Engineering Works, which was established in Colombo in 1900 by Mr. Arthur Randel, is solely concerned with the sale and repair of cycles, motors, and rickshaws, and is housed in the Hamidia Buildings, Union Place, Slave Island, Colombo. Mr. Randel was educated at Berlin, and after passing through the Handelsschule, joined the engineering firm of Messrs. Wolff & Co., Magdeburg, which he left to take up a position on the staff of Albrecht & Co., Braunschweig. After an extensive training in all departments of mechanical engineering, and many years' experience with English and Continental firms, he came to Ceylon and started his present business. The depot is equipped with every accessory for cycles, motors, and other vehicular conveyances; and among the articles on view is Mr. Randel's patent (No. 750) rubber-tyred rickshaw, which possesses certain special features insuring smooth running. The motor department is in charge of Mr. Nietzschmann, who is also an expert engineer; and the machinery used in the various processess of engineering is of the best manufacture. The business is about

A. RANDEL.

the only one of its kind in the island conducted solely by European labour, and its central position makes it a convenient resort for cyclists and motorists.

N. S. FERNANDO.

An example of what native enterprise, joined to honesty of dealing, can accomplish is supplied by the past progress and present position of the business popularly known in Ceylon as N. S. Fernando, and founded by the late Mr. N. S. Fernando in 1875. The present business originated in a humble boutique in Bankshall Street, Pettah, Colombo, the stock comprising little more than a miscellaneous assortment of curry stuffs, relieved with a modest stock of groceries. But there was that about this Sinhalese trader which marked the rising man, and which produced the prosperous merchant and native philanthropist. In the first year he opened his boutique he commenced importing foreign merchandise. For a time Fortune refused to smile upon him. Perseverance, however, conquered. Mr. Fernando continued his importations from Europe, and was the first native to introduce paper into the island. The business flourished and expanded in various directions, and in twelve years Mr. Fernando's position and reputation as a business man had become thoroughly assured. His operations having far outgrown the premises in which he made his humble start, the original premises were demolished, and on their site the present large and handsome establishment was erected and opened in 1887. The enterprise displayed in the costly extension of premises was abundantly justified. From the start Mr. Fernando had laid himself out to win the confidence and secure the goodwill of European houses of business, and the result is seen in the magnitude of his dealings abroad. It is estimated that in the first twenty-four years of the firm's existence over 200,000 packages of foreign merchandise, covering a value of some Rs. 6,000,000, were imported, out of which the amount paid for duty alone came to nearly three lakhs (300,000) of rupees. The late Mr. N. S. Fernando was not content with importing from abroad the articles required to improve the standard of living locally. He resolved to build up an export trade also, and set himself, with characteristic energy, to bring the island's products to the notice of foreign countries. Commencing with India, he gradually enlarged and extended his operations. This Pettah house was awarded a medal in the International Exhibition held at Calcutta in 1884 for native products, another at the Ottawa Exhibition in 1883 for Ceylon drugs, and a third for similar products at the London Exhibition of 1885. At all local exhibitions Mr. N. S. Fernando has also been represented, and with never-failing success. With the object of encouraging other native merchants and imparting a needful impetus to trade, he started in 1885 a journal published in the Sinhalese vernacular, entitled *Welanda Mithraya*, or the *Merchant's Friend*. This proved a useful publication as long as it lived, but it had to be discontinued owing to other demands on Mr. Fernando's time.

The late Mr. Fernando was also a devoted Buddhist, and the present partners, together with all the employees, belong to the same faith. He did much to encourage the loyal

N. A. WIJEYESEKERA. INTERIOR OF CASH DRAPERY STORES.
LOADING GOODS. H. S. FERNANDO. SKETCH OF NEW PREMISES.
BANKSHALL STREET ESTABLISHMENT. THE LATE N. S. FERNANDO. BRANCH ESTABLISHMENT.
(Mohandiram N. S. Fernando Wijeyesekera.)

observance of Buddhist ceremonies and festivals, and was always on the look-out for opportunities of benefiting his countrymen and serving their needs. He was instrumental in having "The Arabian Nights Entertainments" translated into Sinhalese for the benefit of his countrymen. In 1898, in conjunction with a co-religionist, Mr. Fernando built a rest-house at Anuradhapura, the ancient capital of Ceylon and a city sacred to Buddhists, for the convenience of pilgrims, which establishment his widow maintains. Mr. N. S. Fernando may also be considered to have been the originator of the Victoria Memorial Eye Hospital, and his portrait in oils hangs at the entrance hall of that institution. He had given a substantial subscription in aid of any movement to ameliorate the condition of the blind, and when Ceylon's Memorial to Queen Victoria took its present shape and form, Mr. Fernando not only readily consented to his subscription being devoted to this object, but supplemented it with another handsome contribution. For his generosity and munificence Sir West Ridgeway, then Governor of Ceylon, honoured him with the rank of Mohandiram; and the native merchants showed their cordial approval of the honour conferred upon Mr. Fernando by presenting him with a gold sword and an illuminated address. To general regret Mr. Fernando did not live to see his self-denying efforts come to fruition. He left a name which will always be held in respect by the Sinhalese, and an example which all classes of the community might follow. The business which Mr. N. S. Fernando built up with so much care is being carried on by the present proprietors, Messrs. N. A. Wijeyesekera, son of the founder, and H. S. Fernando, his son-in-law, on the same progressive lines. The younger generation have already shown themselves to be shrewd business men, also that they are animated by the high principles which distinguished the late Mr. N. S. Fernando.

The firm not only transacts the general business of export and import merchants, but carries on a large wholesale trade in stationery and paper. They are importers of drapery, native drugs (musk, bezoar, and camphor), and exporters of tea and coconut oil, being owners of coconut estates in the Kurunegala district. The drapery and millinery are imported from Europe direct and the silks from India and Japan. The cash drapery warehouse, which the late Mr. N. S. Fernando started, continues to be a popular institution of one of the busiest business quarters in Colombo, the system of cash sales adopted being a strong element in its success. The new building in which the drapery branch is located is fitted throughout with electricity, the showrooms are spacious and well ventilated, and the inspection of the large and varied stock, which is continually being replenished from the best European houses, may here be undertaken in cool and comfortable conditions. Not only does this warehouse supply a long-felt want for the native classes, but it is securing an ever-increasing measure of European patronage. In the stationery department N. S. Fernando has one of the largest stocks in Ceylon, and a wholesale character is given to this branch of the business by the fact that most of the native retail firms purchase their stock of stationery from this house. The traditions of the house are excellent, its financial standing unquestioned, its connection with European houses wide and extensive; celebrated English, Scotch, and Continental houses are represented, and the firm holds the following agencies: William Duff & Co., London; Wiggins, Teape & Co., Ltd., London; Edward Lloyd, Ltd., London; Scott & Bowne, Ltd., London; the Rosmarine Manufacturing Company, London; A. B. Fleming & Co., Edinburgh; Alexander Pirie & Sons, Ltd., Aberdeenshire; Colgate & Co., New York; and F. M. Clements, Sydney. The firm's bankers are the Mercantile Bank of India, Ltd., and the Chartered Bank of India, Australia, and China.

H. DON CAROLIS & SONS.

This extensive furniture business, one of the largest and best appointed in Asia, was founded by Mudaliyar Don Carolis Hewavitarne, who passed away in February, 1906, at the ripe age of seventy-three. Like so many successful undertakings, this business was begun in a very modest way, its first habitat having been a small house in the corner of Keyzer Street, Pettah, Colombo, where operations were started in 1860, when Ceylon was enjoying the palmiest days of the coffee industry. At that time Mr. Don Carolis, seeing the practicability of supplying the planters with solid and artistic furniture in the best European styles and at moderate prices, brought together for the purpose a small band of carpenters from Moratuwa, a township on the south-west coast of the island, which then had a reputation for carpentry and joiners' work. The principal woods used in the manufacture of the furniture by this firm are nadun (Ceylon walnut), satin, ebony, calamander, and jak—which latter assumes with age a rich mahogany colour. In 1886 Mr. Avery, an Australian horsedealer, introduced Ceylon furniture to Australia; and in 1895 an Indo-Afric syndicate was formed in London to carry on a large furniture business with South Africa. This latter undertaking led to the establishment of the firm's steam furniture works in Slave Island, where about 250 skilled workmen are daily employed. By the enterprise and energy of which this development afforded an instance, the firm has acquired a preponderance of the local trade in this line; and improved methods of manufacture, combined with novel designs and a general go-ahead policy, soon spread its fame, not only throughout the island, but also through the neighbouring continent. The firm is now carrying on business with the Straits Settlements, Australia, South Africa, India, Burma, England, and the United States of America; and on the British military occupation of South Africa this firm, among others, was selected to supply furniture for the Government buildings of that country.

The main premises of the firm are at 54, Keyzer Street, and at 52–56, First Cross Street, both in the Pettah quarter of Colombo. The extensive showrooms at these centres occupy a space of nearly three acres, and are replete with furniture of every description, from the finest and most delicately hand-carved cabinets, overmantels, and drawing-room suites to plain solid household and office furniture of every kind. The showrooms, fitted throughout with electric lights and ventilated by electric fans, form quite one of the sights of Colombo. This extensive business is managed by two of the late Mr. Don Carolis Hewavitarne's sons, aided by a large staff of well-trained and experienced assistants. Mr. Edmund Hewavitarne, the present senior partner, has spent some time in Japan, studying the industrial and commercial methods of that country; while Mr. Simon Hewavitarne has introduced many improvements consequent upon a visit to England and the Continent of Europe. About 750 workmen are employed in the different departments of the business, of whom many are well-trained handicraftsmen; and the principal branches of the business are concerned with the supply of furniture, upholstery, rattan and cane goods, and coir matting. The firm imports large quantities of bentwood furniture, lamps, crockery, cutlery, iron beds, spring mattresses, marble clocks, hardware, carpets, plated ware, Chinese matting—in short, all the essentials necessary for the "house beautiful." The Japanese department is one of the largest in Ceylon, and the collection contains exquisitely artistic work. The firm also undertakes house-building and other contract work, both public and private. Messrs. Don Carolis & Sons have obtained gold and silver medals for furniture exhibited at the Ceylon Agricultural Exhibitions, the Indian Industrial Exhibition of 1901, the Paris Exhibition of 1900, and the St. Louis Exposition of 1904.

The timber used for the manufacture of the furniture is obtained locally, and is brought by carts, rafts, or padda boats to the steam mills, which latter are prettily situated on the banks

INTERIOR OF WORKSHOP

SIMON HEWAVITARNE.

EDMUND HEWAVITARNE.

INTERIOR OF SHOWROOM.

THE LATE MUDALIYAR DON CAROLIS HEWAVITARNE.

EXTERIOR OF WORKSHOP.

of the Colombo Lake, not far from the Galle Face. The steam factory, where a 30-horse-power steam engine supplies the motive power, consists of the two departments of furniture making and timber sawing. A free Industrial School is attached to the works, where a large number of boys are taught carpentry. In all Messrs. Don Carolis & Sons pay about Rs. 250,000 (£16,666) a year in wages, and proof that the workmen are well looked after and contented is supplied by the fact that some of the employees count from sixteen to thirty years' service with the firm.

The founder of this large business, the late Mr. Don Carolis Hewavitarne, was a gentleman of pure Sinhalese and Buddhist origin and culture, having received his education at the Buddhist monastery of Raja Maha Vihara, near Matara, in the south of the island. He was an expert in astrological mathematics, and was the first to print the Sinhalese "Astronomical Year Book." He was also a student of Brahmanical and Buddhist spiritual literature. A predominant feature of his life was his devotion to his religion. A staunch Buddhist, he was one of the founders of the Vidyodaya College—an institution for training Buddhist monks—which he supported throughout his life. He was also a large-hearted, open-handed man, the poor, the sick, and the needy finding in him a ready and kindly benefactor. His munificence, in spite of himself, eventually came to the notice of the Ceylon Government, and he was honoured with the rank of Mudaliyar. The last generous act of his life was the setting apart of property worth Rs. 30,000 for the spread of industrial education in Ceylon among Buddhists, by sending suitable Buddhist young men to Japan to learn Japanese industrial methods.

EDWIN PHILIPS.

Mr. Edwin Philips is an instance of a man born in Ceylon, but who has found success in planting pursuits in a neighbouring portion of the British Empire. He first saw the light in Colombo in 1869, and received his education in Ceylon. In 1893 he left his native country for the Straits Settlements, and there secured a position with the Straits Trading Company, Ltd., which has branches all over the Federated Malay States. Some time later he embarked in tin-mining on a small scale. But his true bent was towards the planting business; and when the superintendentship of Tambun Estate, which was planted with Liberian coffee at that time and is now the site of the well-known Tambun mines, became vacant, he managed to secure the appointment. Subsequently he purchased the Plang Estate, which was planted with coffee, from Mr. F. G. Bosanquet for the modest figure of 3,000 dollars. Yet, owing to the declining price of coffee and the unhealthy state of the district, this was considered a bold speculation on the part of Mr. Philips. Shortly afterwards he took up his residence on the property, and thinking that two strings to a bow were better than one, he planted Para rubber between the coffee at various distances. Rubber planting at that time was entirely experimental, but this new departure proved very successful.

Seven years later Mr. Philips was in a position to place a consignment of sheet rubber in the Singapore market, which fetched the record price of 425 dollars a picul (about 133 lbs.), that is, at the rate of 6s. 11½d. per lb., according to the London rate of exchange at the time. This is the highest price yet obtained for

EDWIN PHILIPS.

sheet rubber from the Federated Malay States; and the transaction naturally attracting the attention of capitalists, Mr. Philips received many offers for the estate. For the time being Mr. Philips resisted all these temptations. But after a while, owing to the many attacks of malarial fever he had sustained, and the absolute necessity for a change from the continued hardships he had endured and battled against single-handed, he eventually made up his mind to part with the estate, and sold the property to the Asiatic Rubber and Produce Company, Ltd., for £10,000. Mr. Philips then made a tour through Japan to recruit his shattered health, and concluded his health-seeking with a visit to his native land, after nearly thirteen and a half years of strenuous labour in the most unhealthy parts of the Federated Malay States. Mr. Philips is now the proprietor of the Eastfield and Kanthan Estates in Sungei Siput, Kuala Kangsar district, Perak, in the Federated Malay States, which he intends to fully utilise by planting both properties with rubber as the main product, and coffee, cacao, and different other products as catch crops. Mr. Philips has large interests in agricultural and mining companies in Malaya, and owns several valuable houses in the State of Perak.

MOUNT LAVINIA GRAND HOTEL.

This hotel, owing to its elevated situation on a knoll at the extremity of a projecting point of the sea-beach on the west coast, about seven miles by rail or road from Colombo, commands a grand view, and is a favourite seaside resort with visitors to Ceylon, the residents of the capital, and the public generally. The sea-bathing in perfectly safe conditions to be enjoyed off the rocks and sandy beach at this spot forms a special attraction. The building is commodious and comfortable in all its appointments, and the establishment is noted for the excellence of its cuisine — a major consideration with visitors whose appetites are whetted by the sea breezes. A specialty of the management is the provision for the needs of travellers in the form of tiffins and dinners, and the wants of these are catered for with particular care. Situated on one of the healthiest spots in the neighbourhood of Colombo, the hotel, with its up-to-date arrangements, is peculiarly suited for the rest and recuperation of invalids and sufferers from the debilitating effects of the city climate. The spacious verandahs in front of the building directly face the ocean and receive the full benefit of the prevailing inshore breezes. The internal disposition of the establishment also ensures coolness as well as comfort, the apartments all being spacious and well ventilated. In the large and lofty principal dining-room 150 guests can be accommodated with ease at one time; and the drawing-room and other public rooms are all on the same scale of amplitude, while the private apartments and bedrooms are airy and comfortable, and in all their appointments up to the standard of a first-class hotel. The building is lighted throughout by electricity, the current being supplied by a small power station in the grounds. Visitors in search of recreation will find that the fine billiard-room contains two excellent tables, or they can take more vigorous exercise in the tennis-court, or scramble about the rocks, or indulge in a stroll along the smooth sandy beach. There is also good sea-fishing to be obtained at the very doors of the hotel. The Mount Lavinia railway station adjoins the grounds of the establishment, and a frequent service of trains is maintained between this point and Colombo, the journey either way occupying from fifteen to thirty

MOUNT LAVINIA GRAND HOTEL. THE DINING SALOON.

minutes ; while, if the road route be preferred, it will be found to pass through picturesque and interesting native villages, being flanked also for the greater part of the seven miles by the superior residences of the wealthier citizens of Colombo. The management of the hotel is in the capable and experienced hands of Mr. C. H. Link, who has a wide and well-deserved reputation as a caterer.

GEORGE FREDERICK NELL.

Motor-cars and cycles have for some time past taken a place in the popular pastimes of the more affluent members of the different communities in the island, but not until recently has their importance as a safe and speedy means of locomotion when travelling on business been recognised. With their introduction the necessity arose for establishments for the repair and maintenance of motor vehicles, so that the motor and cycle trade of Colombo is of some importance. Notwithstanding this, there are only a few motor and cycle engineering works of any consequence in the town, and of these the one owned and directed by the subject of our notice has gained a foremost place as a result of the exercise of industry combined with the possession of the advantages of natural intelligence and a thoroughly practical training. Mr. Nell is the eldest son of Mr. Paul Nell (engineer and tea expert, Ceylon), and a grandson of Mr. Louis Nell, retired Queen's Advocate (in Switzerland). He was born in 1879 at Matale, and was educated at Trinity and St. Paul's Colleges. After completing his education he joined his father's engineering business at Nawalapitiya, and went through a course of training in mechanical engineering, adding to this by further experience gained in India. He then became junior partner and working manager of the firm of P. Nell & Son, proprietors of the Ceylon Cycle Works, Slave Island, Colombo, and in 1898 he started in engineering business on his own account, and from a comparatively small beginning his business increased rapidly to what it is to-day, and at his works, which are situated in Union Place, Colombo, all manner of engineering is carried out in all its branches. He is the sole proprietor and working manager, and, as he resides on the premises, is in a position to devote personal attention and give supervision to all work entrusted to his firm. His principal assistant is Mr. W. O. Edema, late of the motor staff of Sir Thomas Lipton, while in addition he employs over a score of well-trained and experienced mechanics. In the motor, cycle, typewriter, and general engineering departments every make of machine is being dealt with, from small repairs to the practical rebuilding of motor-cars, cycles, &c., all work being done entirely on the premises.

G. F. NELL.

Up-to-date machinery is frequently introduced, and recently a specially imported screw-cutting and surfacing turning lathe for motor-car work was added. The future prospects of the "Union" Cycle and Engineering Works are very bright, and there is every likelihood of its becoming the most important of its class in the island. The question of extending the premises has already forced itself upon the proprietor's consideration.

F. X. PEREIRA & SONS.

The business of direct importation of drapery and millinery from various European countries, under the above title, is carried on at Ridgeway Buildings, Pettah, Colombo. The firm was founded in 1888 by the late Francis X. Pereira, a native of Tuticorin, Southern India, in Main Street, Pettah, in a modest way. The premises were afterwards enlarged with the growth of the business, and in November, 1905, the firm removed to Ridgeway Buildings in First Cross Street, where some 45 hands are now employed. The firm was specially appointed drapers to Sir West and Lady Ridgeway when the former was Governor of Ceylon. This business, now one of the important native houses of Colombo, is the outcome of adaptability and industry, and was built up in the face of many and great difficulties and the fierce competition of Moorish shopkeepers. The founder's honesty, sterling business qualities, and invariable courtesy soon brought their reward, however, and Mr. Pereira, before long, had the satisfaction of feeling that he had succeeded in the keen rivalry. Under his energetic management the establishment forced itself into prominence, attracting the attention and the patronage not only of all classes of Ceylon, but even of the European community. Lady Ridgeway was a regular customer of the establishment during her husband's six years' term of governorship, and on leaving Ceylon she caused a testimonial to be forwarded to Mr. Pereira, expressing her entire satisfaction with her dealings with his establishment.

Some conception of the present well-stocked, yet commodious, premises may be derived from the accompanying illustrations. From these it may be seen that the building affords ample scope for the demands of a large and fully-equipped establishment. Upstairs is a gentlemen's tailoring department, which is under the supervision of able and experienced hands. Downstairs there is a gentlemen's outfitting department; adjoining is a fancy-goods department, also displays of electro-plated ware and jewellery; while the rest of the building is occupied by the ladies' drapery and millinery departments, the ladies' dressmaking branch—which is a special feature of this establishment—and the well-stocked stationery department. The various showrooms, one of which is shown in the accompanying illustrations, are stocked with the latest and most attractive goods, imported direct from Europe.

In March, 1906, Mr. F. X. Pereira died at his native place, leaving his business in Colombo to his five sons. The business is consequently now carried on under the title of F. X. Pereira & Sons, the eldest son, Mr. I. X. Pereira, conducting the business. The portraits of the partners are reproduced elsewhere.

S. K. LAWTON & CO.

The photographic business of Messrs. S. K. Lawton & Co., now carried on at Jaffna and Colombo, was established by Mr. S. K. Lawton, a Tamil of Jaffna, in that town in 1876. For some years before that time, however, he had been an amateur photographer, and had acquired some knowledge of the photographic process of that time, in spite of great obstacles,

EXTERIOR. THE LATE F. X. PEREIRA. I. X. PEREIRA (PRESENT OWNER). INTERIOR.

K. R. LAWTON.

for he resided in a village 200 miles from the nearest photographer. The first few years after the establishment of the business was uphill work, but gradually Mr. Lawton's work became appreciated outside Jaffna, a branch was opened at Colombo, and the business has steadily progressed. Mr. Lawton was the first to introduce the half-tone process into Ceylon, and in this branch of the business the firm's customers are not confined to the island. Mr. Lawton has been joined in the business by his son, Mr. K. R. Lawton, and has from time to time contributed articles describing some of his inventions and improvements to British photographic publications. The firm has now a large connection, and has supplied a considerable number of the photographs reproduced in this volume.

S. K. LAWTON.

W. E. BASTIAN & CO.

This firm of wholesale and retail paper merchants, stationers, commission agents, exporters and importers, was established in Colombo in 1904 by two natives of Ceylon, Messrs. W. E. Bastian and C. James Mathew—of the well-known firm of Messrs. C. Mathew & Co., Colombo—and these gentlemen continue to be present proprietors and conductors of the business. The operations of the firm are under the direct control of Mr. W. E. Bastian, assisted by his brother, Mr. W. Martin Bastian, and a staff of seven hands. The lines of business include the import of paper, printers' stores, and office accessories on an extensive scale, Japanese curios and artware, soaps, perfumery and toilet requisites, patent medicines, watches and jewellery, china and crockery, toys and fancy goods. The firm makes a specialty of paper and general stationery, which are supplied to the wholesale trade as well as retailed. The legal and notarial professions particularly patronise this firm, and the specially prepared brief-paper with Messrs. Bastian's "three-star" watermark is much in demand with them. Printing is also undertaken by the firm.

C. MATHEW, W. E. BASTIAN AND W. M. BASTIAN.

A fair export business is also carried on by the firm in Ceylon produce, which is consigned to different parts of the United States

A. E. DE SILVA, HIS RESIDENCE AND PLUMBAGO STORES.

of America, Japan, and other centres of the world. Messrs. W. E. Bastian & Co. are, besides, importers of goods from various parts of the globe. Their bankers are the Hong Kong and Shanghai Banking Corporation. The showrooms of the firm are at No. 84, Four Cross Street, in the Pettah of Colombo.

Mr. W. E. Bastian was born in Colombo in 1876, and, after receiving his education at the Ananda College, in his native city, joined a local mercantile firm of paper-merchants in the capacity of manager, which post he held for a number of years and relinquished only to set up in business on his own account. The rapid growth of the present business under his management, within the short period it has existed, is an indication of his capacity and integrity. Mr. Bastian is a Buddhist by religion, and enjoys an important standing in the local community.

A. E. DE SILVA & CO.

This business was originally established in the year 1877, under the style of U. D. S. Gunasekere, the offices being located in the Pettah, Colombo. In 1887 Mr. A. E. de Silva joined Mr. Gunasekere in partnership ; and on the death of the latter he continued to carry on the business under the old name. The alteration to the present title was made only two and a half years ago. The firm deals in every description of Ceylon produce—principally plumbago, desiccated coconut, fibre, cinnamon, and tea. The main export business is done with the United Kingdom and the Continent, through the firm's agents in London, Hamburg, and other European ports. The firm's stores are situated at Castle Street, Borella, Colombo, where plumbago is largely handled for shipment abroad.

Mr. de Silva, who is the sole proprietor of the business, is the owner of large estates and town properties. In coconuts he owns over 1,500 acres, the more important estates under this head being Delgolla (650 acres) and Kirivaula (325 acres), in the Kurunegala district, and Koshena (340 acres), in the Chilaw district. In cinnamon he owns about 400 acres, and in rubber he is opening up about 1,000 acres in the Kalutara district. He also owns about 200 acres bearing cacao. For the manufacture of brush and mattress fibres Mr. de Silva is erecting some fully equipped mills.

Mr. de Silva is a member of the Turf Club and a committee member of the Orient Club. He is also a member of the Plumbago Merchants' Union and of the Agricultural Society. His Colombo residence is "Stephanotis," Flower Road, Cinnamon Gardens, and his country seat is Aniakande, near Ragama, on the main railway line and in the Western Province.

W. D. CAROLIS.

Founded on a small scale in 1879, at Welikade, Colombo, by Mr. W. Don Carolis, the tannery has, in course of time, grown to be the largest of its kind in Ceylon, and by dint of industry and perseverance its proprietor became one of the leading native merchants and landed proprietors in the island. Owing to want of space for extension, the establishment was removed to Tannery Lane, Bambalapitiya, where the present buildings—comprising three drying-sheds, a general store, tanning factory, fancy leather factory, material store, and salt and raw hide stores—cover nearly five acres, the whole representing a flourishing industry. The skins are procured from all parts of Ceylon, the butchers of Colombo supplying the bulk of the pelts. The hides are placed in lime-pits, and then scraped, scoured, and wrangled. In the next and principal process—that of tanning—four kinds of native bark are used, namely, ranauara, rewa—which is found in Ceylon as well as imported from India—the mangrove bark, and the ehela bark. Both the latter kinds are collected by the villagers in the country districts and sold to the works.

FANCY LEATHER TANNING SHED. BAMBALAPITIYA TANNERY DRYING SHED.
THE LATE W. D. CAROLIS. W. D. CAROLIS, JUN.
THE LEATHER STORE. THE TANNERY,

The leather turned out consists of grey leather (cowhide), sole-leather (buffalo), prepared goat-skins, sheep's skin and fancy leather. The latter is peculiarly suitable for boots and shoes, and a great deal of it is sold in Colombo. A total of about 10,000 skins are treated every month at this tannery, and a large export trade with London, China, Germany, and America is transacted. In 1900 the firm exhibited at the Paris Exposition and obtained gold, silver, and bronze medals for their leathers, while at the St. Louis Exhibition of 1904 they won two silver medals. They have also been awarded various silver medals at local exhibitions. The firm's head offices are at No. 34, Second Cross Street, Pettah, Colombo; and they possess a leather store at 18, Kayman's Gate, Pettah; a store for hardware, paints, building requisites and ironware —all imported direct from manufacturers in England and the European Continent—at 16, Sea Street, Pettah; and the Oriental Boot Depôt—where boots and shoes are manufactured on the premises and sold retail—at 33, Main Street, Pettah. They have also a branch at 33, Colombo Street, Kandy, a leather store and tannery at Deiyanawilla, and a general store—for leather and hardware—at Galle.

The firm claim to be the largest importers of English and Continental leather and shoe materials in Ceylon. The founder died in October, 1903, and the business is now carried on by his eldest son, Mr. Charles Don Carolis, and his younger brother, Mr. W. D. Abraham, the former of whom is the present head of the firm. Besides the tannery business, the firm owns the Black Pearl estate in the Kelani Valley, planted with coconuts, tea, and rubber, and the coconut estate of Hediyatte, in the Kalutara district; also a large number of house properties in the town. They are sole agents in Ceylon for the boot and shoe dressings for the Nubian Manufacturing Company, Ltd., London.

PURE ICE AND AERATED WATER MANUFACTORY—J. W. FERNANDO, AND VIEWS (INTERIOR AND EXTERIOR) OF THE FACTORY.

THE PURE ICE AND AERATED WATER MANUFACTORY.

This business was founded seven years ago, on the existing site, as a mineral-water manufactory, and an ice-making plant was added in 1901. About 50 hands are at present employed in the various departments of the factory. The ether process is adopted in making the ice, while the aerated waters are bottled by steam machinery of the latest design. The essences used in the manufacture of mineral waters are of the best quality, and the chemicals employed have been declared by the local analysts to be absolutely free from all organic matter, the popularity of the beverages manufactured testifying to their wholesomeness and excellence. Mr. James Walter Fernando, the managing partner of the business, was born at Colombo in 1860, and was educated at St. Thomas's Boys' School, in the city. He was for some time on the staff of the New Colombo Ice Company, and latterly joined Messrs. J. P. Morton & Co., in the business of the Galle Face Ice Factory, which he left to take charge of the above concern. Four other partners are associated with him in the business, which has now developed into a sound and substantial condition, being under the distinguished patronage of His Excellency the Governor. The offices and factory are situated at Union Place, Slave Island, Colombo.

ARTHUR J. FERNANDO & CO.

The firm of Arthur J. Fernando & Co. was established in 1891 at Norris Road, Pettah, Colombo, by Arthur Joshua Fernando, as auctioneers and brokers. This business was continued for three years, when the present mercantile concern was started. Messrs. Arthur J. Fernando & Co. deal in all kinds of Ceylon produce which is brought on the local market, and export largely to the United Kingdom and all parts of the Continent of

A. J. FERNANDO.

Europe, where the firm have their own agents. Mr. Arthur J. Fernando, who is the sole proprietor of the business, was born in 1850 at Colombo, and educated privately. He commenced his business career with Messrs. J. M. Robertson & Co. as chief clerk, and left that firm to start on his own account as auctioneer and broker. At Fernando & Co.'s stores in Norris Road, cocoa is prepared for shipment, and fibre and coir is baled ready for export, about 50 hands being employed in this work.

Mr. Arthur Fernando owns several coconut estates, notable among which are Diyature, in the North-Western Province, the superintendent being Mr. G. H. Hindle; Metiwela, also in the North-Western Province, and superintended by Mr. Vanderwall Fernando; and Arthur's Seat, near Colombo, where the superintendent is Mr. G. A. Bartholomeusz. Mr. Fernando, who is a landed proprietor in Colombo and Nuwara Eliya, is a member of the Agricultural Society. His private residence is "Dorlynn," Havelock Town, Colombo.

SAMSON A. GUNAWARDANA & CO.

This firm of general merchants, commission agents, exporters and importers, was founded not long ago by Mr. Samson A. Gunawardana, who continues to manage the business. The showrooms and general offices are situated at 74, Second Cross Street, in the Pettah of Colombo, while a stores department is maintained at Wattala, in the neighbourhood of the city, and at Galle. The business is both large and varied, and includes the export of every description of Ceylon produce, and the import of soft goods, piece-goods, crockery, china, porcelain, cement, hardware, cutlery, estate requisites, and wines and spirits. The firm is agent for the celebrated brand of whisky, "House of Lords," bottled by MacDonald & Muir, Glasgow, and also represents a number of leading companies and mercantile concerns in different parts of the world. It has agencies in the United Kingdom, the Continent, the United States of America, and other centres of the globe. Among the exports of the business are plumbago, gems, coir yarn, fibres, coconut, copra, cinnamon, cardamoms, spices, essential oils, rubber, and tea.

Mr. Gunawardana, the manager and proprietor of the firm, was born at Galle in the year 1868, and after receiving his early education at Central School, Galle, entered the service of Government, which he left to set up in business. He is a Sinhalese by nationality, and belongs to a respectable and ancient family of the Southern Province. Mr. Gunawardana's private residences are River View, Wettala, Colombo, and Thistle Court, Galle.

THISTLE COURT, GALLE. SAMSON A. GUNAWARDANA.

"BUGGALOWS." ABDULHUSEN SHAIKH JEEVUNJEE. THE STORES.

A. PATE & SON.

This business of carriage-builders, veterinary surgeons, saddlers, and mail-coach proprietors is carried on by Mr. C. H. Pate, under the above title, in Union Place, Slave Island, Colombo. This business was established as long ago as 1855 by Mr. A. Pate, father of the present proprietor. There is stabling for 80 horses on the premises, and loose boxes are also provided. Mr. Pate is an importer in a large way of Indian and Australian horses, and employs about 150 men altogether in his establishment. The firm holds the mail contracts between Ratnapura, Rakwana, Balangode and Kegalla. They also have branches in Kandy and Nuwara Eliya. Messrs. A. Pate & Son are coach-builders to His Excellency the Governor of Ceylon, and they have gained the following awards for vehicles and leather goods : Three gold and two silver medals for the best four and two-wheeled carriages and the best leather work, including harness, boots, and shoes, at the Agri-Horticultural Show in Colombo, 1891 ; and a silver medal at the Nuwara Eliya Agri-Horticultural Show in 1897 for the best harness, boots, and shoes. The firm keeps a register of the names of gentlemen throughout the colony who are desirous of purchasing or of disposing of horses. Special attention is also given to the veterinary department, and a large farriery business is done.

C. H. PATE.

A. H. S. JEEVUNJEE & CO.

Messrs. Abdulhusen Sheikh Jeevunjee & Co., importers, exporters, and general merchants, started in business at 14, Keyzer Street, Pettah, Colombo, in 1903, the headquarters of the firm being at Musjid, Bunder, Bombay. The partners are Messrs. Noorbhoy, Tyebally, Mahomed Ally, & Hussenally Abdulhusen, of whom the first named is the senior partner. Their business mainly consists of the importation of rice, suitable to the requirements of the Ceylon trade, from Indian ports, Burma, and the Straits, which is distributed among native and European merchants and estates in the island. Close upon 200,000 bags of this commodity are turned over every year. Dried fish in huge quantities is imported from the firm's branch at Male, in the Maldive Islands, the sales amounting to 60 tons a month. This is carried in the firm's own native sailing vessels, known as "buggalows." In addition, every description of grain and cereals is imported for the native trade. Flour comes from Bombay The exports comprise areca nuts, tea, cardamoms, coconut oil, and Ceylon produce of every description. All the partners are members of the Borah community and Mahomedans. They have branches at Calcutta, Cuttack, and Jatni in India, and Male in the Maldive Islands.

DON DAVIT & SONS.

The firm of Don Davit & Sons was founded by A. W. P. Don Davit de Silva, in 1875, at Galle, for the importation of spice and foodstuffs from India. At the commencement only a small trade was done, but after four or five years the business

SIMON DE SILVA. FORAGE WORKS, COLOMBO. DON DAVIT.

THE FAMILY.

OFFICE STAFF, COLOMBO.

THE BUNGALOW AT GINTOTA, NEAR GALLE. FORT OFFICE, GALLE
OFFICE STAFF, GALLE.
COCONUT OIL YARD. EXTERIOR OF STORE, GALLE.
INTERIOR OF STORE, GALLE.

became firmly established, and the importation of rice from Calcutta was also undertaken. By degrees the business was extended, and soon the trade mark of the firm became well known all over the country, and a very large trade was done in rice, imported from all Indian ports, as well as from the Straits Settlements and the Federated Malay Straits. Sugar, another article in which the firm deals largely, comes from Austria and Hamburg; while flour is imported from Victoria and Southern Australia, all kinds of grains and cereals from India, and coconut oil is largely dealt in. Another commodity in which the firm does a big trade is barbed wire for fencing purposes, and they have made a specialty in horse-food, of which they are the largest native importers. Some idea of the magnitude of this business can be gathered from the fact that they import, on an average, 50,000 bags of rice a month and 40,000 bags of horse-food a year. In Galle High Street, Messrs. Don Davit have a rice depôt and grocery store, and the general store and head office are also situated in that town. They have branches at 49, 51, and 69, Fourth Cross Street, Colombo, and at Lower Chitpore Road, Calcutta, and also at Cocanada.

At Galle the firm has a large yard where coconut oil, which is bought up from various small dealers, is filtered by special machinery, after which it is exported to England, the United States, and the Continent of Europe generally. Other articles of export dealt in by this firm are desiccated coconut, citronella oil, cinnamon oil, coir yarn, rope, poonac, fibres, and copra, principally to Denmark, the United Kingdom, and the United States. At Hikkaduwa, in the Southern Province, the firm owns a large coconut estate.

The founder of the firm was the son of a local merchant, who started business with his father at Tangalla, in the Southern Province. He is an ardent Buddhist, and renewed and equipped the temple at Ahangama, as well as the school at Gintota. He is a great friend of the poor, and is ever ready to help deserving cases which call for the exercise of charity. An admirable feature of the business is that there is a benevolent fund made up from a certain percentage of the general turnover, and every year some 5,000 poor people are clothed and fed on a special almsgiving day. Mr. A. W. P. Don Davit, the senior partner, presides over the Galle House, Mr. A. W. P. Simon de Silva manages the Colombo branch, and Mr. A. W. P. Baron de Silva is general manager for India. The junior partners, who are smart business men, were educated at local colleges, and Mr. Simon de Silva is a member of the Theosophical Society, besides being a keen sportsman.

A. S. IDROOS.

Mr. A. S. Idroos, merchant tailor and outfitter at the Galle Face Hotel, commenced business in and outside that hotel in a small way twenty-five years ago, and now has a large connection, supplying not only residents, but travellers making Colombo a calling-place, and among the latter his customers include members of the nobility of various nations. He employs about 20 experienced hands, and supplies all kinds of garments, both military and civil; and also exports ready-made clothes to India, the Straits, and Australia. His representatives board all ships arriving at the port to obtain orders from the passengers.

A. S. IDROOS.

CEYLON SPINNING AND WEAVING MILLS.

Although Ceylon is not a manufacturing country, by the enterprise and forethought of energetic and commercial men, large factories for the conversion of raw material into articles of local consumption have been established in and about Colombo. Conspicuous among the successful businesses engaged in local manufacture is that carried on under the title of the Ceylon Spinning and Weaving Mills at Wellawatte, on the south coast railway line near Colombo. These mills were established at this spot in 1888 by Messrs. Darley, Butler & Co., under the management of Sir William Mitchell, for the purpose of spinning and weaving different kinds of cloth and cotton goods. Here Colombo cloth, Lanka tweeds, drills, shirtings, sheetings, towels, tarpaulins, tents, awning, and many other kinds of cotton goods are made for the local market. The cotton in its raw state is chiefly imported from the cotton-growing centres of Tinnevelly, Adoni, and Coimbatore and districts, Southern India. The factory employs about 600 Sinhalese, Tamil, and Mahomedan workpeople, who are brought over from South India. The mill contains 9,600 ring spindles and preparation from Messrs. Dobson & Barlow, of Bolton, Lancashire, and 250 looms manufactured by Messrs. Wm. Dickinson, of Blackburn, and Messrs. Henry Livesey & Co., of Blackburn, while the engines and boilers come from Messrs. A. W. Smith, of Glasgow. All these firms rank amongst the best makers of machinery for cotton manufacture and steam driving.

The present owner of the mills is Mr. Ahmedbhoy Habibbhoy, who acquired the business in 1899 from Messrs. Darley, Butler & Co. Mr. Habibbhoy resides in Bombay. He was born of a rich family, and his father was the leading member of the Khoja community. He is a Jamindar, and sole proprietor of several villages in the Salsette district. He owns very large and valuable landed properties in India and Ceylon, including more than a dozen ginning and pressing factories in Bombay and Madras Presidencies and the North-West and Central Provinces of India. He is the sole proprietor of the Victory Spinning Mills in Bombay, besides owning the Ceylon Spinning and Weaving Mills at Wellawatte. In addition to his other businesses, Mr. Habibbhoy is the managing director of the Bank of Bombay, having been connected with the direction of that institution since the founding of the new Bank, in 1867, and at present fills the office of vice-president. Besides being the head of the Sunni Khoja community, and a liberal Mahomedan, he is the managing trustee and chairman of the school founded by his brother, the late Mr. Khan Mohammed Habibbhoy, who endowed it with three lakhs and a half of rupees, in addition to a house worth more than a lakh. At this institution about 700 boys are given free education, without any distinction of caste or creed.

The mills at Wellawatte and the general management are in charge of Mr. James Hatton, of Bolton, Lancashire, England, in which industrial centre he received his training; and the chief accountant and general assistant is Mr. Sulahuddin A. S. Tyabji, of Baroda, India. The factory buildings cover five acres, and about twenty acres of compound are attached, on which latter the firm has been carrying on extensive cotton-growing experiments. The seeds used for this purpose are those known as Sea Island and Egyptian cotton seeds. The firm pays about Rs. 75,000 (£5,000) per annum in wages, the daily rates ranging from 12½ cents to 25 cents

CEYLON SPINNING AND WEAVING MILLS: AHMEDBHOY HABIBBHOY (PROPRIETOR), JAS. HATTON (MANAGER), SULAHUDDIN A. S. TYABJI (ASSISTANT MANAGER), GENERAL VIEW OF MILLS AND ENGINE-ROOM.

CEYLON SPINNING AND WEAVING MILLS CARDING ROOM, SHOWING MACHINES, BLOWING ROOM, ROVING AND RING ROOM, AND WEAVING DEPARTMENT.

(2d. to 4d.) for boys and girls, 30 to 50 cents (about 5d. to 8d.) for women, and for men 50 cents to one rupee (8d. to 1s. 4d.). Most of the present workpeople have been trained by the firm; and they soon attain astonishing dexterity, while, the employment being steady and constant all the year round, they remain with the firm for years. Although the manufactured cloth is mainly sold locally, a portion of the output is also exported to Madras and Calcutta. All the principal stores used in the mills and by the hands are imported from England and Bombay. To guard against fire, the manager has formed a well-trained fire brigade from amongst the workpeople, who act under the directions of the engineering staff in case of an outbreak. The firm contracts with the Ceylon Government for the supply of cotton goods, providing all the materials used by the Prison and Convict Departments. The town office and showroom are at No. 35, Main Street, Pettah, while the mills are accessible from the Wellawatte railway station. These mills constitute the only spinning and weaving works in the island, thus solely representing an important industry.

HOOSENBHAI MAHOMEDBHAI MOOSAJEE.

Mr. H. M. Moosajee, a member of the Borah community and by faith a Mahomedan, was born in Karachi, Bombay Presidency, in 1874. The name of Moosajee is a well-known and familiar one in India, Moosajee & Co.'s livery stables and posting yard in Karachi being considered one of the finest in the country. The business has been in existence since 1861. The establishment covers over four acres of ground, and 150 horses and 125 conveyances of all descriptions are stabled there. The company has also a carriage-building establishment, in which they employ over 200 men and where carriages are built according to all up-to-date styles. They invariably furnish State carriages and conveyances for high civil and military functions, their attention to customers being testified to by this fact. Messrs. Moosajee & Co. are also contractors, stevedores, and dubashes, and did business in this connection with the Mombassa-Uganda South African Railway Company, whilst for a lengthy period—at the time Messrs. Adamjee & Co. were their Ceylon agents—they were large exporters of Indian and Ceylon produce to Adelaide, South Australia. They have a branch of their livery stable business at 9, Union Place, Slave Island, Colombo, of which Mr. H. M. Moosajee is the owner. He is the son of the head of the firm, Mr. M. Moosajee (a native of Cutchmandvi), and has had a thorough training in the business. He entered his father's establishment at the age of seventeen, and for a number of years he managed the whole concern. He has found it necessary to increase his stock to cope with the public demand, and is a large importer of Sindh cattle. Shortly he will commence business in Ceylon also as stevedore and dubash, a line in which he has had considerable experience. He is a member of the Bombay Union Club of Colombo. In the accompanying photograph Mr. Moosajee is shown seated in his carriage.

THE LIVERY STABLES. H. M. MOOSAJEE. THE CARRIAGE YARD.

CARIMJEE JAFFERJEE.

The extensive range of business conducted under the above name has a somewhat scattered field of operations. While the head offices and the firm's Colombo store for matches are at Fourth Cross Street, kerosene oil is stocked at Kochchikadde at Messrs. Bois Bros.' stores, specially set aside by the municipality for the storage of oil. Then the rice stores are at Prince Street, Pettah, the cracker stores in Bambalapitiya, and the Mangalore tile stores in Wolfendahl Street. Again, there are branches at Galle, Tuticorin, and Calcutta, as well as at Male, the capital of the Maldive Islands, and St. Louis, Mauritius; also agencies at Bombay, Karachi, Cutchmandvi, Mangalore, Calicut, Cochin, Cocanada, Gopalpore, Cuttack, Puri, Rangoon, Penang, Singapore, Hong Kong, Kobe, Yokohama, and Adelaide. The firm exports coconut oil, cardamoms, tea, copra, coir, cowries, shells, areca nuts, nutmegs, and other produce to Bombay and Calcutta; and imports rice from India, Burma, and Penang, also beet-sugar, ready manufactured for the market, as well as sugar-candy, from Austria and China. Groceries of every description are imported from Bombay; cereals, grain, moong, and such-like articles from India, Singapore, and China; flour from Adelaide and Southern Australia generally; paper, for packing and wrapping purposes, from Liverpool and Bombay; dry fish from the Maldive Islands, as well as coir, shells, tortoiseshells in their raw state, coconuts, copra, oil, and other products of the coconut-palm from the same source. Similar products are also received from the Nicobar Islands; and the firm employs its own fleet of six ships, called "buggalows," to carry these products from the islands to Colombo. Some 75 hands are engaged in their stores.

Mr. Jafferjee, of Cutchmandvi, Western India, originated the firm in Ceylon in 1831, and was the pioneer of the Maldive Island trade. His business was first established at Galle, and he removed to Colombo when the latter place was made the port of call. On his death, in 1880, his son, Mr. Carimjee Jafferjee, who had travelled extensively in India and the eastern islands, took over the business. Mr. Carimjee Jafferjee was born at Cutchmandvi in 1850, and joined his father's business when quite a boy. He is now the sole proprietor of the firm, being assisted in the business by his eldest son. The latter was born at Karachi in the year 1884, and educated at the Royal College, Colombo. Both father and son belong to the important community of the Borahs, and are devout Mahomedans. Mr. Carimjee Jafferjee built the Karimee mosque at Fourth Cross Street, Pettah, Colombo, and has founded various schools in his native town of Cutchmandvi. One of the leading men of the Mahomedan community, he is pioneer of various native societies. He is also a large contributor to charities, both public and private, and subscribed liberally towards the Lady Havelock Hospital. His private residences in Colombo are at Fourth Cross Street, Pettah, and Essai Villa, Bambalapitiya.

S. L. NAINA MARIKAR.

The business of the Victoria Drapery Stores, Turret Road, Cinnamon Gardens, Colombo,

CARIMJEE JAFFERJEE.

INTERIOR OF OFFICE.

COUNTRY RESIDENCE, JAFFER VILLA, NUWARA ELIYA.

THE OFFICE.

"BUGGALOW."

S. L. NAINA MARIKAR, HIS VICTORIA DRAPERY STORES AND PRIVATE RESIDENCE.

was started a few years ago by Mr. Sulyman Lebbe Naina Marikar, who was born in Colombo in 1868, and educated at Wesley College, in his native city, and it is now carried on as a proprietary concern. In 1888 Mr. S. L. N. Marikar took over the management of the drapery and outfitting business of his late father, Mr. M. L. M. Sulyman Lebbe (who died in 1892), in the Main St., Pettah, a business started as early as 1856. Under the present owner the business has increased largely, that circumstance necessitating the opening of a gentlemen's outfitting and drapery establishment at Nos. 15, 15B, and 36A, Main Street, Pettah, where also are sold piece-goods, wholesale and retail. The Victoria Park branch is a high-class ladies' outfitting establishment, carried on entirely on European lines. The firm imports dress goods and all kinds of drapery and mercery from England, Germany, Hong Kong, and Japan; and the stock carried is valued at £13,000. Altogether some 25 hands are employed. Mr. Naina Marikar is patron and principal supporter of the New Moor Street "Madrasey Mohamedhan" School, Colombo, for the teaching of Arabic, Tamil, and English. His private residence is "Muirburn," Turret Road, Cinnamon Gardens. All the premises occupied by the firm are the owner's private property.

JANOO HASSAN.

The firm of Janoo Hassan, the head office of which is at Khand Bazaar, Bombay, has been

JANOO HASSAN.

established there for more than thirty-five years. The Colombo branch at 9 and 10, Keyzer Street, was only started in 1898. The other branches are at Akyab, Amritsar, Alleppy, Balasore, Berhampore, Bimlipatam, Bodasakurru, Bezwada Bardoli, Calcutta, Chittagong, Cuttack, Chandbali, Calingapatam, Cocanada, Cochin, Calieut, Cuddalore, Dhoraji, Delhi, Dhamtari, Gopalpore, Haveri, Jellasore, Jharsuguda, Jatni, Karachi, Masulipatam, Madras, Midnapur, Navsari, Negapatam Puri, Rangoon, Rajahmundry, Sambalpur, Secunderabad, Soro, Trivandrum, Vellore, and Vizianagram. The firm is among the largest importers of rice in the island, its turnover totalling some 400,000 bags per annum. Besides rice, which comes from India, Burma, and the Straits, all kinds of grain, paddy, and gram are imported from India, as well as bones for purposes of manure and poonac for cattle food. Among the principal exports of the firm are coconut oil, areca nuts, cardamoms, and tea.

A. E. S. JEEVUNJEE.

Mr. A. E. S. Jeevunjee, who was born, educated, and trained in Bombay, carries on business as a general agent, importer, and exporter at 37, Keyzer Street, Pettah, Colombo, his head offiee being at 65–67, Satar Oosgali, Mandvi, Masjid Bunder, Bombay, where he trades under the name of Esmailjee Sheikh

Jeevunjee. Operations were commenced in Ceylon in 1900, and the business consists of the import of rice (especially coolie and raw rice from the Indian coasts), which is supplied largely to the tea estates of the island, and of all kinds of grains. The firm's export business consists mainly of transactions in areca nuts, tea, cardamoms, coconut oil, and practically every other kind of Ceylon produce. The firm's import of rice now reaches close upon 360,000 bags per annum. Mr. A. E. S. Jeevunjee is a member of the Borah community.

H. A. MALLUM.

Mr. H. A. Mallum, of Nos. 58 and 59, Fourth Cross Street, Colombo, is the local representative of Mr. Issup Ahmed Mulla, a leading importer and general merchant, doing an extensive business all over the East. The head office is at Cuttack, and there are branch offices at the three capital towns of the respective Presidencies of India, also at Balasore, Puri, Rahama, Jatni, Delang, Bhutmandy, Chandbally, False Point, Jambo, Kopelas Road, Kenderpore, Kendrapara and Jalpore Road. The business includes the import of rice, principally from Calcutta, Rangoon, Cocanada, Penang and Singapore, and the export of coconut oil, coir, yarn, fibre and copra to Mauritius and the South African ports. A

H. A. MALLUM.

large business is also done in supplying rice to the tea estates (Ceylon), and to the other Colombo merchants. Mr. H. A. Mallum comes of a respected Mahomedan family in Rander, in the district of Surat, in Bombay Presidency, and has a fair knowledge of English. His forefathers served as captains and chief officers on sailing ships all over the world, long before the introduction of steamships or steamers. Mr. H. A. Mallum is the agent of "Anjumane Islam" of Rander.

NATIONAL DAIRY COMPANY.

The National Dairy Company, whose head office is at Kalbadevi Road, Bombay, was established in 1898 by the proprietors, Messrs. P. V. Dalvi, S. J. Pandia, and V. V. Vasanjee. The firm are manufacturers of butter and cream. Their dairy farm is situated in Gujerat, in the Bombay Presidency, where all the latest and most up-to-date machinery is used in the manufacture of the cream. After the cream has been prepared at Gujerat it is forwarded by train to Bombay, where it is made into butter and packed into ½-lb., 1-lb., 7-lb., 14-lb. and 28-lb. tins ready for export, the monthly output being 40,000 to 45,000 lbs. A very large and important trade is carried on by the firm with London, South Africa, Mauritius, Bangkok, Hong Kong, Shanghai, and the East generally.

Mr. P. V. Dalvi is the managing partner of

C. AMIJEE. INTERIOR OF OFFICE. A. E. S. JEEVUNJEE. THE STORE.

the Colombo branch, which is situated at No. 70, Second Cross Street, Pettah. In Ceylon alone the monthly consumption of the firm's dairy produce is between 10,000 and 12,000 lbs. In January the sale amounted to 17,296 lbs.; while in Rangoon, where another branch has been established, a similar amount is sold monthly. Merchants, hotels, and up-country estates throughout the island are supplied by the National Dairy Company. The company was awarded a silver medal in the Bombay Art and Industrial Exhibition of 1904 for the excellence and purity of its butter. Besides the increasing trade in Ceylon, an extensive business is carried on in India, where, besides providing many of the merchants, the company holds the contract for the supply of butter to the Imperial forces.

MOOSAJEE MOOLA EBRAMJEE.

Moosajee Moola Ebramjee was born at Karachi, India, in 1869 (the year 1288, Zilkad 7, of the Mahomedan Era). At the age of eighteen he left his home and commenced his commercial career at Quetta, Beluchistan, where he remained for one and a half years. Finding the place overcrowded, and that there was not much scope for business, he left the city in August, 1889, and came to Colombo and started business in a small way. Now, at the end of seventeen years, he has increased his trading transactions to such an extent as to necessitate his having two places for his trade. One is at 122, Bankshall Street, Pettah,

M. M. EBRAMJEE.

Colombo, where Mr. Ebramjee sells a variety of merchandise, such as cutlery, stationery, haberdashery, biscuits, conf·ctionery, fancy goods, clocks and watches, &c., imported from England, Germany, Austria, and Japan. In his other shop (No. 92A), also in Bankshall Street, he stocks very largely raw rice, grain and foodstuffs of all descriptions, sugar, crackers, dates, &c., imported from India, Rangoon, and the Far East. These he sells only wholesale. He is also the largest importer of dry fish from the Persian Gulf and India. His European correspondents are Messrs. Stafford, Hill & Co., London, and Messrs. J. Jacobi & Co., Vienna, and he is also the sole agent in Ceylon for these firms. Mr. Ebramjee is a member of the Borah community, and a Mahomedan in faith.

GULAM HOSSEN SHAIKHTYEB & CO.

This firm owns the Mohamedi oil mills, which are situated at 193, Grandpass, Colombo, and are the principal native mills of the kind in Ceylon, the working premises covering three acres of ground. The business was established in 1890 for the manufacture of coconut oil and poonac (a cattle food and a by-product of the oil manufacture). The produce of the coconut-palm, in the shape of copra, is bought in the planting districts, principally in Negombo, Kurunegala, Galle, and Matara, and brought by rail and canal to the mills. There a miniature railway carries the copra from the huge padda boats at the landing stage across the extensive yard to the cutting machinery on the ground-

THE NATIONAL DAIRY COMPANY.

THE BUTTER STORE. R. C. GEORGE. THE GROUP.

G. H. SHAIKHTYEB. THE MOHAMEDI OIL MILLS. S. T. ABDOOLALY.

floor of the huge mill buildings. Here it is cut into fine pieces. The pieces are taken up by screw elevators, and brought overhead into huge hydraulic presses, in which they are subjected to a pressure of 2½ tons. After passing through several further squeezing processes and being filtered, the pure oil for the market is obtained. This is then bulked in huge barrels (which are made on the premises, of teak imported from Burma) and is then shipped to England, America, and India; while the residue is worked into poonac, or cattle food, and packed into bags of about 1 cwt. each for despatch to all parts of the world.

The oil mills give employment to some 300 hands; while the power is supplied by an engine, made by Marshall & Sons, of 90 horse-power, and deriving steam from water-tube boilers which work to a pressure of 100 lbs. to the square inch. A repairing shop, fitted with lathe, drilling machines, and other appliances, copes with all difficulties arising from mishaps to the machinery and necessities for renewals.

Mr. G. H. Shaikhtyeb, the father of the present proprietor of the business, Mr. S. T. Abdoolaly, was one of the first members of the Borah community, an enterprising mercantile section of the Ceylon Mahomedan population. He came to Colombo about 1860, where he started business in Fourth Cross Street, which was afterwards transferred to the existing premises at Grandpass.

P. N. KAPADIA.

Mr. P. N. Kapadia, of 112, Fourth Cross Street, Pettah, Colombo, commenced business thirty years ago as a general merchant, importer, and exporter. At the present time the

P. N. KAPADIA.

principal items of import are wheat flour from Australia, India, and California, and kerosene oil from the Standard Oil Trust. The turnover in these commodities averages 50,000 bags and 120,000 gallons per annum respectively. Other articles of import are bran and pollard from India, oilmen's stores from England and the Continent, sugar from Austria, the imported goods being supplied to local merchants and estates and to the military and general shipping in wholesale quantities. The firm exports chiefly cardamoms, which are bought direct from local brokers and shipped to Bombay on a very large scale, sometimes to the extent of 300,000 lbs. a year. A big trade is also done in tea, the firm exporting close on 1,000,000 lbs. per annum. Mr. Kapadia is a Parsee and a native of India. His early business training he received as accountant to Messrs. Bapty Bros., Ltd., at their flour mills in Bombay, and he took the Ceylon business over from his father in 1891.

M. K. SALDIN & CO.

This firm, which carries on business as importers, exporters, and commission agents, at 94, Fourth Cross Street, Pettah, Colombo, was established in 1896 by Mr. M. K. Saldin, son of Mr. O. Saldin, who died in the present year, and was formerly well-known as the editor of the Malay newspapers, the *Alamat Lankapuri* and the *Wajah Selong*. The firm has agencies all over the United Kingdom, the Continent of Europe, China, Japan, &c., and imports largely cotton and woollen goods of every description, iron and metals, haberdashery and other fancy goods, &c., mostly from the United Kingdom, Belgium, Germany,

M. K. SALDIN.

Holland, and Japan. An extensive trade is also done in crockery and glassware, the whole of the native trade in these goods being supplied by this house. Different kinds of Ceylon produce are exported, these being bought in the cheapest local market. The firm also owns the Milsom Drapery Stores at 21, Main Street, Pettah, where every class of ladies', gentlemen's, and children's outfits is supplied and tailoring is carried on. Mr. Saldin, who is a member of the Malay community, is the grandson of Captain Saldin, of the Ceylon Rifle Regiment.

R. PESTONJEE.

Mr. Ruttonjee Pestonjee, a member of the Parsee community, hailing from Bombay, carries on business as general merchant and commission agent at 16, Keyzer Street, Pettah, Colombo, and the variety of the goods in which he deals is remarkable. Commencing business in 1899, he is now a large importer of Indian, Australian, and American flour, which is supplied to local bakers and merchants, and of rice from India and Burma. He deals also in American pepperil drill, which is the chief material used in the manufacture of the clothing universally worn in the colony, in American carriages. Japanese rickshaws, wines, spirits, beer, &c., while the principal articles of export are cocoa, cardamoms, tea, desiccated coconut, and fibres, which are sent to the United Kingdom and Germany. The London agents are Jeremiah Lyons & Co., 4, Lombard Court, E.C., and Messrs. Oldridge, Salmon & Co., Ltd., Fenchurch Avenue, E.C., the New York representatives being the New York Export and Import Company, Front Street.

W. TAMBIPILLY & CO.

This firm of general merchants and manufacturers' representatives was founded at Kandy in the year 1876. After four years of brisk business there, the establishment was removed to Colombo, where it continues to the present time, the offices and showrooms being located at 19 and 20, Keyzer Street, Pettah. A branch establishment at Jaffna was opened in 1895, and continues in a flourishing condition. The principal line of business is the import of Manchester piece-goods and fabrics, also hardware, and the export of Ceylon produce. The firm is agent for Messrs. Goodlass, Wall & Co., Ltd., paint

R. PESTONJEE.

THE STORE. OFFICE STAFF. THE STORE INTERIOR.

manufacturers, Liverpool ; Messrs. John Moreton & Co., Ltd., hardware manufacturers,

W. TAMBIPILLY.

London and Wolverhampton ; Messrs. S. and C. Nordlinger, Manchester ; Messrs. A. Binda & Co., papermakers, Milan, Italy ; and many other business houses in Great Britain, on the European Continent, in Japan, and elsewhere ; representing also merchants in all the principal cities of the world.

MAGANLAL NATHALAL.

This firm, the only Bombay Hindu firm in the rice trade in Ceylon, has its Colombo branch at 36, Keyzer Street, Pettah. It was established in 1905 by five partners, and the head office is at 16, Amratollah Lane, Calcutta. Rice is imported in large quantities from various ports on the Indian Coast, the Straits Settlements, and from Burma, for sale to Colombo merchants and others. The firm proposes shortly to embark largely in the kerosene oil and flour trade in addition to the above. All the partners are trained and experienced men in the trade.

J. RUSTOMJEE.

The business carried on under the name of J. Rustomjee at 113, Bankshall Street, Colombo, was established in 1883 at Colombo and Bombay. Originally the firm, who are general merchants, commission agents, importers and exporters, traded under the style

J. RUSTOMJEE.

of Adamjee Lukmanjee & Co., and the alteration to the present name was made in

MAGANLAL NATHALAL.

INTERIOR OF GRAIN STORE.

THE STORE.

ISMAIL VILLA. MOHAMED LEBBE MARIKAR HADGIAR MOHOMED ISMAIL.

1905. Grains of all descriptions are imported from India and China, sugar from Austria, and sugar-cane and candy from India, while the principal export is tea. The firm has branches at Bombay, Calcutta, Rangoon, Cocanada, Hong Kong, and Singapore, and supplies kerosene oil to the Government by contract.

MOHAMED LEBBE MARIKAR HADGIAR MOHOMED ISMAIL.

This gentleman was born in Colombo in 1869, and educated at the Wesley College in that city. He commenced his commercial career as an exporter of Ceylon produce to European and foreign countries and importer of foreign and English goods, which combined business he carried on for fifteen years. He retired from commerce in 1904, on the death of his father, of whose estate he was appointed executor, and recommenced business in 1905 by becoming the broker for Messrs. Service, Reeve & Co., of Colombo and London, for which firm he buys all kinds of Ceylon produce, such as desiccated coconut, plumbago, copra, fibres, and cardamoms. He also acts, generally, as guarantee broker for the native merchants, with whom he has built up a large and substantial trade for Messrs. Service, Reeve & Co., in piece-goods, hardware, and other commodities.

Mr. Ismail owns various coconut estates in the Mirigama, Ratnapura, Hanwella, and Kelani Valley districts, as well as house property in many parts of Colombo. He also inherited large valuable properties from his father, Mr. I. L. Mohamed Lebbe Marikar Hadgiar. He is the brother of Mr. M. L. M. Zainu Deen, M.M.C., brother-in-law of the Hon. Mr. Abdul Rehiman, M.L.C., and nephew of Mr. M. I. Mohamed Alie, J.P., Persian Consul in Colombo. He is a member of the Orient, Lawn and Recreation Clubs, as well as of the Havelock Golf Club, Colombo, in connection with which latter he won the Championship Cup for 1905. He was at one time a prominent figure on the Turf, and still retains his interest in racing. He is an excellent billiard player, and has travelled in Europe as well as Egypt and India. His private residence is Ismail Villa, in the Bambalapitiya suburb of Colombo.

T. A. J. NOORBHAI & CO.

This important firm of general merchants, importers, exporters, shippers, and ship-owners, well known throughout the East, was originally started by the present owner's grandfather in Bombay, and he opened the Colombo branch in 1889, in the present premises in Keyzer Street, Pettah, which now form the head office for Ceylon. The firm are amongst the largest grain importers in the island, as well as being extensive importers of piece and cotton goods from India generally; while they export all kinds of Ceylon produce to India, the Continent of Europe, and the United States of America, as well as to the various British colonies, all produce being shipped on the firm's own account. Messrs. Noorbhai were the first to open up steam navigation between Ceylon and the Maldive Islands; but the service was discontinued on account of political differences and the want of encouragement from the Government. The firm also at one time owned the Ceylon Spinning and Weaving Mills at Wellawatte; and they are now about to open up, in Colombo, a large cotton mill, on up-to-date modern lines, in anticipation of the development of the cotton-growing capacities of the island. For this purpose the firm have already acquired large tracts of land in the North Central Province. The firm owns stores in Keyzer Street, Fourth Cross Street, and Maliban Street, in the Pettah quarter of Colombo; and altogether about 150 hands are employed in the business. The firm also have their own fleet of sailing vessels, with which trade is carried on with the neighbouring islands.

Mr. Noorbhai is a liberal supporter of schools and charities, and one of the best-known figures in Colombo commercial circles

NAMASIVAYAN MUDALIAR RATNASABAPATHY.

Mr. N. Ratnasabapathy is the son of Namasivayan Mudaliar, of Colombo, who was at one time a member of the defunct firm of Messrs. Wilson, Ritchie & Co., besides being the owner of large property in Colombo. Allied by birth with some of the leading Tamil families of Ceylon, he was born at Colombo in 1858, and educated at the Colombo Academy (now the Royal College). He started business as a broker in connection with the Colombo firm of Messrs. W. M. Smith & Co. in 1882, and in 1886 joined Messrs. Bosanquet & Co., and after twenty years' service he is still employed as chief broker and confidential adviser to the latter firm. He has an expert and unique knowledge of all Ceylon produce, and conducts all transactions for the firm in the sale and purchase of piece-goods and produce. Mr. Ratnasabapathy holds a half share, with his brother, in the valuable Kadukande estate, of some 800 acres, in the Western Province, and wholly owns, besides, several estates of over 1,000 acres in the North-Western Province, all fully planted with coconuts. The produce of these estates is sold locally. He is also a landed proprietor in Colombo and Jaffna, and has travelled all over India. Mr. Ratnasabapathy is the father of ten sons and two daughters. The eldest son is now being trained in Manchester for a commercial career, while the second is studying at New College, Oxford, with the view of entering a learned profession. Mr. Ratnasabapathy is married to a daughter of the late Mr. E. Dorosamy, Proctor of the Supreme Court of Ceylon, and son of a late well-known member of the Legislative Council. Mr. Ratnasabapathy *père* is a trustee of various leading Hindu temples, and a member of the Ceylon University Association. His father was instrumental in the erection of a large Hindu temple at Jaffna, which he endowed with a large sum of money for the feeding of the poor. All Mr. Ratnasabapathy's children have been educated locally at the Royal College, Colombo. His private residence is Jaffna House, Ward Place, Colombo.

M. L. M. ZAINU DEEN.

This Moorish gentleman, who was born in Colombo, received his education at Wesley College in that city. He is a general merchant and commission agent, as was his late father, I. L. Mohamed Lebbe Marikar Hadgiar. Mr. Zainu Deen started business in 1886 at 105, Main Street, in the Pettah quarter of Colombo, and has since removed to 101, 102, and 103, Hamidiah Buildings, Pettah, where he has his office and extensive showrooms for exhibiting various samples of English and Continental goods. He imports largely piece-goods, haberdashery, millinery, hardware, crockery, glassware, enamelled-ware, and general merchandise from London, Germany, Austria, Japan, and other parts, on orders for his numerous native customers, with whom he has extensive dealings. He also exports large consignments of Ceylon produce, such as hides, horns, cocoa, fibre, oils, and other products of the coconut-palm of the island, which come from various estates and local dealers. These exports are principally consigned to Messrs. Durant, Radford & Co., Ltd., 5 & 6, Billiter Avenue, London, E.C., who are Mr. Zainu Deen's agents. This gentleman has been a member of the Municipal Council of Colombo for the Pettah Ward (the business centre of native merchants) since 1900, he having been thrice selected for the honour by his numerous constituents.

M. L. M. ZAINU DEEN AND FAMILY.

MOOSBHOY SHAIKH HIPTULLABHOY ABDULALLY.

This firm of general importers and exporters have their business premises at 101 and 102, Fourth Cross Street, Pettah, Colombo. The proprietor, Mr. M. S. H. Abdulally, was educated in Bombay, and arrived in Ceylon in the year 1875, where he joined his uncle's and father's business—that of S. T. Abdulally, of 108, 109, Fourth Cross Street, Pettah—and he afterwards took over the business in his father's name in 1882. His father died in 1897, and Mr. M. S. H. Abdulally then started the present firm of M. S. H. Abdulally, general buyers of all Ceylon produce. The principal articles imported by the firm are rice from Calcutta, Burma, the Straits Settlements, China, and Karachi, grain and curry stuffs from India generally, sugar from Austria, and fish, cowrie and tortoise shells, raw coconuts, and copra from the Maldive Islands. The trade with the islands is carried on by the firm's own fleet of "buggalows" (sailing vessels of about 300 tons burden). The export trade of Ceylon produce is also important, being mainly transacted with Penang, the United Kingdom, India, Africa, and Mauritius. Branches of the business have been established at Male (Maldive Islands) and Calcutta, while agencies exist in India, Burma, Hong Kong, Yokohama, Kobe, Singapore, Penang, Zanzibar, Mombassa, Mozambique, Delagoa Bay, St. Louis (Mauritius), and at Durban, Natal.

Valuable estates planted with rubber, tea, coconuts and cinnamon are owned by this firm, the principal property being Gulshenna Ally in the Kelani Valley, consisting of 300 acres. In the management of his business Mr. M. S. H. Abdulally is greatly assisted by his eldest son, who was born in 1886 and educated at St. Thomas's College, Colombo. Mr. M. S. H. Abdulally is also a landed proprietor in Colombo and Kurunegala (Ceylon) and India. He is a keen supporter of all Mahomedan schools and charities. His private residence is in the Bambalapitiya suburb of Colombo.

HASSENALLY DAWOODBHOY AND OFFICE.

HASSENALLY DAWOODBHOY.

Mr. Hassenally Dawoodbhoy, whose head office is at No. 44, Fourth Cross Street, Pettah, Colombo—with a branch at Bombay—is a wholesale merchant and commission agent, dealing in various classes of English and foreign commodities, such as piece-goods, stationery, cutlery, haberdashery, jewellery, perfumery, hosiery, glassware, hardware, clocks, watches, umbrellas, soaps, playing-cards, musical instruments, oilmen's stores, iron safes, toys, carriage bells and lamps, harness, and Japanese goods. He is a native of Morvi, a first-class State in Kathiawar, India. Like all the other Indian merchants in Colombo, he first started business in Ceylon on a small scale. Owing to his ability, insight, and perseverance in his line of business during the twenty years it has been established in Colombo, he has succeeded in converting a small business into a large and flourishing one. He has agencies in London and Paris, Milan, and Solingen; also in Japan. Mr. Dawoodbhoy accepts agencies for the sale of manufactured goods, and invites correspondence in connection with that line of business.

RUSTOMJEE AND CO.

The firm of Rustomjee & Co., bakers and confectioners, was established in Colombo

THE BAKERY INTERIOR.

TEA SALOON.

RUSTOMJEE AND CO.'S BUILDING.

in 1875 by Mr. Rustomjee Muncherjee. In 1884 the business was taken over by Mr. L. P. Billimoria, and became known as the Ceylon Bakery. The head office and bakery are at 38, Chatham Street, Fort, Colombo. The firm are well-known manufacturers of all kinds of biscuits, confectionery, and bread, and possess the only electrically driven machine for the manufacture of biscuits in the island, the latter comestibles being turned out in many shapes, varieties, and sizes. The bread, made by hand, not only has an extensive local sale, but is also supplied to far up-country districts. Large contracts are also held with the various local stevedores and ship-chandlers for the supply of bread to the shipping of Colombo. Messrs. Rustomjee & Co. are noted for their catering for weddings and entertainments of all kinds, wedding-cakes being a speciality of the firm's manufacture. They are also bakers and confectioners to His Excellency the Governor of Ceylon. Altogether the firm employs from 80 to 100 employees ; and besides the central factory in the Fort, the firm has a branch at Rifle Street, in the Slave Island quarter of the city. The whole concern is under the managing directorship of Mr. Cowasjee Merwamjee Nilgiria, who was born at Ootacamund, Madras, was educated in India, and came to Ceylon in the year 1896. He is a member of the National Association of Master Bakers and Confectioners of England and Ireland. His private residence is at 45, Union Place, Colombo. In his leisure he is a devotee of sport, cricket being his favourite pastime, and he is a member of the Bloomfield Cricket Club.

E. G. ADAMALY & CO.

This important firm are general merchants, landed proprietors, importers and exporters, and agents in Ceylon for the Maldivian Government. The partners in the business are Esufali Mohamedbhoy Allibhoy, Gulamhussen Mohamedbhoy Allibhoy, and Adamaly Mohamedbhoy Allibhoy, all brothers. The firm are the largest importers in Ceylon of rice, sugar, flour, matches, kerosene oil, Maldivian produce, and grains. Their importations of rice alone for the year 1905 amounted to nearly 400,000 bags, obtained from different parts of India, Burma, and the Straits Settlements. Many landed properties in the different wards of Colombo, Kandy, and Nuwara Eliya are owned by the firm ; and, owing to the growth of their business, they have lately purchased the Smallpass Stores from Messrs. Aitken, Spence & Co., also two more houses adjoining their office at the Pettah, Colombo, for the sum of Rs. 60,000 and Rs. 75,000 respectively. The Smallpass establishment will be converted into a rice store, equipped with machinery and with all the appliances for cleaning, sieving, and whitening the imported rice for local marketable purposes ; while the newly-acquired premises will provide more extensive offices for the various departments of the business. The firm owns, in the Avisawella district, the Fairfield estate of about 300 acres in extent, where rubber, tea, and cinnamon are planted.

MOHAMEDBHOY ALLIBHOY.

SMALLPASS BRANCH OF ADAMALY AND CO.'S BUSINESS, ALSO OUTBUILDINGS AND BUGGALOW TRADING WITH MALDIVE ISLANDS.

Messrs. E. G. Adamaly & Co. transact a very large export and import business with the Maldive Islands, and own several "buggalows" for carrying cargoes to and from these centres of settlement. The proprietors' grandfather was the first to institute trade between this outlying group of islands and Western India some seventy-five years ago. The firm also has large interests in the Nicobar Islands, from which coconut and other produce of the coconut-palm are obtained in exchange for the necessaries of life, the business being entirely transacted by barter, there being no money currency in these islands.

In Ceylon, Messrs. E. G. Adamaly & Co. possess the monopoly of the supply of sugar manufactured by the China Refinery Factory of Hong Kong. Branches of the business have been established at Male, in the Maldive Islands, Bombay, and in the Nicobar Islands, and agencies throughout India, Burma, China, and the Straits Settlements. The firm contributes to the revenue of the Ceylon Government, in the shape of Customs duty, as much as Rs. 60,000 monthly.

The new premises of Messrs. E. G. Adamaly & Co., situated in the heart of the city of Colombo, embrace all the requirements of a town and country house as well as a business establishment. They are isolated from other buildings by two main thoroughfares, as well as by lands belonging to the firm on either hand, and therefore receive light and ventilation from every side. The building is almost entirely rock-work, and presents a bold aspect, the appearance of solidity being combined with graceful design. The façade is that of a two-storeyed building. From the basement rise pillars of hewn granite, on which arcades of Porebunder rock are turned. The first and second storeys also rise arcade above arcade, and the edifice is crowned with balustrades and cornice. The house occupies a frontage of 80 ft. with a depth of 200 ft., and the basement contains offices, apartments, and stores. A corridor runs through the centre of the basement—with the offices at the entrance and store-rooms to the right and left—and finally leads to a space from which rises a richly designed staircase. On the first and second floors are drawing-rooms, boudoirs, dressing-rooms, and other apartments. A tower rises from the centre of the building to a height approaching 50 ft., from the top of which a fine view of the Colombo harbour and of the principal buildings in the city may be obtained. The woodwork of the building is of teak, imported from India, and the interior is tastefully fitted throughout with incandescent gas lamps. It is one of the most substantially built edifices in the Pettah quarter, as well as one of the most pleasing, and is situated most conveniently in the busiest quarter of Colombo.

THE HEAD OFFICE.

R. J. V. DE S. WIJEYERATNE.

Mr. Lindemullege Richard Joseph Victor de Silva Wijeyeratne is the son of Mr. Robert de Silva Wijeyeratne. Mr. Wijeyeratne, sen., was a Notary Public of Colombo, but did not practise his profession, preferring to adopt a commercial career. In doing so he followed the traditions of his family, for his ancestors on the male side for several generations were timber merchants. The subject of this sketch was born at Colombo on September 12, 1879, and received his education at the Royal and St. Joseph's College. In 1900 he passed the examination of the London College of Preceptors. In 1901 he joined his father in business, and upon the death of his father in 1904 he started on his own account, his operations being mainly confined to contracting for timber, building materials, &c. He is one of the largest contractors for the supply of these goods, and amongst his transactions is the supply of timher and building materials to His Majesty's Government Stores, Ceylon Government Railway Department, the Colombo municipality, &c. His stores, which cover nearly five acres of ground, are situated at St. Joseph's Street, Grandpass. To this centre all kinds of local timber are brought by canal and road from the up-country and low-country forests, and there it is sawn into the requisite sizes. At Mr. Wijeyeratne's stores boats used for conveyance of heavy goods, &c., by canal and river, called padda boats, are built. In the canal which runs through the premises where he has his stores there are docks constructed for the purpose of storing timber which requires to be kept in water for the purpose of seasoning the wood. Bricks and tiles are made at kilns at Wellampitiya, Ambatella, and other places, and are brought down to this centre in the firm's own padda boats by the canal.

Mr. Wijeyeratne is the co-proprietor of the Central Grocery and Wine Stores, 114, Main Street, Pettah, where all kinds of oilmen's stores, Continental wines, spirits, fancy goods, &c., imported from Europe and other places, are disposed of. It is intended shortly to open up an export trade in local produce. Mr. Wijeyeratne is one of the part owners of the

PARTNERS IN THE FIRM OF ADAMALY AND CO., ALSO HEAD OFFICES AND OFFICE STAFF.

BRICK AND TIMBER YARD. R. DE S. WIJEYERATNE. "CLIFTON."
OFFICE AND TIMBER SHED. R. J. V. DE S. WIJEYERATNE. SAW PIT.

well-known coconut estate Hapugahatenne, of nearly 700 acres, in the Veyangoda district, besides owning various properties in Colombo and elsewhere. Another of Mr. Wijeyeratne's interests is a plumbago business which he started this year in conjunction with Messrs. P. D. S. and F. G. S. Wijeyeratne, his cousins. He is a member of the Catholic Union of Ceylon, the Catholic Club, and the Ceylon Agricultural Society. His residence is "Clifton," Horton Place, Colombo.

JAMES DE ALWIS.

Mr. James de Alwis, son of Abraham de Alwis, late actuary of the Ceylon Savings Bank, was born at Colombo in 1878, and educated at St. Thomas's College. Entering the Government service, he was, and still is, attached to the Colombo Kachcheri, but in addition he is a planter and owner of coconut estates in the Western Province, as well as of house property in Colombo. He is a member of the Turf Club and an honorary member of the Sinhalese Sports Club. His private residence is "Milview," Skinner's Road South, Colombo.

F. W. RODRIGUE.

This gentleman is the proprietor of four hotels in Colombo, namely, the British India,

F. W. RODRIGUE.

the Royal, the Metropolitan, and the Mansion Hotels. The British India Hotel, the largest of these, is situated in Upper Chatham Street, and commands a fine view of the Indian Ocean, while at the same time being one of the most comfortable hotels in the Fort. The site being suitable, but the building not being all that the proprietor would like, Mr. Rodrigue intends to pull down the building and replace it by one of the most modern and up-to-date edifices in the city. With the idea of obtaining as much up-to-date information as possible in regard to the building of a first-class hotel of the most modern style of architecture, and replete with the latest improvements relative to ventilation and general convenience, Mr. Rodrigue recently visited the Homeland. When the proposed rebuilding is completed, this establishment will be one of the handsomest and most comfortable of its kind in Colombo.

The Royal and Metropolitan Hotels are both situated in the Pettah quarter of Colombo, the former standing at the corner of Main Street. At both a brisk trade is carried on, the management of each sparing no pains to ensure the comfort and tastes of its patrons, both as regards accommodation and the supply departments.

The Mansion Hotel, situated in the Grandpass suburb of Colombo, is a thoroughly up-to-

JAMES DE ALWIS.

THE TURNOUT. THE RESIDENCE.

date establishment, containing a large range of bedrooms, retiring rooms, a fine billiard-room, a smoking-room, and an extensive dining-room. A feature of this hotel is its wide and cool verandah—so desirable a provision in the East. Another attraction is the grounds, planted with handsome ornamental plants, fruit-trees, and flowering shrubs, and containing a spacious tennis-court. The electric tramcars halt at this hotel. On Saturday evenings a band is engaged to play at this establishment during dinner.

Besides being the proprietor of these four hotels, Mr. Rodrigue carries on the business of a caterer, having had wide experience in this line and holding the contract for supplying the Army and Navy. He also owns several large rubber plantations in the Kelani Valley, not far distant from Colombo.

WILLIAM DIAS.

Mr. William Dias is the head cashier of the Mercantile Bank of India, Ltd., Colombo. He was born in Colombo on March 24, 1863, and is the son of the late Mr. Don Julius Dias, military contractor and landed proprietor, of Colombo. He was educated at the Wesley College, Colombo. On leaving school in 1884 he entered the Chartered Mercantile Bank of India, London, and China, as a clerk; and, rising through all the various departments, he acquired an entire knowledge of banking. In 1903 he was appointed to the important position of head cashier, which he still holds. This was then a unique appointment, as up to that time the post had been confined strictly to Jaffna Tamils. He was the first and only Sinhalese shroff in Colombo.

Mr. William Dias is the owner of several valuable planting estates, the most notable being in Salpiti Korale, in the Western Province. He is also the owner of several properties in the city of Colombo, including bungalows in Cinnamon Gardens. His private residence is Beatrice House, Retreat Road, Bambalapitiya, a southern suburb of Colombo. Mr. Dias is a member of the Young Men's Christian Association, Sinhalese Literary Society, the Gnanaprobodha Association, committee member of the Ceylon Mutual Provident Association, and hon. treasurer of the Wesley College Old Boys' Association, besides being connected with the management of several benevolent institutions. He is a member of the Wesleyan Church. He married Sophia, daughter of the late Mr. Abraham Perera, of Navala, a well-known landed proprietor and arrack-renter.

A. S. F. WIJIGOONERATNE.

Mr. A. Simon Fernando Wijigooneratne, Mohandiram, was born at Mount Lavinia. He commenced business in 1876 as a wine merchant and dealer in oilmen's stores at 63, Main Street, Pettah, and he now imports every variety of wine, spirit, &c., from France, Spain, England, and Germany. The principal commodities dealt in by the firm are jams, butter, tinned fish, tinned meat, and biscuits. Barbed wire, Portland cement, and iron safes are also sold in this cosmopolitan store. Mr. Wijigooneratne, who has branches at 31, Kayman's Gate and Union Place, Slave Island, in 1899 built and fitted up a library for medical students and presented it to the Government. In 1899 he was made Mohandiram by Sir West Ridgeway, and he is the owner of a good deal of property in the Fort, the Pettah, and the Cinnamon Gardens, Colombo. In referring to his many charities, mention should be made of the fact that he contributed most of the cost of the large preaching hall at the Hendala Leper Asylum, is a warm supporter of Buddhist temples and schools, and contributed handsomely to the Victoria Memorial Hospital Fund. He resides at Catherine Villa, Kynsey Road, Colombo. Mr. Wijigooneratne was married in 1895 to a young lady of a respected family named Hewadewagi Ango Fernando, and the issue of the union is five children, of whom

WILLIAM DIAS, MAITLAND HOUSE, BEATRICE HOUSE, AND LAUREL COTTAGE.

MEDICAL LIBRARY. THE BUNGALOW. THE FAMILY.
A. S. F. WIJIGOONERATNE. STORES INTERIOR. STORES EXTERIOR.

the eldest is a son named Peter. The other four are daughters, named Catherine, Roseline, Eugine, and Agnes.

ADRIS MENDIS WICKREMESINGHE SENANAYAKE, Mohandiram.

This gentleman, generally known as Adris Mendis, is a native of Kosgoda, near Galle, having been born in the year 1855, and received his education at the Wesley College, Colombo. Starting business in 1876 as a general merchant at Maradana, he afterwards removed to his present residence, Pretoria Villa, De Saram Place, Cinnamon Gardens. He deals largely in cinnamon, coconut, copra, and cinnamon oil, which products are mostly grown on his own estates in the Southern and Western Provinces. Mr. Mendis is the Government lessee of the Maradana cinnamon gardens belonging to the Crown, and also owns several planting estates with fully equipped and residential bungalows, stores, distilleries, and factories. He is one of the wealthiest landed proprietors in Colombo, owning many houses, some of which are amongst the best-known residences in the city. He also owns considerable property at Galle, Kalutara, Bentota, and other places in the island, and is the managing director of the firm of Adris Mendis & Co., Kosgoda. On all occasions of loyalty being celebrated by public demonstrations, Mr. Mendis has taken a prominent part; and during the last twenty years or more he has spontaneously, and often at great expense, contributed largely to the adornment of the city, notably during the Queen's Jubilee celebrations and the welcome to the Duke and Duchess of Cornwall. Mr. Mendis is known as an able snake-doctor, and has saved many lives. He takes a keen interest in the Colombo Agri-Horticultural Society, and during recent years has carried away over a hundred prizes at the different shows. He is an ardent Buddhist, being a prominent member of the Buddhist Defence Society, Vice-President of the Theosophical Society, and the Manager of the Rajapakse Buddhist College at Kosgoda.

MOHANDIRAM A. MENDIS.

MR. AND MRS. LUCAS FERNANDO AND FAMILY.

In 1903 the titular rank of Mohandiram was conferred upon him by His Excellency the Governor in recognition of his many public services.

R. G. KOELMAN.

This gentleman is an auctioneer, broker and commission agent of Colombo. The business he conducts was founded in the city in 1872 by his father, Mr. E. J. Koelman, under the title of Jensen & Co. Mr. R. G. Koelman joined the firm in the year 1901, and the entire management was taken over by him on the death of his parent in the year 1904. The present head of the business was born in Colombo in 1885, and was educated in Ceylon.

TAMBO SOCKANÂTHAN.

Mr. T. Sockanâthan was born at Colombo in 1863, and is the son of Mr. M. Super Tambo, of Colombo, a broker and landed proprietor. Mr. Sockanâthan was educated at St. Thomas's College, and, on leaving school, started in business in 1883 as clerk with Messrs. Mackwood & Co., Colombo. In 1885 he joined the firm of Messrs. Charles Mackwood & Co. as broker, and in 1899 joined the Bank of Madras as head cashier, which position he has filled ever since. The staff under his personal supervision includes about twenty shroffs and tellers. Besides being a landed proprietor in Colombo, Mr. Sockanâthan is the owner of estates in the Hendala district and other parts, which are principally planted with coconuts. He is a member of the Hindu Sivite community, Agricultural Society, and the Social Reform Union. His private residence is in Checku Street, Colombo.

T. SOCKANÂTHAN.

FELIX JOSEPH LUCAS FERNANDO.

This gentleman is the son of Hettiacandege Joseph Fernando, of Moratuwa, a descendant of a much respected and rich family of the Vellando Kula caste, who was one of the chief arrack-renters and landed proprietors

"NORWOOD" BUNGALOW.

MR. AND MRS. WIJEYERATNE.

of Colombo, Kandy, and other places from the year 1860, and held the Colombo arrack rents for nearly thirty-five years. Mr. F. J. L. Fernando was born at Moratuwa, and educated privately and at St. Thomas's College, Colombo. He joined the Ceylon Medical College and passed his first professional examination. He then discontinued his studies, to assist his father in his large and growing business. He began planting coconuts in 1880, and, on his father's death in 1890, he took over the deceased gentleman's affairs. At the present time he is one of the leading planters and landed proprietors in Ceylon. It is notable that nearly all the estates he owns to-day have been planted by himself. Rukkatene and Pathara estates, in the North-Western Province, which extend over more than 3,000 acres of fully planted land, are convincing proofs of Mr. Fernando's energy as a cultivator. Yadehigedere, Yalawe, Kahatawille, and Katukande, in the same province, are others of his best-known estates, while on his Kingswell Park estate, near Veyangoda, there is a residential bungalow. The produce of his estates, mostly consisting of copra, tea, and cinnamon, is sold in the local markets. He intends embarking upon the cultivation of rubber-trees in the Kurunegala district.

Besides being a planter on a large scale, Mr. Fernando also owns several plumbago mines in the Pasdun Korale, Kalutara district, and Kurunegala, which are worked by lessees. He also owns house properties in Colombo and Kurunegala, of which his private residence —"Norwood," Layards Road, Havelock Town —and "St. James," Colpetty, are the more important. In 1886, he married a daughter of Adittawanse Lindamullege Juan de Silva, Mudaliyar, of Moratuwa, and later of Colombo. Mr. Fernando's eldest daughter, Mary Catherine Jane, is married to Mr. E. R. F. de Silva Wijeyeratne, a rising junior in the legal profession in Colombo.

JOHN CARL KOELMAN.

Mr. John C. Koelman, son of Mr. E. J. Koelman, planter and estate-owner of Kalutara, was born at Colombo in the year 1879. After receiving his education at the Royal College, Colombo, he started learning planting under Mr. Edwin Koelman, on Ossington Estate, Kalutara. Having thus acquired the requisite knowledge, he took charge of his father's property in that district, and remained a planter for eleven years. On the death of his father he sold the plantation to the Dimbula Valley Tea Estates Company and removed to Colombo, where he has since set up in business as broker and commission agent. He is the proprietor of an estate in the Kurunegala district and owner of landed property in Colombo. He is a member of the Turf Club, and at one time ran his own horses both at Colombo and in Nuwara Eliya. His recreations are chiefly riding and hunting. His private residence is "Airydale," Havelock Town, Colombo.

CATHERAWALOE GNANASAKARAM.

Mr. Gnanasakaram, son of the late Mr. Suppramaniam Catherawaloe, was born in

CATHERAWALOE GNANASAKARAM.

Colombo in 1861, and was educated at St. Thomas's College in that city. He commenced his business career in 1879 as assistant cashier of the Oriental Bank at Kandy, and some little while after was transferred to Colombo as assistant to his father, who was chief shroff (cashier) of the Colombo Bank. Subsequently he became joint head cashier of the new Oriental Bank at Colombo, then head cashier of the Hong Kong and Shanghai Banking Corporation, in the same place. Twelve years ago he joined the staff of the National Bank of India as chief cashier, which position he continues to occupy. He is a Hindu by birth, and a landed proprietor in Colombo and other places in the island. He is also a member of the Turf Club. His private residence is "Mangalagiri," Kynsey Road, Cinnamon Gardens, Colombo.

PETER DE ABREW.

Mr. Peter de Abrew, son of William de Abrew, was born on April 2, 1863, in Colombo. He was educated at the Colombo Academy (now the Royal College), and joined his father in business, with whom he had his commercial training. He then started in business on his own account as a produce merchant, and in 1904 was appointed by the Government of Ceylon to the office of Assistant Commissioner at the St. Louis Exposition, U.S.A., of 1904, for the purpose of specially looking after the development of commerce. He returned to Ceylon in 1905 and joined the firm of Messrs. Volkart Bros. He is a Member of the Royal Asiatic Society, Fellow of the Imperial Institute, manager and one of the trustees of the Musaeus School for Buddhist girls, and secretary of the Ceylon Social Reform Society. Mr. de Abrew has travelled much, having visited Europe in 1894 and in 1903, when he toured Italy, Germany, and Austria. His private residence is in McCarthy Place, Cinnamon Gardens, Colombo.

PETER DE ABREW.

"ST. JAMES."

MICHAEL J. DE JONG.

Mr. Michael J. de Jong, dental surgeon at the Colombo Dental Surgery, Norris Road, Pettah, Colombo, proprietor of the City Perfumery at the same address, and of the Arcade Pharmacy, in the Fort of Colombo, received his early education at the Royal College and St. Benedict's Institute, Colombo. He proceeded afterwards to the Edinburgh University in order to complete his course of study in dental surgery at the Edinburgh Dental Hospital. He returned to Ceylon in 1902, where he established a large practice in the particular branch of the medical profession for which he qualified. The City Dispensary was originally founded by the firm of Philip T. de Jong & Sons. But since Mr. Michael de Jong took over the business in Norris Road in 1903, he has started a branch in the Fort, known as the Arcade Pharmacy; and in both of these establishments every description of chemical and druggist's sundries are stored, and a large wholesale and retail business is carried on. The City Dispensary is one of the oldest establishments of its kind in Colombo, and has a considerable share of the wholesale druggists' trade of the island. Mr. de Jong is a member of the Orient Club, the Catholic Club, and the Automobile Club of Ceylon. He is a keen motorist, and possesses an 8-horse-power Darracq and a 12-horse-power four-cylinder Thor car. His private residence is "St. Joseph's," Rosmead Place, Cinnamon Gardens, Colombo.

DON PHILIP A. WIJEWARDENE, Mohandiram.

The timber trade of Colombo is an extensive one. It cannot well be otherwise with a growing town, which is extending its borders all round, and is at the same time replacing the single-floored buildings of a past age with modern ones of architectural pretensions. In this trade, among the most prominent, if not absolutely the chief, are Mr. Alexander Wijewardene's timber yards. These are situated in Seddewatte, the headquarters of the timber trade. Mr. Wijewardene, whose photograph we give, is very young in years, but brings considerable natural talents and business acumen to his work. He has had a good college education, and has served an apprenticeship under his father, the late Don Philip, Mohandiram, whose career is dealt with further on. He started thoroughly conversant with everything connected with the trade, and he easily keeps the position his father won for himself as the chief supplier of timber to the Government, including the Railway, the Public Works Department, and the Harbour Works. But the timber trade, large as it is, has not been enough to fill all the energies of the present youthful proprietor. He has in consequence started brickmaking works, and has very extensive kilns. His is just now the largest brick and tile store in Colombo. Among the more prominent buildings for which Mr. Wijewardene supplied the timber, brick, and tile are the Victoria Eye Memorial Hospital, the administration block of the General Hospital, the Technical College, the new Supreme Court buildings, and the Public Works Offices now in course of construction. Even this scarcely ends the list, for Mr. Wijewardene has found the means to embark upon a contract to supply bulls and cart-drivers to the municipality. He has in consequence over 200 draught bulls in his yards for everyday use, and nearly 400 coolies are engaged every day in driving the carts and in other works connected with this contract. Into the day's work, too, come the concerns of a coconut estate, a young plantation of 600 acres.

Mr. Wijewardene was, in 1905, given the rank of Mohandiram, in recognition of the good work done by him in his dealings with the Public Works Department.

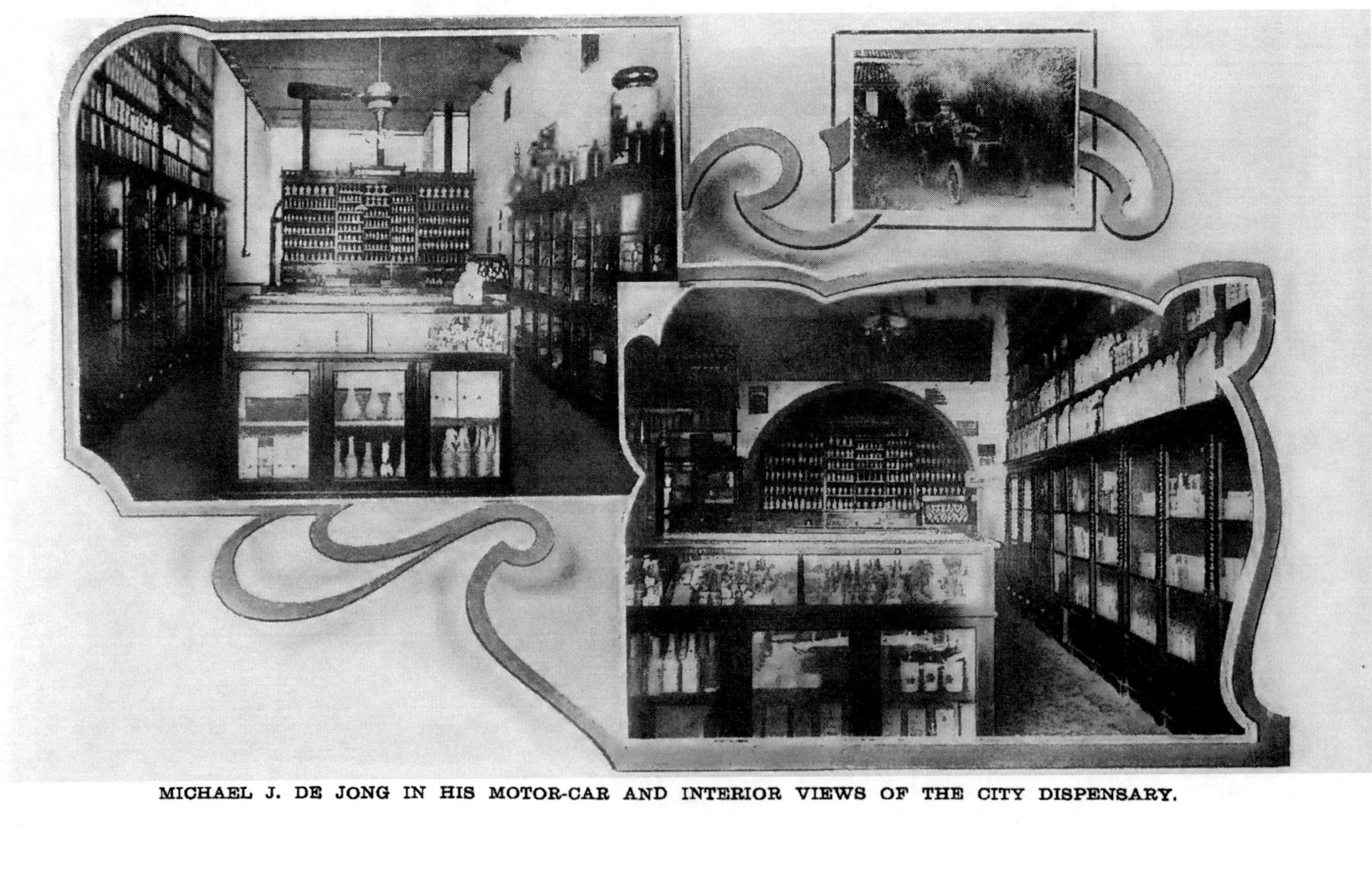

MICHAEL J. DE JONG IN HIS MOTOR-CAR AND INTERIOR VIEWS OF THE CITY DISPENSARY.

DON PHILIP A. WIJEWARDENE. BRICK STORES, GRANDPASS.
TIMBER YARD, SEDDEWATTE. MUNGELWELI ESTATE, PUTTALAM.

CATHIRAVALOE NAMASIVAYAM.

Mr. Cathiravaloe Namasivayam is the chief cashier of the Hong Kong and Shanghai Banking Corporation, Colombo. He was formerly connected with the Ceylon Government Railways as head shroff of that department. He comes of an old and respected Tamil family, and his father, Mr. S. Cathiravaloe, was connected with banking business for nearly half a century, having been the chief cashier of the old and new Oriental Bank Corporations. Mr. Cathiravaloe was the founder of the Chattrum (curative home for the poor) at Keerimalie—which place is well-known for the curative effects of its mineral springs—and also of a vernacular school in Jaffna. Mr. Namasivayam is a wealthy landed proprietor, and owns extensive estates in different parts of the island. He recently published a book of "Interest Tables," which has a large circulation in mercantile circles.

CATHIRAVALOE NAMASIVAYAM.

THOMASZ CORONALIS WIJEYEWARDENE.

Mr. Wijeyewardene, son of the late Don Elias Wijeyewardene, Mohandiram of Gonawella, Sina Korale, was born in 1863, and was educated at the Royal College, Colombo. After completing his school career, he took to planting at an earlier age than usual, under his father's direction. Afterwards, in company with Mr. J. D. Vanderstraaten, he traded in coconuts for about two years. After his father's death, in 1892, he devoted himself solely to the planting business. He has recently commenced opening a rubber estate of 500 acres, called "Brooks Mere," at Kalatuawa, in the Sabaragamuwa Province. He owns the coconut estates of Gonawella, in the Western Province, and Alauwa, in the North-Western Province. The produce of his estates was formerly supplied for desiccation to the merchants of the Fort of Colombo, but is now sold in the shape of nuts in the local markets.

Mr. Wijeyewardene owns extensive paddy fields in the Sina Korale district, which, up to very lately, were cultivated by himself. He also owns lands nearly three-quarters of a mile in length, bearing an extensive outcrop of plumbago, which he now intends mining and bringing to Colombo to be cured and finished. He owns house property at Gonawella, where the old family residence—"Homewood"—is situated. In 1898 he married Louisa, second daughter of James Edmund Jayatillike, Mudaliyar, late President of Baddegama.

J. V. ATAPATTU, Mudaliyar.

This gentleman, who has filled the responsible and onerous position of station-master at the Colombo Fort Railway Station for ten years, is a descendant of one of the ancient aristocratic Kandyan families. He was born on November 17, 1868, and was educated at the Royal College—then the Colombo Academy. He entered the Government service in 1879 as a clerk in the Railway Department, and proving himself eminently satisfactory in the discharge of his duties, he rose rapidly to the position he now holds. In this post Mr. Atapattu enjoyed the rare opportunity of having charge of the arrangements on the occasion of the arrival at and departure from the Fort Station of the Duke and Duchess of Cornwall and York (now the Prince and Princess of Wales), when these royal persons, on their visit to Ceylon in 1901, journeyed by train to the interior of the island. On that occasion the station was superbly decorated according to Mr. Atapattu's own design, and under his personal direction, the beauty of some of the devices, the quaintness of others, and the strikingly brilliant and pleasing effect of the *tout ensemble*, eliciting the admiration of the royal visitors, to whom he was presented by the then Governor (Sir West Ridgeway), and by whom he was highly complimented. Mr. Atapattu's decorative work was also warmly eulogised by the local Press, each of the local newspapers devoting considerable space to appreciative and detailed description of the gorgeous and emblematic display at the Fort Station. No less than forty "living pictures" were included in a scene representative of Sinhalese typical characters. An illustration in the section on Railways conveys an idea of the magnificence of the display. For his services in connection with the visit of the Heir Apparent and his spouse, Mr. Atapattu

MUDALIYAR J. V. ATAPATTU AND FAMILY.

T. C. WIJEYEWARDENE AND FAMILY. THE BUNGALOW.
T. C. WIJEYEWARDENE. REAPING PADDY.
THRASHING PADDY.

N. D. S. SILVA, HIS RESIDENCE AND TURNOUT.

received the rank of Mohandiram, having then, as the Governor remarked on conferring the honour, rendered "excellent and efficient service" to the Government in the Railway Department for twenty-two years, "and especially useful service in connection with the recent royal visit." Mr. and Mrs. Atapattu had the honour of being invited to the reception held at Queen's House in connection with the visit of the Duke and Duchess of Cornwall and York. On Coronation Day the Fort Station was again decorated by Mr. Atapattu in similarly gorgeous fashion, and a photograph of the display sent to the Prince of Wales was acknowledged by Mr. Chamberlain (then Secretary of State for the Colonies) in appreciative terms.

In 1903 Mr. Atapattu was advanced to the rank and dignity of Mudaliyar, when he was again highly complimented by the Governor (Sir West Ridgeway) on his length of service, and upon having gained "the esteem and regard of the merchants and the rest of the community of Colombo." It was a sad blow to Mr. and Mrs. Atapattu to lose their only daughter, Edith, in 1904. The child had taken a prominent part in the reception of the Duke and Duchess of York at the Fort Station in 1901, by strewing flowers and burnt paddy in the path of the royal visitors. In expressing her sympathy with the parents in their bereavement, Lady West Ridgeway wrote that she well remembered how gracefully the little girl performed her part. The accompanying illustration showing the group of the Atapattu family includes six sons—Douglas and Edgar, promising boys of school-going age, and Eric, Victor, Guy and Bertie, eight, five, four and three years of age respectively.

Once again, in January, 1906, the Fort Station burst out into a blaze of decorative glory, the occasion being another royal visit to Ceylon. Mr. Atapattu repeated his past successes, and the result elicited general admiration, and led to his presentation by the Governor (Sir Henry Blake) to the august visitor, the Duke of Connaught. The Mudaliyar has a passion for gardening, evidence of which is afforded by the attractive collection of flowers, shrubs, and fruit-trees, besides vegetables, in the ground attached to the Fort Station. Possessing a widely-known personality and the general esteem of the community—both in his official position and his private capacity—Mudaliyar Atapattu is, no doubt, on the high-road to further promotion in the Government service.

N. DON STEPHEN SILVA.

Mr. Nanayakarage Don Stephen Silva is the second son of the late N. D. P. Silva, to whom lengthy reference is made in another part of this work. He was born at Colombo in 1881, and educated at St. Thomas's and St. Joseph's Colleges. Entering his father's office in Colombo he received a business training there, but when Mr. Silva, sen., died, the subject of this sketch went in for planting coconuts, rubber, tea, and cacao. His best-known estates are Bambarabotuwa in the Ratnapura district, planted with tea, and Ambatella and Wanaskelle in the North-West Province, planted with cacao and rubber respectively. In addition, he owns extensive house property in Colombo, and will shortly go into partnership with his elder brother under the name and style of N. D. P. Silva & Co. He is a member of the Orient, Turf, Catholic, and Lawn Clubs, and of the Catholic Union, and he lives at the Orient Club, Colombo.

FRANCIS JOSEPH ALLES.

This gentleman is the chief cashier of the Colombo branch of the Chartered Bank of India, Australia, and China. He was born on

FRANCIS JOSEPH ALLES, COLOMBO VAISYA CHETTIES (LADY AND GENTLEMAN), TERNON HOUSE, AND THE BUNGALOW.

THE HON. MR. AND MRS. S. C. OBEYESEKERE AND FAMILY.
"HILL CASTLE."

October 4, 1868. A member of the Vaisya Chetty community, the smallest of the various communities of the island, and the majority of whom are Roman Catholics, Mr. Alles is the only son of Anthony Alles and Lucia Rosairo. He was educated privately and at St. Benedict's Institute, Colombo. Having obtained at the latter institution a sound commercial education, he left school in December, 1884, and in the following month began to help his father, who was the guarantee broker to Messrs. Whittall & Co., one of the leading commercial houses in Ceylon. The young fellow's abilities were soon discerned; and in a few months he was offered, and accepted, the storekeepership of the firm, in conjunction with the post of assistant-broker. On the death of his father on February 14, 1889, Mr. F. J. Alles assumed the sole management of the broking branch of Messrs. Whittall & Co.'s business. On February 4, 1895, he married Theresa, youngest daughter of the late Simon Nonis, of the Colombo Customs. On July 1, 1892, the Chartered Bank opened a branch in Colombo, and, on the recommendation of Messrs. Whittall & Co., Mr. Alles was appointed to the important and responsible post of chief cashier of that bank in Ceylon. Since his elevation to that position he has notably extended the very profitable native business of the bank. He was the first of the Vaisya Chetty community in Colombo to obtain a post such as he holds, all bank shroffships in Colombo having been previously monopolised by wealthy and influential Jaffna Tamils. He is a staunch Roman Catholic.

A. S. F. JAYASEKERE, Mudaliyar.

Aluthewhee Seadoris Fernando Jayasekere is a native of Kalutara, who commenced business as a general merchant along with his cousin, and is to-day proprietor and senior partner of the firm of C. Mathew & Co., the well-known stevedores and ship's chandlers, as well as of the firm of A. S. F. Jayasekere, merchants and general importers, of 7, Fourth Cross Street, Pettah, Colombo, and Railway Bridge Road, Kalutara. He owns coconut plantations and paddy lands, and house property in the Kalutara district. He was appointed Arachchi in 1897, Mohandiram in 1899, and Mudaliyar in 1905. He is a member of the Agricultural and Theosophical Societies, and also of the Sinhalese Sports Club, and a liberal supporter of other sporting organisations.

MUDALIYAR A. S. FERNANDO JAYASEKERE.

COLOMBO: PROFESSIONAL AND SOCIAL.

THE HON. MR. S. C. OBEYESEKERE, M.L.C.

Mr. Obeyesekere is a scion of one of the oldest and proudest of Southern Province families, the members of which have invariably held high office, and have been leaders of native society for generations. He is a son of the late D. B. F. Obeyesekere, Mudaliyar of the Talpe Pattu in the Southern Province, and Cornelia Susannah Dias Bandaranaike, and younger brother of the late Hon. James Peter Obeyesekere, M.L.C., and was born on February 12, 1848. His education was obtained at the Colombo Academy (now the Royal College) and St. Thomas's College, where he passed through a highly successful collegiate career. He carried off the majority of the first prizes, and in 1866 he achieved the then rare distinction of passing in the first class the entrance examination of the Calcutta University. He obtained the first-class diploma two years later. Completing his course at St. Thomas's College, he was apprenticed to the late Advocate C. A. Lorenz as a law student, and at the Proctor's examination in 1872 he headed the list of successful candidates in every subject, being specially complimented by the President of the Board of Examiners, Sir Edward Creasy, on the excellence of his papers and his general ability. In addition to being a member of the Legislative Council, Mr. Obeyesekere is a member of the Central Irrigation Board, and also a member of the Royal Colonial Institute and of the Committee of the Ceylon branch of the Royal Asiatic Society. He does not practise, but occupies his time in tending his various properties. His hobby is agriculture and cattle breeding, and he has followed both with practical business results. He favours old farming methods, only discarding these for modern innovations when they show a distinct advantage, taking tropical circumstances into consideration. He was prominent in the movement for the establishment of an agricultural society, being of opinion that such an organisation would be the means of bringing back to the land the peasantry who had migrated to the towns. He has estates and landed properties all over the island, and the former are model places, to be found principally in the Western and North-Western Provinces. His town residence, Hill Castle, is well known, and his country seat at Badulla is of a truth the residence of an old Ceylon squire. He is a supporter of practically all Ceylon charitable institutions, and is a patron or office-bearer of almost every club and association, learned or social, and the leader of the Sinhalese community. He is a member of the Legislative Council and of the executive committee of the Ceylon branch of the Royal Asiatic Society, an incorporated trustee of the Church of England in Ceylon, a member of the executive committee of the Friend-in-Need Society of Colombo, and Vice-President of the Board of Agriculture, Ceylon. He was also one of the party who proceeded to England to present the address of the Legislative Council to His Majesty King Edward on the occasion of the Coronation. Mr. Obeyesekere's wife is the second daughter of the late Hon. James Alwis, M.L.C., and Florence Dias Bandaranaike, who was a sister of the late Sir Harry Dias. His eldest daughter married Don Solomon Dias Bandaranaike, the Maha Mudaliyar; his second is wedded to Dr. W. C. Pieris, whilst the youngest assists her mother in doing the honours of the house. He has one son, Forester Augustus, who is a graduate of Trinity College, Cambridge, a member of the Inner Temple, and reading for the Bar.

DON SOLOMON DIAS ABEYEWICKREME JAYATILEKKE SENEWIRATNE RAJA-KUMARUN KADUKERALU BANDARANAIKE, C.M.G.

This gentleman, better known as Don Solomon Dias Bandaranaike, the Maha Mudaliyar of Ceylon, is a leading member of the Sinhalese community. He is aide-de-camp to the Governor, and in this capacity he is necessarily an intimate member of the Governor's household. He is a direct descendant of one of the most ancient families of the island, represented by the first six of the names he bears, the next two having been assumed by special authority of the Government in 1882, to commemorate his investiture with the rank of Mohandiram of the Governor's Gate by His Royal Highness the late Duke of Clarence, when, as Prince Albert Victor of Wales, His Royal Highness visited Ceylon. Mention is made of this incident in the famous "Cruise of the *Bacchante.*"

MAHA MUDALIYAR DON SOLOMON DIAS BANDARANAIKE.

The Maha Mudaliyar is the son of Don Christoffel Henricus Dias Abeyewickreme Jayatilekke Senewiratne Bandaranaike—who was Mudaliyar of the Governor's Gate and of Siyane Korale East, also Justice of the Peace and Unofficial Police Magistrate—and grandson of the Don Solomon Dias Bandaranaike who is mentioned in the second volume of Tennent's "History of Ceylon." The Maha Mudaliyar was born at Veyangoda in 1862, and educated at St. Thomas's College, Colombo. At the age of nineteen, his collegiate course being completed, he betook himself to the study of public affairs. Having been, as already stated, invested with the rank of Mohandiram of the Governor's Gate in 1882, he made himself thoroughly acquainted with the duties of a chief towards the Government and of a Sinhalese gentleman towards the people of his country, and eventually succeeded his father in the office of Mudaliyar of Siyane Korale East. Nine years later he proceeded to England on six months' leave, this being his first trip to Europe. On his return the then Governor of the island, Sir Arthur Havelock, invested him at Queen's House with the rank of Maha Mudaliyar. He is also a Justice of the Peace for the whole island.

In 1897 he again visited England, this time as an official representative of Ceylon at the Diamond Jubilee celebrations, and received the medal awarded in commemoration of this event. In 1902 he once more figured as a representative of Ceylon in England, the occasion being the Coronation of the present King, and then received his C.M.G. and the Coronation medal. Since his return to Ceylon he has fulfilled his numerous public duties as well as followed agricultural and stock-raising pursuits. As a breeder of large stock he is prominent throughout the island.

The Maha Mudaliyar owns extensive coconut plantations in the Western Province, and has opened a tract of land for rubber-planting. He is also the proprietor of considerable house property in Colombo, Nuwara Eliya, and Veyangoda. In 1898 he married Daisy Ezline, eldest daughter of the Hon. Mr. S. C. Obeyesekere, M.L.C. He is a Fellow of the Royal Colonial Institute and of the Imperial Institute, life-member of the Royal Asiatic Society, also a member of the Board and the Committee of

"HORAGALLA" WALAUWA. THE MAHA MUDALIYAR'S RESIDENCE.

THE MAHA MUDALIYAR, HIS WIFE AND FAMILY.

WHITE HOUSE.

MUDALIYAR AND MRS. SOLOMON SENEVIRATNE.

the Agricultural and Horti-Agricultural Societies and the Turf Club. He is, besides, a member of the Orient and Kennel Clubs, Vice-President of the Sinhalese Sports Club and the Poultry Club, committee member of the Nuwara Eliya Gymkhana Club, and a member of the Sports Club, St. James's Square, London. His recreations are riding and shooting, while his hobbies are horticulture and agriculture, which latter occupations, however, he pursues in practical fashion. His country residence, "Horagalla," at Veyangoda, is the hospitable home of a thorough country squire, and typical of the first native gentleman of Ceylon.

SOLOMON SENEVIRATNE.

Mr. Solomon Seneviratne is the son of Don Hermanis Seneviratne, Mohandiram of Siyane Korale, and grandson of Don Carolis Seneviratne, Mudaliyar of Kalutara, while his great-grandfather was Don Louis Seneviratne, Mohandiram of the same place. Our subject was born at Colombo in 1849, and educated at Queen's College and the Colombo Academy, after which he entered the Government service and was attached to the accountants' branch of the Audit Office as early as 1874. Five years later he became head clerk of the Grain Commission, and in 1883 Mudaliyar of the Ratnapura Kachcheri. In 1887 he became Mudaliyar of Pasdun Korale, and in 1890 of Salpiti Korale; while a year later he was appointed Itinerating Police Magistrate and Acting Deputy Fiscal for the Western Province. In 1893 he received the appointment of Atapattu Mudaliyar of Colombo and the Western Province, and in 1895 Mudaliyar of the Governor's Gate; and for his faithful services in different official positions he has been awarded a gold medal by the Government. In 1891 he married Charlotte, youngest daughter of C. H. Dias Bandaranaike, J.P. for the island and Mudaliyar of Siyane Korale, and sister of the present Maha Mudaliyar. He resides at White House, Ward Place, Colombo, and his country seat is "Kandehena," Veyangoda. He is a member of the Agricultural and Horticultural Societies, and he delights in his leisure hours in studying the ancient history of Ceylon.

WILLIAM CHRISTOFFEL PIERIS SIRIWARDHANE.

Dr. William Christoffel Pieris Siriwardhane, the son of Mr. J. M. P. Pieris Samarasinhe Siriwardhane, J.P., and Mudaliyar of the Governor's Gate, was born in 1867 at 40, Silversmith Street, Colombo. He received his early education at St. Thomas's College, Colombo, proceeding afterwards to the Marischal College, Aberdeen, where he became senior medallist in pathology and bacteriology, obtaining at the same time a certificate of highest distinction in the same subjects, and gained distinctions in materia medica and physiology under such well-known masters as Professors Hamilton, Cash, and McWilliam. He also gained a diploma in mental diseases from the Medico-Psychological Association of Great Britain and Ireland. In 1894 Dr. Pieris Siriwardhane graduated as M.B., C.M., after which he had charge, as Medical Officer, of some of the Orkney Islands for about one year. He then returned to Aberdeen University and walked the chief Scottish hospitals. In 1895 he returned to Ceylon, where he became Senior House-Surgeon of the Colombo General Hospital for one year. He afterwards successively filled the positions of District Medical Officer at Dikoya (1897), District Medical Officer at Rakwana—which post he filled with great credit for five years—Deputy Assistant Colonial Surgeon, District Medical Officer at Panadure, Third Visiting Physician of the General Hospital, Colombo, Lecturer in Clinical Medicine at the Ceylon Medical College, and District Medical Officer at Haputale. In 1905 he returned to Panadure, where he took charge of the hospital and district, and also became Judicial Medical Officer, in which latter office he experienced very heavy criminal work. He

DR. AND MRS. WILLIAM CHRISTOFFEL PIERIS SIRIWARDHANE.

is a member of the British Medical Association, a contributor to the *Ceylon Medical Journal*, and a member of the Turf Club. Dr. Pieris Siriwardhane is a keen sportsman, his chief recreations being hunting, angling, and cricket. He married Ethel Mildred, the second daughter of the Hon. S. C. Obeyesekere, M.L.C., and is the father of one son. The doctor's private residence is "Homeleigh," Panadure.

J. F. D. BANDARANAYKE.

Mr. Johannes Franciscus Dias Bandaranayke comes of a family which may be said to be one of the, if not the oldest of the noble families of Ceylon. Mention is made of members of this family in the very earliest Dutch and Portuguese records, and references to their descendants are frequent in later documents. The family was founded by an Indian officer of high standing who, serving under the kings of Kandy and bearing the name of Nilaperumal, was made high priest and ordered to take the name of Bandaranayke as early as 1454. The Bandaranayke family appears in practically every record existing, but it will suffice to state that Don Franciscus Bandaranayke was made Mudaliyar of the four Pattus after the original Mudaliyars had fled to Kandy in the war between the Dutch East India Company and the Kandyans. He married the mother of Louis de Saram, second Maha Mudaliyar of the Governor's Gate, and his son, Don Conrad Peter Dias Bandaranayke Wijeyewardene, was Maha Mudaliyar of the Governor's Gate and Governor of the four united Pattus, and married Louise Jeronimus. He also was the recipient of two gold medals from the Dutch Government in recognition of his services. Don Conrad's son, Johannes Franciscus Dias Bandaranayke, who was Mudaliyar of the Governor's Gate, was born in 1789 and married Louisa de Saram, daughter of the Maha Mudaliyar of the day. His son, Don Conrad Peter Dias Bandaranayke, was born in 1827 and became Mudaliyar of Alutkuru Korale South and afterwards Mudaliyar of the Governor's Gate and Maha Mudaliyar. He married the daughter of Valentine de Saram, the Maha Mudaliyar, and the subject of this sketch is the sixth of their sons. Born in 1862, he was educated at St. Thomas's and Royal Colleges, and in 1888, he took charge of his father's planting affairs and has been engaged in planting operations ever since. He administers the whole of the estate at the present time. The principal estates belonging to the family are Udupila in the Siyane Korale, comprising 500 acres planted with cocoanuts and fully equipped; Bandarawatte in the Heneratgoda district, 300 acres in extent; and various other estates in the neighbourhood as well as house property at Colombo, Peradeniya, &c. The family resides at the Maha Walauwa, Green Street, Colombo, but Mr. Franciscus Bandaranayke, who married in 1902 Somawati, daughter of Kepitipole Ratemahatmaya of Matale, resides on the Udupila estates.

MUDALIYAR JOHN LOUIS PIERIS SRIWARDHANA.

This gentleman is the son of Mr. J. M. P. Pieris Sriwardhana, Mudaliyar of the Gate and of Siyane Korale West, Justice of the Peace for the Western Province, landed proprietor, and estate owner. Mr. John Louis Pieris Sriwardhana was born in Colombo in 1852, and educated at the Colombo Academy (now Royal College). He entered the Surveyor-General's office in 1876, and was favourably mentioned by that officer in his Administration Report for 1885 in connection with the maps drawn for the London Exhibition. Mr. Pieris Sriwardhana became Mohandiram (Lieutenant) of the Gate 1882, Mudaliyar (Captain) of Alutkuru Korale North in 1887, and Mudaliyar (Captain) of the Gate in 1902. In 1892 he acted as Deputy-Fiscal of Negombo, and in 1894 was appointed Shroff of the Colombo Kachcheri.

Mr. J. L. Pieris Sriwardhana is the author of several Sinhalese works, amongst which "Giniwura"—Sinhalese folk-lore in verses—"Malpata"—stanzas on various topics—and a play entitled "Sanduwati," are the most important. Both his father and grandfather held the offices

MUDALIYAR JOHN LOUIS PIERIS SRIWARDHANA.

of Mudaliyar for Siyane Korale, and his ancestors are descended from the chiefs of Deraniyagala. In 1895 he married his cousin, Florence Eliza, younger daughter of Maha Mudaliyar Conrad Peter Dias Bandaranaike; and he retired on a pension from the Government service after twenty-nine years of work. He is a landed proprietor and estate owner in the Western Province. His brother, Mr. Paul E. Pieris Sriwardhana, is the well-known scholar and District Judge of Kalutara.

FELIX R. DIAS BANDARANAIKE.

Mr. Felix Reginald Dias Bandaranaike, second son of the late Rev. Canon Samuel William Dias Bandaranaike, of Colombo, and Cornelia Susanna, daughter of Don Solomon Dias Bandaranaike, Mudaliyar of Siyane Korale East, was born at Colombo on July 26, 1861. He was educated at St. Thomas's College and the Colombo Academy, and proceeded to England in 1882. He entered Trinity Hall, Cambridge, where he graduated as B.A., LL.B. (Law Honours), in 1885, and took the degrees of M.A., LL.M., in 1889. He read in the chambers of Mr. H. F. Dickens (now K.C.), son of the distinguished novelist, and was called to the English Bar at the Inner Temple in 1887. Returning to Ceylon in 1888, he was admitted as an Advocate of the local Bar, and shortly afterwards (1889) he was appointed Police Magistrate and Commissioner of Requests of Gampola and Nawalapitiya. In January, 1893, he became a member of the Attorney-General's Department, and was confirmed as Crown Counsel for the island in July, 1893. He acted as District Judge of Colombo from August, 1897, and as Additional District Judge from December, 1898, which latter appointment was made a permanent one as from July 1, 1906. He is a member of the Royal Colonial Institute and of the Orient and Ceylon Turf Clubs. His recreations are riding and boating, and at the University he rowed in the college eight. He is largely interested in agriculture, particularly tea and coconut planting. In April, 1890, he married Annie Lucy, third daughter of the late Hon. Mr. James Alwis, M.L.C., and Florence Dias Bandaranaike, and has three children, Reginald Felix, Annette Lena, and Samuel James Felix.

DON WILLIAM CHAPMAN DIAS WIJEWARDHANE BANDARANAYAKA.

Mr. William Chapman Dias Wijewardhane Bandaranayaka is the eldest son of the late Rev. Canon Samuel William Dias, and nephew of Sir Harry Dias, Puisne Judge of the Supreme Court of Ceylon, and stepbrother of the late Hon. James Peter Obeyesekere. He was born on June 9, 1860, and educated at St. Thomas's and Royal Colleges. He first intended joining the legal profession, but abandoned this idea and took charge of his ancestral estates, which include Pinnagolla, Puwakwatte, and Udagama, all planted with coconuts, in the Veyangoda district, of which the produce goes to the desiccating mills at Veyangoda. In addition he owns the Maligatenne estate at Kadugannawa, planted with tea and cacao, and estates in the Kalutara, Kurunegala and Matara districts, and house property in Colombo. He lives at "Buona Vista," a stately old Dutch residence at Mutwal, Colombo. In 1896 he married Rachel Lelavati Asmadale, niece of the late Hon. T. B. Panabokke, Kandyan Member of the Legislative Council, and has two children, Copleston and Rani.

MR. AND MRS. DON WILLIAM CHAPMAN DIAS WIJEWARDHANE BANDARANAYAKA AND FAMILY.

"ROTUNDA."
THE LATE MRS. S. W. DIAS BANDARANAIKE.

THE LATE CANON DIAS BANDARANAIKE.
MR. AND MRS. FELIX R. DIAS BANDARANAIKE AND FAMILY.

PETER DE SARAM. MR. AND MRS. PETER DE SARAM AND FAMILY.
CLARICE VILLA, WELISARA. L. W. DE SARAM.

PETER DE SARAM.

Mr. Peter de Saram comes of one of the most ancient and honourable Sinhalese families, and is the son of Johannes de Saram, Mudaliyar of the Governor's Gate and Interpreter to His Excellency the Governor, and Henrietta, daughter of Godfried Philipse Panditeratne, Maha Mudaliyar of his day and first Sinhalese representative in the Legislative Council upon its formation. The De Sarams have been Maha Mudaliyars in the annals of Ceylon for hundreds of years, and at the inception of the English rule Louis de Saram, a member of the family, held that position. Numerous medals, diplomas, and grants from the Government, signalising the excellence of the services rendered to various administrations by their ancestors, are in the possession of the present members of the family. Mr. Peter de Saram was born at Colombo in 1852, and educated at St. Thomas's College under the Revs. — Bennett and James Bacon. In 1873 Sir Charles Peter Layard took him into the Colombo Kachcheri, where he remained two years, after which he became Acting Mudaliyar of Alutkuru Korale South. In 1876 he was confirmed in that appointment, and nine years later Sir Arthur Gordon appointed him to a cadetship in the Ceylon Civil Service. He was then attached to the Colombo Kachcheri until 1891, was Extra Office Assistant to the Government Agent, and acted on several occasions as Office Assistant and Police Magistrate of the Western Province and as Municipal Magistrate at Colombo. During his occupation of these positions Sir Arthur Havelock specially selected him to hear all gambling cases in Colombo. He was a member of the Commission to inquire into cocoa thefts, together with Mr. Lascelles, the Government Agent of the Central Province, and Chairman of the Ceylon Planters' Association. In 1902 Mr. de Saram was appointed Itinerating Police Magistrate for the Western Province, and is still a member of the permanent Civil Service. He is a member of the Royal Asiatic Society and of the Agricultural Society. He owns the beautiful plantations called Florence Estate, in the Welisara district. His town residence is "The Synagogue," Colpetty; and his country seat is Clarice Villa, Welisara. In 1877 he married Ellen Florence, eldest daughter of the late Hon. Mr. James de Alwis, M.L.C., and Florence Dias Bandaranayke. Of his family, the eldest, Mr. Lionel de Saram, is a Proctor of the District Court of Colombo; whilst his daughter Clarice married Dr. Valentine Gooneratne, son of the veteran Atapattu and Gate Mudaliyar of Galle. The second daughter, Beatrice, married Mudaliyar Louis Arthur Dassenaike, of Hapitigam Korale and Mirigama.

LOUIS ARTHUR DASSENAIKE, Mudaliyar.

The Dassenaike family is an ancient one, and for many generations its members rendered valuable assistance to the Dutch East India Company, for which they received due recognition. The heads of the family for five generations have in turn been Mudaliyars of Hapitigam Korale, and the subject of this sketch is still the Chief Headman.

Henricus Lucius Dassenaike, the father of Mr. L. A. Dassenaike, served the Government for a period of over thirty-five years, and in 1895 acted for the Maha Mudaliyar. Mr. Dassenaike's grandfather, Don Cornelis Dassenaike, held the appointments of Mudaliyar of the Hapitigam Korale, Mudaliyar of the Governor's Gate, Justice of the Peace, Deputy Coroner, Interpreter and Translator to the British Resident, Mudaliyar of the Residency, and chief of the Dalada Maligawa. To go back still farther, his great-grandfather was Don Johannes Dassenaike, while his great-great-grandfather, Samaradiwakara Wickremesinghe Dassenaike, was the recipient of two gold medals from the Dutch East India Company

THE RESIDENCE.

MR. AND MRS. L. A. DASSENAIKE AND CHILD. THE LATE MUDALIYAR H. L. DASSENAIKE.

MUDALIYAR L. A. DASSENAIKE AND STAFF OF HEADMEN

for faithful services rendered to the Company on various occasions. Mr. Louis Arthur Dassenaike was born in Colombo in 1869, educated

MUDALIYAR L. A. DASSENAIKE.

at the Royal College, and entered the Government service in 1891, being engaged at the Colombo Kachcheri. Previous to 1896, when he was appointed to his present position as Mudaliyar of Hapitigam Korale (Mirigama), he worked in different capacities, and in 1905 he was appointed Mohandiram of the Governor's Gate. His district covers some 84 square miles. He has charge of the police in his district, is Inquirer into Crimes, Chairman of Village Committees, and Revenue Officer, and in 1903 he acted for the Deputy Fiscal of Colombo. He is a member of the Agricultural Society, Horticultural Society, Turf Club, and Sinhalese Sports Club, owns various coconut estates at Mirigama (where he has his residence), and in other districts. He also possesses house property both at Mirigama and in Colombo. Mr. Dassenaike has one son, Arthur Lee Dassenaike, who was born on May 12, 1903.

EDWIN DE LIVERA.

The family of which Dr. de Livera is a descendant is an ancient one, and members of it have held high and important positions. One of its members was David de Livera, Mohandiram of Hewagam Korale. This gentleman had a son Franciscus, who was Mudaliyar of Alutkuru Korale North, and who married Charlotte Fredericka, daughter of Simon de Livera, Mudaliyar of Hewagam Korale. The issue of the marriage was Edwin, the subject of this sketch, who was born in Colombo in 1849. During his scholastic career at the Colombo Academy Dr. de Livera won the Jijeebhoy scholarship of the Calcutta University in 1870. In 1873 he went to Glasgow, graduated as M.B.C.M., and he returned to Ceylon in 1878 and was appointed Assistant Colonial Surgeon, Puttalam. He held various medical appointments subsequently, the last one being in 1900 as Colonial Surgeon of the North-Western Province and of Sabaragamuwa. He retired from the service on pension in December, 1906. Dr. de Livera is a member of the British Medical Association and of the Kurunegala Agricultural Society. In 1897 he married Eliza Alexandra Speldewinde, daughter of Dr. J. A. Maartensz, of Batticaloa, and is now residing at Castle Dene, Kandy.

DR. AND MRS. E. DE LIVERA.

DON E. W. DE L. WIJEYEWICKREME SENEVERATNE TENNEKOON.

Mr. Don Edwin William de Livera Wijeyewickreme Seneveratne Tennekoon, Mohandiram of the Governor's Gate, is the third son of the late Julius Ernest de Livera, Kachcheri Mohandiram of Colombo, and Jane Maria, daughter of Louis de Livera, Atapattu Mudaliyar, Colombo Kachcheri, and Mudaliyar of the Governor's Gate, and granddaughter of Don Carolis de Livera, First Atapattu of Colombo, a gentleman who, in addition to the distinction named, held the rank of Maha Mudaliyar of the island, and who was decorated in 1804 by the first Governor of the colony, Sir Frederick North, with a large gold medal and chain for useful services rendered to the British authorities. On the paternal side the grandfather of the subject of the sketch was Don David de Livera Tennekoon, Chief Translator of the Colombo Kachcheri and Mudaliyar of the Governor's Gate. Mr. Tennekoon was born at Atapattu Walauwa, Barber Street, Colombo, and educated at St. Thomas's College. From 1894 to 1897 he administered his father's planting and other properties, which are situated in all the Korales of the Western Province. In the latter part of October, 1897, he entered Government service, being appointed First Native Writer of the Colombo Kachcheri by the Hon. Mr. A. R. Dawson, the Government Agent. In 1901 he acted as Second Translator and Shroff Mudaliyar of the Colombo Kachcheri, and in 1902 he was appointed Chief Shroff of the Ceylon Savings

Bank by Mr. R. W. Ivers, the Acting Colonial Secretary, which position he still occupies. On November 9, 1906, on His Majesty's birthday, he was honoured by Government with the distinction of Mohandiram of the Governor's Gate. On the occasion of his investiture His Excellency Sir Henry Blake gave him permission to wear the gold medal awarded to his grandfather on all public occasions. His Excellency addressed him as follows on the investiture: "Mr. de Livera, you have rendered long service in a responsible office, and you have always been a thoroughly good and faithful member of society. I have much pleasure in conferring on you the rank of Gate Mohandiram." Mr. de Livera is a member of the Ceylon Turf Club and of the Poultry Club, and resides at the old family seat called the "Deweni Maha Walauwa" at Wolfendahl. This historic residence has been occupied by three successive Maha Mudaliyars of the De Saram family, who were all Mr. de Livera's maternal ancestors. He married on November 9, 1900, Venetia Nillie Theodora, second daughter of Henricus Lucius Dassenaike, Mudaliyar of Hapitigam Korale and of the Governor's Gate, and sister of Mudaliyar Louis Arthur Dassenaike, of Hapitigam Korale and Gate Mohandiram. They have three children—viz., Nelly Margaret Evelyn, Venetia Myrlin, and William Vernon. Mr. de Livera has three brothers—viz., Louis de Livera Tennekoon, Mudaliyar of Siyane Korale West; Julian Richard de Livera Tennekoon, draughtsman, Surveyor-General's Office; and Henry Stewart de Livera, Proctor, District Court, Colombo; and two sisters, Jane and Annie de Livera.

THE RESIDENCE. MR. AND MRS. EDWIN DE LIVERA.
DON EDWIN WILLIAM DE LIVERA WIJEYEWICKREME SENEVERATNE TENNEKOON.
(Mohandiram of the Governor's Gate.)

L. C. DE F. W. T. SAMARAKKODY.

In the Saka year 1675, corresponding to A.D. 1750, in an account given of King Kirti Sri Rajasinha, of Kandy, translated by Paul E. Peiris, N.A.C.C.S., barrister-at-law, appears the record of the return of the embassy which the king had sent to Siam, and amongst the officers delegated to meet these ambassadors figures the name of Samarakkody, the Udagampaha Adigar, from whom the subject of this sketch is descended. The Adigar's descendant was Johan de Fonseka Samarasundere Seneviratne Samarakkody, who was the Mudaliyar of Hewagam Korale under the Dutch administration. His eldest son, Paulis, was Mohandiram in the same Korale, and his second son, Andris, who married the sister of Don Abraham Dissenaike, second Mudaliyar

MUDALIYAR L. C. SAMARAKKODY.

of Hewagam Korale, was Atapattu Mohandiram of Colombo in the same government. Louis, grandson of Johan de Fonseka Samarakkody, was attached to the Colombo Kachcheri as Clerk and Commutation Assessor. He married Francina, daughter of Paules de Livera Weerakon, Mohandiram of Hapitigam Korale, and their son, Louis Charles de Fonseka Wijeyewickkrame Tillekeratne Samarakkody, whose name heads this sketch, was born at Colombo in 1840. He received his education at Colombo Academy and St. Thomas's College, and entered the Government service in 1861, attached to the Court of Requests, Colombo, as sworn Translator. He also served in the Colombo Kachcheri, and became Mohandiram of Alutkuru Korale, South, and then was appointed Mudaliyar of the Kegalla Kachcheri. He was President of six Village Tribunals in three different Korales, and was appointed Mudaliyar of the Governor's Gate in 1883. Twelve years later he retired from Government employ, after thirty-eight years of continuous service. In 1871 he married Cornelia Fredrica, the daughter of Jacobus Dionysius de Silva Siriwardene, Atapattu Mohandiram of Colombo (whose grandfather, David de Silva Siriwardene, was Mudaliyar of Rayigam Korale, and whose father, Simon de Silva Siriwardene, was Maha Mudaliyar). Of the sons of this marriage, Charles Henry Augustus is Mudaliyar of Pasdun Korale East; Charles Peter, a Mohandiram of the Governor's Gate, is a planter, who is married to Anne Kathereen, daughter of John Nicholas Dissenaike Tillekeratne, Mudaliyar of Matara; Charles Edwin is a Proctor of the District Court of Colombo; and Charles William is a senior student of Wesley College, Colombo. Mr. Samarakkody has three daughters—Charlotte Henrietta, Mary Elizabeth, and Jane Cicilia. Amongst his family possessions, Mr. Samarakkody treasures a gold medal given to his uncle Carolis de Fonseka Tillekeratne Samarakkody, Mudaliyar, by Governor Sir Robert Brownrigg in 1818 for his meritorious services to the British Government during the Kandyan rebellion, and a Jubilee gold medal presented to him by Governor Sir West Ridgeway. He resides at "Lovedale," Jampettah Street, Colombo.

THE SAMARAKKODY FAMILY.

HENRY A. PERERA, Mudaliyar of Colombo.

Mr. Henry Aloysius Perera Seneviratne Palhiyawadana Wijeyegunawardana, better known as Henry A. Perera, Mudaliyar, comes of an ancient family, which is said to have emigrated during the time of the Portuguese occupation from Matale, in the Central Province. His father was Abraham Perera Seneviratne Palhiyawadana Wijeyegunawardana, planter and estate owner, of Colombo, whose father was a Mohandiram of Alutkuru Korale; while his mother was the daughter of Mohandiram Abeyasingha, of Alutkuru Korale North. Born at Colombo in 1855, Mr. Perera was educated at St. Benedict's Institute and St. Thomas's College. Entering the Government service in 1876, he was attached to the Colombo Kachcheri, and became Kachcheri Mohandiram in 1884 and Mudaliyar in 1889. In 1894 he was appointed Mudaliyar of Colombo, Salpiti Korale North, and Ambatelempahala, and to act as Atapattu Mudaliyar until 1895. In April, 1899, the Ceylon Government presented him with a gold medal for services rendered in repressing crime in his district, and in 1903 he was conferred the rank of Mudaliyar of the Governor's Gate. He is a wealthy landowner, owning coconut estates in the Siyane Korale and other parts of the Western Province, and house properties in Colombo. In 1886 he married Emily Josephine, youngest daughter of Paulus G. Abeyasinghe Weerakoon Basnayake, Mudaliyar of the Guards, Colombo. He resides in

THE PERERA FAMILY. WASALA WALAUWA. H. A. PERERA.

H. A. PERERA.
(Mudaliyar of Colombo.)

MR. F. R. ELLIS, C.M.G., MRS. ELLIS,
(Government Agent, Western Province.)
MUDALIYAR PERERA, AND HIS STAFF.

Palhiyawadana Wasala Walauwa at Kotahena, is a member of the Agri-Horticultural Society and of the Poultry Club. He is also a member of the Catholic Union and Chairman of the Village Committees of Salpiti Korale North and Ambatelempahala.

JOHN ATTYGALLE.

The family of Attygalle is very ancient. It was settled in Madapata for many generations, the whole of Madapata being until recently owned by the family. The name is derived from Atigale, a village near Henwille, in Hewagam Korale. On the maternal side Dr. Attygalle is descended from the well-known Kotalawale family of Rayigam Korale, one of whom was Atapattu Mudaliyar of Colombo about 1780. This family traces its origin to a high personage who came to Ceylon during the time of King Rajasinha, the parricide. He appears to have rendered some important service to the Sinhalese in connection with the building of Nalha Devala in Kandy, and he was well rewarded and appointed to a high office in Sabaragamuwa. Dr. Attygalle was born on January 13, 1842, at Madapata, and was educated at St. Thomas's College and the Royal College, Colombo. After his course at these institutions he proceeded to Calcutta, at the expense of the Ceylon Government, to study medicine. He afterwards went to England, and obtained the degrees of M.R.C.S. of London and M.D. of Aberdeen, and was practically the first Sinhalese to study Western

JOHN ATTYGALLE.

medicine. Returning to Ceylon in 1866, he accepted a Government appointment. Having served the Government in various capacities, he retired from the position of Colonial Surgeon in 1898, after continuous service for thirty-two years, receiving a well-earned pension. His hobby has always been the study of native medicine and matters connected with Sinhalese history and literature. He married Charlotte, daughter of Philip Karunaraine, the Interpreter Mudaliyar of the District Court of Kandy, whose ancestors received the Brownrigg medal during the Kandyan hill campaign. Of his sons, Dr. J. W. S. Attygalle, now at Gambulla, is a well-known member of the medical profession; while Messrs. Theodore and Henry Attygalle are officers in the Ceylon Police Force; Mr. R. V. Attygalle is a Proctor of the Supreme Court of Colombo; and the youngest son, Clarence, is studying medicine. The eldest daughter married Mr. Thomas Dunuwille, son of the Colombo Advocate; and the second daughter, Adeline, married Mr. Harry Ellawalla, son of the late Kandyan Member of the Legislative Council; while the third daughter, Eugenie, married Mr. James Alfred Corea, Mohandiram of Madampe. The family residence is now "Eversleigh," Kuruwe Street, Colombo.

DONALD OBEYESEKERE.

The son of the late Hon. Mr. J. P. Obeyesekere, Member of the Legislative Council, Mr. Donald Obeyesekere, was born at Battadolla Walauwa, Veyangoda, in 1880. After attending St. Thomas's and Royal Colleges, he went to Trinity College, Cambridge, in October, 1898, where he studied

J. A. COREA. THE ATTYGALLE FAMILY. H. ELLAWALLA.

DONALD OBEYESEKERE.

THE BUNGALOW

especially law and moral sciences, passing the first part of the law tripos in 1900 and the political economy special in 1901, and the second part of the moral sciences tripos in 1902. He was President of the Indian Majlas at Cambridge during the October term of 1901. Entering the Inner Temple, he was called to the Bar in November, 1903. During his stay in England Mr. Obeyesekere spent a considerable time at the Royal Agricultural College, Cirencester. In 1904 he was one of the official visitors of the Ceylon Government to the St. Louis Exhibition, and on his return to Ceylon he was admitted an Advocate of the Supreme Court, and has practised as such at Colombo ever since. He is a thoroughgoing sportsman. While in England he won the Freshmen's Boxing Tournament at Cambridge, took a keen interest in all sporting matters, being an enthusiastic rider to the South Devon Hounds and Holcombe Harriers, and went in largely for riding and cricket. The variety of his interests can be judged when it is stated that he is a member of the Turf Club, of the Agricultural Society of Ceylon, a Fellow of the Royal Colonial Institute, a member of the Royal Agricultural Society of England, and the originator and chief promoter of the Social Reform Society, which aims at the retention of old customs, habits, and characteristics of the ancient Ceylon civilisation, with the admission of only such Western methods as are expected to prove unmixed benefits. In addition to his legal practice, Mr. Obeyesekere is a planter on a very large scale, and actively interests himself in all matters relating to the development and improvement of agricultural methods in the island. He resides at "Ascot," Victoria Park, Colombo, and in May, 1906, he married Edith, eldest daughter of the late John Henry Perera, of Kuruwe Walauwa and Wolfendahl, Colombo.

TUDOR RAJAPAKSE.

Few men have been better known in Ceylon than the late Sampson d'Abrew Wijegooneratne Rajapakse, Mudaliyar of the Governor's Gate and Justice of the Peace for Ceylon, who is the father of the subject of this sketch. The late Mudaliyar did more for education than perhaps any other native of Ceylon, and his educational charities remain a perpetual monument to him. He was born in the village of Welitota, in the Southern Province, being descended from B. D. A. Rajapakse, who was Mudaliyar of the Grand Ronda, and his father and grandfather and other ancestors were Mudaliyars before him. On his mother's side his ancestry may be traced to Carlo de Meranda, who was the first interpreter and Chief Mudaliyar of the Maha Badda. The Ceylon Medical College, amongst other educational institutions, owes a great deal of its success to the late Mudaliyar, and practically every college in the island has some prizes and scholarships given by him; while his name was always associated with important public movements in the interests of education or of Buddhism, and his purse and personal influence were ever ready to facilitate such movements.

Mr. Tudor Rajapakse was born at Welitota in 1868, and educated at St. Thomas's College and afterwards under the private tuition of Mr. Cull, the Principal of the Royal College. In 1889 Sir Arthur Gordon appointed him Mudaliyar, and in the following year he was elevated to the position of Mudaliyar of the Governor's Gate. He is a planter on a very large scale, owning estates at Negombo, at Welitara, and in various parts of the Western Province, which are planted with coconuts and cinnamon and fully equipped with bungalows, stores, &c. He also owns much house property at Colombo, and his own residence in that city is "Gatherum," De Saram Place. He has two country seats, one the Maha Kappina Walauwa

T. D. N. D'A. W. RAJAPAKSE. MUTTUWADIYA BUNGALOW, NEAR NEGOMBO.
MAHA KAPPINA WALAUWA. THE "GATHERUM" BUNGALOW.

at Welitara, and the other near Negombo. In 1898 he married Frances Lily, second daughter of J. D. S. Rajapakse, Mudaliyar of Negombo. He is a member of the Royal Asiatic Society, sits on the committee of the Colombo Museum, is a member of the Agricultural and Horticultural Societies, and of the Orient, the Turf, the Lawn, and the Nondescripts Cricket Clubs, as well as Vice-President of the Sinhalese Sports Club. He is an ardent horseman. A Buddhist by faith, he built and endowed the temple at Welitara and the assembly of the Amarapura sect of Buddhist priests, of whom he is a most benevolent patron. He is the founder of the Rajapakse College, which he built at his own expense on his own land and freely endowed. Recently he spent a year in a visit to England and the Continent.

The Mudaliyar's pedigree as quoted from "Ceylon in the Jubilee Year" is as follows :—

Genealogical Table showing the descent of S. D. A. Rajapakse, Mudaliyar of His Excellency's Gate and Justice of the Peace for the island.

B. D. A. Rajapakse, Mudaliyar of the Grand Ronda.

|

A. D. A. Rajapakse, Mahawidana Mudaliyar of Welitara District, married daughter of Lewis Mendis Wickramanayaka, Atapattu Mudaliyar of Maha Badda.

|

A. D. A. Rajapakse, Mudaliyar of Mutwal and Welisera District, married Caroline de Soysa Vijayasiriwardana.

|

S. D. A. Rajapakse, Mudaliyar of His Excellency's Gate and Justice of the Peace for the island.

Genealogical Table tracing the descent of S. D. A. Rajapakse (through his mother) to Carlo de Meranda, First Interpreter and Chief Mudaliyar of the Maha Badda.

Carlo de Meranda, First Interpreter and Chief Mudaliyar of the Maha Badda.

|

Solomon de Meranda, First Interpreter and Chief Mudaliyar of the Maha Badda.

|

Susana de Meranda, married Solomon de Sosa Rajapakse, Kappina Mudaliyar.

|

Caroline, married A. D. A. Rajapakse, Mudaliyar of Mutwal and Welisera Districts.

|

S. D. A. Rajapakse, Mudaliyar of His Excellency's Gate and Justice of the Peace for the island.

S. R. DE FONSEKA.

Simon Richard de Fonseka Warnasuriya Wijeyatunga Samaranayaka is the son of Carolis de Fonseka, Mohandiram, who was married to Welhelmina de Fonseka, a member of the same family. She was the daughter of Selestinus de Fonseka, Mudaliyar of Kalutara, whose father was Johannes de Fonseka, Mudaliyar, the recipient of a gold medal from Governor North, in 1819, for meritorious services rendered during the early period of the British occupation of the island. Carolis de Fonseka, above-named, was the son of Solomon de Fonseka, who was married to Selestina, the daughter of Renoldus de Anderado, Mudaliyar, and grandson of Pedru Fonseka, Mohandiram and Interpreter to the Oppertroofd of Kalutara in the Dutch service in 1760. Simon Richard de Fonseka was born in 1854, and entered Government service in 1873. In 1886 he was appointed Chief Clerk of the Provincial and District Road Committees, Western Province. He married, in 1883, Louisa, the eldest daughter of Juan de Silva Jayasingha, and has six children, viz. : Simon Richard, law student, Lydia Florence, Lionel Stanley, prosecuting his studies in England, Muriel Letitia, Louisa Bridget, and May Elain. In 1892 he was invested with the rank of Mudaliyar by Sir Arthur Havelock. He lost his wife in 1902. The

MUDALIYAR T. D. N. D'A. W. RAJAPAKSE. THE LATE MUDALIYAR S. D'A. W. RAJAPAKSE.

THE FAMILY. MUDALIYAR S. R. DE FONSEKA.
GOLD SHIELD. "ST KEVINS" BUNGALOW.

family is descended from Don Michael de Fonseka, Adigar. Don Michael de Fonseka is mentioned in Baldeus' "Description of Ceylon, 1672," and was married to the daughter of Don Manuel de Anderado, Adigar. In 1658, under Admiral Ryckloff van Goens, Don Michael de Fonseka accompanied his father-in-law in the expedition under which Jaffna was taken by the Dutch. Baldeus and other early writers speak of Don Manuel de Anderado as having rendered signal service to the Dutch.

A NATIVE PHILANTHROPIST—THE LATE CHARLES HENRY DE SOYSA, J.P.

The De Soysas of Ceylon are a family of philanthropists, held in the highest esteem by their countrymen especially, and generally by all in the land. At Moratuwa, where is the country seat of the family, there is no institution, whether religious, educational, or philanthropic, but owes its origin and maintenance mainly or wholly to their largeheartedness. Nor are their benefactions merely parochial or confined to one community, but are designed for all sorts and conditions of men, and have their objects throughout the island. The Alfred Model Farm, the De Soysa Lying-in Home and Medical Museum, and the Bacteriological Institute in Colombo, and Holy Emmanuel Church and Prince and Princess of Wales's Colleges at Moratuwa, all owe their existence to the De Soysa family. At Panadure, Marawila, and Hangurangetta are churches, hospitals, and schools, built by the De Soysas. Numerous roads and wayside resting-places in various parts of the island have the same beneficent origin. In times of famine and flood and during epidemics they have always been to the fore in the support of relief funds, and their munificence has been at times extended to deserving institutions abroad.

The most prominent member of the family was the late Charles Henry de Soysa, J.P., of Alfred House, Colombo. Born on March 3, 1836, he was the only son of Jeronis de Soysa Dissanayake, Mudaliyar of the Governor's Gate, and Francesca de Soysa Lamaetenie (*née* Coorey), of Moratuwa. His constitution was never very robust from childhood. After early training under the Rev. Dr. J. MacVicar, he was placed for a few years at St. Thomas's College, Colombo, under the Rev. J. Baly, subsequently Archdeacon of Calcutta. On leaving college the young man served an apprenticeship on his father's coffce and coconut plantations, which were then managed by his uncle, the late Mudaliyar Susew de Soysa. It is said that even at this time his meagre allowance of pocket-money was often spent in benefactions—an indication of his inborn charitableness. At the age of twenty-seven he married Miss Catherine de Silva, the only daughter of Mr. Jusey de Silva (afterwards Knight Chevalier of the Order of Gregory the Great), of Moratuwa. The alliance was in every way happy, and the union of the sole heirs of two wealthy families contributed to the expansion of the resources of an already considerable estate.

Although shy and reserved by nature, Mr. de Soysa was, at the age of thirty, already a prominent man in the island. His modest disposition and kindly hospitality, coupled with a generous enthusiasm for good works, had gained him the love and esteem of all classes of a somewhat heterogeneous community. Europeans, Burghers, Tamils, and Moors were counted among those who learnt to appreciate the worth of this model Sinhalese gentleman. In a sense, Mr. de Soysa was a public man of the first degree, in that he was one who devoted his energies and wealth to the good of the people. The amelioration of the conditions of life in Ceylon was his chief care and ambition.

To elevate the masses by providing them with education, to relieve suffering humanity by supplying medical aid, to advance the material prosperity of his countrymen by the introduction of new methods and scientific appliances, were no inadequate manifestations of patriotic feeling. And it is surprising that so much of this good work was accomplished within the brief space of tén years; for Mr. de Soysa conceived and carried through his best and permanent work within the seventies. At his old college, of which he lived to be a trustee, he not only endowed a Chair of Divinity, but also gave an impetus to the teaching of science by providing the necessary apparatus. At Moratuwa, for many years, he liberally supported the parish schools. In 1871 he established the Alfred Model Farm in Colombo, an experiment which proved fruitless from various causes. On September 14, 1876, he founded the Prince and Princess of Wales's College at Moratuwa, an institution which to-day affords efficient instruction to about a thousand scholars of both sexes. In the alleviation of suffering Mr. de Soysa never tired. During an outbreak of enteric fever in an outlying village, he himself supervised the distribution of food and medicine supplied at his own expense. Numerous poor patients were supplied with medical aid gratis. He did much to create a supply of trained Sinhalese midwives, and as a further aid for suffering womanhood he opened at Colombo, in 1879, the De Soysa Lying-in Home.

He was a patron of letters and arts, and liberally encouraged native carvers, sculptors, and other craftsmen with commissions for execution. For the benefit of the Moratuwa carpenters he was instrumental in starting, in 1879, the Moratuwa Co-operative Company, an institution which, for want of management, had to be wound up in a few years. In 1884 he formed the Ceylon Agricultural Association, continuing to act as its president until it was transformed into the National Association. In its older form the association had done much useful, if unostentatious, work in the promotion of scientific cultivation among native capitalists, and thus became the precursor of the Ceylon Agricultural Society, which has recently been inaugurated under the presidency of Sir Henry Blake.

On its private side, the life of Mr. de Soysa grew ever more and more charming. He was pre-eminently the country squire of his neighbourhood. His affability was proverbial; he was accessible to his poorest fellow-man, and the brute creation was always his care, while nothing gave him greater pleasure than the sight and company of children. Many a man now remembers with gratitude what a day at Alfred House meant for him in his childhood. At Christmastide in Moratuwa this children's friend excelled himself, for then—in the seventies—Mr. de Soysa and his family of seven sons and seven daughters regularly spent the season at their country-house, the Walauwa, and all Moratuwa and his wife visited them, bearing the customary offering of a handful of betel leaves, a mark of the highest respect in Ceylon. For days high festival was kept; the callers were legion; there was open table; and the children's hearts were made happy with toys. To the villager a visit to the Walauwa was in itself a liberal education, for there he had plenty of sights to see—the curios, the furniture, the horses, the cattle, the poultry.

Mr. de Soysa was a lover of animals. His stud contained some of the finest horses in the island, and his experiments in stock-breeding produced some of the best results locally obtained. He owned several elephants, too, which were trained for useful work. In his menagerie of pets almost the only remarkable omission was the dog, a significant fact in view of his untoward end. Such was his

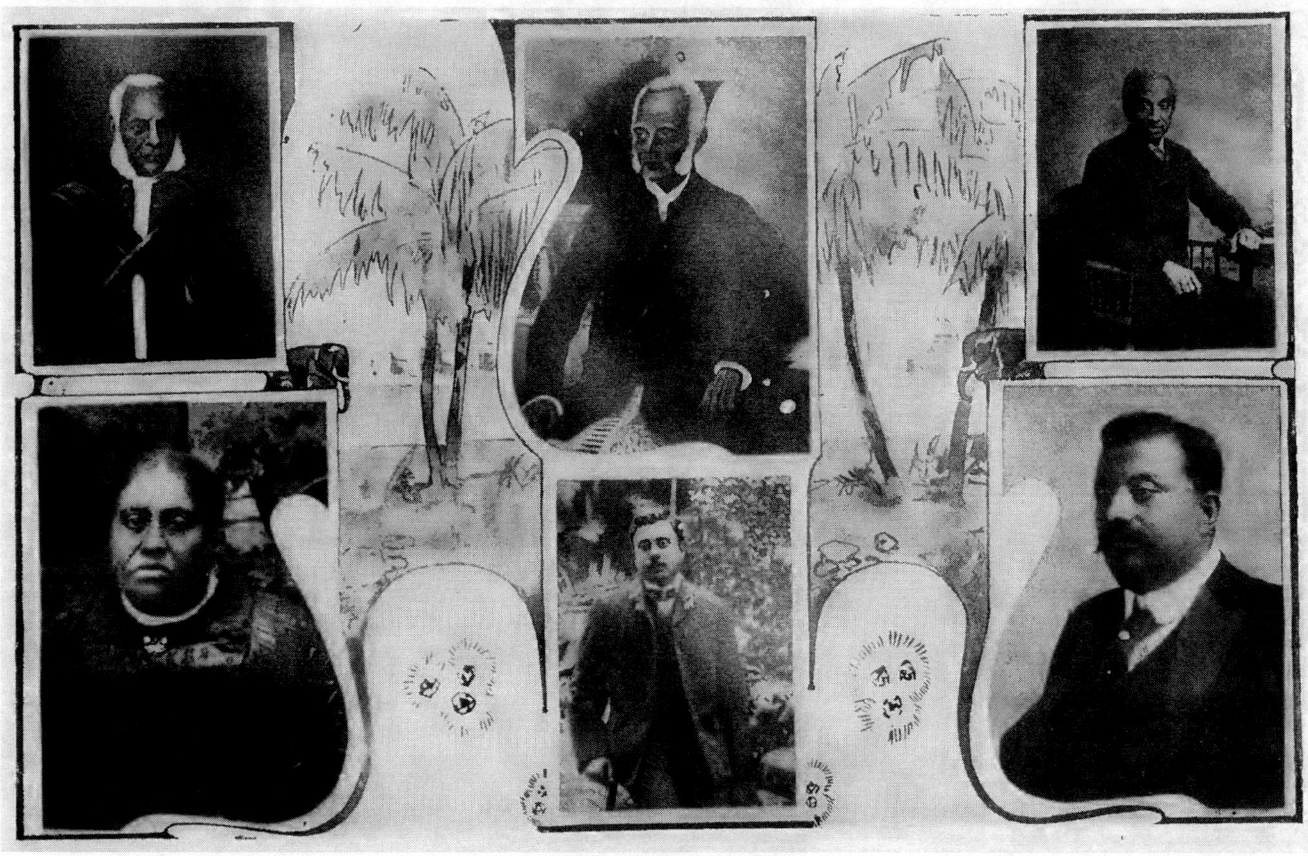

THE DE SOYSA FAMILY.

THE LATE MUDALIYAR SUSEW DE SOYSA. LADY DE SOYSA.

THE LATE MUDALIYAR JERONIS DE SOYSA. ERNEST DE SOYSA. (Youngest son of the late C. H. and Lady de Soysa.)

THE LATE C. H. DE SOYSA. J. W. C. DE SOYSA. (Eldest son of the late C. H. and Lady de Soysa.)

influence over animals, that once, with merely a bunch of plantains in his hand, he placated and got under control an infuriated elephant which had broken loose from its keeper.

Next to his humanity and humility, the predominant traits in Mr. de Soysa's character were his broad-mindedness and intense loyalty. A zealous member of the Church of England, his sympathy was not confined to that communion. Many a Buddhist priest was his friend, and all Christian denominations shared in his benefactions. In 1870 he entertained in lavish style the Duke of Edinburgh, the first Prince of the blood royal of Britain that visited the shores of Ceylon, and the Alfred Model Farm was so named in honour of the Sovereign's sailor son. The college at Moratuwa commemorates the visit to Ceylon of his present Majesty when Prince of Wales; and in the local celebrations of the Jubilee of our late Queen-Empress Mr. de Soysa took a prominent part.

Mr. de Soysa visited England in 1886, and during a six months sojourn in Europe he put his time to the best use in sight-seeing, and in the inspection of farms, manufactories, and philanthropic institutions, making substantial donations towards the last named.

Unhappily, Mr. de Soysa was bitten by a mad dog, and died of hydrophobia on September 29, 1890, in the prime of life. As may be inferred from this short account of this good man's life, the mourning for him was truly national. A correct estimate of the universal grief was made by Dr. Copleston, Bishop of Colombo (now Metropolitan of India and Ceylon), when from the pulpit he exclaimed, in the words of King David, "Know ye not that there is a prince and a great man fallen this day in Israel?" Soon after Mr. de Soysa's death his relict was raised to the rank of widow of a Knight Bachelor in recognition of her deceased husband's life-work; and Lady de Soysa, with her eldest son, Mr. J. W. Charles de Soysa, J.P., Mudaliyar of the Governor's Gate, still carry on the good work initiated by the late philanthropist and previous heads of the family.

1. ALFRED HOUSE. 2. INTERIOR OF THE INSTITUTE.
3. THE BACTERIOLOGICAL INSTITUTE. 4. DRAWING-ROOM, ALFRED HOUSE.

JERONIS WILLIAM CHARLES DE SOYSA.

This scion of a prominent Ceylon family is the son of the late Mr. Charles Henry de Soysa and Lady de Soysa, and was born at the De Soysa Walauwa (ancestral home), Moratuwa, in May, 1865. He was educated at the St. Thomas's and Royal Colleges, Colombo, and Trinity Hall, Cambridge, England. He took his B.A. degree in 1889, and on a visit to England ten years later became an M.A. In 1890 he returned to the island to manage, in conjunction with Lady de Soysa, the affairs of his late father. Mr. de Soysa conducts one of the largest businesses in Ceylon, he being a planter of coconuts, cacao, tea, rubber, and cinnamon, as well as an exporter, importer, and general merchant. The head offices of his business operations are at No. 4, Queen Street, Fort, Colombo. On her own part Lady de Soysa owns a large number of coconut estates in practically every part of the island, and her son is hardly behind in the number of estates under his own control. The products of the coconut estates are, for the most part, either copra or desiccated coconut, which latter are treated in large desiccating mills at Slave Island, Colombo. Of the De Soysa tea estates, that of Maturata, near Nuwara Eliya, under the superintendence of Mr. W. K. G. Saunders, is one of the best known. Mr. de Soysa also started rubber-planting at Kadugannawa and at Kosgama on the Ratnapura road, as well as on his Paradise Estate in the

J. W. C. DE SOYSA'S CINNAMON MILLS, AND VIEWS OF THE DRYING PROCESS, THE CUTTING OF THE PRODUCT, AND THE DESICCATING MILLS.

VIEWS OF J. W. C. DE SOYSA'S CINNAMON OPERATIONS—THE PEELING, THE STORES, AND THE QUILLING.

Sabaragamuwa Province, and at Galpotagama. He was the first to start cotton experiments in the island, having introduced the *Caravonica* cotton-bush from Queensland, and he intends to start planting this variety on a very large scale in the North-Western Province. The improvements he has carried out during the past three years have given him confidence that cotton will more than merely succeed in Ceylon. Then, again, his firm owns the largest cinnamon plantations in the island, and plants this spice by itself only, having nearly 3,000 acres under cultivation near Moratuwa, as well as areas at Salawa and Kuruwitta. At stations on all these estates the cinnamon is peeled and baled ready for transport.

The late Mr. Charles Henry de Soysa, the founder of the business owned by the family bearing the name, was a great believer in coffee, and owned some 150 estates, of which nearly 10,000 acres had been cultivated when that industry collapsed. He was, of course, very hard hit, but with characteristic energy he started planting coconuts, tea, and cinnamon, and more than re-established himself in a very short time. Formerly the coconuts and copra from the De Soysa estates were exported, but now the produce is sold locally. Fibres—bristle, mattress—and, in fact, all kinds of produce of the coconut-palm are dealt in, and the firm has started very large and extensive rope and cable making factories at Negombo, for which expensive and up-to-date machinery has been introduced. Mr. de Soysa also owns very large and valuable plumbago mines in the North-Western Province, among them the famous Sir Visto mine at Dodangaslanda.

Mr. de Soysa is a Justice of the Peace for the whole island, and a Mudaliyar of the Governor's Gate, as well as the officer commanding "R" Company of the Ceylon Light Infantry. He is a trustee of the Prince of Wales's College, Moratuwa; Warden of the Church of Holy Emmanuel, Moratuwa; Patron of the Moratuwa Association, Friend-in-Need Society, and Sunday School Union; Patron of the Colombo Friend-in-Need Society; and also a member of the Orient Club. He represented the Ceylon community at the Diamond Jubilee celebrations in London in 1897, and in the same year founded and endowed the De Soysa Bacteriological Institute, Colombo, which is now presided over by that eminent scientist, Dr. Aldo Castellani. Mr. de Soysa is now building the Princess Louise Hospital at Moratuwa, of which the foundation-stone was laid by Her Royal Highness Princess Louise of Schleswig-Holstein early this year (1906). His Colombo address is Alfred House, Colpetty, and his country seat is the De Soysa Walauwa, Moratuwa. Shooting and racing are the sporting pastimes most favoured by this gentleman. He ran horses extensively between 1890 and 1895, winning the Governor's Cup at Nuwara Eliya, and was the owner of the well-known horse Melrose. He is a member of the Ceylon Chamber of Commerce. It may be noted as an interesting fact in regard to the rise of value in the lands owned by the De Soysa family, that about the year 1860 the Government offered the whole of the cinnamon gardens to the late Mr. Jeronis de Soysa at 5s. an acre, whereas the value of the land on which Alfred House stands to-day would alone be reckoned cheap at £1,000 sterling an acre.

ALFRED JOSEPH RICHARD DE SOYSA.

Mr. Alfred Joseph Richard de Soysa is the second son of the late Mr. Charles Henry de Soysa, J.P., and Lady de Soysa, of Alfred House, Colombo, and was born at Brodie House, Bambalapitiya, on February 15, 1869. He was educated at St. Thomas's College, Colombo (1878), Prince of Wales's College, Moratuwa (1880), and the Royal College, Colombo (1884–1886). In July, 1886, he proceeded to England for further education at the private institute of Highbury House, St. Leonards-on-Sea, where he distinguished himself as a runner by winning the silver challenge cup for the 220 yards race at Highbury House school sports in 1888. He also took a great interest in school theatricals. From Highbury House he proceeded, in 1888, to Trinity Hall, Cambridge, with a view to obtaining a degree in music. He had to return to Ceylon in 1890, after his father's unexpected death, and assisted in the management of the estate. About this period he became a member of the Royal Asiatic Society. He is the sole owner of large estates, covering in all 3,210 acres, planted with coconuts, rubber, and tea, in the North-Western, Central, and Sabaragamuwa Provinces, viz., Kirimetiana, Keenakelle, Horatapola, Diadora, Paragamana, Medarawakka, Madawalatenne, Tatuwelakande, Kuda Oya, and Kottugoda paddy fields of 79 acres in extent. He is also part-owner of the tea estates of Hapugasmulla and Marigold in the Central Province, and of the Kuteriyawalla Estate in the Western Province, the latter planted with cinnamon and coconuts. He is a member of the Colombo Harbour Board, having been nominated to that position by His Excellency the Governor in 1898, and is also a member of the Turf Club of Ceylon. In 1893 he founded and endowed the Jusey de Silva ward at the Lady Havelock Hospital, in memory of the late Chevalier Jusey de Silva, his maternal grandfather. He was one of the largest contributors to and collectors for the Indian Famine Fund in 1897, and subscribed Rs. 5,000 to the Inundation Relief Fund of Colombo, 1904. On February 4, 1892, he married Mary Margaret, daughter of Mr. and Mrs. L. David de Silva, of Henley House, Cinnamon Gardens. Mr. de Soysa's private residence is "Glen Aber," Bambalapitiya, and his Colombo office is at No. 4, Queen Street, Fort, while he has a country residence on the Kirimetiana Estate, Kurunegala. He is a landed proprietor in Colombo and Kandy, and is a gentleman held in high esteem throughout the island. He is an ardent motorist.

EDWIN LIONEL FREDERICK DE SOYSA.

This son of the late Mr. Charles Henry de Soysa and Lady de Soysa was born at Alfred House, Colombo, in 1871. He was educated at the Royal College, Colombo, and at Scaithliffe, Egham, Surrey, England. After his training at the latter institution he proceeded to Trinity Hall, Cambridge, and there finished his education. He returned to Ceylon on the death of his father to assist in the management of the family estate. During his Cambridge course he rowed, hunted, and went in for racing, taking part, as a gentleman rider, in the Cottenham races, near Cambridge. Soon after his return to Ceylon from England he started racing on his own account, his first horse being an Australian filly named Effie, of 14 hands, which won his first race in a field of seven horses. Afterwards he owned many horses which made themselves famous on the Ceylon turf. Amongst the various winners owned by Mr. de Soysa, Jack o'Lantern annexed the Governor's Cup in 1896, also the Turf Club and the Fort Plate in the same year, and again won the Governor's Cup in 1897; while his horses also ran first for the Governor's Cup at Madras and the Cooch Behar Cup at Calcutta. Other lights of his stable have been Midget, Portion, Magna Charta, Ena, Leah, Comewell, Young Surprise, North British—winner of the Governor's Cup in 1899—and Merloolas. The last-named was the best horse of his year in Australia, and won the Sydney Cup there. He was bought by Mr. de Soysa for £2,000 sterling, and the bargain proved a good one, for he won the Governor's Cup, Ceylon, in 1900. Mr. de Soysa built his new racing stables at Colpetty in the year 1905, and at present has a number of horses in training there, among the most important of which are Footprint, Semele, Wizard, Reply, and Ural. He is a very popular sportsman and a member of all the racing institutions in Ceylon. In regard to breeds of horses suitable for racing in the island, Mr. de Soysa is strongly in favour of English griffins in preference to Arabs, maintaining that English horses can run in more than one class, whereas Arab griffins can only be entered in one. He hopes to see the English griffin scheme introduced by the Turf

MR. AND MRS. A. J. R. DE SOYSA AND CHILDREN, THEIR RESIDENCE "GLEN ABER," CARRIAGE AND MOTOR-CAR, AND VIEW OF COCONUT ESTATE WITH BUNGALOW.

MR. AND MRS. E. L. F. DE SOYSA, THEIR RESIDENCE, BUNGALOW, STABLES, AND RACING TROPHIES.

Club before long. Mr. de Soysa's racing stables are prettily built, and contain luxuriously fitted loose boxes, as well as sheds for carriages, hacks, saddlery, and so forth. It may be mentioned that in the first year of his racing career Mr. de Soysa won 23 out of 25 races, and in the second year 19 out of 21.

This gentleman has very large interests in the planting line, he being the owner of the coconut estates of Karakuwe, Potuwille, Dunkannawa, Welihena and Keenakelle in the Western Province, and Gladyland, Hempitagedera, Boddimulle, and Heinulle in the North-Western Province, as well as the tea and rubber estate of Lantern Hill, in the Dolosbage district. He is also part owner of Marigold tea estate in the Maturata district; and in the Kandy district he owns Nyanwatte, Tennekumbura, and Lechmini estates. His tea estates, which are fully equipped with modern factories, are superintended by Mr. J. D. Mendis. Mr. de Soysa is also a plumbago merchant, and owns various mines in the Southern Province. He was married at St. Michael's Church, Colombo, in 1898, to Caroline, daughter of the late Mr. and Mrs. Jeronis Pieris, of "Elscourt," Cinnamon Gardens, Colombo. His private residence is "Rheinlands," Colpetty, Colombo; and his business address 4, Queen's Street, Fort, Colombo.

THOMAS HENRY ARTHUR DE SOYSA.

Mr. T. H. A. de Soysa is the fourth son of the late Mr. Charles Henry and Lady de Soysa, and was born at the De Soysa Walauwa, Moratuwa, in 1874. After being educated at the Prince of Wales's College, in his birthplace, and the Royal and St. Thomas's Colleges, Colombo, he joined the office staff of his late father in 1892. In 1898 he took over the management of the Kandy agency of the business, but started on his own account in the same year. Mr. de Soysa is a proprietary planter, general merchant, and mine-owner, and his estates produce coconuts, tea, rubber, cinnamon, and citronella. He owns plantations practically in all parts of the island, and on his Keenakelle estate, in the North-Western Province, is one of the largest and best equipped fibre factories in the island. The Keenakelle fibre mark and the Kadirane cinnamon mark rank high in the market in Europe. He has now also recommenced plumbago mining on a large scale, having equipped his mines with powerful steam pumping and lifting gear. At the Diyatalawa Mills, Slave Island, Colombo, and the Carbon Stores, Wellawatte, all the yield from these mines and his estates is being stored prior to being made ready for shipment. Mr. T. H. A. de Soysa is the sole proprietor of this business, the head office of which is at No. 2, Canal Row, Fort, Colombo; and his exports, which mainly consist of coconut-oil, cinnamon, cinnamon chips, desiccated coconut, copra, coconuts, plumbago, tea, rubber, cardamoms, cocoa, citronella oil, coir yarn, bristle and mattress fibre, reach all parts of the civilised world.

Mr. de Soysa's residence in Colombo is Brodie House, while his country residences are on his Attiville, Kalutara, and Kadirane estates, Negombo. Mr. de Soysa is a member of various local clubs. In 1899 he married the only daughter of the late Mr. S. P. Abeyawardena, M.M.C., of Galle.

WALTER DE SOYSA.

This gentleman is a son of the late Mr. Charles Henry de Soysa and Lady de Soysa, and

MR. AND MRS. WALTER DE SOYSA.

was born in 1880 at the De Soysa Walauwa, Moratuwa. He received his earliest scholastic education at the Royal College, Colombo; and after private training at Fermain, Hastings, England, proceeded to Trinity Hall, Cambridge. He afterwards became a member of the Inner Temple. He is the owner of the coconut estates of Keenakelle, in the Negombo district, Micadawatte, at Veyangoda, and Limpias-watte, at Panadure, from all of which copra is exported. Mr. de Soysa is a landed proprietor in Kandy, and has always been an ardent sportsman. When at Cambridge he played cricket for Trinity Hall, and he is also well known in the hunting field. His London address is 16, Kensington Hall Gardens, S.W., and his Colombo habitat is Alfred House, Colpetty. He married, in 1904, Maria Micada Piedra, daughter of Señor Don Agosto Albo, of Limpias, Santander, Spain, and Señora Dona Catarina de Gruchy (Crimea). Mrs. de Soysa is a grand-daughter of Señor Don G. de Bernales-Albo, Carlist banker, General of the Revolution and Grandee of Old Castile.

L. W. A. DE SOYSA.

Mr. Lambert Wilfred Alexander de Soysa, sixth son of the late Charles Henry and Lady Catherine de Soysa, was born at Alfred House, Colombo, in 1884, and educated first privately, and afterwards at the Royal College, Colombo, and Prince of Wales's College, Moratuwa. In 1903 he went to England to take a course of studies at the Royal Agricultural College at Cirencester, Gloucester, and there he graduated M.R.A.C. in December, 1905. Mr. de Soysa was President of the Royal Agricultural College International Club for two years in succession. On leaving the college he travelled extensively in Europe, especially investigating agricultural methods in various countries. He returned to his native land in the middle of 1906, and has taken up planting, bringing the extensive knowledge gained in Europe to bear upon the cultivation of Ceylon products. It should be mentioned that during his stay in England he took a certificate in chemistry, and at his present home he intends to have a laboratory fitted up in connection with his planting operations, which will be carried on upon an up-to-date, scientific basis. The estate of Olaboduwa, in the Rayigam Korale, planted with coconut and rubber, is his property, as well as portions of the well-known estates of Keenakelle and Dambuwa. Mr. de Soysa is a member of the Royal Agricultural Society of England as well as of the Ceylon Agricultural Society, and also the Social Reform Society and the Ceylon National Association.

SOLOMON FERNANDO.

Dr. Solomon Fernando, son of Silvester F. Karuneratne, of Moratuwa, was born in that place in 1850, educated at Kotta Christian Institute, the Colombo Academy, and Queen's College. Afterwards he studied medicine at Calcutta, where he received a gold medal for botany. Proceeding to Aberdeen University, he graduated M.B., C.M. and L.R.C.P., and L.R.C.S. of Edinburgh. After working for some time in the Aberdeen Royal Infirmary he returned to Ceylon and entered the Government service as assistant to the Principal Civil Medical Officer at Colombo. He paid a second visit to Great Britain, this time as delegate to the International Congress on Hygiene, where

ESTATE BUNGALOW.

ESTATE VIEW. WILFRED DE SOYSA. ANOTHER ESTATE VIEW.

THE BUNGALOW.

DR. AND MRS. S. FERNANDO AND FAMILY.

he read a paper on Ceylon sanitation, and was presented to the late Queen as well as to the Prince and Princess of Wales. Returning to

S. FERNANDO.

his native island, he took over the medical charge of the jails in Colombo, was lecturer to the Ceylon Medical College in botany and zoology, and finally retired from his profession in 1898. Settling in the capital, he became a member of the Municipal Council for the Kotahena ward, and sat for two terms. On his retirement in 1906 the Council passed a special vote of thanks to him for his services. He owns coconut estates in the Negombo, Chilaw, and Puttalam districts; is a member of the British Medical Association, of the Royal Asiatic and Agricultural Societies, a director of the Colombo Y.M.C.A., and a local preacher of the Wesleyan Congregation. In 1887 he married Fanny Georgina Catherina, eldest daughter of Lady de Soysa, and he resides at "Sigiriya," Bagatelle Road, Colombo.

CHARLES MATTHEW FERNANDO.

The career and position of Mr. C. M. Fernando, Crown Counsel, affords an instance of a man who has won his way to distinction in the premier Crown Colony of Britain by the worthy employment of brilliant intellectual gifts. He is the son of Andrew Fernando and grandson of Andrew Fernando, Mudaliyar of Colombo. He was born in the chief city in 1866, and was educated there, first at St. Benedict's Institute, afterwards at the Royal College. His scholastic career was characterised by exceptional brilliancy. Among other distinctions he won the Fifth-form Scholarship, was first in the Cambridge Local Examination, won the Shakespeare and Turnour Prizes open to all Ceylon, and gained the Government English University Scholarship of the value of £200 per annum, and lasting for three years. In 1883 he passed the London Matriculation First Division, and the Intermediate in Arts of the London University, First Division, in 1885, being the first Ceylonese student to pass that examination. In the same year he proceeded to England, joined St. John's College, Cambridge, and was entered as a student at Lincoln's Inn. In 1886 he won the prize for law at St. John's College, Cambridge, and in 1888 passed the Law Tripos with honours in the second class. Having obtained the Cambridge degrees of B.A. and LL.B., he was called to the Bar in London in 1888. In the following year, on his return to Ceylon, he was admitted an Advocate of the local courts. In these courts he practised until 1897, when he was appointed Acting District Judge at Kurunegala. Owing to ill-health he removed to Kandy, where he was appointed Crown Advocate. In 1901 he became Acting Crown Counsel at Colombo, in which appointment he was confirmed in 1903. He is in charge of the administration of the new Waste Lands Ordinance, as legal adviser, and has appeared in all the principal cases in connection with this legislation, notably the Dehigama and Adipola cases. He has also appeared with success in some of the most important criminal trials in Ceylon within the last six years, notably the Ambalayoda riot and the Mavanella murder cases.

C. M. FERNANDO AND FAMILY, AND TWO VIEWS OF HIS RESIDENCE, "NETHERTON."

In 1893 and 1894, in conjunction with Mr. Walter Pereira, K.C. (now Solicitor-General), Mr. C. M. Fernando edited the reports of the cases of the Supreme Court of Ceylon. Mr. Fernando was one of the founders of the Ceylon Law Students' Union. For six years he was a member of the Colombo Municipal Council, and for two years served on the Kandy Council. He was Secretary of the Ceylon National Association from 1892 to 1895. He was created a Justice of the Peace of the Western Province in 1896, and is now, by virtue of his office, a J.P. for the whole island. He is a member and Councillor of the Royal Asiatic Society both of Ceylon and England, a member of the Provisional Road Committee of the Western Province, President of the Maradahana Literary Association, member of the Orient Club, and a committee member of the Catholic Club. In historical research Mr. Fernando has made a unique name for himself, and is one of the best authorities in Ceylon on cognate subjects; and in this connection it may be mentioned that Mr. Fernando is the author of the "History of Ceylon" included in this volume. In 1904 he proceeded to Europe as the bearer of a special communication from the Catholics of Ceylon to the Duke of Norfolk to protest against the religious terminology of the King's Oath, and was received in special audience by the Pope. Besides contributing to the *Journal of the Ceylon Asiatic Society*, *Spolia Zeylanica*, and other journals, he is the translator of the "Nikaya Sangarawa," a valuable Sinhalese history of Ceylon, written in the fifteenth century. In 1901 Mr. Fernando married Jane Maria, the third daughter of the late Charles Henry and Lady de Soysa. His hobbies are music and numismatics.

HILARION MARCUS FERNANDO.

Dr. H. M. Fernando, one of the leading medical men of Colombo, is the son of Mr. Andrew Fernando and a brother of the well-known Advocate, Mr. C. M. Fernando, concerning whom a notice appears above. Dr. Fernando was born at Colombo in 1864, and educated at St. Benedict's Institute and the Colombo Academy (afterwards the Royal College). His career at school, as afterwards at the University, was of exceptional brilliancy, very few Ceylonese having attained distinction in such a measure. At the Academy he gained the Queen's Scholarship of the fifth form; in 1881, the first scholarship in the Junior Cambridge Local; in 1882 the Mathematical and the Turnour Prizes; and in 1883 the English University Scholarship, obtaining first-class honours in the Senior Local Examination, with other distinctions. He obtained twenty-seventh place in honours in the London Matriculation, and was awarded one of the

H. M. FERNANDO.

Gilchrist Scholarships for Indian students. In 1883 he entered University College, London, and was second in the Medical Entrance Scholarship for 1884. He obtained the gold

"THE PRIORY." DR. AND MRS. H. M. FERNANDO AND FAMILY.

medals for physiology, medicine, forensic medicine, and midwifery, and the Tuke medal for pathology, as well as a silver medal for materia medica. He was Atchinson Scholar in 1888, and was elected a Fellow of University College in 1890. At the London University he passed the preliminary scientific examination for the M.B. degree, also the intermediate scientific examination in 1884, and obtained second place in first-class honours in zoology, as well as third place in honours in botany. He passed his intermediate M.B. examination in 1886, obtaining a gold medal, besides first-class honours, in physiology, and first-class honours in organic chemistry; also the degree of Bachelor of Science with first-class honours in physiology. Graduating as M.B. at the London University in 1888, he gained second place with first-class honours in medicine, as well as the gold medal, and second place with first-class honours in forensic medicine, also a gold medal. In 1889 he passed the M.D. (Lond.) examination, qualifying for the gold medal.

Dr. Fernando returned to the island in 1890, and was appointed Registrar of the Medical College and Government Analyst in 1891. He also became Superintendent of the De Soysa Lying-in Home, and carried on his duties at that institution until 1897. He then proceeded to Bombay to study and to report on the bubonic plague for the Ceylon Government, with a view to organise preventive measures. On his return he was appointed Second Physician to the General Hospital. In 1898 he again visited England, this time for the purpose of studying bacteriology; and on his return to Ceylon in 1899 he became Senior Physician to the General Hospital and Lecturer in Medicine at the Ceylon Medical College. He first started and opened the De Soysa Bacteriological Institute, and was Director of that institution for some time. He reported to the Government on the outbreak of malarial fever in Galle, and has read and contributed various papers to the British Medical Association, both in England and Ceylon, on "Malaria and its Prevention," also on leprosy, dysentery, and other subjects of interest in tropical medicine. He is also the author of various medical reports. He is a Council member of the British Medical Association, and was at one time Hon. Secretary and President of the Ceylon Branch of that body. He is Vice-President of the Ceylon University Association, and a member of the Royal Asiatic Society, also of the Orient and Turf Clubs, and is on the Board of both the Agricultural and the Horticultural Societies. His hobby is agriculture, and on his Notting Hill estate, in the Kurunegala district, he carries on the cultivation of cotton from Sea Island seed on a large scale. In 1891 he married Mary Frances, second daughter of the late Mr. Charles Henry and Lady de Soysa. His town residence is "The Priory," Union Place, Colombo, and his country residence Boragodde, Negombo.

FRANCIS PERERA.

Mr. Francis Perera is the eldest son of the late Mr. Simon Perera, M.M.C., his mother being the daughter of Mudaliyar Wijesekera, one of the largest capitalists and planters of the Southern Province of Ceylon. He was born at Galle in 1875, and educated, firstly, at the Richmond College in that centre, and afterwards at the Royal College, Colombo. He started business as a planter and plumbago merchant at an early age, but has now abandoned the latter branch of production and devotes himself entirely to the supervision of his plantations. He owns coconut properties in the Negombo district, and the fine estate of Wallahandua in the Southern Province, consisting of 800 acres planted with tea, cinnamon, and rubber, and comprising a fine bungalow, on which are a fully-equipped factory, peeling station, and stores—as well as the Bedikantota estate of 700 acres in coconuts at Hambantota, besides various other plantations in rubber and large tracts of paddy lands in the Southern Province. In conjunction with Mr. Joseph Frazer, the visiting agent of his properties, Mr. Perera is fully employed in supervising the work on these estates, besides looking after his numerous house properties in Galle. Mr. Perera is a member of the Municipal Council of Galle, as well as of the Galle Cricket and Gymkhana Clubs, also of the Turf Club, Orient Club, and

FRANCIS PERERA.

Agricultural Society of Colombo. In 1906 he married the fifth daughter of the late Charles Henry and Lady de Soysa. His residence, "Closenberg," which stands on a peninsula jutting out into Galle Harbour, is one of the beauty spots of the Southern Province.

WILLIAM HENRY DE SILVA.

This gentleman, who takes a most active interest in the municipal affairs of Colombo,

W. H. DE SILVA.

was born at Moratuwa in 1868. He is the son of Lindemullege Andris de Silva and Warnekulasooriye Mahapata bedi Lindemullege Bastiana Silva, and is descended from Thakura Arthedevage Aditya (the Colonel of the Guards), who was granted Moratuwa by King Bhuvaneka Bahu VII. This warrior's son became a Christian, together with King Don Juan Dharmapala, and was known as Pedru de Silva, Mudaliyar. He is mentioned for gallantry, by the Portuguese historian Delonto, during the siege of Colombo by Mayadunna.

Dr. W. H. de Silva was educated at the Prince of Wales's College, Moratuwa, and St. Thomas's College, Colombo. He subsequently studied for two years at the Ceylon Medical College; and in 1889 he proceeded to Marischal College, Aberdeen, Scotland. Having determined to devote himself and his talents to the medical profession, he pursued his studies at the Scottish University with ardour, and became senior medallist in bacteriology and practical pathology, besides obtaining first-class honours in eight subjects and second-class honours in seven subjects of study. Having obtained the degrees of M.B. and C.M. (Master of Surgery) in 1892, also a diploma in medico-psychology, he spent a year in London and Paris, during which time he officiated as Clinical Assistant at the Royal Eye Hospital in the former city and at the Pasteur and Galezoski Eye Institutes

MR. AND MRS. F. PERERA AND FAMILY.
THE FERNERY, "CLOSENBERG" BUNGALOW.
RUBBER ESTATE. FRANCIS PERERA'S RESIDENCE.

in Paris. He returned to Ceylon in 1893, and was appointed Lecturer to the Ceylon Medical College, in connection with which he at present holds the lectureship in materia medica and ophthalmology. Dr. de Silva was the Secretary of the Ceylon Branch of the British Medical Association, and held office as Vice-President of that body last year (1905). He was married, in 1896, at St. Michael's Church, Polwatte, to Julia, daughter of the late Mr. C. H. and Lady de Soysa. He took a prominent part in the establishment of the Queen Victoria Memorial Eye Hospital at Colombo, acting as joint-secretary, with Sir Allan Perry, of the public fund raised for founding the institution, and collecting the largest subscription ever got together for any charitable purpose in Ceylon. The first meeting with the object of founding this memorial was held in 1902, the foundation-stone was laid in 1903, and the building was completed in 1905, at the cost of nearly two and a half lacs of rupees. Appropriately enough, Dr. de Silva was appointed Senior Surgeon in charge of the hospital, a post he still retains. Dr. de Silva proceeded again to Europe in 1901, this time as representative of the Medical Association on the occasion of the annual meeting of that body held at Cheltenham, England; and, taking the opportunity of continuing his studies in Edinburgh, he obtained the degree of F.R.C.S., afterwards visiting several eye clinics on the Continent. He has been a member of the Colombo Municipal Council since 1902, representing the Colpetty Ward, and, whilst holding that position, he was instrumental in obtaining for the southern suburbs the extension and laying out of the piece of open ground known as the Havelock Park. Always interesting himself energetically in public health matters, such as sewage disposal and water supply and dust questions, he has come to be looked upon as the representative of up-to-date sanitary progress in the Council, being a member of the Standing Committee on Sanitation and Markets. Among his varied activities in other directions, he is one of the Directors of the local branch of the Young Men's Christian Association, is a Councillor of the Ceylon branch of the Royal Asiatic Society and of the British Medical Association, a member of the Orient and Turf Clubs, a representative of the Anglican Synod, and a Lieutenant in the Ceylon Volunteer Medical Corps.

Dr. de Silva owns estates planted in coconut, cinnamon, rubber, and cacao, of which the principal ones are Pallanchena Farm, in the Negombo, and Monravia, in the Kegalla district. He is also proprietor of large areas in Kandy and Colombo. His private residence is "Nellidith," Bambalapitiya—one of the finest houses in Colombo, of which an illustration is given above.

"NELLIDITH."

LOUIS H. S. PIERIS.

Mr. Louis Henricus Susen Pieris, Barrister-at-law and Advocate of the Supreme Court of Ceylon, was born at Caldecott, in the Colpetty division of Colombo, on June 4, 1879. He is the son of Louis Pieris and Cecilia Elizabeth de Fonseka, the latter a direct descendant of Anderado Adigar, mentioned in the history of the Dutch period in Ceylon. The family, on the side of both parents, is closely connected with some of the best-known names in the island, and, through Eugeltina, the wife of the late Mudaliyar Susew de Soysa, came into direct touch with the family of that name, as mentioned in the life-sketch of the late Charles Henry de Soysa, under the heading "A Native Philanthropist," given in another part of this book. Mr. L. H. S. Pieris was educated at St. Thomas's College, Colombo, where he studied under Dr. Copleston, the present Metropolitan of India. Mr. Pieris then proceeded to London, and entered Gray's Inn, and he was called to the English Bar during the Michaelmas term of 1900. In the following year he returned to Ceylon, and was sworn in an Advocate of the Supreme Court of the island. Being heir to broad acres, he divides his time between the law and the supervision of his many plantations. His country residence is Grosvenor Gardens, Kandy. Having devoted the last eighteen months of his stay in London to the study of the conditions and requirements of the Eastern market, he obtained an insight into these subjects, which he now utilises in his business as a producer. In particular he has given great attention to rubber, which he has planted extensively.

Mr. Pieris is a member of the Ceylon Turf Club and the Orient Club, and is a very popular young man in the local community, a popularity largely shared by his wife, Selina, a particularly gifted young lady, the youngest daughter of Lady de Soysa, of Alfred House, Bambalapitiya, Colombo. Of this union there are three children—Phœbe Catherine Cecilia, Louis Charles de Soysa, and Beryl Selina. Mrs. Pieris's work with the brush is among the choicest attractions of the Whist Bungalow, the celebrated residence of Mr. and Mrs. Pieris at Mutwal. It deserves mention that she was the first Sinhalese lady to compete in the annual exhibitions of the Ceylon Society of Arts. She studied painting—in oil and water-colours—as well as sculpture, under Messrs. Ortel, Miller, and Rost, and from 1896 has been a regular exhibitor at the "salons" of the Ceylon Art Society, by which body she has been awarded no less than eighteen certificates, prizes, and medals for her work. That her tastes are distinctly creative no better evidence could be afforded than her "Wedding-Cake," a most unique and ingenious specimen of artistic and mechanical work in fine wood and glass work, which, as will be seen from an accompanying illustration, is unrivalled as regards originality of design. The chief feature of this marvellous *chef d'œuvre* is the representation of the historic

WHIST BUNGALOW. INTERIOR OF WHIST BUNGALOW. MRS. PIERIS AND BABY.
MR. AND MRS. LOUIS H. S. PIERIS AND FAMILY. THE DRAWING-ROOM.

MRS. LOUIS H. S. PIERIS'S STUDIO.

THE WEDDING CAKE.

satin-wood bridge at Peradeniya, Kandy, but recently dismantled, and it may be left to the imagination to conjure up the ever-memorable and consecrated associations this bridge has for the young couple. This model spanned the spacious reception hall at Alfred House from side to side. The suggestion of water underneath the bridge is most artistically conveyed by a paving of huge mirrors, out of which grasses and moss seem to grow. Swans gliding among lotus flowers or preening their feathers on the bank give realistic touches to the scene, which is rendered vivid by electric lights. The cake itself, the bridal emblem, is ensconced in a huge pearly nautilus, which is drawn by a pair of white swans, Cupid being the charioteer; and by means of a hidden mechanical contrivance, the swans glide over the water to greet the bride and bridegroom (Mr. and Mrs. Pieris) amid an outburst of music.

THE WHIST BUNGALOW.

No description of Colombo would be complete without reference to Whist Bungalow, Mutwal, the Colombo residence of its proprietor, Mr. Louis H. S. Pieris. Away from the stir and bustle of the business quarters of the city, and occupying an ideal site in the northernmost suburb, this delightful residence also has local historical associations. Its praises have been repeatedly sung. Tennent, Digby, and Cordinor, among others, have written of the beauty of the situation, and of the times when this historic dwelling was in the heyday of its glory. As it stands to-day, in surroundings of true tropical charm, the house combines historic tradition with modern taste, comfort, and convenience in a manner enchanting to the visitor to this beautiful spot. It was designed on a large scale, and the spacious reception-rooms speak of the days when our ancestors knew how to entertain generously and the motto with regard to guests was "the more the merrier." Merry indeed were the doings in that roomy residence in the days of yore—the early times of the British occupation of Ceylon—and need there was then not only for the majestic banqueting-halls and card-rooms, but also for the large, old-fashioned wine and provision cellars of solid construction, which are still in a state of perfect preservation. Capacious, too, are the sleeping apartments, to which the fine old roysterers of that long bygone time retired, when at last their prolonged merry-makings were brought temporarily to a close. The stables and coach-houses —the latter now filled with the most modern type of carriages, while in the former are to be seen the best breeds of horses—are all on the same scale of magnificence. Then glance over the ten acres of ground attached to, and surrounding, the bungalow, and the ravished eye lights upon handsome trees and ornamental shrubs and masses of many-hued flowers spread out in gorgeous and dazzling profusion, yet in orderly design, among which the regal rose is especially conspicuous; while equally pleasing to the sight is the fruit-garden with its wealth of tropical trees and shrubs, each bearing its own luscious and richly coloured burden. An exquisite lawn hems the majestic Kelani river, with all its seductive suggestions of pleasant boating parties. What could be more delightful than this outlook over the expanse of water, shimmering under the almost too brilliant sunshine, which stretches away westward and on the shore of which the house stands! On this side you see the broad delta of the Kelani river, while yonder is the shining sea. And surely that is an enchanted islet which lies, crowned with a wealth of foliage, in the broad mouth of the Kelani river! Turn northward, and the coconut groves that stretch along the coast in that direction come into the range of vision. Or look southwards, and admire the picturesque disorder of the fishermen's huts grouped under the tall coconut palms, with a small Buddhist temple in their midst. The spot is truly a haven of peace and retirement, in which the jaded and overwrought mind is soothed and lulled into contentment with the very monotony of the rank luxuriance of its natural beauty.

Professor Ernst H. Haeckel, the great naturalist, in his book "A Visit to Ceylon," published in 1883, devotes a considerable portion of one chapter to a rapturous description of the attractions of this beauty-spot of Colombo. He also explains that "the hungalow derived its extraordinary name from the circumstance that its first owner, an old English officer at the beginning of the century [the nineteenth], used to invite his friends out to this remote villa to indulge in whist on Sunday evenings. As the strict observance of the English Church is, of course, strongly averse from such an employment on Sunday, these jovial meetings were kept a profound secret, and the whist parties and drinking bouts in the isolated bungalow seem to have been uproarious in proportion to the satisfaction of these jolly comrades at having escaped the dreary tedium of an English Sunday and orthodox society." The Whist Bungalow was, in short, a convenient retreat for these roystering Sabbath-breakers. Later on the bungalow was enlarged and decorated and the grounds laid out in ornamental style by a subsequent owner, the well-remembered Sir Richard Morgan. The place is reminiscent of the life of that versatile genius, one of the group of meteoric men that shot into local prominence in the early fifties—C. A. Lorensz, James Stewart, and men of their ilk. Professor Haeckel, with portentous gravity, states that on the decease of Sir Richard his spirit refused to quit the scene of his former glories. The bungalow thus added to its historic fame by becoming haunted, and fearsome scenes were rumoured to take place in the building every night. With bated breath the tale was told of uproarious ghostly revels, of which the spirit of Sir Richard was master and in which winged demons and fiends with fiery eyes participated. Owing to these nightly performances the bungalow remained empty and shunned until a certain Stipperger acquired it. Being of a practical and non-superstitious turn of mind, the new owner at once set to work and routed the supposed ghostly denizens—which proved to be beings no more supernatural than wild cats, bandicoots, and flying foxes. Stipperger restored the neglected house and garden, and it was in its condition of renewed order and beauty that Professor Haeckel saw the spot and became enchanted with it. As the guest of Stipperger at the bungalow for a fortnight, he enjoyed every opportunity, not only for becoming imbued with the beauty of the place and studying the flora and fauna of the vicinity, but also for learning the traditions attached to the house.

A far earlier account of this remarkahle dwelling is given in an exceptionally interesting old book entitled "A Description of Ceylon," of which only a very few copies are said to be extant. It was written by the Rev. James Cordinor, M.A., who had been chaplain to the garrison of Colombo, and was published in London in 1807. The reverend gentleman gives the following account of the "Whist Club," from which the house derives its name: "The bungalow where it [the Whist Club] is held is beautifully situated about four miles north-east of Colombo, at the mouth of the Calanyganga, which there receives the name of Mootwal. The club consists of twelve members, chosen from among the most respectable inhabitants of the place. They give dinners in rotation, and generously invite twelve strangers. Some of the members, whose characters are celebrated for extensive hospitality, assemble a still greater number of guests. The entertainment is always liberal, and the assembly never fails to be animated with the highest share of convivial delight. The company repair to the villa about one o'clock in the afternoon, and play cards, read, or otherwise enjoy the country until four, when dinner is announced. At half-past five, or at six o'clock, they rise from table, make a circuit in their carriages or on horseback, and reach their respective houses before it is dark."

Among the more recent visitors to the Whist Bungalow was Lord Llandaff (the Right Hon. Henry Matthews, Q.C.), who, when passing through Ceylon, found his way to the spot to renew his acquaintance with the house where he was born and spent his childhood. Lord Llandaff was, as may be well expected, delighted to revisit the scene, and he found in every gnarled trunk a source of happy recollections and a beauty born of cherished memories where none till then was suspected. His visit gained for the present proprietor a very useful friend, for Lord Llandaff's acquaintanceship was of the utmost service to Mr. Pieris during the latter's stay in England.

W. G. ROCKWOOD.

One of the most brilliant and most popular of the sons of the soil of Ceylon is Dr. W. G. Rockwood, who has for the last forty years maintained the high reputation of being foremost in the island both as a surgeon and as a physician. What is still more deserving mention, his reputation has not been confined to his native land. Both in the adjacent continent and in England his name is well known and is held in high repute among those who are themselves eminent in the medical profession. Appreciation from such men as Beck and Stonham, Sutton and Barlow, Lord Lister and Sir Frederick Treves, must be reckoned praise indeed. And such appreciation has fallen to the lot of the distinguished, yet reticent and retiring, subject of this notice. This same characteristic of reticence has rendered it difficult to obtain at first hand full particulars of Dr. W. G. Rockwood's remarkable career. But though he will not speak of himself, his achievements are widely and generally known, and there are many who are eager to sound his praises. At a time when grave illness has rendered necessary the complete retirement of this master of medical science from the active practice of his profession and the discharge of the duties he

W. G. ROCKWOOD.

has so long, so faithfully, and so skilfully performed, it is especially fitting that his great services should, to some extent, be recorded in permanent form. The following particulars, though not giving a complete picture of the man and his history, are in every respect accurate and authentic.

Dr. Rockwood was born in Jaffna, in the northernmost province of the island, on March 13, 1843. After some four or five years' attendance at the Vimbadi Boys' School in the place of his birth, he went over to India and entered the Presidency College at Madras. Having passed the matriculation examination of that institution and gained a scholarship, he entered the Madras Medical College. Five years later—that is, in June, 1886—he graduated in medicine and surgery, and then returned to Ceylon. He had hardly been two months in the island when he was admitted to the Government Medical Service and appointed medical officer of Puttalam. Two months later he was sent to his native district (Jaffna) on special duty in connection with an outbreak of cholera. In 1867 he returned to Puttalam as medical officer, and remained there until about the middle of 1875. During this term of service two notable events of his life took place. One of them was his marriage with Miss S. Muttukumara, which took place in 1871, and this accomplished and popular lady happily still presides over the doctor's household. The other was his gaining the ments; and I fully believe that in any English or Scotch University he would have carried the highest honours. The man is no ordinary one, and I expect our Inspector-General will be glad to get hold of him for one of our posts in Southern India." But Dr. Rockwood, happily for so many in Ceylon, preferred to devote his conspicuous abilities to the service of the land of his birth. When he returned from taking his degree at Madras he was stationed at Hambantota for some eighteen months as medical officer, and was then sent to Gampola in the same capacity.

In January, 1878, came the turning-point in Upon his retirement from the Government service, in March, 1898, Sir West Ridgeway, then Governor of Ceylon, in recognition of his long and distinguished services in connection with that institution, appointed Dr. Rockwood Consulting-Surgeon to the General Hospital, an office which was specially created for the occasion and to which Dr. Rockwood is, up to now, the only person who has received an appointment. As a further mark of appreciation, Sir West Ridgeway appointed Dr. Rockwood a member of the Legislative Council of Ceylon, the highest honour of a public kind that can be conferred in the

DR. DAVID ROCKWOOD'S BUNGALOW.

degree of Doctor of Medicine of the University of Madras. This degree was not only a high distinction in itself, but it brought him special honour, inasmuch as he passed in the first class and received a rare compliment from the Board of Examiners. "I have lately had," one of them wrote, "on behalf of the Madras University to examine a man of the name of Rockwood, from Ceylon, for the degree of Doctor of Medicine, and certainly was quite unprepared to meet a candidate for medical honours of this country so remarkably proficient. My fellow-examiners concur with me that two-thirds at least of the students at home do not come up to Rockwood in their attain-

his professional career, for in that month, on the death of Dr. Koch (another eminent son of Ceylon), he became Surgeon-in-Charge of the General Hospital of Colombo, an appointment in which he continued for some five years, adding to it, at the same time, the office of Lecturer in Surgery and Midwifery at the Ceylon Medical College. In 1883 his duties of Surgeon-in-Charge ceased, but he continued in the office of surgeon of the hospital. The following year he went to England on leave, and while there took the opportunity of obtaining the diplomas of M.R.C.S. and M.R.C.P.

Honours of another kind quickly followed

island, and one which is eagerly resought whenever the term of appointment expires. In Dr. Roekwood's case, when the period of five years was completed, the Governor appointed him again for a further similar period, thus stretching the gubernatorial prerogative to its utmost. Dr. Rockwood proved a wise and useful councillor. He took a wide interest in all public questions, especially those connected with sanitation and railway extension. He spoke but seldom, but then always with point and effect. At the beginning of 1906 failing health compelled his retirement from the Legislative Council.

Dr. Rockwood was a frequent visitor to

Europe, his trips thither, however, being taken for purposes of health rather than holiday-making, and for purposes of study and observation more than either. He was President of the Ceylon branch of the British Medical Association, and in 1902, during a visit to England, represented the local branch at the annual meeting of the parent Association, held that year at Manchester. This sketch may appropriately conclude with the hope that Dr. Rockwood, though compelled to give up the active discharge of duties and responsibilities, may long be spared to his family, his friends, and his country.

WILLIAM PAUL RODRIGO.

This well-known medical practitioner and specialist is a son of Mr. Hendrick Rodrigo, of Kotta, and was born at that place in 1868. He received his school education at the Royal College, and subsequently pursued his special studies at the Ceylon Medical College. He graduated as licentiate in 1887, and in April, 1893, was appointed House Surgeon of the Kandy Hospital. He has also filled various offices under the medical department at Medagama, Kitulgala, Welikade, and elsewhere. In 1896 he resigned the Government service and commenced private practice at Dehiwela, and in 1900 he proceeded to England, and in the following two years obtained the degrees of D.P.H. (Cantab.) and M.R.C.S. and L.R.C.P. (Lond.). At King's College Hospital he engaged in special work in bacteriology, at the Chelsea Hospital in special diseases of women, at the Westminster Hospital in eye diseases, and at the City Royal Hospital in chest troubles. Returning to Ceylon in 1903, he was nominated Director of the Colombo Bacteriological Institute. This appointment, however, was not confirmed by the Governor, and, in conjunction with Dr. Gandevia, Dr. Rodrigo was instrumental in working a movement for the construction of a consumptive hospital as a memorial to the late Queen Victoria, in opposition to the eye hospital then proposed. Dr. Rodrigo is a specialist in consumption, and in connection with his bacteriological researches has studied leprosy. In December, 1903, he proceeded to Bangkok, Siam, and practised there in partnership with Dr. Tilleke. But ill-health obliged him to return to Ceylon in the following year, after having made a study of the Ross cure for leprosy at Rangoon; and he has since practised his profession at Colpetty and Bambalapitiya, Colombo. In 1898 he married a daughter of Mr. M. Goonetilleke, Chief Mudaliyar of the Kandy Kachcheri, Mudaliyar of the Governor's Gate, and Justice of the Peace, the lady being also a sister of Mr. H. E. Tilleke, Attorney-General of Siam. Dr. Rodrigo is a member of the British Medical Association, Fellow of the Royal Institute of Public Health, a member of the Turf Club, and President of the Colpetty Cricket Club. His private residence is "The Shrubbery," Bambalapitiya.

CHARLES WALTER VAN GEYZEL.

Dr. Charles Walter Van Geyzel, the son of Dr. John William Van Geyzel and Anne Ursula Thomasz, was born at "The Surgery," the family residence, in Prince Street, Pettah, Colombo, in 1853, and was educated at the Colombo Academy (now the Royal College) in that city. After his course at this institution he studied medicine for three years (1872–75) at Calcutta. He then proceeded to Edinburgh University, where he graduated in 1878, obtaining the degree of M.B., C.M. On his return to Ceylon he entered upon private practice. He obtained his M.D. Edinburgh in 1880, and has now been practising as a general physician for nearly thirty years. His extensive practice did not permit him to take up any Government appointment or lectureship. He was nominated by the Government a member of the Municipal Council of Colombo in 1903, was renominated in 1906, and this position he still retains. In 1882 he married Emma Eliza, daughter of Mr. J. H. Ferdinands, Proctor of Kandy, and a niece of the late District Judge of Colombo, Mr. Charles Lambert Ferdinands. His private residence is "The Grange," Union Place, Colombo. He was one of the first members of the British Medical Association of Ceylon, but had to resign owing to the strain of private practice. At one time also he was a member of the Orient Club, Colombo. He is an elder of the Dutch Presbyterian Church at Wolfendahl; and, on the side of sport, is an honorary member of the Colts Cricket Club.

GEORGE THOMASZ.

This gentleman is the son of Henry Emmanuel Thomasz and Frances, daughter of John Taylor, late chief assistant to the Director of Public Instruction in Ceylon. He was born in Colombo in 1861, and educated at the Colombo Academy (now known as the Royal College). After his course at this institution he entered the Medical College at Colombo, and passed out as a licentiate. In 1883 he proceeded to Edinburgh, and qualifying as L.R.C.P. and S. in 1884 at that University, took up work as a surgeon at the infirmary in the Scotch capital. He returned in the same year to Ceylon, and was appointed Resident-Surgeon of the Colombo General Hospital. He also administered the hospitals at Galle, Matara, Hambantota, and Kandy, had charge of the medical work of the jail as well as the judicial departments, and the sanitary supervision of the districts. In 1897 he proceeded again to Scotland to pursue his medical studies, and worked at the London, Bath, and St. Peter's hospitals. He applied himself especially to the investigation of calculose diseases at the Chelsea Hospital, the diseases of women at the Middlesex Hospital, London, as well as to the study of cancer and ear, nose, and throat affections. On his return to Ceylon in 1898 he was appointed Senior Surgeon of the Colombo General Hospital. In 1905 he again visited England to represent Ceylon at the Leicester Medical Congress, and on his return to the island retired from the public service on a pension. He now carries on private practice

MRS. GEO. THOMASZ AND CHILD.

in Colombo. Dr. Thomasz is the author of a treatise on the "Causes of Elephantiasis in Ceylon," and through the medium of the British Medical Association, of which he is a member, he contributed a paper on "Badges on the Cord," a subject which had hitherto not received treatment at the hands of any writer. During his six years' service at the General Hospital he performed some four thousand major and minor operations. In 1890 he became Surgeon-Lieutenant in the Ceylon Light Infantry, and later obtained his Captaincy. In 1905 he was appointed Surgeon-Major commanding the Medical Staff Corps. Dr. Thomasz is a member of the Orient and Turf Clubs and patron of the Colombo Rovers' Cricket and Athletic Club. His recreation is golf. In 1890 he married Blanche, daughter of Charles Vanderwall, of Kandy. His private residence is "Corona," Colpetty, Colombo.

JONATHAN HOMER.

Dr. Jonathan Homer was born on September 13, 1878, at Jaffna, and educated at St. Thomas's

College, Colombo, where he had a brilliant career. He was Duke of Edinburgh's Scholar, Victoria Gold Medallist, and held other distinctions. Entering the Ceylon Medical College as a Rustomjee Jamsetjee Jeejeebhoy scholar, he was successful in obtaining his licence in medicine and surgery, also taking the medal in medical jurisprudence. He was appointed Senior House Physician at the General Hospital, Colombo, and after two years' service was transferred as first medical assistant to the Superintendent of the Lunatic Asylum, Colombo; he resigned his Government appointment to adopt private practice, and is at present so engaged at Borella, Colombo.

E. V. RATNAM.

This medical gentleman is the son of Inspector S. Elliyatamby, of the Public Works Department, Singapore, and was born at Jaffna in 1876. He was educated at the Central College, Jaffna, and the Jaffna College, and at the former he won the Junior Wesleyan Mission Scholarship of his year. He then entered the Ceylon Medical College, became a licentiate in 1900, was successively appointed Second House-Surgeon at the General Hospital, Colombo, Resident Surgeon at the Kandy Hospital, Resident Medical Officer of the Borella Convict Hospital, and, in 1902, Senior Resident Surgeon of the General Hospital, Colombo. In 1905 he resigned the Government service, and commenced private practice by opening a hospital at Maradana, in the capital, together with a dispensary, with a branch establishment at Old Moor Street, in the Pettah quarter. His practice has now become extensive.

He married a daughter of Mr. C. S. Chitty, a landed proprietor of Colombo. He is a member of the British Medical Association, Vice-President of the Maradana Literary Association, member of the Tamil Union Cricket Club, and Vice-President of the Rovers' Cricket Club. His favourite pastimes are cricketing and riding.

V. O. WRIGHT.

Dr. Victor Oswald Wright, son of the late John Wright, head clerk in the Colombo Police Department, was born at Colombo on May 8th, and was educated primarily at Royal College, Colombo. On the completion of his educational career he took a three years' course of study at the Ceylon Medical College, and in 1890 went to Aberdeen University. In 1893 he graduated M.B., C.M. there, became assistant to an Aberdeenshire practitioner, and afterwards walked the London hospitals. He returned to Ceylon in 1893, and in the following year became House Surgeon at the Colombo Hospital. After holding this position for about twelve months he paid a short visit to England. Ever since his final return to Ceylon in 1894 he has been in private practice and has also taken a great deal of interest in the Ceylon Volunteer Medical Corps, of which he became Surgeon-Lieutenant in 1895 and Surgeon-Captain in 1902. He is a member of the British Medical Association and of the Catholic Club. He is a good musician, and is the conductor of the Glee Club, and his other recreations are cricket, tennis, and billiards. He married, in 1897, Eleanor, daughter of the late Charles van Langenberg, of Colombo. He resides at "Bon Accord," Bambalapitiya, and has two sons and four daughters.

WILLIAM A. PASSÉ.

Grandpass is a thickly populated native suburban quarter of Colombo, consequently the Grandpass Dispensary, founded by Dr. Passé in 1894, and owned and conducted by him, is a busy resort for the afflicted. A large

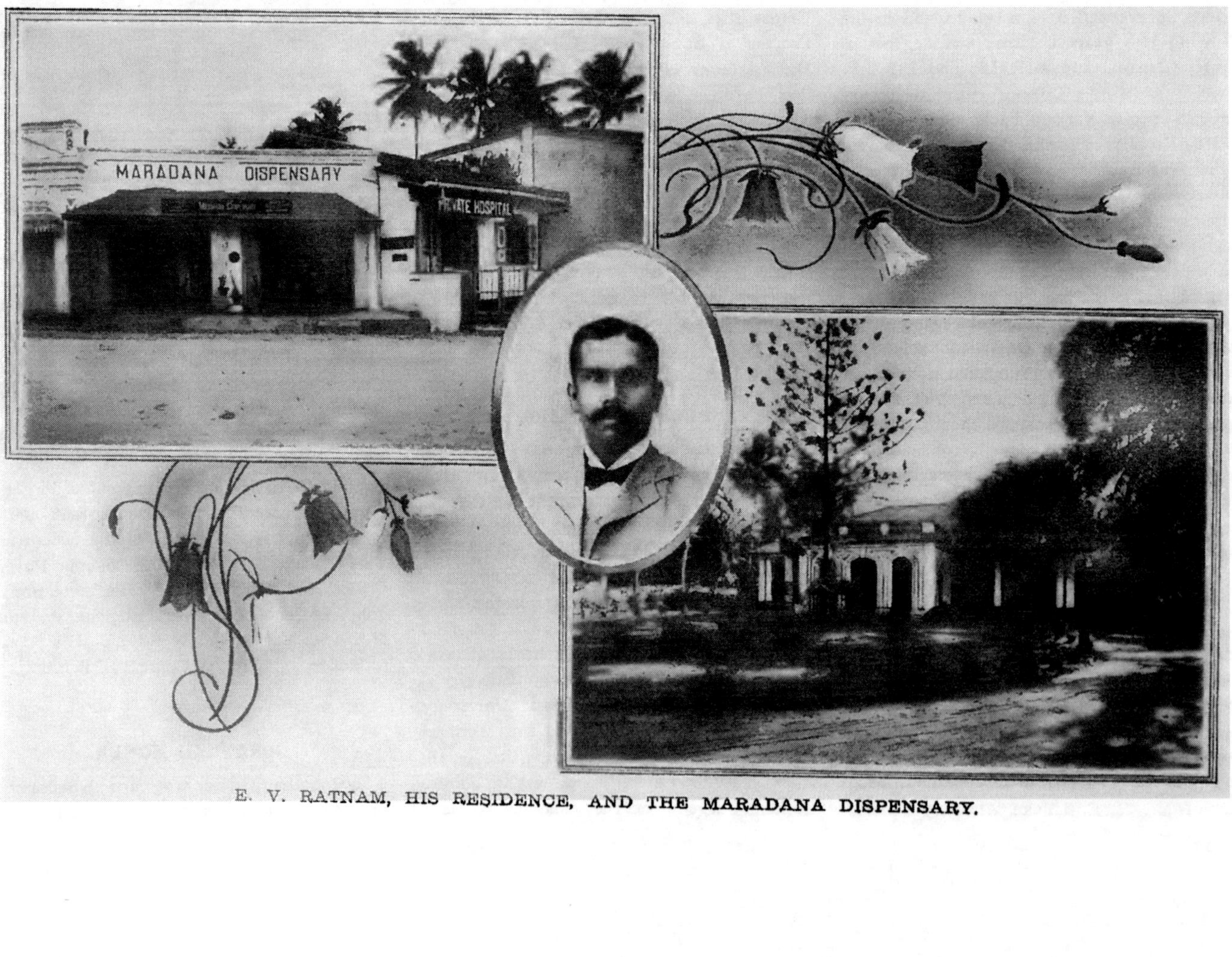

E. V. RATNAM, HIS RESIDENCE, AND THE MARADANA DISPENSARY.

WILLIAM A. PASSE, HIS ASSISTANTS, TWO VIEWS OF GRANDPASS DISPENSARY, AND A VIEW SHOWING HIS BUNGALOW.

crowd of poor people is always to be seen waiting here at all hours of the day and night for their turn to be treated by the doctor. As he himself is a native of Colombo, having been born in the city in 1860, he is especially qualified for dealing with local cases. Dr. Passé is a general practitioner, and treats all kinds of diseases. He is a licentiate of the Ceylon Medical College, also L.R.C.P., L.R.C.S. and L.M. of Edinburgh, and L.F.P. and S. of Glasgow. In January, 1889, he entered the Government service of Ceylon as Sub-Assistant Colonial Surgeon, from which position he was promoted, four years later, to that of Deputy-Assistant Colonial Surgeon. On December 31, 1893, Dr. Passé resigned his Government appointment.

P. M. MUTTUKUMARU, M.B., C.M.

Dr. Muttukumaru was born in November, 1865, and was educated at St. Thomas's College and the Medical College, Colombo. He graduated M.B. and C.M. at Aberdeen University in 1893, and was awarded the medal in practical pathology, as well as first-class certificates of merit in practical zoology and

P. M. MUTTUKUMARU.

clinical (surgical) note-taking; also second-class certificates in anatomy, embryology, and osteology, operative surgery, and practical physiology. On his return from England in 1894 the doctor settled in Colombo, and he now has an extensive practice in the city as well as in the adjacent villages. His address is Colombo.

The doctor is especially proud of having received the following testimonial from the Institute of the Brothers of the Christian School:—

"M. Philip Marian Muttukumaru,
M.B., C.M.

"The Brothers of the Christian Schools deem it to be a duty of gratitude to their benefactors to offer up fervent prayers to the Author of every perfect gift, in order to draw down upon them the blessing of the present life and the rewards of the life to come. Wherefore, as a token of our gratitude for your charity and devotedness to our Communities of Colombo, the Novitiate, and St. Benedict's, and knowing that your piety sets value upon all spiritual goods, we beg to announce to you that your name has been entered upon the roll of Benefactors of our Institute. You are, by this letter, made participator in the prayers recited daily by the Brothers and their pupils for living Benefactors; and after death you shall also partake of the pious suffrages offered daily, and of the Communion made each month, by the members of our Institute, in favour of deceased benefactors.

"Given at Paris this eighteenth day of October in the year of our Lord, One thousand nine hundred, as witness our hand and the seal of our Institute.

(Signed) "Father Gabriel Marie,
"Superior-General."

THE LATE PHILIP SEBASTIAN BRITO.

On April 9, 1906, the medical profession of Ceylon lost one of its most prominent members, and the Tamils one of their leaders, by the death of Dr. Philip Sebastian Brito, son of Philip Britopulle, Shoff Mudaliyar and Notary Public of Puttalam, and brother of Advocate Christopher Brito, retired District Judge of Batticaloa—a man well known in Ceylon for his legal acumen and his profound scholarship. Dr. Brito may be reckoned one of the pioneers of that rapidly increasing body of Ceylonese who win distinction, academic and professional, in a European field. After being educated at the school of the Christian Brothers and at the Royal College, Colombo, he left Ceylon for Great Britain and entered himself at the Aberdeen University. His career was a most brilliant one, for not only did he become the honoursman of the University, and obtain his M.B., C.M., but he was selected to fill the positions of Emeritus Lecturer and Demonstrator in Practical Anatomy, and Regius Professor of the Institutes of Medicine. In London Dr. Brito became a member of the Royal College of Surgeons, England, and competed with success for the Fellowship, he being the first Ceylonese to attempt to secure this high professional distinction. Unfortunately he was unable to complete the full course owing to ill-health, which necessitated his return to Ceylon. Prior to this Dr. Brito, in conjunction with Dr. W. Sterling, M.D., D.Sc., wrote an original dissertation on the digestion of blood by the common leech, and on the formation of hæmoglobin crystals. Arrived in Ceylon after an absence of ten years, the late Dr. Brito was appointed Lecturer in Physiology, Biology, and Histology at the

THE LATE PHILIP BRITO.

Ceylon Medical College. He made a most successful lecturer, and carried forward on local ground the brilliant reputation he had made in the West. A striking mark of his independence of mind was a successful attempt he made at this period to harmonise Eastern and Western systems of medicine. A profound knowledge of Ceylonese drugs, derived from a long course of study, led him to the conviction that there were many purely indigenous drugs worthy of the notice of European practitioners. His views had considerable weight with the profession, with the result that his specific for malaria and other native drugs are now regularly made in Europe, and are obtainable in the Ceylon pharmacies. On relinquishing his post of Lecturer at the Ceylon Medical College, Dr. Brito undertook the duties of Assistant Colonial Surgeon of Puttalam. Here he suffered from repeated attacks of fever, and these led to complications which ended a valuable life at the age of forty-nine. Dr. Brito, it may be added, was born at Madampe on April 7, 1856. He came of an ancient Tamil family of the Colombo Chetty community. He married first Miss Cecilia Charlotte Rajamuttamma Savundranayagam (eldest daughter of Mr. G. P. Savundranayagam, of the Madras High Court Bar), by whom he had four children. By his second wife, Miss Harriet Ondatje, a sister of Mr. N. N. S. Aserappa, police magistrate of Negombo, he had two children.

JAMES RICHARD WEINMAN.

Mr. J. R. Weinman, the subject of this sketch, is the son of the late Mr. John Weinman, who married a Miss Julia de Wolf. Johannes Weinman, the grandfather of John Weinman, was a native of Potsdam, and took service under the Dutch East India Company in Ceylon. Jan de Wolf, whose great-granddaughter Julia was, was a native of Amsterdam, and arrived in Ceylon on December 15, 1783, on board the ship called the *De Zao*. Mr. Weinman was born at Peradeniya, and educated at the Colombo Academy. He read law under the late Charles Ferdinands, Solicitor-General, and the late Hon. James de Alwis. He practised as an advocate for many years in the Metropolis, but since 1902 has filled high judicial office. He was for one year Commissioner of the Court of Requests, Additional Police Magistrate, and Additional District Judge, Colombo, and for the last three years, with a small break, has been District Judge of Colombo.

In 1883 he married Maude, daughter of the late Charles Johnson. Recreations—tennis and walking. Lives at Barnes Place, Colombo; has three sons, amongst the keenest and finest young sportsmen in practically every field of sport in the island.

MRS. J. R. WEINMAN. J. R. WEINMAN. MR. AND MRS. J. R. WEINMAN AND SONS. THE BUNGALOW.

FREDERICK DORNHORST.

Mr. Frederick Dornhorst is a member of the Burgher community of Ceylon, having descended from ancestors of German nationality who settled in the island in 1791. He was born on April 26, 1849, and was educated at the Colombo Academy, now Royal College. He commenced life as a member of the teaching staff of his *alma mater*, and counts among his pupils some of the most distinguished and prominent men of Ceylon. In 1874 he entered the legal profession as an Advocate of the Supreme Court, and very early manifested the brilliant and versatile qualities which have marked his career as a lawyer and public man. He acquired an extensive practice almost immediately, not only competing successfully with the leaders of the day, but soon rising to the highest eminence in the profession. There has been no *cause célèbre* during the last twenty-five years and more in which he has not appeared as counsel; and by force of his varied learning, great powers of advocacy, and extraordinary personal magnetism, he occupies a commanding position both at the Bar and in the general community. He is extremely popular throughout the island, not the less so because he has consistently rejected the allurements of office. One of the objects of political ambition in Ceylon is a seat in the Legislative Council, but Mr. Dornhorst, to the regret of his countrymen, has resisted every attempt to send him there. Nevertheless, his brilliant talents and caustic oratory have always been at the disposal of the public whenever any great emergency required their exercise. He was called to the English Bar, the Benchers of the Inner Temple having, in view of his distinguished career as a lawyer, granted him a dispensation from several terms. One of the New Year Honours conferred by His Majesty the King in 1903 was the appointment of four members of the Ceylon Bar as King's Counsel, and Mr. Dornhorst was, of course, one of them. His years sit lightly upon him, and it will be a long time yet before the people of Ceylon will cease to benefit by the exercise of his great abilities and the example of his unique personality.

ANTONY PETER SAVUNDRANÂYAGAM.

To Mr. Antony Peter Savúndranâyagam belongs the honour of being the first Ceylonese to obtain the degree of Master of Arts of the London University, and indeed the whole of his educational career was one of marked distinction. He is a scion of one of the ancient families of Jaffna, several members of which were notable scholars. His grandfather, for instance, was a Tamil Pundit and grammarian, and was the Interpreter Mudaliyar of the Supreme Court, while his father, Mr. G. P. Savúndranâyagam, of the Madras High Court Bar, was not merely well versed in law, on which subject he published several works, but was also a Tamil poet and grammarian. The legal traditions of the family are also noteworthy. They are not only sustained by the career of his father, who was an Advocate of the High Court of Madras and Government Examiner in Law, but also by his uncle, M. G. S. Arianayagam, who was a Judge of the High Court of Travancore, and by his cousin, M. A. M. Mutunayagam, the present Attorney-General of that State. It was on February 27, 1880, that the subject of this sketch was born. He attended first the school of the Christian Brothers, and afterwards the Colombo Royal College. Mr. Savúndranâyagam's natural ability is shown by the fact that he passed the Junior Cambridge Local Examination when only twelve years old, and in his fifteenth year obtained first-class honours in the first division. At sixteen years of age he passed the London University Matriculation in the first division, a year later the Intermediate Arts Examination in the first class, while at nineteen years of age he obtained his Bachelor's degree. At the close of his course at the Royal College, where he was successful in carrying off seven prizes, among them being the Turnour Prize, given to the most advanced student in the whole college for the year, Mr. Savúndranâyagam went to England as a Government University Scholar, and became the research prizeman and scholar in the comparative philology of Latin and Greek of University College, London. The thesis which he had to write in this competition, entitled "Representatio in the Oratio Obliqua of Cæsar," in the opinion of Dr. J. P. Postgate, M.A., D.Litt., Lecturer in Classics, Trinity College, Cambridge, and examiner for the scholarship, "seemed to be of a soundness and value that would justify its being given to the world." It was in 1904 that he gained the distinction mentioned in the opening sentence, and the same year he was called to the Bar at the Inner Temple. At the close of his four years' stay in England Mr. Savúndranâyagam returned to Ceylon and became an Advocate of the Supreme Court. He is also engaged at present, with the approval of the Government, in translating into English the untranslated portions of Voet's "Commentaries on the Pandects."

CHARLES PERERA SENEWIRATNE GOONETILLEKE.

This gentleman, best known as Charles Perera, is the son of Paulus Perera and Dona Maria Pinto. Mr. Paulus Perera was a member of the Municipal Council for the Maradana Ward of Colombo, Notary Public, and President of the Notaries' Association. Mr. Charles Perera was born in Colombo in 1860, and was educated at Professor Bernard's private academy, afterwards passing successively through the Wesley College, St. Thomas's College, and

AVONDALE HOUSE, EXTERIOR AND INTERIOR.

MR. AND MRS. JAMES PEIRIS, AND VIEWS OF THEIR RESIDENCE, "RIPPLEWORTH."

Royal College (then the Colombo Academy). After his collegiate course he took up the study of law, and was articled to Mr. (afterwards Sir Charles) Layard, formerly Chief Justice of the Colony. In 1880 he became Proctor of the District Court of Colombo, and two years later a Proctor of the Supreme Court and Notary Public. He has since practised for the most part in Colombo. In 1883 he succeeded his late father as elected member of the Municipal Council for the Maradana Ward of Colombo, and has since sat in the Council continuously. He was a member of the bench of magistrates for the city, since abolished. Senior member of the Municipal Council, Mr. Perera has always figured as a staunch champion of public opinion, and the acknowledged spokesman and leader of the elected, or unofficial, party in the Council. Having a thorough knowledge of municipal finance, sanitation, and civic affairs generally, and possessing the confidence of the ratepayers, his public utterances are always received with attention. Essentially combative, he has, on more than one occasion, fearlessly opposed single-handed the whole of the Council. He was a member of the Standing Committee of the Council on Public Questions from 1887 to 1902, and is now on the law and various other committees. He is a member of the Royal Asiatic Society, a member of the Public Institute of Health of Great Britain and Ireland, member of the Orient Club, the Sinhalese Sports Club, and various other sporting institutions, as well as a committee member of the Maradana Industrial School. His residence Avondale House, Maradana, is one of the finest bungalows in the city, being fitted with all the most modern improvements in ventilation and lighting, including a special electric installation and a special cool-air chamber for purifying the air in the house and manufacturing ozone. Mr. Perera owns various coconut estates in the Western Province, and also takes great interest in the development of the cotton industry. Few of the citizens of Colombo are more popular, more progressive in ideas, or more in touch with the masses than Mr. Charles Perera of Maradana.

JAMES PEIRIS.

This gentleman, who gained high scholastic honours in England, is a leading member of the legal profession of Ceylon as well as an owner of considerable planting estates. He is the son of T. Martinus Peiris and Apolonia (*née* De Soysa), and was born at Colombo in December, 1856. At the Royal College, then known as the Colombo Academy, where he received his schooling, he became prize scholar, and won the English University Scholarship in 1878. Proceeding to England, he pursued his studies as foundation scholar and exhibitioner at St. John's, Cambridge, and graduated first-class in both law and moral science, being shortly afterwards elected McMahon Student of Law. He became President of the Cambridge University Union Society, and took an active part in the debates of that body. Having chosen the law for a profession, he was called to the Bar of Lincoln's Inn in 1881. He returned, however, to Ceylon in 1883, and has practised at Colombo ever since. He acted as Crown Counsel of the Western Province of his native island for some time, and as District Judge at Galle; he has been a member of the Colombo Municipal Council since 1898, as representative of the Slave Island Ward, being an active worker on the Public Works Committee of that body. When residing in England he was a member of the National Liberal Club, London. He is a member of the Orient Club, Colombo; Vice-President of the Sinhalese Sports Club; Vice-President of the Ceylon Social Reform Association; Treasurer of the Society for the Propagation of the Gospel, Ceylon; and member of the Standing Committee of the Church of England

Synod. He is also a Fellow of the Royal Colonial Institute. His chief recreation is taken on horseback.

As a planter, Mr. Peiris owns a half-share of the Vilpotha and Walehena estates in the Chilaw district, of 400 and 300 acres respectively, planted with coconuts; also Nadukelle, in the Chilaw district, of 140 acres; and Palangamuwe, in the Ruanveli district, of 100 acres. He is, besides, part-owner of Dambakande in the Western Province, of 250 acres, which is planted in coconut, tea, and cinnamon; while, in the Ratnapura district he owns the coconut and rubber estate of Kandegame, as well as the tea and coffee estates of Ellawatte and Kahambeliya, in the Haputale district. All the copra and tea from these estates is sold locally. Mr. Peiris's country seat is Ellawatte Bungalow, Haputale, and his Colombo residence is "Rippleworth," Turret Road, Cinnamon Gardens. In 1889 he married Grace, eldest daughter of Jacob De Mel, and has four children. He is a Justice of the Peace for the whole island.

NAMASIVAYAM MUDALIYAR TYAGARAJA.

Mr. Namasivayam Mudaliyar Tyagaraja, of Tyaga Nivasa—a beautiful residence, occupying a little over four acres of ground, and situated in Ward Place, Cinnamon Gardens, Colombo —was born in 1859, in Colombo. He is the son of Namasivayam Mudaliyar, a landed proprietor and in his day one of the leaders in Colombo among the Tamils, being always prominent in all Tamil movements. Mr. Tyagaraja was educated at St. Thomas's College, Colombo; and in 1881 he proceeded to England and entered Christ's College, Cambridge. In January, 1888, he was called to the Bar at Lincoln's Inn. In April of the same year he returned to Ceylon, and was admitted to the Ceylon Bar in May. He has now retired from actual practice at the Bar in order to devote his time to the management of his landed property. He is the owner of large estates in the Negombo, Chilaw and Puttalam districts, and part-owner of extensive properties in the Kurunegala district. Principal among these latter properties are: Kattukande, of 800 acres, in the North-Western Province, planted with coconuts; Wiliogama, of 300 acres, also in the North-Western Province; Sindiriamulla, of 300 acres, in the Chilaw district; Giviwella, of 200 acres, in the Kurunegala district; and Battulua, in the Puttalam district. In Colombo Mr. Tyagaraja owns several valuable properties, besides his private residence in Ward Place, namely, at Cargills, Cinnamon Gardens, "Fern Bank" and "Fern Lodge" in Rosmead Place, and a building plot in Barnes Place. He is a member of the Hindu community, President of the Tamil Union Cricket and Athletic Club, President of the Colombo Vivekananda Society, and was also a member of the Royal Asiatic Society. Mr. Tyagaraja took a prominent part in connection with the Jaffna Railway. When a candidate for the Legislative Council he was strongly supported by a large majority of Hindus and Tamils of Ceylon; and he will probably again appear in that character.

Never backward in the support of charitable institutions, Mr. Tyagaraja was one of the prominent speakers at the meeting held in Colombo to consider what fitting form the intended local memorial to Queen Victoria should take, and is a committee member of the Victoria Memorial Hospital. He was the largest contributor among the Tamils towards that institution, as well as towards the establishment of the Lady Havelock Hospital. His father built one of the best and largest temples in Jaffna, and contributed extensively to several local charities, principally in Jaffna. His son is now a trustee of the Jaffna temple. Mr. Tyagaraja has travelled in Europe and India.

N. M. TYAGARAJA'S BUNGALOW.

BENJAMIN WILLIAM BAWA.

This gentleman, whose father was the late Mr. A. Bawa, Proctor of the Supreme Court, was born at Galle in 1865. He attended St. Thomas's and Royal Colleges, where he was successful in gaining the Ceylon Local Scholarship in 1880, and one of the Junior Cambridge Local Scholarships in 1881, as well as the Rajapakse Shakespeare Director's and Turnour Prizes. He passed the Senior Cambridge Local Examination in 1882 and 1883, obtaining a second class on each occasion, and was second to Dr. H. M. Fernando when he took the University Scholarship. Upon the completion of his college career he studied law under the Hon. Mr. James Van Langenberg, M.L.C., and was called to the Bar in August, 1887. For some time he practised at Kegalla and afterwards at Colombo. In 1903 he went to England, entered the Middle Temple, and was called to the English Bar in June, 1904. He is a member of the Council of Legal Education, and a member of committee of the Orient, Turf, Lawn, and Nondescript Clubs, as well as of the National Association. For many years he has actively interested himself in the Volunteer movement. When at college he was a member of the cadet corps, and in 1899 he received his commission as Second Lieutenant in the Ceylon Light Infantry, being promoted Captain in 1905, in command of "Q"—the legal—Company. Whilst in England he passed the School of Instruction for the Auxiliary Forces at Chelsea. Recreations—riding, tennis, cricket, and golf. He lives at Chapman House, Darley Road.

J. A. VAN LANGENBERG.

Mr. James Arthur Van Langenberg, the son of the Hon. Mr. James Van Langenberg, Advocate of the Supreme Court of Ceylon and member of the Legislative Council from 1876 until his death in 1886, and of Maria Susan Toussaint, was born at Kandy on March 2, 1866. In 1885 he became a member of the Inner Temple, and a year later entered Merton College, Oxford. He was called to the English Bar in January, 1888. Returning to Ceylon, he was admitted an Advocate of the Supreme Court, and has practised as such at Colombo ever since. From 1905 to 1906 he acted as Solicitor-General, and in 1904 was a Member of the Legislative Council for six months. In connection with the Volunteer movement he obtained a second lieutenancy in the Ceylon Light Infantry on February 20, 1899, became Lieutenant in January, 1902, obtained his company a year later, and since February, 1905, he has commanded the cadet battalion with the honorary rank of Major. He married Ethel, daughter of J. W. Van der Straaten; is a member of the Orient Club and of the Council of Legal Education. His residence is "Merton," Guildford Crossing, Colombo.

H. A. LOOS.

Mr. Hermann Albert Loos, son of the Hon. Mr. F. C. Loos, Member of the Legislative Council, to whom allusion is made in the Legislative Section, was born at Colombo in 1865, and after being educated privately in Ceylon he went to England as early as 1879, entered the City of London School, and afterwards studied at University College, London, and Gonville and Caius College, Cambridge, where he graduated in 1887. In the same year he was called to the Bar at the Inner Temple, and returning to Ceylon he was admitted an Advocate of the Supreme Court, and became private secretary to Mr. Justice Clarence. He commenced practice on his own account in 1890, then joined the Attorney-General's Department as Acting Office Assistant and Additional Crown Counsel, and in 1899 he was appointed Additional Crown Counsel for the island. In 1903 he was permanently appointed Office Assistant and Crown Counsel and is now the senior Crown Counsel of the colony. In conjunction with Mr. Hector Jayewardene he edited the Supreme Court

H. A. LOOS.

THE BUNGALOW.

C. TIRU-NAVUK-ARASU. "MAHENDRA" BUNGALOW.

Reports. He is a contributor of reports of important cases of general interest of the Supreme Court of Ceylon, and of the legislation of the year to the Society of Comparative Legislation of England. In 1906 he acted as District Judge of Colombo. He is a member of the Voetlights, Orient, Lawn, and Turf Clubs, and has been captain of the Nondescripts Cricket Club almost from its very beginning, and is a keen cricket and tennis player. In 1891 he married Minnie Evelyn, eldest daughter of Dr. E. S. Gratiaen, Colonial Surgeon, of Colombo, and he resides at "Glenesk," Flower Road, Colombo.

CARTEGESAR TIRU-NAVUK-ARASU.

This gentleman, son of Cartegesar of Kokvil, Jaffna, was born at Jaffna. His father was employed as a clerk under Government in the Jaffna Courts. He received his early education in the Jaffna Central School; and while he was a student there, in the year 1879, he won a Queen's Scholarship tenable for three years in the Royal College, Colombo. He passed the matriculation examination of the Madras University in 1879. Early in 1880 he joined the Royal College (then the Colombo Academy) and won another Queen's Scholarship in 1881, tenable for three years, by securing a high position in the Junior Cambridge Local Examination. In 1884 he passed the matriculation examination of the London University. He was a law-student under the Hon. Mr. P. Ramanathan, C.M.G., K.C., and was enrolled as an Advocate in 1892. He practised for several years at Jaffna, and since 1906 he has settled down permanently in Colombo.

The subject of this sketch is descended from an ancient and well-known family of Jaffna. His father was the youngest son of Coomáravél and a grandson of Rájanáyaga Mudaliyár, who, in his turn, was the son of Sangarappillai and the grandson of Tillainâyaga Mudaliyar. On his mother's side, he is the grandson of Sittampalam, the grandson of Veerakatti Udayar, who was the great-grandson of Peria Tamby Udayar. In 1896 Mr. Tiru-Návuk-Arasu married, in Colombo, Taiyal-Náyaki, the eldest daughter of the Hon. Dr. W. G. Rockwood, M.D., M.R.C.S., who was twice nominated as Tamil Member of the Legislative Council of Ceylon. She is a great student of Sanskrit literature, her special study being the Bhagavat-Gita, which is an exposition of the Hindú Vedantha philosophy. Mr. Tiru-Návuk-Arasu practised as an Advocate for several years at Jaffna. Since 1906 they have permanently settled down in Colombo at their residence, "Mahendra," Barnes Place, Cinnamon Gardens.

WILLIAM ALFRED GOONE-TILLEKE.

Mr. William Alfred Goone-Tilleke—or as he prefers to call himself, Mr. Tilleke—is the

W. A. G. TILLEKE.

eldest son of the late Chief Mudaliyar, Mr. Moses Goonetilleke, of Kandy, who was a Justice of the Peace for the Central Province and also held the high rank of Gate Mudaliyar. On both sides of his parentage he has inherited the turn for scholarship, being descended from two of the ablest scholars that Ceylon produced in the last century. His father's brother, the late Mr. William Goonetilleke, was well-known as a linguist, being master of the French, German, Dutch, Italian, English, and several Asiatic languages; and was also an able lawyer. This uncle was, however, best known as editor and proprietor of the *Orientalist*; and he was twice nominated by the Kandyan people, at monster meetings, as the Sinhalese Representative in the Legislative Council of the island. Mudaliyar Louis Wijesinghe, a maternal uncle, was also a distinguished Oriental scholar, and has often been referred to by European Orientalists, including Professors Childers and Rhys Davids, as having been of great assistance to them in their works. He is perhaps best known as the translator of the Mahavansa (the ancient Sinhalese Chronicle) from the Pali text into English prose—work undertaken and completed by him at the request and cost of the Ceylon Government, Sir Arthur Gordon (now Lord Stanmore) having specially selected him for the task.

Mr. W. A. G. Tilleke, the subject of this notice, was born in 1860, was educated at St. Thomas's College, and was subsequently an undergraduate of the Calcutta University. He was for some time editor of his college magazine as well as a prominent member of the College Debating Club. Soon after leaving college, he entered upon the study of the law, and in June, 1884, he passed one of the severest examinations for admission into the legal profession, Chief Justice Burnside, who directed the tests, being then bent upon raising the standard of legal education. Out of nineteen students who presented themselves at this particular examination only two satisfactorily answered the questions set by the Chief Justice preparatory to the final examination. After admission to the Ceylon Bar, Mr. Tilleke practised in Kandy, where, in 1885, he was elected a Municipal Councillor, and was, during the two years following, a Magistrate of the Municipal Court. Mr. Tilleke left Ceylon about seventeen years ago and travelled through India, Burma, and the Straits Settlements, finally settling down in Siam. At the present time he holds the important position of Attorney-General of Siam, which he has now filled for ten years.

HECTOR ALFRED JAYEWARDENE.

The senior of six brothers, of whom five have entered the legal profession, Mr. H. A. Jayewardene was born at Colombo in July, 1870. He received his education at the Wesley and Royal Colleges, and was afterwards articled to the Hon. A. de A. Senewiratne, M.L.C., and Advocate of the Supreme Court. Having been called to the Bar as an Advocate of the Supreme Court in May, 1893, Mr. Jayewardene chose his native city as the sphere for the practice of his profession, and has since worked his way up in the Colombo Courts. He is the President of the Law Students' Union and a member of the Council of Advocates. He was appointed Editor of the New Law Reports of the Supreme Court of Ceylon on the retirement of Mr. P. Ramanathan, K.C., C.M.G., in 1905, which are issued under the authority of the Government. In 1899 Mr. H. A. Jayewardene was elected member for the New Bazaar Ward in the Municipal Council of Colombo, following on the retirement of Mr. Walter Pereira, K.C. He is the author of "Law of Mortgage in Ceylon," a member of the Orient and Turf Clubs, President of the Grandpass Literary Association, member of the District Road Committee of the Western Province, and member of the Friend-in-Need Society. His private residence is Jayewardene Walauwa (ancestral home), Grandpass. He owns the well-known Mudukatuwa estate of 800 acres, near Negombo, which was granted by Government to his greatgrandfather, Don Adrian Jayewardene, for military services

JAYEWARDENE WALAUWA, GRANDPASS, THE ANCESTRAL HOME OF THE JAYEWARDENE FAMILY.

MR. AND MRS. E. W. JAYEWARDENE. E. W. JAYEWARDENE IN HIS OFFICE.
THE BUNGALOW. MOHANDIRAM'S WARRANT.

rendered to the first British Governor of Ceylon.

EUGENE WILFRED JAYEWARDENE.

Mr. Jayewardene is a son of James Alfred Jayewardene, Proctor, and a great-grandson of Don Adrian Wijesinghe, Mudaliyar, who rendered signal services to the English during their wars with the Kandyan king (1800–1815). This scion of a well-known Sinhalese family of Colombo was born at Kalutara on June 11, 1874, and was placed at the Royal College, Colombo, at an early age, where he had a very successful career. He left college in 1893 to follow the profession which his brothers and father before him had chosen to adopt—the profession of the law. His term at school was remarkable for the brilliant distinctions which he successively achieved, first showing promise of great talents and parts by winning the Queen's Scholarship in 1888, whilst in the fifth form, and adding to this success in the years that followed by gaining the Cambridge Junior Local Exhibition in 1889, the Turnour Prize in 1891, the prize offered by the Director of Public Instruction, also in 1891, the Todd Prize in 1893, and the prize subscribed to by the Old Boys' Association of the college in 1892. Mr. Jayewardene was engaged in editing the *Royal College Magazine* while at that scholastic establishment, and also enrolled himself in the cadet battalion attached to that institution. He still interests himself largely in the affairs of his *alma mater*, and is the hon. secretary of the Old Boys' Association, which includes a number of distinguished *alumni* of the college. Passing out of the school in 1893, Mr. Jayewardene read for the law, and qualified himself as a student-professional by successfully taking up the preliminary examination in 1894, with a "special mention" to his credit. After a further course of study he passed his intermediate examination in 1895; and two years later he graduated in law by passing the final examination, with similar results as in the case of his first venture, the Council of Legal Education on this occasion commending him highly for the excellence of his papers. He was called to the Ceylon Bar, and admitted and enrolled an Advocate of the Supreme Court of the island in August of 1897. During his apprenticeship for the usual six months preceding his enrolment, he acted, part of the time, as private secretary to Mr. Justice Grenier; and he entered upon practice at the Bar immediately upon his admission.

Mr. Jayewardene has since worked his way to the forefront of the legal profession in Ceylon; and by his forensic eloquence and sound knowledge of the various systems of law which obtain in the colony he has constituted himself one of the luminaries of the Bar, not only of the metropolis, but of the island's courts in general. He is well known as a keen combatant, a finished speaker, and a lucid expounder of legal perplexities, and has been time and again retained as counsel by litigants in remote parts of the island. Among the *causes célèbres* in the legal history of the colony in which Mr. Jayewardene has prominently figured may be mentioned the Peiris will case, in which property to the value of nearly two million rupees was under dispute, the De Mel murder case, and the famous Dehigama land case, which last-named dragged on for over three years. In 1897 the Government of Ceylon engaged Mr. Jayewardene's services to help in the revision and comparison of the new Criminal Procedure Code with the old edition of 1883 and the corresponding Indian codes, and to collate law and statutes referring to the duties and responsibilities of native headmen. He is a member of the General Council of the Bar, and has often been appointed an examiner of candidates for both branches of the legal profession. In 1906 he was appointed Acting Additional District Judge, Police Magistrate, and Commissioner of Requests for Colombo.

Mr. Jayewardene is a landed proprietor in Colombo, and owns the coconut estates of Talgahawatte in the Chilaw district and Kumbaloluwa (200 acres) in the Veyangoda district. He married, in 1905, Agnes Helen, daughter of the late Don Philip Wijewardene, Mohandiram of Seddewatte, who owned very extensive plantations and residential properties in numerous parts of the island.

Mr. Jayewardene received his commission as Second Lieutenant of the Ceylon Light Infantry ("F" Company), in August, 1904, and qualified himself for a captaincy in July of the following year, being attached at present to "F" Company of the local Volunteer force. He is also a member of the Ceylon Volunteer Rifle Association. A man of many-sided activities and apparently inexhaustible energy, he is Vice-President of the Sinhalese Sports Club, a member of the Orient Club, the Turf Club, the Lawn Club, the Victoria Golf Club—all in Colombo—and the Galle Gymkhana; while he has an honorary connection with the Nondescripts Club and the Bloomfield Athletic and Sports Club of Colombo. His recreations are chiefly golf, tennis, and riding. His private residence is Park House, Park Street, Cinnamon Gardens, Colombo.

LIONEL WRIGHT.

Dr. Lionel Wright, of Jaela, is a gentleman of versatile talents. He was the first Ceylonese to take to music as a profession after studying for quite another calling. He was born in 1860, and received his early school education in Ceylon, first privately and afterwards at Colombo Academy and Wesley College. His father was the late Mr. John Wright, who carried on business as a dispensing chemist in Colombo, and whose name was a household word amongst the Burghers, rich and poor alike. Upon the completion of his college course in Ceylon Mr. L. Wright entered Edinburgh University in 1880, and was so thoroughly painstaking whilst there that his note-books on chemistry, botany, and physiology were in common use by the students "cramming" for exams. From his boyhood days he displayed an intense passion for music, and during his residence in Edinburgh he composed the "Dalmeny Waltz," dedicated to the late Countess of Rosebery, and another composition of his, "Humoresque," was played by the Lyceum orchestra. He also organised an orchestra of his own and conducted others

L. WRIGHT.

in different parts of England, where he lived for some years after the completion of his University course. In 1895, after an absence of fifteen years, he returned to Ceylon at the request of his aged father, and served as relieving Medical Officer in various up-country stations, and on three occasions acted as Sanitary Officer of Colombo. He was, however, being gradually wooed back to music, and finally threw in his lot with that art entirely by becoming Professor of Music at St. Joseph's College. Whilst there he trained an orchestra, composed a Mass and several beautiful hymns, and did much for the choir. In 1902 he resumed the practice of medicine at Jaela, and has been there ever since. Mr. Wright is also an expert amateur photographer and a keen chess-player. He is a member of the Royal Photographic Society of England, of the Hale Chess Association, and of the local Photographic Society. In 1902 he married Antoinette Gertrude, daughter of the late Mr. Austin Fernando, planter, of Kurunegala, and he has one son and one daughter.

L. M. MAARTENSZ.

Lewis Matthew Maartensz was born in 1876 and educated at St. Thomas's College. He studied law under the Council of Legal Education, and in 1898 was admitted and enrolled an Advocate of the Supreme Court, and practised in Colombo. From July, 1901, he acted as Crown Counsel, and was confirmed in that appointment in 1906. His private residence is "St. Leonards," Flower Road, Colombo.

G. S. SCHNEIDER.

Mr. Gualterus Stewart Schneider, son of G. Frederick Schneider, of Colombo, and grandson of Captain G. Schneider, a military officer in the service of the Dutch East India Company, and afterwards the first Surveyor-General of the colony under the British administration, was born in Colombo in 1864. He received his education at St. Thomas's College, and was an assistant master there for nearly thirteen years, after which he studied law, and was admitted an Advocate, and was called to the Bar in 1898. He practised in Colombo, where he is now one of the best-known figures in legal circles. In 1900 he was appointed Law Lecturer to the Council of Legal Education, and he holds that position at the present time. He is a member of the Society of Advocates and of the Orient and Turf Clubs, and in 1904 he married Glencora Barnes, eldest daughter of Mr. Henry Potger, District Engineer of the Public Works Department. His Colombo house is "Lakshminie," Kynsey Road, and he owns the fine rubber estate Fullarton, in the Kalutara district.

G. S. SCHNEIDER. "LAKSHMINIE." MRS. G. S. SCHNEIDER.

WILLIAM WADSWORTH.

Mr. William Wadsworth, of Jaffna, was born on November 8, 1875. He is the youngest son of the late Charles Mailvaganam Wadsworth, who was headmaster of the C.M.S. Training Institution at Copay, Jaffna. Mr. Wadsworth, jun., was educated at the Grammar School at Copay, and at St. John's College, Jaffna, where he took his degree of Bachelor of Arts of the Calcutta University in March, 1897. Having passed the examination for clerical service under the Government in 1895, he was appointed to a post in the General Treasury, Colombo, in 1897. This post he resigned after three months, and was admitted a student-at-law. He won the scholarship awarded on the results of the intermediate examination by the Council of Legal Education. In September, 1901, he was called to the Ceylon Bar, and is now practising his profession in Co ombo. He acted as Crown Counsel for the island for three months from November, 1903. In April, 1904, he married Clarissa Alagamuttu, youngest daughter of the late Mr. Arthur Edwards, of Vadukoddai, Jaffna.

FREDERIC JOSEPH DE MEL.

This son of Mr. Jacob De Mel, a scion of the well-known Vidanelage family, was educated at the Royal College, Colombo, and St. John's College, Cambridge, at which latter University he graduated with honours in arts and law in 1900. Passing his final examination, he was called to the Bar at the Inner Temple in January, 1901, being then the youngest member of that branch of the legal profession. As junior counsel to Sir Robert Reid, the present Lord Chancellor of England, Mr. De Mel held his first brief in the case of Beale *v.* the Great Western Railway, which was heard before Lord Chief Justice Alverstone. After making a prolonged tour in Europe, where the picture galleries proved a great attraction, Mr. De Mel returned to Ceylon and started legal practice. In 1905 he took the degree of Master of Arts of Cambridge.

Mr. De Mel is a member of the Voetlights, the Agricultural, and the Asiatic (Ceylon) Societies, and of the Turf, Orient, Kennel (Ceylon), National Liberal (London) and Cambridge University Liberal Clubs. In keeping with the family traditions, he is a member of the Synod and a strong supporter of the Church of England. His main recreation is riding. In 1905 he married Cissy, the daughter of Mr. Louis Peiris, of the Whist Bungalow, Colombo, and Bowelikada, Kandy. Mrs. De Mel is well known in Ceylon art circles, being an exhibitor in water-colours and sketches, for which she has obtained numerous prizes. She is also a prominent member of the Poultry Club, besides being one of the finest pigeon fanciers in the island.

MRS. F. J. DE MEL IN SINHALESE NATIONAL DRESS. MR. AND MRS. F. J. DE MEL. A PRIZE WINNER.

ARTHUR WILLIAM ALVIS.

Prolixity is the common failing of memorials in the East; yet when the Burgher community approached Sir West Ridgeway with a memorial desiring the appointment of Mr. Arthur Alvis to represent them in the Legislative Council, they deemed it sufficient to urge, in the course of two brief paragraphs, no more than that he was a respected member of the Burgher community, commanding the respect and confidence of that and the other communities in the colony, and a man of prominence in the legal profession. To the Ceylonese, Mr. Alvis's career is at once an example and an inspiration. It is also a guarantee of what a Ceylonese, unaided by patronage, and sometimes thwarted by influence, may achieve. Mr. F. Dornhorst, K.C., at a public dinner given in Mr. Alvis's honour at the Orient Club, a few years ago, bore willing testimony to this. Mr. Alvis is a type of all that is best and much that is hopeful in the community to which he belongs.

Arthur William Alvis, who was born on June 16, 1856, is the elder and only surviving child of Francis Daniel Alvis (late of the Queen's Advocate's Department), and his wife Louisa de Run. Both the families are amongst the oldest and most respected in the community. He was educated at St. Thomas's College, where his progress, wrote Warden Bacon, "was most marked"—so much so that the Warden thought it his pleasant duty to publicly compliment him on the excellence of his papers. In 1871 he passed the matriculation examination of the Calcutta University. In 1873 Sir Edward Creasy broke the old, easy current of admission into the legal profession by prescribing a preliminary examination of a high standard for proctor students. Mr. Alvis was the first subject of the experiment. The Chief Justice on this occasion made the following note in his own hand, and directed the Registrar to have it recorded: "Mr. Arthur Alvis.—This gentleman has passed, his examination in English, History, and Virgil very well, and is quite fit to be a law student." In 1878 Mr. Alvis was enrolled a Proctor of the District Court. He subsequently became a Proctor of the Supreme Court. In January, 1879, he was appointed Notary Public. He was for many years Examiner in Conveyancing of candidates for the rank of proctors of the Supreme Court and notaries, and has been and is still a member of the Ceylon Council of Legal Education. Mr. Alvis made his entrance into municipal life in 1889. Mr. H. J. C. Pereira, the well-known Ceylonese Barrister-at-Law, one of his oldest friends, proposed his election as member of the Municipal Council for the Kollupitiya Ward. Mr. H. H. Cameron, Mayor and Chairman of the Municipal Council, thus refers to this incident in his Administration

"NEWLANDS," EXTERIOR AND INTERIOR. ARTHUR ALVIS IN HIS LIBRARY.

Report: "On April 25, 1889, Mr. Arthur Alvis was elected in Mr. Maitland's place. On this election both the Council and the ward which Mr. Alvis represents are much to be felicitated, and, indeed, the general admission of the acceptability of the candidate may be taken as a sufficient reason in this instance for the absence of competition." The *Ceylon Examiner*, referring to the election, said: "Mr. Alvis is a young Proctor of proved ability and probity, and commands an extensive legal and notarial business."

Failing health compelled Mr. Alvis in 1890 to abandon Colombo for a time for the drier atmosphere in the north of Ceylon. Very shortly after his arrival in Jaffna the Government appointed him Police Magistrate and Commissioner of the Court of Requests of Jaffna and Mallakam. He also acted on several occasions as District Judge. In 1893 Mr. Alvis resumed his practice at the Bar, and was soon plunged into public life once more, he having been elected member of the Municipal Council for the Fort Ward. He remained in charge of those interests till 1902. Whilst a member of the Council he was selected to sit almost in every committee, and he was for many years also member of the Council's Standing Committee. During his visit to Europe in 1897 he devoted time to the study of what is latest in sanitation, sewerage schemes, the modern methods of housing the poor, &c. When he retired from the Council the *Ceylon Observer* urged that his experience and ability would find greater scope for usefulness in the Legislative Assembly. The *Ceylon Standard* endorsed the suggestion, and said: "There is no man in Colombo who has a higher reputation for probity than Mr. Arthur Alvis. He is an honourable gentleman. We know perfectly well that the work of the local Municipal Council has been but the very smallest of beer to those who have opinions which are not confined to the majority of the trivial matters which are brought before them. Mr. Alvis was wasted at the Town Hall. The *Ceylon Observer* suggests that he would be better fitted for work as a Member of the Legislative Council. We fully endorse our contemporary's opinion."

Mr. Alvis is an enthusiastic Freemason. He was initiated in 1880, and has filled the Master's chair, Sphinx Lodge, 107, I.C. (about the oldest Lodge in Ceylon), more than once. He was one of the founders of Connaught Lodge, No. 2,940, E.C. He is Comp. R.A. Lanka Chapter, Mark Master Mason, Most Excellent Master, Royal Select, and Super-Excellent Master, Ceylon Council, No. 21 (Cryptic degrees). He has received the allied degrees of St. Lawrence the Martyr, Knight of Constantinople, Knight of the Red Cross of Babylon, also the 18° at the Victory Chapter, Rose-Croix (London). He was installed Preceptor and Prior, Colombo Preceptory, 164, E.C., in 1902, acted as such during the whole of 1903, and has been elected again to fill that office. He is also Vice-President, Ceylon Law Students' Union, member (one of the original) of the Orient Club, one of the oldest committee members of the Ceylon National Association, Vice-President of the Chums' Athletic Club, one of the three directors of the only Ceylonese motor-car company in the island, and committee member of a number of institutions, *e.g.*, St. Thomas's Old Boys' Association, Colombo Library, Colombo Law Library, Law Society of Ceylon, &c. In 1882 Mr. Alvis married Madeline, fourth daughter of Mr. J. B. Daniel, of "The Grove," Madampitiya; and of his two daughters—both of whom were educated in England—the elder is married to Mr. Thomas Forrest Garvin, Advocate, Supreme Court, Ceylon. Mr. Alvis resides at "Newlands," Polwatte, Colombo.

JOHN ADRIAN ST. VALENTINE JAYEWARDENE.

The third of five brothers who have entered the legal profession, Mr. J. A. St. V. Jayewardene was educated at the Royal College, after which he studied law and passed

MRS. J. A. ST. V. JAYEWARDENE. "CHÂTEAU JUBILEE." J. A. ST. V. JAYEWARDENE.

MR. AND MRS. CHAS. PEIRIS. "HIGH CROSS" BUNGALOW. THE MILLS.
"CARLSHOLME" BUNGALOW.

C. DE S. BATUVANTUDAVE.

DON ANDRIES DE S. BATUVANTUDAVE.

THE BUNGALOW.

the Bar final examination in 1900, heading the list of the successful candidates in both tests. He won scholarships both at St. Thomas's College and as a law student, besides carrying off the prize essays of his year. He was admitted an Advocate of the Supreme Court in March, 1901, and practised for three years at Galle.

In 1904 Mr. Jayewardene proceeded to England, and, in April of the following year, appeared before the Privy Council in the case of Poonma *v.* Arumogan (Ceylon). He joined the Inner Temple, and was called to the English Bar in July, 1905. After travelling on the Continent, he returned to Colombo, where he has since practised. Mr. Jayewardene is a Fellow of the Royal Colonial Institute, a member of the Society of Advocates, President of the Smallpass Association, a former secretary of the Law Students' Union—which presented him with a valuable set of law works on the occasion of his being called to the Bar. He is a member of the Orient Club. His recreation is tennis. In 1906 he married Ethel Charlotte Irene, only daughter of Mudaliyar and Mrs. Francis William Tillekeratne Dyssanayake, of Matara, and a descendant of one of the oldest Southern Province families in Ceylon. His private residence is "Château Jubilee," Ward Place. He owns coconut and paddy plantations in the North-Western and Southern Provinces. Besides being the author of "The Law of Partition of Ceylon," and "Roman-Dutch Law of Ceylon," Mr. J. A. St. V. Jayewardene contributed the able review of the constitution and laws of Ceylon which is published in another part of this book.

C. DE SILVA BATUVANTUDAVE.

Mr. Charles de Silva Batuvantudave, son of the late celebrated Pundit, D. B. de Silva Batuvantudavè, was born in Colombo, Ceylon, in 1874, and educated at the Royal College, Colombo. After studying law in his native isle, he went to England in 1897 and studied law there, and was called to the Bar at Gray's Inn in June, 1901 On his return to Ceylon he was admitted and enrolled an Advocate of the Honourable the Supreme Court of Ceylon, and practises in Ceylon. He is a member of the Royal Asiatic Society, is on the Committee of Oriental Studies, a member of the Orient and Turf Clubs, vice-president of the Maradana Literary Association, vice-president of the Colombo Theosophical Society, member of the Hardwicke Society in England, secretary of the Social Reform Society, and one of the secretaries of the Ceylon National Association. He is a student of the Sanskrit and Pali languages. His recreations are golf and tennis.

CHARLES PEIRIS.

Mr. Charles Peiris was born at Colombo in the year 1860, and was educated at the Royal College, then known as the Colombo Academy. After leaving school he studied law, and articled himself to Mr. A. O. Joseph, a leading legal practitioner in his time. Mr. Peiris was enrolled a Proctor of the District Court of Colombo in 1882, became a Notary Public in the following year, and in 1902 was admitted a Proctor of the Supreme Court of the island. He commands a large practice, and is well known in the metropolitan Bar, as well as in several out-station courts.

Mr. Peiris is the proprietor of large property in Colombo, and is also the owner of several coconut and rubber estates in the Western, North-Western, and Sabaragamuwa Provinces, of an aggregate acreage of over 2,000. The more important of these plantations are: Serapis, Orange Grove, Carlsfield, Mukalane, Galmoruwa, Sunnymead, Fruithill, and Duncannaike. The produce from these estates is generally sold locally, and one of the principal lines of business transacted is in the manufacture of fibre and yarn, a well-equipped factory being erected on Serapis estate for this purpose.

Mr. Peiris is a member of the Orient Club, the Turf Club, Colombo Poultry Club, Ceylon Agricultural Society, Colombo Agri-Horticultural Society, and the Planters' Association of Kurunegala. He is also a committee member of the Incorporated Law Society of Ceylon. He married, in 1887, Annie, eldest daughter of the late Mr. and Mrs. Jeronis Peiris, of Colombo, and on her death he married Maude, third daughter of Mr. and Mrs. Jacob De Mel, of Villa De Mel, Colombo. Mr. Peiris's private residence is "Carlsholme," Cinnamon Gardens.

E. R. F. DE SILVA WIJEYERATNE.

Mr. Edward Robert Francis de Silva Wijeyeratne is the son of Robert de Silva Wijeyeratne, Notary Public, of Colombo. Born at Moratuwa in 1878, he was educated at the Royal and St. Joseph's Colleges, studied law, and became a Proctor of the District Court of Colombo in August, 1901, and has practised his profession there ever since. In 1906 he married Mary Catherine Jane, eldest daughter of F. J. Lucas Fernando, of Norwood, Havelock Town. He owns coconut estates at Veyangoda and elsewhere, is a member of the Catholic Club and Catholic Union, and his town residence is "St. James," Colpetty.

MR. AND MRS. E. R. F. DE S. WIJEYERATNE.

A. C. G. WIJEYEKOON.

Mr. Abraham Charles Gerard is the son of Mr. Abraham Andrew Stephen Wijeyekoon. He was born on May 5, 1878, and educated at Royal and Wesley Colleges. He proceeded to England in 1898, and was called to the Bar at Gray's Inn in 1901, and returned to Ceylon the same year. He was enrolled as an Advocate of the Supreme Court in 1902. He was appointed to act as Municipal Magistrate and Additional Police Magistrate of Colombo in 1903, Acting Police Magistrate of Colombo, 1904, Acting Crown Counsel, 1905, and Additional Crown Counsel, 1906. His recreations are tennis and walking. He lives at "Ballater," Castle Street.

LAMBERT LOUIS PIERIS.

This scion of a well-known family, the son of the late Mr. Jeronis Pieris, was born at Colombo in 1867 and educated first privately, afterwards at St. Thomas's College, Colombo. He joined his father in planting in the Negombo District and afterwards in Kurunegala, thus enjoying opportunities for acquiring a thorough knowledge of planting in all its branches. In 1896 he started as a planter on his own account, and now owns the estates of Danawkande at Heneratgoda, which is planted with coconuts and tea to an extent of 500 acres and contains a tea factory; also the Halwatte, Kehelkande, and Udupila estates, all near Heneratgoda, where rubber has been opened up to a large extent. He owns, besides, coconut estates in the Chilaw District. The produce of all these estates is sold in the local market.

Mr. Pieris has extensive house property in Colombo and Dehiwela, his city residences being "Fern Bank," Park Street, and St. Cuthbert's, Dickman's Road. He has travelled extensively in England, France, Switzerland, and Italy. In 1900 he married a daughter of Gate Mudaliyar J. A. Mendis Jayawardene, of Moratuwa. He is an amateur photographer, and is also fond of shooting and hunting.

E. A. A. J. JAYEWICKREME.

Mr. Edmund Alexander Amadoru Jayesuriya Jayewickreme, of "The Firs," Gregory's Road, Cinnamon Gardens, Colombo, was born at Hambantota on May 4, 1872, and educated at Trinity College, Kandy, and Royal College, Colombo. In 1894 he joined the Surveyor-General's Department and resigned the Government service in May, 1903, after

COCONUT ESTATE.

LAMBERT L. PIERIS

MR. AND MRS. L. L. PIERIS AND DAUGHTER.

ESTATE BUNGALOW.

"FERN BANK."

serving as an officer of the fixed establishment at various stations in the Southern Province. He is now in practice as a surveyor and leveller, besides owning and superintending coconut estates in the Chilaw District, and coconut, cinnamon and rubber in the Kelani Valley. He is a member of the Ceylon Poultry Club and of the Ceylon Agricultural Society. He is the eldest son of Samuel Harmanis Jayewickreme, retired Mudaliyar, late Shroff of the Kurunegala Kachcheri, and Caroline Sophia, eldest daughter of the late Christian Samaraweera Jayesuriya, Mudaliyar of Magam Pattu, Hambantota district. He married, on

E. A. JAYEWICKREME. MR. AND MRS. E. A. JAYEWICKREME AND CHILD. "THE FIRS" BUNGALOW.

May 7, 1903, Helena Margaret, fourth daughter of Mr. Jacob and the late Mrs. De Mel, of Villa De Mel, Cinnamon Gardens. They have one child, Helena Marjorie De Mel Jayewickreme, born April 10, 1904.

BARON DE LIVERA.

Baron de Livera, son of the Rev. Andrew de Livera, C.M.S., of the Southern Province, was born at Colombo in 1853, and educated at Kotta Christian Institute. He commenced business at the Colombo Wharf, and to-day owns the Cargo Boat Despatch Company, which is fully described in another part of this work. On December 29, 1877, he married Nancy, daughter of Charles de Abrew Rajapakse, Ayurvedic medical practitioner and Oriental scholar, of Colombo. His eldest son, Charles Andrew, was educated at the Royal College, and is now a law student; and his second son, James, is the principal assistant in the business of the Cargo Boat Despatch Company. Altogether he had five sons and five daughters, of whom two daughters are deceased. Mr. de Livera's private residence, "The Anchorage," at Wellawatte, is one of the finest buildings in the suburbs of Colombo, and he also owns "Eden Grove," a Cinnamon Gardens mansion, as well as other house property in Colombo. He has coconut estates in different parts of the island. Formerly he was a member of the Standing Committee of the Anglican Synod, and is the treasurer and a committee member of Christ Church and St. Luke's Church. Baron de Livera is also a member of the Agricultural Society.

RICHARD STEUART PIERIS.

Mr. Richard Steuart Pieris, who is the oldest son of the late Mr. Jeronis Pieris, of "The Firs," Cinnamon Gardens, Colombo—who died in 1894—was born at Moratuwa in 1858. He received his early education at the private academy of Professor R. Burnett, at Colombo, and shortly afterwards proceeded to England, where he entered the Chiswick Collegiate School, London, whence he passed into Cheltenham College. Returning to Ceylon in 1877, on the completion of his studies, he started to learn planting on his father's estate at Maturata, and at the end of three years established himself as a planter on his own account, going in largely for the cultivation of tea, Liberian coffee, and coconuts. He is the owner of the estates well known as the Maragolla group, in the North-Western Province which are nearly 1,000 acres in extent, and where tea, cacao, coconuts, and rubber are produced. He also owns the coconut estate of Bullanella, of 200 acres, in the same district, and is part-proprietor of the Agra Elbedda tea estate in Agrapatna, Dimbula district, of 276 acres, superintended by Mr. A. Ashton, as well as of the Agratenne estate in the Badulla district, of about 900 acres, of which Mr. J. Duncan is the superintendent. He is also the proprietor of several other coconut plantations of varying areas, from 75 to 300 acres each, scattered in the Chilaw and Kurunegala districts. Cinnamon is grown on some of Mr. Pieris's low-country estates, and this spice, as well as the produce from his other

BARON DE LIVERA.

THE FAMILY.

"THE ANCHORAGE."

"EDEN GROVE."

properties, is generally disposed of in the local market.

In addition to owning the above plantations, Mr. Pieris also controls several large plumbago mines, of which the better known are those of Walpolla, Meegahatenne, and Wandagahena, the former being situated in the Wattagama district, while the latter two are in the Kalutara district of the Western Province. The plumbago from the mines, like all other products of Mr. Pieris's properties, is sold in the local market; but until recently this mineral output was exported in large quantities to the Continent of Europe.

RICHARD LOUIS DE FONSEKA PIERIS. "BROOMHILL" BUNGALOW. R. S. PIERIS.

Mr. Pieris' private residence in Colombo is at "Broomhill," Green Path, Cinnamon Gardens, while he has country seats at Agrapatna and Bandarawala. He is the proprietor of a good deal of land in the capital city. He is a member of the Church of England, while, as a keen sportsman, he belongs to the Turf Club. He was an ardent cricket and football player in his younger days, and is devoted to hunting and shooting. In 1886 he married Adeline Winifred, daughter of the late Mr. Simon Reynold de Fonseka, Proctor and landed proprietor, of "River View," Kalutara South. The eldest son of this union is Mr. Richard Louis de Fonseka Pieris, who was born at Colombo in 1889, and educated at Queen's College. This son proceeded to England in 1900 to prosecute his further studies at Hartfield College, Eastbourne, and has now entered Trinity College, Glen Almond, where he is preparing for Oxford. Mr. Pieris's second son, Lionel Fonseka, who is at present pursuing a term of instruction at the Training College, Colombo, also expects to complete his higher education in England.

DON PHILIP MOHANDIRAM AND HIS FAMILY.

The municipal limits of Colombo on the northern side end at the river Kelani, and from this extreme limit runs a road, inwards along the river, and this road is the centre of Seddewatte, or Orta de Seddewatte, as it was known in older times. This "garden of silk," as the name implies, is one of the survivals of the days when sericulture was more prevalent than it is now. The industry has entirely died out in Seddewatte, and in its place has grown up the timber trade. Huge logs are floated down the river in rafts, and these find a temporary home in Seddewatte till carted away by building contractors to all parts of the town. The timber king here was Don Philip Mohandiram, who died in 1903. He built up an enormous trade in timber. He was the chief purveyor to Government, and his yards supplied all the wood required by the Public Works Department for bridges all over the island. He supplied also all the building timber wanted by the military garrisoned here, and he, besides, undertook enormous contracts for timber during the building of the southern arm of the breakwater. This last contract was a hard one to fulfil, but Don Philip never once failed, and the success with which he discharged his liabilities earned for him the honorary title of Mohandiram from the Government.

In private life Don Philip Mohandiram was a quiet and unobtrusive man. He was possessed of a large amount of house property in Colombo, and he was the soundest man, financially, of all the wealthy natives. Nevertheless, he lived a most retiring life. A staunch Buddhist, he observed the rigorous requirements of that religion as to almsgiving most rigidly. His charities knew no bounds, and among his many unostentatious works of the kind is a Buddhist temple which he built for the use of the many hundreds of indigent

THE LATE DON PHILIP WIJEWARDENE.
(Mohandiram.)

"KOHOMBE" ESTATE, CHILAW.

WALAUWA, SEDDEWATTE.

MRS. DON PHILIP WIJEWARDENE.

people who lived around his mansion and his timber-yards. He was heartily seconded in all his efforts by his wife, a lady of most estimable and attractive personality. She survives him to-day. His business has passed into the hands of his eldest son, Mr. Don Philip Alexander Wijewardene, who was created a Mohandiram in 1906. Mr. Wijewardene, jun., has brought a college education to help him in his work, and while keeping to the place in the timber trade his father earned by dint of hard work and shrewd calculation, he has added to that business by opening a brick store, which already is the largest in the island. The second son of the family, Mr. Louis Wijewardene, is of a mechanical turn of mind, and has considerable working knowledge of electricity. He has his engines and dynamos to help him in this hobby. He has just fitted a coir fibre mill at Mirigama, one centre of the coconut industry, and has some fine machinery there. The rest of the family number five sons and two daughters, one of the latter having just been married to Mr. E. W. Jayawardene, one of the rising young advocates of Colombo. Mention should also be made of the third and fourth son, Messrs. D. R. and D. E. Wijewardene. The elder of the two is reading for the Bar, while the other means to adopt medicine as his profession.

HENRY A. PIERIS.

Prominent among the owners of land in Colombo and various country districts is Mr. Henry A. Pieris. "Elscourt," Turret Road, Colombo, where he resides, is situated in pleasant sylvan surroundings. Mr. Pieris is largely interested in the industry of growing coconuts—the "Consols of Ceylon planting"—having an estate of 800 acres in the Kurunegalà district devoted to the cultivation of this product. This property is a model of its kind, the soil being fairly drained without being allowed to become arid. Here the average number of plants, at intervals of 24 ft. apart, is sixty to the acre. The nuts are plucked once in two months, and the result of a "plucking" is about 200,000 nuts. After the kernels have been dried on the estate, the copra thus obtained is sent in bags by rail to the Colombo brokers for sale, the railway station of Kurunegala, on the Northern line, being distant not more than 2½ miles from the plantation. The plucking is done by contract, the work being performed by Tamil coolies imported from India. It is satisfactory to learn that no trouble is experienced with this class of labourers. The Sinhalese villagers, however, who are occasionally employed, are not found to be reliable. Mr. Pieris visits his Kurunegala estate once in two or three months, and a report on the operations carried on there is prepared every month. Under the will of his late mother Mr. Pieris inherited several other valuable properties situated in various parts of the city of Colombo, also coconut estates in several plantation districts. As the coconut industry promises to continue in its present flourishing condition—a ready market existing for all that can be supplied in this leading line of production—the outlook for this gentleman's planting business is very promising.

Mr. Pieris also owns considerable house property in Colombo, consisting principally of bungalows let on monthly tenancies, mostly to Europeans. Among these properties are "Rosebank" and "Fincastle" in Cinnamon Gardens, also a block of 19 acres in the same locality. He is, besides, the owner of "The Firs" (now St. Bridget's Convent), "The Tent" (the habitat of the Girls' Friendly Society), and, in Colpetty, of "Fairlight" and "Leyland House," a seaside boarding establishment; also of "Luke Place" and "Bon Accord," two bungalows near the Wellawatte toll bar. Under his mother's will Mr. Pieris is also entitled to certain large mills, covering about six acres of land, called the Victoria Mills, now in the occupation of Messrs. Crossfield, Lampard & Co., with the adjoining bungalows,

"ROSEBANK." "FINCASTLE." "FAIRLIGHT."

THE COPRA SHED.

VIEW FROM "THE UPLANDS" BUNGALOW.

H. A. PIERIS'S ESTATE RESIDENCE.

THE ESTATE BUNGALOW.

"THE UPLANDS" BUNGALOW, KANDY

one of which is the Chemical Laboratory of the Government Analyst, Mr. Kelway Bamber. He has, besides, proprietary interests in other residential blocks of land; while at Kandy he owns the well-known health resort "The Uplands," for many years the residence of the late Mr. Alexander Philip, who was secretary of the Planters' Association. This bungalow commands a fine view of the charming surrounding hill-country at this celebrated beauty-spot. Mr. Pieris is in the prime of life, and is a man of great energy and strenuous business habits; but he finds his hands too full with his own business to have time for taking part in public affairs. His hobby is horticulture, and he is a member of the Agri-Horticultural Society of Ceylon.

PRINS AND BRITO.

The legal gentlemen who established and still carry on the firm of Prins and Brito, legal practitioners, notaries, and conveyancers, are Francis Albert Prins, jun., and Christopher Maloji Brito. The former is the son of the well-known Mr. F. A. Prins, the veteran Proctor, J.P. and U.P.M., of Matala. He was born at Colombo in 1869, and after being educated privately he was articled for the study of law under Mr. Hector Van Cuylenburg. In May, 1892, he was enrolled a Proctor of the District Court of Colombo, and was admitted a Proctor of the Supreme Court and Notary Public in 1897. Mr. C. M. Brito is the son of Mr. Christopher Brito, Advocate of the Supreme Court of Ceylon. He was educated at the Royal College, and received his legal training under Mr. P. Ramanathan, K.C., late Member of the Legislative Council and Solicitor-General. He became a Proctor of the District Court in 1893 and of the Supreme Court and Notary Public in 1906.

J. V. NUGARA.

Among the medical practitioners of Colombo is Dr. J. V. Nugara, of 96, Fourth Cross Street, Pettah, who founded his practice in the year 1870, having previously held an appointment in the Ceylon Medical Service for five years. At the present time Dr. Nugara is practising in Colombo and its suburbs, having an extensive connection among the Parsees and Bombay merchants. Dr. J. V. Nugara was born in Ceylon in the year 1848, and was educated at St. Thomas's College, Colombo. He is a practitioner in all ordinary diseases, and is also a Registrar of Births and Deaths.

J. V. NUGARA.

PLUMBAGO

By E. MANNHEIMER, A.M., T.I.M.E.

PLUMBAGO, which is the Latin term for graphite, has, during the past few years, come into considerable prominence in Ceylon, and to-day forms the chief mineral product for purposes of export, and ranks fifth in the list of articles which help to make up the outward trade of the island. The mineral is a form of carbon constituted largely of matters of organised nature drawn principally from the vegetable kingdom, and really represents vegetable growth, which, through various actions and forces of nature, such as moisture, heat, friction, pressure, electricity or magnetism, has in course of time become mineralised. It is found in various shapes and conditions more or less definitely crystallised, foliated, columnar, needle-shaped, or of massive substance; in fact, it may be said that graphite, next to the diamond, is the most highly crystallised form of carbon, and even the diamond when burned will become pure graphite. It is found in various places in the island, and occurs mostly in the granulites and some of the crystalline limestones of Ceylon, but only when it is discovered in beds or veins running parallel to the foliation planes of the virgin rock does its quantity, substance, and quality make it of use for commercial purposes. It is often found mixed with quartz, mica, felspar, and pyrites of various descriptions, but more often in its pure natural state, the veins running from two inches to over six feet in thickness. Before going into the history of the plumbago industry in Ceylon, it may be stated that Ceylon is by no means the only place in the world where this mineral is found and worked for commercial purposes. Cumberland at one time was the main producing country for graphite, and the Cumberland black lead and pencils attained a universal name for excellence and purity. Bavaria, more especially the Passau district, Bohemia, the United States of America, Mexico, and especially the Ural Mountains of Russia, as well as the Biakal ranges of Central Siberia, and, lastly, Canada, furnish an abundance of the mineral, but in no case has it yet been shown that any of these countries can produce an article of the purity and quality of Ceylon plumbago. Although graphite in Ceylon has only come into prominence within the last twenty-five years, it must by no means be understood that the mineral was unknown in former days. As far as European records are concerned, we find that Robert Knox, who wrote in 1681, mentions the existence of the mineral; whilst even at a somewhat earlier period the Dutch Governor, Ryklof Van Goens, in 1675, writing to his successor, Governor-General Jan Maatsuyker, mentions the existence of veins of "potloot" in the hills and several parts of the maritime provinces, describing it as a product of quicksilver, and the discovery was deemed so important that a military guard was placed over the mine, which was said to have existed in the vicinity of Colombo. It also appears that the last king of Kandy saw the possibility of drawing revenue from the mining of plumbago, and the fact of one of his officers superintending the working of the mineral near Kegalla seems to point in that direction.

There is no record that the mineral was exported from the island earlier than 1825, and the first known shipment consigned to Mr. Joseph Dixon, the founder of the great American Crucible Company, left the island in 1829, and Colonel Colebrooke, one of the Commissioners in Ceylon affairs, stated in his report that provision had been made for the delivery of cinnamon and black lead in the Kandyan provinces (which then included the seven Korales) at fixed rates. The first official mention of plumbago occurs in 1831, when it was included in the list of articles liable to export duty, the rate being 10d. per cwt., and in the year 1832 the revenue accruing to Government from that source amounted to £22 18s. 6d. sterling. There are various causes which combine to make the Ceylon plumbago a profitable article for commercial enterprise, and there are several reasons why the mineral obtained from other countries cannot successfully compete with it. One of these reasons may be that the cost of labour in mining, cleansing, and forwarding the mineral must be far more excessive in foreign countries, but the very fact that Ceylon plumbago is so much superior to any other turned out gives it an undoubted advantage over everything else in the market.

The Ceylon article is very refractory. One might take a piece of local plumbago with sharp needle-like projecting angles and subject it to heat which would melt steel, and yet one would find that the very finest points after that trial would not have been affected in any way. The sight of the mineral in its virgin bed in a plumbago mine is an exceedingly striking and pretty one. It is found in beds in a pure state, removed in lumps, and a selection of these forms the "prime lump" of commerce. The formation most common in a pure state is that of laminated crystals elongated at right angles to the side of the vein, if that vein is not more than four to six inches wide; but when the vein widens the crystallisation often radiates from numerous centres, and the sight then is a very beautiful one. The foliated variety is equally valuable and more brilliant, but it is rarely found in any quantity. The acicular form of crystal is not apt to be as pure in the lump, but is useful for most purposes. The granulite variety, the purest of all, is of little use for crucibles, but with suitable manipulation produces the finest grades for electrotyping and lead pencils, and is unequalled for lubricating purposes.

Pure plumbago is free from grit when pulverised and rubbed between the fingers, and the polish, used in the same way, is instantaneous and very bright, being like a darker shade of polished silver.

Turning to statistics, we find that in the year 1834 plumbago to the quantity of 2,582 cwts. was exported, valued at Rs. 12,000. In 1836 the quantity had risen to 12,644 cwts., valued at Rs. 14,663; in 1839 it had dropped to 423 cwts., valued at Rs. 490; whilst in 1846 it was again some 25,000 cwts., valued at Rs. 30,000. The highest export of this early period was obtained in 1869, when the amount despatched reached 226,131 cwts., valued at Rs. 890,000. During the subsequent years up to 1884 the industry kept on fluctuating, and whilst 1883 saw the then high-water mark with 262,773 cwts., valued at Rs. 2,627,737, it dropped the following year to 182,000 cwts., valued at Rs. 1,825,000.

As graphite is principally used in the manufacture of crucibles as well as stove lead and pencils, the expanse of the British and American steel trade, the introduction of the steel and wire gun, the steel armour of the modern warship, and the numerous steel machinery built up for the purposes of peaceful construction or military and naval armaments, naturally necessitated an increased amount of plumbago for purposes of crucibles, and spurred the industry in Ceylon to greater effort. We find the output steadily rising, until the remarkable boom of the last year of the nineteenth century saw the export of 616,380 cwts., or nearly 31,000 tons, and fortunes were made; but, sad to relate, more fortunes were lost in the wild and mad speculation which followed that period. It should here be stated that the figures of value given before the period of 1884 are calculated on the reckoning of Rs. 10 to the pound sterling. After the excitement of the close of the nineteenth century the inevitable slump followed; numerous mines closed down, and in 1900 the shipments fell to 383,240 cwts., or 19,162 tons, showing a decrease of 233,140 cwts., or 11,657 tons, on the previous year. This naturally had the result of materially steadying the market, restoring confidence, and, of course, increasing exports, and the following figures more than eloquently speak for themselves:—

Year.	Export.
1901	22,663 tons
1902	24,775 „
1903	23,943 „
1904	25,787 „
1905	31,395 „
1906	35,183 „

Prices, too, although not reaching the fancy figure of Rs. 1,000 per ton (at this stage Rs. 15 to the pound) of 1899, have steadied considerably, and have been very satisfactory, ranging from Rs. 525 to Rs. 650 in the higher grades, and Rs. 205 to Rs. 420 in the lower grades of the article. The Government at various times exacted royalties at different rates from the export of plumbago, but latterly the royalty has been Rs. 5 per ton on all graphite shipped. The island's best customers throughout have been the U.S.A., with the United Kingdom as a fair second. The following table will show the principal countries of distribution during the periods 1905 and 1906:—

Country.	1905.	1906.
United Kingdom ...	8,256 tons	9,383 tons
Belgium	2,763 „	3,201 „
Germany	5,534 „	6,362 „
America	13,116 „	15,495 „
France	147 „	239 „
Russia	143 „	62 „
Japan...	1,155 „	130 „

Plumbago is mined in various parts of the island, the principal mines being situated in the Pasdun and Rayigam Korales of the Kalutara district and in the Kelani Valley of the Western Province, the Dodangaslanda, the Maduragoda, and the Ragedere, as well as the Paragoda and Galagedara portions of the Kurunegala district of the North-Western Province, at Udugama, Ambalangoda, Morawak Korale, Weligama, and other portions of the Southern Province, in the Kegalla and the Ratnapura districts of the Sabaragamuwa Province, in portions of the Matale district and the Maskeliya district of the Central Province. The industry gives employment to, roughly, 16,700 males and 3,750 females, with dependents numbering another 15,000, making a total of about 36,000 people. There are innumerable so-called pits all over the island, but only comparatively few proper mines on a large scale, and, generally speaking, mining is carried out on very primitive lines, and is open to a great deal of improvement in every direction. Wherever an outcrop of plumbago or mica occurs on the surface, the procedure is to sink a trial shaft in the shape of a parallelogram, varying in size, generally 8 ft. by 6 ft., which traverses the soft shale and earth formation, following the vertical vein until it strikes the solid rock. This portion, of course, necessitates timbering, and this is carried out by means of roughly sawn planks which, placed against the sides of the shaft, are held in position by vertical pieces, which in turn are supported by transverse quarterings either drawn from centre to centre or dovetailed along the corners of the shaft into the vertical supports. After a certain depth has been reached in this fashion, and rock has been met, timbering is done away with, and a tunnel is driven at right angles from the shaft in almost any direction in which a vein of plumbago may appear. This tunnel, again, will end in a small platform, from which a second shaft is sunk to a lower level, and in this manner, sinking and driving on various levels, a depth of nearly 800 ft. has been obtained in some of the principal mines. It is, however, to be regretted that in most mines no system whatever is followed, and when a vein is struck it is the miner's sole endeavour to follow up that vein, work it out in the quickest time possible, not paying the slightest regard whether his drive may go upwards or downwards, whether it may contain sufficient fresh air or not, whether it may be 7 ft. or 2 ft., and in this fashion most of the older pits are a collection of rabbit warrens, adits, tunnels, drives, shafts, jumbled together without rhyme or reason, and the labour wasted and time thrown away must have been enormous. The rock is drilled by hand in the vicinity of a vein in holes varying from 1 ft. to 6 ft. in depth. These holes are fired by means of blasting powder or dynamite charges, and after allowing sufficient time for the fumes to clear away, the *débris* clearers will swarm in, remove the loose matter to the foot of the nearest shaft, where two barrels on a chain drawn round a wooden winch or roller supply the means of hoisting it to the next level, when it will be carted along the tunnel to the foot of the next shaft, again hoisted, and thus, in a succession of cartage and hoisting, go to the mouth of the pit.

In fairness to the industry, it must be stated that the Sinhalese mine owner of to-day (provided he is of progressive mind and educated) is fully alive to the wastage of time and labour going on, and a great deal of money has of late been spent in steam hoisting, lifting, and pumping gear of elaborate description, and on light trolley lines for the conveyance of matter from inside the pit to the sheds at the foot of the mine.

The greatest enemy of the miner in Ceylon is water, either from internal springs in the rock or from the effects of the monsoon rains, and this water is apt to rise with alarming suddenness, driving the men from their work, flooding the mine, and suspending operations for almost half the year. If there is no pumping gear and the season keeps wet, and no appreciable impression can be made by mere baling by hand, the mine is abandoned, and there are to-day hundreds of valuable properties which might be worth millions to the owners if worked on proper scientific lines. With the introduction of steam machinery and powerful pumps, the aspect of mining in Ceylon will soon be changed, the cost reduced considerably, and the output increased in proportion; and it is encouraging to note that the younger generation of mine owners are steadily working in that direction. The industry is practically in native hands, and that is Sinhalese. Most Europeans who have tried have failed by going at it on too big a scale, from want of knowledge and from totally misunderstanding the ways of local labour. Yet there are several European mines, or, at least, under European management, which are very flourishing to-day.

The labour employed in the mines is Sinhalese throughout, and the best workmen are those drawn from the Southern Province, where the occupation is practically hereditary in the family, the father teaching the son as he has been taught by his own father before. The labour is mostly drawn from villages surrounding the mines, and in most cases these men own small paddy fields which have to be cultivated; and this was responsible for the introduction, years and years ago, of the twenty-four hours' shift: that is to say, a man would be sent into the mine at six o'clock in the morning, would work till six at night with one interruption of one hour only, and then after a further hour's rest was supposed to work right through till six o'clock the following morning. As the atmosphere inside these mines, which are extremely badly ventilated, was anything but pleasant, it could hardly be expected that a labourer could do justice to his employers in the second half of his twenty-four hours' shift, and it is to be hoped that mine owners will learn to see the iniquity and uselessness of a system which calls for impossibilities from the working men, and under which no man could do justice to his employers. A few of the progressive owners have done away with this and are now working the men at shifts of twelve hours.

Wages vary very much. The head cooly, or underground-section captain, may be paid anything from 75 cents to Rs. 1·50 cents per day of twelve hours; strikers and drillers from 45 to 70 cents, and general hands from 30 to 50 cents. Women and children, who are engaged in sorting and sizing the material in the sheds outside the mine, and are mostly the relatives and dependents of the mine workers, are paid from 15 to 30 cents per diem.

The work undoubtedly is very hard; the changes of temperature from the stifling, moist heat at the workhead at the lowest level to the upper-level galleries, which are very draughty and cold, and the dry heat outside, are apt to ruin the best constitution; and yet there is comparatively little illness amongst the workpeople, and phthisis or pneumonia is almost unknown. Formerly the mines used to be the gathering-place of criminals of the worst type, but this has been checked of late by the owners, and is not nearly as bad as the local public is apt to believe. It is not necessary to go into the method by which the plumbago is cleaned and freed from mineral substances after it leaves the mine, as this is fully illustrated in the numerous photographs which follow this article, and which are fully described under their respective heads. It only remains to be added that the industry has received a new impetus from the formation of the Plumbago Merchants' Union, which is fully described elsewhere. This organisation tends to safeguard the interests of the industry, which undoubtedly has a tremendous scope, and which in the future is sure to expand on lines to-day practically undreamt of in the island of Ceylon.

PLUMBAGO MERCHANTS.

THE MINING INDUSTRY.

THE PLUMBAGO MERCHANTS' UNION.

The history of this Union is synchronous with the growth and development in Ceylon of the plumbago industry—that is, mining, curing, and shipping of the mineral known as plumbago. This mineral, since its first appearance in the form of an article of export in 1832, has, as is shown in Captain Mannheimer's article, slowly developed until it has become the most extensive native industry in the island, giving employment to a large proportion of the native labour force available. As the trade in plumbago gradually came to be recognised as an important asset by the native capitalists of Ceylon, the necessity for safeguarding their interests became obvious as a matter of course. A beginning being made with informal meetings of the leading merchants, held when permitted by the fluctuations of the market, an association of plumbago merchants was

PLUMBAGO MERCHANTS' UNION.

formed, which first met in 1888 to consider how best the interests of the trade would be conserved by united action. This association continued its scope of usefulness until 1900, when, under the name of the Plumbago Dealers' Association, it formally espoused the welfare of the industry, under the beneficent influence of the phenomenal rise of the value of the mineral in that year, which averaged as much as Rs. 1,200 (£80) for a ton of the best quality. Thereafter, the association did useful work until 1905, when it assumed the name of the Plumbago Merchants' Union, and established itself on a footing firmer than before. The Union holds meetings at regular intervals, the scope of its business embracing all practicable measures to insure fair and just treatment to all engaged in the trade. It is supported by all interested in the industry; and, judging from the whole-hearted energy with which the work of the Union is carried on and the enthusiastic welcome with which it has been received by the general public, it promises to continue as a tower of strength for the plumbago merchants.

In justification of its representative character, the Union is under the patronage of the Hon. Mr. S. C. Obeyesekere, representative of the low-country Sinhalese in the Legislative Council, the President being Mr. H. B. Fernando, a veteran in the local plumbago trade. The other officials are Mr. R. A. Mirando, Vice-President, and Messrs. C. P. Seneviratne and A. Mendis, hon. secretaries. With a membership of 82 well-known native merchants and miners, the Union has its office in Chatham Street, one of the principal thoroughfares of the Fort of Colombo, a location which constitutes a convenient business centre for all interested in the trade. Messrs. N. D. P. Silva, W. A. Fernando, and U. D. S. Gunasekara are the acknowledged pioneers of the movement which conduced to the foundation of the Plumbago Merchants' Union, while Mr. Jacob De Mel's connection with it has contributed not a little to add to its present popularity. A representative association of this nature in connection with a staple industry fulfills an important purpose and may be regarded as indispensable to the prosperity of an industry upon which, as is the case with plumbago, depends, in part, the welfare of the premier Crown Colony. As the sphere of the Union's usefulness widens with the passage of the years and the development of the plumbago industry of Ceylon, it may be relied upon to continue to exert a useful influence in promoting the best interests of those engaged in the business of winning this mineral from the earth and preparing and shipping it for the world's market.

DON CHARLES GEMORIS ATTYGALLE, Mudaliyar.

The late Mr. Don Charles Gemoris Attygalle was born at Madapata, in the Salpiti Korale of the Western Province, in the year 1834. When

THE LATE D. C. G. ATTYGALLE, MUDALIYAR, THE WALAUWA AT COLAMUNNE, AND THE MONUMENT ERECTED TO HIS MEMORY AT COLAMUNNE.

COCONUT ESTATE, DODANGASLANDA.

PIT HEAD AT KAHATAGAHA MINE, DODANGASLANDA.

THE POLWATTEPITIYA STORES.

KURUNEGALA REST-HOUSE.

(Presented to the Headmen of the North-Western Province by the late D. C. G. Attygalle, Mudaliyar.)

only twelve years old he joined the staff of the Royal Botanic Gardens at Peradeniya. He remained six years in this employ, at first learning botany, and then engaging himself in practical work at the experimental station. Having proved himself efficient and expert in matters agricultural, he was sent by Government to the Hakgala Gardens at Nuwara Eliya, where he was placed in charge of the cinchona plantation. He spent six years in this new position, vacating it at the end of that period to start planting on his own account. In partnership with one or two others, he purchased and planted some properties in the Kadugannawa district with coffee. The profits accruing from the business becoming considerable, Mr. Attygalle, in company with Mr. D. T. Jayetilleke, and, later, with Mr. N. D. P. Silva, embarked in plumbago mining, and acquired large tracts of plumbago-bearing land in the North-Western Province. Here several well-known mines were opened by the combination, which have still a large annual output. Mr. Attygalle then leased from Government the rents for farming arrack in the North-Western Province, and also planted extensively the properties he had acquired with coconuts, cacao, cinnamon, and cinchona, becoming eventually one of the largest landed proprietors in the North-Western Province. Dodangaslanda, in the same province, which was only a small village at the time he opened up estates and mines in the vicinity, is now a neat little town, and is commonly called "Attygalle" town, on account of his owning so many of the buildings. Chief among other edifices he erected is the bungalow he had designed and built at his expense in the heart of Kurunegala for the convenience of the headmen of the North-Western Province, which is at present one of the architectural features of the town. He has also built many ambalams (halting-places) for the convenience of the public at various places.

Mr. Attygalle was the founder of a number of schools in his province, and he has liberally supported every local charity and charitable institution. Being an ardent Buddhist, he built the temple of Colamunne in the Salpiti Korale, which is one of the grandest of its kind, and to which many thousands resort annually for worship, and built and endowed a large number of other temples in the districts wherein his interests lay. For his philanthropy and public-spiritedness he was created a Mohandiram in 1885, and promoted Mudaliyar in 1900, by Governor Sir West Ridgeway. He married, in 1872, Peternella, daughter of the late Mr. Fonseka Abeykoon, and died in December, 1901, leaving one son and three daughters.

Mr. Francis Dixon Attygalle, who is the third of the family and the only son of the late Mr. Attygalle, now carries on, on behalf of Mrs. D. C. G. Attygalle, who was appointed executrix of her late husband's estate, the extensive business founded by his father. Mr. Attygalle, jun., was born at Colamunne Walauwa, the ancestral residence of the family, in the year 1884, and was educated at Wesley College, Colombo. He joined his father's business in 1904, and is now in sole charge of all the operations. The business of the firm, including both plumbago mining and planting, has grown to very large dimensions, the produce from the mines and estates generally being sold locally. The firm owns the following mines: Kahatagaha group (Maduragoda), Haulpatala, Walakatahena, Wawelhena, Miniranhanda, Dematagaha, Maaragaha, Ragedere, and Paragoda, varying in depth from 500 to 800 ft. and giving employment in the aggregate to over 2,500 men. The mines are all equipped with Worthington pumps, Babcock & Wilcox's water-tube boilers, and other necessary steam machinery and gear, and the mineral raised is collected and transported to the Central Stores at Kurunegala, where it is sold in its raw state by public auction. In the planting business the following estates are included: Dodangtalawa, planted in cacao and rubber; Yagapitiya, Moragolle, Ratenamadde, Battalagodda, Dodangadlande, Balawatalle, Katala, Garuhadola, Koulwewe, Nakiyapotte, and Kirindigala, in the North-Western Province and planted in coconut; the coconut estate of Kahathuduwe and the cinnamon plantations of Madapatha, Baruhatia, Millewe, and Batakattera in the Western Province. The firm also holds on lease from Government several tracts of paddy land in the above provinces, which have recently been brought under cultivation. The firm's collecting and stowing stores are at Polwattepitiya, Dodangaslanda, and Paragoda, in the North-Western Province, while the head offices are located at Punchikawatte, Colombo, with a branch establishment at Kurunegalla.

Mr. Francis D. Attygalle, though still young, has shown marked ability in the conduct of this large business, which, under his direction, is steadily developing and expanding. His private residence is Colamunne Walauwa, in Salpiti Korale. He is a member of the Sinhalese Sports Club and the Lawn Club, Colombo, and a keen all-round sportsman.

NOTE.—As these pages were passing through the press we received the intimation of Mr. Francis Dixon Attygalle's death. The information arrived too late to allow of the necessary corrections being made in the text.—EDITOR.

NANAYAKKARAGE DON PAULIS SILVA.

The late Don Paulis Silva, "the Plumbago King" as he was called, afforded a conspicuous example of a successful man among the native (Sinhalese) community of Ceylon. He came from an old and distinguished family, the Nanayakkaras of the Galle district of the Southern Province of Ceylon. The father of the late Mr. Silva formerly bore the title of the Ven. Sri Sumangala, the Buddhist High Priest of what is known as the Siam sect of Baddegama, who subsequently, however, became a convert to the Christian faith. He married a Sinhalese lady of that district. The second child of this marriage was the late Don Paulis Silva, who was born in the year 1838 at Baddegama, a village about twelve miles from Galle, on the banks of the Ginganga or Gindra river. At the age of eighteen he lost both his parents and was left an orphan. He remained for some time in his native village, and afterwards he sold the small family possessions, and in the company of his brother and two sisters made his way to Colombo, where they have since resided. Hearing of the prospects of the Kurunegala district, Mr. Silva proceeded thither to try his luck. After a few months he went to We-uda, a neighbouring village, where he opened a store for coffee, then the leading product of the island. After spending a few years in this line of business, during which he greatly increased his small capital, he embarked in mining for plumbago. The first mine he opened turned out to be very profitable at his hands, and he subsequently bought many other plumbago lands and opened mines, which all became exceedingly profitable. He next acquired large tracts of land, which he planted with coconut, cacao, tea, coffee, cinchona, manilla, pepper, cinnamon, and cardamoms. And Fortune smiled unceasingly on all his ventures.

He was twice married, his second wife being Pagoda Wijeyasinghe Aratchige Dona Isabella Wijeyasinghe, a descendant of one of the oldest Kotta families, whose ancestor held the office of Adigar (king's chief minister) to his Majesty Dharma Parakrama Bahu IX., king of Jayawardhanapura (Kotta). To this ancestor the king granted a sannas (a royal grant of land) in the year A.D. 1505 in recognition of his services. This sannas is still in possession of Mrs. N. D. P. Silva, the widow of the subject of this sketch. Reference to this sannas is made in the Mahavansa, the ancient Sinhalese chronicle.

Mr. Silva was characterised in business by tireless energy and great ability. But in his sixty-third year his health began to fail, and he passed away in May, 1901. The funeral procession was representative of all the

"WIESBADEN," THE OFFICE, AND THE PLUMBAGO STORE.

MRS. ISABELLA SILVA.

MRS. N. D. P. SILVA AND FAMILY.

THE LATE N. D. P. SILVA.

communities of Ceylon, and was upwards of a mile in length.

Don Paulis Silva was both a friend to the poor and a father to his people. He was an ardent Roman Catholic, and a member of all the Catholic institutions of the island. A mere mention of a few of the numberless good acts done by him would testify to his generous, kind, and charitable character. He founded and endowed a ward in the Lady Havelock Hospital, which is still named after him. The Home for the Aged found in him a staunch supporter ever since it was started. He was one of the principal benefactors of St. Joseph College, the leading Catholic College in the island. He built several churches and schools, and liberally subscribed to every public beneficial institution. The Good Shepherd Convent always found help at his hands. Ever ready to assist the needy and oppressed, he supported about 150 old pensioners month by month during his life. Mrs. N. D. P. Silva, in addition to controlling her late husband's large mining interests, carries on unabated the charitable work of which he was the originator. He was a man who did not in the least care for honours, and thrice refused the distinction of "Basnayake Mudaliyarship."

Of the children of the second marriage, the eldest son is now preparing for the medical profession at the London University, while the second is a student-at-law.

As stated above, the affairs of the late Nanayakkarage Don Paulis Silva, embracing plumbago mining, the cultivation of plantations, and general merchant's business—all on a very large scale—are under the direction of his widow, and Mrs. N. D. P. Silva is the first Sinhalese lady who has assumed the control of so vast a concern, which employs altogether some 7,000 persons. In managing the estate and the various industries connected with it she is assisted by her late husband's two sons by his first marriage. The real property consists of twenty large fully-equipped plumbago mines in full working, many smaller mines and plumbago lands, and numerous plantations of coconut, tea, coffee, cacao, rubber, cinchona, vanilla, pepper, cardamom, and cinnamon, besides other landed property. The "N.D.P.S." brand of plumbago, founded by the late Mr. Silva, is highly appraised in the market.

The head offices of this business are at "Wiesbaden," Colpetty, Colombo; and the local and general stores at New Moor Street, Pettah, Colombo. The plumbago stores and curing yards are at Panchikawatte, Kotahena, and Kurunegala, where 500 hands are employed in sorting, sizing, and curing plumbago, and the general preparation of the mineral for the foreign market. The plumbago is brought to Colombo by rail and by road, the latter transport service being the firm's own property. The large plumbago mines the firm owns are distributed into groups, of which the principal is the Dodangaslanda Group, consisting of ten mines, and including the well-known Andris Silva, Kosgaha Patale, Dehigaha, Suriagaha, Ratamirishena Nos. 1 and 2. These mines have been actively worked for the past fifteen to thirty-five years, and give employment to nearly 4,000 people. They are worked to a depth of 700 ft., and powerful pumping gear is employed to cope with the water. Then there are the Paragoda Group of five rich mines—the Suriagaha, Kosgaha, Nelaulla, Cottagaha, and Rambukkewala—employing altogether nearly 1,500 men, and the Wallagala Group, including the Pandenia, Kahatagaha, and Galpatala, and employing about 750 hands. The two former groups are in the North-Western Province, and the latter in the Sabaragamuwa Province. Besides these large mines the firm owns various smaller mines and plumbago lands in the Southern and Western Provinces.

The plantations of the firm are scattered throughout several provinces. In the North-Western Province there are the coconut estate of Gorakadola, consisting of 700 acres, the largest estate in Maduragoda, the Hollongolla, the Malkaduwa, and the Paragahadeniya estates, besides many smaller properties. In the Western Province, the coconut estates belonging to the firm are the Maliduwakanda, Irahandayawa, Willimbula, Mandawala, and Kitulakelle, and cinnamon and coconut plantations of Rathmalgoda estate in the Panadure district. In the Heneratgoda, Panadure, and Negombo divisions are other estates of the firm planted with cacao, rubber, coffee, cardamom, pepper, vanilla, and cinchona, of which the Woodslie estate is one of the largest in We-uda Korale, while the Ambatale estate is also in We-uda Korale. In the Kelani Valley district the firm owns the Pindeni-Oya estate, which is planted in tea, cacao, and Para rubber, and on which there is a fully-equipped tea factory; also the New Bambarabotuwa tea estate of 1,025 acres at Ratnapura, as well as extensive landed property at Colombo, Negombo, Kalutara, Galle, Kurunegala, Ratnapura, and We-uda. The historic "Teak Bungalow," situated at Kalutara, in the Western Province, was the health resort and country seat of the late Mr. N. D. P. Silva; while at Kalutara the firm owns and conducts the largest arrack store in the island, with forty vats, each of the capacity of 5,000 gallons.

Charles Perera Senewiratne, son of B. J. Perera Senewiratne, Mohandiram, who was born at Pussellawa in 1864, and educated at the Royal College, Colombo, became the late Mr. N. D. P. Silva's principal assistant in 1893; and since the founder's death this gentleman has been the general manager of the business. He is one of the secretaries of the Plumbago Merchants' Union.

N. D. BERNARD SILVA.

Mr. N. D. Bernard Silva is the eldest son of the late Mr. N. Don Paulus Silva, the mining magnate whose career has just been sketched. He was born at Mahara in 1875, and educated at the Royal and St. Thomas's Colleges, Colombo. In 1894 he joined his father in the latter's mining business, and after the latter's death in 1901 he commenced operations in partnership with his brother Stephen. The brothers trade as general merchants and mine owners, under the style of N. D. P. Silva and Co., and their office is at No. 1, New Moor Street, Pettah, Colombo. Mr. Bernard Silva owns the estates of Miriswatte, Udalawella, and Paradise, in the Madampe, Chilaw, and Negombo districts respectively, and is also part owner of the Corokadolle estate in the Kurunegala district, planted with coconuts, as well as the Ambatale estate, in the same district, planted with cacao.

N. D. B. SILVA.

Mr. Silva also recently opened plumbago mines at Mabogodda in the Kalutara district. The produce of his estates and mines, such as copra, cocoa, and plumbago, are sold in the local market. Mr. Silva's favourite recreations are motoring, riding, and shooting. He has travelled in India, England, and the Continent of Europe, and is a member of the Orient, Turf, and Catholic Clubs, Colombo. In 1893 he married Christiana, the daughter of A. Isaac Perera, of Kandana, in the Alutkuru Korale of the Western Province, and his eldest son is Stephen Stanislaus Silva. Mr. Bernard Silva's private residence, Guildford

MR. AND MRS. N. D. B. SILVA AND FAMILY.

MASTER STEPHEN SILVA.

THE BUNGALOW.

House, in Cinnamon Gardens, Colombo, is one of the show-places of the suburbs of the city. He owns various other house properties, both in Colombo and Kurunegala.

GAMAMEDALIYANAGE GABRIEL PHILIP PERERA SENARATNE.

This gentleman, a Mohandiram, better known as G. Philip Perera, is a son of Eusabi Perera, of Pamunugama, an owner of landed properties and plumbago mines, and the sixth great-grandson of Hendrick Perera, Lekama, who lived about 231 years ago, and was much respected by the Dutch Government and the inhabitants of that period of the above-mentioned village. Mr. Perera was born on November 10, 1877, and educated at the Government Training School in Kandy, St. Benedict's Institute, and St. Thomas's College. He owns the coconut estates known as the Dammadda Group, Mellowapitiya, and Badagomuwa, in the North-Western Province, and numerous plantations and paddy fields in the Western Province. He also owns three plumbago mines at Maduragoda, in the North-Western Province, where he employs about 500 men, the arrack rent of Anuradhapura and some toll rents in the Colombo district. Mr. Perera is a generous supporter of St. Joseph's Church and the Sinhalese grant-in-aid school at Pamunugama, whilst at his own expense he built and equipped the English school. By the goodwill and pleasure of the residents of the above-named village, Mr. Perera has been elected year after year as President of the Dharmarakshita Association (social union club at Pamunugama). He takes a great interest in the reading-room of the above association, and most of the religious books were supplied by him. In 1906 the rank of Mohandiram was conferred on him by his Excellency the Governor, Sir Henry Arthur Blake, in recognition of services rendered by him in the cause of education. He married in 1897 Miss Dona Theckla, daughter of Jayacodiaratchige Don Raphial Appuhamy, of Pamunugama, and has three sons and two daughters.

G. P. PERERA SENARATNE'S WORKMEN AT DAMUNAGAHA MINE, MADURAGODA.

VIEW OF THE TUNNEL TO THE MINE AT DAMUNAGAHA, MADURAGODA.

JACOB DE MEL.

The head offices of Mr. De Mel are at 195, Grandpass, Colombo, and he stocks his products at Nos. 10 and 11, Grandpass, also at his Lakeside and Alston stores, at Hunupitiya, Colombo. The firm owns and manages a large number of coconut, cinnamon, and tea estates in various parts of the island, with an aggregate area of 4,792 acres; also large fibre mills at Madampe, in the Chilaw district. The produce from the coconut estates is converted into copra on the plantation, and in this form transported by canal on the firm's own boats to Colombo. The mark "J.D.M." is a well-known one in the copra world, and always fetches high prices.

Mr. De Mel is also the owner of many of the largest plumbago mines in the island, having started as early as 1870 to acquire and work graphite properties. Some of his principal mines are at Dematagolla, Ragedera, and Maduragoda in the Kurunegala district of the North-Western Province, and these have been worked for over thirty years. They are the deepest in the island, running down to 800 ft. in depth. It was at one of these mines that steam-gear for pumping and hauling was first erected in Ceylon. As much as 800 tons of graphite ore have been extracted from the pits in one year. The Thitewelgolla mine at Maduragoda, seventeen miles from Kurunegala, has been worked for over twenty-three years, a depth of over 600 ft. having been attained,

G. P. PERERA SENARATNE, MOHANDIRAM, AND MRS. SENARATNE.

FLORA VILLA.

CHILDREN OF MR. AND MRS. G. P. PERERA SENARATNE

SCHOOL AT PAMUNUGAMA, WESTERN PROVINCE.

(Erected by Gabriel Philip Perera Senaratne, Mohandiram.)

and this was the first mine in Ceylon where artificial ventilation was introduced. The firm also owns a further group of ten mines in full working order in the same district. When raised from the mine, the plumbago is forwarded to the railway station by the firm's own transport, and thence trucked to Colombo. After arrival at the Colombo stores it is cured, sized, and sorted, some 500 hands being employed in these operations. The plumbago thus made ready for the market is exported to London, the United States, and elsewhere, as well as sold in the local market. At the Wattaraka mine, in the Kelani Valley, a twin-shaft section is being worked by very powerful pumping, hauling, and ventilating machinery; and specimens of the ore from this property have been proved by analysis to contain as much as 95 per cent. of carbon. Numerous plumbago lands and mines are also owned by the firm in the Pasdun Korale of the Kalutara district.

The well-known cinnamon plantation at Kadirana in the Negombo district was acquired by Mr. De Mel in 1872 for £15,000 sterling; and subsequently he purchased the Ekelle estate of some 300 acres in extent for £22,000. Various other cinnamon estates in the Kalutara and Colombo districts are also owned by him, some of which were interplanted with coconut when the price of the article fell. More than 1,000 acres in these two districts alone are under cultivation with this spice. Peeling factories have been established on the estates, and at Kadirana bark-oil is distilled. A considerable amount of the cinnamon is exported to London and Bremen.

Mr. De Mel is one of the largest employers of labour in Ceylon, having some 3,000 men and women working in his mines, 2,500 on his estates, and 500 at his various stores in Colombo, making a total of 6,000 hands in all. The wages paid per annum in the mines amount to Rs. 250,000; on the estates, Rs. 200,000; and in the Colombo establishments, Rs. 40,000; making a total annual paybill of over half a million rupees. The rice for feeding this small army of workers is imported by the firm direct from India. The honours gained by the firm at various international exhibitions include medals and diplomas for plumbago and cinnamon at the Indian and Colonial Exhibition, London, 1886; World's Columbia Exposition, Chicago, 1897; Exposition Universelle, Paris, 1900; and St. Louis Exposition, U.S.A., 1904.

The proprietor of this large and varied business, Mr. Jacob De Mel, son of Francisco De Mel and Leonora Peiris, was born at Moratuwa in the year 1839. His father, Francisco De Mel, was also born at Moratuwa, just thirty years previously. The De Mel family come of an old and respectable lineage, which can be traced back to the year 1534. The Walauwa (ancestral home) and garden occupied by Mr. De Mel's ancestor, the Mahavidana Ralahami of Laksapathiya, in the year 1610, is now the property of Mr. Jacob De Mel's eldest grandson, Henry Leslie Jacob De Mel. In his time Mr. Francisco De Mel paid rent amounting to more than £50,000 sterling, for which security had to be given in landed property. During his lifetime this gentleman acquired numerous coconut estates, and he died in 1896 at the ripe age of eighty-six years. The son, Jacob, was educated at both Thomas's and Royal Colleges, and subsequently practised as a Notary Public. He started his successful business career by becoming proprietor of the famous Ragedere mines in the Kurunegala district. By sterling worth and honesty,

PIT-HEAD AND MACHINE-ROOM AT THITEWELGOLLA MINE. GENERAL VIEW OF MINES AT MADURAGODA. ESTATE CATTLE ON NEGOMBO COCONUT ESTATE.

THE LATE JACOB DE MEL, HENRY DE MEL, OFFICE AND STAFF, AND VIEWS OF PLUMBAGO YARDS.

coupled with high business capabilities, he increased his business until to-day he owns one of the largest commercial houses in Ceylon. He has now retired from active participation in the management of the business, which is carried on by his son and nephew. Mr. De Mel was married, in 1869, to Dona Helena Ferdinando, at Holy Emmanuel Church, Moratuwa, and has a family of nine daughters and three sons. One of the best known and highest esteemed gentlemen in Sinhalese society, he is an ardent member of the Church of England. He is also a member of the Anglican Synod and of the Sunday School Union. One of the largest supporters of various charities, he is on the committee of the Victoria Home for Incurables. He endowed the "De Mel Ward" at the Lady Havelock Hospital, and contributed largely to the Victoria Memorial Eye Hospital. He is also on the committee of the Horti-Agricultural Society. Mr. De Mel has trained his own employees, and some of his servants have been with him from thirty to forty years.

Mr. De Mel's second son, F. J. De Mel, was educated in England, and is a B.A. and LL.B. of Cambridge, and a barrister of the Inner Temple. On the day he was called to the Bar he was the youngest barrister in the United Kingdom. Mr. Jacob De Mel's eldest daughter is married to Mr. James Peiris, B.A., LL.M., of Cambridge, who gained first-class honours in Law and Moral Science, and was President of the Cambridge Union Society.

HENRY LAWSON DE MEL.

The legal profession has great attractions for the educated among the rising generation in Ceylon, as affording promising scope for their cultivated talents, and many of the sons of leading merchants of the island are to be found among those enrolled in the ranks of the learned profession. Mr. Henry Lawson De Mel, the eldest son of Mr. Jacob De Mel, is one of those who chose the law for their walk in life. He was born in 1877 at "Villa De Mel," Colombo, and after the usual course of study at St. Thomas's and the Royal Colleges in his native city, read for law. He was admitted as a Proctor and Notary in 1898, and became a member of the legal firm of Peiris and De Mel. He was appointed a Proctor of the Supreme Court in 1904, but retired from active practice in the law to assume the direction of his father's extensive business. He married, in 1900, Elsie, daughter of Mudaliyar S. H. and Mrs. Jayawickrame, of Kurunegala. Occupying a prominent position in the community, Mr. De Mel is a member of the Orient and the Turf Club, a committee-man of the Ceylon Kennel Club, a member of the Ceylon Poultry Club, chairman of the Social Committee of the Young Men's Christian Association, member of the Literary Committee, also a member of the Anglican Synod and of the Agricultural and Horti-Agricultural Societies, as well as of the Kurunegala Planters' Association and the Colombo Plumbago Merchants' Union. His private residence, "Elsmere," Horton Place, Cinnamon Gardens, Colombo, is a centre of hospitality among numerous friends. Riding and motoring are his favourite recreations; and he has covered thousands of miles in the island on his "Cardillac" car, which he has always driven himself. In the management of his father's large business he is assisted by his cousin, Mr. J. Matthias De Mel.

J. C. DE SILVA & CO.

This firm carries on business as mine owners, shippers, and general merchants, with a city office at 4, Queen Street, Fort, Colombo, and branches at Kurunegala and Dodangaslanda in the North-Western Province. The present owner, who is the founder of the house, is Mr. John Clovis de Silva. This gentleman's full and proper name is Takuratha Deveaddithiya Gaidivasam Lindemullege. The surname of De Silva was taken by his ancestors in the year 1534, on embracing Christianity during the Portuguese rule of the maritime provinces of Ceylon. Mr. J. C. de Silva is about to retire from the business, which is carried on by his son, Mr. D. J. Clovis de Silva, and his nephew, Mr. P. R. Mendis, as joint-managers.

The firm mines and produces plumbago for the local market, and Mr. de Silva also owns the following coconut estates in the North-Western Province: Clovis, St. Clothilda, Galla group, John s Land, Ernest Wood, Henrietta, Christie's Land, Mary Mount, and Potuwewa; also the tea estates of Watumulla, Bodawe, Kehelwatte, and Hulu Ganga in the Central Province. These four latter estates are now being planted with rubber, and well-equipped factories in connection with the new industry have been erected on Bodawe and Watumulla. In the Western Province the firm owns the Gulmnegoda rubber estate and Regidale cinnamon estate. Their desiccating mills at Kurunegala manufacture fine, medium, coarse chips, strips, and other descriptions of desiccated coconuts, as well as bristle and mattress fibre. The firm sells its copra and black tea locally, whilst the desiccated coconut is exported direct to the United Kingdom and the Continent of Europe. The plumbago mines are situated in the Dodangaslanda district of the North-Western Province, the names being Kodigaha, Galwanagollo, Dehigaha, Ratamitishena, and Andris Silva. These mines have been worked for about twenty-five years, and at present give employment to about 1,500 people.

Mr. John Clovis de Silva was born at Moratuwa in 1852, and was married in 1877. He started coconut planting at the age of eighteen; and then successively took over the arrack rents of the North-Western Province, bought the mines at Dodangaslanda, opened estates in tea, and, in 1890, founded the present business. He is a member of the Catholic and Orient Clubs and treasurer of the Catholic Union of Ceylon. His town residence is "Lynn Bank," Cinnamon Gardens; and country seat, "Green Bank," Moratuwa. Mr. D. John Clovis de Silva, son of the founder of the business, and now principal joint-manager, was born in 1885, and was educated at St. Benedict's Institute and St. Joseph's College. He plays cricket and tennis, and is a member of the Nondescripts and Sinhalese Sports Clubs and the Lawn Club. The firm's visiting agent for the producing estates is Mr. B. H. C. Mendis. The firm was awarded a silver medal and diploma at the St. Louis Exposition, 1904, for black tea and desiccated coconuts.

H. BASTIAN FERNANDO.

Mr. H. B. Fernando is one of the most influential members of the mining community of Ceylon. He was born in the year 1859 at Moratuwa, and is a son of H. Abraham Fernando and Nathalia Fernando. After being educated at Moratuwa and at St. Thomas's College, Colombo, he started business in a small way at 76, Colpetty, Colombo, as plumbago merchant, the year being 1877. In course of time he acquired mines, coconut, tea, and rubber estates in various parts of the island, and became one of the leading operators in the plumbago industry. In 1890 he married Emily, daughter of Proctor D. M. Arseculeratne, and retired from the active management of his business in 1905. Mr. Fernando's private residence is at Deyn Court, Colpetty, Colombo. He is a Roman Catholic, and a member of the Catholic Club and of the committee of the Catholic Union. He also belongs to the Orient Club. Mr. Fernando has always interested himself largely in all local charities, and has been one of their principal supporters.

The head office of the business of H. B. Fernando, where are the main stores for the purpose of curing plumbago, are at "Barendeniya," 43, Colpetty, Colombo, and his other establishments in Colombo are Walstan Stores, Borella, and Havelock Park Stores, Bambalapitiya. At all these establishments plumbago from the mines is cured, sized, and sorted, preparatory to export to different parts of the world. The business is managed by Mr. James

J. CLOVIS DE SILVA AND D. J. DE SILVA, AND VIEWS OF THE CLOVIS ESTATE, THE ESTATE BUNGALOW, THE MANAGER'S BUNGALOW, AND THE INTERIOR OF THE FIBRE MILL.

Peter Fernando, nephew of Mr. H. B. Fernando, who is now a partner of the firm. He was born at Colombo in 1879, educated at the Royal and St. Joseph's Colleges, joined his uncle's business in 1898, and took over the whole management at the beginning of 1906. His private residence is "Wilhelmsruhe," Moratuwa. His recreations are billiards, cricket, and tennis, and he is a member of the Sinhalese Sports Club, as well as a member of the Catholic Club.

The firm owns and works some important plumbago properties. At their Kurunduwatte mine in the Galle district, near Dodanduwa, a depth of some 200 ft. has been attained, and nearly 200 people are employed. Here, also, steam-pumping gear is in operation. Other mines belonging to the firm are Mahagama, in the Kalutara district, and Nape, in the Galle district—which latter is reckoned to produce the best plumbago in Ceylon, and has been worked for over twenty years. The Kadirandola group of mines in the Pasdun Korale, where some 300 people were employed, and which had an annual output of about 500 tons, was at one time under the firm's control. Besides dealing with the ore from its own mines, the firm buys very largely in the local plumbago market as well. In the Colombo stores alone some 400 people are employed in curing and sorting the various grades of the mineral. This product is exported in large quantities to the United States, Germany, and the United Kingdom. For exhibits of plumbago, the firm won a gold medal at the St. Louis Exposition of 1904, and a bronze medal at the Paris Exhibition in 1902.

The coconut estates of Walahapitiya, Letchimi, and Nullunwella, with an aggregate area of 1,200 acres, and situated in the Chilaw and Negombo districts, are owned by Mr. Fernando; while rubber and tea are grown on the firm's Hathmatha estate in the Kelani district, and Dikhene, Peragahahene, and Undupitiyagodde estates in the Kalutara district. The vegetable products of all the estates, whether tea, coconuts, or copra, are sold locally. Although plumbago is the principal line of the business, general mercantile dealings are also transacted. Seventy-five per cent. of all the firm's exports go to the United States of America; and its New York agents are Messrs. Henry W. Peabody & Co., 17, State Street, New York, while its agents in England are Messrs. Arthur Bramwell & Co., 44, Great Tower Street, London, E.C., and Messrs. H. L. Tottenham, 2, Fenchurch Avenue, London, E.C. The import division of the business includes dynamite and detonators from the United Kingdom; and the firm holds the local agency for the National Explosives Company, and also for the British and Foreign Safety Fuse Company. Hoop iron in large quantities is also imported from the United Kingdom. Altogether the firm gives occupation to about 1,200 employees, and the amount paid in wages per annum amounts roughly to Rs. 125,000.

COPRA DRYING. COCONUT HUSKING. COLPETTY STORES.

KANATTE STORES.

THE BUNGALOW. H. BASTIAN FERNANDO.

JAMES FERNANDO. THE FAMILY.

JOHN KOTALAWALA.

Mr. John Kotalawala, mine and plantation owner, born at Bandaragama, near Panadure, in the year 1865, is the son of Mr. J. A. Kotalawala, Notary Public. He was educated at the Royal, St. Thomas's, and Wesley Colleges, Colombo, and, having completed his course of studies, joined the office of the Director of Public Instruction as a clerk. Thence he was transferred to the Police Department; and for saving two lives from drowning while in his new sphere he was complimented by His Excellency Sir Arthur Gordon, then Governor of Ceylon. In 1890 he proceeded to New South Wales to study gold-mining. Returning shortly afterwards to Ceylon, he rejoined the police force, worked his way up, and became the head of the Criminal Investigation Department. In 1896 he married Alice, daughter of Mudaliyar D. C. G. Attygalle, and he resigned his official post to take over the management of his father-in-law's affairs. After the latter's death he continued to manage the estate for the widow. He has now, however, handed over the management of the late Mr. Attygalle's affairs to his son, and commenced business on his own account. He owns large plumbago mines in Rambukewella, Paragoda, Hikkaduwa, and other places, where thousands of men are employed, and he works another mine at Bandigahawatte, in the Kelani Valley district. He is the lessee of

JOHN KOTALAWALA.

the plumbago land well-known as "Morankande," in the Kandy district, belonging to a limited company, called the Rubber Estates of Ceylon. A large quantity of very superior plumbago is dug out here, and hundreds of coolies are employed in the work. Mr. Kotalawala owns coconut and tea estates in the Kurunegala, Kelani, and Kandy districts, of which Pillewe, Padukka, and Godapola are the principal.

Mr. Kotalawala is the largest producer of thorianite in Ceylon, and at his mines in the Galle and Kalutara districts heavy steam machinery is employed for the extraction of this valuable mineral as well as plumbago. He owns 1,000 acres of forest in the vicinity of Galle, where timber is felled and then cut up in large sawmills driven by steam, the logs being hauled to the mills by elephants. This timber is used for the manufacture of plumbago barrels, also for tea chests for estates and building purposes, in which supply trades Mr. Kotalawala is largely interested. The stores in Colombo are situated at Panchikawatte and Kanatte, where some two hundred men and women are employed; and here is brought all the plumbago intended for export. But both plumbago and tea are sold on the local market.

Mr. Kotalawala is also the managing director of the Ceylon-Japan Trading Company, Ltd., which has been recently formed for the purpose of opening up trade with Japan in Ceylon products; and he is now on the point

"FELLOWSLEIGH."

THE SAWMILLS.

INTERIOR OF THE SAWMILLS.

FOREST.

ELEPHANTS AND MAHOUTS.

ELEPHANTS MOVING TIMBER.

of visiting that country to study its commercial institutions. A many-sided man of varied activities, Mr. Kotalawala is a member of the Rational Association of England, and he was a prime mover in the foundation of the Plumbago Merchants' Union in 1905, on the committee of which body he retains his membership. He is a devotee of physical exercise and a pupil of Sandow, and he sees no reason for being ashamed of a proficiency with the gloves. He owns large property in Ceylon, and his offices are at Panchikawatte, his private residence being "Fellowsleigh," Bambalapitiya, Colombo.

A. FERNANDO & CO.

The important native firm of A. Fernando & Co., plumbago mine owners and merchants, have their head offices at Buller's Road, Jawatte, near Colombo. On the retirement of the original proprietor, Mr. A. Fernando—better known as Mr. M. A. Fernando—from active participation in the firm's operations, Mr. Jacob Abraham Fernando, his son-in-law, succeeded to the business, and the latter continues to be the sole managing partner. The firm is extensively engaged in the plumbago mining industry, having under its control the following mines: The Pushena group, the deepest in the three Korales of the Western Province, worked to a depth of 450 ft.; the Aruggammane group, in the Kegalla district of the Sabaragamuwa

PANCHIKAWATTE PLUMBAGO STORES.

Province, which has been worked for two years to a depth of 200 ft., nearly 300 hands being employed in the various pits comprising the group; the Medagode group, also in the same district, which has been recently opened, a depth of over 200 ft. having been reached, and where about 600 men are employed; Panangala, in the Kalutara district of the Western Province, worked for nearly three years and having a depth of about 240 ft., 200 hands being employed and heavy steam machinery (Worthington pumps and 80-horse-power boilers) having been installed; the Kurunduwatte group (partly owned) in the Southern Province, which has been worked for two years, where a depth of 240 ft. has been attained and 200 hands are employed, the machinery including two Worthingtom steam-pumping engines of 80 horse-power; No. 2 group of mines at Panangala, in the Kalutara district, is being now sunk. At this last-named centre of operations Babcock & Wilcox water-tube boilers of 96 horse-power, and Worthington pumps, 14 ins. by 7½ ins. by 10 ins., of 20,000 gallons lifting capacity, with other necessary appliances have been installed, the whole constituting the most powerful pumping-gear plant in Ceylon. The firm also owns various other mines in this district, as well as in the Hewagam Korale of the Western Province. All the plumbago from these mines is brought to Colombo, part of it being sent to the stores at Jawatte to be cured. Here 250 men and women are employed in curing, sizing, and sorting the mineral, the premises and yards covering an area of nearly two acres. The rest of the crude mineral is sold to local curing yards. Coopering is also done at Jawatte, and the cured plumbago is casked ready for shipment or local disposal. In addition to the mines, the firm owns more than a hundred plumbago-yielding lands, some of which are being worked by themselves, while the others are leased to the villagers for working, the firm retaining the ground lease.

Mr. A. Fernando owns several large coconut estates, of which Wewagedera (600 acres), in the North-Western Province, and Kiribaththuduwe and Pitipana (of 300 acres each), in the Western Province, are the most important—the two latter planted partly with cinnamon. At Panaluwa (125 acres), in the Western Province, rubber has been planted, while in the Kurunegala district further coconut-planting

1. JAWATTE PLUMBAGO STORES AND OFFICE.
2. A. FERNANDO
3. J. A. FERNANDO.
4. CLEANING PLUMBAGO, JAWATTE STORES.

JAMES FERNANDO, NATIVE WOMEN WORKING IN HIS PLUMBAGO YARD, AND TWO VIEWS OF HIS HYDE PARK PLUMBAGO STORES.

operations have been started. Mr. J. A. Fernando is a member of the Church of England, and a liberal supporter of Sunday schools and other religious institutions. His private residence is "Fern Dale," Moratuwa, while Mr. A. Fernando resides at Meth Madura, in the same town.

JAMES FERNANDO.

Mr. James Fernando, who succeeded to the business of plumbago mine owners, merchants and exporters established in 1856 by Simon Fernando, Mudaliyar, was born at Moratuwa in the year 1868. After receiving his education at the Royal College, Colombo, he joined the business in 1887, and took over the sole management some six years later. The original premises of the business were situated at Vauxhill Street, Slave Island; but recently the head offices have been removed to 5, Hyde Park Corner, Cinnamon Gardens, though the stores for curing, sizing, and sorting plumbago are still located on the former site. Mr. Fernando's principal mines are situated in the Western and Southern Provinces, and among the more important of these properties are the following: Alukatiya group, worked for three years and having a depth of 150 ft., equipped with Worthington's steam-pumping gear and Babcock & Wilcox's 75-horse-power water-tube boiler, the operations at these mines giving employment to nearly 500 hands; Rambukpotta group, Kiribathera group, Annasigala, and Tunhaula mines, which have varying depths from 150 to 300 ft., and have been opened within the past five years or so, giving employment, in all, to over another 500 hands. These and some 200 other smaller mines owned by Mr. Fernando are scattered over various parts of the Western Province, while in the southern districts of Ceylon this gentleman owns a number of plumbago-yielding lands, which are being worked on his behalf by private prospectors. The Arukgammana mines in the Kegalla district are also properties of Mr. Fernando, and are being worked for him by Mr. A. N. de Silva & Co., over 200 hands and steam pumping gear being employed in the operations. The plumbago from all these mines is brought by cart and rail to the Colombo stores, where it is cured and shipped to the United Kingdom, Germany, the United States of America, and elsewhere, or sold in the local market. For the excellent quality of the plumbago extracted from Mr. Fernando's mines, he was awarded a special silver medal at the Colombo Exhibition in 1893, a gold medal at the St. Louis Exposition of 1904, and another silver medal in 1906.

Mr. Fernando also owns several coconut estates in various parts of the island; while rubber has been planted on his Morankinda property, of 150 acres, in the Kelani Valley and on another plantation of 250 acres near Padukka. Mr. Fernando is a member of the Plumbago Merchants' Union, also of the Turf Club. His private residence is "Sirinevasa," Moratuwa. He is assisted in his business by Mr. M. P. Dissanayake.

HENRY JOSEPH PEIRIS.

Mr. Henry Joseph Peiris, who is the son of the late Mr. Hanwadige Andris Peiris, who died in 1895, was born at Moratuwa in the year 1858. On completing his education at St. Thomas's College, Colombo, he joined his father in business in 1880, and established himself as a general merchant and arrack-renter, owning, at that time, some of the largest arrack farms in the island. When the elder Mr. Peiris retired from the business in 1890, his son assumed sole control of the firm, moving his offices to Consistory Buildings, in the capital, in order to be in a better position to cope with the extensive operations rendered necessary by the growth of the business. With the same purpose, stores for the handling

HENRY JOSEPH PEIRIS AND VIEW OF HIS RESIDENCE.

COOPERING. PLUMBAGO YARD. GABRIEL FERNANDO.

'FAIR LAWN" BUNGALOW, MORATUWA. CLEANING PLUMBAGO.

of plumbago and other Ceylon produce have been established at Katuwakelle in Havelock Town, Colombo. Mr. Peiris is the owner of large plantations and properties in many parts of the island, some of the better known being Mathandey (300 acres), Leehereyagama (400 acres), Dunkana (100 acres), Tambapana (150 acres), Galluneera (100 acres), Danwille (150 acres), Kambukkuliya (500 acres), and Kardepolie (400 acres), all planted with coconut and situated in the Chilaw and Puttalam districts of the Western Province; Dambadeniya (200 acres), Muwanhela (600 acres), also planted with coconut, in the Kurunegala district of the North-Western Province; the Mellewa group, of some 2,000 acres, planted with tea and rubber; Yahalakelle, of 1,000 acres, planted with tea, coconut, and cinnamon; and Bellapitiya, of 500 acres, planted with tea and rubber, in the Kalutara district of the Western Province. All these estates are completely equipped with up-to-date machinery and necessary appliances for the treatment of the produce, while on a large number of them fine residences and bungalows have been erected. All the products from Mr. Peiris's estates are brought to the Colombo stores, where they are cured and made ready for disposal, then either sold in the local market or exported to England. Messrs. Bert & Co., of Ashton Lodge, Tavistock Road, Croydon, act as the firm's agents for the United Kingdom.

In addition to owning the above-enumerated long list of tea, coconut, and rubber estates, Mr. Peiris is also largely interested in plumbago, and is the proprietor of the well-known mines of Pussahena, in the Kegalla district, which have been worked for the last fifteen years, the present depth being 735 ft. Here powerful steam pumping gear with Worthington pumps and hauling machinery are used, the whole of the operations giving employment to over 300 men. At another of Mr. Peiris's mines, Panangola, in the Kalutara district, which has been worked for upwards of ten years and to a depth of 300 ft., heavy steam pumping gear—claimed to be the largest installation of the kind in the island, with boilers of 105 horse-power—is employed. Mr. Peiris also owns and works various mines in the Galle, Kalutara, and Kurunegala districts, the produce from all of which is brought to the Colombo stores and cured, sorted, and sized for disposal in the local market.

Mr. Peiris is a member of the Plumbago Merchants' Union, of the Orient Club, and of the Agricultural Society. He is also Warden of Holy Emmanuel Church, Moratuwa, trustee and treasurer of the church funds, and lay representative to the Synod. He is a Justice of the Peace for the Western Province. His private residence is Oliver Castle, Gregory Road, Cinnamon Gardens, Colombo; and his country seat "Sunnyside," Moratuwa. Mr. Peiris founded the "Andris Peiris Ward," in the Victoria Memorial Eye Hospital, in memory of his late father, to whose memory a tablet is erected in that institution. He is a large subscriber to local charities, and is one of the principal supporters of the Friend-in-Need Society. He built the parsonage of Marawila, in the Chilaw district, and gave grounds and properties to the Holy Emmanuel Church at Moratuwa. In 1888 he married Nancy Charlotte, daughter of Mr. and Mrs. Johannes de Mel, of Melville, Moratuwa.

GABRIEL FERNANDO.

Mr. Gabriel Fernando, who was born at Moratuwa in 1867, is a well-known mine owner, plumbago merchant, and landed proprietor in Colombo and Moratuwa, and carries on business at 74, Colpetty Road, Colpetty, Colombo, where he established himself in 1902. He is the son of Marian Fernando (the eldest brother of Mr. H. Bastian Fernando). He received his education at St. Benedict's Institute, and afterwards entered into business with his uncle, Mr. Bastian Fernando, with whom he received his training in planting, practical mining, and general office and export work. In 1893 he was admitted as a partner with his uncle; but in 1902 he severed this connection in order to set up in business for himself, since which time he has been very successful. At his Kollupitiya store over 250 hands are employed in curing plumbago, which is afterwards shipped abroad on a large scale, as well as sold in the local markets. The establishment has its own coopering sheds, where the barrels are made in which the plumbago is packed for export. At Mr. Fernando's establishment, No. 14, Hunupitiya Lake Road, there is also a curing store, where some 100 people are employed. Mr. Fernando owns several valuable plumbago properties situated in Pasdun Korale (Kalutara district), also several large estates. Chief among the latter are an extensive coconut plantation of 485 acres, known as Mudanapala estate, Kurunegala, in the North-Western Province, the superintendent of which is Mr. A. Perera, and an estate of 115 acres at Homagama, in the Western Province, bearing coconuts and cinnamon, but which is now being devoted to the growing of rubber. Mr. D. C. Wijesingha is the superintendent of this latter estate. Mr. Fernando also owns Kasbawa estate of 100 acres in the Western Province, on which cinnamon alone is cultivated, and on which there is also a peeling station and some smaller properties.

Besides plumbago, nuts and copra are sold locally, also cinnamon by Mr. Fernando; and at the present time cinnamon, copra, coconuts, cocoa, cardamoms, fibre, and tea are being shipped by him direct to various oversea countries, the chief ports of destination being London, Liverpool, Marseilles, Hamburg Antwerp, New York, Vancouver, Adelaide, Brisbane, Zanzibar, and Odessa. Mr. Fernando is also a direct importer of hardware and cotton manufactures from Germany, the United Kingdom, Holland, and the United States of America. At the St. Louis Exposition of 1904 he secured a diploma and silver medal for his plumbago.

Mr. Gabriel Fernando's country residence is "Fair Lawn," which was built in 1855 by his father, and has ever since remained the family residence. His town residence is "Bellwood,' Bambalapitiya. He is a member of the Roman Catholic Church, and also a member of the Plumbago Merchants' Union. He married, in 1895, Josephine Mary, second daughter of the late Mr. D. M. Arseculeratne, Proctor and Notary Public. Mr. Fernando is assisted in his business by Mr. D. C. W. Obeyesekere.

DON SPATER SENANAYEKE, Mudaliyar.

Mr. Don Spater Senanayeke, Mudaliyar, is the son of the late Mr. Don Bartholomew Senanayeke, who died in the year 1878. The former was born at Botale, in the Hapitigam Korale of the Negombo district in the year 1847. After being educated at various schools in Ceylon, he started business on his own account, in the plumbago-mining line, at the early age of eighteen years. He now carries on business as plumbago mine owner, merchant, estate proprietor, and general planter. His offices are situated at "Siri Madura," Castle Street, Cinnamon Gardens, and his stores are located at Kitulotta, Kanatte, Colombo. Mr. Senanayeke is one of the largest mine owners in the island, and controls the mines of Ambepussa, which have been worked for twenty years, and at which steam pumping gear of 34 horse-power is used. These mines give employment to about 3,000 people. Mr. Senanayeke has also commenced operations in mining at Mirigama and Pussehena in the Kegalla district, and the graphite extracted from these and other mines under his control is collected at Ambepussa, on the main line of railway, and thence forwarded to Colombo, where it undergoes the necessary process of curing at the stores, being afterwards sold in the local market. Mr. Senanayeke is the owner of large coconut estates, principally Deobromaya, Deagampola, Lower Kudawe, and Botale in the Negombo district, and Dittawa, Golwena, Neboda-Wadura, Nagahampalawa, and Boyawalana in the Kurunegala district, which aggregate some 2,000 acres in extent, while he is also

MR. AND MRS. SENANAYEKE AND FAMILY. THE RESIDENCE.

MUDALIYAR DON SPATER SENANAYEKE.

(The photograph shows the full dress and insignia of a Mudaliyar. Prominent on the left breast is the jewelled dagger which forms an essential part of the uniform.)

proprietor of other plantations in various parts of the North-Western Province. He owns, besides, a large number of residential properties in Colombo and Kandy.

Mr. Senanayeke was a liberal contributor to the Victoria Memorial Eye Hospital and the Indian Famine Relief Fund, and is a very large supporter of local charities. It was in recognition of these benefactions that Sir West Ridgeway, then Governor of the Colony, conferred on him the titular rank of Mudaliyar. Mr. Senanayeke's town residence is "Siri Madura," one of the most beautiful bungalows in the suburbs of Colombo, while his country seat is Botale Walauwa, in the Ambepussa district. He is a member of the Plumbago Merchants' Union and several other local institutions.

D. D. PEDRIS.

Mr. Pedris, who is a native of Galle, commenced his business career in 1872, interesting himself from the very beginning in plumbago, and starting a drapery establishment later, at Cross Street, Pettah, in Colombo. The latter business soon attained such large proportions that it had to be housed in the extended premises in use at present. Here a brisk business is being done in the sale of piece-goods and in the outfitting line generally. Mr. Pedris's operations in the plumbago business are extensive, and comprise the curing, sale, and export of plumbago. The stores for handling the mineral are at No. 3, Alston Place, Hunupitiya, Colombo, and were established in 1888. Here the plumbago from the different mines belonging to Mr. Pedris is conveyed, and some 125 men and women are employed in sorting and sizing it. At Anasigalahene, in the Kalutara district, Mr. Pedris owns what is practically one of the oldest mines in Ceylon, which has been worked for over thirty-one years, a depth of 510 ft. having been reached. Up-to-date machinery for pumping and hauling, including Worthington and Smith-Vale sinking pumps, has been introduced, and powerful lifting gear, with two 20-horse-power boilers and one of 16-horse-power, is employed. Nearly 500 men are maintained at this mine in either treating the plumbago or transporting it to the railway station at Alutgama, some 20 miles distant. Mr. Pedris also owns other plumbago lands in the Galle district, on which he intends to commence active operations at an early date. He is, besides, the proprietor of extensive paddy fields in the Southern Province, and of residential quarters in both the capital of that province and the metropolis of the Western Province.

Mr. Pedris is a staunch Buddhist, and is on the committee of the Theosophical Society. He is also a liberal supporter of the Friend-in-Need and other local charitable societies. He is a member of the Plumbago Merchants' Union. His hobby is photography; and, as an amateur, he may be well considered an adept in this line of work. He married, in 1882, the daughter of Margris Fernando, Peace Officer of Karandeniya. He is assisted in his business by Mr. W. P. Rupesinghe. His offices are at Alston Stores, Hunupitiya, while his private residence is Vimal Villa, No. 9, Turret Road, Cinnamon Gardens, Colombo.

L. B. A. DE SILVA & CO.

Established at Galle in 1896, the headquarters of this business were removed to Colombo in 1899, the Galle branch, however, being still continued. The firm is chiefly concerned with the mining and exportation of plumbago and Ceylon precious stones; and the present proprietors, Mr. Lianage Bennet Andris de Silva and others, own mines of this mineral in the Ratnapura district, of which the principal are Verelugaha Patalaya, Wadia Patalaya, and Diya Patalaya. These three mines are worked to a depth of about 200 ft., and give employment to some 300 men. The firm also owns and works the Udedeniya plumbago

D. D. PEDRIS AND ALSTON PLACE PLUMBAGO STORE.

L. B. A. DE SILVA, L. B. J. DE SILVA, F. E. DANTANARAYANA, THE OFFICE STAFF, AND VIEWS OF BAMBALAPITIYA PLUMBAGO STORES, LOADING PLUMBAGO FOR EXPORT, AND L. B. A. DE SILVA'S RESIDENCE.

R. A. MIRANDO, PLUMBAGO YARD AND CINNAMON STORES.

mine at Ambepussa, in the Colombo district, and the mines called Dilgaha Patalaya and Kosgaha Patalaya in the Galle district, on each of which several hundred men are employed. In the Colombo stores, where all the plumbago is sorted and sized and cleaned, some two hundred men and women are engaged in the various operations connected with the industry, and the firm does its own coopering, or barrel-making, for storing and packing the cured graphite. The latter is exported largely to the United States and England. The firm's London agents are Messrs. Arthur Bramwell & Co., Ltd., 43-45, Great Tower Street, London, E.C.; while their American agents are Messrs. Kern Commercial Company, 157, Cedar Street, New York. Messrs. de Silva & Co. also export large quantities of Ceylon precious stones to England. Exhibits of Messrs. de Silva & Co.'s plumbago were awarded honourable mention at the Exposition Universelle, Paris, 1900, and the firm gained diplomas at the Galle Exhibition of 1898, as well as a bronze medal and diploma at the St. Louis Exposition of 1904. The head office of the firm is at "Inverberi," Bambalapitiya, Colombo.

MIRANDO & CO.

The offices of this firm are located at 76, Dam Street, Hultsdorf, Colombo, and the principal branches of their business are the handling of plumbago and cinnamon, both for sale on the local market and for export to the various continental ports. The firm's stores are situated at Demettegodde, Colombo, where about 100 people are busily engaged in dealing with the products, which pass through various processes in preparation for shipment.

The firm was originally founded by Mr. Richard Adrian Mirando, in the year 1879, whose operations were mainly concerned with plumbago and cinnamon. At first the firm carried on business as planters and producers of the above-mentioned product; but of recent years it has become a large buyer in the local market of cured articles. The firm owns the Oolooambalama cinnamon estate in the Negombo district, planted with coconut as well, and having an area of 800 acres; the Ratgama, in the Galle district, containing 80 acres; and one or two other minor properties in the Western and Southern Provinces. Large peeling stations have been established on these estates, the prepared cinnamon quills being sent to the Colombo stores for disposal locally or shipment oversea.

Mr. Mirando was born at Colombo in 1854, was educated at the Royal College—then known as the Colombo Academy—and started business in 1879. He is the Vice-President of the Plumbago Merchants' Union, which was founded, in 1905, for the mutual protection and safeguarding of the interests of the local plumbago merchants. He is also President of the Buddhist Theosophical Society, whose object is the propaganda for the spreading and teaching of Buddhism. This society has established one college at Colombo and one at Kandy, and has some 300 schools in different parts of the island under its immediate direction and control. Mr. Mirando's private residence is "Siriwimana," Third Division, Maradana, Colombo.

W. J. FERNANDO.

Mr. W. J. Fernando, who was born at Moratuwa in the year 1842, entered into partnership with Messrs. W. A. & W. M. Fernando in 1867, merchants and plantation owners, under the style of W. A. Fernando & Bros., on the basis of the business that had been established some fifteen years previously by Mr. Philip Fernando, the father of all these gentlemen, at Moratuwa. After continuing in partnership for upwards of twenty-five years, the brothers separated, and Mr. W. J. Fernando set up on his own account at Hultsdorf, afterwards removing his business to Hunupitiya, a suburb of Colombo. The business under his control increasing rapidly and quite out-

W. J. FERNANDO, AND TWO VIEWS OF HIS PLUMBAGO YARD.

growing the inadequate premises in which it was housed at Hunupitiya, Mr. Fernando removed his establishment to Jawatte, near Colombo, in 1899, where it now remains, still expanding in its scope, and employing some 400 men in the operations of the different departments. The stores and yards cover an area of 2½ acres, being replete with every appliance and necessary for the proper handling of the products dealt in, the principal line of business being the curing and exporting of plumbago.

Mr. Fernando owns numerous mines in the Western and Sabaragamuwa Provinces of the island, among the better known of which may be included the Galwallagodelle group of four mines in the Kalutara district, where powerful machinery of 40 horse-power (Worthington pumps) has been installed and about 500 persons are engaged in handling the mineral and extracting it from the pits, which have now attained a depth of 225 ft. Another large mine under Mr. Fernando's control is Kudumirishena, which gives employment to over 150 men. Mr. Fernando also owns a number of other plumbago lands of minor importance in the Sabaragamuwa Province, and also contracts with private mine owners for the output of their pits, while some of his mines are being worked on his behalf by other prospectors. All the plumbago from Mr. Fernando's mines is brought down to the Jawatte stores at Colombo, the transportation being effected either by boat on the Kelani river and Kalu Ganga, or by road direct. Mr. Fernando is chief supplier to the Morgan Crucible Company, of London, of Ceylon graphite, and an extensive business is done in this mineral through Messrs. Aitken, Spenee & Co., of Colombo, who are the local agents for the English firm. The commendations which Mr. Fernando has received for his exhibits of plumbago at various exhibitions in London, Melbourne, and elsewhere, testify to the excellence of the quality of the mineral extracted from his mines. His exhibit of plumbago at the Colombo Museum is especially deserving of notice.

Mr. Fernando has also large interests in the planting line, and owns the estates of Alakolladeniya in the Kurunegala district of the North-Western Province. He is the proprietor as well of smaller plantations in the Sabaragamuwa Province, and is engaged at present in opening up an area of 175 acres in rubber on the property known as Beruwan, Mukulana, in that part. His private residence is "Ferndale," Moratuwa. He is a member of the Church of England, of the committee of the Friend-in-Need Society, of the Moratuwa Sunday School Union, and of a number of other public benefit societies. While his connections in the plumbago business are varied and extensive, he is about the only Ceylonese gentleman who has not identified himself with the Plumbago Merchants' Union of Colombo, or in any way been associated in its membership. He is assisted in business by his son, Mr. P. E. Fernando, and his nephew, Mr. James Abraham Fernando.

W. A. FERNANDO.

The late Mr. W. A. Fernando, a Sinhalese gentleman, who died so recently as the year 1901, was one of the pioneers of the plumbago trade of Ceylon. In the year 1854 he started business as a plumbago merchant in Colombo, where he opened the "Greenside Stores" in Browning Street, now known as Rosmead Place, in the Cinnamon Gardens. From a small beginning, the business, under Mr. Fernando's careful guidance, became one of the most extensive in the line; and its present dealings in the local plumbago market are varied and comprehensive. The rapid increase of the direct export business speaks well for the shrewdness of its present managers; and at the present day large shipments are made to Europe and America, as well as to the Commonwealth of Australia. The premises shown in the accompanying illustrations give a good idea of the nature of the work carried on, as well as the extent of the enterprise. The firm of W. A. Fernando, besides being one of the largest buyers in the local plumbago market, also owns and works mines of its own, the principal ones being at Hikgaha, in the Kurunegala district, Goluwanmulle, in the Galle district, and Himbutamulle, in the Colombo district. The plumbago from these mines, after extraction in the usual manner, is forwarded, by the firm's own transport, by road to the railway stations, and thence by rail to Colombo, where it is received into the stores—of which the principal one is at Rosmead Place, while another, called the "Bremen Stores," is in the Jawatte suburb. At the stores some 300 to 400 men and women are busily engaged in sorting, sizing, and cleaning the plumbago for the market. During this process the mineral is divided into four divisions according to size, each of which is again subdivided into four qualities. Coopering (*i.e.*, barrel making), for the purpose of packing the plumbago, is carried on in the premises, and forms an interesting part of the industry. That Mr. W. A. Fernando's plumbago is of sterling quality is shown by the awards granted to his firm at various international and local exhibitions, as follows: Diploma and medal, St. Louis Exhibition, 1904; diploma, Exposition Universelle, 1900; diploma and medal, Chicago Exposition, 1897; diploma and medal, Indian and Colonial Exhibition, 1886; diploma and medal, Melbourne Exhibition, 1884; silver medal, Governor Gregory's Exhibition, held at the Colombo Museum, 1886; silver medal, Prince of Wales's Exhibition, held in Colombo, 1875; and silver medal, Duke of Edinburgh's Exhibition, held in Colombo, 1860.

On the death of Mr. W. A. Fernando, the business passed into the hands of his son-in-law, Mr. Edmund Clarke de Fonseka, a Proctor of the District Court of Colombo, who resides at "Arcadia," Rosmead Place, Cinnamon Gardens, Colombo, adjoining the principal stores, and in whose capable hands the traditions of the late Mr. W. A. Fernando are worthily upheld. Mr. Don Andris Fernando, who entered the firm's employment in 1898, is the working manager of the business, being assisted in his duties by Mr. Edwin Solomon Rodrigo.

U. D. S. GUNASEKARA & CO.

This firm was originally established in 1877 at Colombo, as plumbago merchants, general produce exporters, and shippers. Mr. U. D. S. Gunasekara, the founder, continued to be the sole proprietor of the firm until his death in 1894, when Mr. A. E. de Silva continued the business till 1904. At the latter date the managerial duties devolved on his son, Mr. Dionysius Bernard Gunasekara, and Mr. Amadoris Mendis, who are the present directors of the firm's operations. Under their control is the Boreluketiya group of mines, in the Kalutara district, which has been worked for over twenty-five years, and where a depth of 210 ft. has been attained, some 200 hands being employed in extracting and handling the mineral; and Kokkumbera group, also in the Kalutara district, which has been worked for upwards of thirty years, and where a depth of 115 ft. has been attained. All the plumbago from the firm's mines is brought to their central stores, Maradana, Colombo, where nearly 70 hands are engaged in curing, sorting, and sizing the plumbago for local disposal and shipment abroad. For the specimens of plumbago displayed at the Indian and Colonial Exhibition in 1884 the firm was awarded a diploma and bronze medal; while at the later exposition in Paris in 1900 their products again elicited admiration and were awarded prizes.

Mr. D. B. Gunasekara has also under his immediate control several cinnamon and coconut estates in the Western and Southern Provinces, of which Kudapalugaswewa (150 acres), in the Chilaw district, planted in coconut, and superintended by Mr. E. A. de Silva, and Nape, in the Matara district, planted in citronella, are the most important. He also owns several minor cinnamon estates in the

THE LATE W. A. FERNANDO, E. DE FONSEKA, E. C. DE FONSEKA, AND VIEWS OF PICKING, SORTING, LIFTING AND PREPARING PLUMBAGO FOR SHIPMENT.

A. MENDIS, D. GUNASEKARA, PLUMBAGO YARD, OFFICE AND STORES, AND PRIVATE BUNGALOW.

Ambalangoda district of the Southern Province, while, as trustee of the estate of the late Mr. U. D. S. Gunasekara, a number of valuable plumbago lands in that province have come under his supervision. Mr. D. B. Gunasekara, who was born at Colombo in 1882 and educated at the Royal College, joined his father's business in 1901. He is a keen sportsman, well known in the local cricket world, and a member of the Nondescripts, Sinhalese Sports, Chums' Football and Athletic Clubs of Colombo, while he has also enrolled himself under the artillery section of the Ceylon Volunteer Force. His partner in business, Mr. Amadoris Mendis, is a son of Mr. Endries Mendis, of Galle, and was born at Ratgama in 1870. After receiving his education at Galle, and latterly at the Royal College, Colombo, he joined the firm as partner in 1904, and has been actively connected with the operations of the house ever since. In addition to his official business, Mr. Mendis also discharges the duties of secretary of the Plumbago Merchants' Union. The head offices of the business are located at Jail Road, Maradana, Colombo, while Mr. Gunasekara's private residence is "Kittyakara," and Mr. Mendis's "The Nook," both in the Maradana quarter of the metropolis.

W. JOSEPH AND A. P. DE MEL.

This firm of plumbago merchants commenced business in 1894 at Rosmead Place, Cinnamon Gardens, Colombo, under the direction of Mr. Joseph De Mel, but have since removed their stores to the present site at Kanatte. The partners in the business are Messrs. Joseph, Peter, and Abraham De Mel, all of whom were born at Moratuwa. The two latter were educated at the Prince of Wales's College in that town. The firm buy their plumbago from the mines direct, as well as from the dealers in the interior and in the local market. After the mineral has been brought to the stores some 100 men and women are employed in curing sizing, and generally preparing it for shipment. Most of the plumbago comes from the well-known Panangela, Kurunegala, and Pasdun Korale mines. The partners reside at Villakone and at Melton, Moratuwa.

Besides plumbago lands, Mr. Peter De Mel also owns the Damunegolle coconut estate, the De Mel Thenne and Godagama estates, and several other properties in the North-Western Province, and is now opening up a rubber plantation in the same province. He is also doing business, in partnership with another, as forwarding and commission agent and general merchant, under the name of Messrs. Mel, Mendis & Co. at Talawakele, Agrapatna, and Lindula, in the Central Province. In the North Central Province the firm own large steam sawmills, where all kinds of Ceylon wood, more especially satin and mille wood, are dealt in. In various parts of the North-Western Province also their sawmills turn out staves for barrels. These articles are sold in large quantities to various dealers in Colombo. At the Kalaoya sawmills sleepers are shaped for the Government Railway Department.

THE BUNGALOW. THE HEADS OF THE FIRM OF W. J. AND A. P. DE MEL. THE PLUMBAGO STORES.

JOHN HENRY ARSECULERATNE.

Mr. J. H. Arseculeratne, the third and youngest son of the late Mr. D. M. Arseculeratne, and well-known Proctor and Notary Public of Colombo, was educated at St. Thomas's College, and joined the well-known firm of his brother-in-law, Mr. H. Bastian Fernando, plumbago merchant, as assistant in 1898. In 1904 he started business on his own account as plumbago curer and exporter, bringing with him a wide experience in every detail of the graphite trade. Plumbago, bought at the pit's mouth as well as in the open

PLUMBAGO CLEANING YARD.
CLEANING PLUMBAGO.

TEMPLE ROAD STORES.
THE BUNGALOW.
THE PLUMBAGO YARD.

market, is brought to Colombo in padda boats on the canals, and then conveyed to stores in carts. Mr. Arseculeratne has two stores for curing plumbago—at the Temple Road Stores in Maradana and the Lake View Stores at Hunupitiya—both in Colombo, where some 100 men and women find employment. The mineral, being cured under skilled supervision, is worked into the various grades. The cured plumbago is sold locally, as well as exported to London, Antwerp, Bremen, Hamburg, New York, and other great trading centres, in all of which Mr. Arseculeratne has his own agents. He is a member of the Plumbago Merchants' Union and the Catholic Club, and resides at "Watersmeet," Mutwal, Colombo.

WIDANELAGE JOHANIS DE MEL.

Mr. Widanelage Johanis De Mel was born at Moratuwa, a town south of Colombo, in 1856, and started business as a plumbago merchant in 1880, in partnership with another member of that well-known family. But, severing his connection with that relative in 1884, he started a business on his own account at Maradana, Colombo, in a modest way, which has now, however, grown to be one of the most important of its kind in the island. A number of stores in Colombo, principally the Melbourne Stores—where the head office is situated—in Hunupitiya suburb, Hunupitiya Stores, and Kanatte Stores, Borella, are owned by Mr. De Mel. At all of these establishments extensive operations are carried on in dealing with plumbago from the time it reaches the yards in its uncured condition, through the sorting, sizing, and curing processes, until it is finally ready for shipment. In these various operations some 400 hands in all are employed. All the plumbago cured by the firm is sold in the local market. Mr. De Mel is not only a large buyer of the mineral in its rough state from minor dealers, who sell the whole of the output of their pits to him, but he also works his own mines in the Mirigama district, and the plumbago from these, as from the other mines, is forwarded to the Colombo stores for treatment and disposal.

In addition to being a mine-owner and plumbago merchant, Mr. De Mel is the proprietor of various coconut estates in the Chilaw and Puttalam districts, and also owns several fine houses in Cinnamon Gardens, Colombo. But his own country residence, known as Melbourne House, is situated in the Moratuwa district, 12 miles south of the city. Mr. De Mel is a supporter of the Young Men's Christian Association, besides being a liberal subscriber to all Church and charitable institutions. He is also a member of the Plumbago Merchants' Union. His eldest son, Mr. Richard Abraham Johanis De Mel, who manages all his father's business, was born at Moratuwa in 1885, and educated at St. Joseph's College, Colombo, and joined his father's business in 1903. Young as he is, he displays a keen business ability. He is a staunch Churchman, and a member of the choir of St. Peter's Church, Moratuwa.

R. MIRANDA & SONS.

This firm, carrying on the business of plumbago and bone-manure merchants as well as of mine owners at 83, St. Joseph Street, Grandpass, Colombo, come from Tuticorin, India, in which town, at 95, Great Cotton Road, they had established a large wholesale and retail business both in oilmen's stores and chemicals and apothecaries' requisites, directly imported from English and American houses, which they still conduct. In 1899, Pius Miranda, the eldest son of Rosario Miranda, Tuticorin, set up at Colombo as a plumbago merchant, buying the mineral in the local market as well as treating the output from his own mines in the Ratnapura district. The plumbago from these and other mines is

WIDANELAGE JOHANIS DE MEL, R. A. J. DE MEL, AND VIEWS OF HUNUPITIYA STORES.

PLUMBAGO YARD. LAZARUS SALEAS MIRANDA. PIUS MIRANDA, OF R. MIRANDA & SONS.

brought by boats to the firm's own wharf on the Colombo Main Canal, and there unloaded and prepared for shipment, some 150 men and women being engaged in the work. All the barrels in which the plumbago is packed are made on the premises. The bone-manure, the business in which is some twenty years older than the firm's plumbago trade, is imported direct from Madras, and then supplied to various local manure factories. Mr. Miranda is the only Indian gentleman engaged in plumbago-mining in Ceylon. He was one of the prime movers in establishing the Plumbago Merchants' union, and is still a prominent member of that organisation. He is assisted in the business by his brother, Mr. Lazarus Saleas Miranda, who is a medical man by profession.

MR. AND MRS. S. D. S. GUNASEKERE AND FAMILY.

S. D. S. GUNASEKERE & CO.

Mr. S. D. S. Gunasekere is the sole partner of the firm of S. D. S. Gunasekere & Co., and up to 1898 he was a partner also in the firm of U. D. S. Gunasekara. In 1899 he commenced business on his own account under the name and style of S. D. S. Gunasekere & Co., at Dematetoda, and in 1901 removed to his present premises at Borella. He was born at Galle, and educated at the Royal College. His parents were Emans de Silva Gunasekere and Soyso de Silva Gunasekere. He had five brothers, one of whom was the late Mr. U. D. S. Gunasekara, the founder of the firm of that name, and five sisters, one of these being the wife of Mr. A. E. de Silva, general merchant and estate proprietor. Mr. Gunasekere is now a large dealer in plumbago, cinnamon, coir, fibre, and cardamoms. He buys plumbago in the local market and cures it at his own stores at Borella, ready for shipment. He employs about 50 men and women at these stores. He has a number of fully equipped cinnamon estates in the Negombo and Galle districts and in the Hewagam Korale. The produce from these is sold at the local markets and the fibre exported to Germany. In 1889 he married Eugenie, daughter of Bastian de Silva Cumarasinghe, general merchant, of Colombo. He is a member of the Plumbago Merchants' Union and of the Ceylon National Association. His residence is Praeminie Villa, Borella.

A. L. MENDIS APPUHAMY.

Allegiawannegey Louis Mendis Appuhamy is a member of the Salagama community, and is a native of Mutwal. He is a descendant of the illustrious poet Allegiawannegey Mobabbale, who flourished during the early part of the sixteenth century, during the reign of the Sinhalese king Senerat, and whose contributions form a valuable addition to the literature of the Sinhalese language. In the latter part of the seventeenth century the family incurred the displeasure of the Sinhalese king then ruling, on the conversion to the Roman Catholic Faith of the representatives of the family by the Rev. Father Joseph Mendez, whose surname those members of the family who were converts then adopted—Mendis being the Anglicised form as it exists now. The converts, having had all their lands confiscated by the king, left the Cena Korale, where they were residing, and settled down at Mutwal, Colombo. Allegiawannegey Louis Mendis Appuhamy, better known as Mr. A. De Louis Mendis, left Mutwal for the planting districts during the palmy days when coffee was the principal planting industry, and surviving the crash which followed the failure of the coffee industry, built his fortunes anew upon the foundations of its substitute—tea. He owns the tea estate known as Handungala estate, situate at Nawalapitiya. A photograph of the bungalow standing upon the estate appears elsewhere. Mr. Mendis owns besides several mining properties, upon which he is prospecting for plumbago. Mr. Mendis is president of the St. Mary's Roman Catholic Church, Nawalapitiya.

A. DE L. MENDIS.

S. SANMOGAM & CO.

Among the very few firms of native merchants of Ceylon who transact their business directly with foreign countries is that of S. Sanmogam & Co., which, unlike other local native firms, deals both in the export and import of goods. Although the firm was established so recently as 1898, owing to the sound manner in which it transacts business and the great satisfaction it gives to its foreign customers, it has already extensive dealings both in export and import lines with the following countries : South Africa, Australia Austria, Belgium, England, France, Germany Holland, Italy, Japan, and the United States.

The firm deals in cardamoms, cinnamon

A. DE L. MENDIS AND FAMILY.

THE RESIDENCE.

S. SANMOGAM & CO.'S ESTABLISHMENT—BALING PRESS, PRIVATE BUNGALOW, FIBRE WORKS AND OFFICES.

citronella oil, cocoa, coconut oil, coconuts, desiccated coconut, copra, fibre, coir yarn, coir rope, mattress fibre, coconut fibre, kitool fibre, Palmyra fibre, plumbago, sapuwood, tea, and other commodities. The telegraphic address of the firm—"Plombagine"—alludes to the mineral which forms a staple product of the island. In this line the firm was awarded a bronze medal for its exhibit of plumbago at the last St. Louis Exhibition. The Colombo offices and general stores of the firm are situated at First Cross Street, Pettah, Colombo; and a good idea of its extensive dealings in the way of fibre is conveyed by witnessing the work carried on in these premises by the enormous number of men and women who are daily employed here throughout the year in order that the goods may be ready for weekly and bi-weekly shipment.

D. P. TAMPOE.

Mr. Daniel Ponnusamy Tampoe is the son of Mr. T. M. Tampoe, retired police magistrate, of Jaffna. He was born at Jaffna in 1872, and received his education at St. Thomas's College, Jaffna. The first part of his commercial career he spent with Messrs. Aitken, Spence & Co., with whom he stayed from 1894 to 1903. He then spent two years planting in the North-Western Province, and in 1905 commenced business in Colombo as commission agent and broker. Since the latter part of 1905 he has been the official auctioneer of the Plumbago Merchants' Union, and in this capacity the bulk of the Ceylon plumbago trade passes through his hands. In addition to this business he has coconut and cinnamon estates at Chilaw, Jaffna, and Kalutara, and at the last-named estate he is now commencing to grow rubber. His offices are in Chatham Street, Colombo, and he resides at Horton Lodge, Horton Place. He is a member of the Turf and Orient clubs, and of the Old Boys' Associations of various leading Colombo colleges. In 1894 he married Charlotte, daughter of Mr. S. T. Muttiah, late of Messrs. Aitken, Spence & Co. His principal assistant in his important business is Mr. H. O. Poppenbeek, of Trinity College, Kandy.

H. O. POPPENBEEK.

THE PUBLIC WORKS DEPARTMENT

NO impressions of Ceylon would be complete which did not include a summary of the history of the evolution of the Public Works Department, next to the railway the most costly and responsible machinery in the island, which has during the last ten years, under the administration of the present Director, the Hon. F. A. Cooper, C.M.G., been brought to a state of the highest development. Indeed, Ceylon owes much of its material prosperity to the thoroughness with which communication was opened up before the advent of the railway by the construction of good main roads. If this development has not been so rapid as some would wish, if it has not exactly kept pace with the impatience of the early pioneers in the planting enterprise, it has been sound. "Slow but sure" is the motto that can be applied to the work of the early days of the Public Works Department. Its road-makers and its bridge-builders understood their business and made the most of the materials at their disposal. In those pioneer days, when Ceylon was in the condition of a rich undeveloped estate and when railway communication was in its infancy, the pioneer and the Government servant living in remote parts of the island were dependent upon three sources of communication—the sea, canals, and the large trunk roads which intersected the country from north to south and from east to west. And the great bulk of the produce had to be transported by road by means of the heavy and cumbrous bullock-carts, the beginning of whose death-knell the twentieth century has sounded. It therefore became a matter of primary importance that the work of road-construction should be thoroughly done, and that the system should be capable of withstanding not only the stress of weather, but the strain of increasing heavy traffic. In the low-country, or what are called the maritime provinces, this work was comparatively of a light and easy description, but in the hill-country the engineering difficulties presented to the earliest of our road-makers were considerable. Many of the most important roads in the island had not only to be cut out of the mountain-side, but provision had to be made for heavy and continuous rainfall, increasing in severity and intensity on the occasion of each successive burst of the monsoon, carrying with it the danger of soil-subsidence or land-slip; they had equally to endure spells of prolonged drought. When these natural difficulties are borne in mind, the successful way in which they were overcome can only be described as marvellous. In the present day, thanks to the energy which has characterised the policy of Government and the administrative efficiency to which the Hon. Mr. Cooper has brought his department, very satisfactory progress has been made toward finality. Shortly after the present Director of Public Works entered upon his duties he reported that the sum allowed for upkeep in recent years had been quite insufficient to maintain the roads in an efficient state, and that on many of the roads there was little or no metal left. In other words, many of the roads were in such an unsatisfactory condition that they required to be entirely re-metalled—that is to say, not re-metalled in the ordinary way, with a little metal put on them here and there, but relaid altogether. The total amount spent on maintenance in the seven years preceding 1896 was Rs. 7,688,864, or an average expenditure of not quite eleven lakhs of rupees a year. So strong a case did the Director make out that a very large increase was necessary to enable the roads to be kept up in a condition fit for traffic, that in 1898 no less a sum than about 13½ lakhs, or 2½ lakhs above the previous average, was allotted for the purpose; since then each year has seen an increase, and the total amount spent on maintenance during the seven years preceding the administration of Sir Henry Blake as Governor was Rs. 10,011,853, or an average of over 14 lakhs per annum. This cost, though somewhat in excess of that obtaining in 1885, is still considerably below the expenditure of 1880, the year preceding the introduction by Mr. Cooper's predecessor of what is generally known as the MacBride system. That the money was well spent, and that it rescued the state of the colony's roads from any reproach of neglect, is generally admitted. In fact, Mr. Cooper's administration may be said to have synchronised with the opening of a new era in road-construction, in which attention was paid, not only to the increase of the mileage of roads of all descriptions, but the existing system was thoroughly overhauled and strengthened and brought up to date, wooden bridges were replaced by iron-work, and everything done compatible with the island's resources to introduce a system of uniformity. The large extensions in railway communication which took place during the administration of Sir West Ridgeway threw additional responsibility on the Department of Public Works in the provision of "feeder roads" for those new railways, and everything was done to increase as far as possible the facilities for using the new railways.

HISTORY.

If railways generally serve the same purposes as arteries in the human system, roads may equally be regarded as the veins, which enable those arteries, in this matter of communication, to discharge their important functions. We discover this correlation existing in the Ceylon Government Railway and the Public Works Department, the two most expensive and most responsible departments in the progressive development of the colony. The history, or evolution, of the Public Works Department, therefore, is interesting as well as instructive. We find that in the year 1815, when the whole of the island of Ceylon came under British rule, there was included in the civil establishments of the colony the Civil Engineer and Surveyor-General's Office. The establishment of that office consisted of the Civil Engineer and Surveyor-General, Mr. Gualterus Schneider, one clerk, one overseer, and six district surveyors. To-day there exists a perfectly organised department, or, rather, out of this modest beginning has sprung three important departments, with which the permanent welfare of the island is more intimately bound up than with any other portion of the administrative machinery. From the Civil Engineer and Surveyor-General's Office has sprung the Public Works Department, the Surveyor-General's Department, and the Irrigation Department, each adequately equipped for performing the work that falls to its portion. In the earlier days of British rule, when the island was under military administration, such road-construction and buildings as were required were executed by the Royal Engineers or other military officers. Mr. Gualterus Schneider filled the office of Civil Engineer and Surveyor-General till 1833, when he was succeeded by Mr. F. B. Norris, who held the appointment till 1850. In 1842 Captain T. Skinner, who afterwards became Major Skinner, and who gained considerable renown as "the Road-maker of Ceylon," was appointed Commissioner of Roads. In 1844 an Ordinance (No. 16) was enacted "for the preservation and improvement of streets, roads, thoroughfares, and public places within towns, and of the public roads, navigable rivers, lakes, and canals of this island." This Ordinance conferred certain powers upon Government agents, the Surveyor-General, Civil Engineer, and Commissioner of Roads, and in 1846 the Surveyor-General's Office became a separate department. In 1848 an Ordinance (No. 8) was enacted "for the purpose of making better provision for the protection and maintenance of roads, and for the improvement of the means of communication by land and by water in the island." By the provisions of this Ordinance the construction, improvement, and maintenance of the means of communication were controlled by provincial and district road committees, of which the Commissioner of Roads, or his representative, was a member. In the same year the Road Ordinance was passed, requiring every able-bodied man between eighteen and sixty years of age to give six days' labour or pay a few shillings as commutation for the maintenance of the roads. Captain T. Skinner succeeded Mr. F. B. Norris as Civil Engineer and Commissioner of Roads in 1850, when the offices of Civil Engineer and Commissioner of Roads were amalgamated. In 1867 by Ordinance (No. 16) it was enacted that "the office of Civil Engineer and Commissioner of Roads shall henceforward be termed the Department of Public Works, and the chief officer shall be termed the Director of Public Works." In the same year Major Skinner retired, after forty years' residence in Ceylon, from the public service, and lived to enjoy his well-earned pension for ten years to the very month. Mr. (now Sir) G. L. Molesworth, M.I.C.E., was appointed Director of Public Works in 1867, and held the appointment till the year 1871. The Technical Staff of the Public Works Department at this time consisted of the following: Office Assistant, Financial Assistant, Architectural Assistant, Officer Commanding Pioneer Force, Irrigation Assistant, Second Financial Assistant, seven provincial assistants, six draughtsmen and framers of estimates, twenty-four superintending officers, seventeen Officers Commanding Pioneers, and one road-tracing officer. On Mr. (now Sir) G. L. Molesworth's retirement, in 1871, Mr. J. R. Mosse, M.I.C.E., was appointed Director of Public Works, which office he held till 1882, though during a portion of this period he was in charge of the Railway Department, Mr. J. F. Churchill, M.I.C.E., acting as Director of Public Works, to which appointment he succeeded in 1882. Retiring in 1885, he was succeeded by the late Mr. R. K. MacBride, M.I.C.E., who held office till 1897, when he was succeeded by the present holder, Mr. F. A. Cooper, M.I.C.E. Mr. MacBride was promoted to a seat in the Legislative Council in 1894, and since then the Director of Public Works has always been included in the official members of Council. Previous to the year 1889 the construction, restoration, and maintenance of irrigation works were under the control of the Public Works Department. By Ordinance No. 23 of 1899 all such works were vested in the Central and Provincial Irrigation Boards, of which the Director of Public Works was *ex officio* a member, and the officers of the Public Works Department rendered the Central and Provincial Irrigation Boards such professional assistance as was required. In 1900 the officers of the Public Works Department were relieved of all executive duties connected with irrigation, and a separate Irrigation Department was formed.

TABLE A.

Year.	Maintenance.	Construction.	Total.	Establishment.
	Rs.	Rs.	Rs.	Rs.
1880	1,932,734	,586,066	3,518,800	336,054
1881	1,688,040	569,238	2,257,278	311,183
1882	1,656,343	336,051	1,992,394	292,575
1883	1,517,054	305,913	1,822,967	268,950
1884	1,350,767	350,370	1,701,137	278,550
1885	1,135,697	780,430	1,916,127	273,151
1886	1,069,018	1,247,785	2,316,803	283,819
1887	1,058,582	1,213,120	2,271,702	315,239
1888	1,134,801	1,110,265	2,245,066	317,835
1889	1,254,907	1,352,683	2,607,590	299,864
1890	1,318,457	1,712,444	3,030,901	345,681
1891	1,438,574	1,539,179	2,977,753	338,358
1892	1,638,690	2,052,906	3,691,596	337,005
1893	1,711,011	2,295,976	4,006,987	340,779
1894	1,710,625	1,720,743	3,431,368	380,027
1895	1,756,001	1,286,889	3,042,890	402,019
1896	1,823,558	1,219,106	3,042,664	385,268
1897	1,726,669	1,838,650	3,565,319	383,682
1898	1,900,307	1,879,467	3,779,774	400,848
1899	2,040,684	2,957,244	4,997,928	415,126
1900	2,029,279	2,684,926	4,714,208	462,262
1901	2,112,905	2,014,060	4,126,965	428,948
1902	2,163,394	2,020,634	4,184,028	439,038
1903	2,240,086	2,615,667	4,855,753	463,488
1904	2,286,812	2,477,932	4,764,744	422,009
1905	2,324,805	1,966,043	4,290,848	410,304

ORGANISATION.

The Public Works Department is in charge of the Director of Public Works. It is one of the scientific or professional departments, and, as distinguished from the Civil Service, its ranks are filled exclusively by officers who have received a distinctly scientific training, and who come out to Ceylon after having obtained some experience in their profession. The Provincial Engineers, whose charges are generally coterminous with the Revenue Provinces, are authorised by the Director as official members of the Provincial Road Committees, of which he is *ex officio* a member himself, though as a matter of fact he never acts as such. The Provincial Engineers of the Central and Southern Provinces are nominated official members of the Municipal Councils of Kandy and Galle, and the Provincial Engineers of the Eastern, North-Western, and North-Central Provinces, and of Uva and Sabaragamuwa are nominated official members of the Local Boards of Batticaloa, Kurunegala, Anuradhapura, Badulla, and Ratnapura respectively. The District Engineers have charges not necessarily coterminous with any other division. Those of them whose headquarters are Local Board towns are nominated members of those Local Boards. The Department has charge of the design, construction, and maintenance of all Government architectural and engineering works, both civil and mechanical, other than those under the control of the Railway, Irrigation, and Postal Telegraphs Departments, and such special work as the Colombo Harbour Works, now being carried out by Messrs. Coode, Son & Mathews. The work of the Public Works Department is conducted at the head office, Colombo, and at the following provincial and district offices :—

TABLE B.

Building.	Cost.	Date.
Colombo.	Rs.	Rs.
General Post Office	351,341	1895
Custom House	112,268	1876
Mutwal Jail	65,890	1892
Supreme Court...	81,885	1860–62
District Court	70,200	
Law Offices	54,856	1882
Museum	199,994	1873
Kachcheri	46,550	
Surveyor-General's Office	65,993	1875
Agricultural School	52,669	
Lady Havelock Hospital	32,400	1895
Police Barracks, Cinnamon Gardens	44,700	1893
Lunatic Asylum	400,000	1888
Victoria Bridge... ... ... (about)	507,143	1895
Police Headquarters ... ... (about)	90,000	1867
Kurunegala.		
Kachcheri	41,752	
Agent's Residence	50,676	
Hospital	30,350	
Puttalam.		
Kachcheri	28,830	1887
Jail	23,734	1872
Chilaw.		
Jail	21,140	
Anuradhapura.		
Hospital	34,889	1892
Badulla.		
Kachcheri	25,680	1891
Court	35,805	1892
Hospital	99,540	1890
Haputale.		
Hospital	69.575	1895
Ratnapura.		
District Judge's House	19,320	1893
Rakwana.		
Hospital	,3,358	1894
Avisawella.		
Hospital	27,684	1894
Malurata.		
Hospital	81,997	1902
Dimbula.		
Hospital	80,863	1901

PROVINCIAL ENGINEERS' OFFICES.

Colombo, Western Province.
Kandy, Central Province.
Jaffna, Northern Province.
Galle, Southern Province.
Batticaloa, Eastern Province.
Kurunegala, North-Western Province.
Anuradhapura, North-Central Province.
Badulla, Uva.
Ratnapura, Sabaragamuwa.

FACTORY ENGINEER'S OFFICE.

Colombo, Western Province.

DISTRICT ENGINEERS' OFFICES.

Colombo, Western Province.
Negombo, Western Province.
Kalutara, Western Province.
Kandy, Central Province.
Matale, Central Province.
Katugastota, Central Province.
Pussellawa, Central Province.
Nuwara Eliya, Central Province.
Dimbula, Central Province.
Dikoya, Central Province.
Jaffna, Northern Province.
Vavuniya, Northern Province.
Mannar, Northern Province.
Pallai, Northern Province.
Galle, Southern Province.
Matara, Southern Province.
Hambantota, Southern Province.
Batticaloa, Eastern Province.
Kalmunai, Eastern Province.
Trincomalee, Eastern Province.
Kurunegala, North-Western Province.
Puttalam, North-Western Province.
Chilaw, North-Western Province.
Dandugama, North-Western Province.
Anuradhapura, North-Central Province.
Mihintale, North-Central Province.
Maradankadawela, North-Central Province.
Badulla, Uva.
Koslande, Uva.
Passara, Uva.
Ratnapura, Sabaragamuwa.
Avisawella, Sabaragamuwa.
Kegalla, Sabaragamuwa.

The Assistant Director of Public Works, Mr. C. A. Lovegrove, A.M.I.C.E., has immediate charge of the work at the head office, which is divided into the following branches : Drawing Office (in charge of a head draughtsman), Correspondence, Accounts (in charge of a financial assistant and accountant), and Store.

For years past the necessity for larger accommodation and better equipped premises has manifested itself, but owing to other more pressing demands on the public purse the construction of new central offices for the Public Works Department has been postponed to this year. This is now being undertaken, and in a short time the department will be housed in a building worthy of its importance. The Factory Engineer, Mr. E. C. Davies, assisted by Mr. G. H. M. Hyde, M.I.M.E., A.M.I.C.E., Mechanical Engineer, has immediate charge of all mechanical and electrical works and the staff of the Government Factory at Colombo. There is also a Superintendent of Works. The 9 provincial engineers are the representatives of the Director of Public Works in the several provinces and, assisted by the 45 district engineers, have immediate charge of all works in the provinces, and in such capacity render assistance to local municipalities, road committees, Local Boards, and other quasi-Government departments. These district engineers are divided into grades: 15 first grade, 26 second grade, 6 third grade. A supernumerary district engineer is employed in place of the officer seconded for duty in connection with the waterworks scheme. Lastly, there are 7 inspectors and 15 overseers. The operations of the Public Works Department may be classified as follows: construction and maintenance of roads, canals, harbours, waterworks, drainage-works, bridges, electric light installations, and the maintenance of harbour tugs, launches, ferry-boats, steam-rollers, cranes, and other machinery in general use by Government departments or in temporary use as plant in the construction of the various works undertaken by the department. In the carrying out of minor works the ordinary methods adopted by the natives to a large extent prevail, whilst in the construction of the larger works steam cranes, dredgers, steam-rollers, cableways, pneumatic riveters, and other modern appliances have been introduced and put to effective use.

The expenditure of the department is classified in the annual estimates as Public Works Annually Recurrent (maintenance of roads, maintenance of inland navigation, repairs to buildings, additions to buildings, repairs to bridges, miscellaneous) and Public Works Extraordinary (new works and buildings, alterations and additions to buildings, special repairs to buildings, new roads, new bridges, repairs of bridges, lands and buildings to be acquired, miscellaneous).

In Table A is given a statement of the expenditure of the Public Works Departmen for the years 1880 to 1905 inclusive, under the headings Maintenance, Construction, and Establishment.

During the period that Mr. Cooper has been the administrative head of the Public Works Department over a hundred new buildings have been completed, and others, including the erection of new central offices for the Public Works Department, and a new central railway station for Colombo, are now in course of construction.

Table B gives a short list of some of the principal buildings erected by the Public Works Department, and the cost of the same.

FISHERIES

THE Ceylon pearl fishery, dealt with in a special article by Mr. James Hornell, constitutes the most important, as it does also the most picturesque, feature of the fisheries of Ceylon. But outside this great industry there are several branches of enterprise which, from their interest and value, call for more than passing reference. A sea-girt isle, with numerous bays and lagoons swarming with fish, and with, in many parts, a well-to-do population near the seaboard to supply a lucrative market for the catches, Ceylon furnishes exceptional opportunities for the practice of the fisherman's calling. It cannot be said, however, that the advantages are utilised to anything like a full extent. In some directions, indeed, there is a degree of apathy shown which would appear remarkable if we did not recall that the Sinhalese is by religious instinct and tradition averse from marine enterprise, and that the remarkable fertility of the island supplies him with many products upon which he can sustain an existence on land without excessive exertion. The fishing industry flourishes best, as is perhaps natural, on the western seaboard about Colombo, where there is a heavy demand for fish of all kinds. Negombo and Chilaw are important centres. The fishermen at these places are a hardworking and enterprising class, and their reputation extends far beyond local limits. The main fishing season is from October to April, during the north-east monsoon. In the other months of the year operations are fitfully conducted owing to the prevalence of the south-west monsoon, which prevents the boats from putting to sea. At this season the men transfer their operations to the rivers and lakes, where an abundance of fish for the most part exists. The system followed on the west coast is described by Mr. S. M. Burrows, Acting Government Agent for the North-Western Province, in his Administration Report for 1905. The chief implements employed are nets known as *ma-del*, *kanni-del*, *katta-del*, *pulun-del*, *suda-del*, *kumbala-del*, and *sola-del*, which are spun by the people themselves. The *ma-del* is used in catching fish of all kinds—big and small. It is usually taken to the sea in a small-sized padda-boat known as the *madel paruwa*, which is specially intended for it. One end remains ashore and the boat rows in a semicircle of about half a mile radius, letting the net into the sea as it goes. The other end is brought ashore. Miniature buoys are attached to a side of the net to make it float, whilst the two ends are fastened on to long thick ropes for the purpose of drawing it ashore, when about fifteen to twenty men are engaged at a time. These men are remunerated weekly according to agreement entered into, whilst they are given small quantities of fish proportionately as an inducement. The net called *kanni-del* is employed in catching large kinds of fish only, such as the shark tribe, *Rhinodon typicus*. The fish anjilawa, katuwalla, huralla, anguluwa, and pannawa are caught by means of the net known as *pulun-dela*. Fishermen who catch fish in rafts called *teppan* make much use of the nets known as *katta-del*, *pulun-del*, *suda-del*, *kumbala-del*, and *sala-del*. At Udappu, Karukkuponai, Toduwawa, and Chilaw much of the fish caught is cured, whilst a large quantity is removed by sea to Colombo by boats which come for the purpose. The rest of the fish is either taken fresh or salted to Kurunegala in pingoes or consumed in the

A NATIVE FISHING BOAT.

district or converted into *kara wala* (dried fish) and *jadi* (pickled fish). Rod and line fishing is largely and widely practised along the coast. A quaint spectacle to be daily witnessed on the Negombo lagoon is a figure wearing a broad-brimmed hat and submerged to the waist, patiently practising the gentle art. Equally familiar are the anglers who post themselves amid the surf on the Colombo foreshore and cast their line just beyond the break of the waves. The favourite quarry of these disciples of Isaac Walton is a small fish which frequents shallow water; but the *mora*, an eatable shark, is sometimes fished for with rod and line. Nets and baited pots are also resorted to in the pursuit of this fish. The most curious method of fishing, however, is that practised on the lake at Pambala. A net called *hin-del* is spread in the lake either by day or night. A canoe is rowed towards it, and meanwhile the occupants of the craft tap the woodwork with a stick. The fish, frightened by the noise, swim off and are caught by their gills in the meshes of the net.

We have spoken of the Negombo fishermen as an enterprising class. The fact is borne out by official records, which tell of long journeys undertaken by these men in pursuit of their calling. One distant centre favoured by them is Mullaitivu, on the extreme north-east coast. A party of from 400 to 500 men annually resort to this part, where, with other fishermen, mainly from Pesalai, in Mannar, they conduct extensive operations. The men are organised in gangs of from twenty-five to fifty, each under a chief fisherman (*Mudalali*). Each Mudalali brings about ten men with him and employs about the same number of Mullaitivu men. They encamp at various places along the coast. Some of them purchase land near their temporary encampments and plant it with coconuts, but these plantations are not so successful as they might be, as they suffer much from neglect during the part of the year when the fishermen are away in their own districts. The boats used are generally their own, but some are hired. They are chiefly large *ballams* about 40 ft. long, and *pathai* boats (flat-bottomed boats of a rectangular shape and about 12 ft. long). The crew of a *ballam* is six or seven men. The nets used by the visitors are a large drag-net, a small drag-net, and two drift-nets. The fish caught are salted and dried, each Mudalali buying about 100 or 150 cwt. of salt for the purpose. When fully cured the goods are sent to Colombo by a native sailing craft, to be sold by the fishermen's Negombo partners. One-third of the profits goes to the principal who advances the money, and two-thirds to the fishermen, any loss in the trade, which is rare, being shared between the Mudalali and the fishermen in the same proportion as the profit. It is supposed to be a profitable investment, the capital invested each year yielding 150 per cent. interest. It is only rarely that there

NEGOMBO FISHING BOAT.

is any loss in the trade.[1] In connection with this fishery it may be added that turtle are occasionally found in the large drag-nets. No systematic efforts are, however, made to trap them, and turtle flesh is never exposed for sale in the local bazaars.

The large tanks and lakes which are a characteristic feature of many parts of the island teem with fish, and the catches constitute a commercial asset of some value. A case is cited by Mr. C. T. D. Vigors, in the Administration Report of the North-Central Province for 1905, of a village which on a tank getting low sold the right to catch fish for Rs. 140. "A more extraordinary sight of its kind than the quantities of fish being caught and removed from Kalawewa in September," says Mr. Vigors, "I have never witnessed. The villagers were camped all round and catching the fish with baskets or by blows with bits of hoop-iron or sticks as they rose gasping to the surface. The catch was being partly dried on the spot and partly hurried away on pingoes and in carts to neighbouring villages to be dried at home."

Some further interesting details on the subject of tank fish are given in the "Manual of the North-West Province" issued by the Government in 1899. "When the water in the tanks fails," says the writer, "the villagers assemble with fishing baskets and catch immense quantities of fish, and this is divided among them according to the village *pangu* (share). The fish seem to have the power of burying themselves deep in the mud or they would soon be exterminated in tanks. I have been astonished to see tanks which a few months before were perfectly dry stocked with good-sized fish when filled." Dealing further with the question of tank fishing, the writer says: "Immense quantities of sprats are caught and dried. There are several fish which are bony and disagreeable. The best kinds are the *lula* and *walaya*. The former is an eel-like fish and grows to about 8 lbs. or 10 lbs. in the rivers and averages 1½ lbs. to 2 lbs. in the tanks. The *walaya* is a fine fish which grows to an immense size and is generally caught with a line and live bait. It has a faint taste of salmon, though the flesh is not firm and flaky. It has a broad, flat head and long, beard-like threads about the mouth, which is furnished with several rows of formidable teeth. I have never heard that any fish here are unwholesome at any time of the year, as some kinds are in the up-country streams." Besides the fish mentioned by the writer, the tanks supply the *kokassa*, an excellent fish for the table, and occasionally the *koraliya*, a fish with the flavour of a good mullet. There are also found there two varieties of stinging fish—the *hunga* and the *ankatta*. Villagers are very frequently stung

[1] "Manual of the Vanni Districts," by J. P. Lewis, of the Ceylon Civil Service.

when fishing, but they invariably carry an antidote to the poison with them, so that no evil consequences follow. In regard to the method of fishing in the tanks, apart from the use of baskets, it may be stated that those who generally fish for the large kinds with hooks fasten several thin rattan canes together, and at the end tie a piece of stout cord, 6 ins. long, with a hook of the ordinary sea-hook kind. This is pushed out into the tank for about 15 or 20 yards and is baited with a small live fish—generally a *tillaya* (Sinhalese), *kendai* (Tamil). The tanks are so full of growing weeds and fallen trees that lines easily get broken, and this rough method of fishing is found to be most effective in securing the fish. Under favourable conditions tank fish have been taken with the artificial fly, but, generally speaking, this method has not been found very effective where tried.

At Bentota, about 38 miles south of Colombo, and Batticaloa, Kotiyar, and other ports on the east coast, edible oysters exist in considerable quantities. Bentota is a pretty little centre, much resorted to by picnic parties from Colombo, and the oysters there are not the least of its attractions. But the bi-valves are too thin and small to have a vogue far outside the limits of the fishing-ground. The east coast oysters are larger. The low salinity of the backwaters which abound hereabout favours development, and oysters are found of great size and excellent quality. It is believed by experts that if oyster culture were carried out on scientific lines a valuable industry might be created. A like remark applies to the sponge trade. The true bath sponge (*Euspongia officinalis*) is found in considerable quantities near Jaffna and in Trincomalee harbour ; but apart from small local sales no effort is made to turn the growth to profitable use.

There is, however, one extensive industry associated with Ceylon fisheries to which the accusation of neglect cannot be applied. The reference is to the important chank trade which flourishes in the north of the island. The chank (*Turbinella pyrum*) is a large and massive shell found in considerable quantities, chiefly along the north-eastern coast between Point Pedro and Mullaitivu and around Jaffna and Mannar. The best shells are collected by divers, but an inferior class of sub-fossil shells is obtained from the sand in the coast line from Jaffna to Elephant Pass. The shells are located by means of an iron probe which the fishermen insert in the sand at likely places.

A FISH KRAAL ON MORATUWA LAGOON.

Chanks are a considerable article of export. In 1905 no fewer than 2,573,820, of the value of Rs. 103,725, were sent out of the country. They went principally to Calcutta, where they are used to meet the ceremonial requirements of the Hindu religion. Some are manufactured into rings, armlets, and anklets to take the place at the funerals of women of the personal ornaments of the female members of their household, the destruction of all jewellery of such persons being enjoined by the precepts of the Hindu faith. Others are made to do service as trumpets used to summon the faithful to worship at the temples. For this purpose right-handed shells, that is to say those in which the spiral is in the reverse direction to that usual, are largely sought for and fetch very high prices. The Government exacts a royalty of one cent. on every five chanks exported. In 1905 the revenue derived from this source amounted to Rs. 5,202.

The *bêche de mer*, or sea slug, to give it its popular name, is another article of export. The fish is a species of Holothurian, of gelatinous composition. Specimens are collected and cut open and dried in the sun and in that form exported to China, where they are in great request for soup-making purposes. *Bêche de mer* soup is reported to possess many virtues, but it has never taken the European fancy to any extent. The bulk of this class of the Ceylon exports goes to the British Indies and the Straits Settlements. In 1905 the united exports to these centres amounted in value to Rs. 23,538.

Though not strictly connected with the subject of commercial fisheries, with which we are dealing, the question of trout acclimatisation may be appropriately touched upon here. The late Mr. Hugh G. Hubbard, of St. John's, Udapussellawa, was the pioneer of the movement for stocking the Ceylon rivers. Assisted by Mr. C. J. R. Le Mesurier and Mr. Hearn, he, in 1880, made his first experiments in trout-breeding. This initial venture was followed by others, and their success encouraged Mr. Le Mesurier, then Assistant Government Agent at Nuwara Eliya, to invite public support for a movement on a large scale. The response was encouraging. Altogether Rs. 3,000 were raised, the amount including a substantial sum from the Local Board, of which Mr. Le Mesurier was Chairman. The rivers were stocked, and as no fishing was allowed it was hoped that the fish would multiply to such an extent that re-stocking would be unnecessary. These expectations, however, were doomed to disappointment. In a few years all trace of the trout was lost. Undeterred by these disappointing results, some ardent anglers in 1892 and 1893 resumed the experiments on their own account, and were rewarded for their enterprise by the successful propagation of the fish. Since then ova have been imported regularly during the first four months of the year. Originally the ova imported were those of the brown trout (*Salmo fario*), but since 1899 the ovum introduced has been that of the rainbow trout (*Salmo irridens*), which stands the climate better than the brown trout. The angler's interests are looked after by the Ceylon Fishing Club, which was founded in 1896. The Governor is President of the organisation, and the Vice-Presidents are the Government Agent, Central Province, and the Government Agent, Sabaragamuwa. It may be added as an interesting concluding fact that the largest trout yet caught in Ceylon scaled over 14 lbs.

ARRACK AND TODDY

CONSPICUOUS amongst the varied uses of the coconut-palm is the drawing out, by means of tapping, of the juice contained in its inflorescence for the manufacture of arrack and toddy. The former is an ardent spirit, and the latter is to the Ceylonese what whisky is to the people of the United Kingdom. Toddy, on the other hand, is a refreshing beverage, non-intoxicating and pleasant, if taken when freshly drawn, and, like the liquid found in the tender coconut, furnishes some measure of relief, not to say sustenance, to the thirsty traveller wandering under the fervid heat of a tropical sun. In some country parts of Ceylon, indeed, the wayfarer is offered a drink of the freshly drawn toddy gratuitously, and in the unpretentious circles of village life it often forms the one medium of conviviality, a medium which is no less appreciatively accepted than liberally and cordially given. With the addition of a little sugar to the liquor, a flavour is given which may be likened to a species of natural aerated water, mild and extremely agreeable; and for this reason it generally goes by the name of "sweet toddy."

But evidently the lack of stimulation and the tameness of this method of dispensing hospitality suggested the fermentation of the juice and the enhancement of its value as a marketable article; and the demand created for it among the peasant and labouring classes encouraged the undertaking of operations on a larger scale. Coconut plantations were leased out and systematic tapping was commenced. Ultimately a firm taste for the liquor was acquired, with the result that the arrack and toddy industry now extends practically all over the island, and may safely be said to be one of the most flourishing trades pursued in Ceylon. It must, however, be noted that the right to distil arrack—except for purely scientific and experimental purposes—is reserved by Government, and disposed of, under conditions and by public auction, to the highest bidder. For this purpose each province is divided into a certain number of farms, and the purchaser of any one of them has the exclusive right to engage in its traffic within the area which he leases out. So great are the possibilities of working these farms profitably that there is keen competition in the bidding, and often Government parts with the rents at phenomenal prices. The system of purchase is by the deposit with the revenue officer of the province of a large amount as security for the proper performance of the stipulations laid down, and instalments thereafter on account, until the entire purchase amount has been liquidated. If the conditions attaching to the rent have been properly fulfilled, the renter gets his discharge and is allowed to draw his deposit; but if any irregularity is noted, the rent is confiscated, and the moneys paid on account are forfeited to the Government. The arrack-renter is, in contradistinction to the wholesale dealer—who is only permitted to deal in liquor in quantities of over 35 gallons—known as the retail trader; and it is his duty to submit to Government a list of the places at which he desires the liquor to be sold. When the rent is sold, these centres of retail—"taverns," as they are called—are specified; and the Government Agent issues a licence to persons nominated by the renter to carry on business at the places indicated. According to the regulations in force the retailer may only sell arrack and toddy at a fixed price, the rate for the former being usually Rs. 4·48 per gallon, or about ninepence per pint. He is also bound by his compact to sell two quarts of the liquor to any one on demand. The renter monopolises the retail trade in his district, and has absolute control over the sale, possession, and removal of the spirit. Wholesale transactions, on the other hand, are attended to by the Government Agent of the province. Illicit distilling and sale of arrack and toddy being rampant, the strictest measures are adopted for the proper checking of all liquor passing into and out of a district, certificates and written orders from the seller, renter, and Government officers being insisted upon for any transportation of the spirit whatever. In this work of supervision the Government is assiduously assisted by the renter, who, having purchased the sole right of retail trade within his district, exercises the utmost care to prevent that right being infringed by others. The system pursued by the renter in the disposal of privileges to tavern-keepers is by accepting security against payment of the instalments, and then supplying the tavern-keeper with liquor at prices varying from Rs. 4·50 to Rs. 6 per gallon, of which Rs. 3·50 is placed to the credit of the quantity of the liquor sold and the balance reckoned on account of the instalments due. Thus, when a few thousand gallons have been furnished to the tavern-keeper, and payment recovered at, say, Rs. 5 per gallon, the excess amount of Rs. 1·50 on each gallon is credited to the purchase-amount of the rent, and the complete sum due for the right of retailing is liquidated. Once this has been effected, the tavern-keeper continues to draw from the renter supplies at the normal price of Rs. 3·50 per gallon, and profits by the difference between the purchase-price and the selling-rate, which, taken in the aggregate on monthly sales, is very considerable. Where the tavern-keeper, however, fails to pay his dues promptly, the renter immediately puts the price up and secures himself by recovering at once the current amounts payable and the arrears by the enhanced rates. Under the Ordinance regulating this industry the possession of arrack in a quantity in excess of one gallon is declared to be illegal, unless the possessor is protected by a Government licence.

The industry, as stated before, is not confined to any particular part of the island, but the greatest activity seems to prevail in the western districts, where some of the largest distilleries are to be found. No restrictions are placed upon the drawing or possession of sweet toddy, but fermented toddy comes in under the regulations of arrack. The process of extraction may be thus described: The flower of the *kitul*—a species of indigenous palm—or the coconut, as the case may be, is bruised and pared at the end, and tied up with strings to keep the pieces together. As the ends become parched, fresh slices are cut off, so as to preserve the bud in a "raw" or open condition. When this has been done two or three times, a little earthenware pot is hung beneath the inflorescence, into which the juice exuding from the bruised flower collects. The instruments usually employed consist of a little wooden mallet for tapping and a small curved knife, which the drawer secures to his person by a belt across his waist. Though the operation appears to be of a very rude and primitive nature, the drawers are particularly dexterous in their work, and often go through a large plantation in the course of a single day. A tight rope connects the trees, which are always planted at equal distances from one another, so that the drawer has no need to descend every time to tap a fresh tree. If the vessel attached to the tree is clean, the juice remains in a pure condition for several days; if a piece of rind from the bark of a *hal*-tree be placed in the pot, fermentation will still further be protracted, or may never occur at all. On the other hand, if a small quantity of the fermented juice be admitted while the liquid is being collected, it will turn the whole liquid sour and fermented. This juice is known as toddy. It is reckoned unlawful to distil liquor from anything but the palm and sugar-cane in this country; and the strong spirituous fermentations which are obtained from rice and other cereals in the South Sea Islands and elsewhere, and which constitute favourite beverages amongst the poorer classes, are practically unknown here. Toddy and arrack are the national beer and whisky of the Sinhalese, though the former may be said to be of very much greater strength under analysis than the refined liquors of the West in point of intoxicant properties. The methods of manufacture are as yet in a rude stage, and elsewhere in these pages will be seen pictures of the apparatus and stills used in the larger distilleries throughout the island.

The chief use to which the sweet or unfermented toddy is put is in the manufacture of a species of crude sugar called "jaggery," which is in great request in the interior districts of Ceylon in the preparation of native sweetmeats and delicacies. The principal consumers of fermented toddy are to be found in the ranks of the poorer population of the towns, who look upon it as a necessary stimulant after a day's hard labour and toil. Though contrary to the principles of the faith of the Sinhalese, there seems to be a growing tendency among the masses to indulge in alcoholic beverages, and at every social function native and imported liquors are freely served. The formation of anti-drinking societies and the organisation of temperance crusades have, it is true, conduced to check the evil in certain measure, but in the interests of their business the renters and those associated with them in the trade have firmly opposed the movement. Government has, in these conflicts of religion and business, to preserve a neutral attitude in terms of its stipulations with the purchasers of the farms; but when the position of the latter has been very severely threatened, it has had to meet the renter half way by the adoption of an excise system, by means of which the officers connected with the special establishment are remunerated by the renter, and Government waives its instalments and recovers on the quantity sold an amount *pro rata*. The conditions at present would appear to indicate a period of great prosperity for the arrack trade, as, owing to the undertaking by Government of heavy public works and railway constructions, the renters are offered a fruitful field for the disposal of their liquid among the large labour forces maintained in connection with the works.

The following table details the amounts received in each year during the past decade by the Government on account of arrack:—

	Rs.
1894	2,358,669·86
1895	2,479,539·65
1896	2,487,769·75
1897	2,812,324·55
1898	2,961,588·76
1899	3,112,324·64
1900	3,233,573·74
1901	3,185,694·94
1902	3,378,219·39
1903	3,413,745·00

The gross receipts of these earnings total up to over Rs. 30,000,000, or nearly two million pounds sterling, a fact which strongly demonstrates the value of the arrack industry as a source of revenue to the Government. So far, the liquor manufactured has only sufficed to supply local demands; but with more modern methods of distillation and bottling, "Ceylon"—as the popular brand of arrack is called—may yet be expected to create for itself a position in foreign markets and a reputation in the great and growing liquor traffic of the East.

THE PROVINCIAL ADMINISTRATIONS

MUCH of the wealth, enterprise, and intellectual and educational effort of Ceylon centres in the capital. But as Paris does not constitute France, so Colombo is far from being Ceylon. Indeed, those who know Ceylon only from a visit to the famous port of call which is the principal seat of government are ignorant of perhaps the leading characteristic features of what is, all in all, the most interesting of the colonies under the direct government of the Crown. They know nothing of the matchless scenery of the mountainous region which covers so large an area in the centre of the island. The vast planting industry which has been built up with British enterprise and capital, and which has brought the island to the highest stage of prosperity, is for them a sealed book. Equally they are shut out from knowledge of the "buried cities," the stupendous tanks and irrigation-works and other remains of the past which attest the grandeur of the ancient Sinhalese civilisation. Nor are they acquainted with the country life of the Sinhalese, which differs as widely from that of the Colombo population as does the life of the Londoner from that of the people of Somersetshire and Devonshire. The whole country teems with special points of interest to the traveller in search of novelty, as well as to the business man seeking fresh avenues for the utilisation of his capital; and for a proper understanding of it, it must be dealt with comprehensively. In this section of the work an attempt will be made to give a picture of each separate administrative portion of the island. For that purpose we shall call to aid all available official information and supplement it with facts which have been collected from other sources. By this means it will, it may be hoped, be possible to bring home to those who do not know Ceylon some idea of the manifold beauties and interest of its separate provinces.

Before we proceed to deal with the administrations individually we may give a brief description of the system under which the provincial government is carried on. Ceylon is politically divided into nine provinces, which are administered by Government Agents, who have under them assistants at the principal centres and subordinate officers whose jurisdiction is limited to the various Korales, Pattuwas, or Peruwas over which they preside. Arranged in the official order of administration, the nine provinces will rank as follows :—

Province.	Capital.
(1) Western	Colombo
(2) Central	Kandy
(3) Northern	Jaffna
(4) Southern	Galle
(5) Eastern	Batticaloa
(6) North-Western	Kurunegala
(7) North-Central	Anuradhapura
(8) Uva	Badulla
(9) Sabaragamuwa	Ratnapura

In order of size their arrangement would appear as under :—

	Sq. Miles.
(1) Eastern	4,036½
(2) North-Central	4,002¼
(3) Northern	3,363¼
(4) Uva	3,154½
(5) North-Western	2,996⅞
(6) Central	2,299½
(7) Southern	2,146¼
(8) Sabaragamuwa	1,901
(9) Western	1,432

A further adjustment of the divisions in respect of population gives the following results :—

	Population.
(1) Western	920,683
(2) Central	622,832
(3) Southern	566,736
(4) North-Western	353,626
(5) Northern	340,936
(6) Sabaragamuwa	321,755
(7) Uva	186,674
(8) Eastern	173,602
(9) North-Central	79,110

Assistant agencies are maintained in the Western Province at Kalutara and Negombo, in the Central at Matale and Nuwara Eliya, in the Southern at Matara: in the North-Western at Chilaw, in the Northern at Mannar, in the Sabaragamuwa at Kegalla, and in the Eastern at Trincomalee. Each province is divided into a number of Korales, which are under the jurisdiction of "Mudaliyars," or native headmen, and the districts under their control are again subdivided into minor groups of villages, under the supervision of "Vidanes" and "Arachchis."

THE EXECUTIVE.

With the inception of British rule representatives of the Crown were stationed at Kandy and the other centres of the island for purposes of conserving the interests of the sovereign Power and of developing the resources of trade and commerce. As during the earlier period of the British occupation the utmost importance was attached to the establishment and building up of a substantial and advantageous intertrade, as the basis of sound and friendly relations with the subject races, the officers of the Government stationed at the various places were naturally designated "Commercial Residents," and were granted Assistants and Deputies to represent them at minor centres in the districts. After a time, however, the title was changed to that of "Collector," the description being borrowed from the neighbouring continent of India. At the beginning of the last century the title was again changed to "Agent of Revenue and Commerce," the representative at Kandy being distinguished as "Revenue Commissioner." About eight years later the terms "Collector" and "Collector of Revenue" were reintroduced; and some time later the title "Agent of Government" was uniformly employed, to be changed, by Regulation No. 6 of 1833, to "Government Agent," which continues to be the official designation. The duties of Government Agents are multifarious, and embrace practically every detail of supervision over the districts they control. They are defined thus in a recent Blue Book: to collect the revenue; to suggest improvements in the mode of collecting it; to superintend agricultural pursuits and the sale of Government waste lands; to hear and settle all disputes arising in the management of the different revenue farms; to exercise a general control in their provinces; and to communicate to the inhabitants the orders of Government. It is also insisted that the Agent shall, from time to time, make circuits through the whole of his province, and acquire a thorough knowledge of the character of the headmen and the situation of the country over which he presides. By the adoption of these measures correct information in respect of the actual state of affairs in every district is obtained, and it is rendered possible for Government to formulate a policy for the more efficient and economic development of the resources of the land. The information obtained in this manner is embodied in the annual Administration Reports of the provinces, by the perusal of which a deep insight is afforded into the present condition of the country. Every Government Agent is, by law, Provincial Registrar of Births, Marriages, and Deaths, Chairman of the Provincial Road Committee and of each District Road Committee, and, by virtue of his appointment, Government Agent in charge of Police, Fiscal of his Province, and a Justice of the Peace for the island. Government Agents of provinces in which Local Boards are established are, by law, Chairmen and Treasurers of the Boards, and those of provinces where a municipal constitution has been introduced Chairmen of the Councils. The only exception is in the case of the Western Province, where a special civil servant does duty as Chairman and Mayor. The Government Agent of the North-Central Province combines judicial with executive functions; and the Agents of the Northern, Southern, and Eastern provinces are also the Collectors of Customs of those provinces. Every Government Agent is in addition Chairman of the Provincial Board of Health. The Government Agents of the Western and Central Provinces are *ex officio* members of the Legislative Council of the island.

Every Government Agent is assisted in his work by an officer called the Office Assistant to the Government Agent, and by one or more cadets, who on joining the Civil Service are attached to the Kachcheris—the local treasuries, revenue offices, and headquarters of the Government Agents—to help them to familiarise themselves with the duties and routine of official work. While the Government Agent is in immediate control of the district circumscribed by the limits of his provincial Kachcheri, he has assistants at the minor centres, who act as his deputies and attend to the execution of his orders and the collection of taxes and general supervision of work in the rural and outlying districts.

All the Government Agents of the provinces meet annually at Queen's House, Colombo, at a durbar presided over by the Governor, at which questions of every description affecting the interests of the population, the development of the country, and the maintenance of institutions and the utilisation of resources, natural and otherwise, of the island, are discussed, and lines laid down for the adoption of suitable and necessary measures for improved methods of control.

THE NATIVE HEADMAN SYSTEM.

The native headman system of Ceylon is, perhaps, the one relic of ancient government which has survived the changed policies and innovations that have been introduced into the country with each successive Power that has presided over the destinies of the country. It is at once an archaic and elaborate system of control, and had the sanctions of the early Sinhalese sovereignty, the tolerance of the Portuguese and Dutch *régimes*, and, in our own times, has the hearty acceptance and approval of the British Government. It may not be inappropriately compared to the old Feudal System of England, for the essential principles of political economy are the same; but in the local system there is the distinguishing patriarchal element, which elects a man to rule his fellows by virtue not only of wealth and influence but also of age, respectability, and social status. As it now exists, of course, the system has been considerably modified, and the right of election, or rather of selection, is vested in the Government, which, by means of its agents and other officers, conducts inquiries into the claims of the candidates, and appoints the one who, in its opinion, is best suited to fill the vacant post on the score of ability and personal popularity with the village or district inhabitants. The fact that those with local influence and landed interests are able to command greater respect than those appointed from outside the district is recognised, and wherever possible full importance is attached to it. It will thus be found that in the ranks of the native headmen a good many will be discovered who have had interests in the districts over which they preside for generations past, and who constitute the influential lairds of the land.

The native headmen are in rank immediately subordinate to the Assistants to the Government Agents, and are concerned in carrying out in detail the orders of the Government in areas which cannot be reached by the European officials owing to difficulties of access and kindred hardships. Their chief duties comprise the supervision of agricultural pursuits; the collection of rates and taxes; the apprehension of criminals or other accused persons who may be "wanted" by the police; the checking of illicit sales of arrack, opium, and other licensed commodities; the suppression of crime; the maintenance of roads and buildings in proper repair; and a general oversight of the people of the place and public affairs. These are, of course, the wider aims and purposes of the system; and, under the organisation, these duties devolve distinctly and separately upon various minor headmen, who are held directly responsible for the performance of their share of work.

The head of the native headman system of the low-country is the Maha Mudaliyar, who generally combines the functions of a native aide-de-camp to the Governor upon State occasions with those of his own duties. Next to him come the "Mudaliyars of the Gate" or "Guard." This term, though peculiar in its English form, is quite common in the East as the designation of a superior officer of the royal household. Cases in point are the expressions "Pharaoh" and "Mikado," which in their respective languages are said to have a root significance of something of the nature of "Sublime Porte." In the local title "Gate" has reference to the Governor's household, and not infrequently it is found in its full form as "Mudaliyar of the Governor's Gate." Ranking below the Mudaliyars of the Gate are the Mudaliyars of the Atapattu, Mudaliyars of the Kachcheris, Mudaliyars of the Korales, and all the other heads of the minor departments of the public service who are entitled to the rank by right of office. Next come the Mohotti

Mohandiram, Mohandirams of the Governor's Gate, Mohandirams of the Atapattu, Mohandirams of the Korales, and all the other *ex-officio* Mohandirams of the various public departments. There are also several other distinctive ranks for special officers, such as "Gravets Mudaliyar," whose limit of jurisdiction is the town and Gravets of the place to which he is appointed; Basnayaka, Padikar, Dadayakkare, and Liyana Mohandirams, whose duties are varied, and who are usually attached to the Governor's establishment. Below the several classes of Mohandirams are Arachchis of the Guard, Arachchis of the Atapattu, Vidane Arachchis, Maha Vidanes, and Vel-Vidane Arachchis; and next to them Kanganies of the Guard, Kanganies of the Atapattu, and Kanganies of the Korales. Last in the scale come Lascoreen attendants of the Guard and Lascoreen attendants of the Atapattu. The titular ranks of Mudaliyar of the Governor's Gate, Mudaliyar, Mohandiram of the Governor's Gate, Mohandiram, and Arachchi are also conferred by the Government on deserving officers of the public service, who then rank with the official holders of the title in the respective classes. The rank of Maha Mudaliyar is hardly anything more than nominal, although at public celebrations and upon State occasions it devolves on the holder of the title to present to the Governor the various native dignitaries. Several of the minor offices are also mere sinecures, and in other cases gratuitous services are rendered by the recipient of the honour in return for his appointment to a post. The officers attached to an "Atapattu" have their jurisdiction over a province, in subordination to the Assistant Government Agents or other officers of the Civil Service: a Mudaliyar presides over a revenue district or "Korale," as it is usually called; a Mohandiram is usually the lieutenant of a Mudaliyar; Arachchis are set over Peruwas, or subdivisions of a district; and Vidanes have charge of a numbered group of villages. In towns where there is a municipal constitution there are Arachchis over the several municipal wards who act as peace officers and are concerned with the collection of commutation and other taxes. Lascoreens are practically a survival of the ancient militia, and are organised on a military scale, with batons and banners and crude "war-music." They are usually requisitioned to attend at the embarkation of the Maldivian Ambassador who annually brings the Sultan's tribute to the Government of Ceylon, and on levee days as personal attachés of the Maha Mudaliyar. Their uniform consists of coat and cap of scarlet or blue cloth, trimmed with yellow or scarlet loops, facings, metal buttons, sword-belt, waist-belt, and hilt and scabbard of tortoiseshell or horn. The Mudaliyars usually wear a long tunic coat buttoned up to the neck, with gold loops and buttons, gold lace spangled sword-belt and sword with gilt hilt and scabbard of silver inlaid with gold. The Maha Mudaliyar's uniform is the same as the Mudaliyars', except that he wears velvet instead of the silk garments donned by Mudaliyars and Mohandirams. The Mohandirams wear uniforms similar to the Mudaliyars, except that their sword-belt is of plain gold lace, not spangled. The Arachchis and Kanganies have silver loops, buttons, and trimmings of gold for the superior ranks, and carry silver-hilted scabbards. The last-named also wear a coloured silk ribbon embroidered with flowers of silver thread instead of the customary silver or gold lace sword-belt.

In the Kandyan districts the designations of native headmen are entirely different, those corresponding to Mudaliyars of districts in the low-country being termed Ratemahatmayas and those immediately below them in rank Koralas. In the Northern and Eastern Provinces these terms are substituted by the titles Chief Mudaliyars, Maniagars, and Udaiyars. The official dress of these Tamil headmen consists of a white turban with silver lace; long tunic coat of white silk with gold loops and buttons; a sash of any optional colour; a sword-belt of gold lace worn over the right shoulder or girded round the waist, and a sword of silver inlaid with gold; trousers and boots or shoes, or the national cloth, wound round the legs, after the fashion of a skirt, with sandals. Moorish chief headmen wear practically the same uniform as the Tamil Mudaliyars, with the exception that a Turkish turban is donned instead of the Tamil headgear, and that a white "sarong" or loose cloth is wrapped around the lower portion of the body. The dress of a Kandyan chieftain has that sartorial amplitude which gives him an extremely ungainly appearance. Over a pair of tight pantaloons, with frilled edges, they have wound round a number of white muslin and gold-figured cloths, in heavy and cumbrous folds, and held together by a broad gold belt, in which is struck a dagger with carved hilt and rich damascening. A large flattened cap of white calico constitutes the head-dress. The coat or jacket is of a Vandyke pattern, made of thin transparent material, with short sleeves, and is surmounted by a richly embroidered and gold-edged tippet. Massive gold chains, amulets, charms, decorations, and a profusion of jewellery and precious stones complete the State dress of a Ratemahatmaya, and make him an awe-inspiring object to behold.

Native headmen of all kinds are permitted to wear, with the sanction of the Governor, medals or similar decorations which they have inherited from their ancestors; and elsewhere in these pages will be found representations of some typical ones, as also illustrations of the warrants and acts of appointment granted to them in the periods of the Portuguese and Dutch or early British occupations.

In the lower ranks of native headmen no salary, or a very insignificant amount if any, is paid; but rewards, from the proceeds of fines of accused persons arrested, are offered them for special services. The Mudaliyars and Ratemahatmayas draw salaries and receive commissions on reporting on Crown lands for sale, on executing cattle vouchers in cases of disputed ownership, and sometimes on collections of taxes and assessment rates. Percentages are also paid on every road-tax defaulter brought to book, for each birth and death reported to the registrar, for pointing out boundaries of Crown lands sold, and on police assessment and sanitary rate recoveries. In addition there is also a "Headmen's Reward Fund," out of which awards are made in recognition of signal and exceptional services in the checking of crime and the maintenance of peace and order.

Side by side with the native headman system is a method of judicature by means of village courts, known as Gansabhawas, councils, and tribunals, under the jurisdiction of presidents and itinerating police magistrates, whose duty it is to hold inquiries into minor cases of hurt, offence, or dispute, and thus save the established courts of law much unnecessary work with trivial and vexatious complaints. The attempt to govern the maritime and interior Sinhalese otherwise than through their own agency has at all times proved difficult, and the necessity for the maintenance of the present system, improved and reorganised as much as possible, is daily increasingly felt. Nor does experience dictate otherwise; for nothing so much pleases the native mind, or goes farther to conciliate it, than the retention of its ancient and time-honoured institutions, of its past sanctions and constitutional usages, and a general and generous recognition of its rights, privileges, and liberties. On the other hand, to meet modern requirements, there is also the necessity for modifications and improvement. That the Government is fully alive to this fact, and is energetically and wisely working towards its fulfilment, there can be little doubt; and the circumstances attending the annual investiture of ranks—usually on the King's birthday at Queen's House—when the Governor personally compliments the recipients and impresses upon them the need for active continuance in their good efforts, tend to point out that due and just recognition follows the labours of the headmen in their spheres of work. In fact, it is not too much to say that the system now forms an indispensable and essential part of the constitution of the country.

WESTERN PROVINCE.

THOUGH smallest in area of the whole of the nine administrations into which the island is divided, the Western Province is the most populous and important. It embraces within its limits the capital, which, with its outlying suburbs, now constitutes "no mean city." But apart from the special prestige attaching to the province by virtue of this circumstance, there are favouring conditions which contribute to its pre-eminence. Its extensive seaboard is the centre of a flourishing fishery, with wide commercial ramifications in other parts of the island; the great coconut-planting industry reaches within its limits its highest development; the lucrative arrack-distilling industry has its principal seat within the province; and some of the most thriving agricultural enterprise (apart from planting) is conducted in districts which are a part of the area. In no other province is there such a wide diffusion of commercial enterprise; in none is the population more advanced and prosperous.

The greatest asset of the Western Province is the coconut. Its ubiquity is astonishing to the new-comer even where he has had prior acquaintance with the tropics. From the time he lands on the shore, margined with coconut plantations, until he crosses the boundary of the province he has ever before him the graceful fan-like foliage of this king of tropical fruit-bearing trees. Of a total acreage of 396,000 under cultivation, no fewer than 280,000 acres are given over to coconuts. It is difficult to over-estimate the influence which this paramountcy of the coconut has on the condition of the people. The fruit furnishes at once a never-failing supply of wholesome food and an abundance of lucrative labour to the inhabitants. Destitution, as the term is understood in Western countries, is practically non-existent. "For those who desire it, work can always be obtained at good wages along the seaboard. The Road Committee returns show that no person now thinks of working on the roads, the obligation to labour being invariably commuted, for 25 cents is still reckoned as a man's wage, and the commutation is calculated on that basis. If there were any difficulty in obtaining work at a reasonable wage, the poorer classes would elect to labour on the roads in preference to paying Rs. 1·50."[1] The prosperity of the province is reflected in the revenue returns for 1905, which were the highest on record. The amount collected during the year was Rs. 2,725,697, a sum Rs. 454,562 in excess of the receipts for 1904 and nearly a million rupees above the return for the year 1888, when the province included the Kegalla and Ratnapura districts, the former of which is now a part of the Central Province and the latter of the Uva Province.

THE LOCAL BOARD, NEGOMBO.

Outside Colombo the most important centre in the Western Province is Kalutara, a thriving town in the heart of an important planting

[1] Report for 1905 of the Hon. Mr. F. A. Crawford, Acting Government Agent.

area south of the capital. The Assistant Government Agent has his headquarters in the town and controls the affairs of the adjacent district, which has an area of 623 square miles and an estimated population of a quarter of a million.

Kalutara has sometimes been called "the Richmond of Ceylon." Parallels of this kind are often amusing, and sometimes irritating; and in this instance more than ordinary violence has been done to artistic truth by comparing this Ceylonese town at the mouth of a great tropical river with the bustling outpost of London, which is built about the "silvery Thames," at this point a sluggish, winding fresh-water stream. Still, it may be admitted that Kalutara is beautifully situated. A long bar intercepts the flow of the river to the sea, and the stream widens out into what to the eye appears to be a considerable lake. The banks of this expanse are covered with tropical vegetation, and the whole scene is most attractive. The view up-river is particularly fine, especially on a clear day, when Adam's Peak shows up in imposing outline in the background.

Kalutara is the seat of the arrack industry. The numerous distilleries contributed Rs. 102,738·32 to the revenue during 1905, an amount which represents nearly one-third of the total receipts of the district. Plumbago mines are also numerous, and a large number of the population are engaged in them. But agriculture is the mainstay of the district. The prevailing love of the coconut as a profit-making agency is here tinctured with a desire to try new avenues of investment. So it has come about that the hard-headed native planters of Kalutara have been drawn into the great rubber speculation, and the authorities in the past few years have been kept busy in surveying and parcelling out Crown lands suitable for the tree which is just now filling such a large place in the eye of the investing world. How far the speculation will succeed in this instance has to be seen. But according to the report of the Kalutara Planters' Association for 1903, it is in the district "that Para rubber has found exactly the conditions of soil and climate that it requires"; and if that be the case, rubber may in course of time vie with coconuts in its power of attraction for the native investor.

MR. AND MRS. A. DE A. SENEVIRATNE AND FAMILY.

At the northern extreme of the province is Negombo, the centre of a fishing trade of considerable importance. The town occupies a somewhat isolated position on a tongue of land thrust out from the mainland towards a narrow, low-lying piece of coast which forms the western embankment of a great lagoon stretching for about a dozen miles in the direction of Colombo. This lagoon is connected by means of a canal with the Kelani Ganga at a point near its mouth, and with that river constitutes the most popular means of communication between the capital and the town. It is certainly a pleasant alternative route to the dusty coach-road along which the visitor perforce must travel if he wishes to proceed by land. The lower reaches of the Kelani river through which the steam-launch passes are very beautiful. The river sweeps to the sea at this point in majestic volume through banks rich in tropical verdure. Villas of wealthy natives peep out amid the trees, relieving by their bright colour the dark green masses of the coconut-palm which here as elsewhere dominates the scene. A turn in the river brings into distant view the masts of vessels riding at anchor in the harbour, with beyond the waters of the Indian Ocean flashing in the sunlight. Another turn, and the launch digs its nose into what at first sight appears to be a dock, but which in reality is a canal some

THE LOCAL BOARD, KALUTARA

twelve miles in length. The work is for the most part a relic of the Dutch occupation. Mynheer, inspired doubtless by the memory of the waterways of his beloved Holland, saw possibilities in this low-lying land with the river as a boundary on one side and the lagoon on the other, and he built the canal with all his native directness. But in the tropics Nature clothes even the straightest lines with grace and beauty, and so it happens that this prosaic canal supplies the medium of one of the most charming water trips that the low-country supplies. The boat passes through plantations whose luxuriant tropical verdure runs to the very water's edge and above furnishes an umbrageous awning through which even the fierce noonday sun cannot pierce. At places where the launch stops crowds of children come with *kurumbas*, or green coconuts, which they offer for sale, and for a few cents there is provided a drink, bright, cool and invigorating, a veritable nectar to the *voyageur* jaded by the torrid heat. About the banks, almost buried in the masses of verdure, are villas of native planters, with here and there a cluster of boutiques, the nucleus of a little settlement. The strenuous life is not for the inhabitants of this favoured region. They lie amid the shade of the palm-groves, looking with lazy curiosity on the launch as it glides along at a rate which never exceeds four miles an hour. The only display of animation is when a barge laden with produce is met with in the canal. Then there is a scurry of feet to tighten hawsers and prepare poles to prevent the violent collision which would be caused by the wash of the launch if these precautions were not taken. Eventually the launch emerges into the lagoon, and then full speed is put on, and for an hour or more the passengers enjoy an exhilarating run against a stiff breeze which sweeps up from the sea. The bellying sails of a number of native craft coming up with the wind lend a touch of picturesqueness to a scene which is otherwise somewhat monotonous owing to the palm-clothed land having now given place to low sand-banks, above which the sun shimmers with tropic intensity. Soon in the distance the spire of a church is visible ahead, peeping up from amongst the trees of a peninsula which at that point breaks the sky-line. Gradually other buildings are discernible, and soon the pretty little town of Negombo is revealed at the head of a creek into which the launch turns. A quarter of an hour later the passengers step ashore at the wharf and pass along the shady road which leads to the town.

FISHING BOATS AT NEGOMBO.

Negombo has an interesting record which goes back to the very early days of the European occupation. The Dutch recognised its importance as an outpost of Colombo, and maintained a strong garrison there, the present-day evidence of which is a fort in a fairly good condition, occupying a dominating position on an eminence between the creek and the sea to the west of the town. Nowadays, when the British dominion is absolute on land and the command of the sea is insured by an overwhelming fleet, Negombo no longer possesses any strategic value. But what it has lost in military and naval importance it has gained in commercial influence. The interests of the place centre in a thriving fishery. As has been stated in the special article on Ceylon Fisheries, the Negombo fishermen are famed throughout the island for enterprise and skill. Numbers of them migrate annually at certain periods to other parts of the island, and the profits on their ventures go to swell the wealth of what is, all in all, a highly prosperous community. The fish locally caught is mostly sent to Colombo, where it commands a ready market. The industry has been greatly hampered in the past by the lack of expeditious means of communication with the capital; but quite recently sanction has been given to a long-projected line of railway which will deprive Negombo of its position of splendid, and undesirable, isolation. The new line will branch off the main Kandy line at Ragama, a station about nine miles from Colombo, and will pass through Ja ela. Eventually it will probably constitute a section of an important railway which will link up Chilaw and Puttalam with the main railway system. Even as a simple branch line it will doubtless serve a very useful purpose by stimulating trade in districts which are languishing for the need of better communication.

Ragama, which has been mentioned as the starting-point of the new railway to Negombo, has an importance of its own from the fact that the place embraces within its area the observation camp for coolies entering the island. On arrival by steamer in Colombo the coolies are at once conveyed to a depôt at the breakwater and are there bathed and fed. Afterwards they are despatched by train to Ragama, where they are detained for forty-eight hours before being allowed to travel to the up-country estates on which they are to be employed. In cases in which the *voyageurs* have come from infected areas in India the detention is for a longer period. The camp is well planned and well serves the purpose for which it is designed—the prevention of the introduction of disease. In 1905 no fewer than 132,690 coolies passed through the camp. This is a far larger number than usual, but there seems every prospect of the stream of immigration being maintained in something like this volume owing to the flourishing condition of the planting industry. Most of the coolies who come over are old hands. The proportion of new labourers in 1905 is stated by the Superintendent of Immigration to have been not more than 1 per cent. This fact shows how popular Ceylon is with the Tamils as a field of labour, and incidentally disposes of the stories sometimes circulated by the ignorant and ill-informed or malicious as to the bad treatment meted out to labourers on the Ceylon estates. Ragama, it may be added as a concluding note, was used temporarily for the internment of some of the Boer prisoners who were sent to Ceylon during the South African War.

THE HON. MR. H. L. CRAWFORD.

From the standpoint of local government the Western Province is a good deal ahead of the other provinces, as is perhaps natural in view of the influence of the life of the capital. There are Local Boards at Kalutara, Negombo, and Minuwangoda, and all are working well. Panadure, a growing town on the coast south of Colombo, should also have a local authority, but the inhabitants shirk their responsibilities, and it seems likely that they will have to be coerced into the acceptance of the rights and privileges of a civilised community. In pleasing contrast to their lack of public spirit is the action of the inhabitants of many of the purely agricultural districts, who have adopted with eagerness and even enthusiasm the system of village Gansabhawas, or village councils, to which special reference is made in the article on Local Government. Animated by this spirit the inhabitants of the Western Province may be expected to maintain the reputation which the area enjoys for advancement and enterprise. There remains, however, one blot upon the fair fame of the province which must be removed before it can enter into the comity of fully civilised communities. That is the exceptional prevalence of serious crime. In 1905 there were 34 cases of homicide as against 23 in 1904, and there were 1,372 serious offences reported as against 1,147 in the previous year. In only 258 cases were there convictions. The situation disclosed by these figures is disquieting. Unhappily, it is characteristic in a measure of the condition of the country as a whole. The Government is being urged to introduce transportation, to the Andamans or elsewhere, as a punishment for those convicted of serious crime, and it is not unlikely that this step will be adopted eventually.

THE HON. MR. HENRY LEIGHTON CRAWFORD.

The Hon. Mr. Henry Leighton Crawford, Government Agent and Fiscal for the Western Province and Member of the Legislative Council, is the son of the Rev. Henry Crawford, a Church of England clergyman. He was born at Jerusalem on November 16, 1855, and after being educated, first at Clifton College and afterwards at Corpus Christi College, Cambridge, he entered the colonial service and went out to Ceylon in 1877 as a writer attached to the Colombo Kachcheri. During the succeeding three years he served at the Kandy, Badulla, and Galle Kachcheris, and was then Acting Police Magistrate of Kegalla, Balapitiya, Matara, Balapitimodara, and Tangalla. In 1883 he was promoted to be Police Magistrate at Kalpitiya and Acting Office Assistant to the Government Agent of the Western Province. In 1887 he was made Acting District Judge, and in 1890 Second Assistant Colonial Secretary. In addition to the duties of this position he acted as Secretary of the Central Irrigation Board in 1893, and in the following year he became Acting Principal Assistant Colonial Secretary, being confirmed in this appointment in 1896. Four years after this he became Commissioner under the Buddhist Temporalities Ordinance of 1889, and in 1904 he was appointed Government Agent of the Southern Province. His present appointment dates from December, 1905. He takes a keen interest in many kinds of sports and games, is the President of the Colombo Cricket Club and of the Chess Club, and for three years he was the croquet champion of the Garden Club, Colombo. Of tennis and rowing he is also very fond.

COLOMBO DISTRICT.

THE COLONIAL PHOTOGRAPHIC COMPANY.

This popular and flourishing establishment was founded as recently as the beginning of 1903, under the management of Mr. Philippe Erdös, who still continues at the head of the firm. The company's premises were specially built to their own plans by the Fort Land and Building Company, and situated as they are just at the rear of the Victoria Arcade, the position is a most central one, alike for residents or visitors to the island. The spacious studio and showrooms are fitted in the latest modern style, and are equipped

THE COLONIAL PHOTOGRAPHIC COMPANY, COLOMBO.

THE CREMATION OF THE LATE F. D. ATTYGALLE

MRS. J. KOTALAWALA. MRS. T. G. JAYEWARDENE. MISS ELLEN ATTYGALLE.

MRS. D. C. G. ATTYGALLE. THE LATE F. D. ATTYGALLE.

with electric fans, private dark-rooms, and every possible convenience for the requirements of their many customers. The principal business they carry on, in addition to portraiture, enlargements, picture-framing, &c., is the supply of all Kodak goods and photographic materials generally, a complete and up-to-date selection of such being stocked. From the very outset the company have gained great popularity, and they now practically hold the monopoly in the island for this class of business. In addition, they do an extensive trade in the developing and printing of plates and films for the many amateur photographers, both resident and tourist, who have occasion for these services. With the rapid increase of business, the staff has needed strengthening from time to time, until at the present it comprises about eighteen hands, which number includes two Europeans.

THE LATE FRANCIS DIXON ATTYGALLE.

A melancholy interest attaches to the views which accompany this sketch. The gentleman whose name figures in the headline, and whose business enterprises are dealt with in another part of the work, was fatally shot on the evening of December 9, 1906, in circumstances which are under judicial investigation at the time of writing. The event caused a great sensation throughout the island, as the murdered man, though quite young, was well known and highly esteemed. Letters of condolence poured in to the deceased's relatives from all parts and from all sections of the community. Amongst others His Excellency the Governor wrote to the unfortunate man's mother deploring his untimely death and tendering sympathy. The public interest in the affair was manifested in the enormous attendance at the funeral. Rarely, if ever previously—in recent years at all events—had such crowds of mourners been seen at the obsequies of a private member of the community. The body was cremated amid all the pomp and impressiveness of the Buddhist ritual. Elsewhere particulars will be found of the late Mr. Attygalle's career; but it may be stated briefly that he was born in 1885 at Colamunne and educated at the Wesley College. His educational career was cut short by the early death of his father, this event rendering it necessary for him to take over his share of the management of his father's estate. Notwithstanding his absorption in business affairs, Mr. Attygalle's interest in his *alma mater* was maintained, and he, besides, continued to show the keenest interest in every form of sport. Although possessed of considerable wealth Mr. Attygalle was most unassuming, and he was liked and respected by all with whom he came in contact. Altogether his was a most engaging personality, and his tragic death forms one of the darkest chapters in the modern history of Ceylon.

THE HOPETOUN STUDIO, SLAVE ISLAND, COLOMBO.

Mr. Adolphus William Andree, the managing proprietor of this, the largest native photographic business in the island, owes whatever success he has achieved in life to his own industry and enterprise. His father was a nephew of the late Mr. C. A. Lorenz and his mother a member of a well-known Jaffna family, and the subject of our brief sketch was born in Jaffna in 1869. His father left Government service to become a professional photographer, and his son inherited the same predilection and, in 1887, joined a ferrotype studio, which was opened by an American in Chatham Street, as chief assistant, remaining there until the business was given up. With the experience thus gained young Andree opened a small studio at his residence in Norris Road, but this proving insufficient as a means of livelihood, he was forced to supplement his income by taking service in the Colombo branch of the National Bank of India, Ltd. In 1893 Mr. Andree married, and started business afresh as a photographer in Union Place, which business, in the course of a few years, he transformed into the present well-equipped studio, his chief assistant being his brother, Mr. Bertie Andree. The present studio is two-storeyed in height, containing the reception and show rooms on the ground floor and a handsome and spacious studio 50 ft. by 25 ft. on the upper floor, with dressing-room attached, and from this studio he has during years turned out much excellent work, which has gained for its proprietor medals and diplomas at the Paris Exhibition and World's Fair held in 1900 and 1904 respectively, while at every Art Exhibition held in Colombo of recent years the judges have marked the good quality of his work by conferring upon him certificates of merit. Mr. Andree makes a speciality of portraiture, and mention should be made of his large and varied stock of Ceylon views and pictorial postcards. He is equally efficient in work by the platinotype process, black and white, and colours. The quality of the studio's carbon work in standard brown, engraving black, sepia, sea green, and red chalk, is also recognised by the increasing popularity of the establishment. On the occasion of the visit of T.R.H. the Duke and Duchess of York (now the Prince and Princess of Wales) to Ceylon Mr. Andree was permitted to accompany the royal train. He holds the sole American rights for photography in bas-relief, and he has also extended his business in the direction of executing half-tone process blocks, blocks on copper, &c., for the pictorial press and book illustrations. During the time of the internment of Boer prisoners-of-war in the colony he brought out a very interesting booklet of views illustrating their life during captivity in the principal camp at Diyatalawa. A similar booklet of views was issued by him in connection with one of the later Pearl Fisheries, before these had passed out of the hands of the Ceylon Government to the Ceylon

A. W. ANDREE'S PHOTOGRAPHIC STUDIO.

LORD NELSON HOTEL. THE RESIDENCE.
M. C. AMOO. A. J. CUTTILAN. KING'S HOTEL, KANDY.

Company of Pearl Fishers, Ltd. Another speciality of the Hopetoun Studio is enlargements, which are executed under his personal supervision and are artistically finished by hand or by the aerograph. In fact, his business is well equipped to execute orders in all branches of the photographic art, including picture-framing in American carved wood mouldings and indigenous woods which specially lend themselves to produce artistic results, such as the rare calamander, ebony, and coconut wood.

M. C. AMOO AND J. A. CUTTILAN.

Messrs. M. C. Amoo and J. A. Cuttilan, proprietors of the Lord Nelson Hotel, Chatham Street, Fort, and of King's Hotel, Kandy, are lineal descendants of the first batch of warlike Malays brought over from the Straits Settlements by the Dutch when they owned Ceylon. These Malays afterwards composed the Ceylon Rifle Regiment. The ancestors of Messrs. Amoo and Cuttilan did yeoman service both for the Dutch and the British in quelling the formidable Sinhalese rebellions and in insuring the final conquest of Kandy. Messrs. Amoo and Cuttilan started business together twenty-five years ago as general contractors for Government, the municipality, &c., and a few years later opened two hotels of their own. Their business capacity, energy, and industry, and their never-failing courtesy towards all with whom they had dealings, brought their reward, and Messrs. Amoo and Cuttilan soon found themselves in a position to expand the various enterprises with which they were connected. Their hotels to-day, the Lord Nelson and the King's, are two of the most popular *caravanserais* in the island—excellently furnished, elaborately fitted and equipped, and run under most capable management—and are largely resorted to by passengers and tourists and the better class of residents in the island.

HENDERSON & NEWTON.

This firm of general commission exporters and importers, carrying on business in Colombo, and having agencies in up-country stations, was established by Mr. Edward Wylie Newton, who was later joined by Mr. William Edward Henderson, a partner in the firm of Henderson & Co. The specialities of the firm are tea, cocoa, cinnamon, fibres, and plumbago, and the principal imports are piece goods and hardware. They hold the agencies for Ceylon for the English Thread Company, Ltd., the Scottish Amicable Life Assurance Society, the General Accident, Fire and Life Assurance Corporation, Ltd., the Oliver Typewriter Company, Ltd., and the Addressograph, Ltd. The firm has special agents in London, Liverpool, Manchester, Glasgow, Hamburg, Amsterdam, Antwerp, Paris, and in other towns in Europe, in North America, South Africa, and New Zealand. Among the registered brands of tea and other food products in which the firm deals are the A1, Regal, Perfection, Orange, Sportsman, Peacock, White Label, White Seal, World, Stag, Gold Label, Gold Packet, Silver Packet, Anchor, Sunset, Dawn, Castle, and Sun, and the Phœnix brand of plumbago.

HENRY PIERIS.

To be a Government contractor in Ceylon is a valuable qualification, and is generally the hall-mark of efficiency of workmanship. Among the best known of Government contractors in Colombo is Mr. Henry Pieris, the subject of this sketch. He is the son of the late Mr. W. F Pieris, who established the business in 1864 and was entrusted both by Government and

HENRY PIERIS.

GROUP OF STAFF.

" DONINGTON."

CHAMBER OF COMMERCE BUILDINGS, COLOMBO.

the general public with works of considerable importance. Among the monuments of the deceased gentleman's skill are the Chamber of Commerce buildings, the Attorney-General's offices, certain wards of the General Hospital, and the Lunatic Asylum; St. James's Church, Kotahena; St. Mark's, Dandiyama; and the Scott and Matthew Memorial Halls. Born in 1879, Mr. Henry Pieris was educated at the Royal College, Colombo, and afterwards he went through a thorough apprenticeship with his father. After a few years he became a partner in the concern, and upon the sudden and untimely death of his father, in 1904, he succeeded to the business. Among the contracts which he has undertaken mention should be made of the Wellawatte Church. He employs about sixty masons and carpenters, and the public and the Government have entrusted him with important works. His first work for the Government was the alteration, improvement, and enlargement of the Government Printing Office. Since 1904 Mr. Pieris has been assisted in his business by his brother, Mr. John Gilbert Pieris, a clever young engineer. He owns a small estate—Talahena—at Kirilapona, near Colombo, planted with rubber, and he has also commenced experimenting in growing cotton there. He comes of a family long identified with Wesleyan Methodism in the island, is a member of that Church, and was formerly steward at the Colpetty Wesleyan Church. He is unmarried, and resides at "Donington," Ward Place, Colombo.

EMMANUEL DE SILVA WIJEYERATNE.

Mr. E. de S. Wijeyeratne, son of Bastian de S. Wijeyeratne, was born in Colombo in 1857, and received his education at St. Benedict's Institute and St. Thomas's College. After his school career he commenced business as a timber merchant in Colombo in 1880, and subsequently he became contractor for the Government and the municipality, supplying various departments, such as the railways and the Colonial Stores, and furnishing besides timber for use in the construction of the Colombo breakwater. He is now also a carting contractor. His timber yards are situated in Skinner's Road South, and cover about an acre of ground. The timber is felled in Crown forests in different parts of the Western Province and conveyed to Colombo by rail, road, and canal, and is sawn into stock sizes and logs. The number of hands employed is between fifty and sixty. Mr. Wijeyeratne is also a landed proprietor, owning the estates Winifred—about 300 acres, planted with coconuts—and Keenewinne, both in Alutkuru Korale North, of the Western Province. In addition he owns tracts of paddy-land and considerable house property in Colombo. He is a member of the Catholic Union and Club, and his residence is Havelock Villa, Havelock Road, Colombo. In 1886 he married Michaela Justina, daughter of William Peter Mendis, late of the Ceylon Public Service, and landed proprietor of Negombo, and granddaughter of Joseph Mendis, Mudaliyar of Alutkuru Korale North. In 1897 he was married a second time, on this occasion to Anne Claribel Mary, daughter of Frederick de Fonseka, Superintendent of Minor Roads, Negombo, and granddaughter of Manuel Fonseka, Mudaliyar of Kalutara. He has seven sons and two daughters, and his son Edmund John Stanislas assists him in the business.

BASTIANKORALLAGEY JAMES AURELIEUS RODRIGO WEERESINGHE GOONEWARDENE.

This gentleman, better known as J.A. Rodrigo, is a leading member of the Sinhalese community

TIMBER YARD. CLIFTON VILLA.

MR. AND MRS. E. DE S. WIJEYERATNE AND FAMILY.

The group above represents MRS. JULIANA DE SILVA WARNESURIYA CURUCULE WIJEYERATNE, wife of the late LINDEMULLEGE BASTIAN DE SILVA WARNESURIYA CURUCULE WIJEYERATNE (third son of the late LINDEMULLEGE JACOB DE SILVA WARNESURIYA CURUCULE WIJEYERATNE), children, grandchildren and great-grandchildren. It is a unique group, as it consists of fifty-nine members of this ancient Sinhalese family taken after the fortieth annual Christmas breakfast given by Mrs. Juliana de Silva Warnesuriya Curucule Wijeyeratne at her residence, "Clanmorris," Grandpass, Colombo.

Bastian de Silva Wijeyeratne, born June 12, 1812; died March 14, 1860. Mrs. Juliana de Silva Wijeyeratne, born December 26, 1825; died February 26, 1905.

Each row reading from left to right, commencing with the row of young children in the foreground.

1. MISS LOUISA DE SILVA WIJEYERATNE (granddaughter).
2. MASTER VICTOR DE SILVA WIJEYERATNE (grandson).
3. MISS ELLEN MARY PEREIRA (granddaughter).
4. MASTER MICHAEL FRANCIS PEREIRA (grandson).
5. MASTER JOSEPH DE SILVA WIJEYERATNE (grandson).
6. MASTER BERTRAM ROBERT FREDERICK DE SILVA WIJEYERATNE (grandson).
7. MASTER CHRISTOPHER EMANUEL DE SILVA WIJEYERATNE (grandson).
8. MASTER JOSEPH LIONEL ANTHONY PERERA JAYASINGHE (grandson).
9. MISS FLORENCE HELEN PERERA JAYASINGHE (granddaughter).
10. MR. DON JOSEPH ARSECULERATNE, Proctor S. C. and Notary (grandson).
11. MR. JACOB DE SILVA WIJEYERATNE, Proctor (son).
12. MRS. ISABELLA DE SILVA WIJEYERATNE (wife of No. 11).
13. MR. MICHAEL FRANCIS PEREIRA, Accountant, Prisons Department (husband of No. 14).
14. MRS. MARIA PEREIRA (daughter).
15. MRS. APROGINIA ARSECULERATNE (daughter).
16. MRS. JULIANA DE SILVA WIJEYERATNE (wife of the late Bastian de Silva Wijeyeratne).
17. MR. ROBERT DE SILVA WIJEYERATNE, Notary Public (son).
18. MRS. CAROLINE DE SILVA WIJEYERATNE (wife of No. 17).
19. MRS. VICTORIA DE SILVA WIJEYERATNE (wife of the late Mathias de Silva Wijeyeratne).
20. Mr. JOSEPH FRANCIS PERERA JAYASINGHE (husband of No. 21).
21. MRS. CAROLINE ANASTASIA PERERA JAYASINGHE (daughter).
22. MR. EMANUEL DE SILVA WIJEYERATNE (son).
23. MISS LILIAN VIOLET CLARIBEL DE SILVA WIJEYERATNE (granddaughter).
24. MRS. CLARIBEL ANNE MARY DE SILVA WIJEYERATNE (wife of No. 22).
25. MR. JOSEPH BONIFACE MICHAEL PEREIRA, Proctor S. C. (grandson).
26. MISS ANGELINA ARSECULERATNE (granddaughter).
27. MISS AGNES DE SILVA WIJEYERATNE (granddaughter).
28. MISS JULIE MARIA PEREIRA (granddaughter).
29. MR. BASTIAN FERNANDO, President Plumbago Merchants' Union (husband of No. 31).
30. MISS CLARIBEL FRANCES MARGARET WEERASOORIYA (great-granddaughter).
31. MRS. ANNE EMILY FERNANDO (granddaughter).
32. MR. GABRIEL FERNANDO, plumbago merchant (husband of No. 34).
33. MASTER GABRIEL LEO MARCUS FERNANDO (great-grandsou).
34. MRS. JOSEPHINE MARY FERNANDO (granddaughter).
35. MISS CHARLOTTE MARY CLARA DE SILVA WIJEYERATNE (granddaughter).
36. MISS MARY ROSALINE DE SILVA WIJEYERATNE (granddaughter).
37. MISS GRACE MARY PERERA JAYASINGHE (granddaughter).
38. MISS WINEFRED CLEMENTINA DE SILVA WIJEYERATNE (granddaughter).
39. MASTER CYRIL SIMON DE SILVA WIJEYERATNE (grandson).
40. MR. EDMUND JOHN STANISLAUS DE SILVA WIJEYERATNE (grandson).
41. MR. EDWARD ROBERT FRANCIS DE SILVA WIJEYERATNE, Proctor (grandson).
42. MR. JOHN HENRY ARSECULERATNE, plumbago merchant (grandson).
43. MR. THOMAS AUSTIN DE SILVA WIJEYERATNE (grandson).
44. MR. ALFRED VINCENT MICHAEL PEREIRA (grandson).
45. MISS MARY PRISCILLA DE SILVA WIJEYERATNE (granddaughter)
46. MR. OSMUND DE SILVA WIJEYERATNE (grandson).
47. MISS EVELYN FERNANDO (great-granddaughter).
48. MR. JOSEPH REYNOLD DE SILVA WIJEYERATNE (grandson and heir).
49. MISS DAISY FERNANDO (great-granddaughter).
50. MR. RICHARD JOSEPH VICTOR DE SILVA WIJEYERATNE (grandson).
51. MRS. LOUISA WEERASOORIYA (granddaughter).
52. MASTER HENRY WINFRED ROBERT WEERASOORIYA (great-grandson).
53. MR. HERMAN PETER WEERASOORIYA, Proctor S. C. and Notary (husband of No. 51).
54. MISS MILDRED FELICIA MARGARET DE SILVA WIJEYERATNE (granddaughter).
55. MR. ALFRED JOHN MATHIAS DE SILVA WIJEYERATNE (grandson).
56. MISS GRACE HARRIET VICTORIA DE SILVA WIJEYERATNE (granddaughter)
57. MR. FRANCIS BENJAMIN DE SILVA WIJEYERATNE (grandson).
58. MISS ADELINE MARGARET PERERA JAYASINGHE (granddaughter).
59. MR. JAMES EMANUEL MAXIMIAN DE SILVA WIJEYERATNE (grandson).
60. MR. DON PETER ARSECULERATNE (grandson, does not appear in the group, being away in England).

ADDITIONS TO THE FAMILY BY MARRIAGE AND THE CHILDREN BORN AFTER THE PHOTOGRAPH WAS TAKEN.

61. MR. LEO PETER FERNANDO (husband of No. 36).
62. MASTER LEO BERTRAM FERNANDO (great-grandson).
63. MASTER ANDREW HILARION FERNANDO (great-grandson).
64. MISS EUGENIE DE SILVA (married to No. 55).
65. MISS VENETIA DE SILVA WIJEYERATNE (great-granddaughter).
66. MASTER FRANCIS MATHIAS CORNELIS DE SILVA WIJEYERATNE (great-grandson).
67. MR. VINCENT FERNANDO (husband of No. 56).
68. MISS STELLA VICTORIA FONSEKA (married to No. 10).
69. MASTER JOSEPH MARSHAL ARSECULERATNE (great-grandson).
70. MASTER LIONEL PETER JOSEPH WEERASOORIYA (great-grandson).
71. MASTER RICHARD AUGUSTUS BERNARD WEERASOORIYA (great-grandson).
72. MISS MARY JANE CATHERINE FERNANDO (married to No. 41).
73. MISS CECILY BEATRICE MARY PEREIRA WIJERATNE (married to No. 25).
74. MASTER JOSEPH HILARION DE SILVA WIJEYERATNE (grandson).
75. MASTER TITUS CYRIL MICHAEL DE SILVA WIJEYERATNE (grandson).

NAMES OF DECEASED MEMBERS OF THE FAMILY WHO DO NOT APPEAR IN THE GROUP.

76. MR. MATHIAS DE SILVA WIJEYERATNE (eldest son).
77. MR. GABRIEL DE SILVA WIJEYERATNE (grandson).
78. MR. ALFRED CYPRIAN DE SILVA WIJEYERATNE (grandson).
79. MR. DON MARSAILLES ARSECULERATNE, Proctor and Notary (husband of No. 15).
80. MISS ANGELINA ARSECULERATNE (granddaughter).
81. MISS ROSALINE ARSECULERATNE (granddaughter).
82. MISS ALICE ARSECULERATNE (granddaughter).
83. MISS MARY ARSECULERATNE (granddaughter).
84. MRS. MARGARET HENRIETTA ARSECULERATNE (first wife of No. 10).
85. MISS JOSEPHINE MARGARET ARSECULERATNE (great-granddaughter).
86. MR. CHARLES FELIX LUCAS DE SILVA WIJEYERATNE (grandson).
87. MR. JOHN ALEXANDER DE SILVA WIJEYERATNE (grandson).
88. MR. ALEXANDER JOHN DE SILVA WIJEYERATNE (grandson).
89. MR. JACOB DE SILVA WIJEYERATNE (grandson).
90. MISS JANE MARIA PEREIRA (granddaughter).
91. MISS ELLEN MARIA PEREIRA (granddaughter).
92. MR. CHARLES MAURICE MICHAEL PEREIRA (grandson).
93. MR. JOHN STANISLAUS MICHAEL PEREIRA (grandson).
94. MR. EMANUEL CYRIL MICHAEL PEREIRA (grandson).
95. MRS. MICHAELA JUSTINA DE SILVA WIJEYERATNE (first wife of No. 14).
96. MR. MARCUS JOHN PERERA JAYASINGHE (grandson).

NAMES OF DECEASED MEMBERS OF THE FAMILY WHO APPEAR IN THE GROUP.

1. MRS. JULIANA DE SILVA WIJEYERATNE (wife of the late Bastian de Silva Wijeyeratne). Died February 26, 1905.
2. MR. ROBERT DE SILVA WIJEYERATNE, Notary Public. Died July 16, 1904.
3. MRS. VICTORIA DE SILVA WIJEYERATNE, wife of the late Mathias de Silva Wijeyeratne. Died April 1, 1904.

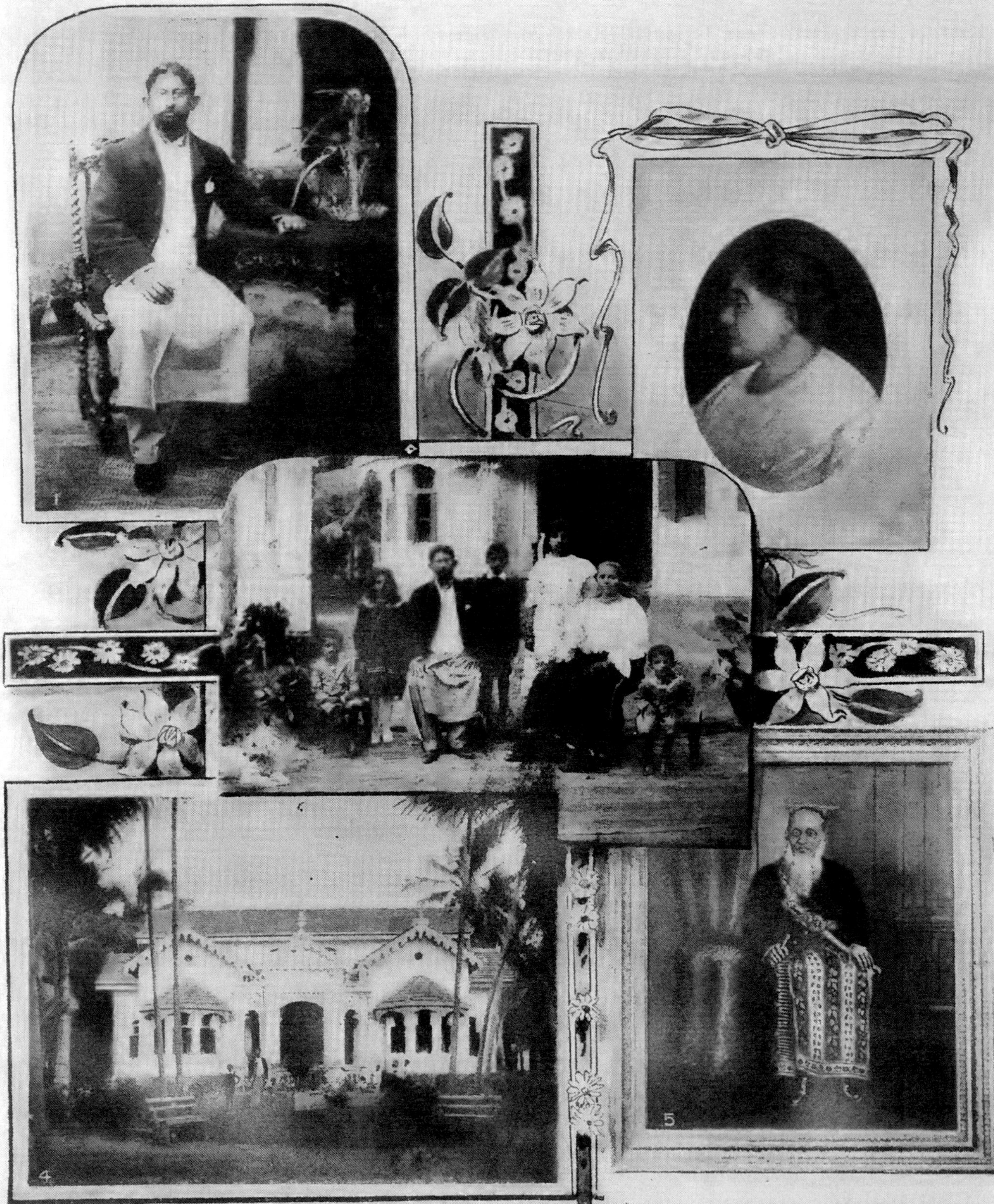

J. A. RODRIGO. J. A. RODRIGO'S MOTHER.

MR. AND MRS. RODRIGO AND FAMILY.

"VILLA THEODORA." J. A. RODRIGO'S FATHER.

of the Govi Wansa (caste). He was born on October 12, 1862, and is the eldest son of B. Johannes Rodrigo Weeresinghe Goonewardene, Mohandiram, and of Halehapperumegey Lucia Fonseka Goonesekere, who is the eldest daughter of Hendrick Fonseka Goonesekere (Peace Officer, Hendella Peruve) and Agida Fonseka. Mr. Rodrigo's grandparents were B. Jaconis Rodrigo and Suraweera Aratchigey Dona Helena, whilst his great-grandparents were Bastiankorallagey Juan Rodrigo and Paliawadene Aratchigey Christina Perera. Mr. Juan Rodrigo is a son of Davit Rodrigo, who was popularly known as Kahene Seeya, grandson of Isaac Rodrigo, and great-grandson of B. Bastian Rodrigo. Amongst the offices which Mr. B. J. Rodrigo W. Goonewardene, father of the subject of this sketch, held, in addition to the titular rank of Mohandiram, were Fiscal's Officer, Vidane Aratchi, Registrar of Births, Marriages and Deaths; Division Officer, inquirer into crimes and sudden deaths in his district; and Moopoo of the Roman Catholic churches of Uswetekeiyawe and Nyacakande.

Mr. James Aurelieus Rodrigo, the subject of this sketch, was educated at St. Benedict's Institute, and on completion of his scholastic career he officiated for his father in various capacities, afterwards commencing business as a general merchant and planter. Subsequently he joined Messrs. Don Joseph, Don Paul, and A. J. Perera, a firm engaged in farming the Government arrack rents, which now owns the rents at Jaffna, Mannar, Mullaitivu, Vavuniya, Negombo, and Kurunegala. Shortly others will be added at Trincomalee, Anuradhapura, and Puttalam. In addition to this business Mr. Rodrigo owns extensive coconut estates, such as Galpotte (in the Kurunegala district), Ambecadeville (Chilaw district), Mundalam (Puttalam district), and Julean Estate (Hendella), and several smaller estates in various districts. He has a cinnamon estate at Hendella and paddy-lands at Bopitiya and in other parts of the Western Province. He manufactures copra and sells it locally. In 1892 Mr. Rodrigo married Dona Theodora, eldest daughter of D. Don Hendrick and Bastiankorallagey M. Rodrigo, sister of Messrs. Don Joseph and Don Paul of Boditiya, in Pamunugame, and he has three sons (one having died in 1897) and two daughters. "Villa Theodora," Hendella, n Alutkuru Korale South, is his residence.

ABRAHAM PERERA GOONATILLAKE.

Mr. A. P. Goonatillake is the son of D. J. G. Goonatillake Dadayakkara, Mohandiram of Halgampitiya, near Veyangoda, and Donna Anna, daughter of D. Carolis Kahandawa. He was born in 1872 and educated at the Royal College. He entered the service of the Government in 1895, being attached to the Deputy Fiscal's Office at Colombo. He resigned in order to take over his father's planting business in 1897. Amongst his coconut estates are Higgolla, Fancy Field, and Indigolla, in the Veyangoda district, as well as the fine estate of Kolongasyaya, in the North-Western Province, which comprises about 300 acres fully planted and equipped, and on which he is about to plant rubber. Copra is at present turned out from this estate, whilst the produce from the other estates is sold as nuts to the Orient Mills, Veyangoda. About 100 hands are employed by him, and he is personally engaged in supervising the work. He has, in addition, about 30 acres of paddy-land, both at Halgampitiya and Metiangane (adjoining the Kolongasyaya estate), in the Kurunegala district; and at the Paris Exhibition in 1900 he was awarded the gold medal for paddy and dry grains. He obtained a similar

A. P. GOONATILLAKE.

D. J. GOONATILLAKE.

DONNA ANNA KAHANDAWA GOONATILLAKE.

"FANCYFIELD" APIARY. PADDY FIELDS.

"FANCYFIELD."

medal at the St. Louis Exhibition in 1904, a silver medal as an extra award for paddy at the Colombo Agricultural Show in 1899, and in the same year, at the Agri-Horticultural Show, a silver medal as first prize for dry grains. He also won a silver medal, second prize, for coconut oil at the Colombo Agri-Horticultural Show in 1899, and a bronze medal at the Paris Exhibition for the same product. Mr. Goonatillake is a member of the Agricultural Society and the Kennel Club. His hobby is bee-keeping, and he has over fifty hives, including two colonies of Italian bees. From these hives he obtains about 200 lbs. of honey each year. He takes a keen interest in his hobby, and is always experimenting for new results. He is fond of shooting, and finds plenty of scope for this sport on his Kolongasyaya estate.

W. A. DEP.

Mr. William Alfred Dep, of Kurikotuwa estate, Veyangoda, is the eldest son of the late Mr. Charles Dep, and grandson of the late Mr. Arnolis Dep (Reuter) of Colombo. He was born at Veyangoda on June 4, 1882, and was educated at St. Thomas's College, Colombo. On the completion of his educational career in 1899 he studied coconut planting, and at present he is a coconut planter and owns landed properties. He is a keen agriculturist and has been the lucky recipient of many prize medals at various agri-horticultural shows held in the island, notably obtaining awards for his fine exhibits of coconuts, of which he is the possessor of a good selection. Mr. Dep joined the Ceylon Volunteers in 1899 as a cyclist and signaller, and is a member of the C.V.R.A., and a marksman in rifle-shooting. He has offered a valuable silver cup for presentation for target-shooting among the members of the Ceylon Volunteer Force under favourable conditions. He married, on December 12, 1906, Miss Louisa Susana Tudugalle, eldest daughter of the late Mr. Don Abraham Tudugalle, and a niece of the late Mr. Don Philip Wijewardane, Mohandiram of Seddewatte, Colombo.

W. .A. DEP.

MORATUWA DISTRICT.

CHARLES PETER DE SILVA.

This gentleman, a brother of the well-known Dr. W. H. de Silva, M.M.C., of Colombo, was born at Moratuwa in 1866, and was educated at St. Thomas's College, Colombo, and Prince of Wales's College, Moratuwa. He joined the Ceylon Survey Department in 1888, and became Assistant Surveyor. Resigning his post under Government, in 1892 he established the Ceylon Survey Agency, with head offices at Moratuwa, which is the only institution of its kind in Ceylon. The staff of the agency consists of 7 field surveyors, 2 civil engineers, 8 draughtsmen, and a number of clerks, besides 50 other hands. The professional assistants are all trained at the Technical College and further instructed directly in their work by Mr. de Silva himself, under whose personal direction the business is carried on. Work is being performed by the agency practically in every part of the island Mr. C. P. de Silva is captain of the Moratuwa Cyclists' Union, Vice-President of the Rawatawatte Association and a committee member of the Moratuwa Sunday School Union. He is also Lieutenant of "R" Company of the Ceylon Light Infantry, and is an all-round sportsman and athlete. His private residence is Carlton House, Moratuwa. He owns various estates planted with coconuts, cinnamon, and rubber, of which Silvatenne, Johanawatte, and Mellewagare, in the North-Western Province, and Ekele and Batapandura in the Western Province, are the more important. He is also a partner of the well-known Kudaganga tea and rubber estate in the Kalutara district. In 1892 Mr. de Silva married Johana Josline, daughter of Mr. Manuel De Mel, of "Melrose," Moratuwa.

PHILIP PERERA SENEVIRATNE ABEYESINGHE PALHIYAWADENA WIJEYEGUNAWARDENA.

Mr. Philip Perera Seneviratne Abeyesinghe Palhiyawadena Wijeyegunawardena, better known as Philip Perera, Mudaliyar, comes of an ancient Vellala Sinhalese family, which is said to have emigrated from Matale in the Central Province during the time of the occupation of Ceylon by the Portuguese. His father was Abraham Perera Seneviratne Palhiyawadena Wijeyegunawardena, planter and estate owner, of Colombo, and his grandfather was a Mohandiram of Alutkuru Korale. His mother was the daughter of Mohandiram Abeyesinghe, of Alutkuru Korale North. Born at Colombo in 1851, he was educated at St. Benedict's Institution and the Colombo Academy (now Royal College). In 1871 he entered the Control Department of the Military Establishment at Colombo, and two years later he was attached to the Colombo Kachcheri as translator. In 1885 he was appointed Mohandiram of Salpiti Korale, and in 1892 was promoted to be Mudaliyar of Salpiti Korale. From 1893 to 1905 he was Deputy Fiscal of the same district, and in 1897 was Acting Atapattu Mudaliyar. In July, 1897, the Ceylon Government presented him with a gold medal for meritorious services, and in 1902 the high rank of Mudaliyar of the Governor's Gate was conferred upon him. He is a wealthy landed proprietor, owning coconut estates in the Colombo and Kalutara districts, and house properties there and in Colombo. In 1882 he married Clementina Matilda, the only daughter of John Henry Corea Abeyekoon, Justice of the Peace and Mohandiram of Kalutara. He resides at Salpiti Korale, Wasala Walauwa. He is Chairman of the village committees of Salpiti Korale and a member of the Horticultural and Agricultural Societies. He is in possession of several medals and other awards for exhibiting fruits and other local products.

MUDALIYAR PHILIP PERERA.

H. B. PEIRIS.

Mr. Hanwedige Bastian Peiris comes of the well-known family of that name, and is the brother of Mr. H. J. Peiris, of whom an account appears in another part of the volume. He was born at Moratuwa in 1860, educated at Holy Emmanuel Church School and Prince of Wales's College, and articled as student-at-law with Mr. A. O. Joseph, Proctor of the Supreme Court at Colombo, but gave up his studies to take up planting under his father, his first appointment being that of superintendent of Yahallekegalle estate, of which he opened up the greater portion. In 1897, a year after his father's death, he took over the management of his own estates, and having acquired extensive knowledge in the cultivation of coconuts, cinnamon, and tea, he planted the whole of his father's properties. His own estates are Katubette, where he usually resides, Neeamba and Walpitemulle in the Veyangoda district, and Ekela in the Ja-ela district, the last-named having always turned out the best known cinnamon in the market. Other estates owned by this gentleman are Kumarekatuwe in the Chilaw district and Mandalay in the Puttalam district. In 1891 he married Jane Helena, eldest daughter of Mr. Joseph Mendis, manufacturer and timber merchant, of Moratuwa.

MR. AND MRS. H. B. PEIRIS AND FAMILY.

KATUBETTE BUNGALOW, MORATUWA.

W. R. DE SILVA.

The late Mr. William Robert de Silva, the son of Jasentu Liane Don Arnoldis de Silva, teacher of the Wesleyan Mission, was born at Ambalangoda in 1865. After his scholastic training he became land registrar of Kegalle Kachcheri and subsequently was transferred to Kalutara as second clerk, but resigned the Government service in 1897 to look after his wife's estates. He owned Graceland estate, Kadigamuwe, Budankumbure, and Negaviluwe, planted with coconuts and situated in Chilaw and Puttalam districts, besides much landed property at Colombo. He married, in 1897, Caroline Engeldina Francesca, youngest daughter of the late Mr. H. Andris Peiris, and it is sad to have to state that both Mr. and Mrs. de Silva died within two years of each other—in 1904 and 1906 respectively. They left a family of four young children, three sons and one daughter, who now reside at "Grace Lyn," Moratuwa, under the care of their uncle and guardian, Mr. H. Bastian Peiris.

HUGH DE MEL.

H. DE MEL.

Dr. Hugh De Mel, a leading Moratuwa medical practitioner, is the son of the late Rev. Francis De Mel, incumbent of St. John's Church, Panadure, and Christ Church, Horetuduwa. He was educated at St. Thomas's College, where he passed the senior local Cambridge examination in 1893. He entered the Ceylon Medical College during the same year, and went to Edinburgh for further study in 1899. There he graduated as L.R.C.P. and L.R.C.S., as well as L.F.P. and S. of Glasgow. After working at Edinburgh Infirmary and London Hospitals he returned to Ceylon in 1901, and was appointed District Medical Officer of Dolosbage. In the following year he resigned this appointment and took up private practice at Moratuwa, where he has been ever since. He is a member of the British Medical Association and of No. 1, St. Mary's Chapter of the Grand Lodge of Scotland, and of the Moratuwa Association.

W. A. PEIRIS.

Mr. William Augustine Peiris, youngest son of Mr. H. A. Peiris, and younger brother of Messrs. H. J. and H. J. J. and Bastian Peiris, was born at Moratuwa in 1880 and educated at Prince of Wales's and St. Thomas's Colleges. In 1900 he went to England and travelled extensively both in the United Kingdom and Europe. Upon his return to Ceylon he commenced planting on Yakahelle estate as well as on his late father's properties in the Chilaw district, where he acquired knowledge of coconut, tea, and cinnamon planting. He is now

THE CHILDREN OF THE LATE W. R. DE SILVA. THE LATE MR. AND MRS. W. R. DE SILVA.
"GRACE LYN," MORATUWA.

"BELVEDERE" BUNGALOW. THE RECEPTION-ROOM.

THE DRAWING-ROOM. MR. AND MRS. W. A. PEIRIS AND INFANT.

managing his own estates, the principal of which are Yahalakelle, 200 acres in extent, Ratmalwewe and Millawa, of 150 acres each; and all these are planted with coconuts and fully equipped with bungalows and stores. He intends opening up some 200 acres of rubber, and owns house property at Moratuwa and Colombo. His beautiful residence, "Belvedere," Moratuwa, lately completed, is one of the finest and best appointed country seats of the Western Province. The interior arrangements are on the latest English lines, the walls, dado, and floors being formed of a most delicate and pleasing series of pictures in mosaic, for which the materials were specially imported from England. For the way in which the designs have been carried out credit is due to Mr. A. L. Marikar, the architect. Mr. Peiris is a member of the Agricultural Society, and captain of the Moratuwa Cyclists' Union and corporal of the "R" Company, Ceylon Light Infantry, Moratuwa, and takes a keen interest in everything connected with cycling. In 1903 he married Fanny Ada Caroline, eldest daughter of the late S. P. Soyza, of Moratuwa.

M. ARNOLIS FERNANDO.

Mr. M. Arnolis Fernando is a successful business man whose philanthropy has developed in proportion to his business. He is the son of Marreyeke Juanis Fernando and Silappu Perumage Angela Fernando, and was born at Moratuwa on August 12, 1850. He was educated at the Buddhist school in his native town and then had instruction in all the different departments of planting under Mr. Hendrik Cooray, at Panadure, in the Rayigam Korale. About 1886 he started business on his own account, and is now the senior partner in the firm of A. Fernando & Co., of which a sketch appears on another page. Mr. Fernando is the largest and most influential plumbago merchant in the island, and the firm owns the largest and deepest mine in Ceylon, which is situated at Pusihena, and is 400 ft. deep. Mr. A. Fernando is a staunch Buddhist, and has done much to improve Buddhist education. He built entirely the Lunawa Buddhist temple, and generously supports the Buddhist school at Peliandelle, near Moratuwa, to which he has also presented a set of manuals of Buddha's teaching, whilst the road from Lunawa station to Princess Louise's Hospital, which he built at a cost of Rs. 2,000, is a permanent and useful monument to his philanthropy. He married, in 1886, Wanaku Wattewaduga Angela Fernando, and their family consists of two daughters and two sons, and they have also adopted a daughter. "Methmedura," Mora-

"METHMEDURA" BUNGALOW, MORATUWA.

THE BUNGALOW. DR. AND MRS. GUNESEKERE AND CHILDREN.

tuwa, is their residence. He is a member of the Buddhist Association and Vice-President of the Moratuwa Association.

JAMES SOLOMON GUNESEKERE.

Dr. J. S. Gunesekere, L.M.S., is the eldest son of Mr. D. J. R. Gunesekere, of Ambalangoda, Ceylon, and was born in 1858. He married, in 1893, Lucie Dora Amadore Jayasuriya, eldest daughter of Mudaliyar S. H. Jayewickreme, of Kurunegala, and granddaughter of the late Mr. Christian Amadore Jayasuriya, Mudaliyar of Magam Pattu, in the Southern Province of the island, and has a daughter and son. Mr. Gunesekere entered the Ceylon Medical College, Colombo, in 1879, and having passed out as a licentiate, he was appointed medical officer in charge of the outdoor dispensary at Moratuwa in 1886, and Sub-assistant Colonial Surgeon in 1889. This position he resigned in 1896 and then established himself in private practice in Moratuwa. The doctor owns landed property in the Kurunegala and Galle district. He is a member of the British Medical Association and of the Ceylon Agricultural Society.

J. S. GUNESEKERE.

G. M. SILVA.

Mr. Gregory Marcelleine Silva, the son of S. Andres Silva, plumbago and timber merchant, of Moratuwa, was born in 1866, and educated at St. Mary's School and the Royal College, Colombo. He was articled as student-at-law with Mr. H. J. Canakeratne, barrister-at-law, and was admitted a Proctor of the District Court in 1889 and of the Supreme Court and as Notary Public in 1900, since which time he has practised as such in Colombo. In conjunction with the late Francisco De Mel he was instrumental in founding the Moratuwa Association, of which he was the first secretary and is still an active member. He owns coconut estates in the Western Province and plumbago mines in the Avisawella district and the Kelani Valley, and is also a member of the Colombo Arrack Syndicate, of the Ceylon National Association, and of the Ceylon Planters' Association. His residence is "Roseville," Moratuwa.

J. S. DE SILVA.

Dr. Joseph Sebastian de Silva, the son of T. A. A. G. Lindemullege Jacob de Silva, merchant and landed proprietor, of Moratuwa, was born there in 1873. His scholastic

DR. AND MRS. J. S. DE SILVA AND INFANT.

THE BUNGALOW.

training he received at St. Sebastian's School, Moratuwa, and the Royal College, Colombo. Commencing in 1892, he took a three years' course of study at the Ceylon Medical College, at the completion of which he went to Aberdeen University, where he graduated M.B.C.M. He next attended University College, London, and obtained the D.P.H. of Cambridge, and from 1900 to January, 1901, he worked at the Pasteur Institute in Paris. He further studied at the Lister (then Jenner) Institute of Preventive Medicine at Chelsea. Returning to Ceylon in 1901, he was appointed Acting Third Physician of Colombo General Hospital, and afterwards Director of the De Soysa Bacteriological Institute. Later he was Assistant Medical Officer of Health of Colombo and Lecturer in Hygiene at the Ceylon Medical College until 1904. In August of that year he again visited the United Kingdom, this time going to the Rotunda Lying-in Hospital in Dublin, where he made a special study of midwifery and diseases of women. In the following year he returned to Ceylon, and has been in private practice at Moratuwa since that time. He is a member of the Ceylon branch of the British Medical Association and of the Catholic and Turf Clubs, Colombo. In 1905 he married Gala Lily Beatrice, fifth daughter of Mr. John Clovis de Silva, of Colombo. He resides at "Green Bank," Moratuwa.

J. S. DE SILVA.

SOLOMON PETER SOYSA.

The late Mr. Solomon Peter Soysa was the son of Domingo Soysa, planter and arrack renter, of Moratuwa (who was the brother of Jeronis de Soysa, Mudaliyar of the Governor's Gate), and was descended from one of the oldest Moratuwa families. Mr. S. P. Soysa was born on July 17, 1854, and was educated at Royal and St. Thomas's Colleges, and then joined the business of the late Charles Henry de Soysa as assistant. By steady application to his work he was raised to the position of general manager of what was then the largest business concern in the island, and was entrusted with a general power of attorney over the whole of the proprietor's affairs. He assisted in building up this huge concern, and for many years was practically Mr. de Soysa's right-hand man. On his death he was appointed the guardian of his minor children; he was also the executor of the will of the late Mr. Susew de Soysa, Mudaliyar. Mr. S. Peter Soysa took a business trip to Europe in 1889, returning on the death of Mr. Charles de Soysa, in 1890; and after five years he commenced business on his own account at No. 2, Canal Row, Fort Colombo, as a planter and general plumbago merchant and arrack-renter, holding the rents for the Uva Province and several parts of the Western Province. He married, in 1883, Dora Caroline, the eldest daughter of the late Mr. A. T. Weerasooriya, Proctor of the Supreme Court of Galle. Mr. S. Peter Soysa died on June 15, 1906, and was accorded one of the most imposing funerals in the recent history of the island. His eldest son, Wilfred Leopold Peter, was born in 1885, and educated at Prince of Wales's and Wesley Colleges, and commenced a planting career under his father. On the death of the latter he

S. PETER SOYSA. THE FAMILY.
THE BUNGALOW. TEA ESTATE.
TEA FACTORY.

DR. H. I. AND MRS. FERNANDO AND CHILD.

THE RESIDENCE.

took charge of his father's business affairs. The second son, Albert Hildebrand Theodore, is still a student at Trinity College, Kandy, while Fanny Ada Caroline, the eldest daughter, is married to Mr. William Augustine Peiris, of whom a biographical sketch is given elsewhere in the volume. There are two other daughters, Ellen Maria Adaline and Elsie Lilian Charlotte, both being minors. On the estates of the late Mr. Peter Soysa are grown tea, coconut, rubber, and cinnamon. Of the properties the best known is Ingiriya, in the Rayigam Korale of the Kalutara district, which covers an area of 1,600 acres and is equipped with tea factory, bungalows, stores, peeling station, &c. A large area of Para rubber is now being opened up. The Carolina estate in Dodanduwa district of the Southern Province, and Dangomu Kanda in the same province, as well as Lapotawa, near Negombo, are some of the best-known coconut estates. Besides these he owns a considerable amount of house property in Colombo and valuable plumbago mines and smaller plantations in various parts of the island. His residence, "Lynn Grove," Moratuwa, is a fine one. He is a member of the Kalutara Planters' Association, of the Agricultural Society, of the Moratuwa Association, and of the Friend-in-Need Society, and is also a member of the Turf Club, Colombo.

HENRY ISAAC FERNANDO.

Dr. Henry Isaac Fernando is the youngest son of Mr. W. A. Fernando, Government

H. I. FERNANDO.

contractor, of Moratuwa, and he was born at that place in 1875. His education he received at the Prince of Wales's College, where he won an exhibition in connection with the Cambridge Junior Local Examination in 1890, and two years later he passed first class in the Matriculation Examination of the University of Calcutta. Entering the Ceylon Industrial College in the following year, he became a licentiate there. In 1899 he was appointed First Assistant at the De Soysa Bacteriological Institute, under Dr. H. M. Fernando, M.D., B.Sc., when that institution was first opened. After occupying that position for two and a half years, he became House Surgeon of the Civil Hospital, Kandy, and resigned the Government service in order to practise privately at Moratuwa. In 1903 he married Gresilda Leonore Wilhelmine, eldest daughter of Mr. W. J. De Mel, of "Melbourne," Moratuwa. He is a member of the Moratuwa Association and of the British Medical Association, and is chief Circuit Steward of the Wesleyan Methodist Church at Moratumutta, Moratuwa, and General Secretary of the Ceylon Methodist Union. He is a lecturer of the St. John Ambulance Association at Panadure and at the Moratuwa Women's Union.

N. D. D. H. THOS. WIJEYESEKERE APPOOHAMY.

The family of Nayakkariyawasan Daluwattetama Don Henry Thomas Wijeyesekere Appoohamy has for some generations past been connected with the maritime customs of the Southern Province in the Dutch and early British administrations and with the arrack and areca nut industry. The grandfather of the subject of this sketch was Don Matthys Wijeyesekere Appoohamy, dealer and general trader of Tellewatte, and his father, Don Cornelis, carried on business on similar lines.

Don Henry Thomas Appoohamy was born at Amhalangoda in 1855, and educated at St. Thomas's College, after which he entered the Government service, being attached to the Kegalle Kachcheri in 1876. After holding various other appointments he retired in 1897 and is now a planter and landed proprietor, owning estates in various parts of the Western and Southern Provinces, as well as paddy-lands and house property at Moratuwa and Colombo. In 1885 he married Elizabeth Laura, second daughter of Johannes De Mel, of Melville, Moratuwa. He was formerly churchwarden and member of the synod for St. Peter's Church, Koralewelle, is a member of the Moratuwa Association and of the Agricultural Society, and resides at Elizabeth Villa, Moratuwa.

H. T. WIJEYESEKERE APPOOHAMY'S RESIDENCE.

HANWADEGE JOHN JACOB PIERIS.

Mr. H. J. J. Pieris was born at Moratuwa in 1863, and received his early education at the Church Missionary School at Kotta, afterwards completing his studies at the Prince of Wales's College, Moratuwa. He joined his father in the planting business in 1884, and opened up the Talagala estate, in Rayigam Korale, which produced coconuts, tea, and cinnamon. In 1892 he commenced arrack-farming, acquiring the arrack rents for Badulla, Colombo, Kandy, Kurunegala, and other places. Since 1896 he has conducted business on his own account as planter, estate-owner, arrack-renter and landed proprietor. He owns a number of planting estates in the North-Western Provinces ; and he is also one of the foremost horticulturists in the Western Province, being the proprietor of a fine model fruit garden of some 20 acres at Kanangwille, where the various kinds of fruits, both tropical and others, are grown. At the present day he owns the arrack rents for Colombo and the Siyane and Hewagam Korles, and farms the arrack rents for Kandy for the years 1907–8. He is also a part owner of the Panangkelle and Pusihena plumbago mines.

Mr. Pieris married a daughter of Mr. D. J. J. Goonewardene, of Galle, whose father and grandfather were both Mudaliyars of the Governor's Gate. Among his benefactions is the presentation of a ward to the new Princess Louise's Hospital at Moratuwa. His private residence is Wilmott Lodge, Moratuwa, and he is a member of various

THE BUNGALOW.

MR. AND MRS. H. J. J. PIERIS AND FAMILY.

BULLOCK HACKERY.

local and horticultural and agricultural societies.

K. J. DE SILVA.

Dr. K. Justin de Silva, of Moratuwa, is the son of K. Selaris de Silva, merchant, of Ambalangoda. Born in 1868, and educated at Wesley College, he entered the Ceylon Medical College in 1889, and in 1894 was appointed District Medical Officer at Narammulla. After holding various appointments he became Assistant Superintendent of the Lunatic Asylum, Colombo, and in 1905 was appointed Medical Officer of Moratuwa, which position he still holds, besides practising privately in the same place. He is a member of the British Medical Association and of the Moratuwa Association, and he is an enthusiastic tennis player. He married, in 1903, Annie Helena Margaret, daughter of W. J. Fernando, of "Ferndale," and his residence is "Milliville," Moratuwa.

DR. AND MRS. K. J. DE SILVA AND FAMILY.

K. J. DE SILVA.
(Now established in private practice at Moratuwa, after twelve and a half years' service in the Ceylon Medical Department.)

JOSEPH MATTHIAS DE MEL.

The scion of one of the best known families of Panadure and Moratuwa, Mr. J. M. De Mel is the grandson of Mr. Francisco De Mel, who is still known as the "Grand Old Man" of Moratuwa and who was born in 1809. Mr. Francisco De Mel founded the Moratuwa Association and became its first President. He was a staunch member of the Church of England, warden of the Holy Emmanuel Church, Moratuwa, from the day of its consecration, and the builder of St. Peter's Church, Moratuwa. Mr. Manuel De Mel, the father of the subject of this notice, like his brothers, Jacob and Johannes, dealt extensively in coconut, cinnamon, and plumbago. On his retirement, in 1898, his only son, Joseph Matthias, assumed control over his affairs.

Mr. J. M. De Mel was born in 1867 and educated at St. Thomas's College, Colombo, and at Trinity College, Stratford-on-Avon, England. After completing his studies and visiting the Continent, he returned to Ceylon, where he took over the management of his father's affairs and became joint-manager of the firm of Jacob De Mel. He is the owner of Heenmeliagera, Horagasoya, Kolamunuoya, and Isabelwatte estates, planted with coconut, consisting of 470, 275, 250, and 64 acres respectively; Imbulgaswadia estate, planted with cinnamon, covering 105 acres; and Davelendiri Mukalana, planted with rubber, containing 292 acres; and part owner of Pambela, Pamblea Pahalawatte, and Thoduawe estates, planted with coconut, containing 108, 90, and 500 acres respectively, and Kudaganga estate, planted with tea and rubber, containing 186 acres. In 1900 he married Lizzie, the daughter of Francisco Fernando, a brother of the well-known mining magnate, H. Bastian Fernando. The Church of St. Luke's, Moratuwa, which was built by his father, is Mr. Matthias De Mel's special care. In 1906 he opened a large plumbago yard and stores at Moratuwa, chiefly to provide employment for the poor, and several men and women find work there in the various branches of preparing plumbago for shipment. Mr. De Mel's private residence is "Melrose," Moratuwa.

THE MORATUWA CYCLISTS' UNION.

The formation of this organisation dates back to 1898. It was established primarily for the purpose of encouraging cycling in the Moratuwa district and neighbourhood, and the promoters also had as one of their aims the drawing together socially of the members, who are recruited from both sexes. The club has been a great success, and as the members wear uniform consisting of white coat buttoned to the neck, white trousers, white shoes, black cap, black and red corded, with club monogram on cap and club badge on the top pocket, they present quite a picturesque appearance when on parade. Since the club's formation the members have on several occasions escorted notabilities who have visited Moratuwa, including Sir Joseph West Ridgeway, G.C.M.G., K.C.B., K.C.S.I, P.C., &c., Sir (then the Hon. Mr.) Everard F. im Thurn, C.B., C.M.G, in 1902, and His Excellency Sir H. A. Blake in 1904. The club gatherings, including picnics and other social functions, form a very popular feature of the club's operations. The principal officials of the Union are: Patrons, His Excellency Sir Everard F. im Thurn, C.B., C.M.G., Mr. J. W. C. de Soysa, M.A., J.P., and Mr. E. L. F. de Soysa; President, Mr. J. G. C. Mendis, M.A. Cantab.; Vice-Presidents, Mr. Solomon Fernando, J.P., U.P.M., and Mr. W. H. Soysa; Senior Captain, Mr. C. P. de Silva; Captains, Messrs. W. A. Pieris, C. E. A. Dias, and H. E. de Alwis; Honorary Treasurer, Mr. C. M. A. Soysa; Honorary Secretary, Mr. Henry M. Pieris.

THE BUNGALOW. PLUMBAGO YARD. J. MATTHIAS DE MEL, SEN.
ST. LUKE'S CHURCH. J. M DE MEL, JUN. J. FRANCISCO DE MEL.

PETER DE SILVA WIJEYERATNE.

Mr. P. de Silva Wijeyeratne, son of Mr. Gabriel de Silva Wijeyeratne, Government contractor, was born in Colombo on January 2, 1868, and was educated at the Royal College, Colombo. At the conclusion of his scholastic career he opened a business as Government contractor for the supply of building materials for the Government Stores, the Army Ordnance Department, and the Royal Engineers. His business progressed, and in 1905 he commenced the additional business of a Government landing and shipping contractor. In 1907 he still further extended his interests in the commercial world and entered the plumbago trade, joining Messrs. F. G. de Silva Wijeyeratne and R. J. V. de Silva Wijeyeratne at 3, Castle Street, Colombo, reference to which business is made in the sketch of the career of the last-named gentleman. In 1901 Mr. Wijeyeratne married Eleanore Anne Eveline, daughter of Mr. and Mrs. J. C. de Silva, of "Lynnbank," Alston Place, Colombo. He resides at "Homeleigh," Castle Street, Colombo. The family to which the subject of the sketch belongs is traced back to Matthew Silva, a resident of Moratuwa in the far-away days when that now thriving suburb of Colombo was a mere cluster of houses. Matthew Silva was a Buddhist, but, influenced by the example of his sister, who abjured Buddhism for Christianity on her marriage, he was baptized. Some time afterwards he married a young lady of Mutwal, of the Karawe community. Matthew Silva had as issue a son named Pedro and a daughter. Pedro de Silva also married a young lady of Mutwal, and had as issue four sons and nine daughters. The eldest was named Paules Silva, who was President of St. John's Church, Mutwal, the second was Jacob de Silva, the third Miguel de Silva, and the fourth Augustino de Silva. Jacob de Silva was given the rank of "Patabendi" in recognition of services rendered, by letters patent dated January 25, 1828. The letters patent were signed by the Hon. Robert Boyd, Commissioner of Service. Lindamulegey Jacob de Silva Warnasuriya Curucula Wijeyeratne (Patabendi) was twice married, first to Balapuwadugey Isabella Mendis, by whom there were two children, Adrian and Augustino, and second to Bodiabaduge Agida Perera, by whom he had the following children: Pedro,

THE DESCENDANTS OF THE LATE GABRIEL DE SILVA WIJEYERATNE AND MRS. MARIA DE SILVA WIJEYERATNE.

The names are given in the order of back row right to left, middle row left to right, front row right to left.

1. Peter de Silva Wijeyeratne (son), merchant and contractor.
2. Mrs. Ellen Agnes Dharmaratne (granddaughter).
3. Anthony Perera Dharmaratne (husband of No. 2), Notary.
4. James Bernard Mendis (son-in-law, husband of No. 30), Pension Clerk, Treasury, Ceylon.
5. Francis Gabriel de Silva Wijeyeratne (son), merchant and contractor.
6. Dr. Charles Gabriel Peries, M.B., C.M., L.M. (grandson).
7. Charles Stephen Leitan (husband of No. 27), Notary.
8. Leo Hugo Peries (grandson).
9. John Francis Peries Gunawardene, Mudaliyar (husband of No. 26), Shroff, H.M. Customs.
10. Emmanual Francis Peries Gunawardene (grandson), Landing Clerk, H.M. Customs.
11. Joseph Gabriel de Silva Wijeyeratne (grandson and heir), student-at-law.
12. Master Gerald Anthony de Silva Wijeyeratne (grandson).
13. Master Austin Bernard de Silva Wijeyeratne (grandson).
14. Philip Neri de Silva Wijeyeratne (son), merchant.
15. Peter Perera (husband of No. 20), assistant, tutorial staff, St. Joseph's College.
16. John Bonifacio Fernando (son-in-law), dealer in oilmen's stores, liquor and wine merchant.
17. Joseph Louis Fernando (grandson), medical student.
18. Miss Elizabeth Justina Fernando (granddaughter).
19. Miss Josephine Mary Fernando (granddaughter).
20. Mrs. Lucy Mary Perera (granddaughter).
21. Mrs. Lucy Philomel de Silva Wijeyeratne (wife of No. 14).
22. Miss Agnes Mary Adeline de Silva (granddaughter).
23. Joseph de Silva Wijeyeratne (eldest son and heir), merchant.
24. Justine de Silva Wijeyeratne, now known as Sister Mary Mount Carmel (daughter), Nun, Good Shepherd Convent, Kotahena.
25. Mrs. Maria de Silva Wijeyeratne (wife of the late Gabriel de Silva Wijeyeratne, President of St. Joseph's Church, Grandpass).
26. Mrs. Engeltina Peries (daughter).
27. Mrs. Cecily Mary Leitan (granddaughter).
28. Mrs. Josephine Peries (wife of No. 6).
29. Mrs. Henrietta Laura de Silva Wijeyeratne (wife of No. 5, daughter of Dr. Charles Stephen Kirtisinghe, Negombo).
30. Mrs. Mary Ignacia Mendis (youngest daughter).
31. Mrs. Eleanore Anne Eveline de Silva Wijeyeratne (wife of No. 1).
32. Joseph Egbert Thomas Patrick de Silva Wijeyeratne (grandson).
33. Eric Finbar Patrick Thomas Mendis (grandson).
34. Burtyl Mary Gwendolyn Frances Mendis (granddaughter).
35. Elsie Leitan (great-granddaughter).
36. James Vivian Herbert Mendis (grandson).
37. Wilfred Pius Peries (grandson).
38. Dunstan Maurice Leander Mendis (grandson).
39. Irene Blanche Mary Elizabeth Peries (great-granddaughter).
40. Ethel Philomel de Silva Wijeyeratne (granddaughter).
41. Eldred Vernon Philip de Silva Wijeyeratne (grandson).
42. Eugenia Mary Constance Perera (great-granddaughter).
43. Gladys Mary Ursula de Silva Wijeyeratne (granddaughter).

DEATHS IN THE FAMILY.

Mr. Gabriel de Silva Wijeyeratne, President of St. Joseph's Church, Grandpass, and son of Warnasuriya Curucula Wijeyeratne Lindamulegey Jacob de Silva, Pattangetyn of Mutwal. Mrs. Catherine Fernando, wife of J. B. Fernando. Mrs. Maria Pavistina de Silva Wijeyeratne, wife of Joseph de Silva Wijeyeratne.

CARGO BOATS. MR. AND MRS. PETER DE SILVA WIJEYERATNE AND CHILD.
"HOMELEIGH." PLUMBAGO STORE.

Anthony, Bastian, Gabriel, and three daughters. About the time of his second marriage Jacob de Silva Warnasuriya Curucula Wijeyeratne (Patabendi) left Mutwal and went to Grandpass, where he started business as a timber merchant, continuing his operations until his death, on February 12, 1830. His business is being carried on by most of his descendants to this day.

The portrait group accompanying this sketch includes forty-three members of this ancient Sinhalese family, the picture having been taken after the thirty-sixth annual Christmas breakfast given by Mrs. Maria de Silva Wijeyeratne in 1906, at "Ellerslie," Rosmead Place, Cinnamon Gardens, Colombo. In the group are Mrs. Lindamulegey Maria de Silva Wijeyeratne, daughter of Thakura Artha-Deva Aditya Guardiawasan Lindamulegey Pedro de Silva, born on August 11, 1836, wife of the late Lindamulegey Gabriel de Silva Warnasuriya Curucula Wijeyeratne (born December 30. 1816), President of St. Joseph's Church, Grandpass, and fourth son of Lindamulegey Jacob de Silva Warnasuriya Curucula Wijeyeratne (Patabendi), children, grand-children, and great-grandchildren.

Three members of the family do not appear in the group, namely, Edward Joseph Peries (grandson), an engineer, at present in England, Charles Wolston Percival Peries (great-grandson), son of Dr. C. G. Peries, and Dunstan Charles Hector Leitan (great-grandson), son of Charles Stephen Leitan, who are infants in arms.

AN HISTORIC CLAN.

Around the western seaboard of Ceylon cluster many traditions of foreigners who came to the island either as invaders or as servants or guests of the reigning dynasty. One story worth the telling as an illustration of the diverse distant sources to which some of the inhabitants trace their ancestry relates to the family of Thakura Artha-Deva Aditya Guardiawasan Lindamulagey. The members of this family are the descendants of a colony of Kshattriyas of the great Aryan race seated in Rajputana in India, who, migrating from Jeypore, settled in Ceylon in the thirteenth century. The Sinhalese kings employed these Kshattriyas in military positions of trust, and the above names represent the names of the distinguished warriors of the particular clan so employed during different periods, according to the custom in Ceylon of prefixing the names of great ancestors to individual names. "Thakura," the first prefix, is taken in commemoration of the great warrior Thakura, who slew the usurper of a Sinhalese throne (Mahavansa, pp. 312, 313, 314). The Sinhalese king Bhuvaneka Bahu VII. granted to Aditya, one of the ancestors of the clan, and a descendant of Thakura, by a Maha Sannasa, certain fields and appurtenant high land, and the Moratuwa proper, now an industrious, populous, and wealthy suburb twelve miles from Colombo (see drawing marked A), to enable Aditya to take charge of the outpost, and to guard the coast against the landing of the South Indian Moors to help Mayadunna.

The son of Aditya, Thakura Artha-Deva Aditya Guardiawasan Lindamulagey Pedro de Silva, was baptized in the Catholic Church by the Portuguese military chaplain (A.D. 1538–1545), and was given the surname of De Silva by his sponsor, Captain de Silva, of the Portuguese army. It may be explained that the giving of Portuguese surnames by the military officers was a general custom in Ceylon during the Portuguese occupation.

The flag (marked B) is the flag of the Kshattriyas, and is retained by the clan. Up to the present time the flag is used by cavalry regiments in Rajputana. The crest (marked C) is the crest of the clan, and represents the five weapons of war of the ancient warriors. The accompanying translation of an *ola* document sheds light on the history of the clan, and is of historical value. The full history of the clan appeared in a brochure called "Aditya Wausa," in the Sinhalese language, printed by Messrs. H. W. Cave & Co., in 1903, at the cost of Mr. Thakura Artha-Deva Aditya Guardiawasan Lindamulagey John Clovis de Silva, of Green Bank, Moratuwa, and edited by Mr. Thakura Artha-Deva Aditya Guardiawasan Lindamulagey Gabriel de Silva.

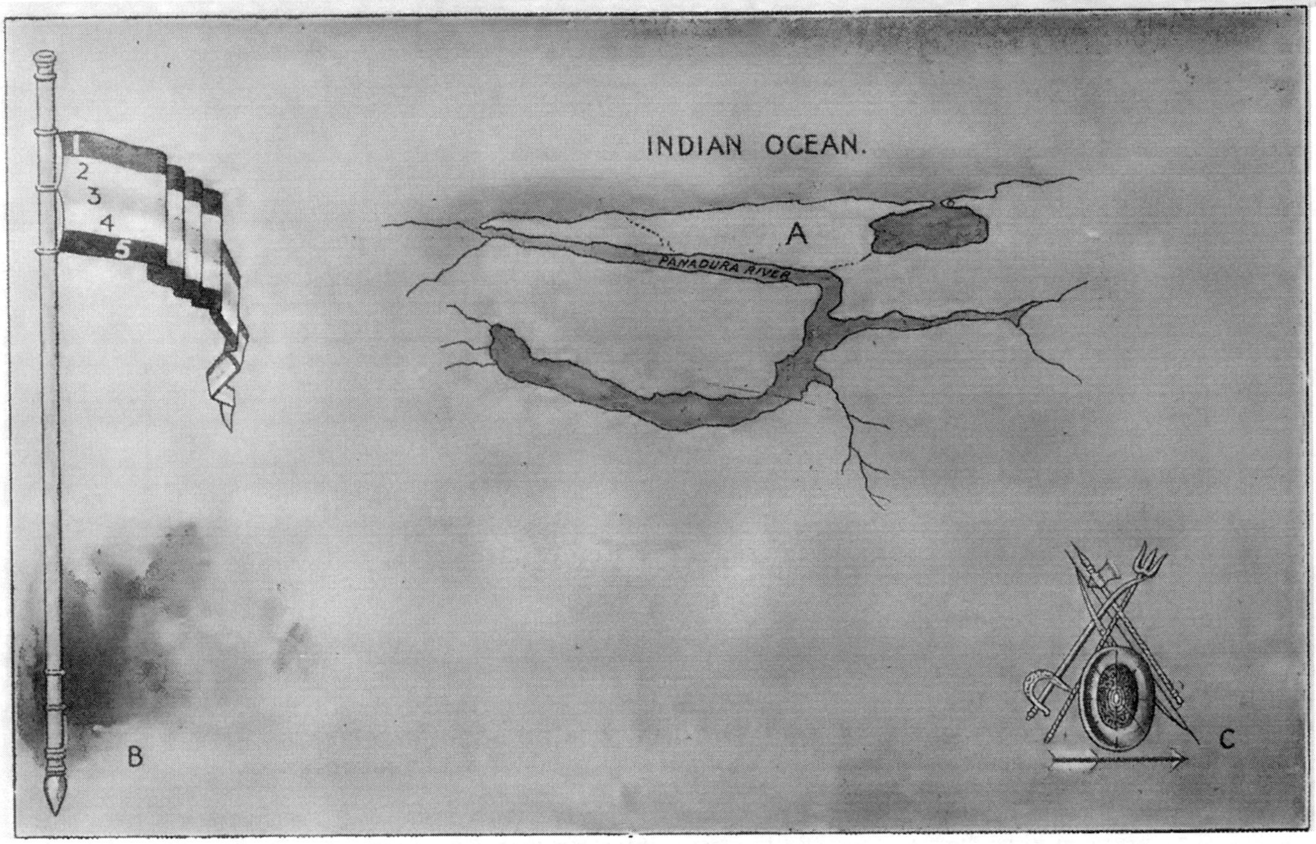

A. DIAGRAM SHOWING THE ORIGINAL SETTLEMENT AT MORATUWA OF THE ADITYA.
B. BANNER OF THE ARYAN KSHATTRIYA ADITYA. C. CREST OF THE ADITYAS.
(1, Blue; 2, Gold; 3, Red; 4, White; 5, Purple.)

The Translation of the old Ola.

The following instructions were given to us by our father in his old age, complaining of loneliness, when lying ill with a pain in his right arm, consequent, according to him, on an arrow-wound received in battle.

The Portuguese at present are once more the trusted allies of us Sinhalese people. There may come a time when these relations may give place to enmity. It is right and proper and due to our family honour that we should be loyal to our Sinhalese kingdom—we who, coming from afar, have received support from the royal treasury—and to the royal dynasty, which has conferred on us rank and honours and lands upon sannas.

The above and what follows he ordered to be committed to writing.

A colony of Kshattriyas of the Aryan race came over from the Rajput city of Jeypore in India and settled in a village in the vicinity of Hastisailapura; they were being supported by the treasury (mint), and employed Nilakarayas for service in their fields and granaries.

At this time, an army of Mallawas and Malays, having come under the pretext of worshipping at the shrines, began to plunder the country. Upon the orders of King Parakrama Bahu, Prince Vijaya Bahu employed the Kshattriyas to destroy them and to guard the Northern outposts from time to time against further invasion.

Thakura, the warrior and slayer of the usurper Mitta, was employed by the next king to instruct and train the army in warfare.

Of his descendants, in later times, your grandfather, who is of the line of the Kshattriya Artha-Deva, was married in binna to [a member of] the Rankotdivela Walauwa family in Four Korales. I was the only child born to my mother.

On the day I was first fed with rice, the five kinds of weapons were placed around me, and I was given the name Aditya, belonging to the nobles of the Suriyawansa of the Arya Kshattriya race. This my mother told me. I grew up, known as Aditya Bandara, and was taught in my youth the art of war by my father. At this time a prince, who had quarrelled with his royal father, came from Yapahu, and lay concealed in the Rankotdivela Walauwa, and together with me learned the art of war.

On leaving, this prince took away with him his wife and his daughter Chandravati, and with them my maternal uncle's daughter, Siribara Kuda Menike. After some time a messenger brought a letter to my grandfather, and took me away to Jayawardhanapura, where I was placed under the king above-mentioned, who had succeeded to the throne under the title of Bhuvaneka Bahu. At this time it was found out that Mayadunna and Rayigam Bandara, the brother princes, had sent men in disguise to Jayawardhanapura to assassinate the king. I took my oath, and was appointed to guard the royal dwellings and palace, and in the course of this employment it was my duty to accompany the king, armed, wherever he went.

Now the son of the Princess Chandravati, who had married Prince Vedhaya, grew up and dwelt in the palace. The fair princess, his mother, was accompanied by my cousin Siribara Menike on her way to and from the baths, but I had no opportunity of open converse with my cousin. In some of these visits I was ordered to go as escort.

The verses which we wrote one another from time to time, compiled in the work known as Siribara Malaya, together with the Maha Sannasa, I entrust to your care. In order to prevent the succession to the throne of the son of the Princess Chandravati, fortresses were built at Sitawaka, and on the banks of the Kelani Ganga. During this time, when making search for gifts of cloth which had been presented by the Portuguese to the members of the royal household, the king came upon our love-letters in verse, and showed his favour to me by getting us married, and invited my grandfather, father, and relations to his court.

While they were in Jayawardhanapura, hearing that Mayadunna was about to invade Jayawardhanapura with an army of Moors and Sinhalese which he had got together, the Portuguese and the Sinhalese armies, in which were my grandfather, father, and myself, fought them a great battle at Gurubabila, and proceeding to Sitawaka, burnt down the fortress, and gained a great victory; in this battle, however, both my grandfather and father were killed. At the request of a Portuguese gentleman, Captain de Silva, whose friendship I had made in battle, you, who were born when the flag of victory was raised, were baptized by the name of Pedro de Silva, being called Pedro after the priest who baptized you, and De Silva after the captain.

While the Portuguese were in alliance with the king, a great feast was held in celebration of the victory, and on the suggestion of Captain de Silva I was invested with a sword at the royal palace, and the wearing of the sword was made hereditary in my family. The flat and meadow land of Moratuwa lying between the sea, the river, the grove, and the ferry as the four boundaries, Mahakumbura, Bogahakumbura with its appurtenant high land of Mahawatta, our Sovereign Lord Bhuvaneka Bahu granted to me upon a Maha Sannasa.

At this time I was appointed head of the regiment told off to protect the palace to insure the security of the king and Prince Dharmapala, and this regiment was called by the Portuguese name of "Guardia."

Some time after the termination of the war, when I was occupied in digging the well for your sisters, I failed to promptly carry out a royal order, and was condemned to death. You will remember how my family in fear carried to the king in procession the new water of the new well, and reminded him of your father's brave deeds in the past, and obtained for me pardon from the king, who then named me Lindamulegey.

I charge you to send for my sons, who are performing military service at Ruanveligoda, to cultivate and improve the lands held under the sannasa, to live in peace with your brothers and sisters, and to bury me when I die in this Mahawatta by the side of your mother's grave.

MR. AND MRS. A. H. GOONETILLEKE.

PANADURE DISTRICT.

ARTHUR HECTOR GOONETILLEKE.

This gentleman, son of Simon Goonetilleke, Proctor, of Kalutara South, was born in 1875, and educated at St. John's School, Kalutara, and St. Thomas's College, Colombo. He read law under the Council of Legal Education, and, after being articled for three years, was called to the Ceylon bar in 1895 as Proctor of the District Court. He commenced practice at Kalutara in 1899. In 1900 he removed to Panadure, where he continues to practise, and has built up a large practice. In 1902 he became a Proctor of the Supreme Court and in 1903 Notary Public. Mr. Goonetilleke is a member of the Panadure Association, the Ceylon Law Society, the Agricultural Society, and the Orient and Turf Clubs. He owns several coconut and rubber estates, as well as considerable house property at Kalutara and Panadure. In 1902 he married Alice, third daughter of Mr. D. J. Wijesinghe, of Colombo, landed proprietor and mine-owner.

MR. AND MRS. J. W. DE SILVA AND FAMILY.

WARNAKULASOORIYA MAHAPATEBENDY LINDAMULLAGE JOHN WILLIAM DE SILVA.

This gentleman was born on August 18, 1855, at Moratuwa, and is the fourth son of the late Mr. Abraham de Silva, landed proprietor, and the late Mrs. Balapuwaduge Justina Mendis. He was educated, firstly, at the Moratuwa Wesleyan and the Government Central Schools, Kandy, and lastly, at Wesley College, Colombo. At the last-named institution he pursued a brilliant career, winning—besides many college prizes—the "Gogerly Scholarship," tenable for two years. He is also an undergraduate of Calcutta university. On February 16, 1887, he married Cecelina Leanora, daughter of Mr. M. S. Goonewardana, of Westland House, Panadure, and is now the father of five daughters and two sons. Mr. de Silva was a teacher at the Wesley College for some time, but afterwards chose the law for his profession, and was called to the Ceylon Bar in November, 1885. In 1893 he was granted a warrant to practise as a notary in English and Sinhalese, and in the year 1904 was admitted a Proctor of the Supreme Court. He is now one of the senior members of the Bar at Panadure, and commands a good practice. Mr. de Silva takes an active part in religious matters, being a prominent member of the Wesleyan Methodist Church and a lay preacher. He is a Sunday-school superintendent, and was for some time a circuit steward. He has also often sat as a lay representative in the annual synods of his Church. He is frequently invited by the clergy of other churches to address public meetings, a testimony to his broad views as a Christian as well as to his oratorical powers. He is one of the best known and most popular of the public speakers amongst the Sinhalese, and has many times, from religious, temperance, and political platforms, addressed large audiences with great persuasive effect. He is the editor, proprietor, and publisher of a Sinhalese monthly religious magazine styled the *Golden Garland*, which is supported by the clergy and laity of almost all the Christian Churches in the island.

PETER ALFRED GOONERATNE.

Mr. Peter Alfred Gooneratne, son of Moses Pieris Gooneratne, Mudaliyar of Panadure, was born in Colombo in 1862. At the close of his scholastic career at the St. Thomas and Royal Colleges in that city, he was articled to Advocate and Crown Counsel P. D. M. Ondaatje, with the view of following the legal profession. After three years of preparatory work he was admitted to the Ceylon bar in 1885 as Proctor of the District Court, and commenced practice at Panadure and Kalutara. He is now the senior member and leader of the Panadure bar. On various occasions he has acted as Police Magistrate and Commissioner of Requests at Panadure. He was one of the founders, and at one time the President, of the Panadure Association. Being an ardent follower of Buddha, he takes great interest

P. A. GOONERATNE AND ALFRED COTTAGE.

in Buddhist education and charities. Mr. Gooneratne owns five estates, planted in cinnamon, coconuts, and rubber, in the Western Province, as well as house property at Panadure and Colombo. His private residence is Alfred Cottage, Panadure.

F. A. WIJEYESEKERA.

Francis Alfred Wijeyesekera is the son of Don Arnolis Andris Wijeyesekera, Interpreter Mudaliyar of the Honourable the Supreme Court of Ceylon, and Johanna Victoria, daughter of Manuel de Fonseka, Mudaliyar of Kalutara, of whose family sketches appear on another page. He was born in 1867, and educated at St. Thomas's College, where he passed the Cambridge local examinations, junior in 1882 and senior in 1884. In the former year he took the *proxime accessit* to the Government exhibitioners. He went to England in 1888, and studied there for eighteen months. After his return he served as senior French lecturer at the Royal College, under Principals Marsh and Harward. In 1894 he was appointed Inquirer and Fiscal's Officer in the Pitigal Korale, and in the following year Justice of Peace and Unofficial Police Magistrate, and in the next year Salt Inspector and Deputy Fiscal at Puttalam. His next appointment was that of President of Siyane Korale West in 1900, to which was added Alutkuru Korale South in 1900; and in 1902 he became Acting Police Magistrate and Commissioner of Requests for Chilaw and Marawila, President of Salpiti Korale in the same year, and Itinerating Police Magistrate for Negombo and Kalutara and Acting District Judge for these places and for Chilaw in 1903. He is now President of the village tribunals of Salpiti Korale. In 1905 he made a second visit to England, and is now keeping terms at Lincoln's Inn with a view to being called to the English Bar. He resides at Nugegoda, Salpiti Korale, and is a member of the Agricultural Society. He read before St. Benedict's Old Boys' Association papers on "The Headmen System of Ceylon" and "The Prevention of Crime," and these were afterwards published. He has also written contributions to various magazines on local topics. In 1893 he married Dorothy Juliana, eldest daughter of the late Gate Mudaliyar Ambrosius de Rowel, and they have two sons, Leopold Rowel and Quintilian Emmanuel Lowe.

MR. AND MRS. F. A. WIJEYESEKERA AND FAMILY.

THE BUNGALOW.

CLARENCE PEDRO FONSEKA.

Dr. Clarence Pedro Fonseka, of Palm Grove, Panadure, is the son of Francis Fonseka, merchant, of Panadure, and Appolania Gooneruardene Fonseka. He was born in 1856 at Moratuwa, and educated, primarily, at St. John's, Panadure, and afterwards at St. Thomas's, Colombo. In 1876 he gained the Government Scholarship, and thereupon entered the Ceylon Medical College, and in 1881 he passed his final examination as Licentiate of Medicine and Surgery. In 1888 he married Leonora Fernando, daughter of Simon Fernando Sri Chandrasekara Mudaliyar, and is now the father of three daughters and six sons. The doctor has held many important positions, among which may be mentioned that of First District Surgeon at Pussellawa, in 1881; District Medical Officer at Lindula, in 1883; Sub-Assistant Colonial Surgeon at Beruwella, in 1889; and Sub-Assistant Colonial Surgeon and Judicial Medical Officer at Panadure in 1889. From this last official post he retired in 1903, and he now enjoys a large private practice. Dr. Fonseka has always been a liberal supporter of charities and charitable institutions, and not the least of his many benefactions is the

THE FAMILY GROUP. C. P. FONSEKA. THE BUNGALOW.

gift of the outdoor dispensary at Panadure to the Government, which establishment has been the means of supplying a long-felt want to the public of that place. He is a member of the British Medical Association, the Panadure Association, and the Agricultural Society. Dr. Fonseka is the owner of two estates, one at Panadure, on which cinnamon is grown, and the other, named Higahalande, in the district of Ratnapura, which produces rubber. He is a landed proprietor in Colombo and Panadure, the premises now occupied by Messrs. Lewis Brown & Co. belonging to him.

DANIEL JOHN FERNANDO.

Mr. Daniel John Fernando, the son of Johannes Fernando, of Miniwangodde and Wellawatte, was born at Miniwangodde, in the Negombo District of the Western Province of the island, in the year 1854. He received his education at the Government and Wesleyan Schools, Negombo, finally finishing at the Wesley College, Colombo. Passing out of the region of pupilage, he continued at the college as a teacher for some time. Later he erected buildings in Colombo and Colpetty, the administration of which took up so much of his time that he found himself compelled to relinquish his teaching duties. In 1898 he removed to Panadure, and there started desiccating mills, fully equipped with all modern steam machinery, including a 12-horse-power engine and boiler manufactured by Turner. Mr. D. J. Fernando is the only manufacturer of desiccated coconut in this district, and, as may he imagined, does a large and important trade in that line, employing in all about 75 hands. The coconuts are brought from his own as well as from outside estates, chief among his own estates being Delduwe, near Kalutara, consisting of about 1co acres. He also owns various smaller estates near Wellawatte and Panadure. Mr. D. J. Fernando is a landed proprietor in Colombo, Colpetty, and Miniwangodde. His private residence and office address is Mill Cottage, Panadure. He is a member of the Panadure Association and of the Anglican Church. He married, in 1882, Maria, daughter of George Felsinger, of Colpetty, and the issue of this marriage is two sons and one daughter. The latter is the wife of Mr. D. L. Wickramasinghe, of the Attorney-General's department.

DON JAMES ALFRED ABEYRATNE.

This medical gentleman, son of Don David Abeyratne, Mohandiram of the Governor's Gate, of Colombo, was born in the capital in 1874, and was educated at the Royal College in that city. He subsequently entered the Ceylon Medical College, Colombo, where he qualified as licentiate in the year 1900. He was appointed House-Surgeon of the General Hospital, Colombo, and afterwards successively filled various medical posts at Kandy, Badulla, Negombo, Avisawella, and other centres in the island. In 1904 he resigned from the Government service to commence private practice at Badulla. A year later he removed thence to Panadure, his present habitat. Dr. Abeyratne is a member of the Ceylon Agricultural Society and of the Panadure Association. His private residence is "Ferndale," Panadure; and he owns various small estates in Salpiti Korale, Alutnuwera, and at Badulla, as well as house properties at Colombo. Dr. Abeyratne's younger brother, Don Herod Stephen, was also educated at the Royal College, Colombo. He afterwards entered the Vidyodaya Oriental College, Maligakanda, where he made a special study of the Sinhalese language, with the result that he became sub editor of the Sinhalese newspaper *Lakrivikirana*. He is the author of several books, among which may be mentioned "Jinarajawansa," an account of the life of Gauthama Buddha; "Buddha-Edahille," the Buddhist hymn-book; and "A Treatise on Medical, Social, and Sexual

EXTERIOR OF MANICA MILLS, PANADURE.

INTERIOR OF DESICCATED COCONUT MILLS AT PANADURE. THE BUNGALOW.

D. J. FERNANDO. MR. AND MRS. D. J. FERNANDO AND FAMILY.

Sciences." He has also annotated the following books of Sinhalese literature: "Kusa Jataka Kavya," "Ummagga Jataka," and "Pujawaliya," for the use of higher classes in vernacular schools. Other literary work in which he has engaged includes a fully illustrated treatise on the science and practice of midwifery, dealing with Eastern and Western methods of treatment, and a series of text-books of geography in Sinhalese, with maps and diagrams, for the use of vernacular schools; also a comprehensive English-Sinhalese dictionary.

THE DISPENSARY, PANADURE.
THE BUNGALOW.

DON JAMES ALFRED ABEYRATNE AND DON HEROD STEPHEN ABEYRATNE.

G. DON JULIS APPU HAMI.

This gentleman, the son of a native agriculturist of the Salpiti Korale, was born at Kesbewa in 1853. Having completed his schooling, he commenced to trade in a humble way by collecting cardamoms and selling them in the local market in Colombo. Endowed with keen commercial instincts, he prospered, and subsequently opened trading stores at Ratnapura and Badulla, and supplied rice to a number of planting estates. In the flourishing times of the coffee industry he bought up and collected all the coffee he could obtain from the Uva Province, and having acquired a warehouse in Colombo, supplied some of the leading firms of the Fort with this article. This business spelt prosperity for Mr. Don Julis, and he purchased a great deal of property both in the town and the country. His office is in Gasworks Street, in Colombo, where a large import trade in rice and general merchandise is carried on. Mr. Don Julis owns some valuable house property in and about Colombo, warehouses in the Pettah, and coconut estates at Pitigal Korale, in Kurunegala, and Veyangoda.

He started plumbago-mining in 1896, and owns the Kutikande mine in the Sabaragamuwa Province, also the Kottiyawatta mine in the Rayigam Korale, employing altogether some 450 men. He is, besides, part-owner of the well-known Panagala mine. He possesses a charming town residence named Charlie Villa, in Maitland Crescent, Colombo, and a country residence at Panadure.

Mr. Don Julis is a member of the Ceylon Plumbago Merchants' Union and the Panadure Association. As an ardent Buddhist, he founded a school near Panadure, which he presented to the Theosophical Society. He is entirely a self-made man, having built up his present fortune by his own unaided efforts.

A UNIQUE ASSOCIATION.

Of the many time-honoured associations in Ceylon, the Rodrigo Family Friend-in-Need Society of Panadure is, perhaps, the most unique. It is sixty-seven years of age, and its existence has welded the family together, and strengthened that kinship with the bonds of a common interest. The membership roll contains the names of 57 members of the family, who take an active interest in the work of the society, and the fact that 90 per cent. of the annual expenditure is on account of those outside the family strikingly demonstrates the broad philanthropy which underlies the movement.

The founder was Johannes Rodrigo Lokumahatmaya, whose name is revered by many who are acquainted with the society's energies. After working out the details he called together other members of the family, who enrolled themselves as members. The society was formed with a threefold purpose, viz., to help the poor and the members of

THE FAMILY.   G. DON J. APPU HAMI.
THE BUNGALOW.   THE RESIDENCE, COLOMBO.

MEMBERS OF THE RODRIGO FAMILY FRIEND-IN-NEED SOCIETY OF PANADURE.

the Rodrigo family in their distress, to render pecuniary assistance towards the education of the children, and to promote a sense of unity in the Rodrigo family.

To start the society on a sound basis, the original members contributed 406 pagodas (Rs. 304·50) as donations, and fixed an annual subscription. The funds came in freely, having regard to the circumstances of the colony sixty years ago; afterwards the necessary legal formalities were undertaken and a notarial deed attested by Carolis Rodrigo was drawn up. The names of all the original members of the society are inscribed on this document, with the addition of a few others, and it is a matter for regret that not one of these gentlemen is alive to affirm the usefulness of the society. As the society progressed, its funds were increased with a view to extending its usefulness. Money was lent to outsiders at 12 per cent., and was readily taken, the usual rate of interest at that time being from 15 to 30 per cent. The income of the society was composed of the interest on the moneys lent, produce of the society's landed property, and donations and subscriptions of the members.

It was felt that there was a larger sphere of usefulness before the society, and, therefore, in 1854, the members made use of the reserve funds in their private enterprises and paid double the rate of interest others paid, besides their respective subscriptions. Small sums of money at low rates were lent the poor, to keep them in their work or in the various enterprises in which they were engaged. The society, of course, had its bad debts, and on its fiftieth and sixtieth anniversaries several of these, totalling Rs. 5,051·44, were allowed to lapse. No goods have ever been sold in distraint of payment, nor has anyone been sent to jail at the instance of the society. The income increased, in spite of these losses, and from a very small beginning the pension list has grown to about 1,500 per annum. In addition to providing these pensioners with rice, clothes, and money, the children of the poor in the Rodrigo family have been educated by the society, their daughters have been assisted in marriage, traders have been helped in their businesses, and in all cases of distress the society has even been ready with aid in money and kind.

Two of the outstanding events in the history of the society may be mentioned. In 1866, when the famine oppressed Ceylon, the society spared no pains to afford relief to all on its books, besides helping several thousands of others. The other instance was in 1897, when a relief fund was opened for the famine-stricken in India, and the society was enabled to forward a handsome donation.

During its existence Rs. 35,162·37 have been expended on the poor, and at the close of the year 1905 the credit balance stood at Rs. 16,594·83. Eleven members of the Rodrigo family have been educated through the instrumentality of the society and all hold responsible positions under Government.

The society has acquired a burial-ground close to the Panadure Courts for the exclusive use of the Rodrigo family, and this will serve as a perpetual memorial of the family. Mr. David Rodrigo is the present President, to which office he was called in 1885, and Mr. Thomas Rodrigo has been its Secretary and Treasurer since 1894. By ardent and willing work the latter has, to a great extent, raised the society to the position it occupies to-day. His term of office marks the halcyon days of the society's life; its usefulness has extended and its financial position has been placed on a far sounder basis than was formerly the case.

CYRIL CHARLES ARNOLD JANSZ.

This gentleman, the second son of the late Mr. J. W. Jansz, of the Ceylon General Treasury, was born at Colombo in 1856, and educated at St. Thomas's College in that city. After passing the first examination in arts of the Calcutta University, he left college and was for some time engaged in educational work in Colombo. In 1880 he was appointed First Assistant-Master at St. John's School, Kalutara, becoming Headmaster of that institution in 1881. In the following year he accepted the headmastership of St. John's School, Panadure, which institution, at that time, was conducted under the Society for the Propagation of the Gospel in Heathen Lands. In 1887 the school was registered as a High School. Since then it has been steadily advancing, and now occupies a prominent position among the educational establishments in the island.

In 1883 Mr. Jansz married Amelia, daughter of Mr. Hilary Donald Jansz, late Crown Proctor of Galle, and in 1885 Mrs. Jansz opened a Girls' School in Panadure, which has gradually grown into the present Girls' High School. In the year 1891 Mr. Jansz took the Boys' School over as a private concern, and has since then been the Principal of these two schools. The number on the list in the Boys' School is 375 and in the Girls' School 150. There are two separate boarding establishments, one for boys and the other for girls. The prominence to which these schools have attained is evidenced by the result of the Cambridge Local Examinations held in December of last year, at which—all the leading Colleges and High Schools in Ceylon competing—St. John's Boys' High School secured a First Class in Honours and the first place in the order of merit for Ceylon in the Senior Examination, and a First Class in Honours with the third place in the order of merit in the Junior; while, among the Girls' Schools, St. John's Girls' High School obtained the second and third places in order of merit in the Senior Examination and the third place in the Junior. The secular subjects taught in the schools are, in addition to the usual English subjects, history, geography, French, Latin, Greek, mathematics, physical geography, botany, and drawing. Distinction has been won at the Cambridge Local Examinations in religious knowledge, English, arithmetic, Latin, mathematics, geography, physical geography, and botany. An interesting feature of Mr. Jansz's work is that in the highest form the two sexes are taken in one class. This, we believe, is the only attempt at co-education in Ceylon. While a student at St. Thomas's College, Mr. Jansz was the editor of the college magazine. He has been a churchwarden of St. John's Church, Panadure, for nearly twenty-five years, and has been a member of the Standing Committee of the Ceylon Educational Association ever since its inception. We may mention, in passing, that Mr. Jansz's eldest daughter, Miss Evelyn Jansz, is a pianist of some repute and an Associate of Trinity College, London.

ANDREW SIMON GOONEWARDENE.

Dr. A. S. Goonewardene, M.R.C.S. Eng., L.R.C.P. Lond., is the fourth son of Mr. M. S. Goonewardene, planter and landed proprietor, and one of the most respected citizens of Panadure. The doctor was born in 1873 at Westland House, Panadure. He was educated at St. John's School, Panadure, and

MR. AND MRS. C. C. A. JANSZ AND FAMILY.

THE RESIDENCE. ST. JOHN'S COLLEGE, PANADURE.

A. S. GOONEWARDENE AND FAMILY.

entered the Ceylon Medical College in 1893, winning a Government Scholarship at a competitive examination. He thus followed the same professional course as his eldest brother, Dr. J. H. S. Goonewardene. After a successful career at the Medical College, the subject of this notice obtained the diploma of licentiate

A. S. GOONEWARDENE.

in medicine and surgery, and succeeded to the post of House-Surgeon and House-Physician of the General Hospital, Colombo. In 1898 he started as a private practitioner in his native town. He proceeded to England in 1904, and entered University College, London. After a course of studies at that institution, he obtained the diplomas of M.R.C.S. Eng. and L.R.C.P. Lond. He then proceeded to Ireland, and spent some time at the Rotunda Hospital, Dublin. Returning to Ceylon in 1906. he resumed practice at Panadure. He is a Wesleyan Methodist, and his private address is "The Eclipse," Panadure.

MRS. JEREMIAS DIAS.

Pattinihannedige Warnadeeptya Kurukulasuriya Selestina Rodrigo, widow of the late Mr. P. Jeremias Dias, is a daughter of the late Solomon Rodrigo—renter and landed proprietor, and a prominent member of the well-known Rodrigo family of Panadure—and was born at Nalloor, in Panadure. Her husband was a member of the old and respected Dias family of Panadure, and was the elder of the two sons of the late Mr. Haramanis Dias, a well-known and respected native merchant of his time. Mr. Jeremias Dias was educated at the local Government English School, and started a business of his own with a limited capital when he was a mere youth in his teens, and by sheer hard work and steady perseverance, added to those high qualities which are essential to a successful man of business, and which he possessed in an eminent degree, rose to the enviable position he enjoyed at the time of his death, which took place in March, 1902, at the comparatively early age of fifty-four. Mr. Dias was a manufacturer of arrack and renter throughout the island, and farmed the arrack-rents of Colombo, Panadure, Kalutara, Kandy, Badulla, Nuwara Eliya, Anuradhapura, Siyane and Hewagam Korales, Negombo, Puttalam, &c. He was one of the largest shareholders in the arrack farms syndicate, in the formation of which he took a leading part, and for the success of which he was mainly responsible. He was also the owner of valuable house property in the towns of Colombo and Panadure, and of several planted estates, besides plumbago-lands in Kurunegala, Ratnapura, and Ruanwella. He took a prominent part in the formation of the Panadure Association, of which he was President at the time of his death. Mr. Dias was a staunch Buddhist, and by his death the entire Buddhist community of Ceylon has lost a warm supporter and ready helper and Panadure one of her greatest sons. He was well known for his liberality, and as a supporter and contributor to all funds for the spread of Buddhism, a cause to which he devoted thousands of rupees annually. He took a keen interest in all public charities and charitable institutions, was the head "dayaka" of Rankot Vihara, the beautiful temple at Panadure, and did a good deal towards the improvement of that temple. Finally, he established a "Parivena," or college for the education of priests.

Mrs. Dias continues to take a keen interest in religious and charitable institutions, and has given a valuable plot of land for additional buildings for the Rankot Vihara besides undertaking to build a Dharmasala or preaching-hall in it.

The renting portion of the business has been taken over by the eldest son, Mr. Harry Dias; but the manufacture of arrack, which is carried on in all its forms, in addition to the management of the estates, is still under the control of the widow. The store-houses, capable of storing over 60,000 gallons of arrack, are situated at Panadure. Among the more important estates belonging to the family may be mentioned the following: Horeketta, at Horana, planted with coconuts and cinnamon; Good-hope and Pinehill, in the Panadure district, both planted with rubber; Sirikandura estate, in the Kalutara district, planted with tea and rubber, covering 650 acres, on which also is a fully-equipped tea factory; Pelpola Kumbura, a paddy-field of over 120 acres, near Panadure; besides a considerable number of valuable smaller lands and fields. The produce of all these estates is sold locally.

Mrs. Jeremias is the mother of four sons and four daughters. The sons are: Harry, born in 1875; Arthur Vincent, born in 1886; Edmund Wilson, born in 1888; and Charles Martin, born in 1898. The eldest daughter,

THE BUNGALOW.
THE DISTILLERY.

THE ARRACK STORE.
INTERIOR OF THE BUNGALOW.

Lilian Vilisia, is married to Mr. Abraham Perera, landed proprietor and estate owner of Panadure; the second daughter, Ellen Maria, is married to Mr. Thomas de Silva, B.A., of the Kandy Kachcheri. The sons were educated at St. John's School, Panadure, and afterwards at St. Thomas's College, Colombo, and they are now assisting their mother in the management of the family estates. The eldest son, Mr. Harry Dias, who married, in 1903, Milly, daughter of Mr. S. T. Gunawardana, Mudaliyar of Pasdun Korale, Kalutara, is manager of all the Buddhist Schools in the Panadure district, is a member of the Theosophical Society and the Young Men's Buddhist Association, and President of the Panadure Association. He is also part owner of the arrack-rents of the Colombo district, in conjunction with Mr. H. J. J. Peiris. His favourite pastimes are tennis and cricket. The second son, Mr. A. V. Dias, is the Treasurer of the Panadure Buddha Sangama, a society for the propagation of the gospel of Buddha; while the third son, Mr. Edmund Wilson Dias, has taken to planting.

CHARLES EDWARD ARNOLD DIAS.

Mr. Charles Edward Arnold Dias, the eldest son of Arnold Dias and Apalonia Soysa, was born at Panadure in 1878, and received his education at St. John's High School in that town and St. Thomas's College, Colombo. After his school career he was apprenticed with the firm of Messrs. Volkart Bros., Colombo, with whom he received his commercial training. On the death of his father, in 1900, he assumed control over the deceased gentleman's affairs. In 1903 he married Beatrice Frances Catherine, fifth daughter of Mr. and Mrs. Jacob De Mel, of Horton Place, Colombo. Of this marriage there are two children, a daughter and a son. His father, Arnold Dias, who was born in 1849, was the second son of Haramanis Dias, the leading arrack-renter and citizen of Panadure. Mr. Haramanis Dias was mainly instrumental in building and endowing the Buddhist temple, Rankot Vihara, in Panadure. He possessed considerable landed property, and dealt largely in arrack. His charitable works included the establishment of the public dispensary at Bandaragama and the public baths at Panadure. He also constructed several minor roads in his native district, and always contributed handsomely to public charities. On several occasions he declined public honours. The late Mr. Arnold Dias, besides being a merchant carrying on a large arrack export trade with Madras, was an arrack dealer on a large scale. He also owned valuable landed properties, the principal being Midellamullahena and Maha-

MRS. ARNOLD DIAS AND FAMILY.

CHARLEY VILLA. MONUMENT ERECTED TO THE MEMORY

THE LATE H. DIAS. OF THE LATE HARAMANIS DIAS. THE LATE ARNOLD DIAS.

MEMBERS OF THE DIAS FAMILY. ARRACK READY FOR EXPORT.

wela, planted with coconut and cinnamon, both in the Kalutara District. His arrack exhibits always attracted attention, and won him silver medals at the Paris and Colombo Exhibitions in 1900 and a gold medal at Galle in the same year. Besides these, he was awarded several other medals at different times for arrack and other agricultural products. He was a public-spirited gentleman who evinced a keen interest in public affairs. He died on the eve of being created a Justice of the Peace and being included among the recipients of the following Birthday Honours. A fine polished Aberdeen granite and marble monument, erected to his memory, adorns the churchyard of St. John's, Panadure, of which he was a warden for several years.

Mr. C. E. A. Dias carries on the arrack trade built up by his father and grandfather, subsidising annually fourteen arrack distilleries. He has gained silver medals for arrack and spirits at Colombo, Heneratgoda, and Moratuwa Exhibitions, and was awarded a special silver medal for these manufactures at the St. Louis Exhibition in 1904. All these were the highest awards for arrack. He is also engaged in planting and general mercantile business. Taking a more than ordinary interest in agriculture, which is, indeed, his hobby, he has established an experimental garden at his Wavulugala estate, Horana, where he is planting rubber. Mr. Dias is the Vice-President of the Panadure Agricultural Society, a member of the Colombo Agri-Horticultural Society, Colombo Agricultural Society, the Ceylon Turf Club, and the Ceylon Poultry Club. He has won several medals and prizes for agricultural products and poultry at the shows and exhibitions held at Colombo, Kandy, Galle, and Heneratgoda. He is captain of the Panadure section of the Moratuwa Cyclist Union. His recreations are tennis, cycling, and shooting. His private residence is Charley Villa, Panadure.

Mr. Vincent Silvester Apalonius Dias, brother of Mr. C. E. A. Dias, and born in 1880, is a licensed surveyor and leveller, having been trained at the Technical College, Colombo, also a partner of the Ceylon Survey Agency. Mr. H. W. J. Dias, another brother and born in 1883, is a broker for Messrs. Peak Bros. & Winch, of Colombo. These two latter members of the family were educated at St. John's High School, Panadure, and Prince of Wales's College, Moratuwa. Both are enthusiastic volunteers, being members of the "R" Company (Moratuwa) of the Ceylon Light Infantry. Their favourite recreations are cricket, tennis, shooting, and cycling.

S. H. B. KURUPPU.

Simon Hendricus Bartholomeus Kuruppu, son of Don Hendrick Kuruppu, Notary Public and Registrar, of Bandaragama, and of Dona Caroline Kotalawala, was born in Panadure in 1863, and educated at Colombo Academy and St. Thomas's College, where he passed the Junior Cambridge Local Examination. He subsequently took over the appointment of assistant to the editor of the *Buddhist* (Mr. Wijeyesinghe, the well-known translator cf the Mahavansa), and occupied it from 1885 to 1887. He served articles with Mr. A. de A. Seneviratne, late M.L.C. and now District Judge, and in 1903 became a Proctor of the district of Kalutara, practising first at Kalutara and then at Panadure, where he still carries on his profession. Mr. Kuruppu is Chairman of Buddhist Temporalities in the Western Province, a member of the Royal Asiatic Society, the Advisory Board, and the Ceylon National Association. He is also a landed proprietor, owning house property and coconut, cinnamon, and rubber plantations in the Rayigam Korale, the largest of the latter being the Stagmoor estate. He married, in 1898, Violet Rosalind, daughter of Cornelis Wijeyesinghe, Interpreter Mudaliyar, Matara Courts. His residence is "Piyarance."

S. H. B. KURUPPU.

MAHAWADUGE CORNELIS PERERA.

This son of the well-known landed proprietor and arrack-renter Mahawaduge Mathes Perera, of Panadure, was born at Wekade, Ceylon, in 1872, and educated first privately and afterwards at the Royal College, Colombo. He studied planting on the Sorane Group in the Rayigam Korale, and soon acquired a complete knowledge of tea, cinnamon, and coconut cultivation. In 1893 he started planting on his own account, and in 1896 engaged in the distillation of arrack. He now owns two large distilleries at Wekade and wholesale stores at Panadure. The manufacture of arrack is carried on at Wekade in all its stages, and from Mr. Perera's stores in Panadure the spirit is distributed among the leading arrack-renters. To supply the large demand for the spirituous beverage, he is obliged to buy large quantities from various other manufacturers in addition to the output from his own distilleries. In fact, he is one of the largest dealers in arrack in Ceylon. He owns parts of the arrack-rents of various districts.

In the vicinity of Panadure Mr. Perera owns some fifty coconut and cinnamon properties, including the large tea estate of Cecilton in the Balangoda district, where a large factory for making up the leaf has now been put up, and another estate, Rosemont, on which there is a fully equipped factory, which not only deals with the tea grown on the property, but also with that of surrounding estates. All the produce of the estates is sold in the local market, and some 600 hands are employed on the plantations. Mr. Perera is Vice-President of the Panadure Association and a member of the Agricultural Society. He is of the Buddhist persuasion, and is the founder and supporter of several Buddhist schools. In 1896 he married Cecilia, fourth daughter of Mudaliyar Simon Fernando Sri Chanderasekera. His private residence is "Mentmore," Panadure.

MERENNEGE MATHES SALGADO.

Mr. M. M. Salgado, arrack-renter and general merchant, is the son of Abraham Salgado, merchant, of Pingwella, near Panadure, on the coast south of Colombo. He was born in 1860, and educated at the Wekade Industrial School. At an early age he joined his father in the produce business and for nearly ten years carried on operations at Kandy. In 1887 he obtained the local military contract for food-stuffs. He commenced the farming of arrack-rents, in company with others, in 1897, and subsequently successively acquired the rents for Anuradhapura, Ratnapura, and Panadure. Mr. Salgado stills carries on a large contract business with the military authorities, besides having bakeries at Kandy, Nuwalapitiya, Hatton, Talawakelle, Diyatalawa, Badulla, and Kurunegala. At the last-named place he has also opened a well-equipped medical dispensary. His arrack stores at Panadure have a storage capacity of nearly 50,000 gallons, and the arrack is collected here and sent out to the various centres as required. Besides the military department, Mr. Salgado also supplies, on contract, various

THE PRIORY. THE BUNGALOW, PANADURE.
M. C. PERERA. ARRACK STORES. MR. AND MRS. M. C. PERERA AND FAMILY.
ARRACK DISTILLERY.

THE FAMILY. INTERIOR OF ARRACK STORE. M. M. SALGADO EXTERIOR OF ARRACK STORE. THE BUNGALOW.

hospitals and jails with rice, bread, and vegetables, spirits, and oilmen's stores. Mr. Salgado's Colombo office is at No. 16, Prince Street, Pettah; his private residence is Salgado Villa, Panadure, and he owns houses in Kandy and other places. He is, as well, the proprietor of many coconut, tea, and cinnamon estates, chief of which are the Richarddale and Graceland. He is, besides, a part-owner of the Royal Hotel, Kandy. Mr. Salgado is a committee-member of the Panadure Association and the Ceylon Agricultural Society. A subscriber to the Buddhist belief, he built the temple at Pingwella, of which he remains the principal supporter and director. He married the sister of Domingo Dias, of Panadure, and has four daughters and two sons.

PONNAHANNEDIGE DOMINGO DIAS.

This gentleman is the third son of the late Covis Dias, a well-known general merchant of Panadure, near Colombo, and a grandson of the late Cornelis Dias, also a merchant and influential resident of the district. His mother was Hewa Fonsekage Hellena Fonseka; and his three brothers are named respectively Jinoris Samuel, Andris, and Jeremias, his five sisters being Solona, Leanora, Selestina, Missiona, and Jane Isabella Dias. Mr. P. D. Dias was born at Panadure in 1853, and received his education at the local Government school. In 1895 he married Dovisina Leanora, sister of Dr. Henry Cooray, and the only daughter of the late Mr. Mendis Cooray, a mine-owner and Government contractor of Horetuduwe. At the age of twenty Mr. Dias started business as an assistant to his father. Subsequently he acquired shares in the toll, arrack and liquor rents, and opened several hotels and liquor-shops. Of the latter the principal ones are the Hill View Hotel at Nawalapitiya, of which Mr. Dias is sole proprietor, the Castle and Royal Hotels at Kandy, and liquor-shops at Maskeliya and Hatton, of which four latter establishments he is the principal owner. From 1883 to 1897 he was general manager and shareholder of the arrack-rents of the Central Province, and since 1898 he has been the principal arrack-renter of the Panadure district. In 1896 he turned his attention also to planting, and he is now the owner of several estates planted with tea, coconut, and rubber in the Western Province and the Kurunegala district. Mr. Dias also owns house property in Panadure and Kandy, five plumbago-lands in the Ratnapura district, and other plumbago-lands and mines in Pasdun Korale, in the Kalutara district. Of his plantations the chief are Monera-endu-kanda at Kalupahana, Batalawattegode at Pelpola, Titte-eta Mukalana, in Salpiti Korale, and Helgama, in Kurunegala. "Siri-madura," his beautiful residence at Panadure, standing in seven acres of ground, was built by him in 1900.

Mr. Dias is Treasurer of the local Agricultural Society, and a member of the Panadure Association and of the Ceylon Agricultural Society. A staunch Buddhist, he is a trustee of several Buddhist temples, also founder of the Dharmasala (preaching-hall) of Uduwatte in the town of Kandy. Besides having spent large sums of money on schools, he contributed a sum of Rs. 1,000 towards the acquisition of Buddhagaya in India, now the centre of Buddhist activity, where stands the sacred Bo-tree under which Prince Siddhartha became Buddha (the enlightened). Mr. Dias is also a leading supporter of Rankot Vihara, the principal Buddhist temple in Panadure. Large sums of money were contributed by him towards the building of this vihara, and

MR. AND MRS. P. D. DIAS AND DAUGHTER. THE DRAWING-ROOM. THE BUNGALOW.

GIKIYANAKANDE ESTATE.

1. Tea Factory. 2. The Bungalow.
3. Tea Pluckers at Work. 4. View of the Estate. 5. Coolies.

the "simawa" (monks' confession-hall) appertaining to it was erected solely at his expense.

KALUTARA DISTRICT.

JOHN EDWARD DE SILVA SURIYA BANDARE GOONEWARDENE.

Mr. John Edward de Silva Suriya Bandare Goonewardene, known as J. E. de Silva, is a son of Gabriel de Silva, merchant, of Colombo, and Caroline, daughter of Dr. Cornelis Werakoon. An early member of the family was Balthazar de Silva, Mudaliyar, who was a Thombo-holder and Sabandu in the beginning of the Dutch occupation. This Mudaliyar was a direct descendant of Suriya Bandara, a general in the army of King Rajasinha, of Sitawake, and fought in the battle at Mullanyuwa with the Portuguese forces at which the commander Diego de Mel was taken a prisoner. The subject of this sketch was born in Colombo in 1853, and educated at St. Thomas's College. He studied law under the late Mr. C. D. Lorenz, Advocate, and entered the Government service in 1873 as a translator in the Colombo Kachcheri, under Sir Charles Peter Layard, K.C.M.G. He became Mohandiram of that office and acted as Mudaliyar of several Korales, after which he was appointed President of the village tribunals of Alutkuru Korales North and South and Hapitigam Korale. He had a good training in the Colombo Kachcheri under Sir Frederick Richard Saunders, K.C.M.G. In 1896 he was created a Mohandiram of the Governor's Gate. In 1900 he was Acting Police Magistrate of Kalutara. In 1903 he was created a Justice of the Peace for the District of Negombo by the Governor, Sir Joseph West Ridgeway, G.C.M.G., K.C.B., in honour of his Majesty the King's birthday of that year. Since July, 1906, he has been Police Magistrate and Commissioner of the Court of Requests of Kalutara. He married Cecilia Maria, daughter of John Perera, Tide Surveyor of H.M. Customs. He owns properties in Colombo and Negombo districts as well as residential property. He is a member of the Royal Asiatic and Agricultural Societies of Ceylon. In religion he is a Buddhist. His country house is Cecilia Cottage at Wellampitiya. He belongs to an ancient Goigama (Vellala) family.

THE GIKIYANAKANDE ESTATE.

This fine estate is the property of the Right Hon. Lord Elphinstone, in whose family it has been since the land was first purchased, in 1844, by the Right Hon. John Lord Elphinstone. The development of the estate to its present high state of perfection has been gradual. In 1879 a small portion of the estate—six acres—was under Liberian coffee, 1,446 acres were citronella grass, scrub, &c., and 1,750 acres forest. The remaining 28 acres represented cleared but unplanted land. In 1880 the coffee area had extended to 162 acres, 6 acres were planted with tea, 4 with cocoa, and 600 with citronella grass. There were also 800 acres of abandoned grass and 1,600 acres of forest. By 1894 the tea area had increased to 552 acres, and Liberian coffee (partly interplanted with tea) covered only 30 acres. The remainder of the estate was thus apportioned: clearings, 15 acres; guinea grass (for cattle), 15 acres; forest, about 1,435 acres; and scrub, 1,183 acres. The late Lord Elphinstone visited the estate in 1881 and made a careful inspection of the whole. In a memorandum which he made at the time appears the following note: "*India Rubber*—Evidently suits soil and climate. This now to

THE RESIDENCE.

MR. AND MRS. J. E. DE SILVA AND FAMILY.

J. E. DE SILVA.

GIKIYANAKANDE ESTATE.

1. View of New Rubber Clearings.
2. Michie-Golledge Rubber Machine.
3. Tapping Rubber-Trees.
4. Rubber Clearings.

be tried (Mr. Porter considers the Para variety might succeed)." This reference to the product which is now playing so important a part in the development of Ceylon was almost prophetic. The estate to-day takes a leading place amongst the rubber-producing properties of the tropical world. Some of the rubber-trees upon the estate are fourteen years old, and the yield has attained very considerable proportions, while the quality is attested by the facts that at the St. Louis Exhibition in 1905 "Gikiyanakande" was awarded a silver medal for its exhibit, and that at the Peradeniya Rubber Exhibition in 1906 one gold and two silver medals were given in respect of the rubber produced on the estate. The exact position to-day as regards rubber cultivation is as follows :—

Para rubber-trees planted through the ten fields from four to fourteen years old			18,339
Do.	do.	1903 ...	15,576
Do.	do.	1904 ...	71,214
Do.	do.	1905 ...	111,437
Do.	do.	1906 ...	27,149
		Total ...	243,715

The tapping of the rubber-trees commenced on February 13, 1902 ; 630 trees were tapped during that year, and some 300 lbs. of dry rubber were harvested. In 1906 no fewer than 8,258 trees were tapped, and the total yield of dry rubber was 16,221 lbs. This is a considerable quantity, but it is not merely the volume of the output which gives the rubber cultivation of the estate a leading place in the rubber world, for the prices obtained for the Gikiyanakande produce have always ruled high. The estate produces annually about 370,000 lbs. of tea ; but to how great an extent the tea interests have become overshadowed by rubber will be seen by the following table representing the acreage as it is to-day :—

	Acres.
Area planted with tea	543
Area planted with rubber	1,000
Area planted with grass	27
Total ...	1,570

The manager of the estate is Mr. G. H. Golledge (Mr. A. Glennie, acting), and Lord Elphinstone's agents in Ceylon are Messrs. Leechman & Co.

JOSEPH VICTOR WEERASINGHE.

Mr. Joseph Victor Weerasinghe, District Engineer, Kalutara, member of the Local Board and District Road Committee, Kalutara, is a son of D. H. Weerasinghe, of Kalutara, and Sophia, daughter of Don Nicholas Abeysekere. He was born in 1874, and was educated at St. John's School, Kalutara, and St. Thomas's College, Colombo. He entered the Public Works Department as apprentice in the Government factory in 1891 and in 1895 became head overseer. In 1899 he was Inspector, and during 1900 was Acting District Engineer, Ambanpitiya, and later of Dandugama. He was District Engineer at Mannar in 1903, and served in the same capacity at Diyatalawa the following year. Subsequently he was for a short time in the Provincial Engineer's Office, Colombo, and became District Engineer of Kalutara in 1905, a position he still occupies. In 1902 he married Maria Caroline, daughter of D. C. Tudugalla, of Seddewatte.

MR. AND MRS. J. V. WEERASINGHE AND FAMILY.

E. E. MODDER.

Dr. Eugine Ellis Modder is the son of John William Modder, late proprietor of the Galle Face and Royal Hotels, Colombo, and Caroline Frances Anjou, whose father was formerly Secretary of the Court at Jaffna. Born in Colombo, in 1855, he received his education at Colombo Academy, and studied medicine at the Ceylon Medical College. After graduating as licentiate of that institution he became successively House Surgeon of the Colombo and Kandy Hospitals, and was Medical Officer at Gampola and Matale during the outbreak of cholera. Later he held appointments at Colombo, Chilaw, and Kurunegala, after which he proceeded to the Royal and Western Infirmary, Glasgow, and in 1885 he took the degree of L.F.P.S. there. Upon his return to Ceylon he held numerous appointments in the Civil Medical Department, and in 1904 he was appointed medical officer of the first grade and given charge of the Kalutara district, and this position he still occupies. He has been a member of the British Medical Association for more than twenty years, both in England and in Ceylon, and he is a member of the Orient Club. A valuable treatise on the native disease known as paranghi written by him was published by the Government, and he has also contributed articles to the *Journal of Tropical Medicine* and the British and Indian medical journals and Ceylon medical journals on the bacteriology of paranghi, and other medical subjects. In 1882 he married Elizabeth Sofia, daughter of Charles Kalenberg, Proctor of Negombo, and in 1896 he married a second time, the lady being Edith Alice Maud, daughter of Mr. James Hugh Spronle, of Kandy. His eldest son, Vyvil, is in the Locomotive Department of the

E. E. MODDER.

Ceylon Government Railways, and his second son is in the Bengal Forest Department. Dr. Modder resides at "Bridge View," Kalutara.

J. Y. G. A. JAYEWARDENE.

The first authentic record of the family from which Mr. John Vincent Gomis Abeyesinghe Jayewardene comes occurs in the name of Weerakonhettige Marthalis Gomis Abeyesinghe Jayewardene, his great-great-grandfather, who held the office of Director of the Government Gardens in 1796, and received the rank of Malwatte Mohandiram from Governor Sir Frederick North. His son Matthes served under General Steuart on a monthly allowance of five pagodas of gold, and accompanied Sir Frederick North to the Kandyan Court at Dambadeniya with a retinue of fifty followers. This officer conveyed letters seventeen times to the court at Kandy, and afterwards accompanied Collector Wood with a body of his men, fighting against the insurgents at Attenegalle, and he and his men subsequently served under Colonel Hook at Kurunegala. He received the office of Dadayakkare Mohandiram from Sir Robert Brownrigg on April 22, 1812, and for the services above stated was presented with a sword of honour, duly inscribed and authenticated by the Hon. Robert Boyd, Commissioner of Revenue in 1824. His son Paulus succeeded him as Dadayakkare Mohandiram, receiving the appointment from Sir Edward Barnes in December, 1824, and the present Mudaliyar's father, Simon, was appointed in 1867 as Mohandiram of the Padikare Nile by Sir Hercules Robinson. His mother was Johanna Christina, third daughter of Don Joseph de Silva Wijayasundara Goonesekera, Mudaliyar of the Atapattu of Colombo.

Mr. J. V. G. A. Jayewardene was born at Colombo in 1861, and educated at St. Benedict's Institute and the Colombo Academy. In 1881 he was attached to the Queen's Advocate's Office as acting Mudaliyar, and acted as Interpreter of the Supreme Court in 1884. Thereafter he held various other appointments under Government, and was in 1895 appointed Interpreter of the Supreme Court. In November, 1900, he was appointed Mudaliyar of Rayigam Korale by Sir West Ridgeway, and also held a deputation as Deputy Fiscal of that Korale. In March, 1902, he was transferred as Mudaliyar of the Panadure and Kalutara Totamunes. When Mudaliyar of Rayigam Korale he was presented by the planters and other residents in the district, under the authority of His Excellency the Governor, with a gold medal set in jewels for his valuable services. He is a planter of coconuts and Para rubber, and a cultivator of paddy, and goes in for the growing of Egyptian, Australian, and local fruits. His estate, Llewellyn, in the Kalutara district, as well as his family seat known as "Dadayakkara Walauwa," in Siyane Korale, is fully planted with rubber and coconut. He is chairman of nine village committees, a member of the Ceylon Branch of the Royal Asiatic Society, of the Ceylon Agricultural Society, and of the local Friend-in-Need Society.

CYRIL A. L. ORR.

Cyril Albert Ledulx Orr is a descendant of a surgeon who came to Ceylon with the British forces in 1796, and was stationed at Colombo. His father is Edward Orr, Proctor, and his mother Eliza, daughter of John Ledulx, of the Customs, Colombo. He was born at Kalutara, in 1871, and educated at St. Thomas's College. He studied law, and became Proctor of the Supreme Court and Notary Public in 1902, and practises at Kalutara. He is an unofficial member of the Local Board, a member of the District Road Committee, and captain of the

CYRIL A. ORR.

Kalutara Town Cricket Club, as well as an honorary member of the Kalutara Sports and Cricket Club.

ALFRED JAMES BAWA.

Mr. Alfred James Bawa, the third son of Mr. Arthur H. Bawa, Proctor of the Supreme Court, and Georgina Matilda, daughter of

ALFRED JAMES BAWA.

J. T. Ablett, Esq., of Colbrooke Row, Islington, London, was born in 1870 at Kandy, and was educated at St. Paul's School, Kandy, and at

MR. AND MRS. J. V. G. JAYEWARDENE AND FAMILY.

THE MUDALIYAR'S SWORD AND MEDAL.

THE BUNGALOW.

MUDALIYAR J. V. G. JAYEWARDENE.

MUDALIYAR J. V. G. JAYEWARDENE AND HIS STAFF OF NATIVE HEADMEN.

MR. AND MRS. H. A. PIERIS AND FAMILY.

MUDALIYAR H. A PIERIS.

THE DRAWING-ROOM.

the Royal College, Colombo. He commenced his commercial career as an assistant with Messrs. Lewis Brown & Co., but his inclination was towards the study of the law, which he, however, was unable to follow owing to the death of his father at that time. In 1889 he began planting on the tea estate of Lavant, in the Kelani Valley district, under Mr. F. J. Wright, and here he continued for thirteen years. He then joined the Galatura group of tea estates in the Ratnapura district, conducted under Messrs. Finlay, Muir & Co., of Colombo, and afterwards was Assistant Superintendent on Maddagedera, Bentota, estate belonging to the same firm. In July, 1905, Mr. Bawa took charge of the Elladuwa estate in the Kalutara district. This property, consisting of 596 acres, and planted with tea and rubber, belongs to the Dimbula Valley Tea Company. It possesses a fully equipped factory, with a Hornsby-Akroyd oil engine and sirocco drying machine. Black tea, which is the special product of this estate, is shipped to the United Kingdom in large quantities, the trade mark "Elladuwa" being well known in the tea world, and the annual output is about 70,000 lbs. Mr. Bawa has already opened up 396 acres in Para rubber, and the area planted for this product is steadily increasing. Mr. Bawa also grows coconuts, interplanted with tea. In 1905 Mr. Bawa married Martha Elaine, the second daughter of Wilfrid Van Twest, of the Customs, Colombo. He is very fond of sport, especially cricket, golf, tennis, and hunting. He is a member of the Kalutara Cricket and Sports Club and the Kalutara Planting Association.

H. A. PIERIS SIRIWARDHANA, Mudaliyar.

Mr. Henry Ashmore Pieris Siriwardhana, Mudaliyar, is the son of the late Mr. J. M. P. Pieris Siriwardhana, J.P., Mudaliyar of Siyane Korale and of the Governor's Gate, and Susan Elizabeth, daughter of Don Solomon Dias Bandaranaike, Mudaliyar of the Governor's Gate. He owns considerable estates at Kelani, Heneratgoda, and Mirigama. He married Eliza Harriet, daughter of Mr. H. L. Dassanaike, Mudaliyar of the Governor's Gate and of Hapitigam Korale, and they have two sons and one daughter—Henry Ashmore, Louis Augustus, and Eliza Irene Augusta. Mr. Siriwardhana, who is Mudaliyar of Hewagam Korale, is one of five sons, all of whom have distinguished themselves. One of them, Mr. John Louis Pieris Siriwardhana, is Mudaliyar of the Governor's Gate and an author of several Oriental works; Mr. William C. Pieris Siriwardhana holds the degree of Bachelor of Medicine; Mr. P. E. Pieris is a Master of Arts, Cambridge, Barrister-at-law, and District Judge of Kalutara; and Mr. D. G. Pieris Siriwardhana is a Mohandiram of the Governor's Gate and a proprietor planter.

T. PIERIS MUDALIYAR ARSECULERATNE DISSANAYAKA.

Mr. Theodore Pieris Mudaliyar Arseculeratne Dissanayaka was born at Kalutara in 1845, and educated at St. Thomas's College, Colombo. He entered the Government service as a volunteer attached to the district court of Kalutara and filled various positions until in 1878 he became Deputy Fiscal of Panadure. He was head clerk and Deputy Fiscal of Kalutara from 1881 to 1905, when he retired from the service on pension. He married, in 1870, Anastasia Juliana, eldest daughter of Mr. Perera, Interpreter of the district Court of Kalutara, and in 1895 he married a second time, the bride being his first wife's sister. His eldest daughter, Anna Regina, is married to Nichol Francis Fernando, contractor, and

MUDALIYAR THEODORE PIERIS. THE BUNGALOW.

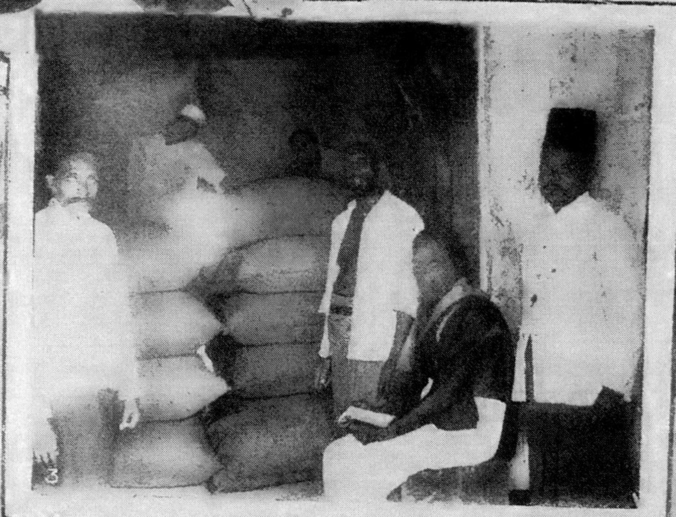

J. B. M. PEREIRA.

RICE GODOWN.

ARRACK STORES.

"ALVERSTONE."

MRS. J. B. M. PEREIRA.

proprietor of the Empire Hotel, Kandy. The subject of this sketch resides at Nutmeg Grove, Kalutara.

JOSEPH BONIFACE MICHAEL PEREIRA.

Mr. J. B. M. Pereira is the eldest son of Michael Francis Pereira, accountant in the Prisons Department, and of Maria de Silva, daughter of the late Lindamulage Bastian de Silva, general merchant, of Colombo, and grandson of Martinus Pereira, Mudaliyar of Kalutara. He was born on May 14, 1878, in Colombo, and educated at St. Joseph's College. Deciding to adopt the legal profession, he studied law, and was admitted a Proctor of the District Court of Colombo in 1902. In 1906 he was enrolled a Proctor of the Supreme Court, and practises in Colombo, being the senior partner of the firm of proctors practising under the name and style of Pereira & Perera. In addition to his professional duties Mr. Pereira carries on the business formerly owned by his father-in-law, the late Mr. W. J. B. Chas. Perera. This business is arrack-renting, dealing in precious stones, rice importation, &c., and is an extensive one, carried on in various parts of the island, but principally in the Kalutara district. Mr. Pereira is the present renter of the Three Korales arrack farm, and is co-proprietor of the Kalutara and Ratnapura arrack-rents. As regards the rice business, a large trade is done with Southern India, the bags of rice being conveyed to Beruwela in Mr. Pereira's own schooners and sold locally. In the precious stone department Mr. Pereira has dealings with some of the leading English jewellers and dealers and also most of the leading local firms. Mr. Pereira owns several small coconut estates and some paddy-land, besides house property of considerable value in Colombo. In 1905 he was married to Cecily Mary Beatrice, elder daughter of the late Mr. W. J. B. Perera, a well-known general merchant and arrack-renter of Kalutara. Mr. Pereira is a member of the Agricultural Society, the Ceylon Law Society, the Catholic Union and Club, and a director of the Central Grocery and Wine Stores, Ltd. His offices are No. 126, Hultsdorf, Colombo, whilst his country residence is Walgama Estate, Pannipitiya, about fifteen miles from Colombo, and his town residence is "Alverstone," Temple-road, Colombo.

NEGOMBO DISTRICT.

WALTER NICHOLAS STRAUBE ASERAPPA.

Mr. W. N. S. Aserappa, son of P. L. Aserappa, of the Public Works Department, and of Mary Magdalene, daughter of Peter Jurgen Ondaatje, landed proprietor, was born in 1867, and educated at St. Thomas's College. He studied law under Mr. T. E. de Sampayo, K.C., and became a Proctor of the Supreme Court in 1892. In the following year he commenced practice in Colombo, and has acted frequently as Deputy Fiscal and Municipal Magistrate and as Public Prosecutor in the District Court, Colombo, in the Supreme Court, and in various parts of the island. In 1904 he was Acting Tamil Member of the Legislative Council, and during the same year was Itinerating Police Magistrate of Negombo and Kalutara, whilst since January, 1905, he has been Police Magistrate and Commissioner of Requests, Negombo

MR. AND MRS. W. N. S. ASERAPPA AND DAUGHTER.

W. N. S. ASERAPPA, P.M.

He is also Additional District Judge of Negombo and Visitor to the jail there. He is a member of the Y.M.C.A., and was Recording Secretary until 1904. Formerly, too, he was President of Voetlights (an association of advocates who have joined the Bar since 1889). He is at the present time a member of the Colombo Branch of the Royal Asiatic Society and of the Board of Agriculture Agricultural Society. In 1893 he married Julia, daughter of Advocate Samuel Arnold Allegakoon, of Jaffna. He is a Tamil, belonging to the Colombo Chetty community (Vaisya caste). He has in his possession a sword presented by H.E. Governor North (afterwards Earl of Guilford) in 1800 to Abram Rodrigo Muttukrishna, Mudaliyar of the Governor's Gate and head of the Chetties (Tamils) in Colombo, this gentleman being an ancestor of Mr. Aserappa on the maternal side. The social parties and balls given by Simon Chenniah, Mudaliyar, one of which was honoured by the presence of H. E. the Governor (Sir R. W. Horton) and family, were mentioned in the official *Gazette*.

JAMES GRENIER DRIEBERG.

Mr. J. G. Drieberg, son of Mr. J. S. Drieberg, Commissioner of Requests and Additional District Judge, Colombo, was born in 1872, and educated at St. Thomas's College, where he passed the Cambridge Local Junior Examination and the entrance examination to the Calcutta University. In 1886 he went to Glasgow, and was apprenticed to Messrs.

J. GRENIER DRIEBERG.

Nevin and Hadden, civil engineers, with whom he served three years. Returning to Ceylon, he was appointed to the Public Works Department, and held the positions of District Engineer at Puttalam, Anuradhapura, and Kalutara, and since 1902 has been District Engineer at Negombo. He is an A.M.I.C.E., a member of the Orient Club, and a cricket and tennis player. In 1904 he married Agnes Eleanor, daughter of the late Sir Samuel Grenier, Attorney-General of Ceylon.

M. H. MIRANDO.

Magina Marcelis Henry Mirando is the son of Magina Andrew Paul Mirando, Mudaliyar, and Anna, daughter of Walisinghe Juannis de Silva, planter, of Negombo, and grandson of Marcus Mirando, medical practitioner of Megalle, in Galle district. He was born in 1870, and educated at the Wesleyan Mission High School in Negombo and Royal College. In 1896 he entered the Government service, attached to the District Court of Negombo as native writer, and became translator to the same court two years later. In June, 1904, he was appointed Mohandiram of Alutkuru Korale North, and is Inquirer into Crime for the judicial division of Negombo. He has various coconut estates in his Korale, house properties at Negombo, and ancestral holdings at Megalle in the Southern Province. In 1902 he married Nancy Maria, the eldest daughter of Hundiram Simon de Zylva, planter and plumbago merchant, of Kurunegala. He is a Buddhist and the Secretary of the Negombo branch of the Agricultural Society.

WILFRED MARTIN RAJAPAKSE.

Mr. Wilfred Martin Rajapakse is the second son of Mudaliyar John de Silva Rajapakse, of whom a biographical sketch is given on another page. He was born at Colombo in 1868 and educated at Royal College, after which he was articled for the study of law to Mr. Fredk. Dornhorst, K.C. In 1890 he became a Proctor of the District Court, and in 1894 of the Supreme Court, and a Notary Public. He has practised his profession at Negombo ever since, and has on various occasions acted as District Judge, Commissioner of Requests, and Police Magistrate at Negombo. He is a member of the Agricultural Society, and resides at "The Retreat," Negombo.

In 1892 Mr. Rajapakse married Catherine, daughter of B. Mendis, of Colombo. Amongst his possessions are the coconut estates of Pothode, Walahapitiya, and Bandirippua in the Negombo and Chilaw districts.

M. H. MIRANDO, MOHANDIRAM. MR. AND MRS. M. H. MIRANDO AND FAMILY. THE RESIDENCE.

THE RESIDENCE. THE ESTATE BUNGALOW.

W. M. RAJAPAKSE. MR. AND MRS. W. M. RAJAPAKSE AND CHILDREN.

"KIRTHINWASSA." MRS. KIRTHISINGHE. K. S. KIRTHISINGHE. F. G. WIJEYERATNE. MRS. WIJEYERATNE. DRAWING-ROOM.

C. L. DE ZYLVA.

Mr. Charles Lionel de Zylva was born at Negombo in 1876, and educated at St. Thomas's College. After a short mercantile career he took up planting, and is now visiting agent of the estates of the late John Leo de Croos in the Negombo and Chilaw districts as well as general manager of the planting operations. He resides at Palansane Mill estate, near Negombo. Mr. de Zylva is a keen volunteer, and in 1894 joined "A" Company of the C.L.I. as private. He transferred to "B" Company at Negombo as lance-corporal, and after passing the N.C.O.'s examination, was promoted sergeant in 1898. Going to England with the Coronation contingent, he obtained the Coronation medal. In 1902 he was appointed second lieutenant, passed his examination for captain in 1903, and was promoted Lieutenant Commanding Negombo Detachment, or what is now "M" Company, of the C.L.I. He was the first Ceylonese Volunteer officer to take part in the Staff ride of 1905, and he passed the D.I. examination in topography, tactics, and engineering. He is the grandson of Edward Lorensz de Zylva, who took part in quelling the Kandyan rebellion, and now holds as an heirloom the sword presented to his ancestor by the British Government.

KURUKULA SURIYA CHARLES STEPHEN KIRTHISINGHE.

Dr. Kurukula Suriya Charles Stephen Kirthisinghe is the son of K. S. Philip Gabrielle Fernando Kirthisinghe, Korale Mudaliyar of Negombo, and K. S. Pholorencia Fernando, and the grandson of K. S. Susey Fernando, merchant, of Negombo. He was born in 1856 and educated at St. Thomas's College, after which he took a course at the Ceylon Medical College, and having distinguished himself in medicine and midwifery, started practice at Negombo in 1882. He has been a member of the Local Board there continuously since 1903, and was on the Board on several occasions previously. He is a member of the Agricultural Society and President of the Negombo Union Club. In 1883 he married K. S. Marie Josephine, daughter of K. S. John Leitan, Mudaliyar, of Chilaw, and his only daughter, Laura Henrietta, married, in 1906, Francis Gabriel de Silva Wijeyeratne, landed proprietor and contractor, of Colombo.

D. DON JOSEPH.

Mr. Dekirikawege Don Joseph, son of D. Don Henrik, of Bopitiya, Pamunugama, Ja-ela, was born in 1818, and educated at St. Patrick's, Jaffna, and St. Benedict's, Colombo. He then joined his father in business, and very early took over the arrack-rents for Mannar and did a large trade in dried fish. After remaining there for two and a half years he went to Kurunegala to superintend his father's estates and plantations, and when his father died, in 1899, he took over his own share of the estates and of the arrack-rents. To-day he owns the rents for Manabar, Mullaitivu, Vavuniya, Negombo, Kurunegala, Trincomalee, Anuradhapura, and Puttalam. In all the afore-mentioned places Mr. Don Joseph has his own stores for the distribution of arrack. His principal store is an enormous building at Kalutara, and from there and from Panadure arrack supplies are principally drawn. He also owns numerous estates all over the country, of which Dangolle, Kotakanda, Galgoda, and Wyandane, in the North-Western Province, fully planted with coconuts, are the chief. There are also tracts of paddy-land and other similar plantations as well as house

D. DON JOSEPH.

MR. AND MRS. D. DON JOSEPH AND FAMILY.

THE RESIDENCE.

GROUP OF D. DON JOSEPH'S MANAGERS. ARRACK STORE AT KALUTARA.

ARRACK EXHIBIT.

property at Mannar, Trincomalee, and Kurunegala, belonging to Mr. Don Joseph. He has a magnificent country residence, called Henry Villa, at Bopitiya, in the Alutkuru Korale South. In 1899 he married Victoria, daughter of Mr. Domingo Rodrigo Weerasinghe Goonewardene, and the youngest sister of Mr. Nicholas Rodrigo Weerasinghe Goonewardene, of Bopitiya. He is a Roman Catholic, and his recreations are fishing and motoring. The joint managers of his business are J. Don Manuel and J. D. Nicholas.

MUDALIYAR J. DE S. RAJAPAKSE. MAGDALENE HOUSE.

J. DE S. W. S. RAJAPAKSE.

Mr. John de Silva Wijeyegooneratne Samaraweera Rajapakse, Mudaliyar and Justice of the Peace, is the son of Augustine de Silva Rajapakse, planter and landed proprietor of Mutwal, and Celestine, daughter of Simon Mendis Amarasekere, and the grandson of Simeon de Silva Samaraweera Rajapakse, Mudaliyar, of Naotunna, Galle district. He was born at Mutwal in 1841, and educated at St. Thomas's College, after which he entered the Government service and was attached to the Kurunegala and Negombo Kaccheris, where he reached the position of Shroff Mudaliyar. After twenty-two years' service he retired in 1892. For twelve years he was an elected member of the District Road Committee, and member of the Local Board, also for twelve years, of Negombo, and for three years of the District Road Committee at Colombo. He now devotes himself to the supervision of his estates, which are planted with coconuts, cinnamon, and paddy. These comprise the estates of Koshena and Andi Agarag group in the Pitigal Korale South, 475 acres in extent, and Horahena and Lilydale, as well as four smaller plantations in the Negombo district. He also owns some house property in Colombo. He is a Roman Catholic, and in 1861 he married Mary Magdalene, granddaughter of Francis Mendis Abeyesekere, Mohandiram, of Negombo. Of his sons, the eldest, Alexander Edmund, is Mudaliyar and a proprietary planter at Katunayake, Wilfred Martin a Proctor of the Supreme Court at Negombo, and Walter Benjamin a planter in the Negombo district. His daughter, Agnes Jemima, married Fred de Zoysa, Proctor and notary, of Colombo. His second daughter, Frances Lily, married Tudor Rajapakse, Gate Mudaliyar, of Colombo; whilst the youngest daughter became the wife of John Edward de Zoysa, Proctor of the District Court at Negombo.

A. E. DE S. W. S. RAJEPAKSE.

Alexander Edmund de Silva Wijeyegooneratne Samaraweera Rajepakse is a son of John de Silva W. S. Rajepakse, Mudaliyar, J.P. He was born in Colombo in 1866, and received his education at the Wesley and Royal Colleges, Colombo. He attended the Ceylon Agricultural School for a period of three years, and, selecting agriculture as a profession, commenced work on his father's Horahena estate. He experimented largely with manure on several coconut estates in different parts of the island, and the results of these experiments are published by Messrs. Freudenberg & Co., of Colombo, in pamphlet form. At present he is buying artificial manures alone to the value of over Rs. 10,000 annually, and a similar quantity is purchased for his father's estate. Mr. Rajepakse is considered by Government to be the only graduate of the Colombo School of Agriculture who has actually carried out successfully the aims of the school, viz., up-to-date planting on scientific lines. Besides his own estates, Amandolame and Hebilbaddere in the Negombo district, Bathgampola and Tabbowa in the Chilaw district, Irebadegame in the Kurunegala district, and several small plantations, he holds

MR. AND MRS. A. E. DE S. RAJEPAKSE AND FAMILY. MUDALIYAR A. E. DE S. RAJEPAKSE.

THE RESIDENCE.

leases of several well-known and extensive estates, amongst the principal ones being Kadirane estate (cinnamon and coconuts), comprising about 1,000 acres, and Kalu Kenda estate (coconuts), in the Negombo district, and Kakiriscanda and Kohilewagure estates (tea and coconuts) in the Southern Province. Mr. Rajepakse manufactures copra and the famous S.D.A.R. Kadirane brand of cinnamon, the former being sold locally and the latter exported to England. He has obtained numerous medals of gold and silver, and certificates for his produce at local and foreign exhibitions, the principal being two medals and diplomas each for cinnamon and cinnamon oil at the St. Louis Exhibition (1904), and the special gold medal offered by the Ceylon Agricultural Society at the Agri-Horticultural Society's Show held in June, 1906, for the best collection of products of the district which could be sent to London by the Ceylon-Government as the Ceylon Imperial Institute exhibit. In recognition of his having adopted agriculture as his sole pursuit after leaving the School of Agriculture, he was awarded the rank of Mohandiram in 1903, by the then Governor, Sir West Ridgeway, whilst in 1906 His Excellency Sir H. Blake elevated him to the rank of Mudaliyar. In doing this His Excellency said: "I have had your name brought before me for the excellent work you have done in your district. You have given your time and your money in the encouragement of what I consider the most important work done in Ceylon, that is, the improvement of agriculture amongst the people of the country. It is a great pleasure to me to acknowledge your good work by conferring on you the rank I now bestow, that of Mudaliyar. I hope that you will live long to continue the good work you have done before." Mr. Rajepakse is Chairman of the Katunayeke branch of the Ceylon Agricultural Society and a member of the Colombo Agri-Horticultural Society. He married, in 1889, Alexandra Alece Engeltina, daughter of John Alexander Mendis Rajepakse, Mohandiram. He has both a town and a country residence, the former being "Rajepakse Walauwa," Mattakulle, Colombo, and the latter at Kadirane.

WILMOT EDGAR LEEMBRUGGEN.

The family of Leembruggen has been settled in Ceylon for nearly two hundred years. Henricus Leembruggen, son of Johan Leembruggen, of Leyden, and Wilhelmina Bloteling, was born in Leyden in August, 1721, and died in Colombo in 1782. By his fourth marriage, with Susanna Maria Runsdorff, he had a son, Casparus Henricus, who was born on June 21, 1782. Casparus married Maria Elizabeth Adelaide, daughter of Count

W. E. LEEMBRUGGEN.

Guillame Joachim du Bois de la Saussage, a Captain in the Wurtemburg regiment, and afterwards Magistrate of Ambalangoda. These were the parents of Gerrard Hendrik Leembruggen, who married Elizabeth Gertrude Ribey, and the subject of this sketch is their son. He was born at Jaffna in 1856, and educated at Jaffna College and at Matara, after which he entered the Ceylon Medical College in 1875, and became a licentiate in 1878. He was then appointed Sub-assistant Colonial Surgeon at Avisawella, and served in various other medical appointments in the island. In 1889 he went to Edinburgh, where he obtained the degrees of L.R.C.P. and L.R.C.S., as well as L.F.P.S. of Glasgow. He worked for some time at the Royal Infirmary, Edinburgh, and Middlesex Hospital in London, and returned to Ceylon in 1890, when he was appointed District Medical Officer of Moratuwa and afterwards Assistant Colonial Surgeon at Gampola. In 1900 he accompanied the Ceylon contingent to the South African War as Medical Officer. On his return to Ceylon he was appointed Assistant Colonial Surgeon of Negombo, in medical charge of the judicial district as well as of the civil hospital and jail. He is a member of the British Medical Association, and an official member of the Negombo Local Board. In 1882 he married Ruth, daughter of the former Crown Counsel, Louis Nell, of Ceylon, and now of Switzerland; and their eldest daughter, Lucilla Gertrude, in 1903 married Arthur, son of Sir Cecil Clementi Smith, P.C., late Governor of the Straits Settlements.

DR. AND MRS. W. E. LEEMBRUGGEN AND FAMILY.

JOHN EDWARD DE ZOYSA.

Mr. J. E. de Zoysa was born in Colombo on July 26, 1878, and is the son of the late Edward de Zoysa, Mohandiram and Superintendent of Colombo Cinnamon Gardens, and Superinten

MR. AND MRS. J. E. DE ZOYSA AND FAMILY.

"GRACE LYNN."

THE WALAUWA.

THE CARRIAGE.

THE MILLS.

MR. AND MRS. JAMES PERERA AND FAMILY.

THE RESIDENCE.

C. J. EDERISINGHE.

dent of minor roads in the Cinnamon Gardens, and Sophie, daughter of William Mendis Karuneratne, brother-in-law of the late Sampson Rajapakse, Mudaliyar of the Governor's Gate, of Welitara. The family have held this rank and office for three generations, Mr. de Zoysa's father, grandfather, and great-grandfather having all possessed the distinction. Mr. de Zoysa was educated at the Royal College, and after passing his junior and senior Cambridge Local Examinations he read law, and was made a Proctor of the District Court of Negombo in 1902. He is now in practice at Negombo. He is a member of the Ceylon Law Society and of the Agricultural Society, and is treasurer of the Negombo Union Club. He married, in 1903, Lucy Grace, daughter of J. de S. Rajapakse, Mudaliyar and J.P., of Negombo. He has his residence at "Grace Lynn," Negombo.

CECIL JERONIMUS EDERISINGHE.

Mr. C. J. Ederisinghe is a son of Mr. B. J. Ederisinghe, who was formerly Coroner of Alutkuru Korale, and Rupina, daughter of P. Perera Amoratunga, of Kandane. He was born in the year 1877, and was educated at St. Benedict's Institute. He studied law, and in 1898 became a Proctor of the District Court, and is now in practice at Negombo. His residence is "Casa Nova," Negombo. He owns a coconut estate in the vicinity. He is a member of the Ceylon Law Society.

JAMES PERERA AMARATUNGE ABEYERATNE SIRIWARDENE.

Mr. James Perera Amaratunge Abeyeratne Siriwardene, Mohandiram of Kandana Alutkuru Korale South, generally known as James Perera Appuhamy, is the son of Isaac Perera Appuhamy. He was born at Kandana in 1876, and educated at Colombo, after which he commenced coconut-planting, and has followed that pursuit ever since. His principal estates are Miriswelwatte at Madampe, Udullewelawatte at Chilaw, Labbole and Bopitiya in the North-Western Province. All these are fully planted and equipped, and Mr. Perera owns also close upon two hundred smaller plantations in other parts of the Western Province. At Weligampitiya he has a fine cinnamon plantation, called Kapuwatte, fully equipped for the working of cinnamon, as well as large areas of paddy-land and house property at Ambalandegge. He is a partner in the arrack-

JAMES PERERA, MOHANDIRAM.

renting business of his brother-in-law, D. Don Joseph, and on his Kandana estate there are mills for the manufacture of fibre of every description. In 1904 Sir Henry Blake appointed him Mohandiram in recognition of his many public charities. He gave the school at Mattumagalle, and is a generous supporter of the Church. In 1901 he married Dona Victoria Beatrice, daughter of the arrack-renter Hendrick Appohamy, of Bopitiya, and he resides at Amaratunge Walauwa, Kandana.

M. P. GOMEZ & CO.

This is a firm carrying on business at various centres, the head branch being at Ratnapura. It was founded in 1889 by M. P. Gomez and Caitan Silva, natives of Tuticorin, in India, who came to Ceylon and started business on a small scale as wine and spirit merchants and proprietors of oilmen's stores and a bakery. Later, branches were opened at Balangoda, Avisawella, and Negombo. The business gradually increased, and now the firm maintains a well-equipped, attractive restaurant and oilmen's stores, and deal in glass-ware, crockery, electro-plate, patent medicines, drapery and outfitting, millinery and haberdashery, besides maintaining an aerated water manufactory and boot emporium. They are about to add a bakery at Negombo and another branch at Pelmadulla. Fancy goods and oilmen's stores, &c., are imported direct from England. The businesses at the present time at Negombo and Ratnapura are the largest mercantile concerns of the island in their respective districts. The firm has a general store at Colombo where goods are kept and despatched to its different branches. The partners are M. P. Gomez, senior, Caitan Silva, junior; M. G. Gomez, Gabriel Gomez, P. G. Gomez. They own house property at Negombo, Chilaw, Ratnapura, &c.

T. PERERA, Mohandiram.

Mr. Thomas Perera Wijeyeratne, known as Mr. Thomas Perera, Mohandiram, is a native of Veyangoda, and was born there in 1871. He received his education at Wesley College, after which he devoted himself to planting pursuits. He resides at Pattalagere estate, near Veyangoda, and has various smaller properties of which the produce in the shape of coconuts is sold locally. In 1903 Sir West Ridgeway appointed him Mohandiram. He is a staunch friend of Buddhist education, and has founded two Buddhist schools of which he is the manager and the principal supporter. He also built a school and presented it to the Government. He married the daughter of Mr. D. T. Jayewardene, Chief Vidane Arachchi of Galgamuwa. He is a member of the Committee of the Theosophical Society, and of the Buddhist Defence Committee, and has contributed articles on various topics to the *Sanderesa*.

D. L. WIJEWARDENE.

The Mirigama district is one of the centres of the coconut industry, but the desiccating and fibre mills there have not been always a great success. To Mr. Louis Wijewardene, a young and energetic planter, has fallen the task of reviving this backward industry there. He comes of a family already famous for making rapid progress in the business world, for he is the son of Don Philip, Mohandiram, the "timber king" and millionaire of Seddewatte, and the brother of Mr. Alexander Wije-

M. P. GOMEZ & CO., NEGOMBO, STAFF AND STORES.
M. P. GOMEZ.

THE MILLS (INTERIOR).
THE ENGINE-ROOM.

D. L. WIJEWARDENE.
THE MILLS.

wardene, who manages his father's timber business. From a very early age Mr. Louis Wijewardene showed an aptitude for engineering and mechanics. While still at school he was a proficient photographer, and as soon as opportunity presented itself he devoted himself to practical electrical work, with the result that he has his own generating station at his home at Seddewatte, from which the house and grounds are extensively illuminated. His taste for machinery led him to establish mills at Mirigama, which have already received a large share of patronage. At the time of writing 80 cwt. of coir fibre is the normal weekly output, and this will probably be considerably increased as time goes on. In a short period the mills, which are used only for the fibre trade, will be utilised for desiccating purposes also. Every modern appliance, including electric light and all the latest machinery, is in operation there.

Born in 1885, Mr. D. L. Wijewardene was educated at St. Thomas's College, and started in business about a year ago. It is interesting to note that Mr. Wijewardene is a proficient artist in etching and silvering on glass, and has frequently exhibited specimens of his work at the annual shows of the Ceylon Art Exhibition, carrying away prizes of Rs. 50 each on two occasions. One particular piece of his handiwork, comprising the emblem of the country and group of Ceylon-grown fruits, silvered on glass, was highly commended.

W. S. W. SOYSA.

Mr. Warusahenedigay Samuel William Soysa is the son of Warusahenedigay Andris, of Panadure, and Kariyakarawana Patabendi Maha Widanelagay Dona Augustina Ferdinando, daughter of Kariyakarawana Patabendi Maha Widanelagay Isaac Ferdinando, of Moratuwa. He was born at Colombo, in 1872, and educated at Prince of Wales's and St. Thomas's Colleges. For some time he was manager of Diyatalawa Mills, Slave Island, for Lady de Soysa, where he superintended the copra-manufacturing and cocoanut oil departments. In 1899 he joined Mr. T. H. A. de Soysa as partner in his business, but left him in 1903 to devote himself to planting. Amongst his estates, Catherine Valley in the Weligama district, and Maeliya and Ja-ela estates in the Ja-ela district are the most important. The latter is a specially fine estate, and the produce from it is of exceptional quality. Copra and cinnamon from his properties are sold at local markets. Mr. Soysa is a member of the Agricultural and Horticultural Societies and of the Turf Club; he is also a member of the Church of England Diocesan Temperance Committee and Religious Inspection Board. He built and equipped the Maeliya Anglo-Vernacular Mixed School. In 1900 he married

W. S. W. SOYSA.

Kate, daughter of Mr. John William Samarawera, of Weligama and Dodanduwa, and they have two sons and two daughters. Their country residence is at Ja-ela, and their town house Montague House, Bambalapitiya.

N. E. DE CROOS.

Nicholas Emanuel de Croos is the only son of the late John de Croos, landed proprietor and merchant, of Negombo. The family originally came over from Tuticorin, in India, and settled at Colombo and Galle during the time of the Dutch occupation. The late Mr. John de Croos, who was one of the largest merchants, landed proprietors, and arrack-renters of Ceylon, was well known in all business circles, a pillar of the Catholic Club and Catholic Union, and universally respected for his innumerable charities, contributions to schools, and assistance to the needful generally. He died in June, 1906. His son, Nicholas Emanuel, was born at Negombo in 1880, and educated at St. Mary's High School and St. Thomas's and St. Joseph's Colleges. He commenced business operations as arrack-renter of Ratnapura, and to-day owns the rents for Chilaw as well as a share of the Colombo rents. He has huge arrack stores at Kalutara and at Chilaw, and draws his supplies from the former place. His main possessions are coconut estates, and he is one of the largest landowners in the Western Province. His principal properties are St. John's Yaya, 1,300 acres in extent, in the Western Province; Kandangamuwa and Dewilapitiya in Mirigama; Noel's Meed at Katukenda; and Kahateville in the Chilaw district. Close to his town residence at Negombo are the Nicsford group and Thornwood estates, and on the latter he has one of the finest country residences ever erected in the island. His plantations in cinnamon and coconuts are ninety-two

N. E. DE CROOS.

in number, besides which he owns a large amount of house property at Colombo and Negombo. Mr. de Croos's grandfather in former years used to export the world-famed brand of "Ekella" cinnamon, but the produce of the estates at the present time is sold locally. As many as 600 men and women are employed daily in Mr. de Croos's operations. Since 1905 he has been an elected member of the Negombo Local Board, and he is a member of the Catholic Club and of the Catholic Union, and President of the Negombo Town Cricket Club. He used to play tennis and football, and has lately become a keen horseman. In 1904 he married Mary Agnes, daughter of Anthony de Croos, of Negombo, and has one daughter, Barbara Noeline. His town residence, "Barbeton," is one of the finest residences in the Western Province.

THE LATE JOHN DE CROOS. MRS. JOHN DE CROOS.
MR. AND MRS. N. E. DE CROOS AND CHILD.

THE DRAWING-ROOM, "BARBETON."

"BARBETON."
COCONUT-PALM AT NOEL'S MEED.

KELANI VALLEY, &c.

J. P. ANDERSON.

Mr. James Patrick Anderson, planter, in charge of Glassel estate, Dehiowita, and visiting agent in the Kelani Valley and surrounding districts, is the son of Mr. James Anderson. Born on October 26, 1865, near Newcastle, he was educated at St. Andrews and Edinburgh Academy, and he went out to Ceylon when he was twenty-one years of age. He bought a share in the Glassel estate, a property of 870 acres, which was afterwards sold to the Panawal Tea Company. Situated at an elevation of only 200 ft., the average annual crop is 310,000 lbs. of tea, and the coolies employed on the estate number 800. He is the Chairman of the Kelani Valley Planters' Association, and a member of a number of the clubs of the island. In addition to his interest in the Glassel estate, on which rubber has been planted during the last few years, he owns half-shares in the Maldeniya and Aludiniya estates, and is financially interested in others. He is fond of golf, shooting, and fishing.

S. E. O. RANSOM.

Mr. Spencer Edward Oliver Ransom, Superintendent of the Atherfield estate, is the son of the late Mr. O. Ransom, formerly of Bury St. Edmunds, Suffolk, but latterly a Ceylon planter. He was born on August 13, 1882, at Deltota, in the island, and received his education at St. Edward's School, Nuwara Eliya, and at Richmond, Surrey. He learnt planting under Mr. E. M. le Feuvre, Midlands estate, Rattota, and afterwards was on the Delta estate, Pussellawa, before taking up his present position. The Atherfield estate embraces 540 acres, of which 300 are planted with tea, half that area with rubber, and the balance is jungle. Three hundred and fifty coolies are employed upon it, and the annual crop of tea is estimated at 140,000 lbs. The estate is owned by the Atherfield Tea and Rubber Co., Ltd., of which Messrs. Bosanquet & Co. are the Colombo agents. Mr. Ransom's recreations are golf, cricket, and shooting.

DOUGLAS GEORGE LUMSDEN.

The son of Mr. J. J. F. Lumsden, senior Member of the Legislative Council of the North-West Provinces, India, Mr. Lumsden was born on September 28, 1874, at Gorakpore, North-West Provinces. He was educated privately, and came out to Ceylon in 1898, and learned tea-planting under Mr. John Fraser, of the Abbotsford estate, Nanu Oya, with whom he remained for seven years. Afterwards he was for sixteen months with Mr. G. D. Brabazon, on the New Peacock estate, and he then took charge of the Dehiowita estate, as superintendent. This estate, which is owned by Messrs. J. F. and R. V. Millington and R. Asplane, has an acreage of 348, of which 260 acres are planted with tea and 52 acres with rubber. The labour force consists of 280 coolies. Mr. Lumsden's recreations are football, tennis, and shooting. He was one of the detachment sent to London by the Ceylon Planters' Volunteer Corps on the occasion of the King's Coronation.

ANDREW DUFF JAMIESON.

This son of bonnie Scotland has had a varied career. The son of Mr. Thomas Jamieson, of the Caledonia Railway, he was born in December, 1872, at Laurencekirk, Kincardineshire. He received his education at the public school in his native place. He next served for some time on board the Royal Mail Steamer *Magellan;* and upon his return to Scotland he again entered the service of the Caledonian Railway Company, and remained with that company for three years. At the expiration of that period, in 1901, he accepted a position under the Ceylon Government Railway. He first commenced work on the Coast line, was two years on the Northern line, and at the present time he holds a responsible position on the Kelani Valley line.

EDMUND INGOLDSBY MASSY.

Mr. E. I. Massy was born on April 26, 1875, at Tipperary, Ireland, and educated at Trinity College, Stratford-on-Avon, Warwickshire. For three years after his school career he learned land agency work in Dublin, and came out to Ceylon in 1897. He went as a creeper on the Chapelton estate, Bogawantalawa, and after staying there for six months went as *sinne dorai* (assistant) on St. Leonards estate, Udapusselawa. Having joined the first Ceylon contingent who went to South Africa, he was away from the island for eighteen months, and received a medal with three bars for Dreifontein, Johannesburg, and Cape Colony. On his return from the war he went to England and returned to Ceylon after six months to take charge of Wellington estate temporarily. Mr. Massy again went to England with the Coronation contingent, and, returning to the island, was appointed assistant of Haldummulla estate. He held this position for thirty months, after which he went to Sunny Croft estate, Kelani Valley, for nine months, and finally obtained his present position as superintendent of the Pambagama estate. This estate of 1,440 acres—of which 607 are planted with tea and 193 with rubber, and 400 acres of which it is intended to plant with rubber—yields an annual crop of 370,000 lbs. of tea, and employs about 1,000 coolies. It is 800 ft. above sea-level and belongs to the Sunnygama Tea Estates Company, Ltd. The local agent is Mr. W. Forsyth. The subject of this sketch is the son of the late Colonel George Eyre Massy, of Limerick, Ireland. He is a member of the Kelani Valley Planters' Association and Club and the Ruanwella Club, and a corporal of the Ceylon Mounted Rifles. His recreations are cricket, tennis, and golf.

A. H. ROE.

Mr. Alfred Henry Roe is the superintendent of the Dewalakande estate, Dehiowita, Kelani

A. H. ROE.

Valley. He is the son of the late Mr. Peter Roe, of Queen's County, Ireland, and was born in Ireland on January 31, 1858. He was educated at the Abbey, Tipperary, and at Watts's College, Portarlington, and in 1877 arrived in Ceylon and joined the Kalaboda group of estates, Kotmale, as a creeper (pupil), and successfully served on estates in the Elkadua and Dimbula districts. He has been during the past twelve years in the employ of the Ceylon Tea Plantations Company, Ltd., low-country estates. Dewalakande estate is about 900 acres in extent, consisting of 552 acres of tea and rubber, and 348 acres of rubber only, and has a labour force of 800 coolies. Mr. Roe is a keen sportsman, plays golf, tennis, and cricket, and is fond of shooting. Formerly he was a member of the Ceylon Planters' Corps.

G. H. HALL.

Mr. George Herbert Hall was born at Lancaster on February 16, 1877, and received his education at King's School, Warwick. Intending to enter the medical profession, he studied medicine and chemistry for a few years, but relinquished the idea and came out to Ceylon to learn tea-planting in February, 1898, as a creeper, under Mr. J. I. Hall, his brother, of Ernan estate, Kelani Valley. He remained there nearly a year and then spent a few months on Yogama estate, and subsequently was upon Polatagama and Weoya estates. He is now the superintendent of Erracht estate, Dehiowita, Kelani Valley, which comprises 744 acres, of which 501 have been opened up and planted with tea and rubber, gives employment to about 600 coolies, and belongs to the Clunes Estate Company of Ceylon, Ltd. He is also a member of the Ceylon Planters' Rifle Corps.

E. KYNASTON.

Mr. Edward Kynaston is the son of Mr. E. Kynaston, of London, and was born on March 5, 1860, at Sydenham, Kent. He received his education at Tonbridge School, and went out to Ceylon in the year 1879. He first worked on one of Messrs. Carey, Strachan & Co.'s estates, and took up planting as a profession, and has been engaged on various estates all over the island. He is now the superintendent of the Lavant estate, Yatiyantota, Kelani Valley, and has also charge of Taldua tea estate. The area of the former is 1,100 acres, fully planted with tea and rubber. About 700 coolies are engaged in producing the annual output of 260,000 lbs. of tea, and Messrs. Gordon Fraser are the Colombo agents. Mr. Kynaston is a member of the Kandy Club, Ceylon Turf Club, the Kelani Valley Planters' Association, and the Kelani Valley Club, and is a part shareholder in the Sitawika Rubber Estate, Kelani Valley.

HARRY DE MEL.

This gentleman, who is a Proctor practising at Avisawella, was born on February 5, 1869, at Moratuwa, and educated at the Royal College. Adopting law as a profession, he was articled to Mr. Walter Pereira, K.C., and called to the Bar in June, 1897. He practised in Colombo for a short time, but in 1898 migrated to Avisawella, and has remained there ever since. He is married to Laura, daughter of Mr. D. J. R. Goonesekera, and has three children — two sons and one daughter.

PRIDEAUX BYRDE.

The superintendent of the Avisawella estate, Avisawella, in the Western Province, Mr. Byrde is the son of Mr. F. W. Byrde, a veteran planter. Born on February 3, 1879, at Dimbula, Ceylon, he was educated at Monkton Combe College, Bath, England. At the close of his school career he came to Ceylon to learn planting under his father, and has been on the estate of which he now has charge for the last ten years. The acreage of the estate, whose elevation is from 200 to 700 ft., is 600 in all, of which 425 is planted with tea, 75 witb rubber, while the remaining portion of land is in a jungle state. The coolies employed amount to 300 in number.

W. A. ELWELL.

Mr. William Arthur Elwell, superintendent of the Sapumalkande estate, Dehiowita, is the son of Mr. R. R. Elwell, an English solicitor. He was born on March 21, 1880, at Lighworth, Wiltshire, and received his education at the Sir William Borlase School, Marlow. He went to Ceylon in October, 1897, and became a creeper under Mr. J. M. Patterson at Allagolla, Udapussellawa. After remaining there a year he became assistant superintendent at Allakolla estate, Madulkelle, and has since been upon the Elston estate, Puwakapitiya, the Allakolla estate, and the Kabragalla estate, Maturata, before taking up his present appointment. The Sapumalkande estate is one of the finest properties in the Kelani Valley, and is owned by Messrs. W. J. Smith and S. L. Harries. It is 1,200 acres in extent, of which 500 acres are fully planted with tea and interplanted with rubber, and 700 acres are fully planted with rubber; 700 coolies are employed upon the estate, and the annual crop of tea is 231,500 lbs.

FRANK HENRY LAYARD.

Mr. Frank Henry Layard, superintendent of the Ganapalla estate, Yatiyantota, was born on April 18, 1872, at Colombo, and educated at Elizabeth College, Guernsey, and St. Anne's, Redhill. He studied law for a time, but ultimately abandoned the idea of embarking upon a legal career, and came out to Ceylon in November, 1888. He learned planting under Mr. E. P. Willisford, Hangran Oya, Nawalapitiya, for one year, and then spent three years on the Mahaousa estate, Madulkelle. Afterwards he had charge of a division of the Blackwater estate, Galboda, and of Penrith estate, Avisawella. Finally he was entrusted with his present charge. The estate has an acreage of 1,084. Of this area 620 acres are planted with tea and 300 acres with rubber; the remainder is uncleared land. Some of the rubber-trees are over three years old. The estimate of the crop of tea on the estate this year is 340,000 lbs. Eight hundred and seventy coolies are employed on the estate. Mr. Layard, it may be added, is the son of the late Mr. Henry William Layard, one of the pioneers of coffee-planting in Ceylon. He is married and has two sons, both of whom are being educated at his old school—Elizabeth College, Guernsey. Mr. Layard is a Justice of the Peace and Unofficial Police Magistrate for the Kegalla district. He is a member of the Kelani Valley Club, of the Colombo Club, and of the Ceylon Turf Club. His recreations are riding, tennis, cricket, golf, and shooting. He is also an ardent Volunteer, having served for fourteen years in the Ceylon Mounted Infantry, and since then in the Ceylon Planters' Rifle Corps.

ALBERT JAMES MARTIN.

This gentleman hails from Australia. Born at Coburg, Victoria, on July 24, 1869, he was educated at the Church of England Grammar School at Melbourne. Leaving school, he joined an insurance company for six years, after which he served in a sawmill for two years in the Australian bush. Mr. Martin then left his country, arriving in Ceylon in August, 1894, to enter the Farnham estate, Kelani Valley, as a creeper, and stayed there for a few months. Afterwards he went to Laxpanagalla, and later still to Benachie estate. He stayed at the latter estate for a year, and then went to the Veralupitiya estate, where he worked for two years. In 1898 Mr. Martin was made the superintendent of the Penrith and Logan estates in Pumakpitiya, Kelani Valley, where he has been ever since. The estates consist of 722 acres planted with tea and 55 acres with rubber, and the elevation is 150 ft. above sea-level. The number of coolies employed is 750. The proprietors of the Penrith and Logan estate are the General Ceylon Rubber and Tea Estates, Ltd., whose general manager in Ceylon is Mr. W. Forsythe.

The subject of this sketch is the son of the late Mr. John Martin, insurance manager, of Melbourne. His recreations are golf, tennis and cricket.

J. A. ANDERSON.

Mr. James Alexander Anderson, superintendent of the Yogama estate, Dehiowita, is the son of Mr. James Anderson, a well-known Ceylon planter, and was born on November 5, 1879, at Maskeliya. He was educated at Gordon College and Marischal College, Aberdeen, and came out to Ceylon in 1898, and was assistant on the Bandarapola estate, Matale, and was afterwards on the Atherton estate, Kotmalie, and the Rondura group, Wattawella, before going to the Yogama Estate. The last named property embraces 1,380 acres, of which about 450 are fully planted with tea and 800 with rubber, and the remainder has been cleared for tea-planting. The annual tea crop is 230,000 lbs., and in gathering this and attending to the rubber a thousand coolies are employed. The estate belongs to the Panawatte Tea and Rubber Estates Company, Ltd., and Messrs. Whittall & Co. are the Colombo agents. Mr. Anderson is a member of the Kelani Valley and Kandy Planters' Associations, and of the Kelani Valley Club and the C.M.R., and his recreation is tennis.

A. L. BAINES.

Mr. Alexander Lachlan Baines, the superintendent of the Densworth estate, Dehiowita, is the son of Mr. Henry Baines, solicitor, of Oxford, and Alice, daughter of Mr. John Browning. He was born at Oxford on October 14, 1877, and received his education at King Henry VIII. School, Warwick. He came out to Ceylon in 1896 as a creeper under Mr. John Tilley, Galkandewatte Estate, Talawakelle, and remained there about twelve months. Subsequently he was four years S.D. on the Le Vallon group, Nilambe. During the late war in South Africa he served for eighteen months with the first Ceylon contingent, and received a medal with bars for Dreifontein, Cape Colony, Johannesburg, and Diamond Hill. He then returned to Le Vallon estate, and was afterwards on the Peacock Hill estate for three years before taking up his present appointment. The Densworth estate is 547 acres in extent, 346 acres being planted with tea and interplanted with rubber, and the annual estimate is (at present) 160,000 lbs. of tea and 2,000 lbs. of rubber, in obtaining which over 400 coolies are engaged. The estate is the property of Messrs. Cooper, Cooper & Johnson, for whom Messrs. Gordon Fraser are the Colombo agents. Mr. Baines is a keen sportsman, and is a member of the Gampola Club, the Taldua Club, and the Kandy Sports Club. He is captain of the Taldua Cricket Club, and has played in Association and Rugby football for Kandy and Gampola Clubs.

ARCHIBALD COCHRANE.

Mr. Archibald Cochrane owns and has charge of the Kitulgala estate, Kelani Valley, and is also the superintendent of the Gonagamma estate. He was born on February 21, 1876, at Galashiels, Scotland, and educated at the Edinburgh Academy and in France. He came out to Ceylon in 1897, and joined the Fordyce group of estates as assistant under Mr. J. G. Palmer. After a training extending over two years, he took charge of the Fruithill estate for seven years, and then assumed control of the estate with which he is at present associated. The estate embraces 265 acres fully planted with tea, 40 acres planted with rubber, and 20 acres which are in course of being opened up. The annual crop of tea is 100,000 lbs., and 200 coolies are employed. The Gunagama estate is 300 acres in extent—200 acres being planted with rubber, and the remainder is being opened up. His recreations are tennis and shooting.

RAWLEIGH MANSEL DAWKIN.

Born in April, 1851, at Cardiff, Mr. R. M. Dawkin, manager of the Eila Tea Company, Yatiyantota, was educated at the local Grammar School and at Bath. He joined his brother-in-law in his business as ship broker and coal merchant and came out to Ceylon in 1877, travelling round the Cape by the *Negrizolla* sailing ship, an Italian vessel. His intention was to embark upon a commercial career, but a visit to the planting districts suggested to him that life on an estate would be pleasanter than desk work in Colombo. The opportunity offering, he took charge of Uplands estate, in the Kandy district. Subsequently he was associated with estates in the Deltota district, Dimbula and Dolosbage. In 1885 he migrated to the Kelani Valley, and has been in the district ever since. The Eila estate, of which he now has charge, has an acreage of 716, fully planted with tea and interplanted with rubber, 25 acres fully planted with rubber, and two other clearings, about 83 acres in extent, in course of preparation for rubber planting in the coming season. The crop of tea this year is estimated at 250,000 lbs. Seven hundred Tamil coolies are employed upon the estate. Mr. Dawkin also has charge of the Kanangama estate, Dehiowita. He is a member of the Kelani Valley Club. His recreations are golf, tennis, and cricket.

WILLIAM AUGUSTUS WEEREKOON.

Mr. W. A. Weerekoon, son of John Weerekoon, Mudaliyar, of Kurunegala, was born 1878, and educated at St. Thomas's College, where he was successful in the local Cambridge senior examination. He also secured the Victoria gold medal and mathematical prize (for the whole of Ceylon), and in 1899 passed the subordinate examination for the Civil Service. He first entered the Colonial Secretary's Office, afterwards being attached to the Batticaloa Kachcheri. In 1900 he became Acting Office Assistant to the Government Agent of the Southern Province at Galle. Subsequently he occupied similar positions at Ratnapura, Batticaloa, and in the offices of the Government Agent of the North-Western Province and Northern Province, and in 1904 was again transferred to Ratnapura. In

MR. AND MRS. W. A. WEEREKOON.

1906 he married Cecilia Augusta, daughter of D. S. Daundesekera, Mudaliyar, of Ratnapura, who is a grandson of the second Mudaliyar of the Guides to the British Army in 1815.

BOMBAY UNION CLUB.

From Bombay to Colombo is a somewhat far cry, but the inhabitants of the great capital of Western India are enterprising, and they go far afield in search of trade openings. So it happens that there is a pretty considerable community of Bombay merchants and traders in Colombo and they are able to form their own institutions of a social or religious character. One of the former class is the Bombay Union Club, which was organised in 1905 by some prominent members of the community for purposes of social intercourse and recreation, and for discussions on trade matters. The club, which is open to all races and creeds—Hindus, Mahomedans, Parsees, etc.—received in its initial stages generous support from leading Bombay merchants, including Messrs. Framjee Bhicajee & Co., Carimjee Jafferjee, E. C. Adamaly & Co., T. A. J. Noorbhoy & Co., J. Rustomjee, and others. The club-house is in Prince Street, Pettah, in the heart of the native business quarter. It is a commodious building, supplied with all the usual requisites for comfort and entertainment, and having, besides, an excellent library and reading-room, furnished with all the latest periodicals and papers. At the club social meetings are held periodically, and in addition to these gatherings excursions are organised to points of interest in the neighbourhood of Colombo. The club membership numbers thirty-five and additions are constantly being made to the roll. Mr. H. Dinshaw acts as the secretary of the club, and to him and a few other members, notably Messrs. J. C. Thakore and C. H. Bharucha, the credit for its successful organisation is due. It should be added that additional members are elected by the votes of the existing members.

H. DINSHAW.
(Secretary.)

D. DON PAUL.

Dekirikawege Don Paul, second son of D. Don Hendrick Appuhamy, brother of Don Joseph, was born at Bopitiya in 1882, and educated at St. Benedict's Institute and St. Joseph's College. He then joined his brother in business, taking charge of the arrack-renting department at Trincomalee and Jaffna, and is now a full partner in the concern. His own principal estates are Hendala in the Western Province and Diyabawa and Labukande in the North-Western Province, and he has smaller estates in the Western Province and near Mannar, as well as tracts of paddy-fields and house property elsewhere. He is a member

THE MEMBERS, BOMBAY UNION CLUB.

MITLAND COTTAGE. D. DON PAUL AND FAMILY.

of the Catholic Club, of the Sinhalese Sports Club, and of the Negombo Union Club. Whilst at college he was a noted football player, and he continues to be an enthusiastic cricketer and tennis player. He lives at Mitland Cottage, Bopitiya.

THEODORE PENNYCUICK ATTYGALLE.

This gentleman, who is a son of Dr. J. Attygalle, retired Colonial Surgeon, M.D. Aberdeen, enjoys the distinction of being the only Sinhalese who occupies a position in the higher ranks of the Ceylon Police Force, as a Superintendent of Police, Unofficial Police Magistrate, and a Justice of the Peace. Born on May 3, 1876, at Puttalam, and educated at Royal and St. Thomas's Colleges, where he passed his Cambridge Local Examination with honours, he joined the Ceylon Police Force as inspector on August 22, 1899. In 1903 he was promoted for meritorious service from the rank of an inspector of the third grade to the position of Assistant Superintendent in charge of the Criminal Investigation Department. Three years later he was again promoted, attaining to the rank of Superintendent, and being placed in charge of the Western Province Police Stations. When Their Royal Highnesses the Prince and Princess of Wales visited Ceylon he was placed in charge of the personal bodyguard of police which accompanied the royal visitors while they were in Ceylon. He has been frequently commended and rewarded for useful service rendered in the suppression of crime in Ceylon. Mr. Attygalle is a member of the well-known, influential and ancient family of the same name in the Salpiti Korale. He married, on December 13, 1906, Constance Valerie, daughter of J. Abeysekere, Mudaliyar of the Governor's Gate, and of Alutkuru Korale, South-Western Province. His recreations are tennis, billiards, and riding. As a member of Bonnie Doon Lodge (S.C.) he is one of the very few Sinhalese Masons in the island.

NORTH-WESTERN PROVINCE.

THIS province shares with its southern neighbour the advantages which proximity to the premier province and an extensive seaboard confer. In area it is only fifth on the list and in population fourth; but judged by the criterion of revenue collections, it occupies third place — and this despite the fact that a greater part of the area is without railway communication, while the roads, apart from the coast road, are not of the best. The prosperity of the province is due in the first place to its coconut industry, which is a great and growing one, and in the second place to its flourishing fisheries, which give lucrative employment to large numbers of the population. When the railway is extended, as it probably will be at no distant date, to Puttalam, in the north of the administrative area, a great impetus will be given to trade, and the province will play an increasingly important part in the commercial development of the island. Already, in spite of the disadvantages referred to, marked progress is being made. In 1905 the revenue collections were Rs. 1,760,704·48, or Rs. 141,384·33 in excess of those of the previous year. This figure constitutes a record, and the fact that the position was reached is the more remarkable as the year was one of serious drought. In his Administration Report for 1905 Mr. S. M. Burrows, the Government Agent, asserts that the coconut enterprise is the source of this prosperity. "The rush into coconuts throughout the year," he says, "has been astonishing, and not confined to capitalists and outsiders. The villager is beginning to appreciate the value of his high lands, and is slipping into coconuts after his own fashion." The outward evidences of the improvement in the condition of the people are very marked.

THE CHILAW LOCAL BOARD.

R. N. THAINE.
(A.G.A., Puttalam.)

"Nearly all the large bazaars are growing; and in many cases more pretentious and capacious boutiques are taking the place of humbler

A CHILAW VIEW.

ones. This is obviously an important criterion of prosperity, and it is occurring in spite of a long drought, which shows that the purchasing villager is not so dependent on his grain as he was, and finds paying employment on coconut gardens and estates." Side by side with "the rush into coconuts," there has been, Mr. Burrows notes, a rush into rubber. "It is early yet to say what the position of rubber is to be in this province. If a rainfall of 80 ins. is required, it is obvious from the excellent rainfall chart published by the Surveyor-General that only a small portion of the province falls within the required zone, for the 80-in. limit passes diagonally across the province from south-west to north-east, and Kurunegala is barely within it; but that it will do splendidly in the south-east and south sections of the Kurunegala district seems to be proved by the success of Delwita and Muwankande estates, and a great deal of land in that direction is being placed under rubber as rapidly as labour and drought will allow; but the latter part of 1905 was disastrous to rubber plantation, and some plantations have had to be planted three and four times over."

The chief centres in the province are Kurunegala, on the eastern confines of the area, Puttalam in the north, and Chilaw in the south. Each constitutes the headquarters of a revenue district. Kurunegala, the largest of the three towns, had a population, in 1901, of 6,483. Its affairs are directed by a Local Board. Recently some important works and improvements have been carried out in the town—in July, 1905, a new market for meat, vegetables, and fish, costing Rs. 11,165·07, excluding the value of the land. Adjoining the markets a new park has been commenced and fully planted up with a variety of palms and selected ornamental trees under the capable superintendence of Mr. J. K. Nock, of Hakgala Gardens. A scheme of town drainage has also been carried out. A feature of the lake at Kurunegala is a growth of "weed" (of flat formation, in great islands 7 ft. to 9 ft. thick). This is obnoxious in many ways, and its removal by mechanical means is being effected. Puttalam, the second of the three districts, covers an extensive area, and its interests are largely maritime. In the great expanse of the Puttalam lake—so-called although it is in reality a vast lagoon—fisheries are prosecuted by a hardy and intelligent race of fishermen, who are, to a large extent, adherents of the Roman Catholic Church, which, planted here in the days of the Portuguese occupation, has gained a strong hold on the inhabitants. On the low-lying marshy lands which fringe the coast hereabouts there are extensive lewayas in which vast quantities of salt are annually produced by means of evaporation. The salt in its turn is used for the curing of fish, and thus strengthens what may be regarded almost as the staple industry of the district. But here, as elsewhere, homage is paid to King Coconut to an increasing extent and annually great tracts of land are being taken up for this most productive of tropical fruits. "The demand for land suitable for coconut-planting," says Mr. F. Bowes, the Assistant Government Agent, in his report on the district for 1905, "can be estimated by the fact that the average price of the 1,207 acres sold during 1905 was Rs. 33·5-8 per acre, while the highest price realised was over Rs. 202 per acre. It is only twenty years since persons planting coconuts on the mainland were regarded as pioneers, and encouraged by a generous system of leases." The salt collection to which reference has been made is

LOCAL BOARD, PUTTALAM.

the main source of the revenue of the district. In 1905, of a total sum of Rs. 962,090·80 collected, no less than Rs. 801,920·61 was m

THE ROMAN CATHOLIC CHURCH AT MARAWILA, CHILAW.

TOWN HALL, KURUNEGALA.

THE RESIDENCY, KURUNEGALA.

TANK SCENE, KURUNEGALA.

respect of salt. The total collection for the year was 313,114 cwts., but large as that amount is, there is no doubt that it falls very far short of the quantity that might be secured if a more scientific system of collection and improved conditions of storage were introduced. The third district, Chilaw, differs little in its general features from its northern neighbour. The town of Chilaw is a centre of considerable historical interest. It was an important place in ancient times—the seat of a petty kingdom. From the period of the Portuguese occupation onward it has figured conspicuously in Ceylon annals. But these are faded glories, and Chilaw now bases its title to fame upon the fact that, like its southern neighbour, Negombo, it is an important fishing centre, and contributes no small share of the fish supply of the capital.

The North-Western Province has an evil reputation for unhealthiness. Malarial fever, to adopt the words of Mr. S. M. Burrows, the Government Agent,[1] is "the curse of the countryside." Periodically epidemics sweep through the villages, causing heavy mortality, and paralysing the activities of the community. The Government have done much by the establishment of dispensaries and the gratuitous distribution of quinine to lessen the evil, and other influences appear to be producing improved conditions. "I believe," says Mr. Burrows, "that our system of elementary education, conducted on increasingly sensible lines, is having, and will have still more in the future, a marked effect on the health of the people. It gives the boys a good walk twice a day; it teaches them manly exercise in the shape of drill and games, while it may be hoped that gardening will gradually be added to the curriculum; and they are taught the rudiments of hygiene and sanitation. These latter subjects will doubtless be taught better as better trained masters come forward, and I should like to see a special effort made to inculcate the evils of drinking. As it is, you can nearly always, in a crowd of village boys, pick out those who go to school from those who do not by their physique and bearing." Still, the situation cannot be regarded as satisfactory when we find that there were 153 births and 182 deaths in Chilaw in 1905, and that the Assistant Government Agent could yet say that "the health of the town has been good throughout the year, except for fever."

[1] Administration Report, North-Western Province, for 1905, p. F. 2.

KURUNEGALA DISTRICT.

S. N. B. M. T. B. LEWIS MOONEMALLE.

Semasinghe Navaratne Basnayeke Mudianselage Theodore Barcroft Lewis Moonemalle is a descendant of Basnayeke Mudianse, who was Rate Lekam (which means Chief Collector of Revenue) at Moonemalle, in the Kandyan provinces, and son of John Marcellus Lewis, a Proctor of the Supreme Court and landed proprietor. This gentleman married Mary Ann, a daughter of that well-known figure in Kandyan life, John Graham Jayetileke Hulugalle, who also was a Proctor of the Supreme Court and landed proprietor, Kurunegala, and whose wife, Dorothea Peternella, was a member of the Tennekoon family, who were Ratemahatmayas of Pannala, in the Kandyan provinces. Mr. Moonemalle was born in Kurunegala, educated locally by the Rev. H. C. Hancock and at Trinity College, Kandy, studied law under the well-known K.C., Mr. T. E. de Sampayo, and became a Proctor of the District Court, Kurunegala, in 1890, of the Supreme Court in 1897, whilst he has on several occasions acted as District Judge and Police Magistrate. When only thirty-eight years of age the Secretary of State appointed him a member

JOHN MARCELLUS LEWIS MOONEMALLE. MARY ANN MOONEMALLE.
JOHN GRAHAM JAYETILEKE HULUGALLE. DOROTHEA PETERNELLA HULUGALLE.

THE RESIDENCE. THE HON. MR. MOONEMALLE AND FAMILY.

of the Legislative Council to represent the Kandyan community, and he took his seat in July, 1906. He is President of the Kandyan Association in the North-Western Province, is on the Board of the Agricultural Society, and a member of the local branch, honorary treasurer of the Kurunegala Library, and Justice of the Peace and Inquirer in the Kurunegala district. He came into prominence in public life in connection with the agitation for the Waste Lands Ordinance in 1896, and headed a deputation to the Governor and procured some important land concessions for the Kandyan people of the North-Western Province. In 1898 he married Enid Jocelyn Catherine, daughter of Frederick Jayetileke, late District Judge of Kalutara. The Hon. Mr. Moonemalle's ancestral seat is the Walauwa at Moonemalle, and his town residence is Mitford House, Kurunegala.

GODFREY EDWARD MADAWELA.

Mr. Godfrey Edward Madawela is the son of Madawela, Basnaike Nilame, notary public and landed proprietor, of Madawela, in the North-Western Province, and Ranmenike, daughter of Chandarasekere Gooneratne Tenekoon Herat Mudianselage, Banda of Walgama. Born in 1878, he was educated at St. Thomas's College and Trinity College, Kandy, where he passed first in the arts examination of 1897. He then studied law under the Council of Legal Education, and was admitted a Proctor of the District Court of Kurunegala in 1901, and has practised as such in that town ever since. He owns coconut plantations and tracts of paddy-lands at Mahakeliya and Madawela, in the district in which he has his legal practice. He married, in 1903, Frances Alexandra Elsie, second daughter of Mr. C. E. Tenekoon, resides at Florinda House, Kurunegala, and has one son and two daughters. He is keenly interested in agriculture in the island, and is a member of the Agricultural Society.

MR. AND MRS. G. E. MADAWELA AND FAMILY.

E. G. GOONEWARDENE AND FAMILY.

"OLD PLACE."

R. E. DIAS BANDARANAYAKE.

Mr. Reginald Edward Dias Bandaranayake is the son of Dr. William Dias Bandaranayake, of Hencratgoda, and nephew of the late Maha Mudaliyar Conrad Pieter Dias Bandaranayake. He was born in Kandy in 1878, and received his scholastic education at St. Thomas's College, and afterwards took a course of study in surveying at the Technical College, becoming qualified as a surveyor in 1902. He then joined the Irrigation Department as a sub-inspector, but resigned that position two years later in order to commence practice as a surveyor at Kurunegala, and during the past three or four years his professional connection has developed considerably. He owns several coconut estates as well as tracts of land in the North-Western Province, and resides at Damhaliyadda, near Wariapola. He married Flora Ethel, eldest daughter of C. E. Tenekoon, R.M., in 1906.

MR. AND MRS. R. E. DIAS BANDARANAYAKE AND INFANT.

EDWARD GREGORY GOONEWARDENE.

Mr. E. G. Goonewardene is a son of Don Johannes Goonewardene, landed proprietor, of Galle, whose ancestors are said to have come from the Ratnapura district of the Sabaragamuwa Province, and who married Donna Johanna Wickkramanayake. He was born in Galle in October, 1858, and received his education at Galle Central School and at St. Thomas's College. After passing the Calcutta University Matriculation Examination in 1875, he was articled to Mr. F. W. de Vos, Proctor of Galle, for the study of law. In 1880 he was enrolled as a Proctor of the District Court of Galle, and in 1884 of the Honourable the Supreme Court of the Island of Ceylon and a Notary Public, whilst in the following year he transferred his practice to Kurunegala. Now he is one of the most respected inhabitants of the district, and has a very large practice there. He acted in 1905 as District Judge, Commissioner of Requests, and Police Magistrate of Kurunegala, and also as Additional District Judge of Kegalla. Mr. Goonewardene is the senior unofficial member of the Local Board, on which he has had a seat for the last twenty years, a member of the District Road Committee, a Committee member of the Kurunegala Planters' Association, and a member of the Agricultural Society and of the Ceylon National Association. On his estate, Bambaragodde, he has planted coconuts and rubber, and in addition to this property he owns others in different parts of the district. He married, in 1885, Mary Evangeline Ada, sister of the Hon. Mr. Moonamalle (daughter of the late Mr. J. M. L. Moonamalle, Proctor, and granddaughter of the late Graham Jayatilake, Proctor, who was at one time Hullugalle Ratemahatmaya). His eldest son, Mr. E. G. M. Goonewardene, is a student at St. Thomas's College and captain of the College Cricket Eleven. It is a notable fact that when Mr. Goonewardene married his was the first known marriage of a low-country Sinhalese with a daughter of the Kandyan nobility. It may also be mentioned that he is the only brother of Mr. D. G. Goonewardene, J.P., Unofficial Police Magistrate and Crown Proctor of Galle.

THE LATE DINGIRI KUMARIHAMY. (Mother of C. E. Tennekoon.) THE LATE MRS. S. JAYETILLEKE. THE LATE MRS. C. E. TENNEKOON.

CHAS. E. TENNEKOON AND FAMILY.

THE LATE S. JAYETILLEKE. (Mudaliyar of the Governor's Gate.)

WIJEYESUNDARA GUNARATNA TENNEKOON HERAT MUDIVANSELAGE CHARLES EDWARD TENNEKOON ENNARUWA.

Mr. Tennekoon was born at Ennaruwa in 1851, educated at St. Thomas's College, and entered the Government service in 1871, being attached to the Registrar's Office, Kurunegala. He became President of various Village Tribunals in the province, Ratemahatmaya of Wanni Hatpattu in 1876, and since 1879 has held the appointment of Ratemahatmaya of Dewamedi Hatpattu. He is Revenue Officer for his district, Inquirer into Crime, &c., a member of the Agricultural Society, and a well-known pillar of the Church of England in the district. In 1880 he married Elizabeth Florinda, daughter of the late Mr. S. Jayetilleke, Mudaliyar of the Governor's Gate and J.P. of the district of Kurunegala. His only son, Charles Wilmot, is now studying law, and of his three living daughters, the eldest, Flora Ethel, married Reginald Edward Dias Bandaranayeke of Heneratgoda, and the second, Frances Alexandra Elsie, married Godfrey Edward Madawela, Proctor of Kurunegala.

HENRY LEONARD COX.

Mr. H. L. Cox, who has charge of the North-Western Rubber Company's property, was born at Rugby, and is the fourth son of Arthur Russell Cox, of Old Bank, Rugby. He was educated at the public school, and commenced his business career with a West Indian merchant in Mincing Lane. He came to Ceylon in 1896, and spent six years learning the business of a planter under that veteran, Lieut.-Colonel Gordon Reeves, at Madulkelle. He then acquainted himself with the treatment of rubber on the estate Kepitigalle, of which he had temporary charge, and since 1904 has had charge of the property named above. At an early age he joined the 2nd Warwickshire Volunteer Regiment, and became a member of the Ceylon Planters'

Rifle Corps on its formation in 1900, being one of the second contingent which went to South Africa for active service. After the disbandment of the force he remained in South Africa, and on visiting England later was attached to the Gloucestershire Regiment. He returned to Ceylon and resumed his planting occupation, and is now a keen member of the Ceylon Mounted Rifles. He is very fond of hunting, although his duties do not permit of his following the sport. He is a committee member of the Kurunegala Planters' Association and a delegate to the parent association at Kandy.

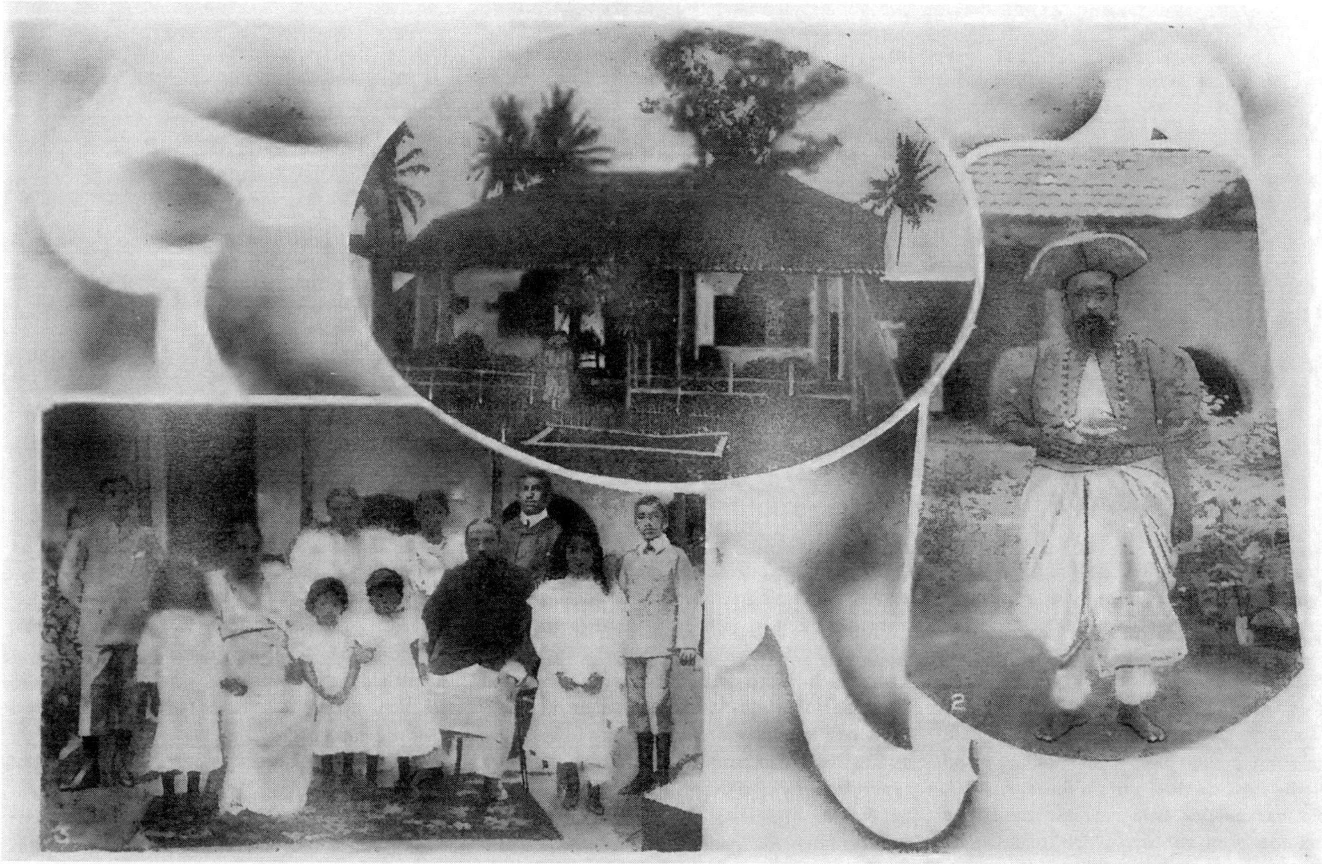

WEHARA WALAUWA. J. G. TENNEKOON.
MR. AND MRS. J. G. TENNEKOON AND FAMILY.

KANDEGEDIRA WIJESUNDERA GUNERATNA TENNEKOON HERAT MUDIYANSILAGE JOHN GRAHAM TENNEKOON.

This gentleman is the Ratemahatmaya, Inquirer, Registrar of Marriages, and Chairman of Village Communities, Hiriyala Hatpattu. He is the son of Tikiri Banda, Korala of Angomu Korale, and of Bogolle Dingiri Menika Kumarihami, and was born at Agaranda in 1863. He was educated at St. Thomas's College, Colombo, where he passed the Cambridge Junior Local and the Calcutta Matriculation Examinations, and at the completion of his education in 1887 he entered the Government service as extra clerk, Land Registry, Kurunegala. The following year he was appointed assistant Gansabhawa clerk at the Kurunegala Kachcheri, and passed the Government clerical examination in the same year. In 1889 he was appointed to the Kandy Kachcheri, and in 1894 became chief clerk, Kegalla Courts. Two years subsequently he was appointed second clerk, District Court, Kurunegala, and President of the Village Tribunals, Hiriyala Hatpattu in 1898, whilst in 1900 he was made Ratemahatmaya. In 1889 he married Ellen Georgiana, daughter of Joseph de Silva Jayasundera, Mudaliyar, and of Denagomuwa Walauwa Tikiri Kumarihami. He has nine children—three sons and six daughters. Mr. Tennekoon's residence is Wehera Walauwa, Kurunegala.

THE NORTH-WESTERN RUBBER COMPANY, LTD.

This company, founded early in 1905, took over the Pitiakande group of estates, comprising some 1,670 acres of land situated on the Kandy - Kurunegala road, in the district of Kurunegala, North-Western Province, at an elevation ranging from 300 to 1,500 ft. above sea-level. A considerable acreage was opened up in coconuts and cocoa, also tea, some ten to thirteen years ago, and the trees made very considerable growth, especially the coconuts, the soil being for the most part of that light and sandy nature which is suitable for these products. About 400 acres of tea were planted at the same time. This grew well from the commencement, and has paid for the upkeep of a large acreage planted with coconuts. The latter are now partly in bearing, and are giving a very fair annual crop of good nuts, which are turned into copra on the estate, the produce selling at top prices. Owing to the increased demand for oils for edible and other purposes in the home market, this product now forms a very valuable asset of the estate. In regard to cocoa the crop harvested during the past four or five years proves this to be a further source of income. In 1904 a small experimental clearing of thirteen acres was planted with Para rubber, and the trees have shown remarkable growth, the land being suitable for the tree.

PITIAKANDE ESTATE.

PITIAKANDE TEA FACTORY. THE ESTATE BUNGALOW.

At two and a half years of age the majority of the trees measured from 12 to 15 ins. in circumference 3 ft. from the ground. As soon as the new company took over the estates the felling and clearing of heavy forest reserve was put in hand, and during the south-west monsoon of 1905 some 70 acres were planted with Para rubber from plants and seed obtained from one of the best estates in the Kalutara district, the old cacao-fields being at the same time interplanted with rubber, which made good growth from the first. Extensive nurseries were laid down about this time, and early in 1906 large tracts of forest land on the south side of the estates were felled, cleared, and planted, the total area amounting to some 430 acres. Favoured with good rains, the rubber in these clearings made very rapid growth. It being an understood thing that young rubber grows faster and better in clean land, weeding has all along been paid special attention to. This has in no slight measure helped to produce the good results indicated. It may be stated that these clearings have been reported upon by leading valuers and planters as comparing very favourably with the best in the island. At the commencement of 1907 the remaining forest reserve, together with other recently purchased land adjoining the estates, amounting in all to about 300 acres, has been cleared, and will be planted in the near approaching monsoon in April and May. There is a large permanent staff of Tamil labour, numbering close upon 700 coolies, who have their work cut out day by day to keep the estates in good order. These coolies are supervised by a European assistant working under the manager. This assistant has again under his control numerous conductors and native clerks, who attend to the details of the numerous works. There is a good factory for the manufacture of tea, which turns out some 120,000 lbs. per annum. A dispensary, with a resident dispenser, is situated in the middle of the group, and is the means of keeping the labour force in good health during the trying season of the year. The company also owns other up-country tea property.

JONATHAN EDMUND DE SILVA JAYASUNDERA.

Mr. J. E. de Silva Jayasundera, a brother of the well-known planter, Denagomuwa, was born at Kurunegala on June 28, 1872, and educated at St. Thomas's College and Wesley College. He read law under the Council of Legal Education, was admitted a Proctor in 1898, and practises at Kurunegala. He is also a planter, and owns the estate Royston in Ranawana, besides other properties planted with coconuts, and stretches of paddy-land in the district, and house property in Kurunegala. He is fond of sport, is a member of the Kurunegala Tennis Club, and of the Library. His wife, Alice Maud, whom he married in 1896, is a daughter of Henry Karnaratne, Mudaliyar of Kurunegala (a native of Bentota, in the Southern Province), and his fine residence, "Park View," is one of the show places of the district.

A. A. DE ZILVA.

Mr. Alfred Adam de Zilva (born October 22, 1865) is the only son of Francis Ebenezer de Zilva, Government schoolmaster at Galle, Kurunegala, Kandy, and Colombo, who in turn was the second son of Adam de Zilva, one of the best known merchants and exporters of Ceylon produce, and also a resident of Galle. Mr. de Zilva was educated at the Central School, Galle, and at the Government School,

MR. AND MRS. J. DE SILVA JAYASUNDERA AND CHILDREN. "PARK VIEW."

2 Z*

Kandy. He commenced his career as a planter on June 1, 1884, on Nella Oolla Estate, in the Galagedara district, under Mr. W. H. Cowley.

DYNEVOR ESTATE BUNGALOW.

In March, 1885, he went as assistant to Mr. P. A. Brain, and in July, 1886, he transferred to Dynevor Estate as assistant to Mr. Edmund Scott, where he worked for over ten years. In December, 1896, he took over charge of Pitiakande estate, and worked there till March 31, 1904. On February 1, 1904, he took over charge of Dynevor estate—the property of the Bambrakelly Estates Company, Ltd. Dynevor is situated on the Kandy-Kurunegala main road, about eight miles from Kurunegala. It comprises 343 acres, fully planted with tea, rubber, coconuts, cacao, and several other minor products. On the property stand a beautiful bungalow and large stores equipped with machinery for curing crops. The labour force employed on Dynevor numbers about 200 Indian coolies, and in addition a large force of Sinhalese labourers. Mr. de Zilva has been twice married. On October 15, 1896, he was united to Julia Sophia, eldest daughter of the late Mr. James Vanderslott, then Superintendent of Dea Ella Estate, in the Galagedara district, and sister of Mr. W. L. Vanderslott, present superintendent of Dea Ella estate. His second wife, whom he married on May 5, 1904, was Daizy Marian, daughter of Mr. C. F. Van Buren, a well-known Proctor of Galle. By his first marriage he has three children—two daughters and one son; and by his second marriage he has three sons. Mr. de Zilva is an ardent horticulturist, and at the last Agri-Horticultural Show of the North-Western Province, held at Kurunegala in 1906, he secured no less than two gold medals for the best tea and the best collection of estate produce, and seven bronze medals for vegetables, poultry, &c. He is an enthusiastic member of the Kurunegala Planters' Association and also a member of the Agri-Horticultural Society, North-Western Province. He is an enterprising planter and a keen sportsman.

GEORGE WM. DODANWELA GOONERAT ATAPATTU WAHALA HERAT MUDIANSILAGE UKKUBANDA.

This gentleman, known as George Wm. Dodanwela, is a son of Kiri Banda, Korala of Dodanwela Walauwa, and of his wife Kumarihamy, and was born in 1849 and educated at Trinity and St. Thomas's Colleges. He entered the service of the Government as early as 1869, holding various positions in the Land Registrar's Department, and acting as translator of sannas and other old documents. Later he became President of the village tribunals of Wanni Hatpattu, part of Dewamedi, Hiriyala, and Weudawili Hatpattus, and Ratemahatmaya of Hiriyala, and in 1885 Ratemahatmaya of Dambadeniya Hatpattu, retiring on pension in 1902, after thirty-three years' unbroken service. At the present time he holds the office of President of the Provincial Committee under the B.T. Ordinance. Mr. Dodanwela was twice married, in the first instance to Ranawana Palihana Walauwa Kumarihamy, and a second time to a sister of the Hon. Mr. Hulugalla, Adigar. By his first wife he had one son, Matthew, who is now President of Gangaboda Pattu, in the Southern Province, whilst by his second wife he had one daughter, Helen, who married Mr. B. Holangoda Nugawela, grandson of the Dissawe of Harispattu. She died on May 27, 1905, leaving one daughter, Muriel, who is at present at the Hillwood Girls' School, Kandy. Mr. Dodanwela owns various estates planted with coconuts, and tracts of paddy-land in the North-Western Province. The more important properties are Dikirilawa, of 300 acres, and Deduruoya, of 125 acres. Mr. Dodanwela is President of the Provincial Committee on Buddhist Temporalities of the North-Western Province and a member of the Agricultural Society. His residence is Helen House, Kurunegala.

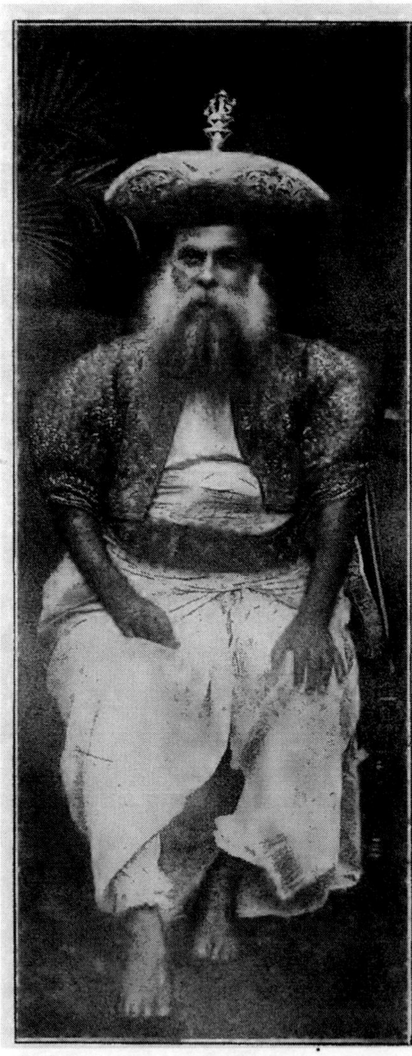

DODANWELA RATEMAHATMAYA.

CHARLES PETER MARKUS.

Mr. C. P. Markus, son of Dr. Markus, M.R.C.S., Assistant Colonial Surgeon, Kandy, and of Agneta Charlotte, daughter of Ferdinand, head clerk of the Kurunegala Kachcheri, was born in 1854. He was educated at St. Thomas's College, passing in the first class the Calcutta University matriculation, and was later articled for the study of law to Mr. Gerald de Livera, B.A. Oxon., barrister-at-law and Deputy Queen's Advocate, North-Western Province. He was made a Proctor of the District Court in 1886, and on different occasions acted as District Judge, Police Magistrate, and Commissioner of Requests. Formerly Mr. Markus was an elected member of the Local Board, and at the present time is a member of the Provincial Road Committee, a member of the Ceylon Law Society, a committee member of the Agricultural Society, and honorary treasurer of the Agricultural Shows. He owns the cacao and coconut properties of Rhenil and Hewapole. In 1879 he married Eveline, daughter of Mr. J. V. Daniels, Secretary of the District Court of Kurunegala, and resides at Carlsruhe. His eldest son, Chas. Hugh, who was educated at St. Thomas's College, is now a Proctor of the Kurunegala District Court and in partnership with his father. Of his daughters, Helen married Proctor Alfred Schokman. Mr. Markus was instrumental, and the principal worker, in getting the Kurunegala Library on to its present footing, and was honorary secretary of the institution for several years.

A. DE SILVA JAYESUNDERA.

Mr. Alfred de Silva Jayesundera is the eldest son of Joseph de Silva Jayesundera, Mudaliyar, of Kurunegala, and of Denagamuwatikiri Kumarihami, daughter of Lokubanda, Korale of Kempitiya Walauwa, in the Kegalla district. This was one of the earliest marriages between a low-country Sinhalese gentleman and a lady of the Kandyan aristocracy. Joseph de Silva Jayesundera, Mudaliyar (better known as Joseph de Silva), was a respectable low-country Sinhalese of the Colombo District, who came and settled down in the Kurunegala district early in the fifties, and served the British Government faithfully in different capacities for a period of nearly forty years. He was an able detective, and rendered meritorious services to Government, as the following testimonial will show :—

[TRUE COPY.]

"Joseph de Silva Jayasundera was my interpreter for the three years during which I was Magistrate of Kurunegala. I found him to be one of the most active and useful native officers I have ever met ; indeed, without his assistance it would have been almost impossible for me to do the work which had been entrusted to me. Although frequently exposed to considerable hardship and privation, he always carried out the instructions given to him honestly and thoroughly, and I should be sincerely glad to hear that Government had recognised his services by giving him a promotion which I can honestly say I believe to be well deserved.

"(*Signed*) F. R. ELLIS.

"*January* 6, 1880."

The ancestors of Mr. Jayasundera on his mother's side originally came from India in the year 236 of Buddha, *i.e.*, 308 B.C., when a slip of the historic Bo-tree was brought over to Ceylon from India to be planted at Anuradhapura. They settled in the village Bodhipala Game, now called Denagomuwa, from *dena*, a coffin. (There is a tradition that the coffin containing the corpse of Maliya Dewa Tera, the last of the Arhats, was halted here on its way to Raja-maha Vihara for the cremation ceremony.) The surname of the family, Bodhi-Guptha (*bodhi*, a bo-tree ; *guptha*, guardian), supports the above statement. One of the ancestors of the family was Dena-

C. P. MARKUS AND FAMILY.

THE BUNGALOW.

A. DE S. JAYESUNDERA.

MRS. J. DE S. JAYESUNDERA.
ALFRED HOUSE.

gomuwa Dissawa, under the Kandyan rule. His son, Kempitiye Mohatalehami, was concerned in the Kandyan rebellion of 1818, and was, in consequence, banished for high treason in 1819. His lands at Denagomuwa were confiscated, but he was subsequently pardoned, and his lands restored to him in 1826 by Governor Sir Edward Barnes. This Kempitiye Mohatalehami had only one son, who was Lokubanda Korale of Kempitiya Walauwa, the maternal grandfather of Mr. Jayesundera. Mr. Jayesundera was born at Wehera Walauwa, Kurunegala, in 1868, and was educated at Matale and St. Thomas's College, Colombo. He entered the Forest Department of the Government service in 1890, and was Forest Officer at various places in the Central Province until 1892, when he passed the Government clerical examination, and obtained employment in the Accountant's Office in the Ceylon Government Railways. He resigned his Government post in 1893 to take over his mother's estate at Denagomuwa. He has devoted his time to planting ever since. He plants coconuts and catch crops, such as plantains, country vegetables, &c., and has lately been experimenting with cacao and Para rubber. His magnificent estate at Denagomuwa, extending over 500 acres (including paddy-lands), fully planted with coconuts, is one of the finest and heaviest-bearing estates at Polgahawela. He manures the trees solely with cow-dung and ash, which are easily procurable on the estate, and which in his opinion is the safest manure for coconut-trees, although it is not so rich as artificial manure. The nuts of the estate are sometimes turned into copra and sold to European buyers in Colombo, but at present he supplies nuts to the Orient Company mills at Veyangoda. The plucking of the nuts is done once in two months. The permanent staff of coolies on the estate are Indian Tamils and low-country Sinhalese, but the greater part of the labour is procured from the neighbouring villages. The paddy-lands, about 150 acres or more in extent, are regularly cultivated for the "Maha season," which is done in the months of June and July every year. Some of the more fertile fields in them are at times cultivated twice a year—both for the "Yale" and "Maha" seasons. The paddy granaries at the old Walauwa, Denagomuwa, numbering about fifteen, are always full, and Mr. Jayesundera is one of the few Sinhalese gentlemen in the island who uses his own country rice. Another large estate of 200 acres owned by this gentleman is Katupitiya, in the Weudawili Hatpattu of the North-Western Province. He owns house property at Polgahawela, is a member of the Agri-Horticultural Society, Kurunegala, and manager of the Polgahawela Buddhist Mixed School. He was formerly Inquirer into Crimes, Dambadeniya Hatpattu (his district). In 1898 he married Madugalle Tikiri Kumari Hami, youngest daughter of Madugalle Basnaike Nilame, of Eriagame Walauwa, Peradeniya, and grandniece of the late Advocate Dunuwille, of Kandy. His residence is at Denagomuwa Walauwa, Polgahawela.

E. G. DE SILVA JAYASUNDERA.

Mr. Everard Graham de Silva Jayasundera, known as E. G. de Silva, is the brother of Mr. Alfred de Silva Jayasundera, of Denagomuwa. He was born in 1875, and educated at St. Thomas's College, after which he studied surveying privately. In 1894 he joined his brother as a planter, and five years later he entered the Government service as a clerk attached to the Kurunegala Kachcheri, and had charge of the Land Acquisition Department for the Northern Railway construction. In 1901 he was permanently appointed to the native department, and since 1904 has been President of Dambadeniya Hatpattu, and holds

THE FAMILY. MR. AND MRS. E. G. DE SILVA JAYASUNDERE.

his two courts at Polgahawela and Narammulla. He is an Inquirer into Crime, a member of the Agricultural Society, part owner of the estates under his brother's management and of house property at Polgahawela. In 1899 he married Ada Emily Beatrice, the eldest daughter of Graham de Silva Seneveratne, Mudaliyar, and they reside at Polgahawela.

MR. AND MRS. FRED DANIELS AND CHILD.

FREDERICK NELL DANIELS, M.L.B., M.D.R.C.

James Valentine Daniels, formerly the Secretary of the District Court, Kurunegala, and his brother Frank are well-known figures in contemporary Ceylon history. They rendered valuable military services during the Kandyan rebellion of 1848 by carrying despatches to and from Kandy and accompanying the troops to Kurunegala. On April 9, 1867, Fredk. Nell Daniels, son of the former, was born. He was educated at Trinity College, Kandy, and later at the Royal College, Colombo, and after serving his articles of apprenticeship as a student-at-law under his brother-in-law, Mr. George Schokman, Crown Proctor and Justice of the Peace, Kurunegala, he passed out as a Proctor of the District Court, started practice at Kurunegala in December, 1889, and soon gained a lucrative business. He passed out as Proctor of the Supreme Court in 1897, and was admitted Notary Public in 1905. He is an elected member of the Local Board, nominated member of the District Road Committee, a committee member of the Library, Tennis, and Cricket Clubs, Secretary of the Law Library, and Honorary Treasurer of the Agricultural Society, Trustee and Hon. Secretary of Trustees of Christ Church, and a manager of schools. He joined the Volunteer force as a private in 1886, resigned owing to his inability to attend drills, rejoined in 1892, obtained his commission in 1893, and since 1903 has been Captain commanding the "G" Company of the Ceylon Light Infantry. In addition to his legal profession he is a planter of coconuts, cacao, and rubber, and his estates, Elogowapitiya, Wehera, and Delta, are well known in the district. He is also part owner of the Kurunegala Dairy, which supplies the hospitals and town with milk and butter. He married Eileen, daughter of Mr. J. H. Sproule, the well-known lawyer, Justice of the Peace, and member of the Municipal Council of Kandy, and resides at "Eastfields," Kurunegala.

PUTTALAM DISTRICT.

RICHARD CHARLES DE SILVA, Dissanayake Mudaliyar.

Mr. R. C. de Silva is the only son of Sellahewage Don Bastian de Silva, landed proprietor, of Matara, and Dona Carlina, daughter of Mr. Don Mathes Jayawickreme, landed proprietor, of Matara. He was born in 1864, and educated at Galle Central School. In 1888 he entered the service of the Government in the Fiscal's Office at Kurunegala, and became Shroff Mudaliyar of Kurunegala Kachcheri in 1900, whilst in 1906 he was appointed Mudaliyar of Puttalam Pattu. He is Revenue Officer and Inquirer into Crime, &c., for a district of nearly 122 square miles in area and 9,000 inhabitants. In 1885 he entered the ranks of the Ceylon Light Infantry, and became Lieutenant in 1904. He is the only native and administrative chief who is also a Volunteer officer. Mr. de Silva owns the Bamunugedere estate in the Kurunegala district, and several others, fully planted, and some house property. He married, in 1899, Alice Grace Amadore Jayesuriya, second daughter of S. H. Jayawickreme, Mudaliyar, of Kurunegala. He has the Coronation medal. His residence is "The Walauwa," Mundel, Puttalam.

MUDALIYAR R. C. DE SILVA. MR. AND MRS. R. C. DE SILVA.

PATTUWE WALAUWA. MUDALIYAR R. C. DE SILVA AND HIS STAFF OF NATIVE HEADMEN.

MR. AND MRS. CASIE CHITTY AND FAMILY. CARMEL COTTAGE.
A. M. C. CASIE CHITTY.

THE RESIDENCE. J. W. P. SENATHIRAJA.
MR. AND MRS. SENATHIRAJA AND FAMILY.

A. M. C. CASIE CHITTY.

Mr. Aloysius Mount Carmel Casie Chitty is the son of Simon Casie Chitty, of the Ceylon Civil Service, District Judge of Chilaw, and author of the Ceylon Gazetteer and other publications. He was born in 1853, and educated at the Colombo Academy and St. Thomas's College. He was then articled for the study of law to Mr. John Ferdinand Prins, Proctor, Supreme Court, Colombo. In 1877 he became a Proctor of the District Court of Chilaw, and is now practising his profession at Puttalam. In 1882 he was admitted as Notary Public in English and Tamil, and was for many years an elected member of the Local Board of that town. He owns the Palachola, Perukkuvattan, Periyakulam, and Mary Ann coconut estates, besides extensive paddy-fields at Pallankandel and Ponparippo in the district. He married, in 1878, Isidora, great-granddaughter of Simon de Rosairo, merchant, of Kalpentyn, and again, in 1889, Mary, daughter of Manuel Muttukumara, and he resides at Carmel Cottage, Puttalam.

J. W. P. SENATHIRAJA.

Mr. John Wirt Ponniah Senathiraja, younger brother of Advocate Senathiraja, of Colombo, was born in Jaffna in 1863, and educated at St. John's College, Jaffna, where he passed the Madras Matriculation Examination, and was reading for the First Arts Examination for nearly two years. Having in the meanwhile passed the Government Clerical Examination, he was in the service of Government for about two years. Leaving Government service, he was articled to Proctor W. P. Ranesinghe, of Colombo, and read law under his brother, Advocate Senathiraja. He was admitted a Proctor of the District Court, Colombo, in 1893, and became Crown Proctor, Puttalam, in 1894. In the year 1897 he was enrolled a Proctor S.C. and Notary Public, and is now a Justice of the Peace and an Unofficial Police Magistrate. He is also a member of the District Road Committee, Puttalam; Ceylon National Association; Ceylon Law Society; Agricultural Society, Puttalam; Friend-in-Need Society, Puttalam; and a Prison Visitor. He married, in 1898, Anne Sellamma, daughter of Mr. John Caitan de Coste, Government salt storekeeper at Puttalam. Mr. Senathiraja is the leading Proctor at the Puttalam bar, and he owns, amongst others, the coconut estates Sirambiadi (200 acres) and Katekadu, Puttalam district.

SUSEPILLAI MUDALIYAR P. VANDERKOEN.

Mr. Susepillai Mudaliyar Philip Vanderkoen, son of Susepillai Mudaliyar, of Mannar, and Mary, daughter of Savarimuttu Superanamiam, Mudaliyar, of Jaffna, was born in 1864, and educated at St. Patrick's, Jaffna, and St. Joseph's College, Trichinopoly. Upon the completion of his college training he took charge of his father's planting and farming affairs at Mannar, but in 1888 he entered the Government service as Udaiyar (Mohandiram) of Mantac North (Mannar), and general storekeeper there in 1894. He became salt storekeeper at Kalpitiya and Puttalam, and in 1902 was made District Mudaliyar of the former place as well as Salt Superintendent there. He is a Justice of the Peace and Unofficial Police Magistrate, and a member of the Agricultural Society and the Public Service Mutual Provident Association. He married, in 1889, Ann, daughter of Emanual Sinnatamhi, of the Jaffna Kachcheri, and resides at "The Mansion," Kalpitiya. His eldest daughter, Gertrude Sophia, married Francis Xavier Nicholas, of Jaffna.

S. M. P. VANDERKOEN. THE BUNGALOW

L. A. DE ROSAIRO'S BUNGALOW.

LONGINUS ANTHONY DE ROSAIRO.

Mr. L. A. de Rosairo, son of John Louis de Rosairo, of the District Road Committee of Puttalam, and of Mary, daughter of Emmanuel David, a landed proprietor of the district, was born in 1859, and educated at St. Mary's School, Negombo. Previous to adopting coconut-planting he assisted Mr. D. M. de Rosairo, who was Mudaliyar of Kalpitiya, in his official duties, acting for him on various occasions. He eventually commenced coconut-planting, and owns Mutwal, an estate at Kalpitiya, which is famous throughout the island for the excellence of its copra. In addition he is the owner of some house property. In 1880 he was appointed Registrar of Births, Marriages, and Deaths. He married in the following year Seraphina, daughter of D. M. de Rosairo, District Mudaliyar, Kalpitiya, and has one son, who assists him on the estate. His residence is "Rosebank," Kalpitiya.

ADAM MUTTUKUMARA.

Mr. A. Muttukumara, son of Robert Melho Muttukumara, Assistant Shroff of Puttalam Kachcheri, and Johanna, daughter of Kurunata Pulle, and grandson of Adam Cadiravela Pulle, Mudaliyar of Kalpitiya, was born at Mampuri in 1872, and educated at the Royal College. He read law and became a Proctor at the District Court, Puttalam, in 1897, and in 1898 was elected a member of the Local Board. He is also a member of the Ceylon National Association and the Agricultural Society. He owns the Serambiadiutcham estate, fully planted, and resides at "Cyrilhurst." He married, in 1903, Sarah, daughter of the Hon. Dr. Rockwood, Colombo. Mr. Muttukumara's cousin, Emmanuel Anthony, who was the son of Solomon Foenander Muttukumara, Notary Public and landed proprietor of Puttalam, and Mary, sister of the well-known Advocate Brito, was educated at the Royal College, and after serving articles with Advocate Brito and Proctor Edward Prins, became Crown Proctor, Puttalam, and Justice of the Peace in 1889. His career, however, was cut short by his comparatively early death in 1895.

E. A. MUTTUKUMARA.

WILFRED ADAM MUTTUKUMARA.

Mr. W. A. Muttukumara is a son of Manuel Muttukumara, salt storekeeper and proprietary planter, Puttalam, and of Cecilia, daughter of Manuel Davidupulle, of Katakadu. He was born in 1880, and educated at St. Benedict's Institute and afterwards at St. Joseph's College. He studied law privately and under the Council of Legal Education, and became Proctor of the District Court, Puttalam, in 1903. He is a member of the Ceylon National Association, the Catholic Union, the Catholic Club, and is Secretary to the local Agricultural Society. His residence is Cecilia House, Puttalam. Mr. Muttukumara, jointly with his brothers and sisters, is the owner of several coconut estates, notably the one at Alancuda, of 400 acres more or less, fully equipped. He also owns tracts of paddy-lands and house property. The family of which he is a member is much respected,

W. A. MUTTUKUMARA.

and his sisters married to Proctor A. M. C. Casie Chitty and Mr. M. J. Paul de Coste, of the Forest Department, respectively.

CHILAW DISTRICT.

JAMES EDWARD COREA.

The Corea family is descended from Vikrama Sinha Mudaliyar, who was the Commander-in-Chief of the forces of the great king of Sitavaka, Mayadunna, in his wars against the Portuguese, which nation had been given a footing in Colombo by the weak-minded king of Kotta, Bhuvaneka Bahu, brother of Mayadunna. When the Portuguese commander, Don Diego de Ataide, was besieged in Colombo in 1564 A.D. by Mayadunna and his son Rajasinha (called by the Portuguese writers Raju), the Portuguese chronicler De Couto says that his countrymen were reduced to great want by the tactics of Vikrama Sinha Mudaliyar, who intercepted all their supplies. "Raju's Field-marshal (Mestre de Campo), Bicaruasinga, repeatedly cut off the convoys which were despatched by Don Diego" (De Couto, Decade VIII.), After the death of Mayadunna, Vikrama Sinha Mudaliyar was treacherously murdered on the secret orders of Rajasinha (Rajavaliya). De Couto, in recording this event, describes Vikrama Sinha as Rajasinha's "Chief Mudaliyar and Master of the Camp, from whom he had learnt the art of war, and who had rendered him such faithful service." Upon the murder of Vikrama Sinha his two sons sought safety in Colombo, where King Dharmapala was reigning over the kingdom of Kotta under the protection of the Portuguese, who were commanded by an officer named Don John Corea de Baretto. There they were baptized under the names of Dominicus Corea and Simon Corea, and received a Christian education, and grew up among the Portuguese in the company of the young Prince Konappu Bandara, whose father, Virasundara Bandara, of Peradeniya, had also been murdered on the orders of Rajasinha, and who had been baptized in the name of Don John, and afterwards became king of Ceylon under the title of Vimala Dharmasuriya. When Rajasinha was laying vigorous siege to Colombo, this prince volunteered to win over the Kandyans to espouse the cause of their lawful sovereign, Donna Catherina (who had been driven out of her kingdom by Rajasinha, and was then living under the protection of the Portuguese at Mannar), and to cause them to harass the king from the hill-country. When Rajasinha had been totally defeated by Don John and slain in battle (A.D. 1592), the Portuguese conceived the idea of marrying the young Kandyan queen to a Portuguese officer (Pedro Lopes de Sousa), in order by that means to gain the mastery of the whole country. This was naturally resented by Don John and the Kandyans, who, led by Don John, turned their arms against the Portuguese. Donna Catherina was rescued from the Portuguese and married Don John, who was thereupon received with acclamation as king of Kandy. At this crisis Dominicus Corea Vikrama Sinha and his brother Simon left Colombo, and offered their services to the comrade of their youth, Don John Vimala Dharmasuriya, who welcomed them with joy, and raised Dominicus to the rank of a prince (see Philalethes' "History of Ceylon," chap. vi.), and appointed him a State Secretary (Mohottala). In 1594 Dominicus Corea successfully led the forces of Vimala Dharmasuriya against the Portuguese commander, Don Jeronymo de Azevedo. Subsequently, in 1597, he was captured in battle and quartered as a rebel by Azevedo (De Couto, Decade XI., Fana y Sousa, Ribeiro). The younger brother rose to great eminence under Vimala Dharmasuriya. De Couto narrates (Decade XII.) that the king in directing a campaign "in the direction of Galle and Matura . . . despatched a prince of his named Madune Pandar and the rebel Simao Correa (brother of Domingos Correa Bicarnasinga, whom Don Jeronymo had ordered to be executed), who had assumed the title of king of Sitavaka." Later, when Vimala Dharmasuriya's successor, King Senerat, made peace with the Portuguese in 1609, Simon accepted service under the Portuguese Governor, and was specially nominated by the Viceroy of India (Azevedo), for his "experience and valour," to the command of the native troops of the Portuguese, and was appointed the Dissawa of Seven Korales (Antonio Bocarro's "Decada 13 da Historia da India." See also *Ceylon Review*, vol. iii., p. 9, and the Rajavaliya), in which post he died in 1615. The present members of the family trace their descent from Dominicus Corea Vikrama Sinha, after whom three generations attained to high rank in the Sinhalese Government. In 1619 Vikrama Sinha Mautri was created a prince, and appointed to the Governorship of Uva. His son was Vikrama Sinha, Mudaliyar of Peliyagoda in 1630, after whom came (A.D. 1650) Vikrama Sinha, Dissawa of Puttalam (see "Parangi Hatane," a Sinhalese poem commemorating the Portuguese wars). When the Portuguese were finally displaced by the Dutch, Christoffel Corea-Vikramasinha entered their service as Mohandiram of Hapitigam Korale. His son Louis was Padicara Mohandiram, an officer appointed by the Dutch Government to arrange for the safe conduct and provisioning of their frequent embassies to the Kandyan court. A Dutch act of appointment, under the hand of Governor Van der Graaff, dated March 20, 1788 (now in the possession of C. E. Corea-Vikramasinha, Proctor, of Chilaw), records the nomination of Christoffel Corea to succeed his father, Louis Corea. Christoffel Corea, the Padicara, was invited to Kandy by the Sinhalese king at the commencement of hostilities with the English in 1803, with promises of favour and promotion to high rank, but died shortly after he reached Kandy, leaving three children, of whom the eldest, Abraham, became Mohandiram of the Chilaw district. The second, Johannes, was Mudaliyar of Alutkuru Korale, and was included in the list of "First-class Sinhalese" prepared under the regulations for the selection of jurors when the system was first introduced in Ceylon; the third was Simon, who succeeded his brother as Mudaliyar of Alutkuru Korale, and was also appointed a Justice of the Peace. Abraham's son Christoffel was Mudaliyar of the Chilaw District, and has left four children: James Edward, Mudaliyar of Chilaw; Allan and Jumeaux, proprietary planters; and James Abraham,

MUDALIYAR J. E. COREA. MR. AND MRS. J. E. COREA AND FAMILY. THE RESIDENCE.
THE MOTHER OF MUDALIYAR J. E. COREA. MUDALIYAR J. E. COREA AND NATIVE HEADMEN.

Proctor. Johannes had one son, Simon, who was Mohandiram of the city of Colombo. His only surviving child is a daughter. Simon Corea-Vikramasinha, J.P., Mudaliyar of Alutkuru Korale, had five children, of whom Charles Edward was Proctor of the Supreme Court, Henry Richard was Mudaliyar of Alutkuru Korale, George Edmund was a Master of the Royal College. The other two, Jumeaux and Simon, have left no descendants. Charles Edward has left three sons, the eldest of whom, Charles Edgar, Proctor, is the unofficial leader of the Chilaw Bar, a member of the Royal Asiatic Society, and Chairman of the Chilaw Association. In 1899 he was elected by the various native associations in Ceylon and a public meeting in Colombo to proceed to England as a delegate of the people of Ceylon to lay before the Imperial Government a representation against the Waste Lands Ordinance. The second son, Alfred Ernest, is a physician, and the youngest, Charles Edward Victor, is an Advocate of the Supreme Court. The Mudaliyar Henry's only son, James Alfred, is Mohandiram in the historic town of Madampe, in the Chilaw district. Winzer, the eldest son of George, is an officer in the Government Police, and the second son, Frederick, is a Proctor at Negombo.

In addition to the hereditary rank of Prince conferred on Dominicus Corea-Vikramasinha by King Vimala Dharmasuriya, the family have acquired from the Dutch and English Governments the following Patabendi titles: Abhayaratna, Gunasekera, Vikramasundara, Vijayasekera. The living members of the family, however, only use the simple surname Corea, and sometimes Corea-Vikramasinha.

James Edward Corea Abhayaratna Vijayasekera, Mudaliyar, Pitigal Korale, North Chilaw, was born on December 2, 1865, and educated at the Colombo Academy, now the Royal College, and entered the Government service in 1887, being attached to the Provincial Road Committee at Kurunegala. In 1888 he was appointed to the District Road Committee, Chilaw, and in 1899 became Mudaliyar, Pitigal Korale North, and has held that office ever since. He is also the Inspector of Coaches and Inquirer into Crimes of the Chilaw District, and in charge of the rural police in Pitigal Korale North. He is the Chairman of the Village Committee and President of the Council of Irrigation, and is a landed proprietor and planter, owning extensive estates. Among others he possesses the Karrukkuwa, Tittakada, and Tambagalle coconut estates in the Chilaw District, as well as large tracts of paddy-lands. He is a member of the Committee of the Agricultural and Horticultural Society. In 1888 he married Frances Eleanor Terentia daughter of D. C. Ameresekera, Proctor of the Supreme Court of Kurunegala. His ancestral home and country residence is the Walauwa at Karukkuwa, whilst his official residence is the Korale Walauwa at Chilaw.

MR. AND MRS. J. A. C. COREA AND FAMILY.

JUMEAUX ARTHUR CHRISTOFFEL COREA.

Jumeaux Arthur Christoffel Corea, the third son of the late Johannes Christoffel Corea, Mudaliyar, Chilaw, was born at Chilaw in 1873, and educated at the Wesley College. In 1893 he entered the Ceylon Survey Department, and four years later passed the licensed surveyor's examination. He commenced practice at Chilaw as licensed surveyor and leveller, is holder of the Surveyor-General's special licence to survey Crown land and fiscal's licensed surveyor for the districts of Kurunegala and Chilaw, and is a member of the Chilaw Association and the Chilaw Tennis Club. In 1902 he married Adeline Beatrice Lucy, daughter of the late Don Condrad Ameresekera, Proctor, Supreme Court, Kurunegala, and their children are (1) Ordella Beatrice Claribel; (2) Eulalie Hypatia Adelaide. Mr. Corea is interested in and owns coconut estates in the villages Puliyankadawara Alutkurumulla and Villattawa, Karukkuwa, Ernuwila, and Kirimetiyana, tracts of fields in Kirimetiyana, and building lots within the Local Board limits of Chilaw.

PERCIVAL ALLAN COREA.

Mr. P. A. Corea is the second son of the late Johannes Christoffel Corea, Mudaliyar, Chilaw, and brother of Mudaliyar J. E. Corea, Chilaw He was born at Karukkuwa, in 1870, and educated at Wesley College. He is a planter,

London College of Preceptors' examination, and winning the junior mathematical prize. He read law, was admitted a Proctor of the District Court in 1906, and now practises at Chilaw. He is a member of the Ceylon National Association and of the Chilaw Association, Vice-President of St. Mary's Literary Association, and sub-captain of the Moratuwa Cyclists' Union.

grandfather of the subject of this sketch, who was born in 1848. Mr. Amarasekere was educated at the Colombo Academy, and learned administrative and revenue work under his uncle, Johannes Christoffel Corea, Mudaliyar of the Pitigal Korale. He was appointed Deed Clerk, Puttalam Kachcheri, in 1872, and held acting appointments as Mohandiram and Kachcheri Mudaliyar from 1873 to 1874. In 1874 he was Mohandiram, Kurunegala Kachcheri, and in 1881 he was President of the Village Tribunals

MR. AND MRS. P. A. COREA AND FAMILY.

T. M. FERNANDO. THE BUNGALOW.

owning a number of coconut plantations, including Mugunuwattewara. He is also proprietary superintendent of the ancestral property called the Karukkuwa Walauwa estate, and is a member of the Chilaw Association. He married, in 1899, Cicely Augusta, daughter of the late George Edmund Corea, Secretary of the District Court of Negombo.

THOMAS MATTHEW FERNANDO.

Mr. T. M. Fernando is the son of the late Romuald Fernando, landed proprietor, of Mount Lavinia. He was born in 1883, and educated at the Royal and St. Joseph's Colleges, passing the Cambridge Local Junior Examination, the

J. C. A. E. KULATILAKE.

James Charles Amarasekere Ekanayake Kulatilake, known as J. C. Amarasekere, Mudaliyar, is a descendant of one Attanayika, who was one of the ministers of King Rajasinha II. Attanayika's sons and grandsons, Ekanayika and Amarasekere, held the office of Protector of the Boundary between the Sinhalese and Dutch Governments and Basnayake Nilame of Kelani Dewale respectively. Their descendant, Francis Amarasekere, is mentioned in records as a Mohandiram, under the Dutch *régime*, at Gotatuwa, and he was succeeded by his son, who was Mudaliyar of Hapitigam Korale in 1760. The latter's son was Mudaliyar of the same Korale in 1785, but his son did not hold office. He was the

of Weudawili and Dewamedi Hatpattus, North-Western Province. He became Mudaliyar of the Pitigal Korale South in 1885, in 1899 was appointed Inquirer into Crimes, and in 1903 Justice of the Peace and Unofficial Police Magistrate, Chilaw district. He is Revenue Officer for his district and Chairman of the Village Committees. He owns a great deal of property, amongst his coconut estates being Peniheleyagama, Dunkanawe, and Dampitiya, fully planted and equipped, whilst he has paddy-lands and house property in the Chilaw district. Mr. Amarasekere is on the committee of the Agricultural Society, and greatly interested in education. In 1880 he married Louisa Lily, daughter of Cornelis de Silva Munesinghe Dessanayake, Mudaliyar of Kandy Kachcheri,

FAMILY GROUP. MUDALIYAR J. C. AMARASEKERE.

THE BUNGALOW. MUDALIYAR J. C. AMARASEKERE AND HIS NATIVE HEADMEN.

and a second time Margaret, his deceased wife's sister. He has three sons and three daughters. He resides at Natandiya Walauwa, Pitigal Korale Central.

T. J. COOKE.

Mr. Thomas James Cooke is the son of Nathaniel James Cooke, who was formerly

THOMAS JAMES COOKE.

Government doctor of Chilaw and afterwards Government Proctor and Justice of the Peace, and Louisa Arnoldina, daughter of Johannes Nicolas Pieris, Deputy Fiscal of Chilaw. He is the grandson of James Cooke, of H.M.'s 19th Regiment of foot, stationed at Colombo, who married there in 1806. Born at Chilaw in 1849, he was educated at Colombo Academy,

NATHANIEL JAMES COOKE.

after which he was articled for the study of law to Mr. Cecil Morgan, Government Proctor of Colombo. He became Proctor of the district Court of Chilaw in 1870 and of the Supreme Court in 1877. On various occasions he acted as District Judge and Police Magistrate, and became Crown Proctor in 1883, Justice of the Peace and Unofficial Police Magistrate in 1888, and retired from active practice in 1901. He was formerly a member of the Local Board and of the District Road Committee. In 1876 he married Emma, daughter of Alexander Carron, of Negombo, owns coconut estates in the district, and is a Proctor of the Chilaw District Court.

MR. AND MRS. J. A. COREA AND CHILD.

JAMES ABRAHAM COREA.

Mr. James A. Corea is a brother of Mudaliyar Corea, of whose family a full account appears on a preceding page. He was born in 1875, and educated at the Wesley College, where he passed the Calcutta University matriculation examination. He read law under the Council of Legal Education, and became a Proctor for the district in 1902 and practises at Chilaw. He is a member of the Chilaw Agricultural Society and Chilaw Association. He married his cousin, Agnes Eveline Rhoda, daughter of Proctor Charles Edward Corea, in 1902. He owns coconut estates in the Chilaw district.

THE LATE W. J. E. W. A. A. A. DE ROWEL.

By an instrument dated Colombo, 1763, the Dutch Governor, Lubbert Baron Van Eck, appointed Anthony Rowel Maha Vidane and Mohandiram of Alutkuru Korale, and in the same year, for services rendered in the Kandyan expedition, he was, on the recommendation of Jan Jurgen Faber, made Mudaliyar of the same district. Miguel, the third son of Anthony, succeeded his father as Mohandiram of the same district, and Waruakulaweerasuriya Jayatilleke Elias Waruakula Aditiya Arsenelaitta Ambrosius de Rowel, the subject of this sketch, was the son of Miguel's son Carolis, Notary Public. He was born at Waikkal in 1844, and after being educated privately, he assisted his father in his notarial duties and in the supervision of his coconut and tobacco plantations. In 1871 he succeeded his father as Notary Public, was appointed Mohandiram of Pitigal Korale South in 1876, Titular Mudaliyar in 1887, and Mudaliyar in 1895. Two years later he became Justice of the Peace and Unofficial Police Magistrate of Chilaw, and in 1902 was made Mudaliyar of the Governor's Gate. He was a member of the Agricultural Society and of the District Road Committee, and before his death, which took place in November, 1906, he was specially commended by the Governor for his faithful services. He married, in 1872, Maria, daughter of Robert Lowe, of Marawila, and their eldest daughter, Dorothy Juliana, married F. A. Wijeyesekere, J.P. and U.P.M. and Presi-

MUDALIYAR W. M. DABERERA. MUDALIYAR W. M DABERERA AND NATIVE HEADMEN.
THE LATE GATE MUDALIYAR DE ROWEL. THE RESIDENCE.

dent of the Village Tribunals of Salpiti Korale, while Rosalind, the second daughter, is married to W. Martin Daberera, Mudaliyar of Pitigal Korale South, for a notice of whom see p. 745.

J. A. E. COREA, L.M.S.

Dr. James Alfred Ernest Corea, of Chilaw, is the son of the late Charles Edward Corea, Abeyeratne Wijeyesekere, who was a Proctor at Chilaw, and the grandson of the well-known Mudaliyar of Alutkuru Korale. He was born at Chilaw in 1870, and received his education at the Royal College, after which he took a course

J. A. E. COREA AND FAMILY.

of study at the Ceylon Medical College, extending over five years. After he had qualified at that college he held Government medical appointments successively at Elkaduwa and Kandy, but he resigned the Government service in 1899, and has since then practised his profession privately at his native town. In 1897 he married Letitia Grace Alice, daughter of Mudaliyar J.C.H. Seneviratne, of Marawila.

GAMAMEDELIANAGE SIMON PERERA.

Mr. G. S. Perera, a native of Talahena in the Negombo district, was educated at St. Benedict's Institute, and joined his uncle, K. D. Juan Appoohamy, in the arrack-renting business, becoming manager of the rents at Jaffna and elsewhere. In 1895 he took up planting, commencing in the Chilaw district, and is now part owner of Rajakadaluwa, an estate of 250 acres, and owner of Naladarankaduwe and Market View estates, which comprise about 350 acres, Ferry estate and others, in addition to about 50 acres of fully-bearing paddy-lands.

G. S. PERERA.

The whole of the estates are fully equipped, and copra is manufactured for the Colombo market. He was appointed in 1896 Registrar of Births, Marriages, and Deaths for Pitigal Korale North. Mr. Perera married twice, his first wife being the widow of the late G. D. Miller, and his second wife a daughter of the late Proctor Nawaratua, Supreme Court, Negombo, and granddaughter of Nawaratua, Mudaliyar of Puttalam. He takes a keen interest in educational matters and founded the Benedicta Girls' School at his Rajakadaluwa estate.

JAMES ALFRED COREA, Mohandiram.

Mr. J. A. Corea, a descendant (eleventh generation) of Wickremasinghe Bandara, chief of Seven Korales under the Kandyan emperor (1520–60), is the son of Henry Richard Corea, Mudaliyar of Alutkuru Korale North, and Cornelia Wilhelmina Perera, and the grandson of Simon Corea, who was a younger brother of Abraham and Johannes Corea, whose ancestry is given in the sketch of Mudaliyar J. E. Corea. The subject of this notice was born at Negombo on November 23, 1871, and received his education at St. Thomas's College, Colombo, after which he learned planting under his father. In 1899 he became Mohandiram of Madampe (Pitigal Korale Central), and still holds that office. He owns Potuwille and Mugunuatuwane, both fully planted with coconuts, as well as house

GOVERNMENT AGENT COREA AND NATIVE HEADMEN.

MR. AND MRS. J. A. COREA.

COREA COURT.

MOHANDIRAM J. A. COREA.
(Government Agent.)

property at Madampe and Colombo. He is a member of the Chilaw Association and the Agricultural Society. On June 7, 1906, he married Eugenie Sarah Matilda, third daughter of Dr. John Attygalle, retired colonial surgeon, of Colombo, and resides at Corea Court, Madampe.

W. A. J. FERNANDO.

Mr. W. A. J. Fernando, Notary, of Chilaw, is the third son of the late Mr. W. A. Fernando, who was a descendant of a respectable Karawa family of Chilaw who lived in the early forties. His father having died when he was an infant three months old, he was brought up as the youngest of a family of three children by his mother, the late Maria Madelena Fernando. When he was old enough to attend school he was admitted to St. Mary's School, Chilaw, where he acquired a thorough knowledge of the Tamil language, which helped him in a considerable degree in after-life. On leaving school young Fernando was apprenticed to the then practising notary of Chilaw, but this gentleman died within a very short time, and his successor in office was entrusted with the care of the young notarial student, and by him he was trained. On the death of his last master Mr. Fernando applied to Sir Arthur Elibank Havelock, the then Governor, and was appointed a Notary Public of the district of Chilaw on August 18, 1891. Mr. Fernando married Miss Lucy Fernando, the eldest daughter of Mr. W. G. Santryago Fernando, a native medical practitioner and a wealthy resident of Chilaw. Mr. Fernando has built a neat and commodious house at the Chilaw end of the Colombo-Chilaw road, known as Laura Villa, where Mr. and Mrs. Fernando, with their seven children, are now residing. Mr. Fernando is an unofficial member of the Local Board of Chilaw, which fact testifies to the popularity and esteem in which he is held by all classes of residents of Chilaw. Amongst Mr. Fernando's landed estates Puwalle and Kanpiculia are the principal ones. He also deals in copra on a large scale, and in many ways contributes to the prosperity of the people of Chilaw.

J. P. FERNANDO.

Mr. Joseph Peter Fernando, son of Mr. Manuel Joseph Fernando, landed proprietor and peace officer of Chilaw, at a very early age commenced coconut-planting, and now owns some of the best known estates in the Chilaw district. Amongst these, Ellapahale, of 436 acres, Kohungahakotuwe, of 120 acres, and Winifred Villa estates are the most important. He has numerous other smaller plantations, both near Puttalam and Chilaw, and on all his properties copra is manufactured. He is also a partner in the arrack-rents for the Chilaw district together with Mr. N. E. Croos, of Negombo, and he has fine arrack stores at Chilaw, from which the spirit is sent all over the district. He is the senior elected member of the Chilaw Local Board, and has been Coroner for the district for fourteen years. He is a member of the Roman Catholic Church, and married a daughter of the well-known planter Mr. Philip Perera. His town residence is Sandringham House.

J. C. H. SENEWIRATNE.

James Caulfield Herat Senewiratne, Mudaliyar, comes of a very ancient Sinhalese family, whose members have held the Mudaliyarship of Madampe (which originally had jurisdiction over the whole of the Pitigal

LAURA VILLA. W. A. J. FERNANDO AND FAMILY.

MR. AND MRS. J. C. H. SENEWIRATNE. THE RESIDENCE.

Korale), from the time of its establishment to the life of the father of the present sketch. Every member of the family has held the office. During the Sinhalese monarchy the Senewiratne Mudaliyar was greatly esteemed by the king, as is evidenced by the fact that in 1758 the then head of the family was rewarded for his services with a large grant of lands in Madampe, lands which are still in the possession of the family. He was also given the title of "Hami," and shortly afterwards the Madampe Korale, of which he was the Mudaliyar, and which embraced the whole of the present Pitigal Korale and parts of the Kurunegala and Puttalam districts, became a Dutch province. In 1764 he was succeeded as Mudaliyar of the Korale by his son, who was, by a Dutch Act dated July 21, 1764, made an officer of the Dutch Government, with the title of "Moodliaar in Koraal van de Pittigal Corle in van de pattoes naggam, mendi Pattoe, oothere, Yatugaha, Makandura, Ratdolane in Welpalle," by which it will be seen that his jurisdiction extended over the entire Chilaw district and a considerable portion of the Kurunegala district. This Mudaliyar was succeeded by his son, who is called Don Gerrit Senewiratne in an old Dutch document of 1773. His son was Don Johan Carlo Herat Senewiratne Mudaliyar, whose son, Don Barend Herat Senewiratne Mudaliyar, of Pitigal Korale and Demala Hatpattu, was the father of the present holder of the Mudaliyarship. Thus has this office been held in hereditary succession by members of the Senewiratne family from the time of the Sinhalese kings.

James C. Herat Senewiratne was born at Madampe in 1850 and educated at the Colombo Academy under Dr. Boake. He entered the Registrar's Office, Colombo Kachcheri, in 1880, and in 1881 was Shroff Mudaliyar of the Kegalla Kachcheri. He retired from service in 1902, having been shortly before invested with the rank of Mudaliyar for life, on the recommendation of several members of the Civil Service, including Mr. W. E. Davidson (who is at present Governor of the Seychelles) and Mr. Bertram Hill, who were both Assistant Government Agents of Chilaw. The former wrote officially to the Government as follows :—

"I now renew . . . my strong recommendation that the rank of Mudaliyar be bestowed on Mr. J. C. H. Senewiratne . . . I certify that in personal character, private means, ancestry, and connections Mr. Senewiratne is eminently worthy of the rank of Mudaliyar."

And Mr. Hill, in recommending Mr. Senewiratne for appointment as Mudaliyar of Pitigal Korale, placed on record that he "is a trustworthy officer of good family and qualified both by education, birth, and territorial influence to hold the place so long held by his ancestors."

He married Nancy Gertrude, daughter of Philip Panditisekere, Mudaliyar of the Salpiti Korale and the Governor's Gate. Mr. Senewiratne resides at "The Towers," Marawila, and is one of the largest landowners in the district. He has the coconut estates of Marawila (700 acres), and Irenawila (820 acres), and the Iratakulana estate (500 acres), the Henepole estate (400 acres), and many others in the Chilaw district, fully planted and equipped. He also owns Balabowe, in the Veyangoda district, and extensive paddy-lands, as well as house property, &c. He is a member of the Chilaw Association and of the Royal Asiatic Society.

W. M. DABERERA.

Waruakulasuriya Martin Daberera, Mudaliyar of Pitigal Korale South, is the son of

W. Sylvester Daberera, landed proprietor of Marawila, and Celestine, daughter of Carolis de Rowel, Notary Public. He was born in 1880, and educated at St. Joseph's and Central Colleges, Colombo. In 1900 he was appointed Fiscal Marshal of Pitigal Korale South, and Inquirer into Crime and Death for the same Korale two years later. He acted as Mudaliyar on various occasions, and succeeded his father-in-law in that position in November, 1906, and is at present the youngest Mudaliyar in the service. In 1902 he married Rosalind Prudentia, youngest daughter of the late Ambrosius de Rowel. He is Deputy Fiscal for his district, Chairman of Village Committees, Revenue Officer, &c. He owns some fine coconut estates in the Chilaw district, and manufactures copra there. He has also a fine modern steam fibre mill at Talwille, in Pitigal Korale Central, where sixty men are employed in the manufacture of all kinds of fibres, rope, and yarns. He owns house property and stretches of paddy-lands in various parts of the island, and his official residence is Wasali Walauwa, Waikhal district, Chilaw. He is fond of cricket and football.

W. L. FERNANDO.

Mr. Waruakulaweerasuriya Lodvin Fernando, Registrar, is the son of W. Roman Fernando, registrar and landed proprietor of Marawila, and Celestine Lowe, cousin of the late Gate Mudaliyar; and his grandfather and great-grandfather were both Mohandirams. He was born in 1858, became Registrar of Births, Deaths, and Marriages for Ajatacalau Pattu in 1884, and held that office until 1899, when he resigned his official position to devote himself to planting. He is one of the leading planters and best known men in the Chilaw district. His properties include Kudamanewaria, Battuloya, Dunkanawe, Narawila, Bandurawe, and Weerahena, all in the Chilaw district, as well as Kunbukgamulle in the Kurunegala district, and some fifteen smaller properties, all fully planted and equipped for the manufacture of copra, which is sent by canal to Colombo, where it is supplied to the leading European firms. He owns also paddy and forest lands and house property, and presented a large tract of land for the erection of the Convent at Marawila. He married Agnes Emerintina, daughter of Warunakula Aditta Arasanilaitta Alvino Lowe (who was appointed Mohandiram of the Northern division of Chilaw in 1854, Mohandiram of the Southern division and Coroner in 1858, Mudaliyar of Pitigal Korale North in 1869, and Mudaliyar of the Governor's Gate in 1881), and Michaela, daughter of Manuel Fonseka, Mudaliyar of Kalutara Totamune, and a descendant of the Andrado family, of which the history is given in the biographical sketch of Mudaliyar Simon de Fonseka. His eldest son, William Rovino, born in 1883, was educated at St. Joseph's College and Lorenz Tutory at Colombo, and now assists his father in the planting business. The second son, Alfred, is attached to the Treasury Department at Colombo, and the third son, Cyril, is a student at St. Joseph's College. The eldest daughter, Winifred Charlotte, married W. Timothy Fernando, son of W. Savriel Fernando, planter, of Marawila. Mr. Fernando resides at Winifred House, Marawila.

J. A. DE S. W. GOONESEKERE.

James Alexander de Silva Wijeyetunge Goonesekere is the son of J. J. de Silva, Gravet Mohandiram of Colombo, and Johanna Dias Bandaranaike, daughter of the well-known Gate Mohandiram Malwane, Don Adrian Dias Bandaranayke. He was born in 1867, and educated at the Royal College. He

THE LOWE WALAUWA. THE LOWE FAMILY GROUP.

W. L. FERNANDO. TIMOTHY FERNANDO.

W. L. FERNANDO AND FAMILY. WINIFRED HOUSE.

THE BUNGALOW. J. A. AND MISS DE SILVA GOONESEKERE.

commenced coconut-planting in 1890, and now owns several coconut lands in the villages of Marawila and Mudukatua. He is also superintendent of Mudukatua, an estate of 300 acres, fully planted and equipped. He manufactures copra, which is sent along the canal to the Colombo market, and buys coconuts in large quantities from neighbouring plantations. He is a member of the District Road Committee, the Chilaw Association, and the Agricultural Society. He married, in 1891, Evangeline Henrietta, sister of Proctor C. E. Corea, of Chilaw, and lives at Marawila Walauwa, Marawila

M. A. LUDOWYK.

Dr. Martin Alexander Ludowyk, son of M. A. Alexander Ludowyk, late head clerk of the Galle Municipality, and of Juliet Eleanor, daughter of Jacob Jerard Kern, postmaster of Galle, was born in 1867, and educated at Galle Central School and St. Thomas's College, Colombo. He entered the Ceylon Medical College, 1888, and passed out licentiate in 1893. Subsequently he held various medical appointments, amongst them being that of Medical Officer in charge of the Boer prisoners-of-war at Hambantota. In 1906 he was appointed District Medical Officer, Chilaw, where he has charge of the hospital and of the medical judicial work of the district. He is a member of the Local Board of Chilaw and of the

DR. LUDOWYK'S BUNGALOW.

British Medical Association. He married, in 1894, Joyce Constance, daughter of Vincent Van Dort, deputy postmaster, Colombo.

C. W. MUNASINHA.

Mr. Charles Welikole Munasinha Dissanayake, Proctor of the District Court of Chilaw and Vice-President of the Chilaw Association, was born in 1864. He received his education at Trinity College, Kandy. From 1882 he was engaged for ten years in the planting industry, after which he was apprenticed for the study of law with Mr. J. R. Weinman, now District Judge of Colombo. In 1895 he became a proctor, and has practised his profession as such ever since. He is a member of the Polonnaruwa Munasinha family. His grandfather, Don Simon, was the son of Polonnaruwa Munasinha and the sister of Panditharatna Appuhamy, who was selected by Rajadi Rajasinha, king of Kandy, as tutor to Prince Muttusamy; and he afterwards became Dissawa of Uva district. Don Simon Munasinha Dissanayake went to the Kandy district in the year of Waterloo, and was selected by the English Government along with Dassanayake Mudaliyar for the purpose of conciliating the people of the Uva district in the rebellion of 1818. The latter was killed and Don Simon only escaped because of the artifice of the woman of the house where he resided. She rolled him in a large mat and placed this in a corner of the room with another rolled mat on it, and in this way he escaped detection. He was appointed Lekam of the Kandy district, and his son, Don Cornelius de Silva Munasinha Dissanayake, the father of the subject of this sketch, served the English Government for forty-five consecutive years, and has lived in retirement on his pension for the last twenty-seven years. In 1848 he served in the capacity of Interpreter Mudaliyar to the officer commanding the forces in the rebellion of 1848, and fulfilled similar duties to H.R.H. the Duke of Edinburgh upon the occasion of his visit to the Kandy district in 1870. He still holds the titular rank of Mudaliyar. Mr. C. W. Munasinha's mother is Wilhelmina Welikole, daughter of David Welikole, and granddaughter of Kirawella Anthony Welikole, Mudaliyar, a descendant of Kirawella Ralahamy. He holds extensive properties in the Chilaw and Puttalam districts. Francis Welikole Munasinha Dissanayake is one of the five sons of Cornelius de Silva Munasinha Dissanayake, Mudaliyar. He was born in 1866 and educated at Trinity College, Kandy. Until 1904 he was engaged in mercantile pursuits, but since that date he has been engaged in planting in the Chilaw district. He married Angilina Elizabeth Ameresekere Ekanayake Teulabilleke, sister of James Charles Ameresekere Ekanayake, Mudaliyar.

P. J. M. FERNANDO.

Ponanperumage John Mariano Fernando is the son of Miguel Fernando, President of St. Joseph's Church, Wennappuwa, and peace officer. His grandfather, Andrew, held the same position, as did also his great-grandfather, Daniel Fernando, brother of Eustacius Mohandiram of Wennappuwa. He was born in 1876 and educated at St. Patrick's, Jaffna, where he was a theological student. He then joined his father in planting, and after the latter's death, in 1900, he was appointed Constable Arachchi of Wennappuwa, and still holds that position. He is the owner of some fine coconut estates,

FAMILY GROUP. CHARLES MUNASINHA. FRANCIS MUNASINHA.

P. JOHN MARIANO FERNANDO.

GROUP OF TENNIS PLAYERS.

MR. AND MRS. P. J. M. FERNANDO.

the principal ones being Issanmeditte, in the Chilaw district, and Wanamewala and Kattinahana, in the Kurunegala district. He also has paddy-lands and house property at Wennappuwa, and manufactures copra. He married, in 1902, Bertalina, daughter of the late John Fernando Muppu, and in 1906 he was appointed as the President of St. Joseph's Church, Wennappuwa. He is patron and founder of the Wennappuwa Tennis Club, and has lately presented the members with a fine tennis-ground and pavilion.

SOUTHERN PROVINCE.

IN its broad aspects the Southern Province closely resembles its Western neighbour. It is a coast province, with as its chief centre an important port—Galle—and having within its limits large areas of fertile land upon which important planting enterprises are conducted. Progress, however, has not been so rapid nor are commercial interests so highly developed as in the case of the Western Province. Indeed, judged by the standard of revenue, the Southern Province has actually retrograded in the past few years, as the following table clearly shows :

Year.	Revenue.
1894	Rs. 1,150,759·70
1895	1,502,682·61
1896	1,525,656·91
1897	1,536,421·57
1898	1,514,460·68
1899	1,659,440·47
1900	1,599,481·11
1901	1,164,042·12
1902	1,354,723·23
1903	1,382,040·57
1904	1,275,223·25
1905	1,450,224·12

Various causes have contributed to the shrinkage of revenue receipts revealed above, but the main cause undoubtedly has been the diversion of trade to Colombo. Time was when Galle challenged the maritime supremacy of the capital, and seemed likely to beat it in the struggle, but with the completion of the harbour works at Colombo trade was gradually but surely drawn westwards, to the detriment of Galle, whose trade in time was reduced to very insignificant proportions. Now her wharves are deserted and "Ichabod" seems to be written upon a shipping trade whose traditions go back to the days of Solomon. If Galle's state is a perilous one from the standpoint of marine commerce, there is no reason to be despondent as to the position of the province. In the last five years the revenue has shown a marked tendency to increase, and this, it is believed, is no transient phenomenon. The great possibilities of the country are being recognised, and industry is feeling the vitalising influence of new capital. Rubber prospectors in particular have been quick to discover the advantages which the province offers for the exploitation of this most promising of tropical agricultural products. Land has been eagerly taken up at various points along the coast where the climatic and other conditions are exceptionally favourable. The Government land sales in 1905 were the largest for many years. In that year 2,162 lots were disposed of, and the revenue profited to the extent of Rs. 175,903·7 by the transactions. The "boom" still continues, and it seems probable that within a few years the Southern Province may become one of the most flourishing centres of the new industry.

In the matter of general trade the prospects of the Southern Province are also distinctly promising. The plumbago industry "is advancing by leaps and bounds," to use the words of Mr. C. M. Lushington, Government Agent. Not merely in the town of Galle but along the roads converging on Galle, and along roads leading to the various stations, may be seen the sheds and stores in which the plumbago is picked, sorted and packed for export. "The stores," says the authority from whom we have quoted, "are of all sizes, varying from the humble shed of the villager to the large stores of the wholesale dealer and exporter in which plumbago is picked, sorted, and packed into bags and barrels, and out of which may be seen emerging long lines of grimy men, women and children, whose faces, arms, and bodies shine in the sunlight from the coating of plumbago-dust with which they are covered." [1]

Another thriving industry is that associated with the preparation of coir for the market. In the coast villages "all day long may be heard the 'hammer, hammer, hammer' of women employed in beating the husks, and all along the roads may be seen men, women and children cleaning or twisting the coir into yarn. At some places the cord is twisted into stout cordage for shipping purposes, at others the yarn is woven into matting ; but the greater part of the material is exported in great bales. Fishing gives full employment to men and boys all round the coast ; lace-making is carried on by the women, and gemming and gem-polishing are also practised. The arrack industry, too, is an important one. In the Galle district there are 33 distilleries and there are 5 in the Matara district. The quantity of arrack distilled in 1905 amounted to 114,215 gallons, of which 81,461 gallons were removed to other districts. The industry gives employment to 1,320 men.

[1] Administration Report of the Southern Province for 1905.

The coast scenery of the Southern Province is very fine. It struck Haeckel, the great German naturalist, who visited Ceylon in 1881–82, more than anything he saw outside the beautiful hill districts. In his work "A Visit to Ceylon" he paints in glowing colours the picture which is unfolded to the traveller on the road between Colombo and Galle. "A most beautiful feature of the Galle and Colombo road," he says, "are the numerous river mouths which intersect the cocos wood, and the wide lagoons which stretch between them, particularly along the northern portion from Colombo to Kalutara. The former lords of the island, the Dutch, were so delighted with these waterways, which reminded them of their native land, that they adapted them to a regular system of canals and neglected the land roads. . . . Since the English made the capital high-road, the water traffic has fallen into desuetude. But they still afford a succession of pleasing pictures to the traveller as he is hurried by, with their banks covered with dense thickets of bamboo and lofty palms, and their pretty little islands and rocks ; the tall coconut palms tower above the undergrowth like 'a forest above the forest,' as Humboldt aptly describes it. The undulating hills in the blue distance supply an appropriate background, while here and there the high heads of the mountains are visible, and loftiest of all the noble cone of Adam's Peak. At the mouths of the larger rivers, several of which are crossed on the road, the smiling landscape assumes a graver character ; the sombre mangroves are a particularly conspicuous feature. The shore of these estuaries is generally thickly covered with them, and their aerial roots form an impenetrable tangle. Formerly they used to be infested with crocodiles, but the progress of civilisation and agriculture has driven these reptiles up the rivers. The finest of the rivers is the noble Kalu

Ganga or black river, which I afterwards explored for the greater part of its length. The lower reaches are as wide as the Rhine at Cologne. At the mouth stands Kalutara, a large village and the terminus of the railway. At the southernmost end of Kalutara a magnificent banyan-tree grows across the high-road like a triumphal arch. The aerial roots of this huge tree have taken hold on the soil on the opposite side of the road and grown to be large trunks, and these and the main trunk form a lofty Gothic vault, which is all the more striking because a number of parasitic ferns, orchids, wild vines, and other parasitic plants have overgrown the stems. Not far from the shore near Kalutara I found on a subsequent visit another wonderful tree, an indiarubber tree, of which the snake-like roots, twisted and plaited till they look like a close lattice, form a perfect labyrinth."

THE FORTIFICATIONS, GALLE

To the south-east of Galle is Matara, lying a little to the westward of Dondra Head, the most southerly point in Ceylon. Matara in Dutch times was an important trading port, and attracted to it much of the cinnamon trade of the Southern Provinces. Many remains of the Hollanders are still to be seen, notably an old Dutch redoubt on the right hand of the Nilwella Ganga, which here enters the sea. Matara still retains its commercial reputation, and about the town are many flourishing plantations. Dondra Head, a long promontory covered with coconut palms, is famous as a place of pilgrimage, and yearly thousands of natives are attracted to its temples. "These sanctuaries," says Haeckel, "have been alternately dedicated to Buddha and to Vishnu, varying with the supremacy of the native Sinhalese or their Malabar conquerors. Only three centuries ago the principal temple was an Indian structure of great magnificence, and so large that, as seen from the sea, it looked like a town of some extent; it was decorated with thousands of columns and statues and with gold and precious stones of every description. In 1587, however, all this splendour was destroyed by the Portuguese barbarians, who sent home enormous quantities of the precious spoil. It is possible to judge of the vast extent of this gigantic temple from the quantities of broken pillars which stand up from the soil. In one corner of the precincts a large dagoba is still standing, and close to it several Bo-trees, or sacred fig-trees. The remains of a smaller temple are to be seen at the extreme end of the narrow tongue of land which forms the southerly termination of Dondra Head. These are octagonal porphyry pillars, standing up lonely and neglected on the bare granite soil, and sprinkled by the spray from the ocean surf which breaks all round them. Looking westwards from this advanced foot of rock, the eye glances along the palm-grown strand towards Matara, eastwards towards Tangalla; on the north the view is shut in by the dense forest, while to the south it is unlimited over an infinite extent of ocean. The ship our fancy sends across the waters to the South Pole will find no land that the foot of man has ever trodden, and beyond that land again it would have far, very far, to sail before it reached another shore. If the ice-bound continents of the South Pole did not lie in the way, it would navigate unhindered the whole Southern hemisphere of the globe, and see no land till it should reach Mexico, near Acapulco, on the northern side of the equator." Beyond Dondra Head a tract of hot, barren shore begins, varied by stretches of salt marsh which extend beyond Hambantota as far as Batticaloa.

The Southern Province is divided into three districts, each named after the town at which the official headquarters are established. These divisions are Galle, Matara, and Hambantota. The Galle district, the largest of the three, has an area of 652¼ square miles, and an estimated population, on January 1, 1905, of 607,602. Its interests are mainly agricultural, but, as has been indicated, manufactures are extensively pursued, and sea fisheries are actively prosecuted along the long line of sea coast which the district possesses. The fishery enterprises have markedly increased in importance since the completion of the railway opened distant markets to the Galle fishermen. Indeed, such has been the impetus given to local effort, that the complaint is made "that it is getting very difficult for residents of Galle and other towns to secure fish of good quality for local consumption, and that the prices paid at Galle (at all events for the European population) are quite as high as those paid in Kandy, Gampola, Nuwara Eliya, and Badulla, to which the choicest fish are transported by rail. It is not possible now to obtain a good piece of sea fish for less than 50 cents per pound, and I believe the price in Kandy is only 30 cents."[1] In the Matara district the agricultural interests are of the first importance. It is estimated that about one-fifth of the total population (estimated at 213,840) are engaged on the land. About 40,000 acres are under rice, and there are 20,000 acres under citronella. The Weligam Korale is the seat of the citronella oil industry. In this area there are no fewer than 276 distilleries. Sea-fishing here, as in the Galle district, gives employment to a large number of people during the north-east monsoon, and is highly profitable. The Hambantota district is the least promising and most sparsely populated portion of the province. With an area of 1,013 square miles its estimated population in 1905 was only 111,107. Agriculture here largely takes the pernicious form of chena cultivation. This wasteful system flourishes in spite of all official efforts to discourage it. In the more legitimate walks of agricultural enterprise the district makes but slow progress. Nevertheless, land is being taken up, chiefly for coconut, citronella, and paddy cultivation, and it is estimated that there are now altogether 25,000 acres planted with coconut, areca-nut, and other fruit-bearing trees. The citronella industry here, as in the adjacent district, flourishes. There are 160 distilleries in the area, affording occupation to a large number of people. The sea also brings its harvest, while on the marshy lands of the coast salt is collected in considerable quantities by primitive methods. The last mentioned industry is hampered by the lack of proper appliances, and annually great stores of salt are wasted simply because it cannot be gathered in in sufficient time. Yet, in spite of all shortcomings, the collection in 1905 amounted to 164,532 cwts., and in the ten years ending 1905 the gatherings yielded 699,624 cwts.

In the Southern Province the system of village tribunals and councils has worked well, and a really intelligent interest is taken by the inhabitants in the work. There appears to be much encouragement for the future in the way in which these local governing organisations are being worked. On the other hand, the black shadow of criminality which overhangs a considerable part of the island is here seen in its deepest shades. Commenting on a report furnished by the Superintendent of Police of the province, Mr. C. M. Lushington, the Government Agent, shows in his Administration Report for 1905 that in the municipality of Galle and the four Gravets (or surrounding districts) the proportion of "true cases" of serious crime—that is, of cases which were found on investigation to have a substantial basis—was as 1 to 49 of the tax-paying community. In other words, there is one case of serious crime in a single year for every forty-nine males between the ages of eighteen and fifty-five living within the four Gravets. "Is it possible for any words to convey to the mind a more lurid picture of crime?" asks Mr. Lushington. As to the causes of this excessive criminality, the Superintendent of the Police in his report on which Mr. Lushington comments makes these significant remarks: "The growing independence of the villagers, especially of the lower castes, has been accompanied by a steady decline in the power and influence of the headmen. For many years the headmen have, through causes beyond their control, been growing less and less equal to the task of maintaining order. Lawlessness has been the result and, being very little checked, has naturally bred and increased until the whole village population has in many places become lawless, partly in self-defence, for in such places it is necessary for the villager to be armed and to be ready to defend himself and his property, especially at night, against the bad characters who abound. The extent of this lawlessness and the powerlessness of the headmen are well illustrated by the fact that the constable arachchi of Ratgama is the only headman who has been able to collect evidence against the bad characters in his district, with a view to their successful prosecution under Section 83 of the Criminal Procedure Code. Elsewhere no witnesses have dared to come forward." This reads like an extract from the report of a resident magistrate in Ireland during the land war. It certainly is a remarkable statement to find in an official document relating to a British colony which is often cited as a model of good government. Until a radical change has been effected it will be impossible to take a hopeful view of the future of the community in which such lawlessness as that described exists.

[1] Mr. C. M. Lushington, Government Agent Southern Province, Administration Report for 1905.

GALLE

There is hardly a place in Ceylon which, in connection with European occupation, possesses so much interest and offers such a fruitful field for the student of the more recent history of this island as the sleepy little town of Galle. For Galle has seen many vicissitudes and has changed hands more than once. First the Portuguese established themselves here, after many a hard fight with the natives; and then, just as the settlement had begun to prosper under this rule, the Dutch ousted the previous invaders. The Dutch held the place

LLOYD'S SIGNAL STATION AT GALLE.

for over a hundred and fifty years, to lose it in turn to the English at the time of the initiation of the present rule in the island.

The present town of Galle consists of two parts, the one situated within the belt of the

H. R. COCHRANE.
(Galle Manager, Mercantile Bank of India, Ltd.)

old fortifications, known as the Fort, the other embracing the outer town, and populated solely by the native section. The fortifications of Galle, as erected by the Portuguese and Dutch, even to-day, after a lapse of over three hundred and fifty years, present a grim, warlike, and imposing appearance, affording no room for doubt that the sea-rovers of these two nations knew how to build. The stone facing of the bastions, harassed by wind and waves for centuries, is in as good preservation as at the time of the erection of these massive defences.

From the present jetty, which juts into the harbour from a point of the fortified part of the town, the whole of the Master Attendant's shipping stock-in-trade may be seen in picturesque disorder. The main gate of the "water bastion" forms the principal point of admittance within the walls. On the side facing the water a British coat-of-arms of comparatively recent date, wreathed in fine representations of maidenhair fern and ivy, surmounts the ponderous stone gateway of some 45 ft. in thickness; inside, and above the interior gateway, is another finely executed coat-of-arms, dated 1668, and consisting of a shield with the letters V.O.C. (*Veveenigde Oost-Indische Companie*—Dutch East India Company). This shield is supported by two lions rampant, and is surmounted by a cock, the emblem of the town of Galle, the date being MDC.

To the left of this gateway is the old Dutch storehouse (*Packhuis*), where now the District Court, the club, and various Government offices are domiciled. The present police-station occupies the exact spot where the first Portuguese fort, "Aleza," used to stand, of which now only the upper and lower bastions, the covered way, and the portcullis remain. This fort was called by the Dutch "Swart Punt," which became "Schwartz Bastion" in English. This part of the fort dates from the year 1580. Where, in former days, tier upon tier of threatening guns pointed out to sea, an old muzzle-loader of King George's times, on a crazy layette, and two more modern muzzle-loading four-pounders now form the whole armament for the defence of Galle. *O tempora! O mores!*

After Fort Aleza, the next bastion, described as "Acker's Sloot," was built in the year 1789, and named after the birthplace of William Jacobzoon Coster, who took the fortress of Galle from the Portuguese in the year 1640. The whole of this bastion, together with the houses facing it, which formerly comprised the factory surgeon's house, hospital, and invalids' garden, is now occupied by the offices of the Master Attendant, the Kachcheri, and other Government departments. Further along the sea-front are the Eolus and Utrecht bastions, at which latter spot is a magazine in perfect preservation, and bearing the inscription, "A. J. Galle den 1st Z.B.E.R. (September) 1787." Next is a minor bastion on which now stands a windmill, by means of which sea-water is raised into a small reservoir, from which the carts for watering the streets are filled. Close by, and inside another bastion, is located Lloyd's Signalling Station, with a tall, tapering shaft, to which thousands of passing vessels report themselves in the course of the year. The finest section of the fortifications—the "sea bastion"—was originally built by the Portuguese in the shape of a single wall, and afterwards enlarged by the Dutch, and converted into a formidable defence of the town and fort from the land side. This bastion, on account of its size, was divided by the Dutch into three parts, known as the "Sun," "Moon," and "Star" bastions, these titles being retained to the present day. The beauty, grandeur, and solidity of this work, with its glacis, embrasures, slopes, and cunningly covered ways, are very striking. In the centre of the "sea bastion" a quaint clock-tower—forming a prominent landmark of Galle—was raised in 1883 by public subscription "to the perpetual memory of Peter Daniel Anthonisz, M.D., a native of Galle, in testimony of his skill and benevolence in relieving human suffering."

Modern-day requirements necessitated the cutting of a new gateway through the massive walls at the end of the "Sea Bastion" on the land side, and this opening now constitutes the principal entrance to the fort. The whole of the reclaimed land which now comprises the race-track, just outside and over against this gateway, and stretches in a green expanse to the railway station, used to be under water in former times. Thus, the fortress of Galle was practically surrounded by water in those days, being only connected with the land by the narrow strip represented to-day by the Matara road.

GALLE MUNICIPALITY.

In common with the metropolis and the "mountain capital" of Ceylon, Galle—the chief town of the Southern Province—possesses a municipal constitution. The system has been in existence now for over forty years, and has proved of the greatest utility in the improvement and development of the town. The constitution is governed by the terms of the Ordinance No. 7 of 1887, and its objects and purposes are practically the same as those of its sister councils. As explained elsewhere, the Government Agent of the Southern Province is *ex officio* the chairman of the Galle Municipality, and the Council comprises besides four nominated and five elected members. The area under the control of the municipality is in extent a little below seven square miles, with a population, according to the last census, of 37,165. This area is divided into five wards, viz., Fort, Kaluwella, Galupiadda, Hirimbora, and Kumbalwella. The roads have a total mileage of thirty, and in the Fort and in the principal residential wards lighting by means of kerosene oil is in vogue, though recently it has been proposed to erect a gas plant by subsidising a private company. The Fort Ward is supplied with good water from the Bikke reservoir, about two miles distant from the fort, while the other wards are supplied with drinking water from wells situated about three miles from the fort. The bed of the Bikke reservoir is 30 ft. above the level of the Fort Ward, has a depth of 30 ft., and covers 2½ acres. The work of construction began in 1890, and was completed about twelve years later, the total cost being Rs. 73,448·64. There are 3 hydrants and 11 standposts in the fort, which are open from 5 a.m. to 11 a.m., and from 3 p.m. to 7 p.m. The system of drainage is poor, but sufficient for local needs, surface drains connected with underground barrel drains, which open out into the sea, existing in the fort, and surface drains leading into artificial canals, which again finally empty themselves into the sea, serving the other parts of the town.

The chief officers connected with the Council are the Secretary, the Superintendent of Works, and the Sanitary Officer. Important works are in hand for the supply of water, the lighting of streets, the establishment of mortuaries, maintenance of burial-grounds, roads, and buildings in proper repair and condition; and for these and other projected schemes loans have been taken from time to time from Government to finance the constructions. The revenue for the year 1905 amounted to Rs. 104,897·25 and the expenditure to Rs. 110,473·50. The following comparative statement is useful as showing the receipts and disbursements for the ten years previous:—

Year.	Revenue. Rs. Cts.	Expenditure. Rs. Cts.
1894	77,471 96	73,417 68
1895	70,905 96	75,572 15
1896	70,009 98	68,053 28
1897	72,014 14	79,321 69
1898	80,797 16	83,164 72
1899	83,862 45	79,923 25
1900	95,249 19	81,923 92
1901	83,192 74	94,009 28
1902	91,652 67	92,535 45
1903	92,886 64	88,115 81

EDMUND ROWLAND JAYETILLEKE GOONERATNE.

The family of which this gentleman is a descendant was one of the oldest Sinhalese families in the Southern Province, originally coming from the hill-country in the interior. Don Bastian Jayetilleke Gooneratne, who was the last Atapattu Mudaliyar of the Southern Province under the Dutch rule, was appointed

THE FAMILY. MUDALIYAR E. R. GOONERATNE. CERTIFICATE OF APPOINTMENT. THE BUNGALOW.

by Governor North to the same office under the British rule. His son, Don David, the father of the present Mudaliyar, was the Mohotty Mudaliyar of the Galle Kachcheri. On his mother's side Mr. Gooneratne is descended from the late Maha Mudaliyar Conrad Peter Dias, his mother having been Miss Catharine Cecilia Dias Bandaranaike.

Mr. E. R. J. Gooneratne was born in Colombo on May 6, 1845, and was educated at St. Thomas's College, shortly after that institution was founded by Bishop Chapman. The young man entered the Government service in the year 1865, as translator at the Galle Kachcheri, and rose steadily through all ranks. He was appointed Acting Extra Assistant to the Assistant Government Agent at Matara, and also held an appointment as Police Magistrate at Balapitiya. Subsequently he became Registrar of Lands at Galle, and he retired in 1897, after thirty-two years of unbroken, honourable service in the employment of the Government. In 1883 the Governor, in recognition of his services, appointed him Mudaliyar of the Governor's Gate, and a Justice of the Peace in 1896. During the year 1887 he travelled extensively in Ceylon, India, and Siam ; and in 1897 he proceeded to England as one of the representatives of the Ceylon Government for the Jubilee celebrations of that year. In connection with this occasion he was presented to the late Queen Victoria and the present King. After a visit to France he returned to Ceylon, and has since devoted himself to literature and planting.

He is a life member of the Royal Asiatic Society, the secretary in Ceylon of the London Pali Text Society, and the editor of several works in Pali. At present he is engaged in writing an English translation of one of the Sacred Texts of Buddhism. He is a manager of a Buddhist school, and has built, at his own expense, several residences for priests of the ancient faith. His family residence is known as the Atapattu Walauwa, a building erected at the end of the eighteenth century by his grandfather. Mr. Gooneratne first married (in 1873) a daughter of Mudaliyar J. V. Ilangakoon, of the Weligam Korale, secondly a Miss Tillekeratne. He has three sons and two daughters. He owns several coconut, cinnamon, and tea plantations in the Galle, Matara, and Hambantota districts.

FREDERICK E. ABEYESUNDERE.

Mr. Frederick Emmanuel Abeyesundere is the son of Don Pemyano William Abeyesundere, who was one of the leading native planters and landed proprietors of the Southern Province, also contractor to the Peninsular and Oriental Steam Navigation Company when Galle was still the port of call of Ceylon. He was a member of the Municipal Council of Galle. In 1898 he was invested by the Pope with the Knighthood and Insignia of the Order of St. Gregory the Great, and the inhabitants of Galle presented him with a gold shield, set in rubies, in honour of the occasion. The family formerly resided at Bentota, but during the Dutch occupation lived at Bope, in the Galle district. Mr. Frederick Abeyesundere was born at Galle, in 1868. He was educated at the Royal College, Colombo, and afterwards joined his father in the business of a marine contractor, whose office is in Prince's Street,

THE LATE CHEVALIER W. ABEYESUNDERE.
F. E. ABEYESUNDERE.
PRESENTATION GOLD TABLET.

VILLA LUCILLA.
MR. AND MRS. F. E. ABEYESUNDERE AND FAMILY.

FRED'S RUHE.

ESTATE BUNGALOW. — THE CHURCH. — CITRONELLA FACTORY. — TEA FACTORY

Pettah, Colombo. On the death of his father, in 1899, he took over the management of the business.

Some of the best estates of the Southern Province are owned by Mr. Abeyesundere, amongst which are Diwulana, in the neighbourhood of Galle, where coconuts, tea, rubber, and cinnamon are grown, and Fred's Ruhe, in the Dodenduwa district, of 1,200 acres in extent, which contains a fine estate bungalow, a fully equipped tea factory, and a citronella oil factory. On the same estate is the Church of Our Lady of Lourdes, which was built by his father, and where the latter lies buried. Mr. Abeyesundere's Malambekelle and Kahambiliagodakelle estates in the Kalutara and Ambalangoda districts are now being opened up in rubber. The produce of all these estates is sold in the local market. Mr. Abeyesundere owns extensive house property in various towns in the island, principal amongst which are Villa Lucilla, his private residence, as well as William's Lodge, and the Britannia Restaurant at Colombo. Mr. Abeyesundere is a member of the Municipal Council, Galle, Southern Province; and he also belongs to the Agricultural and Horticultural Societies, the Royal College Union, the Catholic Club, and the committee of the Galle Gymkhana Club. In 1892 Mr. Abeyesundere married a daughter of Proctor Adrian Sirimane, Justice of the Peace and Unofficial Police Magistrate of Balapitiya.

CHARLES EDWARD DE SILVA.

This well-known Galle medico is a son of the late Mr. Andris de Silva, landed proprietor, of Mirissa, in the Matara district. The doctor was born at Mirissa in 1868, and was educated successively at All Saints' School, Galle, and St. Thomas's College, Colombo. He joined the Ceylon Medical College in 1886, and in 1890 proceeded to England, where he studied at the College at Newcastle associated with Durham University. He then obtained the degrees of M.B., B.S. of Durham, and L.R.C.P. of London, and M.R.C.S. of England in 1891. After a term of work in the Newcastle Infirmary, he returned to Ceylon in 1891, and in the following year was appointed to the post of Health Officer to the Galle Municipality. In addition to his official occupations he has a large private practice at Galle.

Dr. de Silva resides in his own house at "The Firs," Middle Street, Galle. He is a member of the British Medical Association, the Galle Gymkhana Club, and the Ceylon Agricultural Society. In 1896 he married a daughter of Proctor S. R. de Fonseka, of "River View," Kalutara. Dr. de Silva owns the cocoanut, rubber, and tea estates of Mount Pleasant and Kadabeddewatte, in the Galle and Weligama districts.

ALEXANDER REGINALD SENEWIRATNE.

This gentleman, who is the son of the Rev. A. C. Senewiratne, of the Church of England at Hambantota, was born at Galle, in 1863, and educated at Richmond College, in 1895, and Royal College, Colombo, from 1896 to 1902. He passed tbe Cambridge Local Junior and Senior Examinations with honours, and joined the ranks of the Royal College Cadets in 1899. On the formation of the Richmond College Cadet Corps, in 1902, he became Second Lieutenant, and was promoted First Lieutenant in 1903. He is at present one of the Assistant Masters at Richmond College.

EUGENE GODFRED DIAS ABEYSINGHE.

This gentleman is a son of the late Rev. Abraham Dias, advocate of the Supreme Court of Ceylon, and who was a direct descendant of Maha Mudaliyar Nicholas Dias Abeysinghe, who flourisbed about the middle of the eighteenth century. Mr. E. G. Dias Abeysinghe was born in Colombo in 1868, and was educated at the St. Thomas's and the Royal Colleges in that city. He joined the Surveyor-General's Department in 1887, and remained in that employ for eleven years. He was then appointed District Mudaliyar of Bentota, which position he has beld ever since. In 1903 he was made J.P. for the district,

MRS. C. E. DE SILVA. THE BUNGALOW. C. E. DE SILVA.

THE LATE MUDALIYAR DIAS ABEYSINGHE. THE FAMILY. MUDALIYAR E. G. DIAS ABEYSINGHE.

and he acted as President of District Tribunals on various occasions. Mr. E. G. D. Abeysinghe has been twice married, successively to daughters of Mr. A. J. Perera, of Kotugoda Walauwa, in the Negombo district. He owns coconut estates and house property in the Kalutara, Negombo, and Colombo districts. He is a member of the Galle Agricultural Society; and in his capacity as Mudaliyar of the Bentota-Walallawiti Korale he exercises fiscal jurisdiction over a district of some 146 square miles, containing a population of 42,000 people.

CHARLES EDWARD DE VOS.

Mr. C. E. de Vos is the eldest son of the late Mr. William Edward de Vos, Crown Proctor at Galle, and was born in that town in 1871. He was educated at the Central and All Saints' Schools, in that centre, and afterwards at the Royal College, Colombo, where he won the University Scholarship of 1888, and left a brilliant college record behind him. In 1890 he proceeded to University College, London. He afterwards joined the Middle Temple, and matriculated at St. Peter's College, Cambridge, where he graduated in mathematics in 1894. He was called to the Bar in June of the same year. In 1895 he returned to Ceylon, and was admitted an advocate of the Supreme Court. He practised for two years at Colombo, and

THE CHURCH TABLET.

now carries on his legal business at Galle, where he was appointed Crown Advocate in 1899. He is President of the Y.M.C.A. and steward of the Gymkhana Club. He is a keen chess, tennis, and billiard-player. He is a landed proprietor, and resides at No. 26, Middle Street, Galle.

HENRY DE SILVA AMARASURIA.

Mr. Henry de Silva Amarasuria, the son of Thomas de Silva Amarasuria, Mohandiram, of Galle, landed proprietor, planter, mine-owner, and arrack-renter, and Donna Christina Jayasooria, was born at Unawatuna, near Galle, in 1872. His education began at All Saints' School, Galle, and was completed at the Royal College, Colombo. He then, for one year, served as Assistant Master at the Mahinda College, Galle. His next step in life was to engage in planting on the Monrovia estate, under his father. Having thus acquired a thorough knowledge of the methods of cultivating tea, coconut, and cinnamon, he took over the charge of the well-known Citrus group of estates in 1894. These properties he planted fully with the above-mentioned three products, and here he has also essayed the cultivation of the rubber-tree. Mr. Amarasuria personally superintends the work on these various estates, some of which are his father's properties.

The more important of these properties are

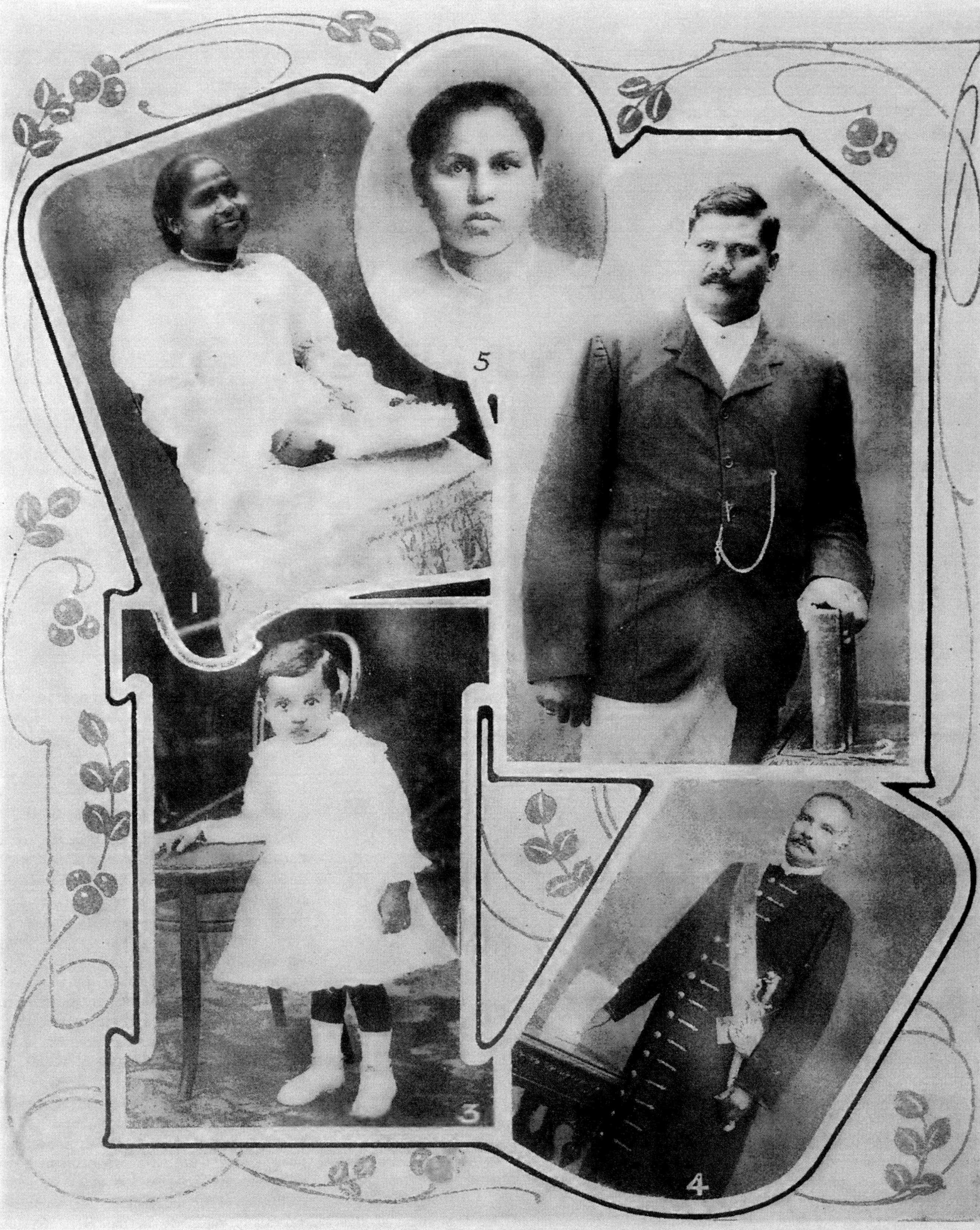

MRS. HENRY DE S. AMARASURIA. MRS. T. DE S. AMARASURIA. HENRY DE S. AMARASURIA.
T. DE S. AMARASURIA, MOHANDIRAM.

MONROVIA FACTORY, THE TEA FACTORY, AND THE WALAUWA.

the Citrus group, of some 750 acres, of which about 150 acres are planted with Para rubber; Olympus, in the Baddegama district, of 243 acres, planted with tea, coconut, and rubber; Monrovia, in the Dodanduwa district, of 950 acres, planted with tea, coconut, cinnamon, and rubber; Belligalena and Kooroologalle, in the Morawak Korale, of 240 and 620 acres respectively, planted with tea only. All the estates have residential bungalows, also stores and manufactories, turning out black teas, which are sold in the local market, where the marks of the various estates are held in high esteem. The boxes in which the teas are packed are also put together on the estates. The factory on the Citrus estate is an especially fine building, entirely erected of stone, and fitted with most modern machinery. The products of the coconut-palm collected on the estates are sold in the shape of nuts, while the cinnamon is peeled and baled ready for the market. Mr. Amarasuria owns considerable house property at Galle. He is a member of the Galle District Planters' Association, the Galle Gymkhana Club, and the Ceylon Agricultural Society. He was elected an Honorary Member of the Committee of Oriental Studies in 1906. Mr. Amarasuria is recognised as an authority on coconut cultivation, and his notes published in 1906 on this subject by Messrs. Freuedenberg & Co. were well received by the public. in 1901 he married Caroline, the youngest daughter of K. C. Juanis de Silva, merchant of Galle and Gintota.

THE ALBION PRESS. INTERIOR.

THE ALBION PRESS OFFICE, GALLE.

This establishment came into existence on September 2, 1867, the want of a printing-office being felt at that time, when Galle was the principal port of call of the island, and as such was pregnant with mercantile importance. The start was made with but modest pretensions, supported as the establishment then was by local patronage only; and although Galle has since fallen in value and estimation in the eye of the shipping public owing to the transference of the sea-borne trade to Colombo, this press, through dint of perseverance, has won its way steadily into the patronage of the mercantile and planting communities throughout the island, as well as that of the mercantile circles of the southern port, until it may now claim to be the premier establishment of its kind in the south of Ceylon, and daily continues to extend the reputation it has made for itself. With a machine, a press, three hands to work them, and a binder, the originator, Mr. M. Armstrong, entered upon his printing business; and, with the hope of extending his operations lucratively, he shortly afterwards exhibited for sale stationery, fancy goods, electro-plated ware, and such-like commodities. This auxiliary business proving remunerative, it has been gradually extended. Mr. Armstrong was assisted in his initial work by a Mr. H. J. Barton, both being present on the opening day. The progress of the establishment was gradual, but steady, and dated from the moment the presses first began to work.

Mr. John G. Bogaars, a nephew of Mr. Armstrong, and the present managing proprictor, was introduced to the establishment in 1882 by his uncle; and when the latter died he left in his relative an able and energetic successor. Mr. Barton continued in the business until his death, in 1894. The Albion Press now gives employment to nearly thirty hands, chiefly drawn from the surrounding villages—all skilled workmen; and many of the hands now holding service in the smaller printing-houses in the south were trained in this establishment. The printing department has grown in working capacity and efficiency, and has not only found favour with the local mercantile firms and the planting community of the island, but has also secured the patronage of the Galle Municipality, as well as that of many of the Local Boards and Road Committees of the colony. The bindery branch is well equipped and ably worked, while the stationery and fancy goods department supplies many of the needs of the Galle public. The Albion Press is situated at the junction of Lighthouse and Pedlar Streets, the principal thoroughfares of the town. Arrangements are being made to work the machinery with steam power.

K. C. JUANIS APPOO.

This firm of general merchants, importers, exporters, and commission agents, who have their head offices at 92, 93, and 94, High Street, Galle, was established in 1880 by the present proprietor. The firm imports rice and flour from India and Burma, sugar from London and Bombay, dry fish from Bombay and Pondicherry, and exports coconut oil and coir yarn, mainly to India. They are the Galle agents for Messrs. E. G. Adamaly & Co., and several other Calcutta and Coconada mercantile firms. They import about 100,000 bags of rice annually and employ about 100 persons. Their branch in Colombo is at No. 92, Fourth Cross Street, Pettah. Mr. Juanis Appoo is an earnest Buddhist, and has built a Buddhist school at Gintota, which he solely maintained [illegible] years and afterwards handed over to the Government. He also built a Buddhist temple

JUANIS APPOO. THE BUNGALOW. JUANIS APPOO AND FAMILY.

at Gintota. His eldest daughter married Mr. W. J. de Silva, Proctor, of Ambalangoda, and the youngest married Mr. Henry Amarasuriya, the well-known Galle planter. Mr. Appoo owns considerable house property at Galle, as well as two fine estates in the Matara district, planted with tea and rubber. He resides at Gintota.

PATRICK FRANCIS XAVIER ANANDAPPA.

This gentleman was born in Colombo, on March 17, 1867, and was educated at St. Benedict's Institute, Colombo. He joined the Colombo branch of the Mercantile Bank of India in 1887, and remained in the city office of that institution until 1896, when he was

P. F. X. ANANDAPPA.

appointed Shroff (Head Cashier) of the Galle branch, which latter position he still holds. He is the secretary of St. Paul's Reading Room, Galle. Mr. Anandappa's private residence is Ananda Villa, Calegana, Galle. In 1897 he married Clara, the daughter of Antony de Rosairo, Mudaliyar of Puttalam, and grand-daughter of Simon Cassi Chetty, late district judge of Chilaw.

ARTHUR ALFRED DIAS ABEYSINGHE.

Mr. Abeysinghe is a scion of an illustrious family of the Southern Province, being the great-great-grandson of Don Nicholas Dias Abeysinghe, Maha Mudaliyar of Ceylon in the Dutch period. His great-grandfather, Don Abraham Dias Abeysinghe, rendered invaluable services as Guard-Mudaliyar of Galle during the early part of this century; and his grandfather, also Don Abraham Dias Abeysinghe, ruled with considerable ability the people of Wellaboda Pattu and Weligam Korale. His father, a distinguished detective, who died in 1905, was Administrator of Police for the whole of the Southern Province for a period of over twenty years.

The subject of this sketch was born at Galle on February 2, 1880, and was educated, from 1892 to 1897, at the Royal College, Colombo, where he passed the Cambridge local examinations with great credit. He subsequently obtained the diploma for teaching from the Department of Public Instruction, and joined the staff of the Richmond College, of which institution he is now a Senior Assistant Master. In 1893, while at the Royal College, he joined the Cadet Battalion as a private, and in 1902, on the formation of the Richmond College Cadet Corps, he became First Lieutenant, succeeding to his captaincy in 1903. He is now commanding a company of about seventy-five cadets. Mr. Abeysinghe holds the following certificate from Colonel Vincent, C.M.G., Commandant of the Ceylon Volunteer Force:

"Mr. Arthur A. Dias Abeysinghe has been an officer in the Cadet Battalion Ceylon Light Infantry since the battalion was formed, in November, 1902, and has commanded the Richmond College Company at Galle, with the rank of Captain, since March, 1903. Mr. Abeysinghe has taken part in many annual camps of exercise and is a keen Volunteer officer who takes an interest in his work and in the company he commands, and is well up in his drills.

"(*Signed*) A. C. VINCENT,
"Lieut.-Colonel, Commandant
"C. V. Force, Colombo.
"*18th August*, 1905."

HUGH HAMILTON BARTHOLOMEUSZ.

This scion of a legal family and son of Proctor John Daniel Bartholomeusz, of Badulla, was born at Haldummulla in 1884, and educated at the Royal and St. Thomas's

H. H. BARTHOLOMEUSZ.

Colleges, Colombo, where he passed with honours in the Junior and Senior Cambridge Local Examination. He was editor of the *St. Thomas's College Magazine*, and assistant secretary of the College Debating Society. In 1902 he began to read law under the Council of Legal Education. He was admitted an Advocate of the Supreme Court of Ceylon in April, 1906, and commenced practice at Galle. He is one of the most zealous workers on the committee of the Y.M.C.A. and the I.O.G.T.

JAMES SAMUEL EDMUND PERERA.

This gentleman, son of Mr. S. Perera Abeyewardene, of Galle, and Matilda, daughter

JAMES E. PERERA.

of the late Christian Jayasuriya, Korale Mudaliyar of Magam Pattu, was born at Galle in 1880. After being educated at the Richmond College, Galle, and the Royal College, Colombo, he read law, and subsequently became Proctor of the District Court of Galle in 1904, commencing practice in his native town the same year. He is a member of the Galle Gymkhana Club and the Ceylon Agricultural Society, also a sergeant in the "I" Company of the Ceylon Light Infantry. On his estates, Janbugaha, Karayaldeniya, and Kitulagoda, in the Galle and Matara districts, coconuts, citronella, cinnamon, and tea are grown, and he also owns large tracts of paddy-fields in the Tangalla district. His private residence, Herton Lodge, Magalle, near Galle, is the site of the residence of a former Dutch Governor.

HENRY ARNOLD KEEGEL.

Dr. Keegel is the son of the late P. L. Keegel, of the Ceylon Police, who was descended from a Dr. Keegel, who, under the early British rule, was Medical Officer of

Jaffna. His mother was the daughter of the late John Giffening, first Burgher Member of the Legislative Council of Ceylon, and a Proctor and Public Notary of Colombo. Dr. Keegel was born at Colombo on December 31, 1854, and was educated at the Central School at Galle, afterwards being a private pupil, at Kandy, of Professor John Hill, formerly of the Training College at Winchester. He

H. A. KEEGEL.

finally entered the Ceylon Medical College in 1872. At this last-named institution he won the Gomaraswamy Prize in 1873, the Government Prize in 1873 and 1874, and the Rajapakse Prize in 1875. He became a licentiate of medicine, surgery, and midwifery, and was appointed a Sub-Assistant Colonial Surgeon at Kandy in the same year. After holding several appointments under the Government, he proceeded to Edinburgh in 1883, where he obtained the diplomas of L.R.C.P. (Edin.), L.F.P., and S.G. After walking the Edinburgh Royal Infirmary and the Western Infirmary, Glasgow, the young medico returned to Ceylon in 1884. He was appointed a Deputy-Assistant Colonial Surgeon in 1885 and an Assistant Colonial Surgeon in 1887. In the island he successively held various posts at Kalutara, Colombo, Anuradhapura, and Jaffna; and on the outbreak of plague in 1896 he was appointed to the chief medical and sanitary charge of Colombo Harbour, remaining Port Surgeon and Assistant Colonial Surgeon until 1903. On many occasions he received the thanks of the Government for specially excellent services. In 1904 he was appointed to the charge of the Government Civil Hospital at Galle, and subsequently acted as Colonial Surgeon of the Southern Province, being stationed at Galle.

Dr. Keegel is the Foundation Secretary of the Ceylon Branch of the British Medical Association. He was editor of the *Ceylon Medical Journal* from 1887 to 1889, and has been a contributor to various medical publications. By virtue of his official position he is a member of the Galle Municipal Council. A Mason of the eighteenth degree, having been admitted a member of the "Coromandel" Chapter, No. 27. E.C., he is a founder of the Grand Lodge of Masons at Galle, and is a Past Master of Lodge Bonnie Doon, 611, S.C., also a Past Grand Officer of the Grand Lodge of all Scottish Freemasonry in India, besides being a Past Master of the Allied and Cryptic Councils of Ceylon. He is also a Knight of Jerusalem and of Malta. His hobby is literature.

JUSTUS SEXTUS WIJESINGHE JAYEWARDENE.

The youngest of the talented group of six brothers of whom Mr. Advocate Hector A.

J. S. JAYEWARDENE.

Jayewardene is the senior, Mr. J. S. W. Jayewardene was born at Colombo in 1881. He was educated at the Royal College, where he pursued a most distinguished career, carrying off nearly all the prizes, exhibitions, and scholarships of his time. Besides being President of the Royal College Literary Club, he was co-editor of the *Royal College Magazine*. He left the college in 1900, and read law under the Council of Legal Education. He passed out, and was admitted an Advocate of the Supreme Court in 1904. He is now practising at Galle. Mr. Jayewardene has published an analysis of "Holland's Elements of Jurisprudence," and he is rapidly becoming one of the leading legal practitioners in the Southern Province. He is a member of the Grandpass Association He owns estates in the Marawila district as well as various house properties in Colombo.

EDWIN LUDOVICI.

This medical gentleman of Galle is the son of Mr. Edwin Ludovici, retired secretary and assistant-chairman of the Colombo Municipality, whose ancestors came from Amsterdam, in Holland, and Mark Elbeck, in Germany, and emigrated to Ceylon during the reign of the Dutch East India Company. One of these progenitors became a military surgeon after the British forces completed their occupation of Ceylon, at the beginning of the nineteenth century. Dr. Ludovici was born at Colombo in 1865, and was educated at the Colombo Academy (afterwards the Royal College). He studied medicine in the Ceylon Medical College, Colombo, and became a licentiate in medicine and surgery in 1887. He was appointed District Medical Officer at Teldeniya, then Sub-Assistant to the Colonial Surgeon at Colombo, and subsequently, in 1894, Assistant-Superintendent of Vaccination at Galle. He resigned from the Government service in 1897, and commenced private practice at Galle, which he still carries on at No. 20 and 20A, Middle Street, where there is also a large dispensary. The doctor is a member of the British Medical Association and the Galle Agricultural Society, and is secretary of the local Gymkhana Club.

E. LUDOVICI.

Since 1899 he has represented Ward No. 1, the Fort, as an elected member in the Municipal Council of Galle.

FRANCIS ALLES.

Dr. Francis Alles was born at Galle in 1869, being the second son of the late Mr. Marian Alles, the broker of Messrs. Vanderspar & Co., who carried on an extensive business at Galle during the seventies. Dr. Alles's grandfather held the position of head of the Christian Chetties at Galle. The doctor was educated at the Catholic School, Galle, and afterwards pursued a course of studies at the Royal College, Colombo. At the latter institution he obtained distinction in Latin and English in the Cambridge Local Examination. Joining the Ceylon Medical College in 1888, he became a licentiate in 1893. Then followed appointment by the Government to the position of House Physician of the General Hospital, under Dr. Gavin; and subsequently Dr. Alles held the following appointments from time to time, viz., Resident Medical Officer, Convict Hospital, Colombo; Medical Officer, Welikade Jail; Additional Port Surgeon, Colombo; and Medical Officer, Agrapatna. In 1901 Dr. Alles proceeded to Europe; and in the following year he obtained the triple qualifications of Edinburgh and Glasgow. After gaining a practical knowledge of his profession in different hospitals in Europe, he returned to the island, and was then appointed Port Surgeon at Galle, and, in 1905, Judicial Medical Officer at Galle. His present office is that of District Medical Officer at Badulla. He is a member of the British Medical Association and of the Catholic Union and Club, Colombo. In 1899 he married a daughter of the late Chevalier William Abeyesundere, of Galle.

DAVID GEORGE GOONEWARDENE.

Mr. D. G. Goonewardene is a well-known lawyer of Galle. He is the son of Don Johannes Goonewardene, landed proprietor, of that town, and a brother of Mr. E. G. Goonewardene, a well-known lawyer at Kurunegala, in the North-Western Province. He was born at Galle in 1863, and educated at the Galle Central School, proceeding afterwards to the Royal College, Colombo. For a short period he was in the Government service, attached to the Kachcheri (Administrative Provincial Office) at Badulla. He resigned this position to take up the study of law, and was articled to his brother at Kurunegala. He was enrolled a Proctor of the District Court of Galle in 1888, and became a Notary Public and Proctor of the Supreme Court in 1897. He was appointed Crown Proctor in 1899, which office he still holds, besides engaging in private practice at Galle. He is a senior Proctor of the Galle Lower Bar, as well as the senior member of the Municipal Council, on which latter body he has represented various wards since 1893. He has acted on different occasions as Police Magistrate, and is a J.P. and Unofficial Police Magistrate for Galle district. He is a trustee of All Saints' Church, a member of the Galle Agricultural Society, besides being vice-president of the Galle Reading-room. In 1897 Mr. Goonewardene married a daughter of Mudaliyar Adrian Peries, of Kalutara. He is the leading resident of the Sinhalese community at Galle, and is closely connected with the progress and general welfare of the town. His private residence is "The Mound," Galle.

CLARK, SPENCE & CO.

This, the chief of the European mercantile firms in the Southern Province, was established in Galle in 1860. The business, consisting of the export of all kinds of Ceylon produce at the southern port, as well as the import of coal and other articles of commerce, is one of the most extensive in the island. The principal articles of export are plumbago—which

THE BUNGALOW. DR. AND MRS. FRANCIS ALLES AND FAMILY. THE PORCH.

THE BUNGALOW.
MRS. D. G. GOONEWARDENE.
D. G. GOONEWARDENE
THE OFFICE.

the firm collect in their large stores on the outskirts of Galle, where it is prepared, graded, and classified according to quality—coir yarns, citronella and coconut oils. These materials are shipped mainly to the United Kingdom, the Continent of Europe, the United States of America, and Australia. Besides carrying on the business of general merchants, the firm are agents for Lloyd's, as well as for numerous shipping, underwriting, and insurance companies. They are affiliated with the well-known business firm of Aitken, Spence & Co., of Colombo.

EXTERIOR OF CLARK, SPENCE & CO.'S STORES.

E. COATES & CO.

This, one of the oldest mercantile firms of Galle, was originally established in that town under the title of Charles Shand & Co. About the year 1860 it became Alexander Reid & Co., who traded as general merchants, exporters, importers, and ship-brokers. Messrs. Reid & Co. in their turn were succeeded in 1866 by Delmege, Reid & Co. In 1893 Mr. E. T. Delmege became the sole proprietor of the business, and the present firm succeeded him in 1897. The firm, besides holding various other agencies, are the Galle representatives of the British-India Steam Navigation Company and of the Asiatic Petroleum Company. Messrs. E. Coates & Co. export coconut and citronella oil, the latter of which is manufactured by the planters in the province, collected at the firm's stores, and, after being thoroughly filtered, made ready for shipment. The test used for oil is the well-known Schimmel's spirit test, and the firm have acquired a high reputation for the excellence of their oil exports. They employ some 50 hands on their premises. The partners of the firm are members of the Chamber of Commerce.

Mr. Edward Coates, the senior partner, after having received a commercial training with a Liverpool firm, came to Ceylon in 1876, and joined the firm as a junior assistant, eventually purchasing the business right out in 1897. Mr. Samuel Hage Titley is also a partner in the concern. The exports are principally shipped to the United Kingdom, New York, Hamburg, and various Australian ports.

E. COATES.

ABRAHAM DIAS ABEYESINGHE.

This Proctor of Galle is a son of the late Rev. Abraham Dias Abeyesinghe, who was Colonial Chaplain and Rector of All Saints' Church, Colombo. The latter reverend gentleman was a direct descendant of Nicholas Dias Abeyesinghe, who was Maha Mudaliyar under the Dutch Government about the middle of the eighteenth century. The present Mr. Abeyesinghe was born in Colombo in 1874, and was educated at St. Thomas's College. He then read law under the Council of Legal Education, and passed as a Proctor of the District Court in 1899, being now engaged in legal practice at Galle. In 1903 he married a daughter of Gate Mudaliyar E. R. Gooneratne, of Galle, and resides at Guardia Walauwa, in Galle, the ancestral home of his family, erected in 1712.

A. DIAS ABEYESINGHE.

CHARLES P. HAYLEY & CO.

This firm, which is one of the few European concerns in the town of Galle, was established in 1878, and carries on business as exporters of Ceylon produce, general shippers, and estate agents. They export plumbago, tea, cinnamon, cinnamon oil (both from leaf and bark), citronella oil, lemongrass oil, coconut oil, rubber, and coir yarn. Of the last-mentioned article they are the largest exporters from Ceylon. The coir yarn shipped by the firm is principally directed to their London correspondents, Messrs. Harrison & Johnson, of

CHARLES P. HAYLEY & CO.

1. C. P. Hayley.
2. Coiling Coir Yarn.
3. Coir Yarn for Shipment.
4. Coir Yarn Baling Press.
5. Coir Yarn Store.
6. Rubber Nursery, Hillside Estate.
7. Rubber Mangle, Hillside Estate.
8. Tapping Rubber.
9. Young Rubber Trees.

No. 9, Trinity Square, E.C.; and their marks are well known in Hamburg, Genoa, Venice, Trieste, Amsterdam, Rotterdam, Antwerp, Havre and Marseilles. In addition, Messrs. Chas. P. Hayley & Co. maintain direct shipments to Adelaide, Melbourne, Sydney, Brisbane, Dunedin, Christchurch, Lyttelton, Hobart, and Shanghai. They count the chief and oldest importers throughout Australasia among their regular correspondents. The coir yarn is received from native dealers, who, in turn, collect it in small quantities from the villagers. After being sorted and classified, it is packed into ballots, coils, or bales for export. Some 200 men and women are engaged in the operations of the firm. Messrs. Hayley & Co.'s private test for citronella oil enables them to aim at a higher standard of quality than that required to satisfy the ordinary well-known Schimmel test; but adulteration is so freely practised by the natives that unfortunately they have often to be content with the minimum standard of purity. Their exhibits for yarn and essential oils at the Chicago, Paris, and St. Louis Exhibitions have, in all cases, been awarded gold medals.

Mr. Charles Pickering Hayley was born in 1848, and came to Ceylon in 1869. In 1893 and 1901 respectively, his sons, Alec C. Hayley and Stewart Pickering, Hayley joined him as assistants, and the former, in the beginning of 1905, was admitted a partner in the firm. Mr. C. P. Hayley is largely interested in the Southern Ceylon Tea and Rubber Company. He is Consular Agent for Austro-Hungary, a Government nominated member of the Galle Municipal Council, a member of the committee of the Galle Planters' Association and of the Ceylon Agricultural Society, and a member of many of the clubs in the island. The firm are members of the Chambers of Commerce of both Galle and Colombo. Mr. Hayley also owns tea and rubber estates in the vicinity of Galle.

MUDALIYAR D. A. GOONERATNE AND SONS. THE RESIDENCE.

MATARA DISTRICT.

DAVID ABRAHAM WIJEYEWICKREME GOONERATNE, Mudaliyar.

As early as in 1706, in the Thombo, the registration book kept by the Dutch authorities, in which names of persons and other particulars regarding them were entered, there appears the name of Gooneratne, that of a respectable and well-known family of Matara, in the Southern Province of Ceylon. In the year 1792 the Dutch Government appointed a member of the family Mudaliyar of a division of the Matara district in that province, and in 1801 the British ruler (Governor North) appointed another member of the family a Pattu Mudaliyar in the Hambantota district. Don David W. Gooneratne, who was a landed proprietor on a large scale, and a respected resident of Matara, in the south of the island, died there in 1846; and his son, the subject of this sketch, was born there in 1835. The latter was educated at the Government school at Matara, and afterwards at St. Thomas's School, Colombo, under the late Mr. J. R. Blake. He entered the Government service at an early age, and held appointments as Interpreter to the Courts at Matara and Tangalla, and that of the Deputy Queen's Advocate at Galle. He was head-clerk of the Fiscal Office of the latter town in 1861. Three years later he was made Mohotty Mudaliyar of the Galle Kachcheri. He filled the office of Deputy-Fiscal at Matara, held the additional appointment of Kachcheri

Mudaliyar and Assistant Superintendent of the prison at Matara, and on Queen's birthday, 1892, was made a Mudaliyar of the Governor's Gate.

In 1898 Mr. Gooneratne retired from the Government service, after forty-four years of unbroken, faithful performance of his duties, during which he won the universal respect of both the Government and the public. He now resides at the well-known Walauwa of the family at Matara, where he is a warden of St. Thomas's Church at Nupe (Church of England). He is a member of the Irrigation and District Road Committees of Matara.

Mr. Gooneratne owns estates planted with cinnamon and coconut in the Matara district. In 1872 he married Georgiana Caroline, daughter of Hendrick de Saram Wijeysisiwardene, Mudaliyar of Weligam Korale. One of his sons is a Proctor of the District Court at Matara, and the other a President of the Village Tribunal, Wellaboda Pattu. His daughter is married to a grandson of the late Mudaliyar of Weligam Korale. In 1904 Mr. Gooneratne was honoured by a special visit from H.R.H. Princess Louise of Schleswig-Holstein, accompanied by Sir Henry and Lady Blake.

EDWARD JUSTIN BUULTJENS.

The son of Proctor John Buultjens, of Matara, in the south of Ceylon, Mr. Edward Justin Buultjens was educated privately under the Rev. J. S. Lyle, and subsequently at St. Thomas's College, Colombo. At the latter institution he won the Calcutta University entrance prize. Leaving school, he was articled to Mr. J. H. Ernst, of Matara, for the study of law, and became a Proctor of the District Court in 1886. He has practised his profession at Matara ever since. He was on the Local Board for that town for some time. Mr. Buultjens owns extensive estates planted with coconut, cinnamon, and citronella, as well as tracts of paddy-fields. He is now opening up plantations in rubber.

E. J. BUULTJENS.

DAVID MARTIN SAMARAWEERA.

Mr. David Martin Samaraweera, the sixth son of Weligama Samaraweera Patabendige Don Theodoris de Silva, notary public and estate owner, and Donna Carlina Abeyewickreme, is one of the most important planters south of Galle. He was born at Ahangama in 1855, and after a private educational training he acquired a thorough knowledge of coconut, cinnamon, and citronella planting on his father's properties, the Induramawille and Rosmead estates. In 1882 he took over from his father the Mulanehewa Udukare estate, quite a small

D. M. SAMARAWEERA'S CITRONELLA FIELDS, ENGINE TANK, AND BARRELS.

MOHANDIRAM D. M. SAMARAWEERA AND FAMILY, THE RESIDENCE, AND MOTOR CAR.

property, and started planting on his own account. In course of time he has acquired considerable properties, and now owns the Charley Mount estate, 1,000 acres in extent, at Udukare in the Weligam Korale; the Hulandaivu estate of 700 acres in the Morawak Korale; the Johnny Dale estate, 75 acres, at Malinbedde, in the Weligam Korale; and the Miriswatte estate of 300 acres at Tangalla, as well as various other smaller properties in the Southern Province. Upon these estates are grown coconut, cinnamon, and citronella principally, but also a small amount of tea. At Charley Mount gumming has been carried on with great success, alexandrites totalling 2,856 carats having been found there, including the largest stone ever found in Ceylon, which realised Rs. 50,000. His father was the first planter to grow citronella in the Southern Province, and the subject of this sketch has gone in largely for cultivating this commodity, and was awarded a silver medal at Matara and at the St. Louis Exhibition for exhibits of citronella and citronella oil. Sir Arthur Gordon appointed him Mohandiram in recognition of his services in the organisation and distribution of relief to the distressed after the flood at Denepitiya in 1889. He has been Deputy Coroner of Weligam Korale since 1884, and became inquirer into death for the same district in 1897. He has now, however, resigned all his official appointments, and devotes himself entirely to planting affairs. He is a Buddhist, and is the manager of the Siddaritta Buddhist School at Weligama and of the Mirissa Buddhist School for Girls. He is also a trustee of several Buddhist temples, and a member of the Theosophical Society and the Ceylon Agricultural Society. He married in 1882 Widanegé Donna Gimara, daughter of Widanege Don Danister de Silva, planter and merchant, of Nalalagame, and they reside at Sirimadura, which was built by Mr. Samaraweera ten years ago. Their only son, John Martin, who was born in 1889, was educated at Royal College, Colombo, and is now undergoing private tuition preparatory to taking up planting, and their daughter, Lydia Margaret, married Walter Jayawickreme, Proctor, of Galle.

SAMSON ABEYESOORIYA.

Samson Abeyesooriya is the son of Thepanis Abeyesooriya, planter, of Weligama, where the family has been resident for generations past. Born at Weligama in 1881, he was educated at Richmond College, Galle, and privately by Mr. Lee, of the City College, and Mr. Harry Fernando, B.A. (Lond.). He entered the Ceylon Medical College in 1899 for the purpose of studying medicine, but when his father died, in the same year, he had to relinquish his studies and take over the management of the deceased gentleman's estates. He plants coconuts on several properties in the Matara district and at Talgahawatte, and citronella at Mahahena. He also has large tracts of paddy-lands under cultivation, and the produce of all his own estates, as well as large quantities which he buys from other planters in his district, are disposed of to merchants in the island. He has also established a regular trade in Ceylon produce with New Zealand, especially in Ceylon lace, which is made to his orders by local women and exported to D. O. Mackley, Wellington. Recently he has commenced prospecting for precious stones, for which purpose he has leased valuable land in the Morawak Korale. In 1904 he married Winifred Hannah, only daughter of J. A. Lewis, formerly Assistant Colonial Storekeeper at Colombo. The beautiful little planted island known as Ganduwa, in Weligama Bay, belongs to him, and it is his intention to build a bungalow on it.

MR. AND MRS. SAMSON ABEYESOORIYA AND INFANT.

GERALD EDMUND KEUNEMAN.

This gentleman is the son of Jurgen David Bartholomew Keuneman, Proctor, of Matara, in the Southern Province of the island, whose ancestors arrived in Ceylon some two hundred years ago, in the days of the rule of the old Dutch East India Company. The members of this family have followed the legal profession for several generations. Mr. G. E. Keuneman was born at Matara in 1849, and was educated at the Government school in that town, also privately, finishing his school career at the Colombo Academy (now the Royal College), Colombo. He was then articled to a local practitioner for the study of law, and became a District Court Proctor in 1874, and a Proctor of the Supreme Court in 1877. He has practised his profession in his native town ever since. Mr. Keuneman has acted as District Judge and Police Magistrate of that place on various occasions, and was the senior member of the Matara Local Board till 1903, when he resigned. In 1876 he married Alicc Harriet, daughter of John Henry Ernst, of Matara. Mr. Keuneman's eldest son, Gerald Percival, who was born in 1882 and educated at the Royal College, Colombo, as well as under the Council of Legal Education, has been a member of the Bar since 1904, and has joined his father in practice. While at the Royal College, Mr. Keuneman, jun., was captain of the College Football Club, and is a good tennis player. Mr. Keuneman's (sen.) daughter married Crown Counsel L. Maartensz, of Colombo. The second son, Arthur Eric, who was born in 1885, is now at Pembroke College, Cambridge, and has entered Gray's Inn, London, for the study of law. He was the University scholar for the year 1905. Mr. Keuneman, sen., was the first elected member of the Local Board of Matara. He is also a member of the District Road Committee of that place.

G. E. KEUNEMAN. ERIC KEUNEMAN. OLD CHINAWARE. G. P. KEUNEMAN.

VALENTINE DAVID GOONERATNE.

This gentleman, the eldest son of Mudaliyar E. R. J. Gooneratne, of Galle, was born in 1874, and was educated at All Saints' School, Galle, and at St. Thomas's College, Colombo. He joined the Ceylon Medical College in 1894, and passed out in 1900 as a licentiate. He entered the Government service by accepting the post of House-Surgeon of the Galle Hospital. In 1901 Dr. Gooneratne resigned from Government service and commenced private practice at Matara, where he is now one of the leading practitioners. In 1906 he married Clarice, daughter of Mr. Peter de Saram, Itinerating Police Magistrate of Welisera. Dr. Gooneratne owns extensive coconut plantations and paddy-fields in the Southern Province of the island.

ALFRED ERNST BUULTJENS.

This, the younger son of Mr. John Buultjens, of Matara, was educated under the Rev. Mr. Lyle, and afterwards at St. Thomas's College, Colombo, at which institution, in 1883, he won the Government University Scholarship and various other prizes. Proceeding to England in 1884, he entered St. John's College, Cambridge, and took the degree of Bachelor of Arts in 1887. He returned to Ceylon in 1888 and was appointed Principal of the Ananda College, the Buddhist institution in Colombo, founded in the previous year, as well as Manager of all the Buddhist Theosophical Schools in the island at that time. During his principalship of the college the attendance was more than quadrupled. He was editor of the *Buddhist*, the official organ of the Theosophical Society; but in 1899 he resigned the post and started planting coconuts and citronella on his Silverdale estate, in the Matara district.

Taking up the study of law in the following year, he was called to the Bar in 1904, sworn in as an Advocate of the Supreme Court, and commenced practice at Matara. Mr. Buultjens has acted on various occasions as Police Magistrate and Commissioner of Requests. He has temporarily retired from legal practice and recommenced his planting pursuits on his Silverdale and Batadela estates in the vicinity of Matara, and now cultivates coconuts and citronella, from which latter product he manufactures oil on a large scale in a well-equipped factory on the latter estate. He also owns house property and tracts of paddy-lands in the Matara district. Mr. Buultjens is a life-member of the Royal Asiatic Society, and has contributed to its literature various papers, mainly Dutch translations. He has also translated portions of the Visuddhi Magga from the Pali tongue into English. He is also a member of the Ceylon Law Society and of the Agricultural Society. In 1897 he married Sylvia Blanche, daughter of Mr. H. D. Andree, accountant of the Savings Bank, Colombo. His town residence is "Berylyn," Matara.

V. D. GOONERATNE.

THE DRAWING-ROOM.

MRS. V. D. GOONERATNE.

CITRONELLA FACTORY AND FIELDS.

MR. AND MRS. A. E. BUULTJENS AND FAMILY,

NORTH - CENTRAL PROVINCE.

In area, this is the largest of the nine provinces; in population it is the smallest. A vast proportion of the 4,047 square miles which constitute the administrative area is covered with forests or "park country" in the north-west, north, and south-east districts, and this territory is almost uninhabited. The general surface of the province consists of gentle undulations, with here and there isolated peaks or short ranges of hills. The south of the province forms the extreme north-eastern verge of the great central mountain zone of Ceylon, of which Ritigala (2,536 ft.) may be taken as the extreme sentinel, and is the highest ground intervening between the mountains of the Central Province and the very similar hills of Southern India. The inhabitants, about 70,000 in number, are Sinhalese, "approximating in manners, feelings, and appearance to the Kandyan Sinhalese. All the castes common to the Kandyan kingdom are to be found, with one or two castes peculiar to this province. Every man is a cultivator or proprietor of land, whether by caste he is a blacksmith, a goldsmith, a potter, a washer, or a tom-tom beater. None are dependent on their craft for a living, and it is only the two last-named castes who devote any attention to their hereditary business. They are generally remunerated by land. Thus the people of a Vellala village will give a piece of land to some dhobies on condition that they wash for them and attend on occasions of ceremony; so it is with the tom-tom beaters. The Kandyan Sinhalese is before all things a cultivator; all shopkeeping and trade in produce is in the hands of settlers, either low-country Sinhalese, Tamils, or the ubiquitous Moors."[1]

LOCAL BOARD, ANURADHAPURA.

Historically, the North-Western Province is the most interesting of the nine territorial divisions. As the great centre of early Sinhalese civilisation and power, it is a country of intense attractiveness to the student of the past. The spider now weaves its web amid the ruins of the ancient palaces of Anuradhapura and the temples of Polonnaruwa, and ancient Mihintale, which once looked down on a scene of teeming life, is now the centre of a wide-spreading jungle. But even time and the influences of the weather in a tropical country have not sufficed to wipe out the evidence that this country once supported a vast population. Not only do the immense ruins, fully described by Mr. J. Still in the special article on Archæology, attest this, but we have convincing proof of the fact in the marvellous irrigation system, monuments of which, after the lapse of centuries, still exist in the shape of stupendous tanks and mammoth embankments. This irrigation system was of great antiquity. Careful students of ancient Sinhalese history consider that there is strong reason to believe that in the fifth century B.C. Vijaya and his followers found irrigation works formed by the aborigines (Yakkus) who preceded them. However that may be, there can be no doubt, says Mudaliyar Wijesinha, the translator of the Mahavansa, "that the country was everywhere studded with tanks and ponds in the days of the former kings, and that there was neither lack of water nor population to till and cultivate the land." The ancient Sinhalese irrigation system is lucidly described by Mr. R. W. Ievers, M.A., in the valuable official Manual of the North-Central Province. "As the North-Central Province, although apparently flat, is in reality undulating," says this writer, "the ancient tank-builders took advantage of this conformation to make chains of tanks in the valleys. The bund, or embankment, was made to run into high ground on each side of a valley, the capacity of the tank depending not only on the catchment area, but also on the height of the high ground on either side, so far as it allows the embankment (*re-kanda*) to be raised. The spill (*vana*) was usually placed at the extremity of the embankment, and was either 'natural' (*i.e.*, where the surplus water flowed over rock or the natural surface of the high ground at the end of the bund), or 'artificial,' where an outlet was provided of masonry or rough-hewn stone. The surplus water from the spills of the upper tanks, and from the fields cultivated under them, supplied the lower tanks. The smaller tanks were fed either by canals of varying length, leading from the great storage tank, or from anicuts on the rivers, or by rain-water drainage. The great storage tanks of Nuwarakalawiya (such as Kalawewa, Padayiya, Huruluwewa, Maha Vilachchiya, Maha Kanaderawe) were formed by throwing an embankment across the valley of some large stream or streams, and dam-

[1] "Manual of the North Central Province, Ceylon," p. 89.

ming up the waters. All the storage tanks in Tamankaduwa (*e.g.*, Minneriya, Giritale, Kawduluwewa, Topawewa, Demitelakulam) were supplied by great canals taking the water from the Matale hills. In case of many, if not all storage tanks, it has been found that canals supplied them, even where they dammed rivers and streams. Many of these canal systems remain to be investigated."

In process of time these splendid works fell into disrepair. Much controversy has arisen from time to time as to the causes which produced the decay of this wonderful system which the genius of the ancient Sinhalese built up. The Central Irrigation Board, in their elaborate report issued in 1888, expressed the view that the ruin resulted from the abolition of the *rajakariya* or forced labour system. But Mr. Ievers, after a careful examination of the subject, asserts emphatically "that it was the perversion of compulsory labour from one of its chief original purposes, and the neglect to enforce it for legitimate works under the later kings, and by the British Government adopting their system, which occasioned the decay of agriculture and the wasting of population."[1]

Whatever the source of the mischief may have been, the deplorable effects of the neglect were beyond dispute, and the Government took a very wise step when they took the question of tank restoration in hand. It is not necessary here to detail the various stages of the prolonged and somewhat tedious discussions which preceded the adoption of a definite policy. It suffices for our purpose to note that the culminating point in the movement was reached in February, 1888, when Sir Arthur Gordon, the then Governor, in the presence of a great assembly of the leading men of the province and many visitors, laid the foundation stone of a memorial commemorating the restoration of the Kalawewa tank of the Yoda Ela canal, at a total cost of Rs. 645,833. This great public work has restored to usefulness one of the most splendid and historic of the ancient reservoirs. Walawewa has been identified with the Lake Megisba of Pliny, though it is thought that Minneriya may dispute the claim. It is mentioned in the Mahavansa as amongst the tanks which King Parakrama Bahu I. repaired in the twelfth century. The modern history of the tank begins in 1832, when an official inspection of the work was made by Major Forbes and Mr. George Turnour. Mr. Turnour subsequently described the ancient spill wall as "one of the most stupendous monuments of misapplied human labour in the island." But he wrote without adequate knowledge, and the best refutation of his view is the fact that in the restoration work the ancient spill has been retained untouched. An interesting account of the tank was given by Mr. Fisher, Government Agent, in a report written at the period of the restoration. "This magnificent reservoir occupies," he wrote, "a very commanding position in the south of the province, and just to the north of the Dambulla rock. It receives the drainage of 240 square miles of mountainous country by three inflowing streams—the Beligamu, Dambulu, and Mirisgoni Oyas—which combine and issue at the great breach forming from this point the Kala Oya river, which widens to 800 ft. when flooded. The rills of the sluices are 400 ft. above sea-level, and all the land lying on both banks of the river, till the sea is reached, is practically within the scope of the tank, its irrigating power being only limited by the discharge of the sluices and the quantity of water stored. The bund of the tank, which is 5½ miles in length, is thrown across the valleys of the three streams already mentioned. It is of stupendous size, the height in places being 65 ft., the base width 250 ft., and the top width 20 ft. The whole face of the bund is covered by a stone revetment, appropriately designated *relapanawa*, or 'ripple band' by the Sinhalese, its purpose being to resist the action of constant wave play, which would inevitably eat into and destroy any dam not similarly protected. The bund is pierced by four sluices, three placed in the Kalawewa and one in the Baluluwewa bund. The first of these supplied Yoda Ela, running north to Anuradhapura, and beyond into the Vilachchiya Korale; the second served all lands lying immediately below and in front of the tank; the third was placed at a higher level to water about 800 acres of high land, also in front of the tank; and the fourth supplied from Baluwewa a second Yoda Ela, leading in a westerly direction for about 16 miles, and irrigating some thirty villages lying on the left bank of the Kala Oya river down to its junction with the Siyambalagamu Oya. . . . The area of the tank with 20 ft. head of water is 4,425 acres, its cubical capacity 1,907,000,000 ft., and its contour 32 miles."

Outrivalling the Walawewa tank in natural charm is the famous Minneriya Lake, situated in the south-east portion of the province. Its sylvan beauties were acclaimed by Sir Emerson Tennent, who likened the great expanse of water, with its hills and overhanging woods, to Killarney "warmed and illumined by an Eastern sun." The tank was formed by Maha Sen, A.D. 275, and 200,000 acres of ground were brought within the scope of the scheme. The whole of the ancient irrigation system of the North Central Province is well worthy of attention, alike from the standpoint of the scientific investigator and the curious traveller who wishes to make himself acquainted with the monuments of an ancient civilisation.

The capital of the province, the headquarters of the administration and the chief centre of what business life there is, is Anuradhapura. This is now an insignificant town, with a population only of 3,672, but it is a centre of absorbing historical interest. Its many splendid relics of antiquity are described at length by Mr. Still in the Archæological section of this work, and it is not necessary to deal further with the subject here. A brief reference may, however, be made to the history of the city as the seat of the Sinhalese power. Authorities are divided as to the exact date at which Anuradhapura was founded, but there is little question that it must have been very considerable in size when fixed upon as a capital, 437 B.C. "For the king appointed a Nagaraguttika to regulate municipal affairs, under whom were 500 low-caste men as scavengers, with 200 night watchers or guards, whilst 150 others superintended the carrying of dead bodies, with as many more at the cemetery."[1] Fa Hian, the Chinese Buddhist pilgrim who visited the city in the reign of Mahahama (415–434 A.D.), describes it "as being inhabited by numerous magistrates, nobles, and merchants engaged in foreign commerce. The houses were handsome, and the edifices well ornamented. The streets and roads were broad and straight, and at all the crossings were built lecture rooms or halls for preaching in." In the ninth century the city was seized and plundered by the Malabars, but the damage done was to some extent repaired. In the reign of Mahinda V. (1001 A.D.) the invaders

W. C. PRICE.
(Provincial Engineer)

[1] "Manual of the North-Western Province," p. 140.

[1] "Manual of the North-Central Province," p. 23.

from India sacked the city, and from this attack the place never entirely recovered. Knighton, in his "History of Ceylon," cites the following poetical description given by a native writer of

G. S. SAXTON.
(Government Agent.)

the aspect of the city before this second assault upon it: "This magnificent city is refulgent from the numerous temples and palaces, whose golden pinnacles glitter in the sky. The sides of its streets are strewed with black sand, whilst the middle is sprinkled with white; they are spanned by arches of bending wood bearing flags of gold and silver, whilst vessels of the same metals containing flowers are observed on either side. In niches placed for the purpose are statues holding lamps. Elephants, horses, carts, and multitudes of people are ever to be seen passing and repassing. There are dancers, jugglers, and musicians of all kinds and of all nations, the latter performing on chank shells ornamented with gold. The city is 4 *gaws* (16 miles) in length from north to south, and the same in breadth from east to west. The principal streets are Moon Street, Great King Street, Bullock Street, and River Street, all of them of immense extent, and some containing 11,000 houses; to enumerate the smaller ones would be impossible." King Parakrama Bahu restored the city in the twelfth century, but the seeds of decay had been sown, and the efforts of this resourceful ruler only tended to prolong for a time the active life of the place. Its deposition from its high estate was doubtless hastened by the growth of the rival capital of Polonnaruwa. With the record of Parakrama Bahu's restorations Anuradhapura vanishes practically from history. "The date of its actual abandonment is unknown. A few scattered notices of its name occur in connection with the Bo-tree, around which a few priests are said to have continued in residence, much in the same way as we found them when, in 1833 A.D., a small settlement was made and a resident European officer camped in the ruins of the ancient capital."[1]

At festival times—the full moons of May, June, and July—great crowds of pilgrims from all parts of Ceylon and from India visit Anuradhapura to worship before the sacred Bo-tree. "There are no houses for their reception, but under the grand umbrageous trees of our park-like environs they erect their little booths and picnic in the open air. As the height of the festival approaches the place becomes instinct with life; and when there is no room left to camp in, the later comers unceremoniously take possession of the verandahs of the public buildings. So orderly is their conduct, however, that no one thinks of disturbing them. . . . These 20,000 people from all parts of the country come and go annually without a single policeman being here; and, as the magistrate of the district, I can only say that anything to surpass their decorum and sobriety of conduct it is impossible to conceive." These words in praise of the peacefulness of the pilgrims, written by Mr. Liesching, a prominent Government official, in 1870, were rudely falsified in 1902, when a serious riot, resulting in the destruction of much property, broke out amongst the pilgrims. The outbreak caused a great sensation at the time, but investigation proved that it was the work of a few agitators, who were associated with the so-called Buddhist revival, and the general body of pilgrims had no lot or part in it. Nevertheless, the commendable reputation for peacefulness which the festival had always enjoyed was shattered, and since the authorities have deemed it necessary to keep a careful eye on the gatherings. Apart from religious pilgrims Anuradhapura is annually visited by increasing numbers of travellers from all parts of the world, attracted thither by the fame of the "buried cities." A Government rest-house supplies accommodation for the visitors, and the resources of this establishment are about to be reinforced by the establishment of a refreshment-room at the railway station.

In a recent Administration Report of the Government Agent is given an admirable description of the province from the point of view of material progress. "The general condition of the province," says the writer, "may be described as moderately prosperous now, with every prospect of much greater prosperity in the not very distant future. At present, with the exception of the town of Anuradhapura, and a few bazaars here and there along the principal roads, which are inhabited by mixed populations of Tamils, low-country Sinhalese, and Moors engaged chiefly in trade, the province is inhabited by an agricultural population collected together in small communities called 'villages,' each under its tank, and each separated from the other by a more or less extensive tract of forest and jungle. These communities are at once primitive and exclusive; the customs and ideas of hundreds of years ago still prevail; the 'village' is the villager's world, and all intrusion from outside is regarded with the utmost jealousy. There are about 1,100 of these villages in the province, with an average population of about 75 in each. Owing to the care which Government has bestowed upon the province since its creation, some thirty years ago, and more especially to the restoration of the village tanks, which has afforded a fairly constant and abundant supply of water both for cultivation and domestic use, the ravages of disease have been arrested, the people have been rescued from starvation, and they are now well-nourished and thriving. It is true that the climate is still unhealthy, the death-rate high, and that fever and parangi in their various forms still prevail; but these diseases are no longer so severe as once they were, and the people have more stamina to resist them. There is no destitution, and even the pinch of want is rarely felt. In most villages there are considerable surplus stocks of food-stuffs. The people possess large numbers of cattle, of which, however, they make but little use. A certain number of the buffaloes are trained for ploughing, and a small proportion of the black cattle are sold to traders for the Colombo and up-country markets; but, generally speaking, the cattle roam about untended and uncared for. Practically no use is made of the milk, which might be a valuable source of food supply.

"It is obvious that the future large development of the province cannot be expected from this primitive and conservative population They have all they require to satisfy their simple wants, they are perfectly contented and happy with their lot, and it is well that they should remain so. Besides, even were they energetic and progressive, their numbers are too few; they have at the most liberal computation not more than 75,000 acres under permanent cultivation under them, and there are upwards of 2,000,000 acres of forest and jungle still to be reclaimed. It is rather to the enterprising Tamil and to the intelligent low-country Sinhalese, from the congested districts of the north and south respectively, as well as to capitalists, both native and European, that we must look in the main for the opening up of the country. With rich soil to tempt them, and so many fields of enterprise to

[1] "Manual of the North-Central Province," p. 30.

be explored, there is every ground for hope that men of the right stamp will begin to be attracted as soon as the Northern Railway[1] has made the country accessible and the restoration of the magnificent ancient irrigation works—with which the country is intersected in all directions—has made appreciable progress. One or two of these, such as Kalawewa and Minneriya, have already been restored; others, such as Nachchaduwa and Maha Galkadawala, are under restoration, and several others have been, or are being, surveyed. No sudden transformation is to be expected, but progress can hardly fail to be sure and steady. Already the population and trade of the town of Anuradhapura have increased enormously, while the numerous inquiries regarding lands available for sale or lease which are received from outside the province prove that its possibilities are attracting attention in many quarters."

HORATIO THOMAS CARTWRIGHT.

Mr. H. T. Cartwright is a son of Mr. William Joseph Cartwright, who has settled at Bordeaux, France, since 1870, and is interested in the wine business there. The subject of this sketch was born in March, 1876, at Bordeaux. After receiving his education partly in France, partly in England and in Germany, and his technical education at the Ecole de Commerce et d'Industrie, at Bordeaux, he joined the engineering department of the Great Northern Railway, King's Cross, London, where he worked and received his training as an engineer for a period of five years. In 1899 he came to Ceylon to fill the position of Assistant Engineer of the northern extension of the Ceylon Government Railway. After the completion of the line Mr. Cartwright was made a District Engineer of the railway. Availing himself of a six months' furlough on October 3, 1905, he went home, and returned on April 3, 1906, and was appointed Acting Resident Engineer of the Northern line—which is his present position.

[1] This line is now open.

SINNACUTTY SAMPANDER.

Mr. S. Sampander, Crown Proctor of Anuradhapura, is a native of Trincomalee. Born in 1865, he was educated at the Wesleyan Mission School at that town, and passed the matriculation examination of the Madras University. He studied law, articling himself to Advocate Allegakoon, and having passed his test for proctorship, he was admitted Proctor at the District Court of Jaffna, where he practised for a short time. In 1896 Mr. Sampander went to Anuradhapura to practise, and in the following year he was appointed Crown Proctor. In 1892 he married a daughter of Kuttutambi, saltstore keeper of Jaffna. He is a member of the Local Board, the District Road Committee, and the Agricultural Society. Mr. Sampander has acted on various occasions—for nearly eight years—as Police Magistrate and Commissioner of Requests.

SOORIYAKUMARA WANNISINGHE MUDIYANSERALAHAMILLAGE LOKU BANDA.

In the year 1683 of the era of Saka the reigning king of Kandy granted certain lands, by a royal sannas, to one of Loku Banda's ancestors, known as Palipana Loku Nilame, in consideration of the valuable assistance rendered by him in defeating aggressors in the Southern Province. In 1760 the then reigning king granted to Sooriyakumara Wannisinghe Nuwarawewa Bulankulame Mudiyanse, the great-grandfather of the subject of this sketch, a vast tract of land in the North-Central Province, called the Nuwasagama Pattuwa, as a nindagama by a royal sannas. The family of Loku Banda to this day reside on the land granted to their ancestors. Mr. Loku Banda, whose father was the Shroff Mohandiram of the Anuradhapura Kachcheri, and grandfather, Ekanayaka Bandara, Ratemahatmaya of Kalagam Palata, was born at Bulankulame Walauwa in 1863. After receiving his education at Trinity College, Kandy, he entered the public service in 1883, being attached to the Anuradhapura Kachcheri, and was appointed Deputy Coroner eleven years after in recognition of faithful service rendered. In the following year he filled the position of Ratemahatmaya of Nuwaragam Palata and Inquirer into Crime. Mr. Loku Banda is now Chairman of the Village Committee and member of the Provincial Road Committee, member of the Agricultural Society, and holds the important and responsible office of President of the Atamasthana Committee, under the Buddhist Temporalities, by right of being the head of the Nuwarawewa family, as provided by the Ordinance. The sacred Bo-tree planted at Anuradhapura, it may be mentioned here, was brought from Magda (India) to Ceylon in 289 B.C. by an ancestor of Mr. Loku Banda amongst others, and the chiefship of the district has ever since been in his family. In 1884 he married Kahanda Tikirikumarihami, daughter of Veragama Kahanda Punchi Bandara, Registrar of Matale (East). Having taken a prominent part in the construction of the Northern Railway, the Government of Ceylon was pleased to present him with a medal worth Rs. 1,000.

S. W. M. BULANKULAME LOKU BANDA, RATEMAHATMAYA.

EASTERN PROVINCE.

OWING to the difficulty of communication, the Eastern Province is one of the least known portions of the island. There is no railway nearer than the mountain line of the Central Province, and the only roads of importance are from Badulla to Batticaloa, and from Anuradhapura and Dambulla to Trincomalee. Visitors from Colombo to Batticaloa, the capital of the province, if they are not wealthy motorists, have to choose between a long railway journey to Bandarawela, followed by an exhausting coach journey over many miles of dreary road, and a trip by sea occupying about three days. In the circumstances the province rejoices in a splendid isolation, which seems likely to become more marked now that Trincomalee has been abandoned as a naval station. The province is largely coastal in character. Its seaboard extends from Kokkilai in the north to the Kumbukkan river in the south. It has an area of 4,036 square miles and a population of 183,237. For administrative purposes the province is divided into two districts—Batticaloa, with an area of 2,871 square miles and a population of 153,522, and Trincomalee, with an area of 1,165 square miles and a population of 29,715.

ROCKS IN DUTCH BAY, TRINCOMALEE.

Batticaloa first figures in history in connection with the arrival of the General Joris Spilbergen in Ceylon, when, on May 31, 1602, he landed in the neighbourhood of this town and made it the base of his operations. The fortress built by the Portuguese was taken in the year 1638 from the Lusitanians by the General Heer Adam Westerwolt, and delivered to the emperor of Ceylon. It is probable that in the period prior to the advent of the European Powers very little was known of these districts of Ceylon, and the description by one of the Dutch Governors of Trincomalee of this portion of Ceylon as a totally uncultivated and wild solitude, and the suggestion that it should be colonised by Chinese and Japanese immigrants, serve to indicate that, with the wave of civilisation and foreign influence advancing rapidly over and across the west, the aboriginal tribes of the island were forced to seek shelter in the fastnesses of the Eastern Province, where, to this day, may be seen all the rough and untamed works of Nature—the dangerous denizens of the forest, the gigantic, but valueless, forest trees, and the "wild man" of Ceylon—growing and flourishing side by side in all their pristine savagery. Indeed, long years of occupation have made the eastern districts of Ceylon the home of the Veddah, where he still lives the primitive life uninterruptedly, except for the visitation, sometimes, of a "cute" and commercial Tamby, who seeks to barter the honey and the products of the chase which the Veddah trader specialises for the cheap gewgaws and imitations of German manufacture which are the stock-in-trade of these pedlars.

Trincomalee is mentioned in Johann Jacob Saar's "Account of Ceylon" (1647–1657 A.D.) as a well-fortified place with an excellent harbour. In 1639 a fortress was raised there, which was carried by the British in their second war. From the earliest times its advantageous position on the great sea route has made it a well-known port of call, and successive Powers which aimed at the conquest of the island first directed their attention to the capture and retention of this strategic base. There is a tradition that the Hindu temple there, which juts out into the sea, has within it a *via sacra* to the world beyond; and until recently fanatics, in the excess of their zeal, were wont to cast themselves into the abyss of the ocean below, from the terrace of the shrine, in the belief that they would thereby attain their emancipation. A strange superstition is that in the time of British conquest a foreign soldier, who had made his way into the "holy of holies" without the necessary purification, was hurled into the waters below, and may still be seen at certain times cursing his fate and striving to return.

Trincomalee, as has been noted, has been deposed from its once proud position of the premier naval station in Indian waters. Its downfall has been brought about by "the new strategy, which demands the relinquishment of isolated outposts which in time of peace are a source of expense and in time of war a cause of weakness." However much force there may be in the theories underlying these principles, it is a subject of regret that this splendid position, with its grand harbour, should no longer be actively identified with the Navy. Time will probably bring its revenges, and Trincomalee will once more take its place on the list of Navy stations. Meanwhile, the place may be commended to visitors as one of the most beautiful and interesting spots in the whole of Ceylon.

The Batticaloa district is famous for its irrigation system. Within the area are situated many fine tanks, which for many centuries have played a leading part in the agriculture of the area. The Dutch recognised their value and improved them in many ways, but they suffered from subsequent neglect, and it remained for Sir Henry Ward to initiate a series of measures which, carried to completion in the term of office of later Governors, have restored the system to something like its old usefulness. The Government Agent of the Eastern Province, in a recent report on this subject, makes an interesting reference, which may be quoted :

"Most people in Ceylon," he says, "have heard of the great irrigation works of the Batticaloa district, and of the vast extents of paddy-land irrigated by those works, but it requires a personal visit to the district to enable one to realise what figures fail to convey to the mind. A drive along the south-coast road from Kalmunai to Karunkoddittivu in Akkarai Pattu, a distance of 14 miles, and thence along the road to Sakamam tank, comes to one as a revelation. On the east side of the road are densely populated villages situated in coconut gardens, with here and there a large estate. On the west side of the road, almost as far as the eye can reach, is a vast stretch of paddy-land extending without a break, not merely for the 14 miles mentioned, but north and south of that distance. Nor is that the only stretch of paddy-land. All along the western shore of the Batticaloa lake are vast tracts of paddy ; along the north-western side of the Badulla road are the tracts irrigated by Rugam tank and its connected works, extending practically to the Naddur lake."

The Eastern Province is a paradise for the sportsman. Game of all kinds abounds in almost every part of it. The topic is of such perennial interest that it even peeps up at times in the prosaic pages of the official report. Thus, the Assistant-Government Agent of the Trincomalee district in his report for 1901 wrote :

"Game seems as plentiful as ever ; elephants, buffaloes, sambur, spotted and red deer, and pea-fowl are met with in almost every jungle throughout the district. It is remarkable that though year after year the number of snipe shot in the Tamblegam tract of paddy-fields is counted by the *thousand couples*, the number of these migratory birds never seems to diminish, and I think there have been more snipe during the present season than in former years. Bears and leopards are also numerous, one young sportsman bagging four bears and one leopard at a water-hole in a single night's watch."

NORTHERN PROVINCE.

ONE of the five original revenue divisions, minus only Nuwarakalawiya, added in 1873 to the North-Central Province, the Northern Province, from its commanding position, close to India, has played a prominent part in the history of Ceylon. Successive waves of conquest have broken upon the island from this quarter, and through its ports have proceeded some of the earliest European adventurers who were the pioneers of the movement which finally resulted in the "all British" occupation. Religious zeal, too, has set its stamp upon the area. On these northern shores landed Buddha when he came from India to preach the doctrine of Renunciation, and in his footsteps followed many of his leading disciples. Christian missionary effort many centuries later took the same line of advance. St. Francis Xavier's assistants planted their flag here, and afterwards the great missionary himself prosecuted his self-sacrificing labours on the inhospitable coast of the Jaffna peninsula. Still later the leading Protestant missions established themselves in the area, founding on enduring lines great colleges and schools, and adding to the tradition which conspicuously marks this province out as a centre of successful missionary effort.

In the prehistoric ages the northern and north-western portions of Ceylon were inhabited by the *Nagas* ("serpents"), on whose account that portion of the island acquired the name of *Nagadipa*, or the peninsula of the Nagas. Recent investigations have served to establish the fact that the word "Naga" did not apply so much to a species of the serpent tribe as to a race of people who deified the reptile and practised ophiolatry, and who were, therefore, contemptuously or otherwise, distinguished from the rest of the island's inhabitants by this generic term.

F. H. PRICE.
(Government Agent.)

From the account in the Mahavansa, the Sinhalese metrical chronicle mentioned in the Historical portion of this work, of a visit to Buddha by a deputation of Nagas, it is reasonable to assume that they possessed an advanced and a complete social and political organisation with distinct and independent kings of their own, who sat on "gem-set thrones," and constituted an important power at that early period of the island's history (*circa* 581 B.C.).

In the reign of the king Devanampiya Tissa (307–267 B.C.) the branch of the sacred Bo-tree is said to have been debarked at the haven of the north and a magnificent vihara erected on

STREET IN JAFFNA.

the spot where the relic rested, and Prince Rama, one of the escorts of the mission, was granted the whole of the districts of Jaffna and Trincomalee in recognition of his services to the church in this connection.

According to local traditions it is believed that a certain princess of the Choli dynasty of South India, who was born with a horse's head, was advised by the sages to repair to Keerimale, near Kankesanturai, the present terminus of the Northern railway line, where, having bathed in the sacred springs, she recovered her human shape. Subsequently a minstrel named Yalpannen came over from the continent and was granted the whole of the northern districts, which he called after himself, the term "Yalpana" being afterwards corrupted by foreign invaders into "Jaffnapatnam"—the city of Jaffna. In the hymns of Sampanta-murti and Suntra-murti, entitled Tevaram, reference is constantly made to the prosperous and flourishing condition of Jaffna in the early days of Sinhalese sovereignty, and it is said that "gold, pearls, precious stones, areca-trees, mango-groves, plantain-bushes, peacocks and apes" abounded everywhere. The first comprehensive account of the peninsula, however, is to be found in Mayilvakanam's "Yalpana Vaipawa Malai."

Jaffna has been, with few breaks, an exclusively Tamil country, and even when Sinhalese invaders carried their arms into the country they did not long possess it, but were repulsed by reinforcements which arrived from the neighbouring continent. It was the last stronghold of the Portuguese, the capture of which by the Dutch brought to a close the Portuguese era in Ceylon; and when, 175 years later (A.D. 1795), the British wrested the fort from the victors, it sounded the death-knell of the Dutch power in Ceylon.

The latter-day Jaffna is a very different place to the Jaffna of even a few years ago. Wealth is circulating and diffusing a spirit of independence amongst "the masses." The matter is touched upon in this passage from a recent Administrative Report of the Government Agent:—

THE LAGOON, JAFFNA.

"Great changes are going on in Jaffna native society, which are bitterly resented by the conservative part of the population. The (so-called) 'low castes' are becoming more rich, and having acquired property, most of them naturally decline to follow the old customs, by which they were prohibited from wearing jewels, riding in carriages, using tom-toms for marriages, and other social functions. Many of the low-caste Nalavalas and Covias become converts to Christianity, and the Vellalas know that the next step in the progress of the converts will be that of wearing jewellery and assuming Vellala customs. Hence arise petty prosecutions and squabbles and cases in court and demand for police prosecution, and often real riots and bloodshed."

That the improved condition of the people, of which these ebullitions are the outward and visible sign, is not confined to the capital is attested by the observations of the Government Agent in another report: "The villager in the Mannar district would a year or two ago," he writes, "have been unable to give the name of any article of food outside the very limited list of food stuffs which he and his forefathers have depended upon for centuries. The very existence of other varieties was unknown, even in the Mannar town, until quite recent years. An increased standard of comfort has, however, spread in the district, and 'luxuries' are now known and appreciated. The Moormen are the commercial travellers, and appeal successfully to the popular change, exchanging biscuits, condensed milk, and aerated waters for paddy, tobacco, and chillies." In a subsequent report the same point is emphasised: mud huts, we are informed, are being replaced by stone houses, more jewellery is worn than of yore, there are more vehicles in use and money generally is more plentiful. One idiosyncrasy of the people is their fondness for tea. At Jaffna there are tea shops (three) at the station, at the market, at the Courts, at the Kachcheri, and they are run at the festivals—in fact, wherever people congregate. The charge for a cup of tea is 1 cent, or 3 cents if more than the usual quantity of milk is required.

Next to the food supply, tobacco cultivation ranks highest as the most important interest in the province. "Jaffna cigars" are a by-word amongst the European residents of the island; but the locally grown tobacco, during the period of the Dutch occupation and also in the early period of British rule, had a good market in spite of a duty of 25 per cent. per candy, with an additional charge of ten janams for brokerage. In an official letter dated October, 1798, Colonel Barbut, the Collector, mentions that "tobacco purchased here last year at 30 rixdollars the candy was sold by merchants at Nagore at a profit of 50 per cent." He adds: "I leave you to judge on the profits that may arise from sending the Jaffna tobacco to Achen and Pulo Pinang, where I am informed the Malays overrate it so greatly that they will not purchase any other tobacco so long as there is a pound of it to be had." In recent years, practically the only demand for Jaffna tobacco has emanated from India, and even that has fallen off. Experts express the opinion that the locally grown leaf is of excellent quality, and that the methods of planting and irrigation are sound, but that the plucking is erroneous and the curing injurious to flavour. The leaf is actually made rotten, and hence the difficulty experienced in keeping the cigars for any length of time.[1] In 1902 a trial was made of curing the Jaffna tobacco to suit European markets, but the experiment does not appear to have had any encouraging results. Nevertheless, it is believed that there is a great future for Ceylon tobacco if the right methods are pursued, and the requisite amount of capital and energy is put into the enterprise.

ECCLESIASTICAL SEMINARY, JAFFNA.

THE FORT, JAFFNA.

The Northern Province is divided into three districts—Jaffna, Mullaitivu, and Mannar. Mullaitivu is comprised in the district historically known as the Vanni, a great tract of forest-clad country 1,864 square miles in extent, 71 miles long, and 60 miles broad. After the break-up of the Sinhalese power the Vanni was under the dominion of a number of petty kings of Tamil origin. These princelets maintained their independence in the face of the aggressions of the Portuguese, but the country succumbed to the Dutch, though the conquerors found their new subjects very troublesome ones. The Hollanders established a fort and founded a town at Mullaitivu, and this became the headquarters of the British administration on the transfer of the Dutch sovereignty in 1796. In the earlier years of British rule the Vanni was administered by means of Aumildars, and for some time it was under the charge of an officer subordinate to the Collector at Trincomalee, a Madras civilian whose title was "Collector of Trincomalee, Batticaloa, and the Wanny." In 1806 the Vanni was separated from Jaffnapatam and Mullaitivu was established as the capital. The administration underwent various changes until it was finally settled on the existing lines.

The Vanni country is thinly populated, and its interests, apart from the fisheries, which are conducted by outsiders, are entirely agricultural. The area is almost entirely covered with jungle. "Viewing the country from the top of one of the high rocks . . . nothing is seen but a sea of forest on all sides of different shades of green, with here and there a dark mass rising out of it, indicating the site of another rock of the same description. On the horizon are the outlines of one or two

[1] Administration Report on the Northern Province for 1901.

blue hills—Mihintale or some other rock of the North-Central Province. Not a village is to be distinguished, but in some places a slight break in the forest shows the position of a tank and its paddy-fields. Travelling along the roads, which for the most part pass through thick jungle, one is sometimes oppressed with the monotonousness of the forest, particularly where it is, as in some places, composed almost entirely of one or two species of sombre-looking trees, such as palai and virai. This is especially the case on the main road to Jaffna, where, as the jungle has been cleared back to some distance on each side of the road, there is little shade. The forest scenery on some of the minor roads, however, and on the old road to Mullaitivu is often very picturesque, with long vistas through trees standing like a series of columns on either side of the road, some of them with curiously twisted trunks. Every shade of green, from the darkest in some of the foliage trees to the brightest in the grass which covers the road, flecked with sunlight, combines to add to the effect. . . . As a rule it is impossible to get any extensive view of the landscape owing to the thickness of the forest. The exception is the maritime Pattus, where there are lagoons and plains bordered by large stretches of paddy-fields. . . Looking across the lagoons one sees a long stretch of water bordered on the horizon by a line of forest, to which distance gives a bluish tint. Sometimes in the bright sunlight the atmosphere seems to dance, and sky and water to merge into one in the far distance, with clumps of trees suspended as it were in mid-air, the general effect being very much that of a mirage. A sunset or sunrise seen across this flat country is often very fine."[1]

The chief characteristic of the inhabitants of the Vanni is want of energy. They never think of manuring their fields. Their ploughing is done in the most perfunctory fashion, and, except in the populous villages of the maritime Pattus, the Vanni villager cannot be got to work for hire, even though he may be in want of money, as he considers it beneath his dignity. They are also extremely conservative. Even though it is sometimes plainly to their advantage to begin sowing their fields at an earlier date than that fixed by custom, it is almost impossible to get them to do it, as "it is not the custom," and this is considered quite sufficient reason for their neglect. The people, too, are intensely superstitious. There is considerable belief in charms and witchcraft. Ulcers and other diseases are ills attributed to sorcery. On one occasion an ola was found fixed on a gate with an invocation to Siva written under a mystical figure, the object of the charm being to cause a separation between the inmate of the house and his wife. Mr. Price records that "acts of this kind are of frequent occurrence, and the village people fully believe in their efficacy." He appears to have thought the practice a serious one, and to have endeavoured to put a stop to it, for not long afterwards he seized what he calls "about 900 diabolical olas" in the possession of a man addicted to witchcraft, and bound him over to keep the peace for it.[1]

KING'S HOUSE, JAFFNA.

The Mannar district of the Northern Provinces, like the Vanni, presents many points of peculiar interest. The district has an area of 400 square miles. It includes the island of Mannar, which is separated from the mainland by a narrow channel, and seems to be a prolongation of the reef which, extending from Teniturai on the Indian coast, forms Ramisseram and Adam's Bridge. The history of Mannar is interesting. There must have been Tamil colonies at a very early period, and somewhat later, though still early in the history of the island, there was a Sinhalese colony at Mantottai. "There is a tradition of an Arab conquest of Tirukesaram, as Mantottai was called before the Sinhalese era, and there is no doubt that in very early days indeed—perhaps as early as the time of Solomon—Arab traders frequented the sacred city. Mr. Nevill says (I do not know on what authority) that from 100 B.C. to 700 A.D. this part of the world was ruled by the Maharajahs of Zabedj ; and it is not improbable that Sinbad himself may have seen the temple, which is said to have rivalled that at Ramisseram, but of which now very few traces are left."[2] The Portuguese effected a settlement in Mannar, and it was here that in 1545 the great massacre of Christian converts made by St. Francis Xavier took place at the bidding of the fanatical king of Jaffna. In 1658 the Dutch captured the island from the Portuguese, and were in turn ousted by the British in 1795 or 1796.

The district is divided into three administrative areas—(1) Mannar Island, (2) Mantai, (3) Musali—each under a superior headman, called Adigar. Each of these is subdivided into two or more, and each subdivision is placed under an Udaiyar, who is the immediate superior of the police, Vitanais—officials who exercise the functions of both police and revenue officers over one or more villages, according to their size or importance. In the Musali district is situated Silavatturai, the headquarters of the Pearl Fishery. "In ordinary times there are only a few boutiques and fishermen's huts and double rows of tulip-trees which mark the streets of the town which spring up when there is a fishery. . . . The only existing public building is a large store, part of which is used as a rest-house—a single room. There is a vault, or strong room, in which to lodge the rupees collected during the fishery. . . . There are several wells and an

[1] "A Manual of the Vanni Districts, Ceylon," by J. P. Lewis, of the Ceylon Civil Service, p. 9.

[1] "Manual of Vanni," p. 263.

[2] "Mannár," a monograph by W. J. S. Boake, C.C.S., Assistant Government Agent of the district, p. 6.

experimental coconut garden, which bears well, and there is no reason why it should not be extended. The land here is somewhat raised above the sea, and the deposits of oyster shells are in many places several feet in thickness. An attempt was made some years ago to utilise these deposits, and a shipload was

HINDU TEMPLE, JAFFNA.

exported to England, but the venture was not repeated. The Persian Gulf oysters are larger and thicker and better adapted for the button trade than our oysters, and they are not worth removing for making lime, even for manure—at least, I suppose this to be the case." [1]

Mannar has come prominently to the front of late in connection with the scheme for linking up the Ceylon railway system with that of India. The subject has for years been under consideration, and many schemes have from time to time been mooted. The latest, which is still under consideration hy the authorities, contemplates the construction by the Ceylon Government of a line from Madawachi or Vavuniya on the Northern line to the end of the island of Mannar. To meet this line the South Indian Railway Company would extend their existing line on the island of Rameswaram to the end of the island, a distance of 13 miles. The bridging of the intervening space between Rameswaram and the island of Mannar, it was suggested by the company, should be accomplished by means of a steam ferry, which would take the train bodily across from the terminus of one line to that of the other. But this proposal does not seem to commend itself to the consulting engineers of the Colonial Office, and has been abandoned. An earlier proposal, which emanated from the Ceylon Government, was that a viaduct should be built over Adam's Bridge, and a material link be thus forged with the Indian peninsula. But the South Indian Railway Company rejected this scheme on the score of the enormous cost it would involve. It is estimated by Mr. Neville Priestley, the agent of the South Indian Railway Company, that an expenditure of at least 300 lakhs would be involved in the construction of the 21-mile viaduct that would be necessary, and that to cover the interest charges on this sum an income equivalent to Rs. 2,200 a mile a week for the 21 miles would have to be earned. This is a rate far beyond the probable earning capacity of the line. The earnings of the South Indian Railway in 1905 were Rs. 222 a mile a week, and on the busiest section of one line—the Cuddalore-Trichinopoly section—the earnings do not exceed Rs. 355 a mile a week.[1] Nevertheless the bridging of Adam's Bridge, probably with the help of the Governments interested, is one of the possibilities of the near future, and when that day arrives Mannar, and indeed the whole Northern Province, will enter upon a career of commercial prosperity undreamt of by early rulers of the province, Dutch and British. One result of the carrying out of even the modified scheme will be to bring into the range of the programmes of visitors to Ceylon the world-famed Hindu temples of the island of Rameswaram, which at present are very difficult of access from the Ceylon side.

[1] Mr. W. J. S. Boake's monograph on "Mannár," p. 70.

[1] Memorandum on the Proposed Indo-Ceylon Connection, by Mr. Neville Priestley, Agent of the South Indian Railway Company, Ltd.

THE BISHOP OF JAFFNA.

The Right Rev. Dr. Henry Joulain, O.M.I., Roman Catholic Bishop of Jaffna, was born at Poitiers, in France, on September 24, 1852, and received his education at the Montmorillon and Poitiers Seminaries. He joined the Congregation of Oblates of Mary in 1880, and was ordained priest at Poitiers in 1875. He arrived

RT. REV. DR. H. JOULAIN, O.M.I.
(Bishop of Jaffna.)

in Ceylon as a missionary in 1880, and from that year until the present time he has laboured unremittingly as such. He has been Bishop of the diocese since 1893.

WILLIAM RUTHERFORD BOGLE SANDERS.

Mr. William Rutherford Bogle Sanders, the District Judge of Jaffna, was born in Calcutta on October 29, 1856, and educated at St. Peter's School, the Collegiate School, Edinburgh, and the Edinburgh University. He was appointed

W. R. B. SANDERS.

to the Ceylon Civil Service in 1879, and on December 15th in that year arrived in Ceylon, and was attached to the Galle Kachcheri. On August 4, 1881, he was transferred to Kandy. In May, 1882, he was made Extra Assistant at Badulla to the Government Agent, Central Province. In the following year he officiated as Acting District Judge. Subsequently he filled positions at Batticaloa, Anuradhapura, Gampola, Colombo, and Haputale. On January 1, 1888, he was appointed Police Magistrate, Chilaw, and in March of the same year was Acting Police Magistrate, Jaffna. After serving here and elsewhere in a magisterial capacity, he was, on May 1, 1896, gazetted District Judge, Ratnapura, Subsequently he officiated at Kegalla and Negombo, and after a period of leave was appointed District Judge, Jaffna. In 1902 he acted for a time as Government Agent in addition to discharging his other duties. He went on leave in 1904, and on his return served for a time as Commissioner of Requests. On April 14, 1905, he was appointed District Judge, Kalutara, but on December 7th of the same year he reverted to his old post at Jaffna.

THE HON. MR. AMBALAVANAR KANAGASABAI.

The Hon. Mr. Ambalavanar Kanagasabai, son of Superamaniam Ambalavanar, was born at Tellepalai, in the Jaffna district, in 1856, and educated first privately and afterwards at Madras University, where he graduated in Arts in 1878 from the Christian College. He then studied law under Mr. C. L. Ferdinands, Deputy Queen's Advocate, and was called to the Bar in August, 1882, when he commenced practice at Jaffna. He is now the leader of the Bar there, and has always identified him-

HON. MR. A. KANAGASABAI AND FAMILY.

THE RESIDENCE.

self with movements of every description for the welfare of the people of Jaffna. As an instance of this it should be stated that he was largely instrumental in bringing about the construction of the Northern Railway. In February, 1906, the Secretary of State appointed him member of the Legislative Council for the Tamil community, in which capacity he represents the interests of one million people. In 1885 he married Kamatchi Ammal, daughter of Sangarapillar Kanagasabai, and his residences are Kailaiwalauwa at Tellepalai, Jaffna, and "Green Bank," Jail Road, Colombo. He is a member of the Royal Asiatic Society and of the Agricultural Society, is on the Board of Education of Ceylon, President of the Board of Directors of the Hindu College, Jaffna, a member of the committee of the Victoria Home for Incurables, and the President of the Board of Directors of the Jaffna Commercial Corporation.

J. M. HENSMAN, B.A., Fellow of the University of Madras.

Mr. James Muthiah Hensman was born on November 24, 1849, at Jaffna, and is the son of the late Rev. John Hensman, incumbent of the C.M.S. Church at Kopay, Jaffna. He was educated at Chundicully Seminary, Jaffna, and Kumbakonam College, Madras, where he passed the B.A. degree examination of the Madras University in English, mathematics, ethics, history and Tamil, under Principal W. A. Porter, M.A. Cantab. In 1870 he joined the Madras Government educational

J. M. HENSMAN.

service as assistant in the Second Grade College at Calicut. Subsequently he was headmaster of various Government High Schools and Second Grade Colleges, after which he was promoted to the first lectureship in English and mathematics in the Government First Grade Colleges, Rajahmundry and Kumbakonam, successively. He also held for considerable periods the acting principalship of the foregoing two colleges. He then became Inspector of Schools for a short time, and retired from the service in September, 1904. He has returned to Jaffna, where he has lived in retirement ever since. He is the first President of the Jaffna Association. He married Elizabeth, the eldest daughter of the late Mr. E. Rogers, Arasaratna Mudaliyar of Jaffna, and resides at Sandilipay, near Jaffna. He has three sons and two daughters.

KANAPATHYPILLAI SIVASITHAMPARAM.

This gentleman was born in 1877, and educated at Trincomalee Wesleyan Mission High School and the Hindu College, Jaffna. After passing the entrance examination for the Calcutta University at the last named institution, he entered the Ceylon Medical College in 1899, and passing out in 1904, became House Surgeon at the Kandy Hospital. Later he acted as Medical Officer at Anuradhapura and he is now House Surgeon at Badulla. He is a member of the British Medical Association and of the Local Board at Anuradhapura.

VISUVANATHER CASIPPILLAI.

Mr. V. Casippillai, Proctor of the Supreme Court of Ceylon and Notary Public of Jaffna, was born at Jaffna on February 12, 1849. He is the son of V. Visuvanather, landed proprietor, and Aiyathaippillai, daughter of C. Visuvanather, of Jaffna. Having been educated at the Chundicully Seminary, Jaffna, he became an undergraduate of the Madras University in 1867. He was articled to Mr. Advocate C. Brito, B.A., with the view of qualifying himself as proctor. He passed as Proctor of the District Court of Mannar in 1876, and was admitted at the Supreme Court of Ceylon in 1879. He practised in Mannar till 1882, when he began his practice in Jaffna, where he still practises. He was admitted a notary public authorised to practise in the English and Tamil languages. Mr. Casippillai married in 1882 Parupathippillai, daughter of C. Mootatamby, and has by her (who died in 1893) a son named Arulambalam, who is a law student, and a daughter named Rasamma. In addition to the practice of law, Mr. Casippillai is a planter and agriculturist, and owns two fully-planted coconut estates, viz., Ariyalai estate, of about 500 acres, and Vettilaikkeny estate, in Veddukkadu, of about 300 acres. He has also another estate at Pallai, which is just being opened and is to be planted with coconuts. Besides these estates he owns about 150 acres of paddy-lands and several other coconut and Palmyra gardens. He is a director of the Jaffna Commercial Corporation and the Jaffna Trading Company, Ltd., Manager of the Hindu College, Jaffna, and Secretary of "Saivaparipalana Sabai" (a Hindu society), and Vice-President of the Jaffna Association.

V. CASIPPILLAI.

F. G. SPITTEL.

Dr. Frederick George Spittel, Provincial Surgeon of the Northern Province, stationed at Jaffna, and residing at Abbot's Lodge, was born in Colombo on January 26, 1853, and educated at the Colombo Academy (present Royal College). After obtaining the licence of the Ceylon Medical College, and having served as Sub-Assistant Colonial Surgeon, he proceeded to Scotland and obtained the diploma of the Royal College of Physicians and Surgeons, Edinburgh, and of the Faculty of Physicians and Surgeons, Glasgow. Returning to Ceylon, he was appointed Deputy-Assistant Colonial Surgeon in 1885, and afterwards served as Assistant Colonial Surgeon at Gampola, Kurunegala, Matara, Galle, Anuradhapura, and Colombo. He was afterwards appointed Colonial Surgeon of the Northern Province. He married Zilia Eleanor, daughter of Henry Frederick Jansz, of Galle. He has three sons and five daughters, and of these the eldest son, Richard Lionel, obtained the licence of the

DR. AND MRS. F. G. SPITTEL AND FAMILY. F. G. SPITTEL. ABBOT'S LODGE.

Ceylon Medical College, and after being appointed House-Surgeon of the General Hospital, Colombo, proceeded to London to obtain British qualifications there. The second son, George Knox, is qualifying as a surveyor in the Technical College, Colombo.

JOSEPH CHERUBIM.

Mr. Joseph Cherubim, commission agent, is a well-known Jaffna personality. He is a son of the late Mr. M. B. Cherubim, who was also a commission agent, and was born on September 23, 1868. He received his education in St. Patrick's College, Jaffna, and since he commenced business, in 1890, has taken up agencies for the British India Steam Navigation Company, Ltd., the Standard Life Assurance Company, the British Dominions Marine Insurance

JOSEPH CHERUBIM.

Company, Ltd., the Ceylon Company of Pearl Fishers, Ltd., and Cameron & Co.'s Tile Works, Travancore. He has two brothers, Messrs. Norbert E. M. Cherubim and Victor E. Cherubim, who assist him in the business. Mr. Cherubim married Anne Magdalene, daughter of the late Mr. P. S. Sandrasagra, agent B. I. S. N. Company, Ltd., Jaffna, and resides in Main Street, Jaffna. Mr. and Mrs. Cherubim are grandchildren of the late Mr. Don Philip Sangarapillai Mudaliyar Cherubim, and grand nephew and niece of the late Mr. Sandrasagra Mudaliyar Saverimutto, Mudaliyar, Mudaliyar of the Governor's Gate and Knight Chevalier of the Order of St. Gregory the Great.

T. NAGALINGA, Mudaliyar.

Mr. T. Nagalinga, Mudaliyar, of Point Pedro, in Jaffna, was born in 1861, and received his

THEYVAM NAGALINGA, MUDALIYAR.

education in the Grammar School at Point Pedro. His father, Theyver, was in his day not only a leading merchant and shipowner at Point Pedro, but one of the pioneers of the planting industry of the Jaffna district, and a great friend to the European planters in the north of the island. His paternal grandfather, Theyver Kanagaraya, Mudaliyar, was the Maniagar of Point Pedro. His paternal great-grandfather, Varunakula Sooria, Mudaliyar, his maternal grandfather, Kathirkama Singa, Mudaliyar, and his maternal great-grandfather, Kathirkama, Mudaliyar, were also titular Mudaliyars, and the present occupant of that title is following in his ancestors' footsteps in setting an example of loyalty and public spirit. Upon the completion of his scholastic career he entered commerce, and is now a leading merchant, shipowner, and landed proprietor of Point Pedro. So great has been his financial success that he is said to be the richest man in the Northern Province, and it is gratifying to be able to state that he has been both judicious and generous in giving of his means for public objects. He is the largest contributor to the proposed Ridgeway Memorial Hall in Jaffna. He has been the leading supporter of the reading-room in his native town. He has for long played a conspicuous part as a peace-maker in his district, successfully averting strife in caste and other disputes on many occasions. He was raised to the rank of a Mudaliyar on November 9, 1903, in recognition of his public spirit and valuable services. It is worthy of mention that Sir West Ridgeway paid a visit to Point Pedro on March 12, 1902, at the instance of the Mudaliyar, who accorded His Excellency a magnificent reception, with which he was so much pleased that he expressed his personal thanks to the Mudaliyar, adding that he would have been very sorry if he had left Ceylon without seeing so important and prosperous a town. The Mudaliyar and his brother-in-law, Sithamparam Maniccum, are in partnership, and own a large fleet of boats which trade between Jaffna and India. These include the barques *Pakialetchmy* (about 300 tons), *Thirunadarajasivakamasundary* (about 250 tons), *Dhoney Dyalnayagy* (about 150 tons); schooners *Parupathapakialetchmy* (about 100 tons), *Sinnaparupatham* (of about 50 tons); and brig *Sivagangapuravy* (about 120 tons). Mr. Nagalinda in 1880 married Theyvanaipilly, daughter of the late Punniar Sidamparam, a leading merchant and shipowner, and they have three sons, named Sithamparappilly, Theyvapilly, and Krishnapilly, and seven daughters.

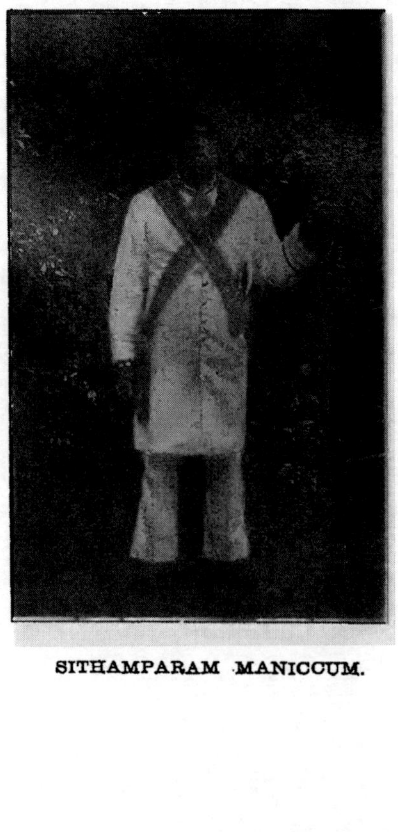

SITHAMPARAM MANICCUM.

HENRY ALEXANDER PATRICK SANDRASAGRA.

Mr. H. A. Patrick Sandrasagra is the son of Mr. J. N. Sandrasagra, Superintendent of Minor Roads, Jaffna. His grandfather was the first Gregorian Knight in Ceylon, having been decorated by Pope Leo XIII. He was a personal friend of Sir Wm. Gregory, the Governor of Ceylon, and possessed several medals and other decorations conferred upon him at various times. The subject of this sketch was born on June 12, 1875, and educated at St. Patrick's College. He afterwards studied under the Council of Legal Education, and was called to the Bar in 1898 as an Advocate of the Superior Court, Jaffna. He has been practising there ever since. Mr. Sandrasagra is married to Josephine, daughter of the late Mr. Simon Cherobin.

ISAAC TAMBYAH.

Mr. Tambyah is a son of Mr. T. A. Tamby Pillai, head clerk of the New Dimbula Tea Company, Ltd., Agrapatnas. Born on August 19, 1869, at Jaffna, he was educated at St. John's College, Jaffna, and St. Thomas's College, Colombo. He held the Divinity Scholarship from 1877 to 1891, and was Liturgy Prizeman. During his sojourn at St. Thomas's Mr. Tambyah edited the college magazine. On the termination of his collegiate career he studied under the Council of Legal Education, and was called to the Bar in 1899. He practised in Colombo until 1901, when he removed to Jaffna, where he has been ever since. Mr. Tambyah, besides being a brilliant lawyer, is a well-known writer. He was the founder of the *Ceylon Review*, and edited that publication until it was sold. He is at present editor of the *Ceylon Law Review* and Tambyah's Reports. He is the author of the "Digest of the Law of Contract and Commentary on the Ceylon Penal Code." Besides, he has edited collections of poems by various writers and the "Garland Verse Collection" of Ceylon. Mr. Tambyah is married to Mangalanayagam, daughter of Mudaliyar J. W. Barr Kumarakulasinghe. Mr. Tambyah is proprietor of Burleigh House, Jaffna, an old Dutch residence built 150 years since.

VENASITAMBY MURGASUPILLAI.

Mr. Venasitamby Murgasupillai, planter, of Jaffna, is the son of Venasitamby, property owner of that town, and Kathergasi Pillai. He was born in Jaffna in 1865 and educated at Batticotta College. Upon the completion of his scholastic career he went to Singapore, and spent twenty-one years there in the service of the municipality, commencing as Inspector and rising to be Chief Inspector of Roads. He then retired on pension and returned to his native town, where he is at present engaged in the superintendence of his estates. He was also President of the Hindu community of Singapore for a period of eleven years, and represented them on the occasion of the visit of Their Royal Highnesses the Duke and Duchess of York in 1901. He married Selvakanmany, daughter of J. Tillainather Pillai, Mudaliyar Maniagar of the Jaffna district. He resides at Sherman Lodge,

V. MURGASUPILLAI.

Vanarponai, Hindu Town, near Jaffna, and his family consists of three sons—Valupillai, Ratnavalupillai, and Kathiravalupillai.

CATHIRKAMAR MURUGASER SINNAYAH, Mudaliyar.

This gentleman, who is Shroff at the Jaffna Kachcheri, is the son of Kathirgamar Murugaser, landed proprietor, of Jaffna. He was born in 1854 and was educated, first, at the Batticotta High School, Jaffna, and then at the Kumbakonam College, in South India. Upon the completion of his college career he entered the Ceylon Government service, passed the necessary examination, and in 1876 became a clerk in the Public Works Department at Ratnapura. After holding various other

MUDALIYAR CATHIRKAMAR MURUGASER SINNAYAH.

Government appointments he was promoted to his present position. He is also an Inquirer into Crimes, hon. treasurer of the Jaffna Agricultural Society, one of the directors of the Jaffna Hindu College, a member of the executive committee of the Jaffna Friend-in-Need Society, manager of an Anglo-Vernacular School at Anacotta, and a member of the District Road Committee, Jaffna. He married Sivagamy Pillai, daughter of Kartegasa Udiyar, and he has one son and one daughter, the latter being married. His residence is named "Srivasa," Anacotta, Jaffna.

WILLIAM MATHER.

This gentleman was born at Jaffna on May 10, 1851, and received his education at

WILLIAM MATHER.

the Vaddukodde English High School in that town. Entering commercial life, he worked his way by dint of diligence and perseverance through the positions of clerk, book-keeper, and accountant and cashier, and finally commenced business on his own account under the style of William Mather & Son, and the firm now holds the agencies for the Ceylon Steamship Company, Ltd., the Basel Mission Tile Works, Messrs. Walker, Sons & Co., Ltd., and the Oriental Government Security Life Assurance Company. Mr. Mather is also the managing director of the Jaffna Commercial Corporation, Ltd., of which he was the founder. He married Eliza, daughter of Mr. J. R. Arnold, editor of the Jaffna *Morning Star*, and author, poet, &c., and their family consists of six sons and four daughters. Of these the eldest son, Edward Mather, is a partner in his father's business, and married a daughter of Dr. William Paul. Solomon Mather, the second son, who is a merchant, married a daughter of Proctor S. T. Arnold. The eldest daughter, Margaret Thangamma, married Mr. R. M. Rajasooryar; the second daughter, Jane Nallamma, married Mr. R. N. Samuel; Harriet Muttaparanam, the third daughter, married Mr. C. T. Hastings; and the youngest daughter, Alice Anna, married Mr. S. M. Edwards.

R. H. LEEMBRUGGEN.

Mr. Robert Henry Leembruggen is the son of the late Mr. G. H. Leembruggen, retired Inspector of Police, and was born at Jaffna on November 12, 1844. He received his education at the Wesleyan Central College, Jaffna, and entered the service of the Education Department of the Government in March, 1866, his first appointment being that of headmaster of the Matara boys' English school. This position he filled with great success for thirteen years, and he then became Principal of the Female Seminary, Colombo. In 1885 he ceased to be a schoolmaster, and between that year and 1889 was successively chief clerk in the Chief Resident Engineer's, the Attorney-General's, and the Colonial Secretary's offices; and in February, 1892, he was appointed Inspector of Schools, a position from which he has now retired. He is a member of the Friend-in-Need Society, Jaffna, and Vice-President of the Jaffna Central College Old Boys' Association, and was at one time an honorary member of the Colts' Cricket Club. As recreations he is fond of boating and fishing, &c., and he resides at "The Nutshell," Jaffna. He married Helen Catherine Mabel, daughter of John Arnold Wakefield Vanzyl.

R. H. LEEMBRUGGEN.

V. M. MUTTUKUMARU.

Mr. Vyra Muttu Muttukumaru, Secretary of the Local Board of Health and Improvement of Jaffna, is the second son of Dr. V. Muttukumaru, of Anaikkoddai, Jaffna, and Thaiyalmuttu, daughter of S. Merwin Murugasapillai, of Vannarpannai, Jaffna. He was born on December 15, 1875, and had a distinguished scholastic career at St. Patrick's College (Jaffna), Royal College (Colombo), and St. Xavier's College (Calcutta). In 1892 he passed the Cambridge Junior Local Examination, being the first in Ceylon to pass in shorthand and book-keeping. In the latter subject he not only passed, but also obtained distinction. In the following year he passed the Cambridge Senior Local Examination, when he gained the only distinction of the year in arithmetic in all the colonies. In 1897 he passed the First in Arts Examination of the Calcutta University in the First Division, and gained a Government Scholarship. He further gained two silver medals for general proficiency in the junior and senior F.A. Classes of St. Xavier's College, Calcutta, respectively, and a gold medal in the B.A. Class for English, mathematics, and science. In 1898 he became Acting Assistant-Master of the Royal College, Colombo, and three years later became first assistant to the Principal of the Central College, Colombo. In August, 1906, he was appointed Secretary of the Local Board of Health and Improvement of Jaffna, and he still holds that position. He is the proprietor of a coconut estate 186 acres in extent and of 40 acres of paddy-land. He married Soma Suntharavally Ammal, daughter of the late Dr. M. Candyah, of Nallur, and they have one daughter, Siva Yogavally Ammal. Their residence is at Temple Villa and Chilambu Walauwa, both at Nallur.

V. M. AND MRS. MUTTUKUMARU.

TAMBIAH STRONG COOKE.

Mr. Tambiah Strong Cooke, Proctor, of Jaffna, was born on November 13, 1863, at Batticotta, Jaffna. He was educated at Jaffna College, and after being a student there he became a master of the college, and occupied that position for some time, assisting in the meanwhile his grandfather, Mr. N. Strong, in his printing establishment at Manipay. Abandoning these appointments, he was articled for the study of law, and was called to the Bar in August, 1901, and since that date has practised his profession in his native town. He has varied and extensive interests, being director and secretary and proctor of the Jaffna Trading Company, director and proctor of the Commercial Corporation, and proprietor of the Jaffna *Morning Star*, as well as owner of several paddy-fields and coconut plantations. He is an ardent Wesleyan Methodist, and is a local preacher, circuit steward, and Sunday-school superintendent for that Church in Jaffna.

TAMBIAH STRONG COOKE.

In addition he is the Treasurer of the Y.M.C.A., and member and Treasurer of the Law Library. He has been twice married, and he has five sons and one daughter—Franklin Kunaretnam and Thomas Jeyaretnam by his first wife, Harriet Tampoe; and Magonn Durairetnam, Albert Arasaretnam, Anna Retnam, and Parson Chelvaretnam by his second wife, Ethel Rosammah Tambiah.

M. G. GEDDES.

Mr. Melville Gordon Geddes, planter, of Pallai, N.P., near Jaffna, is the son of the late John Gordon Geddes, proprietary planter and manager of many of the leading estates in the peninsula, who arrived in Ceylon half a century ago and joined Messrs. J. W. Ritchie & Co. Born at Jaffna in 1867, Mr. Geddes, jun., went Home for his education, which he received at Wickham Park School and the Academy, Edinburgh. He returned to Ceylon in 1886 and commenced coconut-planting, and has made consistent progress until now he is a large proprietary planter, and owns the Tanmakenny estate, 320 acres in extent, and fully planted with coconuts, and, in addition, manages for Major Forbes, the owner, the Mogamally and Karandi estates, each of which embraces 300 acres. He has been resident at Pallai for twenty-one years, during which period he has made two visits to England. It is interesting to note that Mr. Geddes is the first planter in the Jaffna district who has tried planting Ceara rubber. The plants are from one to two years old, and the older trees are 9 ins. thick. Mr. Geddes employs a good number of coolies permanently, and during the cultivation period village labour is employed. He married Lilie, daughter of Henry Rayner, Esq., of Ealing, London, and he has two sons and two daughters, the eldest son, Douglas Gordon, being at present at Harrow, Rickmansworth. He is a member of the Ceylon Agricultural Society and resides on his estate.

GURUSWAMY NATHANIEL HUNT TAMPOE.

Mr. Tampoe is a son of Mr. T. M. Tampoe, retired Police Magistrate and Acting District Judge. Born on June 21, 1879, at Jaffna, he was educated at the Central College, Jaffna, St. Thomas's College, Colombo, and Trinity College, Kandy. At the last-named institution he passed first in arts at the Calcutta University examination. He studied under the Council of Legal Education, and passed as Proctor of the District Court, Jaffna, on March 26, 1902. He is still practising in Jaffna. Mr. Tampoe is married to Mary Rutnam, daughter of the late Dr. Wm. Paul, resident surgeon of the Friend-in-Need Society, Jaffna. There are two children of the union—one son and one daughter. Mr. Tampoe is a brother of Mr. S. D. Tampoe, Advocate, of Jaffna, and of Mr. D. P. Tampoe, of Colombo. A third brother is Mr. A. McGown C. Tampoe, I.C.S., the first Ceylonese to pass the Indian Civil Service Examination.

SABARAGAMUWA PROVINCE.

THE province of Sabaragamuwa occupies a position sandwiched in between the North-Western, the Western, and Southern Provinces on the one side, and the Uva and the Central Provinces on the other. It is last in the order of official importance, eighth in size, sixth in population, and seventh in revenue-earning capacity. It derives its chief interest in the eyes of the outside public from the fact that it is the great centre of the gemming industry for which Ceylon has been famous since the earliest times. The gems are found in the detritus in the rivers and brooks, and in the peaty soil of the valleys. The system of mining is primitive. The earth, when dug up, is put into wicker baskets and washed in wooden troughs, under the vigilant supervision of a foreman, who is usually the proprietor of the mine. The industry is for the most part in the hands of Moormen, and fabulous stories are told of the wealth which has been amassed by these individuals, but it is believed that the mines are not so productive as they once were. Rubies and sapphires are the chief stones sought for, but nearly all precious stones except diamonds, emeralds, and turquoises are found. The general belief is that the mines are not so productive as they once were; but that there are still unrevealed possibilities in mining in the province is indicated by the recent discovery of thorianite in the vicinity of Ratnapura. This valuable mineral product has so far not been found in very large quantities, and it is early yet to say whether a paying industry can be established. The reports of experts, however, are encouraging, and acting upon them licences have been taken out by Colombo firms for working the mineral. The initial mining operations have been fairly successful. Mr. G. S. Saxton, Government Agent, in his Administration Report for 1905, speaking of the mining work, says: "I went to see the working on and near Kondaragala,

THE RESIDENCY, RATNAPURA.

and it was interesting to see the mineral found within 18 ins. of the surface soil in one particular place. The deposits seem to be in patches here and there, which are very difficult to locate in dense jungles." Mr. Saxton also mentions that agents of Colombo firms were buying quantities of thorianite from villages, "of which," he adds, "I have no doubt a great deal came from Crown land." The gemming in the province is worked under a system of Government licensing. In 1905 the number of licences issued was 455, a figure which represents an increase of 162 over that for the previous year. During 1905 sixteen leases of Crown land were sold for Rs. 5,042, that sum representing one-fifth share, which, according to the custom of the country, is the proportion of the value of the proceeds rightfully belonging to the proprietor of the soil.

Gemming and mining by no means absorb all the commercial activities of Sabaragamuwa. The province is more and more coming to the front as a field for planting enterprise. The plantation of rubber here, as in the adjacent provinces, proceeds apace. The following figures, supplied to the Government agent by the Sabaragamuwa Planters' Association, of land to be opened during the season 1905–6, show how extensive are the operations in this direction: Rakwana 1,223, Balangoda 380, Ratnapura and Pelmadulla 6,037—7,640 acres planted through tea; Rakwana 555, Balangoda 110, Ratnapura 2,361—3,026 acres. It is probable that the figures for the Ratnapura district would be even larger than they are were it not for the fascination of gemming. The expectation that valuable deposits may some day be found on land prevents owners from planting it up with permanent products.

VIEW IN THE RATNAPURA DISTRICT.

Ratnapura, the capital of the province, is a town of about 4,000 inhabitants, situated in the centre of a picturesque and highly cultivated district on the banks of the Kalu Ganga river. The scenery in the immediate vicinity of the town, especially on the Pelmadulla side, is very beautiful, and has been likened by travellers to that of North Wales. But the town itself is somewhat disappointing. A charming old tank in the heart of the town, an old Dutch fort, the headquarters of the administration, a bazaar, and some pretty bungalows scattered about in the park-like valley constitute its chief features. The river is a fine stream and is navigable to this point. There is a considerable traffic upon it, barges being floated down with produce to Kalutara at the mouth. Haeckel, who made the journey down stream on the occasion of his visit, gives an enthusiastic description of the river scenery. "The sombre masses of overhanging dark green trees and the black colour given by the fringing thicket to the water near the banks have given its name to the Kalu Ganga, or Black River. The water itself, when the river is low, is a dark, blackish green, but when it is full the colour is yellowish or orange-brown, in consequence of the quantities of yellow or reddish loam brought down by the rains. On the shore itself abrupt rocks and grotesque groups of stones, overhanging boughs, and trees torn up by the roots, supply a marked and delightful foreground to the landscape. The distance is filled up by the sublime outlines of the mountains, swathed in blue mist and appearing much higher than they really are. The chief part of the river's edge looks as if it consisted entirely of vegetation; aralia and terminalia, dillenia and bombax, rubiaceæ and urticaceæ predominate. The dark green of this thicket is pleasingly varied by the bright green of the bamboos; their orange and yellow canes stand in thick clumps from forty to fifty feet high, and the elegant feathery leaves hang over the water like tufts of ostrich plumes. Cocoa and areca palms, talipot and kitool, with here and there a plantation of banana and cassava, betray the existence of inhabitants, and prove that the shores of the river are not such a wilderness as might be supposed from the thicket that fringes its bank. Occasionally, though more rarely, solitary native huts stand on a rocky promontory of the shore; and more rarely still the white cupola of a dagoba reveals the existence of a village."

The Kegalla district, which is an Assistant Government Agent's charge, has an area of 642 square miles and a population of 188,791. About one half the Sinhalese population is engaged in agriculture, chiefly paddy, chena, coconut, plantain, and areca-nut cultivation. Mining here, as in the Ratnapura district, is an important industry. There are in the area 34 plumbago mines, nearly all of which are in

H. B. HELLINGS.
(Government Agent.)

the hands of low-country Sinhalese. Plumbago coolies are usually men from the low-country, and have earned a bad reputation for lawlessness. Kegalla is the only town in the district

VIEWS IN SABARAGAMUWA.

1. Ratnapura. 2. The Shadow of Adam's Peak—Sunrise View from the Summit. 3. Adam's Peak—Another View from the Summit.
4. 5. River Scenes at Ratnapura. 6. Ruanwella.

in which there is a local Board of Health. Dehiowita and Yatiyantota are "small towns" under the control of the Board of Health.

RATNAPURA DISTRICT.

WILLIAM DAVID CONSTANTINE SAMARADIWAKARA ABAYAGUNASEKARA TILLEKERATNE.

This gentleman, who is more generally known as W. D. Tillekeratne, Mudaliyar, is the son of Don Moses Tillekeratne, who held the offices of Kachcheri and Court Mudaliyar of Ratnapura, and was born in 1850. After receiving his education at St. Thomas's College and having passed the Government Clerical Examination, he entered the service of the Government at the Ratnapura Kachcheri in 1870. Subsequently he held the offices of Record Keeper, Native Writer, and Head Clerk of the District Court, and in 1887 was appointed Kachcheri Mudaliyar, which post he fills at the present time. He is Secretary of the Friend-in-Need Society, Sabaragamuwa, Treasurer of the Local Agricultural Society, a member of the District Road Committee, and a landed proprietor owning coconut plantations, paddy-lands, and house property.

W. D. TILLEKERATNE.

G. M. CRABBE.

Mr. George Mortimer Crabbe was born at Elkaduwa, near Matale, Ceylon, but was educated in England, privately and at Dawlish, South Devon. Before coming to Ceylon, in 1887, he was for two years engaged in farming in New Zealand. Upon his arrival in Ceylon he started coffee and tea planting under the late Thomas Mackie on the Great Western estate, Dimbula, and he opened up El Teb, Captain Gordon's estate. In 1895 he went to Malangi in Nyassaland as Manager of the Nyassaland Coffee Company, but he returned to Ceylon two years later, and since then up to the present time he has been in charge of the Mahawella estate, Ratnapura. Formerly he held the office of Chairman of the Ratnapura Planters' Association, and he is now Chairman of the United Sabaragamuwa Planters' Association. Always having taken a strong interest in the welfare of the neighbourhood, he was one of the prime movers of the agitation for a railway to Ratnapura. He is a member of the Committee of the Ceylon Planters' Association, of the Ceylon Planters' Labour Committee, of the Provincial Road Committee, and of the District Road Committee, and he is a great advocate of land settlement arising out of the Waste Lands Ordinance.

The Mahawella estate is situated in the Kuruwiti Korale of the Sabaragamuwa Province, two miles from Ratnapura. It was planted with tea in 1897 and has now 650 acres under cultivation. By systematic and careful cultivation the estate has continued yearly to give increased yields, and the yield is now 600 lbs. of tea per acre, and Mahawella now ranks as one of the cheapest producing estates in the low-country. In 1899 rubber was planted in a small way, but the trees that have been tapped have given good results, and since 1902 rubber has been systematically planted, and now 350 acres have been covered with the product. Thus there are altogether 1,000 acres cultivated, and the prospects for the future are very bright.

GEO. M. CRABBE. THE ESTATE BUNGALOW.

CHARLES FREDERICK DHARMARATNE.

The son of Mr. John Alexander Dharmaratne, Proctor of the District Court, Kalutara, the subject of this sketch, was born in 1870, and educated at St. John's School, Kalutara, and St. Thomas's College, Colombo. He was articled to the study of the law to Mr. George Alexander Dharmaratne, Proctor, of Colombo, and became a Proctor of the District Court,

GEM PITS. WASHING GRAVEL FOR GEMS.

Kalutara, in 1895. In 1897 he transferred to Ratnapura, where he still practises. Mr.

C. F. DHARMARATNE.

Dharmaratne is a member of the Local Board and of the Agricultural Society.

PETER CHARLES FERNANDO WANIGESEKERE GOONEWARDENE.

The subject of this sketch is the son of Mudaliyar T. F. W. Goonewardene, of Panadure. Born in 1879, he was educated at St. John's, Panadure, and the Royal College. He passed the Cambridge Local Examinations, and took a first class in the London College of Preceptors' Examination. Adopting the law as a profession, he became a Proctor of the District Court, Ratnapura, in 1904, and still practises there. He is a member of the Ceylon Agricultural Society, as well as of the local Agricultural Society.

P. C. F. GOONEWARDENE.

MAHIPALA AKRAKKURUPPU WICKREMESINHE BASNAIKE MUDIANSE RALAHAMILEGE WILLIAM ALEXANDER ABRAHAM EKNELLIGODA.

The subject of this notice is the son of Mr M. A. W. B. M. R. J. W. Eknelligoda, whose family sketch appears in another portion of this volume. Born in January, 1826, he received his education at the Colombo Academy under Rev. Dr. Boake. After his school career in 1847 he was made Ratemahatmaya in the Sabaragamuwa Province, a position which was held by his grandfather and father before him. Later he was appointed Deputy Coroner for the Nawadun and Kukulu Korales, and subsequently Ratemahatmaya of Kuruwiti Korale when the final division of the province took place. In 1880 he was appointed Dissawa by Governor Sir Arthur Gordon. Mr. Eknelligoda retired from public service a short time after.

WM. ALEXANDER A. EKNELLIGODA, DISSAWA. PHILIP A. CHAS. EKNELLIGODA. MOLLAMURA KUMARIHAMY. DELWALA KUMARIHAMY.

P. W. DIAS. THE STORE. MR. AND MRS. P. W. DIAS AND FAMILY.

He was presented with a special medal for services rendered by him to the Prince of Wales when in Ceylon by arranging an elephant kraal in the Kegalla district for His Royal Highness's amusement. He is also the possessor of a beautiful ring given by the Tsar of Russia when the latter paid a visit to Ceylon, and of a gold medal presented to his ancestors by Sir Robert Brownrigg in 1818 during the last Kandyan rebellion. Mr. Eknelligoda is at present residing at Eknelligoda Walauwa, Kuruwiti, in the Sabaragamuwa Province, looking after his ancestral plantations and properties. In 1854 he married a daughter of Delwala Wijeyekoon, Mudianse Korala Mahatmaya, a landed proprietor of Nawadun Korale, and his only daughter is married to Mr. Abeyekoon Rajapakse Dissanaike Mudianse Mollamura, late Police Magistrate of Gampola. Mr. Eknelligoda has an adopted son, Philip Andrew Charles, who is Kachcheri Mohandiram at Anuradhapura. Mr. Eknelligoda was made J.P. and U.P.M. for the province on his retirement, and is Basnaike Nilame of the Maha Samas Dehiwale (temple) near Ratnapura. He is also a trustee of Buddhist temporalities in the province.

P. W. DIAS & CO.

This business was established at Ratnapura in 1901 by Mr. P. William Dias, a native of Panadure, who had formerly carried on business as a general merchant at Matale and Kandy. At Ratnapura a large trade in wines, spirits, oilmen's stores, drapery, planting requisites, &c., is done with the planting community and the general public of the neighbourhood. In 1903 the firm opened a very fine billiard-room in the town, containing an excellent full-sized Thurston table, and it now forms a popular resort for all sections of the community. The business was started in a very small way, but by careful attention to details Mr. Dias has already worked up a splendid connection. In addition to this business he owns coconut plantations in the Rayigam Korale and in the Panadure district, as well as house property. He married, in 1901, Cecilia Violet, daughter of L. Francisco Fernando, of Panadure. The manager of the Ratnapura store is Mr. D. L. Wanigaratne.

J. VAN DENBERG.

Mr. James van Denberg is the son of Mr. Charles van Denberg, late Crown Proctor of Ratnapura. Born in 1871, he received his education at St. Thomas's College, Colombo, where he passed the Senior Cambridge Local Examination, obtaining second class honours and distinction in mathematics. For some time he was an Assistant Master at the Royal College, but later he studied law and entered the legal profession, becoming a Proctor of the District Court in 1899. Since 1906 he has been Crown Proctor of Ratnapura. He is a member of the District Road Committee and of the Sabaragamuwa Lawn Tennis and Cricket Clubs, and he resides at Bar House, Ratnapura.

BAR HOUSE.

KEGALLA DISTRICT.

FRANKLIN LUSHINGTON.

Mr. Franklin Lushington, the superintendent of the Houpe estate, Pelmadulla, is the son of the late Sir Franklin Lushington. He was born on December 28, 1876, in London, and was educated at Charterhouse School and Jesus College, Cambridge. On quitting the University he adopted a medical career, but after studying for some time abandoned the medical schools, and came out to Ceylon in 1897 and joined the Kellie group of estates at Dolosbage. Subsequently he became associated with the Ceylon Tea Plantations. The last estate on which he was employed was Mundumana. He quitted this to take up his present appointment on the Houpe estate, the acreage of which is 1,500. The area is all unopened ground, and the intention is to clear it for the planting of rubber.

F. LUSHINGTON.

Mr. Lushington's recreations are tennis and cycling.

MAPITIGAMA KULATUNGE WIJEKOON MUDIYANSELAGE WILLIAM TUDOR MAPITIGAMA BANDA.

This gentleman, who is the Ratemahatmaya of the Galboda and Kinigoda Korales, was born at Dilkandura, and educated at the Buddhist English High School at Colombo and at Trinity College, Kandy. He joined the Government service as third clerk in the District Road Committee's office at Kegalla and was then appointed engineer and lock-up keeper at Pelmadulla. Afterwards he filled a Government office at Balangoda, and finally received his present position. Mr. Mapitigama is a son of Edwin Francis Mapitigama, Rate-

WILLIAM TUDOR MAPITIGAMA, MRS. MAPITIGAMA, AND FAMILY GROUP.

mahatmaya of Mardaniela, and of Muthumenike, daughter of D. D. M. Delkandura, Korale of Nawandum Korale, in the Sabaragamuwa Province. He is married to Semasinghe Nawaratne Wanniayaka Mudiyanselage Dingri Amma Kumarihame, daughter of the Hon. S. N. W. Hullugale, Adigar. Mr. Mapitigama owns paddy-fields and coconut estates in the Sabaragamuwa and North-Western Provinces

CENTRAL PROVINCE.

WHETHER regarded from the standpoint of historical association, wealth, or attractiveness, the Central Province is the most important of the nine administrative areas into which the island is divided. It includes Kandy, the capital of the ancient Kandyan kingdom, and embraces the richest portions of the area which owed allegiance to the later Sinhalese dynasty. On the commercial side the great planting industry, which finds its principal home in the districts hereabouts, gives the province a proud pre-eminence. As a health centre, too, the province is famous. In the glorious mountain region stretching away to Adam's Peak in one direction and Pidurutalagala on the other is found a climate bracing and exhilarating, in conjunction with scenery scarcely to be equalled in the world for romantic beauty.

The early history of the province is treated at some length in the historical chapters of this work, and it is unnecessary to again traverse the ground. Nor is any detailed reference called for to the native life of the area, in view of the admirable and exhaustive view of Kandyan life and manners in the special article by Major Modder which will be found elsewhere. Our concern must be chiefly with the modern aspects of the Central Province. First to call for notice is the planting industry, which has covered a country which was once for the most part an impenetrable jungle, the resort of herds of wild elephants, with smiling plantations which give constant employment to tens of thousands of labourers. To Sir Edward Barnes belongs the honour of being the pioneer of planting in the Central Province. That shrewd and far-sighted ruler, having opened road communication between the hill country and the coast, was not content to allow his labours to be barren of results. In 1825 he opened a coffee plantation near Kandy, and his example was followed by Mr. George Bird, who the next year started coffee planting on extensive lines near Gampola. Little further was done for some years, but in 1837 great activity was shown, and soon the country was in the thick of a "boom." There was mad speculation in land on the part of all sorts and conditions of people,

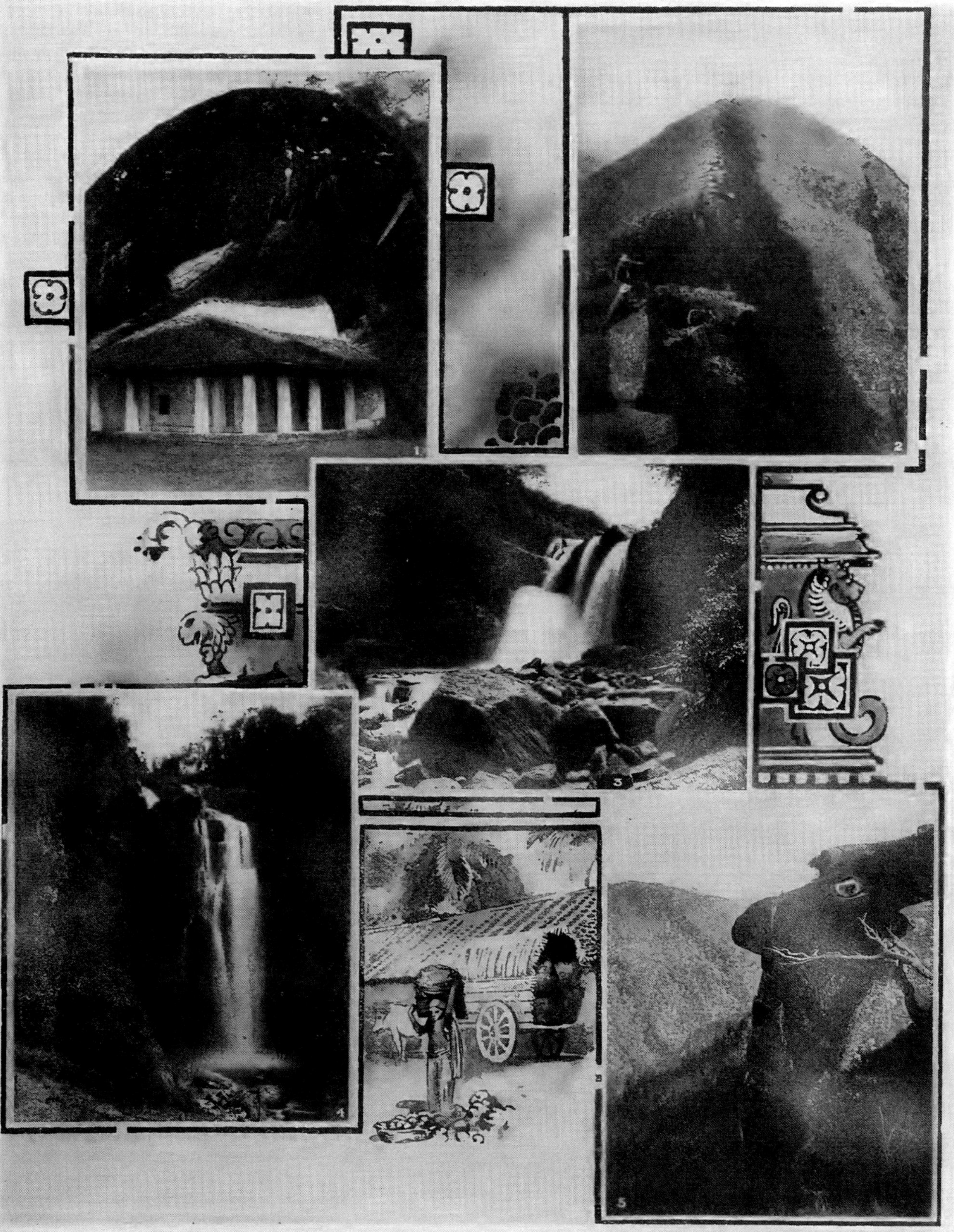

KAIDUGALA TEMPLE, PERADENIYA. MATURATA.

WATERFALL AT RAMBODA. KIRKOSWALD FALLS, BOGAWANTALAWA. MATURATA. (Another view.)

THE LOCAL BOARD, MATALE.

from the Governor downwards. In 1845 the financial crisis in England reacted gravely on the planting industry, and widespread ruin was wrought. Not for ten years did

THE RESERVOIR, KANDY.

the country recover from the blow, and then, confidence being restored, the coffee industry took a new and vigorous lease of life. The opening of "the Wilderness of the Pearls"—Dimbula, Dikoya, and Maskeliya—under the auspices of Sir Hercules Robinson, led to the highest level of prosperity being reached in 1868, 1869, and 1870, in each of which years the exports slightly exceeded 1,000,000 cwts., of a value in European markets of not less than £4,000,000 sterling, against 34,000 cwts., valued at £120,000, exported in 1837; a marvellous development in thirty years of a tropical industry.[1] The opening up of the famous Dimbula district took place as early as 1843. It was begun from Nuwara Eliya by Captain Pallisser, of the Ceylon Rifles, who had a hunting box at Radella, and who planted there a few coffee bushes by way of experiment. The growth of the plants was so good that the plantation, which was at first merely a plaything, became a reality. Meanwhile a second sapping had begun from another direction, and overlapped the ridge, and a third party had followed the river from the low-country. These three focuses of action were gradually extended, and the jungle was, so to speak, eaten away. The progress made was rapid,

H. J. P. SAMARASEKERE.

and it was the more astonishing as there were no roads, and Kandy, 40 miles away, was the nearest place at which provisions could be purchased. "Between 1869 and 1879," says Mr. John Ferguson in his valuable work from which we have already quoted, "over 400,000 acres of Crown land were sold by the Ceylon Government, bringing in more than £1,000,000 sterling to the revenue, and of this 100,000 acres were brought into cultivation with coffee, at an outlay of not less than from 2 to 2½ millions sterling, almost entirely in the upland districts referred to." The appearance of the leaf disease, a fungoid growth dignified by scientists with the imposing name *Hemilcia vastatrix*, worked a disastrous change in the situation. The story of its discovery as told by a leading Dimbula planter is interesting. "The disease," he says, "began in 1869, curiously enough in one of the most outlying districts of the province, upon the estate of Mr. Keith McLellan. This gentle-

[1] "Ceylon in 1905," by John Ferguson.

man, after walking through his estate, noticed some orange-coloured dust on his coat. He thought nothing of it at the time, and on arriving at his other estate near Kandy got his servant to put the coat out to air on the tea bushes, which at that time were planted quite up to the bungalow. It was afterwards noted that this estate was the first on the Kandy side to be attacked. No doubt Mr.

THE JUBILEE MEMORIAL, KANDY.

KANDYAN CHIEF WITH HIS HEADMEN AND STAFF.

McLellan's coat was the medium which conveyed the disease to the estate. Once the disease got hold, it spread like wildfire through the country. Nevertheless, the coffee industry was not for a time markedly injured. In 1878, a dry season well suited to the coffee growth, the planters picked a bumper crop in spite of the disease. By 1881, however, all was dust. You might say that the depreciation of property in eighteen months, divided amongst 1,000 proprietors, was £12,000,000 sterling. The blow was a tremendous one, but we recovered from its effects, thanks to tea. It was in the early eighties that we

THE LAKE AT KANDY.

began to experiment with tea in large quantities, mostly in the lower districts. By 1883–84 it was made clear that we would have to go into it in Dimbula, and by 1890 we could see our way quite clear to handsome profits. The years 1890–96 were a period of abounding prosperity. In 1896 the fixing of exchange came as a severe blow to us, and this, with over-production, led us to consider measures for the protection of our interests. The formation of the Thirty Committee was the outcome of the movement. This body was charged with the duty of taking steps to promote the introduction of tea into foreign parts. On its recommendation the tea cess was imposed—this being, I imagine, the only instance on record of a trading community taxing themselves for purposes which were outside the scope of their ordinary operations. Between the failure of coffee and the absolute success of tea we had been planting cinchona as an experiment, and the history of the cultivation of this tree is perhaps one of the most extraordinary things in the history of agricultural operations, because the cinchona is

GENERAL VIEW OF KANDY.

a delicate growth, very liable to damp off, and it was never supposed that large areas could be cultivated profitably. However, as events proved, the assumption was erroneous. Great tracts of land were planted with remarkable results. In 1887 the output of cinchona bark reached 15,000,000 lbs., the result being that we knocked the price of manufactured quinine from a maximum of 24s. down to a minimum of 8½d. I have no hesitation in saying that the history of rubber will to a very large extent repeat the history of cinchona, excepting perhaps that we shall have a little more prescience in dealing with the inevitable over-production."

Regarded as a playground and health resort, the hill districts of the Central Province are without a superior in the tropics. The Ceylon Government Railway, which traverses the area from end to end, smooths the path of the intending visitor, who in a few hours of comfortable and even luxurious travel can penetrate to the heart of a country which a century ago was a land of terror, and which at a much later period was regarded as an inaccessible

THE LAKE AT KANDY.
(Another view.)

wilderness. The train journey is one of the most interesting in the world. You pass from the palm groves of Colombo and its tropical heat to a country where the rose and other typical English flowers grow in profusion, in a climate which resembles that of a perfect English summer. *En route* you have a glorious succession of panoramas of mountain and vale, of tea gardens and forest-clad slopes, of winding silvery rivers and tumbling waterfalls. The very cuttings of the line on the higher ground contribute to the interest of the traveller, for they are covered with a soft green mantle of maidenhair and other delicate ferns, which in England are usually associated with the carefully tended stove-house.

There are many centres of attraction in this beautiful land, but pride of place belongs to Nuwara Eliya, the great sanatorium of the island. The district in the early part of the century was only known to the villagers of Uva, who resorted there to search for gems and work iron ore. In 1819 some Europeans visiting the locality for purposes of sport were greatly struck with the beauty of the scenery and the excellence of the

THE HON. MR. J. P. LEWIS (GOVERNMENT AGENT) AND KANDYAN CHIEFS.

KANDY.

1. Children Playing. 2. A Street Water Stand. 3. Elephants having their Morning Bath. 4. Elephant and Attendant. 5. The Market. 6. By the Lake. 7. A Lake Scene. 8. In the Bazaar. 9 Elephant returning from Water.

SUPERINTENDENT'S BUNGALOW, HORNSEY ESTATE, DIKOYA.

climate, and their favourable report led in 1828 to the establishment on the site of the present town of a military station and a sanatorium for the troops. In 1833 the place was adopted as the headquarters of the administration of the then Nuwara Eliya district. Thereafter its fame grew, and with it the size of the township. Bungalows were built, shops were opened, and all the usual adjuncts of a popular resort were one by one added. Now the station can boast of several first-class hotels, a residential school for European lads—the only one in the island—a pretty English church and other places of worship, clubs, golf-links, racing, tennis, croquet and hockey grounds, and reading-rooms and libraries. A pretty ornamental lake, named after Sir William Gregory, during whose governorship it was constructed, is another of the features of the place. Finally, there is Queen's Cottage, the modest summer residence of the Governor. Many beautiful excursions are open to the visitor to Nuwara Eliya. He may, if a mountaineer, climb False Pedro,

GARDEN ON HORNSEY ESTATE.

DOLOSBAGE, VIEW FROM DATIE OYA. RIVER SCENE AT GAMPOLA.

KNUCKLES. MATURATA.

or essay Pidurutalagala, the highest peak in Ceylon; if less active and ambitious, he may wander amid the sylvan beauties of the forests which environ the place about, or he may drive to the Rambodda Pass, 7,000 ft. above the sea, and feast his eyes with a view of incomparable loveliness. Also within compass of a morning's excursion is a visit to the Hakgala Botanical Gardens. The gardens are situated at an elevation of 5,600 ft., in a beautiful position about 6¼ miles from Nuwara Eliya on the Badulla road. The view from a vantage point in the gardens is one of the grandest in Ceylon, extending over the Uva amphitheatre to the Haputale, Namunukula, and Madulsima ranges. Immediately at the back of the gardens the grand Hakgala rock rises 1,300 ft. above the surface

COLONEL BYRDE.

of the gardens, and forms an imposing background. On the whole there are few places which have within easy reach so many points of interest as Nuwara Eliya.

The province generally has greatly prospered in recent years. Its revenue has increased by nearly Rs. 1,000,000 in the last decade. In 1905, the total amount paid into the Treasury was Rs. 3,890,350, a record collection. For administrative purposes the province is divided into the following three districts: Kandy, Nuwara Eliya, and Matara. The town of Kandy is the only populous centre in the province which is endowed with a full municipal constitution. The larger towns of Gampola, with a population of 3,791, Nawalapitiya, with a population of 3,454, and Hatton and Dikoya, with a population of 2,341, are under the administration of a Local Board in each place. The affairs of Nuwara Eliya are looked after by a Board of Improvement, while Matale has a Local Board.

KANDY DISTRICT.

COLONEL H. BYRDE.

There are few better known public men in the Kandy district than the gentleman who is the subject of this sketch. For many years, either as a leading planter or an official, he has been a conspicuous figure in the life of the community. His career has been of a most varied character. Educated at the Elizabeth College, Guernsey, he passed into the Royal Military College, Sandhurst, in January, 1853, and went satisfactorily through his final examination there in July, 1854. On August 11th following he was gazetted ensign in the 57th Regiment (West Middlesex), and joined the depôt at Birr and Parsonstown, Ireland. In January, 1854, he proceeded to Malta with the draft, and joined the reserve companies, and on June 2nd in the same year proceeded to headquarters in the Crimea in charge of a draft. He served in the trenches before Sebastopol, and was present with his regiment at the attacks on the Quarries on June 7th and 13th, and shared with the storming party in the attack on the Redan on June 18th. He also participated in the second attack on September 8th. In October he proceeded with his regiment to Odessa, and was present at

THE DUKE'S FACE FROM THE HORNSEY ESTATE, DIKOYA.

the bombardment and capture of Kinburn, at the mouth of the river Dneiper. In November he returned to camp in the Crimea, and after the signing of peace on March 30, 1856, embarked with his regiment for Malta. He was promoted Captain in 1857, and received the Crimean medal with clasp and the Turkish medal. In May, 1858, he proceeded with headquarters, *viâ* Suez, to Aden, and joined the left wing, the headquarters going on to Bombay. In January, 1859, he joined the Staff College at Sandhurst, and retired from the service in January, 1860, by the sale of his commission as Captain. In March of the same year he proceeded to Ceylon and engaged in the cultivation of coffee until 1867. Afterwards he was in business until 1873. In 1861 he was elected Secretary of the Planters' Association, and he was Chairman during the years 1862, 1863, 1864, 1866, 1867, and 1868. In February, 1869, he was re-elected Secretary, and continued in that office until June, 1873. In 1866 he was elected a member of the Kandy Municipal Council, and continued to serve on that body until June, 1873. In July of that year he was appointed Secretary of the Council, and held that position until August 31, 1906. In 1883 Colonel Byrde, in addition to his duties as Secretary, acted as Superintendent of Works, and in that capacity was in charge of the works for the supply of water to the town. In 1881 Colonel Byrde joined the Ceylon Volunteers as Captain. Subsequently he was promoted Major, and he became Lieut.-Colonel in 1892. He retired from the corps in 1904 with the rank of Honorary Colonel.

THE HON. MR. E. ROSLING.

The Hon. Mr. Edward Rosling, the Planters' Member of the Legislative Council, is one of the best known and most popular members of the planting community. Like many other men who have made big reputations on the island, he "drifted into planting." Born in December, 1863, and educated at Queenswood College, Hampshire, he studied for the Indian Civil Service, but owing to ill-health failed to pass the examination. In 1886 he went on a pleasure trip to the colonies, visiting in turn the Cape, Tasmania, New Zealand, New South Wales, and Victoria. Returning to England, he started away again almost immediately for Ceylon, where he proposed to enter upon a planter's career. He landed in Colombo in January, 1887, and worked upon an estate as probationer until May in the following year, when he went home and married. In December, 1887, he was once more on his way to Ceylon, and has been associated with planting enterprise on the island ever since. In 1897 he became Chairman of the Dimbula Planters' Association, and in 1900 was elected Chairman of the parent Association. In the following year he was re-elected, and in November, 1902, he was chosen as the Planters' Representative on the Legislative Council. In March, 1907, Mr. Rosling proceeded on a well-earned holiday to England.

HANWELLA RUBBER AND TEA ESTATE.
RAMBONG RUBBER. TAPPING RUBBER. THE BUNGALOW.

ATGALLA TEA ESTATE.

The Atgalla estate, Gampola, is owned by the Ceylon Tea Plantation Company, Ltd., and the resident manager is Mr. G. C. Bliss, who has been there since 1893. It is situated between 1,700 ft. and 1,800 ft. above sea-level, and comprises 450 acres under tea cultivation, of which 200 acres are interplanted with Para rubber, as well as 75 acres planted with rubber only. The yearly output from the estate is 250,000 lbs. of tea, and another 150,000 lbs. made from leaf bought from small growers also passes through the estate factory. Mr. Bliss has recently returned from Burma, where he visited the only rubber estate in that country, and was much impressed with the good growth of the rubber planted there.

EDGAR TURNER.

The twenty-fourth Chairman of the Planters' Association, and its Secretary for several years, Mr. Edgar Turner's is a well-known figure in Ceylon planting circles. Born in 1862 in Ipswich, of a family which has played a great part in the modern history of the Suffolk town, Mr. Turner, after an education received at the Ipswich School, went to Mincing Lane to learn tea-tasting. A heavy premium was demanded in those days; but in the spring of 1884 he had to leave London owing to an accident at athletics, and three years elapsed before he was allowed to do any work. Mr. Turner came out to Ceylon in 1887, and lived for five months with Mr. N. M. Home, on Woodstock, Ambegamuwa. He then took up

E. TURNER.
(Secretary, Planters' Association, Kandy.)

a billet on Rahatungoda under Mr. P. E. Sewell, and has lived in Upper Hewaheta ever since. He helped to start the Maturata and Hewaheta District Planters' Association in 1896, and became Hon. Secretary in 1897, Chairman in 1898, and again served as Hon. Secretary in 1899. He has been a member of the Thirty Committee since 1897, and last year he visited South India as one of the two Labour Commissioners sent over by the Association. Mr. Turner married, in 1889, the daughter of the late Mr. R. J. Ransome, of Ipswich. Mr. Turner is giving up the secretaryship of the Planters' Association to take up the visiting agent's work for Messrs. Bosanquet & Co.

NEW PERADENIYA ESTATE.

This is an important estate owned by the Ceylon Land and Produce Company, Ltd., and managed by Mr. R. Anderson, who resides on the property. It consists of 454 acres of land situated near Peradeniya, 414 of which are cultivated. Here tea and rubber are intermixed, and there are a few acres of cacao plantation. The yield of tea annually is about 275,000 lbs., whilst a large amount of leaf, averaging about 750,000 lbs. yearly, is bought from the smaller growers. The factory machinery on the estate is capable of dealing with 3,000 lbs. of leaf daily.

The company owning the estate was formed in 1884, and since they took over the property from private owners there have been many changes. Sugar was planted first, only to be discarded in favour of coffee, which in its turn was superseded by tea and rubber. The resident manager, Mr. Anderson, has had twenty-six years' experience of planting, twenty-two of these having been spent on this estate. He is a Highlander from Kincardineshire. He came out to Ceylon to take up planting in 1880.

WILLIAM DUFF GIBBON.

For over half a century Mr. W. D. Gibbon has been a planter in Ceylon, and he is now the oldest in the island, having celebrated the jubilee of his local residence in 1905. He landed on Ceylon shores at Point-de-Galle on September 24, 1855, and at this time there was neither telegraph nor railway, and letters and passengers alike were dependent on the horse coaches for conveyance between Colombo, Kandy, and Galle. There were no hotels, with the exception of those only equal in comfort and cleanliness to a very second-rate rest-house of the present day. Coffee was then the great product, though the planting area was small in comparison with what it now is. Mr. Gibbon is a Scotchman, having been born at the Manse of Lonmay, Aberdeenshire, in July, 1837. His father had been a minister of the Established Church of Scotland for fifty-three years, whilst his mother's father and grandfather (Duffs) had been clergymen of a church near Banff for ninety-five years. Mr. Gibbon was educated at Banff Academy and Aberdeen Grammar School, passing from there to Marischall College and the University of Aberdeen. He was only eighteen years of age when he left college to sail for Ceylon with his brother-in-law, Mr. R. B. Tytler, and his planting career was commenced on the Madulkelle estate, in the Kelebokka district, under "Donald Stewart," who subsequently became the planting "King of Coorg." Mr. Gibbon subsequently took over the management of Oonoonagalla estate, and at a still later date added to his responsibilities the management of Madulkelle. In 1858-59 he took charge of Hoolankanda, of 800 acres, for Mr. Tytler, remaining there until 1864, when he moved to Oodewelle in the Hantane district. After a period of about six years' residence in this district Mr. Gibbon was appointed visiting agent for Messrs. J. M. Robertson & Co. to the estates in their books in the neighbourhood, and also attorney for Mr. R. B. Tytler, and agent for his properties. In consequence of the heavy and continuous work he removed to Kandy, where he became agent for the British North Borneo Company and for Messrs. Dent Bros. & Co., of London. Mr. Gibbon is still an active worker, visiting estates in the remotest quarters of the island. Mr. Gibbon is one of the oldest members of the Planters' Association, and a quondam Secretary. He was elected Chairman in 1878

W. D. GIBBON.

and Acting Secretary in 1899. He has been a member of the Provincial and Road Committees and of the Kandy Municipal Council, whilst during the period of Sir West Ridgeway's governorship Mr. Gibbon was made a Justice of the Peace, and was also nominated to act as Planting Member of the Legislative Council. He married Katherine, daughter of the late Mr. Andrew Murray, of Allatnan, Aberdeenshire, and has three sons and three daughters.

HINDUGALLA AND SHRUBS HILL ESTATE.

This estate, situate near Peradeniya, is owned by Mr. H. A. Webb, and consists of 643 acres. Of the area 543 acres are planted with tea, and in addition a few old rubber-trees (about sixty) on the estate being planted between. There is a factory on the estate to

THE FACTORY. THE BUNGALOW. HINDUGALLA ESTATE, PERADENIYA.

deal with the output, which, including bought leaf, amounts to about 300,000 lbs. yearly. An interesting feature of the estate is the bungalow, which is a very old one, its history dating back to the old coffee days in 1850. Mr. Webb, who is a Gloucestershire man, has been out since 1884, but previous to that he was for three years in Assam. His brother, Mr. E. Webb, is a partner in the estate.

NORWOOD ESTATE.

The Eastern Produce and Estates Company are the proprietors of this estate at Dikoya, which is under the management of Mr. R. H. Eliot, who also inspects the other estates of the company. This company is the largest in the island, owning a gross acreage of 16,000 acres, 12,000 acres planted with tea, 2,000 with rubber, also cloves, nutmegs, pepper, vanilla, cinchona, &c. The company owns eighteen estates. They are in thirteen different districts of Ceylon, three being in the low-country. The acreage of the Norwood estate is 880 acres, 731 of tea and the remainder jungle. The output is about 400,000 lbs. annually, the whole being dealt with at the estate factory. The total annual output from the whole of the estates is 4,600,000 lbs. of tea and 25,000 lbs. of rubber.

NORTH COVE ESTATE.

The North Cove estate in the Bogawantalawa district, near Hatton, is owned by Mr. Thomas Farr, who was born in Norfolk, and whose ancestors built Cove Hall, Suffolk. He was educated at Fauconberg Grammar School, Beccles, and at Uppingham and London. He came to Ceylon in 1870 and joined his only

THOMAS FARR AND PACK OF ELK HOUNDS.

friend in the island on a coffee estate in the Haputale district. Later he worked for Messrs. George Steuart & Co., the head of the firm being then Mr. Alfred Wise, and in 1891 he built the bungalow in which he now resides. The factory and machinery were erected some four years earlier. He had purchased in 1879 Government land, which he planted with coffee, cinchona, and finally tea, 240 acres of which yield about 500 lbs. to the acre. In 1897 he sold a quarter share of this. He is very fond of big game hunting, and has a large and varied collection of trophies. A fact which is interesting is that Mr. Farr came out to Ceylon before the opening of the Suez Canal. He journeyed from England to Alexandria by the P. & O. *Pera*, went by rail to Suez, and from here he proceeded by P. & O. boat *Mooltan* to Galle.

DARAWELLA ESTATE.

The Anglo-Ceylon and General Estates Company, Ltd., are the proprietors of this estate, of which Mr. E. Hamlin is the resident manager. The estate is situated above the village of Dikoya, and encloses an area of about 596 acres of tea plantation, 31 acres of timber and grass, and 48 acres of waste land. The average output of tea annually from here dealt with at the estate factory is about 298,000 lbs. Mr. Hamlin has been in Ceylon since 1887, and previous to that he was twenty-three years in India, where he still owns property. He has been on the Darawella estate for the past twelve years. He is an all-round sportsman and an enthusiastic follower of golf, of which game he is an adept, he having won the Championship Cup in 1893. He is President of the Dikoya and Maskeliya Cricket Club, and also the Ceylon Nursing Association, and is an artist of repute, his excellent work with the brush having won for him many medals. He has over 120 water-colour pictures hung in his bungalow. He has taken great interest in rifle shooting, and was commandant of one of the best shooting battalions in India, and which won the Bangalore Cup in 1881.

KUDA OYA ESTATE.

The Kuda Oya estate, Dikoya, within about 3 miles of Hatton, comprises 522 acres under cultivation of tea, 34 acres of fuel, and 177 of waste land. An average of about 200,000 lbs. of tea is obtained yearly, a large and complete factory having been erected on the estate for the purpose of dealing with this. The estate belongs to the Tea Corporation, a London Company, and is managed by Mr. Alex. Wardrop, who resides on the estate. He has been in Ceylon since 1878, but on the Kuda Oya estate only about a year. He is a member of the Kandy and local clubs, and J.P. and U.P.M. for the Hatton-Nuwara district.

WANARAJAH ESTATE.

This estate at Dikoya is owned by the Wanarajah Tea Company of Ceylon, and managed by Mr. Keith Rollo. It has an area of 1,060 acres on which tea is planted and 70 acres of forest and timber. The output of tea is dealt with at a very fine and up-to-date factory on the estate. In earlier days this estate was one of the best in Ceylon for cinchona. Mr. Rollo is a native of Aberdeenshire, Scotland, from whence he came to Ceylon thirty-nine years ago for coffee planting. When coffee failed he tried cinchona, and finally tea.

BATTALGALLA ESTATE.

Mr. G. C. R. Norman manages the above estate for the Battalgalla Estate Company, Ltd., who are the proprietors. The estate is situated in the Dikoya district, and about a mile away is the Hadley estate, of which Mr. Norman is also manager. He came out to Ceylon in 1872, and has been on these estates for thirteen years. Previous to that he was engaged in coffee planting until that industry failed. The combined estates are composed of 635 acres of tea plants and 41 acres of grass and timber land. The average annual output of tea is about 250,000 lbs., and this is dealt with at a beautifully equipped factory on the estate.

DIKOYA ESTATE.

The Dikoya estate is owned by Messrs. T. L. and G. R. R. Villiers, for whom Mr. W. H. Graham is the resident manager. There are about 353 acres of tea plantation on the estate, which produce about 170,000 lbs. of tea annually. There are also 45 acres of jungle and timber. Mr. Graham first came to Ceylon, in 1877, in the old coffee days, and returned home in 1880. He came again to Ceylon, however, in 1890, and has resided here since. He is an ardent golf player, and is the hon. sec. of the Dikoya and Maskeliya Cricket Club.

ABBOTSLEIGH ESTATE.

This estate in the Dikoya district, about three miles from the town of Hatton, is surrounded by pretty scenery, one of the many vistas being a glimpse of the famous Adam's Peak which is to be obtained a few yards from the bungalow. The estate is managed by Messrs. E. F. Fuller and J. E.

THE BUNGALOW. THE FACTORY. ABBOTSLEIGH ESTATE, HATTON.

C. J. ACTON'S BUNGALOW.

Biddell. The yearly output of tea from the 824 acres set apart for its cultivation is 350,000 lbs., and is of a fine quality. In addition to this land there are 179 acres of jungle and timber and 63 acres of grass. All the tea is prepared in the local factory.

GONAGALLA ESTATE.

The Lanka Plantations Company own the estate of the above name in the Dikoya district, and Mr. J. G. Palmer resides there and manages for them. There are 850 acres of tea plantation and 88 acres of jungle. The average output of tea from this estate each year is about 400,000 lbs., and all of this is made in the factory on the estate. Coming to Ceylon in 1877, Mr. Palmer first took up coffee planting, later trying cinchona, and for the past eighteen years has tended the Gonagalla estate.

ORWELL GROUP ESTATE.

At Gampola there are two estates which form the above group, and these are under the management of Mr. C. J. Acton, who resides on the spot. Mr. Acton came out to Ceylon in 1892, and has held this group for the past six years. He is a native of Worcestershire. The estate comprises about 430 acres, and yields an annual output of about 170,000 lbs. of tea. This is from 410 acres, the remaining 20 acres being planted solely with rubber. With the tea are planted 25,000 rubber-trees. In addition to the output from the estate close upon 250,000 lbs. of leaf are annually purchased from small growers, and the whole is dealt with at the factory on the estate.

THE SCOTTISH CEYLON TEA COMPANY, LTD.

This company, whose London office is 16, Philpott Lane, E.C., owns seven estates, most of these being in the vicinity of Dikoya. Mr. David Kerr is their manager and resides on the Strathdon estate, Dikoya. The estates, districts, and acreage are: Invery and Waterloo, Dikoya district, area 513 acres, planted area 483 acres; Strathdon, Dikoya district, total 304 acres, planted 292 acres; Abergeldie, Lower Dikoya district, total 193 acres, planted 180 acres; Benachie, Lower Dikoya, total 338 acres, planted 297 acres; Lonach, Lower Dikoya, total 421 acres, planted 301 acres; Mincing Lane, Maskeliya district, total 194 acres, planted 183 acres; total area 1,963 acres, planted 1,736 acres. On the Invery and Waterloo, Strathdon, Lonach, and Mincing Lane estates there are factories. The average output annually per acre is 450 lbs., the total being 778,000 lbs. Of the total acreage 1,720 acres are planted with tea, 27 with timber, &c., and 216 are covered with jungle, &c.

Mr. Kerr has been associated with the company since it was formed in 1889. He first came to Ceylon as a coffee planter in

DIKOYA PLANTERS.

KEITH ROLLO, Wanarajah. H. ELLIOTT, Resident Manager, Norwood Estate.
WM. GRAHAM, Dikoya Estate. G. C. R. NORMAN, Battalagalla Estate.
E. G. PALMER, Gonagalla Estate. E. HAMLIN, Darawella Estate.

1874. He is a general visiting agent for other companies in the island both in tea and rubber, is a member of the Royal Colonial Institute, and a member of the Nuwara Eliya and all the local clubs.

THE BUNGALOW, FRUIT HILL ESTATE, HATTON.

JAMES ROBERT WIGHT.

Mr. James Robert Wight, Manager of the Kandy Branch of the National Bank of India,

J. R. WIGHT.
(Manager, National Bank of India, Kandy.)

is the son of Mr. Thomas Wight, of Dumfriesshire. He was born in 1867 in that county, and at an early age entered the Inspector's Department of the Royal Bank of Scotland. In this capacity he served for three years at Sanquhar and at the head office at Edinburgh, thus gaining valuable experience in banking. In 1888 he joined the National Bank of India, and before coming to Ceylon served for fifteen years in the East. In 1900 he came to the island and took up the position he now holds. In 1906 he married Edith, daughter of the late Mr. Sanderson.

FRUIT HILL ESTATE.

In Dikoya, near Hatton, the Lanka Plantations Company, Ltd., own the above estate, Mr. Gerald P. Walker being the resident manager. The area of the estate is 237 acres of tea plantation, which yields about 95,000 lbs. of tea annually, this being made at the estate factory, which is equipped with a plant of the most modern design. Mr. Walker came out about four years ago. He is a member of the Ceylon Mounted Rifles and the local clubs.

NATIONAL BANK OF INDIA, LTD., KANDY.

W. J. NOBLE.

The Rev. Walter J. Noble is the Wesleyan Methodist minister at Hatton, his special work being performed amongst the Tamil coolies engaged on the numerous tea estates in the district, which is a most important one, more tea being forwarded from the station at Hatton than from any other district in the island, and the goods traffic is second only to that of Colombo. The church, which was established in 1890, had a small beginning, but it has progressed rapidly, and to-day the services (English) are attended by Protestants of all denominations. An excellent work is being done on broad-minded principles by the staff, which consists of five catechists. There are about 22 schools, with about 800 children on the books, in the district, whilst the membership in this particular section is 160, most of whom are converts, or children of converts, from Hinduism. From Mr. Noble's bungalow a clear view is obtained of Adam's Peak, which is some 13 miles distant.

CHAS. VANDERWALL.

Mr. Chas. Vanderwall, who is of Dutch descent, was born in Kandy in 1848, and is the son of a leading advocate in that town. On completing his education, which he received at the Colleges Trinity (Kandy) and St. Thomas (Colombo), he adopted his father's profession. He passed his tests, and became a Proctor in 1869. For the first two years he practised in Nuwara Eliya, afterwards going to Kandy, where he is still in practice. He is noted for the manner in which he handles land cases.

By the death of Mr. Vanderwall's father in 1869 the profession suffered no slight loss, as he was at that time looked upon as the leading advocate of Ceylon.

H. HUYBERTSZ.

Dr. Henry Huybertsz, of Kandy, is the son of Mr. J. E. Huybertsz, landed proprietor, and is descended from a Danish naval surgeon who settled in the island during the Dutch occupation. He was born on May 13, 1861, at Colombo, and received his education at

H. HUYBERTSZ.

the Royal College. In 1879 he proceeded to Edinburgh for further medical study, and in 1885 took the degree of L.R.C.P., and afterwards practised for some time in Edinburgh and the Shetland Islands. Upon his return to Ceylon in 1887 he entered the Government Medical Department as Sub-Assistant Colonial Surgeon. He became successively Assistant Colonial Surgeon at Haputale and Kandy, and since 1902 he has been Assistant Colonial Surgeon at the last-named place. He married Miss Noble, daughter of Mr. David Noble, during his stay in Scotland. He is a member of the British Medical Association.

JOHN WILHELMUS SAMUEL ATTYGALLE.

Mr. Attygalle, M.B. and C.M. (Aberdeen), D.A.C.S. Civil Medical Department, District Medical Officer, Gampola, is the eldest son of Dr. John Attygalle, M.D. (Aberdeen), M.R.C.S. (Eng.), retired Provincial Surgeon, Southern Province of Ceylon. He was educated at St. Thomas's College, Colombo, and after his course there entered the Ceylon Medical College in 1888. He passed the first professional examination and proceeded to Scotland to join the University of Aberdeen, where, after obtaining honours in zoology, materia medica, anatomy, surgery, pathology, and medical jurisprudence, he

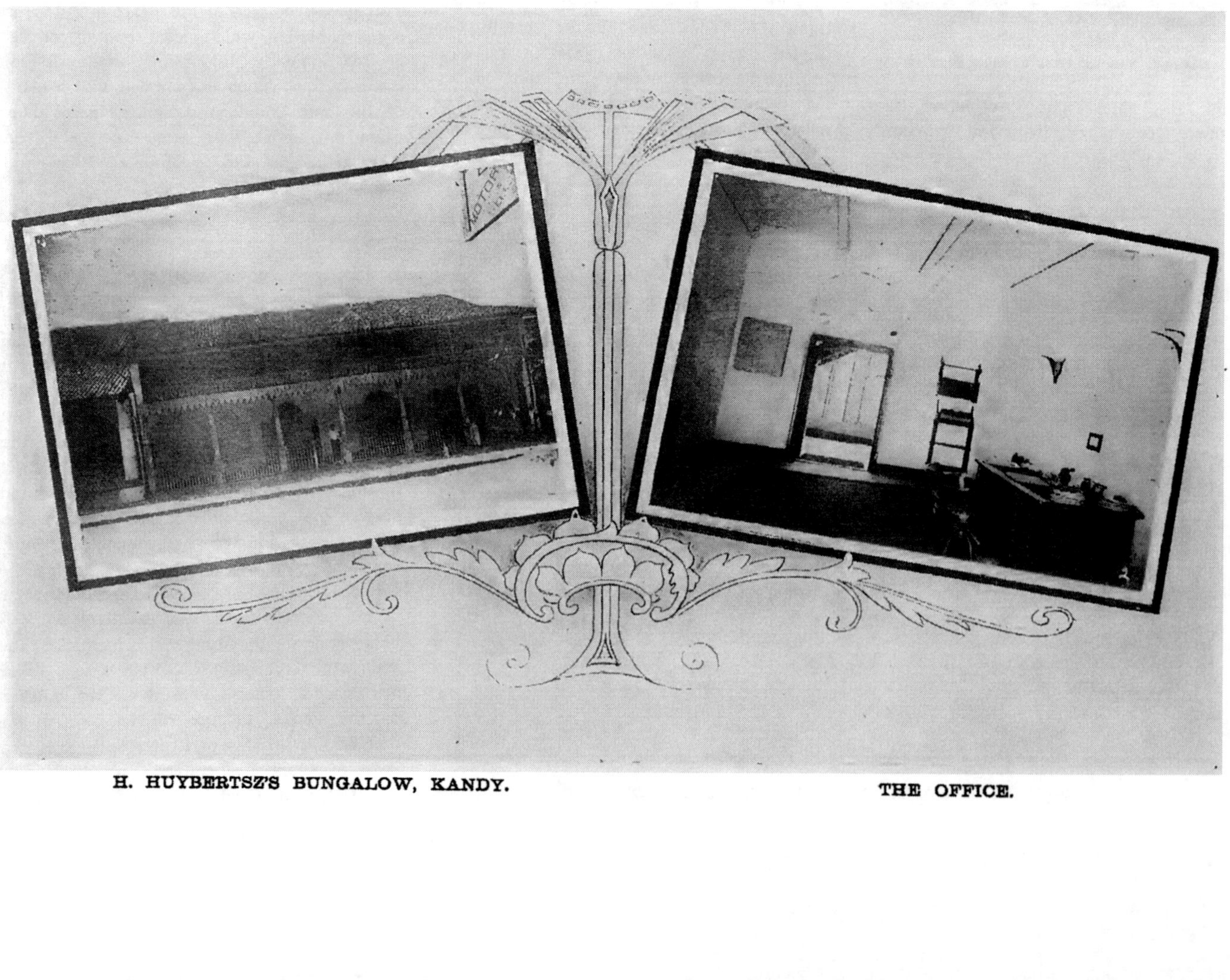

H. HUYBERTSZ'S BUNGALOW, KANDY. THE OFFICE.

DR. AND MRS. J. W. S. ATTYGALLE AND CHILD, THE BUNGALOW, AND THE DRAWING-ROOM.

graduated as Bachelor of Medicine and Master in Surgery. Later, after attending a course of lectures at the Royal Asylum, Aberdeen, he obtained the diploma, by examination, in psychological medicine of the Medico-Psychological Association of Great Britain and Ireland. He held several posts, subsequently, as assistant to medical men in the Midlands of England, and was afterwards appointed junior house-surgeon to the Northampton Infirmary, which post he held for eighteen months. He is a member of several medical societies, chief of which are the British Medical Association and the Röntgen Society, London.

The doctor returned to Ceylon in August, 1897, and joined the Civil Medical Department on January 1, 1898. He was appointed Surgeon-in-Charge of the Police Force, Colombo, and Honorary Surgeon to the Victoria Home, with the rank of Deputy Assistant Colonial Surgeon. At one time he was a lecturer at the Ceylon Medical College, and also held the lecturership in pathology and the post of anæsthetist to the General Hospital, Colombo. He was also lecturer in biology, medical jurisprudence, toxicology, and demonstrator of anatomy on various occasions. After eight and a half years' service in Colombo, Dr. Attygalle was sent to Kandy as Assistant Superintendent of Vaccination for the Central Province, which office he held for three months, being then appointed District Medical Officer, Gampola, and ranking as officer of the first grade in the Civil Medical Department.

The subject of this sketch is one of the committee of management of the Victoria Masonic Temple, and is a prominent and high Mason, being a Past Master of Lodge Bonnie Doon, 611, S.C., Past King of the Royal Arch, Chapter 107, S.C., Past Worshipful Master of the Cryptic Degrees Council, No. 23, Past Thrice Illustrious Master of the Allied Degrees Council, No. 21, of England and Wales. He is also a member of the Preceptory and Priory, holding high office. He was one of the founders and first secretary of Grant Lodge, Galle, 2,862, E.C.; founder and First Senior Warden of Connaught Lodge, 2,940, E.C.; and is a member of Sphinx Lodge, 107, T.C., in connection with which he held the office of organist for several years. He is also Past Grand Steward and Past Director of Ceremonies of the Grand Lodge of all Scottish Freemasonry in India. His chief recreation is music.

EDWIN BEVEN.

Mr. Edwin Beven is a lawyer, and, with one exception, is the oldest practitioner in Kandy. Born at Chilaw, in the North-Western Province of the island, he received his education at St. Thomas's and the Royal Colleges. He commenced to practise in 1864 at the District Court, Kandy, but later he became a Proctor of the Supreme Court. In 1872 he was appointed a member of the Town Council, and occupies a seat at the present time, having served almost continuously for a third of a century. Joining the Ceylon Light Infantry Volunteers as a private, he was steadily promoted until, in 1905, he retired with the rank of Lieutenant-Colonel. He holds the long service medal and the V.D. Mr. Beven is a member of the Provincial Road Committee. He has two sons in the Civil Service, one holding the additional

EDWIN BEVEN.

district judgeship and magistracy of Kurunegala, and the other the position of Office Assistant to the Government Agent of Batticaloa.

GEORGE P. HAY.

Dr. George Powell Hay was born at Nuwara Eliya in 1874, and received his college training at St. Thomas's College, Colombo. He then entered the Ceylon Medical College, and, having passed out as a licentiate, joined the s.s. *Valdivia* as surgeon to the German Deep Sea Expedition, under Professor Cuhn, of Leipsic. In this capacity he made a cruise of the Indian Ocean and the East Coast of Africa. After this he went to Edinburgh, and graduated L.R.C.P. and L.R.C.S., as well as L.F.P. and L.F.S. of Glasgow with honours. He practised at Blantyre and other places in Scotland, and visited the Straits Settlement in 1900. Returning to Ceylon in the same year, he started as a private practitioner in Kandy. Dr. Hay is a member of the British Medical Association, the Orient Club, the Automobile Club, and the Kandy Sports Club, and is also President of the Kandy Rovers' Club and of the Kandy Cyclists' Union. He married, in 1900, Ernestine, daughter of Mr. B. O. Dias, Proctor of the Supreme Court. As early as 1891 he joined the Ceylon Medical Staff Corps as a Volunteer, and became colour-sergeant; but after ten years he transferred to the combatant ranks, and is now Lieutenant of the Ceylon Light Infantry and attached to "H" Company, Kandy. Dr. Kay's residence is Fountain House, Kandy.

THEODORE CECIL VAN ROOYEN.

Mr. T. C. Van Rooyen, Notary Public, Proctor of the Supreme Court and Justice of the Peace, was born in Colombo. After being educated at the Wesley and Royal Colleges of his native city, he was articled to the late Hon. James Van Langenberg, father of the present advocate of that name. On the completion of his articles, and having passed his examinations, he commenced practice in Hatton in the year 1885, and at the present time he commands an extensive practice, numbering amongst his *clientèle* the majority of the tea-planters of the district. He is a member of the Local Board (senior unofficial), and holds a commission in the Ceylon Light Infantry as Lieutenant, and is the officer in command of the Hatton detachment.

SAMASTA WICKRAMA KARUNATIAAKA ABHAYAWARDANA BHUWANASEKERA JAYASUNDARA MUDIYANSE RALAHAMILLAGE TIKIRI BANDA PANABOKKE.

This gentleman, a descendant of one of the most ancient of aristocratic families in the island, was born in 1846 at the ancestral residence, Panabokka, a village in Kandupalata, Udunuwara. He was educated at the Kotta Institute and the St. Thomas's College, Colombo, and entered the Government service at the age of twenty-two as an officer in charge of the rural police in the Central Province. Four years later, on March 4, 1872, he was appointed Ratemahatmaya of Udunuwara, the Inspector-General granting him a year's leave of absence to take up this appointment provisionally, on account of meritorious services. About this time he was also selected to commence the working of the village tribunals, this district being the first in which this system was tried under the British Government. Mr. Panabokke in 1873 was made President of the Village Tribunals of Udunuwara, and a year later of the more important division of Uda and Pata Dumbara. This appointment he held until February, 1881, when he resumed his former post as police-inspector. During a two years' leave he

THE RESIDENCE. THE LATE HON. MR. T. B. PANABOKKE.
T. B. PANABOKKE, JUN. MRS. T. B. PANABOKKE.

availed himself of the opportunity to study law, and in 1886 was appointed Ratemahatmaya of Pata Dumbara. Two years subsequently he was transferred to Udapalata. In 1889 he was selected to represent the Kandyans as an unofficial member of the Legislative Council, and in 1897 he was chosen by the same community to represent them at the Jubilee celebrations of Queen Victoria. On his retirement he was appointed Police Magistrate and Commissioner of Requests of Gampola, afterwards being transferred to Matale. He retired from service in 1899, and died in December, 1902. Mr. Panabokke was responsible for several literary works. He edited the text of the "Niti Nighanduwa," a treatise on Kandyan law, translated into Sinhalese from the original, the "Megadhuta" of the famous Indian bard Kalidasa, was the author of a review of Sir Edwin Arnold's "Light of Asia," and a contributor to the *Orientalist*. He came of a very old family, one of his ancestors having received royal recognition during the reign of King Parakrama Bahu for services rendered to the court of Goa. The family own several temples which are richly endowed. The best known of these is the Pusulpiti Vihara.

Tikiri Banda Panabokke, son of the late Hon. T, B, Panabokke, M.L.C., was born in March, 1883, and was educated at Trinity College, Kandy, and Royal College, Colombo, from 1902 to 1906; he read for the Bar, and in 1904 he carried off the first scholarship for the Proctors' intermediate students. In June, 1906, he was first in order of merit in the Proctors' final examination, and later in the year was admitted a Proctor of the District Court of Kandy. He is now in practice at Gampola. In June, 1906, he married Keppitipola Mantri Kumarihamy, a daughter of Monarawila Keppitipola, Ratemahatmaya.

JAMES ROBERT JAYETILEKE.

Mr. James Robert Jayetileke, Secretary of Kandy Municipal Council, started life as a teacher of mathematics. He was born in 1872, and it was whilst attending Colombo Royal College that his special aptitude for mathematics first showed itself, and during that period he was the winner of several Government exhibitions and the Ceylon Mathematical Prize, and took first class honours in the Cambridge Local Senior Examination, with distinctions in classics and mathematics. At the conclusion of his college training he received the important appointment of Senior Mathematical Lecturer at St, Thomas's College, a position which he held from 1893 to 1906, during which period St. Thomas's College held the reputation of being

J. R. JAYETILEKE.

the leading institute in the island for mathematics. Mr. Jayetileke vacated this position to take up the secretaryship of the Kandy

Municipal Council in the latter year. He is a devotee of chess, the "king of games," and won a correspondence game, which lasted nearly two years, against the Ceylon Chess Club, the only chess club in the island.

DR. AND MRS. H. C. SENEVIRATNE AND DAUGHTER.

H. C. SENEVIRATNE.

Dr. H. C. Seneviratne, of Kandy, was horn at Matara in 1859. He is a son of I. de S. Seneviratne, headman of Kandy, and was educated at Colombo Academy, now Royal College, where he passed the Calcutta matriculation examination in 1877. He studied for a year at the Ceylon Medical College, and afterwards went to Madras University, where he graduated L.M.S. three years later. In 1883 he entered the Ceylon Government Medical Service, and five years later he went to Aberdeen, where he graduated M.B. and C.M. in 1889. Upon his return he was again in the Government service until the year 1906, when he commenced private practice at Kandy. He married, in 1897, the eldest daughter of C. Jayetileke, Proctor, of Kandy.

NEVILL BUDD JANSZE.

Mr. Jansze was born in Kandy in 1879, and educated at St. Thomas's College, Colombo. His education complete, he studied for the legal profession, and having successfully passed his final examination, was admitted a Proctor of the District Court of Kandy in March, 1891. He became a Proctor of the Supreme Court in May, 1906. His favourite recreation is tennis, and he is the Vice-President of the Rovers' Club, Kandy.

EDWARD LIONEL WIJEGOONEWARDENE.

Mr. E. L. Wijegoonewardene, a Proctor and member of the Town Council, Kandy, is a native of Colombo, having been born there on December 8, 1879. After the completion of his scholastic course at Trinity College, Kandy, he studied law, and became a Proctor of the District Court of Kandy in 1903. His father, who was also a native of Colombo, became a planter at Kandy, and subsequently owned many estates in different parts of the island. Mr. E. L. Wijegoonewardene, in addition to his legal practice, is also a planter, is the owner of considerable house property in Kandy, and is now starting rubber-planting. He takes a prominent part in the public life of the town, was at one time President of the Kandy Temperance Society, and is a member of the University Association of Ceylon. Being a staunch Buddhist, Mr. Wijegoonewardene takes a strong interest in all works connected with Buddhism, and is a member of the Central Provincial Committee under the Buddhist Temporalities Ordinance, while a good deal of his spare time is devoted to cricket. He is in partnership with Mr. F. L. Goonewardene, a Proctor of the Supreme Court and Notary Public, and they confine their practice to the Kandy district.

E. L. WIJEGOONEWARDENE.

J. W. DE HOEDT AND FAMILY. THE BUNGALOW.

Mr. Frederick Llewellyn Goonewardene, Mr. Wijegoonewardene's partner, is a Proctor of the Supreme Court of the island and a Notary Public. Born on September 16, 1880, he was the youngest Notary Public and Supreme Court Proctor when he was enrolled in June, 1906. His education he received at St. Thomas's College, where he was junior and senior classical prizeman, and acted as editor of the college magazine and captain of the college cricket club. He was articled for the study of law in October, 1899, was called to the Bar in 1903, and was enrolled Supreme Court Proctor and Notary Public three years later. He is the youngest son of Mr. J. R. Goonewardene, who was formerly in the Government service, and is the owner of considerable house property in the Central Province. He is keenly devoted to sport, and at the present time is a member of the Ceylon Colts' Cricket Club and of the Sinhalese Sports Club. In 1901 he was one of the players selected to take part in the Colts *v.* Hon. H. L. Wace's XI.

J. W. DE HOEDT.

Dr. J. W. de Hoedt is the eldest of the two sons of Mr. James Peter de Hoedt, headmaster of St. John's College, who was an accomplished scholar, well known for his facility for coaching pupils for the clerical and Civil Service. He was born at Jaffna on September 22, 1856, and after he had been educated at St. Thomas's College, Colombo, he entered the Medical College there. Upon the completion of the collegiate course he obtained his licence, and occupied a position in the Government service for eight years. He then proceeded to Aberdeen University to prosecute his medical studies further, and in 1891 he took the degree of Bachelor of Medicine and Master in Surgery with second-class honours. Shortly afterwards he returned to Ceylon, and went to Haputale, and then Lindula, and eventually he was Assistant Colonial Surgeon in charge of Kandy Hospital. He married, in 1881, a daughter of Proctor Charles Strantenberg, and has three sons. The eldest of these is studying electrical engineering in London, England, and the other two have taken up planting in the island.

WALKER, SONS & CO., LTD.

The Fairfield Ironworks, Ward Street, Kandy, belonging to Messrs. Walker, Sons & Co., Ltd., is the oldest business firm in Kandy, and has been established since 1854. The firm opened business in Kandy, afterwards branching off into Colombo. They have several departments, including engineering, printing, stores, general, and motor garage. The co-managers are Messrs. R. Wilson and W. A. Goodman, and the staff consists of three Europeans and 89 natives.

WALKER, SONS & CO., LTD.—KANDY PREMISES.

VETTIVELU SARAVANAMUTTU, Mudaliyar.

Mr. Sarâvanamuttu is a Proctor in practice in Kandy. He is a native of Jaffna, where he was born in 1876. He was educated locally and in India, and passed his University examination in 1898. He got through his final examination in 1904, and commenced practising in Kandy the same year.

V. SARAVANAMUTTU'S BUNGALOW, WALTER LODGE.

SAMUEL ARTHUR OWEN.

Samuel Arthur Owen was born at Bristol in the year 1874 and educated there. He was engaged on the dispensing staff of the Royal Infirmary and obtained his L.S.A. degree, afterwards being employed as a dispenser at Clifton and Bath and at St. Mary's Hospital, London. He arrived in Ceylon in 1896, having been appointed manager of the dispensing department of W. Jordan & Co., at Talawakele. He was afterwards manager for J. Wilson & Co., at Agrapatnas, and has been carrying on the business of a dispensing chemist and general merchant since 1902 at Ward Street, Kandy. He was elected for Ward 4 on the Kandy Municipal Council in 1906, and is also a member of the Ceylon Agricultural Society. When camphor was first taken up in the island he and Mr. Nock conducted a series of experiments in connection with the distillation of camphor at the Government Experimental Gardens at Hakgala.

GEO. E. DE MOTTE.

Mr. G. E. de Motte, surveyor and leveller, is the son of Mr. C. A. de Motte, formerly Chief Clerk, P.W.D., but now retired. He was educated at Trinity College, Kandy, and afterwards at a private school and at the Colombo Technical College. At the last-named institution he obtained the diploma in surveying and levelling. During six years he has built up a good practice at Kandy, and he holds the Surveyor-General's special licence to practise surveying at Kandy.

G. E. DE MOTTE'S BUNGALOW.

WALTER DE LIVERA.

Mr. Walter de Livera, son of Franciscus de Livera, Mudaliyar of the Governor's Gate and Justice of the Peace, and a brother of Dr. de Livera, Colonial Surgeon of the North-Western Province and Sabaragamuwa, was born at Colombo in 1863. After being educated at the Royal College he became private secretary, first to the late Sir Harry Dias and afterwards to Sir Archibald Campbell Laurie. In 1898 he was appointed Police Magistrate and Commissioner of Requests at Chilaw and Marawila, and since 1902 he has occupied a similar official position at Gampola and Nawalapitiya. He is a member of the Orient and Turf Clubs and of the Agricultural Society. His wife, whom he married in 1898, is one of the most charming of Ceylon ladies. She is the sister of Solomon Dias Bandaranaike, C.M.G., Maha Mudaliyar. In 1894 she travelled to England with Bishop Copleston, now Metropolitan of India, and was presented to her late Majesty Queen Victoria by Lady Ripon, and for several years was one of the best known figures in English society. After travelling extensively she returned to Ceylon and married Mr. de Livera in 1898. Their little daughter, "Princess" de Livera, is a young lady of extraordinary attainments. She was a contributor to local papers at the early age of seven years. Her descriptive sketches, written in simple childish language, are real gems for children's literature. Her special talent for music and singing (which she has studied from the age of four under Miss Whitehead, the Professor of Music in Ceylon and Medallist, R.A.M.), is a fruitful source of pleasure to her

WALTER DE LIVERA. "THE ORCHARD" BUNGALOW. MISS "PRINCESS" DE LIVERA. MRS. WALTER DE LIVERA.

friends. On one occasion she attracted the notice of Their Excellencies Sir Henry and Lady Blake, who were delighted with her rendering of "The Morris Dance" and her singing of a song soon after her seventh birthday, when the above photograph was taken of her. Both Mr. and Mrs. de Livera are passionately fond of horticulture, and Mr. de Livera has made a name for rice culture, and their home at Gampola, as well as their country seat, "The Orchard," Veyangoda, bears ample proof of the success of their efforts in the cultivation of flowers.

C. ARACHIGE HAMY.

Mr. Costan Arachige Hamy, son of C. Carolis Appohami, landed proprietor, of Kalutara, was born at Kandy in 1837. In 1851 he joined the firm of R. D. Gerard and went to England with his employer, and shortly after his return to Ceylon he became superintendent of the firm's coffee estates, Kent and Ambokka, in the Matale district, besides opening up various other estates in Matale East. When coffee declined he returned to Kandy and commenced contracting in 1880 on the railway extension to Bandarawela and the South Coast line. He continued in this business for fourteen years and then retired; and at the present time he devotes himself to public affairs and the supervision of his various properties. He owns considerable house property at Kandy, and tea, coconut, and rubber estates. He is an elected member of the Kandy Municipal Council and a member of the Agricultural Society.

C. A. HAMY.

KAHAVITA DON JERONIMUS PERERA ABAYASEKARA, Mohandiram.

This gentleman was born in Kandy on September 6, 1855, his parents (Sinhalese of the agricultural or Goigama caste) having settled in Kandy during the latter part of the forties, at the time when the coffee industry was at its height. He holds an appointment in the clerical service at the chief Government Office—the Kachcheri—in Kandy, and for long and faithful service (over twenty-five years) under the Government he was, on June 7, 1900, invested with the rank of Mohandiram. The investiture was performed at Queen's House, Colombo, by His Excellency Sir Joseph West Ridgeway, then Governor of Ceylon. Mr. Abayasekara married, on June 30, 1887, Magdalen Eliza Perera Samarasekera, the youngest daughter of the late D. C. B. P. Samarasekera, Mohandiram of Udugampola in Dasiya Pattu of Alutkuru Korale, in the Western Province. He is a Roman Catholic, to which faith his wife was converted from Buddhism prior to marriage.

S. M. DON PETER SENANAYAKA.

Senanayake Mudalige Don Peter Senanayaka is the son of D. S. Senanayaka, Arachchi of Kandy, and owner of coconut and cinnamon plantations in the Rayigam Korale and landed property at Talpitiya and Kandy, and Collector and Distraining Officer to the Kandy Municipality, and Mary Magdalen, daughter of Kudeligamegay Don Andries Perera, of Wadduwa

FAMILY GROUP. THE BUNGALOW. D. P. SENANAYAKA.

He was horn at Kandy in 1873, and educated at Trinity College there. On completing his education he was for some time Additional Clerk in the Public Works Department, joining the Kandy Municipality in 1892. His appointment was fixed in 1895, in 1897 he became Second Inspector, and subsequently he was appointed Chief Inspector, a position which he still holds. In 1900 he married Cecilie, daughter of H. Paulis Perera Samarasekera, Mohandiram, of Colombo. He has four children—Violet Beatrice, Edith Margaret, Charlotte Gertrude, and Dionisius Gilbert. Mr. Senanayaka is a Buddhist, and resides in Trincomalee Street, Kandy.

GEORGE FRANCIS SOYSA.

Mr. G. F. Soysa is the third son of the late Harmanis Soysa, landed proprietor and one of the leading and most enterprising native (low-country Sinhalese) coffee planters of his day, and Dona Johanna Ferdinando, daughter of the late Don Joseph Ferdinando, of Moratuwa, in the Western Province of the island. He was born at Moratuwa, and educated at Trinity College, Kandy, in which town he resides. In the seventies his father owned the once famous Hatale coffee estate, in the Kandy district, consisting of a thousand odd acres. He is part owner of the Hapugastenne estate, partly planted with tea and cinchona, in the Maskeliya district, of 601 acres. He also owns coconut and cinnamon plantations in the low-country districts of the island, and is possessed of house property at Kandy. He lives at Cross Street, Kandy, and is an elected member of the Kandy Municipal Council for Ward No. 3.

GEORGE FRANCIS SOYSA.

GABRIEL EDWIN MUTHUKRISHNA.

Gabriel Edwin Muthukrishna is a son of Christopher Joseph Muthukrishna, Mudaliyar, and grandson of Abram Manuel Muthukrishna, Mudaliyar of the Golden Gate. He was born at Kandy in 1865, and educated at Trinity and St. Thomas's Colleges. He became Clerk to the Kandy Municipal Council in 1883, Municipal Court Interpreter in 1888, and Additional Shroff in 1892. In 1905, after acting as Assistant Secretary, he became Shroff to the Kandy Municipality. He married, in 1888, Adaline Maud Jane, daughter of Abram Muthukrishna, Mudaliyar, of Colombo. He resides at "Gem Lodge," Peradeniya Road, Kandy.

SPENCER S. CASIECHITTY RAJAWAJIKERE, Mudaliyar.

Mudaliyar Spencer Sparling Casiechitty is in charge of the special-class railway station at Hatton. He has worked on the Ceylon Government Railways since 1873, when he was employed at the Colombo terminus. He has obtained his present post by diligent attention to his duties. At the time of the Allagala slip he was stationmaster at Peradeniya Junction, where he had charge of the trains for about three months. He received his education at St. Thomas's College, Colombo. His family is a very old one, and of high caste; the majority of his relatives have held high positions in the island. His father was J. P. Casiechitty, Mudaliyar of the Seven Korales and of the Kurunegala Kachcheri, and afterwards of the Hapitigam Korale, serving for thirty-three years. His grandfather, Caspar Casiechitty, was Shroff, Kurunegala Kachcheri, for several years, whilst his great-grandfather was the Rev. Franciscus, Colonial Chaplain, St. Thomas's Church, Colombo, and his maternal grandfather Chief Kachcheri Mudaliyar at Jaffna until the time of his death. Of his other maternal relations, his mother's stepbrother was Chief Tamil Interpreter to the Governor, Mudaliyar of the Governor's Gate, and head of the Christian Chetties in Colombo. His uncle, Manuel Casiechitty, is a retired Government servant and a landed proprietor, Kandy, and William Casiechitty is a Colombo merchant. His wife's relations also held important offices, her maternal grandfather being Colonial Chaplain, Colombo, Dr. William Ondatjee being Colonial Surgeon, and Nicholas J. Ondatjee is Mudaliyar of the Governor's Gate and Chief Interpreter to the Queen's Advocate. A relation of her mother's, M. Morgappah Wanigaratna, is

MUDALIYAR SPENCER S. CASIECHITTY.
(Station Master, Hatton.)

Chief Tamil Interpreter to the Governor, Mudaliyar of the Governor's Gate, and head of the Christian Chetties, Colombo. Mr. Casiechitty possesses two excellent certificates from Mr. W. T. Pearce, General Manager of the Ceylon Government Railway, one recommending him for the rank of Mudaliyar and the other notifying his appointment. He has been twenty-six years in the railway department of Government service.

A. R. CASSE LEBBE.

This gentleman is a descendant of Arabs who settled in Beruwala, near Colombo, in ancient times. He owns some valuable moonstone mines and also some gem lands. As a general merchant and dealer in precious stones Mr. Lebbe enjoys a unique reputation. He is a member of the Society of Arts, and for the excellency of his gems and for the best specimen of gold workmanship he was awarded a gold medal at the Agri-Horticultural Show held in Kandy in 1902. He is an expert judge of all kinds of precious stones and pearls, and supplies gems to patrons in all parts of the world, either on approval or in execution of order. He employs a staff of expert goldsmiths, and all kinds of jewellery are turned out under his personal supervision. He is patronised by the principal Government officials and leading residents. He

A. R. CASSE LEBBE. THE BUNGALOW.

is the fortunate possessor of a photograph of H.R.H. Princess Louise of Schleswig-Holstein inscribed with her autograph.

H. B. ANDRIS & CO.

This firm, carrying on the business of jewellers and gem merchants, dealers in Ceylon curios (principally Kandyan knives, daggers, swords, Dutch boxes, and old ivory works), Kandyan art work (viz., tea sets, flower vases, trays and boxes), hand-made Ceylon laces, &c., at 9, Trincomalee Street, Kandy, was established in 1897 by Mr. H. B. Andris, a native of Galle. The firm make a speciality of ancient Sinhalese jewellery, as well as articles of modern workmanship executed by their own workmen and imported from England and India. They also deal in silver and brass wares, Ceylon precious stones (principally rubies, sapphires, cat's-eyes, aquamarines, alexandrites, tourmalines, and moonstones), and Australian opals and African diamonds. At present they possess an uncut blue sapphire which weighs 365 carats and an amethyst which weighs 2,800 carats, found at Ratnapura. They always have on hand a fine selection of Ceylon pearls from local fisheries. They keep in stock articles in ivory, ebony, calamander, coconut, porcupine quill, tortoiseshell, and a good collection of old Dutch china. They obtained various prizes and medals for the excellence of their gold, silver, and carved work at the Uva Agricultural Show held in 1905. At the last Rubber Exhibition at the Botanical Gardens, Peradeniya, they exhibited a beautiful silver carved elephant covered with Ceylon precious stones. Visitors to Kandy should not fail to visit the establishment, which is generally patronised by the leading residents, tourists, and the planting community.

H. B. ANDRIS. H. B. ANDRIS & CO. (Interior of Shop.)

WYRAWANTHER WEERASINGHAM.

Mr. Wyrawanther Weerasingham, the Shroff (Cashier) of the National Bank of Kandy, comes of an old Jaffna family. He was born in 1855, and after being educated at Jaffna, Chemdikuli Seminary (now St. John's College), he went to Colombo and received a private commercial training under his uncle, who was Shroff of the Oriental Bank. Mr. Weerasingham became the Shroff of the New Oriental Bank at Kandy in 1884, and eight years later, when the Kandy branch of the National Bank was opened, he was appointed to the position he now holds.

W. WEERASINGHAM.

QUEEN'S HOTEL, KANDY.

One of the most popular hotels up-country is the Queen's Hotel, Kandy, and the increasing patronage of European visitors has rendered its enlargement necessary. It was opened in 1849 and was improved and enlarged about ten years ago, but although it is capable of accommodating 150 visitors the hotel is to be still further enlarged by the addition of fifty rooms during the next twelve months. The Queen's is beautifully situated 1,700 ft. above sea-level and commanding the magnificent Kandy lake. Every modern convenience is in use there, and the fact that it is quite close to the station renders it the more suited to the needs of visitors and others with little time at their disposal. With the advent of the motor-car its importance has increased, as it is eminently suitable for being the starting-point for Anuradhapura, Trincomalee, and all other points of interest in the island. It is owned by the Kandy Hotels Company, Ltd., the directors of which are Messrs. Joseph Fraser (managing director), R. Morison, W. Shakespeare, and F. M. Mackwood.

J. P. BURDAYRON.

The Queen's Hotel, Kandy, which has an almost world-wide reputation, is managed by Mr. Burdayron. This gentleman was born in 1864, and has had a varied and extensive experience of hotel management. Having served in different capacities in many well-known hotels, Mr. Burdayron is known by a

QUEEN'S HOTEL, KANDY.

1. Queen's Hotel. 2. Verandah. 3. Billiard Room. 4. Reading Room. 5. Dining Room.

large circle of acquaintances, and as among other positions which he has filled is that of

J. P. BURDAYRON.

chef, he is particularly well qualified to manage such an important house as the Queen's Hotel.

SCHOKMAN & CO.

Messrs. Schokman & Co., of Dikoya (two miles by road from Hatton), are stationers, printers, and importers, auctioneers and commission agents, transacting a large business. The firm was established in 1892 by Cecil E. Schokman, and is now carried on by this gentleman's son, who is the sole proprietor. All kinds of business are transacted by them, though special attention is paid to estate work of all descriptions.

AHAMADO LEBBE.

In the accompanying illustration embodying the salient points of a memorial to Government is given the history of the family of which Mr. Ahamado Lebbe is a descendant. It will be seen that Mr. Lebbe traces his ancestry back to King Seyda Kady Marikar, who ruled an independent State in Southern India about three hundred years ago. Two members of the family migrated to Kandy in the time of King Narendra Sinha and settled there, and one of them, at the king's instigation, contracted a marriage with the daughter of the only gem merchant in the country, who was nicknamed "Thanihadakara-Seeya." This merchant was granted an ola sannas by the king, Rajasinha II., for a block of land situated in Trincomalee Street, Kandy. This property has remained in the family during the two hundred and fifty years which have elapsed since the grant. Apart from the distinction conferred by the facts narrated, the family of Mr. Ahamado Lebbe has another title to honour. It is associated, through a son-in-law of one of the Madura kings, with the memorable defence of Arcot by Clive in 1751. When the supplies and ammunition of the little garrison were running low, the young prince helped to replenish the depleted stocks, utilising his own ships for the purpose. For these valuable services he was granted a gold medal by King George II., to be worn by himself and his descendants. In later times, after the British conquest of the Kandyan provinces, the members of the family were associated with the police force both at the ancient Sinhalese capital and Colombo.

HATTON HOTEL.

The Hatton Hotel, which is a new building, has rapidly become popular with the hundreds of tourists and holiday-makers who visit the beautiful district which surrounds it. Of recent years Hatton has become a favourite resort with holiday-makers, and this is not to be wondered at when it is stated that it is situated four thousand odd feet above the sea-level, and has a bracing climate with a mean temperature of 66 degrees. Every year hundreds of

AHAMADO LEBBE.

THE HATTON HOTEL.

European and native people from Colombo visit Hatton to recuperate, and for these the Hatton Hotel caters admirably, the charges being moderate and the European management by Mr. Werther satisfactory in every way. Hatton can be conveniently visited *en route* to Nuwara Eliya, and is the starting-point for the ascent of Adam's Peak, to which Buddhists from all over Asia make pilgrimages to see the sacred footprints of the founder of their faith.

NUWARA ELIYA DISTRICT.

RALPH GEORGE CARTE, A.M.I.C.E.

Mr. R. G. Carte is the District Engineer, Nuwara Eliya. He was born at Southsea in 1867, and was educated at Portsmouth Grammar School and St. John's College, Cambridge. In 1893 he was appointed by the Secretary of State as District Engineer, having gone through his articles with Mr. H. Percy Boulnois, M.I.C.E., late City Engineer of Liverpool. Mr. Carte is a member of the Ceylon Engineers' Association and the Nuwara Eliya United Club.

THE HON. MR. J. M. CAMPBELL.

The Hon. Mr. J. M. Camphell occupies "Mahagastota," Baker's Farm, Nuwara Eliya. He came to Ceylon in 1870, remained a year, then went to South Africa, spent a period there, and returned to the island in 1880 and took charge of the Moray estate, Maskeliya, his brother's property. When the latter died Mr. Campbell inherited the property. He was elected in 1897 Chairman of the Planters' Association, the most important association in the island, and later in the same year he became member of the Legislative Council for the planters, serving the full term of five years. He is a member of the principal clubs in Ceylon, a Lieutenant in the Ceylon Mounted Rifles, and was one of the Volunteers who attended King Edward's Coronation in England in 1902. He is the general manager in Ceylon of the Anglo-Ceylon and General Estates Company, Ltd.

DONALD McKINLAY MURRAY.

Mr. Donald McKinlay Murray, the manager of the National Bank of India at Nuwara Eliya, was born in the year 1878. He was educated at the Dollar Academy, Dollar, Scotland, and entered the London office of the National Bank of India in 1898. In 1902 he came to the Colombo office, and after three years' service was transferred to Nuwara Eliya.

FRANK GRENIER.

Dr. Frank Grenier, the Assistant Colonial Surgeon, of Nuwara Eliya, is the son of Mr. G. Grenier, I.S.O., Registrar, Supreme Court, Colombo. He was born in Ceylon in 1868, and was educated at St. Thomas's College, Colombo, where he secured the Government University Scholarship in 1887—a distinction worth £150 a year for four years. He took his B.M. and M.S. degrees and first-class honours at Edinburgh, and competed for the gold medal in surgery, which is open only to a select few. It was in 1892 that he obtained his first appointment under the Ceylon Government, and in 1903 was appointed medical officer in charge of Nuwara Eliya. He has been specially selected by the Ceylon Government to proceed to England shortly for research work in connection with tropical medicines.

BARBARA LAYARD.

Miss Barbara Layard, of Grimsthorpe, Nuwara Eliya, is a member of a well-known family, and is herself a familiar figure in Ceylon life. She was born at Bagatelle, Colombo, in 1834, in a house which since the visit of the late Duke of Edinburgh has been called Alfred House, and is now occupied by Lady de Soysa, a Sinhalese lady. Miss Layard's father, Charles Edward Layard, together with his brother Henry (father of the late Sir Henry Austin Layard, discoverer of Nineveh), came out to Ceylon in the beginning of the last century and joined the Ceylon Civil Service. He married, in 1804, Barbara Bridgetina Mooyaart, daughter of the last Dutch Governor of Galle, by whom he had twenty-six children. His eldest son, Sir Charles Peter Layard, was appointed to the Ceylon Civil Service in 1827 and served for fifty years, the last forty-three years without himself or his wife visiting England. He ultimately retired in 1877. Their nine children were sent home for

MISS BARBARA JANE LAYARD.

their education, and their only son, Sir Charles Peter Layard, Chief Justice of Ceylon, retired only this year (1906).

Miss Layard is the last and only surviving

child of her parents, and is universally known in Ceylon as "Aunt Barbara," from the fact that 225 persons living are entitled to call her aunt. Her grandfather, the Right Rev. Dean of Bristol, could claim nearly 600 lineal descendants, which is quite a record family. She is an able water-colour artist, landscapes being her speciality, and was a pupil of Paul Naftel.

H. U. LEEMBRUGGEN.

Dr. Henry Ullrich Leembruggen is the son of Caspar Henry John Leembruggen, Surveyor of Colombo, and of Matilda, daughter of James Koch, of Jaffna. He was born at Matara, in 1875, and was educated at the Royal College, Colombo, after which he studied medicine at the Ceylon Medical College, of which he became a licentiate in 1899. He was Medical Officer, Alutnuwara Hospital, 1899–1900, Medical Officer to the Boer prisoners-of-war camp, Diyatalawa, 1901–2, and in medical charge of the prisoners-of-war camp, Urugasmanhandiya, whence he was sent in 1903 in medical charge of the transport *Templemore* with the repatriated prisoners of war to Durban. He was next appointed District Medical Officer, Aranayaka (1904–5), proceeded to Scotland, and became a licentiate of the Royal College of Physicians, Edinburgh. He worked at the Infirmary and the Hospital for Sick Children, Edinburgh, and at University College Hospital, London. Returning to Ceylon in May, 1906, he was appointed District Medical Officer, Pussellawa, and promoted an officer of the second grade. In 1902 he married Evelyn Muriel, eldest daughter of Gerard E. Leembruggen, Superintendent of Surveys, Colombo.

H. U. LEEMBRUGGEN, L.M.S., L.R.C.P.E.

J. P. E. RYAN.

Mr. J. P. E. Ryan, of Glenomera, Talawakele, is one of the best known proprietary planters of the Dimbula district. He comes of an old planting family which has continuously owned land in the district for fifty years. Mr. Ryan is at present proprietor of 1,350 acres, 880 of which are in Dimbula, under tea, and 450 in Gampola, planted with rubber. A keen agriculturist, Mr. Ryan has been conspicuous in all movements having for their object the improvement of the planting industry. It was largely to his active initiative that the successful Rubber Exhibition was held—an exhibition which marks an epoch in the history of planting in the island. Mr. Ryan is a man of cultured literary tastes, and a work from his pen describing, under the title of "Curry and Rice," the popular aspects of Ceylon life, is shortly to be published.

CHARLES RYAN.

At the 115th mile on the railway from Colombo and at the 22nd mile along the Government high-road from Nawalapitiya to Nuwara Eliya is situated the St. Clair Factory. It produces yearly half a million pounds of tea

THE FACTORY, ST. CLAIR ESTATE, TALAWAKELE. CHARLES RYAN. THE FALLS, ST. CLAIR ESTATE, TALAWAKELE.

of the highest quality, the "mark" being well known on the London and Colombo markets, and St. Clair teas, as purely commercial exhibits, were awarded medals at Chicago and St. Louis Exhibitions. Besides being equipped with the very latest form of motive power and other up-to-date machinery, the factory is provided with its own railway station, and the magnificent St. Clair Falls in the immediate neighbourhood are the admiration of all travellers. The factory serves one of the finest privately owned groups of tea estates in the island. It was formed out of virgin forest in the early sixties as a coffee plantation by Messrs. James and Patrick Ryan, the father and uncle respectively of the present owner, Mr. Charles G. Ryan.

C. A. KALENBERG.

Dr. Charles Allan Kalenberg, the Government Medical Officer, Lindula, was born at Negombo in 1866, and educated at the Royal College, Colombo. He attended the Medical College, and in 1891 he went to Edinburgh and passed through the College of Surgeons and the College of Physicians. He took the degrees L.R.C.S. and L.R.C.P. of Edinburgh, and the L.F.P. and L.F.S. of Glasgow, in 1892, whilst on leave, afterwards returning to Ceylon. He entered the Government service in 1890, and was appointed to his present position in September, 1906.

ARTHUR LLOYD PEREIRA.

Dr. Arthur Lloyd Pereira, Medical Officer in charge of the hospital, Dimbula, was born on June 21, 1873, at Colombo, and educated at St. Thomas's College, Colombo. He entered the Ceylon Medical College in 1892. After a successful career he obtained the L.M. and S., Ceylon, and entered the Government medical service in 1897. He proceeded on leave in 1905, and after a course of study at Edinburgh obtained the triple qualifications of Scotland, viz., L.R.C.P., L.R.C.S. (Edin.), L.F.P., L.F.S. (Glasg.).

ARTHUR LLOYD PEREIRA.
(Government Medical Officer, Dimbula District Hospital.)

C. A. KALENBERG'S BUNGALOW, LINDULA.

MELTON ESTATE, DIMBULA.

This estate is situated at Talawakele, Walaha Valley, Dimbula, and is owned by Mrs. Wiggin. It consists of 200 acres, all under tea cultivation, and the annual output is 120,000 lbs. Mr. G. W. R. Wiggin is the resident manager, and with his brother works the Bambrakelly and Dell estates, which belong to a family company. Bambrakelly was first opened up in 1872 with coffee. Then cinchona was experimentally planted, and finally, tea, the annual yield of the latter at present being 250,000 lbs. On this and the Dell estates there are 480 acres of jungle which hereafter will be used for camphor. The average price realised for tea from this estate is 8d. to 9½d. per lb. Mr. Wiggin, who comes from Gloucestershire, is one of the oldest and most experienced planters in the island. He is a staunch Conservative, and maintains his connection with the Junior Carlton and Conservative Clubs in London.

MAYFIELD ESTATE.

The Mayfield estate is situated in Dimbula, about 4½ miles from Hatton. It is owned by the Mayfield (Dimbula) Tea Company of Ceylon, whose manager, resident on the estate, is Mr. H. L. Armstrong. There are 700 acres of land planted with tea and about 239 acres of timber, &c. Mr. Armstrong came to Ceylon as a planter in 1892, and has been on the Mayfield estate for the past nine years. He is an enthusiastic member of the Ceylon Planters' Rifle Corps.

TROUP ESTATE, TALAWAKELE.

Mr. G. Anderson, sen., the proprietor of the Troup estate, Talawakele (the derivation of "Troup" is from Troup, on the coast of Banffshire, belonging to the heir of the late Mr. Garden Campbell, of Glencoe fame), is the oldest resident planter in his district. His connection with the locality extends as far back as 1865, when he migrated from the North of Scotland and commenced coffee planting in the island. His venture in its earliest years was remarkably successful. In one year alone (1872), when coffee was at its best, he and his partner reaped a profit of £6,500. Eight years later, however, there was a crisis in the coffee trade, and the crop on the Troup estate was barely sufficient to

FACTORY, FERHAM ESTATE..

DISTANT VIEW, ST. ANDREW'S ESTATE, WITH FACTORY.

THE BUNGALOW, FERHAM ESTATE.

cover the cost of cultivation. Mr. Anderson, who was in the Old Country at the time, had to return to the island post-haste and make a new start. Coffee having failed, he devoted his attention to tea and cinchona cultivation on the same estate, but it took ten years to clear the ground and plant tea all over the area. At the present time the whole of the estate, which is situated about 1½ miles from Talawakele, is 358 acres in extent, and the yield in 1905 was 194,000 lbs. of tea. Mr. Anderson is the son of Captain Anderson, who sailed under Nelson's flag.

FERHAM AND ODDINGTON ESTATES.

At Talawakele, Dimbula, Mr. W. C. Oswald manages the Ferham estate for Mr. Thomas Fairhurst, and is also part owner of the Oddington estate, which adjoins. He lives on the former property, having taken up his residence there in 1894. Previously, from 1887, he was in the Ouvah Company, Badulla, and before that had had six years' experience in the tea trade with F. S. Long & Co. in Mincing Lane. The yearly output of tea from the 350 acres of cultivated land which comprise the combined estates is 200,000 lbs., equal to 570 lbs. per acre; and the product being noted for its fine quality, the London price always rules high. In addition to the cultivated area there are 25 acres on which timber, needed for estate purposes, is grown. The elevation of the estate is from 4,300 ft. to 5,100 ft. Machinery of the latest pattern is installed at the factory on the estate. Mr. Oswald is an expert in the manufacture of tea, and his advice is often welcomed by the owners of other estates who wish to improve the quality of their productions. Mr. Oswald is a committee member of the Dimbula Planters' Association, and is a member of the Agras and Talawakele Clubs. He is a native of Croydon, Surrey.

ST. ANDREW'S ESTATE.

This estate, owned by Mr. Thos. Fairhurst and managed by Mr. J. P. Blackmore, is situated at Talawakele, in the Dimbula district, and is about 287 acres in extent, 273 being planted with tea and the balance with timber, &c. The average output of tea from

ST. ANDREW'S FACTORY.

the estate is about 115,000 lbs. per annum, and the whole of it is dealt with at a factory on the estate, which is fitted throughout with the most up-to-date machinery. The estate is visited periodically by Mr. Oswald, of Ferham estate. It is situated between 3,500 ft. and 4,200 ft. above sea-level. About two years ago close upon 2,000 rubber-trees were planted among the tea-bushes, and some of these are progressing in promising fashion.

WALKER & GREIG.

In the above we have the present-day style of one of the oldest firms in the island. Mr. John Walker, who came out to Ceylon to a sugar plantation, eventually found his way up to Kandy, where in 1854 he founded the firm of John Walker & Co., carrying on business as engineers and general merchants, and met with a full measure of success, his coffee-pulping machine being one of the best known in the island. Advancing with the times and to meet the requirements of the coffee planters of Uva, he opened in the sixties a branch business in Badulla and Haldummulla. The style of these two branches became Walker & Wilson, but in 1874 changed to Walker & Greig. With the growing importance of Haputale the old workshop at Haldummulla was closed and removed to the top of the pass, where the business was carried on, the firm eventually removing into their present premises at Haputale. Badulla workshop likewise underwent reconstruction, and now occupies an imposing building in that town. About the year 1873 the head office (John Walker & Co.) at Kandy started a branch business in the Dikoya district in a small

WALKER & GREIG'S STORES.

1. Badulla. 2. Haputale. 3. Tillicoultry. 4. Dikoya.

store close by their present striking and well-stocked premises at Glencairn, also a branch business at Craiglea, Dimbula, which they took over from the firm of Messrs. Lee, Hedges & Co. About the same time they started building a store at Tillicoultry, Lindula, and in 1876 took over the business of Gordon Massie & Co., at Devon, Dimbula, and Agrakande, Lindula, transferring the Craiglea store to and incorporating it with that at Devon. In the early eighties Mr. John Walker retired from the firm of John Walker & Co., taking over the various up-country businesses, and—leaving Kandy to his brother William—carried them on under their present style, viz., Walker & Greig. With the death of Mr. John Walker in 1888, the business passed into the care of trustees, and was eventually managed and bought from the trustees by Mr. John Walker, son of the founder of the firm. Slowly but surely business has prospered in spite of the ups and downs of coffee, and with the coming of tea as the chief product we find in Walker & Greig one of the most prosperous firms up-country. The old buildings have passed away. The firm have been and are steadily marching forward with the times, erecting premises worthy of our successful tea districts, where their stores are replete with everything from the proverbial needle to an anchor, and their workshops fitted to turn out structural and all sorts of ironwork and machinery suited to the requirements of the tea world.

RAGALLA AND HALGRANOYA ESTATES.

These estates, comprising together 912 acres of tea, 150 acres of timber, and 15 acres of cinchona, are owned by the Ragalla Ceylon Tea Estates, Ltd., and give an annual yield of over 550 lbs. per acre. They are in the Udapussellawa district, and are under the superintendency of Mr. Edward Ellice Nicol. Mr. Nicol was born at St. Vincent, West Indies, and was educated at Christ's Hospital (the Blue Coat School), London. His business career was commenced with Messrs. Lewis & Peat, Mincing Lane, London. He came out to Ceylon in 1871, and worked under Mr. Burnett, at Spring Valley, Badulla. Later he worked for nineteen months under Mr. C. E Spooner, son of Professor Spooner, of Veterinary College, London. Subsequently he was engaged on other estates—Lunugallon, Haputale, for fourteen years—until thirteen years ago, when he started on the Ragalla, which was then under the agency of the Galaha Ceylon Tea Estates & Agency Company. Mr. Nicol has been thirty-five years in the island, and only once during that time has had a trip to England, for six months.

LAURENCE ROBERT PEEL.

Mr. Peel came out in 1873 as a coffee planter, afterwards devoting his attention to cinchona, and later to tea. For twelve years he was occupied on the well-known Sheen estate in the Pundalu-oya district. He gave up planting about three and a half years ago, his intention being to go home. He is a well-known all-round sportsman. He has kept a pack of harriers, and followed racing pretty closely, having ridden at meetings frequently in the seventies and eighties.

A NEW CEYLON INDUSTRY.

Ceylon enterprise in the past few years has been conspicuously displayed in many directions where agricultural interests are concerned, but from a manufacturing standpoint the progress made has not been great, perhaps because of the absorption of capital and energy in the great tea and other industries directly associated with the land. Gratifying evidence, however, is forthcoming that the natural aptitude of the Sinhalese for mechanical work is no longer to be neglected. At Talawakele, in the heart of the beautiful country which stretches from the Kelani Valley to the Province of Uva, is situated a thoroughly up-to-date engineering establishment, which, remarkable to state, is turning out machinery representing the very last word of mechanical inventiveness in the domain of plantation rubber manufacture. The concern to which we refer is that of Messrs. Brown & Davidson, Ltd. Established in 1897 by the two gentlemen whose names appear in the present title of the firm, the business for some years was of a general character, and in its comparatively limited sphere was highly successful. But the partners, both men of wide knowledge and experience in British engineering work, and endowed with more than a common share of national "grit," were not content to act merely as the suppliers of the miscellaneous needs of a great tea-planting district. Looking ahead, they saw in the rise of the rubber industry a great opportunity and they seized it, with the result that to-day they enjoy almost undisputed supremacy in the domain of plantation rubber machinery manufacture. Already their fame has gone out to the great rubber-producing world. In the Straits Settlements the volume of the business done on the rubber estates has necessitated the opening of a branch business. More extraordinary still, orders for the supply of rubber machinery have reached Talawakele from distant Mexico; and this is only in the infancy of the enterprise. It needs no prophetic instinct to see that a great future awaits the firm, with the inevitable expansion on an enormous scale of the demand for plant for the manipulation of rubber.

A few words now as to the character of the machinery which Messrs. Brown & Davidson are manufacturing. For the purposes of clearness a brief description of the process of preparing rubber from latex (the fluid exuded from the tree) must be given. On arrival at the factory the latex has to be strained in order to eliminate mechanical impurities. This is done most effectually by a straining machine, consisting of a rapidly revolving basin which drives the impurities on to cotton and enables the latex to be drawn in a pure state through a pipe at the side. After being so treated the latex is stored in large galvanised tanks, and afterwards is coagulated. The freshly coagulated rubber is soft and spongy, and contains, in addition to the indiarubber particles, varying quantities of resins, proteids, &c. To eliminate these it is passed between the rollers of a machine, the two rollers of which revolve at a slightly different speed, with the result that the material is subjected to a kneading and stretching process, and so is in a condition that the impurities may be removed by copious washing. When these operations are complete the rubber is turned out in irregular sheets with a rough, uneven surface. These are then put through the finishing rollers of a second washing machine, which turns out the thin strips commonly known as "crêpe."

The crêpe rubber undergoes a drying process, the operation being carried through by the use of Passburg vacuum driers which work on the well-known principle that the lower the atmospheric pressure the more easily is water evaporated. Vacuum-dried rubber has a much softer and more elastic feel, and is more suitable for blocking than that dried slowly in the usual way.

In order to convert crêpe or any other form of rubber into blocks of any desired thickness from 2 ins. to 12 ins., the ratchet screw blocking press shown in the illustration has been designed. Block rubber, besides being more convenient for packing and shipment than other forms, has the additional advantage that it exposes the least possible surface to the air, and that in this form the liability to stickiness and tackiness is reduced to a minimum; while the great pressure to which the material is subjected improves its quality as regards nerve and resiliency. Besides manufacturing direct from the latex, it has been found possible to secure a large quantity of valuable rubber from bark shavings with the use of suitable machinery. The machines used for this purpose are in many respects similar to the washing machines, but differ from them in that they work with more of a grinding action. It is said that on some estates the whole cost of tapping is paid for by rubber recovered in this way.

The machinery necessary in the above pro-

BROWN & DAVIDSON, LTD., TALAWAKELE.

1. GENERAL VIEW OF WORKS. 2. MR. GEORGE BROWN. (Managing Director.) 3. A PRESS FOR MAKING BLOCK RUBBER. 4. A MACHINE FOR MAKING CRÊPE RUBBER. (Patented and manufactured by Brown & Davidson, Ltd.)

cesses is all supplied by Messrs. Brown & Davidson, Ltd. The perfect models now on the market are the results of years of careful thought and experiments conducted in intimate touch with rubber production in all its stages. When first brought prominently to the notice of those interested in the rubber industry at the great Rubber Exhibition at Kandy in 1906, they created a lively interest, and besides handsome encomiums from experts, won for the firm five gold medals, one silver medal, and five diplomas. Short as is the time which has elapsed since that epoch-making exhibition, further progress has been made in the elucidation of the problems which underly the effective and economical extraction and preparation of rubber. In fine, Ceylon, through the agency of this enterprising firm, is distinctly leading the way in this important matter.

Hereafter possibly its laurels may be wrested from it by European and American rivals, but nothing can deprive it of the distinction which attaches to pioneers in the field of valuable invention.

GRAND HOTEL, NUWARA ELIYA.

There are few hotels in the East which command the advantages of this well-known hostelry. It is situated 6,200 ft. above sea-level, in a magnificent climate, and in close proximity to golf-links which are said by experts to be the best east of Suez. There is excellent trout fishing in the vicinity, and visitors to the hotel will find themselves in close proximity to the railway-station, post and telegraph offices, clubs, and racecourse. Mr. Loesch, the manager, has had great experience as a caterer. He was for some time the manager of a hotel in Hamburg, and also served for several years as a purser in the service of the Hamburg American Company. Since he undertook control at Nuwara Eliya the Grand Hotel has been doubled in size on his persistent representations, and this enlargement has been thoroughly justified by results. Finality, however, has not yet been reached. A further improvement is imminent which will again double the size of the building. It will then contain accommodation for 200 people, with 120 bedrooms, two-thirds of these being double and the remainder single bedded. The building will be two-storied, most of the bedrooms being upstairs. The drawing and dining rooms will cover 2,500 square feet. An electric plant will be laid down for supplying the premises with power for lighting purposes, fans, &c. The bathrooms and conveniences will be of the most modern design, with hot and cold water laid on and the floors and walls tiled. The

A. LOESCH.
(Manager, Grand Hotel.)

GRAND HOTEL, NUWARA ELIYA.
FRONT VIEW. SIDE VIEW.

alterations will be carried out in sections, so that the hotel business will not be interfered with in any way. Amongst the visitors who have stayed at the Grand can be numbered many well-known personages, including the Duc d'Abruzzi (brother of the Italian sovereign), Leopold of Saxe-Coburg-Gotha (nephew of King Edward), the Grand Duke of Saxe-Weimar, Prince Reuss XXXIII., the Maharaja of Kapurthala, and Sir Thomas Lipton. On one day there were as many as sixteen English, French, German, and Belgian titled people in the house. Letters of appreciation have been received from many of these. The hotel stands on 17 acres of ground, and there are 7 acres of kitchen garden, whilst there is a private dairy pleasantly situated on high land.

S. T. SORIS, THE PEDRO VIEW HOTEL, THE VEGETABLE GARDEN, AND INTERIOR OF THE STORE.

PAUL SORIS & CO.

This firm was established in a small provision store at Nuwara Eliya, in the year 1869, by Mr. Paul Soris, a native of Tuticorin, in Southern India. The business increased rapidly, and Mr. Paul Soris was succeeded by Mr. S. T. Soris, his eldest son, who is now carrying on a flourishing concern, importing direct from England and the Continent, as well as dealing with larger commercial houses in Colombo. The firm have a first-class general store and supply the planting community with provisions, stores, liquors, &c. A special feature of this business is the sale of fresh English vegetables, of which they are practically the largest growers in Ceylon, the produce being obtained from carefully cultivated lands of their own. They supply all the leading hotels and shipping companies, including more particularly the Norddeutscher-Lloyd line. They have branches at Badulla and Bandarawela. There are five partners; Mr. Sinna Tamby Soris is the senior, and the others concerned are Messrs. Augustin, Silvester, Croose, and Jacob Soris, all brothers. The vegetable gardens cover fully ten acres, and the seeds for them are imported direct from England and Australia. The firm have won thirty-two prizes for vegetables at the local agri-horticultural shows. Messrs. Service Reeve & Co. represent the firm in London.

ST. EDWARD'S SCHOOL, NUWARA ELIYA.

This well-known educational establishment enjoys a well-deserved reputation throughout the island, and even beyond its confines, as an institution for the training of British boys. Situated in a very healthy and invigorating climate, it has from the health standpoint advantages possessed by few schools in the East. But it does not by any means rely for its support exclusively upon the attractiveness of its position and environment. Besides furnishing an education exactly on the lines of a first-grade school in England, it supplies a school atmosphere of an altogether British character. Two distinct classes are catered for: (1) those who cannot and who do not wish to send their boys Home, and (2) those who intend sending their boys Home later on, and who wish them to have experience of school life beforehand. That the facilities offered by the establishment are appreciated is abundantly clear from the stream of boys who are constantly passing through the school. They come not only from all parts of Ceylon, but also from India, where, even more than in Ceylon, opportunities for the healthy and wholesome training of European boys are few and sometimes altogether wanting. The school has been in existence since 1888. It was started by the Rev. J. E. B. Brine, to provide a first-grade school for the sons of Europeans only. Mr. Brine retired at the end of 1898, and the management is now in the hands of Mr. H. H. Phelp, M.A. Durham. Assisting him is a competent staff, including Mr. E. T. Davis, B.A. London, and Mr. G. E.

Gee, Brasenose College, Oxford. The Rev. C. P. H. Reynolds, B.A., Corpus Christi, Cambridge, takes Scripture. The establishment is under Government protection. The school buildings are commodious and stand in about ten acres of ground. They occupy one of the best sites in Nuwara Eliya and have the advantage of an abundant and pure water supply. The sanitary arrangements are regularly inspected by the Government inspector. The training given ensures a sound English education on the most approved modern lines. Great attention is given to athletics, the boys' games being considered almost as important as their work. The boys have the use of the fine ground of the Nuwara Eliya Cricket Club, which is one minute's walk from the school. Adjoining this is a good football ground. The boys play the Association game and hockey regularly. Generally speaking, the school is conducted on the soundest and most efficient lines, and deservedly stands high in the estimation of the European residents of the island, many of the most influential of whom have allowed their names to be included in the list of references.

W. JORDAN & CO.

Mr. Wm. Jordan, the founder of the present firm, arrived in Ceylon in the early seventies, and took up coffee planting on one of the then principal estates in the Dimbula Valley. Having a keen eye for business, he started the above firm, over thirty-five years ago, in a rather small and unpretentious way, yet supplying a long-felt want in the district. Each year since the inception of the business has been one of progress, and now it ranks as one of the largest and oldest established firms of general merchants outside of Colombo. The methods adopted by this firm are most up to date, and are fully appreciated by a large and still increasing *clientèle*. The business is run on the departmental system, each section being in charge of a fully experienced European, assisted by a native staff. The London office, which was opened several years ago, is in charge of Mr. Wm. Jordan, assisted by his son, Mr. Wm. Jordan, jun.

H. KEMISH.

Mr. Kemish is the manager and engineer for Messrs. C. A. Hutson & Co., estate engineers, of Kandapola district and Colombo, at their Kandapola branch. He was born in Norfolk and educated at York, afterwards being apprenticed to Messrs. F. Savage & Co., of King's Lynn. He served his time with this firm and then proceeded to Lincoln, where he was engaged at the engineering works of Ruston, Proctor & Co. He came out to Ceylon in 1893 to take up an appointment under Messrs. Hutson, and was for two years employed at their Colombo works. For the past twelve years he has been in charge of the Kandapola branch.

W. JORDAN & CO.'S STORE, TALAWAKELE.

G. W. LINDSAY WHITE.

Mr. G. W. Lindsay White, of "Daisy Bank," Nuwara Eliya, has been in Ceylon for the past sixty years, his parents having settled at

"DAISY BANK" AND TEA ESTATE.

G. W. LINDSAY WHITE.

H. J. PERERA SAMARASEKERA, MOHANDIRAM, AND FAMILY.

Kandy. He was educated at Trinity College, Kandy, and the Colombo Academy, and started his business career on a coffee plantation when sixteen years of age. He settled at Nuwara Eliya in 1864, and took up agricultural pursuits. Fifteen years ago he commenced tea cultivation, and he owns the Westward Ho! and Unique View estates, which consist of over 300 acres of tea plantation. He has also a large interest in the Ceylon Brewery, and is one of the largest landowners in Nuwara Eliya. Mr. White is a member of the Ceylon Turf Club and the United Club of Nuwara Eliya.

SAMUEL GODFRIED KOCH.

Mr. S. G. Koch, the Post and Telegraph Master at Nuwara Eliya, is a member of an ancient and respected Burgher family whose ancestors, four generations ago, settled in the island during the period of the Dutch occupation. He was born at Jaffna on October 23, 1862, and having finished his education he joined the Telegraph Department in May, 1879. The department was at that time worked by the Indian telegraphs. After acting as a signaller for a period of about eleven years, he was appointed Deputy Telegraph Master at Kandy in 1891, and after being in charge of various offices in the island he was specially selected for Nuwara Eliya. He has been in the telegraph service now for twenty-nine years. and is in the special class, which is composed of six senior officers of the department. The office at Nuwara Eliya is fitted with the duplex apparatus and the Wheatstone automatic transmitters, &c., for clearing pressure in telegraph business. Mr. Koch is of a genial disposition, and is ever courteous and willing to do all in his power to serve the interests of the public generally.

S. G. KOCH.

H. J. PERERA SAMARASEKERA, Mohandiram.

Mr. H. James Perera Samarasekera, of "The Unique," Pussellawa, known as Mohandiram H. J. P. Samarasekera, is a son of Hettikankanange Don Bastian Perera Samarasekera, Peace and Division Officer of Talpitiya North at Panadure, and of Donna Maria, eldest daughter of Illeperuma Arachige Don David Wijeratne and Habbakkala Kankanange Donna Apalonia Haminey, and granddaughter of Colomba Etul Cotté Illeperuma Arachige Don Daniel Wijeratne and Ponsuge Bastiana Haminey, and grandson of Hettikankanange Louis Perera, Corporal of Lascoreens in the Rayigam Korale, which appointment was granted to him in 1828. Born at Talpitiya in 1855, Mr. H. J. P. Samarasekera was educated at Wadduwa and at St. John's School, Panadure. He acquired various toll rents in the Central Province, starting also in business as a planter of cinchona and tea later. He is the proprietor of the Edward Hill estate in the Pussellawa district, fully planted with tea and equipped with a factory, and of a coconut plantation in the low-country. At Pussellawa—which is his place of residence—he also carries on business as a general store and wine merchant under the style of H. J. Perera & Son. On November 9, 1906, he was created Mohandiram by Sir

"THE UNIQUE."

THE STORE.

EDWARD HILL TEA FACTORY.

THE TENNIS COURT AND CROQUET LAWN.

Henry Arthur Blake for the valuable services rendered to the public in the interests of education, of which he is a great supporter, the C.M.S. Girls' School at Pussellawa being his gift to the district. He also holds the office of Inquirer into Sudden Deaths for the Pussellawa district. In 1880 he married Sophia Evelyn, daughter of Leylwala Don Christian Lianage, planter, of Pussellawa, and of Mestiage Donna Simona Haminey. His eldest son, Joseph, is a partner in the firm of H. J. Perera & Son, and manages the business. His second son is being educated in the Ceylon Medical College; of the remaining three daughters and two sons, the latter are being educated at Trinity College, Kandy, and two of the girls in Colombo. All the members of the family are enthusiastic tennis and croquet players, and own a fine private tennis-court and croquet-lawn near their residence. The two eldest sons have also been members of their respective college cadet corps.

Mohandiram Perera Samarasekera is a member of the Pussellawa Planters' Association, and so is his eldest son. He is also a member of the Ceylon Agricultural Society, and takes great interest in planting matters. He is also the Patron of the Pussellawa Sports Club, which was founded in 1898.

MR. AND MRS. W. P. THURING AND DAUGHTER.

WALTER PETER THURING.

Mr. W. P. Thuring, stationmaster, Talawakele, was born on December 18, 1860, at Kirinde, Southern Province, and educated at the Royal College, Colombo. He is the son of the late Dr. J. L. Thuring, of Colombo, and Adolphina Elizabeth, third daughter of Willen Caen, and grandson of Captain Thuring, of the Netherlands East India Trading Company, and Wilhelmina, daughter of Philip Zelpha, an *Opperkoopman* in the Dutch Service. He commenced service in the Ceylon Government Railways in 1881 as a clerk, and since then has passed through every grade of service to his present position as a stationmaster in the first class, to which post he was appointed in 1905. He married in 1890 Drucilla Sophia, daughter of Peter Van Langenberg, Secretary of the District Court of Kegalla.

SANQUHAR ESTATE.

The above estate is situated near Gampola, in the Pussellawa district, and is under the direction of an able resident manager in Mr. C. W. R. Tyler. Of the 728 acres which the estate comprises, 605 are under cultivation, 475 being planted with tea and 130 with rubber. There is a factory on the estate in which the 250,000 lbs. of tea which represent the annual output are dealt with. Some of the rubber was planted in 1903. Mr. Tyler has been about eighteen years in the island, and has held the Sanquhar estate post for the past twelve years. He comes from near Sittingbourne, Kent, and is heir to the property known as the Lynsted Lodge estate, in extent some 500 acres, including some valuable fruit land and large houses. His father, Colonel Tyler, J.P.—who is the only officer alive of the forty-four officers who served with the Buffs in the Crimean War—is now living on the property.

ASCOT ESTATE.

The Ascot estate, in the district of Pussellawa, near Gampola, has an acreage of 149 acres, all under cultivation, tea and rubber being planted. The proprietors are Messrs. A. L. French and F. W. Wintle, the latter being the managing partner and living on the estate. The annual crop, with bought leaf, from this estate is about 200,000 lbs., and it is manufactured at the factory which is situated there. Until 1906 tea was the sole product under cultivation, but now rubber has been planted. Mr. Wintle arrived in Ceylon in 1888, and came to Ascot estate in 1899.

MIDDLETON ESTATE, DIMBULA.

Messrs. A. V. and J. H. Renton, who came from Edinburgh, are the joint proprietors of the Middleton Estate, Dimbula, which lies about a mile from Talawakele. They have 230 acres entirely under tea cultivation, and the average output is 135,000 lbs. a year. They also own the Talankanda estate, where 250 acres under tea cultivation yield on an average 175,000 lbs. a year. Going out to Ceylon as long ago as 1875, Mr. A. V. Renton, the manager of the Middleton Estate, commenced coffee planting at Talankanda. The Middleton estate was also at one time planted with coffee, but when coffee died out Mr. Renton devoted his attention to tea, with the success outlined above.

MATALE DISTRICT.

JOSEPH FRASER.

This gentleman, who is now the visiting agent of estates 45,000 acres in extent, has been connected with the planting industry of the island for many years. He arrived in Ceylon in 1872, and took up the position of assistant on the Pikkandi estate, and six years later he became manager. In 1886 he became part proprietor of the estate, which shortly afterwards was turned into a private company, the subject of this sketch holding half the shares. The adjoining estates of Sylvakandi and Kinrara were purchased and included in the company's area. All these properties had been planted with coffee, the earliest planting dating from 1842, but since the coffee failure

PITAKANDA ESTATE, MATALE.

1. The Bungalow. 3. The Factory. 2, 4. Views on the Estate.

of 1884 the whole area has been gradually planted with tea, and during the last three or four years rubber has been planted at the lower elevations. These estates, which cover about 1,500 acres, are situated at elevations of from 1,500 to 3,000 ft. above sea-level, and they are at present managed by Mr. Fred. H. Fraser, the son of the subject of this sketch. Since 1891 Mr. Fraser, sen., has been principally occupied visiting and reporting on various estates. He is the visiting agent for the McRosihaugh, Kepitiagalla, Ouvah, Spring Valley, Hunusigiria, Duff Nayabidde, Velliekellie, Pelmadulla, Mahawali, and Woodend estates, as well as many more belonging to the Associated Company, Liptons, Ltd., the Colombo Commercial Company, Ltd., and other private concerns. He is also the managing director of Pitakande and Neboda Tea Companies and the Kandy Hotels Company, and is a director of the Agra Tea Company, and of the Grand Central, Darampitiya, and Hayganya Rubber Companies.

KOTUAGEDERA ESTATE.

In the low-lying flats of the Matale Valley, about a mile and a half from Matale town, are to be found 200 acres of land known as the Kotuagedera estate. Of these 200 acres 197 are under cultivation, tea being produced, and rubber has just been planted. The tea is manufactured at the factory on the estate.

W. A. TYTLER'S ESTATE BUNGALOW.

The estate is owned by A. M. Hurst. For the past five years work on this land has been superintended by the resident manager, Mr. W. A. Tytler, whose father was one of the pioneers of planting in Ceylon, and a notable man of his time. During the last thirty-three years Mr. Tytler has seen the cultivation of coffee, cinchona, cacao, and tea, and has had six years' experience of coffee-planting in Mysore, and spent two years in Australia. Furthermore, he served with the first Ceylon contingent of Volunteers in the South African War, and is at present on the reserve of the Ceylon Volunteer forces. Under him work at the estate makes good progress. About 150,000 lbs. of tea is the average output of the estate yearly.

LOCHNAGAR ESTATE.

The Lochnagar estate, which includes Lawrence-Watte, lies in the Matale Valley, about five miles from the town of Matale. It is an important plantation, with an average annual output of tea amounting to about 160,000 lbs., and a production also of rubber and cacao. Of the total area of the estate, 410 acres are planted with tea, rubber being intermixed in 320 acres, whilst cacao is grown in a smaller degree. The total acreage cultivated and uncultivated is 763 acres. Mr. William Milne is the proprietor, and he is a gentleman hailing from near Aberdeen, N.B., who can fairly be regarded as one of the pioneers of planting in the district in which he labours. He is one of the oldest residents in the Matale Valley, having been a planter there for the past thirty years.

WILLIAM MILNE'S BUNGALOW.

WARAKAMURE ESTATE.

The Warakamure estate, in the Matale district, was one of the pioneer estates planted on chena (scrub covered) land. Situated in the low-lying flats of the Matale Valley, it was opened up by Mr. Harry Storey, nephew of the owner, Mr. Edward Storey, of Lancaster, at a time when the planting of such land was looked upon as a very risky experiment, as it was then thought that tea would only flourish on forest land. The result, however, more than justified expectations, and the estate at the present time is one of the heaviest yielding in the island, the yearly output amounting to between 750 and 850 lbs. of fair medium made tea per acre,

THE WARAKAMURE ESTATE.

View on Warakamure. Estate View. The Factory (Interior). The Factory. The Bungalow.

The estate stands about 1,300 ft. above sea-level, and Mr. Storey's bungalow is charmingly situated on a rise, and commands an extensive view of the beautiful surrounding country. The soil is reddish-coloured and deep-holding, but is mixed with ironstone pebbles on the small hills. During the hot weather the temperature rises as high as 90° or 92° F., and the lowest night temperature is about 61°; while the average day temperature is about 80°. Mr. Storey is an expert big game shot, and is regarded in the island as an authority on this branch of sport. At his bungalow the writer was privileged to see his unique collection of horns, a number obtained during a three months' big shoot in British Central Africa being particularly fine.

BANDARAPOLA ESTATE.

This group of estates, comprising, as it does, Bandarapola, Mundeniya, Godapola, Epelamulla, and Gansarapola, is situated in the centre of the fertile valley of Matale. The factory of the group is only four miles by cart road and two miles by riding road from the Matale railway-station, post and telegraph offices, &c., and is amongst the finest and most up-to-date in the colony. It is the property of the Bandarapola Ceylon Company, Ltd., whose head office is in 16, Philpot Lane, London. Mr. James Anderson is resident manager and has a staff of assistants. The total area of the property is 2,500 acres, of which 1,088 acres is in tea, giving heavy yields, 224 acres in cacao, and 1,020 acres in rubber of various ages from three and a half years downwards. The factory, of which the accompanying photograph gives a very good view, turns out close on 700,000 lbs. of tea yearly, and is equipped with all the latest machinery. The motive power is a 30-ft. water-wheel, a large steam-engine and a 17-horse-power Campbell oil-engine. Recently a patent fuel installation was introduced into the dryers and steam boiler, to do away with the burning of firewood. A wire shoot carries the green leaf down from the outlying divisions, saving an immense deal of labour. The manager's bungalow is a large and commodious building. It is one of the few upstair bungalows in the planting district. One of the pictures gives a panoramic view of a part of the estate with the coolie lines in the foreground and the manager's bungalow to the right; and another picture shows one of the rubber fields, with the manager and one of his assistants in the foreground. The company paid 7½ per cent. dividend in 1905 and 1904, after writing off a large sum for depreciation of machinery, &c., and 10 per cent. was paid in 1903 after setting aside £2,000 for extensions, as well as the usual 10 per cent. for depreciation of buildings and machinery. The shareholders look forward to much larger returns when the rubber comes into bearing.

MARAKONA ESTATE.

About four miles from the town of Matale, at Ukuwela, is a large estate of the above name, owned by Messrs. J. C. Deverell, R. A. Bayford, and T. C. Owen, and managed by Mr. L. R. Rudd. Adjoining this is another estate, Gooroola Ella, owned by the same three gentlemen and Mr. Rudd, and managed also by the last-named gentleman. Mr. Rudd, in addition to this, has private properties at Kadugannawa, Dimbula, and Heneratgoda, on which tea, rubber, coconuts, and cocoa are grown. All are entirely private, and comprise a total acreage of about 1,860 acres, and on each there is a factory. The Marakona estate covers 600 acres, all of which are cultivated, 295 being planted with cacao and rubber intermixed, and the remainder with tea. Gooroola Ella is planted throughout with rubber. The annual output of tea from Marakona is about 100,000 lbs. and of cacao about 1,500 cwts. Mr. Rudd has resided on the estate from the year 1896, but he has been in Ceylon since 1878.

GOOROOLA ELLA ESTATE RUBBER CLEARING.

THE BANDARAPOLA ESTATE, MATALE.

1. The Bungalow. 2. Rubber Clearing. 3. The Factory. 4. General View.

THE BUNGALOW. KENNETH J. HARPER. THE MOTOR-CAR.

WIHARAGAMA ESTATE, MATALE VALLEY.

The Wiharagama estate, which is situated in the Matale Valley, two and a half miles from the town of Matale, is 650 acres in extent, of which 500 acres are under cultivation. The products of the estate are rubber, tea, vanilla, cacao, and pepper; but cacao, rubber, and tea are the most important, the annual yield of these being—Para rubber, 3,500 lbs.; Castilloa rubber, 1,000 lbs.; and other rubber 1,000 lbs.; tea, 30,000 lbs.; and cacao 350 cwts. Mr. Kenneth J. Harper, the manager, who went out to Ceylon to take up planting in 1904, is an old student of Pembroke College, Cambridge. In addition to managing the Wiharagama estate, he is a part owner in the adjoining estate of Meegahawela. He is a keen sportsman, and divides his interest in leisure hours between motoring, shooting, and riding.

CARTIAS ARIYA-NAYAGAM.

This gentleman was born August 1, 1878, and was educated at St. Thomas's College, Colombo. Having passed the senior local (Cambridge) examination, he read law under the Council of Legal Education, and in January, 1901, he passed his examination, being admitted a Proctor in October of the same year. He is now in practice in Matale.

CARTIAS ARIYA-NAYAGAM.

Mr. Ariya-Nayagam is a member of the Ceylon National Association, the Agricultural Society, and the Matale Local Board.

THE GROVE, UKUWELA.

The Grove, Ukuwela, is one of the finest cacao plantations in the island. The estate, which belongs to Messrs. C. C. Barber & Co., is situated about four miles from Matale and twelve from Kandy, and covers 300 acres, 50 of which are planted with Para rubber alone, varying in age up to ten years. Pepper is also grown through various parts of the estate and yields a good return. The unfailing success which has attended every exhibition of the cacao grown on this estate is a striking proof of the high quality of the product, the awards numbering five gold medals, including awards from the Colonial and Indian Exhibition, London, 1886, and the St. Louis Exhibition, 1904, and two special prizes. In addition, the estate has received silver medals and other honours for its products. In 1902 a chocolate and cocoa manufactory, the only one in the East, was built on the estate, with a success which has increased yearly, and now makes an extension of the plant imperative. The advantage of being able to turn the fresh cured bean into the manufactured article on the spot results in a pure and unadulterated cocoa being placed on the market under the name of Barber's "Ne Plus Ultra Cocoa," which obtained a gold

C. C. BARBER & CO.'S ESTATE.

1. Drying. 2. Washing. 3. Cocoa Gathering. 4. Cocoa-tree in Crop. 5. C. C. Barber. 6. Cocoa and Chocolate Factory.

medal at the St. Louis Exhibition on the only occasion it was exhibited out of the island. Mr. C. C. Barber resides on the estate and supervises both the field work and the manufacturing operations.

DANIEL JOSEPH.

Mr. Daniel Joseph, who carries on the business of commission agent and general trader, originally intended to enter the legal profession, and was articled to Advocate Franciscus, at Badulla, on completing his education at St. John's College. He abandoned the law, however, and entered the service of the Government in 1869, being attached to the Irrigation Department at Batticaloa. Resigning this position in 1874, he commenced business as a commission and forwarding agent, his principal work being to carry coffee from the estates. In 1884 he removed to Matale, and planted cacao and coconuts, owning two estates, the Garden of Eden and the Malivotte. He also contracts for forwarding, and buys local produce on commission. He has been a member of the Local Board since 1887 and a Justice of the Peace since 1903. He is a member of the Ceylon Planters' Association of the Matale District, and is also on the Board of the Ceylon Agricultural Society, besides filling the position of secretary of the Matale branch. Mr. Joseph has been closely associated with various public movements, such as the extension of the railway to Jaffna, the abolition of the paddy-tax, &c., and is one of the leading members of the Tamil community. He is the son of Muttatamby, and grandson of Supramaniar Mudaliyar, Maniayar of Badamurachi (of Nallur, Jaffna), and was born in Jaffna. He married, in 1880, the daughter of E. R. Arasaratnam, Mudaliyar, and a second time, in 1904, his late wife's sister. His eldest son is Sanitary Inspector under the Municipality of Perak, Federated Malay States, and the eldest daughter is married to Proctor J. A. Aiyadurai, of Hatton.

MATALE ESTATE.

Tea is the principal product of the Matale estate, which is situated four miles from Matale town, in the Matale Valley. Three hundred acres of the estate are under cultivation, and at the time of writing another hundred acres are being opened up. The yearly output of tea amounts to 100,000 lbs., while smaller quantities of cacao and rubber are also yielded. Mr. J. C. Tribe, the resident manager, has been planting in the island since 1893, and has been on the Matale estate for about eight years. He hails from Devonshire, and his favourite sport is shooting

LILY VILLA, MATALE. MR. AND MRS. DANIEL JOSEPH AND FAMILY.

UVA PROVINCE.

UVA, or Ouva, as it was anciently called, is one of the most interesting of the nine provinces into which Ceylon is divided. Three of the sixteen holy places of Buddha are situated within the area. The province was the scene of some of the most stirring warfare associated with the Portuguese occupation and the Kandyan rebellion during the early period of British rule, and within its limits are to be found some of the most beautiful scenery in the island. The province has an area of 3,154 square miles, with a population of about 190,000, and comprises seven chief headmen's divisions, each under the care of a Ratemahatmaya. These divisions are divided into thirty Korales, and these again are subdivided into 162 Arachchi divisions, comprising 914 villages. The planting interest is strong in Uva. In the districts of Badulla, Madulsima, Monaragala, Haputale, New Galway, and Udapussellawa are nearly 200 estates, employing upwards of 40,000 coolies. "In the very earliest historical times the district formed part of the Ruhunurata, or southern kingdom of the Sinhalese, which lay between the Mahaveli Ganga and Kalu Ganga rivers on the north and west and the sea on the south. The upper portion of this division, which included Upper Uva, was called 'Malaya.' In later times Uva, or rather a portion of what is now called Uva, was a Dissavony of the Kandyan kingdom, as were also Bintenna and Welassa, which are now incorporated into the district known as Uva. It is probable that, owing to its remoteness from the capital and its difficulty of access, this portion of Ceylon was generally under the rule of powerful chiefs, who paid merely a nominal allegiance to the Kandyan throne, while for a short period the king's brother occupied the position of a senior independent sovereign with his capital at Badulla."[1] The Portuguese made desperate but unsuccessful efforts to effect a lodgment in Uva. An expedition under Constantine de Sânivalle occupied the district and burnt and sacked Badulla, but they shortly afterwards met with a most disastrous reverse, and never again entered the area. When Uva came into the possession of the British, in 1815, it was placed under the control of an Assistant Resident, with combined revenue and judicial duties, who was subordinate to the Resident at Kandy and to the Board of Commissioners for the Kandyan province. Two years later a formidable rising against the British dominion took place within the administrative area. The whole population took up arms, and a stubborn resistance was offered to the British forces sent to suppress the movement. Eventually British power and resolution triumphed, but it was at the cost of many valuable lives and the sacrifice of great material interests. The country was terribly wasted in the effort to reduce the rebels. Indeed, it is considered doubtful whether even to this day the district has entirely recovered from the exhaustion which supervened upon the war. Military forts were maintained for a time at Fort Macdonald, Ettampitiya, Badulla, Passara, Alupota, and Kotabowa, but they were one after another abandoned, and now there is not a single British soldier maintained in the area. The military rule necessitated by the rebellion gave place to the usual civil administration under the Kandyan Board of Commissioners. When this body was abolished, in 1832, the Central Province was formed, and an Assistant Agent was established at Badulla. In 1886 the system was superseded by the creation of Uva into a separate province.

BADULLA CHURCH.

BADULLA CHURCH.
(Another View.)

LAW COURTS, BADULLA.

The natural beauty of Uva has been extolled by many writers. It is a combination of swelling upland and sheltering vale, with, in places, great stretches of park-like country. Parts of it have been likened to Sussex, and, indeed, there are tracts which are reminiscent of the glorious southern downs. Owing to the conformation of the country a curious phenomenon is witnessed during the period of the south-west monsoon. While on one side of the mountain range which divides the province there is mist and storm, on the other there is brilliant sunshine and a dry air. This strange natural effect is graphically described by Sir Samuel Baker in this passage from his work, "Eight Years in Ceylon": "From June to November the south-west monsoon brings wind and mist across the Nuwara Eliya mountains. Clouds of white fog boil up from the Dimbula valley like the steam from a huge cauldron and invade the Nuwara Eliya plain through the gaps in the mountain to the westward. The wind howls over the high ridges, cutting the jungle with its keen edge, so that it remains as stunted brushwood, and the opaque screen of driving fog and drizzling rain is so dense that one feels convinced there is no sun visible within at least a hundred miles. There is a curious phenomenon, however, in this locality. When the weather described prevails at Nuwara Eliya there is actually not one drop of rain within four miles of my house, in the direction of Badulla. Dusty roads, a cloudless sky, and dazzling sunshine astonish the thoroughly soaked traveller, who rides out of the rain and mist into a genial climate as though he passed through a curtain. The wet weather terminates at a mountain called Hakgala. . . . This bold rock, whose summit is about 6,500 ft. above the sea, breasts the driving wind and seems to command the storm. The rushing clouds halt in their mad course upon its crest, and curl in sudden impotence around the craggy summits.

[1] "Manual of the Province of Uva," by Herbert White, Esq., of the Ceylon Civil Service, p. 2.

The deep ravine formed by an opposite mountain is filled with the vanquished mist, which sinks powerless in its dark gorge; and the bright sun shining from the east spreads a perpetual rainbow upon the gauze-like cloud of fog which settles in the deep hollow. This is exceedingly beautiful. The perfect circle of the rainbow stands like a fairy spell in the giddy depths of the hollow, and seems to forbid the advance of the monsoon. All before is bright and cloudless; the lovely panorama of the Uva country spreads before the eye for many miles beneath the feet. All behind is dark and stormy, the wind is howling, the forests are groaning, the rain is pelting upon the hills. The change seems impossible; but there it is, ever the same. Season after season, year after year, the rugged top of Hakgala struggles with the storms, and, ever victorious, the cliffs smile in the sunshine on the eastern side; the rainbow reappears with the monsoon, and its vivid circle remains like the guardian spirit of the valley."

This picturesque description may appropriately be supplemented by Sir Emerson Tennent's rhapsody on the wonderful view presented to the traveller from the Pass of Ella. Says this talented writer in his well-known work: "Perhaps there is not a scene in the world which combines sublimity and beauty in a more extraordinary degree than that which is presented at the Pass of Ella, where, through an opening in the chain of mountains, the road from Badulla descends rapidly to the lowlands, over which it is carried for upwards of seventy miles to Hambantota, on the south coast of the island. The ride to Ella passes for ten or twelve miles along the base of hills thickly wooded except on those spots where the forest has been cleared for planting coffee. The view is therefore obstructed, and appears at one point to terminate in an impassable glen; but on reaching this the traveller is amazed at discovering a ravine through which a torrent has forced its way, disclosing a passage to the plains below, over which, for more than sixty miles, the prospect extends unbroken by a single eminence, till, far in the distance, the eye discerns a line of light, which marks where the sunbeams are flashing on the waters of the Indian Ocean."

SCENE NEAR THE MARKET, BADULLA.

THE LAKE, BADULLA.

As has been previously indicated, there are three centres of exceptional antiquarian interest in Uva. One of these is Bintenne, or Mahiyangana, famous for its shrine, which, according to legend, was built while Buddha was yet alive. "In point of antiquity," says Sir Emerson Tennent, "Bintenne transcends even the historic renown of Anuradhapura." This view is enthusiastically supported by Mr. White, who writes lovingly and sympathetically of the traditions of this famous spot. "Mahiyangana," he says, "is literally the *alpha* and *omega* of the Mahavansa. It is referred to in the first chapter and in the last chapter, and continually throughout the chronicle, always with the greatest reverence as one of the most sacred of the sixteen sacred places of Ceylon. Kings innumerable repaired the fabric of the dagoba, and endowed the shrine with lands and villages. A long procession of figures this shrine has seen for well-nigh 2,500 years—founder and disciples, Buddha and dévos, priests and kings, pilgrims and warriors, peaceful embassies and hostile troops, and shaven monks from far-off Siam."[1] Near Bintenne is Horaborawewa, one of the

[1] "Manual of Uva," p. 25.

vast tanks of the ancient Sinhalese period. Tennent gives a description of it which can scarcely be improved upon. "It is," he wrote, "a stupendous work. A stream, flowing between two hills about three or four miles apart, has been intercepted by an artificial dam drawn across the valley at the point where they approach; and the water thus confined is thrown back till it forms a lake eight or ten miles long by three or four wide, exclusive of narrow branches running behind spurs of the hills. The embankment is from 50 to 70 ft. high, and about 200 ft. broad at the base. But one of the most ingenious features in the work is the advantage which has been taken in its construction of two vast masses of rock which have been included in the retaining bund, the intervening spaces being filled up by earthwork and faced with stone. In order to form the sluices it is obvious that the simplest plan would have been to have placed them in the artificial portion of the bank; but the builders, conscious of the comparatively unsubstantial nature of their own work, and apprehensive of the combined effect of the weight and rush of the water, foresaw that the immense force of its discharge would speedily sweep away any artificial conduits they could have constructed for its escape, and they had the resolution to hollow out channels in the solid rock, through which they opened two passages, each 60 ft. deep, 4 ft. broad at the bottom, and widening to 15 or 20 ft. at the top. The walls on either side still exhibit traces of the wedges by which the stone was riven to effect the openings." The tank was restored by Government in 1870, and now irrigates 236 acres of paddy-land.

The second of the sacred places of Uva is Kataragama, a shrine of great antiquity, situated in a sparsely-populated country about forty-five miles from Hambantota and sixty from Badulla. "The sanctity of the spot is due to the tradition that Karthikaya, the Mars of Hindu mythology, to whom the temple of Kataragama is dedicated, halted on the top of the highest of the seven hills on his return homeward to Mount Kailasa, the abode of his father, Siva, the Destroyer, after conquering the Asurs, or Titans. Here also the god found his consort, known locally as Valliamma, in whose honour a special temple has been built at Kataragama. . . . Tradition also connects Kataragama with the *Ramayana* as being the place of meeting of Rama with his queen Sita, the rescue of the latter from the stronghold of Rama. . . . Singularly enough the Mussulmans of India also profess reverence for Kataragama, and have built a mosque there, alleging that a Nebi of great sanctity discovered in the neighbourhood the fountain of life, of which whoever drinks becomes immortal! The fountain is now sealed, and its site unknown, which is the more to be regretted as no fountain or well of any kind is to be found for probably twenty miles round about!"[1] From time immemorial crowds of pilgrims

THE MARKET, BADULLA.

[1] Administration Report of Mr. T. Steele, Assistant Government Agent at Hambantota.

HAPUTALE WATERFALL. BO-TREE IN THE ENGLISH CEMETERY AT BADULLA. BADULLA FALLS.
TREES IN THE FORT AT BADULLA. THE TEMPLE, BADULLA.

1. E. H. Mellor. 2. Alfred Scovell. 3. Alexander Louis Kirk. 4. B. Heathcote. 5. G. O. Trevaldwyn. 6. Bryce J. Wylie. 7. J. W. Balfour Paul. 8. J. R. Barclay. 9. Arthur William Bissett. 10. J. G. Veall. 11. C. W. Beattie. 12. John J. Robinson. 13. Channing Esdaile. 14. J. H. B. Cockburn. 15. James Duncan. 16. John Rettie. 17. George Thain-Davidson.

have annually resorted to Kataragama in the hot, dry months of June, July, and August. Approached through a barren, desolate country, in which the only water supply is that obtainable from the Menik Ganga river—a stream which is frequently dried up in the months indicated—the pilgrimage has ever been one which has put a great physical strain upon the devotees. "The evil effects of the festival are many," says Mr. Steele, whose deeply interesting account of the shrine we have quoted. "The frequency with which it has been the source of epidemic disease has created feelings of terror in all the districts through which the pilgrims travel, and those of Uva and Hambantota in particular. Too often the waysides have been strewn with corpses of men, women, and children who have perished on their ill-fated journey. Those who die, indeed, are taught to look upon such a death as a true *euthanasia*, a certain passport to a better life; but the unfortunate villagers, to whose homes contagion and infection are carried, have little reason to share ecstatic views, and may well call the pilgrimage a scourge." The scenes that occasionally occurred in connection with the festival and pilgrimage were very distressing. One outbreak of cholera in 1858 is vividly described by Mr. Steele. "Regardless of the rites they had travelled so far to take part in, regardless of the closest ties of kindred or friendship, the panic-stricken pilgrims fled for their lives, leaving in many cases their companions to perish by the waysides and spreading pestilence wherever they went. Like wild-fire cholera spread from hamlet to hamlet, from station to station. It was piteous to see forlorn women forsaken by their husbands, their children dying beside them, wailing in all the agony—short-lived but incredibly passionate — of Oriental grief, and recalling forcibly the awful scene of bereavement recorded in Scripture: 'In Rama was there a voice heard, lamentation, and weeping, and great mourning, Rachel weeping for her children, and would not be comforted, because they are not.'" In late years the number of pilgrims has greatly fallen off,[1] and the careful regulations of the Government have prevented the repetition of terrible episodes such as that which Mr. Steele so powerfully depicts.

[1] In 1905 the Government allowed only 2,000 people to proceed on the pilgrimage.

Uva was at one time a country famous for big game. It was the chief scene of the exploits of the redoubtable Major Rogers, who in the course of his lifetime is reputed to have shot at the very lowest estimate 1,400 wild elephants. Major Rogers was not only a great sportsman; he was an indefatigable administrator. He either traced or constructed nearly all the roads in the province; he built most of the rest-houses, and kept in repair all the civil and military buildings in the district, and single-handed carried out the no easy task of arranging the commutation of the gram tax.[1] His end was tragic. On the evening of June 7, 1845, he was sheltering with some brother officials in a house at Haputale. After a time he stepped into the porch to see if the storm showed any signs of abatement. At the same moment there was a brilliant flash of lightning, and he fell to the ground dead. He was buried in Nuwara Eliya, and it is a singular

[1] "Manual of Uva," p. 111.

fact that his tomb was some time later struck by lightning.

The early development of Uva in the forties fills an interesting chapter in the history of the province. Under the stimulating influences of the coffee boom, a large area of Crown land was taken up in 1841. In 1842 and 1843 there were also considerable sales. Amongst the earliest estates opened up were Baddegama or Spring Valley by Sir William Reid; Kottagoda by Dr. Galland, Staff Surgeon at Badulla; Gowarakelle, Nahavilla, Weyvelhena, Cannawarelle, and Dikbedde or Ettampitiya. The crisis of 1845 brought to a general close the rash speculation of which these land transactions in Uva were a part. Sir Emerson Tennent notes that two estates in Badulla which had cost £10,000 were sold for only £350, and that the Hindagalla plantation, which cost £10,000, produced but £500. Since that period planting enterprise conducted on rational business lines has made great headway in Uva, and the estates there are amongst the best in the country.

LOCAL BOARD, BADULLA.

Badulla, the capital of Uva, is a pretty little town encircled on three sides by the Badulla-Oya (river), which is spanned by an iron bridge erected in 1867 during the construction of the Batticaloa road. The place is situated in a charming valley, on one side of which towers the lofty mountain range which shuts Uva in from the Nuwara Eliya plains. The town and its environs are well wooded, and the traveller approaching it from the higher ground looks down on a sea of foliage. The most conspicuous objects which meet the eye are Judge's Hill and bungalow on the right-hand side, and on the left the new hospital and the market. Between these two buildings stands the schoolroom of the Wesleyan Mission, and a little farther on on the same side are the police-barracks and the Kachcheri and Court-House buildings, which occupy the site of the old fort. Below the Kachcheri stands the Ambalam and a monolith commemorating the formation of the Horabora tank, as well as a portion of an old stone sluice brought from the same place, while at the junction of the old Kandy road and the Nuwara Eliya road stands, in a beautiful situation, the rest-house. To the left of the rest-house and at the foot of the old ramparts is St. Mark's Church, which was erected by public subscription to the memory of Major Rogers. The building is situated at the head of a small square esplanade. At the opposite end of this are the Roman Catholic Church and schools and the jail, which was built on the site of an old royal granary. Behind the jail lies the racecourse. This was much improved and enlarged in 1889 and a grand stand was added, while in 1890 an artificial lake was formed in the centre of it, and a new cricket ground made in front of the grand stand. To the north lies the Experimental Gardens, managed as a branch of the Botanical Gardens of Peradeniya and Hakgala. The Residency, the official dwelling of the Government Agent of the province, is a building standing in extensive, well-timbered grounds. Near it is the Town Hall, which was built in 1886, and has since been greatly improved. The building possesses a small stage, and is used for dances, concerts, and public meetings. At the entrance to the town along the Batticaloa road is the Mutiyangana vihara and dagoba, and some distance off along the Batticaloa road is the Kataragama diwala. These, with a curious little structure called Sinnasana, the King's Seat, near the entrance to the last-named temple, serve as reminders of the fact that Badulla was at one time a centre of considerable religious activity. It only remains to be added, to complete the description, the details of which are borrowed from Mr. White's useful "Manual," that the affairs of the town are administered by a Local Board which was established in 1870.

The most recent history of the province is an almost unbroken record of prosperity. The revenue of 1905 amounted to Rs. 206,816, which was Rs. 26,926·33 in excess of that of the previous year. The province is sharing in the enterprise associated with the development of the rubber industry. Extensive acreages have in the last few years been opened up under the stimulus of the Government decision to make grants of large tracts of land on exceptionally favourable terms for the experimental cultivation of the product in districts where it had not been previously tried.

HERBERT WHITE.

The Government Agent of the province, whose official career is sketched elsewhere in the volume, has acquired a position of enviable distinction in connection with the

H. WHITE.
(Government Agent.)

literature of Ceylon. The excellent official "Manual of the Uva Province" was compiled by him; he edited the second edition of the "Ceylon Glossary," and jointly compiled the revised edition of the "Legislative Enactments of Ceylon, 1900." He has also contributed learned papers to the Oriental List and the *Journal of the Royal Asiatic Society*, Ceylon branch. But his greatest work was the compilation of the "Ceylon Manual." This work is a mine of information on all matters pertaining to the island, and is absolutely indispensable for purposes of reference. Though first issued only in 1904, it has already a recognised place in standard literature relating to the colonies. Mr. White, who is a son of the late Mr. Frederick Thomas White, a well-known Chancery barrister, the joint author of White and Tudor's "Leading Cases in Equity," was born in London on August 25, 1857, and was educated at Shrewsbury School. He is married to Louisa Mary, daughter of the late Mr. E. C. Bousfield, of the Isle of Wight. He is a member of the Grosvenor Club, Devon Street, Piccadilly, of the Colombo Club, and of the Sheringham Golf Club, Norfolk. His recreations are tennis and golf.

A. J. WICKWAR.

Mr. A. J. Wickwar, Superintendent of the Topographical Survey, was born on January 1, 1871, in Ceylon, and educated at St. Cuthber

A. J. WICKWAR.

Grammar School, Newcastle-on-Tyne. His official connection with the island dates to 1889, when he received an appointment on the unfixed establishment of the Surveyor-General's Department. In 1897 he joined the permanent staff as thirteenth District Surveyor, a position he shortly afterwards exchanged for that of Assistant Superintendent. On April 9, 1901, he acted for the Superintendent of Surveys, and on June 25, 1904, on that position becoming vacant, it was conferred upon him. Mr. Wickwar is a member of the Hill Club, Nuwara Eliya, and of the Badulla Club. His recreations are golf, tennis, and shooting.

D. C. KOTALAWELA.

A popular and influential member of the Sinhalese community in the Uva Province is the gentleman whose name figures above. He is the largest landed proprietor in the Uva Province, and owns besides much property in the Central Province. He enjoys, moreover, the rank of Mohandiram. Born in 1847 at Undugoda, Rayigam Korale, his early life was spent at Kalutara, where he was educated. In 1864 he bought the Uva and Central Province toll rents, and continued to hold them until 1894, when he retired, leaving his eldest son to acquire the rents. Mr. Kotalawela is a generous supporter of Buddhist educational and charitable institutions, and has done a

MUDALIYAR AND MRS. D. C. KOTALAWELA AND FAMILY.

"PIYA NIVASA."

great deal for Badulla, with which town his father, Don Carolis Kotalawela, merchant and landed proprietor, was intimately associated. The subject of this sketch is married to Sudu Menika Wijekoon, by whom he has had four sons and two daughters. The eldest son, Don Henry, twenty-one years of age, was educated at Royal College. He has the oversight of his father's estates, and also manages the toll rents. The other children are Don James (nineteen years), Don William (sixteen years), Don David (six years), Nandavathi (seven years), and Lily (four years).

THOMAS SCOVELL.

The Batgodde estate, Haldummulla, is a compact property situated at an elevation of from 3,200 to 5,200 ft. The acreage is 210, and it is all planted with tea. The soil is of a superior character, and the annual crop is a heavy one, aggregating 100,000 lbs. The property belongs to Mr. Thomas Scovell, the son of Colonel E. W. Scovell, of the 96th Regiment of Foot. Mr. Scovell was born in London, and educated partly in London and partly on the Continent. He came out to Ceylon in 1872, and joined the Viharehana estate, Marakele district, which partly belonged to his father. After spending two years on this estate he went to the Adam's Peak estate, Maskeliya district, of which he was part proprietor. Here he remained for twenty-four years, witnessing in the interim the decline and fall of coffee, the planting of cinchona, and the rise of tea. When he first went to the district there were very few estates. There was no railway beyond Gampola, and the cart road to the district stopped about 7 miles from the Adam's Peak estate. In 1898 Mr. Scovell quitted Maskeliya and went over to the Dimbula district, taking charge of Derry Clair estate, of which he was also part proprietor in the coffee days. The property was planted with tea under Mr. Scovell's supervision from Maskeliya, and it was in his charge until 1907. Mr. Scovell is married to Ida Helen, daughter of the late Mr. J. H. Wynnel Mayow, the well-known planter, who was proprietor of the Batgodde estate. After Mr. Mayow's death Mr. Scovell became the owner of the estate. Mr. Scovell is proceeding Home on a holiday, and during his absence his brother, Mr. Alfred Scovell, will have charge of the property. Mr. Scovell is a member of the Haputale Planters' Association, and is churchwarden of St. Margaret's, Forest Creek. His recreations are tennis, golf, shooting, and oil painting.

J. W. BALFOUR PAUL.

This gentleman is superintendent of the Cullen estate, Badulla, and has charge of the Cobo estate, while he also supervises the Oodoowerre estate, of which he is proprietor. He was born on June 4, 1873, at Edinburgh, and educated at Sedbergh, Yorkshire. His friends contemplated for him a military career, but the idea was eventually abandoned, and he came out to Ceylon in 1893 to commence a career as a planter. He first joined the Broughton estate, Haputale, but after a year's probationary service transferred to the Lunugala estate, on which he remained for eighteen months. Finally he received his present appointment on the Cullen estate. On the formation of the first Ceylon contingent he volunteered for service, and remained with the force until the action at Pretoria. He was then, with three others, appointed orderly to the Second Mounted Infantry Brigade Staff. He was seriously wounded at Nooitgedacht, his injuries necessitating the amputation of his left arm. Trooper Kelly, one of the other three orderlies, was killed, and the remaining two were wounded. Mr. Paul was invalided home after the Nooitgedacht fight, and remained for some time recruiting his health, which had been greatly shaken by his wound. In December, 1901, he returned to Ceylon, and resumed his position on the Cullen estate. In the Ceylon contingent Mr. Paul first held the rank of corporal, and he rose to the position of quartermaster-sergeant. At the present time he is Lieutenant and Quartermaster in the Ceylon Mounted Rifles.

C. W. BEATTIE.

Mr. C. W. Beattie, Superintendent of the Telbedde estate, Badulla, is a Scotsman hailing from Insch. Born in October, 1874, he was educated locally and at the Aberdeen Grammar School, and came out to Ceylon in 1896. Joining the Sarnia estate, he served there for three years, and subsequently for about a year was associated with the Rahanawatte and Narangalla estates. In 1902 he joined the Telbedde estate, and has been engaged on that property ever since. The estate has an acreage of 1,000, of which 600 acres are planted with tea and 70 acres with rubber. The estimated annual crop of tea is 250,000 lbs. About 500 coolies are employed in the working of the property. Apart from the ordinary planting business, a large cattle establishment and a dairy are worked in connection with the estate, and these supply produce to the inhabitants of Badulla town and the neighbourhood.

GEORGE THAIN-DAVIDSON.

Mr. George Thain-Davidson, the superintendent of the Dambatenne group of estates, Haputale, is a son of the late Rev. Dr. Thain-Davidson. He was born in July, 1871, in London, and educated at Mill Hill School. At the close of his educational training, he went out to California and did ranching for a few years. In 1896 he came out to Ceylon and joined the Inverney estate, Dikoya. After serving on this and other estates he accepted an appointment upon Messrs. Lipton's Panilkande estate, Morawak Korale. In January, 1906, after a period of leave at home, he was appointed to the charge of the Dambatenne group of estates, also owned by Messrs. Lipton. These have an acreage of 1,247½, most of which is under tea, though there is a small area in cardamoms and coffee. The original estate was, as regards half its area, cropped with coffee; the remainder was virgin jungle. The old coffee land was brought under cultivation for tea, and the jungle was also gradually planted with tea. The annual crop of tea is estimated at 700,000 lbs., and the labour force consists of 1,400 coolies. The elevation of the group is from 4,200 ft. to 6,200 ft.

STEPHEN PERERA.

Mr. Perera is a Proctor of the District Court, Badulla. The son of Mr. D. E. Perera, merchant, of Badulla, he was born on August 1, 1877, at Colombo, and educated at Royal College. He prosecuted his legal studies under the auspices of the Council of Legal Education, and was called to the Bar in 1901. Since that year he has practised in Badulla. Mr. Perera is a landed proprietor in the Uva Province. His recreations are tennis and riding.

STEPHEN PERERA.

VEALL & CO.

This is a well-known Badulla firm, doing a considerable business as importers of general merchandise, estate tools and requisites, stationery, and hardware, and as printers and machine rulers. The proprietor, Mr. T. G. Veall, was born at St. Austell, Cornwall, and came to Ceylon in 1886. He is a Lieutenant and Quartermaster in the Ceylon Planters' Rifle Corps, and formerly held a commission in the C.L.I.V. He enjoys a considerable reputation as a marksman. He was a member of the Ceylon Volunteer Force Team which competed at the Southern India Rifle Association Meeting at Bangalore in 1904, and was also one of the Ceylon Planters' Rifle Corps Team which competed at the same centre in 1906. Individually he has won many prizes for rifle shooting. Mr. Veall's recreations are rifle shooting, golf, tennis, and croquet.

ALFRED SCOVELL.

This gentleman, who is the proprietor of the Beauvais estate, Haldammulla, is the son of Colonel E. W. Scovell, 96th Regiment of Foot. He was born in London, and educated privately in England and at Heidelberg, Germany. He was for five years employed in the Australasian Bank, London. At the end of that period he received an appointment to go out to the Melbourne office of the bank, but relinquished the position in favour of a planting career. He went out to Ceylon in 1876, and joined Mr. Derry Clair as assistant. At the expiration of a year he took charge of his own property, Forest Hill coffee estate, Madulsima. He ultimately sold out and returned to England; but he was soon back in Ceylon, enlarging his planting experience by supervising in succession several estates in the Upper Kelani Valley. He has had very wide experience in tea cultivation, and considers that the Haputale district is the best suited to that class of planting, the soil being good and the climate very healthy. The Beauvais estate is situated at an elevation of from 4,000 to 5,000 ft., and it comprises an area of 243 acres under tea. The annual estimated crop is 100,000 lbs. Mr. Scovell is a member of the Haputale Planters' Association and of the Taldna Club. His recreations are music and oil painting. On two occasions he won the Governor's prize for oil painting.

BRYCE J. WYLIE.

The superintendent of the Kalupahani estate, Mr. Bryce J. Wylie, comes of a well-known planting family. His grandfather was Mr. George Bird, a pioneer in the coffee planting enterprise, and his father, Mr. W. B. R. Wylie, was manager and coffee planter for Messrs. Keir, Dundas & Co., Kandy, and the contractor for the railway extension to Haputale. Mr. Bryce Wylie was born at Kandy in December, 1860, and sent Home for his education. Returning to Ceylon in 1877, he joined the Gonavy estate (all coffee), and remained there for about eighteen months. He then took charge of the Patigama estate, and continued in the position of superintendent for about eight years. Subsequently he went over to the Haldummulla estate in 1887. This was originally a coffee estate, but on the collapse of coffee the property was replanted with tea. Mr. Wylie also had charge of the Idulgashena estate, another coffee property which was placed under tea when the crash came. At a later period Mr. Wylie had the supervision of the Kalupahani estate and of the Ormiston estate, which he planted with tea after coffee had failed. Since 1896 he has been engaged in opening up the Oakwell estate, which consists of 267 acres under tea and 245 acres under rubber. The Kalupahani estate has an area of 396 acres under tea. The produce from this estate has sold in England at 7½d. per pound. Mr. Wylie is a member of the Haputale Planters' Association, and of the Ceylon Planters' Rifle Corps. His recreation is tennis.

B. T. HEATHCOTE.

Mr. B. T. Heathcote, the superintendent of the Sherwood estate, is a son of Mr. T. B. Heathcote, solicitor to the Duchy of Cornwall. He was born in May, 1880, at Betchworth, Surrey, and educated at Bradfield College. He came out to Ceylon in 1899, and joined the Blair Athol estate, Dikoya. After serving there for one year he transferred to the Kelvin estate, Haputale, where he gained two and a half years' further experience. Then he took charge of the Sherwood estate, a property situated at an elevation of from 3,800 to 5,500 ft., and having an acreage of 500, of which 450 acres are planted with tea. About 300 coolies are employed upon the estate, the agents for which are Messrs. Cummerbatch & Co. Mr. Heathcote's recreations are tennis and shooting.

G. O. TREVALDWYN.

Mr. G. O. Trevaldwyn, the superintendent of the Wiharegalla estate, Haputale, is a son of the Rev. B. J. Trevaldwyn, Rector of St. Martin's-by-Looe, Cornwall. He was born on June 22, 1880, in Warwickshire, and educated at Coleshill Grammar School, at Kelly College, Tavistock, and in France and Germany. He came out to Ceylon in 1899 and joined the Ardlaw estate, Agrapatnas. After a probationary service of nine months he was appointed assistant on the Ramboda estate, Ramboda, under Mr. de Lemos, and served in that capacity until 1904, when he took charge of the estate. He remained for one year, and then accepted the superintendency of the Hillbodde estate, Pussellawa. Finally, in 1906, he obtained the position he now fills. The Wiharegalla estate is at an elevation of from 2,500 ft. to 5,000 ft., and has an acreage of 929. Of this area 648 acres are planted with tea and 75 acres with rubber. The estimated annual crop of tea is 285,000 lbs., the average price of which, in England, is 8d. per pound. The owners of the property are the Duff Estate Company, Limited, and the local agents are Messrs. George Steuart & Co. Mr. Trevaldwyn is a member of the Haputale Planters' Association and of the Ceylon Planters' Rifle Corps. His recreations are tennis and shooting.

MILITARY AND VOLUNTEERS

FOR military purposes Ceylon is a Major-General's command, and the normal garrison consists of a battalion of infantry, four companies of artillery, and two of Royal Engineers. There is also an efficient Volunteer force. At the present time, however, the regular troops in the island consist of a battalion of Madras Infantry (the 75th Carnatic), one company of Royal Artillery, one company Ceylon and Mauritius Royal Artillery, half a company of Royal Engineers, with details of the Army Service Corps, R.A.M.C., Army Ordnance Department, and Army Accounts Department. Thus it will be seen that the only white soldiers in the island are one company of Royal Artillery and half a company of Royal Engineers, the reductions having been made during Mr. Haldane's tenure of office as Secretary for War. It is noteworthy that during the early part of 1906 the defences at Trincomalee, which had been continuously maintained since the commencement of the British occupation in 1796, were abandoned and the old fort there was dismantled. The substitution of the Carnatic native troops for the Worcester Regiment dates from January, 1907.

In the early years of the nineteenth century, when Ceylon was governed as a military settlement, the colony had a Lieutenant-General commanding, a full staff, four regiments of British infantry, besides two Ceylon Rifle Regiments, a corresponding force of artillery and engineers, and a troop of cavalry. In 1823 the military portion of the population, including wives and children, was returned at 5,852, out of a total of 751,210 for the island. Twelve years later the military numbered 6,227, in 1838 5,705, and in 1845 4,626. In 1864 the number had decreased to 2,981, and cost the colony £137,743, as against £92.850, when the military was one and a half times as strong numerically. It was at this time

BRIGADIER-GENERAL R. C. B. LAWRENCE.

(Officer Commanding the Troops in Ceylon.)

that Lord (then Mr.) Cardwell raised the colony's contribution for military, numbering only 2,738, to £100,000 and over, and spent a large sum besides on military works out of colonial surpluses. At the present time the colony pays three-quarters of the cost of the garrison, as long as that amount does not exceed 9½ per cent. of its revenue—revenue for this purpose excluding profits made by the Ceylon Government Railway and sales of land. In 1885, in return for a military contribution of Rs. 600,000 (£40,000) per annum, it was stipulated that the colony was to have a force of 400 regular soldiers, the number estimated as being required for colonial purposes as distinct from Imperial requirements. The actual cost of the 400 was Rs. 516,000 (£34,000), but the Lords of the Treasury put the balance of Rs. 84,000 (£5,600) down as a contribution for naval expenses. This the Colonial Office resisted, and it has never been countenanced by the Ceylon Legislative Council, although the payment by the Government of the whole sum was sanctioned. The Imperial Government has always maintained a good many more than 400 military in Ceylon. In March, 1888, the detachment of troops stationed at Galle was entirely withdrawn. The Home authorities, in addition to dismantling the batteries, wished the ramparts also to be thrown down, but the townspeople objected. Since then both Colombo and Trincomalee have been strongly fortified, but, as has already been stated, the defences at the latter place have been abandoned. At Colombo three batteries, one at Mutwal Point, a second on Galle Face Esplanade, and a third south of the fort, have been erected at the colony's cost (£24,000), the Imperial Government agreeing to pay £37,000 for the guns for them. The Ordinance fixing the colony's contribution at 9½ per cent. of the general revenue was passed in 1898.

It may be interesting to note the fluctuations in the cost of the military in the island during the last quarter of a century from the following table:—

NET COST OF MILITARY TO COLONY.

1880	£76,330
1885	40,000
1890	50,000
1895	109,787
1905	153,728

The low cost in 1885 and 1890 is due to the fact that Sir Arthur Gordon was instrumental in obtaining a reduction of Rs. 400,000 (about £26,500) in 1885, at the time of the financial crisis of the colony, and this continued until the new arrangement of fixing the cost as a proportion of the revenue was made in 1901. Part of the increase is due to the appreciation of the rupee from 1s. 1½d. to 1s. 4d., and in this connection it is singular that, although in the past the Governments of India and Ceylon had given compensation when the value of the rupee depreciated, this has never been done for military officers serving in Ceylon.

Practically speaking, the whole of the garrison is stationed at Colombo, the only up-country station where a military force is maintained being Kandy, the mountain capital, where a detachment of infantry is stationed. Diyatalawa is used as a camping-ground, and manœuvres are carried out there every year. Curiously enough there is no memorial in the island to those who fell or died of disease during the Kandyan wars.

The troops are at present under the supreme command of Brigadier-General R. C. B. Lawrence, and Major C. R. Ballard is the Chief Staff Officer, Deputy Assistant Adjutant, and Quartermaster-General; while the officers of the details of troops are as follows: Royal Artillery, Colombo, Staff-Lieut.-Colonel J. R. B. Davidson, O.C.R.A., Captain W. B. Anley, Adjutant, and Captain E. B. Scott, I.G. and R.F.; 93rd Company, Major R. G. Merriman, D.S.O., Captain H. C. Reeves, Lieutenants R. S. Bunbury, C. J. Russell, and G. F. C. White; Ceylon and Mauritius R.A., Major C. W. Richardson, officer commanding; No. 3 Company, Captain A. J. H. Keyes, Lieutenants J. G. Gale and C. V. S. Skrimshire, Subadars Cader Miskin and Mul Raj, Jemadars Dasuel Khan and Bhagirat; Royal Engineers, Lieut.-Colonel L. Jones, Surveyor A. D. Geddes, Major R. F. Edwards (Nuwara Eliya), Captain L. J. N. Neville, and Lieutenant R. R. Hyslop; 75th Carnatic Infantry, Lieut.-Colonel M. E. O'Donoghue (commandant), Major S. B. Graham (second in command), Major T. Ffrench, Major H. W. C. Colquhoun, Major E. E. Beddek, Major G. L. P. Clarke, Captain A. W. N. Raven, Captain A. T. Kirkwood, Captain H. Miller, Lieutenant E. L. Robinson, Lieutenant N. A. Worlledge, Captain C. V. Ommanney (Adjutant), Lieutenant D'A. M. Fraser (Q.M.), Captain S. A. Ruzzak, I.M.S. (Medical Officer); Army Service Corps, Major W. J. S. McCormick, Captain B. L. Beddy, and Captain C. H. Bingham (Diyatalawa); R.A.M.C., Lieut.-Colonel G. H. Sylvester, S.M.O., Lieut.-Colonel C. A. Lane, Captain E. C. Hayes, and Lieutenant C. R. Millar; Army Ordnance Department, Captain O. B. Harter, Lieutenant H. J. Jones, and Captain D. Coar; and Army Accounts Department, Mr. H. G. Duneher, First-class Assistant Accountant, and Captain the Hon. O. F. H. Napier.

MAJOR E. J. HAYWARD.
(Ceylon Mounted Infantry.)

VOLUNTEERS.

CEYLON rejoices in the possession of a small but compact force of Volunteers, embracing artillery, mounted infantry, and infantry. All told, the numbers do not reach 2,500, but what the force lacks in numbers it makes up in efficiency. In few parts of the Empire, indeed, do the citizen soldiers more conscientiously perform their duties than in the island. The history of the force dates no farther back than 1881. In that year, following upon the establishment of a Rifle Club in the previous year, a notification was made in the *Government Gazette* that the Lieut.-Governor (Sir John Douglas, K.C.M.G.) had granted the requisite permission for the raising of a corps of Volunteers. Thirteen days later (on April 13th) Mr. John S. Armitage was elected Commanding Officer of the new corps, and on the 13th May the appointment was notified of an Adjutant in the person of Captain George Gwatkin, of the 3rd Battalion Welsh Regiment. The ranks of the corps were speedily filled. By the end of August the enrolments numbered 1,103. Sir James Longden, the Governor, held the first inspection of the corps on November 26, 1881, and the first official inspection by Major-General Sir George McLeod took place on September 23, 1882. In 1883 a company was started at Kurunegala, in the North-Western Province, and three years later a second company was raised at Galle, in the Southern Province. In 1888 a further important development took place in the shape of the raising of a corps of Artillery Volunteers, and in 1890 the bearer company came into existence. In 1891 an infantry company was raised at Badulla, and a cyclist company was formed in Colombo. The next year saw the formation of new companies and detachments of infantry at Batticaloa, Matara, Negombo, and Hambantota, and a company of Artillery Volunteers at Trincomalee. The latter, and a similar corps raised at Galle, were disbanded in 1902. Meanwhile a company of Mounted Infantry had been enrolled at Kandy (on July 12, 1892), and had been a great success. An important change in the constitution of the force was made in May, 1896, when an officer of the Army, recommended by the War Office, was appointed paid Commandant and Inspecting-Officer in the room of the unpaid Commandant who up to that period had officiated. The force was then composed as follows:—

Ceylon Artillery Volunteers ...	129
Ceylon Mounted Infantry ...	110
Bearers	50
Cyclists	5
Ceylon Light Infantry	868
	1,162

The Jubilee year 1897 saw in London a representative detachment of Ceylon Volunteers, including 9 Artillery, 15 Mounted Infantry, and 26 Infantry. A still greater stirring of patriotic ardour was occasioned in 1900, when, on the outbreak of the war in South Africa, a complete company of mounted infantry, numbering 129, fully equipped at the colony's expense, was despatched to assist the British forces operating at the seat of war. The contingent, on arrival at Cape Town, proceeded by train to the Modder River, and marched thence to Poplar Grove, where it was met by Lord Roberts. Subsequently it took part in the engagement at Dreifontein. Later it marched to Bloemfontein with General Roberts's column, and to Pretoria with General Ian Hamilton. The detachment subsequently took part in the following engagements: Johannesburg, Pretoria, Diamond Hill, and Wittebergen. In 1901, in recognition of the services rendered, H.R.H. the Duke of Cornwall presented the Ceylon Mounted Infantry with regimental colours, and at the same time decorated the members who had served in South Africa with medals. A second contingent of Ceylon Volunteers, consisting of 103 infantry, in April, 1902, was embarked for South Africa, and was subsequently utilised in the garrisoning of a defensive post called Brandt Kop, to the south of Bloemfontein. On the conclusion of peace the detachment re-embarked for Ceylon.

PRINCE OF WALES'S COLLEGE CADETS.

CAPTAIN B. HORSBURGH.

One important result which flowed from the feeling caused by the war was the formation of a corps of Rifle Volunteers by the planters. Numbers flocked to the standard of this corps, and by 1902 the roll bore no fewer than 798 names. The older corps also felt the inspiring influence of the period, as the accompanying figures, showing the strength of the various branches, testify :—

Ceylon Artillery Volunteers ...	162
Ceylon Mounted Infantry	128
Bearers	73
Cyclists	14
Ceylon Light Infantry	1,104
Ceylon Planters' Rifle Corps ...	693
Cadet Battalion	418

In May, 1902, the Ceylon Volunteers sent a deputation numbering 102 men, representing all branches, to London to attend the King's Coronation ; and a further tie with the Sovereign was established in 1904, when His Majesty was graciously pleased to assent to become the Honorary Colonel of the Ceylon Volunteer force. Also associated with the year 1902 is the formation of a battalion of cadets drawn from the various schools and colleges in the island.

RICHMOND COLLEGE CADETS.

In its earliest years the force was armed with the long Snider rifle. This was replaced in 1890 by the Martini-Henry, and there was a further change in 1899, when the entire force was rearmed with Martini-Enfield rifles and carbines taking the service 303 cartridge. In 1892 the khaki uniform was provided and has ever since been worn. Camps of exercise are periodically held in connection with the Volunteers. The earliest camp was in September, 1890, at Urugasmanhandia, and that place witnessed a yearly gathering until 1902. In 1903 the camp was moved to Diyatalawa, and as this centre is popular it is intended to have the annual gatherings here in future. The Artillery Volunteers have annually a coast camp of instruction.

LIEUTENANT E. B. CREASY.

The cost of the Ceylon Volunteers in 1905 was Rs. 244,000. The force in that year had a total strength of 2,479 and an efficient strength of 1,821. The force consisted of the following: 9 field officers, 2 adjutants, 34 captains, 33 lieutenants, 32 second-lieutenants, 9 surgeons, 3 chaplains, 380 n.-c. officers, and 2,162 privates, besides 18 permanent staff n.-c. officers. The strength of the various elements of the force was as follows:—

Permanent Staff	21
Ceylon Artillery Volunteers... ...	129
Ceylon Mounted Rifles	135
Ceylon Light Infantry	1,077
Ceylon Volunteer Medical Corps ...	67
Ceylon Planters' Rifle Corps ...	594
Ceylon Planters' Rifle Corps Band	39
Cadet Battalion, Ceylon Lt. Infantry	417
Total	2,479

LIEUT.-COLONEL RICHARD HILLEBRAND MORGAN, V.D.

Richard Hillebrand Morgan—the eldest son of Sir Richard Francis Morgan, Queen's Advocate, Attorney-General, and for some time Chief Justice of Ceylon—was born in Colombo in 1845, and educated, in the first place, at the Colombo Academy (now the Royal College) and afterwards at St. Thomas's College. In 1858 he proceeded to England, and there pursued his studies at Cheltenham College till 1863, when he entered St. John's College, Cambridge, where he took his degree in Arts in 1866. He was called to the Bar at Lincoln's Inn in 1868. In the same year he married the eldest daughter of Mr. Adolph Coqui, proprietor of large property in Natal and one time a member of the Legislative Council of that colony. On his return to England from Ceylon, in October, 1868, he was admitted an Advocate of the Supreme Court of the island, and has practised there ever since. On different occasions he has acted as Police Magistrate of Colombo, also as District Judge of Colombo and Kandy.

Lieut.-Colonel Morgan has always taken a lively interest in local military matters. From 1863 to 1867—that is, during his University career—he was a member of the Cambridge University Rifle Volunteers. In 1881 he received his commission as First Lieutenant in the Ceylon Light Infantry Volunteer Corps, in the formation of which regiment he took an active part. He obtained his company in 1886 and the substantive rank of Major in 1897, having for two years previously held the honorary rank of Major. He was promoted Lieut.-Colonel in 1904, and took command of the regiment in January, 1905, when the decentralisation scheme came into force. Lieut.-Colonel Morgan has attained the distinction of being one of the very few officers who have attended every camp of exercise since the formation of the Volunteer Corps. He wears the Jubilee medal, which he received at Buckingham Palace from the hands of His Majesty the King—then Prince of Wales—and the long service decoration. He visited England again in 1879, 1885, 1889, and 1897, and on the last occasion he was in command of the Diamond Jubilee contingent from Ceylon.

Apart from his military duties, Colonel Morgan has many interests. He was a member of the Council of Legal Education, and is often chosen as an examiner of law students. He is a member of the Ceylon Turf Club and the Ceylon Agricultural Society and President of the Ceylon Light Infantry Athletic Club. It may here be mentioned that in his undergraduate days he went in for rowing, and was a good sprinter. Colonel Morgan's town residence is "Caldicote," Kollupitiya, and his country residence is on the Moonemabai estate in the Kelani Valley, on which he grows coconut and rubber.

CEYLON VOLUNTEER LIGHT INFANTRY (MORATUWA SECTION).

LIEUT.-COLONEL HECTOR VAN CUYLENBURG.

Lieut.-Colonel Van Cuylenburg, the son of P. H. Cuylenburg, who was Assistant Colonial Surgeon in the Colonial Medical Department at Kalutara, was born on January 23, 1847, and was educated at St. Thomas's College and Queen's (now Royal) College, Colombo. Deciding to take up law as a profession, he was apprenticed to Charles Ambrose Lorenz. In 1868 he was called to the Ceylon Bar and in 1876 was engaged by the Queen's Advocate of the day as Crown Proctor. He has paid several visits to England, during one of which he became a member of Gray's Inn. In 1903, having been detained in London longer than was expected, he applied to the Council of Legal Education for special leave to go in for the final examination, taking up all four sections at the same time, and passed successfully. He is the proprietor of the *Ceylon Independent* (mentioned in the Press section of this book); and, apart from his arduous journalistic, legal, and military duties, he is a member of the Royal Asiatic Society of London and Ceylon, Fellow of the Royal Colonial Institute, a Justice of the Peace for the island, a member of the Institute of Journalists, a member of the Agricultural and Horticultural Society, a member of the Ceylon Law Society (of which he was one of the founders), a member of both the Orient and the Turf Clubs, and President of the Bloomfield Athletic and Sporting Clubs.

Mr. Van Cuylenburg takes a keen interest in military matters. On the inception of the Ceylon Light Infantry, in 1881, he enlisted as a private and soon became a lance-sergeant in that corps, in the latter part of the same year being promoted to First Lieutenant. In 1895 he was made Captain, in 1900 Hon. Major, and in 1905 Hon. Lieut.-Colonel, being at the present time second in command of the regiment. In conjunction with Captain Berwick, he was instrumental, in the year 1882, in raising a corps, called "The Devil's Own," composed of legal and medical gentleman. Conspicuous in his devotion to volunteering matters, he has attended almost every camp in the colony since the inauguration of the force, and has been identified with every volunteering movement in the island from the establishment of the corps. In 1886 he shot at Wimbledon, and again in 1894 at Bisley, for the Queen's Prize, as an individual competitor in each case. He has served under all the officers commanding since the raising of the Volunteer Corps.

Mr. Van Cuylenburg was one of the official visitors to the St. Louis Exhibition in 1904, and on his return he submitted a most interesting report to the Government on the subject "How to Push Ceylon Tea." Besides travelling in America and visiting Europe, he has toured India. His private residence is Charsley House, Colombo, a well-known centre of Colombo hospitality.

1. LIEUT. C. P. DE SILVA. 2. CAPT. F. H. DE VOS (C.L.I.). 3. DR. HAY. 4. R. G. SAUNDERS. 5. LIEUT. R. H. MORGAN. 6. LIEUT. SENEVIRATNE. 7. LIEUT. L. G. BROHIER. 8. DR. E. MODDER. 9. CAPT. T. G. JAYAWARDENE. 10. COLONEL R. H. MORGAN. 11. MAJOR J. VAN LANGENBURG. 12. CAPT. E. H. JOSEPH. 13. H. R. H. VAN CUYLENBURG. 14. DR. W. H. DE SILVA. 15. CAPT. W. DIAS. 16. LIEUT. S. A. MARTIN. 17. LIEUT. C. L. DE ZYLVA. 18. CAPT. F. W. DANIELS (C.L.I.). 19. LIEUT. R. C. DE SILVA. 20. DR. BAWA (the Port Surgeon). 21. T. C. VAN ROOYEN.

CAPTAIN THEODORE GODFRED JAYAWARDENE.

Captain T. G. Jayawardene, of the Ceylon Light Infantry, is the son of James Alfred Jayawardene, Proctor, and Cornelia Matilda Wijekoon, both of Colombo. He first saw the light of day in the capital city on June 17, 1872, and was educated at the Royal College. On leaving school, in 1889, he was apprenticed to the Public Works Department. In 1895 he was appointed Assistant Government Factory Engineer. He was in charge of the construction of the General Post Office, Colombo, under Mr. H. F. Tomalin, the architect. He also had charge of the erection of the Diyatalawa Camp buildings. In 1900 he was appointed a District Engineer of the Public Works Department. He is an associate member of the Institute of Mechanical Engineers.

Military matters have always had a keen devotee in Captain T. G. Jayawardene. In 1889 he joined the "F" (Public Works Department) Company of the Ceylon Light Infantry, and within six months he had qualified himself for officership. In 1890 he became a corporal, in the following year sergeant, in 1896 Second Lieutenant, in 1897 Lieutenant, and in 1900 captain. On several occasions he has acted as Adjutant to the regiment. Captain Jayawardene is greatly interested in rifle-shooting; and in 1903 and 1904 he accompanied teams to Bangalore (India), where the annual Rifle Meeting of the Southern India Rifle Association is held. He was one of the three officers who won, in 1903, Lalbagh Cup, offered for competition by the Southern India Rifle Association. In Ceylon he has won the National Rifle Association medal and various other regimental trophies. He holds the position of Honorary Secretary to the Ceylon Volunteer Rifle Association.

In 1905 Captain Jayawardene married Caroline Lena, the second daughter of Mudaliyar Attygala. His private residence is "Emile Ruhe," in Borella, a suburb of Colombo.

JUSTINIAN PERERA RAJAPAKSE.

Mr. J. P. Rajapakse was born in Colombo in 1882, and educated at the Royal and St. Joseph's Colleges. On leaving school he chose the legal profession, and was articled to Mr. O. Van Hoff. However, after passing his Notary Public examinations, he retired from the legal practice and entered upon a commercial life. He is an export agent for his father's firm, and deals largely in Ceylon produce, as well as importing cloth and piece goods. Besides this, he is engaged in mining plumbago, thorite, and thorianite, and is the owner of several valuable estates, chief among which are Hulukelle in the Madampe district, of 250 acres; Welbode in the Central Province, of 400 acres and planted with tea, superintended by Mr. C. L. Davis, and on which there is a fully-equipped factory; and Curaçao in the Gampola district, of 80 acres, planted with cacao. Mr. J. P. Rajapakse is also a landed proprietor in Colombo and suburbs, owning some valuable properties, among which are Hilly House, Hill Street, Marylebone, Wellawatte; "Sunnybank," Kotahena; Palm Court, Chetty Street, Pettah; "Agincourt," Borella; Eltham Cottage, Bambalipitiya; and "Roslin," St. Sebastian Street; besides "Ferncliffe" in the town of Kegalla, Sabaragamuwa Province. He is a member of the Royal Asiatic Society and Catholic Union. Taking a keen interest in matters military, he is Second-Lieutenant in the Ceylon Light Infantry, and has charge of the "B" Company of the Technical College.

SAMUEL ALGERNON MARTIN.

Mr. S. A. Martin, son of the late John Martin, planter, of Chilaw, and Harriet Jane, daughter of Mr. N. J. Cooke, late District Judge, was born in 1879. He was educated at St. Thomas's College, Colombo, passed his junior Cambridge local examination, studied law under the Council of Legal Education, and, being admitted a Proctor of the District Court, now practises at Chilaw and Marawila. He was the promoter of the Chilaw section of "M" Company of the Ceylon Light Infantry, and at present holds a commission as Second-Lieutenant. He is a keen sportsman. He married, in 1903, Zillie Elfrida, daughter of Mr. Horace de Kretzer, Landing Surveyor, Colombo Customs.

HECTOR RICHARD HENRY MORGAN VAN CUYLENBURG.

The eldest, and only, son of Lieut.-Colonel Hector Van Cuylenburg, V.D., Mr. H. R. H. M. Van Cuylenburg, was born in Colombo in 1875. On his mother's side he is the grandson of the late Sir Richard Morgan, of Colombo. He was educated at St. Thomas's College, and later proceeded to England, where he underwent private tuition at Cheltenham. On leaving school he adopted the law as his profession, and became a member of Gray's Inn, London. In 1884 he returned to Ceylon, and in 1902 joined the *Ceylon Independent*, one of the leading daily newspapers of Colombo and owned by his father, as assistant editor. Like his father, Mr. Van Cuylenburg takes a keen interest in all military matters, and in 1888 he joined the Ceylon Light Infantry as a ranker. In 1890 he was promoted to the rank of lance-corporal, and during this period he became champion shot of "B" Company, which distinction he continued to hold for three years longer. In 1891 he became corporal, in 1892 sergeant, 1893 sergeant-drummer, 1896 Second Lieutenant, 1900 Lieutenant, and Captain in January, 1906. He has represented his team at the regular annual Rifle Meeting at Bangalore and also against the Singapore Volunteers. In 1894, 1895, and 1898 he was an individual competitor at the shooting competitions at Bisley. Mr. Van Cuylenburg is also a member of the Ceylon Volunteer Rifle Association.

He has visited England on several occasions, and while there he was a member of the Snodland, Paddington, and Gray's Inn Cricket Clubs, being captain of the last-named. He was also secretary of the Gray's Inn Musical Society. In Ceylon he is a member of the Nuwara Eliya Cricket Club and the Orient Club, and was Vice-President of the Maligakande Literary Association in 1896. He is a well-known billiard player and the winner of many London trophies. In 1898 Mr. Van Cuylenburg married Marion Amelia Miall, daughter of J. J. Miall, Esq., of Maida Vale, London. His private residence is Charsley House, Cinnamon Gardens, Colombo.

CONCLUSION

BEFORE the last pages of this work pass into the printers' hands it is fitting that acknowledgment should be made of the services rendered from many quarters in the arduous task of producing "Twentieth Century Impressions of Ceylon." To His Excellency Sir Henry Blake, the Governor of Ceylon, we are deeply indebted for the sympathetic interest he has displayed throughout in our operations, and for the permission he gave us to publish his name as a patron of the work. The late Sir Alexander Ashmore, Lieutenant-Governor of Ceylon, also placed us under a great obligation by the readiness with which he extended official encouragement and support to our labours; and we have to thank many other high officials for assistance courteously and freely given, amongst them the General Manager of the Ceylon Government Railways (Mr. G. P. Greene) for travelling facilities for our representatives, and for the loan of photographs and documents; the Surveyor-General (Mr. P. D. Warren) for furnishing us with a number of interesting photographs relating to the work of his department; the Acting Government Printer (Mr. H. M. Richards) for the loan of official publications; the Acting Director of the Colombo Museum (Mr. Gerard Joseph) for assistance given in consulting old works relating to Ceylon and in the selection of suitable illustrations; and the scientific staff at Peradeniya (Dr. J. C. Willis, Mr. Herbert Wright, and Mr. H. F. Macmillan) for advice and co-operation in the preparation of matter relating to the botany of Ceylon. We have also to thank our numerous contributors, including the Hon. Mr. H. C. Nicolle, Sir Allan Perry, M.D., the Hon. Mr. Francis Beven, M.L.C., the Hon. Mr. P. Arunachalam, Mr. H. T. S. Ward, Director of Irrigation, Mr. John Still, Mr. Kelway Bamber, Mr. C. M. Fernando, Captain J. A. Legge, Mr. Adrian St. V. Jayewardene, Mr. Edward W. Perera, Dr. A. K. Coomaraswamy, Mr. James Hornell, Mr. Edgar Turner, Mr. H. B. Smith, Mr. E. Mannheimer, Mr. W. A. Julius, Mr. H. W. Mills, and Major Frank Modder, for the many valuable monographs which, individually, are of striking interest, and which, collectively, give the volume a high distinction as an accurate and comprehensive survey of modern Ceylon. Further, our acknowledgments are due to the Ceylon Press—notably to the Hon. Mr. John Ferguson and also to his son, Mr. R. H. Ferguson, editor of the *Ceylon Observer;* Mr. F. Crosbie Roles and Mr. H. Woosnam Mills, editor and co-editor respectively of the *Times of Ceylon;* and to Mr. J. Scott Coates, editor of the *Ceylon Independent*, for the kindly and generous treatment that has been extended to the work throughout the period of preparation. Nor must we omit to express our gratitude to our printers, Messrs. Unwin Bros., Ltd., of the Gresham Press, Pilgrim Street, London, E.C., who have given to this work, as to other volumes of the Greater Britain Series which they have produced, a degree of painstaking care and attention which has contributed in no small measure to the excellent artistic effect achieved. Finally, we have to recognise the loyal and valuable services of Mr. Somerset Playne, our Manager, and the other members of the staff—services rendered under trying conditions of climate and in the presence of difficulties of no ordinary kind arising out of the preparation of a great literary work in a centre where meagre facilities exist for such an enterprise.

LLOYD'S GREATER BRITAIN PUBLISHING COMPANY, LTD.,

Reg. Lloyd

LONDON, *May*, 1907.

GENERAL MANAGER.

TABLE OF RELATIVE CEYLON TIME

COLOMBO time is about five hours and twenty minutes ahead of Greenwich time, and under the standard of Indian time. When it is noon at Colombo the time registered at other centres in different parts of the world is shown in the following table :

I.—Forenoon.

Place	A.M.
Aberdeen	6.32
Aden	9.41
Alexandria	8.38
Amsterdam	7.00
Athens	8.15
Barbados	2.41
Berlin	7.33
Berne	7.10
Boston, U.S.A.	1.56
Brindisi	7.52
Brussels	6.57
Buenos Ayres	2.47
Cabul	11.16
Cairo	8.45
Calais	6.48
Cape Town	7.54
Chicago	0.50
Christiania	7.23
Cincinnati	1.02
Constantinople	8.36
Copenhagen	7.30
Corinth	8.12
Dresden	7.35
Dublin	6.15
Durban	8.43
Edinburgh	6.27
Florence	7.25
Geneva	7.04
Genoa	7.16
Gibraltar	6.19
Glasgow	6.23
Greenwich	6.40
Guatemala	0.38
Hamburg	7.23
Havana	1.11
Herat	10.49
Hyderabad	11.13
Jerusalem	9.02
Kandahar	11.02
Khartoum	8.50
Kiev	8.43
Kingston (Jamaica)	1.33
Lahore	11.37
Lima	1.32
Lisbon	6.03
Liverpool	6.28
London	6.39
Madeira	5.34
Madrid	6.25
Manchester	6.31
Marseilles	7.01
Martinique	2.36
Mecca	10.16
Mexico	0.04
Monte Video	2.56
Montreal	1.46
Morocco	6.09
Moscow	9.10
Munich	7.26
Naples	7.37
New York	1.44
Nicaragua	0.57
Odessa	8.44
Ottawa	1.38
Panama	1.22
Paris	6.49
Pernambuco	4.21
Perth	7.56
Philadelphia	1.40
Quebec	1.55
Rio de Janeiro	3.49
Rome	7.30
Sierra Leone	5.48
Simla	11.49
Sofia	8.14
St. Petersburg	8.41
Stockholm	7.52
Suez	8.50
Teheran	10.05
Toronto	1.24
Trinidad	2.32
Tunis	7.24
Valetta	7.38
Venice	7.29
Washington	1.31
Zanzibar	9.18

II.—Afternoon.

Place	P.M.
Adelaide	3.55
Amoy	2.33
Bangkok	1.39
Batavia	1.47
Benares	0.12
Brisbane	4.52
Hobart	4.30
Hong Kong	2.17
Honolulu	8.09
Malacca	1.29
Manila	2.44
Melbourne	4.20
Nagasaki	3.20
Pekin	2.26
Penang	1.22
Rangoon	1.06
Saigon	1.47
San Francisco	10.30
Shanghai	2.43
Singapore	1.35
Vancouver	10.26

TABLES OF CURRENCY

THE present value of some obsolete coins used in the early Portuguese and Dutch periods is thus appraised :—

One pagoda or star pagoda	=	Rs. 4·50
One copper fanam ...	=	about 10 cents
One stuiver	=	„ 2½ „
48 stuivers = 1 rixdollar	=	Rs. 1·13
96 stuivers = 2 rixdollars	=	Rs. 2·25
One half fanam... ...	=	about 5 cents
One half pice	=	„ 1¼ „
One challie	=	„ ¾ cent

By the minute of Sir Wilmot Horton, dated September 26, 1863, the rupee was wrongly put into circulation at two shillings, the half-rupee at one shilling, and the quarter-rupee at sixpence. The earlier monetary system under the British rule included rixdollars, fanams, and pice; but in 1825 pounds, shillings, and pence were introduced, and nearly fifty years later (1872) the decimal currency was adopted, which is the present legal tender. British sovereigns and half-sovereigns are in circulation, at fifteen and seven-and-a-half rupees respectively. The coins now in use in the island comprise the rupee, fifty-cent piece, twenty-five-cent piece, ten-cent piece, five-cent piece, one-cent piece, and half-cent piece. The quarter-cent piece, of similar size to George III.'s third of a farthing, was current a few years ago, but is now out of circulation. The rupee is the same as the British India coin; but the other pieces are struck expressly for the island's use. All these latter bear on their obverse His Majesty's effigy, with inscription, "Edward VII., King and Emperor"; and on their reverse impression the representation of a talipot palm (*Corypha umbraculifera*), with inscription, "Ceylon," date of the year, and value of the piece in English, Sinhalese, and Tamil.

The following table shows the relative value of the rupee and its subdivisions, and their sterling equivalents :—

Silver.

One rupee = 100 cents	=	1s. 4d.
Fifty cents = half rupee ...	=	8d.
Twenty-five cents = ¼ rupee ...	=	4d.
Ten cents	=	1⅗d.

Copper or Mixed Metal.

Five cents	=	⅘d.
One cent	=	4/25d.
Half-cent	=	2/25d.

The Government note issue includes the following amounts :—Rs. 5, Rs. 10, Rs. 20, Rs. 50, Rs. 100, Rs. 500, Rs. 1,000 and Rs. 10,000.

TABLES OF NATIVE WEIGHTS AND MEASURES

SINHALESE DRY AND LAND MEASURES.

1 Amunam	=	4 pelas.
	=	40 lahas or kurunis.
	=	8 parrahs.
	=	5 bushels.
	=	20 pecks.
	=	160 quarts or seers.
1 Pela	=	10 lahas or kurunis.
	=	2 parrahs.
	=	1¼ bushel.
	=	5 pecks.
	=	40 quarts or seers.
1 Laha	=	4 quarts or seers.
1 Parrah	=	5 lahas or kurunis.
	=	20 quarts or seers.

The extent of land is generally indicated by the amount of seed necessary for sowing it; and the area surveyed is computed by the amunam and its minor divisions, the pela, the laha, and the parrah. Thus, "five amunams" of land would mean an area over which that quantity of grain might be sown. The following are the principal measures of land survey with their equivalents in the standard table of measures :—

1 amunam's sowing extent	=	2½ acres.
1 pela's „ „	=	2 roods and 2 perches.
1 laha's „ „	=	10 perches.
1 parrah's „ „	=	1 rood and 10 perches.
1 quart's „ „	=	2½ perches.

These measures vary in the different provinces, and depend to a great extent upon the character of the soil, the strength of the wind, the description of seed sown, and the supply of water. The usual measures of land in the Jaffna district are :—

12 kulis = 1 lachcham.
24 lachchams = 1 acre.

TABLE OF DISTANCES.

The "fathom," of two yards, is the commonest measure of distance.

The "hoo" cry indicates the distance at which a piercing shout may be heard at the farthest limits, or, approximately, a range of about five hundred yards.

The "gawwa" is nearly the length of four statute miles.

NATIVE MEASURES OF CAPACITY.

in the household usually comprise the "bottle" for liquids; the "bundle" for firewood, straw, grass, herbs, and greens; and the "seer" or "measure" for grain and other loose foodstuffs.

LINEAL MEASURE.

The "span," used in measuring cloth or similar goods, is the length of the outstretched fingers.

The "cubit," of eighteen inches, is used in the measure of superficial area.

LIQUID MEASURE.

In liquid measure the gills and gallons are the same as in the Imperial system; but a distinctive measure, the leaguer, of one hundred and fifty gallons capacity, is largely used in the arrack trade.

INDEX

Abayasekara, Kahavita Don Jeronimus Perera, Mohandiram, 819
Abbotsleigh Estate, 809
Abdulally, Moosbhoy Shaikh Hiptullabhoy, 501
Abeyesinghe, Abraham Dias, 768
Abeyesooriya, Samson, 773
Abeyesundere, Frederick E., 755
Abeyratne, Don James Alfred, 672
Abeysinghe, Arthur Alfred Dias, 764
Abeysinghe, Eugene Godfred Dias, 758
Adamaly, E. G., & Co., 503
Administrative Establishments, 106–138
Agriculture, 355
Aitken, Spence & Co., 437
Alakesvara, The Life and Times of, 40
Albion Press Office, Galle, 762
Alexander, Edward Bruce, 134
Allegacoon, Rasiah William, 104
Alles, Francis, 766
Alles, Francis Joseph, 518
Alles, Dr. F. R., 132
Alston, G. H., 454
Alvis, Arthur William, 571
Amarasuria, Henry de Silva, 759
American Mission, 281
Amoo, M. C., 646
Anagarika (Hewavitarne) Dharmapala, The, 119, 284
Ananda College, 116
Anandappa, Patrick Francis Xavier, 764
Ancient references to Ceylon, 16
Anderson, J. A., 712
Anderson, J. P., 711
Andris, H. B. & Co., 822
Anthonisz, Richard Gerald, 106
Anuradhapura, 101, 103, 123, 129, 143
Appoo, K. C. Juanis, 762
Appoohamy, N. D. D. H. Thomas Wijeyesekere, 662
Appuhamy, A. L. Mendis, 625
Archæological Commission, 128
Archæology, 139
Ariya-Nayagam, Cartias, 844
Arrack and Toddy, 635–636
Arseculeratne, John Henry, 621
Arts and Handicrafts, Native, 180–188
Arunachalam, Hon. Mr. P., M.A. Cantab., Registrar-General, 97, 135, 323
Ascot Estate, 838
Aserappa, Walter Nicholas Straube, 104, 695
Association, A Unique, 674
Atapattu, J. V., Mudaliyar, 51
Atgalla Tea Estate, 806
Atmaram, M., 460
Attygalle, Don Charles Gemoris, Mudaliyar, 588
Attygalle, Francis Dixon (the late), 645
Attygalle, Dr. John, 534
Attygalle, John Wilhelmus Samuel, M.B., C.M., 812
Attygalle, Theodore Pennycuick, 135, 716
Audit Office, 107
Avisawella, 103

Badulla, 101, 122, 129
Baines, A. L., 713
Balapitiya, 103
Bamber, M. Kelway, M.R.A.C., M.R.A.S., F.C.S., 248
Banda, Mapitigama Kulatunge Wijekoon Mudiyanselage William Tudor Mapitigama, 797
Banda, Sooriyakumara Wannisinghe Mudiyanseralahamillage Loku, 779
Bandaranaike, Don Solomon Dias Abeyewickreme Jayatilekke Senewiratne Rajakumaru Kadukeralu, C.M.G., 522
Bandaranaike, Felix R. Dias, 101, 526
Bandaranayaka, Don William Chapman Dias Wijewardhane, 526
Bandaranayake, R. E. Dias, 721
Bandaranayke, J. F. D., 525
Bandarapola Estate, 842
Bank of Madras, 217
Banks, 216

Baptist Missionary Society, 279
Barnard, Adam Sedgwick, M.I.E.E., A.M.I.C.E., 124
Barnard, Henry Osmond, A.C.H., F.R.A.S. and M.S., 129
Bartholomeusz, Hugh Hamilton, 764
Bartlam, Alfred, 112
Bartlett, Frank, 108
Bastian, W. E., & Co., 481
Battalgalla Estate, 809
Batticaloa, 101, 123
Batuvantudave, C. de Silva, 575
Baumgartner, George Algernon, 102
Bawa, Alfred James, 690
Bawa, Benjamin William, 565
Bawa, Dr. H., 132
Beattie, C. W., 855
Bell, H. A., 104
Bell, Harry Charles Purvis, 128
Beven, Allan, 104
Beven, Edwin, 814
Beven, Hon. Mr. Francis, M.L.C., 98, 301
Bibby Line, 388
Bingham, Percy Moore, M.I.C.E., 123
Bishops' College, 117
Blacklaw, Charles Fettis Scott, 125
Blake, His Excellency Sir Henry Arthur, G.C.M.G., 92
Blazé, Louis Edmund, 118
Bois, Percy, 138
Bois Bros. & Co., 425
Bombay Union Club, 714
Booth, Hon. Mr. L. W., 110
Bosanquet & Co., 435
Bostock, J. H., 196
Botanic Gardens, 136; Hakgala, 136; Heneratgoda, 137
Botany, 161–168
Bournasheff, A. N., 138
Brayne, Charles Valentine, B.A., 102, 108
British Governors of Ceylon, 83
British India Steam Navigation Company, Ltd., 381
British Rule, Ceylon under (1796 to 1906), 60
Brito, Dr. Philip Sebastian (the late), 560
Brock, Harry Ernest, 474
Brodhurst, Hon. Mr. H. W., C.M.G., 107
Brodie & Co., 451
Brokers' Association, Colombo, 368
Brown, Gardiner, 312
Browning, K. C., 131
Buddhism, Introduction of, 22
Buddhism, Past and Present, 284
Buddhist Education, 223
Burdayron, J. P., 822
Buultjens, Alfred Ernst, 774
Buultjens, Edward Justin, 771
Byrde, Colonel H., 805
Byrde, Prideaux, 712
Byrde, William Lucius Walter, 125

Cacao, 242–247
Caffoor, N. D. H. Abdool, 460
Cahill, E., & Sons, 452
Campbell, Hon. Mr. J. M., 825
Campbell, Thomas James St. Albans, 127
Capper, Frank A., 310
Carbery, W. H. B., 104
Cargills, Ltd., 457
Cargo Boat Despatch Company, 387
Carolis, N. Don, & Sons, 476
Carolis, W. D., 482
Carson & Co., 429
Carte, Ralph George, A.M.I.C.E., 825
Carter, Ashley, 125
Cartwright, Henry Thomas, 124
Cartwright, Horatio Thomas, 779
Casippillai, Visuvanather, 787
Castellani, Dr. Aldo, 131
Catholic Mission, Independent, 276
Cave, H. W., & Co., 454
Central College, 118
Central Province, 108, 798
Ceremonial Observances, Native, 189–193
Ceylon Agricultural Society, 360
Ceylon Independent, 313
Ceylon Industry, A New, 830
Ceylon Manure Works, 470
Ceylon Observer, 306
Ceylon Poultry Club, 361
Ceylon Society of Arts, 420
Ceylon Spinning and Weaving Mills, 489
Ceylon Standard, 312
Ceylon Teachers' Union, 120
Ceylon Time, Table of Relative, 864
Ceylon Wharfage Company, Ltd., 387
Chalmers, Albert John, M.D., 130
Chamber of Commerce, 365
Chapman, Thomas Howard, A.M.I.C.E., 123
Chartered Bank of India, Australia, and China, 217
Chavakachcheri, 103
Cherubim, Joseph, 788
Chilaw, 101, 103
Chilaw District, 735
Chitty, A. M. C. Casie, 733
Christie-David, C. H., 267
Church of England, 268
Churchill, Alec Fleming, 136
City College, 116
Clan, An Historic, 667
Clark, Alfred Allen, 127
Clark, Spence & Co., 766
Clark, Young & Co., 444
Clayton, Arthur Gardner, 106
C.M.S. Ladies' College, 116
Coates, E., & Co., 768
Coates, John Scott, 315
Cochrane, Archibald, 713
Cochrane, H. R., 753
Cockerill, Thomas, 111
Coconut Cultivation, 251–254
Colbert, George Arthur, 134
Cole-Bowen, Mervyn, 127
Colombo, 101, 103, 123, 129, 393–404
Colombo Advertiser and Shipping Gazette, 457
Colombo Agri-Horticultural Society, 361
Colombo Apothecaries' Company, Ltd., 450
Colombo Club, 419
Colombo Colts C.C., 264
Colombo Commercial Company, Ltd., 431
Colombo—Commercial: Fort Section, 425–466; General, 466–521; Professional and Social, 521–584
Colombo Croquet Club, 267
Colombo Drainage Works, 136
Colombo Garden Club, 266
Colombo Harbour Works, 134
Colombo Municipality, 404–414
Colombo Museum, 137, 415
Colombo Post and Telegraph Library and Recreation Club, 208
Colombo Rowing Club, 265
Colonial Photographic Company, 643
Colonial Surgeons, 130
Colonial Treasury, The, 213
Commerce, 369
Conroy, James, 107
Constitution and Law, 85–88
Consuls, Foreign, 137
Convent of the Good Shepherd (R.C.), 120
Cook, Alfred Leslie, 133
Cook, Thos., & Son, 206
Cooke, T. J., 740
Cooke, Tambiah Strong, 790
Coomaraswamy, Dr. A. K., D.Sc., F.G.S., F.L.S., M.R.A.S., 178, 180
Cooper, Hon. Mr. Francis Alfred, 97, 122
Corea, James Abraham, 740
Corea, James Alfred, Mohandiram, 742
Corea, James Edward, 735
Corea, Jumeaux Arthur Christoffel, 737
Corea, Dr. J. A. E., L.M.S., 742
Corea, Percival Allan, 738
Cottle, Henry Charles, 106
Coudert, Rt. Rev. Dr. Anthony, O.M.I., 271
Cox, Henry Leonard, 722
Crabbe, G. M., 794
Craib, Dr. J., 130
Cramer, Alfred Charles, 435
Crawford, Hon. Mr. Henry Leighton, 643
Creasy, E. B., 449
Creasy, Edward Becket, jun., 138
Cricket, 262–264
Crosfield, Lampard & Co., 443
Crown, Law Officers of the, 89
Cumberland, Charles Russell, 106
Currency, Tables of, 864
Customs, 369
Customs Department, 110
Cuttilan, J. A., 646

Daberera, W. M., 745
Daniels, Frederick Nell, M.L.B., M.D.R.C. 730
Darawella Estate, 808
Dassenaike, Louis Arthur, Mudaliyar, 528
Davey, William Charles Dyer, 126
Davidson, Edward Ernest, 110
Davies, Edward Campbell, 123
Davies, W. H., & Co., 473
Davit, Don, & Sons, 486
Dawkin, Rawleigh Mansel, 713
Dawoodbhoy, Hassenally, 502
De Abrew, Peter, 513
De Alwis, James, 507
De Croos, N. E., 708
Deen, M. L M. Zainu, 501
De Fonseka, S. R., 537
De Hoedt, Dr. J. W., 817
De Jong, Michael J., 514
De Kretser, Edward, I.S.O., 107
De Livera, Baron, 578
De Livera, Dr. E., 130, 530
De Livera, Walter, 104, 818
De Mel, A. P., 621
De Mel, Frederic Joseph, 570
De Mel, Harry, 712
De Mel, Henry Lawson, 600
De Mel, Dr. Hugh, 655
De Mel, Jacob, 596
De Mel, Joseph Matthias, 664
De Mel, Widanelage Johanis, 623
De Motte, George E., 818
Denham, Edward Brandis, 110
Dennis, Arthur Workman, 125
Dep, W. A., 653
De Rosairo, Longinus Anthony, 734
De Rowel, W. J. E. W. A. A. A. (the late), 740
De Saram, Dr. Allan, 131
De Saram, Peter, 104, 528
De Silva, A. E., & Co., 482
De Silva, Charles Edward, 758
De Silva, Charles Peter, 653
De Silva, D. F., & Co., 465
De Silva, F. W., 105
De Silva, J. C., & Co., 600
De Silva, Dr. J. S., 658
De Silva, Dr. K. J., 664
De Silva, L. B. A., & Co., 614
De Silva, Richard Charles, Dissanayake Mudaliyar, 730
De Silva, Warnakulasooriya Mahapatebendy Lindamullege John William, 670
De Silva, Dr. William Henry, 550
De Silva, W. R. (the late), 655
De Soysa, Alfred Joseph Richard, 543
De Soysa, Charles Henry, J.P. (the late), 538
De Soysa, Edwin Lionel Frederick, 543
De Soysa, Jeronis William Charles, 540
De Soysa, L. W. A., 546
De Soysa, Thomas Henry Arthur, 546
De Soysa, Walter, 546
De Vos, Charles Edward, 759
De Wilton, A. W., 135
De Zilva, A. A., 724
De Zoysa, John Edward, 703
De Zylva, C. L., 698
Dharmapala, The Anagarika (Hewavitarne), 119, 284
Dharmaratne, Charles Frederick, 794
Dias, Charles Edward Arnold, 680

Dias, Mrs. Jeremias, 678
Dias, Ponnahannedige Domingo, 685
Dias, P. W., & Co., 797
Dias, William, 508
Dikoya Estate, 809
Dinapatha-Pravrutti, 319
Dissanayaka, T. Pieris Mudaliyar Arsecu-leratne, 692
District Judges, 101
Dornhorst, Frederick, 561
Dowbiggin, Herbert Layard, 134
Drieberg, Christopher, B.A., F.H.A.S., 112, 356
Drieberg, James Grenier, 695
Dunuwille, William, 104
Dutch occupation, The, 55
Dutch Reformed Church, 279
Dyer, Stanley H., 449

Eastern Province, 109, 780
Ebramjee, Moosajee Moola, 496
Ecclesiastical, 268–292
Ederisinghe, Cecil Jeronimus, 705
Education, 219–224
Education, Buddhist, 223
Education Department 110
Ekanayake, H. J. V., 102
Eknellgoda, Mahipala Akrakkuruppu Wickremesinhe Basnaike Mudianse Ralahamilege William Alexander Abraham, 795
Electrical Department, 124
Elwell, W. A., 712
Emerson, Charles Frederick, 123
Engineers, Provincial, 122
Ennaruwa, Wijeyesundara Gunaratna Tennekoon Herat Mudivanselage Charles Edward Tennekoon, 722
Estates, Labour on, 254
Etherington, Ivor, 307
Evans, Edwin, B.Sc., 111
Executive, The, 637
Executive Council, 94
Expenditure, Revenue and, 215

Fairfield Ironworks, 468
Fauna, 157–160
Felix, John Joseph Pocock, 126
Ferguson, A. H., 306
Ferguson, Hon. Mr. John, C.M.G., 97, 308
Ferguson, J. S., 306
Ferham and Oddington Estates, 828
Fernando, A., & Co., 606
Fernando, Arthur J., & Co., 484
Fernando, Charles Matthew, M.A., LL.M. Cantab., M.R.A.S., J.P., 13, 105, 548
Fernando, Daniel John, 672
Fernando, Felix Joseph Lucas, 511
Fernando, Gabriel, 611
Fernando, H. Bastian, 600
Fernando, Dr. Henry Isaac, 661
Fernando, Dr. Hilarion Marcus, 131, 549
Fernando, James, 609
Fernando, J. P., 744
Fernando, M. Arnolis, 657
Fernando, N. S., 474
Fernando, P. J. M., 749
Fernando, Dr. Solomon, 546
Fernando, Thomas Matthew, 738
Fernando, W. A., 618
Fernando, W. A. J., 744
Fernando, W. J., 616
Fernando, W. L., 746
Festing, Richard Arthur Grindall, 108
Finance, Native Systems of, 218
Financial, 213–218
Finlay, M. T., 138
Finlay, Muir & Co., 425
Fisheries, 632–634
Fletcher, William Wellesley Pole, A.M.I.C.E., 123
Fonseka, Clarence Pedro, 671
Football, 262
Foreign Consuls, 137
Forest Department, 127
Forests, 173
Fort Tennis Club, 266
Fowler, Hon. Mr. G. M., C.M.G., 95, 106
Fox, Howard Orme, 135
Fox, John, 133
Fraser, John George, 135
Fraser, Joseph, 838
Freeman, Herbert Rayner, 109
Freemasons, 419
Freudenberg & Co., 429
Freudenberg, Philipp, 137
Frier, William L., 126
Fruit Hill Estate, 811
Fyers, Charles Cornwallis Meadow, 129
Fyers, H. F. C., 127
Fysh, Dr. Mary Nona, 131

Galaha Ceylon Tea Estates and Agency Company, Ltd., 470
Galbraith, Alexander Norman, B.A., 103
Galle, 102, 103, 129, 753
Galle Face Hotel, Colombo, 466
Galle Municipality, 754
Gampola, 104
Garvin, Dr. T. F., 131
Geddes, M. G., 791

General Hospital Staff, 131
Geographical and Meteorological Features, 154–156
Geology and Mineralogy, 178–179
German Club, 420
Gibbon, William Duff, 807
Gikiyanakande Estate, The, 687
Gillam, George Thomas, 128
Gnanasakaram, Catherawaloe, 512
Godamune, P. B., 104
Golf, 261
Gomez, M. P., & Co., 706
Gonagalla Estate, 810
Good Shepherd, Convent of the (R.C.), 120
Gooneratne, David Abraham Wijeyewickreme, Mudaliyar, 770
Gooneratne, Edmund Rowland Jayetilleke, 754
Gooneratne, Peter Alfred, 670
Gooneratne, Valentine David, 774
Goonesekere, J. A. de S. W., 746
Goonatillake, Abraham Perera, 651
Goonetilleke, Arthur Hector, 669
Goonetilleke, Charles Perera Senewiratne, 562
Goone-Tilleke, William Alfred, 566
Goonewardene, Dr. Andrew Simon, 677
Goonewardene, Bastiankorallagey James Aurelieus Rodrigo Weeresinghe, 648
Goonewardene, David George, 766
Goonewardene, Edward Gregory, 721
Goonewardene, Hawadewagey Palis Fernando Vimala, Mohandiram, 391
Goonewardene, J. B. de S., 104
Goonewardene, John Edward de Silva Suriyabandare, 687
Goonewardene, Peter Charles Fernando Wanigesekere, 795
Government Agents, 107
Government House Establishment, 93
Government, Local, 209–212
Government Railways, 124
Government Stores, 132
Governor's Cup, Winners of, from 1886 to 1906, 260
Governor's Residences, The, 93
Governors of Ceylon, British, 83
Grand Hotel, Nuwara Eliya, 832
Grand Oriental Hotel, Colombo, 452
Grant, Hugh Arthur Grote, 122
Gray, Andrew Paton, M.I.C.E., 124
Green, E. E., F.E.S., F.Z.S., 136
Greene, Geoffrey Philip, 124, 203
Grenier, Dr. Frank, 825
Grenier, Hon. Mr. J. R., 100
Griffin, Dr. C. T., 130
Grove, The, Ukuwela, 844
Gunasekara, U. D. S. & Co., 618
Gunasekere, S. D. S., & Co., 624
Gunawardana, Samson A., & Co., 485
Gunesekere, Dr. James Solomon, 658

Hakgala Botanic Gardens, 136
Hall, G. H., 712
Hambantota, 103
Hami, G. Don Julis Appu, 674
Hampton, John Louis, 129
Hamy, C. Arachige, 819
Hancocks, James Edward, 126
Handicrafts, Native Arts and, 180–188
Harbour Department, 133
Harbours, 373
Hartley, Charles, M.A., 111
Harward, John, M.A., 110
Harward, Theodore, 133
Hassan, Janoo, 494
Hatton, 104
Hatton Hotel, 824
Hay, Dr. G. P., 814
Hayley, Charles P. & Co., 768
Head, Ernest Wilfred, 125
Heathcote, B. T., 856
Hellings, Robert Bailey, 109
Henderson & Co., 473
Henderson & Newton, 646
Heneratgoda Botanic Gardens, 137
Henly, Rev. W., 268
Hensman, J. M., B.A., Fellow of the University of Madras, 786
Hill, Bertram, B.A., 102
Hindugalla and Shrubs Hill Estate, 807
Historic Clan, An, 667
History of Ceylon, 13–59
Hitchings, H. C., & Co., 457
Homer, Dr. Jonathan, 557
Hong Kong and Shanghai Banking Corporation, 217
Hooper, George Ernest, 125
Hopetoun Studio, Slave Island, Colombo, 645
Hopkins, Edward Francis, 109, 110
Hornell, James, 227
Horsburgh, Benjamin, 412, 414
Howison, John, 125
Human, Edwin, A.M.I.C.E., A.I.E.E., 111
Hunter, Thomas Gilbert, 137
Hutchinson, Hon. Sir J. T., Kt., Chief Justice, 99
Hutson, C. A., & Co., 450
Huybertsz, Dr. H., 812
Hyde, G. H. M., M.I.M.E., 123

Idroos, A. S., 489
Immigration, 136
Independent Catholic Mission, 276
Industry, A New Ceylon, 830
Information for Tourists, 204–206
Irrigation, 169–172
Irrigation Department, 129
Ismail, Mohamed Lebbe Marikar Hadgiar Mohomed, 500

Jafferjee, Carimjee, 492
Jaffna, 102, 104, 123
Jaffna, Bishop of, 785
Jamieson, Andrew Duff, 711
Jansz, Cyril Charles Arnold, 677
Jansze, Nevill Budd, 816
Jayasekere, A. S. F., Mudaliyar, 521
Jayasundera, E. G. de Silva, 729
Jayasundera, Jonathan Edmund de Silva, 724
Jayawardene, Captain Theodore Godfred, 862
Jayesundera, A. de Silva, 727
Jayetileke, James Robert, 815
Jayewardene, Don Adrian St. V., 85
Jayewardene, Eugene Wilfred, 569
Jayewardene, Hector Alfred, 567
Jayewardene, John Adrian St. Valentine, 573
Jayewardene, Justus Sextus Wijesinghe, 765
Jayewardene, J. V. G. A., 690
Jayewickreme, E. A. A. J., 576
Jeevunjee, A. E. S., 494
Jeevunjee, A. H. S., & Co., 486
Jordan, W., & Co., 834
Joseph, Daniel, 846
Joseph, D. Don, 698
Joseph, Ernest Henley, 315
Joseph, Gerard Abraham, 137
Joseph, W., 621
Joulain, Right Rev. Dr. Henry, O. M. I., Bishop of Jaffna, 785
Judges, District, 101
Judicial and Legal, 99–105
Julius, V. A., 157, 265
Justice, Administration of, 88

Kalenberg, Dr. C. A., 827
Kalutara, 102, 104
Kalutara District, 687
Kanagasabai, Hon. Mr. Ambalavanar, 98, 785
Kandy, 101, 104, 129
Kandy and the Kandyans, 293–298
Kandy District, 805
Kandyan Law, 87
Kapadia, P. N., 497
Kayts, 104
Kearley & Tonge, Ltd., 470
Keegel, Henry Arnold, 764
Keegel, Dr. H. A., 131
Kegalla, 102
Kegalla District, 797
Kelani Valley, 711
Kemish, H., 834
Keuneman, Gerald Edmund, 773
King, W. S., 449
Kings, The later Sinhalese (A.D. 1197 to 1215), 38
Kingswood College, Kandy, 118
Kirthisinghe, Kurukula Suriya Charles Stephen, 698
Kock, Samuel Godfried, 836
Koelman, John Carl, 512
Koelman, R. G., 511
Kotalawala, John, 604
Kotalawela, D. C., 853
Kotuagedera Estate, 840
Krawehl Coal Company, Ltd., 443
Kuda Oya Estate, 809
Kulatilake, J. C. A. E., 738
Kurunegala, 102, 104, 123, 129
Kurunegala District, 719
Kuruppu, S. H. B., 682
Kynaston, E., 712

Labour on Estates, 254
Labussière, E., 137
Lambert, John, 106
Land Settlement Department, 135
Land Survey, 299
Lascelles, Hon. Mr. A. G., Attorney-General, 95, 105
Law, The, 86
Law Officers of the Crown, 89
Lawrence, Brigadier-General, 95
Lawton, S. K., & Co., 480
Layard, Barbara, 825
Layard, Frank Henry, 712
Lebbe, Ahamado, 824
Lebbe, A. R. Cásse, 821
Leechman & Co., 438
Leembruggen, Garret Edward, 129
Leembruggen, Dr. H. U., 826
Leembruggen, R. H., 790
Leembruggen, Wilmot Edgar, 702
Legal and Judicial, 99–105
Legal Profession, 89
Legge, Captain John Augustus, 134, 373
Legislative Council, The, 95–99

Lewis, Alfred, 122
Lewis, Frederick, 128
Lewis, Hon. Mr. John Penry, 96, 108
Lieutenant-Governor, The late, 94
Lipton & Co., Ltd., 440
Lloyd's Greater Britain Publishing Company, Ltd., 315
Loan Board, 132
Local Government, 209–212
Lochnagar Estate, 840
Longden, Cyril Chapman, 134
Loos, Frederick Christian, jun., 100
Loos, H. A., 565
Loosen, G., 453
Lovegrove, Charles Arthur, 122
Lovett, H. J., 133
Ludovici, Edwin, 765
Ludowyk, M. A., 748
Lumsden, Douglas George, 711
Lund, Charles W., 133
Lushington, Charles Morant, 108, 110
Lushington, Franklin, 797

Maartensz, L. M., 570
Macmillan, Hugh Fraser, 136
Macnamara, Patrick Thomas, 133
Macready, William Charles, 133
Madawela, Godfrey Edward, 720
Maddock, Arthur Edward, 129
Mahavansa, The, B.C. 543–360, 20; B.C. 257–304 A.D., 24
Mahomedan Law, 88
Malay Newspapers, 318
Mallum, H. A., 495
Mannar, 102
Mannheimer, E., A.M., T.I.M.E., 585
Marakona Estate, 842
Marikar, S. L. Naina, 492
Marinitsch, Gustav A., 137
Markar, Mohamed Macan, 138
Markar, Othman Lebbe Markar Macan, 463
Markus, Charles Peter, 727
Marshall, D. R., 217
Martin, Albert James, 712
Martin, Harry Alexander, 107
Martin, Samuel Algernon, 862
Massy, Edmund Ingoldsby, 711
Matale, 104
Matale District, 838
Matale Estate, 846
Matara, 102, 104
Matara District, 770
Mather, William, 789
Mathew, C., & Co., 458
Mayfield Estate, 827
Medical Department, 130, 225
Meier, W. H., 131
Melton Estate, Dimbula, 827
Mercantile Bank of India, Ltd., 218
Meteorological Features, 154–156
Middleton, Hon. Mr. John Page, 100
Middleton Estate, Dimbula, 838
Mihintale, 146
Military and Volunteers, 857
Miller & Co., 456
Mills, Harry Woosnam, 255, 311
Mine Inspection, 137
Mineralogical Survey, 137
Mining Industry, The, 587–627
Miranda, R., & Sons, 623
Mirando & Co., 616
Mirando, M. H., 696
Modder, Dr. E. E., 689
Modder, Major Frank, F.R.G.S., 293
Mohamed Alie, Mohamed Ismail, 138
Mohandiram, Don Philip, and his Family, 580
Montagu, Drogo, 133
Moonemalle, S. N. B. M. T. B. Lewis, 719
Moonemalle, Hon. Mr. T. B. L., 98
Moore, Harold Montgomery, 448
Moosajee, Hoosenbhai Mahomedbhai, 492
Moraes, Dr. H. A., 130
Moratuwa Cyclists' Union, 664
More, Samuel Joseph Cattlon, 129
Morey, W., 138
Morgan, Lieut.-Colonel Richard Hillebrand, V.D., 860
Moss, Edward Lambert Boyd, 128
Motoomull, Topunsing, & Co., 459
Mount Lavinia Grand Hotel, 478
Moysey, Henry Luttrell, 133
Mukkuwar Law, 88
Mullaitivu, 102
Munasinha, C. W., 749
Murgasupillai, Venasitamby, 789
Murray, Donald McKinlay, 825
Murty, J. O'K., 109
Musaeus School, 119
Muslim Friend, 319
Muthukrishna, Gabriel Edwin, 820
Muttukumara, Adam, 734
Muttukumaru, P. M., M.B., C.M., 560
Muttukumaru, V. M., 790

Nagalinga, T., Mudaliyar, 788
Namasivayam, Cathiravaloe, 516
Nathalal, Maganlal, 499
National Bank of India, Ltd., 217
National Dairy Company, 495

Native Agriculture and its Improvement 356
Native Arts and Handicrafts, 180-188
Native Ceremonial Observances, 189-193
Native Headmen System, 638
Native Philanthropist, A, 538
Native Systems of Finance, 218
Native Weights and Measures, 864
Negombo, 102
Negombo District, 695
Nell, George Frederick, 479
Nelson, Horatio William, Registrar, 100
New Peradeniya Estate, 807
Nicolle, Hon. Mr. H. C., 95, 107, 132, 213
Nippon Yusen Kaisha, 384
Noble, W. J., 811
Nock, John Knighton, 137
Nondescripts C.C., 264
Noorbhai, T. A. J., & Co., 500
North-Central Province, 109, 776
North Cove Estate, 808
North German Lloyd's Service, 381
North-Western Province, 109, 716
Northern Province, 108, 781
Norwood Estate, 808
Nugara, Dr. J. V., 584
Nuwara Eliya District, 825

Obeyesekere, Donald, 534
Obeyesekere, Hon. Mr. S. C., M.L.C., 97, 521
Observances, Native Ceremonial, 189-193
Ondatje, Ebenezer Francis, 105
Oorloff, Dr. E., 131
Opium, 392
Orient Company, Ltd., 446
Orr, Cyril A. L., 690
Orwell Group Estate, 810
Owen, Samuel Arthur, 818

P. & O. Steam Navigation Company, 380
Panabokke, Samasta Wickrama Karunatilaka Abhayawardana Bhuwanasekera Jayasundara Mudiyanse Ralahamillage Tikiri Banda, 814
Panadure, 104
Panadure District, 669
Parakrama Bahu the Great, The Epic of, 33
Passe, Dr. William A., 558
Pate, A., & Son, 486
Paul, D. Don, 714
Paul, J. W. Balfour, 854
Paul, Dr. S. C., 131
Pearl Fishery, The, 227-233
Pedris, D. D., 614
Peel, Laurence Robert, 83
Peiris, Charles, 575
Peiris, H. B., 654
Peiris, Henry Joseph, 609
Peiris, James, 563
Peiris, W. A., 655
Peradeniya, Royal Botanic Gardens, 136
Pereira, Arthur Lloyd, 827
Pereira, Joseph Boniface Michael, 695
Pereira, F. X., & Sons, 480
Pereira, Walter, K.C., 105
Perera, Edward W., 60
Perera, Francis, 550
Perera, Gamamedelianage Simon, 742
Perera, Hemendra Seppale, 319
Perera, Henry A., Mudaliyar of Colombo, 532
Perera, James Samuel Edmund, 764
Perera, Mahawaduge Cornelis, 682
Perera, Stephen, 855
Perera, T., Mohandiram, 706
Perry, Sir Allan, M.D. Durham, D.P.H. London, M.R.C.S.E., &c., 130, 225
Pestonjee, R., 498
Petch, T., 136
Peter, Conrad, 466
Philips, Edwin, 478
Pieris, Hanwadege John Jacob, 662
Pieris, Henry, 646
Pieris, Henry A., 582
Pieris, Lambert Louis, 576
Pieris, Louis H. S., 552
Pieris, Paulus Edward, M.A., 102
Pieris, Richard Steuart, 578
Plant, George Frederic, B.A., 102
Plâté & Co., 468
Plumbago, 585-627
Plumbago Merchants' Union, 587
Point Pedro, 103
Police, 134
Polonnaruwa, 149
Population: Races, Religions, Languages, Castes, and Customs, 323
Portuguese Period, The, 43
Post and Telegraphs, 132, 207
Present Day in Ceylon, The, 83
Press, The, 301-319
Pre-Vijayan Period, 13
Price, Fernando Hamlyn, 108, 110
Price, Newton James, 125
Price, Walter Cromwell, 123
Prince and Princess of Wales's College, 117
Prins, G., 104
Prins & Brito, 584
Printing Office, Government, 106
Prisons, 135
Provincial Administrations, 637-856
Provincial Engineers, 122
Public Works Department, 121-124, 628-631
Public Works, Director of, 122
Pure Ice and Aerated Water Manufactory, 484
Puttalam, 103
Puttalam District, 730

Queen's Hotel, Kandy, 822

Ragalla and Halgranoya Estates, 830
Raheman, Hon. Mr. Wapchi Marikar Abdul, 97
Railways, Government, 124, 195-203
Rajapakse, J. de S. W. S., 701
Rajapakse, Justinian Perera, 862
Rajapakse, Tudor, 535
Rajapakse, Wilfred Martin, 696
Rajawafikere, Spencer S. Casiechitty, Mudaliyar, 820
Rajepakse, A. P. E. de S. W. S., 701
Ramsammy, J. N., & Bros., 463
Randel, A., 474
Ransom, S. E. O., 711
Ratnam, Dr. E. V., 558
Ratnapura, 103, 123
Ratnapura District, 794
Ratnasabapathy, Namasivayan Mudaliar, 501
Redemann, Arnold William Bernhard, 137
Registration, 135
Reid, W., 217
Reuter's Telegram Company, Ltd., 443
Revenue and Expenditure, 215
Richards, Horace Martin, 106
Ridout, John Bertram Mais, 129
Ripley & Marshall, 446
Roberts, Thomas Webb, 104
Robertson, J., 133
Robertson, J. M., & Co., 437
Robson, George, & Co., 472
Rockwood, Dr. W. G., 131, 555
Rodrigo, Dr. William Paul, 557
Rodrigue, F. W., 507
Roe, A. H., 711
Roles, Francis Crosbie, 311
Roman Catholic Church, 269
Roman-Dutch Law, 86
Rosling, Hon. Mr. E., 97, 806
Royal Asiatic Society, Ceylon Branch, 423
Royal Botanic Gardens, Peradeniya, 136
Royal College, 111
Royal Pharmacy, Colombo, 458
Rubber, 234-241
Ruins in Ceylon, 143-153
Russell, Thomas Brownie, M.A., 104
Rustomjee & Co., 502
Rustomjee, J., 499
Ryan, Charles, 826
Ryan, J. P. E., 826

Sabaragamuwa, Province of, 109, 791
St. Andrew's Estate, 828
St. Edward's School, Nuwara Eliya, 833
St. Joseph's College, 114
St. Lucia's Cathedral, Colombo, 275
St. Mary's Boys' English School (R.C.), 119
St. Thomas's College, Colombo, 112
Saldin, B. O., 318
Saldin, M. K., & Co., 497
Salgado, Mereannege Mathes, 682
Salt, 362
Salvation Army, 280
Samarakkody, L. C. de F. W. T., 531
Samarasekera, H. J. Perera, Mohandiram, 836
Samaraweera, David Martin, 771
Sampander, Sinnacutty, 779
Sandaresa, 317
Sanders, William Rutherford Bogle, 102, 785
Sandrasagra, Henry Alexander Patrick, 788
Sanmogam, S., & Co., 625
Sanquhar Estate, 838
Saravanamuttu, Vettivelu, Mudaliyar 818
Saunders, Reginald Gibson, 101, 109
Saunders, W. S. T., 454
Savings Bank, 132
Savundranayagam, Antony Peter, 562
Sawer, Alfred Johnson, 137
Saxton, George Shadwell, 101, 109
Scanes, Alfred, 312
Schneider, G. S., 570
Schokman, Dr. George Peter, 130
Schokman & Co., 821
School Gardens, 112
Schrader, Louis William Conrad, M.A., 103
Schulze, Adalbert Theodor, 138
Schulze Bros. & Co., 446
Scott, John, B.A., 102, 108
Scottish Ceylon Tea Company, Ltd., 810
Scovell, Alfred, 855
Scovell, Thomas, 854
Secretariat, The, 106
Senanayaka, S. M. Don Peter, 819
Senanayake, Adris Mendis Wickremesinghe, Mohandiram, 510
Senanayeke, Don Spater, Mudaliyar, 611
Senaratne, Gamamedaliyanage Gabriel Philip Perera, 596
Seneveratne, A. de Alwis, 102
Seneviratne, Dr. H. C., 816
Seneviratne, Solomon, 524
Senewiratne, Alexander Reginald, 758
Senewiratne, J. C. H., 744
Sennathiraja, J. W. P., 733
Shaikhtyeb, Gulam Hossen, & Co., 496
Shipping, Commerce and Customs, 369
Shorthand and Typewriting Institute, 121
Siedle, Louis, 472
Sigiriya, 147
Sihala Samaya, 319
Silva, G. M., 658
Silva, N. D. Bernard, 594
Silva, Nanayakkarage Don Paulus, 591
Silva, N. Don Stephen, 518
Sinhalese Arts and Handicrafts, 180
Sinhalese Power, The Disestablishment of the, 43
Sinhalese Sports Club, 267
Sinnatamby, Dr. M., 131
Sinnayah, Cathirkamar Murugaser, Mudaliyar, 789
Siriwardene, James Perera Amaratunge Abeyeratne, 705
Siriwardhana, H. A. Pieris, Mudaliyar, 692
Siriwardhane, Dr. William Christoffel Pieris, 524
Sivasithamparam, Kanapathypillai, 786
Skeen, F., & Co., 451
Slater, Alexander Ransford, 101
Smith, Francis Jagoe, 106
Smith, H. B., 204
Smith, Richard William, 130
Smith, W., 313
Sockanathan, Tambo, 511
Solomon, John I., B.Sc., 233
Soris, Paul, & Co., 833
Southern Province, 108, 751
Soysa, George Francis, 820
Soysa, Solomon Peter, 659
Soysa, W. S. W., 708
Spence, Hamilton Robert, 127
Spence, Dr. J. B., 131
Spices and other Products, 320
Spittell, Dr. F. G., 131, 787
Sport, 255
Sriwardhana, Mudaliyar John Louis Pieris, 525
Steuart, Geo., & Co., 454
Stevenson, Malcolm, 109
Still, John, 139
Stores, Government, 132
Street, Francis F., 472
Strickland, R. B., 111
Sturgess, George William, 135
Sulavansa, The (A.D. 304 to 1152), 28
Superintendents of Surveys, 129
Surgeons, Colonial, 130
Survey Department, 128
Surveys, Superintendents of, 129
Symons, Charles Edward Hood, 138

Table of Relative Ceylon Time, 864
Tables of Currency, 864s
Taffs, W. H., 313
Tamhipilly, W., & Co., 498
Tambyah, Isaac, 789
Tamil Arts and Handicrafts, 187
Tampoe, D. P., 627
Tampoe, Guruswamy Nathaniel Hunt, 791
Tangalla, 103
Tarrant & Co., 446
Taylor, Henry Asher, 126
Taylor, William Ainslie, 132
Tea Industry, The, 248-250
Teachers' Union, 120
Tebb, Rev. Robert, 276
Telegraphs, Post and, 132, 207
Temple land, 88
Templer, George Dawson, 128
Templer, John Harvey, B.A., 101
Templeton, R. S., 129
Tennekoon, Don E. W. de L. Wijeyewrickreme Seneveratne, 530
Tennekoon, Kandegedira Wijesundera Guneratna Tennekoon Herat Mudiyansilage John Graham, 723
Thain-Davidson, George, 855
Thaine, Robert Niemann, B.A., 103, 109
Theodoris, Don, & Co., 465
Thesayalamai, The, 88
Thomasz, Dr. George, 131, 557
Thornhill, Hayman, 134
Thorpe, William Edward, 110
Thuring, Walter Peter, 838
Tickell, R. E., 136
Tillekeratne, William David Constantine Samaradiwakara Abayagunasekara, 794
Times of Ceylon, 308
Tiru-Navuk-Arasu, Cartegesar, 566
Todd, James Reid, 125
Toddy, 635-636
Toller, Harry Chambers, 128
Tomalin, Herbert Frederick, M.I.C.E., F.R.I.B.A., &c., 122
Tourists, Information for, 204-206
Traffic Department, Government Railways, 125
Training College, Government, 111
Tranchell, Charles Lancelot, 134
Treasury, The Colonial, 213
Treasury, The General, 107
Trevaldwyn, G. O., 856
Trimmer, Rev. G. J., 277
Trincomalee, 103, 104
Tropical Agriculturist, 306
Troup Estate, Talawakele, 827
Turner, Edgar, 254, 807
Tyagaraja, Namasivayam Mudaliyar, 564
Typewriting Institute, The Shorthand and, 121
Tyrrell, Francis Graeme, 134

Ukkubanda, George William Dodanwela Goonerat Atapattu Wahala Herat Mudianselage, 726
Unique Association, A, 674
Unsworth, Herbert George, M.I.M.E., 125
Uva, Province of, 109, 847

Van Cuylenburg, Lieut.-Colonel Hector, 315, 861
Van Cuylenburg, Hector Richard Henry Morgan, 862
Van Denberg, J., 797
Vanderkoen, Susepillai Mudaliyar P., 733
Vanderwall, Charles, 812
Vane, Frederick William, 132
Van Langenberg, J. A., 565
Van Rooyen, Theodore Cecil, 814
Vaughan, Charles Stewart, M.A., 103, 109
Veall & Co., 855
Veterinary Department, 135
Victoria Memorial Eye Hospital, 421
Vigors, Hon. Mr. Charles Thomas Doyne, 96, 107
Viner, John William, 129
Volunteers, 858

Waddell, George, A.M.I.C.E., 123
Wade, Edward Hyde Robert Wybrants, A.M.I.C.E., 126
Wadsworth, William, 570
Wait, Walter Ernest, 135
Walker & Greig, 828
Walker, Hon. Mr. Giles F., 97
Walker, Sons & Co., Ltd., 437, 817
Warakamure Estate, 840
Ward, H. T. S., M.I.C.E., 129, 169
Warren, Philip David, 128
Ways and Works Department (Government Railways), 124
Webster Automatic Packeting Factory, Co-operative Tea Gardens Company, and Maravilla Ceylon Tea Company, 433
Weerasingham, Wyrawanther, 822
Weerasinghe, Joseph Victor, 689
Weerekoon, William Augustus, 713
Weights and Measures, Native, 864
Weinman, James Richard, 101, 561
Wellawatte Boys' Industrial Home and Orphanage, 223
Wendt, Hon. Mr. Henry Lorentz, 99
Wesley College, 112
Wesleyan Methodist Mission, 276
Western Province, 640
Whist Bungalow, The, 554
White, G. W. Lindsay, 834
White, Herbert, 109, 852
Whiteaway, Laidlaw & Co., 456
Whittall & Co., 429
Wickwar, A. J., 853
Widows' and Orphans' Pensio Fund, 132
Wight, James Robert, 811
Wiharagama Estate, Matale Valley, 844
Wijegoonewardene, Edward Lionel, 816
Wijewardene, D. L., 706
Wijewardene, Don Philip A., Mohandiram, 514
Wijeyegunawardena, Philip Perera Seneviratne Abeyesinghe Palhiyawadena, 653
Wijeyekoon, A. C. G., 576
Wijeyeratne, E. R. F. de Silva, 576
Wijeyeratne, Emmanuel de Silva, 648
Wijeyeratne, Peter de Sylva, 666
Wijeyeratne, R. J. V. de S., 504
Wijeyesekera, F. A., 671
Wijeyewardene, Thomasz Coronalis, 516
Wijigooneratne, A. S. F., 508
Willey, Arthur, 137
Willis, John Christopher, Sc.D., F.L.S., 131, 161
Woodhouse, George William, B.A., 101
Wood-Renton, Hon. Mr. Alexander, 100
Wright, C. M., & Co., 448
Wright, Herbert, A.R.C.S., F.L.S., 136, 234, 242
Wright, Dr. Lionel, 569
Wright, Dr. V. O., 558
Wylie, Bryce J., 855
Wylie, Thomas Alexander, 125

Young, Samuel Donnaclift, 138
Young Men's Christian Association, 282
Young Women's Christian Association, 283

APPENDIX

VITAL STATISTICS OF CEYLON.

By ALBERT J. CHALMERS, M.D., F.R.C.S., D.P.H.

THE Vital Statistics of Ceylon, that is, the science of numbers applied to the life-history of the communities of Ceylon with a view to elucidating the problems connected with their life and death, have been carefully studied by Mr. Arunachalam, the Registrar-General, from 1887 onwards. And to his able Reports I am indebted for many figures.

Apparently, the ancient Sinhalese kings did not number their people. The Dutch made a limited census in the maritime provinces, but it was not until 1824 that the first census took place, nor till March 26, 1871, that the first of the regular series of censuses began. Since then it has been taken in the years 1881, 1891, and 1901. The last census is a masterly piece of work, due to Mr. Arunachalam, and to this I am also indebted for much information used in this paper. A census deals with the numbers, ages, sex, and also with the racial, district, town, and village distribution of the people, with their marriages, occupations, education, &c., but it does not deal with their vital statistics fully—especially with their birth-rates and death-rates and causes of death. In the year 1867 the Registrar-General's Department was first started and an attempt was made to find out something about the vital statistics of Ceylon.

It is true that some attempts had been made in that direction by both the Dutch and the English Governments, but they were very imperfect; and even in recent years very little was done till 1887, when Mr. Arunachalam became Registrar-General, and started the registration of births and deaths. This improvement was mainly brought about by the aid of Ordinances No. 20 of 1891 and No. 1 of 1895, by means of which the omission or evasion of registration was prevented. False registration was dealt with, and a statement of the "cause of death," in the usual medical terms, secured. New registration districts were constituted on the 1st of July, 1897, and though amendments and alterations were made up to the year 1900, still, after 1898, the registration of the number of deaths may be considered as fairly good, though errors still creep in, which may be eliminated as time goes on. Unfortunately, the registration of the cause of death is not equally good, for the diagnosis has to be made, in a large number of cases, by people who have not received any medical training; consequently, errors of diagnosis must abound.

The registration of births has much improved of late, due to some prosecutions under Section 289 of the Ceylon Penal Code. The result of this was an enormous rise in the number of births registered. Still, it has to be admitted that the registration of births is not as good as that of deaths.

In these remarks on the vital statistics of Ceylon I propose to confine myself to three points: I. The population of Ceylon; II. The infantile mortality of Ceylon; III. The general death-rate of Ceylon.

I.

In the middle of 1904 it was estimated that there were 3,767,826 inhabitants in Ceylon, and that these were distributed as follows:—

Europeans	6,421
Burghers	24,088
Sinhalese	2,476,349
Tamils	1,000,173
Moors	235,595
Malays	12,002
Others	13,198
	3,767,826

This population is steadily increasing; and the increase is due to, firstly, the excess of immigration over emigration, and, secondly, the increase of the birth-rate over the death-rate.

(1) The Excess of Immigration over Emigration.

In some years this excess has been quite considerable, as, for example:—

1900	95,058
1901	2,260
1902	23,846
1903	15,731
1904	21,056
1905	94,567

These immigrants are composed of Tamil coolies, who come here from India to work on the estates in Ceylon.

(2) The Excess of the Birth-rate over the Death-rate.

The birth-rate is an important matter in every community, and has been the subject of considerable remark in certain countries. In considering these vital statistics of Ceylon, the period 1898 to 1904 is chosen. The years antecedent to 1898 are not considered, because from that year onwards the registration of births and deaths shows a marked improvement on preceding years.

In Ceylon the birth-rate is 38·6 per thousand inhabitants on an average, for the years 1898 to 1904, while the death-rate is only 27·4 per thousand, which is a difference of 11·2 per thousand. This is satisfactory, and compares well with other countries. The racial birth-rate per thousand of the population for the same period is as follows:—

Sinhalese	42·6
Moors	38·6
Tamils	29·7
Burghers	29·5
Malays	29·2
Europeans	27·9
Others	13·1

The excess over the death-rates per thousand is:—

Sinhalese	16·8
Moors	9·3
Burghers	7·5
Europeans	6·8
Malays	1·1

Two races show an excess of deaths over births, viz.: Tamils, 1·4; others 8·7 per thousand.

I think in the case of the Tamils the excess of deaths over births is due to the large number of immigrant coolies, for amongst the Ceylonese Tamils of the Northern Province the average birth-rate is 38·0 per thousand, and the death-rate is 31·3 per thousand, which is an excess of the birth-rate over the death-rate of 6·7 per thousand. And, again, the same people in the Eastern Province have a birth-rate of 44·0 per thousand, as against a death-rate of 31·6, which is a difference of 12·4 per thousand. So that the Ceylonese Tamils alone would, I think, show the same excess of births over deaths as the other races in the island. The community classed as "Others" comprises mainly Veddahs, but is a very mixed series of people, and need not therefore be considered in detail. For these reasons I conclude that the birth-rate of Ceylonese races is quite satisfactory. But though the birth-rate may be satisfactory, still it may tend to raise the death-rate if the children under one year of age die off rapidly. In other words, their death-rate, which is called the infantile mortality, if excessive, will annul the good effects of the satisfactory birth-rate. It is therefore necessary to consider the second portion of this article, viz., the infantile mortality of Ceylon.

II.

The infantile mortality rate of a community is the proportion of deaths of children under one year of age to a thousand births. A low infantile mortality indicates, as a rule, a healthy community, and a high rate the reverse. But sometimes this rate is high when the general rate is low, and then, of course, special causes must account for the height. The infantile mortality of Ceylon per thousand during the last eight years is as follows :—

1898	169
1899	197
1900	178
1901	170
1902	173
1903	164
1904	174
1905	176

The average for the period chosen—namely, 1898 to 1904—is 175 per 1,000 births. This rate compares quite favourably with European countries, but not so favourably with certain colonies, such as New South Wales, New Zealand, and Queensland. Perhaps the Ceylon rate is really a little lower than 175, because the deaths are better registered than the births, and this fact tends to raise the infantile mortality figure. It is not easy to compare Ceylon with other tropical countries, because statistics are not available. In India the rate varies from 200 to 400 per 1,000 according to the district. For example, the Bombay Presidency has an infantile mortality figure of 220 per 1,000 in males and 219 per 1,000 in females. In British Guiana in 1904 it was 201 per 1,000 births. The average number of deaths of children under one year of age in Ceylon for the period selected—namely, 1898 to 1904—is 24,213, whereas the average total deaths is 97,804, so that infantile mortality alone was responsible in that period for an average of 1 in 4 deaths, or 25 per cent. This mortality is not spread equally over the first year of life, but falls most severely on the first week, as can be seen from the following table :—

Age.	Males.	Females.	Total.	Comparison of 1st Week with the rest of the Year.
1. One week and under	6,339	5,257	11,596	11,596
2. Over one week and under three months...	3,843	3,465	7,308	12,614
3. Over three months and under one year ...	2,654	2,652	5,306	

It is thus seen that the mortality of the first week of life approaches closely the total mortality of the remaining fifty-one weeks of the year. The mortality is more heavy on males than on females. The distribution of mortalities among the various races in Ceylon is shown in the following table :—

Europeans...	97
Sinhalese	157
Burghers	195
Tamils	213
Moors	230
Malays	292
Others	296

which may be compared with the racial distribution of the mortality in British Guiana in 1904 :—

Europeans...	87
Chinese	99
Aborigines...	124
East Indians	168
Mixed races	226
Blacks	230
Portuguese	313

The various ways in which the racial influence acts upon the infantile mortality are, I believe :—

(1) Condition of the mother's health before the birth of the child, coupled with the question of an early marriage ; (2) the amount of care bestowed on mother and child during parturition ; (3) whether the child receives breast-milk or has to be fed artificially ; (4) whether the mother really understands how to care for, and bring up, her infant ; (5) whether the sanitary condition in which the race lives is good or bad ; (6) whether the race lives in healthy or unhealthy parts of the island.

I believe that the cause of the rate being so low among Europeans is because most of the above-mentioned points are good.

The infantile mortality of the Sinhalese varies remarkably in different portions of the island, as will be seen from the following table for the year 1905 :—

Eastern Province	356
North-Central Province ...	309
Uva Province	226
North-Western Province ...	218
Central Province	175
Sabaragamuwa	160
Southern Province ...	129
Western Province	118

The first four provinces have a very high death-rate, the second four have a low death-rate. The Northern Province is not considered, because there are very few Sinhalese living therein.

The Burgher infantile mortality is influenced by the fact that many of them live in Colombo, which has a relatively high infantile mortality, and also by the fact that many live in small houses in that town and thus suffer from overcrowding.

The Tamil infantile mortality is high because many of them live in unhealthy and poor parts of the island, and therefore the mother is reduced by disease and by lack of proper food.

Moors are an immigrant race, but so long ago that the Portuguese found them in the island and gave them their name after their co-religionists in Spain and Morocco. They live mostly in the Eastern and North-Western Provinces, which have already been shown to be unhealthy parts of the island. For 1905 the figures are :—

Death-rate.	Province.	Infantile Mortality.
49·3	Eastern Province	297
35·5	North-Western Province	369

These people and the Malays keep their women in seclusion, and therefore they are not so accessible to medical aid as other races. Hence infantile and parturient deaths must be high. Moreover, there is much more chance of faulty birth-registration among these people. All these points help to raise their infantile mortality figure.

Malays are a small race, and many of them live in Colombo, and therefore come under town influence as well as the other peculiar circumstances mentioned above.

"Others" are a very mixed community and need not be considered.

Important as is the racial factor, the region of the island appears even more important, and this I propose to investigate in : (A) Provinces, (B) Districts, (C) Towns.

(A) **Provinces.**—The following table shows the distribution of the infantile mortality in the provinces and at the same time the provincial death-rate for the period 1898–1904 :—

Province.	Infantile Mortality.	Death-rate per 1000 Provincial Inhabitants.
1. North-Central.	269	40·7
2. Uva	213	36·2
3. Northern ...	213	31·6
4. Eastern ...	213	30·1
5. North-Western	208	30·3
6. Central ...	198	28·3
7. Sabaragamuwa	173	30·0
8. Western ...	133	21·9
9. Southern ...	135	24·2

On the whole, the comparison between infantile mortality and general death-rate is remarkable. The Western Province is raised above the Southern probably by the aid of the town of Colombo.

(B) **Districts.**—The districts can be arranged in the same way for the same period, 1898-1904 :—

Number.	Name of District.	Infantile Mortality.	Death-rate per 1,000 Inhabitants.
1	Mannar ...	345	44·0
2	Puttalam ...	294	36·7
3	Mullaitivu ...	280	41·5
4	Trincomalee..	277	35·4
5	Anuradhapura	269	40·7
6	Matale ...	238	36·7
7	Kurunegala ...	222	32·8
8	Badulla ...	213	36·2
9	Batticaloa ...	203	29·1
10	Jaffna ...	198	30·1
11	Kandy ...	196	29·0
12	Ratnapura ...	192	32·1
13	Nuwara Eliya	176	21·5
14	Kegalla ...	162	28·5
15	Hambantota ..	154	24·4
16	Colombo ...	149	22·3
17	Galle ...	136	24·9
18	Matara ...	122	23·2
19	Chilaw ...	120	18·9
20	Kalutara ...	116	22·9
21	Negombo ...	114	18·8

Again it is seen that, speaking generally, the worse the health of the district, the higher the infantile mortality.

(C) **Towns.**—Coming to the consideration of town influence, attention may be invited very briefly to the mortality in Colombo. For further details reference can be made to my report on the sanitation of that town.

The average infantile mortality is 395, which can be compared as follows :—

Ceylon	175
Colombo District	149
Colombo Municipality	395

Or again :—

Colombo Municipality	395
Worst District (Mannar)... ...	345
Worst Province (North-Central)	269

Therefore, Colombo is worse than any district or province ; but there are, I admit, worse townships—*e.g.*, Puttalam Local Board. The infantile mortality in Colombo during the years 1898–1904 is as follows :—

1898	375
1899	328
1900	395
1901	389
1902	360
1903	410
1904	353

The fact that Colombo is worse than the districts and provinces compares with the English rates, 1904 :

England and Wales	145
Large Towns in England ...	160
Rural England and Wales ...	125

Nothing shows this town influence better than its action on the Sinhalese, who form the bulk of the population.

SINHALESE INFANTILE MORTALITY PER 1,000 LOCAL BIRTHS, 1905.

Ceylon	158
Western Province	118
Colombo District	126
Colombo Town	304

The lowest Sinhalese mortality is in the Negombo district, 111 in 1905, and in the Alutkuru Korale North of that district, where it is 94.

Seasonal Influence.—I regret to say that I have not been able to find statistics on this point, but I am inclined to think that the season of the North-East monsoon—*i.e.*, about December, January, and February—is probably the worst, perhaps because of the cold weather conducing to more overcrowding into closely shut houses, which produces worse sanitation, while chills conduce to bronchitis and pneumonia.

Causes of Infantile Mortality.—The four principal causes appear to be :

	Per Cent.
1. Infantile convulsions and diarrhœa ...	35·6
2. Prematurity and debility	23·2
3. Tetanus	20·4
4. Bronchitis and pneumonia	11·1
	90·3

These calculations are made from a list of causes of infantile mortality under one year of age prepared by Dr. Marshall Philip, Medical Officer of Health, in 1903. This list, which really applies to Colombo, appears to reflect the causes of infantile mortality throughout the island, for on making a list of the causes of death for the period chosen, viz., 1898 to 1904, the following are found to be the two principal causes :—

Infantile convulsions	9,503
Premature birth	769

while the average number of deaths of children under one year of age is, as I have said, 24,213. Unfortunately, it is impossible to differentiate between diarrhœa, debility, tetanus, and bronchitis as the causes of death in infants under one year, and deaths due to the same causes in adults. Still, I believe that Dr. Philip's table represents the most potent causes of infantile mortality not merely in Colombo, but throughout Ceylon. Definite information on the point is, I think, very urgently required. The causes may be arranged in a different manner, *e.g.*—

(1) Causes due to the mother's health ;
(2) Causes due to the food ;
(3) Causes due to the lack of care of the child.

(1) *Causes Due to the Mother's Health.*—Prematurity and debility must be largely due to the mother, who may be in a poor state of health, due to poverty, disease, or lack of food.

(2) *Causes Due to the Food.*—The proper food for the infant is its mother's milk, and luckily many infants in Ceylon receive this, which accounts for the low rate of mortality among the Sinhalese and other races in many parts of the island. But in Colombo the use of condensed milk has begun and is spreading ; and it is not a matter to be wondered at that if these tins are left open for some days and the milk is allowed to become contaminated by the action of dust and flies, it really acts as an irritant to the child, with the result that infantile convulsions and diarrhœa are common. Unsuitable food is also often given to the child, *e.g.*, rice water.

(3) *Lack of Care of the Child.*—Under the heading "Lack of Care of the Child" I would put such diseases as tetanus in newly-born children and bronchitis and pneumonia. Tetanus must be due to dirt, and bronchitis and pneumonia to lack of care of the child in cold weather.

Remedies.

The whole subject of infantile mortality is a great social question, and must be dealt with in each district separately, and cannot be discussed in a short article like this. For further information, reference can be made to a paper by myself in the *Journal* of the Ceylon branch of the British Medical Association in 1907, entitled "Some Remarks on the Vital Statistics of Ceylon."

Summary.

(1) Infantile mortality in Ceylon is 175 per 1,000 births, but it may not be as high as these figures indicate because the registration of births is defective ; (2) this mortality is highest in the first week of life, which is nearly equal to the other fifty-one weeks ; (3) it falls mostly on "Others"—Malays, Moors, and Tamils ; (4) the worst province is the North-Central, 269, and the best the Southern, 135 ; (5) the worst district is Mannar, 345, and the best Negombo, 114 ; (6) the principal town, Colombo, 395, is worse than any province or district ; (7) the causes are mostly infantile convulsions, prematurity, debility, tetanus, diarrhœa, bronchitis, and pneumonia, and several of these are preventable ; (8) the prevention is a social question, and should be attempted in Colombo not by the Government, but by the municipality and the people.

III.

Turning now to the third part of the subject, viz., the general death-rate of Ceylon, which is calculated as so many deaths per thousand inhabitants, and is only the crude or general death-rate. No attempt has so far been made to prepare a standard death-rate for Ceylon, its provinces, districts, or principal towns ; consequently, no corrected death-rates and no comparative mortality figures are available. Consequently, also, the comparison of one province, district, or town with another province, district, or town, may be quite erroneous. The important point to be remembered is that in the following figures only the crude death-rates are being considered. The average number of deaths per annum for the period chosen, 1898 to 1904 inclusive, is 97,804, which is 27·4 per thousand of the population. This crude death-rate is undoubtedly high ; and in order to study it, inquiries must be made into the racial incidence, and also into the age and sex incidence, the provincial incidence, the district incidence, and the seasonal incidence. Occupational incidence, unfortunately, cannot be given.

1. **Racial Incidence.**—The racial death-rates calculated per thousand of the racial population for the period 1898 to 1904 are as follows :—

Tamils	31·1
Moors	29·3
Malays	28·1
Sinhalese	25·8
Burghers	22·0
Others	21·8
Europeans	21·1

I have not been able to find any statistics about the death-rate of the Veddahs ; and perhaps this is due to the fact that nowadays they are gradually being absorbed into the Tamils or Sinhalese.

Tamils.—The Tamils head the list. The Ceylonese Tamils live mostly in the Northern and Eastern Provinces, in which the death-rate is as follows :—

Northern Province	31·3
Eastern Province	31·6

which may be taken to roughly indicate the racial death-rate of the Ceylonese Tamils. There are several causes which tend to raise the death-rate of the Tamils :—

1. They live in unhealthy portions of the island.

2. The heaviness with which certain diseases hit them, for example :—

(1) Simple fever,
(2) Diarrhœa,
(3) Dysentery,
(4) Pneumonia,
(5) Remittent fever,
(6) Malarial cachexia,

while these diseases fall more lightly on the other races, and the reason is because the Tamils live in districts where malaria is rife, and diarrhœa, dysentery, and pneumonia prevail. I am, however, inclined to think that enteric fever is one of the great causes of Tamil deaths, because it is possible that enteric fever may be mixed up with what is called simple and remittent fever.

Moors.—The Moor death-rate comes second. About a third of the Moors live in the Eastern and North-Western Provinces, which are unhealthy districts ; consequently they are influenced by enteric, simple and remittent fevers, and by infantile mortality.

Malays.—The Malays are a small population, and their death-rate is very nearly that of the island as a whole.

Sinhalese.—The Sinhalese are by far the greatest proportion of the population, as already shown, but their average death-rate is smaller than that of the island as a whole. The reason is because the majority live in healthier portions of the island, and therefore the influences of the good provinces would keep the racial death-rate down. In fact, some of the districts which are mainly populated by the Sinhalese have the lowest mortality of the island.

Burghers.—The majority of Burghers live in Colombo, and the overcrowding in some of their houses in this city helps, I feel sure, to spread their great cause of death, namely, consumption.

Others are too mixed a community to be commented upon.

Europeans.—Europeans are, of course, immigrants in Ceylon. Many of them pass a medical examination before coming out to the colony. They are also at a very viable age, *i.e.*, one at which the death-rate should fall lightly. They are, as a rule, careful about their sanitation and food, and mostly live in the healthy Western and Central Provinces, and though a large number of them reside in Colombo, still, they live in the better portions of the city, and under more sanitary conditions than the other races. They are, for all these causes, more or less spared from local diseases, and their death-rate comes last of the races in Ceylon. But, though low as compared with other races living in Ceylon, it is high—I might almost say very high—when the facts stated above are considered.

2. **Age and Sex Influence.**—It must be clearly understood that ages are very variable in Ceylon. As a general rule the Ceylonese does not know his age; consequently, it is only a "guess," and, therefore, in considering the age influence on disease, it must be remembered that the statements are only approximate. The following table, with this proviso, indicates the age and sex distribution of deaths in Ceylon, for the period 1898 to 1904, per thousand living of the age and the sex :—

Age in Years.	Males per 1,000 living at given Age.	Females per 1,000 living at given Age.
Under 5	64·2	67·2
From 5–10 ...	11·6	13·9
„ 10–15 ...	9·6	10·2
„ 15–20 ...	9·3	7·2
„ 20–25 ...	9·5	13·7
„ 25–35 ...	12·9	20·1
„ 35–45 ...	20·9	22·3
„ 45–55 ...	32·0	27·0
Over 55	71·1	92·8

It is thus seen that the rate as a rule is higher in the case of females. It is high at five years, and sinks to a minimum at twenty years, from which it rises gradually. The healthiest ages are, therefore, ten to twenty-five.

3. **Provincial Incidence.**—The provincial incidence of death is shown in the following table, calculated per thousand of the provincial population :—

North-Central Province ...	40·7
Province of Uva...	36·2
Northern Province ...	31·6
North-Western Province ...	30·3
Eastern Province	30·1
Sabaragamuwa Province ...	30·0
Central Province...	28·3
Southern Province	24·2
Western Province	21·9

It is as well to clearly understand that the above figures indicate mortality and not sickness rates. For even in the best provinces and in the best districts there may be a considerable amount of sickness from, for example, malarial fever, even though the mortality may be low.

4. **District Incidence.**—The district rate of mortality calculated per thousand inhabitants is shown in the following table :—

Mannar	44·0
Mullaitivu	41·5
Anuradhapura	40·7
Puttalam	36·7
Matale	36·7
Badulla	36·2
Trincomalee	35·4
Kurunegala	32·8
Ratnapura...	32·1
Jaffna	30·1
Batticaloa	29·1
Kandy	29·0
Kegalla	28·5
Galle	24·9
Hambantota	24·4
Matara	23·2
Kalutara	22·9
Colombo	22·3
Nuwara Eliya	21·5
Chilaw	18·9
Negombo	18·8

5. **Seasonal Incidence.**—The island can be divided into a dry zone with less than 60 inches of rain, and a wet zone with over 60 inches of rain. In both zones the first quarter of the year is the worst.

Causes of Death in Ceylon.

As already pointed out, the total number of deaths in Ceylon, on an average for the period chosen, 1898 to 1904, is 97,804 per annum, which is 27·4 per thousand population. This death-rate is made up as follows :—

	Per Cent.
Zymotic diseases	44·6
Parasitic diseases	3·7
Dietetic diseases	0·2
Constitutional diseases	7·8
Developmental diseases	2·9
Local diseases	30·9
Violence	1·9
Ill-defined and not specific diseases ...	7·7

A further analysis of the causes of death is as follows :—

EXPRESSED AS A PERCENTAGE OF THE TOTAL DEATHS.

	Per Cent.
Diarrhœa and dysentery	21·4
Simple, ill-defined, and remittent fevers ...	20·6
Ague	0·1
Malarial cachexia, dochmius, and anæmia	2·8
Puerperal convulsions and childbirth ...	1·2
Cancer	0·2
Diabetes	0·1
Infantile mortality from all causes ...	24·7
General debility, &c.	5·0
Dropsy	2·8
Old age	2·1

The great difficulty about the above distribution of mortality is that it cannot be considered in any way accurate, as a very large number of deaths are not certified to by medical men.

When the Registration Ordinance comes into working, it will be possible for the Registrar-General to distinguish between, firstly, deaths certified to by registered medical practitioners, and, secondly, deaths not so certified, and then, perhaps, more accurate information will be obtained.

The racial distribution of the causes of death is shown in the Table on the following page.

It is now necessary to consider some of the diseases more in detail.

Diarrhœa.—This is the principal cause of death in Ceylon, amounting to 15·9 per cent. of the total deaths. Its racial incidence is as follows :—

	Per Cent.
Sinhalese	18·3
Tamils	12·3
Moors	10·0
Others	9·5
Burghers	9·3
Malays	7·4
Europeans...	4·3

Diarrhœa must indicate contaminated food, *i.e.*, bad sanitation, and, therefore, falls much more severely on the native races than on Europeans. It should be possible, however, in course of years, to diminish this cause of death.

Dysentery.—Dysentery has been carefully studied by Dr. Aldo Castellani, Director of the Bacteriological Institute, Ceylon, who has shown that there are, at least, three kinds—(1) Dysentery, due to Kruse Shiga bacillus; (2) Para-dysentery, due to bacilli isolated by Dr. Castellani; (3) Amœbic dysentery, due to Schaudinn's *Entamœba histolytica*. The racial incidence is as follows :—

	Per Cent.
Tamils	11·0
Europeans...	10·0
Others	8·1
Malays	5·8
Burghers	5·5
Moors	4·9
Sinhalese	2·8

The reason why the Tamil rate is so high is because the Indian Tamil coolies are subject to chronic dysentery. Europeans reside for the most part in Colombo, so I cannot help thinking that they are influenced by the conditions of the town. The Sinhalese appear to have practically a racial immunity in this particular.

Ankylostomiasis.—There appears to have been the greatest difficulty in diagnosing this disease in Ceylon. It was mistaken for Beri Beri, which is a Sinhalese term meaning "*Cannot, cannot*," which being interpreted means that the patient is too ill to do anything. The recognition of the disease has improved very slowly; the average number of cases for the period chosen, viz., 1898 to 1904, is 285—a figure which I believe to be far too small; but latterly this has been fully realised, and a sign of improvement is noted. For example, the number of cases in 1904 was 315, and in 1905 it was 562. I believe this to be entirely a matter of diagnosis. Unfortunately, I am certain that a large number of cases are wrongly diagnosed as either anæmia, dropsy, or malarial cachexia, and perhaps even as other diseases. I should be inclined to say that the number of cases varies from those diagnosed as ankylostomiasis, to a combination of ankylostomiasis, anæmia, dropsy, &c. In other words, I believe that the truth concerning the number of deaths from ankylostomiasis for the period 1898 to 1904 is somewhere between 285 and 6,776, which is the total of the deaths due to anæmia, general dropsy, and malarial cachexia per annum. The disease is probably increasing, but there is no statistical evidence on this point. It is, however, a serious matter, because a large number of persons must be dying every year of the disease, which is curable, if diagnosed in its earlier stages.

Tuberculosis.—For the period 1898–1904 the Registrar-General classifies tubercular diseases into :—

(1) Tabes mesenterica	69
(2) Tubercular meningitis	35
(3) Phthisis	3,262
(4) Other forms of tuberculosis ...	265
	3,631

Consequently, all other forms of tubercular disease are insignificant as compared with consumption (phthisis).

Phthisis.—The disease is slowly beginning to increase not merely in Ceylon, but in many

RACIAL DISTRIBUTION OF THE CAUSES OF DEATH.

Europeans.		Burghers.		Sinhalese.		Tamils.	
Enteric ...	10·1	Phthisis ...	9·7	Diarrhœa ...	18·3	Simple Fever...	17·3
Dysentery ...	10·0	Diarrhœa ...	9·3	Simple Fever	12·0	Diarrhœa ...	12·3
Phthisis ...	6·7	Pneumonia ...	6·6	Enteric ...	7·6	Dysentery ...	11·0
Pneumonia ...	4·7	Dysentery ...	5·5	Phthisis ...	3·8	Pneumonia ...	6·2
Diarrhœa ...	4·3	Enteric ...	3·4	Anæmia ...	3·6	Remittent Fever ...	3·8
Simple Fever...	1·7	Simple Fever...	2·6	Dysentery ...	2·8	Malarial Cachexia ...	2·8
Remittent Fever ...	1·5	Remittent Fever ...	2·3	Puerperal Convulsions ...	1·6	Phthisis ...	1·9
Cancer ...	1·3	Childbirth ...	1·1	Childbirth ...	1·2	Anæmia ...	1·7
Ague	0·6	Malarial Cachexia ...	0·8	Pneumonia ...	0·8	Childbirth ...	0·8
Anæmia ...	0·4	Anæmia ...	0·8	Remittent Fever ...	0·3	Enteric ...	0·7
Malarial Cachexia ...	0·3	Cancer ...	0·7	Cancer ...	0·2	Dochmius ...	0·7
Dochmius ...	0·2	Puerperal Convulsions ...	0·3	Malarial Cachexia ...	0·2	Ague	0·3
Childbirth ...	0·1	Ague	0·1	Ague	0·08	Puerperal Convulsions ...	0·2
Puerperal Convulsions ...	0·0	Dochmius ...	0·1	Dochmius ...	0·06	Cancer ...	0·2
Total ...	41·9	Total ...	43·3	Total ...	52·54	Total ...	59·9

Moors.		Malays.		Others.	
Simple Fever	19·2	Simple Fever...	10·4	Diarrhœa ...	9·5
Diarrhœa ...	10·0	Diarrhœa ...	7·4	Dysentery ...	8·1
Dysentery ...	4·9	Phthisis ...	6·8	Simple Fever...	7·4
Pneumonia ...	3·6	Pneumonia ...	5·9	Enteric ...	6·3
Phthisis ...	3·1	Dysentery ...	5·8	Phthisis ...	6·3
Enteric ...	2·7	Remittent Fever ...	3·5	Remittent Fever ...	1·9
Anæmia ...	2·3	Enteric ...	1·5	Dochmius ...	1·6
Remittent Fever ...	1·6	Malarial Cachexia ...	1·5	Malarial Cachexia ...	1·1
Childbirth ...	1·2	Childbirth ...	1·1	Pneumonia ...	0·9
Puerperal Convulsions ...	0·9	Puerperal Convulsions ...	0·9	Childbirth ...	0·6
Malarial Cachexia ...	0·8	Anæmia ...	0·8	Anæmia ...	0·6
Dochmius ...	0·1	Ague	0·3	Ague	0·2
Cancer ...	0·1	Dochmius ...	0·2	Puerperal Convulsions ...	0·2
Ague	0·09	Cancer ...	0·2	Cancer ...	0·2
Total ...	50·79	Total ...	47·8	Total ...	44·9

other places in the East. The number of deaths in Ceylon is shown in the following table :—

1898	2,889
1899	3,167
1900	3,217
1901	3,390
1902	3,297
1903	3,383
1904	3,488
1905	3,733

It will thus be seen that there is a slow and steady increase from 1898 to 1905. Of course, a portion of this increase may be due to better diagnosis, but it is also to be noted in Colombo, as will be seen from the following figures :—

	Per 1,000 Inhabitants.
Average for 5 years, 1895 to 1899 ...	2·38
Average for 5 years, 1900 to 1904 ...	3·14
Average for 1905	3·65

The last figures are very high. Those for the corresponding period for Bombay are 3·8, for Calcutta 1·9, and for England 1·3.

Consumption hits the Burgher community most severely. The racial distribution is shown as follows :—

	Per Cent. of Total Racial Deaths.
Burghers	9·7
Malays...	6·8
Europeans	6·7
Others...	6·3
Sinhalese	3·8
Moors	3·1
Tamils...	1·9

And this not merely applies to the whole island, but also to Colombo, where most Burghers live. The following table, taken from Dr. Marshall Philip's report, shows these figures :—

Burghers	11·5
Others	10·4
Sinhalese	9·5
Malays	8·8
Europeans	7·8
Moors...	7·6
Tamils	7·0

Further, these facts apply not merely to deaths but to sickness rates. For, from an investigation reported in Sir Allan Perry's Administration Report for 1906, the following figures are found :—

One case occurs in every 666 Burghers.
Do. do. 3,000 Tamils.
Do. do. 4,200 Sinhalese.

It is not, however, so much among the Burghers that the disease is increasing, as among the Sinhalese, Tamils, and Moors, as may be seen from the attached table :—

Year.	Europeans.	Burghers.	Sinhalese.	Tamils.	Moors.	Malays.	Others.
1898	7	46	2,118	537	149	20	12
1899	7	39	2,355	544	193	19	10
1900	7	61	2,384	5c4	218	25	18
19c1	13	52	2,470	618	193	20	24
1902	7	44	2,344	616	246	22	18
1903	10	44	2,443	584	256	21	25
1904	11	69	2,530	580	243	33	22
1905	8	52	2,707	640	262	38	26

Turning now to provincial and district distribution, I select the highest year, 1905, when the Western Province and the Colombo district stand out by far the highest. The Colombo Municipality alone is responsible for 620. I have dealt with the question at some length in my report on the sanitation of Colombo, to which reference can be made, and will only remark here that though it was not possible to find out the incidence of consumption due to real overcrowding, *i.e.*, the number of inhabitants living per room, still it is probable that this overcrowding exists in Colombo, as in Calcutta, and that the dreadful abodes which are called houses-let-in-lodgings and tenements, described in the report, must have a great deal to do with the prevalence and slow increase of consumption in Colombo.

Enteric Fever.—Enteric fever is probably a much underrated disease in Ceylon, and certainly in Colombo. Its increase after registration came into use points to better diagnosis. Many cases of enteric fever must be diagnosed at the present time as simple and remittent fevers, and therefore its deadly influence may be considerable, though not properly known. Nothing but better diagnosis will clear this up. The following table indicates the extremes between which this mortality must vary per race :—

	Enteric only.	Combined Death-rates.
Europeans ...	10·1 ...	... 13·3
Burghers ...	3·4 ...	... 8·3
Sinhalese ...	7·6 ...	... 19·9
Tamils ...	0·7 ...	... 21·8
Moors	2·7 ...	... 23·5
Malays ...	1·5 ...	... 15·4
Others... ...	6·3 ...	... 15·6

Cancer.—Cancer has been and still is being carefully investigated in the island. The Registrar-General puts the average number of deaths for the period 1898 to 1904 at 205 per annum, and the case-rate investigated during 1902 and 1903 gives a rate of 220 per annum. It is apparently commoner in males than in females. The average age is forty years, and the most common form of the disease is epithelioma, in relation with the oral cavity. It may probably be induced by the irritation of betel-chewing or smoking. Sarcoma is rarer than carcinoma. The incidence in the races for the period 1898 to 1904, expressed as a percentage of the total deaths, is as follows :—

Europeans	1·3
Burghers	0·7
Sinhalese, Tamils, Malays, and Others	0·2
Moors	0·1

A fuller account of sarcoma and carcinoma may be found in two papers published in vol. i. of the *Journal* of the Ceylon Branch of the British Medical Association for 1904.

Deaths of Women directly due to Childbirth.—The Registrar-General gives the following diseases as causing the deaths of women at childbirth, under the heading of "Diseases of Women at Parturition" :—

Abortion and miscarriage	36
Puerperal mania	1
Puerperal convulsions	1,106
Placenta previa, flooding	12
Phlegmasia dolens	2
Other and undefined accidents of childbirth...	1,024
	2,181

So that 2,181 deaths out of an average of 138,469 births for the same period take place, or, in other words, one woman dies for every sixty-three children born. Calculating this mortality per 1,000 births in the races for the period 1898–1904, the following table is arrived at :—

Ceylon (all races)	15·8
Malays	19·8
Others	17·2
Sinhalese	17·2
Moors	16·3
Tamils	10·6
Burghers	10·5
Europeans	0·8

Expressed as a percentage of the total deaths of races :—

Sinhalese	2·8
Moors	2·0
Malays	2·0
Burghers	1·4
Tamils	0·8
Europeans	0·1

The deaths of women in childbirth, therefore, were 2·1 per cent. of the total number of deaths in the period 1898 to 1904, whereas in England the rate only works out at 0·7 per cent. Therefore, this mortality is three times higher in Ceylon than in England. It is quite possible, however, that this cause of death will diminish as trained midwives increase in Ceylon.

Diabetes mellitus.—Diabetes is responsible for an average of 168 deaths in Ceylon. In 1905 there were 125 deaths, and they were distributed as follows :—

Sinhalese	72
Tamils	37
Moors	12
Burghers	2
Europeans	2

But this racial distribution is not of the interest that an occupational one would be, for the disease, as is well known, hits the lawyer, the doctor, the schoolmaster, and the merchant more than it does the poorer classes.

Malaria.—It is difficult to estimate the deaths caused by malaria, because, though the Registrar-General gives the following table—

Remittent fever	1,494
Ague...	170
Malarial cachexia	1,068

still, it is definitely known that there must be enteric fever and other diseases mixed up with remittent fever, and that ankylostomiasis and kala azar must be confounded with malarial cachexia. Consequently it is probable that malaria does not cause as many deaths as the figures above would indicate. On the other hand, sickness rates of malaria are very considerable. According to Sir Allan Perry's Administration Report of the Civil Medical Department for 1905 there were—

122,642 cases in the North-Western Province,
69,390 cases in the Western Province,
35,192 cases in the Sabaragamuwa Province,

but, of course, many of these must be relapses and recurrences. In the same year there were the following deaths from malaria in these provinces :—

147 in the North-Western Province,
336 in the Western Province,
171 in the Sabaragamuwa Province,

whereas the total number of deaths in these provinces was as follows :—

13,228 in the North-Western Province,
22,296 in the Western Province,
10,140 in the Sabaragamuwa Province.

Therefore, the percentage of malaria to the total deaths is only about 1 per cent. in these provinces ; while the number, as compared with the provincial population, as shown by the census of 1901, appears as follows : One case in nearly 3 inhabitants in the North-Western Province ; one case in nearly 18 inhabitants in the Western Province ; one case in nearly 9 inhabitants in the Sabaragamuwa Province. So that, though the incidence may be very great, the death-rate is low. The incidence of the different causes of malarial fever is little known. Quartan, tertian, subtertian fevers, and the malignant complications of the latter, known as the comatose type, all occur.

Insanity.—According to Dr. Spence, quoted from Sir Allan Perry's Administration Report, the burden of lunacy in Ceylon is relatively light. He points out that if Ceylon had the same amount of insanity in proportion to its population as Ireland has it should have 20,000 cases of lunacy to support instead of 564 ; in other words, it would have to support about 35 times more lunatics than it does at present. Further, Dr. Spence remarks that the total number of admissions into the asylum for the year 1905 was 171, being the highest on record. He contrasts this with the ratio of admissions, which in England is 6·66 to 6·93 per 10,000 inhabitants, from which he takes 6·8 as an approximate mean of these figures, and estimating the population of Ceylon at 3,800,000, says that in order to have the same proportion, the admissions in Ceylon should be 2,600 instead of 171. He further remarks that notwithstanding the fact that there are a number of insane people retained in their own homes in Ceylon, which may account in part for the discrepancy in the asylum figures, still, he is far from thinking that the proportion of the insane to the total population is anything like so great in Ceylon as it is in England. Mania appears to be the most common form of insanity. The cases in the Colombo Lunatic Asylum at the end of 1905 were—

Mania	267
Melancholia	180
Dementia	82
Idiocy and imbecility	9
Epileptic insanity	24
Alternative insanity	1
Stupor	1
	564

and the number of deaths in the same year was—

Mania	29
Melancholia	25
Dementia	4
Idiocy and imbecility	1
General paralysis	3
Epileptic insanity	4
	66

whereas, the average number of deaths from 1898 to 1904 was 54 per annum.

Leprosy.—Leprosy in the period chosen, viz., 1898 to 1904, accounts for 96 deaths per annum, as against 60 in the period 1891 to 1897. On turning to the Principal Civil Medical Officer's Report we find that there are 493 lepers treated in the Hendela Asylum, but it is well known that there are a number of lepers residing in their own homes.

Old Age.—The ages of native races are very problematical, and old age is a very indefinite term ; therefore the remarks under this heading, however interesting they may be, must be taken with considerable caution. Old age is said to account for an average annual number of 2,073 deaths for the period 1898 to 1904, as compared with 1,355 during the period 1891 to 1897. In other words, for the period 1898 to 1904, old age caused 2·1 per cent. of the total deaths. In 1905, 2,395 deaths assigned to old age were distributed as follows :—

Sinhalese	1,551
Tamils	638
Moors	145
Burghers	26
Malays	25
Others	9
Europeans	1

The provincial distribution is interesting :—

	Deaths from Old Age, 1905.	Average Death-rate, 1898–1904, per 1,000 Inhabitants.
Western	995	21·9
Southern	511	24·2
Central	356	28·3
Sabaragamuwa ..	195	30·0
Northern... ...	153	31·6
Uva	85	36·2
North-Western ...	64	30·3
Eastern	27	30·1
North-Central ...	9	40·7

The provinces arranged according to the greatest number of deaths from old age are almost the reverse of the same arranged in order of the greatest mortality, *i.e.*, in the healthiest provinces the largest number of deaths from old age take place.

REFERENCES.

ARUNACHALAM : Census Report, 1901. Administration Reports, Vital Statistics, 1898–1905. Most of the figures used in this paper are derived directly or by calculation from these reports.

CASTELLANI : *Journal of the Ceylon Branch of the British Medical Association*, 1904, 1905, and 1906.

CHALMERS : Sanitation of Colombo, 1907. *Journal of the Ceylon Branch of the British Medical Association*, 1904.

PERRY : Administration Report, Medical Department of Ceylon, 1905.

PHILIP : Report on the Mortality of Colombo, 1906. Quarterly Reports of the Medical Officer of Health, Colombo, 1903.

PROVINCIAL ADMINISTRATIONS—ADDENDA

In the foregoing pages will be found under various heads a very large number of sketches of prominent enterprises and leading personages in the various walks of life in Ceylon. With every desire to make the classification complete, the Editor has not found it possible, having regard to the effective arrangement of the volume, to introduce all the matter at his disposal. It has accordingly been found necessary to prepare this supplementary list, which carries forward in various directions the survey of Ceylon official, commercial, and social life embodied in the book. It may be claimed that though there may be some sacrifice of the principle of unity in the introduction of these pages, the interest of the volume is enhanced by their inclusion.

THE PLANTING INTEREST.

DAVID FAIRWEATHER.

In the circumstances of this gentleman's career we have brought into striking prominence the spirit of enterprise and adventure which has contributed so much to the success of the great planting industry of Ceylon. Born on March 23, 1859, at Newcastle-on-Tyne, Mr. Fairweather, who was of Scotch parentage, was educated at the old Aberdeen Gymnasium and the Aberdeen University. He went into the timber trade, but soon tired of the prosaic life of a provincial town, and, the opportunity offering, he went out to Calcutta under agreement to serve on a tea estate in Assam. After a brief probationary period he went as assistant to Paneery estate to assist a planter, whom he found to be an old schoolmate of his. This gentleman dying, Mr. Fairweather took charge of the estate, and continued to overlook its affairs until he was compelled to take a trip to Ceylon owing to illness. In 1880 he came to Ceylon and joined the Kandaloya estate, Yakdessa, as assistant. At this period the Ceylon tea industry was in its infancy, and a man with Indian experience was much sought after. It is not, therefore, surprising that the end of nine months found Mr. Fairweather manager of the Sembawatte estate, one of the four estates which formed the nucleus of the extensive holdings of the Ceylon Tea Plantations Company, Ltd., a highly successful enterprise which has paid for many years since its inauguration dividends of 15 per cent. per annum. He remained on the estate for some ten years, and during the latter part of the time acted as visiting agent for some of the company's other estates, among them being the famous Mariawatte estate, Gampola. Terminating his engagement with the company, Mr. Fairweather bought land in the low country and started planting on his own account. After a few years' hard work on this property—the Kanangama estate—owing partly to the difficulty of obtaining additional land from the Crown, and partly to a desire for change, he started on a prolonged tour of a remarkable character, making his way *viâ* Aden and Zanzibar to Mombassa, where he organised a caravan and penetrated—all by himself so far as Europeans were concerned—as far as Uganda and the great inland sea, Victoria Nyanza. He had Stanley's boy, Salley, with him, and travelled into the heart of Africa and back in safety, at a cost of £600, without finding any warrant to take up planting land in the then unsettled state of the country and the backward condition of transport. He saw coffee growing or running wild in some parts, tobacco of fine growth being trampled underfoot near numerous native villages, wide areas under bananas, and splendid timbered country and elevated forest land. His general impression was that with improved communication and settled government there was a great planting future for this part of Africa. On returning to Zanzibar Mr. Fairweather was stricken with fever, but he recovered sufficiently to travel over Mauritius and a great part of Madagascar, then, in despair of getting away otherwise, took passage in a sugar barque to New Zealand, and thence, making his way through the Australian colonies, he at length came to Java. Here, in conjunction with others, he secured 3,000 acres of fine land in East Java. In 1897 Mr. Fairweather, on the invitation

THOMAS PERERA, MOHANDIRAM.

(For Letterpress see p. 706.)

DAVID FAIRWEATHER. VIEW ON THE ESTATE. THE FACTORY. THE BUNGALOW.

of Mr. F. Cass, of the firm of Messrs. Lapraik Cass & Co., of Amoy and Tamsvi, made an interesting journey into the interior of the Southern Province of China to report on the tea industry of Amoy. In the course of a stay of two months' duration he travelled right across the Fukien Province, and made a careful inspection of the tea plantations, with a view to determining the causes which had led to the deterioration of the Chinese tea trade. On his return he submitted a valuable report, in which he elaborated the view that the failure of Chinese tea was due to bad and unscientific methods of cultivation and preparation, over-cropping and consequent exhaustion of the land, and a lack of proper means of transport; and he expressed the opinion that there was little hope of a recovery of the industry unless new land was taken up and an up-to-date system of planting followed. Ultimately he returned to Ceylon and took up land in partnership with his brother. Mr. James Richard Fairweather, who is at present on leave in England, and for whom he is at present acting on the Yatadeniya estate. This fine property, since its purchase from the Crown eighteen years ago, has, under the supervision of Mr. J. R. Fairweather, earned for the shareholders dividends amounting to an average of 25 per cent. for eighteen years. The capital of the company—the Yatadeniya Tea Estates Company, Ltd.—is at present Rs. 190,000, and it has a reserve fund amounting to two-thirds of the capital. With his brother and his partner, Mr. P. J. M. Box, Mr. Fairweather is interested in the following estates: Mabopitiya, Parambe, Nillapalla, Alapalawa, Telijjagoda, and Kankarahena, and is visiting agent for several companies and other estates. These properties, which are planted with tea and rubber, will shortly be associated with the flotation of a limited liability company. Mr. Fairweather is a member of the Colombo Club and of the local Planters' Association. The only recreation he allows himself is an occasional shooting trip.

the Chesterfield estate. At the expiration of this period he went to Travancore, India, as Divisional Manager of the Kunan Devan Hills Produce Company, Ltd.'s, estates, and on his return to Ceylon, after a holiday in the Old Country, he joined the Maddagedera estate, and supervised the Galatura and Halwatura Groups. From Maddagedera estate he was transferred to the general managership of the Hapugastenne Group (2,500 acres) of the Hopewell Tea Company, Ltd., where he remained till the middle of the year 1905, and again went home. On his return to the island at the end of the same year he took up his present appointment. The Durampitiya estates consist of about 2,000 acres, of which 660 are fully planted with rubber, and the remainder has been opened up for the growth of that product. Fifteen thousand coolies are employed upon the property, and in addition a large amount of work is done by contract. Messrs. Carson & Co. are the Colombo agents for the estates. Mr. Angus married Isabella, daughter of Mr. Robert Hall, J.P., of Aberdeen, and he has one daughter and two sons.

WALTER JOSEPH SMITH.

Mr. Walter Joseph Smith is the son of Captain Timothy Smith, of Bolton, Lancashire. Born on March 5, 1859, at Greenwich, he was educated at the Charterhouse School and came out to Ceylon in 1879 as an assistant to Messrs. Whittall & Co. He remained with this firm for two years, and then took to planting, becoming connected in succession with estates in the Matale, Nuwara Eliya, and Maskeliya districts for seven years, and with other estates in the Kelani Valley for eighteen years. He is now planter-in-charge of the Polatigama estate, and visiting agent for other estates in the valley. The acreage of the Polatigama estate is 887, planted with tea, interplanted with rubber. The annual crop is 370,000 lbs. of tea and 8,500 lbs. of rubber. Eleven hundred coolies are employed upon the estate, which is situated at an elevation of from 200 to 400 ft., and which belongs to the Yatiyantota Ceylon Tea Company. The local agents for the property are Messrs. Whittall & Co. Mr. Smith's recreations are shooting and motoring. He is a member of the Colombo Club

D. G. Lumsden. S. E. O. Ransom. G. H. Hall. A. P. Byrde.

(For Letterpress see pp. 711-12.)

A. ANGUS.

Mr. Alexander Angus is the Superintendent of the Durampitiya Rubber Estates, which include Pussela, Kotanagala, and Durampitiya Estates. The son of Mr. Arthur Angus, farmer, of Aberdeen, he was born in that city on October 23, 1867, and received his education at Aberdeen Grammar School. When he was twenty years of age he went out to Ceylon and joined the We Oya Tea Company's estate, near Yatiyantota. He then joined Messrs. Finlay, Muir & Co., and served for nine years upon their estates and two years at and also of the Hill Club, Nuwara Eliya, and the Badminton Club, England.

RALPH OLIVER STEWARD.

Mr. R. O. Steward, part proprietor of the Maldeniya estate, Dehiowita, was born on May 15, 1870, at Walton-on-Thames, and received his education at Twyford and Haileybury, where he was a member of the house eleven cricket team and the Rugby team. He visited France and Germany for the purpose of mastering the languages, and on returning to England studied law. These studies, however, were relinquished, and in 1890 Mr. Steward commenced planting in Ceylon, creeping on the Kelaneiya Estate, Maskeliya. Eight months later he went to Brae Madakelle for five months, and then moved to the Kelani Valley, where he has remained. The acreage of the Maldeniya estate is 618 acres—258 acres of tea plantation, 282 of rubber, and the remainder jungle. There is an annual output of 160,000 lbs. of tea, whilst the rubber is from one to four years old. About 450 coolies are employed. Messrs. Carson & Co. are the agents. Mr. Steward's father was Mr. J. C. T. Steward, solicitor, of London, and his mother a daughter of Charles Turner, a Devonshire gentleman. Mr. Steward is a member of the Kelani Valley Club, the Kelani Valley Planters' Association, the Hill Club, the Ceylon Turf Club, a member of the Ceylon Mounted Rifles, captain of the Taldua Tennis Club.

JAMES SCOTT WILSON.

Mr. J. S. Wilson, son of the Rev. William Wilson, of Kippen, Scotland, was born on April 24, 1873. After receiving his education at John Watson's College at the capital, he was employed in a grain merchant's office for five years. In 1895 he came out to Ceylon and joined the Halwatura estate, Kalutara, and was appointed assistant on the Rasagalla estate, Balangoda, in the following year, and remained there for a period of twelve months. The next five years he was on Galatura estate and various other estates in the island. Mr. Wilson is at present the superintendent of Udabage estate, Yatiyantota, whose acreage is 1,600, out of which 500 are planted with tea and 1,000 with rubber, while the remaining portion is in an undeveloped state. Rubber on this estate was planted in 1903. The annual crop of tea is 230,000 lbs., and the number of coolies is 1,000 Tamils and 500 Sinhalese. The estate, which is from 200 to 1,500 ft. above sea-level, is owned by Mr. G. J. Jameson, while the local agents are Messrs. Carson & Co. Mr. Wilson is a member of the Kelani Valley Club, the Kelani Valley Planters' Association, and the Yatiyantota Tennis Club.

1. E. E. Massey. 2. L. V. Neligan. 3. A. F. B. Smeaton. 4. J. P. Anderson. 5. J. S. Wilson. 6. W. A. Elwell.

A. F. B. SMEATON.

Mr. Arthur Frederick Burn Smeaton, superintendent of the Panawatte estate, is the son of the late Rev. J. B. Smeaton, of Hannington, Wiltshire. He was born in that village on July 13, 1862, and received his education at Magdalen College School, Oxford. He first went out to Ceylon in 1882, and joined the Mipitiakande estate, Kelani Valley. Since then he has had charge of many other estates in the district before taking up his present position. The Panawatte estate is 1,050 acres in extent, and is fully planted with tea and rubber. It is the property of the Panawatte Tea and Rubber Estates, Ltd., of which Messrs. Whittall & Co. are the Colombo agents. A thousand coolies are employed upon it, and the annual tea crop is between 300,000 and 400,000 lbs. Mr. Smeaton is a member of the Colombo Club, Kelani Valley Club, and the Kelani Valley Planters' Association, and his recreations are cricket, golf, tennis, and shooting.

EDWARD TAYLOR GRIGG.

This gentleman, who is the superintendent of the Hemingford group of estates, Pussela, Avisawella, is the son of Colonel E. E. Grigg, Commissioner of Kumaon, India. He was born at Fyzabad, North India, and was educated in England at Bedford Grammar School. He went out to Ceylon in 1891 as a creeper at Pansalatenne estate, Matale, and remained there for two years. He then spent some time at the Yatiwatte cocoa estate and the Atherfield tea estate, and finally joined the Hemingford estates, which are the property of the General Ceylon Rubber and Tea Estates Company, Ltd., and are managed by Mr. W. Forsythe. They embrace over a thousand acres, of which 971 acres are planted with tea and rubber and the remainder with rubber only, and upon them 900 coolies are employed. They are situated at elevations varying from 200 to 1,000 ft., and the output from them last year was 491,000 lbs. of tea. Mr. Grigg married Hilda, daughter of Mr. W. J. Addis, civil engineer, Burmah, and they have one daughter. He resides on the estate, is a member of the

Planters' Association of the district, and of the Kelani Valley and Ratnapura Clubs, and is fond of tennis and riding.

EDGAR SMITH.

Mr. Edgar Smith, of the Waharaka estate, is a son of Mr. Henry Smith, merchant, of Blackheath, London. Born on May 13, 1871, he was educated privately at Blackheath, and then served for three years with Messrs. Gow, Wilson & Stanton, of Mincing Lane, the well-known tea brokers. In 1891 he proceeded to Ceylon and engaged in tea-planting. He was in charge for some time of several important estates in the Kelani Valley district, and finally accepted the position he now occupies.

Mr. Smith is married to Catherine, daughter of the late Mr. Henry Helsham, who was a Captain in the Ceylon Rifles, and afterwards Superintendent of Police, Ceylon. He was for some time Chairman of the Kegalla Planters' Association, which he was instrumental in starting, and of which he was hon. secretary in the earlier years. The Waharaka estate comprises an area of 436 acres under tea and 222 acres under rubber. The estate, which is at an elevation of from 600 to 1,200 ft., produces an annual crop of 250,000 lbs. of tea and 4,000 lbs. of rubber. The labour force consists of 700 coolies.

ARTHUR ASPLIN FRANKLIN.

Mr. Arthur Asplin Franklin, the superintendent of the Eadella group of estates, Polgahawela, owned by Sir Thomas Lipton, is the son of Mr. John Franklin, solicitor, of Brighton and London. He was born on June 21, 1875, at Epsom, Surrey, and educated at New College, Eastbourne. He served for some time under articles to a solicitor, and then was associated with a well-known firm of auctioneers. The opportunity offering, he came out to Ceylon in 1897, and learned planting under Mr. Edgar Smith at Nawalapitiya for ten months. He then for a year took charge of the Amblakande estate, Dolosbage. On the outbreak of the Boer War he went out to South Africa with the first Ceylon contingent, and took part in the engagement at Driefontein, afterwards being taken prisoner. He returned to Ceylon in February, 1901, and took charge of the Hunugalla estate, Kegalla district, until September, 1906, when he accepted his present charge. Mr. Franklin is a member of the Kegalla and Kurunegala Planters' Associations. His recreations are motoring and tennis. The Eadella estate, which is situated at an elevation of 400 ft., has an acreage of 811, planted as follows: Tea, 291 acres; cocoa, 101 acres; coconuts, 172 acres; nutmeg and pepper, 4 acres; and rubber 243 acres (trees from one month to three years old). Between 500 and 600 coolies are employed upon the group.

PERCIVAL GATHOR WOOD.

The son of Mr. G. H. Wood, a Hampshire gentleman, the subject of this sketch was born on March 30, 1872, and educated at Eton. He was destined for the Army, but after a period of study under a crammer abandoned the idea of a military career, and in 1891 came out to Ceylon to learn planting. He was a creeper on the Kelaneiya estate, Maskeliya, for eight months, and then served as assistant on the same estate for one year. Afterwards he was associated with various estates in the Kelani Valley. Then after a brief holiday at Home he returned and took charge of the Wendsfield Park estate, Rangalla, of which he is part proprietor. Mr. Wood is at the present time superintendent of the Nujadurinpolla and also of the Pallagama, Batuwana, and Kadigama estates, which have a combined acreage of 4,000, of which about one-fourth is already planted. The balance will be shortly planted. The Rangalla estate, which is at an elevation of from 1,800 to 4,500 ft., is planted with cardamoms (350 acres), tea (500 acres), and rubber (15 acres). The balance of the estate is undeveloped.

DONALD INGLEBY MACKENZIE.

This gentleman, who is the superintendent of the Ruanwella estate, Ruanwella, was born on December 3, 1872, at Sidmouth, Devonshire, and educated at Rugby. He came out to Ceylon in 1891 and joined the Stinsford estate, Ruanwella, as "creeper." After living on this and other estates he obtained his present position. The estate includes 374 acres fully planted with tea and 298 acres of rubber. The estimated annual crop is 200,000 lbs. Five hundred coolies are employed upon the estate, which is from 200 to 800 ft. above sea-level. The property belongs to the Ruanwella Tea Company, Ltd., the local agents of which are Messrs. Whittall & Co. Mr. Mackenzie, besides the oversight of the Ruanwella estate, has charge of the Moralioya estate, which has an acreage of 304 fully planted with tea, and

1. W. MURRAY. 2. G. COX SCOTT. 3. A. A. FRANKLIN. 4. J. H. LAYARD. 5. D. I. MACKENZIE. 6. E. S. SINCLAIR. 7. EDGAR SMITH. 8. J. E. AITKEN.

which employs a staff of 250 coolies. The owners of this estate are Messrs. Cooper, Cooper and Johnson, and the local agent is Mr. Gordon Fraser. Mr. Mackenzie is a member of the Colombo Club and of the Kelani Valley Club. His recreations are tennis and riding.

MIPITIAKANDE ESTATE.

The proprietors of this estate are Mr. James Cantlay and heirs of the late Mr. James Cantlay, Mr. W. H. Morrison, and Captain Kennedy. The superintendent is Mr. A. W. Cantlay. The property is situated in the Kelani Valley district, and two miles distant from Yatiyanto a railway station. It covers an area of 515 acres, of which 364 acres are cultivated with tea, interspersed with 45,000 rubber-trees, some of which are nine years old. In addition, eighty acres are planted with rubber alone, and the balance is all good land available for the latter product. The estate has a fully equipped factory, in which 180,000 to 190,000 lbs. of tea are turned out annually. Tapping is in progress on the older rubber-trees. Mr. Cantlay has recently invented a machine for drying rubber, which he hopes to patent shortly. The rainfall, which is registered daily on the estate, averages about 200 ins. annually.

JAMES LITTLEJOHN.

Mr. J. Littlejohn, superintendent of Ambadeniya Group estates, is the son of Mr. James D. Littlejohn, retired merchant, of Aberdeen. He first saw the light at Aberdeen, on August 22, 1868. After receiving his education at the Aberdeen Grammar School he joined a bank, and remained there for four and a half years, and at the expiration of that time he proceeded to Ceylon. On his arrival in the island he learned planting under Mr. John Greig, on the Macduff estate at Lindula. Subsequently he joined the Clarendon estate at Nanu Oya, and, after a period of eighteen months, he worked successively on the Mipitiakande estate, at Yatiyantota, the Meddakande estate, at Balangoda, and the Chesterford estate, at Ruanwella, till he was appointed to his present position. The Ambadeniya Group estates, whose acreage is 1,038, are adjacent to the well-known Bible Rock Hill, and are at an elevation of from 880 to 2,600 ft. Rubber trees, which are from six months to three years old, are grown on 788 acres, and the remaining portion of the land is shortly to be opened up with rubber. The estates, in which 250 Tamils and about 100 Sinhalese coolies are employed, belong to the Ceylon Para Rubber Company, Ltd., whose manager is Mr. William Forsyth. Mr. Littlejohn is a member of the Ceylon Planters' Rifle Corps, the Kegalla Planters' Association, the Kegalla Tennis Club, and the Ruanwella Tennis Club. He is fond of tennis and cricket.

CHARLES DUNNING HUNT.

The present superintendent of Udugoda estate, Udugoda, in the Kegalla district, Mr. C. D. Hunt, is the son of Dr. A. D. Hunt, of Devonshire. Born on November 30, 1872, he was educated at Hunnington, Devonshire. At the close of his school career at the latter institution, he studied engineering for two and a half years at Marshall's, Gainsborough, Lincolnshire, but gave up his position there to come out to Ceylon in 1896. On his arrival in the island Mr. Hunt joined and worked on the Mahoysa estate, Madakelle, for four years, after which he was for a year on the Chetnole estate, and subsequently on several other estates till he was appointed to his present position. The Udugoda estate, whose elevation is 750 ft., consists of 1,000 acres, of which 450 are planted with tea and 550 with rubber. The number of coolies, both Tamils and Sinhalese, is 450. The local agents for the estate are Messrs. Geo. Steuart & Co.

MIPITIAKANDE TEA ESTATE.

Colombo. Besides being the superintendent of the Udugoda estate, Mr. Hunt is also in charge of the Hillwana, Markville, Goldina, and Ganegoda estates. He is a member of the Kegalla Planters' Association, and his recreations are riding, shooting, and hunting.

EDWARD STANLEY SINCLAIR.

Mr. E. S. Sinclair, superintendent of the Karandupona estate, Kegalla, was born on September 25, 1874, at Loirston, in Kincardineshire, and educated at the Dollar Academy, Clackmannanshire, and the Aberdeen University. He served an apprenticeship as an engineer for six years, and then came out to Ceylon to learn planting. After a brief training on Rangalla estate, Rangalla, he was appointed assistant on the Bandarapola estate, Matale. On the outbreak of war he proceeded to South Africa with the first Ceylon contingent, and received medal, with five bars, for actions at Driefontein, Johannesburg, Diamond Hill, Wittebergen, and the operations in Cape Colony. Returning to Ceylon in May, 1901, he resumed his old position on the Bandarapola estate. Afterwards he obtained his present appointment on the Karandupona estate. The estate, which is at an elevation of from 800 to 900 ft., has an acreage of 516, of which 300 acres are planted with tea and 176 acres with rubber; the balance is jungle. The annual crop of tea is estimated at 150,000 lbs. Mr. Sinclair also has charge of the Dodantola estate, which has an acreage of 200, of which 100 acres are planted with tea. Mr. Sinclair is a member of the Kegalla Planters' Association, and is hospital visitor representing the Planters' Association. His recreations are riding and shooting.

JAMES EWART AITKEN.

Mr. J. E. Aitken, the superintendent of the Kalagala estate, Aranayke, Kegalla district, was born in September, 1872, at Edinburgh and educated at Kelvinside Academy, Glasgow. He came out to Ceylon in 1896, and after a two years' stay returned Home. In September, 1905, he revisited the island and accepted a post as assistant on the Wadamalle estate, Ramboda. Later he transferred to the Houtville estate, Agrapatna, and finally went to the Kalagala estate in his present position. The estate is situated at an elevation of from 250 to 1,000 ft. There are 106 acres under tea and 200 acres almost entirely planted with rubber. The estimated annual crop of tea is 33,000 lbs., and a labour force of 180 coolies is employed upon the property, which belongs to the Rubber Estates of Ceylon, Ltd. Mr. W. A. Strachan is the visiting agent for the estate.

OSWALD LLOYD PEREIRA.

This gentleman, who is the superintendent of the Cottagalla and Guava Hill estates, Gampola and Kegalla, is the son of Mr. J. C. Pereira, landed proprietor. Born on March 14, 1873, he was educated at St. Thomas's College, Colombo, and Trinity College, Kandy. On leaving college he embarked on planting under his father on the Cottagalla estate. In 1897 he took over the charge of the whole group of estates from his father, who had for twenty-five years previously filled the position of superintendent. The acreage of the estates is 745, and the land is planted with cocoa, rubber, and to a small extent with pepper. The rubber-trees are from three to four years old. Mr. Pereira is married to Lydia, daughter of Mr. Thomas White, late Superintendent of Minor Roads, Ratnapura.

J. C. PEREIRA. OSWALD LLOYD PEREIRA AND FAMILY.
THE BUNGALOW, COTTAGALLA ESTATE.

WATAGODA ESTATE.

This is a Matale Valley estate, six miles from Matale town, of 260 cultivated acres. The remainder of the 333 acres which belong to the estate is not cultivated. Tea and rubber are the products, and the latter, which was planted three years since, is progressing nicely. The annual output of tea totals from 95,000 to 100,000 lbs. The proprietor of the estate is Mr. P. Colquhoun Adams, who has had an all-round and lengthy experience of planting. He is a Devon man, educated at Cheltenham and Heidelberg. He is fond of sport, shooting being his favourite pastime.

ARTHUR EDWARD BARRS.

This gentleman was born on May 24, 1863, at Leicester and educated at Loughborough. He was apprenticed to a broker at Rudes Lane, England, for three years. He came to Ceylon in 1883, and joined Agar's Land Estate, Balangoda, serving there for about three years, after which he worked at the Kalaga estate, Kalutara. Subsequently he was appointed superintendent of the Ambapitiya estate, Kegalla, and still holds that position. The total acreage of this estate, whose elevation is from 500 to 1,700 ft., is 850, of which 570 is interplanted with tea and rubber and

277 with rubber—the trees are from six months to six and a half years old. The annual crop of tea is 26,000 lbs., and the labour force consists of 670 coolies. The local agents are Messrs. Carson & Co., while the proprietor is Mr. R. D. Carson. Mr. Barr's recreations are cricket and tennis.

THE EASTERN PRODUCE AND ESTATES COMPANY, LTD.

This is an important undertaking, owning numerous estates in various parts of the island. The most important of the properties are the Vellai Oya (Lower Dikoya). 1,358 acres, the Norwood (Dikoya), 790 acres, the Meddecombra (Dimbula), 2,554 acres, the Hope (Upper Hewaheta), 1,165 acres, the Matale West (Matale), 693 acres, the Rothschild (Pussellawa), 1,062 acres, and the Sogama (Pussellawa), 796 acres. Altogether the area of the estates owned by the company approaches nearly 13,000 acres.

LANCELOT VICTOR NELIGAN.

Mr. Lancelot Victor Neligan, superintendent of the Troy Estate, Ruanwella, is the son of the late Mr. John West Neligan, gentleman, of Bray Head, Ireland. Born on March 4, 1887, at Eastbourne, he was educated at Bedford Grammar School and at the Royal Medical College, Epsom. On leaving the latter institution he learned farming, but eventually came out to Ceylon and started planting under Mr. H. W. Baily, of Elstone estate, Avisawella. Afterwards he was associated with the Glenesk estate, Avisawella, and the Madampe estate, Rakwana. Finally he was appointed to his present position. The Troy estate embraces an area of 360 acres of tea fully planted and interplanted with rubber, and 120 acres of rubber of from one to two years old. The annual crop is 160,000 lbs. of tea, and there are 40 coolies employed. The elevation of the estate is from 200 to 500 ft., and its owners are the Ceylon Proprietary Tea Estates Company, Ltd., and the managing director in Ceylon is Mr. T. G. Hayes.

ANDREW DUFF JAMIESON.

(For Letterpress see p. 711.)

RUBBER PLANTATIONS, LTD.

East Matale is one of the finest rubber-growing districts in the island, and the estate owned by the above company, of which Mr. J. R. Martin is the superintendent, is not the least promising area given over to the product. The estate has an acreage of 455, the bulk of which is planted. Some of the trees, as our illustrations show, have reached an advanced stage of growth.

THE MAPITIGAMA ESTATE.

The Mapitigama group of estates, which are the property of Mr. J. M. Brace, are situated in the Kelani Valley. They have an acreage of 465, and of this area 423 acres are under tea. Messrs. Lipton, Ltd., are the agents for the group.

WILLIAM MURRAY.

Mr. Murray comes of a well-known planting family. His father was the late Mr. William

ROSS BUNGALOW.

VIEW OF DANGAU ESTATE STORE.
(Paddy fields in the foreground.)

J. R. MARTIN'S DANGAU RUBBER AND COCOA ESTATE.
(Road through rubber plantation.)

THOMAS SCOVELL—THE BUNGALOW AND FACTORY.

(For Letterpress see p. 854.)

MAPITIGAMA ESTATE.

1. GENERAL VIEW. 2. RUBBER TREES. 3. THE FACTORY.

Murray, pioneer proprietary planter, who was a leading figure in the halcyon days of coffee planting. Born on September 15, 1869, he was educated at Boyndie House, Banff, Scotland, and Aberdeen Grammar School. He came out to Ceylon in 1891 and joined his father in planting, and afterwards served on various estates. Ultimately he was appointed to his present position, which is superintendent of Ugieside estate, Undugoda. The total acreage of this property is 400, of which 311 acres are planted with tea and 7 acres with rubber. Rubber is also planted in the ravines. The annual crop of tea is 150,000 lbs. Three hundred Tamil coolies are employed in working the estate, the proprietors of which are Mr. James Gray and the heirs of the late Mr. William Gray. Mr. Murray holds the power of attorney for the owners, and the shipping and selling agents are Messrs. Gordon Frazer & Co. He also looks after the Kalupane estate, which is now being opened up for planting with rubber.

HENRY VINCENT TRINGHAM.

This gentleman, who was born in Ceylon at Nuwara Eliya on February 27, 1884, was educated at St. Edward's School at that place and at St. Thomas's College, Colombo

H. V. TRINGHAM AND HIS MANAGER.

He learnt planting under his father, Mr. W. R. Tringham—a veteran in this line—who is planter-in-charge of the Pen-y-lan estate, Dolosbage, but left him, and was in charge for some time of some plumbago pits at Rakwana. Mr. Tringham later was assistant on Windsor Forest, Malgolla, and other estates, and now he is the assistant-superintendent of the Ambadeniya group of estates, Kadugannawa, Aranayke. He is a member of the Dolosbage Tennis and Athletic Club, Gampola and Lower Kotmale Clubs. He is an ardent sportsman, being fond of tennis, cricket, football, shooting, &c., and holds the cricketing record as a batsman of St. Thomas's College between the intercollegiate schools in Ceylon.

J. D. P. MACLEAN.

Mr. J. D. P. Maclean, superintendent of the Kehelwatte estate, Lunugala, was born on January 2, 1870, in Ross-shire, Scotland, and educated at Inverness College. After completing his education he went to Australia and engaged in sheep farming. He remained there for seven years and then proceeded to Ceylon, joining the Maha Uva estate, Kandapola. From this property he transferred to the Dammeria estate, Passara, acting there as assistant. Later he was associated in the same capacity with the Batuwatte estate. After serving here for

J. D. P. MACLEAN—KEHELWATTE ESTATE AND BUNGALOW.

a year he was given charge of the Yapame estate, and held the appointment for three years. Finally he was appointed to his present charge on the Kehelwatte estate. This property has an acreage of 1,800. Of the total area 600 acres are planted with tea and 200 acres with rubber. The estate, which is owned by the Lunugala Rubber and Tea Company of Ceylon, is situated at an elevation of from 2,000 to 3,000 ft. The estimated crop of tea in 1907 is 320,000 lbs. The labour force on the estate consists of 925 coolies. Mr. Maclean is a member of the Badulla and Uva Gymkhana Clubs. His recreations are shooting, hunting, riding, and racing.

C. E. BONNER.

Mr. C. E. Bonner is the resident manager of the Glen Devon Estate, Udapussellawa. The total acreage of the estate is 482, and of this

C. E. BONNER.

423 acres are under tea. The property belongs to the Anglo-Ceylon and General Estate Company, Ltd., for which Messrs. Aitken, Spence & Co. are the local agents.

Alexander Lewis Kirk.

This gentleman, who is the superintendent of the Pita Ratmalie estate, Haputale, is the son of the late Surgeon-Major Kirk, an old Anglo-Indian officer. At the time of the Mutiny, Dr. Kirk was in charge of the Gwalior contingent. The subject of the sketch, as a child, was a witness of some of the most stirring episodes of that memorable period, including the sack of Gwalior and the siege of Agra. Dr. Kirk and several other of Mr. Kirk's relations were killed during the operations. After his educational training at Bath College, Mr. Kirk took service under the Hudson Bay Company. Eventually, in 1876, he found his way to Ceylon, and joined his brother-in-law, Mr. J. F. Jowitt, on the Eltofe estate, Bogawantalawa. He served on this and other estates for some time, and then—nineteen years since—accepted the appointment which he still holds. The estate, which is at an elevation of 5,000 ft., originally belonged to Colonel Lillie, Surveyor-General of Ceylon, and was purchased eight years since by the Ceylon Tea Plantations Company, Ltd. When Mr. Kirk joined the estate the land was mainly under coffee and tea was in its infancy. By slow degrees the area was brought under tea, and now of a total acreage of 1,605, 1,271 acres are so planted. Half the tea is in full bearing and the other half is young tea. The estimated annual crop is 350,000 lbs., which will be doubled when the young tea comes in. The estate employs 880 coolies. Some of the Kanganies (head men) have been on the estate for thirty years. Mr. Kirk is a member of the Colombo Club, the Kandy Club, and the Badminton Club, England. He was for three years Chairman of the Haputale Planters' Association, and still continues his membership of that body. For ten years Mr. Kirk commanded the Uva section of Mounted Rifles, and holds the Diamond Jubilee and Humane Society's medals; he has saved three lives from drowning, and won many prizes for swimming in his younger days. His recreations are shooting, riding, and motoring. Mr. Kirk is married to a daughter of Lieut.-General Sir John McLeod, and has one son, who is studying for the Navy.

[*For photograph see p.* 851.]

John J. Robinson.

The son of the Rev. C. D. P. Robinson, Rector of St. Martin's, Guernsey, Mr. Robinson, the manager of the Gonakelle estate, comes of a branch of the Robinson family which has as its most distinguished representative the Marquis of Ripon. Mr. Robinson was born in Guernsey on February 19, 1857, and educated at Elizabeth College in that island. He came out to Ceylon in 1875, and joined the Amherst coffee estate in the Udapussellawa district. At the expiration of a year he transferred to the Rangbodde coffee estate, Ramboda, where he remained for about three years. Subsequently he was connected with the East Gourakelle and the Kotogada estates. Finally, in 1880, he took charge of the Gonakelle estate. The property at that time only embraced an area of 300 acres, the whole being under coffee. When coffee failed Mr. Robinson planted cinchona, and in 1885 tea planting was started. New ground was broken from time to time, until the estate reached its present large acreage of 1,830, of which 920 acres are planted with tea, 120 acres with rubber, and 70 acres with cardamoms. The estate ranges in elevation from 1,500 to 5,600 ft. It produces an annual crop of tea of 480,000 lbs., the whole of which is sold in England. The labour force on the estate consists of 900 Tamil coolies. Besides superintending the operations on this important property, Mr. Robinson has opened up on his own account two rubber estates—the Paravilla and the Elbawatte—which are now owned by the Uva Rubber Company, Ltd. He is one of the oldest planters in the district in which he lives, and has seen many changes, notably in the means of communication, for when he took charge of the Gonakelle estate, the railway extended no farther than Gampola, while the road from that place to Passara was only just being made.

[*For photograph see p.* 851.]

Edward H. Mellor.

Mr. Edward H. Mellor, the superintendent of the Westmorland estate, Badulla, the son of Mr. Edward J. Mellor, a retired War Office official, was born in April, 1882, at Bray, Berkshire, and educated at St. Mark's, Windsor. He started life in a solicitor's office, but having no great taste for the law, he came out to Ceylon in 1901 to learn planting. He joined the Mahavilla estate, Dcmodera, but at the end of ten months transferred to the Nayabedde estate, where he remained for three and a half years. Later he was associated with the Madulsima estate, and finally, after a trip home, accepted his present charge on the Westmorland estate. This property, which belongs to Mr. George Taylor, is at an elevation of from 2,500 to 3,000 ft., and has an acreage of 430, of which 325 acres are planted with tea. The estate is worked by a labour force consisting of from 250 to 300 Tamil coolies. Mr. Mellor is a member of the Badulla Club. His recreations are cricket, tennis, and hockey.

[*For photograph see p.* 851.]

James Duncan.

This gentleman, who is the superintendent of the Ury estate, has had a varied experience in planting. Arriving in Ceylon in 1874 at the age of twenty-one—he was born on March 13, 1853, in Glasgow—he served successively on the Haragalla estate, on the Hunasgeria coffee estate group, on the Ballacolla, the Dikapitiya and other estates in the Haputale district, and since 1894 has been in charge of the Ury estate in conjunction with the Mahapahagalla estate. The total area of the property now under Mr. Duncan's supervision is 1,000 acres, of which from 800 to 900 acres are under tea. The crop of tea per acre is 520 lbs., and the yield is being continually increased by high cultivation. Under this system trees from twenty to thirty years old are yielding splendidly. About 1,000 coolies are employed upon the estate. Mr. Duncan has been closely identified with public movements affecting the interests of the planters in the districts in which he has been stationed. He was Secretary for five years and Chairman for three of the Haputale Planters' Association, and in those capacities played a leading part in the agitation for the extension of the railway from Nanu Oya to Bandarawela. During the past three years he has been Chairman of the Passara Planters' Association, and he has actively worked for the extension of the railway from Bandarawela to Passara, a project which bids fair to be shortly accomplished, since orders have been issued for the immediate survey of the line. Mr. Duncan is a member of the Badulla Club. His recreation is tennis.

[*For photograph see p.* 851.]

John Rettie.

The Uva Coffee Company, Ltd., of which the above-named gentleman is manager, is an important commercial enterprise owning a number of estates in Uva. The various estates forming the group are: Glenalpin, Grahamstand, Ballagalla, Rockhill, Hindagalla, Lodgerwatte and Talpitigalla. The altitude of the properties ranges from 1,000 to 1,500 ft. in the case of Talpitigalla to 3,000 to 6,000 ft. in that of Glenalpin. The estates have a total acreage of 4,218, of which 2,371 acres are under tea, 207 rubber, 87 coffee, and 67 cocoa. Of the remaining area 493 acres are set apart for providing fuel and 1,000 acres are classed as reserve. No fewer than 2,224 coolies are employed upon the various estates, and their estimated produce for 1907 is 1,259,000 lbs. of tea, 350 bushels of coffee, and 100 cwts. of cocoa. Mr. Rettie, who was born at Banff, in Scotland, came out to Ceylon in 1874 and joined the Spring Valley Estates Company, Ltd., of which his brother, Mr. A. T. Rettie, was manager. For ten years he remained with this company, and in that period saw the decline of coffee. In 1885, on the retirement of Mr. Lavie, he accepted the charge of the properties of the Uva Estates Company, Ltd. At this time, with the exception of an area of 300 acres which had just previously been planted with tea, the whole of the estates were under coffee, and upon Mr. Rettie devolved the duty of making the inevitable change from coffee to tea cultivation. It was a responsible work which he carried out with great thoroughness and conspicuous success. In 1894 matters had so far advanced that the company found it necessary to erect at Badulla a factory for dealing with leaf grown on their own estates, and for the treatment also of produce from other estates in the neighbourhood which at the time possessed no factories of their own. The establishment stands on a site of four acres owned by the company. It is splendidly equipped with machinery of the most modern type. In one wing of the factory is a steam-engine with four rollers, four dryers, tea sifters, a tea packer, and other appliances. In the other wing is an oil-engine working three rollers, three dryers, &c. The leaf from Ballagalla and Rockhill is conveyed to the factory by wire shoots. In one instance the aerial installation is five-eighths of a mile in length, and it is supposed to be the longest wire shoot in Ceylon. Altogether the output of the factory at the present time reaches the high figure of 600,000 lbs. per annum. Financially the company's position is most sound. The original £10 shares, which stood at only £2 10s. when Mr. Rettie took charge of the properties, are now quoted at £10 10s., and as the prospects of the company are extremely good this position is likely to still further improve in the next few years. Considerable attention is being given to rubber cultivation. On the recently acquired Talpitigalla estate 200 acres have already been planted with this product, and the intention is to increase the acreage to 1,000 in the immediate future. It is worthy of note that the Uva Company is the only company in the district which stands on its original basis with regard to capital, the estates having been all developed out of profits. Mr. Rettie is a member of the Badulla Planters' Association, and was for some time Chairman of that body. He is a member of the Colombo Club, of the Hill Club Nuwara Eliya, and of the Badminton Club, London.

[*For photograph see p.* 851.]

S. H. Bower.

Mr. S. H. Bower, District Engineer, Public Works Department, Badulla, is a son of Mr. J. W. Bower, for

S. H. BOWER.

many years resident engineer of the Lancashire and Yorkshire Railway Company. Born on January 31, 1875, in

Lancashire, he was educated at Warwick School and at Mason's College, Birmingham. At the last-named institution he studied engineering, and received a diploma for the same. He served for three years under Mr. J. D. Leechman, A.M.I.M.E., and then went as assistant engineer to Henley Arden, Warwickshire. Later he was appointed assistant to Mr. Price, the City Engineer of Birmingham. After two years' service in the great Midland city he joined the Public Works Department of Ceylon, and was seconded for service in the Irrigation Department. He served in the Eastern Provinces for three years and at the expiration of that period reverted to the Public Works Department. More recently he was attached to the office of the Provincial Engineer, Eastern Province. Finally, he received his present appointment. Mr. Bower is a member of the Badulla and Uva Gymkhana Club. His recreations are tennis, hockey, and riding.

J. H. B. Cockburn.

Like a good many of his brother planters in Uva, Mr. Cockburn, the superintendent of the Hopeton estate, hails from the land of cakes. He was born on September 17, 1855, at Inverness, and went out to Ceylon in 1873. His first experience was on the Amadova coffee estate, of which he was for some time superintendent. In 1881 he severed his connection with this property and joined the Gallola coffee estates in Lunugala. There he opened the first tea district after the failure of coffee. At the expiration of three years he joined the Uva Bank, but still kept up his planting work. In 1891 he acquired the proprietary interests in the bank. Meanwhile he had occupied himself in opening up the Hopeton tea estate. This property, which is at an elevation of from 2,600 to 2,800 ft., has an acreage of 1,300, of which 1,000 acres are planted with tea. The estimated annual crop is 530,000 lbs., and 1,800 coolies are employed in working the estate. Associated with the Hopeton property are the Amblangoda and Swinton estates, the former of 129 acres and the latter with an area of 200 acres. These were formerly the property of Mr. Cockburn, but they are now, with the Hopton estate, owned by the Lunura Tea Company, Ltd. for which Messrs. Crosfield, Lampard & Co. are the local agents. In connection with the estates is a well-equipped factory supplied with modern machinery. The motive power is at present supplied by water, but a 90-h.p. oil engine is on order, and will shortly be erected in the establishment. Mr. Cockburn is a member of the Hill Club, Nuwara Eliya, and of the Badulla and Passara Clubs. His recreations are tennis and fishing.

[*For photograph see p.* 851.]

J. R. Barclay.

This gentleman, who is a member of a well-known Norfolk family, was born on October 15, 1859, and educated at King's College, London. He went out to Ceylon in 1876, and joined the Hoonagasgeria estate in the Kandy district. After serving a short probation here, he was associated with several estates in the Madulsima and Lunugala districts. Then he took charge of the Koslande estate, and worked upon it for eighteen years, supervising the work in connection with the change from coffee and cinchona to tea. Quitting the estate, he went Home, but his stay was not of long duration. Returning to the island, he accepted an engagement on Messrs. Lipton's estates, and finally was given charge of the Dambatenne group, which property he supervised for four years. At the expiration of this period he again visited the Old Country. Arrived once more in Ceylon, he acquired an interest in the Park estate, of which he is at present the manager. The acreage of this property is 1,100, and of the area 376 acres are under tea and rubber. It is intended to extend both tea and rubber cultivation. Probably an additional area of 200 acres will be cultivated before the end of 1907. At present the annual crop of tea is about 100,000 lbs. The estate is worked by a labour force of 450 coolies. Mr. Barclay is a member of the Colombo Club and of the Nuwara Eliya Hill Club. His recreations are tennis and cricket.

[*For photograph see p.* 851.]

J. F. Fraser.

The superintendent of the Tientsin estate, Mr. J. F. Fraser, is a son of the late Mr. John Fraser, proprietary planter, who owned at one time the Aberdeen estate. He was born at Matale, on Feb. 15, 1866, and was educated at Aberdeen Schools and King's College, Aberdeen. Proceeding to Ceylon in 1887, he served for a short time under his father on the Aberdeen estate, and then accepted an engagement on the Kotiyagalla estate, Bogawantalawa. Afterwards he had charge of the Aldie estate for seven years and of the Nicholloya Group estates, Matale district, for eight and a half years. Finally, in March, 1906, he accepted his present charge. The acreage of the Tientsin estate is 385, of which 325 acres are under tea. The annual crop is estimated at 200,000 lbs. A labour force of 280 coolies is employed upon the estate, which is situated at an elevation of from 4,356 ft. to 4,629 ft. Attached to the estate is an up-to-date factory which has quite recently been built. Mr. Fraser is married to Elsa, daughter of Mr. Adolph Meyer, and has two daughters. His recreations are tennis, billiards, and athletic games.

G. C. Scott.

The superintendent of the Indurama estate, Ruanwella, Mr. G. C. Scott, is a Liverpudlian. He was born on the banks of the Mersey on May 8, 1877, and was educated at Liverpool College. He migrated to Ceylon in 1896, joining the Glengariff estate, Dikoya, as creeper. After serving a short probationary period, he was appointed assistant on the Luccon estate, Maskeliya. Later, he was connected with the Binoya estate, and from that transferred to the Indurama estate. On the outbreak of the South African War he volunteered for active service, and was present with the Ceylon contingent at many important engagements. He possesses the South African medal with five bars. After the war and a spell of much-needed rest at home, Mr. Scott returned to Ceylon and resumed his planting career on his old estate. A little time afterwards he was appointed superintendent on the Promised Land estate, but he finally drifted back to Indurama, of which estate he took charge. The acreage of this property is 428, the greater part of the area being planted with tea

THE TIENTSIN TEA FACTORY AND BUNGALOW.

THE TEA ESTATE. JOHN HILL. THE OFFICE.

interplanted with rubber. Plumbago deposits exist on the estate. One lump of the mineral which was discovered is said to be the largest piece ever found in Ceylon, and its quality is stated by experts to be very high. The annual crop of tea is 200,000 lbs.; in its cultivation and production 300 coolies, all Tamils, are employed. The estate belongs to the United Planters' Association of Ceylon, and its local agents are Messrs. Boustead Bros.

John Hill.

This gentleman, who is the manager of the Keenagaha Ella estate, Balangoda, is a son of the late Sir John Hill, Bart., and is the heir-presumptive to the baronetcy. He was born on June 25, 1869, at Londonderry, County Down, and educated at Harrow. He proceeded to Ceylon in 1887 and served a probationership on the Aberfoyle estate, Rakwana. From this he transferred to the Keenagaha Ella estate, and was there for four years as S.D. Later he was connected with various estates, but ultimately returned to the Keenagaha Ella estate as superintendent. This property has an area of 410 acres, of which 2[illegible]0 acres are under tea and 35 acres tea interplanted with rubber. The annual crop of tea is estimated at 120,000 lbs. Attached to the estate is a factory capable of dealing with 150,000 lbs. of tea annually. Upon the estate stands a tea tree of remarkable size. The trunk measures 4 ft. round, and the tree itself has a circumference of 42 ft. Mr. Hill has made some interesting experiments in the scientific cultivation of tea upon the estate, and is the compiler of Rutherford's "Planters' Notebook." He was a member of the Labour Commission which proceeded to India to investigate matters in connection with the engagement of coolies for the estates. He has been Chairman of the Sabaragamuwa Planters Association, and is the Honorary Secretary of the Balangoda and Rakwana Association. He is a Justice of the Peace, and until lately was an Unofficial Police Magistrate. His recreation is tennis.

Channing Esdaile.

Few planters are better known in Uva than this gentleman, who is the proprietor of the Shawlands estate, Lunugala. Born at Framlingham, in Suffolk, in October, 1834, and with a planting record which extends over a half-century, he is one of the veterans of the industry. He first landed in Ceylon in 1856, arriving in the barque *Francis Barclay*, which of course had made the voyage *viâ* the Cape. His first introduction to planting was on the Rangalla coffee estate, where he served for four years. His Uva experiences date from 1863. He opened up lands in Madulsima, planting coffee. At that time the district was little known, so little indeed that Mr. Esdaile was the first European to embark upon planting within its area. Taking up his quarters in a Sinhalese hut, he lived the rough life of the pioneer; but his enterprise was rewarded, and so well was he satisfied with the locality that he has been associated with it ever since. He had charge of various estates in the Madulsima and Hewa Eliya districts, and meantime bought land and planted coffee. In 1877, before the collapse of coffee, he sold his interests in various properties and went Home *viâ* Australia and New Zealand. After a sojourn in the Old Country he returned to Ceylon, and resumed active work on the Verrellapatna and Shawlands estates, of which he was proprietor. These properties were planted with coffee and cinchona, and it became necessary, owing to the failure of both products, to replant with tea. This work Mr. Esdaile carried out, and when the estates were running on the new lines he sold the Verrella property and took up his residence at Shawlands, where he has been ever since. Under his supervision the Shawlands estate has been greatly extended. It now embraces an area of 1,000 acres, of which 650 acres are planted with tea. Rubber is interplanted with the tea on the lower portion of the estate, and there is a plantation of 50 acres of the same product on ground opened up last year. The estimated crop of tea annually is 260,000 lbs. The leaf is treated on the estate in a factory equipped with a water turbine and a 22-h.-p. oil-engine. Mr. Esdaile is a member of the Junior Constitutional Club, London, and he was one of the original members of the Colombo Club. He is also on the members' roll of the Nuwara Eliya Club. Mr. Esdaile, in addition to his tea interests, is proprietor of coconut properties with a combined area of 350 acres.

[*For photograph see p.* 851.]

W. Stewart Taylor.

This gentleman, who is the manager of the Passara group of tea estates, was born in 1853, in Java, and was educated at Glasgow. Proceeding to Ceylon in 1876, he engaged in coffee planting and in time became one of the largest agents of the coffee estates. The failure of the old Oriental Bank Corporation had for him disastrous financial results. But he continued his planting career, and after serving as superintendent of various estates in the Uva Province he, in 1893, was appointed to his present charge. Originally the Passara estates were planted with coffee and cinchona, and their conversion to tea was carried out under Mr. Taylor's supervision. Of the total acreage of 1903 an area of 500 acres is under tea and 280 acres are under rubber. The estimated annual crop of tea is 230,000 lbs. The labour force consists of 600 coolies, mostly Tamils. In connection with the estate is a factory equipped with the latest machinery and capable of coping with 300,000 lbs. of tea annually. The machinery is worked mainly by water power, but steam power is available in case of emergency. The estate is situated at an elevation of from 1,700 to 4,000 ft. The manager's bungalow is 3,100 ft. above sea level. Mr. Taylor is a member of the Colombo and Badulla Clubs, and he is Chairman of the Passara Planters' Association. His recreations are shooting and golfing.

J. B. Cotton.

This gentleman, who is the superintendent of the Dammeria group of estates, is the son of Mr. John Cotton, farmer, of Nuwara Eliya. Born on July 22, 1854, at Nuwara Eliya, he was educated at St. Thomas's College, Colombo. He started planting under Mr. Greason in 1871, and served successively on various estates in Pussellawa, Haputale, and Madulsima. In 1878 he took charge of the Dammeria estate, and has been connected with the property ever since. The estate has an area of 1,400 acres, 595 of which are planted with tea, 37 with cocoa, and 153 with rubber. The estimated annual crop of tea is 285,000 lbs. On the estate 675 coolies are employed. Mr. Cotton is married and has three sons. His recreation is croquet.

Arthur William Bisset.

Mr. Arthur William Bisset, the superintendent of the Yapame and Kinagoda estates, is a son of the late Mr. James Bisset, J.P. and U.P.M. of the Poonagalla group, Bandarawela. He was born in October, 1872, and educated at Aberdeen Grammar School. He qualified as a chemist, and is a member of the Pharmaceutical Society of Great Britain. Unfortunately, his health became indifferent, and under the advice of his doctors he abandoned his career in favour of an open air life. Proceeding to Ceylon in 1897, he learnt planting under his father on the Lunugala estate, Bandarawela. From this estate, after fifteen months' training, he proceeded to Mount Vernon, Kotagala, remaining there for five years, first as first junior assistant and later as senior assistant. Then he acted for a few months as superintendent on the Osborne estate, Dikoya. Quitting this property, he went to the Rukatenne estate, Bandarawela, and finally was appointed to his present position. The acreage of the Yapame estate is 592, of which 330 acres are under tea interplanted with rubber. The annual crop of tea is estimated at 140,000 lbs. Mr. Bisset is the hon. sec. of the Passara Planters' Association, and is a member of the Badulla Club. His recreation is tennis.

[*For photograph see p.* 851.]

G. H. Sparkes.

The above-named gentleman is the superintendent of the Bogawane estate, Bogawantalawa. The son of Mr. G. B. Sparkes, a retired tea-planter, of Southwick, Sussex, he was born on December 29, 1879, and educated at Steyning Grammar School, Sussex. Proceeding to Ceylon in 1898, he commenced his career as planter on the Bogawantalawa estate. From this property he transferred to the Kirkaswall estate, in the same district. Here he served for three years, and at the expiration of that time took charge of the Bridwell estate. His next move was to the Bogawane estate, of which he has been superintendent ever since. The estate has an acreage of 436, of which 386 acres are under tea. The estimated annual crop of tea is 200,000 lbs. About 300 coolies are employed upon the estate, the elevation of which is from 4,500 to 5,000 ft. The factory attached to the estate is equipped with four rollers, two dryers, one Brown's desiccator, two sifters, two roll-breakers, one packer, and two fans. The motive power is supplied by a turbine of 40 h.p. Mr. Neale's recreations are tennis and hunting.

J. W. Baillie.

Born in November, 1883, in London, Mr. J. W. Baillie, the superintendent of the Bridwell estate, Bogawantalawa, was educated at Brighton. He started life in a London bank, but, tiring of desk work, proceeded to Ceylon in 1902, and commenced planting on the Wanarajah estate, Dikoya. At the expiration of a year he secured an appointment on the Kirkoswald estate. Here he remained for two years, and then accepted his present charge. The Bridwell estate is situated at an elevation of 4,400 ft., and has an acreage of 480, of which 420 acres are under tea. The estimated annual crop of tea is 220,000 lbs. The labour force upon the estate consists of 400 Tamil coolies. Mr. Baillie's recreations are hunting and shooting.

E. M. Wyatt.

This gentleman, who is the manager of the Bogawantalawa estate, Bogawantalawa, was born in Monmouthshire, and educated at the Royal Academy, Gosport. On quitting school, he was engaged for four years in a city office. In 1879 he proceeded to Ceylon and opened up land in the Kurunegala district, planting rubber and new produce. Fever compelled him to leave the district at the expiration of six months. He then started tea planting on the Hope estate, in the Hewaheta district. He remained here for three years, and then went to the Baloya estate, Lower Dikoya, where he served until 1885. From 1885 to 1898 he was in charge of the Elbedde estate, Dikoya. Following this came his appointment to the managership of the Bogawantalawa estate, which he has held ever since. This property, which is owned by Colonel F. M. Mackenzie, C.B., is at an elevation of from 4,300 to 5,000 ft. Originally a coffee estate, it has been planted with tea for the last twenty-two years. It has an area of 615 acres, of which 540 acres are planted with tea. The annual crop of tea is estimated at 325,000 lbs., and in its production a labour force of 525 Tamil coolies is employed. The estate factory is equipped with four rollers, four dryers, two rotary sifters, an oil-engine of 11 h.p., and a turbine of 20 h.p. Mr. Wyatt is married to Laura, daughter of Mr. W. J. F. Brand, late of the War Office. He is President of the Bogawantalawa Club. His recreations are shooting, fishing, and rowing.

T. Gidden.

Mr. T. Gidden, the superintendent of the Campion estate, was born in February, 1857, at Edinburgh, and was educated privately. Arriving in Ceylon in 1878, he started planting on the Galaha estate, and from that transferred to the Katooloya estate. For the last fourteen years he has been in charge of the Campion estate. This property is at an elevation of from 4,500 to 5,000 ft. It has an acreage of 712, of which 632 acres are tea, and 12 acres are new clearings planted with tea. The estimate of the crop of tea for the year is an average of 600 lbs. Upon the estate 700 coolies are employed, and the factory connected with it is equipped with four rollers, two dryers, and other machinery, the whole being worked by a turbine of 40 h.p. Mr. Gidden is a visiting agent for various estates, and has also considerable proprietary interests in tea estates. He is a member of the Junior Athenæum Club, London, and of the Colombo and Kandy Clubs, as well as of all local clubs. His recreations are tennis boating, and racing.

Albert D. Sly.

Mr. Albert D. Sly, part proprietor of the Detenagalla estate, Bogawantalawa, was born on June 5, 1879, and educated at the City of London School. He started life in a shipping office in the City, but after two years' desk work decided for an open-air life and went to California and commenced fruit-farming. Finding this not to answer, he, in 1898, proceeded to Ceylon and started planting on the Barnagalla estate, Nawalapitiya. After serving on this property for three and a half years, he accepted an appointment on the Raxagama estate, Wattagama. He had charge of this estate for fifteen months, and on leaving took charge of the Moratenne estate. At the expiration of thirteen months he transferred to the Detenagalla estate, and has been there ever since. The property embraces an area of 491 acres, of which 302 acres are fully planted with tea. The estimate of the annual crop is 125,000 lbs. There are 335 coolies working upon the estate, the elevation of which is from 2,800 to 3,950 ft. Attached to the estate is a factory equipped with machinery of the latest date, with a turbine to supply the motive power. Mr. Sly is also in charge of Rye estate, of 321 acres, of which 115 acres are under tea. Mr. Sly is a member of the Bogawantalawa Club. His recreation is tennis.

A. M. Maitland.

Mr. A. M. Maitland is a son of the late Mr. George Keith Maitland, a well-known Ceylon planter. He was born in July, 1878, in Ceylon, and educated at Beaumont, England. His planting experiences date from 1898, when he joined the Ingestre estate, Dikoya. Afterwards he served in succession on the Weharegalla estate, Haputale; the Donnybrook estate, Lower Dikoya; and the Theresia estate, Bogawantalawa. From the last-named property he transferred to the Marahela estate. This has an acreage of 363, of which 280 acres are planted with tea and tea interplanted with rubber, 13 acres with coconuts,

THE TEA ESTATE AND BUNGALOW, BOGAWANTALAWA ESTATE.

A. D. SLY, THE BUNGALOW, AND VIEWS OF INTERIOR OF TEA FACTORY.

1. A. C. BONNER. 2. A. DE B. KNOCKER. 3. J. F. FRASER. 4. J. G. GIDDEN. 5. E. M. WYATT. 6. W. STEWART TAYLOR. 7. A. WATT. 8. G. H. SPARKES. 9. A. M. MAITLAND. 10. J. W. BAILLIE. 11. P. P. MIERS.

and 20 acres with rubber. The annual crop of tea is estimated at 160,000 lbs. About 300 coolies are employed upon the estate, which is provided with a factory capable of dealing with 200,000 lbs. of tea. Mr. Maitland is a member of the Balangoda, Darawella, and Bogawantalawa Clubs. His recreations are tennis and shooting.

A. de B. Knocker.

This gentleman, the senior assistant superintendent of the Rasagalla estate, Balangoda, is a son of the late Mr. Edward Knocker, solicitor, of Dover. Born on October 1, 1874, at Dover, he was educated at Westward Ho United Service College, and at Oxford University, where he graduated B.A. Proceeding to Ceylon in 1896, he commenced his career as planter on the Bowlana estate, Deltota. He was afterwards connected with the Maddegama and Kirriemetiya estates, Deltota, and with the Hope estate, Hewaheta, and the Yatederiya estate. From the last-named property he transferred to the Rosagalla estate, upon which he has served during the past five years. His recreations are tennis and shooting.

Arthur Watt.

Mr. Arthur Watt, the manager of the Rasagalla Group estates, is the son of the late Mr. John Watt, retired merchant, of Glasgow. Born on January 7, 1866, at Glasgow, he was educated at Glasgow College. He adopted a career as an architect, but finding the work distasteful, proceeded to Ceylon in 1887 to learn tea planting. He was first under Mr. John Aymer on the Caroondawatte estate, Gampola. In 1888 he bought a share in the Aderapolla estate in the Kelani Valley district, and took over the management of the property. He remained on the estate until 1896, when it was amalgamated with other properties owned by a company styled the Aderapolla Tea Company, Ltd., of which Mr. Watt became manager. Mr. Watt took up his residence on the St. Helen's estate, Dolosbage—one of the properties taken over—and remained upon it until the end of 1905, when he resigned the management in favour of his younger brother, Mr. H. E. Watt. On quitting St. Helen's Mr. Watt accepted from Messrs. Finlay, Muir & Co. his present charge on the Rasagalla estate. This property is a very fine one, with a total acreage of 1,660. Of the entire area 1,159 are planted with tea partly interplanted with rubber. Altogether there are about 8,000 rubber-trees upon the estate their age ranging from six to nine years. The annual crop of tea is estimated at 600,000 lbs. and the annual crop of rubber at 2,000 lbs. A labour force of 1,150 coolies is engaged upon the estate. The estate factory is equipped with machinery of the latest type, and the motive power is supplied by a 80-h.p. tandem turbine. The elevation of the estate is from 1,900 to 2,806 feet. Mr. Watt is married to Catherine Shaw, daughter of Captain James Layard, of the Anchor Shipping Line, and has four children. In the capacity of visiting agent he continues his connection with the Aderapolla Company's estates, and he has besides proprietary interests in various concerns. His recreations are tennis and shooting.

P. P. Miers.

Born on November 9, 1869, in Jersey, this gentleman, who is the superintendent of the Denegama estate, Bogawantalawa, was educated at the Royal Gosport Academy. He adopted the sea as a profession, but tiring of the life, proceeded to Ceylon in 1887 to start planting. He commenced his career on the Dikoya estate, Dikoya, and from that property transferred to the North Cove estate, Bogawantalawa. Later he served on other estates and then went to Cape Colony and engaged in farming. Finding this unproductive, owing to rinderpest and locusts, he, at the expiration of three years, returned to Ceylon (in 1896) and took charge of the Denegama estate and has been associated with that property ever since. The estate has an acreage of 429, of which 319 acres are under tea. The estimated annual crop is 150,000 lbs. The elevation of the estate is 3,450 ft. Mr. Miers is a member of the Ceylon Mounted Rifles, and as lance-corporal proceeded to England with the Ceylon contingent on the occasion of His Majesty's coronation. His recreations are hunting and tennis.

A. C. Bonner.

The above-named gentleman is superintendent of the Kirkoswald estate, Bogawantalawa. His planting experience extends over twenty years, and he has been for fourteen years on the Kirkoswald estate. The area of the property is 877 acres, and of this 800 acres are planted with tea. The annual crop of tea is estimated at 600 lbs. an acre. It is dealt with in a large factory equipped with four rollers, three dryers, two sifters, and one packer. The motive force is supplied by a turbine of 40 h.p. The estate, which is at an elevation of from 4,000 to 5,000 ft., is

RASAGALLA GROUP ESTATES TEA FACTORY.

the property of the Bogawantalawa Tea Company, Ltd., for whom Mr. Bonner acts as visiting agent.

F. S. Hill.

Mr. F. S. Hill, part proprietor of the Wallawe estate, Balangoda, is the son of Mr. Charles Roche Hill, a Devonshire landowner. Born on November 17, 1872, in Kent, he was educated at Tavistock, in South Devon. On leaving school he went in for farming in Cornwall, but soon abandoned this in favour of a planter's life. Arriving in Ceylon in 1891, he served under Mr. G. Ross on the Le Vallon estate, Pussellawa. From this estate he transferred to the Sheen estate, Pundaluoya. After serving there for fifteen months he accepted charge of the Beddegama estate, Madulkelle. Here he remained for two and a half years and then was appointed superintendent of the Aldie estate. He held that position for four years, and then relinquished it to take charge of the Wallawe estate, the proprietary interests in which he had purchased. The property, which is at an elevation of 2,000 ft., has an acreage of 578 of which 260 acres are planted with tea interplanted with coconuts, and 70 acres are new clearings planted with tea interplanted with rubber. The annual crop of tea is estimated at 145,000 lbs. The estate factory is equipped with two rollers, one roll-breaker, one sifter, and an oil-engine of 15 h.p. Mr. Hill's recreations are cricket, tennis, fishing, and shooting. He is a member of the Balangoda Tennis Club.

J. R. Neale.

Mr. J. R. Neale, the superintendent of the Chapelton estate, Bogawantalawa, was born on November 11, 1872, in Surrey, and educated at St. Edward's School, Oxford. Arriving in Ceylon in 1890, he started planting on the Norwood estate. Thence after seven months' training he migrated to Dimbula to the Madacoombra estate, serving there as assistant for five years. At the expiration of this period he took charge of the Chapelton estate. This property has an acreage of 685, of which 536½ acres are planted with tea. The annual crop of tea is estimated at 280,000 lbs. The factory attached to the estate is equipped with three rollers, four dryers, two sifters, and two roll-breakers, the whole being worked by a 25-h.p. Pelton engine. Mr. Neale is a member of the Badminton Club, London, and of most local clubs. He is the Honorary Secretary of the Bogawantalawa Club. His recreations are tennis, football, and cricket.

F. S. HILL AND WALLAWE TEA FACTORY.

MRS. GEDDES. THE COCONUT ESTATE. MELVILLE GORDON GEDDES.

(For Letterpress see p. 791.)

J. B. Lindsay.

The superintendent of the Aldie estate, Bogawantalawa, Mr. J. B. Lindsay, was born in July, 1868, at Edinburgh, and educated at Edinburgh Academy. Proceeding to Ceylon in 1888, he commenced his planting career on the St. Andrew's estate, Maskeliya district. Quitting this estate after two years' probationership, he accepted service under the Ceylon Tea Plantations Company, Ltd., and remained on that company's estates for four years. Subsequently he had charge for two years of the Morahela estate, and from that transferred to the Aldie estate. This property is at an elevation of 5,000 ft., and has an acreage of 477, of which 420 acres are planted with tea. The estimated annual crop of tea is 230,000 lbs. The estate is provided with two factories, one for making tea, and one for withering the leaf. The machinery is worked by a turbine. The labour force upon the estate consists of 450 coolies. Mr. Lindsay was a member of the first Ceylon contingent which went to South Africa, and he received a medal with four clasps for his services. He is a member of the Colombo Club, and of the Turf Club, Bogawantalawa. His recreations are tennis, golf, and racing.

Noel Worship.

Mr. Noel Worship, the superintendent of the Devonford estate, Bogawantalawa, is a son of the late Mr. William Worship, solicitor, of Norfolk. Born on December 25, 1874, at Yarmouth, Norfolk, he was educated at Rugby, and proceeded to Ceylon in 1892 to learn tea planting. He served his probationary period on the Diogama estate, Agrapatnas. Afterwards he was associated with the Morahela estate, which he opened up and planted with tea. At a later period he took charge of the Singarawatte estate, Bogawantalawa, and from that property transferred to the Kew estate, Norwood. Finally he was appointed to his present position on the Devonford estate. This property is at an elevation of from 5,000 to 5,400 ft., and has an acreage of 242, all planted with tea. Two hundred coolies are employed upon the estate. Mr. Worship is a member of the Sports Club, London, of the Hill Club, Nuwara Eliya, and of the Bogawantalawa Club. His recreations are tennis, cricket, and shooting.

PROFESSIONAL AND SOCIAL.

R. A. R. P. W. M. P. B. PALIPANE.

Rajakaruna Ananda Rajapaksa Pandita Wasala Mudiyansele Philip Bartholomew Palipane is a lineal descendant of Palipane who was Dissawa of Matale, Uva, and Seven Korales in rotation. (This Dissawa's elder brother was Dissawa of the Seven Korales. He went with Pilimi Talawwa Dissawa to Batavia on an embassy and both of them died on the passage home.) Palipane Dissawa was presented with lands, situate at Palipane in Harispattu, of the Kandy district, on sannas granted on Friday, in the month of Binera, in the year of Saka 1673, for having written a Bana Book. He distinguished himself at Matara in a war with the Hollanders. The then king being highly pleased with him, named him Palingupana (Crystal Lamp) and bestowed on him by sannas granted on Monday, in the month of Il, in the year of Saka 1683, an eta (tusked elephant), an aliya (elephant without tusks), a cutlass inlaid with gold, a magnificent gold knife, and a gold chain, and many other honourable rewards, and lands situate in the village Owilla, in the Kohonsiya Pattuwa of the Matale district. It may be mentioned that some of these gifts are still in the possession of the family, having been handed down from generation to generation. The following is a translation of the sannas as given in Mr. Lawrie's Gazetteer :—

MR. AND MRS. J. G. C. MENDIS AND FAMILY.
(Prince of Wales's College, Moratuwa.)
(For Letterpress see p. 117.)

Sri—the behest of our Sovereign Lord, the illustrious ruler of Lanka. During the period that Palingupana Rajakaruna Ananda Rajapaksa Pandita Wasala Mudiyansele was with unalloyed loyalty and sincerity of heart rendering his services to the Sublime Great Gate, the royal command was given that he should proceed to Matara to put an end to the distress occasioned to the inhabitants of Matara by the Hollanders, and he, having reverently received the command, proceeded with the powerful host of the Uva Dissavane, and having surrounded the strong fortress which the Hollanders had constructed at Matara, and having waged war without retreating a single step from the field of battle, where the firing was

THEODORE P. ATTYGALLE.
(For Letterpress see p. 716.)

C. M. S. WIJEYERATNE, MAHAWATTE, MADAMPITIYA, GRANDPASS.

THE BUNGALOW. FAMILY GROUP.

MALDENIYA GROUP TEA ESTATE, WITH FACTORY.

(For Letterpress see p. 711.)

P. B. PALIPANE AND FAMILY. P. B. PALIPANE, RATEMAHATMAYA. THE BUNGALOW.

incessant, and having vanquished the enemy and demolished the fortress, returned victorious, and made announcement thereof to the gracious effulgence of Majesty, and (the king) being highly pleased thereat, bestowed on him an eta (tusked elephant), an aliya (elephant without tusks), a cutlass inlaid with gold and a magnificent gold knife, and a gold chain, and many other honourable rewards; and, moreover, ensured to his posterity the undisturbed and permanent possession of the fields Uda Yelamunekumbura, 1½ amuna; Pettadeniya, 5 pelas; Getaberiyadeniya, 2 pelas; Dikdeniya, 3 pelas; Totapalapitiya, 1 pela; Galketiyawa, 1 pela; Walliyawatta, 2 pelas; Amunewala, 2 pelas; Liyangahamada, 2 pelas; Wewaladeniya, 2½ pelas; altogether 6 amunu, 2 pelas, and 5 lahas, with the high and low grounds and other appurtenances, situate in the village Owilla, in the Kohonsiya Pattuwa of the Matale Dissavane. This sannas was granted on this Monday, the fifth day of the decreasing moon in the month of Il, of the year denominated Vrashabha, in the year of Saka 1683; by the command which was given, and which command is the command of his Majesty, and thus it is. 23,461.

This Dissawa had four sons and three daughters. Of the sons, the eldest was Dissawa of Ridigan Pattu, who was removed from his office for showing sympathy during the execution of Ehelapola Adigar's children, and the second was Dissawa of Uda Palata. Loku Banda, son of the Dissawa of Uda Palata and landed proprietor of Palipane, married Bandara Menike, daughter of Madugalle Ratemahatmaya of Dumbara (now Lower and Upper Dumbara), in the Central Province, whose father was Gajanayaka Nilame during the Kandyan *régime*. Their son is the subject of this sketch, and he was born in 1850 and educated at the Kandy Central School. He entered the Government service in 1872, being attached in the first instance to the Kandy Kachcheri. Since 1875 he has held the office of Ratemahatmaya of Weudawili Hatpattu in the North-Western Province, and has the distinction of being the oldest Ratemahatmaya in the service of Government. On various occasions he acted as Kachcheri Mudaliyar of Kurunegala in addition to his own duties. In 1875 he was transferred to the Wanni Hatpattu, the condition of that division being then very unsatisfactory, for the purpose of restoring order. After carrying out the object of his mission he returned to his substantial appointment of Ratemahatmaya of Weudawili Hatpattu, which office he holds up to date. Mr. Palipane is a member of the Agricultural Society. His ancestral home is Palipane Walauwa, in Harispattu, of the Kandy district, and his present residence Palipane House, Kurunegala. In 1876 he married Dorothea Sarah, daughter of Samuel Jayatileke, Mudaliyar of the Governor's Gate, of Kurunegala, and of his sons, the eldest, Philip Clarence, is a planter, and Messrs. Philip Bertram and Cyril William are Proctors of the District Court of Kurunegala, and his daughter, Eugenie Frances, is married to George Henry Taldena, Korala and planter, of Badulla. Mr. Palipane owns extensive property planted with coconuts, large stretches of paddy-land in the Central and in the North-Western Provinces, and house property in Palipane, Kurunegala, and elsewhere, and is the possessor of the gold Jubilee Medal of 1897.

DANIEL JAMES JAYETILEKE.

This gentleman is the son of Mr. Samuel Jayetileke, Mudaliyar of the Governor's Gate, Justice of the Peace, and Unofficial Police Magistrate of Kurunegala. Born in Kandy, he was educated at Trinity College, Kandy, after which he was articled to Deputy Queen's

D. E. JAYETILEKE AND FAMILY.

1. Mrs. D. J. Jayetileke (the late) 2. D. E. Jayetileke. 3. Chas. Fred. Jayetileke. 4. D. J. Jayetileke. 5. Mrs. J. S. H. Edirisinghe. 6. Irene Villa. 7. Master Carlo Jayetileke. 8. Mr. and Mrs. D. E. Jayetileke and Daughter.

Advocate Nell. He became a Proctor of the District Court in 1866, and practised at Galagedara, Colombo, and Gampola. Later he transferred to Ratnapura, and he is now the senior member of the Bar there. In 1868 he became a Proctor of the Supreme Court, and a Notary Public in 1900. He has frequently acted as District Judge, Police Magistrate, and Commissioner of Requests. He owns various estates and plantations and house property, as well as some of the richest precious stone mines in Ceylon. He was a member of the Ratnapura Local Board from its inception until 1900, is a member of the Provincial and District Road Committees, and of the Board of the Ceylon Agricultural Society and of the Sabaragamuwa Planters' Association. He married, in 1875, Josephine Maria, daughter of Mr. S. C. Vanderstraaten, late District Judge of Matara, and resides at Irene Villa, Ratnapura. His eldest son, Daniel Elimore, was born in 1876, and educated at the Royal College, Colombo, where he passed both the Junior and Senior Cambridge local examinations. After studying surveying privately, he practised that profession privately at Ratnapura until 1902, when he turned his attention to law. He became a Proctor of the District Court of Ratnapura in 1906, and in the same year succeeded his father as a member of the Local Board. In 1900 he married Ethel Ruth, daughter of Arthur Emmanuel Daviot, of H.M.'s Customs Department at Colombo. He is a member of the Sabaragamuwa Lawn Tennis Club. Mr. Jayetileke, sen.'s second son, Charles Frederick, is a law student, and his daughter, Irene Alexandra, married, in 1906, the Rev. J. S. H. Ederisinghe, incumbent of St. Paul's Church, Kandy.

ELLAWALA EKANAYAKE RAJEPAKSE BASNAIKE MUDIANSE WILLIAM ELLAWALA.

This gentleman, for some time known as the Hon. Mr. William Ellawala, was born at Ellawala in 1834. He is descended from Loku Nilame, son of Pahala Nilame, a landed proprietor, and at one time an officer in the service of the Kandyan Government. Loku Nilame's son was Banda, who was Korala of the Kukulu Korale of the Sabaragamuwa Province at one time, and married a daughter of Don Bartholomew Kuruppu Wikramasekara Jayawardene, of Panadure. Their son is the Don William Ellawala, the subject of this sketch. Mr. Ellawala was educated first at Ratnapura School, and afterwards at St. Thomas's College, and subsequently was for two years headmaster at the former school. He became Ratemahatmaya of Paranakuru Korale in the Kegalla district in 1862, and Ratemahatmaya of Nawadun Korale, in Ratnapura, in 1865. From 1892 to 1897 he sat on the Legislative Council as Kandyan member, whilst he has also been President of Buddhist Temporalities in the Sabaragamuwa Province, a member of the Local Board, Ratnapura, and of the Provincial Road Committee and the District Road Committee. He married, in 1859, Jane Petronella, daughter of Don Bartholomew Kuruppu Wikramasekara Jayawardene, jun., Mudaliyar. His daughter, Agnes, married Mahawalatena, Ratemahatmaya, of Balangoda. His sons Francis and Harry are referred to in subsequent sketches. Mr. Ellawala's residence is Godigomuwe Walauwa, Ratnapura.

1. Wm. Ellawala. 2. The Late Wm. Ellawala. 3. Mr. Mahawalatena, R.M. 4. Cyril Ellawala. 5. Francis Theodor Ellawala. 6. Miss Sylvia Ellawala. 7. Harry Ellawala. 8. Mrs. Mahawalatena.

FRANCIS THEODOR ELLAWALA.

Mr. F. T. Ellawala is the second son of the Hon. Mr. W. Ellawala, and was born in 1862, and educated at St. Thomas's College. He was successful in passing the Calcutta University Entrance Examination, and on the completion